W9-CUJ-199

Libyan Independence and the United Nations

A CASE OF PLANNED DECOLONIZATION

Libyan Independence and the United Nations

A CASE OF PLANNED DECOLONIZATION

BY ADRIAN PELT

FOREWORD BY U THANT

PUBLISHED FOR

THE CARNEGIE ENDOWMENT FOR INTERNATIONAL PEACE

NEW HAVEN AND LONDON, YALE UNIVERSITY PRESS, 1970

 Library of Congress catalog card number: 72-99836. ISBN: 0-300-01216-0. Designed by Sally Sullivan, set in Linotype Times Roman type, and printed in the United States of America by Vail-Ballou Press, Inc., Binghamton, N.Y. Distributed in Great Britain, Asia, and Africa by Yale University Press Ltd., London; in Canada by McGill-Queen's University Press, Montreal; and in Mexico by Centro Interamericano de Libros Académicos, Mexico City.

CONTENTS

FOREWORD

It is with great pleasure that I welcome the opportunity to write an introduction to Mr. Adrian Pelt's book on Libya. I am particularly glad that Mr. Pelt undertook this study. I would say that Mr. Pelt, advising the representatives of the people of Libya, played a major role in successfully implementing the General Assembly's decision to make the former Italian colony of Libya an independent State.

The role assigned to the Commissioner appointed by the United Nations was an unusually difficult one requiring considerable tact and capacity for innovation. The Commissioner and his team of United Nations officials helped the people of Libya in drawing up a constitution, taking into account their historical, political and other special circumstances. The Council for Libya, established to assist the Commissioner, was a truly unique body as its membership included, not only the representatives of the three Libyan provinces, but also six member States and a representative of the minorities resident in Libya. Thus, there was a broad spectrum of advice available to the Commissioner.

When the political decision was taken to create a unified and independent Libya, many had thought that the country would not be able to support itself financially and that the International Community represented by the United Nations would have to assume a special responsibility, particularly in providing help through the technical assistance programme of the United Nations and the specialized agencies. This responsibility was recognized in successive resolutions of the United Nations General Assembly and of the Economic and Social Council. Resulting from these decisions, a United Nations technical assistance programme of an unusually large magnitude was provided for many years until the discovery of oil freed the country from dependence on external sources for economic assistance. The United Nations and its family of agencies now continue to provide technical assistance largely on a reimbursement basis.

Mr. Pelt has paid well-deserved tribute to the Secretariat staff who had assisted him in his work. The Secretariat, on this as on other occasions, has continued to be a reliable and efficient instrument in the institutional framework of the United Nations. Mr. Pelt felt that this was an essential factor in the success of the United Nations effort in Libya.

About his own role, Mr. Pelt writes with characteristic modesty. However, as his colleagues and the Libyans who knew him will appreciate, much of the credit goes to Mr. Pelt for the successful manner in which United Nations responsibilities were handled in Libya. Throughout his career, Mr. Pelt has brought to his work the outstanding qualities of patience, tolerance, and sincerity. His work in Libya provides another evidence of these high traits.

U Thant
Secretary-General
of the United Nations

PREFACE

The object of this study is to describe the peaceful transformation, under United Nations auspices, of the former Italian colony of Libya into an independent and sovereign State.

In pursuing this object, the author in no way aspires to provide a complete history of Libya. If the next section bears the title "Historical Background," this is only because any account of Libya's coming of age would be incomprehensible to the uninitiated reader without an outline of the main events which brought the country to the particular stage of evolution in which it found itself on 15 September 1948, when its destiny, in accordance with the provisions of the Treaty of Peace with Italy, was entrusted to the General Assembly of the United Nations by the four Powers—France, USSR, United Kingdom, and the United States—who had failed to agree on its future.

Neither does the author present the case of Libyan decolonization as a vade mecum for the untroubled conversion of a dependent territory into an independent State. First of all, the initial happenings which caused Libya's case to be submitted to the United Nations were not so peaceful as all that: they were, at least in part, the aftermath of struggles costly in terms of human life, in which Libya's own peoples had played their part, fighting and suffering in their own cause. Second, the methods and procedures devised and put into practice by the United Nations for the emancipation of Libya were related too specifically to that country's particular conditions to make them universally applicable.

Political freedom for colonial territories, in the present-day sense of the term, has had a long and complex history which is not yet finished. In most cases it has been accomplished through war or revolution, bloody and costly at the time, though only too often lauded solely for their glory and heroism, all agony forgotten or deliberately deleted from the record by those who later tell their story. Each individual case of decolonization has its own characteristics, its own background, its own development, and its own happy—or unhappy—ending. No two ruling empires, no two dependent peoples, are ever the same, and so there are seemingly endless variants in methods and the outcome. Yet, although no two cases are so alike as to duplicate each other, neither are such cases in their generality so dissimilar as to preclude all comparison.

In its final stages, Libya's evolution into an independent State could not have been more free from upheaval. Though the policy both of the United Kingdom and the French Governments was based on a desire to maintain zones of influence to accommodate military bases in the area, neither showed any intention of implementing policy by force. This was particularly true of the United Kingdom. The most that can be said is that the presence of British troops in Tripolitania and Cyrenaica (under separate administrations) had a restraining effect on those elements of the local population which might otherwise have been tempted to make their views known by means of disturbing public law and order while peaceful ways of doing so were at their disposal. This sobering influence was no bad thing. The troops were never used to prevent or control demonstrations, at least not during the two years of the United Nations presence in the country, though on a few rare occasions they were kept at the ready in their barracks. Helpful also in satisfying local aspirations was the fact that in September 1949 the United Kingdom Government granted Cyrenaica internal autonomy, at the same time recognizing the Amir, His Highness Mohamed Idris al-Mahdi al-Senussi, as Head of the local Government. Similarly, in April of the same year, the British military occupation of Tripolitania had made way for a civilian administration, and in 1950 and 1951 organs of local government were established in that territory. At the same time, however, these changes impeded the growth of Libyan unity as powers first transferred to these local organs later had to be retransferred to the federal Libyan Government.

The same considerations applied to the Fezzan, although the situation there was somewhat different. From 1943 to 1949 the French Administration was headed by a Military Governor assisted by three officers, each commanding one of the three administrative subdivisions: Shatti, Sabhah-Ubari, and Murzuq. After the adoption by the General Assembly of the United Nations of Resolution 289 (IV) on 21 November 1949, a transitional regime was instituted to ensure wider participation by the local population in the conduct of public affairs.[1] A chief of territory ("Chef du Territoire") was elected by a meeting of the village chiefs, *Jemaa* (a tradi-

1. General Assembly Resolution 289 (IV) was an omnibus recommendation dealing with the disposal of all the former Italian colonies. Part A dealt with Libya. For the text thereof, see Annex I, pp. 891–93.

tional assembly of heads of family). Assisted by a small administrative council, the chief was responsible for all matters pertaining to the internal life of the Territory. Nonetheless, the supervision of this local administration remained in the hands of a French military authority, some of the members of which belonged to the Corps des Officiers des Affaires Indigènes. Small garrisons manned by troops of the Foreign Legion or by Spahis were stationed in the forts built by the Italian Army in the principal oases. They were responsible for, and occasionally had to be used to maintain, law and order. It was fairly obvious that the fact of the presence of these troops was sometimes used, and especially so in 1948 and 1950, to bring pressure to bear on the population in a sense inimical to the achievement of Libyan unity and independence. But at no time during the United Nations presence did this go so far as armed repression.

To summarize: as from the adoption of Resolution 289 (IV) the Libyans did not need to fight either the British or the French to win their independence, since neither Government intended to remain in occupation indefinitely or to acquire sovereignty over the three provinces. Thus, in contrast to so many other cases of decolonization, Libyan independence, in the end, came about in an organized manner, largely thanks to the organs and procedures conceived and implemented by the United Nations to solve what had been a deadlocked problem, both internationally and nationally. The outcome was the product of constructive international and national thinking, and its success the outcome of equally constructive cooperation on both planes.

When Libya's emancipation is compared with that of other former colonies or dependent territories, one question inevitably arises. It can conveniently be phrased in following terms:

> In the achievement of independence, has the international assistance given to Libya by the United Nations in cooperation with the two Adminstering Powers, and with the Libyan leaders themselves, displayed any specific advantages or revealed any particular shortcomings vis-à-vis the more conventional bilateral process of decolonization where a single colonial power treats directly with the dependent people concerned?

Without attempting to answer the question at this stage of the present study—indeed, the extent to which it can be satisfactorily answered is yet to be seen—one may perhaps say, after nearly twenty years of an independent Libya, and with some justification, that that country's transformation from a colony to a sovereign State can be counted a success for the United Nations plans and the way in which they were carried out. With the possible exception of the case of Somalia, comparisons with the Libyan operation are difficult, if only because the problems and situations encountered there have few, if any, parallels elsewhere. Such comparisons are particularly invidious in the political sphere, since the atmosphere that surrounds an international operation differs markedly from that which prevails between a colonial power and its dependent territory at the moment at which the umbilical cord is severed. By force of circumstances, if not indeed by force of ingrained reflexes, a people yearning for independence will naturally suspect the intentions of its colonial master, no matter how well-meant these may be. On the other hand, the best of masters will normally do no better than strike a balance between his own interests and those of the indigenous population. By contrast, the entire raison d' être of a multilateral decolonization is to ensure that, in the essential process of harmonizing the foreign interests involved with those of the weaker nascent State, the advantage lies predominantly with the latter.

In the economic and social sectors the distinction between what may be called bilateral and multilateral decolonization is even more marked. In substance, the problems are the same in the two cases, but the spirit in which they are tackled is very different. Generally, at the time of severance the economic and social interests of the two sides are thoroughly intertwined. To a considerable extent, they have to be disentangled. The question is, whose interest shall prevail? Here again, the international negotiator will, by the nature of his function, be more inclined to give preference to the emergent State than will the former overlord, although the latter may be in a better position to tender economic and financial aid. Hence, there may be advantages in combining international and national assistance.

The history of Libya's emancipation provides many examples of the way in which the two methods work, cooperating as well as clashing. The author therefore deems it to be one of his foremost duties to make an evaluation, on its merits and as a unique case, of General Assembly Resolution 289 (IV), in which it was first declared that Libya should be constituted an independent and sovereign State by the end of 1951, and of its implementation.

The central theme of this study will, however, be the way in which unity and independence came to pass in Libya, partly—ironically—as a result of disagreements among the major Powers who emerged as victors from World War II (though agreement to disagree also helped), and partly, though by no means least, through the tireless efforts of the Libyan peoples themselves.

Although the story of Libya's progress to independence can to a large extent be extracted from unpublished documents in the archives of the United Nations and from the Organization's Official Records, it has never yet been told as one continuous narrative. There are good reasons why this should be so. Even if the United Nations files were freely accessible, no account based exclusively on this source would be complete. As to the national archives of the countries directly concerned with the United Nations operation in Libya, from which large and important gaps could be filled, these will remain closed to research workers for many years to come. Also, many persons who could have given oral evidence of the part they played in the events described in this study are no longer with us; and few of them left written records behind. Others, still living, who could have provided information, were often reluctant to do so; and even those who were willing sometimes gave biased accounts of the events to which they were privy, as might indeed have been expected.

Understandably, the organization being still young, the United Nations Secretariat has only in recent years established rules governing access to the voluminous files in its safekeeping. There exist, indeed, certain standing instructions which are variably applied according to the political sensitiveness of the subject of which the records treat. One such instruction provides that texts based on unpublished United Nations records and intended for publication must be submitted to the Secretary-General for his approval. At first sight, this sounds perfectly simple, provided there is no doubt whether a particular document or record is still unpublished at the moment at which an author's text is submitted for approval.

The archives of the United Nations Mission in Libya comprise the following categories of documentation:

a. Manuscript and typewritten papers, such as letters, memorandums, legal opinions, records of conversations and private meetings, and the like;

b. Summary records of meetings of the Council for Libya, and its working papers, all in mimeographed form, issued in regular United Nations series with the appropriate reference symbols;

c. Mimeographed documents of the Coordination Committee for the transfer of powers, in which the United Nations Commissioner for Libya met with representatives of the Administering Powers (the United Kingdom and France), of the Provisional Government of Libya, and of the administrations of the three provinces (Tripolitania, Cyrenaica and the Fezzan); and

d. Mimeographed documents relating to meetings of experts on Libyan financial, monetary, and development problems.

The typescript papers and a few manuscript notes—category (a)—come under the standing instructions governing documentation of a confidential nature, except insofar as they may have been reproduced in

United Nations public documents, such as, for instance, the Commissioner's five reports to the General Assembly, or in official publications of the Libyan or other Governments. A large number of them have been used as background material for the Commissioner's reports, sometimes by way of direct quotation in annexes, more often paraphrased in the body of these reports.

When the question arose of the extent to which the former United Nations Commissioner for Libya, as the author of the present study, might make use of unpublished material, it was agreed between the Secretary-General of the United Nations and himself that he submit to the Secretary-General confidential material of a sensitve or controversial nature prior to publication. This has been done, even though some of the material is still sensitive or controversial. The author was free to consult such confidential material to refresh his memory. This was particularly helpful to him in reconstructing the background to many passages in his reports, and he is most grateful to the Secretary-General for granting him this facility, without which it would have been well-nigh impossible for him to write the study.[2]

The use of the mimeographed documents in categories (b), (c), and (d) set a different problem. They were originally classified as "Restricted," and some, though far from all, bore the following caveat: "Restricted documents in this series are for official use only of members of the Council for Libya, their authorized staff, the Commissioner in Libya, and the Secretariat. Such documents may not be given to the Press, quoted, published, or otherwise made public in any way." This would seem to rule out any possibility of their being used in the preparation of this study. However, rule 18 of the Council's rules of procedures provided that: "The Council shall meet in open meetings unless otherwise decided." In fact, most Council meetings held in Tripoli were open to the public, whereas all those held in Geneva for purposes of consultation between the Commissioner and the Council on his reports to the General Assembly took place behind closed doors. Yet controversial points that arose in the course of these consultations were summarized in numerous footnotes, or even at times in two or more footnotes setting out the pros and cons of a given issue, to the Commissioner's published reports. This practice was adopted by common

2. Since the author has avoided quoting or directly referring to records of some of the most confidential discussions he held with Government officials and leading Libyans, some points in the narrative are not dealt with in as much detail as he would have wished. On the other hand, the accessible records cited in the study proved sufficient to cover adequately all the major issues which arose during his tenure of office.

agreement in pursuance of the second sentence of paragraph 5 of General Assembly Resolution 289 (IV), which provided that "To these reports shall be added any memorandum or document that the United Nations Commissioner or a member of the Council may wish to bring to the attention of the United Nations."

Hence the solution of the problem depended upon the meaning attached to the word "Restricted" in 1950 and 1951 and upon the significance still to be attached to it in 1966. At the time of issue the documents in question were made available not only to all members of the Council in the numbers and languages they requested; they were also distributed to all members of the Consular Corps in Tripoli and Benghazi and to the senior officials of the Administering Powers in Tripolitania, Cyrenaica, and the Fezzan. In addition, they had a fairly extensive circulation in Arabic, mainly to the members of the Libyan Provisional Government and National Constituent Assembly engaged in drafting the Constitution. All this added up to some 200 to 250 copies in each of the Council's working languages (English, French, and Arabic). Moreover, the substance of the discussions in the Council as well as its working papers and the reports of the Coordination Committee gained even wider currency through press releases, often quite detailed, issued in English, French, and Arabic shortly after the close of each meeting. Documents relating to operations carried out in Libya by the Technical Assistance Board of the United Nations and the specialized agencies also were widely distributed to the interested Governments, to members and officials of the Provisional Government, and to the Administering Powers, as well as to some scores of informed private citizens with whom the tentative findings of technical assistance experts had been discussed in the company of the latter.

Distribution of the working documents of the Coordination Committee and reports emanating from the Meetings of Experts on financial, monetary, and development problems was at first more restricted; but later their contents reached a much wider public through the Commissioner's reports. The final reports to the United Nations and specialized agencies by the technical assistance experts serving in the country were distributed locally in hundreds of copies in English and Arabic, after review by the agency or agencies concerned and clearance by the Administering Powers or the Provisional Government. Most of them were also, of course, available in French, and many of them were printed and put on sale as United Nations Documents.

When discussions on the Libyan question opened in the General Assembly's Committees in 1950 and 1951 the Chairmen, after consultation with the Secretariat, advised the Committees that all representatives could have access to all Council documents, a complete set being available with the Secretary of each Committee. The Chair's ruling was made when committee members intimated that they might like to see the documents mentioned in footnotes to the Commissioner's first report. The effect was to make all documents connected with the Council accessible to all Member States.

It will be clear from the foregoing that the original intention had been to limit the volume of mimeographed documentation that had to be distributed, rather than to preserve the secrecy of its contents. Without some such restriction, the documents in question would automatically have received the extremely wide distribution given to the documentation of the General Assembly, the Security Council, and the Economic and Social Council. The Secretary-General therefore agreed that all mimeographed documentation in categories (b), (c), and (d) could be regarded as in the public domain for the present author's purposes.[3]

Accordingly, this study is only partly—even though to a large extent—based on direct documentary evidence. But this is thoroughly backed up by memory refreshed by and checked against large numbers of confidential papers. Over and above all this, as adumbrated on page xvii above, a number of people, Libyans and others, have authorized the author to use material, still of a confidential nature, which they have communicated to him privately, either in writing or orally. Most of them are still alive, and if they are not to be compromised, strict discretion must be observed about their identity. This has occasionally caused the author some embarrassment; for, much as he would have liked to give exact references everywhere, he has not always been authorized to do so by his sources, to whom, nonetheless, he is grateful.

Thus, what follows is by no means confined to the printed word; neither is it a mere reworking of United Nations documents. In truth, there is hardly a paper in the archives which does not evoke reminiscences in the author's mind, and, what is more important, prompt him to take a fresh look at his past judgments and actions. What is done cannot be undone; but both actions and judgments call for reassessment and appreciation in the light of hindsight. Accordingly, the reader will find a number of critical comments and second thoughts interspersed among the narrative. Some embody reflections which occurred to the Commissioner at the time but seemed unsuitable for inclusion in his formal reports to the General Assembly, especially as these were written in consultation—often contro-

3. For the benefit of the reader unfamiliar with United Nations practice, a brief account of the way in which the Organization's documention is organized, with the symbols of the several series used as sources by the author, is provided in Annex X, pp. 958–60.

versial—with the Council for Libya. Others are the fruit of retrospection over the past fifteen years; and yet others are illuminated by events that have occurred since Libya achieved independence. Wherever the author, writing today, disagrees with the judgment of the Commissioner, acting in the past, or whenever the former has reached the conclusion that his earlier alter ego consciously made a mistake or unwittingly fell into error, he has said so in the text. This, too, is why he refers to himself as "the Commissioner" in dealing with the events of 1950 to 1952—a device that has made it easier for him to view the past objectively, or at least as objectively as is humanly possible in the circumstances.

In a preface, an author cannot, by definition, look back in detail on events still to be described. Such a global review, and an assessment of the attempt to assess the significance of the events thus reviewed, will, however, be found in the epilogue under the title "Afterthoughts." Nonetheless, while writing in 1964–67 about what happened in 1950–51, the writer could not help being influenced by everything that occurred in the intervening period in Libya, in which he always maintained a profound interest. This was so much the more natural inasmuch as the two years of his life spent in Libya were a challenge to his faith in the value of the United Nations system for the promotion of peace and prosperity, as well as to his conviction that, given sincere peaceful collaboration between all the interested parties, decolonization can be purged of much of the anguish that is its usual attendant and yet brought to a successful and happy ending. The greater the difficulties and obstacles met with in the course of the process, the keener the challenge to overcome them. In the case of Libya, they seemed at times insurmountable; so that, when they were at last resolved, the sceptics were not slow in spreading reports—the product of fertile imaginations—to the effect that Resolution 289 (IV) was the ill-begotten brainchild of a strange alliance between down-to-earth diplomats and idealistic civil servants who had succeeded in concocting a State that not only would not be viable, but would also fail to command the faith of even the Libyan peoples themselves. Those familiar with the history of Libya in the twentieth century know that this legend is false. Events during the transitional period (1950 and 1951), and particularly the way in which the Amir and the Libyan National Assembly took the country's fate in their own hands with increasing firmness, prove that, far from being a myth, Libyan independence and unity are a genuine reflection of national needs and aspirations.

For a better understanding of the account that follows, it should also be noted that there is no logical sequel, though there is a political one, between the intentions the leading victorious allies originally had in mind with regard to Libya and the recommendation in favor of an independent and sovereign State as embodied in Resolution 289 (IV). Italy having been defeated, the large territory of its Libyan colony was left as a political void in a strategically sensitive spot on the south coast of the Mediterranean. To leave this gap open would have meant a constant source of danger to the peace of the area. Power politics, as they were being played at the time, required a new balance of competing forces. Simultaneously, the new United Nations Charter philosophy regarding the treatment of colonial territories had to be kept in mind. Hence, from the end of World War II until the spring of 1949, first in the Council of Foreign Ministers and subsequently in the General Assembly of the United Nations, persistent attempts were made to divide Libya into three zones of influence, under the name of trusteeships, to be assigned to three of the contesting powers. All these attempts failed because of persistent disagreements between the negotiating parties and, in the last instance, by decision of the General Assembly. It was only then, partly for lack of a better arrangement, that the leading allies agreed on a recommendation to the effect that "Libya, comprising Cyrenaica, Tripolitania and the Fezzan, shall be constituted an independent and sovereign State."

As United Nations Commissioner in Libya, the author always kept in the back of his mind the fundamental fact that the purpose of the task entrusted to him was the establishment of a new balance of power in the interest of peace and that the creation of an independent and sovereign Libyan State had emerged from the General Assembly's deliberations as the only politically possible means to achieve that purpose.

At the very moment that the author completed his narrative of that achievement, the Libyan monarchy was overthrown and replaced by an "Arab Republic." It would be as hazardous as it would be premature to foretell what internal and external effects this revolution may produce. Judging by first indications, the internal effect appears to be considerable though not yet quite clear. An estimate of the effect it may have on Libya's international position is even more difficult to make, particularly because the present political situation in the eastern Mediterranean is much more heavily loaded with potential dangers to the peace of the world than was the one prevailing during the years immediately following World War II. It is to be hoped that the new rulers of the Libyan State, by safeguarding its unity and independence, will show themselves aware of the delicate part it has to play in the politics of the Mediterranean region.

Until the coup d'etat of 1 September 1969, except for some local disturbances, Libya, in contrast with other new States in Africa and Asia, had been remarkably free from serious upheavals, and some slow but perceptible economic and social progress had set in. It had become more and more doubtful, however, whether social conditions, in particular, had sufficiently improved to offset increasing tensions between the poor mass of the population, the small class of traditional well-to-do, and the growing number of the new rich. The sudden discovery of oil and natural gas in unexpectedly large quantities and mostly of excellent quality, unavoidably followed by an inrush of great wealth, beneficial to the Libyan economy as a whole but ill distributed and therefore disrupting the country's social structure, urgently required far-reaching countermeasures which were not taken in time. Admittedly a number of economic and social changes, including so revolutionary an innovation as the enfranchisement of women, as well as greatly improved educational and public health facilities made possible and accelerated by the wealth flowing from the oil wells, transformed the face of the country. The new riches have also enabled the Libyan State to slough off the constrictions of foreign subsidies and grants-in-aid which, at the time of its birth, constituted such a heavy psychological mortgage on its initial fund of freedom. However, these changes brought in their train other new and serious problems, the solution of which will severely test the administrative talents and political acumen of the new generation of Libyans who now have taken over the heavy responsibilities of their elders.

In the constitutional field, on the other hand, development had been much faster. The author believes that it is fair to attribute the relative smoothness of the country's political evolution to the people's realization that, in the hour of decision, everyone capable of contributing to the conception of the new State was given a chance of doing so, even though no one had things entirely his own way. Under the guidance of a politically wise and experienced monarch, and using the constitutional provisions for amendment, the federal system of government was in time replaced by a centralized form of government, the original three provinces being replaced by ten main administrative units by Public Law No. 1 of 1963. The choice between a federal and centralized form of State and government, which in 1950–51 had given rise to much bitter strife, was thus resolved peacefully by means of discussion and negotiation carried out in accord with stringent restrictive provisions governing changes in the original Constitution. Both foreign observers and some thoughtful Libyans wonder, however, whether the pendulum of peaceful change did not swing too far, or at least prematurely, in the direction of centralization. Indeed, this move was neither accompanied nor followed by the formation of an all-Libyan body politic or by the organization of a national party or parties. The provincial parties active before the declaration of independence in Tripolitania and Cyrenaica had disappeared after the first general parliamentary election in February 1952 and never were allowed to return. Even after the Constitutional reform of 1963, general elections retained their provincial character.

A potent source of tension is a new form of Arab nationalism, which for several years has been taking an increasing hold on the minds of the younger generation. Emotional outbursts have occurred, since the shattering Arab defeat at the hands of Israel in June 1967, which reveal the existence of a serious psychopolitical crisis, bringing to the surface a long-standing problem which has been lying submerged in the national subconscious, namely, the need for a balanced relationship between Arab and Libyan nationalism.

From the preceding considerations it follows that the Libyan people still face a future fraught with difficulty. Nevertheless, when its present prospects are compared with the conditions under which it came into being, modern Libya can still count itself, to use the words of the Preamble to the original Constitution, blessed by God the Beneficent, the Merciful, the Master of the Universe, under whose supreme guidance its people, with profound trust, determined its Constitution and proclaimed its independence fifteen years ago.[4]

For its part the United Nations had good reasons to be satisfied with its achievement in creating the independent and sovereign State of Libya. Indeed, by recognizing, in accordance with the Charter, the right of the Libyan people to freely determine its future form of government, by assisting and advising it in the process of decolonization and the creation of an independent State, the United Nations, with the help of its specialized agencies and of the Administering Powers, has successfully accomplished the task entrusted to it by the Paris Peace Conference in 1947.

A last question, which the author will attempt to answer in the Afterthoughts, is whether any lessons can be drawn from the experience gained.

4. For the text of the Constitution, see Annex II, pp. 902–21.

ACKNOWLEDGMENTS

Work for or in an international organization is, by its very nature, almost always teamwork. This is particularly true of field missions. As United Nations Commissioner in Libya, I could never have carried out my task successfully without the constant and devoted assistance of the team of Secretariat staff and experts made available to me by the United Nations and a number of its specialized agencies.

This study is also largely the result of teamwork; and although I naturally take full responsibility for the way in which the facts are presented, and for the opinions, judgments, and appreciations expressed, I would be guilty of gross ingratitude if I failed to place on record my warmest thanks to all who have directly or indirectly helped me in preparing and writing it.

In the first place, thanks are due to the Carnegie Endowment for International Peace, which, with the assistance of the Social Science Research Council, made it materially possible for me to embark upon the enterprise, and whose staff in New York and Geneva were always ready with advice, encouragement, and help.

My thanks are also due to the Administration and Secretariat of the United Nations; first, to the Secretary-General for permission to consult, on the conditions mentioned in the foreword, the archives of the United Nations Mission in Libya; next, to the United Nations Office at Geneva and the Library there for their generosity in matters of office space, secretarial assistance, and research facilities; and last but not least to the office of the Resident Representative of the Technical Assistance Board and Director of Special Fund Programmes in Libya, at Tripoli, where I was shown the fullest consideration during my visit to Libya in the winter of 1964–65.

The Libyan Government has more than earned my gratitude for its hospitality while I was engaged in research there during that period, especially for help with the many translations of Arabic documents into English. This is particularly true of the *Proceedings of the National Constit-*

uent Assembly of Libya and related documentation. These were ably and rapidly translated by the Cambridge University Arabic scholars Frank H. Stewart and David E. P. Jackson.

Many Libyans and Italians who played a part in the events of 1950–51 rendered most valuable assistance by helping to verify or to reconstruct such facts, episodes, and situations as did not emerge clearly from the available records. Most of them, though not all, prefer to remain anonymous; but my warmest thanks are due to all.

Among those who were most helpful, and have raised no objection to being named, I would like to mention His Excellency Mahmoud al-Muntasir, President of the Council of Ministers in both the Provisional and the first independent Government of Libya, and now Head of the Royal Diwan, who, under authority from His Majesty King Mohamed Idris al-Mahdi al-Senussi, helped to clear up a number of obscurities surrounding events that occurred before and during the transitional period (1950–51).

The following former members of the Council for Libya contributed appreciably by enlightening me on many points that needed checking: Ali Assad al-Jerbi, Mohamed Bin Othman, Ali Nourridine Unayzi, Mustafa Mizran, and Giacomo Marchino. To these names should be added those of a number of Libyans who played important roles in public life in 1950–52 and later, and who kindly discussed with me during 1964–65 a number of the events recorded in this book: Mansur Bey Qadara, Mustafa Bin Halim, Awni Dajani, Ali Sakhli, Mohieddine Fekini, Mohamed Murabet, Khalid Abul Qarqani, and last but not least His Eminence the Mufti of Tripolitania, later the Grand Mufti of Libya, Mohamed Abul Is'ad al-Alim.

Although I have not gone into detail about events that preceded the Italian occupation or occurred during it, I am most grateful for interviews accorded by the following Italian personages, which helped me the better to understand the period 1912–43 and its immediate aftermath: Guglielmo Rulli, Carlo Giglio, Mario Toscano, Giuseppe Vedovato, and, above all, Enrico de Leone, whose work *La Colonizzazione dell'Africa del Nord* (Padova, Italy: Cedam-Casa Editrice Dott. Antonio Milani, 1960) was most instructive.

I am particularly indebted to three former colleagues from the staff of the Libyan Mission: Thomas F. Power, Jr., Principal Secretary and Personal Representative of the Secretary-General in Libya; Marc Schreiber, Legal Adviser; and Hannah Platz, Private Secretary to the United Nations Commissioner.

Thomas Power, whose name and functions crop up repeatedly in what follows, was among the first to encourage me to write the story of Libyan independence. He subsequently found time among his many official duties to read through the entire manuscript chapter by chapter, and finally scrutinized it as a whole. Thanks to his critical mind and fabulous memory, not to mention his many pertinent suggestions, the work has gained greatly in accuracy and depth, in particular with regard to economic and financial questions and technical assistance in general.

Marc Schreiber kindly checked a number of legal points, while Hannah Platz, who often knew her way about the Mission archives better than the Commissioner himself, proved to be a tireless and highly efficient research assistant, both in Geneva and in Tripoli.

As I wrote in a language other than my own, the editing of the manuscript was of particular importance. I cannot be grateful enough for the scrupulous professional care with which S. W. Bailey, the former Chief of the Language Services at the United Nations Office at Geneva, accomplished this part of the work, and for his stylistic suggestions. In particular, the Historical Background has gained considerably by his contribution. I am also deeply indebted to Sheila Bailey, who compiled the Index.

I must also record my very deep appreciation of the effective and indispensable assistance given in Geneva in the more menial but nonetheless essential fields of typing the manuscript and checking points of detail, by Melissa Cutter, Margot Divorne, Doreen Wicky, Jean Hatfield, Elizabeth Gibson, and Lilian Warry. Melissa Cutter also helped with the research in Tripoli, as did Ida Klein.

Last, there is my wife. I can find no words capable of describing the encouragement, patience, and forbearance she has shown over the almost five years with which she has had to live with the manuscript and the many irritations, inconveniences, and general upheaval in the home which its preparation has, inevitably, entailed.

A. P.

Hermance, Tripoli, Geneva, 1964–69

NOTE ON TRANSLITERATION

The system of transliteration of Arabic personal names followed is essentially that adopted jointly by the Board of Geographic Names of the United States and the Permanent Committee on Geographical Names of the United Kingdom, the so-called "BGN/PCGN" system. However, for the sake of simplicity, all diacritical marks have been eliminated, no attempt being made to distinguish, for example, between the various "s," "d," and "t" sounds for which the Arabic alphabet has separate letters. The same system has been employed for geographical names, except in the case of one or two generally familiar place names; where complete fidelity to the latest preferred map spellings would have required, for instance, "Tarablus" instead of "Tripoli," this has been avoided.

Libyan Independence and the United Nations

A CASE OF PLANNED DECOLONIZATION

HISTORICAL BACKGROUND

As explained in the Foreword, this study is not a history of Libya. It mainly covers events which occurred between the end of World War II and the declaration of Libyan independence on 24 December 1951. More particularly it deals with developments that took place during the years 1948–49 and 1950–51 when first the United Nations General Assembly and subsequently the Libyan people with United Nations assistance were shaping the country's political and constitutional future.

Yet the author must briefly refer to events of earlier periods to answer a question that inevitably comes to the mind of an observer of the Libyan scene: Why were the three territories which comprise the Libyan State so profoundly divided in the past, and what forces and events prepared a basis for union? The answer will help dispel the not infrequent misunderstanding that the Libyan people before 1949 had never considered unification and independence, and that the form of government they chose for themselves was imposed by outsiders.

For hundreds of years, it is true, the history of Libya was of events in separate Tripolitania, Cyrenaica, and the Fezzan; there appears to have been little or no political interplay between the three territories, though several times, and for quite lengthy periods, they were under the same foreign rule. Nor did there exist between them economic ties sufficiently strong to create a sense of common interest. This lack of cohesion remained even after the Arab invasions, when the Arabic language and the Islamic religion spread over North Africa, especially among the coastal urban and the rural Berber populations. When early in 1950 the Commissioner visited the small bilingual or solely Berber-speaking villages near the Libyan-Tunisian border, their inhabitants did not even claim to be a racial or linguistic minority.

The forces which for so long a time had kept the three territories separated were as much geographical as historical in nature.

The vast bulk of Libya's 680,000 square miles lies within the Sahara, the centers of habitation being scattered like islands in an ocean of sand,[1] mostly at oases where subsoil water is available. Rainfall is highly irregular, nowhere plentiful, and droughts are frequent. The Sahara and the Mediterranean meet almost without interruption for more than 300 miles between Misurata and Agedabia, a formidable barrier that virtually separated Tripolitania and Cyrenaica as long as land communications between the two depended on foot or camel transport.

The Fezzan, whose people clustered about three main chains of oases near Sabhah, Murzuq, and Brach, is separated by hundreds of miles of sandy or rocky desert from the coastal settlement of the two other territories. Physical conditions alone, therefore, made human contacts extremely difficult during centuries of Libyan history—in fact until modern technologies and ideologies overcame the barrier.

To this must be added that, because of their geographical separation as well as their different history, before the Arab invasions, the three territories also had different, almost centrifugal, orientations and outlooks on the outside world. For centuries Tripolitania was considered part of the Maghreb. It was for a long time under Roman rule. Its people have looked for political inspiration toward the Near East only since the fairly recent emergence of Arab nationalism. Cyrenaica, on the other hand, originally colonized by Greeks, was inclined to look toward the lands around the Eastern Mediterranean. The Fezzan, in contrast to both, appears to have had a seminomadic life of its own in Mid-Sahara, although camel caravans touching its oases carried merchandise between Central African and European markets via North African ports of which Tripoli was one.

This sketch of the conditions that for so long a period of time prevented a rapprochement of the three territories now comprising the Kingdom of Libya must be balanced by relating a bit more extensively those factors which, in a slow process of evolution, contributed to preparing the ground for eventual unification.

The Arab conquest laid some foundations for a union of the area along the southern shore of the Mediterranean, but its unifying effect was to become recognized only in a later day of nationalistic feeling—the area being for long years split by tenacious tribal and parochial feuds and rivalries. A succession of fourteen occupations over three centuries left no imprint. More important was the effect of Turkish rule after the occupation of Cyrenaica in 1517 and the taking of Tripoli from the Knights of St. John of Jerusalem in 1551. The sea power of the expanding empire of sixteenth-century Turkey gave the inhabitants of the Libyan towns an alternative to

1. See map, Annex XIV.

control by European naval powers so that the Turks were invited to come by their coreligionists. The Turkish rule was rather nominal, confined to garrisons in principal coastal towns and their immediate neighborhood keeping order and collecting some taxes with occasional forays into the countryside. The Sublime Porte required only that the annual tribute be paid.

In 1710, the Turkish Governor of Tripoli, Ahmed Bey Karamanli, broke away from Constantinople. The family dynasty, asserting a feudal autonomy replacing Turkish rule in Cyrenaican towns as well, was known to the Western world for its acts of piracy, which brought upon it a punitive naval foray from the fledgling United States of America. The Sublime Porte reasserted its somnolent, stagnating authority in Libya in 1835, which lasted until the Italo-Turkish War of 1911–12.

Turkish rule was superficially unifying since Libya under a single suzerain had uniform administrative terminology, though the rule little affected the tribes away from the littoral and administrative centers. There the sedentary population showed more appreciation for such protection as the regime brought them. Hence, it is not surprising that an authority like Evans-Pritchard considers the Turkish administration of Libya, and Cyrenaica in particular, "an important influence in [Libya's] development." [2]

Arab nationalism, born of Islamic traditions and influenced by Western ideas and fear of foreign domination, was growing into a virile force violently critical of Turkish rule, but the religion that Turk and Arab had in common remained a strong bond between them. In Libya, at least some of the intelligentsia of the coastal belt were attracted by the Young Turk movement. Tripolitanian, Cyrenaican, and Fezzanese representatives in 1908 went to Constantinople to participate in the Young Turk Parliament. However, when the promises of reform were not observed, with the exception of the right to use Arabic in the courts, enthusiasm soon evaporated. Moreover, when it was learned that the Young Turks planned to abolish the Caliphate and to establish a pan-Ottoman empire under Turkish rule, the Arab world, including Libya, was swept by a wave of opposition, particularly strong among the tribes. Some observers, however, committed an error of judgment when they mistook this opposition for a desire to secede from the Empire. Both in Cyrenaica and in Tripolitania the sedentary population as well as the Bedouin wished to maintain the Caliphate. At the same time they wanted Arab autonomy within a reformed biracial Ottoman empire. It also was at this time that the first indications appeared of a desire

2. E. E. Evans-Pritchard, *The Sanusi of Cyrenaica* (Oxford: Oxford University Press, 1949), pp. 90–101.

to establish closer relationships between the two coastal provinces than had existed before—an expression of nascent Arab nationalism.

One by-product of all this turmoil is worth mentioning: it indirectly obliged the Sublime Porte to enter into agreements with the French and United Kingdom Governments to delimit the frontiers of the territories contiguous to Libya for which they were responsible, if only to eliminate potential additional sources of friction with these powers. This put Libya—previously a vague and variable geographical concept—on the map, in the most literal sense of the phrase, as an identifiable territorial unit. Subsequently, other frontier agreements were concluded between Italy and these powers with a similar effect.

It may be doubted, however, whether Arab nationalism alone would have been a strong enough ferment to bring about any genuine form of Libyan unity if, in the first part of the nineteenth century, another unifying element had not come on the scene: the Sanusiya Order. A description worthy of this order of Islam would exceed the limits of the present study. However, in view of the leading part played by its present Head in the emergence of the Libyan State, a brief summary of the Order's history is indispensable. The author quite frankly draws upon the work of others for this description and analysis.[3]

The founder of the Sanusiya, al-Sayed Mohamed bin Ali al-Senussi, known later as the Grand Senussi, was born at Mostaganem, in Algeria, of a distinguished Sharif family, about the end of the eighteenth century. (His grandson, His Majesty King Idris I, gives it as 12 Rabi, 1202 A.H., corresponding to 22 December 1787.) He traced his descent from Fatima, the daughter of the Prophet. After studying law and theology at the Qaraniniyin Mosque University at Fez, in Morocco, he set out at the age of about thirty to travel the Saharan regions of Algeria preaching the faith. He continued his journey through Tripolitania and Cyrenaica to Cairo, where he fell foul of the local ulema who considered him unorthodox, indeed heretical. He therefore went on to Mecca, where, after some time spent in the company of the Wahhabites, the radical nature of his religious reformism again incited the wrath of the ulema. In 1843 he left Mecca for Cyrenaica—the people of which he had come to know and respect on his outward journey—where he established the Mother Lodge of his Order at al-Bayda, near Cyrene, between Benghazi and Derna. His teachings and proselytizing were not greatly to the liking of the Turks, who had just regained control in Libya.

3. An outstanding authority on Sanusiya is E. E. Evans-Pritchard, whose masterly and comprehensive study contains a mass of information with an immediate bearing on the events of 1950 and 1951. It is commended to the reader interested in the antecedents of Libyan unity and independence. See ibid.

They began to harass him, causing him to withdraw in 1855 to Jaghbub (Jarabub), a small oasis some 30 miles northwest of Siwa, where he died in 1859.[4]

By this time the concepts and organization of the Order were firmly established as they have continued to the present. One may quote to summarize:

> The Sanusiya is an Order of Sufis or, as they are sometimes called, Darwishes. They are Sunni or orthodox Muslims. This means that in faith and morals they accept the teachings of the Koran and the *Sunna,* a collection of traditions about the life and habits of the Prophet, whose example in all matters should be followed by believers. . . .
>
> The Sanusiya is, therefore, a highly orthodox Order. It is not a sect, but a *fraternity.*[5]

> But the rise of the Sanusi movement, a religious revival not unlike the Wahhabi movement, gave a sense of unity and supplied leadership which proved to be Cyrenaica's greatest asset.[6]

> Another thing which Sanusiyah achieved in the area [Cyrenaica] is the creation of a feeling of unity. This was again based on religious ties but eventually it expressed itself in political military and nationalistic aspects. To a certain extent Sanusiyah created a feeling of common interest among its followers in Libya on the economic level, and this was helped by, and in turn helped to cement, other bonds and ties.[7]

The Grand Senussi was succeeded by his younger son, al-Sayed Mohamed al-Mahdi. Under al-Mahdi, Sanusiya flourished exceedingly, *zawiyas* being established from Fez to Damascus, and from Constantinople to India.[8] Al-Mahdi's sway—which was that of a territorial sovereign—radiated from Jaghbub as far as Darfur, Wadai, and Bornu in the south, Bilma and Murzuq in the west, and to the Cyrenaican-Tripolitanian coastal strip in the north. All the oases in the Libyan desert were occupied and cultivated; trade with Tripoli and Benghazi was encouraged; and law and order were maintained among the normally unruly Bedouin of the desert. One is struck by the fact that the rigorous orthodoxy of the Order suited the Bedouin of

4. Nicola A. Ziadeh, *Sanusiyah: A Study of a Revivalist Movement in Islam* (Leiden, Netherlands: E. J. Brill, 1958), pp. 48 ff. and footnotes.

5. Evans-Pritchard, p. 1. Italics added.

6. Majid Khadduri, *Modern Libya: A Study in Political Development* (Baltimore: Johns Hopkins Press, 1963), p. 8.

7. Ziadeh, pp. 45 and 127.

8. A *Zawiya* or lodge is the Islamic equivalent of a monastery and center of learning.

Cyrenaica, who in all essentials were leading a life like that of the Bedouin in Arabia in the seventh century among whom Islam first spread.[9]

Al-Mahdi's fame grew so rapidly and extensively that Sultan Abdul Hamid II began to fear that he would soon exercise more real power than the Pasha in Benghazi. Accordingly, in 1889, the latter appeared at Jaghbub with a body of troops. In the face of this and other threats, al-Mahdi abandoned Jaghbub in 1895 for the village of Jawf in the Kufrah group of oases. Here he was faced with a new danger: the advance of the French from central Africa. He, therefore, moved still farther south to Dar Guran, in the western marches of Wadai, where he built a stronghold at Geru to check the French advance; but, like his father, he never waged an aggressive war, content to pursue, and if necessary to defend, the religious activities of the Order. He died at Geru in 1902 after the French had captured Bir Alali.

Both al-Mahdi's sons were minors; the succession, therefore, went to their cousin, Ahmed al-Sherif. The latter was soon compelled by mounting French pressure to withdraw from Geru. Finding neither solace nor support in the Central Sudan, he returned to Jawf. He had many adherents in Egypt, where he was well regarded by both the British and Egyptian authorities. The fact that France had already recognized the desert as within the British zone of interest, therefore, caused him no anxiety. In the meantime, his young cousin, the son of al-Mahdi, Sayed Mohamed Idris al-Mahdi al-Senussi, the first and present King of Libya, hereafter referred to as Sayed Idris, had settled in Alexandria. Al-Sayed Ahmed al-Sherif soon succumbed to the maneuvers of Abdul Hamid II, with consequences that will be described, together with the later course of Sanusiya, when we deal with the Italo-Turkish war and the Italian occupation of Libya from 1912 until 1942–43.

The decisive element in the development of Sanusiya as it affected, and generally favored, the unification of Libya was its immediate and intense appeal to the proud warrior Bedouin of Cyrenaica. The tenets of Sanusiya inspired fearless and fanatical defenders of the Faith, renowned for ruthlessness and tenacity alike. Not for nothing were they descended from the Beni Hilal and the Beni Suleim warriors. So rigid was their orthodoxy that they were even ready to attack the Turks, who, to them, were not true sons of the Prophet; yet, when the latter were attacked by the infidel Italians, they at once came to their help. It was the tradition of Sanusiya brotherhood that gave them the strength to resist the Italians for nearly twenty years between the two world wars, and led them to drop their internal differences and turn to the grandson of the Grand Senussi as their spiritual and temporal leader.

9. Evans-Pritchard, p. 4.

Lest the reader wonder how a single family could achieve such widespread effects within little more than the span of three generations, it may be added that, at the height of its authority, the Order had no fewer than forty-five zawiyas in Cyrenaica, another eighteen in Tripolitania, fifteen in the Fezzan, and six in the Kufrah oases. In other words, considerably more than half of the 146 lodges in northeast Africa, the Sudan, Egypt, and Arabia lay in what is now the United Kingdom of Libya.[10]

THE ITALO-TURKISH WAR, 1911–12

Accounts of the military aspects of the Italo-Turkish war, 1911–12, since they have already been recorded by various authors, may be omitted from this study, but some of the war's political repercussions are inherent parts of Libya's emancipation.

The significant feature of the fighting was the way in which the Arabs, both in Tripolitania and in Cyrenaica, came unhesitatingly to the help of the Turks. Without the support of and reinforcements provided by both the sedentary people and the Bedouin, the Turks could not have held out for very long. That the Turkish commander in Tripolitania did in fact receive their help was largely due to two men: Chief Kohanad Bey Fashat al-Zawi, and Sulayman al-Baruni, a Berber, the former deputy for Tripoli and the latter deputy for the Jebel Nefusa in the Young Turk Parliament.

Khadduri has explained this closing of the Arab-Turkish ranks in the following words:

> It was the religious tie between Libya and the Ottoman Empire that prompted Libyans to fight with the Ottoman forces, preferring to remain the loyal subjects of a Muslim ruler than to become Europeanized citizens under Christian rule. Thus, when Italy was able to force the Sultan to surrender his sovereignty over Libya . . . the legal transfer of sovereignty . . . seemed meaningless to Muslims, who fought the war not in the name of Ottoman sovereignty over Libya but in the name of Islam.[11]

It was, indeed, the Senussi who in the course of subsequent events bore the brunt of the fighting on the Arab side. As a result of the existence of what Evans-Pritchard has termed a "Turco-Senussi condominium" in Cyrenaica before World War I, the tribes first began to see themselves as a nation through the Sanusiya's relations with the Turkish Administration.[12] Faithful to the Senussi concept of the Islamic creed, to which the separation

10. Ibid., chart, pp. 24–25.
11. Khadduri, p. 11.
12. Evans-Pritchard, p. 98.

of Church and State is incomprehensible, the Order, under pressure of external events such as the growing influence in Africa of Great Britain and France, had become more and more of a theocracy. Thus, when Italy invaded Libya, it was only natural that Turk and Libyan should fight shoulder to shoulder against the common Christian and Western aggressor. It is, perhaps, from this moment that the birth of Arab nationalism in Libya became a policy worth fighting for, the sense of belonging both to one another and to the universal Pan-Arabic movement—a sense that was later to inspire the demand for independence under Senussi rule.

THE ITALIAN OCCUPATION, 1912–23

The events of the next thirty years need not here detain us as long as might be expected, as many of the happenings of this period and their implications for the future Kingdom of Libya will be more comprehensible if they are described or referred to at the proper place in the body of the narrative. However, a few of these events must be highlighted at the outset of this study.

On 13 October 1912, two days before the Treaty of Ouchy was signed, the reigning Sultan, Mohammed V, under pressure from the native leaders, issued a firman granting full autonomy to Cyrenaica and Tripolitania, but entrusting the protection of Ottoman rights to his representatives there. This arrangement became part of the Treaty. Ahmed al-Sherif and the Tripolitanian leaders interpreted this as a declaration of the independence of their respective territories, and therefore, at the urging of Sulayman al-Baruni, pressed on with the war, helped by Turkish troops remaining in the country in violation of the peace treaty.

The Italian Government, on the other hand, interpreted the firman as meaning that the King of Italy would in due course determine the terms of Libyan autonomy and define the status of the Sultan's representative under Italian sovereignty. The Treaty itself was ambiguous, and it soon became apparent that "the Sultan had gone out by the front door only to return by the back." [13] All of this merely added to the confusion, which Arabs and Berbers alike were quick to turn to their temporary advantage. The am-

13. Ibid., p. 114. Pages 112–17 of this work give a penetrating analysis of this obscure diplomatic passage of arms between Italy and Turkey. See also Khadduri, pp. 11–12. De Leone criticizes the Italian Government services of the time for insufficient knowledge of Libya, its people, and their customs. Enrico de Leone, *La Colonizzazione dell'Africa del Nord* (Padova, Italy: Cedam-Casa Editrice Dott. Antonio Milani, 1960), pp. 375–448.

biguity of the Treaty was not the only cause of misunderstanding. The Italians had expected the Libyans to greet them as "liberators" from Turkish "oppression." This was a complete misreading of the situation; it should have been foreseen that the religious bond of Islam would prove far stronger than the Libyans' political distaste for certain aspects of Turkish rule. When they realized their mistake, the Italians embarked upon a major military operation. They overran part of the country without, however, really succeeding in putting an end to resistance, though Sulayman al-Baruni fled to Istanbul in March 1913.

As Khadduri has said, "to occupy the country by force . . . was one thing and to control it was another." [14] Envor Pasha visited Ahmed al-Sherif at Jaghbub, whither the latter had repaired from Kufrah in September 1912, and found little difficulty in persuading him to carry on the struggle in Cyrenaica as the Sultan's representative. After this visit, all official documents issuing from the headquarters of the Order were stamped *al-Hukuma al-Sanusiya*: the Sanusiya Government. Any remaining Italian hopes or illusions that the leader of the Senussi would stand idly by were brutally dispelled, and the long fight was on.

The outbreak of World War I was the signal for a tribal rising in the Sirte and the Fezzan. The war was further marked by increased resistance in Cyrenaica, which had been the scene of much fighting in 1912 and 1913. Had military action been better coordinated between the coastal territories and the inland tribes, Italy's position in Libya might have become untenable. As it was, tribal feuding and Tripolitanian reluctance to accept Senussi leadership weakened resistance.

Unfortunately, too, Ahmed al-Sherif had succumbed to the pressures of the Turkish officers in his camp, who had been infiltrated into Cyrenaica by devious routes and means. By them he was persuaded to declare a holy war on the British and to invade western Egypt. However, he at first hesitated to put his plans into effect. This gave the British in Egypt time to send Sayed Idris from Alexandria to Jaghbub to wean his cousin from his unwelcome advisers. Nevertheless, the latter embarked on the invasion at the end of 1915. At the outset he even achieved some success, but prompt action by the British military in Egypt circumscribed his attacks, and forestalled sympathetic risings among the Bedouin of western Egypt and the Nile valley. By the beginning of 1916, Ahmed was back in Jaghbub, utterly defeated. He handed over military and political control of the affairs of the Order to Sayed Idris and after a vain attempt to play a part in Tripolitania, ceased all activity.

14. Khadduri, p. 13.

This diversion inevitably put an end for a time to serious resistance against the Italians in Cyrenaica, and in 1917, Sayed Idris, supported by a number of Senussi leaders, and assisted by the United Kingdom Government, concluded an agreement with the Italian Government at Akrama, near Tubruq, providing for the cessation of hostilities, the recognition of Italian and Senussi zones in Cyrenaica, with freedom of movement between them, the responsibility of each party for security in its zone, and the disarming of the tribes. At the same time, the Senussi chiefs acknowledged Sayed Idris as Grand Senussi. Shortly thereafter, Ahmed al-Sherif, deeming discretion the better part of valor, and not wishing to embarrass his cousin, secretly boarded a German U-boat at Misurata, eventually making his way to Istanbul. He never returned to his homeland, and from this time on Sayed Idris was undisputed religious and political leader of Sanusiya.

This improvement in relations with the Italians was enhanced when, after the war, Italy, with a more liberal view of colonial policy, exhausted by its efforts and unable to sustain large-scale military action overseas, decided to change its attitude toward Cyrenaica and Tripolitania. Statutes were prepared for the two territories allowing for a limited amount of self-government adapted to the local conditions peculiar to each, including elected provincial parliaments to advise and assist the Italian administration. The Cyrenaican Parliament met five times before it was dismissed in 1923; the Tripolitanian assembly never met at all, apparently because of internal rivalries and dissension—a case of coming events casting their shadow before.

In the case of Cyrenaica, this policy of indirect administration was reflected in the agreement of al-Rajma (Regima), concluded with Sayed Idris in 1920. This replaced the Akrama agreement, and granted Sayed Idris the hereditary title of Amir (Prince), recognized him as the ruler of an autonomous area in Cyrenaica, and guaranteed him sundry perquisites in return for an undertaking that he would disband his forces outside that area. When he failed to carry out this undertaking—being, in fact, in no position to do so without waging war against his own followers—a third agreement was concluded at Bu Naryam in 1921, providing for joint control of the forces in question.

In the meantime, the Italians had been trying to come to similar terms in Tripolitania. There was, however, no local chief or leader whose authority was predominantly recognized throughout the territory. Aware of this weakness, a number of Tripolitanian leaders had endeavored to reconcile their differences by declaring an independent republic, which was to play a significant part in Libyan history. With the government of this Republic, the Italian Government, to the disgust of some of its military leaders in

Tripoli, negotiated the agreement of Kallet al-Zaituna in the spring of 1919, granting it on 1 June a Statute (*Legge fondamentale per la Tripolitania*) providing for a parliament, and granting other concessions conferring some limited form of self-government.

THE TRIPOLITANIAN REPUBLIC, 1918–23

The episode of the Tripolitanian Republic consists of a series of confused and sometimes obscure events, and such accounts as are to be found of them frequently do not correspond with one another.

Evans-Pritchard, writing about them thirty years later, notes that toward the end of World War I, the Arabs were more than ever convinced of Italy's impotence. An Arab republic, founded in 1918, the *Jumhuriya al-Trabulsiya,* theoretically ruled the country through a Committee of Reform at Misurata under the chairmanship of Ramadan al-Shetaywi. In practice, there was little order of any kind.[15]

Khadduri, too, observes that the internal situation was far from satisfactory; for, as in Cyrenaica, Italy's weak position in Tripolitania much encouraged the native leaders to press for independence, whereas the Italians themselves wished to control the country through the native leaders. Nor could the latter, weakened as they were by internal rivalries, organize a resistance movement—a situation fully appreciated by the Italians; which was why they never agreed to make the same far-reaching concessions as they had done in Cyrenaica. Lastly, Khadduri notes that these same rivalries lay at the origin of the decision to appoint a council of four notables, assisted by an Egyptian, Abd al-Rahman Azzam, instead of a single Head of State to govern the new Republic.[16]

Two authors have dealt with the Tripolitanian Republic in great detail: on the Arab side, Sheikh al-Tahir Amad al-Zawi, now living in Cairo;[17] on the Italian side, Enrico de Leone, of the University of Cagliani.[18]

15. Evans-Pritchard, p. 147.

16. Khadduri, p. 21. After World War II, Abd al-Rahman Azzam, as Azzam Bey, became the first Secretary-General of the newly founded League of Arab States, a post he occupied from 1945 to 1952. He later became known as Azzam Pasha, a name by which he is also referred to in this study where appropriate.

17. Al-Tahir Ahmad al-Zawi, *Jihad al-Abtal fi Tarabulus al-Gharb* (*The Holy War of the Heroes in Tripoli*) (Cairo: Imprimerie Tajellah al-Jedidah, 1950), pp. 223–48, 296–330, and 330–31. Available in Arabic only. Sheikh al-Zawi has assured the writer that the documents reproduced in his work are authentic copies of the originals, an assurance that is gladly accepted. Nevertheless, having regard to the fact that no complete English translation of this book exists, the writer has in the majority of cases preferred to paraphrase extracts from it in this historical

Both al-Zawi and de Leone mention Azzam Bey's presence and activities in Tripolitania at this time. The latter alleges that the British were behind Azzam Bey; he also expresses the belief that Azzam Bey acted on Sayed Idris' behalf with their knowledge. Evans-Pritchard states that the Republic was founded at the instigation of the Turks and Germans. From al-Zawi's account, which is confirmed by de Leone, it seems that Azzam Bey became the Republic's moving spirit and mind behind its organization.

Azzam Pasha himself, in a private communication to the author, dated 26 July 1966, said that he was "elected the adviser of *Maglis el Comhour* (Assembly of the People) which had four members to represent the whole country and the sovereignty of the State." He added that "the Republic's declaration of independence (in November 1918) and practically every other document in that period was prepared by me." It is the present author's impression that he was moved above all by a strong sense of Arab nationalism.

Referring to the historical importance of the Tripolitanian Republic, Azzam Pasha quoted the opinion of an educated, middle-aged Libyan with whom, shortly before writing his letter, he had been discussing Libya's struggle for freedom, particularly in Tripoli between 1915 and 1925. The latter had said: "It is all distorted, and . . . the truth about that period with its republic is completely hashed, while it was the seed of independence, the real national struggle which made the Libyans conscious of themselves as an entity of people."

These last words correctly reflect the feelings of most educated Tripolitanians, but they are an exaggeration when applied to the Libyan people as a whole. The Tripolitanian Republic remained in most respects a provincial venture. Hence, a detailed account of it would be at variance with the purpose of this work, which is to deal with Libya's unity and independence as a whole. In any case, the available documentary evidence is too contradictory to allow this to be done comprehensively and objectively. Azzam Pasha was right when he told the writer that he would "find himself now

résumé rather than to quote them verbatim. The paraphrases have been prepared from a translation of the three sections enumerated above, made by Frank H. Stewart of the University of Cambridge, England, who was also responsible for the translation of the *Proceedings of the National Constituent Assembly of Libya* (see Chap. 6, p. 429, fn. 2). Stewart's translation is being deposited in the Library at the United Nations Office in the Palais des Nations in Geneva. The reader may assume, therefore, that where there is no specific reference to another author, the source throughout this section is al-Zawi.

18. De Leone, *La Colonizzazione dell'Africa del Nord*. The Secretariat of the Società italiana per la Organizzazione Internationale in Rome kindly had an English translation made of the relevant parts of Volume II of this book for the writer's use.

and then in trouble digging for the reality." The use in this context of the words "now and then" was an understatement. But it is much to be hoped that one day the full story will be told dispassionately, for in one respect the Tripolitanian Republic created a precedent of fundamental importance for the ultimate establishment of the Libyan State.

So far as it is possible to reconstruct the sequence of events from the two main sources available, the decision to create the Republic was taken on the spur of the moment, when Othman Fuad Pasha, the Commander-in-Chief of such Turkish troops as remained in Libya at the time and the embodiment of Turkish "sovereignty" in Tripolitania, was informed by wireless from Constantinople early in November 1918 that Turkey had surrendered to the Allied Powers. It must be remembered that, as a result of the different interpretations placed on the Treaty of Lausanne (Ouchy) by the signatories, the Arabs in Tripolitania still regarded the Caliph as their sovereign in 1918.[19]

They also continued to receive such small quantities of war supplies as could be landed from German and Turkish submarines. Moreover, Sulayman al-Baruni, the Berber chief, who, after having played a large part in fighting the Italians, had left Tripolitania for Constantinople in 1913, had reappeared in 1915 with a firman from the Sultan appointing him Governor-General of Tripolitania and instructing him to continue the struggle against Italy. The hierarchical relationship between Fuad and al-Baruni is not clear.

The former's orders were to leave Tripolitania with his officers in a German submarine which, indeed, arrived at Misurata to pick him up. Apparently, however, as the result of a series of misunderstandings, and perhaps also because of Azzam Bey's hope of continuing the struggle with Turkish and German assistance, the ship sailed without taking anybody on board.[20] Subsequently it became clear not only that Turkish war supplies would be cut off, but also that the country would be left without a government. In these circumstances, the idea of proclaiming a republic, if only to maintain some sort of order, emerged quite naturally in the course of discussions held between Fuad Pasha and the notables present at Misurata. It was even suggested that he should accept the Presidency, but this offer he declined, while agreeing to the idea of a republic. The heads and leaders of the tribes were then invited on his behalf to hold an assembly in the Al-Majabra Mosque at Misallata to proclaim the Republic. The meeting was held on 16 November 1918. Al-Zawi says that people from all over

19. See Evans-Pritchard, pp. 113–15.

20. Later, Fuad Pasha and a small number of Turkish, German, and Austrian officers and lower ranks surrendered to the French, who handed them over to the Italian authorities for repatriation. See de Leone, pp. 482–83.

Tripolitania responded to the invitation, but according to de Leone there was a good deal of hesitation among some of the Sheikhs, who feared that the proclamation of a Republic might provoke a fresh clash between Arabs and Italians. But both agree that the attitude of the Italian authorities when confronted with this new development lacked consistency.

Fuad Pasha invited Azzam Bey to address the audience on his behalf. The latter, who is an eloquent orator, seems to have made a rousing speech calling for the utmost sacrifices in defense of the homeland and for the Arab cause in general until the achievement of independence and the expulsion of the enemy from the country. He also called for collaboration and solidarity (literally "reciprocated brotherhood" in the Arabic), and ended by proposing the establishment of a "Tripolitanian Republic" under a national government whose writ would run from the Cyrenaican to the Tunisian border. In view of Fuad Pasha's refusal to accept the Presidency, and in the absence of a generally recognized national leader, it was decided to set up a Council of Four. Elections were held forthwith, and resulted in Sulayman al-Baruni, Ramadan al-Shetaywi al-Suwayhili, Abd al-Nabi Bin Khayr, and Ahmad al-Murayyid becoming members of the Council, of which the last-named acted as chairman.[21]

The meeting also elected a Consultative Council of twenty-four members, equitably representing, as far as possible, the tribes and the urban population, as well as a Shari'a Council composed four ulema. All present then in turn swore on the Koran a solemn oath of homage and loyalty to the Republic.

Two days later the Council of the Republic, which established its headquarters at Aziziya in the Gefara plain about half way between Tripoli and Gharyan, announced the proclamation of the independent Republic to the world at large by sending messages to the Head of the Italian Government; to President Woodrow Wilson (referring to his famous Fourteen Principles); to the British Prime Minister (assuring him that Tripolitania looked to England as the protector of small nations); and to the Head of the French Government (reminding him of the deeds of the free French nation in proclaiming liberty).[22]

The opening paragraph stated:

> At 4.30 on Sat. 13 Safar 1337 [18 November 1918] the Tripolitanian nation resolved to set the crown on its independence by proclaiming a

21. Bin Khayr's name is sometime written Bilkhayr.

22. These messages and translations thereof are presumably also to be found in the State archives of the countries concerned.

Republic, in accordance with the views of its great scholars, its dignitaries and notables, and the leaders of the noble warriors in the holy war who have gathered here from all parts of the country.

The message to the Head of the Italian Government contained an additional paragraph to the effect that the Republic's sole ambition was to maintain unity and freedom within its recognized political frontiers, and its only wish to live contentedly and in peace with all nations which did not attempt to infringe its rights. Its Government therefore called upon the Italian Government to recognize it, and to do nothing that would oblige it to continue to fight until its legitimate aspirations were satisfied. The message was accompanied by an appendix setting out the conditions on which the Tripolitanian Government was prepared to discuss peace terms. These must have struck the Italians as impudent, to say the least. The most important of the ten conditions were:

1. An immediate standstill and truce based on the positional status quo.
2. Restriction of the movements of Italian warships and aircraft to the areas occupied by Italian forces.
3. A complete ban on private (presumably foreign) correspondence, and on Italian trade and propaganda in Tripolitania. All Italian entries, exits, and official correspondence and communications, the latter to be exclusively in writing, to be channeled through one point to be designated by the Tripolitanian Government.
4. Complete freedom of action and movement to be reserved to the Government of the Republic, especially in respect of contacts with those countries maintaining consulates in Tripoli (which, of course, included the British, the French, and the Americans).

From the Italian point of view, the leaders of the Republic were rebels, and their proposals were naturally rejected. Subsequently, prices were placed on the heads of some; others were sentenced to political detention. But these measures were suspended shortly afterward and, as a result of more liberal policies introduced by Rome, negotiations were opened with the Republic. Al-Zawi and de Leone, though differing greatly on points of detail, agree that the negotiations ran into serious difficulties. Nevertheless, they eventually led to the agreement of Kallet al-Zaituna.

Neither the foundation of the Republic nor the al-Zaituna agreement appears to have been attended by much success, and it was not long before sporadic fighting broke out, both among the Tripolitanians themselves and between them and the Italians. In particular, in the early months of 1920, Ramadan al-Shetaywi embarked upon hostilities in eastern Tripolitania from his base at Misurata, not only rousing the Italians to retaliation, but also bringing together in the spring of 1920 a number of local chiefs in an alliance pledged to put an end to his pretentious ambitions. Al-Shetaywi was defeated and killed at Banu Ulid, in Abd al-Nabi Bin Khayr's territory, in August 1920, whereupon Azzam Bey, who had been advising him, transferred his allegiance to Bin Khayr. From this moment the Republic was governed by a triumvirate. This incident had important political consequences.

It would be irrelevant to go into further detail, either about Tripolitania's internal difficulties or about the way in which the Italians tried to take advantage of them, in particular by fanning the latent antagonism between Arab and Berber.

What is more important is that the Tripolitanian leaders were slowly learning their lesson. Realizing that to perpetuate their quarrels could only increase the state of confusion that was rapidly moving toward chaos, they agreed in principle to call an assembly of notables in the Jebel city of Gharyan, some 75 miles south of Tripoli, in November 1920.[23] A preparatory meeting held in Aziziya in October 1920 drew up an agenda after a week's work.

Among the decisions taken by the preparatory meeting was one to the effect that a delegation should be appointed to promote peace negotiations between Arabs and Berbers. Moreover, members of the Gharyan Conference were to be elected in such a way as to make the gathering as representative as possible of all parts of Tripolitania. Election arrangements were to be put in hand forthwith. The negotiating delegation did not succeed in reconciling the warring factions, so that when the Conference assembled it was not as representative as its organizers had hoped. In particular, no Berbers attended. Even Sulayman al-Baruni refused to come, despite the fact that Ahmad al-Murayyid sent him a message offering to stand down from the Presidency in his favor.

The Conference, which lasted two weeks, unanimously elected Ahmad al-Murayyid as its President.

The Italian Government adopted a wary attitude toward the meeting, even though it had agreed to its being held.

The Conference took three important decisions.

First, it adopted a resolution asserting that the state the country had fallen into could be remedied only by the formation of a strong government,

23. Evans-Pritchard, p. 147, gives November 1921 as the date of the assembly; de Leone, p. 505, gives November 1920; and al-Zawi, pp. 296–307, states that the preparatory meeting took place in Muharram 1339 (October 1920) and the Conference itself at the beginning of Rabia I, 1339 (November 1920), which seems to be the most likely date.

founded on the principles of Islamic Law, and led by a Moslem personality to be chosen from the people and deposable only on valid grounds and by resolution of Parliament. This Moslem leader should be invested with all religious, civil, and military authority, in accordance with a constitution to be agreed upon by the nation acting through its representatives. He would rule over the whole country within its recognized borders.

Second, the Conference elected a national government of fourteen members, which came to be known in English as the Central Reform Board. It was presided over by Ahmad al-Murayyid, and Azzam Bey appears on the list of members in the capacity of "Counselor."

Third, the Conference resolved to send a delegation, headed by Khalid al-Qarqani, to Rome to inform the Italian Government of the steps it had taken and to secure recognition for the Republic.

As was only to be expected, the Italian reaction was far from conciliatory. In particular, Sayed Idris was told in no uncertain terms that any dealings on his part with the Tripolitanian Republic would be considered by the Government in Rome as equivalent to a breach of the al-Rajma agreement.

Luigi Mercatelli, then Governor of Tripoli, granted permission to the Gharyan delegation to proceed to Rome only with the greatest reluctance. It left Tripoli on 27 February 1921,[24] and was followed a few days later by another delegation "appointed by the Government and charged to support during meetings in Rome, in contrast with the other, . . . the motivations of the promoters of the organic law." [25]

De Leone reports that the first delegation succeeded in arranging a meeting with Luigi Rossi, Minister for the Colonies in the Giolitti Government, on 29 April 1921, but only after it had agreed that a number of Italian officers held as prisoners of war in Misurata should be set free. It was told by the Minister that only deputies freely elected by a local parliament could claim to be the legal representatives of the people of Tripolitania. He also admonished the members to observe and respect the colony's statute.

If al-Zawi's version of these events is to be believed, the Gharyan delegation tried to get in touch with members of the Italian Government and with influential people and parties in various parts of the country, but without success, especially in opening negotiations with the government; only the Socialist Party promised to help, always provided that the Italian prisoners of war were released, which was done. Al-Zawi condemns their liberation as an overhasty act, because according to him the Socialists failed to

24. According to al-Zawi, the delegation sailed in December 1920.

25. De Leone, pp. 506–07. Al-Zawi says that this "antidelegation" left early in 1921.

honor their side of the bargain. Meanwhile, the "antidelegation" traveled around Italy in constant rivalry with its Republican opposite numbers. Both delegations appear to have stayed in Italy for about nine months. After the return of the Republican delegation to Tripolitania relations between Arabs and Italians seem to have deteriorated again.

The decision of the Gharyan Conference to set up a strong government led by a Moslem Prince was more easily taken than put into practice. According to al-Zawi, when it conceived of this office—which was, of course, nothing other than the Amirate of Tripolitania—the Conference had had, he asserts, no particular person in mind to fill it; it had left the choice of leader until the time when the nation would need him.

On the other hand, de Leone asserts that the Italians were from the outset under the impression that the Tripolitanians had Sayed Idris in mind, and this belief made them all the more suspicious.

In July 1921, Mercatelli was replaced as Governor by Giuseppe Volpi, an energetic and capable administrator. It took him some months to find his bearings and to map out a policy acceptable to Rome. In Tripolitania the situation became more and more confused. Warfare between Arab and Berber tribes had broken out again, and the latter had suffered greatly. Volpi tried once more to negotiate a peace, but this only strengthened the Tripolitanian chiefs in their belief that the Italians were too weak to continue the war.

Events were bound to come to a head. On the Libyan side contacts had been established between Cyrenaicans and Tripolitanians. According to al-Zawi, the initiative was taken by some notables from Benghazi, and it was decided that a meeting should be held in January 1922 in Sirte between a delegation appointed by the Amir of Cyrenaica and another representing the Tripolitanian Central Reform Board.

Volpi, on the other hand, having learned about the planned meeting, set about preparing an expedition to take Misurata, the center of resistance in eastern Tripolitania.

The meeting at Sirte was not an easy one. For some years a coldness had prevailed between the parties owing to a number of misunderstandings and incidents. It took several sessions to reach agreement, but finally the following text was agreed upon:

> We, the signatories of this agreement, have met as representatives of Tripoli and Cyrenaica and have resolved, after discussion and thought, on the following articles, which embody an agreement of union and cooperation, in good times and in bad, between Tripolitania and Cyrenaica:

1. We are to unite against our enemy, who is trying to seize our country by force, and against those who are trying to sow dissension.
2. We are to have the same enemies and the same friends.
3. Neither side shall make claims on the other with regard to the aggressions which have occurred until the country is stabilized and its overall [political] structure has been fixed. Both parties must attempt to make peace among the Bedouin. Any further incursions are to be suitably punished by the government whose citizen is the guilty party.
4. Anyone who acts against the community and intrigues with the foreigners is to be executed and have his property confiscated by his government, in accordance with the Islamic Shari'a.
5. Both parties believe that the interests of the fatherland and the necessity of defending ourselves against the common enemy demand a united leadership of the country. It is therefore their aim to elect a Muslim Amir who is to have religious and civil power within the terms of a constitution to be approved of by the nation.
6. The two parties will take the necessary measures to achieve the aim mentioned in section 5. The Amir is to be placed in office by the will of the nation.
7. When the objective mentioned in section 5 has been attained, a constituent council is to be elected from the two parties. This council will establish the basic law and the governmental system of the country. Before this, as a preparatory measure, each of the two parties is to send a representative of the two towns, so that both of them may participate in the country's political activity and in taking the measures necessary to defend the fatherland.
8. The two parties undertake not to recognize the enemy's authority, and to prevent his influence from extending beyond the places to which it is at the moment limited. If war breaks out the two parties will ally to fight the enemy, and neither party shall agree to a peace or an armistice without the consent of the other.
9. If the enemy comes out of his fortresses and attacks one of the regions, the other region is to help the one attacked with the necessities of war, with money and with men, to warn the enemy against continuing his aggression, and, if the enemy does not stop, to attack in turn.
10. A body elected from among the inhabitants of Tripoli and Cyrenaica is to meet twice a year in the months of Muharram [October] and Rajab [April] to examine the country's affairs.
11. It is stipulated that this agreement is to be accepted by the Government of Cyrenaica and the Central Board of Tripolitania.
12. The task of the above mentioned body [Section 10] is to strengthen

the ties of friendship between the two parties and to strengthen this agreement.

Qaar Sirt

. . . 22 Jumada I 1340 / 21 January 1922.[26]

It is noteworthy that Sayed Idris is not mentioned in this text, an omission due as much to absence of agreement between the Tripolitanian leaders on his selection as Amir as to the need for their Cyrenaican counterparts to consult the tribal chiefs. Nevertheless, the Sirte Agreement is of historical importance not only for the reasons given in footnote 26 above, but also because it is the first of a series of agreements, or attempts to reach agreement, which ultimately led to the promulgation of the Constitution of the United Kingdom of Libya on 7 October 1951 and to the declaration of Libyan independence on 24 December of the same year.

When, five days after the Sirte meeting, the Tripolitanian leaders returned to Misurata, they found the city in flames. They immediately sent a messenger to seek from the Cyrenaican delegation military assistance in their struggle against the Italian forces that had attacked and occupied the city. However, no such help was forthcoming, apparently, according to al-Zawi, because the Amir wished first to receive a formal act of homage (Bay'a) from the Central Reform Board.

Meanwhile, on 3 March 1922, a truce had been concluded between this Board and the Italian authorities, and negotiations were opened at the Al-Sharif Hotel in Misurata. However, agreement proved impossible, the Italians wishing to limit the talks to Tripolitania whereas the Central Reform Board insisted on a unified government of Tripolitania and Cyrenaica as conceived at the Sirte meeting. Writing to Volpi on the subject, they invoked as one of their arguments that, before the Italian occupation, the two territories had been administered jointly under Ottoman rule. On this issue the negotiations broke down on 1 April 1922, and fighting was resumed. Aziziya was occupied by the Italians on 25 April, after the Government of the Republic had moved south to Gharyan.

However, even earlier, while still in Misurata, the Central Reform Board, realizing that cooperation between the two territories was becoming more and more necessary, resumed its discussions on the Amirate. The question was hotly debated. One of the main objections to Sayed Idris, according to al-Zawi, was the delay in implementing the Sirte Agreement and the fail-

26. The author has decided to quote this agreement in full, despite what is said on p. 13, fn. 17, because of its paramount importance as the first formal and public expression of Cyrenaica-Tripolitanian cooperation—the forerunner of Libyan unity. The Arabic text will be found in al-Zawi, pp. 296–307.

ure to send immediate aid from Cyrenaica to Tripoli at the time of the Italian occupation of Misurata.

Nevertheless, on 10 April 1922, the majority of the Board came out in favor of the Amirate of Sayed Idris, and it was decided to send a delegation to Adjabiyah to invite him to come to Tripolitania so that he might be publicly proclaimed Amir.[27] Sayed Idris declined, however, on the grounds that the weather was too hot and his health too poor. Indeed, he seems always to have been frail.

It so happened, moreover, that at the moment of the delegation's arrival Sayed Idris was meeting Giovanni Amendola, the then Italian Minister for Colonies. Subsequently, the delegation received a letter from the Amir dated, according to al-Zawi, 15 Dhu al-Quda 1340 (10 July 1922), stating that he had met the Minister and discussed the Tripolitanian question with him, and that it had been agreed that it would not be possible to end the war until the Tripolitanians communicated to the Italian Government their willingness to cease hostilities and come to an understanding with that Government, which, in those circumstances, would be prepared also to cease hostilities. The Amir added that the Minister had said that that was as far as he could go in attempting to bring about an understanding.

When the letter reached Gharyan, the Central Reform Board decided to accept Amendola's conditions, and to inform Volpi accordingly. But the latter did not reply, and the war went on.

The Government of the Republic accordingly came to the conclusion that the only thing to do was to send another delegation to Sayed Idris to offer him the Bay'a.[28]

After the customary introduction, the letter of transmittal went on:

> As Your Majesty well knows, we are still in conflict with the Italian Government, who wish to violate all our rights—legal, political and

27. Again there is some uncertainty about the date of the delegation's departure. Al-Zawi gives mid-Ramadan 1340, Moslem style, and June 1922, Gregorian style. But mid-Ramadan 1340 was mid-May 1922. Evans-Pritchard, p. 153, gives April, and differs also from al-Zawi in saying that the delegation offered the Prince "the Amirate of all Libya." April is the most likely date.

As to the territorial extent of the Amirate offered by the Gharyan Conference, Evans-Pritchard may be right. Indeed the letter of transmittal says: "It [the Central Reform Board] therefore gives its allegiance [*Bay'a*] to Your Majesty as Amir of the two regions of Tripolitania and Cyrenaica." As the Fezzan was part of Tripolitania in those days, the Amirate therefore may have been meant to cover all of Libya. When forty years later the author checked on this point with contemporaries of the events, most of them confirmed this impression.

28. According to Khadduri, p. 22, the delegation was headed by Beshir Bey Saadawi, whose name will appear frequently in the course of this study.

administrative. They have made their strength a justification for intervening in our fate and encroaching on our natural rights; but we are the finest nation known to man, and we will not accept oppression: we will not allow our holy law (shari'a) to vanish, and come what may we will not allow our true religion to be harmed. We have therefore faced all dangers and plunged into successive wars, relying on the strength of truth. [We shall fight on] until the hope of our nation is realized. That hope is to found a constitutional government, led by a Muslim Amir who is to unite religious, political and military powers, together with a representative assembly whose members are to be chosen by the nation. Through this our nation will be saved, our religion perfected, the laws of our judges made sound; our holy law and the glorious tradition of our history will be preserved. . . . The Italians have tried by various means to separate one part of the nation from another, but God has ordained that the two brother regions should be united under a single Amir.

Your Highness comes from the most noble and distinguished of families, and unites in his noble person the finest and most exalted qualities. Because of this, the Central Reform Board, possessing full power granted by the Gharyan Conference, which was composed of the elected representatives of the Tripolitanian nation, has found in Your Majesty a powerful and judicious Amir for the whole nation, and one who is universally trusted and loved. It therefore gives its allegiance (Bay'a) to Your Majesty as Amir of the two regions of Tripolitania and Cyrenaica, which you are to lead to the fulfillment of the noble aspirations we have referred to.

Everyone has wished for a Bay'a to you ever since representatives of the two regions met at Sirte; the delay in performing it has occurred because of the events which have imperilled both the members of the Board and the important men of the region in wide areas around the war zones.

By virtue of this Bay'a Your Majesty has become, God willing, the beloved Amir of the two blessed regions. And when it becomes possible for Your Majesty to visit us—in accordance with the wishes of the nation—a fitting ceremony of Bay'a will be arranged for you.

The letter, which is dated 3 Dhu-el-Hijja 1340 (28 July 1922), was signed by Ahmad al-Murayyid and Azzam Bey, in their official capacities, by thirteen members of the Board, and by eleven notables.[29]

29. The writer has again broken his self-appointed rule (see pp. 13 and 22, fnn. 17 and 26) in the case of the offer of the Bay'a and of the Amir's acceptance thereof, not only because of the intrinsic value of the two documents, but also in order to give the reader an opportunity to compare the terms of the two texts with those of 1950–51 (see Chap. 6, Pt. 1, pp. 458–60).

Sayed Idris hesitated even after he received this offer. Evans-Pritchard describes his attitude in the following terms:

> Before giving a reply he wished to consult Bedouin opinion, for it was on the Bedouin he would have to count were hostilities to break out. To this purpose he called, in October 1922, a large tribal gathering at Jardis al-'Abid. In the following month, under great pressure from his advisers, and still hesitating in his own mind, he accepted the Amirate. It must by this time have been apparent to him that the Italians intended to make war whatever course he took and that he might, in that case, just as well have the Tripolitanian Arabs as allies.[30]

In 1950 and 1951, when discussing the Libyan situation as it was during the summer and autumn of 1922 with Tripolitanian and Cyrenaican contemporaries of these events, the writer found that Evans-Pritchard was fairly close to the mark.

In replying to the Tripolitanian Bay'a, the Amir, after the customary opening courtesies, went on in the following solemn strain:

> I am grateful to receive the petition by which you demonstrated your sincere desire to carry out the objective which you agreed on at the Gharian conference, and for which you have fought faithfully in the Holy War, hazarding your lives and your property for my sake. I accept your petition praying to God that he will fulfill the hopes of this nation and crown all its efforts with success.
>
> Since the unification of the fatherland and its safety are the objectives for which I have always striven, I consider it my duty to accede to your request, and to take upon myself the great responsibility which the nation has seen fit to lay upon me. It is therefore incumbent on me to work with you with all my strength; but do not forget that without your boldness and your efforts I am powerless to achieve anything.
>
> I know that immortality is a quality reserved to nations, not to individuals, and that the great and enduring works are those directed at the general good. I therefore pray to God—blessed and exalted be he—that he may guide us to every action that will benefit the nation.
>
> Every people has the right to direct its own affairs, and men are free from birth. Throughout the various stages of their history our people have shown how great is their love of freedom, and have paid a high price to attain it. No-one is justified in trying to enslave them or to tyrannize them.
>
> You have stipulated that there should be a parliament: such a body is the foundation of our religion, and I shall act in accordance with this

30. Evans-Pritchard, p. 155.

principle. For the moment I wish to confirm the existing state of affairs, until a national assembly meets to draw up a constitution. In view of the zeal, the justice, and the good sense which it has shown, I entrust to the Central Reform Board the continued administration of Tripolitania. I have deep faith in the wisdom of its determined and heroic President, Ahmad al-Marid, of its members and of the noble chiefs who helped this sacred body in its efforts to bear with fortitude the burdens of responsibility in order to strengthen the foundations they have laid for our fatherland.

The letter, which is dated 22 Rabi'I, 1341 (12 November 1922), concludes with the usual valedictory phrases.[31]

To the best of the writer's knowledge, this is the first official document in Libyan history to proclaim the "unification of the fatherland" as an aim of national policy.

The Amir's vision of events to come was right. The Italians indeed meant business both in Tripolitania (including the Fezzan) and in Cyrenaica, and Volpi had little difficulty in persuading the new fascist government, which had ousted its leftish predecessor at the end of 1922, to give him a free hand. This led to the collapse of the first and only Republic of Tripolitania, which nonetheless had two achievements to its credit: that of having made the first political gesture in favor of the independence of Libya; and that of having made the first deliberate commitment to join forces with Cyrenaica and the leader of the Senussi.

The leaders of the Republic did not succeed in surmounting the seemingly irreconcilable differences that reduced their country to a medley of internecine strife. Nor did the Sirte Agreement mean that thenceforward the relationship between Tripolitania and Cyrenaica would be as smooth as the common interests of the two territories demanded. On the contrary, as we shall see, it took the Libyan people many more years of political maturation and much suffering, as well as a favorable external environment, to achieve unity and independence. Nonetheless, the events described here appear to have had at the time a profound effect on the political thinking of the educated classes of both territories. A unique precedent had been created, and a unique opportunity lost, but despite the tragic setbacks of

31. See p. 24, fn. 29. In connection with the Amir's reply, the translator observes that it is typical of the rather archaic tone of the document that the Arabic word used for "parliament" is not one of the several possible modern terms, but *shura,* an expression which evokes the very earliest days of the Caliphate and of Islam. This explains why the Amir considers such a body to be "the foundation of our religion." In the offer, the Tripolitanians used only a modern phrase: *Majlis niwabi*—"representative assembly."

the next two decades, the dream of an independent and united Libya, remote though the possibility of its attainment then appeared, served as a guiding star. For many an older Libyan still living, the events of 1918–23 marked the beginning of his faith in the ultimate achievement of what then seemed an unattainable ideal.

Among the younger Libyan generation, a tendency to underrate the part the Republic played during the early stages of their country's constitutional history is noticeable. Even Tripolitanians sometimes play down its importance because it reminds them of the internecine feuds and rivalries of which, in retrospect, they have no reason to be proud. The Cyrenaicans still resent the memory of the Republic because of the anti-Senussi feelings displayed by some of its leaders. Moreover, comparing the early resistance in Tripolitania with their own heroic struggle in later years, they are perhaps too easily inclined to look upon themselves as the sole precursors of Libyan independence. Hence, both sides tend to minimize the historical importance of the fact that without the Republic there might have been no Sirte Agreement and no Bay'a laying down the basic principles of a unified fatherland, of a national assembly convened to draw up a constitution, of a parliament representing the whole of the Libyan people, and, above all of the Senussi dynasty to watch over the country's destiny. Yet, precisely because of the precedents laid down by the Republic, the concept of a constitutional monarchy was not unfamiliar to those Libyans who at the outbreak of World War II resumed talks about the future of their country, and who, in 1950–51, with United Nations assistance, were called upon to write a constitution and to found an independent State.

THE ITALIAN OCCUPATION, 1923–43

In a few years Volpi brought most of Tripolitania and the Fezzan into subjection. His success, coupled with the departure of Sayed Idris for Egypt, led the Italians to the false conclusion that Libyan resistance was a thing of the past. This wishful thinking was prompted by the knowledge that they themselves had in the country a modern and well-equipped force—composed mostly of Eritreans—the strength of which was estimated at 20,000 men in Cyrenaica alone at the end of 1926.

But the peoples of the Libyan desert and of the Jebel Akhdar had not been born to submission. From Ottoman times they had been notorious for resisting payment of taxes. It was unthinkable to them that they should knuckle under to the new occupiers who coveted their lands. When, moreover, the Italians, aware that the spiritual and material source of Bedouin resistance sprang from Sanusiya leadership, moved to destroy the Order's *Zawiyas,* full-scale guerrilla warfare became inevitable.

When Sayed Idris left the country, command of operations against the Italians in Cyrenaica was assumed by his brother, Sheikh Rida, at the head of a force the strength of which varied from 2,000 to 6,000 men at most. But the conclusion of an agreement between the Italian and Egyptian Governments on 6 December 1925, giving the former sovereignty over Jaghbub and Kufrah, led to the unopposed occupation of Jaghbub in February 1926 and to the loss to the enemy of the tomb-mosque of the founder of Senusiya and the Order's central seminary. This was a terrible blow to Cyrenaican morale, and the Italians quickly followed up their advantage. On 3 January 1928 they captured Sheikh Rida and banished him to Sicily.

But resistance fired by patriotism and religion was by no means at an end. A new leader had already emerged in the person of Sayed Omar Mukhtar, who had started fighting the Italians as early as 1911 under Ahmad al-Sherif. He then joined Sayed Idris in exile in Cairo, where he remained until the latter's return there in 1923. Thereafter, with the Amir's agreement, he returned to the field, gathering around him a band of tribal warriors, who formed a small but extremely mobile raiding force that harassed the Italians for nearly eight years. When Rida disappeared from the scene, Omar Mukhtar naturally succeeded him as the leader of the Bedouin guerrillas.

As the years went by, the fighting became increasingly bitter. The war was not waged by the Italians against all Cyrenaicans—the townsman played a clandestine part [32]—but against the Bedouin of the desert. Even among them, as in all the resistance movements of World War II, there were many who stood on one side. These were mostly sedentary, or at best seminomadic, tribesmen whose long contact with previous administrations had made them particularly vulnerable to repressive action and reprisals. The core of Omar Mukhtar's force was therefore mainly nomadic, and it was in this that its strength lay. Pitched battles, of which the insurgents invariably got the worst, were avoided wherever possible. So successful was this plan of action, and so complete was Omar Mukhtar's authority by night, that "his force constituted the 'nocturnal government' in the territory, collecting the zakat (alms) and other contributions from their countrymen." [33]

As Evans-Pritchard has pointed out, such incessant fighting "cannot . . . be described in the language of text-book logistics in terms of manœuvr-

32. Evans-Pritchard, describing the part played by the Cyrenaican officials in the Italian Administration, aptly adapts Tennyson: "Their faith unfaithful kept them falsely true." *The Sanusi,* p. 163.

33. Khadduri, p. 24.

ing, objectives, and battles." [34] It would therefore be pointless and repetitious to try to trace the course of the campaign in detail. Despite the rebels' bravery and powers of endurance, the impetus of resistance gradually slackened off. For their part, the Italians were learning the hard way, gradually making their performance in the field more effective. Moreover, after the conclusion of the Egyptian Agreement in 1925, they were in a position to seal off the Cyrenaican frontier, and thus to cut off supplies reaching the rebels from Egypt and the Sudan. Civilians who harbored, comforted, assisted, or maintained the guerrillas were punished mercilessly. One by one, the nationalist leaders fell in battle or were made prisoner until, finally, the great Omar Mukhtar himself was wounded in a skirmish on 11 September 1931. Pinned down by his horse, near the tomb of Sidi Rafa, he fell into the hands of the Italians. Graziani, then Italian Commander in Chief in Libya, and already notorious for his harsh treatment of his opponents, cut short a holiday and hurried back to Libya to deal with this valiant warrior himself. Neither his age, nor his honor, nor his wounds availed the old man aught. After a summary trial, he was publicly hanged at Suluq in the presence of 20,000 Bedouin and notables from the cities of Cyrenaica, brought there to learn the lesson of his death. "The resistance died with Sidi 'Umar al-Mukhtar. The remaining fights were twitches of an already lifeless body." [35]

There was no further bar to Italy's occupation of Libya. She did not even try to win the support of the desert folk. In the towns and the coastal plain, under a veneer of collaboration, there was persistent, ingrained antagonism toward the new masters of the country. This was largely the result of the demographic nature of Italian policy in Libya. Large parts of the best arable and grazing lands, which were scanty enough in all conscience, were confiscated to provide small holdings and pasture for the poor settlers from the *Mezzogiorno,* and this deprivation of their traditional livelihood left an indelible stamp on the hearts and minds of the Cyrenaicans. Throughout the steady process of decline, from open hostility through reluctant collaboration to inarticulate submission, the ownership of the land remained one of the main issues.

A tragic aftermath of the process of colonization, which, combined with losses in the field, severely diminished Libya's productive capacity, was the flight of thousands of Libyans, who sought refuge in Egypt and the other Arab countries of the Near East, as well as in the Sudan, Chad, Tunisia, and Algeria. Estimates of the numbers of families involved range from several hundred to several thousand; 2,000 is perhaps the nearest one is

34. Evans-Pritchard, p. 170.
35. Ibid., p. 190.

likely to get to the true figure. These emigrés, who included many leading political and intellectual figures, settled in Alexandria, Cairo, Beirut, Damascus, Constantinople, and even Geneva. They met in groups to indulge in the inescapable and unceasing occupation of all political refugees: the publication of newspapers, tracts, and pamphlets, and the dissemination of propaganda. They kept in touch with the Amir in Egypt. Through their contact with him and with one another they gradually became amenable to patient efforts to convince them that the only hope for the future lay in the common independence of the three territories that made up Libya, beginning with Cyrenaica, in the belief that Tripolitania, and later the Fezzan, would follow.

Sayed Idris has been criticized for abandoning his followers in distress. The writer does not endorse that criticism. Nations struggling and suffering in circumstances like those described here are just as much in need of political leaders serving their interests abroad as they are of military leaders in the field. Had Sayed Idris not gone to Egypt to become a rallying point for Libyan refuges, a symbol of hope for a better future to his suffering people at home, had he not returned as the sole acceptable architect of the State to come, Libya's destiny would in all likelihood have been very different.

Referring to Sayed Idris's departure for Egypt, Azzam Pasha, in the private communication to the author already cited, remarked:

> From that moment [1918] . . . I preached unity with Sayed Idris as "Amir"—and went to him [in Ajdabujah] at the end of 1922—where we profiting of the declaration of Egyptian independence and because Sayid Idris was in great need of a cure, and he may also have [had] other reasons, we travelled together by caravan to Egypt.

The Bedouin had suffered terribly. It is difficult to arrive at accurate figures. According to Evans-Pritchard,[36] between 1911 and 1932 their numbers were reduced by one-half to two-thirds, by death and emigration. Mussolini, as quoted by Evans-Pritchard, stated in his introduction to *Cirenaica Verde* that, Cyrenaica "verde di piante" had become "rossa di sangue." Moreover, their livestock, their sole means of subsistence, was decimated, almost in the literal sense of the word, and what remained of it suffered additionally when driven to the more southern desert pasturelands where there was less grass and frequent drought. When the fighting was over, thousands who had fled into the desert fastnesses of western Egypt and the eastern Sudan returned to join the Libyan Arab Force in 1940.

36. Ibid.

Others had gone to the south and west from Tripolitania and the Fezzan into the French Saharan territories.

The number of Italian immigrants to Cyrenaica had risen to some 40,000 by 1941, with many garrisons adding still further to the numbers, all busy trying to convert the territory into an Italian province, feeding themselves in traditional Italian fashion and exporting to the homeland cereals, wine, fruit, and tuna. The Italian population of Tripolitania had grown from 18,000 in 1921 to 70,000 in 1941, all of them in the coastal strip and the Gharyan hills and nearly half in Tripoli town itself.[37]

As we have already seen, the main Italian economic effort in Libya had as its object the settlement of landless Italian peasants from the poorest regions of Italy, to whom the rigors of the kind of life they were to lead in Africa would come as no surprise. But poor as these settlers had been, in their subsidized new settlements they were better off than the local population. It has been estimated that, in all, Italy spent in Libya the equivalent of some 150 million prewar dollars (at prewar rates of exchange) on public works, utilities, and agricultural development during the thirty years over which it administered the country.[38] And although at first most of this was spent on building up the country's infrastructure, between 1936 and 1942 two-thirds of such expenditure went on agricultural development and land reclamation. Some wealthy Italians with fascist credentials maintained large private establishments, a few of which in Tripolitania were purchased in the normal way, others being acquired through forced sale or expropriation. A small number of Libyans found menial jobs on these estates. Most Italian farmers lived in demographic settlements, which used little or no Arab labor, the Italians working first as hired men of the agrarian "colonization" corporations and then as part owners of the land, of which they were to become full owners after twenty years. (The Italian conquest of Tripolitania having been completed several years before that of Cyrenaica, the colonization of the western province was considerably more advanced in 1943.) Together, these two forms of land occupation accounted for

37. Until 1934, the two territories were administered independently; from 1934 until the beginning of 1939, they were administered jointly as the Italian colony of Libya; and from then until the defeat of the Axis forces in North Africa, Libya was an integral part of metropolitan Italy, of which it formed the southernmost province. The southern desert regions, however, and the Fezzan remained under military administration.

38. See *The Economic Development of Libya* (Baltimore: Johns Hopkins Press, 1960), pp. 26–27. This is a report of a mission of the International Bank for Reconstruction and Development organized at the request of the Libyan Government. Chapter 2 starts with a brief historical background, followed by an account of characteristics of the Libyan economy.

225,000 hectares in the two territories.[39] Hence the resentment felt by the Arabs, despite Italian efforts to improve the living conditions of semi-nomads and Bedouin in the grazing country.

In the economic sphere, local handicrafts suffered severely from competition from Italian products. New agricultural-processing and small consumer-goods plants were set up—but for the benefit of the Italian settlers. Virtually all government jobs, except at the lowest clerical and manual levels, were reserved for Italians.

The indigenous population had practically no access to education and public health services. Secondary education and technical training were neglected. Very few Libyans found a place in the higher ranks of the Italian Administration.

In short, fascist colonial policy was to push the Libyans off the land which was worth cultivating, although this was at best marginal and Italian agricultural and industrial enterprises were enabled to survive only by subsidies, open or concealed. No political rights, no economic benefits, no social progress was even considered for the indigenous population. Nothing was done to prepare the Libyan people for self-government. So except for a few Libyan families who were permitted to hold their ancestral farms in Tripolitania, and a handful of people who were essential to the Italians as a sort of liaison staff for purposes of communication, no Libyans received education or training that would fit them to take an active part in modern society or in government. Hence the—characteristically restrained—comment of the World Bank Mission eight years after independence and after a vigorous program of technical assistance had been in operation for nearly as many years: "As a result, through no fault of its own, Libya has remained heavily dependent on foreign administration and technical personnel, and the training of Libyans to replace them is still the most difficult of all the problems associated with economic development." [40]

Ironically enough, the fascist regime which met its fate during World War II left behind it, though against its intentions, an infrastructure of roads, ports, and public utilities and public and private buildings in the towns. Much of it was suited only to colonial overloads and to subsidized colonial agriculture and industry geared to the fascist economic system. Much was destroyed in the war. However, the British occupation authorities made essential repairs on a care-and-maintenance basis and this gave the new State a valuable physical asset, even if in some respects too costly to be supported by an unsubsidized marginal agricultural economy.

In retrospect, the tragedy of the Italian conquest of Libya is seen to lie in the circumstance that, having entered the colonial stakes too late, Italy

39. Ibid.
40. Ibid.

was in too much of a hurry to pursue a policy of enlightened colonization which, in any case, would have been totally incompatible with fascist ideas and methods.

FOREIGN MILITARY AND CIVIL ADMINSTRATION, 1943–51

The history of Libya during World War II is that of the campaigns in North Africa: the ebb and flow of the fighting in the western desert in 1940–42; the invasion of the countries of the Maghreb in 1942; the net that slowly closed round the Axis forces from east and west after the battle of Alamein; the final expulsion of the Germans and Italians from North Africa in May 1943; the simultaneous advance of the Free French Forces under General Leclerc de Hautecloque from French Equatorial Africa; and, finally, British Military Administration in Cyrenaica and Tripolitania and French Military Administration in the Fezzan.

Both France and the United Kingdom had planned their military occupation as thoroughly as the burden of the conduct of the war in general allowed. Both had the most essential prerequisite for the task—trained human resources and leadership—in relative abundance. The British were able to call on former members of the Sudan Government Service, one of the most efficient, acceptable, and progressive elements of the administrative structure of the Empire; the French on the Officiers des Affaires Indigènes, an elite military corps with much experience in dealing with the tribes in the northwestern and southern Sahara. Thus, neither side was plagued by that frequent bane of military occupation, the difficulty of communication. Arabic-speaking personnel were available in adequate numbers; what is more, their long day-to-day dealings with comparable indigenous peoples had given them a most valuable knowledge of and insight into Arab ways of life and thought.

Of course, both countries had vital strategic and other interests in the Mediterranean area: France, in the western Mediterranean and in her colonies in northwestern and central Africa; the United Kingdom in the eastern Mediterranean, Egypt, Suez, and the Near and Middle East generally. These interests dictated their policies toward the Libyan territories for which they were responsible. It was obviously in their interest to establish friendly relations with the peoples of these territories, who accordingly benefited in the economic and social spheres, especially in education and, to a somewhat lesser extent, in public health services. On the other hand, the strategic aims of the two Administering Powers tended to work against the unification and complete independence of Libya. Had they not, in company with the United States, been determined to keep the Soviet Union from gaining a sphere of influence on the southern shore of the Mediterranean in the years immediately following the war, Cyrenaica, Tripolitania, and the Fezzan might have remained under foreign domination for a long time. As things turned out, the failure of the Big Four to agree on the disposal of the former Italian colonies—a failure that hinged on Libya to a much greater extent than it did on Eritrea or Italian Somaliland—and the consequent reference of the problem to the United Nations brought unity and freedom to Libya much earlier than would otherwise have been the case. These developments are dealt with in detail in Parts 1 and 2 of Chapter 1.

But there is one aspect of relations between the British and the Libyans at this time that must be emphasized. From 1940 onward, there was close contact, both political and military, between the United Kingdom Government and Sayed Idris, then living in Egypt. This led, among other things, to the creation of the Libyan Arab Force; it also entailed certain specific political commitments on the part of London toward the Senussi, who provided the bulk of this useful force. Even though there was some subsequent argument as to the precise scope of these undertakings, they did give Cyrenaica a few years' start along the road to independence.

For various reasons that will be explained in Chapters 1 and 2, parallel developments in Tripolitania moved much more slowly—though plans for them were in existence as early as January 1950—but never reached the same level of implementation. In any case, among the United Kingdom's original ideas for Tripolitania there was no question of recognizing the Amir as Head of Tripolitania, as well.

In Tripolitania, British military administration gave way to civil administration in April 1949; the process was repeated in Cyrenaica in September of the same year. However, in the summer of 1943, with the occupation of Sicily and South Italy, a separate Directorate of Civil Affairs had been set up in the War Office and responsibility in the Army Council for the administration of all occupied and liberated territories formally passed from the Director of Military Operations and the Vice-Chief of the Imperial General Staff to the Permanent Undersecretary.

The Fezzan remained under French military administration until independence, although a measure of local self-government was introduced with the appointment of Ahmed Bey Seif al-Nasr as Chief of Territory in February 1950.

Those interested in details of day-to-day British military administration up to 1947 will find a most excellent source in Lord Rennell of Rodd's work on the subject.[41] Unfortunately, there does not seem to be a corresponding

41. Rennell of Rodd, *British Military Administration of Occupied Territories in Africa, 1941–1947* (London: His Majesty's Stationery Office, 1948). As its title indi-

central source on the French side covering the military administration of the Fezzan.

In conclusion, it must be repeated that the purpose of this historical summary is simply to provide the reader with a very general idea of how the past affected the course of events about to be described. Those who wish to go into the historical antecedents more profoundly are referred to the works cited, though for a complete understanding of the background, access to Turkish and Arab records, mostly untranslated, is essential. Only when all such sources, and the archives of Libya and other interested States, have been thoroughly combed will it be possible fully to document the more recent parts of the story.[42]

---

cates, the book deals also with Eritrea and Italian Somaliland, but the greater part is devoted to Cyrenaica and Tripolitania.

42. The following works and documents, some of which have been cited already, may be of interest to the inquiring reader:

Carl Brockelmann, *History of the Islamic Peoples,* trans. from the German by Carmichael and Perlmann (London: Routledge and Kegan Paul Ltd., 1949).

E. F. Gautier, *Le Passé de l'Afrique du Nord: Les Siècles Obscurs* (Paris: Payot, 1942).

Four Power Commission of Investigation for the Former Italian Colonies, *Report,* Volume III, *Report on Libya.* Mimeographed.

Zeine N. Zeine, *Arab Turkish Relations and the Emergence of Arab Nationalism* (Beirut, Lebanon: Khayat's College Book Co-operative, 1958).

Albert Hourani, *Arab Thought in the Liberal Age, 1798–1939,* issued under the auspices of the Royal Institute of International Affairs (London: Oxford University Press, 1962).

Elisabeth P. MacCallum, *The Arab Nationalist Movement,* Foreign Policy Association, Foreign Policy Reports, *XI* (May 1935).

E. E. Evans-Pritchard, *The Sanusi of Cyrenaica* (Oxford: Oxford University Press, 1949).

Nicola A. Ziadeh, *Sanusiyah: A Study of a Revivalist Movement in Islam* (Leiden, Netherlands: E. J. Brill, 1958).

Majid Khadduri, *Modern Libya: A Study in Political Development* (Baltimore: Johns Hopkins Press, 1963).

Al-Tahir Ahmad al-Zawi, *Jihad al-Abtal fi Tarabulus al-Gharb* (*The Holy War of the Heroes in Tripoli*) (Cairo: Imprimerie Tajellah al-Jedidah, 1950). Translation of the sections used in this Historical Background are from pages 223–48, 296–330, and 330–31, and were translated by Frank H. Stewart of the University of Cambridge, England.

Enrico de Leone, *La Colonizzazione dell'Africa del Nord* (Padova, Italy: Cedam-Casa Editrice Dott. Antonio Milani, 1960).

R. W. Hill, *A Bibliography of Libya,* Department of Geography Research Papers, No. 1 (Newcastle-upon-Tyne, England: University of Durham, 1959).

List of material on Libya in the United Nations Libraries in New York and Geneva.

CHAPTER 1

In Search of Unity

It was commonly said in the Western world during the early 1950s that Libya would never have become an independent State had it not been for the divided counsels of the Great Powers and the assistance of the United Nations. A survey of the facts leads the author to a somewhat different conclusion.[1] Looking back today, it can probably be safely assumed that, had the Great Powers ever succeeded in agreeing on one of their several plans to divide up Libya, the country's unification and independence would have been put back by several years. It is also probably correct to say that, had not the United Nations been called to Libya's bedside, it would have taken the patient longer to recover from his internal and external ills than it in fact did. But when one looks at what happened to the other countries of North Africa, it is difficult to believe that Libya's destiny would have differed from that of Algeria, Egypt, Morocco, and Tunisia, even if Mussolini had not been on the losing side in World War II. Some may argue that Libya could have been split up, and its parts incorporated with its

1. During the Third and Fourth Regular Sessions of the General Assembly, the United Nations Secretariat was supplied with a mass of documentation by the interested parties which was not always objective. When the United Nations Mission arrived in Libya in January 1950, political parties and individuals submitted to it fresh memoranda and petitions, which were often supported by oral statements, relating in particular to internal problems and including efforts made to achieve internal unity and independence. In addition, the Commissioner and his staff, as well as members of the Council for Libya, had numerous private conversations with personalities and notables, a number of which were summarized for the record. Some of this material is in the public domain, but, as already explained in the Foreword, much the largest part is still classified. In addition, there is material on the subject published by organizations such as the League of Arab States or brought to light by private authors and research workers. Hence, like the Historical Background, the present chapter is based only to a limited extent on the writer's original research. To a much greater extent it is the fruit of consulting the writings of earlier authors. The factual information thus obtained has gratefully been used and all sources duly acknowledged. At the same time, the author takes full responsibility for the comments and reflections in the text, which are his own.

neighbors. But was not the question of how to divide it precisely the cause of the major disagreements among the Powers? And would not similar disagreements have arisen between Libya's neighbors had fate pushed it in a direction other than that of unity and independence? There is naturally a good deal of speculation in such reasoning, which certainly does not justify the conclusion that Libya's independence and territorial integrity will never be endangered in the future. One conclusion, however, can safely be drawn; that any threat to Libyan independence is most likely to come either from internal political or social rifts upsetting the country's unit and encouraging foreign intervention, or as the result of a major shift in the political and strategic balance of power in the Mediterranean.

It is because both these potential sources of danger played such an important part during the prelude to Libyan independence, and may yet do so, that it is necessary to examine them more closely.

PART 1. INTERNAL EFFORTS TO ACHIEVE UNITY

In the historical résumé it was briefly shown that, the initial and centuries-old differences in the orientation and evolution of the three territories notwithstanding, successive Arab invasions, once their aftereffects had been consolidated, created an economic, social, and cultural environment in Libya in which, in more recent times, a measure of political cohesion could flourish, provided geographical obstacles and human causes of division were overcome. It will also be remembered that in the course of the nineteenth and twentieth centuries there emerged a specifically Libyan brand of Arab nationalism, tolerated under Ottoman rule, recognized by the Young Turks, and inflamed by the Italian invasion and occupation, which culminated in the Gharyan Conference, at which the Amirate of Tripolitania was offered to the Senussi leader of Cyrenaica for the first time. The offer was accepted, but with the advent of fascism and the resumption of Italian military operations, dreams of independence and unity, even of local autonomy, had to be abandoned until the return of better times. These came with the outbreak of World War II.

Several authors of different nationalities have dealt with the effects and aftereffects of the war on the fate of the Libyan people. For the time being the subject seems exhausted, particularly in respect of the period 1939–49; it will remain so until sources of information still locked up in public and private archives become generally accessible.

One author, Majid Khadduri, of Johns Hopkins University, Baltimore, in his book *Modern Libya,* has most commendably included a comprehensive account of attempts made by leading Libyans to prepare their country for unity and independence.[2] From this it appears that between the two world wars, many of the thousands of Tripolitanian and Cyrenaican refugees living in the countries surrounding their homeland, more particularly in the Near East, had been waging a "war of the pen." [3] Sayed Idris, already considered by many of the refugees as their leader, had himself lived as a refugee in Egypt from 1923 onward. When World War II broke out, Tripolitanian and Cyrenaican refugee leaders met in Alexandria from 20 to 23 October 1939, and decided "to entrust their common leadership to the hands of Sayyid Idris, provided he agreed to appoint a joint committee of Cyrenaican and Tripolitanian leaders which would advise him on all future action that might be taken concerning the liberation of their country." [4] This committee apparently never functioned satisfactorily, made up as it was of people who, on top of their conflicting personalities, held conflicting views about the outcome of the war. Many Tripolitanians, in common with millions of people elsewhere in the world, found it difficult in

2. Majid Khadduri, *Modern Libya: A Study in Political Development* (Baltimore: Johns Hopkins Press, 1963), Chaps. 1–4.

3. One example of this literary war is worth mentioning. From 1930 until 1937 there appeared in Geneva, Switzerland, a monthly review entitled *La Nation Arabe*, Organe de la Délégation Syro-Palestinienne auprès de la Société des Nations, servant les intérêts des pays arabes et ceux de l'Orient, rédigé par l'Emir Chekib Arslan et Ihsan Bey el-Djabri. On several occasions the review dealt with matters concerning the Libyan territories under Italian rule. Particularly noteworthy is a letter published in 1930, No. 7, pp. 22–24, dated Damascus, 2 September 1929, that was addressed by Beshir Bey Saadawi to Benito Mussolini. Beshir Bey signed this letter in his capacity as "Le Président du Comité exécutif [des Colonies Tripolitaines]." The letter was written "A l'occasion des négociations de paix en cours en ce moment entre S.E. le Maréchal Badelo [*sic*, Balbo?] Gouverneur de la Tripolitaine-Barka et le leader Seid Omar El-Moukhtar, commandant les Mouvements guerriers au Djébel El-Akhdar." The letter, which appears to have as its aim the opening of peace negotiations in the two territories, includes the following proposal:

> Si vous avez l'intention de faire régner la sécurité et l'ordre dans cette région et que vos négociations sont en cours avec Seid Omar El-Mouktar [*sic*], nous désirons vivement et avec le plus grand espoir que la paix soit générale et non spéciale pour Barka qui constitue une partie inséparable de la Tripolitaine, et établie sur des bases qui assureront les intérêts des deux parties.
>
> Je suis disposé à réaliser ce voeu d'accord avec mes collègues qui sont à la tête des tribus belligérantes et qui se trouvent actuellement hors de la région dans divers endroits.

The letter was written at a time when things were going badly for the Senussi guerrillas. Nothing came of Saadawi's proposals. See also Khadduri, p. 26.

4. Khadduri, pp. 28–29. Khadduri himself refers in this connection to *The White Book on the Unity of Tripolitania and Cyrenaica* (Cairo, 1949) (Arabic), on p. 26.

1940–41 to believe in a victory for the United Kingdom, then fighting virtually single-handed, and accordingly considered that formally to side with the British at a time when Tripolitania was firmly under Italian control would be extremely hazardous. The Cyrenaicans on the Committee, united under the leadership of Sayed Idris, held a different view, believing that they had nothing to lose and everything to gain. It was a dangerous position to take up. In the light of the two territories' very different geographical positions with regard to the theater of war in North Africa in 1940, there was something to be said for each attitude. One territory was so close to that theater that it was highly unlikely it would not become involved in the fighting. The other was so much further away that it could at that time expect to remain outside the zone of hostilities and hence to have little chance of liberation. Three years later the perspective had completely changed, of course, but Cyrenaica had taken a political lead which Tripolitania did not follow until the end of 1951, when, on the declaration of independence, the distinction between the two positions finally disappeared.

In the summer of 1940, after Italy had entered the war on 10 June, the Commander of the British Forces in Egypt, General (later Field Marshal) Sir Henry Maitland Wilson, formally invited Sayed Idris to ask his followers to join in the formation of a Senussi force. The latter called a joint meeting of Cyrenaican and Tripolitanian leaders in Cairo on 7 August 1940 to discuss this plan.

The invitation of the British military authorities was accepted, and a British-Arab Force (later renamed the Libyan Arab Force), led by a British commander, was organized. It fought under the Senussi flag, and the Arab officers serving in it were commissioned in the name of the Amir Idris.[5] At its greatest strength, it consisted of five battalions supported by a supply depot, and it rendered important ancillary services until the Italian and German armies in North Africa had been defeated.

The inauguration of this force created new differences among Cyrenaicans and Tripolitanians. Some Tripolitanian leaders refused to sign the joint resolution establishing it, insisting that the British must give a firm commitment on the future independence of Tripolitania before they could declare their readiness to join. These dissidents formed a separate committee to seek British support for a Tripolitanian army. Khadduri remarks: "Since the Tripolitanian leaders offered to collaborate with the British on the basis of the same terms as those acceptable to Sayyid Idris without acknowledging

5. E. E. Evans-Pritchard, *The Sanusi of Cyrenaica* (Oxford: Oxford University Press, 1949), p. 227; and Rennell of Rodd, *British Military Administration of Occupied Territories in Africa, 1941–1947* (London: His Majesty's Stationery Office, 1948), pp. 244, 246, 255, and 469.

his leadership, the opposition of the Tripolitanian . . . leaders was reduced in the last analysis to their objection to Sanusi leadership over Tripolitania." [6]

The Tripolitanian attitude was justified, since the British authorities had made a distinction by accepting a commitment to Cyrenaica and refusing one to Tripolitania. This became clear from the British reaction to a demand addressed by Sayed Idris, under pressure from his followers, to the British Minister of State in Cairo in August 1941, in which he asked, in exchange for his support as Amir, the immediate grant of internal independence to Libya. He proposed that:

1. Great Britain grant Libyans internal independence of their country.
2. Libya have its own government headed by a Muslim Amir acceptable to the British Government.
3. Great Britain hold the protectorate over Libya and direct the organisation of its financial and military affairs until it reached a higher social, cultural, and civil level.[7]

This demand for a formal written pledge was unacceptable to the United Kingdom Government in the middle of the war; but, wishing to meet Cyrenaica's wishes as far as its interests permitted, that Government decided, after a further exchange of views, to make public its intentions. Accordingly, the Foreign Secretary, Mr. Anthony Eden (now Lord Avon), made a statement on 8 January 1942 in the House of Commons. This became the basis for British policy toward Sayed Idris; but, as it referred only to Cyrenaica, it confused and bedeviled British policy toward Tripolitania, and hence toward the entire question of Libyan unity, for several years to come.

The Foreign Secretary said:

> The Sayyid Idris al-Senusi made contact with the British authorities in Egypt within a month of the collapse of France, at a time when the military situation in Africa was most unfavourable to us. A Sanusi force was subsequently raised from those of his followers who had escaped from Italian oppression at various times during the past twenty years. This force performed considerable ancillary duties during the successful fighting in the Western Desert in the winter of 1940–41, and is again playing a useful part in the campaign now in progress. I take this opportunity to express the warm appreciation of His Majesty's government for the contribution which Sayyid Idris al-Sanusi and his followers have made

6. Khadduri, p. 33.
7. Ibid.

> and are making to the British war effort. We welcome their association with His Majesty's forces in the task of defeating the common enemies. His Majesty's government is determined that at the end of the war the Sanusis in Cyrenaica will in no circumstances again fall under Italian domination.[8]

Eden's statement did not satisfy the Libyans, as the British had hoped it would. Sayed Idris and his followers were disappointed that it did not include an explicit promise of independence for Cyrenaica after the war. Tripolitanian leaders were critical and suspicious not only because it did not refer to Tripolitania, but also because its reference to Sanusiya seemed to imply prior recognition by the United Kingdom Government of Senussi leadership. Sayed Idris himself, however, took the hopeful view that if the Allies won the war the British would honor their oral promises of independence, at least as far as Cyrenaica was concerned.

In the meantime, Cyrenaica soon became the arena of a bitter struggle in the course of which the country changed hands three times and Benghazi suffered as many as a thousand air raids. The territory was finally liberated by the British Eighth Army under General (later Field Marshal the Viscount) Montgomery in November 1942. Benghazi was captured on 20 November, and Tripoli on 23 January 1943. A few weeks later the whole of Libya was free of Axis forces. On 11 November 1942 General Montgomery, in a message issued simultaneously with the proclamation of British military occupation in Cyrenaica, reiterated the promise to Sayed Idris that "the Sanusis will not again be subject to Italian rule." [9]

The British authorities instituted separate military administrations in Cyrenaica and Tripolitania; under an arrangement concluded on 26 January 1943 between General Montgomery and General Jacques Leclerc de Hautecloque, the French Commander in Africa South of the Sahara, the Fezzan was placed under French military administration as far north as latitude 28° and as far east as longitude 18°. However, as the Four Power Commission of Investigation for the former Italian Colonies stated in Volume III, Part Three, page 12, of its report (see p. 45 and p. 47, fn. 18), there were considerable discrepancies between English and French maps in this respect. The British Military Administration in Tripolitania had no record of any detailed settlement of boundaries.

With the expulsion of the enemy and the return of political exiles and emigrants to the country, leading circles in Cyrenaica definitely turned their

8. Hansard, *House of Commons Debates* (London: His Majesty's Stationery Office, 1942), *377,* cols. 77–78.

9. Khadduri, p. 43.

sights onto the political future of their territory. Sayed Idris's leadership was generally recognized, but the future status of the Province remained uncertain. The Cyrenaican people wanted independence under a Senussi Amirate, with the help and guidance of the British, in recognition of their long years of tenacious opposition to Italian rule and of their more recent services to the British forces during the war. The United Kingdom was still reluctant to give any formal undertakings in writing, limiting itself to oral promises.

The uncertainty of his obtaining any form of written recognition made Sayed Idris unwilling to take up formal residence in Cyrenaica. Although paying occasional visits to his homeland, he continued to guide his people from his residence in Egypt, preferring, as Khadduri says, "to remain outside his country so long as it remained under temporary foreign administration." [10] Although his people respectfully called him Amir (Prince), he was not able to use the title officially, but only honorifically. The British scrupulously referred to him as "The Sayed," and addressed him as "Your Eminence," so as to avoid giving the impression that they were changing the territory's status.

Sayed Idris returned to Cyrenaica from exile for the first time in July 1943 and was received with tempestuous enthusiasm wherever he went. The people clamored for an independent Cyrenaica under the rule of the Sayed as Amir. On each successive visit these claims were made more forcefully, and a rising sense of impatience and frustration made itself felt when the people learned through the press and radio that the Council of Foreign Ministers set up at the Potsdam Conference in 1945 (see p. 58) was meeting with difficulties in trying to agree on the disposal of the Italian colonies.

In February 1945, Cyrenaica's elder statesman, Omar Mansur Pasha al-Kikhia,[11] who during the war had been deported by the Italian authori-

10. Ibid., p. 54.

11. Omar Mansur al-Kikhia of the Cyrenaican family of that name had been educated at Constantinople, as the capital of the Ottoman Empire was then called. His first governmental function was that of Qaimaqam (district officer) of Gialo oasis under Turkish administration. About 1905 he was awarded the title of Pasha by Sultan Abdul Hamid II. He was eventually elected to the Young Turkish Parliament where, together with two others of his countrymen, he represented Cyrenaica. Immediately after the Italian occupation of Benghazi he withdrew with the Turkish officials to Constantinople, which he left in about 1913 for Egypt. Here he participated in a campaign to raise money for the Libyan resistance movement. In 1920 Omar Pasha returned to Benghazi and was appointed adviser to the Italian Governor of Cyrenaica, in which capacity he acted as mediator in negotiations with the Senussi. However, after a while he was arrested and imprisoned by the Italians, though later released. Until 1940 he remained politically inactive. Then the Italians again arrested

ties, returned from exile in Rome. He lost no time in taking the lead, with Sayed Idris' assent, in propagating a policy of self-government under the Amirate of the Sayed, with a representative assembly freely elected by the people and an administration assisted and guided by British advisers. On 15 June 1945 he addressed a letter to Sir Edward Grigg, then British Minister of State in Cairo, submitting a plan for consideration by the United Kingdom Government. According to Khadduri's summary, the plan stated that Cyrenaica should become an independent country allied with Great Britain. Its government should be representative and democratic, advised and financially assisted by the United Kingdom, which would be entitled to station forces on Cyrenaican territory for a fixed period.[12] On the same day, Sayed Idris, in a letter also addressed to Sir Edward Grigg, expressed, in his own name and in that of the Cyrenaican nation, his agreement with this plan.

However, pending an agreement in the Council of Foreign Ministers and the conclusion of a treaty of peace with Italy, the United Kingdom Government was still reluctant to assume any formal commitment going beyond the Foreign Secretary's statement of 8 January 1942.

Subsequently, the National Front (Al-Jabha al-Wataniya), founded in the summer of 1946 by the leading tribal chiefs with the Sayed's consent, addressed a manifesto to the British authorities on 30 November 1946, demanding recognition of the Senussi Amirate under Sayed Idris and permission to form a national government to administer the country in preparation for complete independence.[13] These demands revealed a clear preference for realizing Cyrenaican independence before attempting to solve the question of Libyan unity. Indeed, the older generation of Cyrenaican leaders knew only too well that Italian economic interests in Tripolitania were

---

him and deported him to Rome, where he stayed in forced residence until 1945. As described by Khadduri, he resumed his political activities upon his return from exile. On the declaration of Cyrenaican autonomy in 1949, he was appointed Chief of the Amir's Court (the Diwan) and later Prime Minister of the first Cyrenaican Government. However, as a result of disagreements with the Cyrenaican National Congress, he resigned in early 1950. On one of the first occasions the Commissioner had the pleasure of meeting Omar Mansur at a luncheon at the latter's home, he was solemnly presented by his host with an ivory walking stick. Omar Mansur explained that he had received this gift from the Sultan, Mohammad V, in 1913, in the course of a farewell audience, with the words: "You and your people are heading for difficult times. You will often be in need of support. I make you a present of this stick to lean upon whenever the weight of events becomes too heavy." He then said to the Commissioner, in turn: "From now you will have to carry a weight that may sometimes prove heavy. Hence, I now hand this stick to you."

12. Khadduri, pp. 57–58.

13. Ibid., p. 62.

still powerful. They feared, moreover, that, given a certain pro-Italian tendency in international politics, the future of the western province might take a turn detrimental to their own interests. When, four years later, in January 1950, the writer visited Benghazi for the first time, as United Nations Commissioner for Libya, this fear of a possible renascence of Italian influence still dominated Cyrenaican politics. In particular, the appalling thought that Italian settlers might return to reoccupy the land that had originally belonged to the tribes obsessed most of the older leaders; and it continued for the next two years to exert a considerable influence on the form in which Libyan unity was to be shaped in the Constitution.

But there was a group of younger men in the towns with a broader concept of their country's future. Several of them, having been educated in exile, in particular in Egypt, and having fought in the Libyan Arab Force, were fervent supporters of the League of Arab States and its ideal of Arab unity. They wanted to see Libya join the League as an independent united State under the rule of Sayed Idris as Amir or King. To further this policy they established, on 4 April 1943 and with the consent of the Sayed, who became their patron, the Omar al-Mukhtar Club, named after the old guerrilla leader and hero, hanged in 1931 on Graziani's orders (see p. 29). After some time the Club began openly to criticize the British authorities for granting neither the title of Amir to Sayed Idris nor autonomous powers to a Cyrenaican government. At the same time, it reproached the older leaders for their provincialism and moved closer to the Tripolitanian National Congress (see p. 53) in its policy of promoting Libyan unity. However, it was unable to reach unanimity within its own ranks on the form of the State. The Derna branch of the Club, which from the outset had been more radical in its outlook, stood for complete unity between the provinces, whereas the Benghazi branch was prepared to accept federalism if that would facilitate the achievement of unity. Although more moderate and realistic than its Derna brethren, with whom it soon broke, the Benghazi branch, later rechristened the National Association of Cyrenaica, came more and more to play the part of a progressive but nevertheless loyal opposition in Cyrenaican politics. Vis-à-vis the British authorities, it adopted an increasingly critical attitude similar to that of the Congress Party in Tripoli (see p. 53).

An important event in these circumstances was the arrival of a Working Party, directly responsible to the War Office, which was sent to Benghazi toward the end of 1946. Its task was to draw up recommendations for the termination of the British Military Administration (BMA) and the gradual transfer of power to a Cyrenaican government. The Working Party's recommendations provided, among other things, for three stages of evolution:

1. Termination of BMA within a short time.
2. Establishment of an Arab State under British trusteeship. Adequate financial assistance for not less than ten years. Administrative training of Libyan staff. Promotion of educational and technical development.
3. Establishment of a fully independent State. Possible connection with Tripolitania in a unified Libya insofar as the creation of such a State was consistent with the specific recommendations for Cyrenaica. Recommendation of a treaty of alliance with a major Power.

These recommendations, it will be noted, particularly the second and third, were significant inasmuch as, although they suggested a policy for an independent State of Cyrenaica, they also referred to the possibility of a unified Libya.

The Working Party further recommended that Sayed Idris should take up permanent residence in Cyrenaica and that he should enlarge the Executive Committee of the National Front with the idea of its eventually developing into a Council of Ministers. The report finally made proposals for promoting the country's economic, social, and administrative development, including the Libyanization of the civil service. It was a constructive and progressive policy, and had it been implemented in its entirety, not only with regard to Cyrenaica, as was the case, but also in the direction of possible unification of the two coastal provinces, the United Kingdom might have avoided many of the difficulties it subsequently ran up against in Tripolitania.

Toward the end of 1947 Sayed Idris decided to return permanently to Cyrenaica. One of the first things he did there was to dissolve all political parties, asking them at the same time to form a new united front. Among the adherents of the Omar al-Mukhtar Club this measure of compulsory unification provoked much resentment, because they feared that its purpose was to further an independent Cyrenaica at the expense of an independent Libya. On the other hand, the Peace Conference with Italy, having failed to agree on the future of the former Italian colonies in Paris in 1947, had decided to set up a "Four Power Commission of Investigation for the Former Italian Colonies" (hereinafter referred to as the Four Power Commission) with the object of ascertaining the views of the local populations.[14]

In view of this body's forthcoming visit to Libya, it seemed wise to stop bickering over local differences of opinion in an attempt to reach agreement

14. Treaty of Peace with Italy, Paris, 10 February 1947, Article 23, Annex XI (Joint Declaration by the Governments of the Soviet Union, of the United Kingdom, of the United States of America and of France concerning Italian Territorial Possessions in Africa). See also pp. 67–68 and fn. 51.

on the main issue of national policy. Accordingly, on 10 January 1948 an organization called the National Congress of Cyrenaica (Al-Mutamar al-Watani) was formed under the Presidency of Sayed Mohamed al-Rida al-Senussi, younger brother of Sayed Idris. This body claimed to represent the political views of all sections and groups throughout Cyrenaica, including the Jewish community, which had a senior seat on its Administrative Council. Although composed mainly of tribal chiefs, the Congress also contained politically active townsmen, several of whom held views close to those of the more moderate members of the former Omar al-Mukhtar Club. One of the two secretaries of this united front was Khalil Qallal, a prominent member of the Club since its early days, and destined to play a leading part in the drafting of the Constitution (see Chapters 7, 8, and 10).

One of the first acts of the Congress was to set up a committee to study the questions of the Amirate and the independence and unity of Libya. As early as 12 January, the committee unanimously agreed on a policy that was then approved, on the same day, by the Administrative Council of the Congress. When the United Nations Commissioner arrived in Benghazi two years later, this decision, reconfirmed in the light of United Nations General Assembly Resolution 289 (IV) of 21 November 1949, was communicated to him in the following summarized form:

> Achieving complete independence for Libya with its natural frontiers and to adhere to the unity of Libya on the basis of the acknowledgement of the Amirate of His Highness Sayed Mohamed Idris al-Mahdi al-Senussi and the restriction of the Amirate in the noble Senussi family, the formation of one administration in Cyrenaica and one or two administrations in the western part of Libya, as our brethren in Tripolitania and Fezzan may agree upon, on a federal basis under the Senussi Crown and the National black flag with the white crescent and the five pointed star, and there shall be one currency throughout.[15]

On the same occasion the Commissioner was given an authentic, duly signed copy in Arabic, together with a translation in English, of a memorandum that had been handed to the Four Power Commission on 30 April 1948. A large part of this nine-page statement was devoted to bitter complaints about the treatment Cyrenaica had suffered at the hands of Italy and to an account of the resistance it had put up, to the heavy losses it had suffered in body and soul, and to the severe war damage it had sustained, for which it demanded compensation. The conclusion of this lament left no room for doubt about Cyrenaica's wishes:

15. Decision No. 62, taken by a plenary session of the Administrative Council of the National Congress of Cyrenaica, held on 21 January 1950. The decision was published in the local press of that date.

The only just solution of the problem is to give our nation her independence and to set Italy far away from her. We do not accept any sort of bargaining amongst the covetous countries, nor do we accept such countries to square up their problems on the account of our nation. We refuse this totally. If any solution, inconsistent with our independence is put forward, we will very strongly resist it until the end.[16]

In the final paragraph of the memorandum, in a section entitled National Ambitions, the authors, after repeating their claim to an independent Cyrenaica under the Senussi Crown, concluded: "If, thereafter, our Tripolitanian brothers are desirous of incorporation under the Senousi Crown it would be possible to unify the Libyan countries as one, otherwise Cyrenaica makes reservation for her independence under the crown of her King." [17]

The Four Power Commission faithfully noted this point of view in its report, adding:

"[The great majority of the inhabitants desire independence under the Emir, most of the remainder being willing to accept whatever form of government is agreed to by him.] *
[As regards the future of Cyrenaica, the overwhelming majority of the people interviewed would follow the Emir in any decision he would make, a large number specifying that they would like to be independent.] **
[It is recognised that there will be a need for assistance from some foreign Power. They leave the choice of that Power to the Emir and often suggest Great Britain. Little interest was shown in or desire expressed for union with Tripolitania, and there is general and determined opposition to the return of the Italians.] ***
[The great majority of those interviewed by the Commission expressed their desire for freedom, independence, and the Emirate of the Senussi.] ****

* USA/UK text — ** French text
*** USA/UK/French text — **** USSR text [18]

16. Memorandum dated 30 April 1948, submitted by the General National Congress of Cyrenaica to the Four Power Commission and published in the local press of that date.

17. Ibid.

18. Four Power Commission of Investigation for the Former Italian Colonies, *Report,* Volume III, *Report on Libya,* Part Four, *Cyrenaica,* pp. 67–68. Mimeographed. There is some doubt whether this report was ever published in print, although it was derestricted fairly soon after it had been presented to the Deputies of the Council of Foreign Ministers. It is undated and unorthodox in layout and pagination. In all quotations cited in this study, the square brackets and asterisked footnotes are those of the authors of the report.

Viewed in the light of Cyrenaica's historical past, the attitude adopted by the National Congress with regard to Tripolitania in fact expressed preference for unification with the western territory, clearly qualified, however, by an option for possible orientation in an easterly direction should it be impossible to reach agreement on the mode of unification. Pending a definitive decision on Libya's future, this policy engendered fear and suspicion among the convinced partisans of Libyan unity, such as the members of the National Association of Cyrenaica. These feelings were not assuaged when on 1 June 1949, after further negotiations with London, Sayed Idris announced the desire of Cyrenaica to achieve its national aim of independence and his intention of forming a government based on an elected parliament. He also sought recognition by the United Kingdom Government of his assumption of all functions of government. On the same day, the Chief Administrator of BMA declared that the United Kingdom Government had recognized the Amir as the freely chosen leader of his people, as the head of the Cyrenaican Government. It moreover formally recognized the desire of Cyrenaicans for self-government and undertook to take all steps compatible with its international obligation to promote that desire; expressed its agreement to the formation of a Cyrenaican government with responsibility over internal affairs; and emphasized that in taking these steps it would do nothing to prejudice the eventual future of Libya as a whole.

On 16 September 1949, the Chief Administrator of the BMA issued the Transitional Powers Proclamation (No. 187), which empowered the Amir to enact by edict a Constitution and defined the powers which that Constitution should confer. It also listed the matters in which power was to be reserved to the representative of the Government of the United Kingdom, who was thereafter to be known as the British Resident in Cyrenaica.[19]

While these developments caused joyful reactions in National Congress circles and among the majority of the population, the Omar al-Mukhtar Club interpreted them primarily as a fresh British attempt to establish a separate State in Cyrenaica, a suspicion that persisted at the time of the Commissioner's arrival in Libya.[20] Had Tripolitania and the Fezzan refused to accept the provisos in the decision and memorandum mentioned on pages 46–47, a Cyrenaican State might well have come into being. However, in that case the Cyrenaican avant-garde could not have blamed the United Kingdom, since the fault would have lain with their fellow countrymen.

19. For further details of these events, see first *Annual Report of the United Nations Commissioner in Libya,* General Assembly Official Records (GAOR hereafter): Fifth Session, 1950, Supplement No. 15 (A/1340), paras. 40–47.

20. In the meantime the so-called Bevin-Sforza plan had been turned down by the United Nations General Assembly (17 May 1949). For a full account of these events, see pp. 79ff.

For both internal and external reasons, Tripolitania's attitude to the question of Libyan unity and independence was very different from that which prevailed in Cyrenaica. Contrary to the situation in Cyrenaica, there was no unanimity about Senussi leadership in Tripolitania, where the Order had never commanded anything like massive membership. In the western provinces, most of the Order's adherents were in the Fezzan. On the other hand, there appeared to be a growing conviction that, from a political point of view, Sayed Idris was probably the only leader round whom the large majority of the Libyan people could rally. Tripolitania had no recognized leader of its own, not for lack of able men, but because family feuds and tribal rivalries, antagonisms between the urban and rural populations, and, last but not least, conflicting political outlooks and opinions had so far inhibited the formation of that basic sense of cohesion that is essential, particularly in time of crisis, if a common policy is to be formulated. Indeed, the situation that had forced the Tripolitanian Republic twenty-odd years earlier to establish collegiate instead of one-man leadership still divided the succeeding generation. This time even the modicum of understanding needed to form a collegiate leadership seems to have been lacking. It must also be recognized, however, that many contributory circumstances were far from favorable to the consolidation of public opinion. Tripoli town had been liberated on 23 January 1943, some two and a half years before the war in Europe came to an end. It was not unnatural that during that period BMA should have been reluctant to allow political activity to develop in a territory whose future status would foreseeably become an international issue to be settled by the as then unknown victorious nations, and which in the meantime had to serve as a base for the invasion of Sicily. It therefore discouraged the formation of political parties and the publication of newspapers, though it permitted cultural societies to function.

Distinctions of this kind are easy to define in theory but difficult to maintain in practice. Where was the line to be drawn between politics and culture, particularly in a country like Tripolitania, where the people, Arab and Italian alike, were seething with impatience to know their destiny? There were, indeed, reasons galore for restlessness. Whereas the Italian population in Cyrenaica had been evacuated by order of the Italian military authorities themselves, in Tripolitania a large number of Italians had remained in the Province.[21] When the British occupied Tripolitania in 1943, there were 38,200 Italians there. By 1947, their number had increased to 44,149 (British figures based on the number of ration cards issued), the

21. According to figures supplied to the Four Power Commission by BMA, there were 43,077 foreigners, almost all of them Italians, in Cyrenaica in 1941. In the Commission's report, it is stated that the total Italian community in Tripolitania amounted to 70,000 in 1940–41.

increase being mainly due to births. It is understandable that up to the signing of the Treaty of Peace with Italy in 1947, the Italian population, particularly the fascist element, having until quite recently been masters of the country, should have found it extremely difficult to adjust themselves to their new status of political suspects in the eyes of the indigenous population. Adaptation was made even more difficult by the attitude of the Republican Government in Italy, which, after having expressed in 1945 the hope that Italian sovereignty might be retained in Tripolitania, West Cyrenaica, and Eritrea, referred with pleasure in 1946 to a proposal made to the Council of Foreign Ministers "to make Italy the trustee of her colonies." [22]

While this policy heartened the Italians in Tripolitania, it made the Arab population even more restless than it had been. The Arabs, moreover, resented the fact that they were not protected against the return of Italian rule, as were their Cyrenaican countrymen under the terms of the public statement made by Eden in 1942. To this feeling of political frustration and insecurity must be added the gloom cast by economic depression. The farmer and orchardman could go back to work, though the 1946–47 and 1947–48 harvests suffered from particularly bad droughts, but trade had come to a standstill. Tripolitania as a whole had suffered far less war damage than Cyrenaica, but Tripoli harbor was blocked by shipping sunk in air raids. In any event, for a large part of 1943 the territory was in use as a base for the invasion of Italy. Roads were badly dilapidated, and many buildings were in urgent need of repair. When commercial activity started up again, it was difficult for the urban population to come to terms with the fact that they were no longer living under the Italian regime of heavy subsidies, and therefore in largely artificial prosperity, but under the very down-to-earth "care and maintenance" policy of a temporary military administration; here was yet another source of discontent.

In brief, by the time the war came to an end and BMA could afford to be more liberal in permitting the politically conscious part of the population to give expression to its views, the situation was sadly confused. When the Four Power Commission arrived in Tripoli on 6 March 1948, it found what it called in its report six "Libyan" political parties: the Nationalist Party, the United National Front, the Free National Bloc, the Egypto-Tripolitanian Union Party, the Labor Party, and the Liberal Party.[23] The authors of the report probably used the term "Libyan" in order to distin-

22. *Italy and the United Nations,* prepared for the Carnegie Endowment for International Peace by a study group set up by the Italian Society for International Organization (New York: Manhattan Publishing Company, 1959), p. 39. See also p. 64.

23. Four Power Commission *Report,* Volume III, Part Two, *Tripolitania,* p. 9.

guish these parties from the minority organizations and the Italian parties it subsequently mentioned. It was, however, an erroneous identification, since not one of the six parties had any membership outside Tripolitania, or even claimed to exercise any influence outside the Province, except, perhaps, and to a limited extent at that, in the Fezzan. Indirectly, the authors corrected their error by adding the following comments:

> The first four were formed and recognised by the British Military Administration in 1946. The others started in 1947 and are of considerably less importance. In addition there is the National Council for the Liberation of Libya, formed of Tripolitanian exiles, with its headquarters in Cairo.
>
> The programme of all the political parties regarding the future of Tripolitania is identical, i.e., complete independence, the unity of Tripolitania, Cyrenaica and the Fezzan, and membership of the Arab League. They submitted a joint memorandum to the Commission explaining this programme in detail. The Egypto-Tripolitanian Union Party in addition advocates the union of Libya with Egypt under the Egyptian Crown while the Liberal Party favours the Emirate of Sayyid Mohammed Idris el Senussi. All except the small Labour Party support the National Council for the Liberation of Libya [see p. 52] which acts to some extent as a central organisation for the promotion of the agreed programme. The political parties have expressed friendly feelings towards the Italians living in Tripolitania and stated that they would give them complete equality of rights with the Libyans once independence is attained. The main obstacles to fusion of the parties have been personal rivalries of the leaders and differences on the question of the form of the future State.
>
> The political parties are not democratic in their internal structure and have no social or cultural activities in the territory. The parties do not embrace the mass of the population, especially outside Tripoli Town, and the people as a rule do not have a clear understanding of the implications of the party programmes.[24]

These comments leave the writer with the impression that, perhaps because of wishful thinking, the Four Power Commission underrated at the time of its visit to Libya the strength of conviction of those Tripolitanians who wished to reach agreement with Cyrenaica, and who were in favor of a united Libya under Senussi leadership. Indeed, it is striking to note that in 1946–47 Tripolitanian leaders, like their forbears at the Gharyan Conference, had made a serious attempt to approach Sayed Idris. In June 1946

24. Ibid.

a delegation was sent to consult him in Cairo. The initiative in this action was taken by the United National Front, an organization consisting mainly of urban and rural conservative notables and tribal sheikhs. The delegation was the bearer of a plan aiming at the achievement of Libya's unity and independence under Senussi leadership. The form of government was to be constitutional, democratic, and parliamentary. The country was to seek membership in the Arab League. Sayed Idris agreed to these principles, and the plan was discussed in greater detail between Cyrenaican and Tripolitanian leaders, first in Cairo and subsequently in January 1947 in Benghazi, in his presence. Disagreement developed on such points as the hereditary nature of the Senussi Amirate, regarding which the Tripolitanians made some reservations. Another cause of dispute concerned the composition of a joint committee for promoting the common interests of the country under the Amir's guidance, Cyrenaica asking for equal representation, Tripolitania, as the more populous territory, wishing to be in the majority. What really broke the camel's back, however, was a Tripolitanian demand that any offer of independence or trusteeship made by the Great Powers to either of the two provinces without regard for the wishes of the other should be rejected. Cyrenaica took the line that it would continue to seek unity, but could not bind itself unconditionally, for, if offered a special status, it must accept.[25] Or, to put matters another way, if Cyrenaica were to receive a promise of independence, it would not reject it even if Tripolitania received no similar promise. Behind this issue lay Cyrenaica's chronic fear that in some form or another—for instance, under a trusteeship—Tripolitania might once more come under Italian rule or influence, in which case Cyrenaica had no desire to be tied to Tripolitania by a promise of unity. This failure to reach agreement left bitter feelings on both sides. It also caused profound disappointment among Libyan refugees in Egypt and other countries in the Near East. As a result, and with the help of the League of Arab States, a body known as the National Council for the Liberation of Libya (NCLL) was established in March 1947, with headquarters in Cairo. Its leader was Beshir Bey Saadawi, a Libyan by birth, who had participated in Tripolitanian politics at the time of the Republic and gone into exile as a political refugee after that short-lived State was overthrown in 1923. He had acquired extensive experience and knowledge of international events between the two world wars and during the second one. His last function before heading NCLL was that of adviser to King Ibn Saud of Saudi Arabia. He never lost interest in the cause of Libyan unity and independ-

25. For a detailed account of these negotiations, see Khadduri, pp. 84–95. In later years the Commissioner heard a similar version of these events in the course of conversations with Libyans who had been party to them.

ence, and was a convinced supporter of Sayed Idris as the only man who could bring Cyrenaica and Tripolitania, and eventually the Fezzan also, together in one State. However, in 1947, and even at the beginning of 1950 when the Commissioner met him for the first time, his ideas about the form the future State should assume were still in a formative stage.

The word "Liberation" in NCLL's title was in fact beside the point since Libya had already been liberated. If it was none the less appreciated by many Libyans, this was because of their fear that the country, or parts of it, might be left under foreign domination. Apart from its name as standard-bearer, NCLL's immediate aim was to promote more purposeful and less divergent political thought among the Tripolitanian leaders and to bring about an understanding between them and their Cyrenaican opposite numbers. The March 1948 visit to Libya of the Four Power Commission was indeed a favorable occasion for such a call for unity, but Saadawi's aim of uniting all parties in one organization with a common program remained an arduous task, though he was generally accepted as leader in Tripolitania. In fact, it required the impact of the Bevin-Sforza plan and the violent reaction this plan provoked on 8 and 9 May 1949 to bring the Nationalist Party and the United National Front together in a joint organization under the name of the Tripolitanian National Congress, with Saadawi at its head. From that moment onward, the Congress Party, as it was popularly called, became the leading political factor in Tripolitania. It organized the demonstrations against the Bevin-Sforza plan, as well as the joyful celebrations which followed its rejection by the General Assembly.[26]

The Congress Party leaders, watching, under Saadawi's guidance, the turn of events affecting Libya on the international stage, belatedly came to realize that it was high time they defined their position with regard to Senussi leadership and their relationship with Cyrenaica. In June, therefore, after the declaration of Cyrenaican internal independence, they sent a delegation to Benghazi to present the Party's congratulations to the Amir. The questions of unity and supreme leadership were discussed once more, and although, in view of the decisions to be taken during the approaching Fourth Regular Session of the General Assembly, no formal agreement was concluded, the atmosphere was decidedly happier than on the previous occasion. This improvement in mutual relations was consolidated in July and August when the Amir passed through Tripoli twice on his way to and from a State visit to London. In August, when reviewing its program, the Congress Party reiterated its claim for a united and independent Libya but this time unreservedly agreed to Senussi leadership. Thus, between 1921

26. See fn. 20.

and 1949 Tripolitania had come full circle with regard to the question of a joint Senussi Amirate over the two coastal territories of Libya.

Since the developments just described occurred after the visit of the Four Power Commission, the section of its report dealing with the wishes of the population was out of date by the time it reached delegations to the General Assembly. It is nevertheless interesting to note that on this important matter there was a clear-cut difference of opinion between the French, the United Kingdom, and the United States delegations on the one hand, and the USSR delegation on the other.[27] The three first-named delegations found that the majority of the people interrogated were in favor of an independent and united Libya affiliated to the Arab League. A considerable proportion of them wanted independence at once, while the rest considered that, the country not being ripe for independence, a transitional period under the guidance of a European power—preferably Italy, because it was already well known to the peoples of Libya—was necessary. These three delegations further noted that the population, finding the existing regime intolerable, were unanimous in wanting a quick decision. The Soviet text on the subject noted that some people had expressed fear of reprisals and trouble as a consequence of frank expression of their views, and that, moreover, certain police measures had restricted free contact between the population and the Commission. The USSR delegation also stated that it had received complaints that BMA favored Arab propaganda activities at the expense of those of pro-Italian organizations and individuals. It further noted that local Arabic newspapers published by the British information services had printed proclamations emanating from prominent Moslem religious leaders in Egypt calling on the population to vote for independence, unity, and affiliation to the Arab League. Emigré Libyans, including interpreters working in BMA, expressed strong pan-Arab feelings, while local representatives of the administration, as well as notables, sheikhs, and representatives of leading families, frightened the population with threats against those who entertained pro-Italian sentiments. The USSR delegation also alleged that, according to evidence in the Commission's possession, mudirs and sheikhs issued rationed goods only to those who agreed to oppose the return of Italy, refusing them to those who declined to do so. Finally, it noted that when the Four Power Commission toured the country to ascertain the wishes of the population, it was as a rule preceded by a delegation from NCLL, the members of which told the population how and what to answer to the Commission's questions. It was at about this time, while the Four Power Commission was still in Tripoli, that the Soviet Union addressed a note to

27. Four Power Commission *Report,* Volume III, Part Two, *Tripolitania,* pp. 83–91 and 94.

the Italian Government stating that it was in favor of Italian trusteeship over all Italy's former colonies.[28] Comparison of the two positions shows that both sides, though in different ways, mentioned possible Italian trusteeship. The explanation is that a general election was due to be held in Italy in April 1948. Both East and West, by that time deeply engaged in the cold war, were competing for Italy's favors, the Soviet Union supporting the Italian Communist Party, the Western powers doing their best to strengthen the position of de Gasperi's Government. The fact that both anglers confidently expected their potential prize to be attracted by the same bait is a graphic comment on the feelings prevailing at the time in Italy with regard to the former colonies. In a way, these feelings were understandable, but they had an alarming effect on Libyan leaders and drove them to close their ranks.

This brief account of the attempts made by the leaders of the Libyan territories between 1939 and 1949 to bring them together into one independent State would be incomplete without some mention of the Fezzan. Lying as it does in Libya's remote southwest, its administrative center, Sabhah, being separated from the Mediterranean coast by more than 400 miles of barren wastes, the Fezzan has always retained a character of its own. It was, and still is, by far the least populous of the three provinces. The population is in part sedentary and in part nomadic or seminomadic, living in scattered villages and oases in various parts of the territory. It is naturally the poorest part of Libya and still has a rather low standard of living. According to an estimate made by the French Military Administration (FMA), approximately 90 percent of the population was illiterate in 1948. During the Italian occupation some schools had been built, and with the arrival of the Free French Forces in 1943 a French educational system had been instituted, but education was at a very low level. The main occupation of the Fezzanese at that time was small-scale agriculture entirely dependent on water. As the first French Government report to the United Nations put it: "Everything is on a modest scale, like the country itself." [29]

There were neither political parties nor local newspapers in the Fezzan. The number of people with wireless receivers must have been very small. Surprisingly, this did not mean that the Fezzanese were completely ignorant of events in the outside world. For centuries, one of the main caravan

28. George Henry Becker, Jr., *The Disposition of the Italian Colonies 1941–1951*, Thèse No. 87 de l'Université de Genève, Institut Universitaire de Hautes Etudes Internationales (Annemasse, France: Imprimerie Granchamp, 1952), p. 112, fn. 1.

29. "Annual report of the French Government to the General Assembly concerning the administration of the Fezzan," GAOR: Fifth Session, 1950, Annexes, Agenda item 21 (A/1387, 22 September 1950), p. 4.

routes from Central Africa to the Mediterranean had passed through the Fezzan, as it was served to a large extent by Fezzanese camels and their drivers. Though this traffic had dwindled to almost nothing by the outbreak of World War I, the opening of ports and harbors on the west coast of Africa, among other causes, meant that there remained in the Fezzan a class of traders who, distinct from the farmers, maintained traditional links with Tripolitania. Another line of contact with the coast was the largely seasonal migration of heads of families, who, for lack of local opportunities, were obliged to live temporarily to make a living either in the coastal cities of Tunisia or in Tripolitania. Through these channels, as well as through traveling merchants, news penetrated into the Fezzan so that, as experience proved, there were a good number of politically conscious people there with opinions of their own about the future of their territory in the light of postwar developments. Rather than ignorance, their problem was the difficulty of communication between one oasis or village and another, and hence the impossibility of consulting one another. Up to the arrival of the French, the only institutions were religious in nature; in this connection it is worth mentioning that a remnant of Senussi influence still lingered on from the time when lodges of the order (*Zawiya*) existed in the Fezzan.

At first, FMA showed no tendency to annex the country. The French were there by virtue of the Hague Rules of 1907 and therefore, in principle, on a temporary basis.[30] However, as years went by the impression spread that the French Government wanted to add the territory of the Fezzan, as defined in 1943 by the agreement between General Montgomery and General Leclerc (see p. 41), to one of the neighboring African territories under French administration. They began by establishing traffic barriers and obstacles between the Fezzan and Tripolitania in an attempt to divert trade to Tunisia. Seasonal migration to Tripoli was also made more difficult. This provoked a timid resistance movement which found expression in the formation of a secret society in 1946; its President was Sheikh Abd al-Rahman Bin Mohamed al-Barquli and its Vice-President Mohamed Bin Othman al-Sayd. Both these names will come up again in this study.

30. The so-called "Hague Rules" were adopted at the Peace Conference held at The Hague in 1907. Those applying in Cyrenaica and Tripolitania under British Military Administration and in the Fezzan under French Military Administration comprise Articles 42–46 of Section III (Military Authority over the Territory of the Hostile State) of the Annex (Regulations respecting the Laws and Customs of War on Land) to Convention IV of 1907 respecting the Laws and Customs of War on Land. For the text, see *The Hague Conventions and Declarations of 1899 and 1907,* ed. James Brown Scott (New York: Oxford University Press, for the Carnegie Endowment for International Peace, 1918), pp. 122–27. See also Chapter 2, p. 129.

According to Khadduri's version, in 1947 this movement was penetrated by the French authorities, who arrested the principal leaders.[31] When, three years later, the United Nations Commissioner visited the Fezzan, he was told about these events in much the same words as Khadduri uses. The consequences were nevertheless of a lasting nature, and will be further referred to in Chapter 2. The salient fact is that, notwithstanding all the precautions the French authorities took, they never quite succeeded in preventing travelers from carrying messages back and forth between the Fezzan and Tripolitania. At the same time, the suppression of the society made it more difficult than ever for political opinion to develop and be propagated among the population. It is therefore not surprising that when the Four Power Commission visited the Fezzan in April 1948 it found, according to the Soviet Union text, the following opinions about the future government of the territory: 44 percent of those questioned were in favor of the French Administration (about half of these were Tuareg); 26 percent were for any government; 18 percent were for an Islamic government; and 12 percent were content to accept the decision of the Four Powers. The more detailed French/United Kingdom/United States text also reveals that opinions about the future of the country varied greatly throughout the territory.[32] That a fairly large proportion should favor the French Administration was not surprising, as the social policy of the French authorities had brought improvements which were appreciated by the people. The sedentary Fezzanese who had no political pursuits were also favorably impressed by the sense of security the French occupation gave them against marauding nomads. On the other hand, when the Commissioner visited the territory two years after the Four Power Commission, he found that those, admittedly not many, who had been courageous enough to come out in favor of a united and independent Libya, or similar aims, had had reason to regret their frankness. This aspect of the Fezzanese problem will be discussed further in the next chapter.

To summarize the internal situation in Libya as a whole, it seems undeniable that during the period 1939 to 1949 the movement in favor of unity and independence had steadily gathered momentum; that several major efforts had been made by Cyrenaica and Tripolitania to reach agreement on a mutually acceptable form of unity; that at the center of these efforts the Amir Idris was playing an increasingly important part; but that no constructive results had been achieved by the time the Libyan question was turned over to the General Assembly of the United Nations.

31. Khadduri, pp. 107–09.

32. Four Power Commission *Report,* Volume III, Part Three, *The Fezzan,* pp. 45–48.

PART 2. FOREIGN ATTEMPTS TO PROMOTE OR DISCOURAGE UNITY AND INDEPENDENCE

After having followed the course of the efforts made by the Libyans themselves to achieve unity with the aim of ultimately attaining independence, it is now necessary to analyze in broad outline the policies followed by the Powers which undertook the task of determining the future of the Italian colonies, and, insofar as possible, the motives behind those policies. For the purposes of this study, the analysis will be confined to the case of Libya, except where, for tactical reasons, the destinies of other Italian colonies were linked with it in the course of the negotiations.

The defeat of Italy had brought Libya under British (in Cyrenaica and Tripolitania) and French (in the Fezzan) military administration. These administrations observed, as far as local conditions permitted, the Hague Rules of 1907, that is to say, in principle they were "care and maintenance" administrations (see p. 56 and fn. 30). The Italian Military Armistice of 3 September 1943 and the Additional Conditions of the Armistice transmitted to the Italian Government at Malta in September 1944 said nothing about the fate of Italy's colonies. Section 41 of the Additional Conditions stipulated, indeed, that "The provisions of the present instrument shall not apply in or affect the administration of any Italian colony or dependency already occupied by the United Nations or the rights or powers therein possessed or exercised by them." [33] Therefore, when the Big Three—the United Kingdom, the United States of America, and the Union of Soviet Socialist Republics—meeting at Potsdam in July 1945, instructed the Council of Foreign Ministers (CFM), set up on the same occasion, "to continue the necessary preparatory work for the peace settlements," [34] the road ahead was free of commitments, except for the declared position of the United Kingdom with regard to Cyrenaica in particular and to all the Italian colonies in general. On 21 September 1943, Winston Churchill had said in the House of Commons that Italy had "irretrievably lost her African Empire," [35] and on 4 October 1944 this position had been confirmed by the Foreign Secretary in reply to a member's question.[36]

33. U.S. Dept. of State, *United States and Italy, 1936–1946, Documentary Record,* No. 2669, European Series 17 (Washington: Government Printing Office, 1946), p. 63.

34. Ibid., p. 160.

35. Hansard, (1943), *399,* col. 102.

36. Ibid. (1944), *403,* col. 908.

At the Yalta Conference, in February 1945, there had been some discussion, in view of the forthcoming United Nations Conference on International Organization, which was scheduled to be held at San Francisco from 25 April to 26 June of that year, about the possibility of placing non-self-governing territories under a trusteeship system. It had been agreed not to discuss specific cases; the Conference was to deal only with principles and machinery. As a result, the Charter of the United Nations, drafted and adopted at the San Francisco Conference, contains three chapters relating to colonial problems: Chapter XI, "Declaration Regarding Non-Self-Governing Territories"; Chapter XII, "International Trusteeship System"; and Chapter XIII, "The Trusteeship Council." This was a progressive development of the mandates system and philosophy of the League of Nations and as such was destined to play an important part in the negotiations and discussions on the future of the Italian colonies. The declaration in particular appealed to many governments. It bound Member States responsible for non-self-governing territories "to recognize the principle that the interests of the inhabitants of these territories are paramount, and accept as a sacred trust the obligation to promote to the utmost, . . . the well-being of the inhabitants of these territories." To this end they were, among other things, "to develop self-government, to take due account of the political aspirations of the peoples, and to assist them in the progressive development of their free political institutions, according to the particular circumstances of each territory and its peoples and their varying stages of advancement" (Article 73). Opinions were divided, however, about the merits and demerits of the three forms of trusteeship defined in Article 77, and about Article 81 which provides that "[The administering authority of a trust territory] . . . may be one or more states or the Organization itself." Signed by fifty members on 27 June 1945, the Charter of the United Nations came into force on 24 October of the same year.

Consequently, when the Foreign Ministers of the four Great Powers—the three Potsdam Powers, joined by France—met for the first time, from 11 September to 2 October 1945, in London, to examine the disposal of the former Italian colonies,[37] they were preoccupied not only by their own conflicting aims and interests but also by the problem of how to reconcile them with the spirit and letter of the Charter.

What were their aims and interests? Today, when Libyans discuss the emergence of their country as an independent State, they like to recall with

37. The question of Libya was generally treated together with that of the other Italian colonies—Italian Somaliland and Eritrea—but their eventual disposal was the subject of separate votes by the General Assembly on different sections of the same resolution.

a twinkle in their eye that, fortunately, the presence of oil in the deep layers of the subsoil, though suspected by Italian geologists as early as the 1930s,[38] was still considered in the 1940s as so remote a possibility that it played no dominant part in the postwar discussions. As no other minerals or economically workable raw materials were known to exist, and other resources were so meagre as to make Libya one of the poorest countries in the world, it was obvious that the competition between the principal Powers was not due to the country's economic attractions.

The problem takes on quite another aspect when looked at from the strategic angle, as a glance at the map will show more vividly than a great deal of exegesis. A country with a coastline of approximately 1,100 miles running opposite the "belly" of Europe from Sicily to Cyprus, commanding the middle of the southern shore of the Mediterranean sea, close to which pass the shortest navigable east-west seaways, could not fail to attract the interest of every sailor, soldier, or diplomat with thoughts of world power at the back of his mind. Even airmen, though to them the Mediterranean is more a broad ditch than a sea, feel the same interest, for air bases established on Libya's shores would provide ideal possibilities of reconnoitering and controlling the sea routes, not to mention more far-reaching operations.

Under the conditions prevailing at the end of World War II, the United Kingdom, having lost a good deal of its influence in the Near East, particularly in Palestine and Egypt, naturally looked for compensatory balance to the eastern Mediterranean basin, as close as possible to the Suez Canal. Cyrenaica seemed to it to be one of the best places available. This in itself was enough to provoke the opposition of the Soviet Union which, besides wanting to see the British zone of influence pushed back as far as possible to the west and south, also had ambitions of its own in the area. How else can one explain Stalin's mentioning at Potsdam in one and the same breath the question of trusteeship and his country's desire for some territory from the defeated States? That desire was aimed at the Italian territories. This was confirmed when the Soviet Union proposed itself as trustee for one of the Italian colonies, preferably Tripolitania. To this, Churchill replied: "I had not considered the possibility of the Soviet Union desiring to acquire a large tract of the African shore. If this is the case, it will have to be considered in relation to many other problems." [39] France, so to speak, had but a negative interest in the future of Libya. Her true interest, obviously, was to remain in North Africa as long as possible. Hence, she was not in

38. For an account of Italian efforts to strike oil in Libya, see Ardito Desio, "L'oro nero nel sotto suolo della Libia," *La Via del Mondo, 6* (1960).

39. James F. Byrnes, *Speaking Frankly* (New York: Harper & Brothers, 1947), p. 76.

favor of trusteeship in any part of Libya; but if this proved unavoidable, she would prefer Italy, the former colonial Power, to be the trustee, rather than have a collective trusteeship exercised by the United Nations, as proposed by the United States of America.

The United States, uninhibited by a colonial past, except insofar as it had once itself been an agglomeration of British colonies, took a somewhat more far-sighted view, though without losing sight of its own interests. These consisted of creating peaceful conditions in the Mediterranean by giving Arab nationalism a reasonable chance of expressing itself, by opposing the expansion of Soviet influence in the area, and by strengthening its own position there through the establishment, with United Kingdom consent, of an air base on the Libyan coast near Tripoli.[40]

During the CFM discussions in London in September 1945, the Soviet Union, in view of the military occupation of Tripolitania and Cyrenaica by the United Kingdom and that of the Fezzan by France, demanded that the country be divided into four parts, each to be administered by one of the Big Four, with itself in control of Tripolitania. France, opposing trusteeship as a dangerous precedent for her neighboring dependencies of Tunisia, Algeria, and Morocco, advocated the return of the Libyan territories to Italy. The United Kingdom reserved its position, but irrevocably rejected their return to Italy, evoking its wartime promise that Cyrenaica would never again fall under Italian domination. The United States proposed a ten-year collective trusteeship by the Big Four under United Nations auspices, after which Libya would become independent. According to the United States Secretary of State, "This plan would give assurance that the Italian colonies [including of course Libya] would not be developed for the military advantage of anyone." [41]

At the end of CFM's first session, there was agreement in principle that Libya would be brought under the trusteeship provisions of the United Nations Charter, but there was no agreement on the form of the trusteeship or who was to be the administering authority. The Deputies to the Foreign Ministers were instructed to work out an agreement along the lines of the American proposal, but were unable to reconcile the various demands.

When CFM itself met for its second session in Paris on 25 April 1946

40. For a detailed account of these and following negotiations in CFM on the future of Libya, see *Rapports Officiels du Conseil des Ministres des Affaires Etrangères* (Paris: Imprimerie Nationale, 1946), Vols. I–IV. For a concise but fairly detailed summary thereof, see Benjamin Rivlin, *United Nations Action: Italian Colonies* (New York: Carnegie Endowment for International Peace, 1950); and Becker, *Disposition of the Italian Colonies.*

41. Byrnes, p. 94.

in an increasingly deteriorating cold-war atmosphere, three of the Big Four had changed their positions. The United Kingdom now advocated immediate independence for a united Libya, a proposal enthusiastically greeted by the Arab world. The Soviet Union, well aware of Cyrenaica's desire for a British alliance, and wary of any move that might enhance British influence in the Near East, rejected the British suggestion, proposing instead a complicated collective trusteeship system:

> Pour une période ne dépassant pas dix ans, les colonies italiennes seraient placées sous une régime de tutelle collective de deux Etats dont l'un serait une des Puissances alliées et dont l'autre serait l'Italie. Ces deux Etats seraient par exemple pour la Tripolitaine, l'U.R.S.S. et l'Italie, et pour la Cyrénaique les Etats-Unis (ou l'Angleterre) et l'Italie, etc. L'Administrateur de chaque territoire serait responsable devant le Conseil de tutelle de l'O.N.U.; il serait désigné par le gouvernement de la Puissance alliée en question, son adjoint étant désigné par le gouvernement italien. L'administrateur et son adjoint seraient assistés d'un Comité Consultatif composé de 5 membres, à savoir 3 représentants des Puissances alliées (U.R.S.S., Etats-Unis, Royaume Uni, France) qui ne désignent pas l'administrateur et 2 représentants de la population locale. C'est ainsi par exemple que pour la Tripolitaine, le Comité consultatif pourrait être composé des représentants des Etats-Unis, du Royaume Uni et de la France et de deux représentants de la population locale.[42]

When this was adamantly refused, the USSR discarded the whole idea of individual Big Four trusteeships and, alert to the possibilities that would flow from a communist victory in the impending Italian general elections, supported the return of Libya and all other Italian colonies to Italy, but under trusteeship. The United States, too, had abandoned the idea of collective trusteeship as a potentially dangerous precedent for its own holdings in the Pacific, and now also supported Italian trusteeship over Libya, provided a definite date for independence was set. France, hopeful of retaining the Fezzan, agreed to this suggestion, provided, however, that no such date was fixed. The United Kingdom would agree only on condition that Cyrenaica was excepted and placed under British trusteeship. As each Power had reached the limit of the compromises it was willing to make, CFM was deadlocked, and once again the problem was referred to the Deputies.

42. *Rapports Officiels du Conseil des Ministres des Affaires Etrangères,* Vol. II, p. 16.

At the end of CFM's second session, the United States tabled two proposals, the first requiring Italy to renounce all right and title to her colonies, the second providing for one year's delay as from the date of entry into force of the Peace Treaty, before the final decision on the disposal of the former colonies need be taken.

When the third CFM session opened on 15 June 1946 in Paris, these two proposals were approved by the other three Powers, though on the final solution to the problem all four were still far apart, particularly the United Kingdom and the Soviet Union. The United Kingdom sought to improve upon the procedural aspect of the two proposals by submitting a draft article for inclusion in the Peace Treaty, accompanied by a Four Power declaration providing a choice of solutions: independence; incorporation in a neighboring territory; United Nations collective trusteeship; or trusteeship to be exercised by individual members of CFM. Each delegation found something of its own brew among these various possibilities. The draft declaration also contained a provision stipulating that, in the event of failure to reach agreement, the matter would be referred to the General Assembly of the United Nations, whose recommendations in the matter the Four Powers would agree to accept and implement.[43] It also contained a suggestion that a commission of inquiry be dispatched to the former Italian colonies to ascertain the views of the local population, and to supply the Deputies to the Foreign Ministers with material that would enable them to make recommendations to CFM itself. After the Deputies had studied and slightly revised this proposal, it was approved by CFM and the Four Powers themselves in July 1946 (see p. 45).

The Peace Conference opened in Paris on 29 July. CFM's decision had been a bitter pill for both the Italian Government and its people. As recently as August 1945 the Italian Prime Minister, Ferruccio Parri, and the Minister of Foreign Affairs, Alcide de Gasperi, had respectively written to the United States President (Harry S. Truman) and the Secretary of State (James F. Byrnes), expressing their government's hopes and expectations

> that the sovereignty of Italy might be retained in Tripolitania, West Cyrenaica, and Eritrea, [stating] that there would be no outstanding difficulty in the creation of a strategic zone in East Cyrenaica. Ample facilities would, it was promised, be accorded to Ethiopia in the port of Assab in Eritrea. The creation of a collective trusteeship was urged for Italian Somaliland and adjacent zones.[44]

43. Provision originally proposed by the United States Secretary of State, James F. Byrnes.

44. *Italy and the United Nations,* p. 38. For full texts of these letters, see *United States and Italy, 1936–1946, Documentary Record,* p. 63.

To understand Italy's official policy regarding her colonies after the war and the time it took to evolve, it is also necessary to take into account the state of Italian public opinion on the subject. This has been summarized as follows by the representative study group of Italian scholars responsible for the account of relations between Italy and the United Nations prepared for the Carnegie Endowment for International Peace:

> It is clear that the dissatisfaction shown by Italian public opinion sprang principally from fear that the original rights on which Italian colonization in Africa was based, as well as the conception which had inspired the Italian regime, would not be considered impartially. Thus, it was felt that the Italian presence in Africa was based on original rights of the same nature as those governing other colonial territories. Why, therefore, it was asked, should these rights be contested only in the case of Italy? Others added that the military occupation of Libya, Eritrea, and Somaliland had made it impossible for Italy to show that it too could have advanced in line with the general evolution of the colonial policies that began at the start of World War II.[45]

Two Italian authors, Salvemini and La Piana, had written in *What to do with Italy,* published in London in 1943:

> Eritrea, Somaliland and Libya have been lost as a result of the present war. The pleasure of collecting deserts and sinking money in them has already been too costly for Italy. But from talks with many citizens and residents of Italian extraction in this country [the United Kingdom] we have reached the conclusion that if the old Italian colonies were taken away from Italy and given to someone else, Italians of all parties would consider this loss an unpardonable injustice. The same frame of mind prevails, no doubt, in Italy as well. If colonies are coveted for reasons of prestige, there is no reason why some countries must monopolize this prestige to the exclusion of others. If colonies are desired for reasons of self-interest, there is no reason why some countries may see their interests satisfied and others not.
>
> The only way to deal with the colonial problem is to internationalize the colonies. All colonies should be considered as a trust of the entire world, and they should be put under the surveillance of an international administration in which all countries participate. In this collective trust there must be neither privilege for one nation nor unfavorable discrimination against another. Each must have the right to work and trade under equal conditions.[46]

45. *Italy and the United Nations,* p. 56.
46. As quoted in Becker, pp. 125–26.

Reactions in the Italian press and Parliament during the first year after the war suggest that these two authors, though writing abroad, had correctly gauged the Italian people's feelings. It is noteworthy, however, that they do not seem to have envisaged the possibility of independence for one or more of the Italian colonies.

On 10 August 1946, at a plenary meeting of CFM, the Italian Prime Minister, de Gasperi, nevertheless sounded a note of optimism by stating:

> We note with pleasure that the proposal made to the Council of Foreign Ministers on May 10th, to make Italy the trustee of her colonies, met with some approval. We are confident that such suggestions will prove their worth when the time comes to decide them.
>
> Provided we are not asked to sign away our rights before such a time, we have no objection to postponement and to the continuance of the present military rule in those territories. But we trust that their administration during the year's delay shall be—in accordance with international law—at least partly entrusted to Italian officials even if under the supervision of the occupation Authorities. At the same time we insist that the many tens of thousands of refugees from Libya, Eritrea and Somaliland, who are now living precariously in Italy, or in Concentration Camps in Rhodesia and Kenya, may be allowed to return home.[47]

On 23 September 1946, Ivanoe Bonomi, leader of the Italian delegation to the Peace Conference, addressing the Political and Territorial Commission for Italy, explained Italy's policy with regard to its colonies in the following terms:

> He began by expressing the hope that Italy not be asked to give up its work in the colonies just as it was beginning to bear fruit. In considering the matter of the Italian settlers in those territories, he continued, two factors had to be taken into account: first, that one was dealing with problems of workers and work and, therefore, of economic and social justice, and second, that if the will of the people were to be taken into account, the wishes of those Italians who still resided in Libya, Eritrea, and Somaliland, or who were there as refugees or internees, should not be passed over in silence.
>
> Speaking of the collaboration between Italians and the indigenous people, Mr. Bonomi declared that democratic Italy looked upon the Arab countries of the Middle East with particular friendship and admiration for their progress, and considered renewal of cordial relations to be of

47. *Collection of Documents of the Paris Conference,* Vol. I, Verbatim Records of the Plenary Meetings, Part IV, 9th–28th Meetings, 29 July–15 October 1946 (Paris: Imprimerie Nationale, 1951), pp. 226–27. Mimeographed.

great importance. An Italian trusteeship in Libya would, he continued, furnish the occasion and the proof. As for the provisional administration of these territories, he pointed out that in occupied territories it was customary, pursuant to the rules of international law, to maintain the local administration under the military control of the occupying power. But in Italy's African territories British military administration has completely replaced Italian administration. It was, he concluded, most unacceptable to Italians to bear such conditions for still another year.[48]

The Italian position was further elucidated in a note presented on 4 November 1946 by the Italian Ambassador to Washington, Alberto Tarchiani, to the four Foreign Ministers:

> First, he asserted that, although Italy was according to the draft peace treaty to renounce its sovereign rights in the colonies, the draft did not indicate the legal status to be given the areas. Nor was there any consideration of the situation which would be created in Italy. The draft proposal, therefore, contravened any fair evaluation of the work which Italy had put into the improvement and future development of the colonies. And, as a second point, the Italian government stressed again a definite reservation in the event of a unilateral and unjust judgment.[49]

Hence, Italy's position before the signing of the Treaty was well known. Nor was she alone in advancing her claims. In particular, Brazil wished the colonies to remain in Italian hands and proposed an amendment to the draft declaration to that effect, providing that Italy should be made the trustee of all her former colonies with the exception of Cyrenaica. Other amendments were also proposed. Egypt in particular presented several territorial claims, some of which would have affected her frontier with Libya.[50] The Chinese delegation advocated that Libya be given its independence immediately, or, failing that, be administered by the United Nations under the international trusteeship system. Australia did not want the future of the Italian colonies to be determined by the General Assembly of the United Nations, if the Big Four failed to agree on a solution, but by

48. *Italy and the United Nations,* pp. 39–40. For original text, see U.S. Dept. of State, *Paris Peace Conference, 1946: Selected Documents,* No. 2868, Conference Series 103, Doc. No. 4 (P) (Washington: Government Printing Office, 1946), pp. 204–06.

49. *Italy and the United Nations,* pp. 40–41. For original text, see *Paris Peace Conference, 1946: Selected Documents,* Doc. No. 22, p. 10.

50. Egypt's claims were based on considerations of national security. They related in particular to the Bay and Plateau of Sallum, the port of Bardia on that bay, and the oasis of Jaghbub. See also Chapter 5, Part 5.

those Powers that had contributed to the defeat of Italy. New Zealand, on the contrary, proposed that Italian sovereignty over the colonies be transferred to the United Nations, and the question of their future brought immediately before the General Assembly without wasting another year. Finally, South Africa tabled an amendment similar in spirit to that of Australia. Toward the end of the Conference, the Brazilian and New Zealand amendments were put to the vote and defeated. The others were withdrawn by their sponsors on the ground that the Four Power Joint Declaration, which was to be annexed to the Peace Treaty, contained a provision to the effect that the views of "other interested governments" would be taken into consideration. When the final vote on draft Article 17 (Article 23 in the definitive text) was taken, Australia abstained, the only Power to do so. Indeed, throughout the Conference, the Four Powers had been adamant in refusing to accept modifications to CFM's text on the Italian colonies.

The texts of Article 23 and of the Joint Declaration as they appear in the Peace Treaty read as follows:

Article 23

1. Italy renounces all right and title to the Italian territorial possessions in Africa, i.e. Libya, Eritrea and Italian Somaliland.
2. Pending their final disposal, the said possessions shall continue under their present administration.
3. The final disposal of these possessions shall be determined jointly by the Governments of the Soviet Union, of the United Kingdom, of the United States of America, and of France within one year from the coming into force of the present Treaty, in the manner laid down in the joint declaration of February 10, 1947, issued by the said Governments, which is reproduced in Annex XI.

Annex XI

Joint Declaration by the Governments of the Soviet Union, of the United Kingdom, of the United States of America and of France concerning Italian Territorial Possessions in Africa

1. The Governments of the Union of Soviet Socialist Republics, of the United Kingdom of Great Britain and Northern Ireland, of the United States of America, and of France agree that they will, within one year from the coming into force of the Treaty of Peace with Italy bearing the date of February 10, 1947, jointly determine the final disposal of Italy's territorial possessions in Africa, to which, in accordance with Article 23 of the Treaty, Italy renounces all right and title.
2. The final disposal of the territories concerned and the appropriate

adjustment of their boundaries shall be made by the Four Powers in the light of the wishes and welfare of the inhabitants and the interests of peace and security, taking into consideration the views of other interested Governments.

3. If with respect to any of these territories the Four Powers are unable to agree upon their disposal within one year from the coming into force of the Treaty of Peace with Italy, the matter shall be referred to the General Assembly of the United Nations for a recommendation, and the Four Powers agree to accept the recommendation and to take appropriate measures for giving effect to it.

4. The Deputies of the Foreign Ministers shall continue the consideration of the question of the disposal of the former Italian Colonies with a view to submitting to the Council of Foreign Ministers their recommendations on this matter. They shall also send out commissions of investigation to any of the former Italian Colonies in order to supply the Deputies with the necessary data on this question and to ascertain the views of the local population.[51]

Reference has already been made in Part 1 to the reactions in the field to the Four Power Commission's activities (see pp. 45–47). The Commission was duly constituted on 20 October 1947, and received instructions from the Deputy Foreign Ministers. These left it wide freedom of action, with a few reservations, the principal of which was that it was not allowed to make any recommendations about the final disposal of the former colonies. Hence, the Commission was intended to function as a fact-finding body, but it appears from its reports that its members, probably under the influence of preconceived ideas or, more likely, instructions from their respective governments, differed widely in their appreciation of the facts they learned and the situations they encountered in the course of their travels. They seem also to have been unduly addicted to the practice of hedging, with the result that many paragraphs of their report are inconclusive. For the same reasons, they revealed a true and illuminating picture of the extent to which the policies of the Four Powers still diverged. Yet it is only fair to recognize that the Commission succeeded in assembling a mass of factual material which, at least in the case of Libya, later proved most helpful to the United Nations Mission in that country. From 6 March to 20 May 1948 it heard a considerable number of political leaders, notables,

51. For text of the Treaty of Peace with Italy, see *United Nations Treaty Series, 49* (1950), No. 747. (The *United Nations Treaty Series* is a collection of treaties and international agreements registered or filed and recorded with the United Nations Secretariat.)

and ordinary people in the three territories, not omitting, of course, the heads and other members of the British and French Administrations. In the circumstances, it is not surprising that the members of the Commission went home with conflicting interpretations of many aspects of what they had seen, heard, and read. It is therefore all the more noteworthy that the Commission should have found itself basically unanimous on certain general but important conclusions, though each member maintained his personal evaluation of the underlying facts. The section of the report entitled "Conclusions for the whole of Libya" is divided into two parts: a Western text prepared by France, the United Kingdom, and the United States, with some sections critically annotated by the United Kingdom and the United States and others by France, and a text prepared by the Soviet Union.

The Western text reads as follows:

> The former colony of Libya is now controlled by three different military administrations and the three zones are separated from one another by stretches of desert. There are two main tracts of agricultural productivity (the Jebel Akhdar in Cyrenaica and the Jebel Nefusa and coastal oases in Tripolitania). Each has adjacent grazing lands which thin out towards the south and finally fade into the desert, which is broken only by a few scattered oases.
>
> In Cyrenaica the inhabitants are almost all nomadic. In the rest of Libya the settled and semi-nomadic inhabitants are in the majority. Throughout the territory the population is almost all Muslim, and outside the towns is organized into tribes or tribal sections. The influence of the sheikhs over their tribes is paramount in Cyrenaica, but in Tripolitania it has been weakened by the breaking down of the traditional tribal structure.
>
> The whole territory is poor in natural resources and is dependent upon financial assistance from outside. No part of Libya is economically self-sufficient. Each of the three zones is dependent, though in differing degree, on foreign assistance in administrative, technical, and economic fields.
>
> The homogeneous political and social composition of Cyrenaica, however, provides a good foundation for building up self-government. The population of the Fezzan is too small and its natural resources too poor for the territory ever to become independent.
>
> An overwhelming majority of Libyans are illiterate, and the degree of political understanding is low. At present none of the three zones is politically ready for self-government.
>
> In Tripolitania most of the inhabitants desire immediate independence.

Desire for unity of Libya and membership of the Arab League is also widespread but less strongly emphasized. [Opposition to the return of an Italian administration is widespread] * [Opposition to foreign domination was often mentioned, and many have expressed dissatisfaction with the present regime and resentment against the former one. Individual relations between Italians and Arabs are good] **

* UK/USA text.

** French text.

In the Fezzan, the inhabitants appear to be content with the present administration and to have given little thought to a change of regime, although many would welcome an Islamic government. There is no anti-Italian feeling.

In Cyrenaica a large majority of the inhabitants wish independence under the Emir Sayyid Mohammed Idris el-Senussi, while the remainder would accept any decision he makes. There is no strong desire on the part of Cyrenaicans for unity and they would agree to it only on their own terms. There is strong and determined opposition to the return of the Italians.[52]

The Soviet text reads as follows:

[Libya covers an area of about 1.75 million square kilometres and has a population of approximately 1,150,000. At present, as well as before the Second World War, Libya has been a single unity geographically, ethnically, economically, linguistically, religiously, culturally, and also with regard to the mode of life of its inhabitants. The productive lands of Libya are located along the coast, with a desert hinterland; the overwhelming majority of the population are Arabs; the economic relations of the Territory with the outer world are maintained by sea: the dominant language is Arabic and the prevailing religion is Islam; the bigger part of the population is illiterate and conducts a semi-nomadic and nomadic mode of life; etc. [*sic*]

Local differences accentuated in the post-war period, owing to the artificial political division of this integral Territory, recede into the background before its natural and social unity.

The post-war differentiating factors connected mainly with foreign interests are an obstacle to the normal economic and social development of Libya and are largely counter-balanced by the integrating factors connected with the national interests of the Libyans themselves. This is confirmed inter alia by the fact that the majority of the Libyans which have

52. Four Power Commission *Report,* Volume III, Part Five, *Conclusions for the Whole of Libya.*

been interviewed by the Commission expressed themselves decidedly in favour of the unity of the Territory].[53]

A careful reading shows that these two texts are too subtly shaded, as a result of the national views held by the individual authors, and too fragmented by remarks relating to one territory in isolation, to allow a comprehensive and precise conclusion concerning Libya as a whole to be drawn. Nevertheless, taken together, they give the clear impression that, in the eyes of the investigators, although the majority of the peoples of the three territories were eager to acquire independence and therefore opposed to the return of Italy, the territories were too dependent on foreign aid to be ready for immediate independence.

These conclusions, coming on top of persistent rumors of plans to divide the country, gave the Libyan leaders a nasty shock, complicating as they did the latter's attempts to promote unity. At the same time, the possibility of their problem's coming up for final decision in the United Nations General Assembly engendered new hopes—in the first place the hope that the Big Four would continue to disagree.

The Italian Government, for its part, let the report of the Four Power Commission go unanswered. On 30 July 1948 the Italian Ambassador to the Court of St. James's, Duke Tomaso Gallarati-Scotti, made his Government's comments known to the Deputy Foreign Ministers. These comments read, in part, as follows:

> [not] for years and often not until almost the arrival of the Commission were the pro-Italian elements allowed to express their views and organise their political forces. Under such inevitable handicaps the Commission's work has taken place and this must be taken into account independently from the undoubted good will and the determination of all the Delegates to whom I am very glad to offer today my acknowledgement.
>
> Moreover the Commission of Investigation had been entrusted by the Deputy Foreign Ministers with a limited task: to ascertain locally the situation existing in those territories and the wishes of the populations. It was made up solely of delegates of the Four Powers as the Conference had not accepted the Italian request to allow representatives of the Italian administration to take part in or to express their views during the work of the Commission, whilst the British Military Administration were heard.
>
> Therefore the conclusions of the Commission should be [rounded out] by the contents of the documentation on the territories in which the Ital-

53. Ibid.

ian Government has submitted to the Conference in Paris and later to the Deputy Foreign Ministers.[54]

The signing of the Treaty of Peace brought with it a change in Italy's policy toward what had now definitely become her former colonies. Before the Peace Conference, the Italian Government, with the virtually unanimous support of public opinion in the country, had pressed to be reinstated in her sovereign rights over Libya, Eritrea, and Somaliland. During the course of the Conference, this policy was abandoned in favor of a claim for trusteeship over these territories. From a legal point of view this ambition did not appear impossible of realization. The PeaceTreaty, although obliging Italy to renounce all right and title to her African possessions, had not determined to whom these rights and titles were to be transferred. At the same time, Article 77 in Chapter XII of the United Nations Charter, dealing with the international trusteeship system, prescribes that, apart from two other categories of territory, the system shall apply to "(b) territories which may be detached from enemy states as a result of the Second World War." Moreover, the Charter (Article 81) does not expressly stipulate that the State or States to whom territories can be entrusted under the system must be a member or members of the United Nations, so that Italy could not be barred on the ground that she was not a member (see p. 59). Once the Peace Treaty had entered into force (15 September 1948), Italy pressed the new claim even harder than the earlier one, thus raising hopes among her countrymen in Africa, and at the same time provoking hostile reactions throughout the Arab world. However, Italy also received a good deal of support as clearly emerges from Table 1.

This table is highly instructive. It shows considerable support for the idea of placing the former Italian colonies, or parts of them, under Italian trusteeship. It also shows a marked preference for trusteeship rather than independence.[55] At the beginning of the year of grace that the four major Powers had granted themselves to find a way out of the labyrinth of issues in which they were lost, the extraneous views and suggestions did not carry much weight; but as the year ticked on to its end, with no solution in sight, the situation changed, and the ideas summarized in the table started to mold the shape of things to come.

At the beginning of September, the Deputy Foreign Ministers presented their report, which was, however, published only on 14 September 1948. With the exception of former Italian Somaliland, for which the report recommended Italian trusteeship—a recommendation subsequently ac-

54. As quoted in *Italy and the United Nations,* pp. 44–45.

55. The views of Egypt and Pakistan are specially noteworthy in light of their subsequent membership in the Council for Libya (see this chapter, Part 3, passim).

Table 1.
Summary of Views of Other Interested Governments

Australia	Trusteeship under Britain. If Libya is divided parts should be placed under similar systems of trusteeship.
Belgium	No specific recommendations. Guiding principle should be wishes of the population plus satisfaction to legitimate claims. If independence is not warranted, territories should be put under trusteeship with Powers that played predominant roles in the war in Africa given preference as administrators.
Brazil	Once British commitments to Sanusis were settled, trusteeship under Italy.
Byelorussia	Trusteeship under Italy. No partition.
Canada	Trusteeship under Britain, whether or not territory is divided.
China	Immediate independence.
Czechoslovakia	Trusteeship under Italy. No partition.
Egypt	Independence or trusteeship under an Arab League state, plus border rectifications in Egypt's favor.
Ethiopia	Against return to Italy.
Greece	No recommendations. Concerned solely with the protection of rights of Greek nationals in Libya, particularly fishing rights off coast.
India	Trusteeship under direct UN administration.
Italy	Trusteeship under Italy.
Netherlands	Trusteeship under Italy. A joint trusteeship may be feasible in order to satisfy Sanusi.
New Zealand	Trusteeship under Britain.
Pakistan	United under Sanusi rule, with some form of supervisory international control in which Egypt participated.
Poland	Trusteeship under Italy. No partition.
Ukraine	Trusteeship under Italy. No partition.
Union of South Africa	Territory to be partitioned. Tripolitania under British trusteeship; Fezzan under French trusteeship; Cyrenaica under British trusteeship, or if not feasible under Italian trusteeship.
Yugoslavia	Trusteeship under Italy.

Note: This table summarizes the views of the nineteen interested governments participating in the Peace Conference, as recorded by the Deputies to the Council of Foreign Ministers during the summer of 1948, with regard to the three former Italian Colonies. For the purposes of the present study only the section of the table concerning Libya has been reproduced.

Source: Benjamin Rivlin, *United Nations Action: Italian Colonies* (New York: Carnegie Endowment for International Peace, 1950), pp. 22–23.

cepted by the Four Powers—no agreed solution was put forward for the future of the colonies. In the case of Libya, the Union of Soviet Socialist Republics proposed Italian trusteeship for a period to be defined. France wanted to postpone the decision for yet another year. The United Kingdom and the United States proposed that Cyrenaica be placed immediately under United Kingdom trusteeship, the decision on Tripolitania and the Fezzan to be deferred for twelve months. A last-minute attempt by the Four Powers to come to an agreement, on 13 September, also failed, though the Soviet Union made a not entirely disinterested, though outwardly conciliatory, gesture by abandoning its case for Italian trusteeship and proposing that all three colonies be put under direct United Nations trusteeship, with a chief administrator responsible to the Trusteeship Council and assisted by an advisory committee composed of representatives of the Four Powers and Italy. It was further suggested that this committee should include representatives of the local population.[56] Meanwhile, the international situation had deteriorated to the point where any East-West cooperation was extremely difficult. France and the United Kingdom had never liked the American idea. Now the United States itself liked it no more. The proposal was therefore rejected. It is a moot point what the Soviet Union's motives were in tabling the proposal. One possibility is that it was a last attempt to keep a finger in the pie. However, the USSR must have known that there was little or no chance of the plan's being accepted. Hence another possible explanation is that, counting on rejection, its suggestion was a clever stratagem to show up the United States as having paid no more than lip service to the collective trusteeship system provided for in the United Nations Charter, and to weaken beforehand the position of the three Western Powers in the forthcoming debates in the General Assembly, especially in the matter of their strategic ambitions.

PART 3. LIBYA IN THE HANDS OF THE UNITED NATIONS

Whatever the explanation, on 15 September 1948 the task of determining the destiny of the former Italian colonies passed from the Four Powers to the General Assembly, a body where no veto could prevail, then made up of fifty-eight members taking their important decisions by a two-thirds majority and voting on a basis of equality. From that time on the question was to be tackled in a very different arena under very different rules. The search for a substantive solution would be none the easier for that, though tactically there would be more room for compromise. Above all, unanimity was no longer a prerequisite, and all debates, except those in sub-committees, were public. As far as the parties directly interested were concerned,

56. This proposal closely follows that made by the Soviet Union in CFM in April 1946 (see p. 62). The United States had suggested a similar system in CFM in September 1945 in London (see p. 61).

the transfer of the proceedings to the United Nations gave them an opportunity of pleading their cause before a larger and more accessible forum than had hitherto been the case. This advantage was particularly marked for Italy, though she had no voting rights, as well as for the five political parties and organizations of the three Libyan territories; their delegations were heard in full committee and made numerous contacts with delegates from other countries.

On 21 September 1948, six days after the year of grace expired, the Third Regular Session of the General Assembly opened in the Palais de Chaillot, Paris. Within the context of this study, the Fourth Session, held in the autumn of 1949 at Lake Success, is naturally of greater importance, because of its success in reaching final agreement. But this is not to say that the Third Session can be ignored. Indeed, for many delegations it provided a useful opportunity of studying the vast amount of background documentation, in particular the voluminous report of the Four Power Commission. It also enabled Governments and delegates to exchange views and explore the lie of the land, a valuable process that was made easier by the decision to divide the session into two parts, the first running from 21 September until 11 December 1948 in Paris, the second from 5 April until 18 May 1949 at Lake Success, thus providing more time for consultations. As a result, the United Kingdom and the United States succeeded in agreeing that, as far as Libya was concerned, Cyrenaica would be administered by the United Kingdom under United Nations trusteeship, and that the decision on Tripolitania should be put off until the second part of the session. The Fezzan was not mentioned in this agreement; it seems that although the United Kingdom was ready to support France in its desire to retain that territory within its zone of administration, the United States was opposed to such a policy. France itself maintained its hostility to any idea of an independent Libya. Meanwhile, Italian diplomacy had been successful in mobilizing Latin American sympathy for its cause, sympathy which manifested itself in solid opposition to a British-Soviet attempt to secure immediate consideration of the question. Apparently Italy and its Latin American friends believed that with the passage of time Italy's position vis-à-vis the General Assembly would gain in strength. As events were to prove, this was an unsound gamble, since procrastination also gave the Arab States and their supporters time to build up a case.

On 6 April 1949 the First Committee (Political and Security Questions) of the General Assembly started its debate on the former Italian colonies, in the course of which practically all delegations were to speak, but not before having decided to appoint a sub-committee to examine requests from parties and organizations in the territories concerned to be heard in full committee.

For Libya, the sub-committee recommended that the representatives of five groups be invited to sit at the Committee table:

The National Congress of Cyrenaica;
The National Council for the Liberation of Libya (NCLL);
The National Association of Refugees from Libya and East Africa;
The Association of Libyan Ex-Servicemen; and
The Jewish Community of Tripolitania.

All five declared themselves in favor of unity and independence, opposing the return of any part of Libya to Italy. The National Council, indeed, told the Committee on 27 April 1949 that the splitting up of Libya did not correspond in any way or manner to the wishes of the Libyan people.[57] Not being able, however, to submit a commonly agreed formula for the realization of unity, the impact they made was considerably less forceful than might otherwise have been the case.

The Four Powers—noblesse oblige—were the first to state their views.

John Foster Dulles, speaking as a delegate for the United States of America, pointed out that the task entrusted to the General Assembly was unique in the history of the United Nations and a challenge to its ability to cut the Gordian knot that the Big Four had failed to unravel. He stressed the importance of observing the basic principles of the Charter concerning non-self-governing territories (Article 73), in particular the concept that "the interests of the inhabitants of these territories are paramount" and the obligation "to further international peace and security" (see p. 59). With regard to Libya, he suggested that full independence should be the ultimate aim after a not too long period of trusteeship, the United Kingdom to be designated as trustee for Cyrenaica at least.

Ambassador Chauvel, for the French Government, recommended Italian trusteeship over each of her former colonies as the best solution.

The Minister of State for Foreign Affairs, Hector McNeil, speaking for the United Kingdom, opposed the French proposal, invoking in particular his Government's wartime pledge to Cyrenaica. He declared its willingness, however, to support France's claim to a privileged position in the Fezzan. For the rest, his proposals are summarized in the chart below.

Andrei Gromyko, the delegate for the Soviet Union, after having charged the Western Powers, and the United Kingdom and the United States in particular, with responsibility for failure of the Four Powers to reach agreement because of their strategic ambitions, reiterated the USSR's proposal for direct United Nations trusteeship over all three former Italian colonies.

The Italian Foreign Minister, Count Sforza, while asking that due consideration be given to the valuable contribution Italy could make to the

57. GAOR: Third Session, Part II, 1949, First Committee, 252nd Meeting, 27 April 1949, pp. 134–40.

economic and technical development and welfare of Africa, said that his government would accept, inter alia, in Libya, Italian trusteeship over Tripolitania as "one of the pivotal points in the friendly co-operation between Italy and the Arab nations." [58]

These statements were followed by a lengthy debate in which more than forty delegations took part, suggesting a large variety of solutions, backed up by almost as many draft resolutions. Of these, five proposals relating to Libya are of major interest here because of the support they received. Rivlin summarizes them, concisely and admirably, as follows:

Table 2. *The Five Major Proposals*

United Kingdom (United Nations Doc. A/C.1/446)	1. British Trusteeship for Cyrenaica; 2. Postpone decision on the remainder of Libya [Tripolitania and the Fezzan] until the fourth session of the General Assembly; 3. In the meantime the Governments of Egypt, France, Italy, Great Britain and the United States to prepare, for submission to the fourth session of the General Assembly, the terms and conditions, including the administrative relationship with Cyrenaica, under which the rest of Libya would be placed under the International Trusteeship System; 4. Ten years from the adoption of the resolution, Libya shall achieve independence provided the General Assembly, having reviewed at that time the progress made by Libya towards independence, decided that Libya is ready to assume independent status.
Soviet Union (United Nations Docs. A/C.1/433 and A/C.1/433/Rev.1)	1. Direct United Nations administration under trusteeship agreement for 5 years (originally 10 years); 2. Administrator with full executive powers to be appointed by the Trusteeship Council, to which he would be responsible; 3. Administrator to be assisted by an Advisory Committee of nine: representatives of the United Kingdom, USSR, France, Italy, USA and Egypt, and a European and two Arab residents of Libya chosen by the aforesaid six representatives; 4. Libya to be granted independence at the end of Trusteeship period. (5 years).
India (United Nations Doc. A/C.1/448	To be placed under the international Trusteeship system with the United Nations Organization as the administering authority for a period of not less than 10 and not more than 20 years.

58. GAOR: Third Session, Part II, 1949, First Committee, 241st Meeting, 11 April 1949, p. 31.

Table 2. *Continued*

Latin American Joint Draft Resolution (United Nations Doc. A/C.1/449)	1. Independence in 10 years, provided the General Assembly then decides that this is appropriate; 2. Trusteeship in the meanwhile under terms and conditions to be drafted by the Governments of Egypt, France, Italy, United Kingdom and the USA for submission to the fourth session of the General Assembly.
Iraq (United Nations Doc. A/C.1/453)	Libya to be granted immediate independence.[59]

A comparison of these five proposals shows the extent to which the General Assembly was divided into groups defending various interests or propagating different ideologies and philosophies. Ranging from ten years' trusteeship to immediate independence, with trusteeship itself varying from the collective to the single-Power type, these proposals were so divergent, both in purpose and in method, that they hardly offered an appropriate basis for compromise, particularly under a procedure requiring, for a valid decision by the General Assembly, a two-thirds majority of those present and voting. Nevertheless, efforts to that end were made, mainly among the Latin American, Middle Eastern, and Asian States, which, together, were numerous enough to stand at least a chance of success. However, even they failed. The Latin Americans continued to press for Italian trusteeship, which was difficult for the Arabs to accept, and some of the Asian States showed a marked preference for collective over single-Power trusteeship, in which they saw too many relics of the old colonial system. In these circumstances, the United States proposed the appointment of a sub-committee of fifteen members (Sub-Committee 15) to find a common denominator for the proposals tabled in the First Committee. The Sub-Committee was given until 12 May to complete its task, but the general feeling was that the chances of reaching agreement were small. To many delegations it looked as if the General Assembly had run into a deadlock as bad as that which had hamstrung the Council of Foreign Ministers. This time the main hurdle seemed to be the difficulty of finding a solution capable of commanding the two-thirds majority. Hence the necessity of finding a new compromise acceptable to two or more blocs capable of together meeting that condition. Since the Latin American States formed the largest homogeneous group with a common policy toward the former Italian colonies (eighteen out of the twenty Latin American States), the obvious thing to do was to evolve a formula which these States and as many others as could be marshaled

59. Rivlin, pp. 30–31. Only the proposals relating to Libya are quoted.

would support. In terms of practical politics, this meant giving some degree of satisfaction to Italy's claims. The Government that most eagerly wished to see the deadlock broken was that of the United Kingdom, which was anxious, four years after the cessation of hostilities in Europe, to consolidate its postwar position in the Mediterranean and the Near East. To that end a meeting was arranged between Bevin and Sforza when the latter passed through London on his return from New York to Rome in May. The result of the talks the two Foreign Ministers had on that occasion was the highly controversial Bevin-Sforza agreement. Briefly, this called for:

1. British trusteeship over Cyrenaica;
2. French trusteeship over the Fezzan;
3. Italian trusteeship over Tripolitania as from 1951;
4. Partitioning of Eritrea between Ethiopia and the Sudan; and
5. Italian trusteeship over Italian Somaliland.

The compromise principally affected the original United Kingdom attitude to Libya, more particularly in the case of Tripolitania, which, under the plan, was to remain under British administration, assisted by an international advisory council, for three more years (1949–51). The trusteeships were to run for ten years,[60] and Libya was to become independent at the end of that period if the General Assembly decided that this development was appropriate.

The plan was published in the morning newspapers on 10 May, the very day on which Sub-Committee 15 had planned to start its consideration of the various proposals submitted to its parent body. In Lake Success it was received with very mixed feelings; in Tripoli it was greeted by violent riots. Reactions among delegations to the General Assembly ranged from satisfaction within the Latin American bloc to vehement criticism in the Arab ranks, while in the center many delegates, frustrated by the general inability to find a better solution, were disconsolately resigning themselves to a "better this than nothing" philosophy. A formal source of criticism was the fact that two of the interested Powers had worked out a solution between themselves, whereas the Treaty of Peace signed by both of them had consigned the issue to the General Assembly for settlement. The United Kingdom was held particularly responsible for this derogation. For the Arab States, the plan meant death, administered by a process smacking of neocolonialism, to their ideal of Libyan unity. The following particularly pertinent remark was made by the Saudi Arabian representative in the First Committee: "It was alleged in the Sub-Committee's report that the recommended proposal represented a compromise. If that was so, many delega-

60. The Italian trusteeship over Tripolitania was to last from 1951 until 1959.

tions would be bitterly disappointed, for the compromise would be reached at the expense of the populations whose fate was being decided." [61]

The advocates of the collective trusteeship formula were profoundly disappointed by the prospect of Libya's being partitioned into three territories, each under a single trustee, which to them looked more like protectorates in the old colonial style than wards of the international community. The Soviet Union was bitterly critical, for strategic reasons, and moreover, deeply resentful of the fact that it had been bested in an important sector of the ideological struggle between East and West. Considerations on a higher moral plane also played their part in the debate—for instance, when the delegate of the Philippines warned the Committee that "History would recall the Assembly's decision. It should not be satisfied with an easy solution which was not a just one." [62]

On 10 May 1949, Mansur Qadara, then attending the General Assembly as head of the delegation of NCLL, in which capacity he signed the communication, sent a cable to the Secretary-General of the United Nations which included the following sentence: "Tripolitania people will defend its sacred right for freedom and for opposing with its own life any restoration of Italy's rule." [63]

In the town of Tripoli, according to a dispatch datelined 17 May 1949 from the Cairo correspondent of the *New York Times* (and published in that newspaper on page 8 on 18 May 1949), in which the American correspondent quotes a cable from the Tripoli representative of the leading Egyptian newspaper *Al Ahram,* twenty thousand Arabs took part in a demonstration against the plan to transfer Tripolitania to Italian trusteeship in 1951. The crowd applauded the Soviet Union and inveighed against the British, Americans, and Italians.

61. GAOR: Third Session, Part II, 1949, First Committee, 271st Meeting, 12 May 1949, p. 356.

62. Ibid., p. 359.

63. Early in 1965, while the author was assembling material for use in the preparation of the present study, he had occasion to visit Cairo, where he called on the family of the late Omar Loutfi, who had been Legal Adviser on Constitutional Matters to the United Nations Mission to Libya (see Chapter 2, p. 122 and fn. 13 for a curriculum vitae). Loutfi's family most kindly made all his private papers on the Libyan question available to the writer, with unqualified permission to make such use of them as he saw fit. The papers, which comprise MS, typescript, and mimeographed documents, will hereinafter be referred to as the Loutfi Papers. The text of the two telegrams reproduced above (in part) and on pages 81–82 (in full) are taken from a mimeographed paper, produced by the "Libyan delegation" to the Fourth Session of the General Assembly, in this collection. The writer would like to take the opportunity of expressing his deep gratitude to the family of Omar Loutfi for their generous assistance in this matter.

The *Times* dispatch went on:

> Horsemen from the desert joined the demonstration, calling for independence and a united Libya. There was every evidence, according to Cairo reports, that the movement was spreading throughout Libya. Yesterday demonstrations occurred at Giado, Zanzour, Zliten, Misurata, Azizia and Soukelgoma and similar demonstrations were reported in the same towns and other towns today.
>
> However, the reports so far available indicated there had been little more violence. The total number of injured stands under forty-five.
>
> Americans, British and Frenchmen are keeping off the streets. Yesterday an Italian flag was burned as was a United States flag the day before.
>
> The British are understood to have issued a proclamation emphasizing the difference between the present Italian republic and the Mussolini regime and promising that, after eight years of Italian trusteeship, independence would be granted to Tripolitania.
>
> Carrying out an announced policy of non-cooperation with British authorities, representatives of the National Congress and Libyan Liberation Committee are refusing to obey emergency measures. A general strike continues, and so far as is known here there is no indication that it will be halted for some days.
>
> Most Arab stores and establishments remained closed for the greater part of the day. The Senussi flag has been raised in various cities, principally over mosques.
>
> An organization called the Benghazi Independent Youth has cabled British Foreign Secretary Ernest Bevin that his plan, reached with Italian Foreign Minister Carlo Sforza, is immoral and contradicts Britain's promises to the people of Libya. The message said the disorders in the country were the responsibility of the British Government.

On 11 May, Qadara addressed a second cable to the Secretary-General. This read:

> In connection with our last cable forwarded to your Excellency on 10 May carrying our protest against all British proposals and suggestions submitted with a view to partitioning Libya and placing it under trusteeship with entrusting Italy with administration in Tripolitania at end of 1951, we find it our bounden duty to forward to United Nations text of cablegram just received from Tripoli calling attention to state of unrest, forboding serious disturbances in Tripolitania if British proposals and suggestions are carried through, flouting legitimate demands of Libyan people and ignoring their lawful right to independence and unity.

Text of cablegram as follows:

"We cabled to Bevin and Trygve Lie protesting and remonstrating at that wrong agreement Bevin assured Sforza with population in ferment. Communicate our remonstration any restoration Italian administration our beloved country. (signed) Mizran, President National Party."

And again for the sake of peace and security in this troubled area, we request respectfully that our protest and contents of Tripolitanian cablegram be known to United Nations honorable members.[64]

But when all was said and done the fact remained that the Bevin-Sforza agreement appeared to be the only compromise with any chance of breaking the two-thirds majority barrier. This, at least, was the view held by the majority of Sub-Committee 15 which, ignoring the other draft resolutions before it, took the original United Kingdom proposal as amended by the Bevin-Sforza formula as a basis for discussion. Notwithstanding bitter counterattack from the Arab–Soviet–Asian minority, the outcome was a text, adopted by 10 votes to 4 with one abstention recommending:

1. That Libya be granted independence ten years from the date of the adoption of this Resolution, provided that the General Assembly then decides that this step is appropriate;

(a) that Cyrenaica be placed under the International Trusteeship System, with the United Kingdom as the Administering Authority, without prejudice to its incorporation in a united Libya;

(b) that the Fezzan be placed under the International Trusteeship System, with France as the Administering Authority, also without prejudice to its incorporation in a united Libya;

(c) that Tripolitania be placed under the International Trusteeship System by the end of 1951, with Italy as the Administering Authority, also without prejudice to its incorporation in a united Libya. During the interim period, the present British temporary administration shall continue, with the assistance of an Advisory Council consisting of representatives of Egypt, France, Italy, the United Kingdom, the United States, and a representative of the people of the territory. The Advisory Council should determine its scope and duties in consultation with the Administering Authority.

That the Powers charged with the administration of the three territories take all necessary measures to promote the co-ordination of their activities in order that nothing be done to prejudice the attainment of an independent Libyan State. The Trusteeship Council will be responsible for supervising the execution of this provision;

64. Loutfi Papers.

2. [Relates to Italian Somaliland];
3. [Relates to Eritrea];
4. That agreements and instruments designed to give effect to the foregoing recommendations in accordance with the purposes and principles of the Charter and the provisions of the Treaty of Peace with Italy be submitted for the subsequent approval of the fourth regular session of the General Assembly (except those for Tripolitania, which shall be submitted to the sixth regular session); that the Trusteeship Council, where trusteeship is concerned, and otherwise the Interim Committee, be authorized to represent the General Assembly in working out such agreements, in co-operation with Italy, where Italian interests are concerned and that, in the case of Libya, the trusteeship agreements so to be submitted provide for such adequate inter-territorial administration relationships as will promote the attainment of an independent, unified Libyan State." [65]

It has been necessary to reproduce this particular draft resolution in its virtual entirety because, politically, it constitutes a whole, with the adoption of the proposals concerning one territory mutually depending on the adoption of those concerning the others. The reference to a "unified Libyan State" in the last sentence of paragraph 4 is worthy of note.

When, on 12 May, the draft resolution came up for discussion at a plenary meeting of the First Committee, the opposition was even more vocal, strengthened as it was by the criticisms made by the spokesmen of the interested populations. For Libya, NCLL led the attack. However, all the substantive amendments proposed were rejected, with the exception of Norway's request that the word "provided" in the second line of paragraph 1 be replaced by the word "unless" (with the appropriate consequential changes), thus making Libyan independence at the expiration of the ten-year period quasiautomatic.

The debate in the First Committee, which took its decisions by simple majority, provided a good opportunity for assessing the chances of the resolution's adoption in plenary session by the General Assembly, the more so as the draft was voted upon paragraph by paragraph. The result of the voting on 13 May revealed a precarious situation. The resolution as a whole was adopted by 34 votes to 16 with 7 abstentions, representing a majority of only slightly more than two-thirds. However, the vote on paragraph 1(c) (Italian trusteeship over Tripolitania), on which everything hinged because of the Latin American attitude, was 32 to 17 with 8 ab-

65. GAOR: Third Session, Part II, 1949, First Committee, Annexes to Summary Records, Agenda item 13 (A/C.1/466, 11 May 1949), pp. 27–28.

stentions, or just under two-thirds of the delegations present and voting (abstentions not counting).

In these circumstances, the opponents of the resolution, and the Arab delegations in particular, were encouraged to lobby for the votes of individual delegates to the General Assembly.[66] Indeed, one vote more or less, for or against, could tip the balance. The successful canvasser was Ali-Nourridine Unayzi, at the time an official of the Secretariat of the Arab League and as such a member of the NCLL delegation at Lake Success, and subsequently a member of the Council of Libya (see Chapters 8 and 10). His target was the Haitian delegate, Emile Saint-Lot, whose acquaintance he made—or so he told the present author—by paying him a pretty compliment on a speech he had delivered in favor of Libyan independence during the general debate in the First Committee. Later, Unayzi, actively assisted by Rafik Asha of the Syrian delegation, succeeded in convincing Saint-Lot that the Bevin-Sforza plan might well prevent, and would certainly delay, independence. (A street in Tripoli town bears the name of Sharia Saint-Lot.) In the event, Haiti voted against the paragraph recommending Italian trusteeship over Tripolitania, which was defeated when the vote in the General Assembly was 33 votes to 17, with 8 abstentions, or one short of the required two-thirds majority. In any case, the draft resolution as adopted by the First Committee had been mutilated almost beyond recognition by a deluge of amendments, in particular one deleting the proposal for Italian trusteeship over Somaliland. The end finally came when the Latin American group, having lost interest in the emasculated remains, withdrew its support. The resolution as a whole was accordingly defeated by 14 votes in favor to 37 against, with 7 abstentions (17 May 1949).

The General Assembly was accused of having wasted two months of valuable time at its Third Session in vain attempts to solve the question of the former Italian colonies. It would have been more correct to say that by refusing to listen to the wishes of the inhabitants and by seeking to impose on them a compromise between irreconcilable interests, including the return of the former colonial Power, it taught itself the useful lesson that the solution had to be sought in a direction different from that followed up to that time. This was particularly true in Libya's case.

66. The Libyan delegations were actively lobbying representatives at the General Assembly in the corridors at Lake Success and Flushing Meadows, and in New York hotels. In later years they recalled that when they told John Foster Dulles of their hopes of independence, he had expressed doubts about the wisdom of creating "splinter" States, too small to hope to attain economic viability. The Libyans felt that they had refuted this argument successfully by pointing out that if size of population were to be a criterion, Libya, with over one million, was certainly as much entitled to independence as Iceland, a founding member of the United Nations with a population of only 120,000.

The Secretary-General prophetically noted in his report that: "The debate in the General Assembly on the Italian colonies revealed that the majority of the Members expect to welcome Libya as an independent Member in a few years, and Somaliland perhaps somewhat later." [67]

As the sequel eventually proved, the failure at the Third Session was in fact a case of *reculer pour mieux sauter,* and a Polish proposal that further consideration of the question be postponed until the Fourth Session in the autumn of 1949 was wisely adopted without opposition.

Developments during the interval between the two sessions proved that the lesson had also been understood in London as well as in Rome, and, to a lesser extent, in Paris. On 1 June 1949, the United Kingdom, as mentioned earlier, announced its intention of granting internal self-government to Cyrenaica and of recognizing the Amir as Head of Government, following this up in the autumn by Proclamation No. 187 (see p. 48). Although this measure subsequently complicated the formation of a united Libyan State, an assurance to the contrary notwithstanding, it was nonetheless a move in the right direction. From then on it became difficult for Italy not to recognize that the status of Tripolitania must be raised to a comparable or even identical level. It is apparently in this light that the following statement, issued on 31 May 1949 by the Italian Prime Minister, is to be understood:

1. The Italian Government recognise as legitimate the people's aspirations for self-government and undertake to give their diplomatic support to such aspirations at international meetings;
2. in particular the Italian Government are favourable to the creation in Tripolitania of a government which should be representative of a popular assembly freely elected and representative of various ethnic groups, and with which Italy might enter into relations of close and productive collaboration.[68]

According to the *New York Times* of 3 June 1949, this meant, in non-diplomatic language:

> that Italy be entrusted by the United Nations with the task of organizing and supervising elections in Tripolitania that would lead to the creation of a popular assembly or native parliament that in turn would elect a government within a specified period; that Italy would get the right to

67. *Annual Report of the Secreiary-General on the Work of the Organization, 1 July 1948–30 June 1949,* GAOR: Fourth Session, 1949, Supplement No. 1 (A/930), Introduction, p. xii.

68. *Italy and the United Nations,* p. 48. For full text of statement, see Royal Institute of International Affairs, *Documents on International Affairs, 1949–1950,* ed. Margaret Carlyle (London: Oxford University Press, 1953), p. 745.

> appoint her own experts to advise and guide a new government on the road to autonomy; that the new Tripolitanian State would undertake a policy of collaboration with Italy designed to promote Italian-Arab trade exchanges and permit settlement in Tripolitania of Italian nationals.[69]

While the Prime Minister's declaration did not go far enough to meet the realities of the situation, it too represented a step forward destined to facilitate the discussions at the Fourth Session of the General Assembly.

When this session opened in September 1949, the first debate in plenary meeting showed that independence, with or without an initial period of preparation, was widely recognized as being the only solution for Libya susceptible of commanding a two-thirds majority. The procedure followed was much the same as previously, namely, a general debate in the First Committee, spread over the two hundred and seventy-eighth to the two hundred and ninety-third meetings, with the participation of an Italian representative without the right to vote, and the setting up of a sub-committee (Sub-Committee 17) to draw up a draft resolution. A second sub-committee was set up, as before, to examine requests for hearings from representatives of political parties or organizations in the territories concerned (Sub-Committee 16).

Delegations representing the following Libyan institutions were heard on this occasion:

The National Congress of Cyrenaica;
The National Congress of Tripolitania;
The Independence Party of Tripolitania; and
The Jewish Community of Tripolitania.

The debate, once more embracing the destiny of all three former colonies, began on 30 September 1949. It soon became clear that practically all delegations had lost faith in trusteeship as a suitable solution for Libya, and that there was virtual unanimity in favor of independence. At the same time, wide divergences of opinion seemed to exist about the way in which this should be brought about. The USSR, abandoning its policy of collective trusteeship for Libya, forestalled all other proposals by submitting a draft resolution providing that: "Libya shall be granted independence immediately. All foreign forces and military personnel must be withdrawn from Libyan territory within three months, and all military bases liquidated within the same period." [70]

Hector McNeil, speaking for the United Kingdom, launched the idea of Libya's becoming independent as soon as possible, its backwardness not-

69. As quoted in Rivlin, p. 44.

70. GAOR: Fourth Session, 1949, First Committee, Annexes to Summary Records, Agenda item 19 (A/C.1/487/Rev.1, 7 November 1949), p. 21.

withstanding. The General Assembly should fix a short period during which the United Kingdom and France would continue to administer the territories currently under their occupation and at the end of which they would hand over their powers to the Libyans themselves. This statement left the General Assembly with the impression that the United Kingdom, pressed for time to regulate its position in Cyrenaica, was prepared to make sufficient concessions on the other aspects of the Libyan question to facilitate a solution acceptable to the Latin American and Arab States. This policy called for some further sacrifice from Italy, in exchange for which McNeil urged the Assembly to sanction a special trade agreement between Italy and Tripolitania in order to safeguard Italy's economic interests in that territory. At the same time the United Kingdom still seemed to be prepared to recognize France's special interests in the Fezzan.

France found herself in a difficult position. For reasons already explained, it disliked the idea of a united, independent Libyan State. It also realized that independence for Libya was becoming an increasingly popular solution. Its spokesman, Maurice Couve de Murville, therefore put forward an extremely carefully worded statement on the way in which Libyan independence should be brought about, which was not unlike the British policy for Cyrenaica. Read in retrospect, the statement sounds like a forecast—which indeed it was—of the policies the United Kingdom and France attempted to follow in Libya during 1950 and the first part of 1951.

The relevant passage reads:

> Although many representatives had stressed the importance of the unity of Libya and although the three territories constituting Libya obviously had affinities, those resemblances should not be exaggerated and the features distinguishing and even sometimes dividing Libya should not be overlooked. . . .
>
> The settlement of the whole question, based on the principle of Libyan independence would, therefore, require the creation in the respective territories of separate Governments which should be granted independence as soon as possible, although it might well be impossible to define the period during which the independence would materialize. As soon as those Governments functioned normally, it would be their responsibility to establish the system of association under which they wished to dwell. During the interim period, the occupation authorities would assume responsibility for the administration, and, obviously, the United Nations would reserve the right to supervise the political evolution conducive to the implementation of its recommendations.[71]

71. GAOR: Fourth Session, 1949, First Committee, 279th Meeting, 1 October 1949, pp. 25–26.

The United States of America, through its spokesman, Philip C. Jessup, sided generally with the United Kingdom but submitted a more elaborate draft resolution containing several suggestions which subsequently found their way into the General Assembly's final recommendation. With regard to Libya, the American draft proposed:

1. Libyan independence at the end of three years, during which period the Powers then administering the territories of Cyrenaica, Tripolitania, and the Fezzan should coordinate their activities toward the achievement of Libyan independence;
2. A meeting of representatives of the inhabitants of the three component territories at a suitable time at least one year prior to the date of independence to determine the form of government they desired upon the attainment of independence;
3. An advisory council, consisting of representatives of Egypt, France, Italy, the United Kingdom, the United States, and two representatives of the local population, one from Cyrenaica and one from Tripolitania, to advise the administering authorities as to how assistance might be given to the inhabitants with regard to formation of a government for an independent Libya, and on such related problems as common services. The draft proposed that the Council be empowered to visit the territory, but that its headquarters be outside Libya.[72]

Subsequently, a Pakistani draft resolution, also stressing Libyan unity and independence, suggested the addition of representatives from Pakistan and the Fezzan to the advisory council. An Iraqi proposal called for the immediate proclamation of a united sovereign state of Libya in as short a period as practicable.

India, more precise and to the point, perhaps troubled by its own problems of State-building, insisted on the unification of the three Libyan territories into a single, united independent group, with a constitution to be drawn up by a constituent assembly representative of the inhabitants of the entire group and to be approved by a commission appointed by the General Assembly.[73]

On 1 October 1949, Italy made an important contribution to the debate which is apparent in the summary record of a part of Count Sforza's statement:

72. For the text of the United States proposal, see GAOR: Fourth Session, 1949, First Committee, Annexes to Summary Records, Agenda item 19 (A/C.1/497, 10 October 1949), pp. 23–24.

73. For texts of proposals of Pakistan, Iraq, and India, see ibid. (A/C.1/499, 11 October 1949), pp. 24–25; (A/C.1/489, 3 October 1949), p. 21; and (A/C.1/491, 4 October 1949), p. 22, respectively.

In April 1949, when Italy had asked for trusteeship over the territories in question, it had been because, at that time, trusteeship appeared to be the most appropriate solution through which Italy would have paved the way for the earliest possible independence of those territories. The proof of the sincerity of that intention was borne out by the prompt decision which had been adopted by his Government two months later, when it had declared itself in favour of the immediate independence of the two most progressive territories, namely Eritrea and Libya, as soon as the debates of the previous session had evidenced such a trend of opinion. Italy had therefore immediately withdrawn its request for trusteeship over Tripolitania and Eritrea and favoured their independence.[74]

Reporting the part of his speech dealing with concrete proposals, the summary continued:

With regard to Libya, a unitary state, able to preserve the common historical heritage of its component territories, should be established. Obviously, account should be taken of the different characteristics of those parts and the varying levels of their political maturity. An appropriate federal council should be created to protect their common interests. The Italian Government was well aware of the fact that the events of the second World War had bound two of the three sections of the Libyan territory to the United Kingdom and France. Italy, therefore, acknowledged the necessity for those Powers to assume the transitional task of guiding them towards independence, on the understanding that any action to that end should come within the structure of a future federal unity of Libya, and that Tripolitania should be granted full freedom to dispose of its future. Accordingly, free elections for a constituent assembly should be held in Tripolitania within six months. That assembly should immediately proceed to the appointment of a government, whereupon British Administration should cease. The transitional stage should be supervised by a control commission in which Italy would be one of its members. Following the establishment of such a government, Italy, on equal footing, would negotiate with it an appropriate agreement to safeguard the interests of the Italian minority. Should, however, the transitional period be extended, the powers of the suggested control commission should not be limited to supervising the elections; it should assume the character of an over-all collaboration.[75]

74. GAOR: Fourth Session, 1949, First Committee, 279th Meeting, p. 26.
75. Ibid.

Meanwhile, active consultations were going on both between the Arab and Latin American blocs and among the individual delegations in each of them. The Arabs wanted immediate independence for Libya (this was their main preoccupation during the Fourth Session), but differed about the way in which unity and independence should be achieved.

The Latin Americans, inspired by Brazil, still warm in their support for Italy and again linking the two issues, made it plain that they would oppose all plans for Libyan independence unless the General Assembly agreed to Italian trusteeship over Somaliland. This condition provoked less hostility from the Arab States than at the third session.

The general debate in the First Committee came to an end on 6 October and was followed by four days of hearings of representatives of parties and organizations from the three former colonies. The statements of the Libyan groups differed little from those made seven months earlier, except that there was even greater insistence on unity and independence. As to unity, some progress had been made, as shown in the first part of this chapter, though no tangible result was as yet in sight.[76]

76. U.S. Dept. of State *Bulletin,* Vol. XXII, 29 May 1950, p. 837, gives the following summary of the statements made by the Libyan groups:

> Bashir Bey [Saadawi] spoke for the National Congress of Tripolitania and urged an independent and united Libya which could become a factor for peace and stability in the Middle East. His organization sought an immediate grant of independence to Libya. Omar Sheneib (National Congress of Cyrenaica) also asked for Libyan independence and referred to the impatience with which the Cyrenaicans, under the Emir Al-Senussi, were awaiting full freedom. He argued against too long a transition period and felt that Libya should be unified under the Emir if the Tripolitanians were agreeable. He saw no obstacle to Libyan unity in the British action of granting Cyrenaica internal self-rule and urged early independence for Tripolitania and the Fezzan. Later, another spokesman for the same group read to the Committee a cable from the Emir asking for the complete independence of his country without an interim period. Abdulla Sherif Bey (Independence Party of Tripolitania) demanded the "immediate, integral and complete independence" of Libya. During a transitional period prior to the emergence of a democratic and constitutional government, he felt that a United Nations Committee should supervise implementation of the Assembly's decision.
>
> Mr. Perlzweig (Jewish Community of Tripolitania) made two statements on October 7 and 10. He asked for special safeguards for the position of the Jewish community whose economic and social position was deteriorating and whose safety had been endangered by terrorist acts "stimulated by outside influence." The Jews of Tripolitania, he said, wanted any United Nations commission supervising the transitional period leading to independence for Libya to include a "neutral power" and a representative of the minorities. The General Assembly should also prescribe

Such then was the overall appearance of the Libyan question when the First Committee unanimously decided on 11 October to set up a sub-committee of twenty-one members (Sub-Committee 17) for the purpose of "studying all drafts and suggestions which have been submitted to the Committee or which may be submitted to the Sub-Committee and to propose a draft resolution or resolutions to settle the question of the disposal of the former Italian colonies in Africa." [77]

The Sub-Committee was instructed to submit its report on the three colonies not later than 15 October. This time limit proved far too short and had to be prolonged. The promising consensus about independence for Libya and Italian trusteeship for Somaliland notwithstanding, the elaboration of draft resolutions covering detailed compromise solutions for all three territories took so long that not until 1 November was the report on Libya ready, though the solution for the easiest case of the three—Eritrea—was waiting to be submitted to the First Committee.

No formal minutes of the lengthy deliberations in Sub-Committee 17 (twenty-nine meetings were held between 11 October and 1 November) were taken, but the Secretariat kept an informal record, which is still formally classified. So did a number of delegations; but as it proved difficult for a group of twenty-one representatives accompanied by experts and secretaries to keep secrets, enough reliable information leaked out to provide an account of what transpired.[78]

From a procedural point of view, the discussions in the Sub-Committee were systematized by a French suggestion that the proposals before it be studied subject by subject, instead of resolution by resolution. It was further decided to deal with the three former colonies in the order Libya, Somaliland, Eritrea. The principal subjects that came up in the case of Libya were: independence; unity; the length of the transitional period preceding independence, together with procedures and activities during that

---

that the Libyan government be based on democratic principles, employ proportional representation, and specifically guarantee human and religious rights as well as the right to emigrate. He did not charge that the Jewish community was being persecuted but asked that it be given special assurances that its cultural and religious position be respected and that its economic position be protected.

77. GAOR: Fourth Session, 1949, First Committee, Annexes to Summary Records, Agenda item 19 (A/C.1/498, 11 October 1949), p. 24.

78. For a useful summary, see "Report of Sub-Committee 17 to the First Committee," GAOR: Fourth Session, 1949, First Committee, Annexes to Summary Records, Agenda item 19 (A/C.1/522, 1 November 1949), pp. 25–33. Moreover, an extensive account of these transactions can be found in U.S. Dept. of State *Bulletin,* Vol. XXII, 29 May 1950, pp. 832–59.

period; the role of the Administering Powers during the transitional period; the representation and presence of the United Nations (commissioner and/or council); composition of the council; representation on the council of the local populations, including the minorities; and the functions of the commissioner. Since, in the last instance, all these subjects had to be coherently brought together in one resolution, it was not always possible to have separate discussions on each of them in the order listed. Sometimes they became intermingled, but on the whole the procedure proposed by France proved effective.

On the basic principle of independence, agreement was easily reached. It was more difficult to arrive at a compromise on the length of the transitional period. A USSR proposal that Libya be granted immediate independence was rejected, though the Arab members of the Sub-Committee, Egypt and Iraq, supported the USSR argument. It was, however, vaguely agreed that the period should be long enough to allow for the creation of a Libyan government and administration capable of ensuring a decent life for the people of Libya.

The representative of France believed it would be better not to prescribe a definite time limit, but merely to state that independence should be achieved as soon as possible. The United Kingdom representative, on the other hand, proposed that Libyan independence should be complete within two years, preferably, and certainly in not more than three years. The United States representative suggested that independence follow a transitional period of three years during which the administering authorities would cooperate in setting up a constituent assembly and other governmental institutions. The proposal finally adopted was India's, which suggested that a united, independent State be proclaimed two years after the appointment of a commission of experts whose task it would be to approve a constitution to be drawn up by a Libyan constituent assembly. It was also unanimously agreed that Libya should not be partitioned to form three separate and sovereign States, but should become one independent State, with the form of government to be decided by the inhabitants themselves. As a result of this meeting of minds, the following text was taken to embody the essential recommendations regarding Libya:

1. That Libya, comprising Cyrenaica, Tripolitania and the Fezzan, shall be established as a single independent and sovereign State.
2. That this independence shall become effective as soon as possible and in any case not later than 1 January 1952.
3. That a constitution for Libya, including the form of the government, be determined by representatives of the inhabitants of Cyrenaica, Tripoli-

tania and the Fezzan, meeting and consulting together in a National Assembly." [79]

It will be noted that while paragraph 1 implied unity, the word itself was not used.

Although the Sub-Committee agreed without too much difficulty on the principle that the United Nations should be represented in Libya in order to watch over and give advice on the measures necessary for drafting a constitution and choosing the form of government, the question of whether a commission with executive powers, or an advisory body, or, alternatively, a commissioner with advisory powers, should be sent to Libya for the transitional period gave rise to some discussion. The terms of reference for such a body or person also proved controversial. Suggestions ranged from that of a body empowered to make certain that the Libyan constitution contained the necessary safeguards for human rights and fundamental freedoms, to that of an impartial high commissioner acting as an adviser and assisted by an advisory committee. Some members proposed a council, whose duty it would be, in cooperation with the Administering powers, to settle all questions relating to elections and the establishment of governmental institutions. One member suggested that the United Nations should act as a catalytic agent between the people of Libya and the Administering Powers, and stressed the advisability of appointing a United Nations mediator, or body, to which the people of Libya could appeal.

Thus from the very outset there was disagreement as to whether the General Assembly should appoint a commissioner, assisted by experts, with or without an advisory council, or whether it should set up a commission without a commissioner. Several delegations expressed doubts about the need for a council, believing that it would do to have either a commissioner or a council, and that if both were appointed complications could not fail to ensue. Others maintained that it might be well to have some individual, or an advisory council, to whom difficulties could be referred. The United Kingdom delegate believed that a commissioner should be empowered to co-opt the services of any experts he might need, and found the idea of an advisory council less attractive.

Since no agreement could be reached, a vote was taken on whether it was or was not advisable to set up only a United Nations commission for Libya. The result was negative. The Sub-Committee also rejected the idea that a commissioner without a council should be sent to Libya. After

79. "Report of Sub-Committee 17 to the First Committee," p. 31. For the text of Resolution 289 (IV) as finally adopted by the General Assembly, see Annex I, pp. 891–93.

lengthy discussions, another vote was taken on the principle of appointing a commissioner assisted by a council "to aid and advise him." This proposal, made by the representative of India, was approved, and agreement was reached on the following paragraph to be inserted in the draft resolution:

> 4. That for the purpose of assisting the people of Libya in the formulation of the constitution and the establishment of an independent Government, there shall be a United Nations commissioner in Libya appointed by the General Assembly and a council to aid and advise him." [80]

At the request of the Iraqi delegate, the title of High Commissioner, distasteful to the Arab ear, was changed to Commissioner. This also tallied with the advisory nature of the Commissioner's functions.

Although it was generally understood that the Commissioner would be assisted by a technical staff, a further debate developed about the composition of the Council. On the whole, it was agreed that the Council should reflect the interests of the Libyan people, of the neighboring States, and of the Administering Powers. The USSR representative was of the opinion that the Four Big Powers should be represented on the Council, but a Polish proposal to include the USSR was defeated. An Indian proposal, on the other hand, provided that the Council should include one representative of each of the following countries: Egypt, as a neighbor; the United Kingdom and France, as the Administering Powers; Italy, on the ground that its past experience in Libya would undoubtedly prove useful; [81] the United States of America, which could give precious economic aid; and Pakistan, which had recently acquired independence and whose advice would therefore be of great help. The Indian formula also provided for representatives of Cyrenaica, Tripolitania, and the Fezzan to sit on the Council, and thus constituted the most acceptable compromise between the various points of view expressed. It was accordingly adopted, together with a much contested Guatemalan amendment to the effect that the proposed Council should also include a representative of the minorities in Libya, who would be able to advise the Commissioner on their wishes and interests.[82]

80. "Report of Sub-Committee 17 to the First Committee," p. 31.

81. The United Kingdom was against Italian membership in the Council because of Eden's pledge to the Senussi that Cyrenaica would in no circumstances again fall under Italian administration (see pp. 40–41). It accordingly took no part in the voting.

82. The opposition to minority representation on the Council mainly came from Iraq, Egypt, and Argentina, and appeared to be inspired by fear of "foreign" intervention in Libya's internal affairs. The United Kingdom recognized the existence of a minorities problem in Libya, but considered that representation on the Council would not solve it. Hence, it again took no part in the voting. Since the most numerous minority was Italian, the British pledge to the Senussi played its part on this occasion also.

Having decided that there should be a United Nations Commissioner and a Council to aid and advise him, and having also determined the composition of that Council as well as the mode of appointing its nongovernmental members, the Sub-Committee attempted to define further the relationship between them. India proposed that the Commissioner should "consult and be guided by the advice of the members of his council." Several suggestions were made for clarifying the meaning of these words, but as no commonly acceptable formula could be found, this wording was adopted for lack of a better definition; it subsequently became a constant source of friction between the Commissioner and certain members of the Council, as will be described in more detail in Chapter 4.

The paragraphs inserted in the draft resolution as a result of this further discussion read as follows:

> 6. That the Council shall consist of ten members, namely:
>
> (a) One representative nominated by the Government of each of the following countries: Egypt, France, Italy, Pakistan, the United Kingdom and the United States of America;
>
> (b) One representative of the people of each of the three regions of Libya and one representative of the minorities in Libya;
>
> 7. That the United Nations commissioner shall appoint the representatives mentioned in paragraph 6(b), after consultation with the Administering Powers, the representatives of the Governments mentioned in 6(a), leading personalities and representatives of political parties and organizations in the territories concerned;
>
> 8. That, in the discharge of his functions, the United Nations commissioner shall consult and be guided by the advice of the members of his council, it being understood that he may call upon different members to advise him in respect of different regions or different subjects.[83]

The next point to be determined was the role of the Administering Powers and the relationship between them on the one hand and the Commissioner on the other. It was agreed in principle that any resolution adopted should include a recommendation to the effect that the Administering Powers would continue, during the transitional period, to administer the territories in order to help in the establishment of the unity and independence of Libya; would coordinate their activities to that end; and would render annual reports to the General Assembly on the implementation of the resolution. To these tasks was added, at the request of Pakistan and the United States, the task of cooperating in the formation of governmental institutions. Thus, thanks to the joint efforts of India, Pakistan, the United States, and others, the concept of Libyan unity was explicitly introduced

83. "Report of Sub-Committee 17 to the First Committee," pp. 31–32.

into this paragraph of the draft. At the same time it was understood that neither the Commissioner nor the Council would have anything to do with the current, day-to-day administration of the three provinces.

McNeil, speaking for the United Kingdom, claimed that the Administering Powers should be given sole responsibility for assisting the Libyan people in their evolution toward independence, including the transfer of power toward a duly constituted independent Government, without the interposition of either a Commissioner or a Council. After lengthy deliberation, the various agreements reached found expression in the following paragraph:

> 10. That the Administering Powers:
> (a) Initiate immediately all necessary steps for the transfer of power to a duly constituted independent Government;
> (b) Administer the territories for the purpose of assisting in the establishment of Libyan unity and independence, co-operate in the formation of government institutions and co-ordinate their activities to this end.[84]

This, then, is a brief account of the process by which, through manifold mutual concessions, an almost unanimous solution was found for the main issues concerning Libya's future. The socialist group remained aloof, since the USSR had not been given a seat on the Council for Libya, and because its proposal calling for the withdrawal of all foreign troops from Libya and the liquidation of military and air bases within three months had been rejected. In pursuance of this position, these countries also adopted a reserved attitude toward a United States proposal that Libya be admitted to membership of the United Nations as soon as it became independent. The USSR representative said that his Government would support Libya's candidacy for membership if, when the time came, that country's political status fulfilled the conditions for the admission of new members laid down in Article 4 of the United Nations Charter. The United States proposal was adopted unanimously, appearing in the following wording in the draft resolution:

> 11. That, upon its establishment as an independent State, Libya be admitted to the United Nations in accordance with Article 4 of the Charter.[85]

In the light of the steadily worsening relations between East and West, this unanimity may seem surprising. But although in the view of the USSR

84. Ibid., p. 32.
85. Ibid., p. 32.

the agreed-upon solution was dominated by Western interests to a much too great extent, the USSR presumably wanted to woo the Arab States.

A few details still had to be settled. Opinions differed on the way in which Council and Commissioner should report to the United Nations. In fact, the issue boiled down to determining which of the two would have precedence over the other. The Administering Powers and their friends preferred the Commissioner to report, apparently feeling that they might find an individual—even though his identity was still unknown—easier to get on with than a commission or council. The Arab States, on the contrary, supported by several other countries, attached more importance to reports from a body on which they would be represented. The Pakistani representative suggested, by way of compromise, that the Commissioner, in consultation with the Council, should submit reports to the Secretary-General for transmission to the General Assembly. In the final draft, the members of the Council were given the right to append their observations to the Commissioner's reports, thanks to a further proposal by Pakistan. Thus, in this matter of reporting, an approximate balance was struck between Commissioner and Council, though in practice the former, as the future draughtsman of the reports, enjoyed a slight advantage. This new compromise was expressed in the following paragraph of the draft resolution:

> 5. The United Nations commissioner, in consultation with the council, shall submit to the Secretary-General an annual report and such other special reports as he may consider necessary. To these reports shall be added any memorandum or document that the United Nations commissioner or a member of the council may wish to bring to the attention of the United Nations.[86]

Another question still open was the procedure by which the Commissioner was to be nominated. Several widely divergent formulas were proposed by Pakistan, Egypt, and the United States: nomination by the six governmental members of the Council for Libya, or by the Trusteeship Council (Pakistan); by a committee of nine, including the six mentioned in the Pakistani proposal (Egypt); by a committee of the "Big Four" (United States of America); or by a group of five persons comprising the President and two Vice-Presidents of the General Assembly and the Chairmen of the First and *Ad Hoc* Political Committees (Argentina). The last method was ultimately adopted by way of a separate resolution, with the adjunction that if the group was unable to reach agreement on a single

86. Ibid., p. 31.

nominee, it should submit the names of three candidates to the General Assembly.

Egypt having raised during the Peace Conference in Paris the question of the delimitation of its frontier with the future Libyan State (see p. 66 and fn. 50), the Pakistani member of Sub-Committee 17 proposed that this task be entrusted to the Commissioner assisted by his Council. The USSR representative strongly opposed this proposal, arguing that this was a historical tactic for the partitioning of colonies which, in the case at issue, would encourage attempts to grab areas of Libyan territory. He suggested that any demarcation of Libya's frontiers should be carried out by the future Libyan Government in conjunction with its neighbors. The French, United States, and United Kingdom representatives having also raised objections, the Pakistani proposal was rejected. At a later meeting, the Egyptian representative again raised the question, insisting that, under paragraphs 2 and 3 of Annex XI to the Treaty of Peace with Italy, the question of the adjustment of frontiers, as distinct from delimitation, had been left to the "Big Four," and therefore had subsequently been referred to the General Assembly, together with the other issues involved, on their failure to agree among themselves. In the face of continued opposition, and in the absence of any further action by the Sub-Committee, he reserved the right to raise the matter in the First Committee itself.

Finally, there remained economic, financial, and social problems of two kinds to be settled. First, those (economic and financial) arising out of the Treaty of Peace with Italy (Annex XIV thereto, paragraph 19), and second, those (economic and social) which, prior to independence, would undoubtedly demand attention in the planning and setting up of the Libyan State.

With regard to the first and highly intricate category of questions (which will be dealt with further in Chapter 5), it was decided to insert the following paragraph in the Sub-Committee's report to the First Committee:

> The Sub-Committee had no specific recommendation to offer with regard to this question, but it was the sense of the Sub-Committee that the question of the economic and financial provisions for Libya should be considered and decided upon at the next regular session of the General Assembly, when reports on the subject would have been received from the Administering Powers and, possibly, from the commissioner and his council. The representative of the United Kingdom wished that mention should be made in the report of his right to raise the matter again before the First Committee.[87]

87. Ibid., p. 28.

As to the economic and social problems of the future Libyan State, the Sub-Committee hardly gave them any attention. Indeed, political considerations, one more controversial than the other, had completely dominated its debates, although the report of the Four Power Commission had said bluntly that Libya was "poor in natural resources and . . . dependent upon financial assistance from outside." [88]

The Chilean representative therefore proposed that the Commissioner be authorized to make suggestions to the General Assembly, the Economic and Social Council, and the Secretary-General on the measures the United Nations might take to help to solve Libya's economic and social problems, especially those related to its economic development. The Chilean proposal came in for a good deal of criticism. The United Kingdom expressed the fear that its adoption might serve as a pretext for adding an economic and social secretariat to the Commissioner's staff. The USSR argued that the proposal was tantamount to intervention in the domestic affairs of the new State before it could even ask for assistance. After the sponsor had toned down his proposal by deleting the reference to economic development, it was approved, though the USSR still voted against it. The agreement was included in the draft resolution as paragraph 9:

> 9. That the United Nations commissioner may offer suggestions to the General Assembly, to the Economic and Social Council and to the Secretary-General as to the measures that the United Nations might adopt during the transitional period regarding the economic and social problems of Libya.[89]

When the First Committee took up the report and recommendations of Sub-Committee 17 on 4 November, the sensitive question of Libyan unity once more, and not for the last time in the next two years, became the dominant issue. As one of the first speakers in the general debate, the United Kingdom representative proposed the following four amendments to the draft resolution on Libya:

Section A (with respect to Libya):

(1) Delete paragraph 1, and insert the following:

> "1. That the people of Libya, comprising Cyrenaica, Tripolitania and the Fezzan, shall become independent with a form of union and government to be decided upon by the people themselves as prescribed herein."

88. See pp. 69–71 and fnn. 52 and 53. The quotation is from the French/UK/USA text of the Commission's conclusions for the whole of Libya, but the USSR text, too, tacitly endorses this opinion.

89. "Report of Sub-Committee 17 to the First Committee," p. 32.

(2) Delete paragraph 3, and insert the following:
"3. At a suitable time before that date the representatives of the people of Cyrenaica, Tripolitania and the Fezzan shall meet and consult together freely to decide upon the form of their future union and government, whether unitary, federal or other."

(3) In paragraph 10(*a*), delete the words "a duly constituted independent government," and insert the words "the appropriate organs of government to be constituted in accordance with this resolution."

(4) In paragraph 10(*b*), delete the words "in the establishment of Libyan unity and independence," and insert the words "the people of Libya in achieving independence and the form of union and government they desire." [90]

If these amendments are read in conjunction with the statement of the French representative that is quoted on page 87, it will be seen that the United Kingdom representative could not have made it plainer that the two Administering Powers did not intend in the first instance to promote a united Libya. Their aim apparently was to encourage the creation of three separate States (Cyrenaica, Tripolitania, and the Fezzan) which might subsequently, if they could, form a union among themselves. Compared with the Bevin-Sforza formula, this new policy admittedly reflected some progress in degree of liberality and form of presentation, but in intention it did not really differ from the old idea of dividing up the country into three zones of influence. Of course, Italy's share therein had been considerably reduced, but had the British amendments been adopted, Tripolitania, whether left to its own devices or forming part of a weak Libyan union, would have fallen willy-nilly into the Italian orbit again, with all that that would have meant in friction and clashes between Italian demographic pressure and Arab nationalism. Moreover, the impact of Libyan unity as a stabilizing factor in North Africa and the Mediterranean basin would not have been felt for several years. There is, of course, no gainsaying the fact that the Bevin-Sforza plan as well as this renewed Anglo-French attempt to keep the country divided were in part due to the absence of a clearly defined Cyrenaican-Tripolitanian agreement on unity. Had such an agreement existed, it could not have failed to attract the Fezzan, French efforts to the contrary notwithstanding. Neither could it have failed to carry weight with the General Assembly. But it did not exist; Italy's departure had left a vacuum, and nature abhors a vacuum. The United Kingdom and France were only too willing to fill the void.

It is difficult to say how many delegations perceived the implications of

90. GAOR: Fourth Session, 1949, First Committee, Annexes to Summary Records, Agenda item 19 (A/C.1/526/Rev.1, 5 November 1949), pp. 33–34.

the British amendments at the time. The Libyans present did, as Omar Shenib, then leading the National Congress of Cyrenaica's delegation, later told the author, at least to the extent of realizing that advantage was being taken of the inherent weakness of their position. To some others the amendments appear to have been attractive at first sight. They were certainly attractively presented. Their purpose, the United Kingdom spokesman assured the Committee, was to secure the rights of Libyans to make their own free choice regarding the form of their future government and the method of meeting and consulting together. The draft resolution proposed by Sub-Committee 17, he argued, contained a suggestion about their unity which, perhaps, not all Libyans would like. In fact, it would compel them to adhere rigidly to a single, unified political structure, whereas some might prefer a federation or some other form of association. Admittedly, the three territories could not lead economically viable lives as independent States. They should be free to choose how they would consult with one another, provided their consultations led to the inception of a single, sovereign Libya by the proposed date. Much would depend on what was understood by "unity," which to the inhabitants of Libya was a difficult and involved concept.

The United Kingdom representative also suggested that some Libyans would prefer to be advised by a Commissioner and Council (who, from the point of view of the Administering Powers, might turn out to be rival authorities).

Support for the British position came first from the Netherlands. The United States stood firm behind the Sub-Committee's plan for the three colonies as a whole, but nonetheless supported the United Kingdom amendments regarding Libya. So did South Africa.

The Pakistani representative objected to the provision in the plan for Libya that authorized the Commissioner to call upon different members of the Council, instead of upon that body as a whole, to advise him in respect of different regions or subjects.

The Argentinian representative disagreed with the notion that the Sub-Committee's proposals prescribed a specific type of government for the new Libyan State. The plan provided that Libya should be a single, sovereign State, but that in no way prejudiced the issue of whether it would be federal, confederated, or unitary in form.

The representative of Czechoslovakia opposed the appointment of a Commissioner whose functions were too independent of his Advisory Council. He also opposed the United Kingdom amendments, as he considered that the principle of a united, independent, and sovereign Libyan government was grounded firmly in the wishes of the local populations.

The Indian representative, defending the draft resolution before the

Committee, observed that there was no great difference between the Sub-Committee's proposal and the United Kingdom amendments. Unified Libya would have a choice of forms of government, but it was better to encourage unity from the very beginning, leaving the inhabitants the liberty of abandoning it if they so wished. He invited the United Kingdom to give further consideration to its amendments before pressing them to a vote.

After the Italian spokesman had declared that any kind of exchange between Italy and Tripolitania would promote mutual understanding and agreement between the Italian and Arab peoples, and the Guatemalan representative had stressed the importance of the representation of minorities on the Council for Libya, which would offer them stronger guarantees than a Commissioner, the USSR representative pointed out that the Sub-Committee's report presented only the views of a majority. The attitude of that majority reflected the struggle among various Powers to partition the former Italian colonies. His delegation's draft resolution, still before the First Committee was, on the contrary, intended to ensure the self-determination of the local population while safeguarding the interests of members of the United Nations as a whole. His Government still considered that Libya should be granted independence forthwith. He opposed the United Kingdom amendments, the purpose of which was, in his opinion, to dismember Libya by setting up "puppet governments" like the one already established in Cyrenaica. In conclusion, he once more protested against the installation of the United States air base near Tripoli.

The Peruvian representative strongly supported the Sub-Committee's proposals. In his view, in the case of Libya, "unity," as used in the Sub-Committee's reports, referred to the international legal personality of the State, not to the form of government the people would adopt. He believed that the intention of the United Kingdom amendments was already inherent in the resolution, and that they were therefore redundant. The Liberian representative, on the contrary, supported the amendments.

Thus the debate continued for five days in the course of which opposition to the British amendments steadily grew. Libyan unity remained the dominant factor throughout, but the other issues dealt with in the section of the draft resolution dealing with Libya called forth all the old arguments in support of the old positions.

By 9 November the First Committee was ready to vote. The USSR proposal concerning immediate independence, the withdrawal of foreign troops, and the liquidation of military bases was rejected.

Among the resolutions proposed as amendments to the Sub-Committee's draft, two were of major importance. The first, sponsored by India, proposed that the opening paragraph read: "That Libya, comprising the territories of Cyrenaica, Tripolitania and the Fezzan, shall be constituted into a united independent sovereign State."[91]

The Indian representative explained that his proposed changes were a compromise, as well as a clarification of the Sub-Committee's real intention, namely, that the three Libyan territories should be brought together into a single political unit, but that the unit's form of government should be left for the Libyan people to decide.

The United Kingdom representative, confronted with this proposition, agreed to withdraw his own amendments. In doing so, he made, in the course of his statement, the following observations, here quoted verbatim:

> The Committee will, I know, understand that as I have already more than once attempted to point out, my Government as the Administering Authority has always contemplated certain steps which had to be taken on the road towards the sovereignty of Libya before full unity and independence in that territory could be achieved. As I have already said, I hope quite precisely, we felt that we should as events permitted invest sovereignty in Cyrenaica and that thereafter again as events permitted we should press ahead to endow Tripolitania with a measure of internal autonomy comparable with that which exists in Cyrenaica. Indeed, as I remember telling the Committee, we had already started planning for that situation. As has been plain from the beginning and the representative of the Australian delegation has just pointed out, neither of these events conflicted with the intention of the Sub-Committee or with the intention of the Committee as a whole in regard to the independence and sovereignty of the territory of Libya. Our fear, however, was that the resolution as it emerged from the Sub-Committee did not literally provide room for such steps, although, as [the Australian representative] has pointed out, it was quite plain from the discussions in the Sub-Committee that such steps were accepted by a majority of the members as necessary and practical. I would not want, therefore, to be reproached at a later date or to run any chance of being accused of ill faith through any ambiguity in the resolution upon which we are about to vote or, to be equally honest, through any vagueness as to the intentions of the United Kingdom as Administering Power. Obviously, the Administration must continue to discharge its responsibilities in the period between the adoption of this resolution and the granting of Libyan sovereignty and independence, but the whole Committee must clearly understand that the obligations we have do not extend beyond that period.

91. United Nations Doc. A/C.1/531, 1 November 1949. For text, see GAOR: Fourth Session, 1949, First Committee, 318th Meeting, 9 November 1949, p. 221.

With the creation of Libyan independence our role as administrator is finished.[92]

Subsequently, the Indian amendment, which had been subjected to some change during the discussion, was voted upon by roll call and approved by 51 votes to none, with 7 abstentions. In all fairness, it should be recognized here and now that the United Kingdom statement served its purpose, namely, to avert any misunderstanding as to the policy which the United Kingdom Government had intended, and apparently still intended, to follow in the matter of Libyan constitutional development. The statement did not, however, inhibit the emergence of divergent interpretations about the meaning of Libyan unity and the manner in which it was to be brought about. As events subsequently proved, the statement never could have done so because of certain ambiguities and contradictions in the text of the resolution itself.

The second amendment of substantial significance was submitted by the Chinese representative, who argued that the relationship between the Commissioner and the Administering Powers needed clarification. With this aim in view he proposed an amendment which required the Commissioner to prepare his annual report to the United Nations "in cooperation with [the] Administering Authorities" as well as in consultation with the Council, and also provided that the Administering Authorities carry out certain steps toward the establishment of self-government in the territory "in co-operation with the commissioner." [93]

The second part of the amendment was carried by 50 votes to none, with 6 abstentions, after the first part had been defeated. Two Polish amendments, the first proposing that Libya be declared independent by "1 January 1951" instead of "in any case not later than 1 January 1952," the second seeking to replace France, the United Kingdom, and the United States on the Council for Libya by three smaller States, were also thrown out. Thereafter, each paragraph of the Sub-Committee's text, as amended by the Indian proposal and by the second part of the Chinese proposal, was approved in turn, after which the draft resolution as a whole was adopted by 50 votes to none, with 8 abstentions.

On 19 November 1949, the First Committee's resolution was taken up

92. Typescript text of statement, used by the speaker at the meeting. For official summary of McNeil's statement, see GAOR: Fourth Session, 1949, ibid., p. 222. The use of the words "sovereignty in Cyrenaica" in the above context was, of course, not legally correct, as was understood by the majority of delegations present, the United Kingdom included. But no official correction was ever submitted to the record.

93. For the text of the Chinese draft resolution, see GAOR: Fourth Session, 1949, First Committee, Annexes to Summary Records, Agenda item 19 (A/C.1/528, 5 November 1949), p. 34.

in the plenary session of the General Assembly.[94] During the general debate most of the arguments previously advanced in the First Committee were repeated yet again. However, it also gave delegations an opportunity of expressing their general appreciation or criticism of the work already done, as well as their hopes and expectations about the way in which the resolution would be implemented. The following illustrations of these statements may be of interest.

Iraq characterized the resolution as "an example of the best work that the United Nations could perform in the existing circumstances. . . . No single Member had succeeded in obtaining all he had wished. Yet all the points of view had been . . . so far as possible taken into account." It hoped that "the Commissioner appointed by the General Assembly, advised and guided by a council, would help the people of Libya, in cooperation with the Administering Authorities, to achieve their independence and unity." It "attached great importance to [the] unity of Libya." It believed that Libya was "one, geographically, historically, economically and culturally." [95]

The *United States of America* described the Assembly's recommendation as "one of the most gratifying achievements . . . of the General Assembly. . . . The terms of the draft resolution . . . ensured that the form of the Libyan State and the constitution of its government would be determined by the people themselves. Thus . . . the General Assembly would be fully supporting the Libyan people's right to self-determination." [96]

India believed that the draft resolution "[was] unique in the history of the United Nations . . ." and that "in the matter of the disposal of the former Italian colonies, the General Assembly was acting for the first time not as a glorified debating society, but as a real world parliament with a power of final decision binding upon all concerned. . . . [The] appointing [of] a . . . Commissioner to set up . . . a National Assembly to frame a constitution . . . was the first time the United Nations had taken so momentous a step." [97]

Pakistan noted that "the proposals with regard to Libya commanded a more nearly unanimous support in the General Assembly than [those regarding] the other two former colonies," and that "There had already been indications that [they] commanded the support of all sections of the population of Libya." [98]

94. Adopted by the General Assembly on 21 November as Resolution 289 (IV).

95. GAOR: Fourth Session, 1949, 247th Plenary Meeting, 19 November 1949, p. 266.

96. Ibid., p. 268.

97. Ibid., pp. 271–72.

98. GAOR: Fourth Session, 1949, 248th Plenary Meeting, 19 November 1949, p. 279.

Some governments were relieved. *Lebanon,* for example, pointed out that "Under the stress of [the] reaction of world opinion [to the resolution embodying the Bevin-Sforza plan], the point of view of Italy, and of those who had advocated its claims, had undergone a considerable change. . . . They had come to the current session prepared to agree to the proposal which the Arab and Asian states had from the first enunciated, namely, that the people of Libya were in no need of trusteeship and that they should be granted their independence in as short a time as possible." [99]

Assessments of the prospects for Libyan unity afforded by the resolution were varied.

Peru said that "the question of Libyan unity . . . had been settled in the best possible way," stressing that "Libya's independence was bound up with Libya's unity. But that unity applied to the territory and not the form of government [which] could be unitary, federative, or confederative." [100]

The *Philippines* considered that "the formula recommended for Libya was most satisfactory. . . . It only remained for the General Assembly to make it plain, beyond any possibility of misunderstanding, that it wished to see established one independent and sovereign state of Libya, leaving it to the Libyans themselves to determine their own form of government." [101]

Egypt reminded the General Assembly that "The fate of millions of people in Africa who looked to the United Nations for justice and liberty depended on the decision the Assembly would take. . . . On that decision depended also . . . the prestige of the United Nations." With regard to Libya it was its considered opinion that "the solution proposed was on the whole satisfactory. . . . [But] certain portions of it, concerning both independence and unity, could have been strengthened to great advantage and . . . the rights of the commissioner and the council could have been extended." [102]

Other Governments were highly critical:

Czechoslovakia criticized the proposed composition of the Council for Libya because it included only three of the four Great Powers which had referred the matter to the United Nations. The question of the disposal of the former Italian colonies had been entrusted to the General Assembly because "[the United Kingdom, France and the United States] had approached the problem not from the point of view of the interest of the

99. GAOR: Fourth Session, 1949, 247th Plenary Meeting, 19 November 1949, p. 270.

100. GAOR: Fourth Session, 1949, 248th Plenary Meeting, 19 November 1949, p. 281.

101. Ibid., p. 283.

102. Ibid., pp. 291–92.

peoples of the territories, . . . but purely and solely from the point of view of their imperialist policy." [103]

The *Union of Soviet Socialist Republics* complained that the proposed resolution was merely the old Bevin-Sforza plan "in a slightly more veiled form," of which the United States and the United Kingdom "by new manoeuvres . . . had managed to obtain the adoption by a majority of the First Committee. . . . The British and French military administrations in Libya were already setting up puppet governments. . . . a regime in Cyrenaica under the leadership of Emir el Senussi . . . [in] the Fezzan under the leadership of Ahmed Bey Seif el Nasr. . . . The appointment of a commissioner and a council to assist the people of Libya in preparing a constitution . . . [was] an inadmissible interference in the internal affairs of Libya . . . the people of Libya had not been consulted . . . the proposed Council would include only two representatives of non-colonial powers." [104]

Poland considered it "a well-known fact that the United Kingdom had opposed the establishment of a council to help the people of Libya in the transitional period.[105]

The *Byelorussian Soviet Socialist Republic* charged that the recommendations "did not take into account the desire of the population to obtain immediate independence and to ensure the unity of Libya, which the occupying Powers, the United Kingdom and France, had artificially divided in order better to serve their interests in the post war period." It felt it necessary "to warn the Libyan people . . . that as long as foreign troops and military bases remained on their territory, there could be no true independence for Libya." [106]

The Administering Powers were wary:

The *United Kingdom* recalled that its delegation had "at various stages expressed some doubt concerning the wisdom and realism of certain details of the proposed machinery, particularly where the relationship between the advisory council, the commissioner and the administration was concerned." It "would not disguise the fact that [it] felt something approaching horror about everything approximating to a duality of control, and an even greater fear of checks and balances inserted or imposed at the executive end of any scheme." But "the Administration would cheerfully and fully co-operate with the commissioner and his council." Regarding Cyrenaica,

103. Ibid., p. 274.

104. GAOR: Fourth Session, 1949, 249th Plenary Meeting, 21 November 1949, pp. 292–93.

105. GAOR: Fourth Session, 1949, 248th Plenary Meeting, 19 November 1949, p. 285.

106. Ibid., p. 287.

the United Kingdom "felt sure that the commissioner and his council would not forget that there was an Administration in Cyrenaica, that, by the very nature of the territory and its history, there had to be an Administration, and that the Administration also had its obligations to fulfill under the resolution. Those obligations would be fulfilled; and the Administration, while offering cheerful and eager co-operation, would in its turn expect from the commissioner and his council not rivalry but co-operation and help." [107]

France considered that the resolution "was essentially a compromise formula" but asked "whether it was not a compromise with common sense." As to the definite time limit of two years laid down for Libya's preparation for independence, France regarded this "as unrealistic . . . in the light of the . . . report of the Four Power Commission of Investigation . . . the four members of [which] had been in complete agreement in considering that none of the territories . . . were ready for independence, that [they] were poor and incapable of becoming self-sufficient and that their political education was rudimentary. That evidence had not been contradicted by . . . the representatives of associations considered as representative of the peoples concerned. [Although they] had all stated their desire for independence, . . . [which] had occasioned no surprise . . . [they] had not made any constructive proposals regarding the most important, because . . . the most uncertain and difficult point, namely the best way of achieving that independence. Such was the real problem which the United Nations had to solve." Moreover, "The purpose of . . . the draft resolution, concerning Libya, was to enable that territory to achieve independence in an orderly and dignified manner. . . . The conditions under which the experiment was about to be made were neither the best possible nor the most reasonable. Nevertheless, France would co-operate in the experiment to the full. As a Power administering one of the territories concerned it would continue to administer the territory throughout the specified period, while doing its best to develop institutions of self-government. As a member of the council for Libya, it would co-operate in the consultations provided for between the authorised representatives of the three territories for the purpose of devising a suitable central organisation. . . . It would . . . neglect nothing which might help to implement the General Assembly's resolution once it was adopted." Finally, although France "would be obliged . . . to abstain from voting on the draft resolution as a whole . . . the French government would accept the verdict of the United Nations and, in its implementation, would give all the assistance required of it." [108]

107. GAOR: Fourth Session, 1949, 247th Plenary Meeting, 19 November 1949, p. 267.

108. GAOR: Fourth Session, 1949, 249th Plenary Meeting, 21 November 1949, pp. 295–97.

The foregoing statements [109] foresaw with uncanny precision the problems and difficulties which were to arise in implementing the resolution. Indeed, it was not very long before such issues as the policies of the Administering Powers with regard to the concept and degree of Libyan unity, the role of the Council for Libya, and its relationship to the Commissioner became highly controversial.

When the General Assembly met to take the final vote at its two hundred and fiftieth meeting in the afternoon of 21 November 1949, Section A of Resolution 289(IV) was adopted by 49 votes to none, with 9 abstentions.[110] Thus the Libyan people were given the opportunity of preparing for their independence and determining the form of their future State.

The main theme of this chapter has been Libyan unity. The picture that emerges from the foregoing account can briefly be described in the following terms.

Ignoring, in this context, the episode of the Tripolitanian Republic at the close of World War I, from 1939 to 1949 the Libyan leaders had been trying hard to reach agreement on a form of unity, in particular between Cyrenaica and Tripolitania. Although they had made considerable progress, no mutually acceptable solution had been found. In the process, the idea of unity had become increasingly associated with the concept of independence, but the joining of the two had complicated rather than simplified the problems involved. Hence, under the United Nations plan, it now was up to the Libyan people themselves, with the assistance of the Administering Powers, the Commissioner, and the Council, to elaborate a joint and simultaneous solution for both unity and independence as twin aspects of one and the same problem. Before November 1949, foreign interventions in what was basically an internal Libyan question had been of a contradictory nature; and they continued to be so. Some outside forces had worked for unification. Others had aimed at dividing the country. Their combined effect on the Libyan leaders had been, above all, to make them see clearly the dangers of disunity, and to strengthen their conviction that a common area of understanding had to be found. The following chapters deal with the evolution of this process under the auspices of the United Nations.

109. For a full account of the General Assembly's closing debate, see GAOR: Fourth Session, 1949, 247th–249th Plenary Meetings, 19–21 November 1949, pp. 265–301.

110. The following delegations abstained: Byelorussia, Czechoslovakia, France, New Zealand, Poland, Sweden, Ukraine, USSR, and Yugoslavia. On the same occasion, the General Assembly adopted Resolution 289C (IV), inviting its Interim Committee to study the procedures to be adopted to delimit the boundaries of the former Italian colonies insofar as they were not already fixed by international agreement, and to submit a report together with its conclusions to the Fifth Regular Session of the General Assembly.

CHAPTER 2

Into Action

PART 1. CLEARING THE DECKS

The main issues having been settled, the General Assembly lost no time in adopting a resolution [1] setting up a committee consisting of the President of the General Assembly, two of the Vice-Presidents, the Chairman of the First Committee, and the Chairman of the *Ad Hoc* Political Committee,[2] requesting it to nominate a candidate or, if itself unable to agree on a single name, a list of three candidates, for the post of United Nations Commissioner in Libya.

Shortly afterward, the Secretary-General of the United Nations, Trygve Lie, casually mentioned to the author, then Assistant Secretary-General in charge of the Department of Conference and General Services, that he had put his name forward for the Committee's consideration. It seems that the background to this nomination, as came out many years later, was that the Secretary-General, after consulting his Executive Assistant, Andrew Cordier,[3] and a few others in his inner circle, had come to the conclusion that

1. Resolution 289 B (IV), 21 November 1949. For text, see Annex I, p. 893.

2. Respectively: His Excellency Brigadier General Carlos P. Romulo, of the Philippines; His Excellency M. C. de Freitas Valle, of Brazil; His Excellency the Honorable Sir Muhammad Zafrulla Khan, of Pakistan; His Excellency the Honorable Lester B. Pearson, of Canada; and His Excellency Ambassador Nasrollah Entezam, of Iran.

3. Andrew Wellington Cordier, born on 3 March 1901, was educated at Manchester College, North Manchester, Indiana, and at the University of Chicago, where he received his Ph.D. in history in 1926. After teaching at his college, he studied at the Graduate Institute of International Studies at Geneva in 1930–31, returning therefrom to his post as Chairman of the Department of History and Political Sciences at Manchester, an appointment he held until 1944. During the whole of this period he also lectured in the social sciences at the University of Indiana. In 1944, he was called upon by the United States State Department to serve as an expert on international security. From this assignment it was a natural step to expert membership on the United States delegation to the San Francisco Conference on International Organization (1945). Thereafter, Cordier discharged a number of functions in the Preparatory Commission for the United Nations, finally becoming Executive Assistant to

the writer was the best available candidate. He had been looking not so much for a man with special talents or training as for somebody with all-round experience of international life. Moreover, looking at the nationality distribution of his immediate entourage—invariably a cause of constant concern to the chief executive officer of an international secretariat—Trygve Lie may well have decided that a change therein would not come amiss. However that may be, the Nomination Committee seems to have agreed to his suggestion without much hesitation. For the nominee himself the news was rather disconcerting, as he had serious misgivings about his suitability for an assignment generally considered to be exceptionally difficult and delicate. His knowledge of Libya's history and geography was superficial, he was not a constitutional lawyer, he could neither read nor write—let alone speak—Arabic, and his notions of the Islamic world were limited to generalities. He also protested that, not having had the slightest inkling of his forthcoming appointment and having had his hands full with his departmental duties, he never had paid any attention to the question of the former Italian colonies. Nonetheless, the Secretary-General strongly urged him to accept. Reflecting that the nomination was certainly a mark of confidence and that, after all, this was not the first unexpected international mission he had been called upon to fulfill, he accepted, after some further hesitation. The idea of helping a former colony to acquire independence was, moreover, attractive.

Shortly afterward, on 8 December 1949, the Nomination Committee reported that Adrian Pelt of the Netherlands had been unanimously chosen as its sole nominee,[4] and two days later, at its two hundred and seventy-sixth plenary meeting, the General Assembly, by secret ballot, elected him United Nations Commissioner in Libya. Of the 59 votes cast, 8 were abstentions; of the other 51, 28 were cast for Pelt. Jose Arce of Argentina received 20 votes and Sir Muhammad Zafrulla Khan of Pakistan the remaining 3.[5]

---

the Secretary-General, a position he occupied from 1946 to 1961, holding the rank of Undersecretary. In this capacity, he served as adviser to every President of the General Assembly during these seventeen years. Hence he was at the very hub of General Assembly affairs and the implementation of that organ's decisions. As such he fulfilled several important missions. From 1961 to 1962 Mr. Cordier served as Undersecretary in charge of General Assembly Affairs. In 1962 he was appointed Dean of the Columbia University Graduate School of International Affairs, and in 1968 was made the Acting President of Columbia University.

4. GAOR: Fourth Session, 1949, Annexes, Agenda item 19 (A/1235, 8 December 1949), p. 58.

5. GAOR: Fourth Session, 1949, 276th Plenary Meeting, 10 December 1949, pp. 614–15.

Thus, not only had the vote been far from unanimous in the Commissioner's favor; after his name had been put forward as that of the only official candidate, two other names had been added to the ballot papers, one that of a Latin American who would obviously command the unanimous vote of his bloc, the other that of an eminent Moslem scholar and statesman.

Remembering the strong Latin American support for the Italian position during the debates in the Assembly, the Commissioner feared, despite the good wishes for success conveyed to him on behalf of that body by its President, that he would take up his new duties under something of a handicap. To be sure, the representatives of several Arab countries were at pains to tell him that the nature of the vote had strengthened his position in their eyes, but this was no reassurance to one convinced from the outset that his success would largely depend not only on his strict impartiality, but also, and in even greater measure, on his being looked upon as completely unbiased by all the parties concerned. However, the die had been cast, and the machinery put together by the resolution on Libya set in motion.

Before he even had time to take stock of his new duties, the Commissioner had to cope with numerous visits, meetings, and consultations with Libyan and other Arab politicians who wished to congratulate him and to explain their particular points of view. Many others came to offer advice, or to ask for special attention, like the Jewish international organizations. A high United Kingdom official remarked to the Commissioner's wife at dinner: "Madam, I wish your husband the best of luck, but to be quite frank I am afraid he is going to break his neck."

With these words ringing in his ears, the Commissioner took advantage of the peace of Christmastide to study the antecedents to his new post. Here, briefly, is what he wrote down to clarify the position in his own mind.

If Libyan independence was to be achieved by 1 January 1952, the Commissioner would have to be the driving power behind the scenes. Not only the Administering Powers, but the Libyan groups too might need a certain amount of tactful guidance—perhaps even gentle pressure.

While the Council for Libya should be given every opportunity of advising the Commissioner, it should not be allowed to interfere directly with the Libyan National Constituent Assembly or with the administration of the territories by the Administering Powers.

The most delicate aspect of the Commissioner's duties might well prove to be the maintenance of a clear distinction between his own functions and those of the Council for Libya, the Administering Powers, and the National Assembly, while at the same time trying to prevent friction among them.

The guiding principle to follow, he believed, should be encouragement of the Libyan people in formulating their own wishes and making their own plans without undue interference from himself, the Administering Powers, or the Council, thereby inducing them to take the responsibility for their own future.

As matters turned out, this embryonic concept of the Commissioner's duties was not far wide of the mark, though it proved to be a considerable understatement.

Meanwhile the administrative services of the Secretariat of the United Nations had turned their sights on Libya, and the Commissioner was besieged. The Budget Division of the Controller's Office wanted to discuss provisional estimates of expenditure; the Office of Personnel wanted to know what kind of a secretariat was needed; the Department of Security Council Affairs submitted several excellent and most useful background documents and working papers; the Office of Legal Affairs offered interpretations of potentially obscure parts of Resolution 289 (IV); and the Library sent up a mass of material on the country and the people of Libya.

At the time when the Libyan Mission was being organized, the Secretariat had had four years' experience in mission management, particularly in Palestine, Korea, Indonesia, and Kashmir. Moreover, a number of former League of Nations officials had entered the service of the United Nations and, though League precedents were not always appreciated at Lake Success, the younger organization nevertheless enjoyed the benefit of its predecessor's twenty-year spell of trial and error. In 1943, a group of these League officials had met in London, under the auspices of the Royal Institute of International Affairs (RIIA), to try to pass on to their successors the experience they had gained. Under the Chairmanship of the Right Honourable the Earl of Perth, P.C., G.C.M.G., C.B., formerly Sir Eric Drummond, First Secretary-General of the League, the group produced a report entitled *The International Secretariat of the Future,* published in 1944. The present author, who was a member of the group, ventures to quote two basic statements therefrom: "No attribute is more essential for an international secretariat than ability to gain and hold the confidence of member Governments." "The greater the political importance of the organization, the more will its members demand as a condition of such confidence that the Secretariat should include some of their own nationals." [6]

6. Royal Institute of International Affairs, *The International Secretariat of the Future* (London: Oxford University Press, 1944), p. 17. The other members of the Group were: Th. Aghnides, Greek Ambassador to the Court of St. James's, formerly Undersecretary-General of the League of Nations; Erik Colban, Norwegian Ambassador to the Court of St. James's, formerly Director of the Minorities Section of the League Secretariat; F. P. Walters, formerly Deputy Secretary-General of the League of Nations; J. V. Wilson, Assistant Director of Research at Chatham House, formerly Chief of the Central Section of the League Secretariat; and Robert I. Kull, Secretary.

The logical corollary to these two statements is that members of an international secretariat must be capable of reconciling loyalty toward their own country and loyalty toward the international organization they serve. It further follows that such persons should neither be men without a country nor extreme nationalists. Hence, the concept of international loyalty, which was fostered and put to the test by the League of Nations and incorporated in the Charter of the United Nations under Articles 97–101 (Chapter XV, "The Secretariat"). The RIIA report describes "international loyalty" as follows:

> It is not the denationalized loyalty of the man without a country. On the contrary, it is the conviction that the highest interests of one's own country are served best by the promotion of security and welfare everywhere, and the steadfast maintenance of that conviction without regard to changing circumstances. It is breadth of international outlook, which a well-placed observer aptly describes as "something quite different from the attitude ridiculed by Canning as that of 'a friend of every country but his own.' " "The international outlook required of the international civil servant is," he continues, "an awareness made instinctive by habit of the needs, emotions, and prejudices of the peoples of differently-circumstanced countries, as they are felt and expressed by the peoples concerned, accompanied by a capacity for weighing these . . . elements in a judicial manner before reaching any decision to which they are relevant.[7]

The Commissioner knew from experience that if this spirit of international loyalty was indispensable to the proper functioning of the headquarters of an international secretariat, it was even more so in the case of a mission in the field, especially one whose terms of reference were essentially political. The history of the United Nations Mission in Libya fully bore out that conviction. Detached from its parent secretariat in New York, enjoying an unusually large measure of autonomy, and working in an environment where thousands of ears and eyes hung on its every word and gesture, the Mission as such and every member of its staff had to watch

7. Ibid., pp. 18–19. The "well-placed observer" was C. W. Jenks, then Legal Adviser, now Principal Deputy Director-General, of the International Labour Office in Geneva. The reader who wishes to pursue this subject will find the following works useful: Egon F. Ranshofen, *The International Secretariat—A Great Experiment in International Administration* (Washington: Werthheimer, for the Carnegie Endowment for International Peace, 1945); International Civil Service Advisory Board (ICSAB), *Reports on Standards of Conduct in the International Civil Service,* ICSAB Doc. Co-ord/Civil Service/5 (1954); and Georges Langrod, *The International Civil Service—Its Origin, its Nature, its Evolution* (Dobbs Ferry, N.Y.: Oceana Publications, Inc., for A. W. Sythoff, Leyden, Netherlands, 1963).

their every step, while at the same time safeguarding the freedom of action without which they could not do their duty. In practice, this called for a primary policy of building up mutual trust between the Mission and local officialdom of all types—not only the British and French Administrations, but also the Libyan authorities wherever they existed—as well as the Consular Corps in the three Libyan provinces and the members of the Council for Libya. No less important was the establishment of good public and personal relations with political and religious leaders, urban and rural notables, and the public at large. In a country where mass information media were decidedly underdeveloped, this meant making hundreds of personal contacts both in the towns and among the tribesmen.

In fact, the problem had two aspects. First of all there was the position of the Mission itself. This facet was not too difficult after an initial period of explanation. By strictly adhering to its terms of reference as an advisory, nonexecutive body, and by constantly stating that position in public, the Mission largely succeeded in avoiding serious misunderstandings on this count. The only difficulties that occurred were associated with the rare attempts by one party or another to use the Commissioner for its own particular purposes or, more frequently, the occasions when the Libyans expected him to intervene in the British and French administration of the territories. A polite refusal was generally sufficient to dispel the awkwardness thus created.

The more delicate aspect of the Mission's arrival in its new environment was how to avoid friction between its members and the local population. Tripoli was a crowded city in the early 1950s. In addition to the Arab population of approximately 150,000 and minorities numbering about 50,000, there was a British garrison and a British administration. The Mission needed office space, its members living quarters and restaurants, all for some two years. Later, a similar problem arose with regard to the non-Libyan members of the Council for Libya and their staffs. At first, the Mission staff was housed in a second-class tourist hotel, Del Mehari, beautifully situated on the Mediterranean but without heating and still suffering from wartime dilapidation and lack of amenities. It was January when the advance party arrived, and it happened to be bitterly cold. Electric fires could be used but sparingly, because the power supply was barely sufficient for the city's needs. Open fireplaces, as usual in North Africa, were rare.

To these material inconveniences were added others of a more psychological nature. The lower and middle ranks of the British military and civilian staffs understandably looked upon members of the United Nations staff as intruders who had come to complicate their lives and work, ultimately even to deprive them of their jobs. Another sore point was that the

United Nations salary and subsistence allowance scales produced a higher total income than the British rates. This disparity naturally engendered a certain amount of jealousy which, in turn, made it difficult to establish social relations between those already on the spot and the newcomers.

It became clear that accommodation and rents were one of the most sensitive sources of potential friction. Generally speaking, the better type of villa and apartment was owned by Italians. Many had already been requisitioned and assigned to British military and civilian officials, but there was still a long waiting list of such people, whose families could not join them for lack of quarters. When the United Nations staff began to arrive, some of these villas and apartments, having been derequisitioned in the meantime, were offered to them, but at a considerably increased rent. This caused bad blood on both sides. Anyway, there was not enough housing immediately available for all the staff, whether married or unmarried. Those who were obliged to stay on at Del Mehari started complaining that rents were too high and that the British authorities were not helpful enough in meeting their requirements. Neither complaint was justified. Rents were not unduly high when considered in relation to United Nations incomes, and BMA was doing what it could within the very narrow limits of its possibilities to assist the Mission's administrative officer to solve an admittedly most difficult problem. Even had the complaints been justified, it would have been tactless on the part of staff, and decidedly contrary to the best interests of the Mission's work, to air them in public. As a result, the Principal Secretary to the Mission, as Chief of Staff, with the Commissioner's full support, had to put his foot down. A circular went out to all staff and produced the desired effect.

In the course of the spring the problem was solved as well as circumstances permitted, thanks to the help of BMA, and from that moment social relations improved considerably.

Another problem that demanded attention within the Mission was that of morale. All heads of United Nations and other international missions in the field are sooner or later confronted with this problem, which must be taken in hand at an early stage, before it reaches the point where it impairs the discharge of the Mission's functions. Maintaining an effective sense of order, discipline, and collaboration within an international staff is obviously not quite the same thing as doing so within a staff of a single nationality. As the size of a mission grows there are more and more different backgrounds and outlooks to contend with, a greater risk of clashes of character and temperament, and, above all, a wider range of opinions about the way in which the common task should be carried out. There are also dangers in the area of personal relationships. Besides the gamut of national habits of all kinds there is the problem of married and single, male and female, all suddenly thrown together, often meeting one another for the first time and all unfamiliar with their new surroundings. That is why a mission staff must be forged as soon as possible into a homogeneous team, including the local members, who are not always easy to incorporate.

A mission leader with experience of this special kind of management is familiar with a number of precautions and remedies capable of forestalling or curing the kind of trouble that may weaken morale. First of all, the staff, from top to bottom, must know what it is working for. All members should be fully and intelligently informed, not only of the Mission's terms of reference, but also of the manner in which its job is to be carried out. Hence, rather frequent staff meetings permitting free interchange of opinions and the circulation of internal information bulletins and files including, to the largest possible extent, confidential papers, are essential. It is the author's experience over forty years that the discretion of international staffs, when they are taken into the leader's confidence, can be trusted to a surprising extent. Admittedly, there will be occasional leakages, but these are generally far less serious in their effects than excessive secrecy. In any event, missions of this kind should reduce their confidential files to a minimum.[8] When, in January 1952, the Libyan Mission was dispersed, all papers that at the time had to be treated as genuinely secret were contained in a single envelope. Besides this, there was, of course, much more confidential material, in the sense of its not being suitable for immediate publication (see the Preface, pp. xvi–xx).

Another basic precaution in safeguarding morale is not to accept staff under twenty-five years of age on mission duty in the field, and to choose only people who by nature are stable and capable of standing on their own feet. Mentally unstable people, when set to work in an unusual environment, are bound to create problems. As a matter of fact, even secure people are in need of sympathetic working and social intercourse within

8. In 1932 the author was serving as Deputy Secretary-General of the Lytton Commission, charged by the Council of the League of Nations to investigate the Chinese-Japanese dispute over Manchuria. The Secretary-General was Robert Haas. In August of that year, while a cholera epidemic was raging in the city, the Commission was drafting its report in the Hotel des Wagons-Lits in Peking. It was soon noticed that the Japanese intelligence service was making considerable efforts to obtain a copy of the report. In the prevailing circumstances it was difficult to counter these efforts by orthodox preventive methods. Haas therefore instructed his staff not to hide any papers, but to let drafts, final texts, and even willfully produced false texts lie about indiscriminately in offices and bedrooms. Years later a Japanese diplomat confided to the writer that his country's intelligence officers had been completely baffled and had taken a misleading report for the real one.

a mission's group life, particularly when outside social relations are lacking or superficial. The senior members of a mission staff therefore must set an example by keeping open house for their junior colleagues, who must be made to feel that they belong to one family that is none the less closely knit for being short-lived. This also implies that a chief of mission must at all times be accessible to staff with complaints or in need of advice, private affairs not excluded.

It cannot be claimed that the Libyan Mission was free from staff problems, but they remained the exception to the rule, and the staff's performance as a team was remarkably high. From beginning to end the Commissioner knew that he could always count on all its members even when, as was often the case, the circumstances demanded endurance and exceptional devotion to duty. Without a staff of such caliber the Mission could never have been a success. As for private relations, the Commissioner is still proud of having had the privilege of attending many happy staff gatherings outside office hours and of having given away three brides.

The Secretary-General, who was well aware of the Mission's particular needs, greatly facilitated the selection of the staff by permitting the Commissioner, contrary to established procedure, to choose his own immediate collaborators. In doing so, his criteria were not only personal competence, experience, and integrity as international officials, but also ability to promote the variety of contacts which would have to be maintained with the Administering Powers, the members of the Council for Libya, and other interested parties. Hence the professional staff obviously had to include a Frenchman, an Englishman, and an Arab. Again, considering the part of mediator between Arabs and Latin Americans that the United States had played in preparing the final draft of Resolution 289 (IV), an American too was indicated. Indeed, the Commissioner had an early hunch that he might occasionally have to call on Washington to act as mediator between London and Paris on the one hand and himself on the other. Certain delegates brought pressure to bear on the Commissioner to add an Italian to his staff, but it was clear that to have done so would have irritated the Libyans and made his task more difficult. On the other hand, fully aware of the interests of the large Italian minority in Libya, it seemed to him wise to secure the inclusion on the staff of a national from a country sympathetic to the Italian cause, preferably a Latin American. Since Libya also contained other minority groups, particularly in Tripolitania, such as Jews, Greeks, and Maltese, who had been living there for centuries, it seemed wise to have a person on the staff of Mediterranean origin and specifically in charge of contacts with them. Finally, inasmuch as the Commissioner's principal task was to assist the people of Libya in the formulation of their constitution and the establishment of an independent government, a lawyer with special knowledge of constitutional law and Arab public and personal status (Shari'a) law was indispensable.

Since the Mission staff would have to serve for at least part of the time as secretariat to the Council for Libya, administrative and conference elements, such as translation, interpretation, clerical, and documents services had also to be provided. Arabic, French, and English were fixed as the Mission's working languages.

The inclusion in the staff of economic and social experts was left in abeyance until the need for them could be evaluated on the spot, but the presence as from the day of the Commissioner's arrival in Tripoli of a professional information officer was considered imperative, as was also the need for administrative staff (personnel and financial services). Considering the vastness of the country and the necessity of maintaining frequent contacts between Tripoli, Benghazi, and Sabhah, the capitals of the three provinces, the need for communications by air, road, and wireless had also to be borne in mind. In addition, there was the question of cipher and pouch communications with both United Nations Headquarters in New York and the European Office of the United Nations (as it then was) in Geneva. All these requirements carried a risk of staff and budget inflation. It was therefore decided in principle that specialization of functions should be avoided by giving each staff member, to the extent possible, more than one job to do, and by making staff interchangeable wherever feasible. Local staff was, moreover, to be engaged to the maximum extent, their work ranging from menial tasks to the language and contact services. As a result of this policy, the permanent Mission staff, apart from experts, never amounted to more than forty-nine at any one time. This strength was, admittedly, not always sufficient, and when, in moments of stress, for instance during the second half of 1951, the staff became seriously overworked, additional temporary personnel had to be borrowed from New York or Geneva.

In these circumstances a rational organization of the work of the staff and a logical distribution of duties was of primary importance, first between Commissioner and staff, second within the staff itself. As to the first aspect, it was obvious that the Commissioner, having been appointed by the General Assembly, was responsible to that body alone, and not to the Secretary-General. Hence, he could not be made responsible for any administrative matters even had his political work left him time for such duties. Accordingly, following a practice developed in earlier missions, the staff was regarded as an ad hoc secretariat, created for a special purpose, with its own budget, and placed under the orders of a separate chief, a Principal Secretary, who was directly responsible to the Secretary-General and, moreover, acted as his personal representative in all matters not within the Commissioner's competence. The latter was fortunate enough to find for this key post a young member of the State Department, then serving on the staff of the United States Permanent Mission to the United Nations in New York, Thomas F. Power, Jr.[9]

As the operation developed, Power, who had a truly extraordinary capacity for work, a well-trained talent for administration, and a keen political mind, took on several other functions. In particular, although the post never existed officially, he acted on several occasions, with the consent of the Council for Libya, as Deputy Commissioner. More important, in the spring of 1950 he took charge of the first exploratory technical assistance venture in Libya (see Chapter 9) which, under his direction, grew into a major activity, the counterpart of and closely linked with the country's constitutional development. From early in 1952, after Libya had achieved independence, Power served for three years as Resident Representative of the Technical Assistance Board (TAB) [10] in the country he had come to know so well, thus ensuring a highly desirable measure of continuity.

Next came the Deputy Principal Secretary, Alberto Gonzalez-Fernandez, a Colombian diplomat who, as Deputy Head of his country's Permanent Delegation to the United Nations in New York, had attended the Third

9. Thomas F. Power, Jr., was born at Worcester, Massachusetts, on 15 May 1916. He received his B.A. degree from Amherst College in 1938, and M.A. and Ph.D. degrees from Columbia University in 1939 and 1942, respectively. In 1942 he joined the State Department in Washington as a research specialist. In 1945 he became a specialist for Dependent Area Affairs there. At the San Francisco Conference on International Organization in 1945 he was an assistant committee secretary in the international secretariat. When the United Nations was set up as the outcome of this Conference, he was appointed to the first United States delegation to the Organization (1946), with which he remained, serving in a number of capacities, until appointed Principal Secretary and personal representative of the Secretary-General of the United Nations in Libya early in 1950. After the Mission left the country, Power stayed on until 1955 as Resident Representative of the Technical Assistance Board (TAB). He coupled this function with other duties, namely, United Nations observer with the Libyan Public Development and Stabilization Agency (1952–55); and United Nations Adviser to the Libyan Finance Corporation (1953–55). After leaving Libya, Power became briefly Special Assistant to the Executive Chairman of TAB, then Resident Representative of TAB in Iran (1955–61), from which appointment he was seconded to the United Nations Emergency Force in Egypt as Chief Administrative Officer in 1956 and 1957. From 1961–66 he was Resident Representative of TAB and the United Nations Special Fund (later merged to form the United Nations Development Programme) in Pakistan. In 1966–67 he served as Special Adviser to the Administrator of the United Nations Development Programme, and since early 1966 has been Executive Secretary of the Fund of the United Nations for the Development of West Iran.

10. See Chapter 9 for an account of the composition and functions of this body.

and Fourth Regular Sessions of the General Assembly. Gonzalez, apart from deputizing on many occasions for Power, served as Secretary to the Council for Libya and was in charge of Italian minority questions.[11]

The choice of Gonzalez proved to be a fortunate one. He was a man of tact and excellent judgment who quickly adjusted himself to his manifold functions, soon gaining the confidence of members of the Council for Libya, of official and private Italian circles, of the Libyan leaders, and last but by no means least, of his colleagues in the secretariat. It was largely due to Gonzalez' close collaboration with Giacomo Marchino, the representative of the minorities on the Council, and Roberto Gaya, the Italian consular agent in Tripoli, that the Commissioner's dealings with the highly sensitive Italian minority organizations were conducted on a basis of mutual confidence.

Next in the hierarchy came four political officers, respectively British, French, Egyptian, and Maltese. Their functions were varied and numerous, and called for a good deal of traveling, mainly within Libya. The French officer, assisted by Arab staff, also acted as Information Officer and repeatedly visited the Fezzan; the Maltese member was in charge of relations with the three smaller minorities and served as Deputy Secretary to the Council.[12] The Egyptian political officer had in a way the most difficult task of all, being in charge of liaison with Libyan parties of all tendencies, the

11. Alberto Gonzalez-Fernandez was born at Bogotá, Colombia, on 16 February 1903. At the age of fifteen he moved with his family to New York, where he completed his secondary education and took a course of study in the humanities at Columbia University before going to the Consular Academy in Vienna in 1923. He stayed there until 1926, taking a diploma in international law, history, economics, and foreign languages. In 1926 he joined the Colombian Foreign Service, rising to become Secretary-General of the Ministry of Foreign Affairs in 1943. Subsequently, he was a member of the Colombian delegations to the Chapultepec (1944) and San Francisco (1945) Conferences and to the Second and Third Regular and First and Second Special Sessions of the General Assembly of the United Nations. From 1947 until the time at which he joined the Mission to Libya, he was Colombian Permanent Representative at United Nations Headquarters in New York. Upon leaving the service of the Mission, he joined the staff of the United Nations High Commissioner for Refugees, whom he represented in Bogotá vis-à-vis most of the South American countries until 1958, when he returned to his country's service as Secretary-General of the Office of the President of the Republic. Since then he has served his country as Ambassador at the Holy See, at the Federal Republic of Germany in Bonn, and currently at the Republic of Peru in Lima. Gonzalez' long diplomatic experience, his knowledge of international law, and, above all, his mastery of English, French, and Italian were a great asset.

12. The Jewish minority, which had been in Libya the longest, required special attention at a time when relations between the Arab countries and the new State of Israel were extremely tense. Hence, the Commissioner himself assumed responsibility for relations with the Jewish communities.

League of Arab States, NCLL, and, of course, the Egyptian Government itself. His British colleague had his hands full in maintaining liaison with the two British Administrations, which necessitated his spending part of his time in Benghazi. Once a United Nations radio communications network had been established in Libya, a small branch office manned by one radio officer was opened in Benghazi. This greatly facilitated contacts with the Amir and the British Resident in Cyrenaica, as did also the charter of a United States Army Transport DC-3 (Dakota) aircraft for general service over the length and breadth of Libya, and even for flights to Cairo, Tunis (on Fezzanese affairs), and Rome, and as far afield as Geneva.

The administrative staff consisted of two officers, one who dealt with all purely administrative matters, including office management, housing, communications, etc., which was a heavy job; the other who was in charge of budget and finance, also a more than usually ticklish task.

The Mission was served by three interpreter-translators and two précis-writers, who also functioned at Council meetings and interpreted at and kept records of private conversations. In addition, the original manning table provided for one documents officer (who was also the archivist), six stenographer-secretaries, and two typists. Finally, there were two United Nations guards, seconded from the recently formed corps known as the UN Field Service, in standard light-blue uniform with the UN badge. Their duties varied greatly according to local conditions, and they served as need arose as security men, chauffeurs, transport-service engineers, radio operators, and first-aid men. They even did the typing when the regular staff could not be used.

The small number of expert posts provided in the manning table were as a rule filled only as and when required. There was, however, one exception to this principle, namely, the post of Legal Adviser to the Mission, which from beginning to end was filled by Omar Loutfi, a lawyer of Egyptian nationality.[13]

13. Born in 1907 in Cairo, Omar Loutfi was graduated from the Faculty of Law of Cairo University in 1930. Immediately after graduation, he joined the Ministry of Justice as a state attorney and in 1944 was appointed a judge before the Mixed Court.

In 1946, he was Assistant Counselor of the Egyptian State Council. In 1948–49 Loutfi served as legal adviser to the Egyptian delegation, which, at Rhodes, participated in the negotiations leading to a General Armistice Agreement in Palestine. Later he was sent to the United Nations as Legal Counselor to the Egyptian delegation (1949). In 1950, he was appointed Counselor of the State Council and was seconded to the United Nations mission in Libya as legal adviser. He completed his mission in 1952 and returned to the State Council. During three periods between 1950 and 1962, Loutfi sat on the United Nations Administrative Tribunal.

In 1953, Loutfi was appointed Minister Plenipotentiary in charge of the Department of International Organizations and Legal Affairs in the Ministry of Foreign

Loutfi soon came to play an important part in the Mission's work, not only as adviser on several doubtful points of legal interpretation that arose in the course of the operation, but more particularly because of the assistance he rendered in the drafting of the Libyan Constitution. Loutfi was a man of independent mind and disinterested judgment, who inspired confidence in all around him and discharged his duties as an international civil servant very conscientiously. As will be seen, differences of opinion over the Constitution were frequent, and though Loutfi's advice was not always followed, it was always treated with the greatest respect.

Space, unfortunately, does not allow of individual mention here of other members of the staff who rendered outstanding services to the Mission; and to single out some, ignoring others, would be highly invidious. However, a staff list of the United Nations Mission in Libya, 1950–52, is appended as Annex XIII (pp. 974–75).

The Secretariat having been planned on the above lines, most of the actual appointments followed during February and March 1950. In April, when the Council for Libya was constituted (see Chapter 3, Part 1), the Mission's political and administrative machinery was ready to go into action. Impatient Libyans were already beginning to complain that precious time was being lost, but their feelings were assuaged when, at the beginning of January, an advance logistics officer arrived in Tripoli. (Toward the end of December 1949, an American member of the Department of Conference and General Services at United Nations Headquarters, who spoke fluent Italian, had been sent to Tripoli to make provisional arrangements for Mission housing, office space, and communications, all of which were set up and waiting when the vanguard arrived in Libya on 18 January 1950.)

Affairs. That same year he was promoted to the rank of Ambassador, and served as legal adviser on the Egyptian delegation that negotiated an agreement with the United Kingdom on the Anglo-Egyptian Sudan.

At the United Nations, Ambassador Loutfi attended the Fourth and Eighth Sessions (1949 and 1954) of the General Assembly as Egypt's representative in the Sixth (Legal) Committee.

He attended all sessions of the General Assembly after 1953, and in 1955 he was elected Chairman of the Third (Social, Humanitarian, and Cultural) Committee; in the following year (1956) he served as Chairman of the Fifth (Administrative and Budgetary) Committee. In 1955, he was appointed Permanent Representative of Egypt, and later (1958) of the United Arab Republic, to the United Nations. In this capacity he represented his country on the Security Council, the Economic and Social Council, and the Trusteeship Council.

On 1 January 1962, Loutfi rejoined the Secretariat of the United Nations, this time as an Undersecretary for Special Political Affairs. On 17 May 1963 he died in the Organization's service.

Meanwhile, the Commissioner had convened two informal meetings in New York of the Permanent Representatives there of the six Member States with seats on the Council for Libya, to exchange views on the task ahead. At the first meeting, held on 19 December 1949, he announced his intention of leaving New York for Libya on 12 January to consult the administering authorities on the spot and to sound out both the Libyan leaders and representatives of the minorities about their choice of the four local members of the Council to be appointed by him. It was to be a reconnaissance to enable him to get his bearings and to establish first contacts; no commitments or promises would be made. At the end of the journey the Commissioner would pay a round of visits to the home Governments of the six members. He invited the representatives to provide him with lists of the people in Libya whom they would advise him to consult, although he could not, of course, undertake to limit himself to these. He did undertake to convene the Council as soon as its four Libyan members had been chosen.

On 9 January 1950 the six representatives met the Commissioner again and discussed how and by whom the Council should be convened. The Council as such could hardly begin to function until the four Libyan members had been seated, yet Resolution 289 (IV) called upon the Commissioner to appoint the latter after consulting the other members. It was agreed that this consultation clearly should not constitute an official meeting of the Council, and that it might be held informally in Geneva.

The Commissioner remarked on this occasion that he expected to encounter difficulties in selecting the Council member who was to represent the minorities in Libya. The Egyptian representative thereupon observed that the objective of Commissioner and Council alike should be the unification of the three territories. Not too much emphasis should be placed, in his opinion, on the minority groups in the area.

In the course of the second meeting there was a brief and inconclusive discussion on the seat of the Council.: Two opposing tendencies that had already appeared in Sub-Committee 17 in the General Assembly again manifested themselves. One, represented by Egypt and Pakistan, showed a preference for Tripoli. The United Kingdom and France, anxious to avoid interference by Council members in the internal administration of the territories, wished the Council to meet in Geneva. The United States of America was prepared to compromise. The Commissioner, although anxious to keep in close contact with the Council, reserved his position until after his exploratory visit to the country.

A third informal meeting (dealt with in greater detail on pages 203–

204) was held in New York on 10 March 1950, after the Commissioner's return there. He stressed, as one strong impression he had gained, that the task of the United Nations should not be limited merely to rendering assistance in the formulation of a constitution and the establishment of an independent government. A good deal of attention would also have to be given to economic, social, and administrative problems. Most members agreed with this, but the representatives of the United Kingdom and France made some reservations. The Pakistani member remarked that constitutional development, the transfer of powers, and economic matters should be regarded as the main task of Commissioner and Council, but that in general he was in favor of a broad interpretation of the common task, even if this meant increasing the Mission's budget.

After having reported on his selection of candidates to fill the four Libyan seats on the Council, the Commissioner reverted to the question of the Council's seat. His own headquarters, he announced, would be in Tripoli. Throughout a long discussion, the earlier divergence of opinion persisted. Egypt and Italy favored Tripoli, but Pakistan proposed that in view of the housing shortage in that city, the Council's first plenary session be held in Alexandria, on the understanding that the Council would move to Tripoli as soon as possible; in his opinion, Tripoli was its logical headquarters. No firm agreement was reached, but it was tentatively decided to hold a meeting of the six Member States and the Commissioner in Geneva on 4 April. The latter would subsequently consult all ten members about the date and place of the Council's first formal plenary session. He would also look further into accommodations and other facilities in Tripoli.

In view of the emphasis placed on the need for the display of the most scrupulous objectivity by the Mission toward all interested parties, the Commissioner felt it unwise to take the Mission into Libya on board transport wearing the flag of any of the interested powers. Accordingly, he and his party, having traveled by *RMS Queen Mary* from New York to Southampton, flew by Royal Dutch Airlines (KLM) charter plane to Amsterdam airport. There, by courtesy of Albert Plesman, Director of KLM, they boarded an aircraft bound for Johannesburg, which was specially diverted from its Tunis stopover to Tripoli for the occasion, and which on arrival ran up the blue and white flag of the United Nations. Since at the time KLM had no landing rights in Libya, bad weather was given as the official reason for the diversion.

Before the plane landed at Tripoli the Commissioner received a last-minute telegram canceling a reception arranged for that evening at the

Tripoli residence of the British Chief Administrator, Travers Blackley,[14] to introduce the Commissioner and his wife to members of the local Consular Corps and those members of the British Administration with whom the Mission would be dealing. Instead, the reception would be held next morning. Neither, when the plane arrived after dark, in cold, wet weather, was the Chief Administrator there to meet it as planned. His secretary gave the Commissioner an apologetic note from him, explaining that he had just come out of the hospital, and inviting the Commissioner to drop in for a drink on his way to the hotel. This did not seem a very good inauguration of the close collaboration called for by Resolution 289 (IV), and it later transpired that the plans had been changed for political reasons on instructions from London. The United Kingdom Government had felt it necessary to stress the fact that their Chief Administrator represented a sovereign power responsible for the administration of Tripolitania and that the Commissioner was there only in an advisory capacity. Upon reflection, the latter had to admit that the point was well taken. Indeed, as will be seen, Libyans were only too readily disposed to believe that the Commissioner had come to supersede the British and French Administrators. Sitting and chatting that evening beside a blazing fire at the Villa Volpi, the British Residency, the incident was soon cleared up.

The reception at the airport (which still bore signs of war damage) otherwise went off as planned. The Consuls General or Consuls of countries represented in Tripolitania were all there, as well as leaders of local political parties and associations and representatives of the religious authorities, with whom consultations were to start next morning. Amid flowers and words of welcome—a good omen—the United Nations Mission began its work.

The same evening, to make his position clear, the Commissioner issued a prepared statement for use by the press and radio, the following paragraphs of which have relevance here:

> I should like to take this opportunity to tell you in general terms the purpose of my mission. My terms of reference are clear: they lay down that the United Nations Commissioner will assist the people of Libya

14. Travers Robert Blackley, C.M.G. born on 10 March 1899, was educated at Charterhouse School, England, and Worcester College, Oxford, where he was an Exhibitioner. After serving in World War I, he joined the Sudan Political Service in 1922, in which he saw service in the Blue Nile, Kordofan, and Kassala provinces. He was seconded to the British Occupied Territory Administration in 1940 with the rank of Lieutenant Colonel, being promoted to Colonel in 1942 and Brigadier in 1943. After a tour of duty in Ethiopia in 1941 and 1942, he became British Chief Administrator in Tripolitania in 1943, and British Resident there in 1951.

in the formulation of their constitution and in the establishment of an independent government. The Commissioner is also instructed, after consultation with the Administering Powers, the members of the Council [for Libya] and the leaders and representatives of the political parties and organizations in Libya, to appoint the representatives of Libya in the Council. It is not my function to govern your territory; that remains within the competence of the Administering Powers until you assume it for yourselves.

My first visit to Libya will last three weeks and will be, as it were, an exploration. For the moment my purpose is simply to learn your views and hear your suggestions, particularly with regard to the choice of your representatives in the Council, and to make preliminary contacts with the representatives of the Administering Powers.

On my final return to Libya, about the middle of March, the first task will be to bring the Council together and then to take the first step towards setting up a National Assembly. As you know, the chief task of that Assembly will be to frame a constitution, which will be the charter freely accepted by the people of Libya for the ordering of its future national life. My part in these events will be to advise and guide you, and it is my hope that the constitution, while taking into account the special characteristics of the country, will be based on solid democratic foundations, so that everyone may exercise his civil and political rights in peace and freedom and perform his duties as a good citizen for the benefit of the whole community. In short, it would seem that you should seek the union of the noble heritage of your past with certain methods of the West, in harmonious association. Such an association should contribute to the reconstruction of the country and so promote the economic development and social progress of all its people. . . . In this age in which we live, and in face of the great task awaiting us, we must not count on miracles. Only with hard work, with much goodwill and with a spirit of intelligent co-operation can we merit the assistance of the Almighty in attaining our great and noble purpose.[15]

PART 2.
WHAT THE ADMINISTERING POWERS WERE PLANNING

In the preparation of the three provinces for common independence in a united Libyan State, the policies of the Administering Powers would

15. First *Annual Report of the United Nations Commissioner in Libya,* GAOR: Fifth Session, 1950, Supplement No. 15 (A/1340), Annex I, p. 39.

obviously play a vital part. The Commissioner was soon to discover that, as already indicated, their plans reflected a policy aimed not so much at the union of the territories as at instituting a large degree of autonomy for each of them, presumably to facilitate the creation of spheres of influence. Having studied the records of the Fourth Session of the General Assembly, this discovery came to him more as a disappointment than as a surprise.

In the Commissioner's view, such a policy contradicted both the letter and the spirit of Resolution 289 (IV). To his way of thinking, the Resolution meant, first, that the Administering Powers were from the outset to see to it, in collaboration with him, that governmental institutions were established in each territory of a type that would enable the representatives of the inhabitants, meeting together in a National Assembly, to decide for themselves on the form of the State, and, second, that not later than 1 January 1952 all powers must be transferred to the duly constituted independent Government of that State. He considered it obvious that the prior emergence of one or more of the territories as independent—or even merely autonomous—units would not only jeopardize the possibility of union but would also de facto oblige their representatives to adopt some loose form of federal government without much choice in the matter.

In this respect, the already semi-independent status conferred on Cyrenaica created a disquieting precedent that was in utter conflict with the General Assembly Resolution. As pointed out in Chapter 1 (see p. 199 *et seq.*), the United Kingdom had drawn attention to this contradiction, even going so far as to seek to amend the text of the Resolution to bring it into line with the policy of which the statutory position of Cyrenaica was the result. The General Assembly had refused to follow suit, but without formally challenging the British position. It is not even certain whether all delegations had clearly understood the issue at stake. Hence it was to be expected that British policy with regard to Tripolitania would in broad outline be similar to that pursued in Cyrenaica. France had implied that it would do likewise in the Fezzan. True, these statements had been made before the adoption of the Resolution, except for a declaration made in the French National Assembly on 15 December 1949 by Robert Schuman, the French Foreign Minister, in which he repeated the sense of French policy as explained by the French representative in the General Assembly. Was there any possibility of bringing these policies into line with the Resolution? Much would depend on the attitude taken by the Libyan leaders in the three territories.

It soon became clear that the Administering Powers indeed interpreted the Resolution differently; they held practically the same views as before its adoption, with the result that several months of painstaking and sometimes agonizing negotiations were needed before the United Kingdom and France agreed to modify their respective plans to some extent; even then, their ultimate aims remained unchanged.

Before an account of these negotiations is given, it may be useful to consider the legal status of the United Kingdom and France as the Administering Powers in Libya and the question of to whom sovereignty over the former Italian colony belonged.

From the beginning of their military occupation of the territories in 1943 until the entry into force of the Treaty of Peace with Italy on 15 September 1947, the legal status of the Administering Powers had been governed by the Hague Rules of 1907. As is apparent from footnote 30 in Chapter 1 (p. 56), these rules had originally been conceived to govern the military occupation of enemy territory. Their application in the case of former colonies therefore gave rise to various difficulties. In the case of the three Libyan territories, for instance, the population had not looked upon the British and French forces as enemies, but as liberators whom they welcomed as friends. The immediate pertinence of the Hague Rules to our argument is that they lay down that military occupation of a territory does not imply a transfer of its sovereignty to the occupying power, which may exercise the powers of sovereignty only pending the conclusion of a peace treaty.

Accordingly, as from 15 September 1947, the Hague Rules had ceased to apply in Libya, since there was no longer a state of war between the two occupying powers and their former enemy. Henceforward, their legal status in the territories was determined by Article 23 of the Treaty, which stipulated that, Italy having renounced all right and title to her former territories in Africa, these possessions, pending their final disposal, would continue under their present administration.

At the same time, by failing to specify in whose favor Italy had renounced her sovereignty over the Libyan territories, the Peace Treaty left wide open the question of to whom that sovereignty belonged.

Some Libyans were prone to argue that upon Italy's renunciation of her title to the Libyan territories the latter had automatically become independent. They based their argument on the premise that before the Italians had won sovereignty over Libya, the latter had enjoyed autonomy as a province of the Ottoman Empire. Turkey having renounced its rights over Libya in favor of Italy at the outcome of the Italo-Turkish War of 1911–12 by the two Treaties of Lausanne (18 October 1912, 24 June 1923), and Italy having in turn renounced its rights over Libya in 1947, the Libyan people were now free to exercise sovereignty over their own territories. This theory found no acceptance. Neither did others, according to which sovereignty over the former colonies had temporarily passed to the "Big Four" or to the United Nations.

According to the best legal advice at the Commissioner's disposal, sovereignty over these territories was in fact suspended until such time as, in the case of Libya, an independent and sovereign State comprising Cyrenaica, Tripolitania, and the Fezzan was constituted and the United Kingdom and France had transferred their de facto powers to a duly constituted independent Libyan Government.

Meanwhile Resolution 289 (IV) directly affected these powers by prescribing the purpose for which, as well as the manner in which, they were henceforward to be exercised.

Again, according to the opinion of the Commissioner's legal advisers, the Administering Powers, in agreeing to the terms of Resolution 289 (IV), had accepted responsibility for continuing to administer the territories under their control on 21 November 1949 until the Libyan State was constituted and became independent. Except as otherwise provided for in the Resolution, they had sole responsibility for the internal administration of these territories and the right to perform all acts necessary for the maintenance of peace, order, and good government. It had been stated in Sub-Committee 17 and understood by the General Assembly that the Commissioner would not interfere in the exercise of the day-to-day administrative functions of the Administering Powers.

As of the adoption of Resolution 289 (IV), the basic purpose of their administration of the territories had become that of assisting in the prompt establishment of Libyan unity and independence. The Administering Powers were therefore under an obligation to abstain from any governmental or administrative decisions which would run counter to the achievement of this aim.

Moreover, to the same end, the Administering Powers were to cooperate in the establishment of governmental institutions. This obligation covered the establishment and development of local and regional (or territorial) institutions and of executive, legislative, or judicial organs competent to act for Libya as a whole. The Administering Powers were also to coordinate their activities in this respect; this provision imposed an obligation to consult with one another and take concerted action, and encouraged them to adopt common programs and policies. Action at the territorial level, which if uncoordinated with action in other territories might impede the achievement of the purposes of Resolution 289 (IV), had to be avoided.

The Administering Powers were to initiate immediately all steps necessary for the transfer of power to the duly constituted independent Libyan Government within the time limit fixed by the General Assembly.

They were to cooperate with the United Nations Commissioner in all the foregoing matters. Such cooperation could be effected through the elaboration of specific programs by the Administering Powers conjointly with the Commissioner, or the former could elect to provide the latter with full information about their programs and policies and such steps as they might take to give effect to paragraph 10 of Section A of the Resolution. The Commissioner was entitled to make to the Administering Powers such observations and recommendations on these matters as he found appropriate.

The Administering Powers were to enable the representatives of the local population to meet in the National Assembly, and in general it was their duty to facilitate the performance by these representatives of the functions set forth in the Resolution.

Lastly, they were to permit and facilitate the performance of the functions of the Commissioner and the Council for Libya.

One corollary to this interpretation, the importance of which will emerge later, was that until Libya's independence was proclaimed, the Administering Powers were the sole authorities entitled to represent Libya in international affairs.

Responsibility for establishing whether specific actions by the Administering Powers violated the provisions of Resolution 289 (IV), particularly paragraph 10, lay with the Administering Powers themselves and with the Commissioner and the Council. In the event of disagreement between the Powers and the Commissioner, negotiations were to be carried out in a spirit of cooperation in an endeavor to reach a solution; if disagreement persisted, the General Assembly could be called upon to arbitrate (see Chapter 4, Parts 1 and 2).

BRITISH PLANS FOR POLITICAL AND ADMINISTRATIVE DEVELOPMENT IN TRIPOLITANIA

On 11 January 1950, the eve of his departure for Libya, the Commissioner received a then confidential memorandum from the British Foreign Office with a covering letter from the United Kingdom Permanent Representative to the United Nations in New York. The memorandum outlined the action His Majesty's Government had under consideration for Tripolitania in pursuance of the terms of the Italian Peace Treaty. The covering letter expressed the hope that the proposed action would enjoy the Commissioner's support and said that any suggestions he might wish to make would be welcome.

The memorandum proposed, first, that an executive council be established, consisting of three British members ex officio, namely, the Chief

Secretary and the Legal and Financial Secretaries to the British Administration in Tripolitania; and one or two British officials, five to seven Libyan members, and one Italian member, all to be nominated by the British Chief Administrator. The council's functions would at the outset be advisory, but the Chief Administrator would consult it on all important matters of Tripolitanian domestic policy. Concurrently, electoral rolls would be drawn up in preparation for the election of a legislative assembly, and the Libyanization of the civil service would be speeded up.

Second, it proposed the inauguration, after six months or so, of a legislative assembly consisting of the three British ex officio members of the council, some twenty-five to forty elected members, and about ten nominated members. Minority representation in the assembly was also envisaged. The assembly would have the power to pass bills which would become law when approved by the Chief Administrator. It would not be authorized to discuss such matters as the position of His Majesty's Forces or the constitutional development of Libya as a whole, and the Chief Administrator would also retain the power to enact any measure he deemed necessary for good government. Certain other matters, such as the powers of the assembly itself, could be discussed only with his agreement. When the assembly had been set up, the composition of the executive council would be altered to comprise the three British members ex officio, the rest being chosen by the Chief Administrator from among the members of the legislative assembly. The functions of the council would then approximate more closely to those of a cabinet, and individuals would become identified with, and possibly responsible for, certain groups of departments.

Third, the powers and responsibilities of both the assembly and the executive council would be progressively extended, with a view to their shouldering final responsibility by the date laid down in Resolution 289 (IV).

Finally, the United Kingdom Government expressed the view that regional self-government was an essential preliminary to any progress toward Libyan unity. On the other hand, it recognized its obligation to promote that unity and announced its intention of considering specific action in that sense toward the end of 1950.

It was not until he had been aboard *RMS Queen Mary* for a few days and had time to study the document thoroughly, as well as to ponder over its likely implications, that the Commissioner found he was faced with a plan that was in many respects at variance with his own ideas. However, not yet having explored the situation in Libya at first hand, he did not feel prepared to express a definite opinion. He therefore drafted a reply while still at sea, which, while making clear that his reaction was provisional, expressed doubts about a number of points in the British plan that might conceivably give rise to difficulties. His first line of reasoning ran more or less as follows.

He agreed that there was no time to lose in initiating action to implement the General Assembly Resolution, and considered it sound policy to endow the territories under United Kingdom administration with organs of local government at the earliest possible moment, in order to give the population more experience in handling its own affairs than had hitherto been the case. But on certain other points he hoped to be reassured by the British Chief Administrator in Tripolitania, and afterward by the Foreign Office itself during a projected visit to London.

The Commissioner's first question was whether the proposal to give Tripolitania an executive council and a legislative assembly had been discussed with leading Tripolitanians. He recalled that similar action taken the year before in Cyrenaica, although favorably received in that province, had been criticized in Tripolitania by those local leaders who favored a united Libya.

His second question was whether the French Government had been consulted about the proposal and, if so, what its reaction had been. Might not the proposal incite it to take similar action in the Fezzan, or provide it with a pretext for following an independent course of action, thus endangering the coordination between the two Administering Powers so essential to coherent development of the three territories toward a united and independent Libya?

His third question was what effect the United Kingdom plans for Tripolitania might have on the Council for Libya once that body had been constituted and convened. Would the action contemplated not cause resentment in the Council, which had not been consulted on so important a matter as the establishment of an executive council and a legislative assembly in Tripolitania, and would it not provoke the Council to act henceforward as a suspicious watchdog vis-à-vis the Administering Powers?

In conclusion, the Commissioner expressed the hope that some compromise might be possible between the need to make haste and the need for coherence in the various steps to be taken in preparation for Libya's unification and independence. He ended with an expression of confidence that it should not prove difficult to reach an understanding.

Shortly after his arrival in Tripoli, the Commissioner had several talks with the British Chief Administrator about the United Kingdom's plans. It soon became clear that the Chief Administrator was under strict orders from London to carry out the proposals as soon as possible, with the main emphasis on the form of Tripolitanian autonomy, similar to that already introduced in Cyrenaica, rather than on the achievement of all-Libyan unity. Indeed, he and some of his senior officials had already consulted leaders of Tripolitanian political parties on the subject, and the executive council was to be set up by 1 February 1950. In view of this haste, the Commissioner, in order to avert any possible misunderstanding of his own position, found it inadvisable to wait until he could discuss the matter in London, and on 22 January addressed a *note verbale* to the British Chief Administrator summarizing his views.

In place of an executive council, it would be preferable, he believed, to set up an administrative council to assist the Chief Administrator in matters of internal administration, including economic affairs but excluding all matters affecting the constitutional development of Libya as a whole. By consulting this advisory body on all important domestic matters, the Chief Administrator would be giving the inhabitants of the territory ample opportunity to gain essential administrative experience. The exclusion from its scope of matters affecting Libya's constitutional development would rule out any risk of conflict with the Council for Libya. Neither would there be interference on the part of the Administering Power in the functions of the Libyan National Assembly.

Membership of the administrative council should be provided for on a basis which would allow the views of the Libyan members to outweigh slightly those of the non-Libyans. To this end, the Commissioner proposed that the Council consist of thirteen members, seven of them Libyans. One or two of the remaining six might well be Italian, in view of the importance of the Italian minority to the economic life of the territory, in which case there would be four British members. The Commissioner hoped that this would be acceptable to Tripolitanians,[16] inasmuch as the administrative council would not be dealing with constitutional affairs. Members should in the first instance be appointed for a term of six months, thus making it possible at the end of that period to review experience gained. The Chief Administrator, instead of presiding over the council's meetings, should appoint one of its members, preferably a Libyan, as chairman for the first six months.

The Commissioner believed that the British plan was admirably suited to the quickest possible Libyanization of the civil service.

The rest of the United Kingdom proposals should be held in suspense until the Commissioner had had time to seek advice from his own Council.

Naturally, the British plan was one of the main topics of conversation

16. He soon found that his hopes were illusory.

in Tripolitanian political circles. Characteristically, it engendered strongly mixed reactions. In the many discussions which the Commissioner and members of his staff had with party leaders and with notables, two lines of thought were manifest. On the one hand, most of the younger nationalist leaders considered that the establishment of a local government could well weaken future Libyan unity, since a similar government already existed in Cyrenaica, and, moreover, there were strong indications that the French Government too intended to install one in the Fezzan. This line of thought corresponded to the Commissioner's personal views. On the other hand, many of the older leaders, whose political ambitions had been stifled under Italian occupation, were strongly tempted by the opportunities they saw in the British plan for a resumption of political activity at the territorial level. However, few were prepared to admit that what they liked and what they feared in the British plan would remain inseparably bound up unless it were modified along the lines suggested by the Commissioner.

A good example of these mixed and somewhat confused reactions was provided by a memorandum on constitutional development in Tripolitania during the period of transition submitted about this time to the Commissioner and the British Chief Administrator by Beshir Bey Saadawi, then President of the National Congress Party. The memorandum began by rejecting the Administration's project on the ground that the members of the proposed executive council would not exercise any executive, legislative, or judicial powers over the organization of the government or the State, and that it would include members who were not natives of Tripolitania (meaning Italians). It further protested that the council would be directly subject to the control of the Foreign Office and that it failed to provide for the training of Tripolitanians in the management of their own affairs in the period preceding the transfer of powers as recommended by the United Nations in Resolution 289 (IV).

It went on to make a detailed counterproposal, dealing first with the establishment of an administrative council and then with the methods to be used for Libyanizing the administration.

An administrative council for Tripolitania should be formed immediately and continue to function until a national government of a unified Libyan State had been set up. It should consist of a Tripolitanian president and nine members, including a representative of the Jewish minority. It might if necessary co-opt additional local members, provided that the total membership did not exceed eleven, excluding the president. It would have a permanent secretariat and meet at least once a fortnight. Decisions would be taken by majority vote and the proceedings would be secret. The president and members would enjoy parliamentary immunity except where immunity had to be waived in the interests of justice, but this could be effected only by due legal process.

The powers of the administrative council would embrace all subjects and matters relating to internal administrative affairs, including emigration and immigration of Italians from and into Tripolitania. The council would express its views on these matters and take appropriate decisions by a two-thirds vote of its members, and with the approval of the president, though such decisions would be subject to the Chief Administrator's further approval. The latter would communicate to the council his views on all matters relating to Italian emigration and immigration, on which he might himself take decisions subject to the council's approval. In the event of disagreement on any of these matters between the administrative council and the Chief Administrator, the issue would be referred to the Commissioner and his Advisory Council. In the event of disagreement between the Chief Administrator and the Commissioner, the subject would be referred to the General Assembly of the United Nations, whose decision would be final, as provided for in Resolution 289 (IV).

The administrative council would be entitled to propose draft laws relating to the economic and social progress of the country, to the maintenance of peace, to justice, to the liberty of the individual, and to freedom of thought and religious belief. The council might also propose laws designed to safeguard the legitimate interests of the foreign communities in the territory. The Chief Administrator would be free to reject any proposal or advice offered to him by the council, provided he gave his reasons for so doing. On the other hand, the council would be entitled to enact all bills approved by the Chief Administrator, who would have the right to propose drafts, provided they were referred to the administrative council for opinion. Once approved by the administrative council and the Chief Administrator, the bills would become law.

In cases of emergency, the Chief Administrator would be entitled to issue such proclamations as he might deem fit for the maintenance of peace and good government, but these edicts would remain the responsibility of the British Administration in its capacity as the Power actually exercising authority only until 1 January 1952 at latest. Disputes or disagreements would be settled by the procedure suggested for administrative matters.

Having functioned for six months in the manner described, the administrative council would assume broader legislative, executive, and judicial powers, its president assuming responsibility for the general administration of the territory in collaboration with the administrative council and the Chief Administrator. Each member of the council would take over responsibility for one or more government departments, and would be assisted by an adviser selected from among senior officials occupying key positions in the administration and appointed by the Chief Administrator. The advisers would attend meetings of the council, but would not rank as members. Under this new status the council would deal with emigration from and immigration into Tripolitania.

Where the competent courts passed sentence of death, the case would be examined by the administrative council; but the sentence would not be executed until confirmed by the Chief Administrator.

Large-scale Libyanization of the administration would begin immediately in Tripolitania with the object of training citizens in the management of their own affairs, both in the capital and in the rest of the territory, and both in local government and in other branches of the civil service. No supernumerary or additional posts would be created, in order not to overload the budget. The Chief Administrator might retain in office the necessary number of senior officials to maintain good government, but a number of senior posts would be made available forthwith to Tripolitanians who had already served in the administration for not less than five years. Educational facilities would be provided at once for the training, to university levels, of the largest possible number of Libyan officials during the transitional period. No more foreigners would be appointed, nor would foreigners already serving receive further promotion until after the administrative council had begun to function. Exceptions to these rules might be allowed, provided the Chief Administrator submitted the nominations for appointment or promotion to the administrative council for its approval. In the event of disagreement, such matters would be referred to the Commissioner or his Advisory Council, whose decision would be put into effect.

As will be apparent from its memorandum, the Tripolitanian National Congress Party had genuinely tried to find a basis for compromise between their aspirations and the duties of the British Administration; unfortunately, they had done so in a way which largely conflicted with the letter and the spirit of Resolution 289 (IV). In particular, their proposal amounted to premature diminution of the responsibilities of the Administering Powers and radical modification of the functions of the Commissioner and the Council for Libya, involving their transformation from advisory into arbitral bodies. Above all, their proposals were so exclusively centered on Tripolitania that they would have imperiled the achievement of Libyan unity.

Consideration of the United Kingdom plan thenceforward became a three-cornered business: the British Chief Administrator and the Commissioner, each from his own point of view, discussing it with the party leaders and, simultaneously, with one another in an effort to find a compromise acceptable to all three sides. In talking to the leaders, the Commissioner found some difficulty in making them understand that, by insisting on organs of local government with extensive powers, analogous to those already functioning in Cyrenaica, they would jeopardize their chances of reaching their own goal of Libyan unity. When some of them finally saw the point, they ceased to press their counterproposal, but without formally withdrawing it, for the good reason that others were still urging it. As to his discussions with the Chief Administrator, these made it clear that, if the Commissioner was to reach agreement with the British, he would have to approach higher authority; he therefore decided to return from Tripoli to New York via London. There, with a few members of his staff, he had meetings from 20 to 23 February with the Superintending Undersecretary of the African Department of the Foreign Office and his advisers. In the course of frank and far-reaching talks, a memorandum of agreement was worked out which, without altogether satisfying either party, proved in practice a workable instrument.

The United Kingdom plan was still to comprise three stages:

1. The creation of an administrative council to advise the Chief Administrator on matters of internal administration;
2. The creation of a legislative body competent to legislate on matters of Tripolitanian internal administration; and
3. The Libyanization of the Tripolitanian civil service.

The Foreign Office accepted the Commissioner's suggestion that the advisory body should be called an administrative rather than an executive council. As to its composition, it was agreed that it would include, ex officio, the three secretaries to the British Administration in Tripolitania (see p. 131) and one nominated Italian member. Some difference of opinion persisted about the rest of the membership, but it was agreed that there should be a Libyan majority and that the criterion for their selection must be personal ability rather than party affiliation.

No agreement could be reached on the chairmanship of the administrative council. The Foreign Office felt that the Chief Administrator should preside, whereas the Commissioner was convinced that the council's prestige and educational value would be enhanced if the Chief Administrator were to appoint an independent chairman, himself remaining *au dessus de la mêlée*. In the end, it was decided that the Foreign Office would consult the Chief Administrator in Tripolitania, who in turn would discuss the matter with local Tripolitanian leaders.

It was further agreed, first, that the administrative council's competence would be limited to domestic administrative matters, and that it would not discuss questions affecting the constitutional development of Libya, which would remain the exclusive province of the National Assembly; and second, that the members of the administrative council should be appointed for six months, which would enable its composition and functions to be reviewed at the end of that time in consultation with the Council for Libya itself.

As for the creation of a legislative assembly, for which an electoral law would have to be drafted and promulgated in consultation with the administrative council, elections would be held possibly in June or July. The Foreign Office and the Commissioner agreed that the assembly should number twenty-five to forty members elected directly by the people on a constituency basis, together with the three ex officio secretaries to the British Administration. If need arose, ten nominated representatives would be added. The power to make such nominations was considered necessary to ensure proper representation in the assembly or the executive, including, if appropriate, that of the minorities.

The legislative assembly would be empowered to pass bills, including money bills, subject to approval by the Chief Administrator. It would not be authorized to discuss certain subjects, such as its own powers or the constitutional development of Libya. It might be called the "Administrative Chamber for Tripolitania," and its legislative powers might be extended whenever such extension seemed to be called for. One of its tasks would be to draw up its own organic law, with due regard to the deliberations concerning the independent Libyan government.

Thus, as far as Tripolitania was concerned, by the end of February a reasonable working agreement had been hammered out between the Commissioner and the Administering Power responsible for the territory.

FRENCH PLANS FOR POLITICAL AND ADMINISTRATIVE DEVELOPMENT IN THE FEZZAN

It will be remembered that in his statement in the General Assembly just before the vote on Resolution 289 (IV) was taken, the French representative had said that France considered independence for Libya within two years to be an unrealistic proposal in the light of the report of the Four Power Commission of Investigation for the Former Italian Colonies, and accordingly would abstain from voting. Nonetheless, he had assured members that his Government would accept the General Assembly's verdict as it had undertaken to do in Article 23, Annex XI, of the Treaty of Peace with Italy (see Chapter 1, p. 108).

To understand French policy toward the Fezzan, and to the Libyan question in general, during the ten to fifteen years following the end of World War II, a number of considerations must be taken into account, of which national interest, prestige, fear, and pride were the most important.

The shortest and most convenient caravan route from Tunis to Lake Chad, and therefore from what was at that time still French North Africa to French Africa south of the Sahara, ran through Sabhah (rechristened Fort Leclerc during the French occupation), the administrative center of the Fezzan. By air, too, the shortest route from Paris through former French Equatorial Africa to Madagascar went through that town. Already before World War I, and even more so after, partly as a result of the modernization of several seaports on the western coast of Africa, shipping had largely ousted the traditional caravan traffic through the Sahara;[17] but there were enterprising Frenchmen with visions of crossing the desert in mastodonlike trucks, true desert liners, which, they claimed, would be able to carry cargo and passengers more cheaply than seagoing vessels on the West Africa run. Trial crossings with such trucks had been made from Tunis to Fort Lamy (4,400 kilometers) and a Tunisian company (*La Société tunisienne d'automobiles de transport*) had actually announced the opening of a regular service.

The advocates of continued French occupation of the Fezzan also argued that effective administration, which in their opinion the admittedly competent officers for Arab affairs in the French Army (the *Officiers des Affaires Indigènes*) and the troops under their command could guarantee, was essential to protect the adjacent French territories against Fezzanese nomad marauders (*rezzous*). Moreover, there was a smell of oil in the Saharan air, if French and other geologists were right. Hence the problem of certain disputed sectors of the border, at Ghudamis and Ghat-Sardalas (see Map); in addition there were other reasons which, in French eyes, made rectification desirable.[18]

However, the paramount factor was French fear of the chain reactions which might be triggered in the French Maghreb territories as a result of Libya's gaining its independence too quickly. France did not deny the Fezzan's (or Libya's) ultimate right to independence; but it refused to fix a time limit for its achievement, thus raising the insoluble issue of objectively

17. For a brief account of the main caravan routes to the center of Africa, see Jean Pichon, *La Question de Libye dans le Règlement de la Paix* (Paris: J. Peyronnet et Cie., 1945), pp. 29–37.

18. For the history of French-Libyan frontier problems, see ibid.; Enrico de Leone, *La Colonizzazione dell'Africa del Nord* (Padova, Italy: Cedam-Casa Editrice Dott. Antonia Milani, 1960); and Majid Khadduri, *Modern Libya: A Study in Political Development* (Baltimore: Johns Hopkins Press, 1963).

determining at what stage in its development a people is ready for independence. Since the end of World War II, and in particular since General de Gaulle's famous statement of 30 January 1944 at a meeting of the governors of French African Territories, held in Brazzaville, on the evolution of the *Union française,* nationalist hopes in the French dependencies had been raised high, and in Metropolitan France, Government and public opinion alike were nervous and only too sensitive to the pace of that evolution, which they meant to keep under control.

Two more elements went to make up the French position, one steeped in national sentiment, the other rooted in pride in performance. The first dated from the early part of World War II, when General Jacques Leclerc and his Free French desert columns, fighting under the tricolor surcharged with the Croix de Lorraine, upheld French political prestige and military honor by raiding the Southern Sahara, ultimately occupying the oasis of Kufrah (jointly with British Commandos) as well as the Fezzan, and joining up in southern Tripolitania with General Montgomery's Eighth Army (see p. 41), then poised to embark upon the liberation of Tunisia. The second was the pride which the French Administration on the spot, and its backers in Paris, justly took in the way in which order and security had been restored in the Fezzan after the Italian surrender. They were even more proud of the results they had achieved in raising the Fezzanese standard of living. The majority of the population welcomed these improvements, and was not slow to show its gratitude for them.

All this was known to and rightly appreciated by the Commissioner; but Resolution 289 (IV) having been adopted by the General Assembly, and France having repeatedly pledged itself to fulfill its obligations and implement it in cooperation with the Commissioner, he could not accept the foregoing arguments as valid justification for delaying the required action or for misinterpreting the terms of the Resolution. In this respect, it was his plain duty to apply to French policy the same criteria as to British plans in Tripolitania and Cyrenaica, however much local circumstances might differ from territory to territory.

Of course, had the population in one or more of the provinces convincingly, and by a significant majority, demonstrated its unwillingness to become part of an independent and united Libya, the Commissioner would have been obliged to report to the General Assembly through the Secretary-General that Resolution 289 (IV) could not be applied; such, however, was not the case, even in the Fezzan.

The problem with which he was faced, therefore, was to find out what, officially and factually, French policy with regard to the implementation of the Resolution was going to be. It was true that the French Government had clearly stated its position in the General Assembly before and after the adoption of the Resolution; but various parliamentary debates in Paris had a rather different ring about them.

Since the end of World War II, both Chambers of Parliament had repeatedly shown deep concern about Fezzanese affairs, generally in the wider context of the French position in Africa. For the purposes of this study, two debates are of particular interest; the first because it took place in the National Assembly on 13 December 1949, only three weeks after the adoption of Resolution 289 (IV); the second because it was held in the Council of the Republic on 16 March 1950, shortly after the Commissioner had made his point of view known to the French Government, both orally and in writing.

The first debate was initiated by four interpellations; the second by an oral question. In both cases, the speakers adduced the arguments described above, showing serious alarm about the consequences the United Nations resolution might have not only for the Fezzan, but for the *Union française* as a whole. The observations of two of the interpellators showed that they had not fully mastered the facts they invoked; one assumed, wrongly, that France was exercising a trusteeship over the Fezzan; the other, equally wrongly, referred to the visit of the Four Power Commission of Investigation in 1948 as a referendum organized in the Fezzan by the United Nations in 1948. In each case, the Minister for Foreign Affairs, Robert Schuman, defended the Government's policy by almost identical arguments.

Having been attacked on the ground, among others, that the French delegation at Lake Success had abstained instead of voting against Section A (Libya) of the Resolution on the disposal of the former Italian colonies, 289 (IV), Schuman replied:

> Nous ne pouvions pas voter contre parce que—et cette remarque vise le fond—dans la réglementation qui a été votée, tout n'était pas mauvais et nous ne pouvions pas tout rejeter, notamment l'idée de l'indépendance à atteindre à un moment donné par les différentes colonies italiennes. Nous aurions heurté très gravement les pays arabes et la population arabe des territoires en cause si nous avions eu l'air de vouloir prendre position négativement contre l'idée même de l'indépendance. Or c'était un des éléments essentiels de la réglementation.[19]

In the course of the debate on 16 March 1950 in the Council of the Republic, using the same argument, he added to this by saying:

19. *Journal officiel de la République Française, Débats Parlementaires, Assemblée Nationale,* 1949, No. 110, p. 6822, col. 1 (3e séance du 13 déc. 1949).

on y trouve le principe d'une indépendance, principe que est inscrit dans notre propre Constitution et qui doit être l'objectif essentiel à atteindre dans tous les territoires non autonomes que nous avons à gérer. Ainsi, nous devions éviter de sembler nous prononcer contre ce principe, notamment en ce qui concerne des populations avec l'aide desquelles nous espérons, maintenant, aboutir à des solutions concrètes et positives qui soient favorables en même temps à la France et à elles-mêmes.

Si nous avions émis un vote purement négatif, non seulement cela n'aurait rien changé, mais on aurait pu exploiter dans ces populations une attitude qui aurait pu paraître hostile non pas au principe de l'unité, mais à celui de l'indépendance de ces populations, même à terme.[20]

Speaking to the substance of the problem, Schuman, referring to its history, reminded the National Assembly in particular of the fact that, by virtue of Article 23 of and Annex XI to the Treaty of Peace with Italy, the French Government had been under an obligation to defer to the recommendation of the General Assembly of the United Nations from the moment when the Four Powers had been unable to reach agreement on the future of the former Italian colonies. This was an aspect of the matter the consequences of which many members of the Chamber had apparently not fully appreciated, or had underestimated. The Minister went on to argue that, within the limits of this obligation, the French delegations to the Third and Fourth Regular Sessions of the General Assembly had done their utmost to safeguard France's interest in the Fezzan. He recalled the rejection in May 1949, by a single vote, of the Bevin-Sforza formula, and how, subsequently, the plan for a united Libya had for the first time been launched officially. He formulated French policy from that moment onward as follows:

Dans ces conditions, nous ne pouvions plus maintenir notre revendication visant une mise sous tutelle. Notre préoccupation devait être d'enlever à cette proposition nouvelle ce qu'elle avait de plus dangereux. Il s'agissait, d'une part, du délai trop court pour l'octroi de l'indépendance aux territoires en question—puisqu'on prévoyait finalement un délai de deux ans seulement, alors que nous avions toujours été d'avis qu'il en fallait au moins dix pour permettre à ces populations d'atteindre un degré d'évolution suffisant et donc de s'administrer elles-mêmes. Il s'agissait, d'autre part, d'assurer l'indépendance de chacun des trois territoires, ou du moins de laisser à la population de chacun d'eux la

20. *Journal officiel de la République Française, Débats Parlementaires, Conseil de la République,* 1950, No. 26 C.R., p. 864, col. 1 (séance du 16 mars 1950).

liberté de décider si le territoire devait rester autonome ou être compris dans une entité plus large.[21]

Hence the extreme importance the French delegation attached to the first paragraph of the draft resolution subsequently presented in the First Committee at the Fourth Session of the General Assembly, which introduced the concept of Libyan unity. "Si ce texte avait été voté," said Schuman, "l'unité de la Libye aurait été une obligation et non plus une simple faculté"; for the information of the National Assembly he added: "Le gouvernement britannique, je tiens à le dire, dans toute cette évolution, restait partisan de la séparation des trois territoires, et je n'ai aucun indice qui me permette de penser qu'il ait changé de position sur ce point essentiel." [22] He further concluded that under these circumstances and in the light of Article 73 of the United Nations Charter:

> Quel est le sens de la recommandation?
>
> Nous sommes arrivés à ce résultat—je le dis surtout parce que ce sont des arguments que nous avons à faire valoir et que nous ne serons pas seuls à faire valour auprès d'autres pays—que, dans le texte coté, il n'est plus question de l'unité de la Libye. Nous sommes arrivés à faire éliminer le mot "uni."
>
> Quel est, en second lieu, le fait essentiel?
>
> La volonté des populations intéressées déterminera le statut futur. Vous trouvez l'idée développée tout au long de ce texte. Or, tant que les populations de chacun de ces territoires, pris isolément, n'auront pas donné leur consentement, il n'y aura pas d'unité de la Libye. C'est là l'interprétation officielle.[23]

He ended this part of his statement with the following affirmation: "Argument supplémentaire que nous invoquerons: la consultation de la population du Fezzan en 1948 s'est révélée favorable au maintien de l'autonomie." [24]

The Government having refused a substantive debate, the debate was adjourned without a motion being adopted. But one of the interpellators, Jules Castellani, read out the text of a motion he would have moved had the rules of procedure permitted him to do so. In it, the Government was

21. *Journal officiel de la République Française, Débats Parlementaires, Assemblée Nationale,* 1949, No. 110, p. 6821, col. 3 (3e séance du 13 déc. 1949).

22. Ibid., p. 6822, col. 1.

23. Ibid., col. 2.

24. Ibid. Here Schuman was apparently referring to that part of the report of the Four Power Commission of Investigation for the Former Italian Colonies that dealt with Libya (Volume III).

invited "à ne pas accepter la décision de l'ONU et à reprendre les discussions nécessaires pour tenir compte: 1° Du voeu des populations du Fezzan; 2° Des intérêts de la France et de l'Union française." [25] Subsequently, "le renvoi à la suite des interpellations, demandé par le Gouvernement" was adopted by 333 votes in favor to 272 against: number of members voting, 605; absolute majority, 303.[26]

Having been informed of the gist of these debates, at the end of January 1950 the Commissioner consulted the French Consul General in Tripoli, Roger Chambard, and the Military Governor of the Fezzan, Lieutenant Colonel Maurice Sarazac,[27] about the French Government's plans for the Fezzan. Each of these officials explained that France intended to establish an autonomous administration in the Fezzan under the direction of a *chef du territoire* to be elected by the Fezzanese people.

Colonel Sarazac, in the course of a conversation in Sabhah on 29 January, assured the Commissioner that the Fezzanese did not want unity with the other parts of Libya. He attributed this feeling to unhappy memories dating from the days of the Republic of Tripolitania in 1918–23 (see the historical resume, pp. 13–27). The Republic, said the Colonel, had made its existence felt in the Fezzan only through the collection of taxes and by its failure to maintain order, so that the territory had been swept by a wave of banditry and chaos. He added that although some Fezzanese interviewed by the Four Power Commission had expressed a desire for independence, the population as a whole would rather be ruled by a foreign power, preferably France. Other French officers suggested that the population had suffered from Senussi invaders also in the past, but this was not confirmed in the course of the talks and hearings that the Commissioner and members of his staff subsequently had with large numbers of Fezzanese. The impression gained was rather that in the fighting between French and Senussi the sympathy of the population had been with the latter, although it naturally had suffered in the fray.

When the Commissioner asked what share the Fezzanese would have in

25. Ibid., p. 6821, col. 1.

26. Ibid., p. 6827, col. 2.

27. Maurice Sarazac was born at Liorac, in the Dordogne, on 17 December 1908. He chose the French Army as his career, entering in the normal way through the military academy at Saint-Cyr. In 1940–43, as a Captain, he took part in the Fezzanese, Tripolitanian, and Tunisian campaigns carried out by the Free French Forces under General Leclerc. He was Military Governor of the Fezzan from 1947 to 1950, in which year he was gazetted Lieutenant Colonel and appointed French Resident in the Fezzan, in which post he remained until the early spring of 1951. Subsequently, Colonel Sarazac resumed his distinguished career in Metropolitan France, being gazetted *Général de brigade* in 1963 and *Général de division* in 1966.

the administration of their territory, the Colonel explained the French Government's intentions regarding the future administration of the Province. Delegates elected by representatives of the people of each *mudiriyya* (administrative district) would soon meet in Sabhah as a territorial assembly to elect a chef du territoire. When elected, the latter would have the assistance of six Fezzanese counselors who would have competence in internal affairs, and of two French advisers qualified in financial and legal matters. Certain reserved powers would be retained by the French Administration.

The Commissioner suggested that implementation of this plan be deferred until he had had time to discuss it in Paris. As might have been expected, Colonel Sarazac replied that authority to do so lay not with him but with the Governor-General of Algeria. He promised, however, to transmit the Commissioner's proposal to the French Government, which he did on 31 January.

These conversations convinced the Commissioner that his objections to the plan should be set out immediately and formally in a *note verbale* to the French Government through the intermediary of the French Consul General in Tripoli. In this note, dated 4 February, the Commissioner expressed the view that transfer by the Administering Power, with his cooperation, of a maximum of administrative responsibilities to the local population would be in line with paragraph 10 of Resolution 289 A (IV). It would, however, in his opinion, be contrary to the letter and the spirit of the resolution if the Administering Power were to create political organs susceptible of prejudging the final form of Libyan unity and of putting obstacles in the way of a free choice in that respect by the Fezzanese members of the future Libyan National Assembly.

The Commissioner assured the French Government that he did not merely approve of, but sincerely wished for, the Fezzanese people's participation in the administration of their territory, because it would give them an opportunity of gaining knowledge and experience indispensable to the management of their public affairs and would enhance their sense of public duty. For this reason, he suggested that, instead of electing a chef du territoire in the Fezzan, the French Government should establish an advisory council which would meet periodically and whose opinions, suggestions, and recommendations would be communicated to the Governor of the territory, who would remain responsible for their execution. Understanding that the election of a chef du territoire would nonetheless take place, and probably before 12 February, the Commissioner asked the French Government to postpone this action which would otherwise create a fait accompli.

The French Government replied to the Commissioner's Note in February. It pointed out first of all that France had made it a principle of its policy in Arab territories never to flout age-old customs to which local tribes were deeply attached, a policy which had enabled her to maintain order and meet her responsibilities with a minimum of military force. It was in the spirit of this prudent respect for local customs that the French Government had studied measures appropriate to the adaptation of the Fezzanese to the situation arising from the Resolution. The implementation of this policy in the Fezzan was, in the French view, a guarantee of success for the task the United Nations had assumed with regard to Libya as a whole.

Nevertheless, in order to take into account the Commissioner's observations, the French Government was prepared to spread over a period the systematic inauguration of the local institutions which it planned for the Fezzan. In addition, it promised to take the necessary steps toward a temporary division of administrative functions between the French authorities and the chef du territoire in accordance with the views advanced by the Commissioner.

The French Government felt constrained, however, to point out that the people of the Fezzan had been preparing for some time to elect, on 12 February, one of their countrymen qualified to represent their interests and customs in the spirit of the United Nations Resolution, and to this end certain tribes had already started to move some days earlier. The French authorities had neither reason nor means of postponing the election, which had been announced and awaited for months, and which, moreover, was in complete conformity with the rights of peoples to self-determination recognized in the Charter of the United Nations.

The French Government considered it very probable that Ahmed Bey Seif al-Nasr would be elected. If he were indeed elected, that would reflect, they argued, not French desires, but Fezzanese recognition of the fact that he belonged to a family established for centuries in a country where tradition was supreme.[28]

When the Commissioner arrived in Paris in the middle of February for his consultations with the French Government, the exchange of views on the latter's policy in the Fezzan was continued. In the course of meetings

28. It is indeed a fact that Ahmed Bey's family enjoyed considerable prestige in the Fezzan, although it was not comparable to that of the Senussi family in Cyrenaica. Whether Ahmed Bey would have been unanimously elected Chef du Territoire in February 1950 if he had not been supported by the French Administration is open to some doubt in the author's opinion. There might well have been another candidate had one been allowed to stand. (See pp. 189–99 for evidence in support of this contention.)

at the Quai d'Orsay, attended by Georges Balay, the newly appointed French member of the Council for Libya, a spokesman for the French Government announced that Ahmed Bey Seif al-Nasr had been unanimously elected Chef du Territoire by delegates representing the various regions of the Fezzan, including Ghudamis but excluding Ghat. The delegate from Ghat had not voted because the people of that area considered themselves French citizens and would soon be sending a petition both to the French Government and to the Commissioner asking to be incorporated in French territory (see pp. 189–99 for further developments in this direction).

The French spokesman further explained that the Chef du Territoire would be the chief executive in the Fezzan. He would appoint six Fezzanese counselors, who would have the rank of cabinet minister, to take a hand in the local administration of the territory. He would also have the assistance of French advisers. The French Military Governor in the Fezzan would change his title to French Resident in the Fezzan, and, assisted by an advisory council, would retain powers in respect of such matters as foreign relations, air control, defense, prospecting for minerals, the custody of enemy property, currency, and extradition.

The Commissioner replied that he was in full agreement with the idea that the Fezzanese should be given an opportunity of acquainting themselves with the machinery of administration. At the same time, he considered that the French plan was tantamount to the establishment of an autonomous government in the Fezzan. This would endanger the future unity of Libya and prejudge the form of its government, which was to be decided upon by a Libyan National Assembly. Moreover, the United Nations resolution referred, in subparagraph 10 (a), to a transfer of powers to a "duly constituted independent Government," which could only mean a duly constituted Libyan Government, not a local, regional, or territorial one.

True, he admitted, the form unity should take was still undecided; and he did not rule out the possibility that Libya might become a federal State. Nevertheless, he had reservations about the French plan, particularly about the method adopted for its implementation. He reminded his interlocutor that he had expressed similar reservations about the British plan for Tripolitania, and asked whether it would not be possible for the French Government to apply the same formula as the British authorities were now doing there. Such a modification, he felt, would avert criticism of the French and British Governments in the Council for Libya and later in the General Assembly.

Developing this point, the Commissioner suggested that the French

Resident should continue to administer the Fezzan, that he should appoint the counselors, and that the latter should be given consultative status in administrative matters only. This would enable a number of Fezzanese to familiarize themselves with local administrative problems, but would avoid the danger of a Fezzanese government with executive powers. In this way the French Government would not be laying itself open to a charge of having prejudged the future form of the Libyan Government, a decision for which the Libyan National Assembly was to be solely responsible. While the Libyans, and the Fezzanese in particular, might well prefer a federal form of State, that was in the end a matter for them to decide.

The French spokesman replied that his Government would prefer a federal State, which, he affirmed, would certainly not conflict with the idea of Libyan unity. Federation, in his opinion, was one means of achieving unity, to which the French solution was not inimical. If subparagraph 10 (b) of the United Nations Resolution referred specifically to unity, subparagraph 10 (a) did not presuppose the existence of a single, independent government in Libya. In fact, there was already a government in Cyrenaica, which did not seem inclined to relinquish its authority. As federation could be a step toward unity, the Commissioner's suggestion about administrative counselors and the French plan were virtually identical.

The Commissioner, unable to accept this comparison, pointed out that under the French plan there would be a real transfer of executive powers to a Fezzanese authority, whereas he was only suggesting a transfer of administrative functions to an advisory body.

The French spokesman retorted that the French aim was in fact to transfer administrative powers alone to the Fezzanese, and that cabinet rank was to be conferred on the Fezzanese counselors solely to give them some standing in the eyes of the people. He reiterated that the authors of the United Nations Resolution apparently had not ruled out the formation of local governments, since the text was silent on the subject of the Cyrenaican Government. That, of course, was an argument in support of the French thesis which it was difficult to ignore.

The discussion ended with an assurance from the French spokesman that his Government would reconsider its plan in the light of the Commissioner's observations.

A more discordant note was sounded in the course of the Commissioner's meeting with Henri Queuille, who as French Minister of the Interior had ultimate responsibility for the French administration of the Fezzan. Queuille stated that in his view the election of Ahmed Bey Seif al-Nasr was a clear indication of the Fezzanese desire for independence, and that this introduced a new factor into the situation, having come about since the adoption of the United Nations Resolution. It might be difficult for the French Government to disregard this manifestation of the Fezzanese people's wishes. In this statement, the Commissioner saw the makings of a policy similar to the one the British were contemplating for Cyrenaica, and he promptly challenged it. Subsequently, he learned that the Quai d'Orsay had been rather pleased with this clash of opinions between Queuille and himself since it so clearly demonstrated the internal difficulties they were experiencing in implementing the General Assembly Resolution.

Early in March the Commissioner received a Note from the French Government outlining the measures it had decided upon for the Fezzan in the light of the suggestions made by him during his visit to Paris. According to this communication, Ahmed Bey's council would be an administrative one, composed of three counselors and eight assistant counselors. It would be given charge of matters which would allow its members to familiarize themselves with the practical aspects of public affairs; they would act in consultation with officials of lower rank recruited on the spot. The French Government would ensure that this administrative apprenticeship, in which, it declared, the Commissioner had rightly shown great interest, remained under the guidance of the French Resident. Executive power would rest with him.

This formula, the Note went on, demonstrated the French Government's desire not to prejudge in any way the final form of Libyan governmental institutions.

The Note also informed the Commissioner that on 13 February the Chef du Territoire had chosen his three principal counselors—one each for Justice and Finance, and one for Health and Education together—from among the delegates to the territorial assembly in Sabhah, and that he had also appointed eight assistant advisers.

Whether, in the pursuance of the objectives the French Government was trying to attain, its policy had really changed became even more doubtful when on 16 March 1950 the matter came up again for public debate in the Council of the Republic. On that occasion Robert Schuman was more outspoken on the French—and by implication on the British—position toward the question of Libyan unity:

> Que contient le texte actuel qui, grâce à notre influence, nous est beaucoup moins défavorable que la rédaction initiale?
>
> Ce qui est marqué comme objectif principal à l'article 1er, ce n'est pas l'unité de la Libye. Le mot "uni" ne figure pas dans le texte; il a été rayé à notre demande. "La Libye," y lit-on, "est composée de la Cyrénaique, de la Tripolitaine et du Fezzan." On reconnait donc par là

les trois territoires qui, pour le moment, ont une entité séparée qui subsistera jusqu'en 1952, jusqu'au moment où ils seront constitués en Etats indépendants et souverains et non pas en un Etat unique comme cela était dit précédemment. Cela signifie que l'essentiel de la recommandation, c'est l'indépendance, et non pas l'unité de la Libye.[29]

Analyzing the United Nations Resolution further, quoting paragraphs 3, 4, and 10 (b) thereof, and looking at them once more in the light of Article 73 of the United Nations Charter, Schuman came to the following conclusions:

C'est donc la volonté des populations intéressées qui prime tout; elle est supérieure à la volonté même des Etats qui composent les Nations Unies. C'est là que nous devons mettre en œuvre notre système de défense des intérêts dont nous avons la charge. . . .

Donc, si un des trois territoires est opposé à l'unité, celle-ci ne pourra pas se faire.[30]

It is in this part of Mr. Schuman's statement that one surprisingly comes across an error in quotation on a point of basic importance. The Foreign Minister is reported as having said:

Il est vrai que les Nations Unies ont marqué une préférence pour une Libye unie. C'est à l'article 10, paragraphe *b*, que cela apparait. Il est dit: "Les puissances administrantes—c'est-à-dire la France pour le Fezzan—en coopération avec le commissaire des Nations Unies, doivent:
1. Pouvoir constituer un gouvernement indépendant pour chacun des territoires;
2. Administrer les territoires en vue de faciliter la réalisation de l'unité et de l'indépendance de la Libye." C'est la seule fois où il est question de l'unité. Les Nations Unies désirent donc que l'unité de la Libye se réalise, mais elle n'est pas imposée. Ce n'est pas là l'objet de sa décision. L'élément décisif dans tout ce qui sera fait dans ces territoires, c'est précisément la volonté des populations.[31]

It was obviously the Minister's intention to quote subparagraphs 10 (a) and (b) of the Resolution, the text of which is already familiar to the reader. The difference between the official text of the Resolution and the text as cited in the official verbatim record of the debate in the Council of the Republic, which inaccurately stated that an independent government could

29. *Journal officiel de la République Française, Débats Parlementaires, Conseil de la République,* 1950, No. 26, C.R., p. 864, col. 1 (séance du 16 mars 1950).
30. Ibid., col. 2.
31. Ibid., cols. 1 and 2.

be established for each of the three provinces, is manifest. At the same time, Schuman's integrity being beyond all doubt, his error in quotation was in all likelihood due to poor staff assistance, or possibly to a misreading of the French text of the Resolution (there is certainly no discrepancy between the official English and French versions). Whatever the origin of the error may have been, it had the unfortunate effect of giving the members of the Council of the Republic an entirely wrong impression on an essential point.

It further follows from the Minister's statement that he greatly counted on France's membership in Council for Libya, as well as on negotiations with the Commissioner, to influence the course of events to come. He even referred to a possible reopening of the whole Libyan problem. Nothing could have been more remote from the realities of the situation, but it was exactly what both Chambers of Parliament were driving at.

Indeed, the Council of the Republic adopted the following resolution (no details of the voting are given):

> Le Conseil de la République,
>
> Emu par la résolution de l'Assemblée générale des Nations Unies du 21 novembre 1949 concernant la constitution d'un Etat indépendant de Libye, comprenant la Cyrénaique, la Tripolitaine et le Fezzan;
>
> Constatant que la constitution de cet Etat ne répond ni à l'évolution des populations, ni à leurs aspirations, ni aux conditions géographiques, historiques et économiques des pays intéressés et que, en ce qui concerne le Fezzan, elle va à l'encontre de la volonté nettement exprimée de l'immense majorité de la population et des intérêts français;
>
> Invite le Gouvernement à user de toute l'autorité de la France en vue d'arriver à une solution définitive qui soit conforme aux vœux des populations et aux intérêts français, notamment sur les deux points suivants:
>
> 1. Le sort du Fezzan proprement dit;
> 2. Le sort de la circonscription de Ghadamès et de la région de Ghat-Serdelès.[32]

The first of the debates discussed in the foregoing paragraphs caused the Commissioner no surprise, since French public opinion on the subject was well known to him, and the attitude of the Government had been made clear in the General Assembly of the United Nations.

The position taken by the French Government in the second debate, after his visit to Paris, however, came as a disappointment to him. He had hoped that, in making the concessions previously mentioned, the French Government would also have reviewed the substance of its policy, to bring

32. Ibid., p. 865, col. 2, and p. 866, col. 2.

it more into line with the Commissioner's interpretation of the United Nations Resolution. It was now evident that he had been too optimistic, and that his troubles over the problem of Libyan unity were by no means at an end.

At the same time, he was struck by the oddly unrealistic attitude of both the Government and the majority in the two chambers of Parliament. What had been constantly referred to in the debates as a "referendum" organized by the Four Power Commission had in fact been nothing more than a rather haphazardly conducted consultation of about 700 persons out of a total population of 49,950. Several speakers had argued that during this "referendum" 80 percent of the population had come out in favor of the maintenance of French administration. Nowhere in the report is this percentage mentioned. The French, United Kingdom, and United States members of the Commission had summed up their conclusions in the following words:

> Owing to the haphazard selection of persons to be interviewed, and the chance whereby a majority of the inhabitants of one village were counted as having expressed their views, while in another village, perhaps equally large, only a handful was present, the figures above only show general trends of feeling.
>
> Because of the lack of political consciousness and of public information on the purpose of the Commission's visit, there had been in general no prior consideration of the issues.
>
> Bearing the previous two paragraphs in mind, it may be said that:
>
> (a) There is a widespread desire for an Islamic government, some specifying that it should be free from foreign interference. But there seemed to be doubt in the minds of persons interviewed whether such a solution was a possibility, and a number of people gave the continuation of French administration as a second choice.
>
> (b) The sedentary agriculturalists, especially, are appreciative of French measures of assistance. They desire a strong government to protect them against raiding nomads, and a large majority of them would be quite content for the French administration to continue.
>
> (c) The Tuareg contained in the Fezzan desire to be under the same administration as the majority of their people, who are under French rule.
>
> (d) Members of two Arab nomad tribes of the Fezzan who were heard by the Commission, and whose tribes have grazing and rain cultivation in Tripolitania (viz: Zintan, Megarha) expressed their desire to see the two areas under a single administration, and this view was echoed by inhabitants of Murzuk, villages around Sebha, and individuals in other areas.

(e) There is no anti-Italian feeling and such criticism as there was of Italian administrative methods referred mostly to the war-time period.
(f) The excesses of the Senussi leaders from 1915–1930 are remembered and they are not considered capable of forming a government.[33]

The USSR member had stated his views in the following terms:

During its stay in the Fezzan the Commission interrogated about 700 persons.

The characteristic feature of these interrogations in the Fezzan was that in about half of the localities where the interrogations were made, those interrogated had no definite opinions with regard to the future Government and their statements were according to the formula "either . . . . . . or . . . . . ."

The sole exception were the Tuareg, who constituted about 20 per cent of all those interrogated. They expressed themselves in favour of the maintenance of the French Administration.

As a rule the Tuareg came to meet the Commission on the instruction of their Mudirs and stated that they would abide by the decisions of their sheikhs who, according to the French Military Administration, receive stipends from the Administration. The Tuareg stated that the French Administration treated them well and exempted them from taxes, but that the former Italian Administration also was good to them.

Opinions on the future government

1. In favour of the French Administration (about half of them were Tuareg)	44%
2. For any Government	26%
3. For an Islamic Government	18%
4. Would accept the Four Powers' decision	12%[34]

Whichever of these appreciations came closer to the truth, there was obviously an appreciable feeling in favor of the French Administration in the Fezzan in 1948, even when the views of the Tuareg are ignored. What many Frenchmen were apt to overlook, however, was that since November 1949 the situation had been slowly changing. In 1948 the population had no choice but that of living under French rule or blindly accepting an unknown alternative. In 1950, the United Nations Resolution offered them, in tangible form, a new possibility—that of becoming part of an independent Islamic State. For many Fezzanese the choice was not an easy one but, as

33. Four Power Commission of Investigation for the Former Italian Colonies, *Report,* Volume III, *Report on Libya,* Part Three, *The Fezzan,* p. 47. Mimeographed. See also Chap. 1, p. 57.

34. Ibid., p. 48.

subsequent developments proved, the attraction of an independent Libya under a Moslem ruler was more powerful than even the French Administration on the spot had believed possible.

The two series of negotiations in which the Commissioner had been engaged revealed to him the marked difference between British and French methods of promoting local autonomy. In Tripolitania, the British authorities used indirect tactics, carefully supporting certain political parties and opposing others, in an endeavor to promote controled emancipation; as this process was inevitably slower than even moderate local nationalists wanted, it caused discontent which was not assuaged by British measures in favor of Libyan unity and independence. In the economic and social fields, British policy had been considerably more constructive, particularly in the educational sector, though its implementation was hampered by the "care and maintenance" mentality born of the knowledge that British rule in the territory was not intended to endure.[35]

In Cyrenaica, where the United Kingdom had more immediate and more lasting interests, both its constitutional and economic and social policies had been taken considerably farther.[36]

In the Fezzan, the French Administration, while ostensibly trying to match British policy in Cyrenaica, went about matters in its own way; in practice, it held up constitutional development by repressive measures, the intensity of which varied from oasis to oasis and from village to village, according to the nature (sedentary or nomadic) of the inhabitants and the attitude of the local notables. At the same time, it introduced economic measures which considerably improved living conditions in the territory. The most important of these steps, taken shortly before the arrival of the United Nations Mission in Libya, was to increase, from one-quarter to one-third, the share to which the water-drawer (*jebbad*) was entitled in the income from plots he irrigated for the owners' account. In a country where irrigation from subsoil water was of paramount importance for agriculture, this change in the financial relationship between landowners and drawers of water was a mark of great social progress. This dual French policy, conservative in the political field, progressive in the economic and social sectors, aroused contradictory reactions among the people of the Fezzan, who sometimes presented the Mission with conflicting reports.

Soon after his arrival in Libya the Commissioner began to receive com-

35. "Annual report of the Government of the United Kingdom to the General Assembly concerning the administration of Cyrenaica and Tripolitania," GAOR: Fifth Session, 1950, Annexes, Agenda item 21 (A/1390, 29 September 1950), pp. 37–40.

36. Ibid., pp. 35–37 and 39–40.

plaints to the effect that the French Administration was oppressing the population of the Fezzan.[37] Some, made by Fezzanese living in Tripolitania, were obviously inspired, in language as well as in content, by certain of the Tripolitanian political parties. Others, however, coming from the Fezzan itself, seemed to be genuine. The Commissioner felt obliged, having regard to subparagraph 10 (b) of Resolution 289 (IV), to communicate the more serious complaints to the French Resident in Sabhah.

In a conversation with Colonel Sarazac, during which the Commissioner brought the matter up, the former protested that the allegations were false, and invited the Commissioner to make his own inquiry into the complaint. Lacking both staff and time, the Mission was clearly in no position to carry out such a task, but in the course of numerous public hearings and private talks which its members had with the local population, a sufficient number of specific cases were brought to the Mission's notice to allow of some measure of verification. To determine the administrative responsibility for individual acts was plainly outside the Mission's competence.

The majority of cases of alleged physical "atrocities" turned out to be considerably less grave than the complaints made them out to be. A few cases of beating were confirmed with a fair degree of certainty. Only one really extreme case could be proved, and in this the Commissioner secured the victim's release by drawing the matter to the French authorities' attention. Most complaints were found to have been provoked by administrative sanctions, sometimes excessive, of a corporal nature. In the course of 1950, the number and seriousness of such complaints declined. In 1951, they ceased altogether.

Behind the firmness, not to say harshness, of the French regime, particularly at the junior officer level, there was some anxiety about the attitude of the local population, due to fear of difficulties with the nomadic tribes. This was the outcome of a surprising incident that had occurred at the principal French post, Sabhah. Basically, the local French Administration was organized on the pattern common to southern Algeria, with units of the Foreign Legion and Spahis stationed in fortified places. In the Fezzan, these places were the former Italian forts. In Sabhah, the fort was a rather imposing structure on top of a low hill. The French armed forces in the area patrolled the desert from oasis to oasis, in armored vehicles or on camels, to maintain order by show of force.

One day in 1948, the fort at Sabhah was seized by a handful of villagers from the nearby village of Jadid, led by a self-styled prophet who claimed

37. Similar charges had been brought to the notice of the First Committee of the General Assembly at its Fourth Session in a statement delivered by the NCLL delegation. See GAOR: Third Session, Part II, 1949, First Committee, 252nd Meeting, 27 April 1949, p. 135.

to have received a message from an angel come down from heaven, telling him to take the fort. The French had regarded this man as mentally unbalanced and harmless. The villagers, pretending to be casual laborers reporting for work at first light, calmly mounted the sweeping stairway to the fort, suddenly turned upon and slew the two sentries at the entrance, and swarmed into the fort where the garrison was still asleep. Taking advantage of the fact that the garrison's rifles were stored in racks with a rod passing through the trigger guards and secured with a padlock as a precaution against theft, the villagers succeeded in overpowering the sleeping Foreign Legionnaires, whom they then threw out of the fort. They soon found in the guardroom the key to the padlock securing the stacked rifles, which they seized. However, part of the garrison was quartered below, outside the ramparts. Thus the villagers soon found themselves besieged inside the fort. A small party of Legionnaires crept round the side of the building to a small, unguarded door at the foot of the wall, and forced their way in. They quickly overcame the invaders, most of whom were killed in the melee. By noon, the fort was back in the hands of the Legion, but the news of its initial loss had in the meantime been radioed to Paris, where the Commanding Officer, then on leave, learned the dismaying news. This local skirmish, despite the fact that it had no lasting military effect, badly rattled the French military authorities, who never forgot the experience, and almost certainly impaired Fezzanese respect for the invincibility of the French. Moreover, it had demonstrated that, however confusedly, the mind of the local population was open to ideas of revolt.

The Commissioner learned of this episode quite by accident when listening to complaints, while visiting the nearby oasis, that a number of young men had been killed by the French and their bodies buried in quicklime. Surprised and puzzled, he asked whether there was any possible foundation for this report. The French local commander then explained that the bodies of those killed in that morning's fighting in 1948 had been laid in the desert outside the fort so that they could be claimed by their families. He denied that any bodies had been cast into a lime grave; the unclaimed ones had been buried in the normal fashion outside the fort.

BRITISH PLANS FOR POLITICAL AND ADMINISTRATIVE DEVELOPMENT IN CYRENAICA

As recounted earlier, Cyrenaica had been granted internal autonomy on 16 September 1949, some ten weeks before Resolution 289 (IV) was adopted by the General Assembly.[38] The United Kingdom delegate had

38. For organization of the Cyrenaican Government and its powers, see the first *Annual Report of the United Nations Commissioner in Libya,* paras. 43–49.

said in the First Committee on 30 September 1949 that His Majesty's Government

> could not continue to refuse the people of Cyrenaica its indisputable right to the greatest possible measure of self-government consistent with the international obligations of the United Kingdom Government and with the rights of the General Assembly, under the Treaty of Peace with Italy, to make recommendations on the future of those territories. At the beginning of September the United Kingdom Government had therefore given the Emir of Cyrenaica absolute powers in the internal affairs of that territory within the limits just mentioned and without prejudice to the question of Libyan unity. With the entire approval of the United Kingdom Government and after having consulted his people, the Emir had proclaimed a constitution under which a Government of Cyrenaica would shortly be set up. Faced with a demand from representatives of the people of Cyrenaica for independence—a demand which it could not grant because of its international obligations—the United Kingdom Government, after careful deliberation, had decided that in accordance with the Treaty of Peace with Italy and the terms of the Charter from which its powers derived, it could not do less than grant Cyrenaica that full measure of self-government.[39]

On 9 November 1949, Hector McNeil made a further statement in the Committee, quoted in part in Chapter 1 (see pp. 103–04 and fn. 92).

It is implicit in this statement that the United Kingdom considered itself legally entitled, subject to certain conditions, to grant domestic autonomy or even full independence to the territory of Cyrenaica, Resolution 289 (IV) notwithstanding. Perusing the General Assembly records, one again wonders whether all delegations grasped that implication. Some obviously did; but the majority apparently did not, or tacitly assumed that sooner or later theory would be wedded to practice. Certainly, the Resolution recognized no difference in status, real or potential, among the three territories, for it expressly provided that "Libya, *comprising Cyrenaica, Tripolitania and the Fezzan,* shall be constituted an independent and sovereign State" (author's italics). At the same time, it was silent on the semiautonomous status of Cyrenaica, thus creating ambiguity.

The fact that its adoption deterred neither Cyrenaicans nor British from their plans to make Cyrenaica independent was patently due to the complementary nature of their desires and interests at the time.

The impatience of the Cyrenaicans was understandable. They had been

39. GAOR: Fourth Session, 1949, First Committee, 278th Meeting, 30 September 1949, p. 20.

looking forward to independence ever since the British Eighth Army had driven the Germans and Italians from their territory. Although the United Kingdom Government had promised in 1942 only that "at the end of the war the Sanusis in Cyrenaica will in no circumstances again fall under Italian domination," [40] a promise reiterated in October 1944 by the Foreign Secretary in the House of Commons, the Cyrenaicans considered that the United Kingdom was morally obliged to grant them independence. However, there had been one delay after another. Two years had elapsed between the end of World War II and the conclusion of the Treaty of Peace with Italy; that Treaty itself (Article 23 and Annex XI) provided for a further year to pass while the Big Four tried to agree on the disposal of the former Italian colonies; and yet another year had gone by while the General Assembly was discussing the future. Finally, the terms of Resolution 289 (IV) made it plain that it would probably be two years more before independence arrived, and even then it would entail union with Tripolitania and the Fezzan.

The readiness of the United Kingdom Government to acquiesce in Cyrenaican insistence on independence was equally understandable in the light of the strategic considerations mentioned in the Foreword and the Historical Background. Moreover, when the rejection of the Bevin-Sforza plan ruled out the possibility of British trusteeship over Cyrenaica, the maintenance of Britain's friendly relations with the Senussis called for ready acceptance of the Amir's demands. All the more so as, in return for badly needed financial help, the Cyrenaicans were prepared to allow British forces to remain on their soil. But, however understandable this mutual desire for Cyrenaican independence might have been from the point of view of the two parties concerned, to the Commissioner it was a serious obstacle to the discharge of the duties entrusted to him by Resolution 289 (IV), as he understood them. The gravity of the problem soon became apparent. The first indication he had of it was a paragraph in the United Kingdom memorandum handed to him on the eve of his departure from New York. Though this document dealt mainly with British plans for Tripolitania (see pp. 131–32), it mentioned the self-government already granted to Cyrenaica, announcing at the same time that at the Amir's request His Majesty's Government proposed to add to the powers already transferred a number of others still reserved. It gave an undertaking that the Commissioner would be kept informed before action was taken.

When the latter paid his first visit to Cyrenaica at the end of January 1950, he tried to elicit more information both from the Amir and from the

40. See Chapter 1, pp. 40–41.

British Resident, E. A. V. de Candole,[41] about their intentions; but he came away not much the wiser. A meeting with the Cyrenaican Government confirmed that the Amir had been pressing the United Kingdom Government for the transfer of additional powers; a conversation with the Amir himself indicated that His Highness envisaged the future Libya as a federal State, with extensive local powers for each of the three component provinces and a central government concentrating on certain common services; and an interview with the Resident confirmed that his Government viewed sympathetically the Amir's request for more powers. The Commissioner got the overall impression that a further transfer of powers was contemplated in the not too distant future, and he therefore requested the United Kingdom Government, through the Resident, to defer any such action until he himself could visit London.

Having finished his first tour of the three territories, and having paid visits to Cairo, Rome, and Paris, the Commissioner spent a few days in London on his way back to New York toward the end of February.

At the Foreign Office, the discussions were mainly devoted to British plans for Tripolitania, as described on pages 138–39, but the Commissioner also raised the question of Cyrenaica, to which both sides brought an open mind. As he expected, the United Kingdom position turned out to be that Cyrenaica's case differed from Tripolitania's because of the recognition of the Amir as Head of State and the absence of a minority problem. The Amir had been for long, and was still, pressing for full independence, arguing that Libyan unity could be engineered later under a federal form of government. He would not, the British spokesmen said, agree to any form of union with the other two territories that might entail the risk of a renascence of Italian influence in Libya. Neither would Cyrenaica accept

41. Eric Armor Vully de Candole, C.M.G., was born on 14 September 1901. He was educated at Aldenham School and at Worcester College, Oxford, where he was an Exhibitioner. Just too young to see service in World War I, he entered the Sudan Political Service in 1923, serving in the Education Department until 1928. Thereafter he was District Commissioner in the Berber, Khartoum, and Darfur Provinces (1928–36). He was Resident at Dar Masalit from 1936 to 1944 and Deputy Governor of the Northern Province from 1944 to 1946. In the latter year he was seconded to British Military Administration, in which he served successively as Chief Secretary, Cyrenaica (1946–48); Chief Administrator, Somalia (1948); Chief Administrator, Cyrenaica (1948–49); and British Resident, Cyrenaica (1949–51). Those who seek signs in coincidences may find food for thought in the fact that both the British Chief Administrators in what was subsequently to become the Kingdom of Libya had been Exhibitioners at the same Oxford college. What is more significant is that their long service in the Sudan has made them good Arabic linguists, and endowed them with great experience and understanding of the Arab-Moslem way of thinking and of political trends generally in North East Africa.

numerical domination by Tripolitania. Consequently, the United Kingdom Government was prepared to transfer to the Amir the reserve powers it held, provided the latter would take over its obligation under Resolution 289 (IV) to ensure that Cyrenaica became part of a united Libya not later than 1 January 1952. The United Kingdom neither would nor could transfer any right or title of sovereignty, since it did not itself possess anything of the kind. Hector McNeil's statement before the First Committee of the General Assembly on 9 November 1949 (see pp. 103–04) was adduced in support of this point.

The Commissioner limited himself to pointing out that any transfer of powers would have to be compatible with the terms of the Resolution, a statement of principle with which his interlocutors concurred. Nevertheless, he had the impression that some difference of interpretation persisted affecting the implementation of those terms.

Shortly thereafter, the Commissioner learned from a number of sources that plans for Cyrenaican independence were developing more rapidly than before. He therefore asked the Foreign Office whether he could be acquainted with these plans; and just before his return to Libya in the middle of March he was told that, in response to renewed demands by the Amir for complete self-government and full independence, negotiations were to be started without delay on a treaty or agreement by which the United Kingdom Government would grant independence and financial assistance to Cyrenaica, in return for permission to keep British troops stationed there and an assurance by the Amir that he would assume the United Kingdom's responsibility for implementing Resolution 289 (IV).

It further transpired that no draft treaty yet existed, properly speaking, but only an outline of what might become one. It was also explained that the agreement would state that the independence of Cyrenaica was being granted pending the constitution of the State of Libya in accordance with the United Nations recommendation. It was, moreover, understood that the Amir would undertake to promulgate the legislation required to carry out the recommendation, and that, conversely, he would promulgate no legislation which might hinder its fulfillment. In particular, he would take no action with regard to Italian state, parastatal, or private property that would in any way prejudice final recommendations by the United Nations concerning the economic and financial provisions that might be applied arising out of Article 19 of and Annex XIV to the Treaty of Peace with Italy. The Foreign Office therefore hoped that the interim nature of the arrangements to be negotiated, which covered only the period up to 1 January 1952, would be acceptable to the Commissioner as fully safeguarding the position insofar as the United Nations resolution was concerned.

At this point the Commissioner realized beyond all doubt that the Cyrenaican situation presented a problem far more urgent and far-reaching in both its immediate and its more distant consequences than that created by the British and French proposals for Tripolitania and the Fezzan. Nevertheless, he trusted that, backed by the moral authority of the United Nations, he would be able to bring home to the British Government and the Amir that they were heading straight for an open conflict with the General Assembly and should modify their plans accordingly. At the same time he knew only too well that the spearhead of the drive for Cyrenaica's independence was the Amir, who was not bound by the resolution. His Highness was responsible only to his own people, and if he wished to conclude an agreement with the authority administering his territory, there was nothing the Commissioner could do except strongly advise him not to take such a course.

So the Commissioner decided to probe the issue with both the other parties; and in view of the British Government's obligations toward the United Nations, he decided to spend a few more days in London on his way back from New York to Libya. There he found that the matter indeed boiled down to a difference in interpretation. His Majesty's Government felt that they were on legally sound ground in taking the Resolution to mean that France and the United Kingdom, while obliged—in cooperation with the Commissioner—"to administer the territories for the purpose of assisting in the establishment of Libyan unity and independence," [42] were free to do this by first creating three independent or autonomous local governments which could subsequently unite, if they so wished, to form an independent and sovereign State. The Commissioner, however, believed that, in providing in subparagraph 10 (a) of Resolution 289 (IV) that the Administering Powers, in cooperation with the Commissioner, should "Initiate immediately all necessary steps for the transfer of power to a duly constituted independent Government," and adding in subparagraph 10 (b) that "the territories [were to be administered] for the purpose of . . . the establishment of Libyan unity and independence," the General Assembly had had in mind the constitution of a single Libyan government, not three. He also believed that the word "immediately" was to be construed in its literal sense, at least with regard to the first steps to be taken. In his opinion, it could never have been the General Assembly's intention that the unity of Libya should be achieved by first dividing the country into three parts and then allowing these to merge in a single State. On the contrary: the Assembly had intended that the Commissioner and the Admin-

42. General Assembly Resolution 289 A (IV), 21 November 1949.

istering Powers should together promote the unification of Libya from the very beginning.

But it was not for the Commissioner to dictate the policies of the Administering Powers, although he had hoped that it might be possible, even if much harder than in the case of Tripolitania or the Fezzan, to reach a working agreement on Cyrenaica. If such agreement proved impossible because the United Kingdom Government considered that its strategic interests in the area were too vital to brook delay in granting Cyrenaica independence, he could only declare formally that he neither could nor would accept United Kingdom policy, reporting to the General Assembly that the Resolution had become unworkable. But until matters reached that point he would continue to do his utmost to promote the implementation of the Resolution in the spirit in which it had been adopted.

Fortunately, the United Kingdom had at no time formally pledged itself to grant Cyrenaica independence. Could His Majesty's Government be persuaded that it would be in its own best interest first to cooperate in implementing the United Nations Resolution, and only then to start negotiating, not with Cyrenaica, but with a provisional government for the whole of Libya? That was the paramount issue, on which all would depend.

The Commissioner accordingly began his consultations at the Foreign Office by outlining the situation in which, in his view, the United Kingdom would find itself if it granted Cyrenaica independence despite the fact that, on its own admission, it held no title to sovereignty over any part of the territory.

First, the very act might well start a wave of protest rolling from the Council for Libya right up to the General Assembly.

Second, the United Nations could soundly argue that transfer of any additional powers to the Amir, even short of independence, would be contrary to the spirit, and even the letter, of Resolution 289 (IV). Certainly any transfer of power before the constitution of the Libyan State had been determined by the Libyan National Constituent Assembly would infringe the terms of that Resolution.

Third, it seemed likely, judging by conversations he had had in Paris a few weeks earlier, that the French Government might well follow in the Fezzan the example set by the United Kingdom in Cyrenaica. If so, the brunt of the blame for violating the United Nations Resolution would fall on the British.

Finally, McNeil's crucial statement, though admittedly not challenged at the time, constituted a unilateral declaration, by which many member States, particularly the Latin American and Arab groups, would in all probability not consider themselves bound.

To avoid these unpleasant consequences, the United Kingdom had only to delay action on Cyrenaican independence until the Libyan National Assembly had decided upon the form of the future Libyan State. If His Majesty's Government and the Amir would not agree to any delay, the Commissioner would have no choice but to seek the advice of his Council and then refer the matter to the General Assembly for decision.

Although the Foreign Office did not change its position during the discussion, the Commissioner left London with the impression that an understanding might yet be reached.

The next thing was to get to Benghazi as soon as possible for a second audience with the Amir. During his first audience, on 28 January, the Commissioner had felt himself to be on rather uncertain ground when discussing Anglo-Cyrenaican relations with the Amir; but this time he was on much firmer soil. On arriving in Benghazi on 20 March, he contacted the British Resident to put him in the picture. De Candole had in the natural course of affairs received reports on the London talks; but it was only proper to take no action without informing him. The Resident had little to say, except that he was under constant personal attack in the local press for continuing to decline to hand over the reserved powers. It was hardly fair, he added, and with some justification, to expect the Cyrenaicans to put the clock back in the matter of their dearest aspirations.

The next morning the Commissioner had an audience with the Amir, which lasted more than two and a half hours. The Commissioner felt that, their brief acquaintance notwithstanding, a sense of mutual confidence had started to burgeon between them. He was greatly impressed by the Sayed's personality, finding in him not only a wise and experienced man, but one who could be exceedingly tenacious. In his long and troubled career, the Amir had developed his remarkable gifts of perception and foresight in political matters. He was wary and astute, but at the same time a reliable negotiator capable of putting the general interest before his own. Above all, he was moved by a profound religious sense of responsibility for his people.

The Commissioner's main concern was to find out whether the man opposite him would limit the scope of that responsibility to his Cyrenaican countrymen, or whether, and to what extent, his political vision encompassed the whole of the Libyan people. Having regard to the spiritual and political history of Sanusiya, the Commissioner sensed that he could probably count on the broader vision. He was soon to know the answer to that unspoken question.

To place his problem in the context of Libya's international position, he began by giving the Amir a detailed account of his visits to Washington, Cairo, Rome, Paris, and London. Assuming that His Highness was fully informed about the positions of the French and British Governments, he said that he had found the Egyptians opposed to the formation of separate territorial governments in Libya. The Foreign Minister, Mohammed Salah el-Din, had assured him that Egypt was prepared to support him fully in carrying out his duties as Commissioner. In Rome, in the course of a long conversation with Sforza, he was given a pledge to the effect that Italy had no more colonial ambitions and had abandoned all thought of returning to its former African territories. The Italian Government's current official policy was to encourage its nationals domiciled in Libya to become Libyan citizens, and to protect the interests of those who nonetheless preferred to retain Italian nationality. At the same time, the Commissioner had been waited upon by a number of delegations representing former Italian colonists in Libya whose strong desire to return to their farms there was only too evident. These people plainly had no realization of the extent to which conditions had changed, so that the Commissioner had been obliged to advise them to give up any such hope. On this, the Amir observed that no Italian could be allowed to return to Libya. In Washington, the Commissioner resumed, he had been assured by responsible officers of the State Department that they fully supported the United Nations Resolution and would help the Commissioner in his efforts to implement it.

After having mentioned the British plans for the establishment of an advisory council and legislative body in Tripolitania, with its possible dangerous consequences for Libyan unity, the Commissioner mooted the idea, which was increasingly taking shape in his mind, of setting up a preparatory committee for the Libyan National Assembly. He had already outlined such a procedure in London and Paris, where it had met with little opposition. Such a committee, preferably consisting of a small number of elected men representing all three territories on an equal footing, would admittedly be a novelty in Libyan public life, but it could at least replace the bilateral Cyrenaican-Tripolitanian negotiations which so far had failed to produce agreement on Libyan unity. It would, in the Commissioner's opinion, enable Libyans to exchange views on their country's political future, not as negotiators defending territorial interests, but as planners for the future National Assembly, working out its structure and composition and the manner in which it would go about its duties. The Amir replied that he had no objection to the formation of such a committee, which seemed to him the shortest way of attaining the desired goal.

After this introductory exchange, the Commissioner turned to his main point, expressing concern at the fact that, in his view, the United Kingdom–Cyrenaican agreement determining the territory's almost immediate independence and its future, albeit interim, relations with Great Britain ran counter to the intentions and provisions of Resolution 289 (IV). Indeed, the premature establishment of Cyrenaica as an independent State might well endanger the creation of a united and independent Libya, or at least make it much more difficult. The French Government, too, might well follow the British example and grant independence to the Fezzan. Such a chain of events would undoubtedly provoke a great deal of understandable criticism in the Council for Libya and later in the General Assembly, which might even lead to the Libyan question being reopened, in which case a revival of proposals along the lines of the Bevin-Sforza agreement, granting Italy some kind of privileged position in Tripolitania, could not be ruled out. Other consequences, of secondary significance but not unimportant, might also ensue; for instance, if action taken by Cyrenaica and the United Kingdom made it impossible to implement the United Nations plan, the General Assembly might refuse to make technical assistance funds available to the territory. Again, although the Resolution provided for Libyan membership in the United Nations in due course, this obviously applied to a unified Libyan State, not to a single part of it. The Commissioner also pressed his opinion that the General Assembly had not intended that one part of the country should become independent separately from the others.

In short, the action contemplated by Cyrenaica and the United Kingdom might jeopardize the former's future status both from an internal Libyan point of view and from the international one.

The Commissioner concluded by declaring that he fully appreciated Cyrenaica's impatience after so many sacrifices and so many years of waiting. Nonetheless, he could not but advise both His Highness and the United Kingdom to put off action of the kind they were contemplating until the Libyan National Assembly, or at least the preparatory committee, had made an attempt to carry out the United Nations Resolution.

In reply, the Amir pointed out that any agreement he might sign would provide for its own liquidation by 1 January 1952, thereby implying that by that time Cyrenaica would be free to join, on its own terms, in a union or federation with the other two territories. To this, the Commissioner answered that, the final goal being the attainment of Libyan unity and independence, the achievement of this aim through a National Assembly convened to draft a single constitution for Libya as a whole offered, in his view, a much surer chance of success than negotiations between three previously established independent States.

It was at this point that His Highness disclosed that he was already fully engaged in treaty negotiations with the United Kingdom. Indeed, he said, the latter had submitted to him a draft, though he did not feel free to show it to the Commissioner. He therefore suggested that the latter should ask the British for a copy so that he could advise both parties whether it contained anything that conflicted with the terms of the General Assembly Resolution. Rather taken aback by this request, but at the same time glad of the opportunity it afforded him of taking a hand in events at a critical juncture, he accepted the unexpected invitation, adding the hope that nothing would be signed pending his advice. To this His Highness readily assented.

Later that day the Commissioner informed the British Resident of the Amir's suggestion and request for advice. De Candole, also somewhat surprised, replied that the draft treaty was a confidential document which he could not divulge without authority from the Foreign Office. This, of course, was a perfectly normal position, so the two sat down together, quite amicably, to draft a cable to London. Early next morning the Commissioner had to fly back to Tripoli. When he took leave that evening, the Resident warned him that every Tom, Dick, and Harry in Benghazi knew that a treaty was being negotiated between the Amir and the United Kingdom and that its signing was expected in the near future. He went on to say that in his personal opinion the negotiations might take longer than the people cared to believe, but that any undue delay would undoubtedly cause great disappointment, except perhaps among the members of the Omar Mukhtar Club. The Commissioner agreed that the Resident was right in this, and that if the treaty were not signed some alternative solution would have to be found. The question was: what?

A few days after the Commissioner got back to Tripoli the British Resident there handed him a copy of the draft treaty with Cyrenaica, which apparently he had only just seen for the first time. The Commissioner at once consulted the senior members of his staff, among whom there was unanimous agreement that it would be bad policy for him to limit his comments to critical observations of a legal and political nature. Something much more constructive would have to be put forward, making the problem of Cyrenaican independence part and parcel of the larger issue of Libyan unity and independence as envisaged by the General Assembly. At the same time it was felt that Cyrenaican aspirations would have to be satisfied to some extent short of the granting of independence. The concessions would naturally be made public, and the Council for Libya ought to be given an opportunity of discussing them and, if it so wished, expressing an opinion on them. While accepting the United Kingdom view that constitutional development in Cyrenaica should be above board and of an interim character, it was also considered that, pending Libyan independence, no agreement should be signed between the United Kingdom and

Cyrenaica that mentioned the provision of military facilities and the financial support to be given in exchange. This was a matter that ought not to be raised until a Provisional Libyan Government elected by a Libyan National Assembly had been constituted, and even then such an arrangement might be open to criticism. Indeed, it would be better if all such issues were to be settled between a "duly constituted independent [Libyan] Government," in the terms of subparagraph 10 (a) of Resolution 289 A (IV), and the United Kingdom or any other Government with which an independent Libya might seek to conclude agreements of this kind.

The Commissioner visited London again early in April for talks at the Foreign Office on the basis of this alternative to the contemplated treaty. He made it clear that in proposing it he had gone to the extreme limits of the concessions he could make, and that in doing so he was taking obvious risks, though he was willing to go that far in order to save the United Nations plan in the interest of Libya's future.

The Foreign Office position was that much would depend on the Amir. Should he, after receiving the Commissioner's advice, persist in his request for the transfer of the reserved powers and recognition of Cyrenaica as an independent State, the United Kingdom Government was pledged to meet it, provided it could do so in a form compatible with the United Nations Resolution.

In the course of a long session, most of the earlier arguments were repeated on both sides and reexamined from every possible point of view, real and hypothetical. Gradually it became clear that an understanding might be reached subject to Cabinet approval. An agreement was drawn up which jointly stated that the Commissioner's response to His Highness's request for advice would consist in declaring that it was incompatible with the United Nations Resolution, and inexpedient for the Amir's international position, to insist on immediate transfer of powers still reserved by the British Resident. The Commissioner would recommend instead that the Amir adjust his plans to fit in with the United Nations program for the constitutional development of Libya as a whole. As a first step, His Highness should consult with representatives of the other Libyan territories on the committee proposed by the Commissioner to prepare the way for the Libyan National Assembly, regarding the powers that might, consistently with the Resolution, be transferred by the British Resident to the Amir. The Commissioner would further advise the Amir that, should the preparatory committee find that transfer of these powers before the achievement of *Libyan* independence would not conflict with the Resolution, and provided the Amir pledged himself to accept the fundamental provision for the establishment of an independent and sovereign Libya made up of all three territories not later than 1 January 1952, the General Assembly of the United Nations might, in his opinion, find it difficult to object.

The United Kingdom Government, for its part, would advise the Amir that, although in the circumstances it felt he should follow the Commissioner's advice, it was still prepared to recognize Cyrenaican independence and conclude a treaty to that effect if the Amir insisted. Should, however, His Highness be willing to accept the Commissioner's advice, the contemplated action would be suspended for the time being; but the position would be subject to reexamination if the preparatory committee failed to agree within a reasonable period of time on the fundamental principles of Libyan unity.

It was further agreed that the Commissioner and the Administering Powers would jointly announce, after the first session of the Council for Libya, their plans for the constitutional development of Libya as a whole. It was also understood that the provision of long-term facilities for the defense of the territory should be agreed upon at the same time as the final transfer of power to the Libyan State after having been negotiated in draft form between the United Kingdom and the Provisional Libyan Government with the Commissioner's advice. The counterpart to the provision of these facilities would consist in badly needed technical and financial assistance.[43] This agreement might serve as a model for similar agreements between Libya and other interested foreign powers; and taken together, the body of such agreements would establish the full scope of the international commitments to be undertaken by the future State of Libya as well as the full volume of the assistance it would receive.

Provided these agreements, concluded with the Provisional Libyan Government, were in his view consonant with the Charter of the United Nations, the Commissioner would support them before the General Assembly; he did not, however, consider that body's prior formal approval necessary.

The agreement also recorded the opinion of the Commissioner and of His Majesty's Government that a federal structure for the future Libyan State seemed to be in conformity with its physical conditions and political tendencies, and that the Amir appeared to be indicated as the probable head of such a State.

It goes without saying that this agreement was far from ideal from the Commissioner's viewpoint. But if the Amir accepted his advice, the signing

43. See Chapter 10, The Transfer of Powers, for the way in which this understanding was implemented. For texts of the temporary agreements signed on Independence Day by the duly constituted independent Government of Libya, see Annexes VII and VIII, pp. 948–52.

of a treaty which would have planted a bomb under the United Nations plan for Libya, a bomb the explosion of which might have been fatal for it, would be postponed for at least several months, and perhaps for the entire transitional period.

Nonetheless, the Commissioner appreciated the fact that he had taken a considerable risk, and was fully aware that from the United Nations viewpoint fault could be found with the agreement in several respects.

It could be argued that it would have been better for the Amir to consult the Libyan National Assembly or Provisional Government instead of a preparatory committee. It would have been more correct to communicate the Commissioner's agreement with the United Kingdom Government to the Council for Libya at the beginning of the latter's first session, instead of publishing it after that session had closed. It might have been altogether preferable had the Commissioner not stretched the authority granted to him in paragraph 4 of Resolution 289 (IV) by undertaking to assist the people of Libya in negotiating international agreements between their Provisional Government and foreign States.

To each of these objections the Commissioner believed there was an appropriate answer. The impatience of both the United Kingdom and the Amir would not have brooked putting off consultations with representatives of the other territories until the National Assembly had been constituted or the Provisional Government elected. In fact, the Commissioner's expressed intention of requesting the Council for Libya to advise him in April 1950 on his plan for the constitutional development of Libya put the two parties to a test of severe restraint. As for assisting the people of Libya in the negotiation of foreign treaties when he was only authorized to assist them in the formulation of a constitution and the establishment of an independent government, the Commissioner had undertaken to do so for two reasons. On the one hand there was no one else in a disinterested position to advise an inexperienced provisional government in defending its interests when negotiating agreements of such importance. On the other hand, the preparation of the agreements before the day of independence was vital if the Libyan State was not to be born bankrupt. The staff of the United Nations Mission had become convinced, and their conviction was later shared by competent United Nations experts, that Libya's budget, balance of trade, and balance of payments were all grossly deficitary, a situation which could be redressed only by grants of foreign assistance over several years. Provided satisfactory arrangements could be worked out, balancing future obligations on the part of the Libyan State against reasonable and in any case unavoidable foreign financial assistance, they would, the Commissioner trusted, command a majority in the General Assembly.

His belief that international treaties of the kind envisaged would not need the formal approval of the General Assembly could also be challenged; but he considered that once Libya became independent, it would be free, like any other independent State, to conclude any treaty it found in its interest with any State it wished. Moreover, he was fairly confident that the Constitution that would enter into force on Independence Day would include certain limitations on parliamentary approval of foreign treaties.

When, a week after having acquiesced in this memorandum of agreement, the Commissioner received official confirmation in Tripoli that the British Cabinet had approved it, he was ready to present to the Amir the advice requested by the latter three weeks earlier. The advice followed the lines set forth above, and was accompanied by suggestions for an alternative procedure, also described above.

Would the Amir agree? For him, it was no easy decision, especially as the United Kingdom Government had virtually left him a free choice. The Commissioner, not having had time to get his memorandum translated into Arabic, submitted it in English with a detailed oral explanation. He also seized the same opportunity to raise two other matters connected with the plan for Cyrenaican independence: the Cyrenaican nationality law and the organization of a Cyrenaican army, rumors about both of which had caused a great deal of unrest in Tripolitania, as well as among Cyrenaican partisans of Libyan unity, as reflections of a separatist Cyrenaican policy.

The Amir explained that the purposes of the nationality law were, first, to identify those entitled to participate in the forthcoming elections to the Cyrenaican consultative assembly and, second, to make it possible to provide Cyrenaicans with travel documents, since there was no legal basis for issuing any kind of personal identity document. The law had been in force for several months, and it was too late to repeal it. In fact, it had never been used to establish a separate Cyrenaican nationality.

The Commissioner expressed his satisfaction with this explanation, but suggested that it might be as well to make matters clear by issuing a public commentary on the law.

As for the widespread concern about the organization of a Cyrenaican army, His Highness laughingly observed that in the heyday of the Karamanlis it had been Tripolitania that had made attacks on Cyrenaica rather than the other way around. No aggressive intent lurked behind the creation of a Cyrenaican armed force, which would not exceed six hundred men in strength and would be used to assist the police in maintaining order. It might be considered as the nucleus of a future Libyan army and would not impose a heavy burden on the Cyrenaican budget. He would gladly try to find another name for the body, and would explain publicly its contemplated size and purpose, and would be grateful if the Commissioner could convey his explanations to the Council for Libya if the matter came up there.

As to the advice and suggestions just submitted, the Amir said he would like to study them overnight, consult the British Resident, and discuss them again with the Commissioner the following day.

In the course of an audience with His Highness that evening, de Candole, who had been handed a copy of the Commissioner's advice, fully supported it, as instructed by London.

The next morning the Amir opened his conversation with the Commissioner by saying that he had carefully studied the latter's suggestions as an alternative to an Anglo-Cyrenaican treaty and found them "wise and good for Cyrenaica." He accordingly approved and accepted them.

The Commissioner's relief as he returned to Tripoli can easily be imagined; but it was tempered by awareness of the tasks that lay ahead, such as his collaboration with the Council, the drafting of the Libyan Constitution, the transfer of powers, and last but not least, the economic and social problems to be tackled.

Looking back at the events of the past three months, he noted with mixed feelings that the situation had been more or less successfully adjusted to the pattern envisaged in the General Assembly Resolution. Although none of the adjustments was entirely satisfactory, they appeared good enough in the case of all three territories to serve as a starting point for the main task, the practical organization of an independent and sovereign Libyan State. The next thing to be done was to convene the Council for Libya, the installation of which had been delayed by the difficulty of selecting its Libyan and minorities' representatives, and then, with its aid and advice, to convene a preparatory committee for the Libyan National Assembly.

As almost four months had elapsed since the adoption of Resolution 289 (IV) it was indeed high time to shift public interest from the local to the national scene. The most beneficial effect of the critical period now ended was, perhaps, that for many Libyan leaders it had served just that purpose.

PART 3. WHAT THE LIBYANS WANTED (Mission Interviews)

A general historical account of the hopes, aspirations, and plans of Libya's leaders at the end of the war about the future of their country has already been given. These aspirations must now be looked at in detail in the context of what has just been said about the intentions of the Administering Powers.

Independence and unity, coupled with membership in the League of Arab States, were the common goal of all Libyan nationalists; but most of the latter were still in the dark as to how independence could be achieved, a matter which to a large extent depended on external developments. Even internal unity, an idea cherished by every Arab nationalist, had yet to be defined in political and constitutional terms. And most Libyans still lacked a clear idea of what their country's position would be within the Arab League. Neither could many of them grasp the place it would occupy as a sovereign member of the international community—though all took its membership in the United Nations for granted. This vagueness about the political future was understandable in a people with no practical experience of independent statehood, but it added to the already considerable difficulties of planning for the birth of the future State. Fortunately, as events will show, a few Libyans emerged whose political experience and vision enabled them to view their country's problems lucidly in both their internal and external contexts.

Meanwhile, divisions of opinion on the basic question of the national leadership, a question all the more difficult to resolve as loyalties varied from one territory to another, persisted.

In this respect Cyrenaica was fortunate in having no problem. In the Fezzan, French control discouraged outbursts of rivalry and strife between leading families and tribes and had enabled Ahmed Bey Seif al-Nasr to be accepted—though not so unanimously as the Amir in Cyrenaica—as the territorial leader.

It was in Tripolitania that the political situation was really complex, not to say confused. Since 1835, in which year the Sublime Porte deposed the last of the Karamanli Pashas, themselves of Turkish descent, there had been no local authority but governors representing first Constantinople and later Rome. No local dynasty or family was in a position to claim recognition as the leaders of Tripolitania, although several were in competition for it. In this respect, the situation at the end of World War II resembled that in 1918, at the time of the Tripolitanian Republic, when, for lack of an agreed leader, a Council of Four had by force of circumstances found itself in charge of public affairs. At that time the existence of a Berber minority, though largely assimilated to the Arab majority, had given the Italian authorities a chance to "divide and rule." By 1945, that source of cleavage had almost disappeared, Arabs and Berbers having suffered in common under the harsh Italian colonial rule.

In short, at the moment when the United Nations started operating in the country, Libya had no accepted national leader, no national party or newspaper, no national institution. The only unifying factors were the common language, culture, and religion, those fundamentals in which the

Arab sense of oneness is so deeply rooted, which, notwithstanding manifold and sometimes profound divisions, transcend the boundaries of all Arab lands.

Such was the state of affairs until 21 November 1949. From that date on, almost unexpectedly to many Libyans, a new factor was introduced on the scene in the shape of the United Nations Resolution, with its recommendation that the three territories be merged to form the independent and sovereign state of Libya not later than 1 January 1952. Suddenly, earlier hopes and aspirations were no longer dreams but exciting possibilities which at short notice would have to be translated into political and constitutional reality. Moreover, the Libyan people themselves were called upon to accomplish this.

The Commissioner's first task on arriving in Libya was not, therefore, to find out whether the political parties and their leaders still clung to the ideas they had expressed in 1948 before the Four Power Commission of Investigation for the Former Italian Colonies, and in 1949 to the First Committee of the General Assembly; their loyalty to these basic concepts could be taken for granted, as it had been by the latter body. With only two years in which to complete his mission, the Commissioner was convinced that the most pressing need was to find out whether any plans were being conceived for implementing the Resolution, and in particular for drafting a constitution.

As there was obviously no time to lose, the first thing the Commissioner did when he reached Tripoli was to publish the statement quoted on pages 126–27, in which he expressed his desire to "learn your views and hear your suggestions," emphasizing that "my door will be open to you, and your visits and proposals will be welcome." [44]

Mindful of warnings received before his departure from New York from some of the Libyan representatives, as well as from the Administering Powers, he had been careful to include in his message the phrase, which soon proved to be a very necessary counterpoint to the main theme of his mission: "It is not my function to govern your territory; that remains within the competence of the Administering Powers until you assume it for yourselves." [45]

So almost uninterruptedly from 19 January until 7 February 1950, and again from 17 March until 28 March, using the United Nations plane as an air taxi, the Commissioner interviewed leaders of all parties and minority groups as well as large numbers of private individuals, including leaders of

44. First *Annual Report of the United Nations Commissioner in Libya,* Annex I, p. 39.

45. Ibid.

the three principal faiths, Islamic, Roman Catholic, and Jewish, all over the country. Some of these interviews lasted for several hours. They generally followed a uniform pattern. The Commissioner was accompanied by a few of his staff, all of whom, including the interpreters, were bound by their oath of loyalty to the United Nations, based on Article 100 of the Charter.[46] Discussions were informal—conversations rather than interrogations. Coffee, tea, or nonalcoholic drinks were served, and as that winter was, exceptionally, a cold one, the discussions were generally held cosily around an electric fire, power supply permitting.

During the Commissioner's brief, though frequent, absences from Libya, members of his staff maintained these and other contacts. All in all several hundred individuals were thus given an opportunity of making their views known. Many more were heard in the course of mass meetings, especially in rural areas.

It soon became clear that even among party heads and leading notables, with the exception of those few who had attended the General Assembly debates, there was a good deal of ignorance and misunderstanding about the content of Resolution 289 (IV). As a result of inadequate press and wireless communications and the limited circulation of local newspapers, hardly anyone seemed to have a full and accurate Arabic translation of the Resolution; and the few who did often misunderstood some of its provisions. Admittedly, certain of its parts did leave a great deal to the interpretation placed on them by those who had to work with the Resolution, but its main features were clear enough. Two remedies were immediately applied. First, copies of an Arabic translation of the Resolution were distributed to all visitors, party secretariats, and newspapers, and the text was broadcast over the local British and American (military) networks. Second, the Commissioner and his colleagues made it a rule to open each interview with an explanation of the Resolution, its purpose, and the machinery provided for its implementation during the transitional period (1950 and 1951).

For some time, two major misunderstandings bedeviled efforts to arrive at mutual understanding between the Mission and its visitors, and it was April or May before the situation became clearer, at least to politically conscious Libyans. It was not, however, time wasted, for in the course of the conversations each side learned a great deal about the other's point of

46. Article 100, paragraph 1, of the United Nations Charter stipulates: "In the performance of their duties the Secretary-General and the staff shall not seek or receive instructions from any government or from any other authority external to the Organization. They shall refrain from any action which might reflect on their position as international officials responsible only to the Organization."

view. The meetings also provided members of the Mission with opportunities of becoming personally acquainted with virtually all Libya's leaders and notables as well as with many people in more modest walks of life.

The first and main cause of misunderstanding proved to be that many Libyans, obviously thinking wishfully, sincerely believed that the United Nations had already proclaimed the country's independence and that the Commissioner and the Council for Libya had come to take over from the Administering Powers until a Libyan Government could be established. These people impatiently asked exactly when the British and French "occupation authorities" would be leaving. Others were under the impression that the Commissioner, advised by the Council, had come to establish a kind of provisional government under whose control the British and French authorities would continue to administer the country until the proclamation of independence.

One result of this kind of misunderstanding was that the Commissioner's office was swamped with complaints against the Administering Powers, most of a purely personal and minor nature, but some alleging serious misconduct in public affairs going back for years. Considering that the Commissioner's duties were merely advisory, and that the Administering Powers were, subject to certain limitations, responsible for the government of the territories, the Mission could only adopt a policy of merely acknowledging minor and personal complaints, explaining that they lay outside its competence. In a few cases, however, of complaints which seemed prima facie to have a bearing on the exercise of his duties, the Commissioner, invoking subparagraph 10 (b) of Resolution 289 (IV), asked the administrations involved for information, sometimes suggesting that an inquiry into the facts might prove mutually useful. As a result, a few misunderstandings or points of friction between the Administrations and individuals or political parties were quietly cleared up. At the same time, relations between the Mission and the local representatives of the Administering Powers, which at the outset had been slightly uncomfortable, steadily improved, despite the fact that each had its point of view to defend.

Fortunately, the Mission also had visitors more concerned with the future than with the present or the past. One result was that another kind of misunderstanding came to light. People asked: "Mr. Commissioner, what kind of a constitution are you going to give us?" Generally, this question was followed by firm demands for some kind of a united Libya, although what was meant by "united" varied greatly from one visitor to the next, and quite markedly from territory to territory. In other cases, people came with very pertinent suggestions, and some even submitted ideas for a constitution. One Tripolitanian party leader complained that he had actually prepared a draft of a highly democratic constitution, but that the police, when searching his office after a somewhat unruly incident, had unfortunately confiscated the only copy. Another time, the Sheikh of an important Cyrenaican tribe came to ask for a detailed explanation of the difference in executive powers between the President of the United States of America and the President of the Swiss Confederation. Having listened very attentively, he expressed the opinion that Libya should become a confederation like Switzerland, with the Amir of Cyrenaica as King, exercising powers at least equal to those of the occupant of the White House. Subsequently, he was proudly surprised to discover that he had been something of a prophet. In the Fezzan, discussions were often on a more practical plane, bearing on such matters as who would be responsible in the new State for water supply, taxes, education, and protection against nomadic incursions against the sedentary population of the oases.

As the white DC-3 with its United Nations markings carried him from territory to territory over hundreds of miles of empty desert, the Commissioner observed that, apart from the recognition of a national leader, the issue that loomed largest was the choice between a federal and a unitary State. In this connection, it frequently proved most difficult for Libyans to understand how a State regarded as a single entity in international law could be organized internally on the basis of federated, autonomous parts. To the Arab way of thinking, with its centuries-old concept of an Islamic community inspired by the common religion and language of the Koran rather than by geographic or racial considerations, unity and federation were hardly reconcilable. To conceive of such a reconciliation was particularly difficult for Libyans, who in their political and social thinking were slow to reach the stage of balancing their manifold local loyalties against the broader attachments inherent in national loyalty.

Illustrative of this sort of political schizophrenia were the ideas of those who, although ardent advocates of a united and even unitary Libya, were nevertheless thinking primarily in terms of three territories which would first achieve independence separately, merging only later to form a single Libyan State. Apparently they could not see that the end result might be a far less united State than one initially organized as a federation.[47] The more far-sighted leaders did not fall into this mental confusion, which in any case gradually clarified into a more clear-cut vision. Before the first six months of 1950 were out, the leaders were roughly divided into federalists and antifederalists, with the latter strongest in Tripolitania and the former dominating in Cyrenaica and the Fezzan.

In April, however, when the Council for Libya was due to hold its first session, public opinion had not yet reached that stage of self-clarification.

47. This contradictory attitude naturally suited the Administering Powers in their policy of encouraging local autonomy as a foundation for a future Libyan federation.

A review of the records of three months of continuous consultation (from mid-January until mid-April) shows that almost all the talks focused on three categories of topic:

1. Local problems of various kinds;
2. The form of the future State and its national government, including its leaders. Given the existence, since the previous summer, of a semi-autonomous local government in Cyrenaica and of persistent rumors that the British and French Governments were planning to set up similar governments in Tripolitania and the Fezzan, these problems could not be dealt with apart; and
3. The appointment by the Commissioner of one representative of the people from each of the three territories, and of one representative of the minorities in Libya, to the Council for Libya.

Paragraph 7 of Resolution 289 (IV) instructed the Commissioner, before making these appointments, to consult with the Administering Powers, the representatives of the six non-Libyan Governments on the Council, and leading personalities and representatives of political parties and organizations in the territories concerned.

In order to protect himself against a possible charge of favoring a particular group or individual, the Commissioner requested all parties, organizations, and leading personalities he had consulted in each of the three territories to reach agreement among themselves on one single candidate by 15 March 1950. Except in the Fezzan, where the candidate was elected, developments indicated that he had overrated the people's capacity to reach agreement on one representative person. In Tripolitania in particular, mutual consultation as a means of agreeing on the choice of representatives and leaders proved to be a difficult process which was not eased by reluctance to solve the problem by way of election. In Cyrenaica, the problem was bypassed by the Amir's presenting to the Commissioner a list of eight personalities, varying in background and qualifications, from whom he was invited to make his own choice.

Most difficult of all was the designation of a common candidate to represent the four minorities. Admittedly, the procedures for consultation laid down in the Resolution were not very helpful in this particular case. It was no secret in Libya that the principle of minority representation had been inserted in the Resolution under pressure from Latin American delegations in support of Libya's Italian minority, whose situation was manifestly a delicate one. No less delicate, though for different reasons, was that of the Jewish community. The Maltese and Greek communities, which had been treated by Italy as enemy aliens during World War II, had suffered therefrom, and the representation of their interests raised some special issues. No mention was made, on the other hand, not even by the minority itself, of the Berber people in the Jebel Nefusa and along the Tunisian frontier, most of whom had identified themselves with the Arab-Libyan cause for religious reasons, and as the outcome of centuries of coexistence. From the debates in the committees and sub-committees at the Fourth Session of the General Assembly, it was clear that those concerned about the position of the minorities in Libya had had in mind the Italians, Jews, Maltese, and Greeks alone. However, nowhere in the Resolution were any of these minorities mentioned by name, nor was the meaning of the term "minority" defined. The situation was further complicated by the fact that several Arab delegations had been unsympathetic, if not hostile, to the inclusion of the minority clause, and had given way only to secure Latin American support for the overriding principle of Libyan independence (see also Chapters 2 and 4, p. 94 and pp. 335–50).

An added complication arose from internal divisions within the Italian minority group, which was organized in four associations, parties, and fronts, along political, religious, and economic lines. Early in the deliberations, the Commissioner, after consulting the Administering Powers, had advised the Jews, Greeks, and Maltese to accept an Italian as their common representative. After some hesitation, they had agreed to do so. The problem of choosing one representative for all four minorities therefore consisted in making the Italian groups agree on one person jointly acceptable to the minorities themselves and to the Arabs, particularly those in Tripolitania. If the minority representative on the Council for Libya, whose position would be awkward at best, were to be able effectively to defend and promote minority interests in constitutional and other matters, he would have to enjoy the confidence of his colleagues, particularly that of the three Libyan members of the Council. Fortunately, the Tripolitanians in particular proved in the long run—for political reasons—to be rather more tolerant than the minorities had expected. In Cyrenaica and the Fezzan anti-Italian feeling was much stronger.

The findings of the United Nations Mission in the consultations it carried out throughout Libya can be summarized by territory and topic as follows:

A. MISSION INTERVIEWS IN TRIPOLITANIA

The Mission consulted the National Congress Party; the Liberal Party; the Free National Bloc (Kutla Party); the Egypto-Tripolitanian Union; the Libyan Labor Party; and the Independence Party.[48]

48. The principal spokesmen for these parties in the course of the hearings were: Beshir Bey Saadawi, his Egyptian adviser, Fuad Shukri, and Mustafa Mizran for the Congress Party; Sadok Zaraa for the Liberal Party; Ali al-Faqih Hassan for the Free National Bloc; Ali Rajab for the Egypto-Tripolitanian Union; Beshir Hamza for the

Neither the British Administration nor the Mission itself was ever able to arrive at a reliable estimate of the importance of these parties in terms of their numerical membership or political influence. Neither had the Four Power Commission of Investigation for the Former Italian Colonies fared any better. Some consisted of not much more than a leader, supported by some personal friends.[49] After having observed the scene for some time, however, the Commissioner, and later the Council for Libya, agreed that the National Congress Party was by far the most influential, even though its numerical strength was impossible to evaluate, particularly in the rural areas. As for the leaders of the parties, most were intelligent men; but they varied considerably in breadth of political outlook and in experience. In the latter respect, the National Congress Party leader, Beshir Bey Saadawi, proved unquestionably the most able.

In the course of endless consultations, the leaders, as they came to understand better the machinery of Resolution 289 (IV) and the kind of decisions they would be called upon to make during the next two years, adjusted their positions to this new realization; this helped to clarify the situation.

1. Opinions on the Form of Government

a. The National Congress Party was at the outset in favor of a unified Libya, declaring itself hostile to any form of regional government. One of its arguments was that Cyrenaica and the Fezzan, being poor areas, would be dependent on the more prosperous and more highly developed Tripolitania, which therefore should play the leading part. Later, particularly because of the existing semiautonomous local government in Cyrenaica, the Party came round to considering the possibility of setting up similar local governments in the other two territories, provided that their powers were purely administrative and that they were sanctioned and proclaimed by the Amir of Cyrenaica. Because the Party saw in His Highness the only possible Head of State, it objected to any enhancement of his status in Cyrenaica that might serve the Administering Powers as a precedent for setting up local governments in Tripolitania and the Fezzan, thereby endangering the unity of the future Libyan State.

With regard to the Commissioner's plans for the establishment of an elected committee to prepare the organization of the National Assembly,

---

Libyan Labor Party; and Selim Muntasir, Ahmed Rasim Ku'bar, Abdulla Sharif, and Sheikhs Ahmed Gurza Mizda, Sinni al-Omar Zintan, and Hamida Bin Amor Mizda for the Independence Party.

49. Four Power Commission *Report,* Volume III, Part Two, *Tripolitania,* pp. 9–17.

Beshir Bey Saadawi gave his agreement to this proposal and authorized the Commissioner so to inform the Amir. As to whether representation on the preparatory committee should be equal for each territory, or proportional to its population, Beshir Bey said he would have to consult his Party before he could give an answer.

b. The Independence Party also was against the institution of other local governments. Its leaders felt that the Libyan people should express themselves on the form of government, and especially as to whether Libya should be a monarchy or a republic, through the National Assembly. If the majority preferred a monarchy, the Party felt that the head of Sanusiya would be best capable of uniting nationalists in all three territories; but even then a decision would have to be made as to whether the Amir should be proclaimed king on a personal basis or called to the throne as the head of a Senussi dynasty. The Party agreed to the establishment of a preparatory committee—which it would like to see elected—to lay the foundations for a National Assembly.

c. The Liberal Party was for a united Libya and against the institution of local governments, arguing that the latter would always have a tendency to favor local interests, thus endangering the formation of a united State. It expressed confidence in the Amir of Cyrenaica as future national leader but had not the same degree of confidence in Ahmed Bey Seif al-Nasr as local leader in the Fezzan.

d. The Free National Bloc leaders had prepared an outline of a democratic and republican constitution providing for a united Libya. They advocated the suppression of the existing local government in Cyrenaica and called for the immediate institution of a provisional government for the whole of Libya. Favoring a republic, which would entail the election of a President, the Party expressed fears that the Cyrenaicans might try to impose the head of the Senussi family on the rest of the country.

e. The Egypto-Tripolitanian Union was in favor of union between an independent Libya and the Kingdom of Egypt, federated on an equal footing. It had, moreover, drawn up a reform program, calling mainly for such advances as the Libyanization of the civil service, the adoption of Arabic as the official language, and the repeal of laws discriminating against the Arabs, dating from the time of the Italian occupation.

f. The Libyan Labor Party was strongly in favor of a united Libya and of membership in the Arab League, but felt that the interests of labor, which it complained were suffering from unemployment and low wages, ought to be regarded as more urgent than the question of the form of government. It criticized the National Congress Party as being primarily a party of government officials supported by the British Administration, asserting that it was preoccupied with political issues to the exclusion of economic and social problems.

2. Selection of the Tripolitanian Representative on the Council for Libya

In view of the terms of paragraph 7 of Resolution 289 (IV) the Commissioner systematically brought up in the course of each consultation the selection of the Tripolitanian member of the Council for Libya. In the absence of central leadership, and given the multiplicity of competing parties, this proved to be a particularly ticklish matter.

a. The National Congress Party took the view that, as it represented practically the whole of the Tripolitanian people, although it was prepared to consult the other parties, its own candidate should be accepted as the sole nominee for the territory; this claim was naturally firmly rejected by the other parties.

b. The Independence Party agreed that representation of the whole of Tripolitania by one person was by far the best method, but found it difficult to suggest a method of consultation among the parties to designate this individual.

c. The Liberal Party recommended that the territorial candidate be elected in such a way that the person supported by the largest number of *parties* became the nominee.

d. The Free National Bloc did not believe that interparty consultations would be useful, preferring to nominate its own candidate for the Commissioner's approval.

e. The Egypto-Tripolitanian Union, through its President, also agreed to a single candidate commanding the widest possible backing. Because he feared that if left to their own devices the parties would be unable to reach agreement, the President suggested that each should nominate three candidates to provide a list of fifteen to eighteen names from which party members would vote for the candidate of their choice.

f. The Libyan Labor Party had no interest in this aspect.

In the face of so much divided counsel, the Commissioner, who had originally asked for the name of a single candidate by 15 March, was obliged to extend the time limit to 28 March. Meanwhile he was frequently asked for advice; but he felt strongly that if the Tripolitanian member of the Council was to enjoy the confidence of his countrymen, he would have to be selected by the Tripolitanians with a minimum of assistance from himself.

Finally, at the eleventh hour, the names of seven candidates were submitted, among them Mustafa Mizran, one of the Vice-Presidents of the National Congress Party, and President of the Nationalist Party, affiliated to the former, who enjoyed so much support as to make the Commissioner's choice relatively simple.

It was alleged by the leaders of the other parties that the support for Mizran had been generated by British pressure on the people. It was true that the British Administration had a preference, to which it was entitled, since the Resolution gave it the right to be consulted, but a discreet investigation by the Mission staff revealed that members of the Administration had indeed campaigned for the chosen candidate, apparently with the tacit consent of their superiors. However, there was no proof of pressure having been exerted. Ironically, once appointed, Mizran turned out to be anything but a mouthpiece for British views.

3. Selection of the Representative of the Minorities

As already stated, the selection of one man to represent all four minorities proved the toughest nut to crack. In the light of the reasons for which the General Assembly had introduced the principle of minority representation into its resolution, it seemed politically plausible for the minorities to propose an Italian, all the more so as the Italian minority, being by far the largest and economically strongest of the four, was in the best position to defend the material interests as well as the cultural and spiritual institutions of the other three. On the other hand, it could be argued against an Italian candidate that he would be looked upon as representing the former colonial Power, whereas it was in the interest of the minorities that their representative stand in good favor with the three Libyan members of the Council. This consideration notwithstanding, the Greeks, the Jews, and the Maltese were prepared to agree to an Italian candidate provided that the conditions mentioned on pages 178–79 were met. These, however, proved to be a major stumbling block, as the Italian community was deeply divided into four associations and groups: the Democratic League; the Political Association for the Progress of Libya (which included some Moslem members); Catholic Action; and the Economic Front (which also numbered Moslems among its members). When the consultations came to an end, they disclosed the following positions:

a. The Jewish community was ready to cooperate in the selection of an Italian as the minority nominee provided he commanded substantial Arab support. For its own part, the Jewish community insisted that the future Libyan State must guarantee the security of every inhabitant's life and property.

b. The Maltese community was ready to cooperate with the future Arab authority in Libya, but feared that its interests might not always be adequately defended in the Council if the minority representative were an

Italian. It therefore suggested that the representative be supported by an advisory body on which all four minorities would be represented; if this condition was fulfilled, the Maltese community would agree to an Italian.

c. The Italian groups. Representatives of these groups were consulted jointly, as it was clear that separate consultations would only have aggravated their internal schisms. The Commissioner insisted that the candidate chosen should formally and publicly declare in a letter addressed to him that if designated he would consider himself as jointly representing all four minorities, and also that he would pledge himself to cooperate with the other members of the Council in favor of the implementation of the United Nations resolution establishing a united, independent, and sovereign Libyan State. At this juncture, the question was raised whether "minority" should be defined by religion or by nationality.

Having foreseen that this issue might arise, the Commissioner had sought the opinion of the Office of Legal Affairs at United Nations Headquarters. The Office pointed out that "nationality" as such did not enter into the definition of the term "minority" as unanimously adopted by the United Nations Sub-Commission on Prevention of Discrimination and Protection of Minorities at its Third Session, held from 9 to 27 January 1950. That definition, in part, read:

> (a) . . . The term minority includes only those non-dominant groups in a population which possess and wish to preserve stable ethnic, religious or linguistic traditions or characteristics markedly different from those of the rest of the population;
>
> (b) Such minorities should properly include a number of persons sufficient by themselves to develop such characteristics; [50]

This quantitative standard, the Office of Legal Affairs averred, could only be applied in the light of a particular situation, it being impossible legalistically to suggest any more specific criterion.

d. The Mufti of Tripolitania advised against selection of an Italian.

e. The Independence Party, believing that the largest minority should guide the Commissioner's choice, was not against the appointment of an Italian, though not blind to the objections that might be raised, principally that Italy would then in effect have two seats on the Council.

f. The National Congress Party at first refused to consider the Italians as a minority at all; subsequently it declared that an Italian Jew might be an acceptable candidate. Later still, it accepted a non-Jewish Italian.

50. United Nations, Economic and Social Council Official Records (ESCOR): Eleventh Session, 1950, Commission on Human Rights Report, Supplement No. 5 (E/1681), p. 10, fn. 9.

g. The Secretary of the Tarhuna branch of the *Independence Party,* accompanied by the Party's Secretary-General, came to declare for himself that, although the Party's members had fought the Italians bitterly during the war, that was now a thing of the past. The Party felt that, in view of the adoption by the General Assembly of the resolution on Libyan independence, the Libyans should recognize the fruit of Italian labor in the country and look upon the Italians not as enemies but as fellow citizens with whom they should join in the task of building the country's future. These notables emphasized that such a friendly attitude toward the Italian minority would be patent proof of the Libyans' capacity to assume the responsibilities of independence.

h. A delegation representing the *Greek, Jewish, and Maltese minorities,* that had in the meantime been in consultation with the various Italian groups, reported their conclusion that the internal dissension among the Italian community had so far proved the main obstacle to their own proposal of an Italian candidate. They had agreed on two names, but while the Libyans objected to only one, the Italians could not agree to either.

To escape from this impasse, they suggested that there be two minority representatives on the Council for Libya, one for the Italians, and a second for the other three minorities. The wording of the Resolution, however, precluded any such solution. At last, on 18 March, after having proposed, and then dropped, an Italian gentleman farmer of progressive tendencies, the three minorities agreed on an Italian candidate, Aurelio Finzi, a judge known for his integrity, who belonged to no political party and was First President of the Tripolitanian Court of Appeal. However, as such he was ex officio a servant of the Italian Government.[51] Finzi's nomination was acceptable to the large majority of the Italian community, but not to its left wing, which put forward the name of Giacomo Marchino, the same candidate who had in the first instance been suggested by the three smaller minorities. When, however, the National Congress Party privately expressed a preference for Marchino, who had long experience of local affairs and with whom they felt they could cooperate more effectively, Finzi's chances became doubtful, and the three non-Italian minorities withdrew his candidature. On the other hand, the Italian right wing objected strongly to the left-wing candidate. The British Administration had no preference. It was now late in March, and when, notwithstanding feverish last-minute attempts, no agreement could be reached, all groups reverted to their original

51. In early 1950, the British Administration in Tripolitania still employed about 1,000 Italian officials, who received salaries from the Italian Government equivalent to those paid to officials of equal rank in Italy, as well as an allowance from the British Administration.

positions. The Commissioner thereupon received the names of ten candidates, of whom Finzi had numerically the strongest support. The Commissioner's personal preference was for Marchino, since he seemed to offer the best hope of promoting good relations between the minorities and the Arabs. However, it did not seem entirely fair—and might later have undesirable repercussions in the General Assembly—to appoint as minority representative a man acceptable to the Arabs by rejecting a candidate originally proposed unanimously by the three non-Italian minorities, and one who, moreover, had the support of the large majority of the Italian community itself. The Commissioner therefore decided, albeit reluctantly, to recommend Aurelio Finzi as his candidate for the appointment.

B. MISSION INTERVIEWS IN CYRENAICA

The situation in Cyrenaica was a good deal simpler than in Tripolitania, if only because there was a recognized leader and only two political parties, the National Congress Party of Cyrenaica, representing primarily the rural areas but also the more conservative elements in the towns, and the National Association of Cyrenaica, better known as the Omar Mukhtar Club (see pp. 44–45), both of which the Mission consulted. A third association, the National Youth League, the members of which were mostly young men who supported the more conservative elements in the local government, had become practically inactive by the time of the Commissioner's visit to Benghazi.

1. Opinions on the Form of Government

The constitutional position in Cyrenaica, being much more clearly defined than that in Tripolitania or the Fezzan, in effect complicated the overall Libyan constitutional problem, as became clear from the moment the Commissioner met the members of the Cyrenaican Government.

a. The Prime Minister of Cyrenaica, Omar Mansur al-Kikhia, an elder statesman, stressed that the existence of a Cyrenaican Government was an established fact, and would have to be taken into account in any plans for the creation of a unified Libyan State. While declaring that his Government was wholeheartedly in favor of the principle of Libyan unity, he reminded the Commissioner that Cyrenaica had already been an autonomous province under the Sublime Porte. Moreover, it had earned its right to autonomy by the struggle its people had kept up against the Italian invaders and by the loyal assistance it had given to the Allies during World War II. He also recalled Eden's statement in the House of Commons on 8 January 1942; the announcement on 1 June 1949, by His Highness the Amir, of Cyrenaica's desire for independence; and the Transitional Powers Proclamation (No. 187) issued by the British Chief Administrator on 16 September 1949. Under the Constitution promulgated by the Amir on 18 September, the Assembly of Representatives was to be elected in a few months, at which time the Executive Committee of the National Congress Party of Cyrenaica, which functioned as a kind of advisory body to the Head of State, would be dissolved.

b. His Highness the Amir shortly afterward told the Commissioner, as the latter already knew, that he very much wanted to secure the transfer of the reserved powers still in British hands, in order to achieve complete independence for his territory.

This put the Commissioner in a difficult situation, already described in detail in Part 2 of this chapter. At his first audience, he had confined himself to listening and to tirelessly repeating his interpretation of the Resolution's basic stipulations, namely: "That Libya, comprising Cyrenaica, Tripolitania, and the Fezzan, shall be constituted an independent and sovereign State"; and "That a constitution for Libya, including the form of government, shall be determined by representatives of the inhabitants of Cyrenaica, Tripolitania and the Fezzan meeting and consulting in a National Assembly."

c. The Omar Mukhtar Club. In this connection, the views of the younger generation as represented by the Omar Mukhtar Club were interesting. With the arrival of the United Nations Mission in Libya, the Club had asked permission, on 14 January 1950, to form a new political organization under the name "The National Association" (see p. 44). More receptive to Tripolitanian appeals for union than were the older Cyrenaicans, the members of the Club formed a kind of avant-garde of Libyan unity. This widened the gap between it and both the older group and the British Administration.

When the Commissioner met representatives of the Club in Benghazi, they expressed the opinion that the unity of Libya would present no problem had not the British and French Governments "artificially" created local autonomous governmental institutions to serve their colonial ambitions. The Club was in favor of a united Libya under the Senussi Crown, and although it believed that the Amir was under severe pressure from outside (meaning the United Kingdom), its complete confidence in him was not thereby impaired. As to the existing local government, the spokesmen alleged that it was persecuting the National Association, and that, if there was a certain estrangement between the Association and the Amir, it was due mainly to the "undemocratic" National Congress Party of Cyrenaica, whose Executive Committee advised His Highness.

In the course of the Commissioner's meeting with the Derna branch of the Club, the spokesmen of this group declared that while the National Congress Party gave Cyrenaica priority in the matter of independence, both branches of the Omar Mukhtar Club considered Libyan unity paramount. On that fundamental issue, the two sections were one.

2. Selection of the Cyrenaican Representative on the Council for Libya

On this pressing matter, the Cyrenaican Prime Minister expressed the view that it would suffice for the Amir to designate one man, chosen from a list of names put before him by the Cabinet, for the Commissioner's approval. The Commissioner was obliged to point out that paragraph 7 of Resolution 289 (IV) made it mandatory upon him to hold far wider consultations, and he had no option but to do so.

a. National Congress Party members who were consulted expressed views similar to that of the Prime Minister.

b. The Omar Mukhtar Club (National Association) suggested that the Cyrenaican member of the Council be chosen from among those who had already represented the territory at the Fourth Session of the General Assembly of the United Nations; the Amir needed simply to choose one of them.

c. The Omar Mukhtar Club (Derna branch) had no particular ideas as to how the territorial representative should be chosen. The Commissioner therefore suggested that the two branches of the Club should consult one another, after which he would ask the Amir to receive a joint delegation from them to discuss the matter.

In the outcome, a list of eight names was submitted to the Commissioner by the Amir. Some of the men on this list had been proposed by the National Congress of Cyrenaica, others by the National Association. Further scrutiny revealed that one candidate, Ali Assad al-Jerbi, Minister of Public Works and Communications in the Cyrenaican Government, enjoyed the confidence of both parties as well as that of the Amir and the British Administration. The Commissioner accordingly duly recommended that he be appointed.

3. Selection of the Representative of the Minorities

Cyrenaica having no minorities—all the Italian settlers were evacuated with the German and Italian troops when the latter withdrew from the country—no interest was shown in the selection of a minority representative in the Council for Libya. However, the unanimous feeling was that he should not be of Italian nationality.

C. MISSION INTERVIEWS IN THE FEZZAN

In many respects the situation in the Fezzan differed entirely from that in Tripolitania or Cyrenaica. The territory was less progressive, it was poorer, and in 1950 the population did not exceed 50,000.

In these circumstances, one would not expect to find organized political parties, yet the Fezzanese were not devoid of political consciousness. Matters of common interest were settled by a village council of sheikhs and heads of families meeting together as a *jemaa,* which had some executive authority.[52] Thus the hearings conducted in five different parts of the Fezzan between 29 January and 4 February 1950 differed in form from those held in Cyrenaica and Tripolitania. On arrival at the principal village of an oasis, the Commissioner and his staff were received by the chief *mudir* (district commissioner) who, after an initial exchange of courtesies, would call in his colleagues, the mudirs of neighboring districts, and, finally, various groups of local elders. On a few occasions the elders asked for permission to talk to the Commissioner in the absence of the mudir, obviously in order that they might speak more freely. In such cases, the mudir at once withdrew. In one oasis a French Army lieutenant was present in the local school where the hearing took place, but left when one of the notables present asked him to do so.

52. The *jemaa* is a political institution which has existed throughout Berber territory since time immemorial. It is constituted by a meeting of all the heads of family and notables and is a real assembly of the people. The jemaa has supreme power, which it does not delegate. It is not only a legislative body, but also an executive and sometimes a judicial organ. It is based upon the principle that the people should make and carry out decisions themselves. Under the Italian regime, the jemaa was replaced by a system of *mudirs* (district commissioners); but, when they arrived, the French took care to restore to the jemaa its important role. The following description of the way in which the jemaa, which elected the *Chef du Territoire,* was organized illustrates how the grand jemaa functions. First, the notables and heads of family from each *mudiriyya* (administrative district) selected three men to represent the mudiriyya at the jemaa. In all, fifty-eight such representatives were appointed. (The author is aware that fifty-eight is not divisible by three, but it is the figure given in all the official documentation he has consulted. He has been unable to find any explanation of the discrepancy.) The fifty-eight then assembled at Sabhah, where they proceeded to elect Ahmed Bey Seif al-Nasr, and subsequently, on 15 March, the Fezzanese representative on the Council for Libya. Of the three men chosen in each district, one represented the tribe, one the local (rural) jemaa, and the third the population of the towns. Lastly, it may be added that any person in the Fezzan who owns a house, however small, or a few palm trees or similar property, is looked upon as a notable. Honesty and integrity, rather than notability in the strict sense, were the qualities for which his fellows chose their representative.

1. Opinions on the Form of Government

a. Murzuq, a market township, was the venue for the first hearing. The chief mudir, Hajj Ahmed al-Senussi Sofu, who was later elected first Fezzanese member of the Council for Libya, began by avowing that he had never heard of the United Nations or of its resolution on Libya. This somewhat startling statement prompted the Commissioner to ask the French Military Governor to send a circular to all the villages explaining briefly, but simply and clearly, what the United Nations had recommended for Libya in Resolution 289 (IV), the Commissioner's role, the purpose of his visit, and the need for the Fezzan to designate its representative on the Council for Libya. By way of precaution, the following two paragraphs were added by agreement between Colonel Sarazac and the Commissioner:

> Il est bien entendu que le délégué du Fezzan au Conseil Consultatif n'aura pas pour tâche de gouverner le Fezzan; son rôle sera uniquement de conseiller le Commissaire sur les intérêts et les vœux des Fezzanais et ceci pour l'aider à préparer la Libye pour l'Indépendance avant le premier janvier 1952.
>
> Il est également entendu que jusqu'au moment ou la Libye devient un pays indépendant en 1952, le Fezzan continuera à être administré par la France.[53]

Meanwhile, the mudir described at length the duties of his own office, reminding the Commissioner that under Turkish rule the Fezzan had always enjoyed a large measure of autonomy, with the Seif al-Nasr family playing a leading role for generations. The other mudirs then joined in the conversation and were asked whether they believed the territory was in a position to exercise not only administrative but also economic autonomy. They conceded that such articles as sugar, tea, fats, textiles, and agricultural implements had to be imported, but maintained that what the Fezzan needed above all was security, which one termed "half its very life," and in the second place schools where Arabic would be taught.

Before leaving, the Commissioner stressed the need for the Fezzanese to cooperate with the French authorities pending the proclamation of independence.

53. The above quotation is taken from a typescript copy of the original French version of the circular as agreed upon by the writer and Colonel Sarazac. This copy is now in the United Nations Archives. The Arabic translation was presumably circulated under the letterhead of the French Administration in the Fezzan. The writer has been unable to locate a copy to elucidate this point.

Later it was reported to him that at the public reading of the circular the people had joyfully shouted "Long live unity! Long live Tripolitania! Long live Sayed Idris!" According to the French authorities present, the people had misinterpreted the sense of the United Nations Resolution and had shouted "The French will leave the country!" and other slogans, which had given the demonstration a "pro-Tripolitanian" character. Order, they said, had been easily restored.

b. Gorda, in the oasis of Sabhah, was the scene of the next hearing, in the course of which the following conversation took place:

> *Commissioner*: The Tripolitanians consider the Fezzan to be part of Tripolitania. But according to the General Assembly resolution the Fezzan is a separate territory. Have you a preference for one or the other of these ideas?
>
> *The mudir*: In the past the Fezzan and Tripolitania were one. The administering authorities made a separate territory of it under the aegis of Ahmed Bey Seif al-Nasr.
>
> *A notable*: We are Moslems. We want to be attached to a Moslem country and to other Arab countries.
>
> *Commissioner*: The resolution envisages, without going into any detail, the constitution of an independent and sovereign Libya. What would you prefer, a unitary form of government or a federal state consisting of three local governments?
>
> *Several notables*: The Fezzan, poor in resources and men, ought not to have a government of its own. We seek the union of the Fezzan and Tripolitania within a unified Libya.[54]

c. Jadid, although a village which formed part of the oasis of Sabhah and was therefore close to the headquarters of the French Administration, proved in the course of the Commissioner's meeting with a large group of its notables to be, politically speaking, a case apart. A large part of the people, though not all, appeared to be in a state of chronic opposition to the French as well as to Ahmed Bey Seif al-Nasr; they were led by a notable named Sheikh 'Abd al-Rahman Bin Mohamed al-Barquli. The Sheikh declared that the Fezzanese aspired to a unified Libya comprising

54. This quotation is a translation (from French) of a passage from the minutes of the hearing held at Gorda on 31 January 1950. Such minutes were compiled after every hearing (there were fifty-four in all) by a member of the Commissioner's staff. They exist only in typescript in the United Nations Archives, because there never was any need to make formal United Nations documents of them. On the other hand, there can be nothing confidential about their contents, as all the hearings were conducted in the semipublic fashion mentioned at the beginning of this part of Chapter 2.

all three territories.[55] The Commissioner stressed that if a united and independent country was to be brought into being, it was incumbent upon all Libyans, including the Fezzanese, to reach agreement among themselves, to which those present unanimously assented.

d. Brach, an oasis and the principal center of the Shatti depression, inhabited by almost one-third—17,000—of the population of the Fezzan, was the fourth center in which hearings were held. Opinions there proved to be almost the converse of those expressed in other parts of the Fezzan. The mudir started by declaring that the Fezzan was so weak and so poor that it could only survive under the protection of a foreign flag. Independence was unthinkable, because in the absence of a strong and well-organized central authority, the Fezzan would be wide open to anarchy. The Commissioner explained in reply that the three territories were to become the independent State of Libya, and that a State assumed responsibility for the security and well-being of its people. He asked whether there was reason to doubt that such would be the case under the Libyan flag. The mudir replied that, without foreign protection, there could be no security in the Fezzan because the Fezzanese were incapable of governing themselves.

Another mudir added that the Fezzan could not exist for a single day

55. Toward the end of December 1950, the Commissioner received a copy of a petition, which read as follows:

> Thanks to God—
>
> We, all the members of the Alhadiri family and others living in Sabhah al-Jadid, declare the following:
>
> We had been asked to agree to the election of *Ahmed Bey Seif al-Nasr* as Chief of the territory of the Fezzan, but we refused and did not sign the declaration made by the inhabitants of the Fezzan. Now we expressly declare that we have *given up our previous opposition* and that we have become subject to his leadership and amirate. We are confident that he will forgive us and pardon us especially after this recognition, because he is a *generous* man.
>
> We are therefore submitting to Ahmed Bey this petition and we hope it will meet with his approval.
>
> (Signed) HAMID BIN AHMED aL-HADIRI
> SALEM BIN'ABD aL-RAHMAN OTHMAN aL-HADIRI
> MOHAMED BIN MOHAMED aL-BESHIR aL-HADIRI
> 'ABD AL-RAHMAN MOHAMED aL-BARQULI
> SALEH BIN BESHIR SHIBL
> AL-TAYED BIN MAHFUZ aL-HADIRI
> SALEM BIN HASAN aL-HADIRI
> AHMED BU SALEH aL-ZEYN
>
> 3 December 1950"

This, and other indications, seemed to show that the elements formerly in opposition were becoming reconciled with one another, and that French policy, too, was softening up.

without the protection of a foreign government, that Tripolitania was too far away to serve the purpose, and that the population would prefer the French to stay.

At this point, the Commissioner asked the mudir to bring in the notables who had been waiting outside and inform them of the preceding discussion. One of the notables, an old man, made substantially the same observations as the mudir, explaining that in the past the Fezzan had only too often suffered from nomad raids and from changes in the administration; the security which prevailed at present was too precious to risk yet another change. The French, he asserted, had asked his people whether they would like to have their independence, but they had said "No!" For him, the important thing was that the French Administration had made substantial efforts to improve economic conditions by making loans, parceling out land, and drilling wells, the water from which had made large tracts of land arable.

When the Commissioner asked how one could account for the difference between the views of the men of Brach and those expressed in other parts of the Fezzan, one of the notables repeated that the Fezzan was too poor to pay for an administrative apparatus of its own. According to him, during the three-day interval between the departure of the Italian forces and the arrival of the Free French under General Leclerc, Brach had suffered greatly from an incursion by brigands. In any event, the Fezzan would soon have its own government under Ahmed Bey Seif al-Nasr; moreover, the Fezzanese had promised the French not to deny their protection. From this and similar declarations it seemed that the local French Administration, through a certain show of force, had engineered a kind of unofficial referendum. The Commissioner therefore felt constrained to point out that, under the terms of the General Assembly Resolution, France had undertaken to cooperate in the establishment of an independent Libyan State, which would take in the Fezzan, within two years, and thereafter to leave the territory. A mudir prudently replied that the Fezzanese would wait to see what kind of constitution the new State adopted before deciding whether or not to join it.

During the afternoon the exchange of views continued, first with the notables in private, then with the mudirs present. One of the notables raised the question of taxation. At that time the people paid tax only on the harvest. He wanted to know whether the new State would impose other taxes. This was a matter on which the Commissioner was unable to reassure him, beyond expressing the view that aid to cover a territorial deficit in the Fezzan would obviously have to be provided, either by the Libyan State or by a foreign Government.

When asked by the Commissioner why the people of Brach were content to remain under Christian rule when they could join a Moslem community, one notable replied that it had been a Moslem country, Turkey, which had abandoned them within living memory, an act they had not forgotten.

e. Ghudamis was the site of the last of this series of hearings. The consultations there lasted two days. The Commissioner, having been warned that market outlets and caravan routes were two of the main concerns of the people of Ghudamis, brought the matter up first with the chief mudir, who explained that under Italian rule Ghudamis had been an administrative part of the Fezzan. Now it maintained economic and cultural links mainly with Tunis. The fruits of the harvest were consumed on the spot, and as far as imports were concerned, some came from Tripolitania and some from Tataouine in Tunisia.

With regard to the United Nations Resolution, the mudir expressed the opinion, apparently shared by many of his countrymen, that it meant the establishment of three local governments which would be subsequently brought together by a central Libyan government.

The Commissioner explained why this was not quite his understanding. At this stage, the notables who had been waiting outside were shown in, and the gist of the foregoing conversation was repeated for their benefit. They thereupon made it clear that, whereas in the past Ghudamis had been attached either to the Jebel Gharbi district or to Tripolitania direct, it had always considered itself a part of Libya.

The Commissioner took note of the express desire of the meeting to see that the oasis of Ghudamis was once more incorporated in Tripolitania. It was agreed, however, that for purposes of consultation during the coming months it would be more practical to continue to regard Ghudamis as part of the Fezzan.[56]

2. Selection of the Fezzanese Representative on the Council for Libya

During the Commissioner's visit to Murzuq it had been agreed that the mudirs, assisted by the notables, would initiate a large-scale consultation of public opinion on the traditional jemaa pattern (as explained in footnote 52), region by region, and that the candidate for the Fezzanese seat on the Council for Libya would be chosen by representatives of each region, meeting in Sabhah. It was also agreed that the consultations would have to be completed in four days' time. The mudirs claimed that the cooperation of the French authorities would be needed. Several of those present doubted whether a man could be found capable of serving as the territorial repre-

56. Ghudamis was handed over to the Libyan authorities immediately after the declaration of independence.

sentative. In their humble opinion, there were not many people in the Fezzan with the knowledge and experience required to deal with the matters on which the Council would have to advise the Commissioner. The latter explained that the candidate should simply be a man of sound common sense, known and respected in the territory and well enough informed to defend Fezzanese interests in the Council. Since France would have its own representative on the Council, the Fezzanese should, in his view, be careful to select one of their people capable of effectively presenting their views where these differed from those of the French Administration.

On the Commissioner's subsequent visits to the other oases mentioned above, this procedure was unanimously approved, although in Jadid and Ghudamis a few people voiced the fear that the French authorities might try to influence the voting. The Commissioner relayed these apprehensions to Colonel Sarazac and received assurances that no pressure would be brought to bear.

As we know (see p. 148), the representatives of each region of the Fezzan met in Sabhah as a territorial assembly on 12 February and unanimously elected Ahmed Bey Seif al-Nasr *Chef du Territoire*. Complaints were later received that he had been imposed by the French authorities. One petition, submitted by a group of Fezzanese living in Tripoli, declared: "We Libyans consider that this United Nations Resolution is a gift from the Lord, granting us life after more than thirty years of struggle. We, therefore, hold fast to it, and will never give it up, despite the policy advocated by France, which we would have said represents barbarism in the Twentieth Century, had it not been for the storming of the Bastille." [57] Similar but somewhat less sophisticated complaints were received from Jadid and Ghudamis, but none of them mentioned the name of any other candidate the petitioners might have preferred to Ahmed Bey.

On 14 March, the jemaa met at Ahmed Bey's residence in Gorda, where he gave his approval to its nomination of Hajj Ahmed al-Senussi Sofu, the chief mudir of Murzuq, as Fezzanese representative on the Council for Libya.[58]

Although the Commissioner later received petitions signed by 520 individuals supporting Sheikh 'Abd al-Rahman Bin Mohamed al-Barquli of Jadid, it became clear that, although Sofu had not commanded unanimous support, he had had the backing of the majority.

Ghat had taken no part in the election of the Chef du Territoire, or in

57. Petition bearing thirty-one signatures, dated Tripoli, 18 May 1950, addressed to the United Nations Commissioner in Libya. Typescript. Now in the United Nations Archives.

58. Hajj Sofu was obliged to resign shortly afterward for reasons of health.

that of the representative on the Council for Libya, because, according to the French authorities, the people of that area considered themselves French citizens. The Commissioner did indeed receive a petition signed by 161 sheikhs and notables from Ghat and its surroundings, dated 16 May 1950, declaring that they were Tuaregs and wished to remain under French rule. They also asked that their region be incorporated in French territory. The petition stated that their decision was unanimous, and had been reached freely, no pressure of any sort having been exerted on the signatories.

Ghat remained outside the stream of Libyan political activity until the proclamation of independence. A few months after that happy event, the Amghar led a delegation to wait on King Idris in Benghazi and pledge fealty to the King and the Libyan State.[59] In return, he received assurances of noninterference in local Tuareg affairs. A few Libyan officials returned with the Amghar's party to take up administrative duties in Ghat, and a small Libyan police detachment drawn from the Cyrenaican force was sent there. The French authorities maintained that the boundary of the Ghat-Sardalas area was still undefined, and only in 1955 was a protocol signed delimiting the boundary (see p. 831, fn. 117, item 3). The effect of this demarcation was that a small, sparsely inhabited area, traditionally the grazing ground for a Tuareg subtribe living in southern Algeria, was incorporated in the latter territory.

3. Selection of the Representative of the Minorities

As regards minorities, the situation in the Fezzan was virtually the same as in Cyrenaica. Since there were no minorities living in the Fezzan who were recognized as such, or who demanded recognition, there was little interest in the selection of the minority representative, except for a strong feeling, voiced by Ahmed Bey, that he should not be of Italian nationality.

The Commissioner's conversation with Ahmed Bey took place at Jadid on 24 March, during his second visit to the Fezzan. The Chef du Territoire expressed the hope that the Libyans in general and the Tripolitanians in particular would unite internally for the good of the nation. If the Tripolitanians remained divided among themselves, he would not join them; the Fezzanese would lead their own lives in their own territory, the limits of which, he claimed, included the Gulf of Sirte and parts of southern and western Tripolitania, an extent larger than that agreed upon between Generals Montgomery and LeClerc at the time of Libya's liberation early in 1943 (ct. p. 41). The fact that Ahmed Bey owned a date-palm grove at Sirte was, perhaps, not unconnected with this claim.

59. The Amghar was the Sheikh of the subtribe of that name, which is a member of the larger Tuareg family. Its lands lay astride the Fezzanese-Algerian boundary.

The Commissioner took the opportunity of explaining to the Chef du Territoire his idea of a committee to pave the way for the Libyan National Assembly, which in turn was to draft the Libyan constitution establishing the form of government, and expressed the hope that the Fezzanese would be represented thereon. Ahmed Bey agreed, making it plain that the Fezzanese representatives would closely watch the trend of events and withdraw if disunity among the Tripolitanians persisted. In reply, the Commissioner referred to the Bevin-Sforza plan and said that he hoped for the sake of Libya itself that division of the country would be avoided, so as to avert a return of foreign rule. Ahmed Bey retorted that a return of the Italians would mean war.

About the middle of May the attitude of the Fezzanese toward the United Nations plan for a united Libya became more precise. At that time the Council for Libya, with its Cyrenaican member, Ali Assad al-Jerbi, usually referred to as Ali Bey Jerbi, presiding as Acting Chairman, accompanied by the Commissioner and members of his staff, paid a visit of several days to the Fezzan (see pp. 228–36). The Council met the Chef du Territoire and his advisers, and in the course of this first meeting Ahmed Bey declared his gratitude to the United Nations for granting Libya independence, to France for granting independence to the Fezzan, and to Great Britain for the grant of independence to Tripolitania and Cyrenaica. He announced that he accepted the Amirate of Sayed Idris over the whole of Libya, but made it clear that he did not wish to deal with the Amir through an intermediary. He wanted direct access; anything he had to say to the Amir must go "from mouth to ear."

When asked by Ali Bey Jerbi how he envisaged the role of the Fezzan in the future Libyan Government, Ahmed Bey replied that there should be a government for the whole of Libya, but that the Fezzanese should remain responsible for their own internal affairs. The Fezzan would send representatives to the Libyan National Assembly, since there could be no independence for the Fezzan apart. Independent Fezzan must be linked with Tripolitania and Cyrenaica, for the ideal unity of Libya lay in Allah, and this could not be achieved without the union of all three territories.

The Commissioner, aware of the importance of security in the Fezzan, asked how, in Ahmed Bey's opinion, law and order would be maintained in the future. This prompted an interruption by the Fezzanese Counselor for Justice, Hajj Hamuda Bin Tahir, the Mudir of Jadid, who asked permission to speak frankly. After the visit of the Four Power Commission of Investigation, he said, the people of the Fezzan had for a long time heard nothing about the future of their country. Only when the Commissioner visited the Fezzan in February had the people learned for the first time of the United

Nations Resolution granting independence and unity to the whole of Libya. The Counselor then gave a brief and correct summary of the Resolution as the Commissioner had explained it to the Fezzanese people three months earlier. Although the Fezzan would become part of Libya, the Counselor continued, the Fezzanese had elected Ahmed Bey Seif al-Nasr as Chef du Territoire because it was an isolated territory which needed a leader of its own. The Fezzanese had also elected Hajj Ahmed al-Senussi Sofu as their representative on the Council for Libya. He conceded that Ahmed Bey's authority was not recognized by all Fezzanese, and that there had been a minority candidate for the Fezzanese seat on the Council for Libya, but claimed that the administration which had now been formed under his leadership, and which was already functioning with the advice of the French Resident, as the former Military Governor had by now become, enjoyed the confidence of the large majority of the people.

As to the question of security, he explained that a Fezzanese police force was being organized. While the Fezzan did not wish to sever its relations with Tripolitania and Cyrenaica, it must, because of its geographical situation, have an internal administration of its own. In order to make his meaning clear, the Counselor compared the plan of unifying the three territories of Libya with an attempt to put "iron and eggs in the same basket without breaking the eggs," the Fezzan being the eggs and the other two territories the iron. If Tripolitania and Cyrenaica would agree, and the French Government would assent, to the Fezzan having its own internal administration, the unity of Libya would be an accomplished fact. Although Libya constituted a religious and political unit, the domestic circumstances of the Fezzan differed from those of the other two territories, and the territory would be better placed than the central government to deal with local affairs. The Counselor added that the Fezzanese people's mandate to Hajj Ahmed Sofu embodied the views he had just expressed.

Turning from political to financial affairs, the Counselor expressed the gratitude of the Fezzanese people to France for the help it had provided in the economic field; the Fezzan could not live without outside help. For the time being France was providing that assistance, which covered 90 percent of the territory's expenditure. In the future, the Libyan Government would have to make that deficit good.[60]

60. According to France's report to the United Nations, total receipts for the year 1949 amounted to 31,828,164 (Algerian) francs, whereas total expenditures, ordinary and extraordinary, including non-interest-bearing loans repayable after the harvest, normally in kind, amounted to 47,086,153 francs, thus leaving a deficit of 15,257,989 francs to be covered by the French Government. The estimated deficit for 1950 was 113,470,835 francs, the substantial increase in expenditure being due to "the intro-

Concluding, the Counselor, speaking on behalf of all his people, declared that the Amir was their religious and political leader and that he should be sovereign over all of Libya. However, the Fezzanese would have some requests to make to him concerning their special rights; they were confident that he would give everyone his due.

Thus it was clear that in the space of three months the people of the Fezzan had done a considerable amount of political thinking for themselves.

PART 4. THE END OF THE RECONNAISSANCE: GENERAL IMPRESSIONS

When, at the end of March, the Commissioner's schedule brought his exploratory flying tour to an end, he still felt far from an expert on Libyan affairs—particularly when talking to Libyan leaders or to old hands in the British and French Administrations—but he and his staff had nevertheless formed an overall picture of the situation, of which the salient features were:

1. General readiness, often eagerness, to form a united and independent State, though some confusion and hesitation still marked Fezzanese ideas about the nature of the Fezzan's relationship to that State.
2. Widespread, though not unanimous, feeling in favor of Sayed Idris as head of that State.
3. Gradual polarization of sentiment around two concepts: that of a unitary and that of a federal State:
   a. In Tripolitania, with its instinctive conviction, rooted in history, that the territory and its capital city were the natural political center from which the rest of Libya should be ruled, the urban majority wanted a united Libya under a centralized government with a minimum of local administration. There were, however, signs that the rural population wished still to be attached to local institutions of a regional, municipal, or tribal nature.
   b. In Cyrenaica, where there was fear of domination by the more numerous Tripolitanians, the majority favored a federal State. The wiry Cyrenaican tribesmen, as well as the older sedentary folk, were wary of their more sophisticated brothers in the western territory. Had

duction of new political organs and the execution of the first instalment of the schemes for the construction of new buildings and hydraulic works." Expenditures did not include military occupation costs. See "Annual Report of the French Government to the General Assembly concerning the administration of the Fezzan," pp. 13–15.

not the Cyrenaicans put up a much stiffer fight against the Italians and fought side by side with the British to liberate their country? They considered that Italian influence was still too strong in Tripolitania, and dreaded a return to Cyrenaica of the Italian settlers who had fled to Tripolitania and Italy in 1943. At the same time, an active minority representing the younger urban generation wanted a unitary form of State.

c. In the Fezzan, the desire for local autonomy was at least as strong as in Cyrenaica. But, once the people had become aware—through the circular mentioned on page 190, their consultations with the Mission, and information filtering through from the other two territories—of the possibilities afforded by the United Nations Resolution, the urge to renew old economic links with Tripoli and the Sirte, and the attraction of religious ties with the Senussi, gradually won them over to the idea of a united Libya.

4. Difficulty in exchanging and reconciling views among the peoples of the three territories because of the tenuity of internal communications, inherent in the country's geography, but due also to the policies followed by the Administering Powers. In particular, communication of any kind between the Fezzan and Tripolitania was severely restricted by the French Administration in the former. Links between Tripolitania and Cyrenaica were easier but expensive and time-consuming.

5. Continued preference on the part of the Administering Powers for a confederation so loose as to endanger the full implementation of Resolution 289 (IV) in letter and spirit.[61]

61. When, in September 1950, the Commissioner in his first annual report remarked that during the initial stage (of the transitional period) the Administering Powers had put forward a number of suggestions for the development of constitutional machinery in each of the three territories, offering no proposals for promoting the unity and independence of Libya as a whole, the representative of the United Kingdom on the Council for Libya requested the inclusion of the following footnote, with which the representative of France associated himself insofar as it expressed the view, *mutatis mutandis,* of his own Government:

> His Majesty's Government have always been fully cognizant of their obligations under the General Assembly resolution, obligations which include co-operation with the Commissioner in the execution of paragraph 10. They took the view, however, that, if the objective of a united and independent Libya were to be effectively achieved, the essential preliminary step should be the development of local institutions of self-government in each of the territories for the administration of which they were responsible. His Majesty's Government held that, since the inhabitants of the territories were unpractised in the management of their own affairs and correspondingly unprepared to cope with the problems which would later confront them, any precipitate action on the part of the Administering Power might

Factors 3, 4, and 5 provided an indication that immediate convocation of a National Assembly to elect a Provisional Libyan Government, no matter how desirable, would be premature. Representatives of the three territories obviously first needed a chance of getting together *en petit comité* to talk over what kind of common State they wanted. That would have to be done quickly, in view of the pressure being exerted by the Administering Powers in favor of local autonomy. That was why the Commissioner had been systematically sounding out Libyan opinion on the formation of a preparatory committee. The idea had been well received generally. Although views as to how such a committee should be established were still vague, the Commissioner thought that it might be elected by the existing territorial assemblies or councils, and that it might be made up of equal numbers of representatives from each of the three territories. Indeed, he had become convinced that this last condition was a sine qua non if Cyrenaican and Fezzanese participation was to be ensured, and he hoped that the Tripolitanian political leaders would be able to persuade their followers to accept it as a political necessity. As will be seen, these two points—elective procedure and equality of representation—turned out to be much more serious stumbling blocks than he had expected.

The other outcome of his reconnaissance was of course the nomination, not without considerable difficulty and delay, of the candidates for the four seats on the Council for Libya reserved for the three territories and the minorities. That delay had obliged the Commissioner to take a number of important political decisions without the advice and aid of his Council. It was with a lighter heart, therefore, that he at last called a meeting of the six non-Libyan members of the Council on 4 April 1950 in Geneva to consult them on the filling of the four Libyan seats on the basis of the list of candidates which he commended to the Council, as described earlier in this chapter.

---

commit them to a form of government or a pattern of unity upon which they had been unable to exercise a considered judgment. In the initial stages, therefore, His Majesty's Government designedly confined themselves to putting forward suggestions for the creation and development of local organs of self-government in which the inhabitants might gain experience while at the same time making it clear, as they did to the Commissioner during their first conversations with him in February 1950, that further specific action towards the promotion of unity would follow at a later and more appropriate stage.

First *Annual Report of the United Nations Commissioner in Libya,* para. 234.

CHAPTER 3

Launching the Council for Libya

PART 1. THE CONSTITUTION OF THE COUNCIL

The difficulties experienced in reaching agreement on the seat of the Council for Libya have already been touched upon. The Administering Powers were afraid that if the Council met in Libya their authority would be weakened in the eyes of the inhabitants. The United Kingdom Government was understandably anxious that no impression of dual administration should be given to the peoples of Cyrenaica and Tripolitania, who could not grasp the distinction between the function of the British Administration and that of the Commissioner and the Council. The latter, moreover, included representatives of certain governments which London had reason to believe would be critical of the British Administration, thus, possibly, giving rise to local agitation. Accordingly, while not objecting to occasional Council meetings in Tripoli, Whitehall preferred that its permanent seat be outside Libya. The French Government similarly believed that the aura emanating from Council meetings in Tripoli would spread as far as the Fezzan, and even to neighboring French territories in Central and North Africa, and likewise opposed the establishment of the Council in Libya.

On the other hand, Latin American and Southeast Asian delegates to the General Assembly had told the Commissioner that they would strongly criticize the Council's being seated anywhere but in Libya, although they would not object to its meeting elsewhere occasionally.

The Commissioner believed that it was for the Council to decide where its permanent seat should be. He himself was of two minds about the matter. As he was required to consult the Council on all major issues, it would be convenient to have it within easy reach of his Tripoli headquarters. However, since for reasons of economy one and the same staff had to serve both the Commissioner and the Council, this might impair the efficiency and autonomy of the Mission secretariat. Another important consideration was the convenience of the four local members who, it was to be supposed, would all be living in Libya and who would need to keep in close personal touch with those whom they represented. It did not seem reasonable to expect them to cross the Mediterranean and the Alps whenever the Council met in Geneva, quite apart from the delicate question of who would bear the cost of such journeys.

On 10 March 1950 the Commissioner had had a meeting with the six non-Libyan members of the Council in New York to discuss, among other things, its site.[1] He had then drawn a distinction between the need for a permanent meeting place and that for a venue where they could hold their prescribed consultation to appoint the four Libyan members, suggesting that if there were only four candidates for the four seats, this might well be Tripoli; but if there were a number of candidates for each seat, it might be wiser to meet in Geneva in order to get away from possible pressure from conflicting Libyan groups.

The Pakistani member thereupon suggested that the six non-Libyan members and the Commissioner should meet in Geneva for the sole purpose of choosing the Libyan members, and that the first official session of the full Council might be held in Alexandria. But, in his view, as soon as sufficient accommodation could be found in Tripoli, the Council should move there permanently, given the need for close and continuing cooperation with the Commissioner during the twenty months which were all that remained for preparing Libya for independence.

The United States member feared that if the Council were seated permanently in any one of the three Libyan territories, the other two would regard this as favoritism; and a seat anywhere in Libya would expose the Council to pressure from local interests.

The Egyptian member wondered why the Council should fear pressure. He maintained that it must remain in close touch with the Libyan people at all times. His Government preferred that the Council have its permanent seat in Libya and meet there from the outset.

The Italian member had many highly contradictory interests to reconcile. On the one hand, he favored Tripoli, where he could maintain close contact with his much divided national minority, with Libyan leaders, and with the British Administration. On the other hand, he saw certain advantages in Cairo, where access to the Italian and other diplomatic missions would be easy; moreover, it was the capital of a country that would undoubtedly play a large part in Libyan affairs, and one with which Italy was endeavoring to improve its relations. Similar reasoning applied in his mind to the Arab League. Last but not least, to a man who liked his creature comforts, Cairo offered many amenities that Tripoli lacked.

1. A brief account of this meeting and of the considerations dealt with in the preceding paragraph has already been given in a broader context on pp. 124–25.

The French and United Kingdom members wanted Geneva for the organizational meeting, the second hoping that the full Council might then stay on in Geneva for its first formal session.

Eventually, it was tentatively decided that the constituent meeting should be held in Geneva on 4 April 1950, with the idea that after the constitution of the full Council the Commissioner would consult all its members on the date and place of the first formal session, and that he would also consult the Administering Powers about accommodation and other facilities in Tripoli.

Subsequently, when it became clear that there would be twenty-seven candidates for the four Libyan seats, the Commissioner confirmed these provisional arrangements.

At the constituent meeting, the Commissioner explained the procedures by which the nominations had been put forward. His choices for the three territorial seats were accepted without demur. But his recommendation for the minority seat, Aurelio Finzi, drew objections from the Italian representative, whose Government felt that, in view of the continuing discussion among the Italians in Tripolitania, Giacomo Marchino was to be preferred. It later transpired that the Italian Undersecretary of State for Foreign Affairs had summoned the presidents of the two leading Italian organizations in Tripoli to Rome, together with Marchino, who was able to satisfy all of them, through written assurances, that if appointed he would consider it his duty to defend impartially the interests of all the minorities, including the Italian right-wing groups.

As the Commissioner knew that Marchino was also acceptable to the other three minorities in Libya, he could now with an easy conscience recommend the appointment of the candidate he had preferred from the beginning, feeling reasonably sure that cooperation between the Arab members of the Council and the representative of the minorities would get off to a good start.

At this meeting it was also agreed that the Council should hold its inaugural meeting in Tripoli.

Inasmuch as the personalities and backgrounds of the members of the Council, as well as considerations of national prestige and other interests, obviously affected its work, brief sketches of those involved may help the reader to appreciate the course its deliberations took.

a. *Cyrenaica* was represented by Ali Assad al-Jerbi, already mentioned on page 188, who was born in Derna in 1901, the son of a local official in the Turkish Administration. He had been educated in Constantinople between 1911 and 1923, where he studied medicine. When he returned home, he found Cyrenaica under Italian occupation, but his subsequent career carried no taint of collaboration in this regard, for in matters of this kind Libyans have always made a distinction between *force majeure* and basic loyalties, and Ali Bey Jerbi had always been considered as loyal to his own people. He became successively a schoolteacher (1924); a *mudir* (1927); Secretary for Arab Affairs, a post especially created by the Italian authorities (1936); Mayor of Derna (1940) during the first occupation by the British (a function he resumed when he returned with them in the second occupation); adviser to Sayed Idris in Cairo (1942); Superintendent of Education in Cyrenaica (1944); Deputy Secretary for Development in the British Military Administration (1945); and Minister for Works and Communications in the Government of Cyrenaica (1949). He was also one of the two secretaries of the National Congress Party of Cyrenaica, and the only man on the Amir's list of candidates for the Cyrenaican seat on the Council who enjoyed the support of both the local parties. Fluent in Arabic, Turkish, Italian, English, and French, Ali Bey Jerbi had a pleasant personality, a ready smile, and unfailing good humor. He brought a balanced and liberal judgment to bear on the fulfillment of his Council duties and inspired general confidence and respect.

b. *Egypt* was represented on the Council by Mohamed Kamel Selim Bey, who was of Turkish origin and had been educated at Oxford University. Hence his knowledge of English, which he spoke well, even eloquently, was profound and cultured. Married to a Scottish wife and widely traveled in Europe, he was fluent in Arabic, English, and French. A Wafdist,[2] he had begun his career as private secretary to Zaghlul Pasha, whom he accompanied to London in 1930 for negotiations with the Foreign Office. He was Assistant Secretary to the Egyptian Council of Ministers in 1931, Secretary-General of the Chamber of Deputies in 1933, and from 1938 until his appointment to the Council, Secretary to the Egyptian Council of Ministers. Thus he was a man well versed in political and administrative affairs, both national and international. He was also, unfortunately, highly strung, with the result that his emotions occasionally got the better of him, leading to passionate, even angry, outbursts in the Council, which did a disservice to the cause he otherwise defended so ably. At such times his relations with the Commissioner became rather strained, but tension never lasted long, for Kamel Selim Bey was fundamentally a warmhearted man.

c. *The Fezzan* was represented by Hajj Ahmed al-Senussi Sofu, who was born at Murzuq in 1906 in a family which originally came from Cyre-

2. The Wafd was at that time the extreme nationalist party in Egypt.

naica. Like Ali Bey Jerbi, he was the son of an official in the Turkish Administration, who had subsequently been recognized as Sheikh of the Murzuq area by the Italian Administration in 1914; Hajj Sofu succeeded his father in the latter capacity and retained his function under French occupation. Hajj Sofu was familiar with Shari'a law. He spoke a little Italian in addition to Arabic, but when he came to the Council meeting it was the first time he had visited Tripoli, so far from his own palm trees, his garden, and his two houses. Being a modest and conscientious man, he was in danger of being overwhelmed by his new responsibilities and the mass of documentation presented for his perusal. However, his native intelligence stood him in good stead, and his simple, dignified behavior won his colleagues' respect.

In a letter written to the Commissioner after three months' work on the Council, Hajj Sofu ably analyzed the problems of the Fezzan, which he attributed to ignorance and poverty. Although Islam obliged every man and woman to educate himself or herself, he wrote, the Fezzanese had never been allowed the opportunity of doing so. He urged the introduction of an educational program suited to the needs and finances of the territory, with different kinds of schools for such subjects as trades, handicrafts, and the training of teachers. Poverty was largely due to the geography of the Fezzan, but he felt that prospecting for mineral wealth might solve the problem as it had done in the Arabian Peninsula.

d. France's representative on the Council was Georges Joseph Antoine Jules Balay, born in 1903 at Lyons, the perfect example of a French diplomat. He had had the usual varied diplomatic career, beginning in 1929 as third secretary at the French Embassy in Moscow, and having risen by 1946 to the rank of Envoy Extraordinary and Minister Plenipotentiary in Baghdad. As we have seen, the French Government had on the one hand pledged itself unreservedly to cooperate in the implementation of Resolution 289 (IV), while on the other, by abstaining from the final vote in the General Assembly, it had made clear its belief that it would be premature to proclaim Libyan independence within two years. Balay was therefore in a rather delicate position, but he played his cards with a great deal of subtlety and skill, delaying Libya's progress toward independence as far as he reasonably could without adopting an unremittingly negative attitude. His contributions to the debates were always worth listening to, often sagacious, sometimes constructive.

e. Italy was represented by Baron Giuseppe Vitaliano Confalonieri, born in 1902 at Milan, who graduated in law from the University of Pavia. After having seen military service in the cavalry, he entered his country's diplomatic service in 1925, and reached the rank of Minister in 1948. As a member of the Council he held ambassadorial rank. Italy wanted to build up friendly relations with Libya and other Arab countries. She had renounced colonial ambitions, but she could not afford to neglect the material interests of the Italian minority. There also remained the thorny problem of the ultimate disposal of what was still called enemy property under British custodianship. Confalonieri, by his bonhomie and common sense, succeeded in improving Italo-Libyan relations despite the hostile feelings of many Libyans, especially the Cyrenaicans, toward his country.

f. The Minority representative, Giacomo Marchino, had come to Tripoli in 1919 and started a successful citrus farm in the mid-1920s. Under the Italian Administration he had been Mayor of Tajuri, a provincial oasis town east of Tripoli; Government Commissioner in the Chamber of Commerce; Vice-President of the Economic Council of the Colonial Office; Commissioner of the Agrarian Association; member of the Steering Committee of the Institute of Arts and Crafts; and Vice-President of the Savings Bank of Libya, which had its headquarters in Tripoli. At the same time he had kept more or less clear of politics, and was respected and trusted by the Arabs.

As a member of the Council, Marchino avoided as far as possible going beyond his terms of reference, and went to great pains to abstain from taking position on matters which did not affect the minorities. On the other hand, he conscientiously and with great tact defended all the minority interests entrusted to his care, a task that called for an extensive knowledge of the facts combined with sound political judgment.

g. Pakistan's representative, Colonel Abdur Rahim Khan, was born in 1901, the son of the Speaker of the North-West Frontier Provincial Assembly. After serving as an officer in the British Army in India, he held a secretarial post in the Provincial Assembly and later served in consular offices of the (British) Indian Foreign Service in Kabul, Afghanistan, and Iran. Returning to military duty in 1947, he was gazetted Lieutenant Colonel, and promoted to Colonel in 1948. Having entered the Pakistani Foreign Service in 1947, he spent the following two years as a member of the United Nations Special Commission on the Balkans. Thereafter, he was a member of his country's delegation to the United Nations General Assembly, and at the beginning of 1949 was appointed its Permanent Representative to the United Nations with the rank of Ambassador.

Rahim Khan was a small, dapper, dynamic man who soon made his presence felt in the Council by his drive, initiative, and aggressiveness. In debate he had a tendency to oversimplify the issues and to overstate his case, a habit which, for all his ability, astuteness, and undeniable devotion to the work in hand, sometimes tripped him up. In private life he was an altogether delightful and charming individual.[3]

h. Tripolitania was represented by Mustafa Mizran, who was born in Tripoli in 1897, where he received a Turkish-Arabic education. He spent the earlier part of the Italian occupation in Saudi Arabia and Syria, serving in the Turkish Army during World War I. After a sojourn in Alexandria, he returned to Tripoli in 1919. For some years he pursued his private interests, then became a member of the board of the Moslem secondary school there (1935); Vice-President of the Administrative Commission of the Arts and Crafts School (1938); Adviser to the Municipality of Tripoli (1937–41); Adviser to the Tripolitanian Government from 1941 until the beginning of the British occupation; leader of the Nationalist Party (1947); Vice-President of the National Congress Party of Tripolitania (1948); and by 1950 he had been Director of the Arts and Crafts School for a number of years.

Mizran was a staunch advocate of Libyan unity, but his Tripolitanian background and outlook sometimes made it difficult for him to see eye to eye with his Fezzanese and Cyrenaican colleagues about the form of Libya's future government. Although he kept his feelings within politically acceptable bounds, his suspicion of British and French policy was profound, and he came to form, with the representatives of Egypt and Pakistan, an anti-Western group on the Council. Not being one to mince his words, he always made his position perfectly clear and, right or wrong, stuck stoutly to his opinions.

i. The United Kingdom representative was Sir Hugh Stonehewer Bird, K.C.M.G., born in 1891, a career diplomat familiar with the Arab world

3. On 14 and 15 March 1950, Rahim Khan came to see the Commissioner in New York, after having visited Tripoli, Benghazi, Cairo, Rome, Paris, and London to familiarize himself with the Libyan problem. With regard to the Council's permanent seat, he expressed the belief that the United Kingdom was making a great mistake in trying to get that body to meet outside Libya, and went on to develop the views attributed to him on page 203. He did not consider it necessary to consult the Libyan members on the question; the Commissioner thought otherwise.

Regardless of United Nations regulations governing the payment of travel costs and subsistence allowance to delegates to the General Assembly and United Nations Councils and their subsidiary bodies, which had been communicated in writing to him and all other members of the Council for Libya by the Secretary-General, Rahim Khan wanted the Council to be in session constantly, and not periodically, or "spasmodically" as he put it. The Commissioner formally objected. This was the first sign that the representative of Pakistan conceived the Council as an executive instead of an advisory body—the revival of a battle that had already been fought in Sub-Committee 17.

and its language. He had served in Casablanca, and during World War II was British Minister at Jedda. He had been Ambassador to Iraq before his appointment to the Council. Sir Hugh was a balanced, wise man, rather quiet, who obviously did his best to reconcile Britain's interests in Libya with the aims of the General Assembly Resolution. When illness prevented him from serving on the Council for more than the first few months of its life, he was replaced by his alternate, José Campbell Penney, originally of the Egyptian Civil Service, later of the Sudan Government Service, who had been political adviser to the Chief Civil Affairs Officer in the British Administration in the former Italian Colonies in Africa and, later, political adviser to the British Chief Administrator in Tripolitania. A middle-aged man who spoke fluent Arabic, Penney represented the best type of British colonial civil servant, tactful, soft-spoken, firm in the defense of the British case, but never overplaying his hand and always ready to cooperate whenever possible, even with his opponents.

j. The United States of America was represented by Lewis Clark, born in Montgomery, Alabama, in 1895. He entered his country's foreign service in 1925, qualifying later as a Chinese language officer. Most of his diplomatic career was spent in China, interrupted by several years of service in Paris and Ottawa where in 1945 he served as Consul General and Counselor of Embassy. In 1947, after a year in London, he was retransferred to China (Nanking) with the personal rank of minister, later attaining the rank of career Minister. In 1949 he was an adviser in the United States delegation to the United Nations General Assembly. From 1950 through 1951 Clark served on the Council for Libya with the personal rank of Ambassador. At his retirement in 1957 he was United States Consul General in Algiers.

Although the United States had its largest Mediterranean air base only a few miles to the east of Tripoli, anticolonialism was a historical factor in the framing of its policies. While it had generally supported the United Kingdom's views before and during the debates in the General Assembly on Libya's future, it had done so with some unequivocal reservations. This divergence of views became more marked in the course of the Council's debates, during which Clark exercised a restraining influence on the policies of the Administering Powers, frequently acting as a mediator in a quiet and unpretentious way. In this, he obviously enjoyed the support of the State Department.[4]

4. One night in 1951, at a Ramadan dinner party with Libyan friends, one of them asked the Commissioner the following question: "Less than two hundred years ago the United States were a British colony. They fought hard to free themselves. Today they appear to be on friendly terms with the British, yet nevertheless I still feel in Mr. Clark something of the anticolonialist. How do you explain this, and is

So it came to pass that the Council for Libya met for the first time in the afternoon of 25 April 1950 in Tripoli's Grand Hotel, where the large dining room, its walls hung with oriental tapestries in the Moorish fashion, had been converted into a conference hall. Wooden, straight-backed chairs, admirably designed to keep somnolence at bay during the long sultry afternoons, were set round a horseshoe table, at the head of which first the Commissioner, then, after his election, the Chairman, flanked by their aides, sat looking out over the harbor and the Mediterranean beyond. The Council members took their seats at the table in English alphabetical order of the countries they represented. Interpreters and précis-writers sat in the middle of the room, and during open meetings the public sat in rows near the entrance.

The inaugural meeting was of a ceremonial character, and every important personage in Tripoli had been invited, and was present. Lack of adequate means of communication had prevented the attendance of notables from Cyrenaica and the Fezzan, but the British Resident in Cyrenaica was there, sitting next to his colleague from Tripolitania. The French Resident in the Fezzan was represented by the French Consul General in Tripoli. The Consular Corps, which in those days consisted of the consular representatives of Greece, the Netherlands, and the United States, as well as of France, had all turned out, and the Italian Government was represented. The Qadi, the Mufti, the Bishop of Tripoli, and the Grand Rabbi, together with the leaders of the political parties and minorities and a large number of Arab and Italian notables, made up the rest of the audience.

In an explanatory opening statement, the Commissioner, who presided over the meeting pending the election of a chairman, extended a hearty welcome to the members of the Council on behalf of the Secretary-General of the United Nations, the Mission, and himself, and observed that Resolution 289 (IV) united in a unique fashion four elements—the Libyan National Assembly, the Commissioner, the Council, and the Administering Powers—all essential to the establishment of a duly constituted independent Libyan State. The Council then proceeded to elect its provisional chairman. As a result of previous agreement in favor of the representative of Pakistan, the election went off without difficulty.

Thereafter, each member explained his own particular idea of the way in which the Resolution should be implemented, but no one pushed his

---

he sincere?" The Commissioner tried to answer the question to the best of his ability, though without much success. The question remained the main topic of discussion until the dawn broke up the party. What everyone present seemed to forget, or at least nobody mentioned, was that the Commissioner's own country had itself been fighting to retain its colonies only a few years previously.

point of view to the verge of controversy, and there was little sign of the difficulties which were to arise later.

Immediately after the ceremonial public opening, the question was raised whether the Council's meetings should be public or private. The Cyrenaican, Egyptian, and Pakistani members favored public meetings, whereas the Administering Powers, supported by the other five members, pressed for private meetings, asserting that dissension among members on important issues, if aired in public, would not only confuse and discourage Libyan opinion, but also, perhaps, hamper the implementation of Resolution 289 (IV). In reality, the Administering Powers were afraid that certain members would use the Council to stir up public opinion against their management of public affairs. On the other side there was a strong feeling that to bring out into the open the various problems attending Libya's transformation would have the advantage of helping the people of Libya to form a more knowledgeable view of prevailing difficulties and their possible solutions. Finally, the Council adopted by 7 votes to 3 a French proposal that all meetings should be held in private until the rules of procedure had been adopted.

Five meetings were devoted to consideration of these rules,[5] which had been drafted by the United Nations Secretariat in New York in consultation with the Principal Secretary of the Mission, following normal United Nations practice insofar as concerned the internal conduct of Council affairs. However, given the exceptional relationship between the Council and the Commissioner, the draft rules also contained special provisions, such as: rule 3, empowering the Commissioner to accredit the Libyan territorial and minorities representatives; rule 6, laying down that he would be invited to participate without a vote in Council meetings or to designate a member of his staff to do so if he could not attend in person; rule 11, stipulating that he had the right to request the holding of a Council meeting; rule 16, entitling him to propose items for inclusion in the provisional agenda for each meeting; rule 19, entitling him to attend private meetings of the Council, accompanied by such staff as he might need; rule 25, providing that the Principal Secretary or his authorized deputy had the right to make to the Council on behalf of the Secretary-General of the United Nations any oral or written statements he deemed desirable; rule 10, stipulating that no proposal involving expenditure by the United Nations could be voted upon until the Secretariat had provided an estimate of its financial implications

5. See United Nations Docs. A/AC.32/COUNCIL/W.1/Rev.1, 26 April 1950 (draft rules), and A/AC.32/COUNCIL/R.12, 4 May 1950 (rules as adopted). Mimeographed. See also Summary Records of Council's 2nd to 6th Meetings, United Nations Docs. A/AC.32/COUNCIL/SR.2–6, 26 April–2 May 1950. Mimeographed.

for the United Nations budget; and rule 24, empowering the Chairman of the Council to accord precedence to the Commissioner over other speakers on his list.

The principal issues at stake in the debate were: the Commissioner's presence at Council meetings; the way in which the chairmanship should rotate; the Council's permanent seat; and public versus private meetings.

Rule 18, governing the privacy of meetings, read: "the Council shall meet in private unless otherwise decided in each instance." However, it added that "press communiqués will as a rule be issued at the end of each closed meeting." Rule 20 specified that press releases or oral briefings were strictly subject to the approval of the Chairman or Secretary of the Council. The Commissioner argued in private that both public and private meetings should be provided for; and that the real issue was: on which of the two should emphasis be laid? He believed that public meetings should be the rule. While he recognized that future decisions to meet in private might arouse alarm, he was convinced that the advantages of informing and educating public opinion in Libya outweighed that risk. However, he did not speak in the debate, preferring to let the Council itself take full responsibility for the decision. The Egyptian member proposed that the word "private" in rule 18 be replaced by the word "open"; and, after some discussion, it was decided by a show of hands that open meetings should be the rule, private meetings being permitted by special decision. As a result, at most of the Council's meetings the public seats were pretty full, and many a Libyan there received his first lesson in parliamentary procedure as it affected his country's problems.

The debate on the Council's meeting place (rule 11) was long and dour. The draft provided that "Meetings of the Council may be held as and where its work may require, by decision of the Council itself, at the request of a majority of its members or at the request of the Commissioner. Before the closure of each meeting the Council will decide the place and date of its next meeting."[6] The Administering Powers still objected to a permanent seat in Libya, whereas the Italian and the four local members wanted the Council to meet in Tripoli. The Cyrenaican member wanted it also to meet occasionally in Benghazi, so that his countrymen could familiarize themselves with its work. Various proposals were made, unsuccessfully, and finally the matter was referred to a sub-committee, presided over by the United States representative, which was instructed by the Council to prepare alternative drafts. After a day's discussion, the Sub-Committee came up with two proposals, both providing for the main seat to be Tripoli, with

6. United Nations Doc. A/AC.32/COUNCIL/W.1/Rev.1, 26 April 1950, p. 4.

possibilities of meeting elsewhere. The more precise draft was adopted by 7 votes to none, with 2 abstentions, the Italian representative being absent. As adopted, rule 11 then read:

> In carrying out its responsibilities the Council will necessarily function in Libya and have its principal seat in Tripoli. It will also travel about the country to study local conditions. It will hold meetings in Tripoli or elsewhere in Libya as its work may require.
>
> Nevertheless, being a body of the United Nations, the Council will maintain a seat at the European Office of the United Nations in Geneva to which it will withdraw from time to time to study such information as it has collected and to examine with the Commissioner his reports to the Secretary-General.
>
> Meetings of the Council may be held by decision of the Council itself, at the request of a majority of its members or at the request of the Commissioner. Before the closure of each meeting the Council will decide the place and date of its next meeting.[7]

Practice proved this compromise to be eminently satisfactory. Most working meetings, including several on controversial issues, were held in Tripoli. Members availed themselves of the opportunity to travel about Libya, to get to know local conditions. On the other hand, frictions which developed between the Commissioner and the Council on such matters as consultation on his annual reports to the Secretary-General of the United Nations happily occurred in Geneva, far from the gossiping coffeehouses of Tripoli.

There was another lengthy debate on rule 5, which provided that, at its first formal plenary meeting after adoption of the rules of procedure, the Council would elect from among its members a chairman who would hold office during the first series of meetings, the duration of the series to be determined by the Council. For subsequent series of meetings, the chairmanship would be rotated among the members in English alphabetical order of the names of the states, territories, or groups represented, beginning with the member whose alphabetical order followed next after that of the first chairman. The member whose alphabetical order followed that of the incumbent chairman would be vice-chairman, presiding in the absence of the chairman with the same powers and duties.

The Egyptian representative pointed out that this system would in effect deprive the representatives of Cyrenaica, Egypt, France, and Italy of the chairmanship, and that the Council had not known when it elected the

7. Ibid.

representative of Pakistan as chairman, which they had done on the basis of his personal qualities, that their choice would also decide the order in which he would be succeeded. Selim Bey suggested that the Council follow instead the straightforward alphabetical order, starting with "a."

The United States representative explained that the Sub-Committee had understood that only a *provisional* chairman had been elected so far, that the first official chairman was still to be elected, and that the proposed system of rotation was intended to rule out the possibility of the first chairman's holding office a second time before other members had had a chance of doing so, as might happen if the straightforward alphabetical order were followed.

The provisional Chairman assured the Council that if it were to adopt the procedure proposed by the Egyptian representative, which he himself favored, he would withdraw when Pakistan's turn came round again. He also considered that the term of office should be made more specific than "a series of meetings," and suggested a definite period of two months.

After a recess to allow Arabic translations of these various suggestions to be made, the following text was adopted by 5 votes to 4 with 1 abstention: "At its first formal plenary meeting after adoption of these Rules of Procedure, the Council shall elect among its members a Chairman . . . for the period ending the 30 June 1950. Thereafter the chairmanship shall be held in turn by members of the Council for periods of two months in the English alphabetical order of the names of the states, territories or groups represented." The rule also embodied the provisions governing the office of vice-chairman quoted above.[8]

Objections were raised to the wording of rule 6, which provided that the Commissioner "shall" be invited to participate without a vote in Council meetings. The provisional Chairman suggested that "may" would be preferable, because there might be occasions when the Council would wish to discuss the Commissioner's own actions, in which case it would be better if the Commissioner were not present.

Here the Commissioner intervened, arguing that Resolution 289 (IV) made it incumbent on the Commissioner to consult with and be guided by the Council, an obligation which both sides would find it difficult to fulfill if he were excluded from any of the official meetings. The Council could always confer informally without asking him to attend.

In the end, after members had discussed the matter among themselves, rule 6 was adopted as drafted. The Commissioner felt that the matter was of some tactical importance, because the records of the First Committee

8. Ibid., p. 2.

and plenary debates made it clear that the General Assembly intended the relationship between the Commissioner and the Council to be as close as possible and to involve mutually binding obligations. Accordingly, it was essential that his advisory body should not be able to meet officially behind his back.

Indeed, by the time the rules of procedure had been adopted and Abdur Rahim Khan elected as Chairman for the initial period ending 30 June, the Commissioner felt like a Siamese twin to the Council. His lively brother showed every sign of pushing and pulling in a variety of directions, and their unbreakable link would not permit him (the Commissioner) much freedom to move for himself unless he decided to stand his ground and, when necessary, do some pulling and pushing of his own.

PART 2. FIRST STEPS

Once the rules of procedure were out of the way and the first Chairman elected, the Council settled down to its real business as an advisory body to the Commissioner. He and his staff had prepared three papers for its consideration; a memorandum dated 19 April 1950 on the Commissioner's activities since 10 December 1949; a request for advice submitted by the Commissioner, and dated 15 April 1950, regarding the scope of his work; and a second request for advice, dated 16 April 1950, regarding a plan for the constitutional development of Libya.[9]

However, even before the Council had had time to study its rules of procedure, Abdur Rahim Khan, speaking as representative of Pakistan, had requested that a draft resolution be placed on the agenda and taken up before the Commissioner's report on his activities since his appointment. He proposed that the Council advise the Commissioner to request the Administering Powers to communicate to him, for transmission to the Council, all relevant information on the steps they had taken already or envisaged taking in pursuance of subparagraphs 10 (a) and (b) of Resolution 289 (IV) in connection with the transfer of powers and the promotion of Libyan unity. He also wanted the Council to advise the Commissioner to request them to suspend the enforcement of measures not yet put into effect until the Council had had an opportunity of considering them and tendering their advice via the Commissioner. It was plain that what Rahim Khan wanted was to obtain information additional to that already

9. For texts of papers, see first *Annual Report of the United Nations Commissioner in Libya,* GAOR: Fifth Session, 1950, Supplement No. 15 (A/1340), Annexes III, IV, and V, pp. 40–46.

supplied in the Commissioner's memorandum while at the same time initiating a debate unencumbered by the contents of the memorandum. In brief, he wanted to get to the bottom of British and French intentions. He had a perfect right to do so. It must be presumed that the members of the Council had studied the memorandum, which, it must be admitted, gave in some respects an abridged version of events, particularly with regard to the Commissioner's negotiations with the United Kingdom and French Governments on constitutional development in the territories under their administration. The paper gave a full account of the outcome of these negotiations, but it did not deal in detail with the original plans of the Administering Powers, or with the difficulties with which the Commissioner had had to cope in getting them, at least in part, adapted to his interpretation of the United Nations Resolution. Meanwhile, enough rumors had been circulating to provoke lively curiosity in interested quarters.

By referring to his memorandum, with the object of gaining time for the consideration of his requests for advice, the Commissioner twice obtained the deferment of the Pakistani proposal, the first time by pointing out that the information asked for had already been provided; the second time by informing the Council that the measures for ensuring constitutional development, worked out by the British Administration in Tripolitania and the French Administration in the Fezzan in consultation with himself, were on the verge of being discussed with the local political leaders, and that others were being implemented. He undertook to keep the Council further informed, but when shortly afterward the Pakistani representative again pressed his draft resolution, a debate took place that clearly brought out the suspicions certain Council members entertained about the policies of the two Administering Powers.

After an exchange of views that lasted almost three hours, the Council unanimously adopted that part of the Pakistani proposal asking for information from the Administering Powers. However, the second part, concerning the suspension of the enforcement of measures, ran up against a great deal of opposition inspired by the fear that, time being short, such suspension might delay the implementation of Resolution 289 (IV) as a whole. The sponsor accordingly withdrew that part of his draft resolution.

As a matter of fact, suspicion of British and French policy had already been noticeable when the Commissioner's report on his activities since his appointment had come up for discussion. In a way, of course, the report, reflecting as it did almost four months of activity already accomplished, came like mustard after a meal. It was therefore surprising that the debate was not of a much more searching nature and that no embarrassing questions were raised. Still, it gave the representatives of Egypt and Pakistan an opportunity of expressing their fears that the current policy of the Administering Powers favored the separation rather than the unification of the three territories. In reply, the representatives of France, the United Kingdom, and the United States argued that it seemed logical to establish regional governments which might later merge in a Libyan State. The member for Cyrenaica intervened to make it clear that his territory wanted Libyan unity on a federal basis.

The Commissioner's views have already been expounded in Chapter 2, but at the time it would have impaired his relations with the Administering Powers, with whom he was bound to cooperate, had he spoken as freely as he can today. He therefore kept silent.

The discussion was brought to an end by the Council's agreeing to take note of the Commissioner's memorandum of 19 April without formally voting on it. It was obvious that, had a vote been taken, there would have been a division with an unpredictable outcome.

The Pakistani draft resolution had raised another issue which neither the Commissioner nor any member of the Council had taken up at the time, but which, as everyone around the table realized, would soon come out into the open. What, exactly, had the General Assembly intended in creating the "troika" of the Administering Powers, the Commissioner, and the Council? This would have to be defined, together with their mutual relationships. What was the role of the Council? Was it meant to be a governing or an advisory body? Was its advice binding on the Commissioner, or could he refuse to accept it? Was he to act as the Council's executive arm, or was he entitled to act in his own right? Could the Council use him as an intermediary in calling the Administering Powers to task, as the representative of Pakistan apparently intended to do? These and related questions began to be asked and soon would demand clarification.

In the meantime, the Council had also dealt—though too briefly—with the Commissioner's request for advice as to the scope of his work, which had been prompted by the extreme brevity of the United Nations Resolution about Libya's economic and social problems. Indeed, all it said on the matter was contained in paragraph 9, under which the Commissioner was authorized to offer suggestions to the Secretary-General, the Economic and Social Council, and the General Assembly about the measures the United Nations might adopt during the transitional period regarding such problems. Compared with the emphasis laid on the task of the Commissioner, Council, and Administering Powers in promoting the country's constitutional development, this looked rather thin. The Commissioner was therefore anxious to have the Council's support in taking certain initiatives in the economic, social, and administrative fields, without which the establishment of a viable Libyan State seemed impossible. He therefore put the following question to the Council:

> The Council is kindly requested to advise the Commissioner whether it considers that he and his staff, under the terms of the Assembly resolution, as a major part of their activities should utilize the resources of the United Nations and the specialized agencies to undertake thorough studies regarding the establishment of the administrative services of the future Libyan State and its economic and social development, make recommendations thereon to the Administering Powers, and advise and assist the people of Libya in such matters.[10]

In his explanatory comment, the Commissioner expressed the belief that in addition to the help and advice he might offer to the people of Libya on the constitutional development of their country, it should also be his responsibility to employ all available means to assist them in establishing the necessary machinery of state, including administrative facilities, and the development of their economic resources and social institutions. A program of that kind appeared so much the more necessary as the country lacked trained personnel, was economically underdeveloped, and, budgetwise, had a constant and heavy deficit. Careful studies and plans would be needed not merely for the intervening period up to the declaration of independence, but also for years to come thereafter. The Commissioner did not claim to be able to indicate in detail at that moment the nature of the measures and plans required. He rather hoped that by combining the studies and plans already drawn up by the Administering Powers with the expert advice to be provided by the United Nations and the specialized agencies, a comprehensive development plan could be worked out. Some of the plans would undoubtedly be urgent; others might wait until after independence. But looking at the problem as a whole, there was no time to be lost.

During the debate, the Commissioner received all the support he could have hoped for, and the Council advised him to take the action he suggested. However, its members, though not always for the same reasons, were also sensitive to the possibility that he might tackle economic and social questions without adequately consulting them. Hence, the French representative proposed that sub-committees be set up to deal with the matters which the Commissioner and his staff would be studying. The Pakistani member wanted to be sure that the action proposed by the Commissioner would fall within the compass of that provision of Resolution 289 (IV) which read: "The Commissioner shall consult and be guided

10. Ibid., Annex IV, p. 45.

by the advice of members of his Council." In his reply, the Commissioner left no room for doubt. The member for Cyrenaica wanted to know whether the assistance to be furnished would be in the form of material aid or merely advisory, whereupon the Commissioner explained what United Nations technical assistance—which in those days was in its infancy—really meant. In doing so, he was careful to emphasize that the general principles concerning technical assistance adopted by the General Assembly and the Economic and Social Council stipulated that it could be sought and received only through and by governments of Member States. Since Libya was not yet an independent State, requests for such aid would have to be made by the Administering Powers in consultation with the Commissioner. Although the Commissioner had suggested that part of the studies could be carried out by experts on his own staff, and therefore paid for out of the United Nations regular budget, the foreseeable volume of work was such that it would clearly be preferable in the long run to rely on the United Nations technical assistance system.

As a sequel to this discussion, two sub-committees of the Council were set up: one on the needs and requirements of Libya in the technical assistance field, the other on finding ways and means to finance the requirements of Libya in the technical field. Since the Council had already established a Sub-Committee on Rules of Procedure, and later added two more, on work and travel, and on matters related to the press, it finished up with five sub-committees in all.

These subsidiary bodies met very irregularly, and brought one weakness to light, of which the General Assembly apparently had not been fully conscious when drafting its Resolution, namely, the desirability that members of the Council should be experts in particular fields, or at least include experts among their advisory staff. In the course of the debate in Sub-Committee 17, the expectation had been voiced that the Council would include, or the Commissioner in some way be assisted by, experts, but in practice the way in which the Council was made up to some extent ruled this out; it was hardly to be expected that the Libyan members would be specialists in economic, social, or administrative matters. But some of the six governmental representatives might have filled the bill. In fact, there was no lawyer, economist, or expert in public administration on the Council; most of its non-Libyan members were career diplomats.

Considering the political origins of the Italian colonial problem and the manner in which the General Assembly had dealt with it, such a composition of the Council was, in a way, understandable. However, from the moment the Assembly decided to set up an independent State, it ought to have realized that States are not made purely and simply of constitutions and governments, and that a host of economic and social problems, just as vital as the political ones, have to be solved, particularly in a country as poor and backward as Libya. The United Kingdom and France, with administrations on the spot, were of course in a privileged position. Neither were the Italians lacking either in technical experience or in advice, though this was somewhat out of date. The United States had a fairly large consular staff in Libya, and could always call in experts. Hence, the real sufferers were the members for Egypt and Pakistan, whose small staffs did not include anyone with expert economic or social knowledge.

It will be shown in Chapters 9 and 10 how the absence of such specialists sometimes handicapped the Council, and even provoked in it a feeling of frustration, for which little could be done. Keeping it informed by submitting expert reports, which hardly ever gave rise to a serious discussion, was no remedy. Looking back, one gets the impression that the General Assembly was so taken up by political considerations that the economic, social, and administrative needs of the new State crept into the resolution almost as an afterthought. Fortunately, Libya did not suffer from this lack of emphasis, as ample technical and other assistance was supplied by the Administering Powers, the United Nations, and the specialized agencies.

PART 3. THE COMMISSIONER'S FIRST REQUEST FOR ADVICE ON CONSTITUTIONAL DEVELOPMENT

GENERAL

The Commissioner has already stated why he considered it necessary to establish, as soon as possible, an all-Libyan organ to offset the tendencies of local provincialism and to counteract the policies of the Administering Powers, which aimed at granting autonomy, if not outright independence, to the territories under their control. In addition, he naturally also had in mind the need for an early start on the country's constitutional development, required by Resolution 289 (IV); and it was his considered opinion that this would proceed faster and more effectively if engineered in the first instance by a gathering of limited size rather than by a full-blown National Assembly. It therefore seemed to him that these two considerations should be merged in a single request for advice, namely:

> (2) Selection of a Preparatory Committee of the National Assembly not later than July 1950 for the purpose of recommending the method of election, including composition, of the Libyan National Assembly, and of drafting a constitution.[11]

11. Ibid., Annex V, p. 45.

During his first travels about the country from early February until the end of March, the Commissioner had discussed the idea with the British and French authorities on the spot, as well as with leaders of political parties in all three territories, with the Amir in Cyrenaica, and with the Chef du Territoire in the Fezzan. He had also consulted the Foreign Office in London and the Quai d'Orsay in Paris. Generally speaking, all had been in agreement. With this encouragement, and his growing knowledge of local conditions and opinions, the germ in his mind crystallized into a plan.

As he saw it, it would be a time-consuming, costly, and difficult business to organize elections in a large, thinly populated country with but little experience of such processes. Of course, it then seemed obvious that elections would have to be held some time during 1950, but it would be a particularly arduous task to secure the indispensable cooperation of the three separate administrations in drafting a national electoral law and setting up nationwide electoral machinery. He therefore preferred to make as much use as possible of existing elected bodies. Admittedly, this would mean an election in two stages, but such a process seemed better than relying on a nominated body commanding less authority and prestige either at home or abroad. There was already an elected body in the Fezzan: the assembly of notables (the *jemaa*). In Cyrenaica, elections for an assembly of representatives were to be held in June 1950. And in Tripolitania an elected legislative assembly was on the drawing board. The Commissioner therefore hoped that by the beginning of July there would be three electoral bodies which could elect, or at least designate by some selective process, the representatives of their respective territories on the proposed preparatory committee.

Another major issue was, on what basis were the three territories to be represented on the preparatory committee? The choice lay between equal and proportional representation. It had not taken the Commissioner a long stay in Libya to realize that this was a massive bone of contention among the three territories, which might never have been argued over with such vehemence had the three territories been roughly equal in population and degree of development. But the population of Tripolitania was approximately 750,000, that of Cyrenaica about 300,000, and that of the Fezzan only about 50,000.[12] As the main centers of population were separated from one another by hundreds of miles of desert, communications between them were difficult and tenuous. Quite apart from historical reasons, it was understandable that the Tripolitanians should consider themselves to be

12. These were the generally accepted figures at the time. The 1954 census showed the true populations then to be: Tripolitania, 738,338; Cyrenaica, 291,236; and the Fezzan, 59,315. See Mohammed Murabet, *Facts about Libya* (Valetta, Malta: Progress Press Co., Ltd., 1964), p. 81.

entitled to the leading place in the State-to-be. It was just as understandable that the Cyrenaicans and Fezzanese should fear that their interests and way of life would be threatened by the much larger and more advanced third member of the triad. It was an unfortunate coincidence that these fears strengthened the hands of the Administering Powers in the implementation of their divisive policies. But the Commissioner hoped that once the representatives of the three territories got together, their common interests would reinforce their sense of unity. He therefore proposed that they should be equally represented with five members each.

THE QUESTION OF THE REPRESENTATION OF MINORITIES

Another delicate point was whether the preparatory committee would be made up exclusively of Libyans, or whether it would also include representatives of the minorities. This raised several questions of a political and a legal nature (the problem per se is dealt with in Part 3 of the next chapter). When drawing up his plan, having taken proper legal advice and having listened to many leading people in all parts of the country, the great majority of whom did not want the minorities to be represented on the new body, the Commissioner concluded that it ought to be "entirely Libyan." [13]

TERMS OF REFERENCE OF THE PREPARATORY COMMITTEE

The next problem was the committee's terms of reference. Considering that the main issue would be federalism versus unitarism, the Commissioner felt that it should be one of the first duties of the committee to reach agreement on a recommendation concerning that fundamental question. He therefore suggested that the committee should be requested to make recommendations on the method of election and on the composition of the National Assembly, as well as on the fundamental principles of the constitution to be drafted. This appeared all the more desirable as such a recommendation would help the National Assembly in determining the form of government, the final decision remaining with the latter body as laid down in the United Nations Resolution.

It appeared essential, too, that the committee prepare a draft electoral law, or at least an outline of the methods by which the National Assembly would be elected. Admittedly, the Resolution did not postulate that the Assembly should be elected; neither did it stipulate any other way in which

13. First *Annual Report of the United Nations Commissioner in Libya,* Annex V, p. 46.

it should be constituted. All it said on the point was "that a Constitution for Libya, including the form of the government, shall be determined by representatives of the inhabitants of Cyrenaica, Tripolitania and the Fezzan meeting and consulting together in a National Assembly."[14]

Though the resolution was thus silent about whether the deputies were to be elected, selected, nominated, or designated by some particular method, the Commissioner, having studied the official records of the General Assembly, reached the conclusion—in which he was supported by many Libyans—that it would be in conformity with its spirit for the Libyan National Assembly to be constituted through elections.

Last, but not least, there was the question of timing. It was beyond the Commissioner's power—or anyone else's for that matter—to impose a time table on events to come. On the other hand, the maximum of two years (of which five months had already passed), allowed for the accomplishment of this task, put both the Council and himself, not to speak of the Administering Powers, in a kind of straitjacket. He therefore suggested the following schedule:

1. *June and July 1950.* Elections to be held for the Cyrenaican Assembly (already fixed for early June). In Tripolitania, the Administration would endeavor to hold elections in July, although there were difficulties about the preparations. In the Fezzan, the jemaa could be called together at any time at fairly short notice.

2. *End of July 1950.* It seemed that it should be possible by the end of July to request the three local assemblies to select their representatives on the preparatory committee. In his formal request for advice, the Commissioner intentionally used at this point the word "select," in order not to bind the local assemblies as to the exact procedure they should follow.

3. *Autumn 1950.* The preparatory committee, having—hopefully—by then finished its work, the National Assembly would be elected. It would hold its constituent meeting shortly afterward.

4. *Early in 1951.* The establishment by the National Assembly of a Provisional Libyan Government.

5. *Most of 1951.* The elaboration and adoption of the Constitution by the National Assembly.

6. *Late in 1951.* Proclamation of Independence.

When, on 4 May, this request for advice came up in the Council for the first time, the representative of Egypt declared that this was the most important meeting the Council had held, and that the document before it was the most significant yet submitted to it. He was in favor of elections, but on

14. General Assembly Resolution 289 A (IV), 21 November 1949. For the full text, see Annex I, pp. 891–92.

one condition: that they would be conducted along the same lines in all three territories, preferably using the Cyrenaican electoral law as a model.

The representative of Pakistan did not like the Commissioner's plan. He argued that the National Assembly should be to the highest degree possible typical of the Libyan people, and that the leaders of the different political parties ought therefore to be asked to nominate a number of representatives in proportion to the number of supporters of each. Such a method, even if practicable, would have given the advantage to Tripolitania, and was accordingly unacceptable to Cyrenaica and the Fezzan.

During the ensuing debate, spread over five meetings, the Council members soon took up their positions round the basic points of the Commissioner's plan: election versus selection; equal versus proportional representation; and the issue of minorities representation in the preparatory committee.

The question of the relative competence of the Commissioner and the Council was raised yet again on this occasion. The representative of Egypt, supported by his Pakistani colleague, insisted that no steps should be taken to implement the Commissioner's plan until it had been studied and approved by the Council. The Commissioner agreed that he would consult the Council at every stage of the plan; for the rest, he reserved his position.

The French representative was the first to suggest that it might be better to defer further discussion. While paying tribute to the clarity of the plan and its logical sequence, he feared that it did not make sufficient allowance for contingencies. Its limits were too sharp, and the successive stages too rigid. Moreover, it had certain automatic features which did not seem suited to the kinds of local problem which the Libyans themselves would have to settle; as long as the latter had not clearly formulated their wishes, it would be difficult to give the Commissioner carte blanche. In brief, Balay would have liked to see the decision put off until the Council had made a tour of the country, which was being planned at that moment. In his view, the proposed preparatory committee would look too much like an embryonic Libyan Government. It was clear that the representative of France was playing for time, and in the light of his Government's policy this came as no surprise.

The Egyptian representative, on the contrary, wanted an immediate decision, before members set out on their travels; one of the reasons he advanced in support of his suggestion was that the Council might otherwise find itself confronted with a fait accompli on the part of the Administering Powers.

On the other side, there was a good deal of support for the Commissioner's plan, in particular from the representatives of the United Kingdom, the United States, and the member for Cyrenaica.

The Commissioner himself was torn two ways. On the one hand, he would have liked an immediate decision; on the other, he hoped, perhaps a trifle naïvely, that the Council's visits to Cyrenaica, the Fezzan, and Tripolitania would convince its opponents of the soundness of his plan, so that it would finally enjoy unanimous support. He therefore agreed to the postponement of the debate. Looking back, this was a mistake. Immediate approval of his plan, which seemed possible at the cost of minor modifications, not only would have saved precious time, but might also have avoided or mitigated a number of problems which came up again, greatly magnified, at the end of the Council's odyssey.

After the Commissioner had replied to the points raised, the Egyptian representative said that he would support the Commissioner's plan, provided his wish that the elections be held along similar lines in all three territories was met. He also wanted the preparatory committee to consist of five members each for Tripolitania and Cyrenaica, with one member from the Fezzan.

His Pakistani colleague then pointed out that, if no decision were taken on the Commissioner's plan before the Council left Tripoli, the entire time table of the Administering Powers would be put back; it might even be that the implementation of Resolution 289 (IV) would be delayed to a certain extent. He therefore proposed that extra meetings be held before the Council's departure.

When, however, the United States member formally moved the adjournment of the debate, the motion was carried by 6 votes to 4, thereby frustrating the Egyptian and Pakistani insistence on an immediate decision.

THE COUNCIL'S TRAVELS THROUGH THE THREE TERRITORIES

From the time of their first meeting in the country, the non-Libyan members of the Council had felt the need to familiarize themselves with conditions in the provinces; that was why, as already mentioned, a subcommittee had been set up to work out, among other things, detailed travel plans in collaboration with the secretariat.

So far as Tripolitania was concerned, this was a fairly simple matter, as practically every center of any importance could be reached in one day from Tripoli. Moreover, by the end of April the secretariat had two sedans, a station wagon, and two Landrovers, with a total seating capacity of twenty-two, so that the British Administration had to be asked for help only when worst came to worst.

The same fleet of cars could be made available for travel in Cyrenaica, though the Italian-built coastal road between Tripoli and Benghazi still bore signs of the heavy military traffic which had passed over it during the war. Only a few bridges had been repaired, and in most places motor traffic had to pass through the dry wadis themselves. During the rainy season, whenever the streams were in spate, traffic came to a standstill; but in May and June, the months for which the trip had been planned, the road, though still full of holes, was passable for ordinary cars. As for accommodations, there were very few hotels, except in Benghazi, and most of those were closed, and restaurants were few and far between. Hence, in the rural areas the journey became something of a camping trip.

But when it came to planning the visit to the Fezzan, preparations took on a more adventurous look. This is best illustrated by the request for equipment which the Mission's Administrative Officer addressed to the Executive Officer of the United States Air Base at Wheelus Field, namely: 3 squad tents, 30 cots, 60 blankets, 10 five-gallon water cans, one Lister bag, 30 camp mess kits, 10 fourteen-gallon blankets, 3 folding tables, 6 folding chairs, 6 lanterns, 3 small paulings, and 3 first-aid kits. And this was only part of the equipment to be loaded onto the United Nations plane. It was made perfectly clear that the United Nations would make good any loss or damage.[15]

In order to prepare Council members for the kind of living they had to expect, the Principal Secretary issued a circular pointing out that, while Council members would be accommodated in rooms in the former Italian fort at Sabhah, then serving as headquarters of the French Military Governor and a detachment of the Foreign Legion, some of the staff would have to sleep under canvas. In Sabhah, meals would be served in the Officers Mess, but members were advised to bring their own beverages. In Ghudamis, the party would be housed partly in a hotel, partly in tents; but the circular went on to say that at Ghat the party would be accommodated "simply." A more ominous announcement was that the secretariat would provide DDT bombs. Clothes presented less difficulty, as members had agreed not to bring formal evening wear; informal summer slacks and suits were recommended, but as some traveling might have to be done early in the morning or late at night, members were urged to bring woolen suits and topcoats. Hats, or sun helmets, and sun glasses were also recommended. As there were no banks in the Fezzan, travelers checks could not be cashed, though dollar bills could. It was estimated that about three dollars (approximately 1,000 Algerian francs, the currency then used in the territory)

15. This list follows United States Air Force terminology and will doubtless be familiar to American readers. Indeed, most of the items call for no explanation; but the following three definitions may ease possible mystification: a Lister bag is a canvas water-holder; a "fourteen-gallon" blanket is one of exceptionally large size (on the analogy of a four-gallon Stetson hat); and a pauling is a groundsheet.

per day would cover the cost of food and lodging. Members were also warned that they would find almost no opportunity of buying consumer goods.

The report submitted the Sub-Committee on Travel expressed the view that it would be preferable for members to make their visits to the territories in one single group. This never proved possible in practice, partly for reasons of a personal nature, but partly, also, because certain members had plans of their own; for instance, the representatives of Egypt and Pakistan, accepting an invitation from the Amir, decided to pay a separate visit to Benghazi instead of accompanying their colleagues to the Fezzan and later to Cyrenaica. Another difficulty was that some members would have liked to have formal Council meetings in the Fezzan and Cyrenaica. However, the staff required could be neither transported nor accommodated, at any rate not in the Fezzan. It was therefore agreed that should a meeting have to be held, the members' advisers would lend their services. In the upshot, this never proved necessary.

So much for the preliminaries. The visits to each of the territories will now be described in detail.

A. Tripolitania

Occasionally, there were signs of political activity, in Tarhuna, for instance, where representatives of the National Congress Party and of the Independence Party asked for separate interviews at their respective headquarters. After some discussion, it was decided that the Commissioner and the Council members would hear both parties together, on neutral ground.

The representative of the Congress Party declared that the country had no problems, and but a single aim, namely: the unity and independence of Libya under the sovereignty of the Amir of Cyrenaica. He was sure that the Independence Party—which, he said, represented only a minority of the people—would share that aim. The representative of the latter party thereupon announced its firm support for the United Nations Resolution, and stressed its eagerness to offer the Commissioner and the Council any help that would not conflict with the Resolution.

The Commissioner urged the two parties to sink their differences and to work together for the achievement of their common aim; there was no response to this appeal.

The visiting party had similar experiences in other Tripolitanian towns. The overall impression confirmed what the Commissioner and the Council already knew, namely, that although the Congress Party was the most active and most representative of the political organizations in Tripolitania, the Independence Party was in no way to be underrated as a political force.

B. The Fezzan

The group which finally left for the Fezzan on 13 and 14 May numbered thirty-one people, too many for one flight, so that two had to be made. The Landrovers had been sent on ahead, a somewhat hazardous expedition in itself, though accomplished without serious incident. The French Administration had been helpful in making two command cars available for travel within the Fezzan.

Visits were paid to all the main administrative centers: Sabhah, and the adjacent village of Jadid; Brach, the center of the most populous area of the Shatti depression; Murzuq; Ghat; and Ghudamis. The last two were reached by air, the other three by road, or, more correctly, track. The distance from Sabhah to Murzuq is 148 kilometers, that to Brach 222 kilometers, that to Ghudamis 915 kilometers, and that to Ghat 562 kilometers.

For some in the party, not used to this kind of travel, it was rough going, not so much because the distances were so long as because departures were usually early and returns often late. Meeting and questioning as many people as possible within the short time available in itself demanded constant and tiring mental concentration. It may also be supposed that the nights were not always restful for those accustomed to don silk pajamas before retiring to a comfortable bed, but now obliged to wear that same attire on an army cot. The flies, abundant in daytime, were another source of discomfort. This gave rise to a rather comical incident during a luncheon given the Commissioner and Council members by Ahmed Bey Seif al-Nasr. Presiding cross-legged at the head of a low table, with his guests in the same not always easy position on either side, the host rigorously wielded his fly whisk to drive as many of the insects as possible to the far end of the table, thereby causing acute discomfort to the junior members of the party seated there. Finally, one of the latter, unable to stand it any longer, discreetly pulled a DDT bomb from his pocket, and gave it a few quick but audible bursts. The result was disastrous; in a very short time, he and all around him had their plates full of dead flies. Ahmed Bey remarked drily that the modern inventions of Western civilization were not always suited to simple Saharan conditions.

The visit to the Fezzan lasted from 14 to 21 May. The representatives of Cyrenaica, the Fezzan, France, Tripolitania, and the United States, and the advisers to the representatives of Italy and the United Kingdom, had interviews with the Acting French Resident, the Chef du Territoire and his counselors, and many notables from the region. The Commissioner, owing to pressure of work in Tripoli, could participate only in the visits to Sabhah and Jadid, but even so, he was struck by the change in atmosphere since his two earlier visits.

It looked as if on this occasion the French Administration had lifted all bans on freedom of expression. The result was a much more colorful and varied pattern of opinion—even if fundamentally the same—than he had heard before. What lay behind this change in French policy went unexplained. Some thought at the time that it was a matter of the personal attitude of the Acting Resident, Captain Cauneille, who was replacing Colonel Sarazac while the latter was on leave, but this does not seem likely in the light of overall French policy.[16] Others believed that it was an attempt to sound the true feelings of the Fezzanese people, which were, it was presumed, virtually unknown to the French Administration as a result of its own restrictive policy. These were interesting guesses, but neither was confirmed by any official statement or document. Anyway, there is some evidence that after the Council's visit many of the old restrictions on freedom of expression and movement were reintroduced.

On May 15 the Commissioner and the Council members present had a revealing interview with Ahmed Bey Seif al-Nasr, an account of which has already been given on pages 197–99. The most important features of his statement were his expression of gratitude to the United Nations for its action to promote Libyan independence, and his acceptance of the Amirate of Sayed Idris over the whole of a united Libya.

It was, and still is, the fashion—particularly in Tripolitania—to underrate the intelligence and moral courage of Ahmed Bey, now dead. He certainly was a simple and unsophisticated man, not greatly learned by Arabic standards, or refined. In his younger days he had been a fighter and had led the life of a seminomad. Later he settled down, and became at once respected by the majority of traditionalists among his people and suspected, by the younger generation, which had been touched by Arab nationalism, of pro-French feelings. Politically speaking, he was himself a traditionalist; but he was very much aware of what was going on in his territory. Compared to the prudent position he had taken when the Commissioner had first met him in January, February, and March of 1950, he was almost outspoken in May; that must have taken a great deal of courage and a keen feeling for the political changes in the air. His position at the time of the Council's visit is best illustrated by the declaration just mentioned, and by an additional statement in which he expressed his thanks to France for its

16. Captain Cauneille took over from Colonel Sarazac as French Resident in the Fezzan later in 1950. Having been associated for several years with the Corps des Officiers des Affaires Indigènes, he was an excellent Arabist, and easier to deal with, from the United Nations point of view, than his predecessor.

action in granting independence to the Fezzan and to the United Kingdom for similar action in Cyrenaica and Tripolitania. It would have been difficult for him to be more subtle, because he knew very well that if the two Administering Powers were talking about independence, they were certainly not doing so with the establishment of a truly united Libya in mind. What in fact Ahmed Bey did was to confront them with their own policy statements in order to be able himself to adhere publicly to the ideal of some form of Libyan unity. What that form was going to be, in his opinion, became clear when, in reply to a question from the Acting Chairman of the Council, Ali Bey Jerbi, he said that there should be one government for the whole of Libya, but that the Fezzanese should be left to deal with their own internal affairs. He developed this line of thought by stating that there could be no independence for the Fezzan alone; an internally autonomous Fezzan must nevertheless be linked with Tripolitania and Cyrenaica. Libya should be independent, but the ideal unity was that of God (meaning a common Islamic brotherhood).

After Ahmed Bey had spoken, the Mudir of Jadid and Counselor for Justice made the declaration recorded on pages 198–99.

The French member of the Council expressed his pleasure with Ahmed Bey's very interesting statements about his relations, religious and other, with the Amir; he was equally pleased that they had been made publicly and officially. He asked to what extent the people of the Fezzan shared Ahmed Bey's feelings toward the Amir, adding that France knew the latter well and was not forgetful of the help His Highness had given to the common cause during the recent war. The Counselor for Justice replied that the Amir was their religious and political leader, and would be sovereign over all Libya. However, the Fezzanese would have to ask him to recognize their special interests; they were confident that Sayed Idris would give everyone his due.

Mustafa Mizran, the Tripolitanian member, who was to have at least one separate private interview with Ahmed Bey in the following days, expressed his thanks to the Bey and to the Counselor for what they had said about the unity of the country. All Libyans were brothers, and the Amir would be their King. The Fezzanese would have complete freedom in managing their domestic affairs.

During the party's three-day sojourn in Sabhah and its surroundings, the Tripolitanian and Cyrenaican members had a number of personal conversations with Ahmed Bey, both in private and in the presence of his advisers. These, and their travels and talks elsewhere in the Fezzan, gave them for the first time an opportunity of getting to know the leaders of and living conditions in the Fezzan, which neither had previously visited. Ali Bey

Jerbi brought not only the Amir's greetings, but a message from him expressing the hope that all the leaders of the Fezzan would support him in working toward the unity and independence of Libya. His Highness also sent assurances that, as far as he was concerned, there would be no interference with the local administration. In these meetings the bond of the Senussi faith was reaffirmed, all pledging allegiance on the Senussi flag. Thus, an important by-product of the trip was a distinct improvement in relations between the three Libyan members of the Council; this in turn facilitated collaboration between the three territories.

There had been a number of misunderstandings on the part of the Tripolitanian member about the sentiments of the Fezzanese people. In discussions, particularly in the oases of Brach and Ghudamis in the Northern Fezzan, spokesmen repeatedly spoke of their sufferings at the hands of the Tripolitanians. Mustafa Mizran as often denied that "Tripolitanians" had ever oppressed the Fezzanese. It transpired that the complaints were of long standing, and related to raids by the seminomadic tribes of the southern Tripolitanian hills into the Fezzanese oases. When Mustafa Mizran grasped the true nature of the charges, he assured his listeners that it was the intention that in the future the tribes would be curbed by Libyan police.

When, three days later, the party paid a farewell visit to Ahmed Bey, he said that the Fezzanese were good people and always agreed with one another. No attention should be paid to the minority of dissidents. However, the latter had certain qualities, and he intended to visit those who did not understand the real situation, to explain to them the points about which they were ignorant. The Council need have no apprehensions in this regard.

The next day there was a meeting with the three Counselors—for Justice, Finance, and Public Health and Education—who, apparently feeling quite free to speak their minds, usefully supplemented the general information given the day before by Captain Cauneille and Ahmed Bey. It was on this occasion that Nasir Bin Salem, Counselor for Finance, speaking in the name of the inhabitants of the Shatti depression, the richest and most densely populated region of the Fezzan, with 17,000 inhabitants, said that he had not altogether shared the spirit of the earlier meeting with Ahmed Bey. However, in view of the explanations given during the hearing, particularly about the Fezzan's becoming part of the Libyan State under the sovereignty of the Amir, he was now prepared to accept the Senussi, provided that Ahmed Bey express certain reservations to the Amir directly in order to safeguard the territory's interests.

Later the same day, members received a visit from Sheikh 'Abd al-Rahman al-Barquli, the head of the opposition group, accompanied by a delegation (see pp. 191–92). They had come to say that they were in favor of Libyan unity and the unification of the country, but opposed to Libya's being divided into three parts. They enlarged upon this by asserting that they wanted one single administration with the Amir as King of Libya so that the Fezzan could again be united with Libya as it had been under Italian rule. The Sheikh alleged that the French Administration was encouraging separatist tendencies, was doing everything in its power to nullify the feelings being displayed in the Fezzan in favor of Libyan unity, and was trying to establish a kind of trusteeship over the territory. This was bluntness the like of which had not so far been heard in the Fezzan, except during the visit of the Four Power Commission of Investigation in 1947, when it had had dire consequences for the few Fezzanese who had had the courage to indulge in it.

In Brach, the *Chef-lieu* of the Shatti, where the party met a group of notables, the tone of the views expressed was still much the same as when the Commissioner paid his first visit to this oasis in February. The Qadi recognized Ahmed Bey's authority but did not want the Fezzan to be joined with Tripolitania or Cyrenaica. He wanted the Fezzan to stay under French protection and trusteeship. In reply to questions, he repeated that he recognized Ahmed Bey's authority within the boundaries of the Fezzan, but did not want the territory to be independent. Others present shared these opinions, which according to them were those of all the inhabitants of the Shatti.

Ali Bey Jerbi, speaking as Acting Chairman of the Council, referred to the conversation Council members had had the previous day with the Chef du Territoire, and sketched the position the Fezzan would enjoy in a united Libya. The Qadi replied that if he were free to choose for himself, his choice was made; any other choice would have to be imposed by force.

The French member asked whether this meant that the people of the Shatti were against the idea of a Libyan union or the Amir. The Qadi answered that he wanted neither one nor the other.

Ali Bey Jerbi, speaking both in his official capacity and as a Moslem, said that he regarded the views expressed by Ahmed Bey as decisive, and that the opinions of the people of the Shatti were those of a minority. He was sorry to see his Moslem brothers take such a stand.

Mustafa Mizran gave an assurance that there was no question of the Fezzan being placed under the authority of either Tripolitania or Cyrenaica. The three territories would be like three sons of the same mother. He had no objection to the Fezzan having its own administration, but he wanted the territory to be governed by Moslems.

One of the notables present repeated that the Fezzan wanted to be separate from the other Libyan territories; he himself knew that Tripolitania and Cyrenaica were not really at one on the subject.

At Murzuq, the party was received by a group of men who declared that they were opposed to the nomination of Hajj Ahmed al-Senussi Sofu as Fezzanese member of the Council for Libya. According to them, Hajj Sofu had been chosen by the Administration without any consideration for the wishes of the people; moreover, he harbored separatist ideas. In this connection, it should be noted that before reaching Murzuq the Commissioner had received an anonymous letter from a resident of that place, requesting him to call a private meeting of the leaders of public opinion there. The meeting should not be held in a government building, and government officials such as Hajj Sofu and others should be excluded. It was therefore plain that public opinion in Murzuq was divided, as the Commissioner had perceived during his first visit.

When the Principal Secretary asked the group whether they had been subject to ill treatment or pressure on the part of the French authorities, they were unable to give chapter and verse for any such incidents. It was therefore not clear exactly how opinions in Murzuq were split between supporters and opponents of Ahmed Bey, but it was obvious that the local people felt able to speak much more openly than at the time of the Commissioner's earlier visit.

In Ghat, the Council knew what to expect, namely, that the Tuaregs, who had refused to take part in the jemaa convened for the election of the Chef du Territoire and the Fezzanese member of the Council for Libya, wanted to remain under French rule. Nevertheless, a large group of tribal chiefs, led by the Amghar of the Adjer, were there to receive the party and the Commissioner's personal representative, the Principal Secretary, the Commissioner himself having had to return to Tripoli. After Ali Bey Jerbi, Mustafa Mizran, and the Principal Secretary had explained the purpose of the visit and the meaning of the United Nations Resolution, the Amghar stated that he did not want to be joined to Tripolitania; his people wanted peace, and to remain united with their brothers, the Tuareg of the Adjer, as they were at present. Whenever the Tuaregs had had anything to do with the Tripolitanians there had been difficulties which had forced many of the Tuaregs to flee to the Sudan. He saw no possibility of any agreement between Tripolitania and the Tuaregs. He emphasized that his people wanted the present situation to continue permanently, and that if anyone wanted to change it, they would have to use force. The Tuaregs had always protected Ghat against enemies from without. Furthermore, they had always protected Tripolitanian caravans on their way to the Sudan. But they would never agree to come under an Arab government, any more than they would submit to Fezzanese authority.

A discussion ensued between the Arab members of the Council present and the Amghar as to who was responsible for the bad relations between Tripolitanians and Tuaregs. Then a promise was given that the Tuaregs would keep their autonomy in a united Libya, but the Amghar refused; he even went so far as to say that at the time of the election of the Chef du Territoire he had gone to Sabhah, but had refused to see Ahmed Bey as he thought that he knew his own affairs better than did the latter. "That is all I have to say," he concluded, "and now I shall ask permission to withdraw, for one word is better than ten." [17]

At a second meeting, held later that day, the Council party received seven inhabitants of Ghat who, speaking for themselves and seven others, presented a petition asking that Ghat should be united to Libya. These men apparently represented the local sedentary inhabitants.

Just before sundown, a group of about two hundred sheikhs, elders, and notables, all wearing blue veils from eye to ankle, gathered in a semicircle outside the fort. Peaceable in demeanor, though each man carried sword and either spear or rifle, they were addressed by the Amghar resplendent in his flowing red robes, blue veil, and white turban, who gave his account of the day's happenings. He then asked the Principal Secretary to give the United Nations point of view. Speaking in English, which was then translated into Arabic by a United Nations interpreter, and thence into Tuareg by one of the Amghar's entourage—a process not calculated to ensure accuracy—the latter explained what the United Nations was, the terms of the resolution on Libya, and the purpose of the Council's tour. He laid particular emphasis on the prescription of Libyan unity and the requirement that the Libyans draw up and adopt their own constitution. While the Principal Secretary was explaining the United Nations decision that there should be a unified Libya, presumably within its existing borders, the United Nations interpreter, hearing ominous mutterings, digressed to make it clear to the assembly that it was the Principal Secretary, not he, the interpreter, who was speaking of unity and independence!

At the conclusion of this twenty-minute speech, the Amghar stepped forward in the early twilight, took his place beside the Principal Secretary, and told his tribesmen that, having heard from the United Nations they could now choose: did they wish to support him or the United Nations? In the latter case, he would disappear into the desert. With a roar of approval for their Amghar, the tribal leaders brandished their rifles and spears, and

17. Minutes of hearings at Ghat, United Nations Archives. Typescript.

clanged their swords to punctuate their cheers of allegiance. As the crowd surged forward, the Principal Secretary shook hands with the Amghar, thanked all present for their courteous attention, and withdrew fifty yards to the gateway of the fort where the Council members and staff had been discreetly watching the confrontation. The tall, dignified Amghar strode away into the darkness surrounded by his cheering followers.

It was difficult to weigh the relative importance of the Tuareg's refusal to join a united Libya and the request of the sedentary population to become part of the new State. However, it seemed clear that the nomads in the area were both in the majority and genuine in their refusal to join a united Libya. According to the French Administration, the settled inhabitants numbered no more than five or six hundred; this too seemed an accurate estimate.

The nomad Tuaregs, their martial customs notwithstanding—perhaps even because of them—were in the habit of leaving their civil affairs in the hands of their women, who periodically met in a kind of council. The system has been compared to a matriarchy, though all decisions of war and peace were the prerogative of the men. During one visit they paid to Ghat, members of the United Nations Mission were told a story of a French captain, *un beau garçon,* who in order to establish better relations with this women's council had learned to knit, thus virtually making himself one of them. It was further related that not only was he a very effective administrator; he was also so successful in other directions that after a while his superiors decided that it would be better to transfer him to another post, where his charms were less appreciated.[18]

The party's next and last stop in the Fezzan was at Ghudamis. The problems there were not unknown to the Commissioner and his staff. Local resources were very limited, but the town had always enjoyed a certain importance as a center of trade with Tunis and Tripoli. On his earlier visit, in February, the Commissioner had been met with complaints that all trade links with Tripoli had been cut by the French Administration, and told that the population wanted them restored.

On the present occasion, when the party arrived by air, it was greeted with a demonstration in favor of independence, in the course of which the Amir of Cyrenaica, Beshir Bey Saadawi, and the Arab League were all acclaimed. From the temper of this demonstration it was fairly obvious that, French precautions notwithstanding, the slogans of the National Congress Party of Tripolitania had reached Ghudamis and influenced a fair number of its inhabitants.

This impression was confirmed at a meeting with a group of notables, as

18. The author is indebted to the Principal Secretary for this anecdote and for the account of the confrontation with the Amghar.

well as in the course of a visit to the town itself. A spokesman for the notables made it quite clear that the population of Ghudamis wanted to join an independent Libya.[19]

C. Cyrenaica

While those members of the Council and their advisers mentioned on page 228 were in the Fezzan, their colleagues from Egypt and Pakistan had been paying a visit to Benghazi and other parts of Cyrenaica at the invitation of the Amir. Staying as his personal guests at the Al-Manar Palace in Benghazi, they had several long, quiet talks with the Cyrenaican leader. At the same time, they met many other people, and received a number of petitions expressing a variety of opinions on the local situation and on the future of Cyrenaica itself and Libya as a whole.

On 25 May 1950, the group which had visited the Fezzan left for Cyrenaica. Without being the personal guests of the Amir, they had occasion to see him, collectively and individually, as well as members of the government and party leaders. In fact, their program was in many respects similar to that of the Egyptian and Pakistani representatives; but this tour carried them to the borders of Egypt, whereas the other Council members stopped at Al-Bayda, about 150 miles east of Benghazi.

When the second group arrived in Benghazi, there was naturally a considerable amount of speculation as to what had occurred at the private talks between the Amir and the Egyptian and Pakistani representatives. Political circles were rife with rumors, highly colored by each party's and each man's views on the all-pervading problem of federalism versus unitarism. Perhaps the most objective information, later confirmed by developments, came from those moderately progressive men, of whom fortunately there were more than a few, whose aim was to engineer a practical compromise between the two extremes. Seen from this angle, the conversations between the Amir and the Egyptian and Pakistani members had not produced the result for which these observers had hoped. They had expected that Selim Bey and Rahim Khan, having learned that Cyrenaica preferred federalism whereas many Tripolitanians wanted a unitarist State, would have acted as arbiter and go-between, with the object of reconciling the two positions. According to these sources, who were later proved right, nothing of the kind happened. Both representatives, and especially Selim Bey, had defended the unitarist policy of the Arab League and the Tripolitanian Congress Party, while paying lip service to federalism.

The Council members, who had traveled from Tripoli to Benghazi by

19. For an account of the Commissioner's earlier visit to Ghudamis, see Chapter 2, p. 194.

road, visiting several towns on the way, first met the Amir, and then attended a luncheon given by the Cyrenaican Prime Minister, Mohamed Saqizli, who delivered a brief speech.[20] In this, he drew attention to the territory's special position, acquired first by the contribution it had made to the Allied war effort, second by the fact that it had already had an organized government before the United Nations Resolution was adopted. While Cyrenaica would welcome an association with Tripolitania and the Fezzan in steady progress toward independence within a united Libya, that was primarily for the Libyan people to decide. He expressed the opinion that the will of the Tripolitanian people should be ascertained by elections such as the election of representatives to the Cyrenaican legislative assembly that were to take place on 5 June.

These views were expressed in rather general terms, and accordingly prompted several members to seek clarification; the outcome was issued the next day as the official text of the speech. In it, the Prime Minister explained that for reasons already made clear, Cyrenaica had a right to the leading place when the independence of the country came to be considered. To assert this right, it had shaped its future for itself shortly before the United Nations' decision on the Libyan question was taken. That was why Cyrenaica was what it was, going its own way, maintaining its rights, steadfast in its endeavors, while still disposed to support the implementation of the United Nations Resolution as far as the other parts of Libya were concerned. The Cyrenaicans saw no insurmountable difficulties, provided the intentions of their Tripolitanian brothers were good. Indeed, if the latter could overcome their few personal differences and move resolutely toward the country's revival, in the direction of Cyrenaica, it would be possible to attach the Tripolitanian coaches to the Cyrenaican train. The whole could then steam steadily forward, for the road was clear and the track ran straight. Given those conditions, it was difficult for the Cyrenaican people to understand why their Tripolitanian brothers objected to following their example of holding free elections which would result in the creation of a truly representative body. (The insistence on Tripolitanian brotherhood will be noted.)

A week later, when the party returned to Benghazi, the Prime Minister expressed very much the same ideas in somewhat milder and more optimistic terms.

On 30 May, the day on which the Commissioner joined the party for four days, visits were paid to the British Acting Resident—the Resident himself being on leave—and to the British Educational Adviser to the Cyrenaican

20. Saqizli had recently taken over the Premiership from Omar Mansur al-Kikhia. See Chapter 2, p. 184.

Government. A few days later the party also met the Supervisor of Elections.

The Acting Resident mentioned among other things the difficult budgetary position, which will be discussed in more detail in the later chapters of this study. He also gave some general information about the position of the press. *Al-Watan,* the organ of the Cyrenaican National Association—the former Omar Mukhtar Club—had been suspended by the Cyrenaican Government. The suspension had now been lifted, although the paper had not yet resumed publication as it had not paid the deposit required by the law. Three other papers appeared in Benghazi: *Al-Istaqlal,* with a circulation of about 200; *Barqah al-Jedida,* published by the Cyrenaican Government, with a circulation of about 1,200; and the *Cyrenaican Observer,* published in English, with a circulation of about 850.

From the Educational Adviser the party learned that there were approximately 20,000 children of school age, of whom only about 8,000 actually went to school. The educational system had broken down in 1940; operations had been resumed in 1943 only on a very reduced scale. Most schools had been destroyed, and there was a general scarcity of teachers. Instruction had formerly been given in Italian; only in secondary schools had there been some teaching in Arabic. The result was that there were at the time very few Cyrenaican teachers capable of working in Arabic.

It was interesting that the Council's visit should have coincided with the holding of the elections to the Cyrenaican legislative assembly. The Supervisor of Elections said that the enrollment of voters, numbering some 60,000, had passed without difficulty. Candidates had to be more than thirty years old, voters over twenty-one; the franchise was exclusively male. Candidates had been presented individually, not on party lists; twenty-one had been elected unopposed. All possible precautions had been taken to ensure the freedom and secrecy of the ballot. No difficulties were foreseen in the towns. In tribal areas, where about 90 percent of the population was illiterate, voters would have to cast their vote orally. In Benghazi, there were thirteen candidates for six seats, in the Benghazi tribal district fifteen for seven seats, in Barce two for one seat, in Derna four for two seats, in the Derna tribal district ten for five seats, in the Jebel district twelve for six seats, and so on for the fifty elected seats. Ten additional members would be appointed by the Amir on election day. It had taken three months from the date of the promulgation of the Electoral Law to prepare the elections. As for the voting eligibility of non-Arabs, the Supervisor explained that Jews were considered to be Cyrenaican, as also were Greeks without passports. The same applied to those Tripolitanians, Tunisians, and Sudanese who had resided in Cyrenaica for a prescribed period.

Later, at a reception given by the National Association, which was virtually the opposition party, the Commissioner, accompanied by a few members of the Council and advisers, listened to a number of complaints about the organization of the elections. One was that it had been difficult to enable tribal members living in cities to vote, another that there had been no freedom of association during the electoral campaign—only the holding of meetings previously authorized by the Government, whose permission was not always easily forthcoming. In private conversation, bitter complaints were made about the suspension of *Al-Watan,* a step taken, it was alleged, to hamper the Association's propaganda.

Election day was 5 June. It was estimated that about 80 percent of the townsmen and 66 percent of tribesmen voted. Of the fifty elected members of the Cyrenaican assembly, six belonged to the National Association and forty-four to the National Congress Party. However, several of the latter were sympathetic to the Omar Mukhtar Club, having belonged to it in their younger days. The ten appointed members were generally notables with no pronounced party loyalty, or none at all.

The anniversary of Independence Day (the independence of Cyrenaica, 1 June 1949) was celebrated at Benghazi Town Hall by a reception given by the Mayor. In his speech, the latter declared that the date of 1 June 1949, when the Amir had proclaimed the independence of Cyrenaica, was a turning point between two epochs: one which should not be remembered, except as a lesson, the other just beginning, full of hope for progress. He concluded by acclaiming independent Cyrenaica and its Amir. Libya was not mentioned, except by the Commissioner in his reply.

The Council members visited many other places in Cyrenaica, and almost everywhere the reception was warm and instructive. During a reception in Derna Town Hall, a group of members of the National Association assembled in front of the building, carrying banners calling for the unity of Libya and shouting such slogans as: "No independence without unity"; "No unity without the Amir"; "We do not want the Bevin-Sforza Plan"; "The United Nations resolution must be fully implemented"; "The enemies of unity are the enemies of the nation"; "After our long struggle we cannot accept the overlordship of any foreign power, be it Britain, Italy, or France"; and so on and so forth. Ali Bey Jerbi assured the demonstrators that the aims of the Council were precisely those they had just expressed.

A few days later the party listened to the opposite, profederalist view, expressed by the President of the Youth League in the following broad terms: a united Libya under the Senussi Crown; the maintenance of full autonomy for Cyrenaica within the united Libyan State, which would be characterized by one flag, one crown, and the unified management of foreign policy and representation; each of the three territories to enjoy full autonomy in all other matters, such as defense, currency, budget, education, foreign trade.

Thus it was made plain that not only public opinion in Tripolitania, but that in Cyrenaica also, was still deeply divided. The difference between the two territories was that in Cyrenaica the majority appeared to be for federalism, whereas the opposite was the case in Tripolitania.

The Council's visit by road to the coastal towns and the Jebel Akhdar (the Green Mountain) behind them was an illuminating experience, for members saw the abandoned Italian settlements, only a few of which had been taken up by local farmers, the grazing lands with their scant forage for the Barbary sheep, the upland scrub, and the fringes of the desert. They visited the Greco-Roman ruins at Cyrene and Apollonia on the coast, and saw burned-out hulks of armored vehicles and aircraft scattered about the landscape side by side with ancient Roman cisterns, and, at Tubruq, the modern devastation resulting from the siege, and vessels sunk during the war still lying in the partially cleared harbor.

Houses, community centers, administrative buildings, barracks, barns, and granaries were largely in ruins, partly from the fighting, but also because of subsequent looting, which had stripped them of all their metal and wood (indeed, scrap metal from the battlefields had been a major export in preceding years). Still clearly visible on some of the buildings were Italian slogans, such as "Viva Il Duce," "Dulce et decorum est pro patria mori," "Il Duce ha sempre regione," and other exhortations to the Italian soldiers and colonists to fight and work for Italy and fascism. These fascist slogans were only painted over in 1952, by which time they had become the subject of so much amateur photography and comment by United Nations technical assistance experts and others traveling the Jebel Akhdar highway that the Cyrenaican authorities decided they should be obliterated. This lack of concern about the vestigial trappings of the Italian Empire was typical. While in Benghazi, some members of the Council had visited the Italian monument standing on the edge of the harbor which commemorated the conquest of Cyrenaica and honored the memory of the Italians fallen. When the United States representative asked why it had not been removed, he was told by one of the Palace staff that it would have cost too much in dynamite and clearance.

The party also visited the enormous cemeteries of the Allied and German forces at Knightsbridge, near Tubruq, and explored the small bazaar at Derna, a beautiful and unscathed coastal town, a hundred miles west of Tubruq. Several members had particular interests along the way. At Cyrene the American representative searched for the graves of the archeologists of the Harvard University expedition, whose murder in 1911 had provided the pretext for the first Italian invasion; and at Derna, he tried to locate the site of the United States Marines encampment of 1812. A few years later both places were marked with appropriate tablets presented by the United States Government in memory of its dead. The French representative, however, was frustrated in his wish to visit the Free French war cemetery at Bir Hakim, some miles south of Tubruq. The site was accessible only by a desert track, which wound its way through minefields, a grim legacy of the war. On the day when Ambassador Balay wanted to make his visit, the British District Officer was preoccupied with the election, and professed inability to provide a guide, since the most reliable man had stepped on a mine while making the same trip shortly before, and lost a leg. Alternative guides were considered too inexperienced to guarantee the Ambassador's safe return.

Members of the Council visited the two polling booths in Tubruq on election day; voting was proceeding calmly and peacefully, as it was indeed throughout Cyrenaica. They noted with interest that the largely illiterate electorate came forward one at a time to declare orally their choice, which was then recorded on the electoral roll, while literate members were allowed to mark their own ballot papers.

The party went on as far as the Libyan-Egyptian border post, a desolate checkpoint in the desert, undistinguished by natural features and not far from rusting barbed-wire defenses stretching south into the desert as far as the eye could see. The party had dwindled by this time to the French and United States representatives, the Principal Secretary, and members of the United Nations staff. The others had found, at various points along the way, urgent reasons for returning to Benghazi.

On 9 June, the second group flew back to Tripoli from Benghazi, a great deal wiser, but also more than ever convinced that they had not yet seen a clear picture of what Libyan unity was actually going to be.

On their return, both groups reported to the Council. Their general impressions tallied, except that, as might have been expected, Kamel Selim Bey and Abdur Rahim Khan had paid more attention to those voices which were for a unitarist State, whereas certain of their colleagues had been impressed more by the partisans of federalism.

Rahim Khan and Selim Bey reported that they had enjoyed the Amir's warm hospitality, and that their exchanges during four meetings had revealed complete agreement on every point. They felt that it would not be proper to go into detail about these private talks, but they did report the conclusions they had reached.

In particular, they asserted that not one party, delegate, or individual had expressed any desire but for the unity and independence of all Libya. They had gathered that Cyrenaica wanted a federal unity; but not a single man had urged the independence of Cyrenaica before Libyan unity. They had also been struck by the fact that the Amir was unanimously accepted as the indispensable and undisputed Head of the new Libyan State. Finally, they observed that in Cyrenaica, as in Tripolitania, the immediate interest of the people was centered on a National Assembly, without which the United Nations Resolution would remain a dead letter, as Libyan unity and independence would remain a dream. Concern had been expressed in unmistakable terms about the delay in bringing a National Assembly into being.

All this was, of course, well known to the Commissioner, in particular from the talks with representatives of the Benghazi and Derna branches of the Omar Mukhtar Club recorded in Chapter 2 (pp. 187–88).

Looking back, the author feels—as he did in his role of Commissioner at the time—that a golden opportunity was lost in the course of these events. No others could have played the part of intermediaries better than the Pakistani and Egyptian representatives. Unfortunately, when those progressive Cyrenaicans who had been willing to make concessions saw the two Moslem, non-Libyan members of the Council supporting unitarist tendencies to the hilt, they were thrown back on to a defensive position based on federalism and supported later by Ahmed Bey Seif al-Nasr and his friends in the Fezzan. The outcome of this episode is all the more regrettable, inasmuch as the Egyptian and Pakistani members, who stood for a truly united Libya, could in all probability have procured a considerably more centralized federation than finally emerged. The only people happy with this development were the former adherents of the Bevin-Sforza Plan.

RESUMPTION OF THE DISCUSSIONS IN THE COUNCIL ON THE COMMISSIONER'S FIRST REQUEST FOR ADVICE ON CONSTITUTIONAL DEVELOPMENT: INTERVENING EVENTS

When, on 12 June, the Council resumed its debate on the Commissioner's request for advice on constitutional development, the situation was radically different from what it had been before its members had toured the three territories. The change was indeed so radical that it would be difficult to comprehend without an account of certain events which had taken place in the meantime.

On May 26, Beshir Bey Saadawi had written to the Amir, giving the reasons for which, in his opinion and in that of the National Congress of Tripolitania, general elections were precluded in that territory. Unfortunately, it has been impossible to trace the text of this communication, but the letter by which the Amir informed the Chairman of the Council of its content states that, according to Beshir Bey, "holding elections in several parts of the country within the short period will be burdensome so far as the inhabitants are concerned. H. E. The United Nations Commissioner has been satisfied with this idea. Accordingly, I [the Amir] have agreed that no elections be held in Tripolitania." [21]

At first sight, and for a variety of reasons, the letter caused surprise. Up to the moment when the Council had embarked on its travels, there had been no opposition to the holding of elections. On the contrary, during the first part of the debate, at the beginning of May, the elective principle had been approved. It had also been accepted during the many consultations the Commissioner had had with personalities in the three territories, including Beshir Bey Saadawi himself, when the Commissioner first discussed with them the plan on which his request for advice was based. Why then this sudden change? From that moment to the present, many explanations have been put forward for this volte face on a cardinal issue affecting Libya's constitutional development.

After checking and rechecking, the Commissioner came to the conclusion—and he has had no reason to change his mind since—that the Tripolitanian parties, especially the National Congress Party, feared that the elections might well deteriorate into an embarrassing demonstration of the political disunity and personal rivalries that unfortunately played such a large part on the Tripolitanian public scene. There was also a risk that the elections would show up the gross exaggerations in which the members of all parties without exception had indulged to bolster their prestige and make propaganda for their cause. Another likely reason was genuine alarm lest the elections not be free because of the presence of the British Administration.

However, the third reason sounded less valid than the first two. After all, elections had been held in Cyrenaica on 5 June in the presence of members of the Council. As we have seen, the opposition had criticized the organization of these elections, but there had never been any suggestion that the British Administration had attempted to influence the results. Admittedly, the situation was not the same in the two territories. Cyrenaica had its own Government, even though the British Resident retained a body of reserved powers; Tripolitania enjoyed no such autonomy. On the other hand, the mentality and policies of the two British Administrations were not so far apart as to justify the fear that they would interfere in one case and not in

21. United Nations Doc. A/AC.32/COUNCIL/R.38 and Corr. 1, 13 June 1950. Translated from Arabic. Mimeographed.

the other. Even if fear of such meddling might be a little more justified in Tripolitania, did it provide sufficient justification for suppressing all electoral process? The Commissioner did not think so.

The assurance that Beshir Bey Saadawi allegedly gave to the Amir—that the United Nations Commissioner was satisfied with his proposal—also calls for comment. In fact, the Commissioner was not satisfied at all. He still preferred, and continued to prefer, all opposition notwithstanding, that the members of the preparatory committee, and subsequently those of the National Assembly itself, should be chosen by some elective process. But he also understood that if there were strong opposition to elections, it would be not only unwise, but also well beyond his powers to press the point.

In the meantime, those who were against elections in Tripolitania found themselves in a difficult situation in the Council, as they could not count on a majority to support their new policy. On the face of it, three or four members at best would be on their side. Accordingly, they instigated talks behind the scenes among the representatives of Egypt, Italy, Pakistan, and Tripolitania. The objective of these talks was the conclusion of a deal by which the Libyans, on the one hand, would drop their opposition to a minorities representative (in all probability an Italian) on the preparatory committee; in exchange, the Italian member, as well as the representative of the minorities, would support the Tripolitanian case against elections. These negotiations, prepared largely at the lower level of advisers but subsequently sanctioned by the Council members involved, were concluded before the Council resumed its session on 12 June. The Commissioner first heard rumors to this effect soon after his return to Tripoli from Benghazi. The success of the intrigues enabled the representative of Pakistan to rally a majority for the rejection of the Commissioner's request for advice.[22]

Naturally, a compromise of this kind carried with it certain political risks. One of them was that the Italians, having obtained satisfaction in the case of the preparatory committee, might press similar claims when the time came to discuss the composition of the National Assembly. Mustafa Mizran, who was plainly aware of this danger, therefore asked for and obtained a written assurance from Baron Confalonieri that no such claim would be advanced. Unfortunately for the historian, the text of this assurance can no longer be found.

One more event must be mentioned in this connection. As described in Chapter 2 (pp. 131–39), the British Administration in Tripolitania—with the agreement of the Commissioner and in consultation with the local

22. Fifteen years later, in 1965, when the writer was checking up on these events, several witnesses, who, however, declined to allow their names to be cited, confirmed the accuracy of this account.

political parties, but not without considerable opposition—had set up an administrative council for the territory and had also been trying to organize elections for a territorial legislative chamber. In this context, too, the problem of minority representation—particularly Italian—had arisen first with regard to the composition of the administrative council, and second because of the proposed Italian participation in the elections to the legislative chamber. In the case of the former, resistance had been overcome with the support of the Commissioner; but when it came to allowing the minorities to take part in the elections to the legislative chamber, the opposition grew so strong that these had to be postponed until after independence. There were other factors, too, which militated against the holding of elections, but it was obvious that, after the general fear of British intervention, the minorities problem came next in importance.

The consequence of these difficulties was that the Commissioner could no longer count on a local legislative chamber to elect or select the Tripolitanian members of the preparatory committee. He therefore had to change his plans. Still wishing to safeguard, as far as possible, the principle of an elected committee, he turned to the only elected bodies in the territory, namely, the sixteen municipal councils, which together represented approximately 90 percent of the total population of the territory. He was well aware that this was not an ideal choice; but he was moved by the consideration that it would be highly undesirable to have the Tripolitanian members of the preparatory committee chosen without the benefit of a democratic process when the Cyrenaican and Fezzanese members were to be designated by the representative bodies of those two territories.

However, it is now clear that the idea of calling on the municipal councils was a tactical error. Indeed, popular distrust of British policy was so strong that the revised plan provided its opponents with fresh arguments.

While all this was going on, the Commissioner was also engaged in exploring the possibility of finding a solution for an even more important aspect of the Libyan problem, namely, the rift between Cyrenaicans and Tripolitanians on the form of the future State. The problem was to facilitate a compromise between extreme Cyrenaican federalism and extreme Tripolitanian unitarism. The Commissioner believed that if he could bring the Amir and Beshir Bey Saadawi together at the same table, there might just be a chance of this. He had therefore, with the Amir's consent, suggested to Beshir Bey that he accompany him to Benghazi for the express purpose of discussing this basic issue. He was the more hopeful of success inasmuch as the Amir, though a convinced supporter of federalism, had never taken a rigid position on this issue when it came to discussing details. Beshir Bey, on the other hand, was a shrewd politician, whose main purpose was to engineer a united Libya, a policy of which he had been a life-long supporter and in which he was strongly backed by the Arab League and its first Secretary-General, Azzam Pasha, whose greatest fear was that a federal Libya would be nothing but a tool in British and French hands. Perhaps, then, the Amir's diplomatic skill and Beshir Bey's political sense would enable them to reach a meeting of minds on a degree of federalism capable of providing an acceptable measure of unity.

The Commissioner had come to appreciate Beshir Bey as a well-intentioned man with much political acumen and the vision, though not always the strength of character, of a statesman. One particular weakness was a tendency to cast onto others the responsibility for his own mistakes and misjudgments. This, of course, is not an unknown shortcoming, particularly in politicians, but Saadawi indulged it to the point where it rebounded upon himself—to his detriment. Nevertheless, together with the Amir and Mahmud al-Muntasir, he was one of the leading personalities in Libyan politics during the two years of transition. Unfortunately he was rather susceptible to the influences of others, with the result that not only did he find it difficult to make up his mind, but, having done so, he also not infrequently changed it. This would be reasonable enough in itself, but he often failed to inform the interested parties of what he had done. The pressures exerted upon him by the leaders of the Tripolitanian Congress Party on the one hand and by the Arab League on the other (although Beshir Bey did not always see eye to eye with Azzam Pasha), were apparently so strong that he found it difficult to formulate and stick to a middle policy of his own, which might have made possible an understanding between the two principal Libyan territories in matters of constitutional development.

During the four days (30 May to 2 June 1950) the Commissioner spent in Benghazi, he had three long meetings with the Amir and two with Beshir Bey; unfortunately, however, the three-cornered meeting for which the Commissioner had hoped never materialized. It was quite clear that Beshir Bey preferred to deal with His Highness and the Commissioner separately, in order not to be tied down to any specific commitment. Anyway, it was Beshir Bey who avoided a common meeting. His attitude was the more puzzling in that, fully aware that the Amir was the paramount unifying force in Libya, he supported him as future Head of State. At the same time, he knew very well that the Amir was a staunch advocate of federalism. Surely it would have been in his own best interest to seek an agreement, for failure to do so would have emphasized his subjection to the influence and the pressure of the extreme unitarists?

Apart from this main issue, the Commissioner also seized the opportunity of trying to reach an agreement with Beshir Bey on the internal situation in Tripolitania, especially with regard to the preparatory committee. In this respect His Highness advised and supported him, but, having as yet no official standing in Tripolitania, he had to tread carefully, all the more so as Beshir Bey tried to load on to him responsibilities which he did not yet feel legally competent to assume. An example of this was provided by the issue of whether or not the municipal councils could be called upon to designate the Tripolitanian members of the preparatory committee. Beshir Bey, being himself opposed to the Commissioner's plan, asked His Highness to undertake the obviously delicate task of recommending this procedure; but the Amir refused. Neither had the Commissioner power to make such appointments. In the absence of a government in Tripolitania similar to those in Cyrenaica and the Fezzan, the British Chief Administrator was, in law, the only authority competent to accredit the Tripolitanian members to the committee. This, in the Commissioner's eyes, was one more reason for electing them. Beshir Bey, however, argued that the municipal councils had been set up before the formation of the National Congress Party, under British influence, and that they were therefore unrepresentative of the true wishes of the people. What he really meant, of course, was that they did not consist of men of his choice—trusted party members. Once more the Commissioner tried the way of compromise, suggesting, in agreement with the Amir, that of the five members to be chosen, three should be designated by the municipal councils meeting together, and the two others appointed by the Chief Administrator with the agreement of himself as Commissioner. In putting forward this idea, he had in mind that the two appointed members would be Beshir Bey himself and Mahmud al-Muntasir, if they were not elected by the municipal councils in the first place. Both the Amir and the Commissioner considered that in this way at least two capable and influential men would be certain of seats on the preparatory committee. However, this suggestion drew Beshir Bey's strong disfavor, for he regarded it as highly offensive to be appointed by the head of the British Administration, even with the Commissioner's agreement. Considering the impression such a procedure might have made on public opinion, perhaps he was not altogether wrong.

In all these talks, one more problem occupied the minds of the Amir and the Commissioner, namely, the need to improve collaboration within the Council for Libya between the Cyrenaican and Tripolitanian members, Ali Bey Jerbi and Mustafa Mizran. But collaboration at this level depended, in turn, on an understanding being reached between the Amir and Beshir Bey. As this proved practically impossible, the political relations between the two members were often marked by friction. One question that particularly divided them was that of equality of representation between the three territories; but as it became plainer and plainer that only on this condition could the preparatory committee be convened at all, the issue gradually lost importance as a source of political dispute.

The Commissioner's discussions with Beshir Bey, which were generally frank and open, revealed once again a mistaken idea on the part of the latter about the Commissioner's powers. Beshir Bey took, or affected to take, the line that the difficulties between Tripolitania and Cyrenaica were entirely due to the British Administration in the latter territory and the influence it exercised on His Highness and his Government. He therefore argued that it was the Commissioner's duty to check the trend toward autonomy in Cyrenaica, the extreme form of which he rightly considered to be contrary to the spirit of the United Nations Resolution. He also condemned the attempts made by the British Administration in Tripolitania to establish local organs of government. It was true that these attempts had caused considerable difficulties and delay, but Beshir Bey conveniently forgot that he had himself been in favor of them as recently as February and early March, as has been seen in Chapter 2 (pp. 135–37). The fact was that he had changed his mind for quite understandable reasons; but those same reasons ought to have deterred him from criticizing the same measures at this later stage. He even complained bitterly that, while the Commissioner had originally possessed the power and the will to put an end to these separatist policies, he was no longer in a position to do so. As a result, he added, the Council's work had come to a standstill. That body was gallivanting about the country instead of concentrating on its main task. In the same breath, he argued that it was premature to talk about a federal or a unitary form of government, as the time was not yet ripe to deal with that problem, which should be left until the National Assembly was in session. He refused to see that, on the contrary, the issue had to be settled before the Assembly could be convened. That the preparatory committee was the best means for preparing the ground for such an undertaking, he also declined to admit, arguing that the National Assembly should have been convened at once; but he omitted to say how this could have been done.

In the course of these often painful conversations, Beshir Bey's preference for excluding all electoral processes and appointing the Tripolitanian members of the preparatory committee on the sole advice of the leaders of the political parties became more and more marked. The Commissioner profoundly disliked this prospect, not only because he considered nomination an undemocratic process, but also because he knew from experience how unsatisfactory and time-consuming the necessary consultations would be, particularly in Tripolitania.

It had been planned that Beshir Bey should attend the next meeting with the Amir, but he had politely turned down the invitation. In the circumstances, His Highness offered to attempt to clarify the situation in writing. A written agreement would have to cover both the basic principles governing the future form of the Libyan State and the more immediate question of how the Tripolitanian members of the preparatory committee should be appointed.

The Cyrenaican and Fezzanese positions about the form of State were perfectly clear and well known to Beshir Bey. It was now up to him to define the Tripolitanian attitude. This was the issue at stake, and it was a crucial one.

The day after the Amir's attempt to reach agreement with Beshir Bey, the situation, although no better from the Commissioner's point of view, had at least taken on a certain degree of clarity. Beshir Bey, having once more repeated his unshakable opposition to all forms of election, direct or indirect, had presented the Amir with a list of eight persons who in his opinion were capable of representing Tripolitania on the preparatory committee; five of them should be appointed by the Amir. Among the people on the list were two members of the National Congress Party—the Mufti of Tripolitania as well as Mustafa Mizran; one member of the Independence Party; four men belonging to no party; and the leader of the Egypto-Tripolitanian Union Party (or another member thereof). This at once raised the question whether a member of the Council for Libya (Mustafa Mizran) could at the same time properly be a member of the preparatory committee. Both the Amir and the Commissioner agreed that this was not a desirable cumulation of functions, which might well place the incumbent in politically difficult situations; but there was no legal impediment to it. Standing by his refusal to make the appointments, and agreeing that the Commissioner was not competent to do so, the Amir once more proposed that the Chief British Administrator in Tripoli should designate the five members.

Having weighed the pros and cons of the various solutions, the Amir and the Commissioner came to the conclusion that the best way out of the imbroglio might still be the designation of three members by the municipal councils and the appointment of the two others by the Chief Administrator in agreement with the Commissioner. It was agreed, moreover, that in the final instance the Chief Administrator would have to accredit all five members if they were to enjoy a status comparable to that of their colleagues from Cyrenaica and the Fezzan.

With regard to the form of State, including the form of government, the Amir had defined his views in the following terms. The future government of Libya would be federal, under one crown and one flag; there would be a common currency for the three territories, a common foreign policy, and a unified military command; there would be two capitals, Tripoli and Benghazi, and when the Amir was residing in one he would be represented in the other by a local deputy; the Amir would also have a Fezzanese deputy in that Province; in each of the three territories there would be a local government linked to the others through the foregoing common factors.

Beshir Bey accepted the system but would not promise to make a public statement to that effect—a significant and ominous attitude.

When the Commissioner asked whether the powers allotted to the federal government could be enlarged to take in such sectors as communications, justice, and education, and whether there should not be a federal parliament in addition to the three local chambers, His Highness replied that that aspect of the question had not been studied by the former national congress of Cyrenaica. All that that institution had had in mind was that each of the local governments would be an emanation of its local chamber; but in his own opinion there might be a federal parliament, in the form of an upper chamber, as an emanation of the three local chambers. It was understood that all these matters would naturally come up for discussion in the preparatory committee and eventually for decision in the National Assembly.

Once more the Commissioner arranged a meeting with Beshir Bey in an attempt to draw common conclusions from the separate discussions each had had with the Amir. This time Beshir Bey was more explicit, in that he definitely rejected not only any form of electoral process, but also any intervention by the British Chief Administrator in the matter of the membership of the preparatory committee. What he still refused to admit was that in the final analysis the latter's authority alone was competent to accredit the Tripolitanian members of the committee, unless they took their seats as mere private individuals. He declared that if the Chief Administrator's intervention were not definitely excluded, he would have to reconsider his whole attitude toward the institution of the preparatory committee, maintaining that the appointment of members nominated by the political leaders was the only feasible solution.

The Commissioner reluctantly replied that he would be prepared to examine this method further; but he warned Beshir Bey once again that failure to follow electoral procedures might provoke criticism in the General Assembly of the United Nations. Personally, he was still strongly in favor of elections; but he realized that, being merely an adviser to the Libyan people, he must at all costs avoid giving the impression that he was trying to impose his will upon them.

The next day Beshir Bey, apparently having reconsidered the names of his candidates for membership of the preparatory committee, submitted a shorter list, omitting Mustafa Mizran and one of the independents. Whether the new list was a result of consultation with other political leaders was not clear. In the event, the Amir immediately acknowledged receipt of the letter, declaring that he had no objection to any of those named, and wishing Beshir Bey continued success.

RESUMPTION OF THE DISCUSSIONS IN THE COUNCIL ON THE COMMISSIONER'S FIRST REQUEST FOR ADVICE ON CONSTITUTIONAL DEVELOPMENT: FORMAL DEBATE

It was in the foregoing much changed circumstances, and in an atmosphere quite different from that which had prevailed a month earlier, that on 12 June 1950 the Council resumed its debate on the Commissioner's request for advice on his plan for the constitutional development of Libya. What had seemed acceptable to the majority a month before now came under severe fire from several quarters. Moreover, it could be sensed that the views of several members had crystallized, that the dice had been thrown, and hence that the discussion was virtually pointless. Indeed, it soon transpired that the members for Egypt, Italy, the Minorities, Pakistan, and Tripolitania were now against the Commissioner's plan; and the member for Cyrenaica, though hesitant at the outset, soon joined the opposition, apparently out of a desire not to accentuate more than necessary his past differences with his Tripolitanian colleague.

The representatives of France, the United Kingdom, and the United States were still in favor of the plan, though with reservations.

The member for the Fezzan was absent for genuine reasons of health, and indeed soon after was obliged to resign from the Council.

The main criticism was that too much time had already been lost in establishing the National Assembly, and that the appointment of the preparatory committee by electoral process would only make matters worse. Recourse to the municipal councils, which could have been convened within a few days—thus largely saving the time that would otherwise have to be spent on elections to the legislative chamber—was also opposed on the ground emphasized by Beshir Bey, namely, that they had been elected under British influence and remained under British influence. It was also argued that elections were not prescribed in the United Nations Resolution, which left open the question of how the National Assembly was to be set up by the Libyan people. Even the legality of creating a preparatory committee was contested, since no such body had been foreseen within the framework of the Resolution. The Commissioner, it was added, had no right to propose either the committee or elections to it.

All this criticism led its proponents to the conclusion that the only possible way of appointing the Tripolitanian members of the preparatory committee was through consultations with the leaders of the political parties. The point already made—that only the Administering Power could accredit candidates emerging from such consultations—was not at first grasped; when it was, the competence of the Administering Power was at once contested.

The other side continued to defend the plan, although proposing certain changes, which were embodied in a resolution submitted by the United States representative. This had been drafted at the request of several of his colleagues and commanded the support of eight of them. However, some of these supporters changed their minds when the Pakistani representative introduced a motion of his own.

For the last time, the Commissioner justified his plan on both political and legal grounds, at the same time expressing his willingness to agree to certain changes; but he had the strong impression that he was defending a lost cause.

The United States proposal sought to advise the Commissioner to proceed along the general lines set out in his request for advice. However, it expressed the belief that the preparatory committee's terms of reference needed further study, and that the municipal councils should not be brought into play unless this was specifically requested by the inhabitants. The draft also took note of the willingness of the inhabitants of Cyrenaica and the Fezzan to accept the Commissioner's proposals, and regretted that no corresponding concurrence was so far forthcoming from Tripolitania. It ended by urging the Commissioner to continue his consultations with Tripolitanian leaders with a view to finding some acceptable basis for selecting the Tripolitanian members.

The Pakistani draft resolution, after referring to the United Nations Resolution, requested the Council to express the opinion that immediate action should now be taken by the United Nations Organization in Libya to help the people of that country to meet in a National Assembly. To this end, it was proposed that the Council advise the Commissioner to take the following action:

(a) To request the Amir to *propose* the names of seven representatives from Cyrenaica;

(b) To consult the political leaders in Tripolitania and, after obtaining their views on the subject, propose for the approval of the Council the names of seven outstanding personalities to be invited by the Commissioner to join the Cyrenaican representatives; and

(c) To request the Chef du Territoire of the Fezzan to *nominate* seven representatives to consult with the representatives of Cyrenaica and Tripolitania, all to meet in Tripoli not later than 1 July 1950 and prepare a plan whereby the representatives of the inhabitants of the three territories should meet in a National Assembly for the purposes stated in paragraph 3 of Resolution 289 (IV).

After all those on the list of speakers had been heard, but before the vote was taken, the Commissioner, in view of his special position vis-à-vis the Council, asked once more for the floor. This request was refused by the Chairman (the representative of Egypt) on highly debatable grounds. The ruling was challenged by the United States representative, but upheld by 5 votes to 3, with 1 abstention. The Commissioner's intention had simply been to seek clarification of certain obscurities which might have made it difficult for him to carry out the Council's advice once this had been determined; as it had been made impossible for him to do so, he was obliged to submit a supplementary request for advice the following day.

The United States proposal was put to the vote first and rejected by 6 votes to 2. Since, at this particular meeting, only the member for the Fezzan was absent, some other member must have been out of the room when the vote was taken; but nobody seems to remember today who this was, and as the decision was taken by show of hands, there is no record of individual votes to clear up the mystery. Whoever it was, he must have been a person who realized that he was in a very embarrassing position. The Pakistani draft resolution was adopted by 6 votes to none, with 3 abstentions, the absent member having presumably returned.

Apart from a few minor amendments, the Pakistani representative had agreed to one substantial change, namely, the replacement, in subparagraph (b), of the word "approval" by the word "advice." This was indeed not without significance, since the Council, as a purely advisory body, had no right to approve or disapprove candidates proposed by the Commissioner.

After the voting, Kamel Selim Bey proposed that the Council adjourn for a week to give the Commissioner time to establish the necessary contacts and carry out the consultations in pursuance of the resolution just adopted. This was agreed to. But when the Commissioner insisted on his right to submit a supplementary request for advice on the manner in which he was to conduct the consultations, it was finally decided that the Council should meet again two days later.

Without reacting too dramatically, the Commissioner was nevertheless seriously disturbed about the way in which his plan had been treated. On the one hand, some of its essential features had survived, such as the convening of a preparatory body (although of a different kind), which at least implied recognition that the National Assembly could not be improvised out of nothing. Equally important was the tacit approval of the principle of equal representation for the three territories, without which the committee could never have been constituted. The increase from five to seven members per province was, at first sight, not particularly important, but soon produced certain complications, as will be seen. That its terms of reference had been emasculated to the point of mere preparation of a plan for the meeting of the National Assembly was regrettable, but not fatal. It would in a way make the work of the future committee more difficult, but at the same time it left its members more freedom of initiative and action. The Commissioner was still not without hope that, once the committee got together, a truly Libyan esprit de corps would develop among its members and lead them to draft their own terms of reference. Indeed, once in existence, the preparatory committee would enjoy a unique status, being under no obligation whatsoever to listen either to the Commissioner or to the Council.

The Cyrenaican members would follow instructions received from the Amir, based on his Cabinet's advice and, perhaps to some extent, on that of the British Resident. The Fezzanese would receive instructions from the Chef du Territoire and undoubtedly, though subject to mutual agreement, from the French Resident in Sabhah too. In Tripolitania there was nobody who could give the lead, not even the British Chief Administrator, though the latter might try to influence some of the territory's representatives, who would otherwise listen to their party leaders and probably to many other voices as well.

There remained one part of the original plan, the rejection of which caused the Commissioner serious misgivings: the omission of any reference to the use of an electoral process and the resulting inequalities in the way in which members would be designated in the three territories. His qualms on this point were coupled with fear that a similar disparity in nomination procedures might attend the constitution of the National Assembly as, indeed, certain members of the Council had already adumbrated. He also found it difficult to believe that a nominated National Assembly would not come in for serious criticism at the next General Assembly of the United Nations. One advantage, however, had to be recognized: that in the circumstances prevailing in Tripolitania consultations would require less time than elections. The only faster procedure on hand was the use of the municipal council machinery; but unfortunately this had proved unacceptable.

CONSIDERATION OF THE COMMISSIONER'S SUPPLEMENTARY REQUEST FOR ADVICE

The Commissioner's supplementary request for advice raised two questions.[23] The first related to the composition of the preparatory committee, which, it will be remembered, was to be made up entirely of Libyans. This had not been an original feature of the Commissioner's plan, but had been included to secure the approval and participation of the Amir, of the Chef du Territoire in the Fezzan, and of several Tripolitanian leaders.

Now a new situation had been created. The Council's advice of 14 June [24] took the *whole* of Resolution 289 (IV) as the basis for the action to be taken by the Commissioner in inviting nominations for the new committee, thus including paragraphs 6 and 7 defining the composition and selection procedure the Commissioner was to apply in appointing the four local members of the Council for Libya. The much debated paragraph 3 was also involved. Moreover, in the course of the discussions, several members, in particular the Egyptian and Pakistani representatives, had specifically suggested that the Commissioner should follow the same procedure in his forthcoming consultations. Bearing in mind also what he had learned unofficially about the agreement reached between certain members of the Council, which had produced the majority for the Pakistani resolution, it was fairly clear to the Commissioner that the consultations on which he was to embark might involve the appointment of a minorities representative, probably an Italian subject, to the preparatory committee. It was not clear whether this implication was fully understood, particularly by the Cyrenaican member, at the moment when the vote was taken. Thus the Commissioner found himself caught between his existing understanding about the exclusively Libyan composition of the committee and the possibilities opened up by the advice of the Council. Clarification was required on two points:

First, should the Commissioner consult the Cyrenaican and Fezzanese leaders regarding the possible inclusion of representatives of minorities among the Tripolitanian personalities to be consulted? Second, should he subsequently also consult them on the possibility of including a minorities' representative among the Tripolitanian members of the preparatory committee?

The second issue raised in the supplementary request concerned the criteria and methods the Commissioner should apply in the course of his

23. For full text of the supplementary request for advice, see the first *Annual Report of the United Nations Commissioner in Libya,* Annex XVI, pp. 75–76.

24. Ibid., Annex XV, p. 74.

consultations, a point on which the advice of 14 June was completely silent. This, too, was connected with paragraphs 6 and 7 of Resolution 289 (IV), as well as with the interpretation of paragraph 3 thereof. The Commissioner reminded the Council that the procedures prescribed in paragraph 7 had in particular given rise to a great many time-consuming differences of opinion among the Tripolitanian parties and organizations as well as among the minority groups. He now proposed to avoid such complications by proceeding along the following lines:

1. He would first decide upon the outstanding persons to be consulted;
2. In addition, the Council would provide him with a list of organizations and parties which in its opinion he should consult;
3. He would invite, in writing, each party or organization on the Council's list to present to him within three days a list of seven persons whom the party or organization concerned considered competent and suitable to represent Tripolitania on the preparatory committee;
4. Having received all these lists, the Commissioner would place on the list to be submitted to the Council for its advice those names which appeared most frequently on the party lists;
5. If this first round failed to produce seven names, he would repeat the procedure outlined in (3) until all seven vacancies had been filled by agreed candidates; and
6. The foregoing procedures should not last more than nine days, counting from the date on which the requests for the first lists were dispatched. On the evening of the ninth day the Commissioner would inform the Council whether or not all seven posts had been filled; if not, the Council would advise him how to proceed.

Finally, the Commissioner raised the question, already debated but so far unanswered, of the authority by which the seven agreed Tripolitanian representatives should be accredited or appointed to ensure that they enjoyed a status equivalent to that of their Cyrenaican and Fezzanese colleagues.

When the Council met on 16 June to discuss these matters, it decided, in view of their delicate nature, to sit in private. At the outset, the United Kingdom representative submitted the following draft advice to the Commissioner:

1. That he conduct the required consultations in Tripolitania according to his best judgment and ability, generally following a procedure analogous to, but where necessary modified at his discretion from, that laid down in paragraph 7 of Resolution 289 (IV);
2. That he consult with the Administration in Tripolitania as to how the seven agreed representatives for that territory should be accredited in

order that they might have a status similar to that of the Cyrenaican and Fezzanese members; and

3. That he consult with the Amir and with Ahmed Bey Seif al-Nasr, through the good offices of the Cyrenaican and Fezzanese representatives on the Council, and if necessary by personal contact, about the meeting mentioned in the last paragraph of the Council's advice of 14 June.

The draft ended by requesting the Commissioner to inform the Council of the result of these consultations preferably not later than 21 June 1950.

Penney pointed out that advice of this kind could not and should not cover every detail of the Commissioner's actions. He had therefore provided latitude for the Commissioner to use his discretion in certain circumstances. He reaffirmed the view he had already expressed at an earlier meeting that the only authority competent to appoint the Tripolitanian representatives was the Chief Administrator. Lastly, paragraph 3 of his draft was meant to provide useful clarification of some points that were obscure in the previous advice.

Kamel Selim Bey contested the legal need for having the Tripolitanian representatives accredited by the Chief Administrator. However, he did not press the point—which was shortly to cause some unpleasant complications.

Baron Confalonieri said that he had listened to the Commissioner's request with both satisfaction and sorrow: with satisfaction about the request itself, which proved that the Commissioner intended to consult the Council and to be guided by its advice; with sorrow because the request gave the impression that relations between Italians and Arabs were of the worst, although during the recent visit to Cyrenaica members had been able to see for themselves that even there, there was no hatred of the Italians.

The Chairman also regretted the tone of the Commissioner's request, but wanted to make it clear that he wished the latter to include the minorities in his consultations. He, moreover, would do everything he could to see that the minorities were included among the Tripolitanian representation. For the rest, he considered the United Kingdom draft a simple and well-conceived document, easy of implementation. He foresaw no complications.

Ali Bey Jerbi, referring to Baron Confalonieri's remarks, observed that his was an Arab country with an Arab Amir and an Arab population. Undue political significance should not be attached to the welcome and hospitality extended to members during their visit to Cyrenaica.

After the representatives of Egypt and the United Kingdom had also expressed the hope that a representative of the minorities would find a place among the Tripolitanian members of the preparatory committee, the draft advice was unanimously adopted.

The Commissioner started on his fresh round of consultations the same day.

PART 4. THE COMMITTEE OF TWENTY-ONE: CONSULTATIONS ON MEMBERSHIP [25]

The Commissioner and his staff had been considering for some time what method of consultation and appointment or accreditation they would follow should the Council advise against the use of the municipal councils. Expert opinions had been sought from United Nations legal advisers, in particular as to whether the Commissioner had the power under paragraph 7 of Resolution 289 (IV) to act as he had done earlier in the case of the appointment of the four local Council members (see Part 3, passim). They had answered in the negative, considering that although he could still use the consultation procedure provided for in paragraph 7, his power of appointment had ceased to be effective.

In these circumstances it was clear that, in the absence of any Libyan authority in Tripolitania, and in the light of subparagraphs 10 (a) and (b) of the Resolution, the only course was to follow the Council's recommendation that the Commissioner consult the British Administration in Tripolitania as to how the seven representatives of that territory, once agreed upon, should be accredited to the Committee of Twenty-One (as the preparatory committee was now being called). This might create fresh tension between certain political parties and the Administration, a development which Beshir Bey Saadawi had already foreseen and tried to avoid by submitting his own list of nominees to the Amir. The latter, having no powers in Tripolitania, had had no alternative but courteously to decline to act on that submission. But the fact that he had been invited to act itself reflected the new political climate that was beginning to form. As was shown in the Historical Background, negotiations between Tripolitanians and Cyrenaicans, the latter represented by the Amir, were not without precedent. The new element was that a Tripolitanian leader had invited His Highness to take the lead in an important local political matter because he recognized him as the *Head of a future Libyan State*.

Thus, for the first time, political observers saw the shape of things to come; but the brutal fact remained that the only authority competent to appoint, endorse, or accredit the Tripolitanian members of the Committee of Twenty-One was the British Chief Administrator. It so happened that at

25. With the adoption of the Pakistani draft resolution (see pp. 252–53), the preparatory committee became the Committee of Twenty-One.

that time he was on leave; and his deputy, not unnaturally, deemed it necessary to consult London. However, this became a matter of concern only later. At the time, the consultation procedure took priority over everything else. Fortunately, the Council's advice left the Commissioner sufficient latitude and liberty of action to adapt his course to the new circumstances.

Accordingly, in the evening of 16 June a letter was sent out to fifteen political parties and organizations—the same organizations, except for some unimportant changes, that the Commissioner had consulted about the choice of the Libyan members of the Council. But there was an important difference between the two situations. Earlier, he had had to appoint one representative for each of the three territories and one for the minorities. It had therefore seemed proper to appoint the candidate who, after due consultation with all concerned, appeared to command the strongest support. That this unavoidably left a minority dissatisfied could not be helped.

Now, however, seven Tripolitanians had to be chosen, and it seemed equitable to do so in such a way as to make the group as representative as possible of the various tendencies and opinions of the population of the territory as a whole.

Another difference was that the Commissioner this time had to submit a list of names to the Council for advice. The latter might very well disagree with his proposals. Furthermore, the controversial question of subsequent appointment or accreditation persisted.

The Commissioner's letter in each case solicited the names of seven candidates, not more than four of whom were to belong to the party or group consulted; the rest should be members of other parties or outstanding independent personalities. As time was short, replies were asked for by 19 June; in practice, this was too soon, but the request would, he hoped, create an effective atmosphere of urgency. The communication ended with the hope that this approach would encourage consultation and cooperation, cutting across party lines, and so produce the largest possible area of agreement. A list of all the parties and organizations, including the minority communities, to whom the request had been addressed, was annexed. By 19 June eight lists had been received, but also three refusals to cooperate.

Inquiry revealed that the parties in the National Congress group had not yet submitted their lists (although these had been agreed upon) because they were waiting for the Amir's reaction to their views on minority representation. This showed how much uncertainty still prevailed on this issue. It was obvious that more time would be needed before the Commissioner could report on the list of candidates he had been called upon to submit "to his best judgment and ability."

For the Commissioner and his staff there followed a few hectic weeks of criss-cross consultations with party leaders, members of the Council, the British Administration, and a surprisingly large number of individuals, both party and nonparty, who came privately to advise the Mission against certain candidates or to press the claims of others. At the same time, petitions were coming in from all parts of the Province, supporting or opposing the main issues at stake. It was difficult to find a common denominator in all these views; but certain names came up more frequently than others, and personality seemed definitely to count more than party affiliation. And yet another conclusion emerged clearly: that the people, even in the rural areas, were now much more aware of the broad problems confronting them than they had been earlier in the year.

CONSULTATIONS WITH CYRENAICAN AND FEZZANESE LEADERS

In the meantime, nominations from Benghazi and Sabhah were coming in without apparent hitch; but the efforts of the Cyrenaican and Fezzanese members of the Council to consult their respective leaders on minority (Italian) representation on the Committee of Twenty-One yielded no positive results. Accordingly, the Commissioner, at the Amir's invitation, went to Benghazi on 18 June to try to find a way out of the difficulty through personal contacts. At the request of the Chairman of the Council—at the time Kamel Selim Bey, who refused to make the trip—the Commissioner invited Mustafa Mizran to accompany him, so that he would at least have a representative of the Council majority at his side, who could also bear witness to what transpired, should that prove necessary. The Cyrenaican member, Ali Bey Jerbi, completed the party ex officio.

On arrrival, the Commissioner found that Beshir Bey Saadawi, accompanied by his Egyptian political adviser, Fuad Shukri, had also come to Benghazi. Thus the scene was set for a confrontation, with the Commissioner defending the Council's policy which, as the Amir knew, did not coincide with his personal views. The Acting British Resident also supported the Council's plan, at least as far as minority representation was concerned.

Before leaving Tripoli, the Commissioner had learned from private sources that Mustafa Mizran was carrying a personal and confidential letter to the Amir from Abdul Rahim Khan and Kamel Selim Bey. Its purpose apparently was to convince the Amir that it had been necessary to accept an Italian member on the *appointed* Committee of Twenty-One in order to ensure a majority in the Council for the Pakistani proposal and the rejection of the Commissioner's original plan for an *elected* preparatory committee of fifteen.

During the first interview with the Amir (18 June), the Commissioner explained the differences between the two proposed bodies, the manner of their composition, and the definition of their duties. The mysterious letter was not mentioned. The Amir wanted to know what lay behind the controversy. The Commissioner could only reply with some rather plausible conjectures, the most likely of which was fear of the outcome of elections and, hence, a desire to keep the selection of the committee members in the hands of a few party leaders.

At a second audience the following morning, the Amir mentioned that he had met Beshir Bey Saadawi and his adviser, and also Mustafa Mizran. The personal communication had been handed to him; it had been accompanied by a long exposition. His Highness did not feel free to show or read the letter to the Commissioner; but he gave a broad outline of its contents through the Egyptian United Nations political officer who was acting as interpreter, and asked what the Commissioner thought of it. It appeared that the authors and bearers of the letter had reminded the Amir that since the work of Commissioner and Council would be brought to the notice of the General Assembly through the former's annual report, the motives for the Council's recent decision might be misunderstood. They feared especially that the Administering Powers might suggest that in the prevailing circumstances Libya could hardly be ready for independence by 1 January 1952, and would accordingly ask the United Nations to put the date back, as it had done in the case of Somaliland. Moreover, to strengthen their case, the two Powers could argue that Cyrenaica and the Fezzan had already gone their own way, and that the situation in Tripolitania was ambiguous. The votes of the Latin American States in the General Assembly would be needed to frustrate any such maneuver. This in turn would require the cooperation of Italy, which could best be secured by agreeing to Italian representation on the Committee of Twenty-One. His Highness added that a joint advisory committee he had appointed to go into the matter (see p. 267) had not been convinced by Beshir Bey's supporting arguments. They also believed that the letter reflected only the views of its authors, not those of the Council as a whole. That was why he was thinking of sending a couple of emissaries to Tripoli to give him an eye-witness account of the situation and to get a better idea of the consequences that might be expected to flow from Italian membership of the Committee of Twenty-One. The two emissaries would also be instructed to propagate the Cyrenaican view on federation.

Asked again for advice, the Commissioner replied that the arguments he had just heard had taken him somewhat by surprise. His comments would therefore be neither definite nor final. His first reaction, however, was that the Administering Powers would not take the risk of proposing that independence be postponed, as they must be perfectly well aware that no such proposal would ever command the two-thirds majority required for its adoption. Anyway, as Commissioner, he would himself advise the General Assembly against such a course.

He also expressed his belief that considerations of a more general political nature might well be involved. It looked to him as though the Italian Government was seeking to improve its relations with Egypt, and with the Middle East in general, a praiseworthy enough purpose in itself. It was in the nature of things that Italy should have a considerable interest in the eastern Mediterranean, not least in Libya. It was equally natural that Egypt should have a similar interest; but a rapprochement between the two countries should not be achieved at the expense of the future Libyan State. What disturbed the Commissioner was that Kamel Selim Bey, Abdur Rahim Khan, and Beshir Bey Saadawi seemed disposed, in order to avoid elections at all costs, to make concessions to Italy before even a provisional Libyan government had been established. For one thing, the question of the status of Italian subjects in the future Libyan State had in his opinion been raised prematurely; for this was a matter solely for the Libyan National Assembly. At the same time he did not wish to dramatize the situation. Naturally, the minorities in Libya, including the Italians, were entitled to the privileges and benefits conferred by the relevant provisions of the Universal Declaration of Human Rights, which should be incorporated, insofar as possible, in the Libyan constitution. Negotiations would also have to be initiated to implement the economic and financial provisions of the Treaty of Peace with Italy as they affected former Italian property in what was to become Libya. But no decisions taken in these areas could legally bind the Libyan people as long as there was no Libyan State. In the meantime, the Commissioner felt that one Italian on the Committee of Twenty-One, or even in the National Assembly, would not be in a position to do much harm. A majority in the Council having made this a possibility, it would be politically unwise to oppose it, particularly in view of the forthcoming meeting (the Fifth Session) of the General Assembly. Speaking officially, therefore, he advised the Amir to agree to Italian participation in the Committee of Twenty-One, but at the same time to seek corresponding guarantees to protect Libyan interests. Asked what he had in mind, he suggested, by way of example, a formal promise that Italian representation on the Committee or presence in the National Assembly would not be taken as a precedent for Italy's claiming, after independence, political rights for her subjects resident in Libya. As we shall see, several more meetings, both with the Amir and the Cyrenaican Cabinet and with the Tripolitanian representatives in Benghazi, were necessary before it was decided that the Commissioner should ask the Council for further clarification in this matter.[26]

Seven months after the issue had been settled, and after the Arab delegations to the Fifth Session of the General Assembly, led by Egypt, had severely criticized the setting up of the Libyan National Assembly on the grounds that it had not been elected (see Chapter 5, p. 355 *et seq.*), the Tripolitanian newspaper *Tarablus al-Gharb* published an article that included the full text of the famous, or infamous, letter that had been presented to the Amir on 18 June. The letter was preceded and followed by editorial comment, the closing sentence of which read as follows:

> When Cyrenaica opposed the inclusion of the Italian member in the Committee of 21, Kamel Selim Bey and Abdur Rahim Khan sent a letter to His Majesty the King [*sic*] which was taken personally by Beshir Bey Saadawi with the intention of persuading His Majesty to accept the method of appointment of the Committee of 21 and to discard the idea of election, thus gaining the vote of Italy in addition to the other votes in favour of that appointment.[27]

The letter speaks for itself:

> Tripoli,
> 17 June 1950
>
> His Highness Sayed Mohammad Idrees El Mahdi al-Senousi, may God preserve him!
>
> I have the honour to write to you concerning a matter of very great importance. My colleague, the representative of Pakistan, and I hope that you will kindly look into it, because we fear that it may give rise to some misunderstanding.
>
> Your Highness knows that God has given us victory in our struggle to defeat one plan and to establish another. The plan we fought against and destroyed was that put forward by Mr. Pelt, providing for the establishment of a Preparatory Committee to be selected by the Municipal Councils in Tripoli. The majority of the members of these Councils are illiterate and they are blindly subservient to the Administration. Further-

26. See first *Annual Report of the United Nations Commissioner in Libya,* paras. 151–57. The text of the Council's formal advice on this issue of 24 June 1950 will be found in ibid., Annex XIX, p. 77. See also pp. 268–69.

27. Translation made for internal purposes by the language staff of the United Nations Mission in Libya from the Arabic text published in *Tarablus al-Gharb,* 19 January 1951. Now in the United Nations Archives.

more, the said Committee was to undertake the task of preparing an electoral law and a constitution for a unified Libya. This is a task which may require a year and a half which would mean that the resolution could not be implemented by 1 January 1952. Conditions would thus remain as they are at present. The scheme which we have prepared, however, and whose acceptance we have won by the will of God, provides for the establishment of this Preparatory Committee of 21 members, seven of whom will be selected by Your Highness for Cyrenaica, seven by Ahmad Bey Seif El Nasr for the Fezzan and seven by the political parties in Tripolitania for this territory.

This Committee will convene on 1 July in order to carry out one simple task, namely, to suggest the manner in which the National Assembly is to be established. In our opinion the Committee can accomplish this task in less than ten days and the desired National Assembly can be established before the end of the present year. When the Assembly convenes, its first act, by the will of God, will be to declare Your Highness King of united Libya and Your Majesty will then be able to form your cabinet in the manner that you desire.

At the same time the National Assembly will work on the drafting of a Constitution. This will be undertaken by a Preparatory Committee chosen from among its members, which will prepare a draft of the constitution and submit it to the National Assembly. The advantages of this suggestion of ours are that, firstly, the National Assembly would be created and, secondly, that you would become head of this State in your capacity as King of the country.

The independence and unity of the country would thus be accomplished within the time stipulated in the resolution of the United Nations. Your Highness will see the great advantage this suggestion of ours offers. Our proposal was opposed by the representatives of the United Kingdom, France and the United States. The other four members [the Fezzanese representative being absent] supported it, so that this was a great blow to the enemies of Libyan independence. We would not have been able to reach this happy conclusion, which is in fact a miracle, had we not resorted to a strong plan, which was the outcome of the political ability acquired by us through our long political life. This plan was based upon the idea of gaining the two Italian votes in the Council for the adoption of our resolution, and at the same time winning 22 votes of the Latin-American countries should the matter be placed before the General Assembly of the United Nations. Everything, Your Highness, has a price in the world. The price that we have paid and that was accepted by all the heads of the political parties in Tripolitania was that the Preparatory

Committee should include a representative of the minorities (an Italian). That did not appear to us to involve any harm or prejudice in the attainment of the objective, but Ali Bey Jerbi and Mr. Pelt, the United Nations Commissioner, opposed it on the grounds that Your Highness would never accept an Italian in any Committee or in any scheme, even in Tripolitania where the leaders have accepted this as a price for achieving our aspirations. My colleague, the representative of Pakistan, and myself, out of true sincerity and loyalty, declare frankly to Your Highness that there is no hope whatever of the resolution being implemented and of the Libyan Kingdom being established under your auspices and crown, unless this price is paid and these votes are won. The supreme decision, however, is left to you and after that to the will of God. Please accept our sincere wishes, loyalty and respect.

(signed) Mohamad Kamel Selim
Representative of Egypt in the
United Nations Council for Libya

(signed) Abdur Rahim
Pakistan [28]

The letter was followed by an addendum on much the same lines, though brief, which also explained Beshir Bey's agreement to act as the courier, and was accompanied by a lengthy document entitled "An Explanatory Memorandum Concerning the Constitutional Developments Anticipated in Libya. The Difficulties Facing Elections in Tripolitania Alone." [29]

The publication of these documents six months after the events to which they related was not only a cruel but also an unwise act. It profoundly deepened the rift between federalists and unitarists at the very moment when the National Assembly was embarking upon its work, and it debased the authority of the Council, or at least that of certain of its members. Last but not least, it did a grave disservice to the cause of the Italian minority. Unfortunately, in those days Tripolitanian politics knew neither mercy nor discretion.

The author has dealt with this matter in full in the body of the text, instead of relegating it to a footnote or to an annex, for two reasons: first, because the incident was a disturbing element in the course of Libya's constitutional development, which caused a good deal of embarrassment all round and wasted valuable time and mental energy; second, because it shows clearly how the Commissioner's work was unduly complicated by a maneuver carried out behind his back, though one which, fortunately, proved the exception rather than the rule in his many dealings with all manner of men during his two years' activity in Libya.

28. Ibid.
29. Ibid.

After having heard the various points of view, particularly with regard to the difference between the Commissioner's original plan and the combined import of the Council's advice of 14 and 16 June, the Amir expressed his willingness to cooperate with the Italian minority in the economic field. But he could not agree that the minorities should play any part in the policy making of the constitutional organs. To admit an Italian to the Committee of Twenty-One, and possibly to the National Assembly, meant for him allowing the Italian minority to do precisely that. Furthermore, His Highness argued that it was unusual for foreigners resident in a country to help in drafting that country's constitution. He feared that such a course would be tantamount to granting the Italians in Libya de facto citizen status before Libya had even achieved independence.

In the course of his stay in Benghazi, the Commissioner also had an interview with the Cyrenaican Prime Minister, who was known to favor economic cooperation with Italy in the interest of both sides. Saqizli also felt, however, that as the future status of the minorities in general and that of the Italians in particular had not yet been defined, the latter should take no part in the political life of the country until legislation had been enacted granting Libyan citizenship to all who applied for it. He, too, asked whether, in the Commissioner's opinion, Italian participation in the Committee of Twenty-One and the National Assembly would presage their continued participation in the future Libyan government and parliament. The Commissioner replied that he saw no reason why Italians who acquired Libyan citizenship should not take part in the country's future government. In the meantime, he repeated that Italo-Libyan relations could not fail to improve if, as a gesture of goodwill, the Libyans agreed to admit one Italian to membership in the Committee of Twenty-One. The Prime Minister then suggested that the question of Italian membership on the Committee and the National Assembly could perhaps best be decided by the Libyan members of the former body which, he presumed, would meet as soon as possible.

Meanwhile, Saadawi and Mustafa Mizran had once more expounded to the Amir the reasons why they were in favor of granting the Italians a seat on the Committee, stressing once again that their fear that the Administering Powers might seek postponement of the date fixed for the country's independence was the paramount motive.

The Amir in turn again asked whether the Commissioner believed that failure to include an Italian in the Committee might delay the timely implementation of the United Nations resolution. This time, the Commissioner gave it as his considered opinion that it would be to the advantage of Libya to keep the Italians and their Latin American supporters in the General

Assembly in a friendly mood. He repeated that he found it difficult, for reasons he had already given, to believe that the Administering Powers would propose postponement of independence. He understood the distrust certain Libyans had of their intentions and policies; but such feelings should be kept within the bounds of political reason. In any case, he had never heard the argument adduced before, and stuck to his personal opinion that, if Beshir Bey Saadawi and his friends on the Council had agreed to minority representation, they had done so to gain Italian support against the holding of elections.

At the same time he advised the Amir, now that the suggestion had been made, to accept the Council's modifications of his (the Commissioner's) original plan, including the possibility of there being an Italian on the Committee, and possibly one in the National Assembly. Personally, he foresaw that in the long run neither of the parties directly involved would find the solution to its liking; and he realized that rejection of the Council's advice might do more harm to Libya's interests at home and abroad than one Italian could possibly cause by discussing the country's constitutional future in the company of twenty Libyans. That Italian might even succeed in explaining the minority point of view to his colleagues on the Committee.

While this exchange of views was going on, the Cyrenaicans continued to hold consultations of their own. These went on between the Amir and the joint advisory committee first mentioned on page 261, an ad hoc body consisting of the members of the Cabinet, the head of the Amir's Diwan (Omar Shenib, see pp. 294–95, fn. 49, for biographical note), His Highness' legal adviser, and other counselors. These advisers were loath to express an opinion in the absence of more precise information about the intentions of the Tripolitanian leaders. They had therefore formally proposed that the two emissaries mentioned by the Amir to the Commissioner be sent to Tripoli to elucidate two points:

1. How did the Tripolitanian leaders envisage the consequences of Italian participation in the Committee of Twenty-One? Could it mean giving the Italian residents there rights equal to those of Libyans? If so, their presence might endanger the future State, in which case the emissaries were to point out that Cyrenaica reserved the right to follow a course capable in her view of safeguarding her future against any Italian interference; and
2. What precisely was the Tripolitanian attitude toward a federal shape for the new State? On this point, the emissaries were to make it plain that a federation was the only form of government acceptable to Cyrenaica.

The Commissioner, sensing that a discussion on these issues between the two territories would bring matters dangerously close to the breaking point, suggested that an attempt be made to devise a formula that would protect Cyrenaica from the Italian penetration it feared during the transitional period. What happened after independence, he argued, would depend on the constitution, on the future government, and on such relevant legislation as might be enacted by them—all matters of which the National Assembly would be the sole master. The Amir agreed that the Commissioner should try to work out such a formula with the Cyrenaican and Tripolitanian members of the Council and Beshir Bey, but this attempt failed.

The Cyrenaicans were feeling increasingly uncomfortable in this welter of political maneuvering, and the Amir therefore decided to consult his Parliament. The question of Italian participation in Libya's constitutional development, he told the Commissioner, would affect the country's future for generations to come, and might even have international repercussions. The problem was thus too serious for him to resolve alone. However, he had decided, before approaching Parliament, to seek the advice of the Council for Libya, through the Commissioner, on a specific question which he formulated in the following terms:

> Does the Council for Libya consider that the Italian participation in the Committee of Twenty-One and in the National Assembly does not prejudge the settlement of the legal status of the Italians after Libya has promulgated its constitution and achieved its independence? [30]

The Amir's intention was to communicate the Council's advice to the Cyrenaican Assembly of Representatives in the hope that it would substantially assist all concerned in forming their opinion on the question put to them. With the request in his briefcase, the Commissioner returned to Tripoli.

The Council had difficulty in finding the right answer, taking the best part of two meetings over the task. To facilitate matters, the secretariat submitted a draft advice, the operative part of which read:

> The Council considers that Italian participation in the Committee of Twenty-One and in the National Assembly would not prejudge the settlement of the legal status of the Italians after the promulgation of the Libyan Constitution and the achievement of the independence of Libya.[31]

After amendment, the operative paragraph was adopted on 24 June by roll-call vote, by 7 votes to none with 3 abstentions. It read:

30. First *Annual Report of the United Nations Commissioner in Libya,* Annex XVIII, p. 77.

31. Summary Records of Council's 22nd Meeting, United Nations Doc. A/AC.32/COUNCIL/SR.22, 24 June 1950. Mimeographed.

> The Council considers that Italian participation in the Committee of Twenty-One or in the National Assembly envisaged under paragraph 3 of the General Assembly resolution 289 A (IV) of 21 November 1949 would not prejudge the settlement of the legal status of the Italians, after the promulgation of the Libyan constitution and the achievement of the independence of Libya.[32]

That the member for Cyrenaica should abstain was natural, his leader being the author of the question on which advice was sought. That the member for the Fezzan also abstained was more ominous, as he did so on instructions from Ahmed Bey Seif al-Nasr to the effect that he and his advisers were opposed to any representation of the minorities, and particularly of the Italians, on the Committee of Twenty-One. The third member to abstain was the French representative, who did so on two grounds: that he had opposed the original Pakistani proposal which had led up to the present situation; and that he was without instructions from his Government. On this occasion it looked as if France were following a Fezzanese lead, instead of the other way round.

The members for Egypt, Pakistan, and Tripolitania found the situation simple, straightforward, and to their liking. They had no difficulty in voting for the secretariat's draft. Neither had their Italian colleague. The representative of the minorities seized the opportunity of explaining his affirmative vote to launch a bitter attack on the Commissioner. Marchino even went so far as to declare that the minorities' confidence in the Commissioner's work had been seriously undermined by the latter's attitude. He reproached him for having subtly raised the minorities question in his request of 16 April 1950 for advice on his plan for constitutional development by suggesting that the preparatory committee for the National Assembly should be *entirely Libyan* (cf. p. 222). This, Marchino argued, was a gross misinterpretation of paragraph 3 of Resolution 289 (IV), which provided that the Libyan constitution should be determined "by representatives of the *inhabitants* of Cyrenaica, Tripolitania and the Fezzan meeting and consulting together in a National Assembly." The Commissioner confined himself to the observation that time would show that he had not been the worst friend of the minorities.[33]

The United States member considered that the Amir's question was simple and that there could be but one answer to it. His Highness was asking the Council for an assurance that after the promulgation of the

32. First *Annual Report of the United Nations Commissioner in Libya,* Annex XIX, p. 77.

33. For further comments on the interpretations to be placed on the terms "minorities" and "inhabitants," see Chapter 2, p. 184 and fn. 50. See also Chapter 4, pp. 335–50.

Libyan constitution and the achievement of the country's independence, the Italians would not, as foreigners, be free to participate in its government. The Council could perfectly well give the Amir that assurance. Naturally, if Italians acquired Libyan nationality, in accordance with a law that would, in his opinion, undoubtedly be enacted sooner or later, they would be entitled to take part in Libya's internal affairs on an equal footing with other Libyans; but they would have no such right as Italians. For him, the case for allowing the minorities to take part in the drafting of a constitution and the other preparations for Libyan independence was that there was as yet no Libyan nationality that they could acquire.

The United Kingdom representative, after considerable hesitation, expressed the opinion that Italian participation in the Committee of Twenty-One would in no way prejudge the settlement of the legal status of Italians after independence. But there was a great difference between the Committee and the National Assembly. However, the insertion of the words "envisaged under paragraph 3 of the General Assembly resolution 289 A (IV) of 21 November 1949," which made it clear that the term "National Assembly" could not refer to any postindependence legislature, had enabled him to vote for the advice.

After the vote, the Council, impressed by the intensity of Cyrenaican fears of a possible revival of Italian political influence, and realizing that a similar reaction was to be expected from the Fezzan, informally requested the Commissioner, if he found a suitable opportunity of doing so, to draw the Amir's attention to the fact that even when Libya became independent it would still have to fulfill several important conditions before it could be admitted to membership in the United Nations. One of these was that the country must be governed in accordance with the principles laid down in the United Nations Charter and in the Universal Declaration of Human Rights. This warning, already uttered by the Commissioner himself, did not fall on deaf ears.

Two days later, after having cabled the text of the Council's advice to the Amir, the Commissioner once again took the white plane with the blue markings to Benghazi, where he found that the Amir's advisory committee had been meeting, and indeed was still in session. He was told that there was strong opposition to any Italian participation, and that the committee was having extreme difficulty in reaching agreement. Nonetheless, the next morning he was given a rough English translation of a first draft of an opinion to be submitted to His Highness in favor of minority representation on the Committee of Twenty-One, but excluding all possibility of such representation in the National Assembly—a question which, as we have seen, the Council had intentionally left open.

In the course of an audience, the Commissioner pointed out that the

Council's advice gave the Amir a perfectly clear answer to his question and should accordingly allay all his fears. He also emphasized that the new advice should be read in conjunction with the last paragraph of that of 14 June, limiting the functions of the Committee of Twenty-One to planning the meeting of the National Assembly for the purposes prescribed in paragraph 3 of the Resolution 289 (IV), which meant that it could not apply to any legislature that might be convened after independence. Nevertheless, the Amir put several more questions, and appeared satisfied only when it became clear to him that the Committee of Twenty-One was free to decide whether or not an Italian would be included in the National Assembly, as well as the method of convening that body.

At the same audience the Commissioner conveyed the Council's hope that the Libyan constitution would include the relevant basic principles of the Charter and the Universal Declaration. The Amir gave the most specific assurance that this would be so.

The Amir in turn informed the Commissioner that, to save time, he had abandoned his idea of convening Parliament, falling back on consultations with his advisory committee. By now, the latter comprised the members of the Cabinet, the Council member for Cyrenaica, and the seven Cyrenaican members of the Committee of Twenty-One, five of whom were elected members of Parliament. But he had not yet reached a final decision. In the light of the additional information provided by the Commissioner, however, he was prepared to ask his advisers to reconsider the question of minority representation in the National Assembly. (It appeared that this point was conceded, insofar as Cyrenaica was prepared to leave the decision to the Committee of Twenty-One.)

The essential features of this reply, which the Amir finally approved textually for transmission to Commissioner and Council on 27 June, were:

> (1) The [Joint Advisory] Committee wishes to make it clear that it interprets the advice of the . . . Council for Libya . . . as meaning that neither the Italians nor any other foreign community in Tripolitania or elsewhere will have any right or claim to political representation in any constituent body or governmental organization, and that all they are entitled to is the guarantee of their civil, religious and social rights, according to the constitution, this being in keeping with the rule followed in modern constitutions and in conformity with the United Nations resolution which provided for the establishment of a sovereign independent Libyan State not later than 1 January 1952.
>
> In establishing this interpretation, the Committee hopes that the advice is not intended to have any other meaning.
>
> (2) In view of the foregoing considerations and their consequences, and

of the genuine intention and general feeling that the civil rights of all foreigners should be guaranteed in the future constitution of Libya, and in view of Cyrenaica's anxiety for a speedy implementation of the General Assembly resolution of 21 November 1949, the Committee does not for the present object to a foreigner representing the Minorities in Tripolitania on the Committee of Twenty-One, provided that the Tripolitanians themselves decide to accept him. The Committee of Twenty-One will have the right to determine whether or not foreigners will be represented in the National Assembly.

(3) The Committee cannot accept any responsibility for, nor can it have any part in, any evil consequences that may arise from the Tripolitanians' acceptance of a foreigner to serve with them on the Committee of Twenty-One.

(4) The Committee believes that in this way and in this spirit the Committee of Twenty-One can meet and convene the National Assembly, to which the United Nations resolution has entrusted the power to determine the constitution of Libya. In the Committee's opinion it would be to the general interest for that constitution to have a federal form.[34]

Before the Commissioner left Benghazi to report to the Council, the Amir had strongly advised him to enter into consultations with Ahmed Bey Seif al-Nasr in the Fezzan as soon as possible, in order to obtain his agreement too. A difficulty had arisen between them in the matter. The two leaders had been in touch by cable, and the Amir had asked Ahmed Bey to delay his decision until Cyrenaica had made up its mind. The latter had not complied with this request, but had instructed the Fezzanese representative on the Council to oppose Italian participation in the Committee of Twenty-One, or, a fortiori, in the National Assembly (cf. p. 269). This meant that Ahmed Bey would have to be persuaded to reverse his position, and as this was likely to be a difficult task, the Amir gave the Commissioner a letter for him, recapitulating the conclusions reached by the Amir's advisory committee.

There were other reasons to fear that this new consultation would prove even more difficult than the one that had just been brought to a satisfactory end. The Italian Government had in the meantime requested the French Government to support its attempts to secure representation on the Committee of Twenty-One by intervening with the Chef du Territoire in the Fezzan. This démarche was symptomatic in several respects. It demonstrated the considerable importance Rome attached to the success of its

34. First *Annual Report of the United Nations Commissioner in Libya,* Annex XX, p. 78.

policy. It was an indication of the growing part Ahmed Bey was coming to play in Libyan politics. And, last but not least, it confirmed an impression toward which the Commissioner had been inclining for some time—that Ahmed Bey was beginning to ignore French advice and to act on his own. Although old and sick, he was quite compos mentis. French ophthalmic surgeons had recently operated on him for trachoma, and he was convalescing in a hospital in Tunis. The French Consul General in Tripoli went there to convey his Government's support for Italy's claims, but, as he informed the Commissioner later, met with the strongest objections from the old warrior.

When Ahmed Bey received the Commissioner's message informing him of the Council's recommendation about minority representation on the Committee of Twenty-One, and of the possibility that this might be extended to the National Assembly also, his immediate reaction was strong disapproval. It was the Italians who had driven his tribe from its grazing grounds and reduced their numbers from 6,000 to 300. The tribe had lost their lands, their palm trees, their cattle, and had been obliged to flee to the Chad. Some of his own kith and kin had been killed by the occupiers. Such bitter memories did not encourage him to give the Italians a chance to reenter the political life of Libya. The Consul General had endeavored to persuade Ahmed Bey, but the old man had fallen silent and had sat there weeping, making gestures of refusal the while. As the Consul General was known not to be a sentimentalist, this report was probably no exaggeration.

When the Commissioner, accompanied by the Fezzanese member of the Council, Hajj Sofu, arrived in Tunis, Ahmed Bey was still in the hospital, and Ramadan, the Moslem month of fasting, was not yet over. Consequently, the Bey could only receive the Commissioner after sunset, after the evening meal, at about 10 P.M. Sitting cross-legged on his bed, he was obviously profoundly upset by the prospect of the discussion. The Commissioner therefore took great pains to speak deliberately, giving him a clear and detailed picture of the situation and pressing in particular the arguments which had converted the Amir of Cyrenaica and his advisory committee to acceptance of the Council's advice. Finally, he handed him the Amir's letter. He might just as well have saved his pains, for Ahmed Bey began impatiently to recite his grievances against the Italians. In an excess of passion, he tore open his shirt to display the scars of the wounds they had inflicted on him. He wound up by recalling that a large number of Libyans who had taken an active part in the struggle against the Italians were now exiled in Egypt, the Sudan, Tunisia, and other Arab countries. He was in duty bound to seek their opinion on so serious a matter. This last argument was vigorously supported by a representative of the refugees, Ali Nuri Fekini, who with Ahmed Bey's consent was present at the interview. He was an old comrade-in-arms of the Fezzanese leader, and now claimed that his group should be represented, by six of its members, on the Committee of Twenty-One. The meeting lasted until almost midnight, and ended in complete deadlock.

When the Commissioner returned to the hospital the following evening, he began by asking whether Ahmed Bey had had an opportunity to study the Amir's letter. He replied that he had; but, though now willing to consider the inclusion of an Italian on the Committee of Twenty-One, he felt that he should consult the Amir in person before making a final decision. He therefore intended to visit him in Cyrenaica after the end of Ramadan. This would have entailed considerable delay, and the Commissioner therefore asked whether a meeting with the Cyrenaican member of the Council would not serve as well. Ahmed Bey agreed, but in the end this proved unnecessary.

All the same, he was obviously far from convinced, and complained bitterly that the Commissioner did not appear to appreciate the reasons for his opposition. To make himself better understood, he would relate a tale well-known in Arab folklore: "The Nail of Shams." This he did with all the art of a Scheherazade.

Once upon a time there was a man named Shams, who had reluctantly sold his house because he could not afford to keep it up. But he did so on one condition: that he continue to be the owner of one single nail in the wall of the living room, to which he would always enjoy free access. The buyer, anxious to clinch the deal, agreed to this condition, thinking it of no importance. Soon after the new owner was happily installed, Shams called at the house and hung a small piece of string on the nail. The owner protested mildly, but Shams pointed out that he owned the nail, and as the string was not touching the wall, he had a right to hang it there. Some days later he returned, and replaced the string by a length of stout rope. The discussion about his right to do so followed the same course. The next time he called he tied a sack to the end of the rope. Later again he came back with a dead cat, which he placed in the sack. There was yet another argument, in the course of which he maintained his lawful right to hang anything he wanted on the nail. As day succeeded day, he brought more and more offensive things, which he stuffed into the sack on top of the cat. The house soon became uninhabitable because of the stench, leaving the occupant no choice but to sell the house back to Shams at a fraction of the price he had paid for it. Ahmed Bey concluded impressively by declaring that to him a single Italian in the Committee of Twenty-One would be just like the nail of Shams.

The Commissioner left that night with the feeling that he was slowly gaining ground, but was still far from his goal.

A mere four days elapsed before the final interview, at which Ahmed Bey announced that, although he could neither forget the past nor forgive the harm the Italians had done his people, he would nonetheless accept Italian participation in the Committee. When, however, the Commissioner asked whether this meant agreement to the inclusion of one Italian on the Committee with the proviso that the Committee itself would decide about Italian participation in the National Assembly, Ahmed Bey again reacted vehemently. In no circumstances would he agree to their becoming members of any Libyan body other than the Committee of Twenty-One.

In the course of these long talks, many aspects of Fezzanese life were touched on, including financial matters. In his simple way, Ahmed Bey had a keen sense of sound administration, which to him meant above all financial independence, a practically impossible aim for a country so devoid of natural resources as the Fezzan. Loving as he did to express himself in parables, one night he painted the dangers of financial dependency in the following colors.

There was once a poor man who lived with his son in an old house that was falling to pieces; but he had no money to mend it. In one of the holes in the garden wall there lived a serpent, who sometimes came out at night to snatch one of the man's hens. This angered the man, and he threatened to beat the serpent to death. The serpent said soothingly to him: "I know you are poor, but I am rich. If you let me live quietly in my hole in the wall, I can help you. All you have to do is to come out after sunset and play your flute, and I will bring you a gold piece." The man made the bargain. So things went on for a long time, and father and son led an easy life. Then the man fell ill, and the son, knowing of the bargain, killed the serpent to get hold of its hoard; but he never succeeded in finding the treasure. So the easy life came to an end. The house fell into ruins, and father and son were condemned to work for the rest of their lives as drawers of water for a wealthy landowner. Ahmed Bey looked inquiringly at the Commissioner. "Do you understand?" he asked. The Commissioner was sorry, but he did not. "Well," Ahmed Bey impatiently retorted, "it is simple enough. The serpent was first the Italians, who paid for the Fezzan. Now it is the French. When Libya is independent, shall we still be short of money? If so, who is going to pay?"

Ahmed Bey's rhetorical question was in fact very much to the point;

later, the matter assumed great importance during the negotiation of the financial agreement concerning the Fezzan concluded between the Libyan and French Governments (see Annex VIII, pp. 591–92).

CONSULTATIONS IN TRIPOLITANIA

During the second fortnight in June, the Commissioner had been spending most of his time flying back and forth between Tripoli, Benghazi, and Tunis. Nevertheless, under the Principal Secretary's direction, consultations in Tripoli were actively continued, and by the end of June the last lists of candidates had come in. Twelve parties and organizations had submitted sixty-five names in all.

The lists submitted by five parties—the Egypto-Tripolitanian Union, the Liberal Party, the National Congress of Tripolitania, the Nationalist Party, and the United National Front—were virtually identical. The Nationalist Party had left one place open for a minority representative, and the other four included Giacomo Marchino; these five lists also contained the following names:

Sheikh Abur-Rabi' al-Baruni
Sadek bin Zaraa
Abd al-Aziz al-Zaqalla'i
Ahmed Awn Sawf
Salem al-Murayyid
Ali Rajab

In addition, some fifty candidates had been proposed by leading personalities and notables, who had been consulted under the terms of paragraph 7 of Resolution 289 (IV). Many of these names appeared several times. In all, about one hundred candidates had been proposed. Three parties—the Independence Party, the Free National Bloc (the Kutla Party), and the Political Association for the Progress of Libya—had refused to submit a list despite repeated efforts by the Principal Secretary and several members of the Council to persuade them to do so, either because they were opposed to the principle of the equal representation of the three provinces or because they did not agree with the consultative method of selecting the candidates.

Thus the Commissioner was faced with the difficult problem of assessing the extent of popular support to be attributed to each person on each list, as well as the relative strength of each party. Moreover, the merits and aptitudes of individual candidates and their place of origin had to be taken into account. The situation was further complicated by widespread and profound dissatisfaction with the suggestion that a representative of the minorities, in all probability an Italian citizen, should be included in the Tripolitanian delegation. Opposition was less strong in the case of Jews (except those with a foreign passport), as they were considered as Libyans. Finally, there was outspoken criticism of the principle of equal representation, although most leading Tripolitanians were reluctantly prepared to accept it as the political price to be paid for Cyrenaican and Fezzanese agreement to the convening of the Committee of Twenty-One.

A few days before the matter came up in the Council, the Commissioner, faced with British Foreign Office insistence on its right to be consulted about the selection of candidates under paragraph 7 of Resolution 289 (IV), had submitted the following draft list to the Acting Chief Administrator (the names are listed in order of the volume of support they received):

Sheikh Mohamed Abul Is'ad al-Alim	Mufti of Tripolitania since 1921; born at Suq al-Jum'ah; member of the United National Front; Vice-President of the National Congress of Tripolitania (see also pp. 435–36).
Ahmed Awn Sawf	District Officer at Zawiya; President of the United National Front; member of the National Congress.
Abd al-Aziz al-Zaqalla'i	Member of the Nationalist Party; member of the National Congress; member of the Tripolitanian Municipal Council.
Salem al-Murayyid	Born at Tarhuna; Member of the United National Front; member of the National Congress.
Ibrahim Sha'ban	A prominent Berber; Independent; member of the Tripolitanian Administrative Council.
Ali Rajab	Born at Tripoli; President of the Egypto-Tripolitanian Union Party.
Giacomo Marchino	Minorities member of the Council for Libya (see p. 207).

In the course of consultation, each of these seven names was closely examined, and, although the Acting Chief Administrator did not consider the list very satisfactory, he found it acceptable except for the President of the Egypto-Tripolitanian Union Party, Ali Rajab. Wishing to meet British objections within reason, and also with the time factor in mind, the Commissioner replaced Ali Rajab by Salem al-Qadi, a member of the Tripolitanian Administrative Council and of the Ahliya Court, Mayor of Misurata, and a member of the National Congress.

This meant that there were now two members of the Administrative Council on the list, the other being Ibrahim Sha'ban. The Commissioner therefore replaced the latter by another prominent Berber, Sheikh Abur-Rabi' al-Baruni, a judge of the Shari'a Court of Appeal in Tripoli and a member of the National Congress, before submitting the list to the Council for Libya.[35]

The debate opened on 10 July. The Commissioner's list was criticized in particular by the members for Pakistan and Egypt, who maintained that the inclusion of two names complicated what should have been a simple task. One of them, the Mufti of Tripolitania, had not been proposed by the party to which he belonged, the National Congress of Tripolitania, though he was its Vice-President. The other persona non grata was Salem al-Qadi, another member of the National Congress not proposed by that party. This criticism boiled down to a reproach that the Commissioner had not accepted in its entirety the National Congress list proposed by the five parties mentioned on page 276 in cooperation with the two Council members who now were so critical. A particularly curious situation arose with regard to the Mufti, whom the critics did not want, but whom at the same time they considered too important a person to be removed from the list. The reason for their opposition was that the Mufti was an elderly and experienced man, too independent of mind to bow willingly to party policy when it ran counter to his own views. In the outcome the members concerned reluctantly accepted him, but insisted in return on the reinstatement of Ali Rajab at the expense of Salem al-Qadi. In order not to prolong the debate, and as a gesture of conciliation, the Commissioner agreed to this, and the Council finally advised the Commissioner on 11 July, by 6 votes to none with 4 abstentions, that Tripolitania should be represented by the list of persons he had submitted, as amended during the debate.[36]

As a result of this consultation, six of the seven Tripolitanian members of the Committee of Twenty-One turned out to be members of the National

35. For the revised list placed before the Council, see ibid., Annex XXI, p. 79.
36. Ibid., p. 80.

Congress or of parties affiliated with it. This was a higher proportion than the Commissioner had hoped for, but refusal to accept the Council's advice would have meant a time-consuming conflict, the outcome of which in any case would have been uncertain.

The day after the Council handed down its advice, the Independence Party published a manifesto addressed to the people of Tripolitania, which the Mission language staff considered the finest sample of literary Arabic they had seen since their arrival in Tripoli. In it, the Commissioner was severely attacked, particularly for his insistence on equality of representation between the three territories despite the differences in their numerical strength. This was condemned as contrary to justice and logic; by his action, the Commissioner had dealt a deathblow to the right of the Tripolitanian people to be represented in accordance with its wishes. The manifesto went on to allege that the Committee of Twenty-One was an illegal body as its existence had not been provided for in the United Nations Resolution. It was for the foregoing reasons that the Independence Party had refused to have anything to do with its creation. The manifesto ended by stating that the Party was resolved to defend the rights of the Tripolitanian people to its last heartbeat. But the people must bestir themselves and be vigilant, because times were serious and conditions difficult. There would be no respite unless the people believed in Allah, who would help those who were in the right as He had promised in the Koran: "O ye who believe! if ye help God, He will help you, and will make firm your footsteps." [37]

There could not have been a more dignified way of acknowledging defeat without actually accepting it.

As the Commissioner had communicated to the Council a few days before the lists of those chosen to represent Cyrenaica and the Fezzan, the Committee of Twenty-One was now complete. Its membership was as follows:

CYRENAICA [38]

Hajj Rashid al-Kikhia
Mahmud Bu Hidma
Tayal al Bijou
Hajj Abd al-Kafi Semin
Ahmed Agheila al-Kizza
Omar Shenib
Khalil al-Qallal

37. The Koran, XLVII (The Chapter of Mohammed also called Flight [Medina]), 5–10, trans. E. H. Palmer, with an introduction by R. A. Nicholson and Geoffrey Cumberlege (Oxford: Oxford University Press, 1949), p. 437.

38. The first five representatives were members of the Cyrenaican Assembly of Representatives. One of them, Hajj Rashid al-Kikhia, was its President.

FEZZAN[39]

Ali Maghtuf	Si al-Mahid, Qadi of Ghudamis
Tahir Jerari	Tibuli
Al-Hajj Ali Bedoui	Mohamed Bin Othman al-Sayd
Belqasem Bouguila	

TRIPOLITANIA

Mohamed Abul Is'ad al-Alim	Ali Rajab
Sheikh Abur-Rabi' al-Baruni	Ahmed Awn Sawf
Salem al-Murayyid	Abd al-Aziz al-Zaqalla'i
Giacomo Marchino	

But the question of Tripolitanian representation was not yet disposed of. The issue of appointment or accreditation again raised its irritating head. The Acting British Chief Administrator, anxious not to place too much emphasis on the question of his competence, had hoped for a less formal procedure, and the Egyptian representative had suggested that the Commissioner should take legal advice on the problem. From the latter's point of view, the Council's advice of 16 June implied that the Commissioner himself should appoint the Tripolitanians in pursuance of the recommendation that the procedure provided for in paragraph 7 of Resolution 289 (IV) should be followed. However, from a legal standpoint the situation was not so simple, and in the course of the debate the Commissioner stated:

> that the legal opinion he had received was that, although to be a representative on the Committee of Twenty-One was to exercise a function independent of the administration of the territory, the Administering Powers, under paragraph 10 (a) and (b) of the resolution of the General Assembly, were required to initiate all necessary steps for the transfer of power to a duly constituted independent government, and to administer the territories for the purpose of assisting in the establishment of Libyan unity and independence and co-operate in the formation of governmental institutions; that the designation of the representatives on the Committee of Twenty-One was one of the "necessary steps for the transfer of power" and was also inherent in the administration of the territories for the purposes stated; and that the Commissioner's power of appointment was exhausted upon the completion of his duties under paragraph 7 of the resolution. If no action were taken by the Administering Authority, the

39. The Fezzanese members had not been selected without difficulty owing to divergent tendencies, the existence of which the Commissioner and the Council had observed earlier, particularly during their joint visit to the territory in May 1950.

representatives of Tripolitania would sit as private individuals, and accreditation or recognition by that Power would therefore be useful.[40]

The Commissioner agreed that accreditation (or recognition) would be "useful," without attaching too much importance to it.

The representative of Egypt dissented, emphasizing that paragraph 10 of the United Nations resolution was inoperative in this context. The representative of Pakistan supported this view, arguing that paragraphs 3 and 4 alone were applicable.

In the meantime, it had become clear that the position of the Foreign Office was more rigid and formal than that originally taken by the British Administration in Tripoli.

Subsequently, the Commissioner was informed that, under instructions from London, the Acting Chief Administrator was obliged to submit to his Administrative Council for its advice both the list of selected candidates and the question of their appointment or recognition. By this time, the Council for Libya had tendered its advice to the Commissioner, with the result that, were the Administrative Council to recommend a different list, there would be conflict between the two bodies.

In these circumstances, the Commissioner advised the British Administration in its own interest not to proceed to seek the Administrative Council's advice. If there were agreement between the two Councils, local public opinion would be inclined to look upon the step taken by the British Administration as mere confirmation of the Council for Libya's achievement. In that eventuality, the Administration would lay itself open to the charge of having caused unnecessary complication and delay, and the position of the Council for Libya would be strengthened. If, on the other hand, the two Councils disagreed, there would in all likelihood be a majority in the Council for Libya for standing by its own list and denying the right of the British Administration to intervene. The ensuing conflict should, in the Commissioner's opinion, be avoided. There had already been enough controversy, he felt, over this long drawn-out but inessential issue. Of course, the British Administration was free to waive responsibility for the Tripolitanian delegation, but public opinion would certainly regard such a step as a victory for the Council for Libya. The Commissioner also made it clear that, having reached a compromise with his Council and having agreed with it on a list, even though a far from ideal one, he could no longer support the Administration in the course it proposed to follow.

As to accreditation, his advice was that the Administration accept the

40. First *Annual Report of the United Nations Commissioner in Libya,* para. 170.

Council for Libya's list with a minimum of formality, for instance, by a simple formula of recognition, to which, to safeguard its position vis-à-vis London, it might add a comment to the effect that it disagreed with the consultation procedure recommended by the Council and followed by the Commissioner, and that, in its view, a more representative list could have been drawn up by electoral means.

On 21 July, the Commissioner received from the Acting Chief Administrator a reply conveying the result of his consultation with the Tripolitanian Administrative Council, which he passed on to the Council for Libya.

The Libyan members of the Administrative Council were unanimous in their condemnation of the method used to select the seven Tripolitanian members of the Committee of Twenty-One, calling it "unrepresentative" and even "dictatorial," and observing that in the case of the National Congress candidates, the Executive Committee of that institution had not even been consulted. (This was subsequently denied by Beshir Bey Saadawi.) Their general feeling was that it would have been better, for instance, to have constituted an electoral college from among the elected members of the municipal councils. In this way, the true wishes of the people might have been ascertained. (The Commissioner could not have agreed more, but there had been no point in insisting upon electoral procedure.) They were also unanimously of the opinion that the British Administration should withhold its recognition from the present list. The name of the Mufti found universal favor, but alternatives were suggested by various members for as many as five of the six other names. The British Administration had advised the Administrative Council, however, to confine its suggestions to the minimum considered necessary, and the Libyan members readily appreciated the desirability of reaching a compromise with the Council for Libya in the matter. The list which the majority of the Administrative Council finally agreed to recommend for recognition contained only two changes. It read as follows:

The Mufti of Tripolitania
Sheikh Abur Rabi' al-Baruni
Salem al-Qadi
Ibrahim Sha'ban
Salem al-Murayyid
Ahmed Awn Sawf
Ali Rajab

This list commanded the approval of six out of seven Libyan members of the Administrative Council present. All six were opposed to foreign participation in the Committee of Twenty-One, maintaining the attitude they had adopted over the Tripolitanian Electoral Law.[41] The seventh Libyan

41. The Libyan members of the Administrative Council had opposed foreign participation in the elections to the Tripolitanian Legislative Chamber.

member was opposed to the list in any form, as he disagreed with the principle of parity of representation between Tripolitania, Cyrenaica, and the Fezzan. The Italian member and the Jewish member agreed with the list as amended by the Administrative Council, except for wishing to reinstate the name of Marchino at Ali Rajab's expense. The Acting Chief Administrator concluded by stating that he had informed the Administrative Council that he would transmit their views and recommendations to the Commissioner for such action as the latter might see fit to take.

When it was suggested that the matter be taken up by the Council, the Chairman, Ali Bey Jerbi, pointed out that the letter had been addressed uniquely to the Commissioner, who had submitted no comments on it to the Council. He therefore proposed that the matter not be placed on the agenda. After a brief discussion, the Council agreed—a not altogether correct procedure. As a result of this tug-of-war, the Tripolitanian members of the Committee of Twenty-One never had the same status as their colleagues from the two other territories, but this admittedly did not prove of great importance, either legally or practically, in the Committee's work. What counted was that that body could at last get down to the job.

PART 5. UNDER WAY, 27 JULY–31 OCTOBER 1950

On 25 July, almost six weeks after the Commissioner had first sought the Council's advice on the method of selecting the Tripolitanian delegation, it became at last possible to convene the Committee of Twenty-One. For days the United Nations plane had been standing by to fetch the delegations from Cyrenaica and the Fezzan, and the Mission staff had completed arrangements for servicing the meetings. As subsequent developments proved, a new chapter was opening in the constitutional evolution of Libya.

At this point it appeared as if the Benghazi consultations had yielded an important by-product: an agreement between the Amir and Beshir Bey Saadawi on the form of State. As early as the beginning of June, the Commissioner had impressed upon the leader of the Tripolitanian National Congress that a new situation was developing as a result of the Amir's decision to abandon his plan for an independent Cyrenaica and to play an active part in the common effort to establish a united Libya on the one hand, and of Ahmed Bey Seif al-Nasr's declaration that he was prepared to accept a united Libya with the Senussi leader as Head of State on the other hand. Hence the time had come for Tripolitania and Cyrenaica to reach agreement on the form of State, and thus to eliminate the only serious obstacle to further constitutional progress. Beshir Bey had at first denied the force of this argument, maintaining that existing difficulties between the two territories were due not to their own differences but to the policy of "divide and rule" pursued by the British Administration. However, in the end he came to recognize the facts of life, and after a while began talks with the Amir, of which the Commissioner was kept informed.

Toward the end of July these conversations had reached a stage at which Beshir Bey felt that he could give the Commissioner a more or less detailed account of the agreement reached. He had accepted a federal form of government, the details of which, however, were to be worked out by the National Assembly. Being in an optimistic mood, he expected the Committee of Twenty-One to complete its work in about a fortnight. The National Assembly, he conceded, would require more time. He also hoped that the constitution would be ready before the end of 1950, or early in 1951 at latest. After its adoption, a Libyan government could be formed and powers transferred to it. Indeed, he saw no reason why they should not be transferred to a provisional administration while the constitution was still being drafted. In the meantime a study should be made of the economic problems the new State would have to face.

When the Commissioner asked to whom exactly powers should be transferred, as there could be no *legal* Libyan Government until the constitution had been adopted, Beshir Bey explained that transfers could be made to local administrations which would provide the nucleus for the future Libyan government. To his own dismay, the Commissioner realized that Saadawi once again had been carried away by his impatience for independence to the point of jeopardizing unity. And the fact that the concept of transfer of powers he had just been listening to came dangerously close to the intentions of the Administering Powers caused him serious concern. It was clear that, although the National Congress leader wanted to push ahead as fast as he could, he did not fully understand the constitutional and political risks he was running. For instance, he argued that there was nothing to stop the Amir's being proclaimed King of Libya while the National Assembly was still drawing up the broad lines of the constitution—in other words before its promulgation and the proclamation of independence. Sayed Idris would then have been Monarch of a nonexistent State. Such ideas might have been feasible in a revolutionary situation; they were totally unrealistic under the prevailing conditions. Beshir Bey's ideas about the organization of the federal government were equally vague, and the same was true of his approach to economic, budgetary, and monetary problems, the complexity of which he constantly underrated.

The Commissioner got the impression that, although important progress had been made toward mutual understanding between the Amir and Beshir

Bey about the form of the future State, there was still too much room for political misunderstanding. Even more important was that the constitutional and administrative preparations would have to be carried out in carefully thought-out stages. On the Amir's side, the understanding with Beshir Bey was consistent with Cyrenaica's policy and experience since the end of the war. On Beshir Bey's side, it is no exaggeration to say that there had been an almost complete reversal of policy, a switch from a formal, dogmatic concept of a unitary State to pragmatic acceptance of a loose federation. In the circumstances it was understandable that he should have declined to make a public statement about the conclusions reached in his talks with the Amir (see p. 249). This very refusal made the Commissioner wonder how far Beshir Bey's Tripolitanian followers, who were mostly fervent protagonists of a unitary, centralized State, would go toward endorsing his agreement with the Amir.

About a week after this informative conversation, Beshir Bey had a long discussion with the United Kingdom member of the Council for Libya in which he repeated most of what he had already told the Commissioner, adding, however, a number of highly revealing details.

After having confirmed that he was now committed to the concept of a loose federal State under a Senussi Monarch, in which, however, he personally had no wish to play a part after independence, he declared his opposition to the inclusion of any non-Libyan (Italian or other foreigner) in the Libyan National Assembly. He then proceeded to outline his immediate plans for that body and the Committee of Twenty-One. First, the Committee should draw up a set of basic principles to be followed by the National Assembly when it got down to drafting the constitution in detail. The statement of principles should cover five points: the State should be a monarchy; the Monarch Designate should be Sayed Idris al-Senussi; the form of government should be federal; there should be a central government to deal with certain reserved matters; and there should be but one flag, one army, etc.

As to the establishment of the National Assembly, the Committee should propound the following plan:

1. The National Assembly should consist of sixty members, twenty from each territory;
2. The twenty territorial members might or might not include persons who had served on the Committee of Twenty-One;
3. Non-Libyan members should be excluded, i.e. no foreigners should sit in the National Assembly;
4. The territorial representatives should be selected in Cyrenaica by the Amir, in the Fezzan by Ahmed Bey Seif al-Nasr, and in Tripolitania by

the National Congress Party, both the Fezzanese and Tripolitanian selections being subject to formal endorsement or appointment by the Amir. In Tripolitania, Beshir Bey himself would tour the various districts and select the Tripolitanian members on a proportional basis, so many from each district and so many from Tripoli town. He knew all the leading personalities, and would see to it that tribal leaders as well as townsmen were included.

As to the status of the Committee of Twenty-One and the National Assembly, in his view neither the Commissioner nor the Council for Libya nor the Administering Powers were competent to supervise or direct the proceedings of either. (In this, of course, he was right.) They were free and independent organs which need refer nothing to the Commissioner, though they could ask him for advice when they wanted it.

The United Kingdom member tried to make Beshir Bey understand that he should take a broader view of the situation, in particular with regard to other political parties and to the importance of Italian participation. He also drew Beshir Bey's attention to the illegality of his plans concerning the proclamation of the monarchy, which would endanger the Amir's future position. He pleaded in vain.

This was a typical Saadawi attitude, the fruit of the mentality of the one-party boss, who considered that his party and his views alone mattered. Other parties he considered to be negligible, even despicable. It was true that the National Congress was the largest, the best organized, and the most influential of the Tripolitanian political groups. In fact, it was an agglomeration of parties with identical programs which had federated to form the Congress, though without abandoning their individual identities. But that was not to say that the other parties were not representative of other tendencies and opinions among the people; even less did it mean that the large number of prominent Tripolitanians who belonged to no party at all could be ignored. This, however, Beshir Bey could not or would not admit, and on many occasions—the last being the selection of the Tripolitanian members of the Committee of Twenty-One—he bitterly criticized the Commissioner and the Council for listening to others. From the outset his approach to public affairs had smacked of dictatorship; now he was planning to dominate the political scene in Tripolitania in view of the imminent inception of the Committee and the institution of the National Assembly. That inherently his position was weaker than he pretended was shown by his refusal to agree to elections, an attitude which had forced him to take a step which in the long run was to work against Libyan unity. For, by currying Italian support for his opposition to an elected preparatory committee and an elected National Assembly—a policy for which a few months later he was to be severely criticized in the General Assembly of the United

Nations by his friends from Cairo—he had succeeded in intensifying Fezzanese, and especially Cyrenaican, suspicions of Tripolitanian hegemony and hence of the return of Italian settlers to Libya. That certainly was not in the interests of the Libyan unity for which he was otherwise working so hard.

So far as the Italians were concerned, they had won a Pyrrhic victory: one seat on the Committee of Twenty-One, which allowed them to make themselves heard; but their attempts to secure a place in the National Assembly were doomed to end in political defeat. That they would have gained constitutional guarantees of their minority rights anyway was clear from the Amir's letter of 27 June and later confirmed by decisions of the Committee of Twenty-One and the National Assembly. Thus the notorious Italian-Egyptian-Pakistani deal of early June had many delaying and harmful complications to answer for (see p. 244).

From its first meeting, held in Tripoli on 27 July, the Committee of Twenty-One displayed a tendency to behave as a body with a collective personality of its own. It was the first all-Libyan institution in the country's history, and it was very conscious of its importance as such. Its members, moreover, faithfully reflected the issues that divided the country: unitary versus federal State; equal versus proportional representation of the territories; and elective versus selective procedures. But, these profound divisions notwithstanding, the Committee also showed a determination to bridge them and to establish a plan for convening the National Assembly that they had been called upon to prepare. It even went further than the Council had intended it to do by taking advantage of the general character of its terms of reference; but this belongs to a later part of our story.

At the opening meeting—which was attended by the members of the local Consular Corps, the Commissioner, and members of the Council, as well as a number of notables—the Commissioner said that he was "gratified to witness the first meeting of a body representing all Libya for the first time in the modern history of this country." [42] In reply, the Mufti of Tripolitania, who acted as Dean for the occasion, declared that it was "a happy occasion to speak on behalf not only of Tripolitania but of all Libya, in looking forward to the day when Libya becomes a united, independent sovereign state under the leadership of the Amir of Libya . . . as its king, the symbol of its unity and independence." [43]

42. Ismail Raghib Khalidi, *Constitutional Development in Libya* (Beirut, Lebanon: Khayat's College Book Co-operative, 1956), p. 29. Khalidi's English quotations, of which a number follow in the next few pages, were made by himself from the Official Summary Records of the Committee of Twenty-One, which are otherwise available only in Arabic.

43. Ibid.

For some time public opinion in Libya had been critical of the Commissioner and the Council for having wasted too much time in what people called "procedural palavering"; and this reproach was not entirely unjustified. The members of the Committee of Twenty-One, therefore, by way of reaction, were determined to set a faster pace. They obviously wanted to show their foreign advisers that if things were left in their hands they would move much more swiftly. From the Commissioner's point of view, this tendency was a matter for rejoicing, as it was a far cry from the mentality he had found six months earlier on his arrival, when he had been expected by many Libyans to take the initiative and lead the people to independence. In their desire to encourage this new sense of political responsibility for the country's future, the Commissioner and his staff were careful not to offer any advice unless it was asked for, and even to avoid the slightest appearance of doing so.

It was accordingly decided at a staff meeting to give help only on request. Moreover, assistance was to be divided into practical conference services on the one hand, and advice on matters of substance on the other. The former, without which the Committee would not have been able to meet, were indispensable. They consisted in providing meeting space at the Mission's headquarters as well as the use of the United Nations plane to fly the Fezzanese and Cyrenaican delegations to and from their home territories. The Mission supplied an Arabic typewriter, while the British Administration made an Arabic typist available and provided office furniture. The Administering Powers agreed to pay each Cyrenaican and Fezzanese member a modest subsistence allowance to cover his living expenses in Tripoli, and the local British Administration announced its readiness to make good loss of earnings by the Tripolitanian members. As it was the Committee's intention to hold most of its meetings in public, a United Nations guard was detailed to keep order in the gallery. All these facilities were gladly accepted; indeed, the Committee seemed much inclined to take them for granted.

The question of substantive advice was much more delicate. When the Commissioner asked the Committee whether it wanted the help of his Legal Adviser, Omar Bey Loutfi, or of other professional Mission staff, Loutfi's cooperation and that of Ismail Raghib Khalidi was gladly accepted. Khalidi (the author of *Constitutional Development in Libya*) served as Deputy Secretary of the Committee, assisting Mohamed al-Amir from the Fezzan and Khalil al-Qallal from Cyrenaica who were appointed Joint Secretaries after the Mufti of Tripolitania had unanimously been elected Chairman.

At its second meeting, which in fact was the first working session, the Committee considered the report of a sub-committee set up to draft its rules of procedure, which had taken as its model a simplified version of the Council for Libya's rules. The rules of procedure were approved unanimously, with the addition of two important stipulations to the effect that all decisions of the Committee were to be taken by a two-thirds majority and that fifteen members of the Committee would constitute a quorum. Both these decisions had obvious political significance, as, taken in conjunction, they would provide the best possible protection against any one delegation's trying to dominate the policy making of the Committee with the support of a minority of one of the other two. Even this was not considered adequate by the Fezzanese, who wanted a unanimous vote for important questions, but to this the others would not agree. The Tripolitanians, on the other hand, argued that a simple majority would be enough, but they were defeated by the other two delegations.

A few days later the Committee adopted its agenda, which comprised the following items:

1. Number of members of the National Assembly;
2. Should representation in the National Assembly be in proportion to the number of inhabitants or should it be on a basis of equality for the three territories of Libya?
3. Should members of the National Assembly be elected or selected?
4. How should the members of the National Assembly be chosen if the principle of selection were adopted?
5. Date and place of convocation of the National Assembly.

It will be noted that the question of minority representation in the National Assembly does not figure in the list. It was placed on the Agenda only on 12 October 1950 on the proposal of a Cyrenaican member. In the meantime, at a meeting held on 7 August, the Committee had decided that the National Assembly should be composed of sixty representatives equally divided among the three territories. This disposed of items 1 and 2 of the agenda. The decision was taken by seventeen affirmative votes and 3 abstentions, one member being absent. Khalidi summarized the discussions which took place on these two basic issues in the following terms:

> In the discussion of items 1 and 2, the representatives of the Fezzan and Cyrenaica supported the principle of equality as a basis for the composition of the Assembly. Both delegations argued that such equality was called for by the General Assembly resolution of 1949, which had recognized the existence of the three territories of Libya and had called upon the representatives of those territories to meet in a National Assembly. They reasoned that the composition of the Committee itself was based on the principle of equality between the three territories as

established and sanctioned by the Commissioner and his Council, and they considered this to be a legal precedent for the composition of future Libyan constitutional organs.

The Tripolitanians insisted that no truly democratic body could be established unless it was based upon the principle of proportional representation. They pointed out that the General Assembly resolution made no specific reference to the composition of the National Assembly and, furthermore, that as representatives of the three territories, they were free to adopt any decision which obtained the consent of the majority of the members of the Committee, and certainly one which would be democratic in nature.[44]

As events were to show, this decision foretold the form of the future State.

At the same meeting the Committee began to discuss item 3 of the agenda, i.e. whether the members of the National Assembly should be elected or selected (the latter term in fact meant appointed). Once again the issue proved to be a major stumbling block. The arguments for and against were those which had already been heard in the Council for Libya. But, rather surprisingly, this time it was the Fezzanese representatives who, in the name of democracy, made a stubborn stand in favor of elections, the Tripolitanians maintaining that free elections were hardly feasible while the British Administration was still ruling the country. The Cyrenaicans now sided with the Tripolitanians because "they felt that since elections had been held several months earlier in their territory, and since the short time available would make it practically impossible to hold them in Tripolitania, the idea were best abandoned." [45]

At the end of the discussion the Committee found itself confronting two proposals: the Fezzanese one in favor of elections, and the Cyrenaican and Tripolitanian one upholding the principle of selection.

When the proposals were put to the meeting, neither received the required number of votes. The Fezzanese motion received 13 votes, one short of a two-thirds majority, the other only 4 (three members were then absent). An attempt to persuade the Fezzanese to abstain from voting on the second proposal, after once more having made their point of view clear for the record, failed. At this juncture, the French Consul General in Tripoli, who throughout this difficult period had remained optimistic about the prospects of reaching an agreement, suggested on behalf of Ahmed Bey Seif al-Nasr that the Fezzanese delegation should return to Sabhah for consultations. If the United Nations plane could be made available, the

44. Ibid., p. 31.
45. Ibid., pp. 31–32.

round trip need take no more than five days. The plan looked too good to be true. The Commissioner, who at the time was in Geneva consulting with the Council on the draft of his first annual report, took it up with the French member, and agreed to the use of his aircraft on condition that it should not wait for more than five days at Sabhah to fly the delegation back to Tripoli. On reflection, Ambassador Balay suggested that the plane should not wait at Sabhah at all, to avoid giving members of the Fezzanese delegation the impression that they were under pressure. To this the Commissioner could not agree, whereupon Balay suggested that it might be better for the delegation not to leave Tripoli at all, but for the Committee to break off its work until after the end of the forthcoming (fifth) session of the United Nations. This made the Commissioner explode, diplomatically speaking; he lost no time in telling the French member in forceful terms that under no conditions could he be a party to such an arrangement. How did the French member propose to explain the delay to the Council and to the General Assembly without exposing both his own Government and the Commissioner to a charge of obstructing the Committee's work and thereby frustrating the implementation of Resolution 289 (IV)? The Commissioner then renewed his offer to fly the Fezzanese delegation to Sabhah, where it would be picked up for the return trip on 23 August. There was a calculated measure of bluff in this proposal, which was finally accepted, but it at least ensured that the delegation would be back in Tripoli before the end of the month. However, the delegation brought with it no change of policy. On 29 August, when the Committee resumed its work, the issue of election versus selection was again hotly contested. In the course of the discussion the Fezzanese were openly accused by their colleagues of delaying the work of the Committee under pressure from a foreign Power. At the request of the Fezzanese, a vote was taken on their motion the next day, 30 August. It was lost by 10 votes to 7, four members being absent.

Weeks of valuable time thus had been lost. Private conversations with members of the Fezzanese delegation confirmed the impression that, despite his newfound independence of mind, Ahmed Bey Seif al-Nasr was under heavy French pressure to exploit the issue as a delaying tactic. Since the local French authorities in the Fezzan were unlikely to bring pressure to bear on their own account, the real question was: what policy directives were reaching them from the Government in Paris? Was Paris paying only lip service to the United Nations resolution, following the Commissioner's advice in matters of secondary importance while hanging back from definite steps toward Libyan unity and independence? Discreet inquiries revealed that while the French authorities in Tripoli and Sabhah, and at the Quai d'Orsay, realized that the establishment of a united and independent Libya, including the Fezzan, was an unavoidable development, a contrary trend had been introduced in government and parliamentary circles in Paris, where continued French protection over the Fezzan was apparently the subject of much wishful thinking. The Commissioner had received a foretaste of this state of mind during his official visits to Paris in February and April (see Chapter 2, Part 2), and now a number of signs confirmed this reaction, which had been triggered by two recent developments: an increase in nationalist activities in Tunisia; and Ahmed Bey Seif al-Nasr's declaration of 15 May, in the presence of the Commissioner and several members of the Council for Libya, to the effect that he was willing to accept a unified Libya, including the Fezzan, with the Amir of Cyrenaica as Head of State (see p. 197). This had come as a painful surprise to the French, even to those on the spot, who had never expected the Bey to be so explicit. His action had caused a real shock in Paris; but people there refused to take no for an answer, and from that moment French policy began to harden.

The French reaction took a number of forms. The French Resident in Tunis, accused of not having been firm enough, was replaced, and his successor instructed to act more forcefully. The attitude of the French representative on the Council for Libya became more negative, particularly toward the Commissioner's request for advice on the constitution of a preparatory committee for the National Assembly and on the election of such an assembly. He attempted to minimize the effect of such measures as much as possible without opposing them outright. He resisted any suggestion about the establishment of a provisional Libyan government by the National Assembly, as foreseen in the Commissioner's plan. He complained in private conversation that constitutional development was moving too fast, leaving his Government insufficient time to adjust its policy to changing conditions.

In particular, the French opposed the Amir of Cyrenaica—whom they saw as nothing but a British tool—becoming Head of the Libyan State; they feared that if this came to pass British influence would be carried to the borders of Tunisia, Southern Algeria, and French Equatorial Africa, thus upsetting the Anglo-French balance of power in Africa north of the Equator. This fear grew as it became clearer and clearer that the Amir was the only possible candidate for the Libyan throne and that in both Tripolitania and the Fezzan he was becoming increasingly acceptable as potential ruler of the country. In vain did the Commissioner try to convince the French authorities that the Amir was in fact a man of much more independent mind than they—or for that matter the British themselves—thought. His words made no visible impression. When, on 1 June, accompanied by members of the Council, he visited Benghazi for the first anniversary of the Amir's recognition as Head of the Cyrenaican Government, the Commissioner was called upon, without warning, to address the crowd from the balcony of the Town Hall. To have refused would have been discourteous; moreover, he would have missed an opportunity of stressing the importance of Libyan unity. So he improvised a speech in English, which was translated into Arabic sentence by sentence by his own interpreter, prudently alluding to his hope that one day the Libyan people might proclaim the Amir King of an independent and united Libya. The crowd reacted enthusiastically, the Amir and members of the Government expressed their pleasure; but within the hour the French member of the Council had lodged a verbal, but nonetheless formal, protest with the Commissioner, accusing him of having exceeded his authority. Taking note of the protest, the Commissioner made it plain that he could not consider it justified. Suspecting that the protest and his reply might be communicated to New York, he informed the Secretary-General of the incident; but apparently nothing of the kind happened. However, a week later the French Consul General in Tripoli, known for his sound and balanced judgment of Libyan affairs and of North African matters in general, called on the Commissioner—whether under instructions or in his private capacity was not clear—to tell him that in government and parliamentary circles in Paris the temperature was rising to the boiling point over the North African situation. The Government might even fall on the issue, in which case its successor might be obliged publicly to disavow the United Nations Resolution on Libya, in the vote on which, anyway, it had abstained. France might even withdraw from the United Nations. The Commissioner could not help feeling, without underrating the intensity of French concern, that this was an attempt to intimidate him. However, the limits of his freedom of maneuver were so narrow that he could not afford to deviate from the line of policy he had adopted. So, while taking note of this warning, he continued on his course. After a while tension in Paris seemed to slacken, although as late as 19 August 1950 a highly respected member of the Institut de France and adviser to the Quai d'Orsay on Mediterranean affairs, Jacques Bardoux, submitted to the Assembly of the Council of Europe a motion recommending the Committee of Ministers "to secure action by the European delegates in the General Assembly of the United Nations with regard to an international mandate for Libya." [46] Bardoux in fact wanted the Consultative Assembly to recommend

46. Council of Europe, Consultative Assembly, Second Ordinary Session, 7–28 August and 18–24 November 1950, Documents, Working Papers Part III, Document 76, 19 August 1950 (Strasbourg: Council of Europe, 1950), p. 858.

"that the Commitee of Ministers should instruct the European Representatives of the United Nations Organization, before whom the case has been brought [*sic*] by Mr. Adrian Pelt, the United Nations Commissioner in Libya, to entrust the mandates on these three territories to three European States, as follows:

The Mandate for Cyrenaica, to England,
The Mandate for Tripolitania, to Italy, and
The Mandate for Fezzan, to France." [47]

It will be noted that Bardoux's proposal boiled down to a revival of the Bevin-Sforza plan. In Libya, this became known through dispatches in various European and Arabic newspapers; it raised a wave of emotion, which, however, soon subsided. The motion was referred to the Commission for General Foreign Affairs, which in turn, on 21 August 1950, transmitted it for further study to its Sub-Committee for Overseas Territories. According to information received later from the Secretariat of the Council for Europe, the motion was not followed up.[48]

The Commissioner returned to Tripoli from Geneva on 7 September. Immediately, the Committee of Twenty-One sought his good offices in trying to bring about a change in the Fezzanese position. Notwithstanding a visit to Sabhah and a prolonged talk with Ahmed Bey Seif al-Nasr, his efforts were fruitless. At the same time, the Fezzanese delegation again asked for the use of the United Nations plane, this time to go home for the religious feast of Qurban Bairam. The Commissioner, fearing that they might indefinitely delay their return, granted this request only on condition that they would all be back in Tripoli before the end of the month.

A visit to Paris to confer with the responsible officials at the Quai d'Orsay produced nothing better, although the Commissioner left with the feeling that a change of policy might not be altogether out of the question, and that there was a tendency to allow Ahmed Bey more freedom of action. In these circumstances, there was one more possibility of bringing about a change of policy in Sabhah, namely, by persuading the Amir to send a personal and trusted spokesman to win Ahmed Bey over. Approached in this sense by the Commissioner, who meanwhile had left Tripoli for New York, His Highness decided to send Omar Shenib, the Head of the Royal Diwan (the Amir's personal secretariat).[49]

47. Ibid.

48. Private communication to the author.

49. Omar Shenib was born between 1885 and 1890 in Derna, where he received his primary and secondary education at Turkish schools. He was then appointed clerk in the civil administration of the same town. About 1909 he was appointed *mudir* of

This mission being a purely internal Libyan affair, the Commissioner and his staff kept out of it, except for providing the aircraft. Shenib apparently saw Ahmed Bey at the psychologically right moment, and found the right kinds of arguments, religious as well as political. There was also reason to believe that the British and United States Governments had advised the French Government to change its policy. The Commissioner, for his part, had started to drop hints in the course of private conversations that, if the present situation continued, he would be obliged to report to the forthcoming session of the General Assembly that constitutional development in Libya was being held up by French delaying tactics.

What counsels prevailed in Paris during those weeks it is difficult to say without access to French archives; but the fact remains that on the day after Shenib's return from the Fezzan on 12 October, the Fezzanese representatives on the Committee of Twenty-One explained "that they were prepared to accept the principle of selection for the members of the National Assembly on condition that the chief political parties of Tripolitania, as also that section of the population that did not belong to any party, were represented in the Assembly."[50] The Committee, after a stormy debate, finally accepted unanimously the principle of selection for the composition of the Tripolitanian delegation on the terms laid down by the Fezzanese. The success of Shenib's mission was another indication that Senussi influence in the Fezzan was waxing.

With this major obstacle out of the way, the Committee went on to

---

a rural district near Derna, whence he was transferred in the same capacity to Sallum. When the Turkish officials withdrew from Sallum after the Italian occupation, Shenib accompanied Anwar Pasha to Constantinople and was then sent to serve in his previous capacity in Syria. There he met some of the Tripolitanian refugees, among them Beshir Bey Saadawi, and formed the Tripoli-Cyrenaican Defense Committee, the purpose of which was to publish leaflets and articles in the Arabic press and spread propaganda against the Italian occupation of Libya. He remained in Syria, always in contact with all Libyan personalities in the Arab world and in Egypt in particular, until the outbreak of World War II. In 1940 he was summoned by the Amir to join him in Egypt. Shenib accepted the invitation and became his *Chef de Cabinet.* He played a leading part in recruiting Libyans, who had been made prisoners of war while in Italian uniform, and in forming the Libyan Arab Force, in which he himself became a major. In 1945 he came to Cyrenaica with the Amir. In 1948 and 1949 he was sent as head of the Cyrenaican delegation to the General Assembly at Lake Success. Shenib was head of the Cyrenaican delegation to the Committee of Twenty-One, and later of that to the National Assembly, of which he was also Vice-President. He was Minister of Defense in the provisional Libyan Government. Later he became Minister (head) of the Royal Diwan.

50. *Second Annual Report of the United Nations Commissioner in Libya,* GAOR: Sixth Session, 1951–52, Supplement No. 17 (A/1949), Annex II, p. 72.

discuss minorities. The specific issue under consideration was whether nonnational minorities—minorities whose members were subjects of foreign countries—could be considered as "inhabitants" in the context of paragraph 3 of Resolution 289 (IV) and hence claim representation in the future National Assembly. Without much ado, the Committee agreed that nonnational minorities should not be allowed to participate or to be represented in the National Assembly.[51] In accordance with the Amir's promise to the Commissioner and the Council, the following statement was included in the Committee's records:

> Non-national minorities will not be allowed to participate or to be represented in the National Assembly. There is, however, a genuine intention and a general feeling that all civil, religious and social rights of all minorities and foreigners should be fully safeguarded in the future constitution of Libya. The Committee is confident that this principle will be taken into consideration by the National Assembly when it draws up the constitution, in accordance with the practice of all civilized nations." [52]

THE SELECTION OF THE TRIPOLITANIAN MEMBERS OF THE NATIONAL ASSEMBLY

The day after the Fezzanese delegation's change of heart had enabled the Committee to resume its discussions on the composition of the National Assembly, the even more knotty problem arose of how its Tripolitanian members should be selected. Four possibilities were under consideration, namely, selection by:

1. The Mufti; or
2. The Mufti assisted by two Tripolitanian members of the Committee of Twenty-One; or
3. The Mufti assisted by all the Tripolitanian members of the Committee; or
4. The Mufti assisted by the two Vice-Chairmen of the Committee, i.e. by one Cyrenaican and one Fezzanese member.

The fourth procedure was turned down unanimously by the Tripolitanians, who did not want the other two territories meddling in their affairs. At the same time, it was generally recognized that to leave the selection to the full Tripolitanian delegation would not work out. Choosing two Tripoli-

51. For a more detailed exposition of the meaning of the term "nonnational minorities," see Chapter 4, p. 336 ff.

52. *Second Annual Report of the United Nations Commissioner in Libya,* Annex II, p. 73.

tanians to assist the Mufti was a delicate enough problem in itself, as there was no agreement as to who the two should be or how they should be designated. There remained only the possibility of the Mufti acting alone, which happened to be the procedure preferred by the British Administration. Some Tripolitanian members of the Committee were not too happy about this, as they feared that the Mufti might too readily accede to British preferences. Those who thought so underrated His Eminence's political astuteness. As a matter of interest, some of them would have preferred to entrust the task to the Commissioner, but apart from the fact that he had to attend the Fifth Session of the General Assembly at Lake Success, the latter felt, in the light of past experience, that there was not much reason to expect that he would be any more successful than the Mufti. Indeed, the reverse was more likely to be the case.

Nevertheless, the Committee invited the Commissioner to assist it in finding a solution to the paramount problem of the *method* by which the Tripolitanian members of the National Assembly should be chosen. He at once consulted the leaders of the Tripolitanian political parties and leading personalities in the territory, as well as Ahmed Bey in the Fezzan and the Amir in Cyrenaica, but without success. The main stumbling block was how to divide up the twenty seats among the several political parties in accordance with their relative strengths. These strengths never having been tested by elections, each party could claim to be stronger than its rival. And, naturally, all inflated their true membership. The result was that the Commissioner found himself faced with as many claims for the proportional distribution of seats as there were parties. Finally, the imminence of his departure for New York obliged him to leave the matter in the lap of the Mufti—and in fact in that of the British Administration as well, which once again, though less formally than before, insisted on its right and duty to have a say in the matter.

In the event, the Committee of Twenty-One adopted the following resolution:

> His Highness Sayid Mohammed Idris el Senussi will select the representatives of Cyrenaica; Ahmed Bey Seif el Nasr will select the representatives of the Fezzan; in accordance with unanimous wishes of the Tripolitanian representatives on the Committee of Twenty-One, the representatives of Tripolitania will be selected by His Eminence the Mufti, who will hold the necessary conversations and consultations and will then draw up a list and submit it to the Committee of Twenty-One not later than 26 October 1950.[53]

53. Ibid., p. 72.

The final outcome was a list made up of nine men belonging to the National Congress of Tripolitania or to its affiliated parties, five belonging to the Independence Party and six independents with no affiliation. This was certainly a fairer distribution than that represented by the selection by the Commissioner and the Council of the Tripolitanian delegation to the Committee of Twenty-One itself, which had been top-heavy with National Congress members. The only criticism that could be made of the Mufti's choice was that the proportion of members of the Independence Party was rather high, and that two of their seats might have been given to one member of the small Kutla Party and to one member of the even smaller Egypto-Tripolitanian Union. Such a makeup might have eliminated a good deal of personal bitterness and probably would have won wider support for the Mufti's choice; admittedly, however, it would also have increased the divisions within the Tripolitanian delegation.

The list as it stood was approved by the Committee of Twenty-One by 16 votes to 1, with 1 abstention, three members being absent (Marchino, Sheikh al-Baruni of Tripolitania, and Hajj Rashid al-Kikhia of Cyrenaica). The negative vote was cast by Ali Rajab, and Abd al-Aziz al-Zaqalla'i abstained; both men were from Tripolitania. This meant that only four Tripolitanians out of seven had voted for their own territorial list. When the result became known, it gave rise to protests and public demonstrations. The Commissioner, in Lake Success, received a number of cables, some inviting him to undo the work of the Committee, others suggesting that such protests were mere political maneuvers to prevent the National Assembly from meeting. Although the Commissioner had his own criticism to make of the Committee's work—mainly that the National Assembly would not be an elected body—he believed that the progress it had made was far too important to be set aside. Moreover, of the two years allowed for the implementation of Resolution 289 (IV), ten months had already elapsed, and to start all over again would have jeopardized the acquisition of independence by Libya before 1 January 1952. He therefore congratulated the Committee on its achievement.

The date on which the National Assembly was to be convened also had been the subject of considerable discussion in the Committee of Twenty-One. The Cyrenaicans would have liked it to meet in November. The Fezzanese, still trying to hold up matters at the behest of the French, proposed a date in the first half of January. The Tripolitanians were inclined to share the Cyrenaican point of view, which was also favored by the British Administration. The date finally chosen, 25 November, was therefore a compromise, but a compromise with a vital implication. It had been intended to convene the Council for Libya on 29 November, a date which in the event had repeatedly to be postponed because the discussions on Libyan affairs at Lake Success required the Commissioner's continued presence there. The choice of 25 November was based on the desire of both the British Administration and the majority of members of the Committee of Twenty-One to confront the Council with the fait accompli of the National Assembly's being in session. This stratagem succeeded brilliantly, as the Council met only on 19 December.

Before the work of the Committee of Twenty-One, and hence its existence, came to an end, Omar Shenib, speaking for the Cyrenaican members, requested, as he had done before, that the Committee should state its views on the form of the future State. He himself proposed a federal monarchy with the Amir as King. Bin Othman, a representative of the Fezzan, stated, however, that "any decision of that nature might be regarded as interference in the work of the future National Assembly.[54] The Chairman declared that he had no objection to the Committee's recommending that His Highness the Amir Sayed Idris el Senussi be proclaimed King of Libya. But he believed that it would be better to leave the question of the form of State to the National Assembly. This, again, was one of those soothing compromises at which the Mufti was a past master. There were no objections to his suggestion, but before the Committee dissolved, it decided to send congratulatory messages to the Amir, Ahmed Bey Seif al-Nasr, and the Commissioner to mark the completion of its work.

It was quite obvious that most members of the Committee felt rather pleased with themselves; they had reason to be.

In the meantime, the Amir and Ahmed Bey had made their appointments, giving the National Assembly the following final composition (A/AC.32/Council/R.110):

REPRESENTATIVES OF CYRENAICA

Omar Shenib	Mohamed Ali Sifaat Bu Farwa
Bubakr Bilthan	Abd al-Hamid Delaf
Sulayman al-Jerbi	Rafaa Bu Gheitas
Mohamed Bu Rahim	Hamida Mahjub
Abd al-Jawad al-Furaytis	Salem al-Atrash
Mabruk Geibani	Khalil al-Qallal
Qaylani Laytewish	Tayal al-Bijou
Tahir al-Asbali	Ahmed Agheila al-Kizza
Abdulla Bin Abd al-Jelil Sowaykir	Mahmud Bu Hidma
Hussein Jerour	Hajj Abd al-Kafi Semin

54. Ibid., p. 74.

REPRESENTATIVES OF TRIPOLITANIA

Ahmed Awn Sawf	Ali al-Kalush
Abd al-Aziz al-Zaqalla'i	Abd al-Majid Ku'bar
Munir Burshan	Abdullah Bin Matuk
Ali Tamir	Mohamed Mak al-Hammali
Ahmed As Sari	Ibrahim Bin Sha'ban
Mukhtar al-Muntasir	Yahya Mas'ud Bin Issa
Salem al-Murayyid	Abu Bakr Na'ama
Mohamed al-Mansuri	Mahmud al-Muntasir
Mohamed al-Hinqari	Tahir Karamanli
Mohamed Abul Is'ad al-Alim	Ali Bin Selim

REPRESENTATIVES OF THE FEZZAN

Akermi Bin Oubey	Mohamed al-Amir
Ali Maghtuf	Mohamed Bin Othman
Abd al-Hadi Bin Ramdan	Mabruk Bin Ali
Jarzari Bin Ali	Mansur Bin Mohamed
Sa'ad Bin Midoun	Tahir Bin Mohamed
Bubakr Bin Mohamed	Tahir Bin Qedafi
Ali Saadawi	Sharil Ali Bin Mohamed
Ahmed Tibuli	Fituri Bin Mohamed
Belqasem Bouguila	Ali Bedwi
Ali Bin Abdullah	Senussi Bin Hammad

The few members who resigned later were replaced through a co-option procedure exercised separately within each group.

Several months passed before the Council for Libya found time in March 1951 to discuss the Commissioner's memorandum regarding the work of the Committee of Twenty-One that had been submitted to it on 15 December 1950.[55] The long delay suggests that in the eyes of several Council members this postmortem had lost its significance. Nevertheless, the Committee of Twenty-One came in for severe criticism from the Egyptian, Pakistani, and Tripolitanian members. All three accused it of having exceeded its terms of reference, maintaining that the National Assembly it had created did not meet the requirements of Resolution 289 (IV). The Council had meant the Committee to prepare a plan that would enable representatives of the inhabitants of Cyrenaica, the Fezzan, and Tripolitania to meet in a National Assembly. The Committee had gone beyond that, and the Egyptian representative went so far as to speak of "a breach of trust."[56] According to him, the normal procedure should have been as follows:

55. For text of the memorandum, see ibid., pp. 71–74.
56. Ibid., para. 5.

> three steps would have been taken before the National Assembly came into being: first, the Committee of Twenty-One would have prepared a plan; secondly, the Commissioner and the Council would have examined that plan to see if it was democratic and conducive to the establishment of the duly representative National Assembly required by the United Nations resolutions; thirdly, after the Commissioner and the Council had given their opinions on the plan, measures would have been taken by the Commissioner, in cooperation with the Administering Powers, to set up the National Assembly.[57]

The member for Pakistan asserted that the Committee was responsible to the organ which had created it, and that it had acted irresponsibly by itself implementing the plan it had prepared instead of submitting it to the Commissioner or the Council. He also criticized the Commissioner for not having kept the Committee on the rails.

The United States, United Kingdom, French, Cyrenaican, and Fezzanese representatives defended the Committee's work and commended the way it had gone about its task, including the establishment of the National Assembly.

The Commissioner recalled that, in its advice to him of 14 June, the Council had departed from his original proposal that the National Assembly be elected, but had failed to indicate what method was to be followed in setting it up. Neither had the Council stipulated that the Committee's plan should be referred back to the Commissioner or to the Council. Even had the Council made such a stipulation, neither Commissioner nor Council would have been able to take any executive or administrative action to modify the Committee's plan or prevent its implementation, as their functions were purely advisory. All the Council could have done would have been to hand down one more advice. Despite his own reservations about its work, he did not believe he could rightly blame the Committee. It had accomplished a useful and indispensable task in extraordinarily difficult circumstances.

After three days of rather heated discussion, the debate was closed. No motion was put to the meeting. Once more the proceedings had revealed the existence of profound differences of opinion about the duties and competence of the Council and the Commissioner and their mutual relationship. While the majority of the Council recognized that neither the Commissioner nor the Council could do more than tender advice, a minority claimed the right to construe Resolution 289 (IV) in such a way as to empower the Council to impose its views not only on the Commissioner but

57. Ibid.

even on the people of Libya. More and more Libyans were beginning to resent this attitude, and for the first time the situation held the elements of a divergence of outlook between the United Nations organs—the Council in particular—on the one hand, and certain sectors of Libyan public opinion on the other.[58]

A fortunate sequel to the change in French policy on the selection issue (p. 295) was that from this moment Franco-Senussi relations slowly began to improve. The most apparent effect of this was a strengthening of Ahmed Bey's position. It was no doubt as a result of these closer relations between Sabhah and Benghazi that, for instance, the village of Jadid abandoned its hostile attitude toward Ahmed Bey in December 1950. This relaxation of tension also facilitated the task of the French Administration; more importantly, however, it prepared the ground for closer collaboration between the Cyrenaican and Fezzanese representatives in the National Assembly.

58. Ismail Raghib Khalidi's views on the subject are of interest, since his duties gave him opportunities for close objective observation of the Committee's work. He writes: "To sum up: the decision of the Committee represented a series of compromises on the part of all concerned. The fact that they avoided going into the substance of the United Nations resolution when ruling out procedural difficulties signified the sincere desire of the representatives from the three territories to begin without further delay the task of drafting the constitution. But the Committee's decision was a significant defeat for the advocates of a unitary state and it paved the way for the setting up of a federal form of government. Any other course would have rendered the United Nations resolution ineffective." Khalidi, p. 35.

CHAPTER 4

The Vital Machinery of Resolution 289 A (IV)

PART 1. THEORY

As related in Chapter 2, before leaving New York for Libya for the first time, the Commissioner had tried to construct for himself a working hypothesis of what his duties amounted to (see p. 112). Though his embryonic concept of the task as he then saw it was not far off the mark, he had grossly underrated its complexity.

During the early months of his mission, he and his staff, with legal assistance both in New York and Tripoli, had thoroughly studied the official records of the Third and Fourth Sessions of the General Assembly in an attempt to fathom the whys and wherefores of the relationships established by Resolution 289 A (IV) between the Commissioner, the Council, the Administering Powers, the Libyan people, and, later, the National Assembly and the duly constituted Libyan Government.

These records showed clearly that, broadly speaking, the history of the Libyan problem fell into two periods. The first, starting as far back as the end of World War II and closing with the rejection of the Bevin-Sforza plan, covered the struggle between the Four Great Powers to find a commonly acceptable political solution to the future of each of the three former Italian colonies. The failure to find such a solution was largely due to the growing intensity of the cold war.

The second period covered the spring and autumn of 1949 when, within the precincts of the United Nations, agreement was reached on the principle of independence, at least insofar as Libya was concerned. It was taken up by attempts to find ways and means of translating the principle into effective practice. The outcome was the invention—improvisation is perhaps a better word—of the complex, but reasonably well balanced, machinery described in Part 3 of Chapter 1. To the Commissioner the subject was indeed double Dutch, for the simple reason that until late in November 1949 he had been busy seeing to the internal functioning of the General Assembly, without an inkling that he would have anything to do with Libya. Nobody seems to have thought, while Resolution 289 (IV) was being drafted, of the man who would be called upon to play the leading part in its implementation. Hence, when the general discussion on the disposal of the former Italian colonies opened in the First Committee of the General Assembly on 30 September 1949, the main emphasis fell on the implementation of the principle of independence rather than on the principle itself. The author may, therefore, be forgiven if in this chapter, comparing theory with practice, he deals in detail with those features of the Resolution which subsequently gave rise to controversial interpretations. As recorded in Chapter 1 (p. 88 ff.), three delegations submitted draft resolutions specifying the way in which the plan for Libyan independence should be put into practice.

The Indian proposal was that:

> 1. The territories of Libya shall form a single united independent group, with a constitution to be drawn up by a constituent assembly representative of the inhabitants of the entire group and to be approved by a commission appointed by the General Assembly of the United Nations,
> 2. The commission shall consist of not less than three and not more than five persons to be chosen by the General Assembly from a panel of experts,
> 3. The commission shall study local conditions and lay down a practicable basis for a truly representative constituent assembly for the purpose of drawing up a constitution for the said territories,
> 4. The constituent assembly shall after drawing up the constitution submit it for the approval of the commission,
> 5. When the commission has approved of the draft constitution, it shall report the fact of the approval and send a copy of the draft constitution to the Secretary-General who shall thereupon communicate the same to the present Administering Powers (namely, the United Kingdom and France),
> 6. The present Administering Powers shall, upon receipt of the said communication, take appropriate steps for giving effect to the constitution as approved by the commission,
> 7. All the steps prescribed above shall be completed within a period not exceeding two years from the appointment of the commission.[1]

The Pakistani proposal included the following paragraph:

> [A.1] (d) There shall be established an advisory council consisting of representatives of Egypt, France, Italy, Pakistan, United Kingdom, the

1. GAOR: Fourth Session, 1949, First Committee, Annexes to Summary Records, Agenda item 19 (A/C.1/491, 4 October 1949), p. 22.

United States and three representatives of the local population, one from Cyrenaica, one from Tripolitania and one from the Fezzan. The council shall advise the Administering Authorities . . . as to how assistance might be given to the inhabitants with regard to formation of a government for an independent Libya. The council shall be empowered to visit the territory of Libya and to obtain, with the co-operation of the Administering Authorities, such information as it deems necessary to enable it to discharge its functions. The council shall make an annual report to the Secretary-General, for the information of the Members of the United Nations, on the carrying out of its task.[2]

The United States draft resolution proposed that:

(d) There shall be established an advisory council consisting of representatives of Egypt, France, Italy, the United Kingdom, the United States and two representatives of the local population, one from Cyrenaica and one from Tripolitania. The council shall advise the Administering Authorities as to how assistance might be given to the inhabitants with regard to formation of a government for an independent Libya, and such related problems as common services. The council shall establish its seat outside of Libya at a place to be determined after consultation with the Secretary-General, and shall be empowered to visit the territory and to obtain, with the co-operation of the Administering Authorities, such information as it deems necessary to enable it to discharge its functions. The council shall make an annual report to the Secretary-General, for the information of the Members of the United Nations, on the carrying out of its task.[3]

These and other proposals were referred to Sub-Committee 17, which was instructed to prepare a comprehensive draft covering all three former colonies.[4] The part of this composite draft relating to Libya was subsequently approved by the First Committee subject to a few changes. It follows that, to understand and interpret the Resolution, it is necessary to consult the Secretariat's notes on the deliberations of Sub-Committee 17 and the records of the First Committee; even then, certain passages are open to varying interpretations, mainly because the Sub-Committee did not have enough time to give a final polish to all parts of the machinery it had assembled.

2. Ibid. (A/C.1/499, 11 October 1949), p. 25.
3. Ibid. (A/C.1/497, 10 October 1949), p. 24.
4. For details and nature of the records taken by the Secretariat of the Sub-Committee's deliberations and of the publicity given to them, see Chapter 1, p. 91 and fn. 79.

THE COMMISSIONER AND THE COUNCIL

It will be remembered that when Sub-Committee 17 held its first meeting on 11 October 1949, none of the draft resolutions before it contained any reference to a commissioner, whereas the advisory council was given a more important part to play than was assigned to it in Resolution 289 (IV). The first mention of a commissioner occurs in a proposal submitted by the Brazilian delegation on 13 October 1949, which read as follows:

> *The First Committee*
> *Recommends* that a United Nations High Commissioner be appointed by the General Assembly for the purpose of assisting the peoples of Libya in the formulation of a constitution and the establishment of a government. In the fulfillment of his task, the High Commissioner shall be assisted by an Advisory Council consisting of representatives of France, Italy, Egypt, Pakistan, the United Kingdom, the United States and three representatives of the local population, one for Cyrenaica, one for Tripolitania and one for the Fezzan.[5]

Later, the Brazilian representative defined the terms of reference on the proposed Commissioner as follows: "The sole terms of reference of the Commissioner should be to assist the people of Libya in adopting a constitution and establishing their government." [6] He added, by way of clarification, that he had thought it better not to go into detail, restricting himself to defining the broad responsibilities involved. He also expressed the opinion that:

> the solution of a High Commissioner elected by the General Assembly from a number of people known for their objectivity and sense of justice seemed to his delegation the simplest, and the one most likely to enable the United Nations to achieve its aims. The United Nations agent that would be going to Libya would have *to take quick decisions and act quickly, which a High Commissioner would be in a position to do.*
>
> *To advise the High Commissioner* a committee would be set up, consisting of representatives of the countries directly concerned and of the peoples of the three territories, whose task it would be to express their views on the formation of a government and on the drafting of a constitution.[7]

5. United Nations Doc. A/C.1/SC.17/L.1, 13 October 1949. Mimeographed. Distribution of this document was strictly limited to those taking part in the work of the Sub-Committee.

6. Unofficial translation from the French of the Secretariat's notes of the Sub-Committee's fifth meeting. Typescript. See footnotes 4 and 36 in this chapter.

7. Ibid. Italics added.

It is worth noting here that the United Kingdom representative declared that:

> the idea of a High Commissioner was most attractive . . . the dual aim was to proclaim the existence of Libya as a political entity and to vest the High Commissioner with the authority of the United Nations. . . . The idea of an advisory committee was less attractive. . . . [The High Commissioner] should be empowered to co-opt, and use the services of, such assistants as he might feel he required.[8]

In reply to a point raised by the Pakistani delegation about the precise conditions under which the Commissioner would be free to reject or accept the advice tendered by the advisory committee, the Brazilian representative explained that:

> a High Commissioner elected by the General Assembly would carry great moral weight, *as his authority would not be dispersed as would that of a committee.* He would be responsible to the General Assembly direct, thus ensuring the highest degree of objectivity. On the other hand, the creation of an advisory committee would give the countries concerned also their say in matters.[9]

As mentioned on pages 93–94, the Sub-Committee was unable to reach agreement, and a vote was therefore taken on whether it was advisable to set up a United Nations commission alone, i.e. without a commissioner. The voting resulted in a tie (one member abstaining), and the motion was accordingly lost under the General Assembly's rules of procedure.

On the theory thus propounded by the Brazilian representative, the Commissioner would be the principal agent; the main function of the advisory committee being to allow the countries most directly concerned with the Libyan problem to make their views known.

The following day (14 October 1949), at the request of the United Kingdom representative, the Chairman took a vote on whether the Sub-Committee wished to recommend to the General Assembly that it appoint a commissioner alone. That proposal was also rejected, by 14 votes to 5, with 2 abstentions. The Sub-Committee then approved, by 12 votes to 6, with 3 abstentions, the principle of a Commissioner *and* a Council to aid and advise him, as proposed by the Indian delegation. Thus agreement was reached on paragraph 4 of Resolution 289 A (IV) (cf. p. 94).

During a later phase of the discussion, agreement was reached on another provision, also proposed by India: "In the discharge of his functions, the United Nations commissioner shall consult and be guided by the advice of

8. Ibid.
9. Ibid. Italics added.

the members of his council, it being understood that he may call upon different members to advise him in respect of different regions or different subjects." [10]

The last part of this provision provoked an objection from the representative of China to the effect that the Commissioner might possibly make excessive use of the power of selecting his advisers, but this objection was overruled.

However, the Argentinian representative subsequently made the following statement in the First Committee:

> The sole purpose of that provision was to give the commissioner a large measure of discretion as the Council would certainly number among its members many experts specializing in certain questions. In authorizing the Commissioner to consult with the one or other member of the Advisory Council according to need, it had not been intended to exclude consultations with the other members. In doubtful cases the Commissioner would naturally consult the Advisory Council as a whole.[11]

When the question of who should submit the annual reports to the Secretary-General came up in the Sub-Committee, some comments were made which also shed light on the relationship between the Commissioner and the Council. The United Kingdom representative observed that the main organ created by the United Nations would be the Commissioner; the sole function of the Council would be to assist him in the performance of his duties. Hence it would be preferable for the Commissioner to be the reporting authority. The Guatemalan representative supported this view, arguing that it would not be proper for a report to be presented by the Council apart from the Commissioner, for the latter alone was responsible to the United Nations for Libyan affairs. The Pakistani representative, Abdur Rahim Khan (who later became the representative of his Government on the Council), suggested that:

> the . . . commissioner, in consultation with the advisory council, should present to the Secretary-General an annual report and such special reports as he might deem necessary in order to keep the United Nations informed about the performance of their task. In his [Rahim Khan's] opinion, the key word was "consultation." If one or more members of the council were not satisfied with the views expressed by the . . . com-

10. Subsequently paragraph 8 of Resolution 289 (IV), 21 November 1949.

11. GAOR: Fourth Session, 1949, First Committee, 313th Meeting, 5 November 1949, p. 197.

missioner or by the majority, he or they would be entitled to request that their dissatisfaction be recorded in the report.[12]

The suggestion was adopted by 17 votes to none, with 4 abstentions. Thus it was once again confirmed that the Commissioner would be the principal United Nations agent in Libya, and that it was he who would address reports to the Secretary-General, though in consultation with the Council.

Sub-Committee 17 thereupon decided to set up a drafting group to prepare a text for final agreement. Discussion of the text this group submitted brought to light fresh problems of interpretation. The Chinese representative drew attention to a paradox between the text of paragraph 4 and that of paragraph 8 of what finally became Resolution 289 (IV), pointing out that whereas it was first stated that the Council was to aid and advise the Commissioner, it was subsequently laid down that the Commissioner should consult and seek the advice of the Council. In the first case, the Council would be given the power to aid the Commissioner whether he sought its assistance or not; in the second, the Commissioner was instructed to seek the Council's advice.

The Egyptian representative, attempting to interpret these provisions, understood that the phrase "be guided by it" imposed no absolute obligation on the Commissioner; but it was slightly stronger than "to seek the advice of," the phrase used in the draft before the Sub-Committee. He suggested therefore that the wording of paragraph 4 be made stronger so as to bring it into line with that of paragraph 8.

The representative of Mexico did not agree that there was any inconsistency between the two phrases. In his view, paragraph 4 related to the duties of the Advisory Council, whereas paragraph 8 related to those of the Commissioner.

Rahim Khan observed that paragraph 4 merely provided that the Commissioner should have a Council to advise him; paragraph 8 stated how he should treat that advice. This observation in fact summed up concisely the respective obligations of the Council and the Commissioner. It proved of particular interest in that it was supported by several representatives and aroused no opposition. In brief, paragraph 4 of the resolution dealt with the obligations of the Council, which were to aid and advise the Commissioner. The interpretation of that provision seemingly raised no difficulty. Paragraph 8 dealt with the obligations of the Commissioner, who was required to consult and be guided by the advice of the members of his Council.

12. Unofficial translation from the French of the Secretariat's notes of the Sub-Committee's ninth meeting. Typescript.

Following the discussions in Sub-Committee 17, the Commissioner's legal advisers interpreted this phrase as meaning that the Commissioner was obliged to seek the Council's advice on important issues referred to it. He must also be guided by that advice. Accordingly, they found that, although he was not bound to follow it literally or blindly, he must do so as a general rule; moreover, unless he could adduce very cogent reasons for not doing so, he must follow the main points of the advice which the Council gave him on any specific question. In the event of disagreement between the Commissioner and the Council, it would be for the General Assembly to settle the issue.

It followed from this interpretation that the Commissioner and the Council alike would do well to avoid, as far as possible, any disagreement of a nature so serious as to make it necessary to bring it before the General Assembly for settlement.

According to the letter of the Resolution, the Council collectively did not seem to have been made responsible to any other organ or authority. Whether this omission was deliberate is not clear from the record. Apparently the point was never made. Theoretically, therefore, it could be argued that the Council owed responsibility to no one. In fact, the situation as it developed was somewhat different and rather involved. Six members of the Council had been formally accredited to the Secretary-General by their respective governments, from which they received their instructions. But two of those governments—the United Kingdom and France (notwithstanding the latter's abstention from the voting in the General Assembly on Resolution 289 (IV))—had assumed special responsibilities toward the General Assembly, and under subparagraph 10 (c) of the Resolution were required to make, in cooperation with the Commissioner, annual reports to that body on the steps they had taken to implement its recommendations. The other eight members of the Council, despite differences in status, were all members of a council whose responsibilities had been determined by the General Assembly, and this in itself created a special link between them and the United Nations. The strength of that link was demonstrated by the right granted to them individually under paragraph 5 to add to the Commissioner's annual reports any memorandum or document that they might wish to bring to the attention of the United Nations. A glance at the reports and the numerous footnotes thereto will show that this right was very liberally exercised, even by the Administering Powers.

Furthermore, it must be noted that Egypt, Pakistan, and the United States, as members of the United Nations, had voted for the Resolution determining the future of Libya, an act by virtue of which their representatives on the Council were also bound to see to its implementation. In this respect, Italy, which at the time was not a member of the United Nations, was in a position apart, but even of her it could be said that, as a party to the Treaty of Peace, she had assumed certain duties concerning the future of Libya. Moreover, the Italians domiciled in Libya having been recognized as one of the minorities under the interpretation placed on subparagraph 6 (b) of Resolution 289 (IV), and these minorities as a whole having been granted a representative of their own on the Council, Italy could claim certain privileges for them. The representative for the minorities, it should not be forgotten, was morally responsible to his own committee. The three Libyan members of the Council had in a sense a twofold responsibility, one toward the authorities of the territory they represented, the other, as members of the Council, to the General Assembly, which had created their function. Admittedly, the member for Tripolitania was in a somewhat special position, but even he had been recognized by the Commissioner, by the responsible Administering Power, and by the other five Governments members of the Council as the duly appointed representative of the territory.

To sum up, the concept of a Council for Libya had its strengths and its weaknesses. Although the Council's advisory duties were clear, its responsibility was untrammeled by any fetters of logic or method. Its role had never been properly thought out; nor was it the product of systematic planning. No wonder that no one has hitherto tried to give a comprehensive account of the Council. Yet in practice, its inherent incoherence notwithstanding, the Council functioned as a body with proper rules of procedure and in time even developed usages and traditions of its own. Naturally, each member in the first place defended his own interests—what he thought would be best for his country, territory, group, or party; but the interests of Libya as a whole were never foreign to the Council's discussions and decisions. Moreover, collectively, the Council felt itself to be what in fact it was, a United Nations organ having politically to account for its actions to the General Assembly; and the individual member conducted himself, and chose his words, having in mind not only his instructions, but also the impression his behavior and statements would make on fellow delegates in New York and on the Libyan audience in the public gallery in Tripoli.

THE COMMISIONER AND THE ADMINISTERING POWERS

Under the terms of Resolution 289 (IV), the Commissioner was required not only to consult the Council and be guided by its advice, but also to cooperate with the Administering Powers, which, reciprocally, were to initiate all necessary steps for the transfer of power to a duly constituted

Government of Libya, to administer the territories for the purpose of assisting in the establishment of Libyan unity and independence, and to coordinate their activities to this end (subparagraphs 10 [a] and [b]). All this had to be done as quickly as possible, and in no case later than 1 January 1952. Consequently, according to the Commissioner's legal advisers, the Administering Powers were under an obligation to abstain from any governmental or administrative decisions which would run counter to the accomplishment of this basic purpose.

It must be noted, however, that the Administering Powers had the right to exercise all governmental functions in the territories for which they were responsible, even though the sovereignty of these territories was not vested in them. It was true that Article 23 of the Treaty of Peace laid down that "Italy renounces all right and title to the Italian territorial possessions in Africa," and that "Pending their final disposal, the said possessions shall continue under their present administration"; but on the question in whom the sovereignty of the territories was vested in the meantime, the Treaty was silent. Several theories had been put forward, but none had won authoritative acceptance.[13]

Whatever may be the interest for scholars of such a legal question from the viewpoint of jurisprudence, there was no question but that de facto responsibility for the administration of the three territories was vested solely in the United Kingdom for Cyrenaica and Tripolitania, and in France for the Fezzan. Hence, the two Powers had the right to perform there all acts necessary for the maintenance of peace, law and order, and good government. And from the debates in Sub-Committee 17 it followed that the Commissioner should refrain from interfering with the exercise of the day-to-day administrative functions of the two Powers.

As to the form of their cooperation, this could be effected through the joint study by the Administering Powers and the Commissioner of specific problems; or the Administering Powers might choose to provide the Commissioner with full information about their programs and policies and any steps they might take in pursuance of subparagraphs 10 (a) and (b). The Commissioner's legal advisers considered that, conversely, he was entitled to address to the Administering Powers such observations and recommendations as he might deem appropriate, provided that these related to the purposes specified in the resolution and in his opinion were essential to its implementation. The Administering Powers, however, were not obliged to accept the Commissioner's observations and recommendations.

13. See editorial comment by Josef L. Kunz, in *The American Journal of International Law* (1947), p. 624. For full text of Article 23 of the Peace Treaty, see Chapter 1 above, pp. 67–68.

STATUS OF THE NATIONAL ASSEMBLY

There were two other organs which, without forming an integral part of the machinery, were closely linked with it. One was the General Assembly of the United Nations, the other the Libyan National Assembly. It resulted from the United Nations General Assembly Resolution itself that the Administering Powers and the Commissioner were responsible to the General Assembly; that both were required to submit reports to it; and, implicitly, that the General Assembly would act as the arbiter of irreconcilable differences of opinion between the two sides.

As for the National Assembly, although its duties had been clearly specified, the Resolution said nothing about to whom it was responsible or to whom it was to report. There is nothing in the records to suggest that the matter was ever seriously considered. The reader will at times come across questions on the subject that were never answered. These apparent lacunae very well may have been intentional. Indeed, one gets the impression that the great majority of delegations wanted the Libyan National Assembly to be completely free and independent in carrying out its task, particularly vis-à-vis the Administering Powers. It seems to have been taken for granted that the Assembly owed responsibility only to the inhabitants of the three territories, whom it was to represent. The resolution did not even specify how this representation was to be organized, through many delegations appear to have assumed that the deputies would be elected. The Commissioner therefore read paragraph 3 of Resolution 289 (IV) as meaning that the Administering Powers were not entitled to intervene in the work of the National Assembly. Paragraph 3 also meant, in his opinion, that while he was to be at the National Assembly's disposal to give assistance, aid, or advice, the Assembly was under no obligation to ask for or accept these.

CHECKS AND BALANCES

It will be appreciated from the foregoing that the General Assembly had in effect devised a system of checks and balances, although it cannot be said that the parts to be played by each of the three partners were precisely defined. This, again, was doubtless due to the very short time at Sub-Committee 17's disposal and to the fact that this was the first time in the history of the United Nations that such a system had been instituted, so that there were no precedents to fall back on. To make the system work, two basic conditions had to be met: relations between the three partners must be governed by mutual confidence; and no partner should try to dominate either or both of the other two. The Commissioner in particular had to watch his step, as he was the central cogwheel in the movement, and one of his duties in this role was to hold the balance between the Council for Libya and the Administering Powers.

This account of the legal background of Resolution 289 (IV), viewed in the light of its political history as described in Chapter 1, will, it is hoped, make clear that much was left to the discretion and interpretation of those organs and individuals entrusted with its implementation. The chapters that follow provide ample proof of this.

PART 2. PRACTICE

Had the convoy of States that made up the community of nations during the years 1948–52 been steaming through calm seas, the task of the United Nations in Libya probably would have been much more difficult than it was. In all likelihood the story would then have been front-page news, with all that such treatment implies in the public and in the private sectors of international affairs. But the convoy was passing through a zone of political storms very like the "roaring forties," to use a nautical simile. This is not the place to describe international political developments during those troubled years, when the cold war was at its worst. But the agenda of successive sessions of the General Assembly during that period, including Palestine and the Near East, Greece, Korea and peace in the Far East—to mention only the principal sources of tension—tells eloquently enough that for the world at large, with the exception of the Powers immediately interested, Libya had been relegated to a very minor place.[14] The shift of world interest away from Libya because of tension elsewhere had a double effect—one tending to simplify the task of the United Nations, the other tending to complicate it. The reader will remember that while the disposal of the former Italian colonies was still in the hands of the Council of Foreign Ministers, the Soviet Union had taken a very lively interest in the matter, particularly with regard to Libya. The dissenting opinions expressed by the Soviet member in the report of the Four Power Commission of Investigation for the Former Italian Colonies, seen in the light of subsequent developments, had not only often been to the point, but sometimes

14. Some members of the Mission to Libya will not easily forget the circumstances in which they learned through foreign wireless stations on 25 June 1950 of the outbreak of fighting in Korea, in which the United Nations was to become so closely involved. They were on the point of leaving for the Fezzan, and political circles in Tripoli were seething with excitement. A few hours later they landed on the desert airstrip at Sabhah, where nobody knew anything about this tragic event, and life went on untroubled. The contrast was almost unbelievable.

even prophetic. But later, especially after the adoption of Resolution 289 (IV), which made no reference to the matters with which the USSR was especially concerned—military bases and personnel—Soviet interest waned. Moscow had other fish to fry. Had Soviet interest in Libya continued unabated, the outcome of the United Nations operation might have been very different. A single hypothetical question will serve to show what turn events might have taken. If Soviet policy had entailed active support for the Arab League's and Egypt's demand for a unitary Libyan State dominated by Tripolitania, what would have been the attitude of Cyrenaica and the Fezzan? Would the General Assembly, gathered in Paris in January 1952 for its Sixth Session, have seen a delegation of an independent federal Libyan State taking part in its deliberations? Many more such questions could be asked, but what purpose would such speculation serve? The practical fact that counts in the circumstances was that, with the exception of Soviet interventions in the General Assembly debates of 1950 and 1951–52, i.e. at a time when the Western Powers still commanded a fairly reliable voting majority, the influence of the USSR in the Libyan affair was negligible.

On the Western side of the Iron Curtain the intensification of the cold war had an exactly contrary effect, in that interest in Libya on the part of the United Kingdom, France, and the United States, and, in a different way, that of Italy also, became keener than ever. The United Kingdom was in a hurry to consolidate its political relations with Cyrenaica in order to build a solid foundation for its military bases and other facilities there. France, for political and strategic purposes, was seeking to strengthen its position in the Fezzan in order to slow down the pace of the expansion of Arab nationalism westward. The United States had an interest in furthering Libyan independence, in that it wished to conclude an agreement with the new State regulating the position of the Wheelus air base near Tripoli.[15] Lastly, Italy, having reconciled itself to the idea of its former colony being transformed into an independent State, was impatiently awaiting the time when it would be able to negotiate with the new country agreements for the protection of its economic and financial interests in Tripolitania, as provided for in the Peace Treaty and more particularly in General Assembly Resolution 388 (V) of 15 December 1950 (see Chapter 5; also Annex I, pp. 894–99, for the text of this resolution).

Thus, for reasons of practical politics, none of the Four Powers concerned was in principle opposed to Libyan independence; neither, in the

15. Both the strategic and tactical importance of Wheelus Field declined considerably with the opening of the missile age, but until then it was one of the most important North Atlantic Treaty Organization (NATO) bases in the Mediterranean.

nature of things, was any of the other six members of the Council. Hence independence was never an issue. The complications sprang from two other sources. One was the form of the future State, in particular because the interests of the United Kingdom and France were more closely related to Cyrenaica and the Fezzan than to Libya as a whole. This consideration applied in a sense to Italy also, but was barely pertinent in the case of the United States. The problem of unitarism versus federation therefore runs like a leitmotiv through the Libyan story from beginning to end. Neither the United Kingdom nor France was really interested in a united Libyan State; if anything, both countries were opposed to it, and would have preferred the loosest possible form of federation. The Arab States, on the contrary, with Egypt in the van, wanted a united, centralized State that would be less vulnerable to divisive foreign influence and intervention.

In brief, the international backdrop to the stage on which the drama of Libya's transformation was played out was the Mediterranean and Middle East region, with its Anglo-French-Arab antagonisms, to a much greater extent than the worldwide cold war—though the reverberations of the larger conflict were never out of earshot of the principal actors insofar as they were united through NATO.

Accordingly, it is in the more limited perspective of the smaller of these two theaters of conflict that the events to be described here must be judged and evaluated. One consequence of the general situation was that senior officials in Ministries of Foreign Affairs, even those of the countries directly concerned in Libyan affairs, had to devote the bulk of their attention to more important problems. The same applied even to the Secretariat at United Nations Headquarters. As a result, the Commissioner and the Council in far-off Tripoli were often left to cope with their problems alone, when in more settled circumstances they might have been the victims of an overdose of advice and instructions. Nevertheless, the Commissioner and his staff always found willing ears and helpful minds ready to come to their aid whenever a local crisis put them in real need of assistance. This applies in particular to the Secretary-General's Executive Office and its able chief (cf. Chapter 2, p. 110, fn. 3) as well as to the various specialized agencies. The gratitude of the Libyan team for that help was and is as profound as it is sincere.

Soon after the Council started work it became clear that the relationship between the three partners, and especially those between the Commissioner and the Council, would not be as smooth as the General Assembly had hoped. As we have seen, the Commissioner had from the outset also had his differences with the Administering Powers, but these had been eliminated, at least in part, by negotiation and compromise, and although he was never quite happy about the result, his personal relations with the two Governments never suffered appreciably.

The friction between the Commissioner and the Council was of a very different nature, and in the middle of 1950 he almost reached a breaking point with some of its members. Fortunately, wiser counsels prevailed, and by the time the Commissioner prepared his first Annual Report to the General Assembly, in consultation with the Council, relations had been repaired to the point where effective cooperation was once more possible. Nevertheless, antagonism between certain Council members and the Administering Powers and between these members and the Commissioner continued to cloud the atmosphere. Since the incidents about to be related touch on matters of principle, and were directly connected with varying interpretations of Resolution 289 (IV), it is necessary to deal with them in greater detail than in the general account given in Parts 2 and 3 of Chapter 3.

As early as 26 April 1950, the member for Pakistan had submitted a draft resolution, the first paragraph of which read:

> This Council advises the Commissioner in Libya to request the Administering Authorities in the three regions of Libya to communicate to the Commissioner, for communication to the Council, all information relating to the steps which the said Powers have taken already or contemplate taking in pursuance of paragraph 10 (a) and (b) of General Assembly Resolution 289 (IV).[16]

The second paragraph read:

> Further, this Council advises the Commissioner in Libya to request the Administering Powers in the three regions of Libya to suspend the enforcement of measures not as yet put into operation and referred to above until the Council has had an opportunity to consider these and give their advice with regard to them to the Commissioner for communication to the Administering Powers.[17]

Despite the Commissioner's insistence that the proposal be taken up as quickly as possible, the Council was unable to do so until it had disposed of his requests for advice on the scope of his work and on the constitutional development of Libya—in other words, not before the middle of May. In the meantime, several members of the Council had come to believe that

16. United Nations Doc. A/AC.32/COUNCIL/R.7, 26 April 1950. Mimeographed. For final text, see first *Annual Report of the United Nations Commissioner in Libya*, GAOR: Fifth Session, 1950, Supplement No. 15 (A/1340), Annex VI, p. 46.

17. Ibid.

behind the Pakistani draft resolution there lay a policy with which they could not agree.

As reported on page 216, the Council adopted the first paragraph without too much discussion; the second, however, aroused widespread opposition. The Commissioner himself was against it on the ground that, with only two years to go, the Administering Powers should not be required, unless absolutely necessary, to lose time in reporting on the cooperation they owed to him, not to the Council. Moreover, he saw in it an attempt to exploit him as a channel for censuring or lecturing the Administering Powers. It was perfectly in order for the Council to ask the Administering Powers for such information, and the channel used—the Commissioner—was the correct one. What was not correct was to use the Commissioner to call the Administering Powers to task as if they were responsible for their actions to the Council or to himself, whereas they were accountable solely to the General Assembly.

Such misgivings were heightened in the ensuing debate when the Egyptian member argued that there was a formal link between the Commissioner's duties (a) to consult the Council and (b) to cooperate with the Administering Powers. This chain of reasoning implied that since the Commissioner required the Council's advice on all matters coming within the scope of the Resolution, and since the Administering Powers in turn required his cooperation, the former should not give his assent to any measures the two Powers might propose to take without first referring them to the Council. This was an interpretation with which neither the Commissioner nor the Administering Powers, nor, indeed, several other members of the Council, could agree.

One member after another spoke against the second part of the Pakistani proposal, which its author withdrew after the Commissioner had assured the Council that he would not fail to consult it before consenting to any implementation measure envisaged by the Administering Powers, in discharge of the obligation imposed upon him by paragraph 8 of the Resolution. In giving this assurance for the sake of harmony, he went to the limit of what he could concede without making himself completely dependent on the Council. Yet the debate was inconclusive because it left open the cardinal issue, which was whether, and if so to what extent, the Commissioner was bound by the Council's advice. Meanwhile, in accordance with the advice given to him in the first part of the Pakistani proposal, he addressed requests for information to the Administering Powers, and in July received detailed replies from all three administrations. These he communicated to the Council for its information.[18]

18. See ibid., Annexes VIII, IX, and X, pp. 47–52.

Notwithstanding the up-to-date information thus provided, the Pakistani member submitted, in succession, three more requests for information from the Administering Powers through the Commissioner:

1. Information on the steps taken to implement the Council's advice of 3 May 1950 on the scope of the Commissioner's work;
2. Information on the steps taken to transfer authority to the people of Libya; and
3. Information on the steps taken by the two Administering Powers to coordinate their activities in the promotion of Libyan unity and the formation of governmental institutions.

It was during the consideration of these requests that differences concerning the interpretation of the relationships between the Commissioner and the Council and the Administering Powers came to a head. Two factors contributed to this: the nature of the information sought; and, especially, the way in which the requests were framed.

Before his arrival in Libya, the Commissioner had expected the Administering Powers, in accordance with subparagraph 10 (a) of Resolution 289 (IV), to seek his cooperation in "[initiating] immediately all necessary steps for the transfer of power to a duly constituted independent Government." He had expected the same approach to their obligations to "administer the territories for the purpose of assisting in the establishment of Libyan unity and independence," to "co-operate in the formation of governmental institutions," and to "co-ordinate their activities to this end" (subparagraph 10 [b]).

What in fact happened was that the United Kingdom and France, having their own ideas as to how the United Nations Resolution should be implemented, only communicated to the Commissioner proposals for the establishment of regional governmental institutions which were supposed to develop subsequently into a single government over the whole of Libya. Consequently, the Commissioner's plans for bringing about Libyan unity and independence and those of the two responsible Powers had been far apart from the outset, and it had not been at all easy to find the not altogether satisfactory compromise solution described in Chapter 2.

All this happened before the first meeting of the Council, the members of which had nevertheless been informed of the situation by a detailed memorandum, dated 19 April 1950, submitted by the Commissioner.[19]

Had the critical remarks of the Pakistani representative and his Egyptian and Tripolitanian colleagues been directed toward this central issue in the first place, not only would they have rendered a signal service to the cause of Libyan unity, but they also would have helped to strengthen the Com-

19. Ibid., paras. 60–89, and Annex III, p. 40.

missioner's position vis-à-vis the Administering Powers. Unfortunately, instead of concentrating on the main issue, the three critics spent most of their energies in attacking the British Administration in Tripolitania about important but nonetheless secondary problems, such as education, the Libyanization of the local administration, and the territory's economic and financial situation. Such matters were indeed within the Council's competence, but at the time and in the context of the debate, they were not part of the basic controversy. Moreover, when speakers indulged in attacks over matters of day-to-day local administration—for instance, the difference in the pay of British and Libyan officials in Tripolitania, or the losses caused to local taxicab and carriage drivers by the British military bus services—the Council looked more like a small-town meeting of discontented taxpayers than an assembly of ambassadors whose task it was to watch over the future unity and independence of a nation in the throes of birth. In a fit of disgust the Commissioner told them so to their face, an outburst which, looking back, was neither wise nor fair—at least not to all the members.

The issue at stake was further obscured by the persistence with which the Pakistani representative criticized the Administering Powers for not taking steps to transfer authority to "the people of Libya," instead of sticking to the official language of the Resolution, which spoke of the "transfer of power to a duly constituted independent Government" (subparagraph 10 [a]). Confusion reached its peak when certain speakers complained that the Administrative Council instituted by the British Administration in Tripolitania as a local advisory organ was not a suitable body to receive in due course the powers that would place Tripolitania on an equal footing with Cyrenaica. To hear this from Council members who claimed that their highest political aim was the unity of Libya was indeed bewildering and discouraging.

A tendency to make the Commissioner responsible for the actions of the Administering Powers ran through the debate like a thread. This emerged clearly from the kinds of questions put to him, for example, how did he propose to correct measures allegedly wrongly taken by them? He was also accused both of not having prevented them from taking certain actions, and, conversely, of not having insisted on their taking others. Thus the feeling that an attempt was being made to abuse the machinery set up by the United Nations Resolution grew stronger day by day.

This impression hardened even more when the discussion of the Pakistani requests for information had to be interrupted to enable the Council to take a decision on its program of work, to allow for consultations with the Commissioner on his first annual report to the Secretary-General of the United Nations. It was then that Rahim Khan declared that, before the report was drafted, there should be consultations on the general lines it should follow. This was not the Commissioner's idea of writing his annual report in consultation with the Council, as required by paragraph 5 of the General Assembly Resolution. On the contrary, he told the Council, he would submit a full draft report on which members would be invited to make observations and comments, which he would either accept or reject. Since under the same provision members were entitled to add any memorandum or document they might wish to bring to the attention of the General Assembly, he would gladly join to his report any such material, either as footnotes or as annexes; but he reserved the right to add counter-observations or additional comments of his own where he differed with the content. (This was a rather special mode of consultation, and produced a particular type of report.) In the Commissioner's view this was the logical way of carrying out the General Assembly's directive.

Rahim Khan recalled that the phrase "in consultation with the Council" had been introduced into paragraph 5 at his own suggestion by Sub-Committee 17 when confronted with two conflicting proposals. The United Kingdom representative had thought that the Commissioner alone should submit the report, the Egyptian representative that it would be for the Council to do so. Each side had commanded support from other members of the Sub-Committee. His own proposal had been intended to reconcile the two positions; it had been accepted almost unanimously. He therefore claimed to be the one person qualified to say what it meant.[20] His view was that there should be a preliminary discussion between the Commissioner and the Council on the general lines of the report. When the report had been drafted along those lines, it could be discussed paragraph by paragraph. If no prior agreement were reached on the form, Rahim Khan maintained that the text might have to be redrafted, or the Egyptian representative and he might be obliged to submit a dissenting report. If that proved necessary, the draft report would have to be sent to Karachi, where it would take his superiors some time to examine it and authorize him to submit a separate one.

The Commissioner felt that these arguments supported, if anything, his own thesis. In the end, the Council decided that, in accordance with rule 11 of its rules of procedure, it would move to Geneva in the first half of August to consider the Commissioner's draft report. The discussion on the Paki-

20. It was indeed correct that the member for Pakistan had proposed the insertion of the phrase in question while representing his country on Sub-Committee 17. However, the notes taken by the Secretariat at the time in no way support the contention that the Sub-Committee attached to these words the interpretation he now endeavored to place on them.

stani requests for information was thereupon resumed. Before dealing with this, however, mention must be made of the exchange of letters that took place in May 1950 between Kamel Selim Bey and Abdur Rahim Khan on the one hand, and the Commissioner on the other.

When the Council had decided to suspend its formal meetings for about a month to visit the three territories, as described in Part 3 of Chapter 3, the United States member, by moving that the debate be adjourned, had asked his colleagues not to take a decision on the Commissioner's request for advice on constitutional development (see pp. 224–25). Instead, he had suggested, the Council should simply express general approval of the plan; that would enable the Administering Powers and the Commissioner to get on with things while the Council was away. The members for Egypt and Pakistan had disagreed, considering the United States suggestion as tantamount to the Council's abdicating its main function. A little later they put their dissent in writing, reaffirming their contention that the Administering Powers should act only in cooperation with the Commissioner, who in turn should act only on the advice of the Council as to the steps to be taken to promote the constitutional development of Libya. In their view, any departure from such a procedure would be incompatible with either the spirit or the letter of Resolution 289 (IV). By adding that they knew the Commissioner shared this opinion, they obliged him to take a formal stand, which he did, as related in Part 1 of this chapter.

During the ensuing discussions, the question of the relationships between Commissioner and the Council and the Administering Powers was repeatedly referred to in a way that persuaded the Commissioner that there was either an honest misunderstanding, or, as he became convinced more and more, a deliberate attempt to maneuver the Council into a position where it could control both himself and the Administering Powers.

The representatives of the Administering Powers lost no time in setting the record straight, but, naturally, did so to clarify their Governments' positions rather than that of the Commissioner.

The United States member, trying to pour oil on the troubled waters, reproached all three parties for harboring unworthy suspicions of one another and for laboring under an undue sense of self-righteousness. He urged both the Commissioner and the Council to take into consideration, irrespective of any legalistic interpretation of the United Nations Resolution, the de facto role being played by the Administering Powers, to whom both were free to make suggestions and recommendations, which they could not, however, impose. As a realistic approach to their work, members might show more charity toward one another in interpreting the Resolution. It was not enough to criticize what had been done; it was also necessary to make constructive suggestions for achieving the Council's task.

This last remark was wisdom itself. Unfortunately, from the Commissioner's point of view, the United States representative undid much of the effect of his intervention by going on to say that preparations for the transfer of authority were not moving so fast in Tripolitania as they had done either in Cyrenaica or in the Fezzan, thereby implying that the transfer of powers to local governmental institutions would help the unification of Libya. A further remark that the continued existence of any local institutions set up in Cyrenaica or the Fezzan would depend upon their compatibility with the constitution to be drafted for the whole of Libya, was poor consolation. It was the Commissioner's unfaltering view that the existence of local governments with executive powers could only hamper the country's progress toward unity.

The French representative, following a statement by his British colleague, made a frontal attack on the Pakistani claim that it was the duty of the Administering Powers to discharge their obligations under subparagraphs 10 (a) and (b) in cooperation not only with the Commissioner but also with the Council. He utterly rejected that argument, summarily observing that paragraph 10 was quite specific. It provided for cooperation with the Commissioner but made no mention whatsoever of the Council. It was evident, as the United Kingdom representative had already stressed, that the Administering Powers were responsible for the fulfillment of their obligations under paragraph 10 not to the Council, but to the General Assembly alone. He realized that paragraph 8 instructed the Commissioner to consult and be guided by the advice of the members of the Council in the discharge of his functions; but it must be borne in mind that that paragraph treated of the Commissioner's functions vis-à-vis the Council, whereas paragraph 10 dealt with the functions of the Administering Powers. The latter discharged their obligations in the fields that concerned them in cooperation with the Commissioner, and the Commissioner discharged his, in cooperation with the Council, in the fields that concerned both these parties. In brief, constitutionally speaking, there were no official relations between the Administering Powers and the Council, except through the Commissioner, who must cooperate with the former and be guided by the latter. If that were not so, and the Pakistani representative's ideas were applied literally, the Administering Powers would be unable to take any action at all without first consulting the Commissioner and, through him, the Council, a procedure which could not fail to produce long discussions, delays, perhaps even contradictions. The theory that the Commissioner must always act in accordance with the Council, and the Council with him, was too rigid. The Commissioner could, and indeed must be able to, act independently. He prepared his report to the General Assembly, for example, merely in consultation with the Council, and was free to submit suggestions to the General Assembly, to the Economic and Social Council, or to the Secretary-General as of right.

If the Governments represented on the Council had any observations to make about the Administering Powers, they must make them in the General Assembly, which alone was competent to pass judgment on the way in which the Administering Powers were managing Libyan affairs. The French delegation's attitude within the Council would be to accept any commendation with pleasure and to reply frankly to any criticism. It would do its best, though it was in no way obliged to do so, to satisfy the members of the Council, through the intermediary of the Commissioner. If members wanted information or clarification on certain points, his delegation would transmit their requests to the Administering Power, which would take whatever action on them it deemed fit. That Power did not, however, consider itself bound by the Council's advice or to submit to its criticisms.

The French member concluded by expressing his agreement with the Pakistani representative that confidence was the key to the situation. He feared, however, that constant opposition to the action taken by the Administering Powers was more likely to sow mistrust. That was why he was bound to say—and it was no threat, simply a warning—that if the Council continued in its present frame of mind and persisted in regarding itself as a tribunal before which the Administering Powers could be called to account for their activities, the French delegation would have to part company with it, with all the consequences such a split would entail.[21]

It was at this point in the debate that the Commissioner felt obliged to clarify matters. He started by saying that Resolution 289 (IV) struck a very delicate balance of functions and responsibilities between the people of Libya, the Administering Powers, the Commissioner, and the Council. It had been generally admitted at the time of its adoption that the machinery would not be easy to operate, but he had always believed that by taking a practical view of the situation, by cooperating with each other on a basis of mutual trust, and by respecting each other's duties and functions, the Commissioner and the Council would be able to work out an effective relationship that would enable both sides to serve the interests of Libya to the best of their ability. That belief was now being challenged and might even be destroyed if the Council were to accept the Pakistani member's conception of that relationship. Since the latter had himself raised the issue, both directly and by innuendo, the Commissioner had no choice but to counter the challenge, not legalistically, but in terms of practical politics.

21. For full texts of statements made by the United Kingdom and the United States members, and by the Pakistani member, which provoked the discussion, see the first *Annual Report of the United Nations Commissioner in Lybia,* Annex XI, pp. 53–64.

The Commissioner then proceeded to define the position, as he saw it, in six points:

First, he had been sent to Libya by the General Assembly as a representative of the United Nations, to help the people of Libya to draw up a constitution and to set up an independent government. His assistance was therefore freely offered to the people of Libya, it being understood that the latter were equally free to ignore it if they so wished.

Second, the Council was to aid and advise him in the achievement of his task, and, with the object of promoting the closest possible cooperation between the two, the General Assembly had very wisely made it obligatory upon him to consult and be guided by the advice of the members of the Council.

Third, such advice as the Council might hand down to the Commissioner, either at his request or on its own initiative, was as a rule to be followed, but was not to be considered as binding. The Commissioner was not the Council's executive arm. He acted on his sole responsibility to the General Assembly, and to the General Assembly alone. He did not have to answer to the Council for any of his acts. But if he did decide, after having exercised his best judgment and searched his conscience, to ignore the Council's advice, he would have to justify his action in the General Assembly.

Fourth, the Administering Powers, in cooperation with the Commissioner, were to administer the territories for the purposes defined in the Resolution. They must also, equally in cooperation with him, initiate all necessary steps to transfer power to a duly constituted, independent Government, which meant to a duly constituted, independent *Libyan* Government. The resolution did not mention transfer of authority to the people of Libya, as the Pakistani request for information wrongly asserted.

Fifth, the Administering Powers were not responsible for their activities either to the Council or to the Commissioner, but again only to the General Assembly, to which they had to report. Constitutionally speaking, there were no official relations between the Administering Powers and the Council except through the intermediary of the Commissioner, who had to cooperate with the one side and be guided by the advice of the other.

Sixth, the requirement that he cooperate with the Administering Powers in the administration of the territories for the purposes of the General Assembly Resolution did not mean that the Commissioner shared their responsibility for such administration. He was naturally accountable for any advice he might tender to the Administering Powers, but they were perfectly free to accept or reject it.

In the light of that conception of his position, the Commissioner went on to deal with the questions put to him by the Pakistani representative. In replying to them, he neither defended his position nor justified his actions, for reasons that have been made explicit. He merely provided certain information, in a spirit of constructive cooperation, to put the Pakistani member in a better position to play his part in the Council's task of giving the Commissioner well-founded advice. But before he did so, he made one general point.

In several of his questions, the Pakistani representative had touched upon the relationship between the Commissioner and the Administering Powers, which was defined by the term "cooperation." The Commissioner's idea of cooperating with the Administering Powers was certainly not to make a public announcement every time he agreed or disagreed with them. Such a practice would have destroyed the mutual confidence which must exist between them, as well as between himself and the Council. There was, of course, occasional disagreement between the two former, but it was always possible to reach a reasonable compromise within the framework of the General Assembly Resolution. Most of the differences were brought to the Council's notice through the documentation submitted by the Commissioner. Generally speaking, he did not think it wise to give publicity to minor or passing disagreements, unless it was in the interests of Libya to do so. The Council could, however, rest assured that he would never hide from it any disagreement of real importance.

The Commissioner went on to recall that the Pakistani representative had asked him, in connection with what he called the transfer of power by the Administering Powers to the people of the country during the interim period, whether the steps taken in Cyrenaica and Tripolitania had been the subject of consultation and cooperation with the Commissioner; he had also wanted to know whether the latter had suggested any measures other than those mentioned in his memorandum (on his activities since 10 December 1949) and in his two requests for advice (on the scope of his work and on his plan for constitutional development), and, if so, what had been the reaction of the Administering Powers. He (the Commissioner) had just pointed out that Resolution 289 (IV) provided for the transfer of power not to the people of the country during the interim period, but to a duly constituted independent Libyan Government. In drafting that provision the General Assembly had had in mind the promotion of Libyan unity, for any transfer of power to local governments would unavoidably have created three small autonomous units, whose existence would have prejudiced the liberty of action of the Libyan National Assembly with regard to the constitution and the form of government of the country as a whole.

It had been for that very reason that he had requested the United Kingdom and French Governments to modify their constitutional development plans for Tripolitania and the Fezzan (a semi-independent State had already been set up in Cyrenaica before the adoption of the General Assembly Resolution), which had allowed for a transfer of power to local governments. The Administering Powers had readily acquiesced. He had therefore been somewhat surprised to hear the Pakistani representative, who claimed to be a sincere advocate of Libyan unity, arguing in support of a policy which had originally been that of the Administering Powers, and which, in the Commissioner's opinion, placed Libyan unity in jeopardy. Abdur Rahim Khan was perhaps laboring under a misapprehension. Neither the establishment of an Administrative Council with advisory functions, nor the possible establishment of a Tripolitanian legislative chamber, also with advisory functions, nor the Libyanization of the civil service constituted a transfer of power in any legal sense. They were purely administrative measures, taken with the object of making the Tripolitanians familiar with the conduct of their own internal affairs, which in no way diminished the powers currently held by the British Chief Administrator. The Commissioner's position with regard to those measures, as to those proposed by the Administering Power and the Amir in Cyrenaica, had already, and formally, been made clear to the Council; it would also be explained in the Commissioner's report to the Secretary-General.

In brief, the answer to the Pakistani representative's question was that the Administering Powers had consulted the Commissioner on the steps they had taken to implement the General Assembly Resolution. In certain cases he had agreed with these steps, and in others the Administering Powers had accepted the changes he had found it appropriate to suggest. He had informed the Council of these consultations in his memorandum of 19 April 1950.[22]

Having thus disposed of the issue of principle, the Commissioner seized the opportunity of replying in detail to numerous questions pertaining to local problems put to him by the members for Egypt, Pakistan, and Tripolitania. At the time these seemed important, but looking back it is plain that they had no direct bearing on Libyan unity and independence. They need not therefore detain us here.

Toward the end of his statement, the Commissioner reverted to the central issue, in reply to a question asked by Kamel Selim Bey as to the steps taken by the Administering Powers to bring about the unification of the three Libyan territories. The commissioner pointed out that up to that moment the Administering Powers had been required to do very little in that field, and that he had deliberately refrained from asking them to do anything more explicit, except for the request that they modify their plans for regional constitutional development. The Council would realize that the

22. See ibid., Annex III, pp. 40–44.

few months that had elapsed since the beginning of the year had been devoted to the implementation of paragraph 3 of Resolution 289 (IV). The main preoccupation of both the Council and the Commissioner had been to clear the way for the formation of the Libyan National Assembly. The Committee of Twenty-One had just been set up and would prepare a plan for that purpose. In his opinion, it would have been contrary both to the spirit and to the letter of paragraph 3 for the Administering Powers to take any part in the preparations, except insofar as they were required to do so under paragraph 10.

Before he ended his statement, the Commissioner, referring to a number of matters of local interest raised by the representative of Tripolitania, expressed agreement that certain acts of the British Administration might give grounds for criticism. He did not claim that they were outside the Council's competence; but he did feel strongly that a line must be drawn between problems that were of capital importance for the unity and independence of Libya and those that were not. He urged the Council not to fritter away its time and energies on such minor matters. It had given him much good advice, sometimes all the more valuable in that it had run counter to his own original ideas, but it had also wasted precious time in acrimonious debates on issues only remotely connected with Libya's fundamental interests, or in procedural discussions that could just as well have been settled privately between members or in consultation with the Secretary of the Council. Surely, given a little common sense, it should not be difficult to remedy the situation: all that was needed was for members to approach one another, the Commissioner, and the Administering Powers with a modicum of tolerance for the others' opinions, with a modicum of confidence in the honesty of their intentions, and a modicum of willingness to cooperate constructively for Libya's sake and for that of the United Nations. He did not suggest that the Council should abandon its critical approach. He merely expressed the hope that in the future the Council would view its task from within the framework of the Resolution, see the national and international interests of Libya in their true perspective, and carry on in that frank atmosphere of earnest and honest cooperation without which it certainly could not succeed.[23]

Abdur Rahim Khan was unable to accept the Commissioner's definition

23. The above account of the Commissioner's intervention is based on the Summary Record of the Council's 33rd Meeting, at which it was delivered; see United Nations Doc. A/AC.32/COUNCIL/SR.33, 22 July 1950. Mimeographed. A less vehement version of the statement, the product of the "conciliation" meeting between the Chairman of the Council and the Commissioner mentioned on pp. 333–34, appears as Annex XII in the first *Annual Report of the United Nations Commissioner in Libya*, pp. 64–69.

of his functions, and referred again to the report of Sub-Committee 17 and the light it shed on the meaning of the phrase "in the discharge of his functions the United Nations Commissioner shall consult and be guided by the advice of the members of his Council."

The debate had at least served to show that the difference of interpretation that divided the Commissioner and certain members of the Council was largely confined to the meaning of the last ten words of that phrase. The Commissioner was compelled to repeat that he had never disputed the fact that he was obliged to seek the Council's advice; on the contrary. But he considered that he was to some extent free to accept such advice or to reject it. His obligation to consult the Council must not be identified with an absolute requirement that he follow its advice. Neither the word "guide" nor the word "advice," in his opinion, had any mandatory connotation. Had the General Assembly used the word "decision" instead of "advice," and had it instructed him to be "directed" instead of "guided" by the Council, the situation would have been radically different. But such was not the case.

The member for Egypt, also referring to the work of Sub-Committee 17, recalled that when the functions of the Council had been under study, the question had arisen whether it was to establish direct contact with the Administering Powers and the National Assembly, or whether it was to act through the agency of a neutral intermediary. The latter procedure had been agreed upon, and it was in this that the idea of a Commissioner had originated. The Commissioner had thus come into being after the Council and, in Kamel Selim Bey's opinion, it was clear that he had been put at the disposal of the Council to carry out its decisions and advice. Otherwise there would be no point in providing that he was to consult and be guided by it. The Council was not a nominal institution whose advice the Commissioner could reject or accept as he saw fit. Libya's fate had not been entrusted to one man, but to an international Council with a Commissioner as its chief executive officer.

This, at least, was an implicit interpretation of the Resolution; but in the opinion of the Commissioner and his legal advisers no support for it was to be found either in the report of Sub-Committee 17 or in the notes of its proceedings taken by the Secretariat. If anything, the reverse was true.

Thus the debate once more ended inconclusively, except that the Commissioner and his critics reached agreement on a point of procedure, namely, that their differences should be brought to the attention of the General Assembly. The Commissioner therefore promised that a clear statement of the divergence would appear in his first annual report. A number of governments were bound to be aware of the conflict of interpretation, and the General Assembly was entitled to be informed of it. That body could then decide whether to take up the matter formally. The fact that the report would be submitted only after consultation with the Council would ensure that the interests and opinions of all members were adequately safeguarded.

When, at the end of August, in Geneva, the Commissioner consulted the Council on his first report, a new issue arose about whether he was under any obligation to communicate to the Council the reports which the Administering Powers were to make to the General Assembly in cooperation with him, or at least their gist. Abdur Rahim Khan, supported by several other members, maintained that the Commissioner, when cooperating with the Administering Powers under subparagraph 10 (c) of Resolution 289 (IV), did so in the discharge of his functions as defined in paragraph 8. Therefore he should consult and be guided by the advice of the Council. The Commissioner, disagreeing, declined to amend the sixth paragraph of the report, which read:

> 6. In the following chapters the Commissioner reports the action he has taken both before the Council came into being and, later, with the advice of the Council, in furtherance of the resolution of the General Assembly. The steps taken by the Administering Powers to implement the resolution are the subject of reports drawn up by them in co-operation with the Commissioner."[24]

To this paragraph the Pakistani member appended the following observation:

> All the members of the Council present (except the French, British and the United States of America) have asked the Commissioner:
>
> 1. To give them orally a very brief summary of the contents of the reports which have been drawn up by the Administering Powers in co-operation with the Commissioner.
>
> 2. To inform the Council, in the light of the above-mentioned co-operation, what suggestions he made to the Administering Powers to add to or modify their reports and which of these have been accepted or rejected.
>
> 3. To inform the Council if those reports have been prepared to his satisfaction as Commissioner.
>
> To all these items the Commissioner persistently refused to comply as if the matter should be kept in perfect secrecy from the Council or as if it has no bearing whatsoever on the mission of the Council. The Council

24. First *Annual Report of the United Nations Commissioner in Libya,* para. 6.

was treated as an outsider and although paragraph 8 of the resolution stipulates that, in the discharge of his functions, the Commissioner shall consult and be guided by the advice of the members of the Council,

And although he discharged his functions as a Commissioner by his co-operation with the Administering Powers which prepared their reports to the General Assembly,

And although the report of the Commissioner which is being studied and modified by the Council has been sent to London and Paris and the local administrations in the three zones of Libya and is well known to all of them,

Yet the Commissioner, despite all these facts, persisted in not saying one single word on the items he has been asked about and preferred to keep the Council for Libya in ignorance with regard to the intentions and views of the Administering Powers about their duties and achievements for Libya as portrayed in their reports.[25]

This *cri de cœur* ended by referring the reader to the Council's summary records for a detailed account of the corresponding debates.

The representative of France thereupon requested the following addition to the footnote:

With regard to the above note, the French delegation desires to state:

1. That, as regards the question of form, it would be more truly in keeping with the discussions to say "the following members of the Council: Cyrenaica, Egypt, etc.," than "all the members of the Council present, with the exception of France, United Kingdom and the United States of America";

2. That, on the question of substance, the Administering Powers, under paragraph 10 of the resolution, are required to make a report to the General Assembly, in co-operation with the Commissioner, no provision being made for the intervention of the Council. Moreover, it would seem to be contrary to custom to transmit a document to third parties, much as they may be concerned in the matter, before the body for whom it is intended, namely the General Assembly, has been able to take cognizance of it;

3. That, finally, the wording of the said note does not, in the opinion of the French delegation, take account of the position adopted by the Commissioner in the course of the discussions nor of his efforts to abide by the spirit and letter of paragraph 10 of the resolution.[26]

25. Ibid., p. 2, fn. 2.
26. Ibid.

The Commissioner himself added the following note;

> The Commissioner regrets that he was unable to communicate the draft reports of the Administering Powers to the Council either in whole or in résumé. It was not his intention to withhold information from the Council. He felt that it would be improper to communicate to a third party documents which were not his property and which had been transmitted to him in provisional form and under confidential cover by their authors. It would evidently have been impossible for the Commissioner to have discussed his comments on those draft reports without disclosing their contents, and in the absence of any suggestion by the Administering Powers that he might transmit their contents, he decided that consultation could not be undertaken. The Administering Powers took the view that their reports were addressed to the General Assembly and that, while they were to seek, and had sought, the co-operation of the Commissioner, in accordance with paragraph 10 (c) of the resolution, in the form of suggestions which they might or might not accept, they were neither called upon nor properly entitled to submit them to any person or body other than the General Assembly.[27]

Reviewing the matter today, the author realizes that his attitude was formalistic. However, this was one of the occasions when he found himself caught between two fires. Had he acceded to the Pakistani member's request, the most probable outcome would have been another debate like the one that had ensued in the Council when he was asked to transmit critical remarks to the Administering Powers. For reasons which will be familiar to the reader, he did not feel that it was any part of his duties to act as an intermediary for such purposes. Had the atmosphere in the Council been marked by a greater measure of mutual trust, he might have been able to engineer a working arrangement between the Council and the Administering Powers to cover this particular point; but, regrettably, that proved impossible. He therefore had no recourse but formalism.

In the prevailing circumstances, it would hardly have been surprising had the following paragraph, included by the Commissioner in his draft report to clarify his position beyond misunderstanding, caused a fresh conflagration:

> The resolution of the General Assembly clearly laid down that the function of the Council was to aid and advise the Commissioner, while it was incumbent upon the latter to consult the members of the Council and be guided by their advice. This pre-supposed a marked degree of co-operation and understanding between the Commissioner and the

27. Ibid.

> members of the Council. In fact, the relationship between the Commissioner and the Council has not been uniformly interpreted, with the result that the partnership has been less harmonious than the Commissioner had hoped. Certain members of the Council have advocated an interpretation of the resolution according to which the Council should give direct aid and advice to the people of Libya and should take the Administering Powers to task, instead of confining its efforts to the function attributed to it by the resolution. At the same time, these same members have expressed the opinion that the Commissioner should consider any advice he may receive from the Council as binding upon him. The Commissioner acknowledges that, under his terms of reference, he "shall consult and be guided by the advice of the members of his Council" and that as a rule he should follow such advice. He has always desired and endeavoured to maintain close co-operation with the Council and has always made it clear that he considered it his duty to ask for the Council's advice on any question of importance which might arise in the course of the implementation of the resolution. He has done so from the outset and intends to continue to do so in the future. Advice which the Council has thought fit to tender him on its own initiative has proved of great value. He is fully aware that he must have extremely serious reasons for not following advice given to him by the Council. Nevertheless, the Commissioner believes that he is correct in understanding that, while the resolution obliges him to be guided by the Council's advice, it does not bind him to follow it in each and every case, especially if circumstances and his best judgment were to make it impossible for him to do so. He is not the executive organ of the Council, since he acts under his own responsibility towards the General Assembly and towards the General Assembly alone. Up to now the Commissioner has never rejected advice tendered to him by the Council. However, should the necessity arise, he will keep the Council fully informed and he will have to justify his action before the General Assembly.
>
> The functions which the resolution assigned respectively to the Commissioner and to the Council are different but complementary. They can best be performed in the interest of Libyan unity and independence if mutual confidence, co-operation and understanding prevail between the Commissioner and the Council and if each respects the duties and responsibilities of the other.[28]

However, when the Council reached this paragraph, the Chairman—at the time the member for Egypt—announced that the Commissioner and he

28. See ibid., p. 35, fn. 76, relating to para. 249.

had discussed its subject matter. They had agreed that the issue should be handled in a more conciliatory manner than in the draft report, and the Commissioner had accordingly redrafted the passage, which now read:

> In the course of their labours, the Council and the Commissioner have repeatedly discussed their relationship in the light of paragraphs 4 and 8 of the General Assembly resolution of 21 November 1949. The Commissioner and certain members of the Council interpreted these paragraphs in different ways. The principal point under discussion was whether an advice of the Council is or is not under all circumstances binding upon the Commissioner. After lengthy discussions, the Council unanimously decided on 1 September, and the Commissioner agreed, that no useful purpose could be served by trying to solve the problem by strict legal interpretation and that in order to further a constructive relationship, in the interest of Libya, the only practical solution was for the Council and the Commissioner to co-operate on a basis of mutual confidence respecting each other's views as to their respective duties and responsibilities and to reach agreement from case to case as circumstances might require. The Commissioner is glad to state that so far he has always followed the advice of the Council.[29]

The Commissioner and one of his principal opponents having thus smoked the pipe of peace, the former wished that the Council would bury the hatchet without trace. Unfortunately, this was too much to hope for. The member for France, while appreciating the spirit which had prompted the redrafting of the passage in question, and while gladly recognizing that the new text described exactly relations between the Commissioner and the Council as they then stood, considered that, in order to bring the General Assembly fully into the picture, it would be as well to set forth in detail the facts as the Commissioner had given them in his first version.[30]

This discordant intervention notwithstanding, the new text received the Council's unanimous approval, and from that time on peace was, to a point, restored.

A comparison of the Commissioner's first and second annual reports, and of the supplementary report to the latter, shows that relations between the Commissioner and the Council were indeed better in 1951 than they had been in 1950. The footnotes and annexes in which the Commissioner and members of the Council contradicted one another in their appreciation of certain situations became fewer and somewhat less acrimonious. But they never vanished.

29. This version was incorporated in ibid. as para. 249.

30. Ibid., p. 35, fn. 76, relating to para. 249. See also footnote 28 in this chapter.

The author feels that he here owes the reader some explanation for what may well seem undue repetition in his descriptions of disputes about the relationships between the Commissioner and the Council and the Administering Powers, some of which have already been dealt with at length in Chapters 2 and 3. He has been forced into such reiteration because, as the reader will have noted, the differences arose on each occasion in a different context and on a different issue. Moreover, the intricacies of the author's accounts of these troubles matches the complexity, not to say tortuosity, of the interplay of the three forces in the field, and will thus help the reader visualize and better appreciate the difficulties with which the Commissioner and his staff had to contend in discharging their duties to the people of Libya on the one hand and to the General Assembly on the other, often in trying climatic and material conditions.

PART 3. MINORITIES AND INHABITANTS [31]

This chapter would not be complete without some account of the interpretation and application of the important terms "minorities" and "inhabitants" in the context of Resolution 289 (IV). The first affected the composition of the Council for Libya (subparagraphs 6 [a] and [b]), the second that of the National Assembly (paragraph 3). The essential issue was whether the minorities were or were not to be considered as inhabitants of the three Libyan territories. If they were, they would be entitled to exercise their political rights by taking part in the determination of the country's constitution, including the form of government. If they were not, they would have no right to do so. The issue was therefore of cardinal importance, not only for the Libyans but also for the minorities themselves, and especially the Italian minority. That it was also an extraordinarily

31. Specific references to United Nations documents bearing on the definition of "minorities" and "inhabitants," and cross-references to other relevant parts of this study, have been provided wherever necessary in this part of Chapter 4. In addition, the following documentation can usefully be consulted: (1) "Report of Sub-Committee 17 to the First Committee," GAOR: Fourth Session, 1949, First Committee, Annexes to Summary Records, Agenda item 19 (A/C.1/522, 1 November 1949, para. 21), p. 27; (2) First *Annual Report of the United Nations Commissioner in Libya,* paras. 253–56, and Annexes XXVI and XXVII, pp. 82–83; (3) *Second Annual Report of the United Nations Commissioner in Libya,* GAOR: Sixth Session, 1951–52, Supplement No. 17 (A/1949), paras. 65–66 and Annex II, pp. 71–74; and (4) *Supplementary Report to the Second Annual Report of the United Nations Commissioner in Libya,* GAOR: Sixth Session, 1951–52, Supplement No. 17A (A/1949/Add.1), passim.

sensitive problem in a country in process of decolonization needs no emphasis.

When, in the distant mid-1920s, the author, then a young member of the League of Nations Secretariat, was sent on a rather delicate mission, the Secretary-General, Sir Eric Drummond (later Lord Perth), giving him his final briefing, ended by saying: "Now don't forget that if you are successful, nobody will thank you; if you fail, everyone will criticize you; don't worry anyway, provided failure is not due to a mistake by you." No better advice could ever be given to international civil servants.

In later years this warning rarely echoed more ringingly in the writer's memory than when, as United Nations Commissioner in Libya, he had to deal with minority and related problems. The General Assembly Resolution contained several controversial provisions, but by far the most difficult to interpret and to carry out were those which touched on this aspect of the Libyan problem—paragraph 3, subparagraphs 6 (a) and (b), and paragraph 7.

As has been seen, the question of the minorities originated in the General Assembly's decision that the ten members of the Council for Libya should include a representative of the minorities.

From the outset of the discussions on the disposal of the former Italian colonies the several United Nations organs dealing with the Libyan problem had given the term "minorities" a broad meaning. A perusal of the records gives the impression that this tendency was due in part to a desire to strengthen the position of the former ruling (Italian) population vis-à-vis their new masters, in part to the fact that the word "minority" was a handy way of defining a group or groups of people who were in many respects distinct from the indigenous population among whom they would have to live in the new State. This was in line with the definition devised by the United Nations Sub-Commission on Prevention of Discrimination and Protection of Minorities in January 1950 (see p. 184). Thus, in the absence of any more precise definition, this broad interpretation made no distinction between minorities differing from the majority only in language, religion, or race, and those differing also in nationality. When applied to Libya, this meant that no distinction was made between national (Libyan) minorities, such as Libyan-born Jews, and nonnational (alien) minorities, such as the Italian, Greek, and Maltese minorities. Both categories were entitled to the protection of their linguistic, religious, racial, civic, and other rights, but grave difficulties arose when it had to be decided whether the alien minorities were entitled to exercise political rights. Resolution 289 (IV) being silent on the point, the Commissioner was obliged to make up his own mind, with the aid and advice of the Council, when the meaning of the word "inhabitants" in paragraph 3 had to be determined.

The question was inextricably bound up with that of Libyan citizenship. Legally speaking, there can be no citizen of a country that is still dependent; but the implementation of the Resolution, which called upon the inhabitants of the three territories to determine the country's constitution, including the form of government—a political task—implied that the Libyan people would have to act as "nationals" of their country, exercising their political rights, before independence had been declared.

The proposal that a representative of the minorities be appointed to the Council for Libya was first made by the Guatemalan delegate to the General Assembly, Garcia Bauer, who throughout the discussions in the First Committee and Sub-Committee 17 had shown great interest in the fate of what he called the "Libyan minorities," especially that of the former Italian group (see p. 94 and fn. 82 to Chapter I). As the original purpose of his proposal was merely to give the minorities a voice in the Council—i.e. in an *advisory* body—so that they could make their desires, interests, and views known to its members, the Libyans would have been ill-advised to oppose such an appointment, although some in fact did. The Guatemalan proposal itself came in for some criticism in Sub-Committee 17, mainly from the representatives of Argentina, Egypt, Iraq, and Pakistan, who argued that it was for the Libyans themselves to deal with their minorities, and that it would be better not to mention the problem in the Resolution; but this view did not prevail. Hence, notwithstanding the difficulties the Commissioner had encountered in the course of his consultations, as described in Part 3 of Chapter 2, Giacomo Marchino's appointment was consistent with the General Assembly's intentions.

Meanwhile, as the reader knows, it had become clear that, although the Libyans were willing to cooperate with the minorities in the economic field, and to guarantee them their civic, religious, and cultural rights, there was strong opposition to—even genuine fear of—granting them political rights.

Before embarking upon the consultations preceding the appointment of the minorities' representative to the Council for Libya, therefore, the Commissioner had taken the precaution of consulting his own legal advisers, who assured him that, in their view, the General Assembly's intention, within the sole context of subparagraphs 6 (a) and (b) and paragraph 7, had been that the word "minorities" should be interpreted in the broadest possible sense, in other words, without taking the nationality aspect into account. The Commissioner had followed this advice, and an Italian subject had been appointed.

The question of the meaning of the term "inhabitants" as used in paragraph 3 of Resolution 289 (IV) became acute when, on 16 April 1950, the Commissioner submitted to the Council his request for advice regarding his plan for the constitutional development of Libya.[32] The specific issue was whether, in the implementation of this paragraph, the minorities were to be considered as inhabitants of Libya. The Commissioner, after due consideration of the legal principles involved and lengthy consultations with both the Administering Powers and the leaders of public opinion in the three territories, had, in the comment accompanying his request for advice, suggested that the proposed preparatory committee for the National Assembly (the Committee of Twenty-One) should have an entirely Libyan membership.[33] He was fully aware of the heavy responsibility he had assumed in so doing. Although he had legal advice to support his position, he realized that it could and would be contested on weighty grounds. If, nonetheless, he had come down on the side of exclusively Libyan membership, he had done so both on political and on legal grounds. More than two months of consultations had driven him to the conclusion that, given the strong opposition in Cyrenaica and the Fezzan, insistence on minority representation would endanger the committee's constitution or, at least, unduly delay its convocation. He also had to bear in mind that, under the terms of the United Nations Resolution, his primary duty was to help the Libyan people to bring about an independent, sovereign, and united State before 1 January 1952. It was true that, from the point of view of the organization he served, the protection of minority rights was also a primary duty, but he was convinced that where the two conflicted the independence and unity of the Libyan people must have priority over the more limited question of minority representation in temporary political organs. He had moreover formed the opinion that there were more effective ways and means of securing the rights of the minorities and safeguarding their interests than by insisting on their being represented in Libyan policy-making bodies, where, at best, they could count only on one or two seats. One more consideration to be reckoned with was the fact that in Cyrenaican and Fezzanese eyes the minority problem meant essentially the presence in Tripolitania of some 45,000 Italians. This figure included Italian settlers

32. Paragraph 3 of General Assembly Resolution 289 (IV), 21 November 1949, reads: "That a constitution for Libya, including the form of government, shall be determined by representatives of the inhabitants of Cyrenaica, Tripolitania and the Fezzan meeting and consulting together in a National Assembly." For the text of the request for advice, see the first *Annual Report of the United Nations Commissioner in Libya,* Annex V, pp. 45–46.

33. See Chapter 3, p. 222 and fn. 13.

from Cyrenaica who had left their farms there on Italian military orders at the moment of the Axis collapse in North Africa. Apart from the fear, already mentioned more than once, that these colonists might reoccupy their abandoned farms, perhaps with the connivance of certain pro-Italian Tripolitanian leaders, the Cyrenaicans also harbored a deep-rooted suspicion that in a united Libya they might be dominated by the more numerous and sophisticated Tripolitanians. This twofold anxiety made the Cyrenaicans extremely reluctant to grant the Italian minority any concession that seemed to imply a right to interfere in Libya's political future.

Thus, by the early spring of 1950, the Commissioner was sure that the implementation of paragraph 3 of Resolution 289 (IV), as it was interpreted by the representative of the minorities, would prove not only detrimental to the achievement of the General Assembly's main aim, but also harmful to the true interests of the minorities themselves. Indeed, experience had already shown, and was to be further borne out by subsequent developments, that Italian insistence on securing political rights was intensifying anti-Italian feeling among the Arab population. This was making it even more difficult to arrive at a satisfactory agreement about the common interests of the two groups, which in fact were for the most part, economic, social, cultural, and religious, rather than political, in nature.

In early May, at the outset of the Council's discussion on the proposed preparatory committee, the member for the minorities, subsequently supported by his Italian colleague, had expressed concern about the Commissioner's suggestion that all members of the committee should be Libyans (see pp. 269–70). Hence the necessity, in his view, to define the term "Libyan." Marchino advanced the theory that, the Libyan State having as yet no legal existence, there was no reliable criterion by which Libyan nationality or citizenship could be determined. He further argued that it appeared reasonable to accept the criterion adopted by the General Assembly in referring to "the population of Libya" in Resolution 289 (IV).[34]

According to Marchino, the General Assembly had thus explicitly acknowledged the presence of minorities on Libyan territory, and, by providing for their representation on the Council, had recognized that they formed part of the "population" by reason of their permanent residence in the country, irrespective of their race, religion, or origin.

He therefore asked the Council to specify that the word "Libyan" used in the Commissioner's request should be interpreted in its broadest sense,

34. In fact, the resolution speaks not of the "population" but of the "people" of Libya (paras. 4 and 6[b]). The subtle difference in meaning between the two words is not without importance here, and difficulties of translation may also have played a part.

thus giving the minorities the right to vote in the elections to the Tripolitanian legislative chamber, which, according to the Commissioner's plan, would be called upon to elect or select that territory's representative on the preparatory committee.

It should be noted here that the Commissioner was at that very moment supporting the British Chief Administrator in the latter's efforts to convince the leaders of the Tripolitanian political parties of the desirability of including a representative of the minorities, in the case in point an Italian, in the legislative chamber,[35] which was to deal exclusively with certain matters of local administration but would have no say in Libyan constitutional affairs except for the proposed designation of members of the preparatory committee. He had taken this step in the face of a great deal of opposition from some of the local leaders, in the hope of improving Arab-Italian relations and also in order to give Libya a trump card in future arguments with Italy's friends in the General Assembly. Marchino was now implying, however, that a representative of the minorities, most probably also an Italian, might become an elected or appointed member of a political committee. This was not in accordance with the Commissioner's plan, neither did the implication meet with a sympathetic reception from at least two members of the Council. The Commissioner also knew from his round of hearings that opposition in Cyrenaica and the Fezzan would be considerably stronger than in Tripolitania, and would seriously impair cooperation among the three territories. Whether the implication was in harmony with the intention of paragraph 3 of the Resolution was a debatable point.

The time had therefore come to reexamine the meaning of the term "minorities" in a fresh legal and political context. The issue was no longer the relatively simple one of appointing a representative of the minorities to a United Nations body, the Council for Libya, but that of deciding whether or not it was admissible to elect or appoint such representatives to an entirely different kind of organ, whose function it would be to prepare the Libyan National Assembly and to make recommendations to it about the country's political and constitutional future, including the form of government. The situations differed fundamentally both in nature and in importance.

35. For various reasons, this body never met. For one thing, the Arab members of the Tripolitanian Administrative Council, when considering the provisions regarding eligibility to vote in the draft electoral law, had formally opposed, by 7 votes with 1 abstention, the participation of Italians in the elections, on the grounds that they should not be allowed to vote until they could acquire Libyan citizenship.

In drafting their opinion on this point, the Commissioner and his legal adviser naturally started by studying the history of paragraph 3 of Resolution 289 (IV) as depicted in the Official Records of the General Assembly and the First Committee, and in the Secretariat's informal notes of the discussions in Sub-Committee 17. They found that in the Sub-Committee the Guatemalan representative, José Rolz-Bennett, who had taken over from Garcia Bauer, had suggested that the phrase "including the representatives of minorities" should be inserted after the words "the representatives of the inhabitants of Cyrenaica, Tripolitania and the Fezzan." The United States delegate, as sponsor of the original proposal, had been prepared to accept that suggestion, but during the ensuing discussion certain other members of the Sub-Committee, in particular the Argentinian representative, had opposed the idea. The mover of the amendment had, however, insisted that the right of the minorities to have their say in the preparations for Libyan independence be guaranteed. Thereafter, their representation in Libyan legislative bodies would be decided by the people of Libya themselves. The Indian representative believed, like his Guatemalan colleague, that the minorities should be numbered among the "inhabitants" of the three territories.

Hector McNeil, speaking for the United Kingdom, came out against the Guatemalan suggestion. In a significant statement, he maintained that, despite its thorough knowledge of the inhabitants of the regions in question, his Government could not tell in advance what they wanted or how they would react. The United Kingdom would obviously protect the rights of the minorities insofar as possible. Given the special conditions obtaining in Libya, McNeil was not in a position to say for sure whether the minorities should be granted the usual representation. The hands of the Administering Powers must not be tied, the hopes of the people of Libya must not be frustrated, and the terms of reference of the future Council for Libya must not be restricted by too rigid directives from the General Assembly.[36]

However, no vote was taken on the Guatemalan proposal, and the additional phrase was not incorporated in the Resolution; thus the word "inhabitants" was left in paragraph 3 unqualified and undefined.

36. The above summary of this subtle intervention has been taken from the Secretariat's notes of the Sub-Committee's debates. For the meeting at which McNeil spoke, these were in French, and no official translation into English exists. When approached by the author for an original English version, the Foreign Office, to its genuine regret, found itself bound by the (then) fifty-year rule governing access to State papers. The author has therefore been obliged to prepare his own English text. See also footnotes 6–9, 12, and 47 in this chapter.

There was yet another difficulty. Even had the text of paragraph 3 explicitly included "minorities" among "inhabitants," the problem of what the General Assembly itself had understood by "minorities" in the context of that paragraph—one of particular importance in the light of the arguments advanced by most Libyans against minority (Italian) representation in the preparatory committee and, a fortiori, in the National Assembly—would have had to have been cleared up. For, although some of the minority groups consisted almost entirely of aliens—e.g. the Italians, Greeks, and Maltese—there were also a considerable number of Jews belonging to communities which had been in Libya for centuries. Some had foreign passports, but the great majority considered themselves—and were considered by the Moslem Libyans—citizens of the country. Hence, a difference did exist, and was recognized on the practical plane, between national and nonnational minorities, though both were inhabitants of Libya in the general sense of the word.

Yet another aspect of the problem was whether Libyan nationality could be defined. If it could, those inhabitants who should be considered as aliens could be identified. Italy having renounced all right and title to its territorial possessions in Africa under the terms of the Peace Treaty, the question arose whether it was permissible to deduce therefrom that Italian legislation regulating Libyan nationality had been abrogated, in which case Libyan citizenship could not be defined for lack of a law on the subject. Some people certainly held that opinion. In the Council for Libya, the representative of the minorities had declared on 4 May 1950 that all persons permanently resident in the territory *should be considered as having the status of Libyans,* regardless of race, religion, or origin.

However, the British administration in Tripolitania was still applying, for the control of immigration, the Italian Royal Decree No. 2012 of 3 December 1934 on Libyan nationality. This Decree, which later became Law No. 675 of 11 April 1935 XIII (*Ordinamento organico della Libia*) and was still in force, laid down the general principle that all persons whose place of residence was in Libya and who were not metropolitan Italian citizens or foreign citizens or subjects, were presumed to have Italian Libyan citizenship. Article 33 defined Italian Libyan citizens in the following terms:

> The child, wherever born, of a father having Italian Libyan citizenship, or, if the father is unknown, of a mother having Italian Libyan citizenship; a woman married to an Italian Libyan citizen; anyone born in Libya, wherever his place of residence, who is not a metropolitan Italian citizen or a foreign citizen or subject according to Italian law; children

of unknown parentage found in Libya are presumed to have been born there unless there is any proof to the contrary.[37]

Article 40 stipulated, inter alia, that "Italian Libyan citizens retain their own personal and inheritance status, in the case of Moslems; and their own personal status, in the case of Jews." There were therefore two nationalities in Libya under this law: Libyans, including Jews, had the status of "Italian Libyan citizens," whereas Italians were "metropolitan Italian citizens." Under Article 37, Italian Libyan citizens could, on certain conditions, acquire metropolitan citizenship.

Under Royal Decree No. 70 of 9 January 1939/XVII, incorporating the four provinces of Libya as they then existed as an integral part of the Kingdom of Italy, the status of "Libyan Italian citizenship" was maintained (Article 1). Article 8 revoked the faculty provided by Article 37 of the earlier law for Italian Libyan citizens to acquire metropolitan Italian citizenship. On the other hand, Article 4 introduced a "special Italian nationality" for indigenous Moslems from the four Libyan provinces, acquirable on certain conditions. Libyans who were admitted to this new status were entitled to a number of rights, but they were also subject to certain restrictions (Article 7); in particular, they could not be appointed to posts or functions giving them authority over metropolitan Italians. Hence, at the outbreak of World War II there were three different types of nationality in Libya.[38]

Not having been repealed, these laws were still valid in 1950, and were, as we have seen, applied for certain practical purposes by the Administering Power. Thus, at the time when the matter came up in the Council for Libya in the spring of 1950, those who could be considered as Libyan citizens were clearly identifiable; so, by inference, were the aliens. Consequently, and especially in view of the failure of the General Assembly to make matters clear, it became more necessary than ever to define the meaning of the term "minority" in relation to the term "inhabitants."

It is generally admitted that, to share in the political life of a State, an inhabitant must be a national of that State.

After World War I particular attention was paid to the protection of minorities, and special provisions relating thereto were written into the Minority Treaties ancillary to the Peace Treaty of Versailles. These provisions embodied certain principles, namely, that protection could extend to

37. The English translation of this article, as well as those that follow, including the quotations from Royal Decree No. 70 of 9 January 1939/XVII, was made for internal purposes by the language staff of the United Nations Mission in Libya.

38. To study more closely this particular aspect of the problem, see Annex XI, pp. 961–63.

all the inhabitants of the territory, and that aliens could benefit from it, but a distinction was also made to the effect that, whereas protection of life, freedom, and the practice of religious rites was granted to all the inhabitants of a country, only those members of minorities who were its nationals were entitled to exercise political rights.[39]

Thus, in essence, the Commissioner's legal adviser found that political rights, such as, for instance, those inherent in the functions to be discharged by members of the Committee of Twenty-One or of the National Assembly, should be granted to members of minority groups who were Libyan nationals, but not to members of the same or other minority groups who were aliens.

This carefully prepared legal opinion coincided with the Commissioner's personal views insofar as it advised him against the inclusion in the Committee of Twenty-One or the National Assembly of individuals belonging

39. L. Oppenheim, the eminent international lawyer, in *International Law: A Treatise,* ed. H. Lauterpacht (7th ed.; London: Longmans, Green and Co., 1952), Vol. I, *Peace,* Chapter XI, "The Protection of Minorities," on pp. 651–52, has the following to say on the subject:

> After the First World War, when a number of new States had recently emerged out of the European melting-pot and large portions of territory were changing hands, the system of the protection of minorities received a new impetus. The Principal Allied and Associated Powers were able to stipulate by treaty with Poland, Czechoslovakia, the Serb-Croat-Slovene State, Roumania, Greece, Austria, Bulgaria, Hungary, and Turkey for the just and equal treatment of their racial, religious and linguistic minorities. Subsequently, as a condition of their admission to the League of Nations, similar obligations were undertaken by Albania, Esthonia, Latvia, Lithuania, and Iraq, in the form of unilateral declarations accepted and rendered obligatory by various resolutions of the Council of the League. The relevant clauses in the treaties are substantially the same, and the protection which they are designed to afford may be summarised as follows:
> (i) For the *inhabitants,* protection of life and liberty and the free exercise of religion without distinction of birth, nationality, language, race or religion;
> (ii) In general, for *certain inhabitants,* automatic acquisition, or just facilities for the acquisition, of the nationality of the contracting State;
> (iii) For the *nationals,* equality before the law and as to all civil and political rights, and as to the use of any language. (The Permanent Court of International Justice repeatedly laid down that the prohibition of non-discrimination must operate in fact as well as in law and that a measure general in its application but in fact directed against members of a minority constituted a violation of the Minorities Treaty);
> (iv) Freedom of organisation for religious and educational purposes; and
> (v) State provision for the elementary instruction of their children through the medium of their own language in districts where a particular minority forms a considerable proportion of the population."

See also Chapter 7 below, pp. 542–43.

to an alien minority. At the same time, it admitted the possibility of including someone belonging to a national minority. Under the conditions obtaining in Libya at the time, this would virtually have limited the choice to Jews who did not hold a foreign passport. For some Tripolitanians this would have been much more acceptable than the appointment of an Italian subject. But the Commissioner had to consider also whether a member of the Libyan Jewish community was likely to be considered as a vigorous and successful defender of the rights and interests of the minorities in an Arab country at the very time when thousands of his fellows were abandoning Libya for the new State of Israel, whence large numbers of Arabs had fled, and whose relations with the Arab world were tense. The answer was clearly in the negative.

At the same time, the Commissioner doubted whether the British Administration had been right in maintaining in force, for purposes of its own, an Italian law on nationality after Italy had renounced all right and title to the territory to which that law applied. Moreover, he was impressed by the arguments of those Libyans who found it difficult to agree that, on the verge of independence, minorities should enjoy the same political rights as themselves when a clear distinction had been made between the two categories under Italian rule.

All this brought the Commissioner, in his request for advice, to urge that both the Committee of Twenty-One and the National Assembly should be composed exclusively of Libyans. When the Council's advice implied the contrary, however, he did not feel that considerations of a purely legal nature should stand in the way when the advice was supported by an alliance of Libyans and Italians in the Council, however dubious their motives might have been. The sequel to this part of the story has already been told in Chapter 3, but the last had not been heard of the matter. This awkward issue came up for discussion for the third and last time in August 1950, when the Commissioner and the Council met in Geneva for consultations on the former's first annual report to the General Assembly. The various positions had by then crystallized even more firmly; the same arguments were adduced yet again; but this time both sides had to be particularly careful about what they committed to writing. It would serve no purpose but that of repetition to describe here the discussion that took place, but the author would be failing in clarity if he did not draw attention to the way in which the opposing points of view were expressed in his report.

Chapter VII of the report—"The Constitutional Development of Libya: Consultations with the Council"—contained a factual account of the discussion on the Commissioner's first plan for constitutional development; to this, the Italian member requested the addition of the following footnote:

The representative of Italy draws attention to the democratic inspiration of the resolution of the United Nations in its affirmation that it is for *the inhabitants of the three territories* to formulate the constitution and to determine the form of government. This is contrasted with the attitude adopted by the Commissioner in regard to the composition of a Preparatory Committee, to the exclusion of the Minorities, as it is expressed in the first part of paragraph 133.[40]

To this in turn the representatives of Cyrenaica and Tripolitania jointly requested the addition of the following passage:

> The representatives of Cyrenaica and Tripolitania do not agree with the interpretation of the meaning of the word "inhabitants" expressed by the representative of Italy in the above note and during the Council's discussion of the participation of the Minorities in the Preparatory Committee. Their view was formulated by the representative of Cyrenaica on 29 June as set forth in paragraph 155. In the absence of any official interpretation of the word "inhabitants" the term can be applied only to the Arabs of Libya and not to persons who, as large numbers of members of the Minorities had done, had retained their foreign nationality.[41]

The paragraph 155 referred to in this statement reads as follows:

> At the same meeting, the representative of Cyrenaica stated that he did not agree with the interpretation given by the representatives of Italy and the Minorities to the term "inhabitants." In his opinion, this term, in the absence of any official interpretation, could be applied only to the Arabs of Libya and not to persons who, as large numbers of members of the Minorities had done, had retained their foreign nationality. He stated that the Cyrenaican acceptance of the principle of participation by the Minorities in the Committee of Twenty-One was not based on the interpretation of the word "inhabitants," used in the resolution of the General Assembly, as meaning the whole population of Libya; it was based on the desire of Cyrenaica to co-operate with the Tripolitanians, if the latter considered that the acceptance of a representative of the Minorities would serve the cause of Libyan independence.[42]

When the Council reached paragraph 159, which refers to the selection of the Tripolitanian members of the Committee of Twenty-One, the repre-

40. First *Annual Report of the United Nations Commissioner in Libya,* para. 133, and p. 20, fn. 44.

41. Ibid.

42. Ibid., pp. 23–24.

sentative of that territory found it necessary to request the inclusion of yet another footnote:

> The name of a representative of the Minorities was included in the list, not because the Tripolitanian political parties accepted the interpretation that the word "inhabitants" in paragraph 3 of the resolution of the General Assembly gave the Minorities the absolute right to be included in Libyan political bodies, but as a gesture of good will and as evidence of a desire for peaceful co-operation between the Arabs and the Minorities.[43]

Finally, Chapter IX, "Concluding Remarks," came up for discussion. Here, as the opening passage in the section on the problem of the minorities, the Commissioner had written:

> The settlement of the future status of the Minorities is scarcely less important to the Libyan people than to the Minorities themselves. If the future of the Italian community is particularly delicate, especially in view of its large economic and financial interests, the other minorities, legally and morally, have equal interests to safeguard. All, however, bring a vigour to the life of the country without which its future development would be jeopardized.[44]

To this, the representative of the minorities appended the following comment:

> The Minorities wish to emphasize that their request to participate in the formation of the future Libyan State is founded upon the interpretation of the letter and spirit of the resolution of 21 November 1949, as they emerge also from the discussions preparatory to the resolution.
>
> Their request is motivated by their desire to co-operate with the majority in an atmosphere of agreement and in a constructive spirit, free of any political calculation other than the natural interest of the Minorities in the formation and well-being of the new State.
>
> The problem today is such that it appears necessary to obtain an authentic interpretation of paragraph 3 of the resolution of 21 November 1949, upon which opinions vary. The representative of the Minorities requests the consideration of the memorandum submitted as annex XXVI of this report as a request to the General Assembly for such an interpretation.[45]

43. Ibid., p. 24, fn. 57.
44. Ibid., para. 253.
45. Ibid., p. 36, fn. 78.

To this the Italian representative added:

> The representative of Italy is in agreement with the interpretation given by the representative of the Minorities in Libya of paragraph 3 of the resolution of 21 November 1949, because the Assembly, in using the term "inhabitants," intended not to discriminate among the population. This was confirmed by the fact that the resolution provided that the Minorities in Libya should have a seat on the United Nations Council for Libya, thus stressing that they were entitled to share in the fullest manner in the formation of the new State. In these circumstances, the representative of Italy declared that there is no justification for depriving the Minorities of their political rights at the most important moment, that is, during the formation of the Libyan State.
>
> If the suggestions made by the Commissioner were to be accepted, it would imply the acceptance *ipso facto* by the Minorities to be considered, not as such, but as a foreign community.
>
> For these reasons, the representative of Italy, while associating himself with the decision of the representative of the Minorities to appeal to the General Assembly of the United Nations, expresses the hope that the Committee of Twenty-One, with the advice of the Commissioner, will recognize that the participation of the Minorities in the forthcoming National Assembly is both right and opportune.
>
> The representative of Italy emphasizes furthermore that the parties in Tripolitania—the region in which the Minorities reside—have formally declared to the Commissioner that they favour the participation of the Minorities in the constitutional development of Libya, holding a fruitful collaboration between majority and minority to be indispensable.[46]

Lastly, the United Kingdom representative requested that the following addition be made to the statements of the representative of the minorities and the Italian representative:

> The representative of the United Kingdom wished it to be recorded that the position of his Government as regards the interpretation of the word "inhabitants" was still that stated by the representative of the United Kingdom in the Political Committee in the autumn of 1949.[47]

The intransigent nature of the discussions, and the plethora of footnotes and memorandums appended to his report, strengthened the Commissioner

46. Ibid.

47. Ibid. The reference to the "Political Committee" seems to be erroneous. What Penney probably had in mind is the statement made by Hector McNeil in Sub-Committee 17 on 13 October 1949, summarized on p. 341.

in his conviction that the problem of the interpretation of the word "inhabitants" (and hence the proper implementation of paragraph 3 of the Resolution) was insoluble in the purely legal sense. Indeed, several members of the Council had admitted as much in the course of the debate. He therefore summed up his position as follows:

> The problem is difficult and complex. The Commissioner does not pretend that, during his seven months at work in Libya, he has mastered all its intricacies; even less does he pretend that he has formed a definite opinion on possible solutions. Many considerations of a political, legal, economical, financial, social, cultural and religious nature, must first be weighed. Indeed, it will only be possible to find and to effect an agreed solution as the constitutional development and political organisation of Libya proceeds. The desire of the minority groups for quick decisions and solutions to put an end to the prevailing uncertainty is understandable, but it is the Commissioner's conviction that none of the interested parties would benefit from haste.
>
> Experience indicates that it would be easier to find a solution if the problem were removed from its political context. If an understanding between the Libyans and the Minorities were sought only in the administrative, economic, social, financial, cultural and religious fields, there would be a good chance of solving the problem as a whole. The injection of political considerations such as minority participation in Libyan political bodies during the transitional period may delay both the achievement of Libyan unity and an agreed settlement of the minority problem.
>
> A procedure which might recommend itself both to the Minorities and to the Arab population could be conceived in the form of negotiations, under the auspices of the Commissioner, if so desired by both parties, between a delegation of the Minorities and a Committee appointed by the National Assembly for the purpose of achieving agreement on the clauses to be inserted in the Constitution for the safeguarding of the rights and interests of the Minorities in Libya.[48]

The two sides to the dispute summarized their views in two memorandums annexed to the report, the first of which constitutes the appeal to the General Assembly by the representative of the minorities mentioned in footnote 78 thereto.[49]

48. Ibid., paras. 254–56.

49. Ibid., "Memorandum on the position of the Minorities in Libya, submitted by the representative of the Minorities on the Council for Libya," Annex XXVI, pp. 82–83; and "Memorandum submitted by the representatives of Cyrenaica and Tripolitania on the Council for Libya commenting on the memorandum submitted by the representative of the Minorities in Libya (Annex XXVI)," Annex XXVII, p. 83.

The matter obviously could not remain quiescent. Questions of this nature never do. On 23 October 1950 the Committee of Twenty-One made its recommendation that nonnational minorities not be allowed to participate or to be represented in the National Assembly, adding the rider concerning guarantees of basic human rights quoted in full on page 296.

This rider was heeded by the National Assembly, and when in the course of 1951 it took up the matter in connection with the constitution, a large, though not full, measure of satisfaction was given to the minorities' demands (see pp. 536–47 below).

The way in which the General Assembly dealt with the problems at its Fifth Session will be related in the next chapter.

CHAPTER 5

The Libyan Question at the Fifth Session of the General Assembly

PART 1. THE POLITICAL ISSUES

Toward the end of July 1950, the Commissioner and his staff began to draft the report, which, in consultation with the Council for Libya, he was required to submit to the Secretary-General for transmittal to the General Assembly. The report itself was supplemented by two brief memoranda, both dealing with the work of the Committee of Twenty-One, which were submitted during the General Assembly without prior consultation, as the Council had in the meantime adjourned. These three documents, together with the annual reports submitted by the Administering Powers in respect of the territories for which they were responsible, provided the basis for discussion at Lake Success in the autumn of 1950.[1]

All concerned with the Libyan question were aware that the way in which Resolution 289 (IV) had been implemented during the first eight months

1. 1. *Annual Report of the United Nations Commissioner in Libya,* GAOR: Fifth Session, 1950, Supplement No. 15 (A/1340).
2. "Supplement to the annual report of the United Nations Commissioner in Libya," GAOR: Fifth Session, 1950, Annexes, Agenda item 21 (A/1405, 28 September 1950), pp. 41–43.
3. "Second Supplement to the annual report of the United Nations Commissioner in Libya," ibid. (A/1459/Rev.1, 30 October 1950), pp. 43–44.
4. "Annual report of the French Government to the General Assembly concerning the administration of the Fezzan," ibid. (A/1387, 22 September 1950), pp. 1–34.
5. "Annual report of the Government of the United Kingdom to the General Assembly concerning the administration of Cyrenaica and Tripolitania," ibid. (A/1390, 29 September 1950), pp. 34–41. The gist of items 2 and 3 above was subsequently embodied in the Commissioner's memorandum to the Council for Libya regarding the work of the Committee of Twenty-One; see *Second Annual Report of the United Nations Commissioner in Libya,* GAOR: Sixth Session, 1951–52, Supplement No. 17 (A/1949), Annex II, pp. 71–74.

of 1950 would in all probability provoke a good deal of criticism. Indeed, from the point of view of poorly informed delegations or of delegations with preconceived views unamenable to persuasion, there were grounds and to spare for complaint, in the sense that the General Assembly's intentions, as expressed at the Fourth Session, had not been carried out as expected; or even where the Assembly's wishes had been respected, progress had been too slow. Admittedly, to an outsider, the internal situation in Libya was not readily comprehensible. Such matters as the delay in completing the Council for Libya, the policy pursued by the Administering Powers, the long time it had taken to convene the Committee of Twenty-One, its inception, its composition, the problem of selection versus election, the question of the minorities, the controversy over the meaning of the term "inhabitants" as used in paragraph 3 of Resolution 289 (IV), the convocation of the National Assembly itself, and other points dealt with at length in earlier chapters of this work, supplied more than enough material for critical remarks, adverse comment or, at the least, penetrating questions.

Those with a detailed knowledge of the local scene might have found it easy to state a case for or against the way events had evolved; but how many with such knowledge were to be found in the General Assembly?

The Commissioner therefore considered it right not only to give a detailed account of his own activities and those of the Council, not to mention his dealings with the Administering Powers, but also to encourage members of the Council to exercise their right to embody dissenting opinions in footnotes, statements, or memoranda. The result was a rather unusual type of report, reminiscent of Joseph's coat, in which everyone had an opportunity of making his views known.[2]

The section of the report which he had personally pondered a great deal was Chapter IX, "Concluding Remarks" (pp. 33–37). How could the significance of past events be best summed up; how should future developments be forecast? He decided on a blend of optimism and forceful emphasis on the heavy task still to be tackled.

He couched this dual approach in the following words:

> It is the firm conviction of the Commissioner, after having observed political conditions in Libya for the last eight months, that, notwithstanding serious obstacles and difficulties, but rather counting on the keen

2. The right mentioned was conferred by paragraph 5 of Resolution 289 (IV), 21 November 1949. Despite the author's at times disparaging remarks in the course of this study about too frequent recourse to this procedure by certain members of the Council (see in particular p. 310), he appreciated its usefulness. It had the merit of completing the record of all views held or expressed in the Council, bringing them together between the same covers, instead of their being dispersed in a multitude of documents.

desire of every Libyan to see his country independent in the shortest possible time, the aim of the General Assembly will be attained within the time limit prescribed and perhaps somewhat earlier. It is his sincere belief that, if the Libyan political leaders continue to show the sense of responsibility and constructiveness which they have increasingly displayed over the last eight months, they will reach their goal. It is, of course, indispensable that the Administering Powers continue to administer the territories for the purposes set forth in the resolution. When the Libyan National Assembly has adopted a constitution, including the form of government, the Administering Powers should proceed to take all the necessary steps for the progressive transfer of functions to a provisional Libyan administration. As more detailed measures have to be taken, both within the territorial spheres and on the over-all Libyan level, the co-ordination of the activities of the Administering Powers will become progressively more necessary, particularly in the fields of administration, finance, currency and economy. The Commissioner may have to suggest at a not too distant date the establishment of a standing co-ordination committee, comprising officials of the Administering Powers and perhaps also of the Cyrenaican Government and the Fezzanese Administration, together with an appropriate representative of Tripolitania.

. . . Libya, like any other State, cannot base its independence on the mere constitution of a government. If the new State is to acquire and maintain a stable position in the family of nations, a properly organized and competent administration with a carefully planned budget, supported by a viable economy, is no less essential.

. . . None who have read the preceding chapters will be astonished if the Commissioner expresses the belief that the establishment of an effective administration, a sound financial system, and a viable economy offering the prospect of a gradually improving standard of life for the Libyan people, is certain to take more time than the period set for the achievement of Libyan independence.

. . . This last statement implies no mental reservation regarding the establishment of an independent Libyan State within the time allotted by the resolution. When Libya achieves its independence, it will certainly not be the only independent State in the world requiring assistance to organize its administration and to balance its finances and economy.[3]

The Commissioner was happy to find that no member of the Council disagreed.

3. First *Annual Report of the United Nations Commissioner in Libya,* paras. 258–61.

Soon after the Fifth Session of the General Assembly opened in September 1950, it was decided to refer the Libyan question to the *Ad Hoc* Political Committee, which would deal not only with the reports of the Commissioner and the Administering Powers, but also with such matters as ex-enemy property, war damages, and Libya's boundaries. Technical assistance was to be dealt with by the Second Committee (Committee on Economic and Financial Questions); and the Mission's budget was to be examined by the Fifth Committee (Committee on Administrative and Budgetary Questions).

Before the Council adjourned in Geneva, it decided, against the opposition of the Administering Powers, to delegate the Chairman of the day, Kamel Selim Bey, accompanied by a second member of his choice (who, perhaps not unnaturally, turned out to be none other than Abdur Rahim Khan) to represent it at the Assembly. The *Ad Hoc* Political Committee subsequently decided to invite Selim Bey to take a seat at the Committee table. The Commissioner for his part had invited, by virtue of paragraph 8 of Resolution 289 (IV), the four Libyan members of the Council to come to New York at United Nations expense to advise him there; three of them, Ali Bey Jerbi of Cyrenaica, Mustafa Mizran of Tripolitania, and Giacomo Marchino, the representative of the minorities, accepted. The member for the Fezzan, Hajj Ahmed Sofu, was, unfortunately, ill. (Soon afterward he was obliged to resign for reasons of health.) The Commissioner was in a way glad he could not attend, in the first place for Hajj Sofu himself. He could have rendered a most useful service by providing information on a little-known territory, but, speaking only his mother tongue, and having never attended a General Assembly like his colleagues, he would have been in a most uncomfortable position between the French and Arab delegations.

When, on 9 October 1950, the *Ad Hoc* Political Committee took up the Libyan question,[4] the United Kingdom delegation at once submitted a draft resolution on the economic and financial provisions to be applied in Libya in pursuance of Annex XIV, paragraph 19, of the Treaty of Peace with Italy, and providing, among other things, for the establishment of a United Nations arbitral tribunal.[5] As this was a highly intricate legal and technical subject, the Committee, after having heard a spokesman for the Italian Government,[6] decided to refer the matter to a special sub-committee (Sub-

4. For the complete record of its discussions, see GAOR: Fifth Session, 1950, *Ad Hoc* Political Committee, 7th–17th Meetings, 9–19 October 1950, pp. 41–109; and 80th–82nd Meetings, 13–14 December 1950, pp. 511–34.

5. GAOR: Fifth Session, 1950, Annexes, Agenda item 21 (A/AC.38/L.9, 9 October 1950), pp. 45–46.

6. Italy was not yet a member of the United Nations.

Committee 1), which reported only toward the end of the session. It was also decided that an "observer" (a representative with the right to take part in the discussions, but not to introduce proposals or to vote) for the Italian Government, the Commissioner, and the Chairman of the Council for Libya should attend meetings of the Sub-Committee in an advisory capacity.

From that moment, the *Ad Hoc* Political Committee concentrated exclusively on the five reports before it, though without discussing them in detail, and it soon appeared that the critics were even more numerous and more severe than the Commissioner and his advisers had expected. In part, this was undoubtedly due to genuine concern about the slow pace of implementation of the Resolution, but it was also evident that several delegations had not had time to study their documents thoroughly, with the result that numerous factual misunderstandings encumbered the discussions—a not uncommon phenomenon at meetings of United Nations bodies in general, and an understandable one considering the mass of documents delegations receive, particularly before and during a General Assembly session. The smallest delegations are hardest hit in this respect. Moreover, in the case in point, the consultations with the Council having been particularly slow, the Commissioner had been unable to dispatch his annual report to the Secretary-General until 4 September; accordingly, it was distributed only much later that month. Other delegations obviously came to the Committee table with their minds already made up. Both the Commissioner and the Chairman of the Council—though for very different reasons—often found themselves in difficulty. The delegations which came to their defense—usually ignoring the differences that had arisen between them—were in a minority. Furthermore, the arguments of these delegations were weakened by the fact that they numbered the Administering Powers among them. Broadly speaking, the critics fell into three groups: one led by the Soviet Union; another comprising the Arab States; and the third made up of a number of Latin American delegations which sometimes, but not always, joined forces with the Arab group.

The first two groups, and a few members of the third, still haunted by the ghost of the Bevin-Sforza plan, had a deep-seated suspicion of the intentions of the Administering Powers, in whose policies they saw a renewed attempt to dismember Libya through the creation of separate States and puppet governments. They found support for their misgivings in the Commissioner's report. There was also a tendency to accuse him, and even the Council itself, of having endorsed those policies to some extent, without any understanding on the part of the critics of the reasons that had moved them to do so.

A number of Arab delegations expressed doubts about the usefulness of the Committee of Twenty-One, and practically all the members of this group attacked it on the grounds that it had been appointed, and not elected, and that it was composed of an equal number of representatives from each of the three territories, despite their considerable differences in population. Both these features were condemned as "undemocratic"; no one seemed to appreciate the peculiar local conditions which had in the final outcome made them unavoidable.

The Latin American delegations proved particularly sensitive to the problem of the minorities, just as they had been at the Fourth Session. Listening to their oratory, the Commissioner sometimes got the impression that he was guilty of failing to give priority to minority protection over Libyan independence.

The Latin American delegations proved particularly sensitive to the problem of the minorities, just as they had been at the Fourth Session. Listening to their oratory, the Commissioner sometimes got the impression that he was guilty of failing to give priority to minority protection over Libyan independence.

The socialist countries were mainly concerned about Libyan unity and the presence of foreign troops and military bases on Libyan territory.

As all the criticisms were repeated even more dramatically in the plenary Assembly, there is no point in describing in detail what went on in committee. It should be noted, however, that three more draft resolutions were introduced in the course of the debate. They were summarized in the following terms in the *Ad Hoc* Political Committee's report to the Assembly:

(a) [A passage referring to the United Kingdom proposal for a United Nations Tribunal.]

(b) A draft resolution . . . submitted by the Union of Soviet Socialist Republics at the 8th meeting, providing that the parts of Libya be united in a single State and that legislative and executive organs for Libya be established, and that all foreign troops and military personnel be withdrawn from Libya within three months and military bases dismantled.

(c) A joint draft resolution—submitted by Canada, Chile, Ecuador and Greece at the 11th meeting, which took note of the reports that had been received; recommended that the administering Powers press forward with the formation of governmental institutions for Libya in accordance with the wishes of the people in order to facilitate the establishment of an independent and sovereign Libya not later than 1 January 1952; urged the Economic and Social Council, the Specialized Agencies and Members of the United Nations to continue to assist Libya, through technical and financial assistance, to develop a sound and viable economy; and reaffirmed the recommendation that Libya be admitted to the United Nations upon its establishment as an independent State.

(d) A joint draft resolution . . . submitted by the representatives of Egypt, Indonesia, Iraq, Lebanon, Pakistan, Saudi Arabia, Syria and Yemen at the 12th meeting, which called upon the authorities concerned to ensure the full and effective implementation of resolution 289 A (IV) of 21 November 1949 and particularly to safeguard the unity of Libya and the early transfer of power to an independent Libyan Government, and recommended that a National Assembly representative of the inhabitants of Libya be convened not later than 1 January 1951, and that the National Assembly should set up a Provisional Government not later than 1 March 1951 to which would be transferred all powers exercised by the administering Powers.[7]

In the course of the next few days, both during the debates in committee and in a number of private conversations, the Commissioner and his staff, the Chairman of the Council, and the other three members present at Lake Success had many opportunities of clearing up a number of basic misunderstandings. On one such occasion, the Commissioner, accompanied by the three Arab members of the Council, was invited to attend a private meeting of the Arab group of delegations to answer questions, which enabled him to correct a number of wrong impressions. The Chairman of the Council and his Pakistani colleague were naturally in daily touch with their own and other delegations, sometimes finding themselves in a somewhat delicate position over the selection versus election issue and others. The Tripolitanian and Cyrenaican members were searchingly questioned by every delegate interested in the Libyan problem, and their divergent opinions, taken in conjunction, served to clear up many misapprehensions.

It would have been asking too much to expect complete agreement, but after a week or so the atmosphere in the Committee had cleared sufficiently to make it possible for the twelve sponsors of the third and fourth draft resolutions, joined by India, to get together in an attempt to produce a compromise text. In this they succeeded, thanks to many mutual concessions, though, as subsequent events were to prove, a measure of disagreement persisted on one or two basic issues.

The socialist countries, on the other hand, were adamant, particularly on the withdrawal of foreign troops and the dismantling of military bases; and

7. "Report of the *Ad Hoc* Political Committee," GAOR: Fifth Session, 1950, Annexes, Agenda item 21 (A/1457, 25 October 1950), p. 58.

the first part of the group's proposal in favor of a single Libyan State—i.e. a unitary State in contrast to the loose federation advocated by the British and French—commanded a good deal of Arab support.

The Thirteen Power joint draft resolution read as follows:

The General Assembly

Having resolved by its resolution 289 A (IV) of 21 November 1949, that Libya shall be constituted a united independent and sovereign State,

Having noted the report of the United Nations Commissioner in Libya, prepared in consultation with the Council for Libya, and those of the Administering Powers, submitted in accordance with General Assembly resolution 289 A (IV), as well as the statements of the United Nations Commissioner and the representatives of the Council for Libya,

Having noted in particular the confidence expressed by the Commissioner that the aim of the General Assembly, namely, that Libya should become an independent and sovereign State, will be attained within the time-limit prescribed, with the increasing co-operation of the Administering Powers with the United Nations Commissioner and the mutual co-ordination of their activities toward that end,

Having noted the statements in the above-mentioned report of the Commissioner regarding the needs of Libya for technical and financial assistance both before and after independence, if such assistance is requested by the Government of Libya,

1. *Expresses confidence* that the United Nations Commissioner in Libya, aided and guided by the advice of the members of the Council for Libya, will take the necessary steps to discharge his functions toward the achievement of the independence and unity of Libya pursuant to the above-mentioned resolution;

2. *Calls upon* the authorities concerned to take all steps necessary to ensure the early, full and effective implementation of the resolution of 21 November 1949 and particularly the realization of the unity of Libya and the transfer of power to an independent Libyan Government; and, further

3. *Recommends*

(a) That a National Assembly duly representative of the inhabitants of Libya shall be convened as early as possible, and in any case before 1 January 1951;

(b) That this National Assembly shall establish a Provisional Government of Libya as early as possible, bearing in mind 1 April 1951 as the target date;

(c) That powers shall be progressively transferred to the Provisional

Government by the Administering Powers in a manner which will ensure that, by 1 January 1952, all powers at present exercised by the Administering Powers shall have been transferred to the duly constituted Libyan Government;

(d) That the United Nations Commissioner, aided and guided by the advice of the members of the Council for Libya, shall proceed immediately to draw up a programme, in co-operation with the Administering Powers, for the transfer of power as provided in sub-paragraph (c) above;

4. *Urges* the Economic and Social Council, the specialized agencies and the Secretary-General of the United Nations to extend to Libya such technical and financial assistance as it may request in order to establish a sound basis for economic and social progress;

5. *Reaffirms* its recommendation that, upon its establishment as an independent State, Libya be admitted to the United Nations in accordance with Article 44 of the Charter.[8]

How difficult it had been to reach even this imperfect compromise was revealed by the number of amendments tabled when the *Ad Hoc* Political Committee itself started to discuss the proposal.

The Australian delegation proposed that the word "united" be deleted from the first paragraph of the preamble, thus raising once more the issue which had caused so much trouble the year before (see Chapter 1, Part 3, passim), and which was now more acute than ever because of the suspicions aroused by the policies pursued by the Administering Powers. Selim Bey advised against this change.

The delegation of Argentina wanted a new paragraph inserted recalling the recommendation made in subparagraph 10 (b) of Resolution 289 (IV) that the Administering Powers, in cooperation with the Commissioner, administer the territories for which they were responsible with a view to promoting the establishment of Libyan unity and independence.

Pakistan wanted to insert in subparagraph 3 (b) a phrase making the proposed provisional government responsible to the National Assembly, and to add at the end of the subparagraph a saving clause to the effect that if the National Assembly was itself unable to form a provisional government by 31 March 1951, the Commissioner, advised and guided by the Council for Libya, should at once proceed to set up such a government in consultation with the National Assembly. The Commissioner was opposed to these two suggestions, considering that they would amount to interference in

8. Ibid. The sponsors were: Canada, Chile, Ecuador, Egypt, Greece, India, Indonesia, Iraq, Lebanon, Pakistan, Saudi Arabia, Syria, and Yemen.

Libya's internal affairs, unless his advice was sought by the National Assembly or he considered it necessary to offer advice on his own account.

The United States delegation considered the text of paragraph 4 too imperative, and accordingly wanted the word *"Urges"* to be replaced by the phrase *"Draws the* attention of."

Finally, Israel proposed that subparagraph 3 (a) be amended to read "a National Assembly duly representative of *all* the inhabitants."

Each of these proposals gave rise to considerable debate, but in the end all were withdrawn against a promise by the Committee's Rapporteur that the specific points raised would be clarified in his report to the General Assembly by agreed interpretations. Accordingly, the Committee's report contained the following passage:

> At the 17th meeting, the Vice-Chairman of the Committee made an explanatory statement on behalf of the 13 sponsors of the joint draft resolution . . . , which the Committee agreed should be included in the Rapporteur's report. In his statement the Vice-Chairman stressed the following points:
>
> (a) That the inclusion of the word "united" in the first paragraph of the preamble meant only that the aim of the General Assembly, as expressed in paragraph 10 (b) of Section A of its resolution of 21 November 1949, was to establish Libyan unity and independence; the word was not intended to impose on the Libyan people a unitary State if they did not wish it, nor in any way to prejudge the form of government; the form of State to be created, and whether it would be a unitary or federal State, must be left entirely to the representatives of the Libyan people, meeting and consulting in a National Assembly.
>
> (b) The use of the words "increasing co-operation of the administering Powers" in the third paragraph of the preamble should not be interpreted as implying any criticism.
>
> (c) That, while it was not possible to specify the financial implications of paragraph 4, that paragraph was intended to emphasize the need of the new State for technical and financial assistance to enable it to found its nationhood on a firm economic basis.
>
> (d) Parts of the General Assembly resolution of 21 November 1949 and, in particular, the recommendation regarding the admission of an independent Libya to the United Nations, were reiterated because it was considered helpful to repeat those words which could enhance the morale of the people of Libya.
>
> . . . At the same meeting, the amendment proposed by Australia . . . was withdrawn on the understanding that the above clarification of the

intentions of the sponsors of the joint draft resolution would be included in the Rapporteur's report. The amendment proposed by Argentina . . . was also withdrawn following the withdrawal of the Australian amendment.

. . . The amendment proposed by the United States of America . . . was withdrawn on the understanding that the Rapporteur's report would make it clear that paragraph 4 was intended merely to request the United Nations organs and specialized agencies mentioned to grant requests made by Libya for assistance to the extent that such organs and agencies might be in a position to do so.

. . . The amendments proposed by Pakistan . . . were withdrawn in the interests of unanimity.

. . . The amendment proposed by Israel . . . was withdrawn on the understanding that the word "inhabitants" in sub-paragraph 3 (a) of the joint draft resolution was not intended to have a prohibitive meaning, excluding certain sections of the population from equal participation in the life of the new State, and that it was the desire of the Committee that adequate safeguards for the protection of the rights of minorities should be included in the future constitution of Libya. It was agreed by the Committee that this interpretation should be included in the Rapporteur's report.

. . . The representative of the Union of Soviet Socialist Republics proposed an oral amendment to delete from the third paragraph of the preamble of the joint draft resolution the words "with the increasing co-operation of the administering Powers with the United Nations Commissioner and the mutual co-ordination of their activities toward that end." [9]

When, on 16 November, this compromise resolution came up for discussion in plenary Assembly, it looked for a brief time as if all would be plain sailing.[10]

The first speaker, the representative of France, accepted the draft resolution, although his Government had a number of reservations, based in part on the Commissioner's report. This was a marked improvement on 1949, when the French delegation had abstained from voting.

From this happy moment, however, criticism came hailing down, particularly from the USSR delegation and its supporters, from several Arab States, and from one Latin American State, El Salvador.

9. Ibid., p. 59.

10. For complete record of the discussions in plenary, see GAOR: Fifth Session, 1950, 305th–08th Plenary Meetings, 16–17 November 1950, pp. 393–424 and 436; 325–26th Meetings, 14–15 December 1950, pp. 681 and 684–86.

The Soviet attacks on the presence of foreign troops and military bases in Libya were renewed in even stronger terms than in Committee; but it was again noteworthy that, while several of the Arab and some of the Latin American delegations supported the call for the withdrawal of foreign troops, the majority in both these groups declared that the dismantling of military bases came within the domestic jurisdiction of the future Libyan state. A typical statement was that made by the delegate of Saudi Arabia: "The attainment of the objectives of the General Assembly's resolution of 21 November 1949," he said, "might be hindered by the very presence of foreign troops on Libyan soil." At the same time, he declared:

> We shall abstain, however, from voting on the last part of the Soviet Union draft resolution which contains the words "and military bases dismantled," for we believe it is not within our competence to make such a decision. It is the Libyan people themselves who should decide on such a vital issue.[11]

It was never clearly explained why such a distinction was necessary. Could it be that certain delegations considered that some day the Libyan people might need these bases for their own use? At the same time no one seemed to envisage the possibility that some day an independent Libyan Government, however reluctantly, might find the presence of both troops and bases, in return for financial compensation, essential to balance the new State's budget—a possibility that was translated into reality within the year.

The Arab States' criticism was focused mainly on two points: first, that the Committee of Twenty-One had not been elected and that the National Assembly, as had become known in the meantime, would not be elected either; second, that the three Libyan territories were equally represented on both bodies. The epithet "undemocratic" was again in much demand, and, the explanations given in the Commissioner's report (which he reiterated even more forcefully when called upon to explain his position at the three hundred and sixth plenary meeting) notwithstanding, the inevitability of these two measures was not understood.[12]

11. GAOR: Fifth Session, 1950, 306th Plenary Meeting, 16 November 1950, p. 409.

12. It is not normal United Nations procedure for a Commissioner or other servant of the Organisation in a comparable position to take part in the General Assembly's debate on his report. In the present instance, the President of the General Assembly was requested by the representatives of Lebanon and Iraq to invite the Commissioner to the rostrum to give an explanation of certain matters arising out of his report. The President having put the suggestion to the meeting, and no objection being raised, the procedure proposed by the two Middle Eastern delegations was followed. The Commissioner spoke at the end of the general debate, but the representatives of Syria and Egypt returned to the attack at the next meeting.

As the debate went on, tension mounted, and it became clear that unless the critics were given certain assurances, the fate of the Committee's draft resolution might well be in the balance. Called upon by a number of delegations to give an assurance that future constitutional developments in Libya would be "democratic," the Commissioner reminded the General Assembly that

> the national assembly was appointed, and not elected, very much against my own advice and . . . equality of representation as between the three territories had to be incorporated into the national assembly's set-up as a matter of unavoidable political expediency.[13]

Although he realized that he was hurting the feelings of many Libyans through expressing the opinion held by many others, he nevertheless felt obliged to add that

> since [the National Assembly] is an appointed and not an elected body, there are grave doubts in my mind as to whether it will have the necessary moral and political authority to elaborate a final and definite constitution for Libya.[14]

Subsequent events fortunately proved the Commissioner wrong in this pessimistic appreciation. Looking forward, he continued:

> I have always envisaged the future independent Libya as a democratic State. Hence the future parliament of Libya should preferably be an elected body, that is to say, a body to be elected by the Libyan people as a whole. At the same time, we have to recognise conditions in Libya as they are. As a result of historical and geographical circumstances, Libya is composed of three territories which, although they have a great deal in common—more than enough to constitute a nation united in a single State—have their own local peculiarities, outlooks and interests to which they are attached and which they want to safeguard. This is particularly true with regard to Cyrenaica and the Fezzan.
>
> A problem of this kind is not new. It exists in many other countries, and it has been solved in many other countries. It is my conviction that it can and will be solved in Libya.
>
> There is a third point which gave rise in the *Ad Hoc* Political Committee to what in my eyes was unjustified criticism, namely, the fact that the provisional government is not going to be responsible to the national assembly. In the Committee, I advised against such a responsibility for

13. GAOR: Fifth Session, 1950, 306th Plenary Meeting, 16 November 1950, p. 411.

14. Ibid., pp. 411–12.

the simple and practical reason that, if the provisional government were made responsible to the national assembly, it would be virtually impossible to organise the new State for independence in the short time left. However, this does not mean that in the final constitution the government of Libya should equally not be responsible to the parliament. On the contrary, I consider that this principle of responsibility is an essential feature of a democratic State.[15]

The Commissioner concluded with the following statement of policy:

For all these reasons, it is my intention, on my return to Libya, to suggest to the Council the following advice to be given to the Libyan national assembly and to the Libyan people.

First, that the constitution to be prepared by the national assembly should be considered as a draft to be enacted in a provisional form, but which will require final approval and, if necessary, may be amended by a parliament to be elected by the Libyan people as a whole. Even at the cost of a certain loss of time, I feel this to be an absolutely essential precaution if the Libyan State is to be founded on a stable political basis.

Secondly, that in order to reconcile the two tendencies existing in the country, that is to say, the unitary concept and that of territorial particularism, parliament should consist of two chambers—a small senate composed of elected representatives of the three territories on a basis of equality, and a popular chamber to be elected by the people as a whole. In my opinion, that popular chamber should have among its competencies the sole competence of the State budget.

Thirdly, that the Libyan government should be responsible to the popular chamber.

I trust that the Council for Libya will give me its unanimous support in tendering this advice to the Libyan national assembly and to the Libyan people. The Commissioner and the Council acting together enjoy sufficient authority to make me feel that advice of this kind will be accepted, so much the more as it corresponds to the personal opinion of a great many leading Libyan personalities in the three territories.[16]

The author must admit that, at the beginning of the discussion, he, as Commissioner, had had no intention of making so far-reaching a statement —at least not at a plenary meeting of the General Assembly. For several months he had been convinced that a federal form of government based on a bicameral parliamentary system would in all probability prove not only

15. Ibid., p. 412.
16. Ibid.

the most acceptable but also the only feasible solution to Libya's constitutional problems. He had intended, on his return to Tripoli, to seek the Council's advice on whether he should make a suggestion of this kind to the National Assembly. Hence, it was with considerable reluctance that he made the foregoing statement, which from the internal Libyan point of view was decidedly premature. It would have required—and in fact, as we shall see in the next chapter, did require—a great deal of oral explanation and preparation on the spot, within and outside the National Assembly, before the matter could safely be raised. However, the pressure, in particular from the Arab side, had been such that at the time he felt he had no choice but to act as he did. As matters turned out, the Arab opposition was still not satisfied.

At the next meeting the Arab delegations, led mainly by Syria and Egypt, renewed their attack, choosing the nonelected National Assembly as their target.

The representative of Syria said that "the national assembly should be elected and should not be appointed by anybody. If this body is appointed, it cannot be said to represent the inhabitants of Libya.[17]

The representative of Egypt declared that:

> The statement made yesterday before the Assembly by Mr. Pelt, the United Nations Commissioner in Libya, has not in any way allayed our fears. On the contrary, it has once more confirmed the fact that the national assembly which is to draw up the Libyan constitution will be appointed rather than elected.[18]

Referring to the draft resolution before the Assembly, the representative of Egypt went on to say:

> The interpretation given in the *Ad Hoc* Political Committee and in the Assembly to the words "a national assembly duly representative of the inhabitants of Libya" leaves no room for any doubt whatsoever. These words refer—and they can only refer—to an assembly elected in proportion to the size of the population of the three component units of Libya. They cannot refer to an appointed assembly based on equal representation.[19]

While accepting the Commissioner's asseveration of the previous day that any constitution prepared by such an assembly could only be a pro-

17. GAOR: Fifth Session, 1950, 307th Plenary Meeting, 17 November 1950, p. 414.
18. Ibid.
19. Ibid., pp. 414–15.

visional instrument requiring final approval, and subject to amendment, by a parliament elected by the Libyan people as a whole, the speaker asked:

> But, if that is the case and if that is really our purpose, why do we not begin where Mr. Pelt would like us to end? Why not convene a truly national, representative and constituent assembly without further delay, instead of convening this appointed assembly of sixty members which, though apparently based on the principle of equality, is in fact an expression of the most flagrant inequality? [20]

Notwithstanding this rhetorical appeal, the compromise reached in the *Ad Hoc* Political Committee was still good, no amendment having been tabled to the Committee's draft resolution. At that moment, however, the South African representative committed a grave tactical error, which almost proved fatal, by proposing what he chose to call a minor drafting change in paragraph 4 of the operative part of the draft resolution concerning technical assistance. It was indeed an insignificant matter, but it gave the Egyptian representative an opening, which he immediately seized, for proposing a much more important change. He wanted subparagraph 3 (a) to be amended to read: "That a national assembly duly *elected and* representative of the inhabitants of Libya." [21]

The President thereupon called upon the Commissioner, who, invoking as his main argument the short time left for the completion of constitutional developments in Libya, warned the General Assembly that, if the National Assembly did not meet on 25 November as at present planned—if, on the contrary, preparations had to be made for general elections in a country that had never known anything of the kind—"there would be no National Assembly until far into next year, and in that case [he] must point out that the possibility of achieving independence by the end of next year would become a dream. The date of 31 December 1951 for independence would in that case be out of the question." [22]

The floodgates were now open to a further spate of eloquence for and against the Egyptian proposal. The Commissioner's main argument had apparently made some impression, with the result that the representative of El Salvador was struck by the bright idea of solving the problem very simply by adding two months to the dates of 1 January and 1 April 1951, specified in subparagraphs 3 (a) and (b) of the draft resolution, thus incidentally shortening by a like period the time left for the drafting of the constitution.

20. Ibid., p. 415.
21. Ibid.
22. Ibid., p. 416.

The representative of Egypt said he could not understand why such a mild and restrained amendment as his should have aroused so much opposition. Actually, he argued, it was not an amendment at all. All he was trying to do was to clarify an extremely ambiguous text to make it consistent with what he thought was the view of both the *Ad Hoc* Political Committee and the General Assembly itself, namely, that the Libyan National Constituent Assembly should be an elected, and not an appointed, body.

Fortunately, other delegations fully appreciated the implications of the Egyptian proposal, and the Turkish representative asked the Commissioner to tell the Assembly whether in his opinion it would be possible to organize and hold regular elections within the time limit proposed by the delegation of El Salvador.

The Commissioner seized the opportunity thus presented, first to impress upon the representative of Egypt that by pressing his amendment he ran the risk of doing Libya the greatest possible disservice by endangering a carefully worked out compromise among Libyans from all three territories. As to the question put by the representative of Turkey, his reply was categorically in the negative. If the two earlier dates were changed, as proposed by the representative of El Salvador, then in logic the date of 1 January 1952 fixed for independence should also be put back by two months. But nobody, not even the Egyptian representative, was prepared to act on this suggestion.

Nevertheless, when the Egyptian amendment was put to the meeting, it mustered 24 votes against 20, with 15 abstentions. Accordingly, having failed to obtain the required two-thirds majority, it was lost. But the result was an eloquent demonstration of how strong the demand for an elected National Assembly had been.

The draft resolution, as amended by the South African proposal, was then adopted by 50 votes to none, with 6 abstentions, becoming Resolution 387 (V) of 17 November 1950 (see Annex I, pp. 893–94 for the full text).[23]

Finally, the USSR draft resolution (cf. page 356) was put to the vote. The first paragraph, on Libyan unity, received 23 votes to 21, with 10 abstentions, and was therefore rejected. The second paragraph was voted upon in two parts: the first, reading "that all foreign troops and military personnel be withdrawn from the territory of Libya within three months,"

23. Paragraph 4 of the operative part of the resolution as amended by South Africa reads: "*Urges* the Economic and Social Council, the specialized agencies and the Secretary-General of the United Nations to extend to Libya, in so far as they may be in a position to do so, such technical and financial assistance as it may request in order to establish a sound basis for economic and social progress."

was rejected by 36 votes to 11, with 5 abstentions; the second, reading "and military bases dismantled" was rejected by 36 votes to 7, with 11 abstentions.

There was much to please the Commissioner in the resolution as adopted. In particular, two of the suggestions made in his report had been incorporated in the text: that concerning the establishment of a provisional government; and that providing for the establishment of a standing coordination committee with the task of drawing up a program for the transfer of powers from the Administering Powers to the Libyan Government when constituted. The stress laid on the need for increased cooperation between Commissioner and Administering Powers, and on a greater measure of coordination of their activities, was also welcome.

A point which had not been effectively clarified was the meaning of the word "inhabitants." But the relevant paragraph in the *Ad Hoc* Political Committee's report quoted above (p. 361) ran closely parallel to his own suggestions.[24] In this connection, it was fortunate that the General Assembly's desire that adequate safeguards for the protection of minorities be written into the constitution had been anticipated by a recommendation of the Committee of Twenty-One.

All in all, and notwithstanding the many criticisms visited upon him, the Commissioner returned to Tripoli confident that his position had been strengthened. At the same time, he realized that he might be in for a difficult time over the advice he had undertaken to request the Council to give to the National Assembly.

His difficulties with the Council had played hardly any part in the discussions; in the wider perspective of Lake Success they had looked much less disturbing than in the stuffy meeting room in the Grand Hotel in Tripoli.

Looking back on his statement to the General Assembly, the Commissioner did not regret having made it, mainly for the reasons given on pages 364–65. Nonetheless, he felt that, had time and the pressure of events permitted, it might have been more carefully phrased. As he was to learn, the Amir and many other Libyans, including the whole of the National Assembly, had been seriously perturbed. After his return to Libya it took the Commissioner a few months to live down the unfortunate effect his words had made on them. Only after he had brought leading Libyans to understand his motives in making the statement was the old confidence fully restored.

24. First *Annual Report of the United Nations Commissioner in Libya,* paras. 254–56.

PART 2. ECONOMIC AND FINANCIAL MATTERS

When the problem of the disposal of the former Italian colonies was first referred to the United Nations, the interest of delegations to the General Assembly was centered on its political aspects. Initially, scant attention was devoted to the no less important economic, financial, and social issues.[25]

This lack of balance in envisaging the future of the three territories was further reflected in Resolution 289 (IV). Of its eleven paragraphs, only one (9) dealt with other than political, constitutional, or organizational questions; it is worthwhile quoting it in full, as its brevity typifies the General Assembly's approach at that time:

> 9. That the United Nations Commissioner may offer suggestions to the General Assembly, to the Economic and Social Council and to the Secretary-General as to the measures that the United Nations might adopt during the transitional period regarding the economic and social problems of Libya.[26]

Nevertheless, this proved to be a useful provision as it enabled the Commissioner to make a number of suggestions of an economic, social, and administrative nature without which the preparation of Libya's independence might have been governed by constitutional considerations alone. Last but not least, paragraph 9 allowed a large program of technical assistance to be initiated, as we shall see in the next part of this chapter as well as in Chapter 9.

Reading the Secretariat's notes on the discussions in Sub-Committee 17 at the Fourth Session of the General Assembly, one is struck by the offhand way in which paragraph 9 was conceived—almost as an afterthought. It was the last item on Libya discussed by the Sub-Committee, and it seems as if it might have been overlooked, had not the Chilean representative drawn attention to it, apparently (the notes are not entirely clear about this) in

25. During the second part of its Third Session (5 April–18 May 1949), the General Assembly had adopted Resolution 266 (III), 17 May 1949, that simply recommended that "the Economic and Social Council should, in studying and planning its activities in connexion with economically under-developed regions and countries, take into consideration the problems of economic development and social progress of the former Italian colonies." A year later, as described below, the Secretary-General and the Commissioner raised the economic and social problems of Libya in the Economic and Social Council at its Eleventh Session, and in the General Assembly.

26. Annex I, pp. 891–92.

connection with a United Kingdom proposal concerning the way in which, under the Treaty of Peace with Italy, economic and financial problems bound up with the transfer of sovereignty from Italy to Libya, including the highly complicated question of former enemy property, should be handled.

Without going into the substance of these problems, the Sub-Committee dealt at length with their procedural aspects, and finally decided to include the following paragraph in its report to the First Committee:

> The nineteenth question examined concerned the economic and financial provisions for Libya, arising out of Annex XIV, paragraph 19, of the Treaty of Peace with Italy. In that connexion the representative of the United Kingdom submitted a proposal to the effect that the economic and financial provisions for Libya should be considered at the fifth regular session of the General Assembly. He pointed out that such a study entailed many intricate technical problems; it could best be undertaken by the Administering Powers which would present a report on the whole problem to the next regular session of the General Assembly. Some members of the Sub-Committee were of the opinion that such a study should be made by the commissioner in consultation with his Council and the Administering Powers; others maintained that all matters concerning economic and financial problems should be dealt with by the new Libyan authorities and the interested Governments. The view was also expressed that, inasmuch as the problem of the disposal of the former Italian colonies came within the competence of the United Nations, the settlement of that particular aspect of the problem should be carried out by the United Nations or its agency. The Sub-Committee had no specific recommendation to offer with regard to this question, but it was the sense of the Sub-Committee that the question of the economic and financial provisions for Libya should be considered and decided upon at the next regular session of the General Assembly, when reports on the subject would have been received from the Administering Powers and possibly, from the commissioner and his council.[27]

One of the arguments advanced by the United Kingdom representative in Sub-Committee 17, when he had spoken against requesting the Commissioner to study the problem and report on it at the Fifth Session, was that this would require considerable time and staff. The Commissioner was soon to discover how justified this warning was. The value of the interests

27. "Report of Sub-Committee 17 to the First Committee," GAOR: Fourth Session, 1949, First Committee, Annexes to Summary Records, Agenda item 19 (A/C.1/522, 1 November 1949), p. 28.

involved, consisting of state, parastatal, and private property was considerable. According to Count Vitetti, speaking in Sub-Committee 1 as observer for the Italian Government, the total amount spent by the Italian State in Libya from 1912 to 1942 amounted to more than one billion lire, but no breakdown of this figure was given. As previously mentioned, the estimates of United Nations and World Bank experts were that the amounts were possibly equivalent to about 150 million US dollars at prewar rates of exchange (see p. 31).

The number of individual cases to be handled was thought by Count Vitetti to be as high as 31,000. The legal aspects of the problem were highly intricate. Most of the relevant documentation was to be found only in Italian Government archives. Moreover, part of such documentation left behind by the Italian Administration had been destroyed by acts of war. Virtually all former enemy property was located in Tripolitania and Cyrenaica,[28] and since 1943 had been controlled by a British Custodian of Enemy Property in each of the two territories. In Cyrenaica, where, as we have seen, the whole Italian civilian population had left the country at the moment of defeat on the orders of the Italian military authorities, a large number of abandoned farms had been occupied by the local inhabitants, mostly nomads or seminomads. As both the Italian owners and the Cyrenaican occupants were anxiously and impatiently waiting for an authoritative and final decision as to their respective rights and claims, the United Kingdom felt it to be its duty as the Administering Power to submit a report on the question to the General Assembly. At the same time, according to the passage just quoted from the report of Sub-Committee 17, the Commissioner and the Council also were "possibly" to make known their views on the subject. (On this issue, for reasons already stated, the Commissioner did not submit a request for advice to the Council.) The Commissioner's position was complicated by the fact that the Libyan leaders, as yet unable to protect their interests themselves, to some extent counted on him to act for him. Formally, this was impossible, but as a kind of amicus curiae he could speak for Libyan views and interests, though it was not always easy to do even this, as under the terms of paragraph 10 of Resolution 289 (IV) the Libyan territories continued to be administered by the United Kingdom and France, not only internally, but also with respect to their external relations. It was therefore desirable to reach agreement, especially with the United Kingdom, on certain issues of a procedural and substantive nature. One problem on which no such agreement could be reached was that of compensation for war damage, particularly close to

28. There was practically no Italian private or parastatal property in the Fezzan, only state property.

the heart of the Cyrenaicans, in whose view the problem of reparations was closely bound up with that of former enemy property.[29] This was only natural, as most of Cyrenaica, and in particular the town of Benghazi, had suffered large-scale destruction. The Italian Government, which had paid for most of the damaged property in the first place, did not, however, share this view; neither did the French or British. The concept of reparations for war damages to be paid by the vanquished had no more practicability in Libya than in Western Europe and the British Isles.

To examine some of the basic problems, the Commissioner took onto his staff a Dutch Arabist, the late Professor J. P. Mensing of Utrecht University, who had made a special study of land ownership in Arab countries, to prepare a memorandum on the regulations governing possession and ownership under the Italian regime in Libya.[30] The Principal Secretary of the Mission also devoted what little spare time remained to him to the problem. Most important of all, the Office of Legal Affairs of the United Nations Secretariat put one of its staff onto the same job. But, no matter how useful these combined studies proved to be, they left the Commissioner and his staff with an uneasy feeling that they were insufficiently briefed to face a discussion on the substance of the matter.

The United Kingdom Government, for its part, prepared in the course of 1950 an extensive memorandum accompanied by a draft resolution for submission to the Fifth Session of the General Assembly (cf. pp. 354–55). However, the memorandum was neither final nor complete. In its Annual Report to the General Assembly, the United Kingdom Government noted:

> The question of Italian state and para-statal property and undertakings in Tripolitania and Cyrenaica continues to be examined. It has not, however, been possible to complete the examination of the question of para-statal property and concerns, which present very great complications, and the examination so far made has disclosed the need for further data which are not available in the territories. As a result of the examination which has already been made, however, it would appear desirable that the administering Power should apply to all questions of former Italian property in Tripolitania and Cyrenaica the general rules

29. See the first *Annual Report of the United Nations Commissioner in Libya*, para. 184.

30. "Memorandum on the regulations governing possession and ownership under the Italian régime in Libya," United Nations Doc. A/AC.51/R.1 (A/AC.32/TRIB/R.1), 21 July 1951. Mimeographed. This memorandum, which dealt specifically with real estate, was unfortunately never finished, owing to the untimely death of its author. But even in its incomplete form it proved to be of considerable use to the United Nations Tribunal in Libya (see pp. 384–92).

of international law and procedure applicable in such circumstances, having regard to the interests of all parties concerned.[31]

The Commissioner fully shared these views, especially those expressed in the last sentence of the quotation. To him, the problem was not simply a legal one. It also had important human, economic, and social aspects, and he felt that an equitable solution to it would have a considerable effect on future relations between the Libyan people and the Italian and other minorities living among them.

During the summer the Foreign Office showed the Commissioner drafts of its memorandum and the accompanying resolution; extensive consultations followed, first in Tripoli, later in New York. The Commissioner also had talks on the matter with the Amir, with the Cyrenaican and Tripolitanian members of the Council, and, last but by no means least, with the representative of the minorities.

THE DISCUSSIONS IN THE AD HOC POLITICAL COMMITTEE

As noted on page 354, the *Ad Hoc* Political Committee took up the Libyan question, within the broader framework of the disposal of the former Italian colonies, on 9 October 1950. In the course of his introductory statement, the Commissioner drew attention to the economic problems that the delay in settling the question of former enemy property was creating.[32] Later in the same meeting, the United Kingdom representative, in a lengthy statement introducing his delegation's draft resolution, summarized the issues calling for solution. Subsequently, the United Kingdom delegation issued a detailed statement, amplifying its reasons for submitting the resolution.[33] A few days later, at the Committee's eleventh meeting, Count Vitetti replied to the United Kingdom representative at some length.

This is not the place to go into all the intricacies of this legal cut and thrust. Extensive extracts from the two statements, together with other relevant material, have therefore been relegated to Annex XII (pp. 964–73) for the convenience of the reader specifically interested in the problem.

31. "Annual report of the Government of the United Kingdom to the General Assembly concerning the administration of Cyrenaica and Tripolitania," pp. 39–40.

32. GAOR: Fifth Session, 1950, *Ad Hoc* Political Committee, 7th Meeting, 9 October 1950, p. 42.

33. The draft resolution was circulated as United Nations Doc. A/AC.38/L.9, 9 October 1950. For text, see GAOR: Fifth Session, 1950, Annexes, Agenda item 21, pp. 45–46. The statement was issued as United Nations Doc. A/AC.38/SC.1/L.1, 17 October 1950. Mimeographed.

For the general reader, it is hoped, the following brief summaries will not prove too tedious.

Sir Gladwyn Jebb first made a distinction between points of law and points of fact. Though the provisions of the Peace Treaty did not apply to the former Italian colonies, they might prove useful in solving the latter's problems by analogy. Italian property and property rights in Libya fell into three main categories:

1. State and parastatal property;
2. Rights arising out of local contractual engagements entered into between the metropolitan and provincial governments, for example, those relating to pensions; and
3. Private property, including rights arising out of concessions granted to individuals, some of which had lapsed.

The position regarding immovable property was extremley complex, as the Italian legislation in force at the time of the occupation of Libya by the Allied Armies recognized no fewer than nine different kinds of such property. Moreover, the Italian Government had acquired land by six different methods. Local customs, too, had to be respected.

To complicate matters, the municipal administration had broken down when the Italians left North Africa. The new municipalities set up there had not yet regained all the property belonging to their predecessors, some of which was still under custodial administration.

The situation with regard to parastatal property was even more complex, as it was difficult to reach agreement on the meaning of the term. Again, there were three categories, and every individual case would have to be decided on its merits.

While it was quite out of the question for Libya to meet even that part of the Italian debt which applied to its territory, agreement would have to be reached between the two Governments on Italy's contractual engagements.

Lastly, distinctions had to be made between the rights of persons or undertakings domiciled in Libya, and those of others; and between those whose property and activities were confined exclusively to Libya, and others.

The United Kingdom Government believed that the most practical way of dealing with all these highly technical problems would be for the United Nations to set up an ad hoc tribunal to deal with matters on the spot. This court should be provided with directives in the form of general principles, should base its conduct on the tenets of international law and recognized judicial procedure, and should draw what analogies it could from the legal provisions of the Treaty of Peace with Italy, to which, among other matters, the United Kingdom representative referred specifically.

In his reply, Count Vitetti challenged the validity of the premises on which the United Kingdom draft resolution rested. He denied that the problem of former Italian property in Libya could justly be solved by analogy—i.e. by invoking the provisions of the Peace Treaty relating to Italian property in territories other than the former territories—without rendering Annex XIV of the Treaty nugatory, and argued that the economic and financial obligations imposed upon Italy—for example, the transfer, without compensation, to Successor States of all Italian Government property—were in fact an exception to the general rules of international law.

Furthermore, in Count Vitetti's view, the question of Italian property was indissolubly bound up with that of sovereignty and all rights and claims attaching thereto in Africa, dealt with in Article 23 and Annex XI of the Treaty. (Wherever property had to be ceded under other articles, explicit provision was made therefor.)

The solution proposed in the United Kingdom draft resolution would be neither just nor legal; for the first time in history a State would be encumbered with an indefinite obligation—indefinite because there had been no prior consultation with the Italian Government on the subject. No legal authority in the world would consider so imprecise an imposed settlement to be good in international law. While he was sure that the United Kingdom delegation had never intended to introduce such an unsound principle into international law, that principle was nonetheless implicit in the draft resolution.

Hence the first issue to be decided was whether it was legitimate to impose on his country without its consent new and exceptional burdens.

THE DISCUSSIONS IN SUB-COMMITTEE 1

If anything could have convinced the *Ad Hoc* Committee that this was not a suitable subject for discussion in full Committee, it was this spate of legal argument. Hence the matter was referred to Sub-Committee 1, which comprised representatives of France and the United Kingdom, as Administering Powers; of Greece, which had proposed its establishment; and of Argentina, Belgium, Egypt, and Poland. The observer for the Italian Government, the United Nations Commissioner, and the Chairman of the Council for Libya were invited to take part in the Sub-Committee's work in an advisory capacity.

Before this decision was taken, however, the Iraqi representative asked whether the Libyan people had been sounded on the question of Italian property. In reply, the Commissioner explained that, although he represented the United Nations in Libya, he could not be regarded as representing the Libyan people before the United Nations. That was the duty of the Administering Powers. Nevertheless, the political leaders of that country had made it clear that they counted on him to keep a watchful eye on Libyan interests. In order to be the better able to do so, he had requested the four members of the Council for Libya representing the local population to cross the Atlantic to brief him on any matters—including the issues before the meeting—on which he might lack information or find it difficult to express a personal opinion.

As already indicated, the author has no intention of tracing in this work the tortuous course of the debates, which kept Sub-Committee 1 busy for twenty-eight arduous meetings, or to describe the train of events which it set in motion. Suffice it to say that not until the signature in Paris of an Italo-Libyan Agreement on 2 October 1956, five years after Libya had become independent, were these economic and financial issues finally settled.[34] In the last instance, the agreement was negotiated between the two Governments directly, without the assistance of the United Nations.

To deal with the subject in all its aspects would require an analytical survey of the nature and volume of the different forms of Italian property in Libya, as well as a detailed study of the legal, economic, social, and last but not least, political issues at stake both before and after independence; and an account would have to be given of the negotiations that led up to the exchange of Notes between the United Kingdom and Italian Governments of 28 June 1951 concerning the disposal of Italian private property in Cyrenaica and Tripolitania—never recognized by Libya [35]—and of the work of the United Nations tribunal.

It can be seen from Annex XII that the draft resolution submitted by the United Kingdom on 17 October 1950 consisted of two parts—the resolution proper and an annex. Further information about the United Kingdom's motives for making its proposal will be found in the accompanying statement (see p. 373, fn. 33), in particular in paragraphs 2, 3, 5, and 6.

The gist of the operative part of the draft resolution itself can be stated in the following terms:

1. The economic and financial provisions to be applied in Libya were defined in operative paragraphs 6 to 10 and in the annex (paragraph 1).
2. A United Nations Arbitral Tribunal of three members should be

34. See p. 391 and fn. 53.

35. *Exchange of Notes between the Government of the United Kingdom and the Italian Government concerning the Disposal of Italian Private Property in Cyrenaica and Tripolitania,* Treaty Series No. 62, Cmd. 8312 (London: His Majesty's Stationery Office, 28 June 1951).

appointed to decide by majority vote all questions relating to the application of these provisions, relying on the general principles of international law where the directives laid down by the General Assembly in the annex were inadequate (paragraphs 2 to 5).

3. The Administering Powers were to ask the Tribunal for directions about the disposal of former Italian property; such directions were to be given immediately where no reasonable doubt existed as to the action to be taken (paragraph 4).

4. The social insurance organizations operating in Libya should be the subject of special arrangements to be concluded between Libya and Italy direct (paragraph 6).

5. The Italian Government would continue to be liable for the payment of civil and military pensions (paragraph 7).

6. Libya would be exempt from payment of any part of the Italian public debt (paragraph 8).

7. Subject to certain conditions and exceptions, Italy should return to Libya as quickly as possible any ships in Italian possession that had been owned on 3 September 1943 by Libyan residents (paragraph 9).

8. If Libya granted compensation to its own nationals for war loss or damage, it should grant no less favorable treatment to United Nations nationals owning property or other rights in the country (paragraph 10).

The first two paragraphs of the annex dealt with the transfer to the Libyan State, without compensation, (a) of Italian state property, whether movable or immovable, and (b) of Italian state interests in any undertakings, public companies, and organizations within Libya, transfers in category (b) to be subject to certain limitations.

The third and final paragraph provided that concessions within the territory of Libya which had been granted to individuals by the Italian or former Libyan Governments would be confirmed if it could be shown that the concessionaire had carried out the terms of the concession in full.

As stated on page 351, during the summer of 1950 the Commissioner had been preparing himself for what awaited him in this field at the General Assembly. In particular, the Mission staff had studied the United Kingdom draft resolution with a view to getting it amended, if possible, in order the better to serve certain specific aims brought to the Commissioner's attention by Libyan leaders. He had also consulted the four Libyan members of his Council, the Amir, and the British Administration and Government. On the Libyan side, apart from understandable impatience to see all property questions settled promptly and an end made to the prevailing uncertainty about the country's economic future, he was confronted with a specific request that the British Administration should be asked to realize on the

Italian property in its custody and to apply the proceeds to the payment of war-damage claims. Needless to say, this request enjoyed the full support of the Amir and the Cyrenaican Government. Legally, this was a difficult case to argue, and no support for it was forthcoming either from the Administering Powers or from Italy, or, later on, from any delegation at the General Assembly. Realizing how bitterly disappointed the Libyan people, and especially the Cyrenaican Government, would be at this lack of interest, the Commissioner tried in vain to get them to link the issue instead with the problem of reconstruction and development and thereby strengthen Libya's future requests for financial assistance.

After protracted talks, he drafted a number of suggestions—as an adviser he was not allowed to submit formal amendments—relating to the United Kingdom proposals (for the full text of the suggestions, see Annex XII). Having discussed them with the United Nations Office of Legal Affairs, which had helped with their preparation, the Commissioner soon discovered that some of them were acceptable to the Foreign Office which, however, did not intend to revise its draft resolution. The United Kingdom Government's basic position was that it would not make the General Assembly Resolution more onerous than the Italian Peace Treaty itself. While this was a perfectly comprehensible—indeed honorable—attitude for a signatory to that Treaty, it was not one that could be shared by the Commissioner, whose duty it was to help the Libyan people, who were not party to the Treaty, to build up as strong a State as possible, not only politically but also economically and financially. Confident that in the long run the ill will and resentments of colonial days would die down sufficiently to make Libyans and minorities alike realize the importance of cooperating for their common good, he felt that he was acting in the spirit of Resolution 289 (IV) in insisting on provisions that would ensure fair protection of the economic and financial interests of both. Even if, at the time, such a forecast might have seemed unduly optimistic, it was obviously essential to make a start by setting the economic and financial relations between majority and minority on a sound base. To ensure that this end was achieved insofar as was humanly possible, he took good care to obtain the agreement with him of the three Libyan Council members. It was readily forthcoming.

The Commissioner's suggestions were largely intended to amplify the United Kingdom proposals in the light of the provisions of Annex XIV to the Treaty of Peace with Italy. A brief summary of them follows, to bring the ensuing discussions in the Sub-Committee into proper focus.

After stressing the importance of the problem for the Libyans, and the paralyzing effect, especially on agricultural development, of continued custodianship, the Commissioner framed his primary points as follows:

1. All state property or property interests to be transferred to Libya without compensation.
2. The private property of Italian nationals to remain in the hands of the present owners.
3. Parastatal property, including that in which the Fascist Party held an interest, to be assimilated to state property and treated as such, except for purely managerial interests.
4. The decisions of the Arbitral Tribunal to be binding on all the parties; the court to have special responsibility for establishing whether conveyances of real estate after the outbreak of war were or were not bona fide.

The changes in the draft resolution—apart from drafting emendations—suggested by the Commissioner related to the following points:

1. The principles enunciated in operative paragraph 2 to include those of common and municipal, as well as international, law.
2. A provision to be added to paragraph 4 binding the Libyan Government, should the Tribunal be functioning after independence, to provide it with information about all properties coming within its purview.
3. A new provision to be inserted as paragraph 6 making the Tribunal's decisions binding on all governments concerned both before and after independence.
4. The date specified in paragraph 10, relating to the return of Libyan ships, namely, 3 September 1943, the date of cessation of hostilities, to be brought forward to 10 June 1940, the day on which Italy came into the war. Moreover, since it would be impossible for anyone to acquire Libyan nationality until a Libyan State had been established, such return should apply to all owners resident in Libya at the time (October 1950), rather than to Libyan nationals alone.
5. A new provision to be added, based on paragraphs 9 and 13 of Annex XIV to the Peace Treaty, protecting the legitimate interests of the Italian minority in respect of lawfully acquired property rights and interests.
6. A new paragraph to be added requesting the Secretary-General of the United Nations to study the complex and far-reaching problems of compensation for war damage and to report thereon to the General Assembly at its Sixth Session.
7. Paragraph 1 of the Annex to provide also for the Administering Powers, pending independence, to receive on behalf of Libya, without compensation, former Italian state property. Furthermore, provision to be made for parastatal property belonging to certain specified Italian institutions to be transferred to Libya without payment. It should also be stipulated that all relevant Italian archives of an administrative or technical nature be handed over to Libya.

8. Lastly, a new provision should be inserted as paragraph 3 of the Annex, to the effect that, with certain specified exceptions, all transfers of property and related interests made after 10 June 1940 be deemed null and void.

The reader will find the Commissioner's observations on and explanations of his suggested changes in the full text of his statement in Annex XII (pp. 967–70).

The preliminary issue raised in the *Ad Hoc* Political Committee by the Italian observer came up again in Sub-Committee 1, where the United Kingdom and Italian spokesmen exchanged similar technical legal arguments. It was finally decided to continue the discussion on the substance, deferring for the time being a decision on the legal aspects of the problem. In fact, no such decision was ever taken, but the Sub-Committee did succeed, at the cost of much time and effort, in drafting a report and resolution on the substance acceptable to all its members, with the exception of the Polish representative, who had entered reservations in the course of the debate. Consequently, the draft resolution was adopted by 6 votes to 1.[36]

The observer from Italy, who had brilliantly defended his country's interests while making a constructive contribution to the common task, requested at the end of the Committee's twenty-eighth and final meeting that the following passage be included in the summary record:

> During the course of the discussion, the representative of Italy raised the question of the formal agreement of his Government concerning the text that the Sub-Committee was to draft and stated that his delegation maintained its reservation with regard to the necessity of the consent or the agreement of the Italian Government.[37]

36. "Financial and economic provisions relating to Libya: Report of Sub-Committee 1," GAOR: Fifth Session, 1950, Annexes, Agenda item 21 (A/AC.38/L.70, 11 December 1950), p. 49.

37. *Ad Hoc* Political Committee, Sub-Committee 1, Summary Records of 28th Meeting, 11 December 1950. Typescript. These summary records were drawn up by the Secretariat of the Sub-Committee for its own convenience and that of the members. Like the Sub-Committee's working papers, they have no official standing. Their status is similar to that of the Secretariat's notes of the meetings of Sub-Committee 17 of the First Committee the previous year. Moreover, certain written proposals exchanged across the table seem to be missing from the archives. It would therefore be a hazardous undertaking to try to reconstruct the process by which, article by article, General Assembly Resolution 388 (V), 15 December 1950, was given its final form. It would be simpler and more effective to compare the text as it emerged from the Sub-Committee (the Assembly adopted it unchanged, as we shall see) with the proposals submitted by the United Kingdom delegation and the Commissioner, which, together with the comments of the Italian observer, were gone over virtually

THE DISCUSSIONS ON THE REPORT OF SUB-COMMITTEE 1 IN THE AD HOC POLITICAL COMMITTEE AND IN THE GENERAL ASSEMBLY

The Sub-Committee having thus completed its work, its proposals were now subjected to the acid test of consideration by the *Ad Hoc* Political Committee and the plenary Assembly. In both these bodies, the discussion hinged not so much on substance or form as on the more fundamental issue of whether it was proper for the United Nations to decide matters of such vital importance to the Libyan people before there was a Libyan Government to speak for them in its own right. The pros and cons of the question had to be weighed all the more carefully, since, as drafted, the resolution encumbered the future government of Libya with certain important obligations. The Commissioner earnestly searched his conscience over the matter. On the one hand, the economic and financial provisions relating to Libya formed part of the arrangements for the final disposal of that territory pursuant to Article 23 of the Italian Peace Treaty; and under the terms of Annex XI to that Treaty, it was within the United Nations' power to recommend what those arrangements should be. Moreover, it was obviously in Libya's interest not to delay them. On the other hand, the draft resolution did not altogether meet Libyan hopes and wishes, particularly in the matter of war damage compensation; conversely, it took good care of certain minority interests. This kind of contrast might well hurt Libyan feelings. The Commissioner had never recommended that negotiations on the economic and financial provisions be postponed until after independence, but he had often asked himself whether he should not suggest that they be put off until a Provisional Libyan Government had been formed. However, such deferment would have raised problems of another kind: would a Libyan Provisional Government, while in the throes of independence, stand a fair chance of getting better terms than those being negotiated? Might it not fare worse? How would an improvised, ill-prepared Libyan delegation stand up to skillful and experienced Italian lawyers and diplomats, without the assistance and advice of qualified British and United Nations experts? Able experts were available; but what would their position be as advisers to a provisional government? Having carefully pondered all these considerations, the Commissioner reached the conclusion that it was in Libya's best interest to reach a settlement forthwith. If worst came to worst, an independent Libyan Government could always argue that, having been no party

---

word by word at least twice during the period of more than two months that the Sub-Committee devoted to their consideration.

to the adoption of the resolution, it was not bound by it.[38] It could even disown the suggestions and concessions made by the Commissioner—and for that matter by the United Kingdom—on the ground that they had not been put forward by a duly appointed representative of its own. Admittedly, such a *politique du pis-aller* might lead to a chaotic economic and financial situation. In point of fact, in the first few years after independence, the situation did develop rather along these lines; but in the final outcome, events showed that the Commissioner had underrated the ability of some ministers and senior officials in independent Libya to defend their interests.

When the Sub-Committee's report came up for discussion in the *Ad Hoc* Political Committee on 13 December, the USSR representative asked for time to study it. He was supported by his Polish colleague, who expounded upon his reasons for disapproving of the draft resolution. Both suggested that the debate be postponed, arguing that the General Assembly ought not to dispose of Libyan interests before a Libyan Government was even in existence. The Chairman pointed out that there was not much time for discussion. The report was dated 11 December; it had been distributed on 12 December; and it was due to come up for discussion in the Assembly on 15 December. It was accordingly decided to spend one more day discussing it in committee. The next day, S.K. Tsarapkin, the USSR representative, raised a few objections, to which the Argentinian representative, who had served as Chairman of Sub-Committee 1, replied. The Egyptian representative, who had consistently stood up for Libyan interests in the Sub-Committee, said that he "could not agree that the provisions of the draft resolution would be detrimental to the people of Libya, and he assured the Committee that, if his delegation had thought they would, it would never have supported the resolution.[39]

There being no time for a thorough debate, the discussion came to an end when a USSR proposal that consideration of the matter be deferred for twelve months, i.e. until the Sixth Session, was rejected by 26 votes to 5, with 9 abstentions.[40]

In the Assembly on 15 December Tsarapkin repeated, this time as a point of order, the proposal he had made in Committee. It was defeated by

38. During the discussions in Sub-Committee 1, the Commissioner entered a reservation to this effect with the object of protecting the position of the future Libyan Government.

39. GAOR: Fifth Session, 1950, *Ad Hoc* Political Committee, 82nd Meeting, 14 December 1950, p. 532.

40. Ibid., p. 533. For the full debate on the report of Sub-Committee 1, see GAOR: Fifth Session, 1950, *Ad Hoc* Political Committee, 81st and 82nd Meetings, 13–14 December 1950, pp. 519–34.

44 votes to 6, with 5 abstentions. The operative part of the draft resolution in Part A was then adopted by 47 votes to 5, with 2 abstentions. Part B, dealing with the administrative arrangements for the United Nations Tribunal, was adopted by 49 votes to 5, with 2 abstentions.

The figures were significant, since they showed that practically all the Arab and Latin American States had voted for the resolution, thereby demonstrating that, in their opinion, Sub-Committee 1 had succeeded in meeting the requirements of both the friends of Libya and those of Italy. But this was not to say that the procedure followed for arriving at decisions affecting vital economic and financial interests of a State before a representative government could make its views known was generally considered to be perfect. It left many delegations with mixed feelings: satisfaction at having more or less successfully coped with a difficult and complicated task, imposed on the General Assembly by the terms of the Peace Treaty; and an uncomfortable sense of having done so without Libya's participation in the negotiations as a full partner. The Commissioner shared these feelings, which found expression in two explanations of vote. First the Polish delegate criticized the procedure followed, for the reasons he had given in committee. He was followed by the Egyptian delegate, who praised the substance of the resolution, pointing out in particular that:

> Like all countries which have recently achieved independence, Libya will need foreign capital and labour for some time to come. The Italian nationals who remain there, if they adapt themselves to the new circumstances, can make a valuable contribution to the economic and social progress of the country.[41]

These were indeed words of wisdom, which still apply to many decolonized countries but are not always translated into practice.

If Resolution 388 (V) is compared with the two drafts submitted in Sub-Committee 1 (cf. p. 380, fn. 37), it will be seen that, appreciable differences notwithstanding, its underlying principles largely follow those laid down in the United Kingdom draft resolution. Certain features of the Commissioner's suggestions, such as that on the binding character of the Tribunal's decisions; some provisions designed to protect minority interests; and others relating to the transfer of Italian property, had been incorporated in more or less modified form; but on three important points he had failed to carry the day:

41. GAOR: Fifth Session, 1950, 326th Plenary Meeting, 15 December 1950, p. 686.

1. His proposal that the date of 10 June 1940 be substituted for that of 3 September 1943 for the return of Libyan ships in Italian possession had been set aside, to the detriment of members of the Maltese community in Libya in particular.
2. His proposal that the Secretary-General should study the problem of compensation for war damage had similarly been passed over in silence, presumably in order not to create the impression that the question had any connection with that of reparations, dealt with in Part VI of the Peace Treaty with Italy, or with the economic and financial provisions embodied in Resolution 388 (V). However, the Egyptian delegation incorporated the idea in another resolution dealing with technical and financial assistance to Libya, which was adopted by 40 votes to none, with 1 abstention.[42]
3. Lastly, his suggestion that, subject to certain exceptions, all transfers of property and related interests made after 10 June 1940 be deemed null and void, had also been ignored. For years after independence many Libyans, mainly former landowners, suffered from the failure to make such provision; moreover, in a number of cases, the omission made political refugees hesitate to return to their homeland.

THE UNITED NATIONS TRIBUNAL IN LIBYA

In pursuance of Article X of Resolution 388 A (V), the Secretary-General in due course appointed the following members of the United Nations Tribunal in Libya: Faiz Yöruköglu, President of the Chamber for Commercial Affairs of the Supreme Court of Turkey; Hugo J. L. Wickström, President of a Chamber of the Court of Appeal for Western Sweden and former President of the Mixed Court in Egypt; and Vincente Sánchez-Gavito, Director-General of Political Affairs and of the Diplomatic Service of the Ministry for Foreign Affairs of Mexico and former Legal Counselor of the Mexican Embassy in Washington. The Secretary-General also assigned to the Tribunal a Registrar and the necessary technical staff (Resolution 388 B (V), paragraph 2).

The three judges arrived in Libya in July 1951, and immediately began to draft the rules that would govern proceedings before the Court. The rules of procedure, on adoption by the Tribunal, were communicated to the governments concerned and published.[43]

42. General Assembly Resolution 388 (V), 15 December 1950. For text, see Annex I, pp. 894–99.
43. "Rules of Procedure of the United Nations Tribunal in Libya," United Nations Doc. A/AC.51/R.3, 1 September 1951. Mimeographed.

When the Commissioner, acting on this occasion as representative of the Secretary-General of the United Nations, presided over the inaugural ceremony of the Tribunal in Tripoli on 20 August 1951, he observed that the drafting of the substance of Resolution 388 (V) had been a thorny process. His remarks were summarized as follows:

> Not only was there no agreement between the authors of international law on the exact rules which should govern the economic and financial aspects of State succession resulting from the ceding of a territory, but the ways in which such problems had been solved in recent peace treaties had been very different.
>
> With regard more specifically to Libya, considerable difficulties arose also from the existence of a system of property laws drawn from such widely divergent sources as Koranic law, Ottoman law, Italian colonial law with its special institutions, and military occupation law.
>
> It was not for him to try to interpret resolution 388 (V). Broadly speaking, it decreed that the property of the Italian State in Libya should pass to the Libyan State. On the other hand, the rights of Italian private individuals were to be guaranteed. Within that framework, the resolution dealt with extremely important matters related to the main issue, such as the obligations of Italian social insurance organizations towards the inhabitants of Libya, the payment of civil and military pensions, the return of Libyan ships, Libya's exemption from the payment of any portion of the Italian public debt, and the conditions in which Italian nationals who wanted to leave Libya might dispose of their property. It laid down important principles with regard to the system of concessions and, in particular, those concessions granted through the *Ente per la Colonizzazione della Libia* and the *Istituto della Previdenza Sociale.* In several cases provision was made for special agreements between Italy and Libya to determine the way in which the principles enunciated by the General Assembly should be given effect. Finally, the United Nations Tribunal was set up to facilitate the implementation of the resolution. The Tribunal was empowered to give the parties concerned—that was to say the Italian Government and the Administering Powers, acting for Libya until they had transferred their powers in that respect to the Libyan Government and, thereafter, the Libyan Government itself—such instructions as might be required for the purpose of giving effect to the decisions of the General Assembly. The Tribunal might also be seized by any one of those authorities of any disputes which might arise between them concerning the interpretation of resolution 388 (V). In both cases, the decisions of the Tribunal were to be final and binding.

The United Nations Tribunal was an interstatal tribunal. It could consider disputes only on the request of Governments. Private individuals who wished their rights determined on the basis of the rules laid down by the General Assembly should, therefore, apply to their Governments. [Once] the Tribunal had been seized of the dispute, it would afford the Governments in question an opportunity to present their views in full. The resolution also authorized the Tribunal to request information and evidence from any authority or person whom it considered to be in a position to furnish it.[44]

From 1952 until 1956, successive Annual Reports of the Secretary-General contained a brief account of the Tribunal's activities.[45]

It appears from the report for 1951–52 that the first case submitted to the Tribunal was brought by the Government of Italy against the United Kingdom Government. By a memorial and a request for interim measures dated 22 December 1951, the former sought reinstatement in the administration of its alienable patrimony in Tripolitania and Cyrenaica; the buildings that it wished to use for its diplomatic and consular establishments in Libya; and the buildings that it wished to adapt to the educational needs of the Italian community in Libya. On 18 February 1952, the Tribunal decided that the Libyan Government was to be considered as a codefendant in the case, rejecting a contention lodged by the latter that it lacked jurisdiction, and likewise throwing out the Italian request for interim measures.[46]

On 5 February 1953 the Tribunal ruled on two questions of substance raised in the Italian Government's memorial. It rejected that Government's claim that the administration of the properties constituting its alienable patrimony in Tripolitania and Cyrenaica should be handed back to it. It further ruled that the Libyan Government should abstain from disposing

44. "Summary Record of the Ceremony of Installation," United Nations Doc. A/AC.51/R.4, 1 September 1951. Mimeographed.

45. Respectively:

1. *Annual Report of the Secretary-General on the Work of the Organization, 1 July 1951–30 June 1952,* GAOR: Seventh Session, 1952–53, Supplement No. 1 (A/2141).

2. Ibid., *1 July 1952–30 June 1953,* GAOR: Eighth Session, 1953–54, Supplement No. 1 (A/2404).

3. Ibid., *1 July 1953–30 June 1954,* GAOR: Ninth Session, 1954, Supplement No. 1 (A/2663).

4. Ibid., *1 July 1954–15 June 1955,* GAOR: Tenth Session, 1955, Supplement No. 1 (A/2911).

5. Ibid., *16 June 1955–15 June 1956,* GAOR: Eleventh Session, 1956–57, Supplement No. 1 (A/3137).

46. *Annual Report of the Secretary-General on the Work of the Organization, 1 July 1951–30 June 1952,* p. 163.

of any of the properties involved without obtaining either a prior release from the Italian Government or the Tribunal's authorization.

The Tribunal also rejected the Italian Government's claim for the immediate restitution of the administration of the buildings which it wished to use for its diplomatic and consular services in Libya.

As to the buildings which the Italian Government wished to use as educational establishments, the Tribunal found that the Italian Government had for some time been in possession of the properties in question, and ruled that it was entitled to administer them until the agreements called for by Resolution 388 A (V), Article I, paragraph 5, had been concluded.[47]

On 7 March 1953, the agent of the Italian Government submitted to the Tribunal a request for instructions regarding the institutions, societies, and associations referred to in Article 5 of the Agreement concluded on 28 June 1951 between the United Kingdom and Italian Governments concerning the disposal of Italian private property in Cyrenaica and Tripolitania (see p. 376, fn. 35), involving a total of twenty-three establishments.

On 21 June 1954 the Libyan Government filed its general rejoinder, accompanied by memoranda and documents relating to sixteen of the establishments listed in the Italian request. It asserted, moreover, that it did not consider it necessary to discuss the status of six of the remaining seven establishments, on the ground that they had no property in Libya that could be assigned. As to the seventh establishment, the Libyan Government confined itself to taking note of the Italian Government's recognition that the Libyan Government was entitled to 15 percent of its property.[48]

On 3 July 1954 the Tribunal, treating the Italian request as a dispute, in accordance with Article X, subparagraph 1 (b) of Resolution 388 A (V), ruled that the assignment of the property of three of the establishments to their liquidators was in conformity with Article I, subparagraph 3 (b) of that Resolution. In its opinion, the return of the property of three other establishments to their legal representatives, without prejudice to Article II of the resolution, was in accordance with the terms of that article and of Article I, subparagraph 3 (b), while the terms of the Anglo-Italian Agreement concerning six other establishments were also in accordance with the latter provision. With respect to the other eleven establishments at issue, the Tribunal directed the parties to enter further pleas and to submit additional supporting documents.[49]

47. *Annual Report of the Secretary-General on the Work of the Organization, 1 July 1952–30 June 1953,* pp. 147–48.

48. *Annual Report of the Secretary-General on the Work of the Organization, 1 July 1953–30 June 1954,* pp. 102–03.

49. *Annual Report of the Secretary-General on the Work of the Organization, 1 July 1954–15 June 1955,* p. 108.

On 27 June the Tribunal handed down its final decision on the thirteen remaining establishments. It rejected the plea of lack of competence again raised by the agent of the Libyan Government, and a cognate application, ruling with regard to the substance: that the return of the property of five establishments to their representatives was in conformity with the provisions of Article I, subparagraph 3 (b), of Resolution 388 A (V); that the return of the property of five other establishments to their representatives was not in conformity with those provisions; that the return of the land owned in common by the Italian Government and the *Società Agricola Coloniale della Stampa Emilio de Bono* to the *Società's* representatives was not in conformity with the provisions of Article I, subparagraph 3 (a); and that the release from sequestration of the property of two other establishments was not in conformity with the provisions of Article IX. The Tribunal also ruled that the Libyan Government was entitled again to place under sequestration the property of the establishments referred to under the second and fourth heads above and the land referred to under the third head.

The President of the Tribunal informed the Secretary-General, by a letter dated 5 July 1955, that with the delivery of the ruling cited above there were no cases before the Tribunal.[50]

When the Tribunal was set up in 1951, it was estimated that it would need some two or three years to complete its task. Hence it became necessary for the General Assembly to examine the question of the continuation of its functions at its Eighth Session (1953). The Libyan and Italian Governments considered that it should remain in being for a further period. The President of the Tribunal informed the Secretary-General that cases in hand would keep the Tribunal busy for most of 1954, and that such information as he had been able to obtain suggested that it would probably have to deal with further requests for instructions or interpretations of Resolution 388 (V). The Assembly accordingly decided by Resolution 792 (VIII), adopted on the recommendation of the Sixth Committee on 23 October 1953, that the Tribunal should continue in existence. The Assembly also noted that the Governments of Italy and Libya were negotiating the conclusion of the various agreements provided for in Resolution 288 (V).

After receipt by the Secretary-General of the letter addressed to him by the President of the Court on 5 July 1955, the General Assembly, at its Tenth Session, again reviewed the Tribunal's position in the light of com-

50. *Annual Report of the Secretary-General on the Work of the Organization, 16 June 1955–15 June 1956,* pp. 102–03. (There seems to be a discrepancy between the figure of eleven "other establishments" in the 1954–55 report, and that of thirteen such establishments in the 1955–56 report. It has not been possible to elucidate this mystery.)

munications received from the two Governments concerned. The relevant passage from the Secretary-General's report for 1955–56 reads:

> The position taken by the Italian Government in these communications was that the continued existence of the Tribunal was an indispensable safeguard for the future. The Italian Government also considered that the seat of the Tribunal should be removed to a country other than Italy or Libya. The Libyan Government's position was that the United Nations Tribunal had completed its mission to the extent that it had been possible for it to do so and that, in the circumstances, its continuation was no longer justified. The Libyan Government indicated however its willingness, should a legal dispute arise in the future, to submit such a dispute to arbitration by a duly qualified body.
>
> The respective positions of the Governments of Italy and Libya on the question of the continuation of the Tribunal were fully explained to the Sixth Committee by the representatives of these Governments who, with the approval of the Committee, took part in the discussion of the item. Several representatives of Member States welcomed the spirit of conciliation displayed by the Governments directly concerned during the Committee's proceedings, and expressed the opinion that a solution would be found which would be acceptable to those Governments and consistent with the interests of the United Nations in the matter.
>
> A draft resolution was presented by nine delegations, which was the expression of a full agreement reached by Italy and Libya as a result of direct negotiations. The draft resolution was approved unanimously, after tribute had been paid by the sponsors to the work performed by the United Nations Tribunal in Libya.
>
> The draft resolution, which was adopted on 6 December 1955 by the General Assembly (Resolution 988 (X)), provided, *inter alia,* for the termination of the United Nations Tribunal in Libya on 31 December 1955 and for a transfer on that date of its functions, powers and jurisdiction to an Italian-Libyan Mixed Arbitration Commission consisting of three members. One of these members was to be appointed by the Government of Italy, one by the Government of Libya and the third by the Secretary-General, upon joint designation of Italy and Libya or, in the absence of a joint designation, directly by him. The Commission was to come into existence upon the appointment of the umpire and at least one of its other members. Two of the members of the Commission constitute a quorum for the performance of the Commission's functions and for all the Commission's deliberations a favourable vote of two members is sufficient. The Commission will determine its rules of procedure, includ-

ing the designation of the place or places where its work is to be conducted. The expenses of the Commission are to be borne exclusively by Italy and Libya in equal shares.

In January 1956, the Secretary-General informed all Members of the Organisation of the appointment of the following members of the Italian-Libyan Mixed Arbitration Commission:

Mr. Giuseppe Belli, Attorney of the State, member appointed by the Government of Italy;

Mr. Mohieddine Fekini, Minister Plenipotentiary, legal adviser to the Ministry of Foreign Affairs, member appointed by the Government of Libya;

Mr. Georges Leuch, Chairman of the Appeal Authority for German Assets in Switzerland, former Federal Judge, umpire appointed by the Secretary-General upon joint designation by the Italian and Libyan Governments.[51]

The Mixed Commission never met. The truth of the matter is that while the Italian Government had based great hopes on Resolution 388 (V) and on the Tribunal established thereby, the Libyan Government had never liked either. Indeed, the two Governments had radically different ideas of how the issues outstanding between them should be settled. The Italian Government put its faith in the application of the rule of law. The Libyan Government preferred a political settlement reached through diplomatic negotiations. This was why, as early as 1951, the Provisional Libyan Government had refused to recognize the validity of the exchange of Notes of 28 June of that year between the United Kingdom and Italian Governments (p. 376, fn. 35); the Libyans even regarded the conclusion of this agreement as an unfriendly act.

After independence, during the years 1952–54, attempts to negotiate the various special agreements provided for in Resolution 388 (V) also failed, mainly because of Libyan reluctance to approach the issues from a legal point of view.[52] In the meantime, it had become clear that another grievance that the Libyans, and especially the Cyrenaicans, harbored against Resolu-

51. Ibid.

52. Had Libya had any experienced lawyers of its own, or had it been willing and able to pay the sometimes exorbitant fees demanded by foreign lawyers, things might have been different. This not being the case, a settlement out of court through diplomatic channels was the better course for Libya. During this period of juridical squabbling, the United Nations and its by then ex-Commissioner, generally regarded as the promoters of General Assembly Resolution 388 (V), 15 December 1960, though the United Kingdom had been at its origin, were not altogether popular in certain circles in Libya.

tion 388 A (V) was the absence of any provision under which they could have renewed their claims for compensation for war damage.

In 1955 the Italian Government, understanding the Libyan position and wishing to get its relations with its former colony onto a harmonious footing, agreed to resume negotiations, which by mutual consent were conducted through diplomatic channels. Resolution 388 (V) was quietly shelved. This, admittedly, must be seen as a failure of the legal machinery—though not of the basic principles—set up so laboriously by the General Assembly in 1950; and it must be recognized that the direct approach proved more successful in improving neighborly relations between Italy and Libya. Negotiations opened in October 1955 and were brought to an end on 2 October 1956, on which date Prime Minister Mustafa Bin Halim and Prime Minister Antonio Segni signed the resultant treaty on behalf of the two countries. The negotiations had been conducted by Ali Sakhli, at that time Director of the Royal Diwan, later Libyan Ambassador to Rome, for Libya, and by Ambassador Guglielmo Rulli for Italy. As they told the author many years later, each drove a hard bargain; but, recognizing in each other honest men intent on reaching a realistic agreement acceptable to both parties, they succeeded in hitting it off. Ali Sakhli had received from Bin Halim instructions that left him a large measure of freedom of action. Ambassador Rulli was instructed to forget the old legal arguments and to negotiate a straight political deal. Even the old sore of war damage was healed, with the Italian Government, while refusing to accept formal responsibility on that account, agreeing to pay £1,000,000 sterling and the equivalent of another £1,750,000 in lire as a contribution to the economic rehabilitation of Libya.

While the agreement was approved by the Libyan Parliament in closed session without much difficulty and ratified by the King on 30 March 1957,[53] its passage through the Italian Parliament was much rougher. There was a great deal of criticism, echoed in the press, to the effect that the Government had virtually abandoned all Italian claims in Libya. In reply, the Government argued that for the sake of future Italo-Arab relations it was much more important to live in friendship with Italy's closest Arab neighbor across the Mediterranean than to own a few buildings and some land there. This was a broad-minded and far-sighted attitude, which a majority in Parliament finally came to accept, thus silencing opposition from the Italian minority in Tripolitania.

53. The text of the Agreement was published in the Libyan *Official Gazette,* VIII, No. 5, on 25 March 1958. The Agreement does not appear to have been registered, recorded or filed with the Secretary-General of the United Nations, and so does not appear in the *United Nations Treaty Series.*

The signing of this treaty undoubtedly inaugurated a new era in the relationship between Italy and its former colony.[54]

PART 3.
INITIATION OF TECHNICAL ASSISTANCE FOR LIBYA

Whether in 1950 Libya was an overdeveloped country whose resources had already been exhausted, or whether it has always been underdeveloped, is an interesting bone of contention among historians, archaeologists, and economists. Quoting from classical authors, the advocates of the first theory point out that, as part of the Roman Empire, Tripolitania, or at least the central and western part of that territory, seems to have enjoyed an era of prosperity; it has even been described exaggeratedly as the granary of Rome.[55] Ruins of cities like Leptis Magna and Sabratha, as well as Oea (now the town of Tripoli), suggest, however, that there may have been some truth in these accounts. It is difficult to imagine that these cities can have existed without a hinterland, and indeed the remains of the Roman *limes* have been found, the ruins of what were apparently fortified farms. This line of defensive barrier appears to have started at the Mediterranean coast a little to the east of Leptis Magna and can be followed today as far as Ghudamis; in its time, it probably stretched further into Tunisia.

Herodotus mentions the existence of a people he calls the Macae, who apparently lived west of the Great Sirte:

54. For an account of these negotiations, see also Majid Khadduri, *Modern Libya: A Study in Political Development* (Baltimore: Johns Hopkins Press, 1963), pp. 275–77.

55. Gautier gives the following explanation of what he calls "un préjugé classique":

> L'Afrique *grenier de Rome,* nous avons tous ce cliché-là dans un coin de notre mémoire. Au début de l'occupation française on a fait grand usage de cette citation encourageante. Elle n'est pas fausse; il est très vrai que l'Afrique romaine a porté ce surnom. Mais voici quel était le sens exact, au dire des archéologues: La Rome des empereurs, celle qui assurait à la plèbe "le pain et le cirque," se procurait le pain par un impot en nature sur certaines provinces, *l'annone.* L'Afrique romaine était taxée annuellement d'une quantité de froment calculée pour nourrir la moitié de la plèbe romaine, soit environ 350,000 âmes. Pour un pays aussi étendu, une exportation équivalente aux besoins d'un tiers de million de consommateurs, c'est bien peu de chose, à l'échelle dont se servent les économistes. Et ainsi, que l'Afrique ait été le grenier de Rome, c'est littéralement exact, et, justement pour cela, ça ne signifie rien.

E. F. Gautier, *Le Passé de l'Afrique du Nord: Les Siècles Obscurs* (Paris: Payot, 1942), p. 14.

These people live beyond the Nasamones; but towards the sea-coast, westward, are the Macae. It is the custom of this people to leave a tuft of hair in the centre of the head, carefully shaving the rest. When they make war their only coverings are the skins of ostriches. The river Cinyps rises amongst these in a hill, said to be sacred to the Graces, whence it continues its course to the sea. This hill of the Graces is well covered with trees; whereas the rest of Africa, as I have before observed, is very barren of wood. The distance from the hill to the sea is two hundred stadia.[56]

As a *stadium* in Herodotus's work has been estimated by competent commentators at 99.75 metres, the distance between this forest and the sea cannot have been more than about 20 kilometers, which does not correspond to the distance between Jebel Nefusa and the Mediterranean. (Modern historians identify the River Cinyps with Wadi Chaam near Leptis Magna, a location which makes Herodotus's statement a great deal more significant.) The question therefore remains where this forest was actually situated.

Pliny, for his part, mentions that in his time elephants were plentiful around Ghudamis. On the other hand, Hannibal's elephants came, it appears, from the foot of the Atlas Mountains and the coast of Morocco, where Hanno claims to have seen them.[57] Herodotus seems to confirm this story of what he calls western Libya, now part of the Maghreb, when he says that west of the River Triton the country is full of wild animals and covered by forest.[58] The difficulty in all these accounts is to determine the exact geographical area to which the topics relate, as the name "Libya" was applied in ancient times to a much larger region than is the case today—sometimes even to the whole of Africa.

Other classical authors give similar accounts of the central part of Cyrenaica, and there can be no doubt that such cities as Cyrene, Barqah, and Apollonia, originally colonized by a Cretan people, knew greater prosperity in ancient times than they do today. The Great Sirte, on the contrary, which separates present-day Cyrenaica from Tripolitania, seems always to have been a desert. This distant period in Libya's history is, of course, well outside the scope of the present study. If the author has nonetheless devoted a

56. Herodotus, *History,* Book IV—Melpomene, CLXXV, translated by the Rev. William Beloe (London: Henry Colburn and Richard Bentley, 1830), Vol. II, p. 229.

57. Quoted by Gavin de Beer, *Alps and Elephants: Hannibal's March* (London: Geoffrey Bles, 1955), Appendix A, pp. 91–97, and references 90 and 93 on p. 116.

58. Herodotus, CXCI.

few words to it, he has done so because it is a subject that in his opinion merits thorough examination by scientists and technologists, if only in order to draw what lessons one can from certain techniques practiced by the Greeks and Romans, particularly in irrigation and cultivation. Such a study might also clarify the causes of later erosion and exhaustion of the soil, to the benefit of those living in places which seem to have been richer in the past than they are now. It would be of great interest if one could establish the size and standard of living of the population that once lived within the Roman *limes* of modern Tripolitania.

Economists and agronomists who study current conditions, while sharing the historian's and the archaeologist's interest in the remains of Roman irrigation works, are mostly indifferent to the argument about over- or underdevelopment. For them, modern Libya is an underdeveloped country, whatever it may have been earlier, and it was their opinion, and the results of the Mission's own observations, that the Commissioner echoed in Chapter VIII of his First Annual Report. Similar appreciations supported by facts and figures will also be found in the annual reports of the French and United Kingdom Governments to the General Assembly on the Administration of the territories for which they were each responsible.[59]

In the appraisal of Libya's general economic problems, included in his first annual report, the Commissioner said:

> Libya is an under-developed area with a marginal agricultural economy, basically handicapped by inadequate rainfall and poor soil. Subsoil mineral resources have not been found in commercially exploitable quantity. Great areas of the country are completely desert, but in the coastal regions, and in the oases, irrigation, dry-farming and animal husbandry offer the possibility of a viable agricultural economy. There are off-shore fishing possibilities, particularly in tuna and sponge-fishing, which might be developed further. However, the indigenous population is untrained in the proper utilization of land and the conservation of water, and lacks the material resources and technical knowledge to tap underground water except by simple surface wells. It is believed that the country could grow the crops and flocks needed for its subsistence and for a small export trade by careful dry-farming and by greater and more efficient drawing of water for irrigation. Up to the present, however, the crop surplus for export has been small and irregular, limited not only by

59. See, respectively, first *Annual Report of the United Nations Commissioner in Libya;* "Annual report of the French Government to the General Assembly concerning the administration of the Fezzan"; and "Annual report of the Government of the United Kingdom to the General Assembly concerning the administration of Cyrenaica and Tripolitania."

the lack of human skill and capital resources, but also by recurrent severe droughts. Libyan agricultural products which might be exported are generally of inferior quality and high cost; this is due not only to poor methods of agriculture, but also to a lack of marketing skill and facilities.

. . . Under Italian rule, Libya received from Italy very substantial subsidies and assistance, with small regard to the possibilities of repayment from the resources of the country. Under the fascist administration, the interests of the indigenous inhabitants did not receive the same consideration as did those of the Italian community, with the result that the technical and financial assistance received by the former was less favourable than that granted to the Italian agricultural economy. This explains why today the Arab population of Libya stands in need of as much financial and technical assistance as the United Nations can supply. The various forms of subsidies and exemptions granted to the Italian community brought temporary prosperity to the country. The substantial capital investment, the material improvement and development and the technical skill of the Italian settlers remain as assets for the future of the country.

. . . The cessation of the subsidies, followed by the exhaustion and destruction of war, have brought into sharper focus the substantial adverse trading and fiscal balance of Libya. Because of the deficit, the Administering Powers have had to make substantial grants to the country to maintain its services and economic life, even on a modest scale, with limited rehabilitation and development work. The present Administrations have informed the Commissioner that their combined average annual grants-in-aid in recent years have exceeded 4,750,000 dollars, exclusive of occupation costs. Although the Commissioner is awaiting expert assistance to have these figures properly analysed, it is obvious that the country requires very substantial outside assistance to maintain even its present standards, and yet more for development in the economic and social fields.

A further serious hindrance to the economic life of Libya arises from the almost complete lack of credit and banking facilities following the closure of the Italian banks in 1943 upon the defeat of the Italian forces.[60]

60. First *Annual Report of the United Nations Commissioner in Libya,* paras. 180–83. When the Commissioner wrote this report, indications of the possible occurrence of subsoil mineral resources, in particular of oil, were still so vague that a more optimistic opinion would have been unjustified. Under Italian rule, first indications of the existence of hydrocarbons in the Libyan subsoil date from 1928; they

After having referred to the serious economic problems created by the uncertain status of the considerable amount of property which the Administering Powers continued to treat as former enemy property, particularly Italian state and parastatal property,[61] the Commissioner presented an appraisal of educational conditions:

> During the fascist period, the Libyan people were afforded only limited educational opportunities. A few thousands attended primary schools annually but only a handful received secondary education. Political and financial considerations strictly limited study abroad for the Libyans. A considerable proportion of the curriculum was devoted to the study of the Italian language, which was also used as the language of instruction for many of the classes.
>
> . . . All schools were closed in 1942, with the result that the Administering Powers were faced with the problem of re-establishing public education. They were, however, severely handicapped, even after the cessation of hostilities outside Libya, by a lack of funds and trained teachers.
>
> . . . Primary schools for Arabs were gradually opened in the three territories. At present, the total number of students has risen to about 39,000, not including those in Koranic schools. Approximately 26,000 students are from the Arab population, about a threefold increase since the Italian occupation. Only a few more than 400 Arab students are in secondary schools in Cyrenaica and Tripolitania.
>
> . . . The first post-war secondary school for Arabs in Tripolitania was opened in 1946, and in Cyrenaica in 1948. There are no facilities for higher education in Libya. The existing schools are severely handicapped by lack of equipment and adequately trained teachers although, particularly in Cyrenaica, a number of teachers have been brought in from abroad.
>
> . . . The school population and the standard of education are both inadequate. The former is far below the average in a normal State which may be taken as 20 per cent of the population. To raise it to this level, educational facilities would be needed for somewhat more than 200,000

---

were encountered while drilling for water in the neighborhood of Zliten, in eastern Tripolitania. In 1933–34, while again drilling for water in the same neighborhood, drops of oil were found, though not enough to justify drilling on a commercial scale. For further details, see the article cited in Chapter 1, p. 60, fn. 38. Oil in commercial quantities was found only in 1958, when improved drilling techniques had enabled considerably greater depths to be reached. Large-scale drilling started in 1959.

61. Ibid., paras. 184–85.

> persons. Even if it were assumed that the proportion of the school-age population attending school would be relatively low among the nomadic and semi-nomadic group, the number of students for whom education would have to be provided would considerably exceed 100,000. It must also be borne in mind that the long period without educational facilities has produced a large number of students whose education had been arrested and requires completion.
>
> The Arab population feels keenly the need of education but the present financial resources and the trained teachers of the country are too few to meet it.[62]

Another problem that the Commissioner found most pressing, but to which the Administering Powers had already been paying a good deal of attention insofar as the means at their disposal allowed, was the training of personnel for administrative posts ranging from the clerical to the executive. Without a training program, the policies practiced by both the United Kingdom and French Administrations of Libyanizing the administrative services were bound to remain fruitless. Faced with these needs, the Commissioner, as he reported to the General Assembly,[63] began at an early date to explore tentatively the possibilities of procuring aid through the United Nations and the specialized agencies, particularly under the Technical Assistance Programme which, in its expanded form, had been initiated in 1949 but was not yet in full swing. He soon discovered that there would be few practical ways of aiding Libya until more detailed studies had been made and funds had become available under the United Nations Expanded Programme of Technical Assistance (EPTA). In the meantime, the Secretary-General and the Executive Heads of the specialized agencies, including the Food and Agriculture Organization of the United Nations (FAO), the International Bank for Reconstruction and Development (IBRD), the International Monetary Fund (IMF), the United Nations Educational, Scientific and Cultural Organization (UNESCO), and the International Labour Organisation (ILO), recognizing the special urgency of Libyan needs, assured the Commissioner that they would provide whatever assistance they could.

As related in Part 2 of Chapter 3 (p. 215 ff.), in April, as soon as the

62. Ibid., paras. 186–91. On the subject of education there was a profound difference of opinion between the Italian member of the Council for Libya, on the one hand, and his colleagues from Cyrenaica and Tripolitania, on the other. See again, ibid., fn. 66 to para. 186, and "Memorandum on educational organisation in Libya under Italian administration, submitted by the representative of Italy on the Council for Libya," ibid., Annex XXVII, pp. 84–110.

63. Ibid., paras. 192–201.

Council for Libya had met, the Commissioner had submitted a request for advice regarding the scope of his work. Should he and his staff devote a major part of their activities, making use of the facilities and resources of the United Nations and the specialized agencies, to thorough studies relating to the establishment of administrative services in the future Libyan State and to its economic and social development? Should they make recommendations in this sense to the Administering Powers and to the Libyan people? Or should they limit themselves to giving aid and advice on the drafting of a constitution, on which Resolution 289 (IV) laid so much stress? The Mission staff was from the first in favor of the broader concept, believing that qualified experts from the United Nations family should study Libya's needs and draw up plans for meeting them. To avoid duplication of effort and waste of time, they would make as much use as possible of the planning already carried out by the Administering Powers and of the prewar work of the Italian Government. Many of these studies would naturally need to be adapted to the new circumstances. Some were out of date. Others had had as their object the attraction of capital for investment purposes, an aim that was beyond EPTA's scope and resources. Hence the question at once arose: would Governments or private capital be willing to invest in Libyan ventures or lend money to the future Libyan Government? As to the studies undertaken by the Administering Powers, none had been made on an all-Libyan basis; for obvious reasons they related only to each individual territory or parts thereof. Therefore, although they were still very useful, most of them had to be revised to bring them into line with the wider concept of a united Libya.

It was also clear from the outset that mere studies and plans would not be enough. They would simply provide the necessary basis for requests for international technical assistance or for the elaboration of projects for the execution of which loans might in time be forthcoming from IBRD or the private capital market.

The Commissioner's request for advice on these important problems gave rise to much discussion, not only in the Council of Libya but also in the course of the Mission's daily contacts with Libyan leaders and with representatives of the Administering Powers. Opinions differed greatly; moreover, there was a good deal of misunderstanding of the purposes, techniques, and limitations of technical assistance itself. As a result, the Commissioner came to the conclusion that, before specific requests could be made for such assistance, it was essential that a comprehensive inventory be taken of Libya's immediate and long-term needs, correlated with the probable economic, financial, and personnel potential of the future state.

When he tried to put these ideas into practice, the Commissioner ran into difficulties of a procedural nature. Under EPTA's rules, only governments were entitled to submit requests for technical assistance. Neither the Secretary-General, nor the Executive Heads of the specialized agencies, nor the Commissioner himself could do so. Hence Libya would only be able to submit its requests when a duly constituted Libyan Government had taken office after independence, and even then only when the country had been admitted to membership of the United Nations or the specialized agencies concerned.

But the country's needs could not possibly go unattended until 1952. Hence, two problems called for prompt solution: first, how could technical assistance be obtained without delay? And, second, how could the continuance of technical assistance be ensured during the period between Libya's acquisition of independence and its admission to the United Nations family?

To get out of the impasse, the Commissioner suggested to the Governments of France and the United Kingdom in March and April 1950 that they ask the Secretary-General—in their capacity of Administering Powers responsible for, among other matters, the foreign relations of the three territories—to make available, under the regular United Nations technical assistance program, the services of an expert to make a start on the initial planning; the same expert would subsequently act as coordinator of a comprehensive technical assistance program for Libya. At first, the two Governments did not respond to this appeal, but in June the United Kingdom informed the Commissioner that it wished to put in an application for a comprehensive survey of the economy of Cyrenaica and Tripolitania. This change in British policy was most welcome—all the more so in that initially the local administrations in Tripoli and Benghazi, as well as the responsible departments in London, had shown a hesitancy bordering on unwillingness to cooperate in this field. Lack of familiarity with the newly conceived institution of international technical assistance, an ingrained habit of thinking only in terms of on-the-spot administration, and the embers of antagonism to the idea of a unified Libyan State, seem to have been behind this attitude. Fortunately, the change in the British approach promoted a similar change of policy in Paris.

In the meantime, in May 1950, before this reversal had come about, the Secretary-General, at the request of the Commissioner acting under paragraph 9 of Resolution 289 (IV), had made funds available for the immediate recruitment to the Commissioner's staff of a few technical advisers, including experts in agriculture, currency, banking, administrative and budgetary organization, and problems of land tenure (p. 415). At the same time, he agreed to send to Libya a small reconnaissance unit to make a preliminary survey and formulate recommendations on the planning of studies for a comprehensive technical assistance program. This team visited Libya in July. It was made up of Carter Goodrich, who at the time was in the Department of Economics at Columbia University, assisted by two members of the United Nations Secretariat: William Dean, Chief of the Africa Unit of the Division of Economic Stability and Development at Headquarters, and W. A. Kooy of the Social Activities Division at Geneva. Its terms of reference, given to it by A. D. K. Owen, then Assistant Secretary-General in charge of Economic Affairs, later Executive Chairman of the Technical Assistance Board (TAB), and presently Co-Administrator of the United Nations Development Programme, were: [64] to examine as closely as possible the problems confronting the Commissioner in the economic and social fields and consider with him the possibilities of providing technical assistance under EPTA, having in mind the long-term needs of the country, the Commissioner's responsibilities under Resolution 289 (IV), and the purposes of EPTA as laid down in Resolution 222 A (IX) of the Economic and Social Council (ECOSOC).[65]

Goodrich, as leader of the team, was also instructed to visit, before proceeding to Libya, the Governments directly interested, including the Italian Government, as well as the Executive Heads of the specialized agencies already approached by the Commissioner and IBRD and IMF.

The Goodrich mission stayed in Libya for three weeks. It saw a great number of leading Libyans and, thanks to the United Nations aircraft, traveled widely yet speedily through the country, visiting a number of social, medical, and educational institutions. It also had far-reaching consultations

64. The Technical Assistance Board (TAB), set up under operative paragraph 3 of ECOSOC Resolution 222 A (IX), 15 August 1949, consisted formally of the Secretary-General, as Chief Administrative Officer of the United Nations, and the executive heads of the specialized agencies taking part in EPTA. Later it became a body attended by the deputy executive heads, responsible for technical assistance matters, of the specialized agencies and was presided over by an Executive Chairman, A. D. K. Owen, assisted by a small headquarters staff. Its principal function was to coordinate the activities of the members of the United Nations family in the technical assistance field with a view to preventing overlapping or duplication of effort and to ensure efficient exchange of information between them on all aspects of technical assistance operations. Government contributions to EPTA were paid into a central account of TAB from which the funds for approved agency programs were drawn. With the merger, in 1965–66, of EPTA and the United Nations Special Fund to form the United Nations Development Programme, the concept of technical assistance was, of course, broadened even more. The field offices are headed by Resident Representatives.

65. For full text of ECOSOC Resolution 222 A (IX), 15 August 1949, and Annexes I and II thereto, see ESCOR: Ninth Session, 1949, Supplement No. 1 (E/1553), pp. 4–14.

with representatives of the British and French Administrations as well as with members of the Council for Libya. The report [66] drawn up by the team was subsequently submitted to and accepted by TAB in September 1950, and from then on served as the basic inventory for the future planning of technical assistance to Libya. The substance of its recommendations is dealt with in detail in Chapter 9 of this study.

In the request for the comprehensive survey, which it formally submitted on 13 June, the United Kingdom Government had suggested that:

> a team of experts should survey the economic situation of [Cyrenaica and Tripolitania] and produce a long-term development plan covering the next twenty or thirty years, with recommendations for its implementation by stages. The phases should be based on plans of capital investment so designed as to ensure the minimum initial capital investment required for the progressive financing of succeeding stages from accruing national wealth. Therefore, studies would be required of the approximate cost of recommendations, of the economic and social activities of the inhabitants and of the nature and character of the soil and climate. Studies suggested in the economic field included agriculture, horticulture, irrigation, animal husbandry, soil conservation, forestry, secondary processing industries and the possibilities of low-cost power for agriculture and industry.[67]

The Commissioner suggested to the French Government that it associate itself with the United Kingdom request, as far as the Fezzan was concerned, and was given an assurance that it intended to do so immediately.

In due course, both Governments also applied under the regular technical assistance program for public administration fellowships for a number of Libyans in their employ.

Earlier, the Commissioner had approached UNESCO, which had sent a representative to Libya with whose assistance a draft program for education and training in public administration for the development of a Libyan civil service had been drawn up. A little later, the United Kingdom Government asked UNESCO for assistance in expanding an existing clerical and training program in Tripolitania to enable instruction to be given to 250 trainees simultaneously from October 1950; the request was approved by TAB in the middle of August. UNESCO undertook to recruit a principal and twelve teachers. The major part of the cost of running the school was borne by

66. "Report of the Preparatory Mission on Technical Assistance to Libya," United Nations Doc. TAB/R.57 and Adds.1–4, 24 April 1950. Mimeographed. The report was also circulated as United Nations Doc. A/AC.32/TA.1, October 1950, in the Council for Libya's technical assistance series.

67. First *Annual Report of the United Nations Commissioner in Libya,* para. 204.

the United Kingdom. Again the Commissioner suggested that the French Government take part, to enable students from the Fezzan to attend the courses; but he was told that there were as yet no Fezzanese with sufficient education to profit from them. Knowing the educational position in the territory, the Commissioner was prepared to believe that this was true of the Fezzan proper; but he understood that there were several Fezzanese students in Tunis and Algiers who might have qualified. Why they were not recommended was not clear, unless a sense of competition was involved.

The United Kingdom Government also sought fellowships and scholarships from the United Nations, UNESCO, and FAO for the training abroad of twenty-nine qualified Libyans working in the British Administration, to meet specific needs in the process of Libyanization in Tripolitania and Cyrenaica. Funds being available, the fellowships were granted at once; and on this occasion the French Government joined in, ten fellowships for Fezzanese being awarded by UNESCO to train teachers.

Another sector in which technical assistance was badly needed was public health. At the Commissioner's request, a consultant from the World Health Organization (WHO) visited the three territories in June 1950, to make a preliminary inquiry, the results of which were summed up as follows:

> This preliminary inquiry showed that the chief prerequisite in the Libyan public health field is education. There are no indigenous Libyan doctors and only a few qualified medical assistants. The present educational facilities in Libya are inadequate to prepare students for advanced medical studies. Two Libyans are now studying medicine abroad. A few Libyans are qualified for training as auxiliary medical personnel.
>
> . . . The medical services are assured by a staff of approximately eighty Italian doctors, 60 per cent of whom are members of the Italian Colonial Service, under the supervision of medical officers of the British Administration. The latter pays their salaries plus an adjustment to meet the increased cost of living and this income is supplemented by private practice. The Administration collects contributions at the rate prescribed by the Italian law which was in force at the time of occupation, and these sums are held in suspense to meet their pension and life assurance rights, which rights are preserved by the Italian Government. There is an understandable uncertainty among them about their future. Medical services in the Fezzan are furnished by three French doctors, also in government service. There are eighteen British and foreign doctors in Cyrenaica, and this number will shortly be increased to twenty.
>
> . . . The most serious and immediate task in the field of public health is to make arrangements that will maintain even the existing level of

> services after the independence of Libya. The preliminary survey indicates that there is no possibility of finding qualified replacements for the existing medical staff in the immediate future. The problem will be to retain as much of the existing staff and facilities as can be afforded and to build upon them. There appears to be no source of official international funds for providing supplies or staff. The possibility of aid from private institutions has yet to be explored.[68]

In the light of this inquiry, the Commissioner requested WHO to explore further the possibilities of fellowships for medical assistants (if properly qualified candidates could be found), of securing expert advice on the establishment of health administration (including financing, sanitary codes and related matters, the institution of a system of collecting vital statistics, and a program for maternal and child health care), and of obtaining instructional material for medical assistants and books and periodicals for medical libraries.

So much for the first problem facing the Commissioner. There remained the second, longer-term one. At the time, it was reckoned that Libya would be admitted to the United Nations or to one or more of the specialized agencies in a matter of months after independence; in the event, it was a matter of years.[69]

An item on the consideration of the economic and social problems of the former Italian colonies having been placed on the agenda of ECOSOC's Eleventh Session, in pursuance of General Assembly Resolution 266 (III) (see page 369, fn. 25), the Commissioner, invoking paragraph 9 of Resolution 289 (IV), addressed a communication to that Council, accompanied by a draft resolution intended to promote the solution of these problems. In his memorandum the Commissioner stated:

> The needs of Libya are incontestable. The Libyans lack experience in administering their public affairs. There is a great shortage of trained personnel for such responsibilities. The country is clearly an underdeveloped one suffering from a chronically deficit economy, lacking in subsoil natural resources, while its agriculture is handicapped by inadequate rainfall. Great areas of the country are desert but in the coastal

68. Ibid., paras. 211–13.

69. Libya was admitted to membership in the United Nations, together with fifteen other States, on the recommendation of the Security Council, on 14 December 1955. See General Assembly Resolution 995 (X), 14 December 1955. The sixteen recommendations were put to the vote, by roll call, separately. The recommendation relating to Libya was adopted by 56 votes to none, with 1 abstention (Israel); see in this connection Chapter 11 and Annex XIII.

> regions and oases irrigation, dry farming and animal husbandry offer possibilities for establishment of a viable agricultural economy. However, the Libyans lack both the technical knowledge and material resources to exploit the possibilities of their country. I strongly urge that these gaps should be bridged through the resources of the United Nations, its specialized agencies and Member States, first, through technical assistance and later through financial assistance.[70]

In an oral statement introducing his proposals, the Commissioner first stressed heavily the special responsibility the United Nations bore for assisting the Libyan people not only in drafting a constitution, but also in establishing sound administrative services and practices suited to the needs and resources of the country, and in developing a healthy economy to make the new State viable. He accordingly strongly urged that Member States of the United Nations and the specialized agencies, as well as those organizations themselves, should help Libya first by providing technical assistance, later by making financial assistance available. Since, for lack of time and expert advice, he was not yet in a position to submit specific proposals, he suggested that, in the light of the studies then being carried out, ECOSOC should recommend to the General Assembly, to Member States, and to the Secretary-General that special consideration be given to Libya's needs when the Administering Powers submitted requests for technical assistance. He also reminded the Council that it would be fatal if technical assistance were to be cut off the moment Libya became independent. Special provision would have to be made for an orderly continuing program from then until such time as Libya was admitted to membership of the United Nations and the specialized agencies and so became entitled to submit requests on its own account.

The response to the Commissioner's appeal was as prompt as it was generous. The same day, ECOSOC passed a resolution recognizing that Libya stood in great need of assistance to develop its economy and to set up an efficient public administration. It drew the attention of the Secretary-General and the Executive Heads of the Specialized Agencies participating in EPTA, and that of TAB, to the special need for prompt action, and requested the Secretary-General to present to the General Assembly at its Fifth Session specific proposals for a procedure that would enable Libya to

70. United Nations Doc. E/1758/Rev.1, 12 Aug. 1950. Mimeographed. The memorandum was submitted according to the normal United Nations procedure as "Note by the Secretary-General transmitting a communication from the United Nations Commissioner in Libya and a suggested draft resolution," under item 2 of ECOSOC's agenda. See General Assembly Resolution 266 (III), 17 May 1949.

continue to receive technical assistance in the interim between independence and admission to membership of the relevant international organizations.[71]

While technical assistance on the international plane thus began to take shape, difficulties arose locally. The Libyans had seen Italian experts come and go in large numbers, followed by British and French experts. They therefore felt that technical surveys had been overdone, and that so far they had not seen much practical benefit from them. This attitude was not altogether fair, either to the Italians or to the British and French, but it was understandable enough in a people that for a generation had been largely exploited for the benefit of a colonial Power, only to come later under the caretaker regime of the Administering Powers. Since the Commissioner was convinced that the success of a technical assistance program would to a large extent depend on the enthusiastic collaboration of those who were to profit by it, he arranged for the Libyan members of the Council and a number of leading Libyans and local Italians to meet the Goodrich mission at his residence soon after it arrived.

The discussion that followed was lively and frank, removing a good deal of misunderstanding on the Libyan side while being instructive for the mission. It showed that on the fundamental issue both sides were in agreement to a surprising degree; but it also revealed a wide diversity of appreciation of the methods of implementation. Mustafa Mizran, the Council member for Tripolitania, suggested the following list of topics to be surveyed: agriculture, irrigation, animal husbandry, trade, health, education, administrative training, monetary questions, and budgetary matters; but there was complete disagreement about the priority that should be assigned to each item. Hence, the next morning the Commissioner sent a letter to all those who had attended the meeting, enclosing Mizran's list, and asking each for his comments and his views on their relative importance.

One of the first came from Hajj Ahmed Sofu, the Fezzanese member, who, having always maintained that ignorance and poverty were the main scourges of Libya, gave top priority to education. His preference was for industrial schools and colleges for training teachers, a combination particularly suited to conditions in the Fezzan. He naturally wanted the mission to devote attention to other matters too, particularly in the field of natural

71. For full text of ECOSOC Resolution 322 (XI), 15 August 1950, see ESCOR: Eleventh Session, 1950, Supplement No. 1 (E/1849), p. 61. For an account of the discussion in ECOSOC, see ESCOR: Eleventh Session, 1950, 413th Meeting, 15 August 1950, pp. 339–43. See also first *Annual Report of the United Nations Commissioner in Libya,* paras. 216–22; and "Memorandum from the Commissioner to the Council for Libya on Recent Developments regarding Technical Assistance to Libya," United Nations Doc. A/AC.32/COUNCIL/R.94, 26 August 1950. Mimeographed.

resources, where he clearly hoped for discoveries similar to those made in the Arabian peninsula, especially the presence of oil. But his primary concern continued to be education.

Mukhtar al-Muntasir, writing on behalf of the Independence Party, gave first priority to irrigation, followed by agricultural credits and health services. Education came fourth, animal husbandry fifth, and trade sixth. Administrative training was not mentioned, nor were monetary or budgetary matters, or, for that matter, any topics regarding which Libyans were wary of foreign intervention.

The Fronte Economico della Libia favored the following order: agriculture, irrigation, animal husbandry, trade and commerce.

The Associazione degle Agricoltori della Tripolitania, a mixed Arab-Italian organization, put agriculture first, irrigation second, and animal husbandry third; apparently it was not much interested in the other items on the list. Among its general observations figured a paragraph arguing that technical assistance could be kept to a minimum, both in duration and in amount, since Tripolitania already possessed technical legislation and experience, the result of careful study in the past. Most of the money that would otherwise be spent on technical assistance could therefore, in its view, take the form of direct financial assistance.

This opinion was in fact widely held in Libya, and it was a long time before people learned that technical assistance must precede financial assistance if the latter was to be forthcoming and bear fruit.

The Camera di Commercio expressed more balanced views. It recognized that there were certain basic problems that required preliminary study, particularly in those cases where financial assistance would be required. It also touched on a number of matters, such as taxation, that were in the hands of the Administering Powers, and claimed that there was no lack of technically able men in Libya in the agricultural, industrial, commercial, and financial fields. This was a view particularly prevalent among the Italian section of the population. With regard to the list, the Chamber of Commerce proposed the following order of priority: taxation, animal husbandry, credit and freedom of exchange within and outside the sterling area.

It will be seen from the foregoing that both Arab and Italian circles in Tripolitania were, if not sceptical, at least critical, about the Commissioner's plans for the country's future economic and social development. The basis on which this critical attitude rested can best be described as a universal desire for cash and credit rather than advice. This was not surprising, especially among the Arab population, which, having lived for a generation side by side with the wealthier Italians, craved capital to improve its own standard of living. Moreover, the Italians themselves, and the few Libyans who were familiar with their economic policy as practiced in Libya, still had nostalgic memories of the good old days of official or semiofficial subsidies. The average Italian farmer or small tradesman is particularly hard-working, and those who emigrated to Libya were no exception to the rule, but a long-standing policy of economic featherbedding had blunted their appreciation of the difference between subsidy and investment. But most people were prepared to wait and see what happened. Another thing that emerged from the meeting and the subsequent consultations was that almost all concerned viewed Libya's future from the Tripolitanian angle. Hardly anybody had as yet acquired an all-Libyan outlook in the economic field.

When these questions were considered in the Council, the discussion was, as usual, very frank. In accordance with his normal procedure, the Commissioner had submitted at the end of June a memorandum on the implementation of the Council's advice concerning the scope of his work in respect of studies on the establishment of administrative services in Libya and on the country's economic and social development.[72]

In July, the Pakistani member asked for additional information. The debate opened with a long statement by Selim Bey, who viewed the memorandum with mixed feelings.[73] He liked it because the principles on which the plans were based were sound; he disliked it because their details left much to be desired. He went on to criticize the plans on various grounds. The approach to the problem had been conditioned by a series of requests based on the Commissioner's personal conception of his mission, and on his desire to have comprehensive surveys made of everything Libyan. Some of the items admittedly deserved study, for they were necessary, even urgent. But such an elaborate program as that proposed was hardly essential to help penniless Libya. The outcome of all the requests would be brief visits by experts, who would not be in a position to give authoritative opinions. Selim Bey also attacked the Commissioner for having sought technical assistance instead of financial help. The former was of no use, he felt. What Libya needed was funds to help the country to recover from the ravages of war and the Italian occupation. So far, too, the Commissioner, despite his many requests, had received nothing but empty promises. No funds were available for Libya under the United Nations technical assistance programs. The Commissioner had even admitted that without proper expert advice it

72. For details of the memorandum and the terms of the advice, see first *Annual Report of the United Nations Commissioner in Libya,* Annexes IV, p. 44, and XXIII, p. 80.

73. Council for Libya, Summary Records of 27th Meeting, United Nations Doc. A/AC.32/COUNCIL/SR.27, 12 July 1950, pp. 2–8. Mimeographed.

would be impossible for him to submit specific proposals in the short time at his disposal. Selim Bey thought this a gloomy and uninspiring picture, which was why he did not like the memorandum. What Libya really needed was not flying visits by experts, who merely produced reports, but a few technicians and advisers who would stay in the country to work with the Administering Powers, and later with the government of the new State. Thereafter, the country would need funds to finance a number of vital projects. The member for Egypt ended by expressing the view that there was every justification for concluding that a program of such vast scope, and one so impossible of realization financially, had been drawn up mainly for propaganda purposes, and that some of the Commissioner's requests had been made with the same object, and to create the impression abroad that something useful was being done in Libya. In brief, though the program seemed attractive, it was impracticable and would be fruitless.

These criticisms may appear unwarranted to those familiar with modern international technical and financial assistance programs for developing countries, but in 1950 people with knowledge and experience of such operations were rare indeed.

Most members of the Council commended the Egyptian representative for his remarks, with which they associated themselves, endorsing his suggestions for good measure. One of the two members whose interventions showed that they appreciated the intricacies of the problem was Lewis Clark of the United States, who most ably argued the case for studies before funds. The other praiseworthy exception was the representative of the minorities, Giacomo Marchino, who made a series of sound practical suggestions.

The rest of the debate was largely taken up by statements—lectures might be a better word—by the Commissioner and the Principal Secretary, the latter being more particularly responsible for the technical assistance program, in which they tried to explain the history and the functioning of technical assistance machinery as conceived by ECOSOC, the General Assembly, and the United Nations Secretariat.

In the end, a draft resolution submitted by Abdur Rahim Khan was unanimously adopted. It advised the Commissioner to keep the Council regularly informed of any action taken in the technical assistance field, to include in his report to the General Assembly a full account of Libya's economic and social requirements, and to convey to the Secretary-General the Council's hope that, while observing the requirements of Article 101 (3) of the Charter, he might yet be able to arrange for the recruitment of advisers to the Mission staff in the first place from the countries of the

Middle East.[74] The Council further decided to set up two sub-committees: the Sub-Committee on Needs and Requirements of Libya in the Technical Assistance Field; and the Sub-Committee on Ways and Means of Financing Libya's Requirements in the Technical Field. The resolution further recommended that the two Sub-Committees should consult with and advise, through the Council and the Commissioner, all technical experts visiting Libya. Insofar as possible, Libya's requirements in technical assistance and funds for the implementation of plans resulting from expert inquiries should be examined and implemented in accordance with the wishes of the representatives of the country. The Sub-Committee on Needs and Requirements would, moreover, assist and advise the experts in establishing priorities on the same basis.

On reflection, one gets the impression that what really moved certain members of the Council to speak as they did in this debate was the fear—borne out by events—that the staff of the Mission, with TAB's help and connivance, was about to embark on a program the technical nature of which would make it difficult for the Council to exercise any effective control over its execution. As far as the Administering Powers were concerned, they seemed to fear that United Nations technical assistance activities might—from their political point of view—lay undue stress on the idea of Libyan unity, thus jeopardizing their own more limited regional development plans. At the time, these fears were understandable; but, as the Libyan situation evolved, United Nations technical assistance proposals and those of the British and French Administrations drew closer together, though the two sides never saw fully eye to eye. For instance, one important issue on which they differed arose in the second half of 1951, when a decision had to be taken about federal finances and the cognate problem of customs revenue. That point was a technical one only in appearance. In reality, it was a political issue directly related to the extent of federal unity.[75]

By a happy coincidence, the Sub-Committee on Needs and Requirements was able to meet for the first time while the two United Nations staff members on the Goodrich mission were still in Tripoli. They had almost finished their inquiries, but had not yet begun to draft the mission's report.

74. Article 101 (3) in Chapter XV, *The Secretariat,* reads as follows: "The paramount consideration in the employment of the staff and in the determination of the conditions of service shall be the necessity of securing the highest standards of efficiency, competence, and integrity. *Due regard shall be paid to the importance of recruiting the staff on as wide a geographical basis as possible.*" (Italics added.)

75. See Chapter 7, pp. 521–36 and Chapter 8, passim, for a detailed account of the negotiations.

They were therefore not in a position to recommend an actual program, with priorities, on which they would have first to consult Goodrich himself, who had already left Libya; but speaking personally, they expressed the view that in some cases the allocation of priorities would be a function of the exigencies of time. The mission had taken note of certain obvious needs, such as the establishment of an effective administration, the introduction of a currency and banking system, the institution of agricultural credits, the correction of the country's adverse balance of payments through economic, and particularly agricultural, development, as well as of substantial problems in the educational and public health sectors.

They also stressed the point that study of the main sources of income and of indispensable expenditure was fundamental; no program for the future could be drawn up unless it was known how much money would be available and from what sources. They went on to suggest that the problem could best be solved by establishing all the relevant facts; this was particularly welcome to the Commissioner, as it was the perfect answer to a certain scepticism he had noted when trying to convince local notables and leaders that Libya's budget and economy alike were deficitary. Libyans generally were inclined to suspect that this argument was simply a pretext on the part of the Administering Powers for justifying their continued presence in the country.[76] It took expert advice from people who were neither British nor French (Dean was an American, Kooy a Belgian) to make Libyans accept the fact that their country was really in the red. In the end, it became plain that the meeting had had a sobering effect on the Libyan members of the Sub-Committee, an effect that was reinforced when the Goodrich mission's report was circulated in September 1950. (The extensive program of technical assistance initiated by this report is described in Chapter 9, Part 1, passim.)

After a second meeting, this time with no foreign expert present, the Sub-Committee drew up a report and draft resolution for the Council. The report ended with a list of the subjects which in its view needed the most urgent study. The order of priority was as follows:

76. A typical illustration of the way these suspicions worked is provided by a request made by Selim Bey for a copy of the detailed British Administration budget, so that he could see for himself how the British were spending Libya's money. It was obvious that, as late as July 1950 at best, he still had not realized that the treasuries of the Administering Powers were covering large annual deficits in each of the three territories. In paragraph 182 of his first *Annual Report,* the Commissioner had noted that, according to information received from the Administering Powers, their combined average annual grants-in-aid in recent years had exceeded $4,750,000, exclusive of occupation costs. Subsequently, the accuracy of this figure was confirmed by United Nations experts (see Chapter 9).

Banking and currency
Commercial and agricultural credit
Education
Technical education
Training and education abroad
Public health

This enumeration was remarkable not so much for what it included as for what was missing from it, namely, any reference to matters of administration. This, too, was a difficulty with which the Commissioner had had to cope before, and again it was caused by Libyan suspicions of the Administering Powers. Did not the British and French encourage young Libyans to undergo training for entrance into the administration as a means of maintaining their own nationals in the senior posts? Would they not take deliberate advantage of the selection of trainees to push their friends and protégés and thus avoid having to accept Libyans from the critically minded nationalist parties? However justified these fears might have been, one could hardly blame the Administering Powers for preferring to employ in their service people prepared to cooperate rather than prone to criticize. But as the ultimate goal could not be other than the Libyanization of the administration, the only possible solution was tolerance and reasonableness on both sides. However, these were the very qualities the impatient and suspicious young nationalists lacked. In fact, the problem was never completely solved during the transitional period, though during 1951, as independence drew closer, it became less acute.

When a few days later the draft resolution was considered by the Council, it gave rise to no difficulty except with regard to the final paragraph, in which the Sub-Committee recommended that the Council decide that

> the Sub-Committee [on] Needs and Requirements of Libya in the technical assistance field is authorized to invite Libyans to appear before it to express their views on Libyan needs orally or in writing, in order that it may be in a position better to assist and advise, through the Council and the Commissioner, the technical experts in preparing the priority of the schemes for technical assistance to Libya.[77]

The Chairman of the Sub-Committee, Rahim Khan, introduced this paragraph as if it were of no particular importance. He was at pains to make it clear that there was no question of investigating the way in which the British and French authorities were administering the country. Nor was there any intention of criticizing them on such grounds. The Sub-Committee

77. United Nations Doc. A/AC.32/COUNCIL/R.85, 30 July 1950. Mimeographed.

was simply proposing to hear statements from organizations or individuals well acquainted with conditions in Libya, capable of giving advice and making suggestions which would help it to define the country's needs more precisely. In addition, one or two experts would be needed on the Commissioner's staff to study whatever material became available, and to suggest ways and means of reducing the country's budgetary and economic deficits. It all sounded very reasonable, and would have been so in practice, had all the members of the Council trusted one another.

As matters stood, however, the representatives of the Administering Powers smelled a rat. The British member pointed out that it was not the function of the Council or that of any of its subsidiary organs to collect information by means of a public inquiry. He also drew attention to the risk of duplication of effort or confusion that would be created if the Sub-Committee were to make inquiries in fields which had already been surveyed by experts. He therefore submitted an alternative text for the paragraph in question, proposing that the Council recommend that its members, and in particular those on the Sub-Committee, make a special study of Libya's economic, financial, social, and related problems to put it in a position the better to assist and advise the technical experts in allocating priorities to technical assistance projects. This amendment, which, in fact, was the direct opposite of what the Sub-Committee had in mind, was not unnaturally thrown out.

In an attempt to meet the Administering Powers, Selim Bey proposed that the words "to appear before it" be deleted, at which the United States member proposed that the words "orally or" be removed as well. The Commissioner, considering that the procedure envisaged for the Sub-Committee needed clarification, supported both amendments. The first was adopted, the second rejected. As a result, the resolution as finally carried authorized the Sub-Committee to invite Libyans to express their views on Libyan needs orally or in writing. In the circumstances, the Commissioner reserved his liberty of action. From his point of view there was nothing seriously wrong about the decision, but as a difference of opinion about the Council's competence was involved, it might add fuel to a smoldering fire that needed little to make it flare up. As it turned out, it did neither much harm nor much good, for the simple reason that, with but one or two exceptions, the members of the Council lacked the necessary knowledge of and experience in economic affairs either to question effectively anyone appearing before them or to advise foreign experts. It proved much more practical and fruitful for Libyans and experts to get together directly without the Sub-Committee's intervention. In itself, this was a pity, for it would have been helpful could the Council have played an active and efficient part in the provision of advice on economic and social affairs. However, as has already been observed in the course of this study, to make this possible, the initial choice of Council members would have had to have been guided by different considerations than those which in fact applied.[78]

Reverting to the discussion in ECOSOC, described on pages 402–05, it remains only to be said that the Secretary-General reached the conclusion that the Council's objectives could best be achieved through a General Assembly decision requesting ECOSOC and the specialized agencies to consider Libya as eligible for technical assistance without regard to its membership of any United Nations organization. At the Commissioner's request, therefore, the Secretary-General submitted a draft resolution for the General Assembly's consideration. This recognized that Libya should receive technical assistance in the development of its economy and in the establishment of an efficient public administration and that it should be eligible to receive technical assistance without interruption after attainment of independence. Moreover, it requested ECOSOC and the specialized agencies concerned "to consider Libya as eligible to receive technical assistance under Economic and Social Council resolution 222 A (IX) as soon as it shall be constituted an independent State in accordance with General Assembly resolution 289 A (IV)." [79]

One would not, perhaps, have thought that so simple a proposition would give rise to much discussion, but the proceedings in the Second Committee only served to confirm an impression that was beginning to take shape in the minds of several people concerned with Libyan problems, namely, that the apparent simplicity of anything connected with them was a snare and delusion.

A variety of fears and suspicions were voiced about the practical implementation of the Secretary-General's proposals. The Pakistani representative, supported by his Egyptian colleague, wanted the mention of the establishment of an efficient public administration to be struck out, the second arguing that technical assistance in that field could in practice be manipulated to perpetuate administration by foreign Powers.

A group of Arab States proposed the insertion of a paragraph requesting TAB, when granting technical assistance to Libya, "to be mindful of the economic unity and independence of Libya in conformity with the basic

78. To meet the wishes of the Council, as well as the needs of the public, the Mission secretariat began to issue from this time on a periodical entitled the *Fortnightly Technical Assistance News Letter*. This appeared in the three working languages (Arabic, English, and French).

79. GAOR: Fifth Session, 1950, Annexes, Agenda item 65 (A/1404, 28 September 1950), pp. 1–2.

principles embodied in the Economic and Social Council Resolution 222 (IX) and the General Assembly Resolution 304 (IV)." [80]

The Uruguayan delegation wanted to make sure that if Libya continued to receive technical assistance after independence, this should be provided only at its own request. The same delegation also wished the General Assembly to instruct the Secretary-General "to study, prepare and submit to the Economic and Social Council a draft plan of technical, cultural and financial assistance sufficient to improve the economic and social development of Libya." [81]

It took the Committee one three-hour meeting and parts of two others to reach agreement on the final text of the resolution. Thanks to the sterling efforts of the Chilean representative, Herman Santa Cruz, to bring the parties together, all amendments were withdrawn and an agreed draft put forward which was adopted unanimously. The new text answered the purposes of that submitted by the Secretary-General while at the same time incorporating the principal suggestions made in the course of the debate. To the Commissioner's great satisfaction, the resolution included in its definition of the aims of technical assistance for Libya the improvement of the country's public administration. A few days later, the plenary Assembly approved the resolution by a unanimous vote. All fears that technical assistance would be cut off when Libya became independent were thereby dispelled. Moreover, an assurance was given on behalf of the Secretary-General that he would immediately approach those nonmember Governments that had taken part in the recent Technical Assistance Pledging Conference, which had dealt with the questions mentioned in the resolution, with a view to securing their agreement to its terms.[82]

Thus the way was cleared for the development and execution of the very comprehensive technical assistance program devised for Libya, the full account of which will be found in Chapter 9.

PART 4. MISSION FINANCES

The *Ad Hoc* Political Committee and the Second Committee were not the only places where the stresses and tensions of the Libyan experiment found an outlet during the Fifth Session of the General Assembly. Part of the

80. GAOR: Fifth Session, 1950, Second Committee, 136th Meeting, 10 November 1950, p. 123.

81. Ibid., p. 124.

82. General Assembly Resolution 398 (V), 17 November 1950. For text, see Annex I, p. 899.

game was played in the Fifth Committee in the debate on the budget of the United Nations Mission to Libya and the Council for Libya.

In 1949, before the Commissioner was appointed, a tentative budget for his office in Libya and for the servicing of the Council had been drawn up by the Budget Division of the Office of the Controller at United Nations Headquarters. The estimates as approved amounted to $251,100. Experience, however, soon showed that this was well below requirements. In its report to the General Assembly, the Advisory Committee on Administrative and Budgetary Questions (ACABQ) indicated that the revised figure for 1950 came to $466,600, and that the excess expenditure would have to be met by drawing on the Organisation's Working Capital Fund.[83]

The Secretary-General's report stated that the cost of implementing Resolution 289 (IV) in 1951 was estimated at $619,300. These were large sums for an operation which, in the eyes of certain delegations, simply consisted in writing a constitution and programming a transfer of powers. Fortunately, ACABQ took a more realistic view of the scope of the work, and, although in duty bound to recommend economies, limited its proposed reductions to $37,100. The Secretary-General, having consulted the Commissioner, accepted this recommendation as an overall reduction to be spread over the whole of the estimated expenditure.[84]

The representative of Pakistan in the Fifth Committee immediately started criticizing virtually every item in the budget, from staff costs to transportation, and ended up by proposing a reduction of $104,000 over and above that proposed by ACABQ. A few other delegations followed up this attack. The Egyptian delegate, though not going as far as his Pakistani colleague, nevertheless proposed a total reduction of $90,030. As these criticisms came from Governments represented on the Council for Libya, they were taken as gospel. Only a few members of the Fifth Committee seemed to suspect that they might be inspired by political motives.

Both the Commissioner and the Principal Secretary put up a stiff fight to save what they knew from experience was a carefully calculated and realistic budget. The most dangerous reductions proposed were those in staff and in local transportation. The staff required in 1951—which had in part been engaged in 1950—consisted among others of advisers on such subjects as

83. "Financial implications of the draft resolution proposed by the *Ad Hoc* Political Committee: twelfth report of 1950 of the Advisory Committee on Administrative and Budgetary Questions," GAOR: Fifth Session, 1950, Annexes, Agenda item 21 (A/1479, 2 November 1950), pp. 54–55.

84. Ibid., p. 55; and "Financial implications of the draft resolution proposed by the *Ad Hoc* Political Committee: report of the Secretary-General," GAOR: Fifth Session, 1950, Annexes, Agenda item 21 (A/C.5/392, 26 October 1950), pp. 52–54.

agriculture, the Libyan budget and public administration, and land claims, not forgetting two legal advisers. Had TAB been able to foresee, in 1949 and 1950, Libya's special and urgent requirements, several of these advisers would undoubtedly have been paid out of its funds. But as this had not been possible, and Libya could not wait if it was to become independent by 1 January 1952, the Secretary-General had been obliged to charge a certain amount of technical assistance expenditure to the regular Mission budget (see pp. 399–400). The staff also included four political officers who, apart from other duties, were responsible for daily contacts with the local administrations in the three territories and with the minorities. As, moreover, the Mission staff had to service the Council, which, under its rules of procedure, had English, French, and Arabic as its working languages, a language staff of two interpreter-translators and two minute-writers, with a supporting staff of seven secretaries, was not unduly large. Altogether, the Commissioner and the Principal Secretary had at their disposal an international staff of not more than forty-nine at any one time (i.e. not counting local staff).[85]

Another reduction which, if approved, would have crippled Libya's preparations for independence was the one in local transportation costs, the largest single item of which was represented by an amount of $60,000 a year for the aircraft chartered by the United Nations from the United States Air Force for the Mission's use, crew and servicing included. But, in a vast expanse like Libya, inhabited by widely scattered groups of people, served by only a rudimentary system of land communications, the Commissioner and Council and their staff would have been left high and dry, so to speak, without an airplane to maintain the necessary contacts between the three main centers, Tripoli, Benghazi, and Sabhah, separated from one another as they are by distances varying from 410 to 475 miles as the crow flies. Those Libyans who served on such bodies as the Committee of Twenty-One also needed rapid transport. The United Nations aircraft—a modest DC-3 —was therefore in constant demand for a variety of purposes, and there was general agreement in the field that without it the task assigned to the Mission and the Libyan people could not be finished in the short time available. The same considerations applied to the equally modest radio network set up to enable the Mission to maintain rapid communications between Tripoli and Benghazi as well as with New York through the relay center at the European Office of the United Nations at Geneva.

During the second day of the debate, when it began to look as if a majority might be found to vote for a serious cut in the budget, the Commissioner was obliged to intervene, to remind the Committee of the very

85. For a more detailed account of the Mission establishment and the functions of the staff, see Chapter 2, Pt. 1, and in particular p. 119.

special conditions under which he had to do his duty, and to voice his anxiety about the consequences of the proposed reductions. He drew attention to paragraph 258 in his first annual report, in which he had expressed confidence that the aim of the General Assembly would be attained within the time prescribed, that was to say, that Libya would become independent by the end of 1951—perhaps even a little earlier. He went on to say:

> That confidence had been based on the assumption that he would be given the means with which to carry out his task. The *Ad Hoc* Political Committee had noted his expression of confidence and had asked whether it should be included in the resolution to be submitted to the General Assembly in the near future. He had agreed, as he sincerely believed that confidence to be justified. If, however, the Egyptian and Pakistani proposals were adopted by the Fifth Committee, he would with deep regret have to inform the Chairman of the *Ad Hoc* Political Committee and the President of the General Assembly that his confidence was no longer justified.[86]

The arguments advanced by the Commissioner and the Principal Secretary did not fail to produce the desired effect, not least because the speeches of the Egyptian and Pakistani representatives contained some glaring, easily corrected factual errors. Anyway, the Canadian representative expressed the opinion that "bearing in mind the importance of the enterprise, in which multiple nationalities were uniting to form a new State, the budget was remarkably low and petty criticism would be unworthy of the occasion.[87]

Off the record, the Chairman of the Fifth Committee, the Maharaja Jam Sahib of Nawanagar, a man who knew what he was talking about, quipped that rarely had independence been bought so cheaply.

In the outcome, the joint Egyptian and Pakistani proposals, finally brought down to a cut of $52,930 (over and above ACABQ's figure), were rejected by 25 votes to 6, with 13 abstentions, while ACABQ's proposed cut of $37,100 was unanimously approved. All's well that ends well—but Libya had narrowly escaped the disaster of seeing her independence delayed because of the inadequacy of United Nations funds.

PART 5. LIBYA'S BOUNDARIES

There was one aspect of the question of the disposal of the former Italian colonies which, although not among the most important, proved to be

86. GAOR: Fifth Session, 1950, Fifth Committee, 261st Meeting, 7 November 1950, p. 153.
87. Ibid.

particularly embarrassing to the General Assembly. This was the question of what was called, in the Treaty of Peace with Italy, "the appropriate adjustment of . . . boundaries." Annex XI, paragraphs 2 and 3, thereto, read as follows:

> The final disposal of the territories concerned [Libya, Eritrea, and Italian Somaliland] and the appropriate adjustment of their boundaries shall be made by the Four Powers in the light of the wishes and welfare of the inhabitants and the interests of peace and security, taking into consideration the views of other interested Governments.
>
> . . . If with respect to any of these territories the Four Powers are unable to agree upon their disposal within one year from the coming into force of the Treaty of Peace with Italy, the matter shall be referred to the General Assembly of the United Nations for a recommendation, and the Four Powers agree to accept the recommendation and to take appropriate measures for giving effect to it.[88]

It was the Commissioner's good fortune that this knotty problem was not mentioned in Resolution 289 (IV), and therefore did not come within his terms of reference. In any event, as far as Libya was concerned the matter was not solved until a few years after independence. However, the author has decided to deal with it briefly in this study, not only for the sake of completeness, but also because the question of Libya's boundaries was sometimes raised in his dealings with the French and, especially, the Egyptian Government.

At the Fourth Session of the General Assembly, this matter, like most of the other problems of the disposal of the former Italian colonies, was referred to Sub-Committee 17 of the First Committee, which became the workshop in which the basic resolutions determining their future were forged. The Sub-Committee discussed boundaries at three meetings. The primary issue was whether the General Assembly was competent to deal with the question at all. The debate was not entirely conclusive; however, the Secretariat noted in a memorandum it submitted somewhat later to the Interim Committee of the General Assembly, to which the matter had been referred at the Fourth Session by Resolution 289 C (IV) (see Annex I, p. 893), that: "Representatives who expressed an opinion on the subject generally held the view that the Assembly had no competence under the Charter to delimit or adjust international frontiers." [89]

88. *Treaty of Peace with Italy,* Paris, 10 February 1947. For text, see *United Nations Treaty Series* (1950), Vol. I, No. 747.

89. "Study of procedure to delimit the boundaries of the former Italian Colonies," United Nations Doc. A/AC.18/103, 27 January 1950, p. 11. Mimeographed.

The next question to arise concerned the specific competence of the General Assembly to delimit or adjust the frontiers of the former Italian colonies under the Italian Peace Treaty. The Secretariat had the following to say on this narrower issue in its memorandum:

Several representatives drew a distinction between the General Assembly's competence *to adjust* the boundaries of the former Italian colonies and its competence *to delimit* their boundaries. That a difference exists between adjustment of a frontier and delimitation of a frontier was generally accepted during the discussion. . . .

(i) *Competence to adjust*

The representative of the Union of Soviet Socialist Republics felt that the phrasing of paragraphs 2 and 3 of Annex XI of the Peace Treaty was vague but was of the opinion that the Four Powers, according to the text of paragraph 2, had assumed two tasks: to decide the disposal of the former Italian colonies, and to undertake appropriate adjustment of the boundaries. Paragraph 3, on the other hand, mentioned only the question of *"their disposal."* This was the "matter" to be referred to the General Assembly, if the Four Powers were unable to agree. . . . The representatives of Ethiopia and Poland, at the same meeting of the First Committee, agreed with the representative of the Union of Soviet Socialist Republics. The French representative, in Sub-Committee 17, felt that the interpretation of the paragraph in question was doubtful, but that the Union of Soviet Socialist Republics interpretation could be sustained. The United States representative likewise expressed doubt, at the same meeting, regarding this question and withheld his opinion, while the representatives of Egypt and Pakistan thought that the question of adjustment was referred to the General Assembly by paragraph 3 of Annex XI.

(ii) *Competence to delimit*

At the 323rd meeting of the First Committee, the representative of the United States expressed the view that the Assembly's competence to delimit—as distinct from adjust—was inherent in its authority to dispose of the Italian colonies. At the same meeting, the French representative stated that it was "obviously within the purview" of the General Assembly to delimit the boundaries of the Italian colonies, if some of these were not at present determined or delimited. The representatives of the Union of South Africa and Peru, however, expressed doubt. The Union of Soviet Socialist Republics' representative did not take a definite stand as to whether the Assembly had received authority to delimit the boundaries, but expressed the view that it was entirely unnecessary for the General Assembly to deal with this problem inasmuch as most of the boundaries were already fixed in international agreements, and the question of further delimitation could and ought to be left to the parties concerned.[90]

General agreement was finally reached in Sub-Committee 17, and subsequently in the First Committee, that the task of the General Assembly was to fix a *procedure* for delimiting these boundaries, rather than to delimit or adjust them itself. When, however, in the course of a debate in the Sub-Committee on the proposed Italian trusteeship for Italian Somaliland, the Ethiopian representative announced that his country would not sit on a boundary commission with mediatory powers, as suggested by the United States delegation, to delimit the frontier between Ethiopia and former Italian Somaliland, the matter of boundaries was dropped for the time being.

Nevertheless, delegations continued their discussions in private, and as a result, on 11 November 1950, the delegations of Argentina and Turkey introduced in the First Committee a draft resolution, the operative paragraph of which called upon the Interim Committee

> to study the procedure to be adopted to settle the question of the boundaries of the former Italian colonies in so far as they are not already fixed by international agreement and report with conclusions to the fifth regular session of the General Assembly.[91]

Later, at the Committee's three hundred and twenty-third meeting, the representative of France, stating specifically that he wished it to be made clear that the purpose of the proposed procedure was not to adjust but to delimit the boundaries, suggested that the phrase "to settle the question of" be replaced by the words "to delimit," to which the sponsors of the draft resolution agreed. For the rest, most of the arguments advanced in Sub-Committee 17 were repeated, but the draft resolution as amended was adopted in plenary session without further change.

The matter was thus referred to the Interim Committee for the sole purpose of gaining time at the Fifth Session; but this procedural decision did not meet with the approval of the Soviet Union, which had regarded the Interim Committee from the outset as an illegal body. It accordingly took no part in that committee's work.

The Interim Committee took the matter up in January 1950, but, admitting its ignorance of the various boundary questions involved, asked the Secretariat to study the problems. The result was the memorandum already

90. Ibid., pp. 11–13.

91. GAOR: Fourth Session, 1949, First Committee, Annexes to Summary Records, Agenda item 19 (A/C.1/536/Rev.1, 11 November 1949), p. 35.

quoted. Only on 15 September 1950, however, having delayed further discussion pending information on the proposed trusteeship for Italian Somaliland, did the Committee revert to the question. It then found itself confronted with a draft resolution submitted by the United States, the operative paragraph of which with respect to Libya read as follows:

> That the portion of its boundary with French territory not already fixed by international agreement be delimited, upon Libya's achievement of independence, by negotiation between the Libyan and French Governments, assisted upon the request of either party by a third person to be selected by them or, failing their agreement, to be appointed by the Secretary-General of the United Nations.[92]

However, the Committee did not succeed in reaching agreement on the United States proposal, partly for lack of time, partly because of an Egyptian reservation. Earlier, Egypt had also reserved its position on the study carried out by the Secretariat. In the end, the Committee decided to append the United States resolution in draft form to its report to the Fifth Session of the General Assembly.[93]

On the same occasion, the French representative declared that

> his government reserved the right to put before the Assembly at the proper time the question of the delimitation of the boundaries of its territories and of Libya. The French Government had not thought it necessary to ask for the inclusion of this question as a separate item in the provisional agenda of the fifth regular session of the General Assembly because item 21 (f) of that agenda covered all the specific cases of delimitation of the boundaries of the former Italian colonies. Consequently, the French delegation would state its views on the question when the Assembly considered item 21 (f).[94]

Before we relate what happened at the Fifth Session, something must be said about the substance, at least as far as Libya's frontiers were concerned at the time. Here again the Secretariat's memorandum can be quoted to advantage:

> 6. LIBYA
>
> (a) *Northern part of western frontier* (with *Tunis*)
>
> No claims or questions have been raised with regard to this frontier which is fixed by the Agreement between Turkey and France on 19 May 1910

92. United Nations Doc. A/AC.18/118/Rev.1, 15 September 1950, p. 2. Mimeographed.

93. See GAOR: Fifth Session, 1950, Supplement No. 14 (A/1388), Annex C.

94. Interim Committee, Summary Records of 45th Meeting, United Nations Doc. A/AC.18/SR.45, 15 September 1950. Mimeographed.

along a certain detailed line from Ras Adjadir on the Mediterranean to Ghadames in Tripoli.

(b) *Southern part of western frontier and south-western frontier* (with *Algiers* and *French West Africa*)
No claims or questions have been raised with regard to this frontier which was fixed by an Exchange of Notes between Italy and France of 12 September 1919, rectifying the former boundary somewhat in Libya's favour. The revised frontier runs from Ghadames in a southern direction to Rhat (Ghat) and further in a south-eastern direction along the crest of the mountain range to Tummo.

(c) *Southern frontier* (with *French West Africa* and *French Equatorial Africa*)
This frontier was fixed by the so-called "Rome Agreement" of 7 January 1935, between France and Italy. However, the French delegation, in a notation on the map attached to the report of the Four Power Commission of Inquiry regarding Libya, has pointed out that this Agreement never came into force as it was never ratified, and that it furthermore was formally denounced by the Italian Government in 1938. The boundary in question is therefore, according to this French notation, still governed by the "Franco-Italian Protocol for the delimitation of the frontier between Libya on the one hand, and French West Africa on the other hand, which was signed on 10 January 1924 and which remains in force." This Protocol is not to be found in standard reference books or in articles on Libya. *Martens*: *Recueil Général des Traités* contains, however, the text of a Franco-*British* Protocol of 10 January 1924 fixing this boundary between French Equatorial Africa and the *Sudan.*[95]

95. In the course of the eighty-first meeting of the *Ad Hoc* Political Committee at the Fifth Session, the representative of France said he wished to correct a mistake which had found its way into this paragraph:

> The truth was that the provisions of the Franco-Italian Agreement of 7 January 1935 fixing the boundary of Libya with the French West Africa (later Toummo) and with French Equatorial Africa had never come into force, since that agreement had not been ratified and the Italian Government had denounced it on 27 December 1938.
>
> In those circumstances reference should be made to previous provisions fixing that section of the boundary. Those were contained in the Franco-Italian Agreement of 1 November 1902, since the Agreement of 12 September 1919 dealt only with the boundary between Ghadames and Toummo. According to the Agreement of 1902, the boundary in question was the boundary of Tripolitania indicated on the map annexed to the Additional Statement of 21 March 1899 to the Franco-British Convention of 14 June 1898. That Additional Statement had been completed by a supplementary Franco-British Convention signed on 8 September 1919

(d) *Southern part of eastern frontier* (with *Sudan*)
No claims or questions have been raised with regard to this frontier, which was fixed by an Exchange of Notes of 20 July 1934, between Great Britain and Egypt on the one hand, and Italy on the other, to follow the 25th meridian southward from 22° to 20° north latitude, then westward along the 20th parallel north to the intersection with the 24th meridian east, and southward along this meridian into the boundary between French Equatorial Africa and Sudan.

(e) *Northern and middle parts of eastern frontier* (with *Egypt*)
This boundary is fixed by Agreement between Egypt and Italy of 6 December 1925. The frontier which begins on the Mediterranean coast between the Port of Bardia and Sollum, Bardia being on the Libyan side, follows a certain defined line through the desert plateau of Sollum and Bardia, runs east of the oasis of Djarabub [Jaghbub] and then straight south along the 25th meridian to 22° north latitude.

The Egyptian Government presented a Memorandum to the Paris Peace Conference in 1946 "on the subject of the western frontier of Egypt" and another Memorandum "on the subject of the Djarabub," claiming that Egypt had been obliged to cede the oasis of Djarabub to Italy, by Agreement of 6 December 1925, under pressure by the British Government, in order to fulfil the promises which Italy, at its entrance into the First World War, had received from Great Britain and France about territorial compensations in Africa. The Egyptian Government further claimed that the plateau of Sollum, including the port of Bardia, historically belonged to Egypt and, like the oasis of Djarabub, was of vital strategic importance to the defence of Egyptian territory.

On 19 April 1949, at the 245th meeting of the First Committee during part II of the third session of the General Assembly, the representative of Egypt, in reiterating the Egyptian claims to these two areas—the Sollum Plateau and the Djarabub oasis—also stated that the Egyptian Government "laid claim to the oases of Arcona and Karad in the Siwa area." These two oases do not appear even on available maps.

On 4 October 1949, at the 282nd meeting of the First Committee during the fourth regular session of the General Assembly, the Egyptian representative, referring to the Egyptian Memoranda which had been

---

and by a Franco-British Declaration of 21 January 1924 relating to a protocol of 10 January of the same year. The matter was therefore governed at present by all the texts he had just quoted.

GAOR: Fifth Session, 1950, *Ad Hoc* Political Committee, 81st Meeting, 13 December 1950, p. 529.

presented to the Paris Peace Conference in 1946, and the claims put forward at the third session of the General Assembly, stated that the Egyptian Government had specifically mentioned the Sollum Plateau, the oasis of Djarabub, the two oases of Arknoh and Oweinat, and the Sarra wells. The only Sarra wells found on the available maps or referred to in literature regarding the general area are the Sarra wells which are located in Libya about 200 miles west of the Sudan-Libyan frontier.

The Egyptian representative further stated at the same meeting that Egypt, which made its requests at the same time when three separate trusteeships were being suggested for Libya, felt that it was in a position to negotiate similar frontier adjustments in a spirit of friendship and mutual co-operation with a sister nation, the independent Libya of the future.

On 14 October 1949, at the 9th meeting of Sub-Committee 17 of the First Committee, the Egyptian representative stated that Egypt did not claim any territory, but that it was frequently necessary to fix the frontiers exactly in desert areas.[96]

In a letter to the Secretary-General dated 12 July 1950, the Permanent Representative of Egypt to the United Nations asked that there be placed on the agenda of the Fifth Session an item entitled "The appropriate adjustment of the frontiers between Egypt and the former Italian colony of Libya, with particular reference to paragraphs 2 and 3 of Annex XI of the Treaty of Peace with Italy." [97]

On 26 September 1950, the General Assembly referred this item to the *Ad Hoc* Political Committee for consideration and report.

This demarche by the Egyptian Government stirred up considerable emotion in Libya, particularly in Cyrenaica, mainly because al-Sayed Muhamed Bin Ali al-Senussi, the founder of the Senussi Order (the Sanusiya), known as the Grand Senussi, who lived from 1787 to 1859, was buried in the oasis of Jaghbub, which had also been the first seat of the Order. There, in addition to the Grand Senussi's tomb, were to be found in their time the Order's university and library of some 8,000 volumes. And if the claim succeeded, the oasis would pass to Egypt.[98]

Hence, it was not surprising when, early in September 1950, the Commissioner received a telegram from the Amir of Cyrenaica drawing the

96. "Study of procedure to delimit the boundaries of the former Italian Colonies," pp. 5–7.

97. For relevant documentation, see GAOR: Fifth Session, 1950, Annexes, Agenda item 59.

98. E. E. Evans-Pritchard, *The Sanusi of Cyrenaica* (Oxford: Oxford University Press, 1949), pp. 1–28.

Commissioner's attention to the bad effect the Egyptian step would have on the good relations that existed between the two countries. The Amir contended that any decision adversely affecting Libyan territory that might be taken before the achievement of independence would be unjust and contrary to Resolution 289 A (IV). He added that Libya, and Cyrenaica in particular, would never recognize or accept any such decision before she had attained her sovereignty, or so long as she was unable to defend her interests before the General Assembly through her own plenipotentiary representatives. The Commissioner viewed this reaction sympathetically. At the same time he recognized that the primary responsibility in the matter rested with the United Kingdom as the Administering Power. But he also realized that, given the past history of the case, the United Kingdom Government might find itself in a delicate position vis-à-vis Egypt if it intervened in favor of Libya. He therefore sought and found an opportunity of meeting the Egyptian Foreign Minister in Paris, suggesting to him that Egypt's claim for frontier rectification might be held in abeyance until Libya became independent. In the course of the conversation, Salah-al-Din Bey seemed to appreciate that Egypto-Libyan relations might be endangered if the matter were pressed in the United Nations but said he would have to consult his advisers, who might be prepared to inform the General Assembly that the matter could be put off. However, no firm understanding was reached.

In the event, nothing transpired before the General Assembly opened on 19 September 1950, and the Egyptian claim figured on the agenda as item 59, in the terms just quoted. It was referred to the *Ad Hoc* Political Committee. When the latter took the item up at its eightieth meeting on 13 December, Mustafa Bey briefly restated the Egyptian case, referring in particular to the oasis of Jaghbub and to the Sallum plateau. However, he added that, in view of the friendly relations between the two countries and his country's concern that Libya should become a unified and independent State within the period prescribed in Resolution 289 (IV), the Egyptian delegation would ask the General Assembly, while keeping the item on its agenda, to defer discussion on it until the Sixth Session. The Committee agreed, but no motion to this effect was tabled; the President of the Assembly himself therefore moved an appropriate resolution, which was unanimously adopted the next day. Thus the Amir's demands with respect to the timing of the negotiations were met.[99]

The report of the Interim Committee on the procedure to be adopted to

99. GAOR: Fifth Session, 1950, 325th Plenary Meeting, 14 December 1950, p. 681. The President's draft resolution, as adopted, became Resolution 391 (V).

delimit the boundaries of the former Italian colonies insofar as they were already fixed by international agreement, together with an associated United States proposal, came up at the eighty-first meeting of the *Ad Hoc* Committee, also held on 13 December 1950. The United States draft resolution was a revised version of the one annexed to the report. It recommended that the General Assembly adopt the following paragraph in respect of Libya:

> That the portion of its boundary with French territory not already delimited by international agreement be delimited, upon Libya's achievement of independence, by negotiation between the Libyan and French Governments, assisted upon the request of either party by a third person to be selected by them or, failing their agreement, to be appointed by the Secretary-General [of the United Nations].[100]

A comparison of the two texts shows that the word "fixed" in the first draft had been replaced by "delimited," thus stressing once again the majority view that the General Assembly should not itself adjust or rectify frontiers.

The French representative, though not opposed to the American proposal, did not feel altogether happy about it. In particular, his delegation doubted whether a sufficiently clear distinction had been made between the concepts of delimitation of a boundary by international agreement, demarcation on the spot of a boundary already fixed by a convention, and rectification of a boundary. It followed, in its opinion, that the competence of the United Nations in these various matters had not been precisely determined. This was a matter of regret to the French delegation, he concluded, which considered in particular that paragraphs 2 and 3 of Annex XI to the Treaty of Peace with Italy empowered the General Assembly to make appropriate rectifications in the boundaries of the former Italian colonies. Judging by this intervention, the French Government must have reconsidered and revised its position since the discussion in Sub-Committee 17 a year earlier. What it actually had in mind became clearer when, later in his statement, the French representative recalled that, on 15 September 1950, his colleague in the Interim Committee had reserved his right to draw attention to a special situation existing on the border between the Fezzan and Algeria in the region of Ghat and Sardalas. These oases had been included within the territory of the Fezzan under a Franco-Italian Treaty concluded on 12 September 1919. They were inhabited by Adjer Tuaregs of the Sahara, who, as already mentioned in Part 3 of Chapter 2 (pp. 233–34), had repeatedly expressed the wish to be reunited with their

100. GAOR: Fifth Session, 1950, Annexes, Agenda item 21 (A/1723, 14 December 1950), p. 141.

kindred, the tribesmen of the Djanet (Fort Charlet) region of Algeria. The French Government now wished to inform the United Nations that it reserved the right to settle the question in a friendly spirit by direct negotiation with the Libyan Government.[101]

After the United Kingdom representative had announced his delegation's support for the United States draft resolution, the Egyptian representative declared that his delegation, too, would vote for it, on the understanding that it would in no way affect the boundary between Egypt and the Sudan or that between Egypt and Libya, and that the question of both remained reserved.[102]

The Soviet Union representative having reiterated that, for known reasons, his delegation would vote against any draft resolution dealing with the delimitation of the boundaries of the former Italian colonies, the United States proposal was adopted by 35 votes to 5, with 1 abstention. Two days later, the plenary Assembly confirmed this decision by 44 votes to 5, though not before the USSR delegation had again voiced its objections.[103]

Thus, after a protracted and awkward process in which the subject was bandied back and forth between its various organs, the General Assembly renounced the competence to make appropriate adjustments to the boundaries of the former Italian colonies with which the four Great Powers, unable to reach agreement among themselves, had apparently sought to invest it. Instead, it recommended a delimitation procedure to be carried through by the parties directly interested. Nothing uttered during the discussions in any of the bodies which dealt with the matter made explicit the reasons for this evasive attitude on the part of the Assembly, save for the view, expressed by a number of delegations, that the Charter conferred no powers on the General Assembly in respect of the adjustment of boundaries. A minority rejected this interpretation of the Charter, or voiced misgivings about it; but there the matter rested—yet another unresolved issue.

Reading between the lines of the official records, one gets the impression that most delegations were unwilling to create a precedent that would have granted to the General Assembly the power of adjusting boundaries, one of the inherent attributes of sovereignty, even had this been legally possible under the terms of the Treaty of Peace with Italy.

101. GAOR: Fifth Session, 1950, First Committee, 81st Meeting, 13 December 1950, p. 528.

102. Ibid., p. 529. This reference to the Egyptian-Sudanese boundary was apparently inspired by fear that the procedure recommended by the General Assembly might at some time in the future be invoked as a precedent in respect of that boundary too.

103. GAOR: Fifth Session, 1950, 326th Plenary Meeting, 15 December 1950, pp. 683–84.

As far as the future sovereign State of Libya was concerned, the debates had revealed that, soon after it became independent, Libya would be burdened with two frontier problems, both of which seemed to be more complicated than cases of simple delimitation usually are. Moreover, it followed from the statements made that, whereas the French Government intended to negotiate its claims in accordance with the procedure recommended by the United Nations, the Egyptian Government declined to do so.[104]

104. See Chapter 11, *Independent Libya at the Sixth Assembly (1951–52),* for a brief account of the final disposal of the problem of Libya's frontiers at the Sixth Session of the General Assembly.

CHAPTER 6

The National Assembly Takes Over

PART 1. THE FORM OF STATE AND GOVERNMENT

As recommended, but in effect decided, by the Committee of Twenty-One (though, as an advisory body, the Committee theoretically had no power to take decisions, in practice its recommendations were treated as such), the National Assembly met for the first time on Saturday, 25 November 1950, in the official residence of the former Italian Governor-General, then still known in Tripoli as the Balbo Palace.[1] Significantly, it called itself the National *Constituent* Assembly of Libya (NCAL), in order to make it clear from the outset that it intended to write a constitution, not a mere draft.[2]

1. Air Marshal Italo Balbo was Italian Minister for Air from 1929 to 1933 and Governor-General of Libya from 1933 until 28 June 1940, when he was shot down over Tubruq by Italian antiaircraft fire, probably because he failed to give correct recognition signals.

2. The *Proceedings of the National Constituent Assembly of Libya,* to which constant reference will be made in this and succeeding chapters, were compiled at the time by Sulayman al-Jerbi, the National Assembly Secretary for Cyrenaica (see p. 443). By Western standards they are unorthodox. As the reader will see, verbatim passages and more or less extensive summaries of the debates are not always clearly distinguished or distinguishable. The tone throughout is orotund, the language at times picturesque, the summaries being couched in the rhetorical style favored by most of the speakers. This further increases the difficulty of locating the verbatim passages where they are not clearly marked. At some time after independence, the Arabic originals were published in Tripoli on orders from the Registrar of the Libyan Parliament. Early in 1965 the author sought and obtained from His Excellency Mahmud Muntasir, then Prime Minister of Libya, permission to have an English translation made from the Arabic originals for use in the preparation of this study. The translation is the work of two Arabic scholars at the University of Cambridge, England: Frank H. Stewart and David E. P. Jackson. The NCAL held forty-three meetings in all, between 25 November 1950 and 6 November 1951. The translation, *which exists only in typescript,* runs to 258 pages. To save time, the work was divided between the two translators. Stewart was solely responsible for the first thirty-one meetings and for the first part of the thirty-second meeting (down to the end of the discussion on Article 21 (in section II) of the draft constitution (pages 1–154 of the

The meeting was attended by a large number of notables, by representatives of the two Administering Powers, by representatives of the Commissioner (who was still attending the Fifth Session of the General Assembly at Lake Success), by members of the Consular Corps, and by all but two members of the Council for Libya. The exceptions were the representatives of Egypt and Pakistan, who desired to show by their absence that they did not consider that the National Assembly, as convened, met the requirements of paragraph 3 of Resolution 289 (IV) or subparagraphs 3 (a) and (b) of Resolution 387 (V).

The Assembly met in an atmosphere and in a mood very different from anything that could have been foreseen on 16 April 1950, when the Commissioner had submitted to the Council his first request for advice on his plan for the constitutional development of Libya. At that time it looked as though the Libyan people, moved by a common desire for unity and independence, would unanimously agree on the way in which their goal was to

---

typescript)); Jackson was solely responsible for the remainder (pages 154–258). All references in this study are to this English translation, and will be cited as *Proc. NCAL,* Stewart-Jackson Translation, followed by the number and date of the meeting in question. (It should be noted that the translators refer to "sections," not "chapters," of the draft constitution, and to "sessions," not "meetings," of the Assembly.) A copy of the Arabic originals and one typed copy of the English translation have been deposited with the Library of the United Nations Office in Geneva, Palais des Nations, Geneva, Switzerland, where they can be consulted. The original and four other typed copies of the translation were sent to His Excellency Hussein Maziq, then Prime Minister of Libya, by the author in February 1966. It may be added that the translation has been scrutinized by Ismail Khalidi, who was on the staff of the Mission in Libya, and whose name will be familiar to the reader of the present work, in the light of his direct and expert knowledge of the NCAL's work; he found the translation to be of excellent quality in all respects.

Arabic *Minutes* were also produced of the meetings of the Committee for the Constitution (the Committee of Eighteen) set up by the NCAL. They were compiled by the late Khalil Qallal, who played a leading part in the drafting of the Constitution, and are referred to hereafter in the same way as the Proceedings of the Assembly itself, with the addition of the words "Committee for the Constitution" after the abbreviation *Proc. NCAL.* Practically everything said above about *Proc. NCAL,* including deposition with the United Nations Library in Geneva, applies also to the Committee's Minutes, except that (a) the original comes slightly closer to Western ideas of such records; and (b) the translation, 89 pages long, was entirely the work of David E. P. Jackson.

Finally, the delegation sent by the National Assembly to Cairo in 1951 to make contact with the members of the League of Arab States, as described in detail in Part 4 of this chapter (pp. 487–508), drew up a report entitled *Detailed Report of the Activities of the National Assembly's Delegation to the Heads of Delegations of the Arab States, January to February 1951,* hereafter referred to as *Report of NCAL Delegation to Arab League.* This was entirely translated by Frank H. Stewart. Both the original and the translation have been deposited in Geneva.

be reached. Since then, as we have seen, serious differences of opinion had arisen on several basic constitutional issues. On the one hand, the National Congress Party of Tripolitania, in which a large part of the coastal population of that territory was represented, stood for a unitary form of State and for proportional territorial representation in the National Assembly. On the other hand, most of the people in Cyrenaica and the Fezzan, supported by some in the Tripolitanian hinterland, wanted a federal State and equal representation. At one time during the summer of 1950 the two sides, with the help of the Amir, the Commissioner, and the Council had come close to an understanding, but the cleft had proved too deep and attempts to effect a compromise had come to nothing. Moreover, when, at the Fifth Session of the General Assembly, the delegations of the Arab States took up the unitarist claims of the Congress Party, while at the same time calling for an elected National Assembly, the Libyan people became more divided and confused about these issues than ever before.

As regards the form of State, the partisans of federalism were greatly encouraged by the conclusions reached by the Committee of Twenty-One: for the first time in history, an all-Libyan body had unanimously reached agreement on a plan for an all-Libyan Constituent Assembly. The protagonists of a unitary State, on the other hand, were vehemently critical of those conclusions. Here at least the issue was clear-cut.

The Arab delegations' advocacy of an elected National Assembly, however, caused much perplexity. On the federalist side, the Fezzanese, who had fought a losing battle for elections in the Committee of Twenty-One, were now convinced that they had been on the right track. A similar feeling prevailed among the Cyrenaicans, who in June 1950 had elected their own territorial Assembly of Representatives. Despite all this, faced with unrelenting Tripolitanian opposition, the representatives of both of the other territories had agreed, for reasons of political expediency, to an appointed National Assembly, and they now felt that it was too late to go back on their decision if independence was to be achieved by the end of 1951.

The Congress Party found itself in an even more embarrassing position. For reasons which the author has never been quite able to fathom, the Party leadership apparently failed to reach a timely understanding on this vital issue with the Secretary-General and members of the League of Arab States.[3] The result was that, having opposed the election of representatives

3. Lack of coordination between Tripoli and Cairo or, on a more personal plane, a divergence of views between Azzam Pasha and Beshir Bey Saadawi may well have been the cause of this misunderstanding.

It will be remembered from the Historical Background that the former, Egyptian by birth, and subsequently the first Secretary-General of the League of Arab States, had played a predominant part as Counselor to the Government of the Republic of

to both the Committee of Twenty-One and the National Assembly, the Congress Party leaders were now, to their consternation, under fire from their best friends abroad for having done so. The Congress Party's position might have been eased had it chosen to side with the majority in the General Assembly when it rejected the Egyptian proposal that representatives to the Libyan National Assembly be elected. This action, however, no doubt would have caused a rift between the Congress Party and its friends in Cairo. For a short-time, the Party seemed to dither, but it soon appeared that its leaders, and at least some of their followers, were coming round to the idea that an elected National Assembly might, after all, be better than an appointed one, though the genuineness of this change of heart seemed suspect. Anyway, it was by no means certain that the rank and file would publicly agree to the consequential delay in the date fixed for independence. Some of the Party's opponents went so far as to allege—and continued to do so until the end of 1951—that this change of policy was merely a tactical maneuver designed to keep the issue open until the General Assembly met for its Sixth Session in the autumn of 1951, in the hope that the United Nations itself might take the responsibility of postponing the proclamation of independence pending the holding of a general election. This last speculation gets some support from Khalidi, who says:

> This was an abrupt departure from the position which the Arab representatives on the United Nations Council for Libya and the major political parties in Libya, had taken hitherto. The reasons underlying this change in the Arab attitude may be attributed to the increased opposition, strongly manifested by the Congress Party, which now publicly attacked the constitutional steps taken so far on the grounds that the creation of the National Assembly was contrary to established rules of Parliamentary procedure.[4]

Tripolitania. As such he had shown himself to be an enthustiastic protagonist of a united independent Libya under Senussi leadership. Beshir Bey Saadawi, who belonged to the same generation as Azzam Pasha, was of Tripolitanian origin, and was an elected member of the Gharyan Conference, had also been a warm supporter of the Republic and its policies.

There is no reason to assume that either of the two men ever changed his mind on the basic concept of his policy regarding Libya's future. However, in the years 1950–51 one could hear rumors in Libyan and Arab League circles to the effect that differences of outlook had arisen between them on issues of a tactical nature. In this connection it was only natural that Azzam Pasha, looking at the Libyan problem from Cairo, saw it as a whole while Beshir Bey Saadawi in Tripoli could not fail to be influenced by preoccupations of a provincial nature.

4. Ismail Raghib Khalidi, *Constitutional Development in Libya* (Beirut, Lebanon: Khayat's College Book Co-operative, 1956), p. 37.

Right up to the present day, the author has found it impossible to glean from those who were party to the events precise information as to whether this change of policy originated with the Congress Party itself in Tripoli, or with the Arab League in Cairo. A not unlikely explanation is that it was belatedly initiated in joint consultations between the two, probably during October 1950, when the work of the Committee of Twenty-One was coming to an end (see Part 4 of this chapter, passim).

Fortunately, in this obscure situation there was one matter on which there was virtual unanimity, though for a variety of reasons, throughout the country, namely: recognition of the Amir of Cyrenaica, Sayed Idris, as the one person around whom the Libyan people could rally as a symbol of national unity. That some did so for predominantly religious and traditional reasons, whereas others were moved rather by political considerations, made no difference to the wholeheartedness of their support.

In the Historical Background, a brief account was given of the origins and evolution of the Senussi Order. From an Islamic revivalist movement, it had, before World War I and under Ottoman rule, developed into a kind of theocracy, particularly in the interior of Cyrenaica and to a lesser extent in Tripolitania and the Fezzan. Subsequently, French and British penetration into North and Central Africa, followed by the Italian occupation of Libya, had profoundly affected the Order, forcing it to fight for its life. During the 1930s it had practically ceased to exist in Libya, but its spirit survived, in the person of its leader, Sayed Idris. While in the eyes of many of his followers he was still fundamentally a spiritual leader, circumstances had forced him to play the part of statesman and diplomat, in particular in defense of his people in Cyrenaica. Living in Egypt, he led the political struggle for their liberation from Italian domination, and it was as a political leader that he returned to Benghazi after World War II. When the United Nations decided that Libya should become an independent and sovereign State, Sayed Idris's prestige and authority armed him with considerable influence. This had already been fully appreciated by the United Kingdom Government when it proclaimed him Amir of Cyrenaica in 1949. Elsewhere in Libya his authority was also increasingly recognized. A member of the Department of History of the American University of Beirut has said:

> Still when all is said and done, Sanūsīyah as a state ceased to exist [when finally the Italians occupied all Libya]. Even the rebuilding by the Italian Government of some of the Sanūsī zāwiyas later as a policy of appeasement did by no means lead to the revival of the Sanūsī state.
>
> The liberation of Libya in 1943 at the hands of the allies gave Sayyid Idrīs an opportunity to revive the movement, especially as he had suc-

ceeded in keeping the torch somewhat alive. But when he eventually returned to Cyrenaica as the recognized political leader of the people and the accepted Head of the Sanūsī Order, matters began to take a different course for him. In Cyrenaica he did more or less hold the reins in his hands, but as Sanūsīyah had never been as strong in Tripolitania, his political position there was somewhat challenged. It may be added also that a number of educated people in Libya altogether doubted the advisability of reshaping the new state along pure religious grounds, although such an administration received the support of the masses. The total result of the experience was, as we can see it, that the modern state of Libya needed a new pattern. The tribal Sanūsī body of principles and teachings was probably good for the period between 1843 and 1911, and it was certainly useful in carrying out the struggle against the Italians, but it was not exactly befitting of a modern regime.[5]

It is the great merit of the Amir that he understood the need for this change, and it does even greater credit to his wisdom that he should have succeeded, as King Idris I, in steering a traditional Arab and Moslem society through the initial stages of modern statehood.

For the Commissioner, who had the privilege of watching him accomplish this highly delicate task, he was fascinating to see in action. (The Commissioner's first impressions have been described on pages 164–65.) One might have expected a man in the Amir's position to raise the banner of Arab nationalism to inspire the Libyan people in their progress toward unity and independence. In fact, nothing of the kind happened; the Amir knew his people too well to set a pace which they could not maintain. He carefully took them along at a speed which they could sustain without discomfort, thereby displaying the remarkable restraint that distinguishes the contemplative leader. Indeed, he never took a step forward unless he knew that he could and would be followed. At the same time, his advice was always available. If necessary, he would take the initiative, but even then, as a rule, through well-chosen leaders. Here he was aided by his able judgment of men and situations and by his refusal to take action without searching reflection. But once he had made up his mind it was not easy to get him to change it, though on controversial issues he was always ready to listen to those who differed with him, submitting them to the test of debate when he thought it appropriate to do so.

By manner and comportment he was—and still is—a true leader of the Senussi, faithful to the teachings and traditions of his forebears, a man of

5. Nicola A. Zaideh, *Sanūsīyah: A Study of a Revivalist Movement in Islam* (Leiden, Netherlands: E. J. Brill, 1958), pp. 133–34.

great culture and learning who yet lives simply and austerely. Though physically a frail man, his bearing and manner communicate great dignity, softened in private conversation by a kindly sense of humor and a tranquil, radiant friendliness.

The Commissioner, always conscious of his ignorance of local conditions, soon learned not only to respect Sayed Idris but also, and increasingly, to value his opinions and seek his advice, even if circumstances did not always allow him to follow it. No man in the Amir's position can be without fault, and there were always people, including some of his own most devoted countrymen, ready to criticize his actions and decisions. Nonetheless, it can be said without fear of contradiction that the great mass of his people deeply respect and love him, often to the point of veneration.

Libya, and in particular Tripolitania, was also fortunate in possessing another man of recognized standing in the person of the Mufti of Tripolitania: Sheikh Mohamed Abul Is'ad al-Alim, son of a Qadi, born at Suq al-Jum'ah about 1880 and educated at the al-Azhar University in Cairo. Despite his judicial-religious position, he had not hesitated to play a leading part, first in local and later in national political affairs. As a leading member of the National Front, and subsequently its President, he became Vice-President of the National Congress Party of Tripolitania and thus a follower of Beshir Bey Saadawi. Being also a man of independent mind—a trait which, as we have seen in Part 4 of Chapter 3 (pp. 276–79), made him for some people an unwelcome candidate for appointment to the Committee of Twenty-One—who enjoyed the confidence of many people in other parties and of many independents, and being, moreover, respected in Cyrenaica and the Fezzan, he was the ideal man to play the part of mediator. Because of his strong personality, he was at times severely criticized not only by his own Party but also in the Council for Libya. This antagonism did not, however, prevent his election first to the Chairmanship of the Committee of Twenty-One, and later, unanimously, to the Presidency of the NCAL. (The confidence the Mufti thus enjoyed after World War II was all the more striking as he had been elevated to the supreme office of Grand Mufti of all Libya by no less a person than Benito Mussolini—hardly a recommendation in the eyes of the public. If he later succeeded in overcoming this handicap and, under the British Administration, in winning acceptance as Mufti of Tripolitania, he did so because people were fully aware of his intrinsic integrity. After independence he again became Grand Mufti of Libya, appointed this time by the King.)

Perhaps the most eloquent proof of the measure of confidence he enjoyed was the unanimous decision taken by the Committee of Twenty-One in October 1950 to entrust him with the task of drawing up the list of Tripolitanian candidates to be appointed as representatives of Tripolitania in the NCAL. Admittedly, his list did not command unanimous approval, but had the matter been left to the Tripolitanian party leaders themselves there would probably have been no agreement at all. In the last instance, approval was given by the Cyrenaicans and the Fezzanese, supported by three Tripolitanians.[6] More than anything else, the incident showed beyond doubt that the Mufti was widely respected as a tolerant, liberally minded man with a natural gift for political compromise. The Libyan people owe him a profound debt of gratitude.[7]

A third leader who deserves mention for the part he played in these two crucial years in Libyan history was Ahmed Bey Seif al-Nasr, the Chef du Territoire in the Fezzan, of whom we have already had much to say in Chapters 2 and 3. Admittedly, his influence was limited to the Fezzan, but that is no reason for underrating it; events might have taken a very different

6. At the moment of voting three members were absent (one Tripolitanian, one Cyrenaican, and the Tripolitanian member for the minorities), leaving eighteen members present. Of these, one Tripolitanian voted against the list and one abstained. The sixteen who voted for the list, therefore, were three Tripolitanians, six Cyrenaicans, and seven Fezzanese. (See *Second Annual Report of the United Nations Commissioner in Libya,* GAOR: Sixth Session, 1951–52, Supplement No. 17 (A/1949), para. 2; and also Chapter 3, pp. 297–98, above).

7. After independence, the Mufti withdrew from active politics, although, as the following anecdote demonstrates, he continued to be regarded by large sections of the population as a leader in both temporal and spiritual matters. The United Nations Technical Assistance Mission to Libya once had occasion to call on him for help in a rather unusual situation. The World Health Organization (WHO) was assisting the Maternal and Child Health Centre in Suk-el-Giuma, where the Mufti was still living. The Lebanese doctor in charge of the project, being concerned about the lack of protein in the diet of her pregnant patients, recommended that they should eat fish, which she knew was available at reasonable prices in the marketplace. To her surprise, she ran up against resistance to this suggestion on the grounds that the Koran forbade Moslems to eat the flesh of any creature which had eaten the flesh of man. The doctor countered this argument by explaining that she was not recommending shark flesh, but that of the small fish found in the offshore waters near the town. The patients, unshaken, replied that all fish were forbidden because it was well known that from time to time sailors fell into the sea and were eaten by its inhabitants. Since they could not know for certain whether or not a particular fish in the market had eaten the flesh of a drowned sailor, they must cut out fish entirely. At this point, it was arranged for the WHO expert to call on the Mufti, who was rather amused by the story, at once categorizing it as superstition and a distortion of the Koran. He thereupon issued a statement, which was reproduced in the local press and distributed to the patients at the Centre, making it clear that the prohibitions in the Koran were intended to apply only to the fish of known man-eating species, such as sharks, and not to fish generally. Thus reassured, the mothers-to-be attending the Centre got their protein in the local market.

turn had not Ahmed Bey, besides being a man of character supported by the large majority of Fezzanese, also been a faithful follower of the Senussi leader. What was more, he had a genuine sense of responsibility for the welfare of his people, and the moral courage and independence of mind to do what he could to protect their vital interests. A striking example of his mettle is the declaration he made on 15 May 1950, in the presence of the Commissioner and certain members of the Council, "that he accepted the Amirate of Sayyid Idris el Senussi over the whole of Libya and that he supported it on grounds of Moslem brotherhood and because it would promote the cause of union amongst the people of the country." [8]

Something has already been said on pages 229–30 of Ahmed Bey's character and the suspicions entertained about him, especially in Tripolitania. These suspicions, and the hostility of certain personal enemies, were rooted in the belief that he was in the pay of the French Administration; tribal jealousies also played a part. But it was in the nature of the situation obtaining in the Fezzan that he should be under French influence and that the greater part of the territory's expenditure should be met out of French funds.

Ahmed Bey's lack of refinement or learning was offset by a highly developed native wit, the product of his Koranic schooling and the phenomenal memory of the intelligent illiterate. He had an inexhaustible fund of tales, a veritable treasury of the Arabian Nights, of which two splendid examples have already been given on pages 274–75. His profound knowledge of his own folk, coupled with an innate astuteness, enabled him to hold his own both with the more sophisticated leaders in Cyrenaica and Tripolitania and, as has been seen, with the French Administration.

Such were the three men who, from within or without, were to play the leading parts in the NCAL when it set out along the road to independence.

But the picture would be incomplete without a portrait of the man who, from outside the Assembly, led the opposition inside it: Beshir Bey Saadawi, of whom we have already heard much and of whom we shall hear a great deal more. Beshir Bey, a Tripolitanian by birth, had been active in local politics since the time of the short-lived Republic of Tripolitania. Later he fled the country, taking refuge from Italian colonization in the Near and Middle East, finally entering the service of King Ibn Saud of Saudi Arabia. (He also at some time acquired Saudi Arabian nationality, an act that was to cost him a great deal, since, as will be seen in Chapter 10, it enabled the Libyan Government to expel him from the country for alleged electoral

8. First *Annual Report of the United Nations Commissioner in Libya,* GAOR: Fifth Session, 1950, Supplement No. 15 (A/1340), para. 89. See also Chapter 2, p. 198 above.

misconduct. At that time there was as yet no legal procedure for acquiring Libyan nationality while renouncing another nationality.) After World War I he returned to Tripolitania and resumed the political leadership there. An orator of great eloquence and an efficient organizer with a magnetic, emotional personality, he was a natural demagogue whose influence was felt not only throughout Tripolitania, but also among the younger generation in the coastal cities of Cyrenaica and even in the northern part of the Fezzan. As leader of the Tripolitanian Congress Party, he wielded real power, and there were times, as we have seen, when the Amir and other Libyan leaders, not to mention the Administering Powers, the Commissioner, and the members of the Council, were constrained to heed his words and deeds. The fact that he enjoyed not only the political but also the financial support of the Arab League and its most active member, Egypt, greatly strengthened his position.[9]

Had Beshir Bey, over and above being a very able popular leader, also been a statesman of the Amir's calibre, casting far-sighted policies in the mold of clear-cut plans, the understanding between the two that was always hovering on the brink of realization might truly have come about. (Although it is hazardous to speculate on what might have been, the Commissioner has always believed that in this event the constitution finally adopted would have come closer to the Tripolitanian concept of Libyan unity than it did in fact.) But hopes were either devoured by the Scyllan monster of Tripolitanian ambitions to run the future State or sucked under by the Charybdis of Cyrenaican fears of domination by its more powerful neighbor with its still economically influential Italian and other minorities.

As the reader will be only too well aware, the Commissioner, in his many long talks with the Tripolitanian leader, often had the feeling that personally he was on the point of letting political wisdom prevail over demagogy.

9. There had been a time—when Beshir Bey still professed to favor a loosely federated Libya—when the British Administration had not only tolerated but even encouraged him and his party. It continued to do so during the early part of 1950, when he was in all likelihood receiving material support from British sources. At party meetings and rallies his followers traveled into town in buses or trucks, which would certainly not have been available otherwise. Later in the year, as will be related, he went over to the Egyptian side. The British maintained that this change coincided with the arrival of Fuad Shukri from Egypt in the early summer of 1950. Shukri, who became Beshir Bey's legal and political adviser (it will be remembered that he played a very active part in the drafting of the notorious letter addressed to the Amir by the Egyptian and Pakistani members of the Council described in Chapter 3, pp. 260–65 was regarded as the paymaster of the Arab League, at least for Libya. He was expelled by the British Administration in May 1951 on the ground that he was inciting demonstrations against the Amir on the occasion of the latter's first official visit to Tripoli (see Chapter 8, pp. 611–12).

Then, presumably under pressure from the Arab League or his own extremists, with their chronic suspicions of Anglo-French intentions, Beshir Bey would change his mind, and the game would be back at square one. Such vacillation was short-sighted, for it played straight into the hands of the British and the French and thereby endangered the very unity and independence that the Tripolitanians were so eager to achieve.

Despite what has just been said about the dangers of giving free rein to the imagination, it is tempting, in weighing up Beshir Bey Saadawi's personality and policies, to conjecture what might have happened had the NCAL, under pressure from the Tripolitanians, adopted a unitary form of State. Cyrenaica and the Fezzan then might well have retreated behind the wall of British and French protection for some time to come, leaving the intransigent Tripolitanians to fall again under Italian influence, at least in the economic sphere. Thus for a while Libya would have lived under conditions more or less equivalent to those envisaged under the Bevin-Sforza plan (fear of which was the mainspring of the policy pursued by the Tripolitanian leaders and their backers)—a bone of contention in the Mediterranean heartland. Later, in the wake of the emancipation of the Arab countries of the Maghreb, in the late 1950s and early 1960s, the three Libyan peoples, having thus bought their experience dearly, would presumably have joined forces again in search of unity and independence. In the meantime, oil would have been discovered under Libya's soil. . . . But perhaps it would be more realistic to get back to the more mundane topic of the labors of the NCAL.

The opening meeting of the NCAL was presided over by the Mufti of Tripolitania as its oldest member. In his inaugural speech, the Mufti expressed himself as follows:

> In the name of God Almighty and with blessings and peace on our lord Muhammad the noble prophet and the wise legislator, possessed of an upright character and a merciful heart, does the National Constituent Assembly of Libya open the first of its sessions to establish the future constitution of the Libyan State in accordance with the U.N.O. resolution of 21 Nov. 1949, confirmed in the resolution of the same body issued on 17 Nov. 1950. His Honour then thanked the U.N. Commissioner, the Arab and Islamic states and the U.N. for the valuable help they had all given. He reviewed the struggle of the Libyan nation, how it had persisted in it, and how it had held out until it had gained the freedom, dignity and independence it aspired to. He then went on to say that the Libyan state wished to live on good terms with the whole world. Its desire was to spread peace and deal with its own economic, social and

cultural affairs so that it might share with the nations in establishing peace. He explained that for the nation to survive it must establish a strong constitution which would include certain provisions of Islamic Law. The constitution must avoid particularism and guarantee the citizens freedom of religion. His Honour then finished his speech with a declaration of fidelity and devotion to H. H. the Amir, anticipated King of Libya, and with a salute to Libya.[10]

In the course of the second meeting, held two days later, it was decided, seemingly by way of a tribute to the idea of national unity, to use for votes taken by roll call a nominal list of members in Arabic alphabetical order instead of grouping the names by territory as had been done at the first meeting. Nevertheless, when shortly afterward an ad hoc sub-committee was appointed to draw up draft rules of procedure, it was constituted on the basis of equality—four members from each territory—and thus the principle of territorial equality was once more emphasized.

It did not take the NCAL long to settle its internal organization, though a few procedural decisions were taken that were heavily charged with political significance.

The Sub-Committee on Rules of Procedure sat for a few days at the Commissioner's Headquarters in the Grand Hotel, assisted by his first legal adviser. Rule 2 of the draft it prepared provided that:

> The National Assembly shall draft the Constitution of the Libyan State in accordance with paragraph 3 of the United Nations General Assembly Resolution of 21 November 1949.[11]

The following discussion ensued when rule 2 came up for consideration:

> The Hon. Mem. Abdul Aziz Zagalai' asked whether the Assembly was to produce a constitution or only a *draft* for a constitution, which would then be presented to Parliament. The Hon. Mem. Omar Shennaib answered that Parliament was above the constitution, and that the duty of the Assembly was to produce a constitution, and not a draft for a constitution. The Hon. Mem. Munir Burshan now proposed that the Constitution contain an article to the effect that the Libyan Parliament had the right to amend any article. His Hon. the President said that the Parliament was more powerful than both the constitution and the N.C.A.L. The Hon. Mem. Salem al Atrash rose and said that the Rules of Procedure contained rules and regulations for the workings of the N.C.A.L. and that it would be best to limit ourselves to discussing these

10. *Proc. NCAL,* Stewart-Jackson Translation, 1st Meeting, 25 November 1950.
11. *Proc. NCAL,* Stewart-Jackson Translation, 3rd Meeting, 2 December 1950.

articles, without plunging into constitutional questions. The Hon. Mem. Abdul Aziz Zagalai' said that the Assembly had only plunged into the question of the constitution because the 2nd Article was devoted to this matter. The Hon. Mem. Munir Burshan then asked whether the Rules of Procedure were to be criticized, or merely set forth article by article. His Hon. the President answered that the Assembly had the right to criticize them. The Hon. Mem. Munir Burshan went on to say the members had a right to express their opinions, just as the [Committee for the Constitution] had the right to fix the powers of Parliament. The Hon. Mem. Abdul Zagalai' returned to the question of the competence of the N.C.A.L.; the Hon. Mem. Omar Shennaib answered him with the assurance that its concern was to establish a constitution, not the draft for one. The other members agreed with this.[12]

It is noteworthy that, according to the definitive text of rule 2, the words "including the form of Government" were inserted between the words "the Libyan State" and "in accordance with." [13]

Much more important, however, was the NCAL's interpretation of the substance of the rule, namely, that the Constitution to be drafted was to be final.

It is clear from the debate that, through the press and radio and probably also through private and diplomatic channels, the members of the NCAL had not only attentively followed the discussions at Lake Success, but had also fully grasped the nature of the issues raised there. Their swift decision on the NCAL's competence suggested that they wanted to forestall any attempt the Commissioner and Council might make to advise them in the sense announced by the former before the General Assembly. It also looked as if they wanted to confront the opposition with a fait accompli and, by adopting rule 2 in its definitive form, to serve notice of that intention on all concerned.

Another politically important decision came at the end of the discussion on the quorum. The draft rule concerned provided that: "Thirty-one of the members of the Assembly shall constitute a quorum." [14] The following debate ensued:

The Hon. Mem. Abdul Aziz Zagalai' proposed that the article be amended to read: "Three quarters of the members of the Assembly shall constitute a quorum." The Hon. Mem. Munir Burshan proposed adding

12. Ibid.

13. *Second Annual Report of the United Nations Commissioner in Libya,* Annex V, p. 80.

14. *Proc. NCAL,* Stewart-Jackson Translation, 3rd Meeting, 2 December 1950.

> . . . "provided that all three territories are represented." His Hon. the President remarked that the universally accepted quorum for any body is two thirds. Shaykh Ahmed as Sari objected to the amendment, and asked the President to put it to the vote. This was done, and the proposal of the Hon. Mem. Abdul Aziz Zagalai' was defeated by 50 votes to 5. The article remained in its original form.[15]

In the final English text of rule 12 "thirty-one" was replaced by "two-thirds," and thus a two-thirds majority was substituted for a simple majority. This text differs on an essential point from the record of the proceedings, which states clearly that the rule remained as drafted.

An equally important decision was taken on rule 31, which in draft provided that:

> Decisions of the Assembly shall be taken by a majority of the members present and voting.
>
> If a vote is equally divided, the proposal shall be regarded as rejected.
>
> The Assembly may not take any decision unless a majority is present.[16]

The following discussion took place:

> The Hon. Mem. Abdul Aziz Zagalai' proposed that decisions be taken on the basis of an absolute majority. The Hon. Mem. Muh. al Hankari asked him to change the expression "an absolute majority," if by this he meant a simple preponderance i.e. one vote more than half of the members of the N.C.A.L. The Hon. Mem. Mahmud al Muntasser requested a two-thirds majority. . . . The discussion ended with agreement on the article without any emendation.[17]

According to the second annual report, "The Legal Adviser to the Commissioner, who attended the meetings of the sub-committee [on rules of procedure], recommended that decisions should be taken by simple majority, but this recommendation was overborne by political considerations both by the sub-committee and the National Assembly." [18]

However, the text of rule 31 as adopted reads:

> Decisions of the Assembly shall be taken by a two-thirds majority of the members present and voting.
>
> The Assembly may not take any decision unless a quorum is present.[19]

15. Ibid.
16. Ibid.
17. Ibid.
18. *Second Annual Report of the United Nations Commissioner in Libya,* para. 35.
19. Ibid., Annex V, p. 82.

Here again, the final outcome is at variance with the record of the proceedings, which states that the rule in question was adopted unamended.

It is, of course, possible that, both in this case and in that of the quorum, the NCAL discussed and voted on texts other than those drafted by the Sub-Committee—perhaps as the result of oral amendments not recorded in the Proceedings. Be that as it may, it is obvious that the combined effect of these two rules of procedure was to make it possible for the representatives of any two of the three territories to dominate the NCAL, provided there was no serious absenteeism or abstention from voting, and that each territorial group voted as a solid bloc.

As soon as the Rules of Procedure had been adopted, the Assembly went on to elect its officers, once more following the principle of territorial equality. The Mufti of Tripolitania, whose selection of the proposed Tripolitanian members of the NCAL had caused such turmoil, was now unanimously elected President of that very body. The personal esteem in which he was held had clearly triumphed over political objections. Two Vice-Presidents were also elected: the leaders of the Cyrenaican and Fezzanese delegations, Omar Shenib and Mohamed Bin Othman, respectively. Three secretaries were appointed, one from each of the three territories (Sulayman al-Jerbi, Cyrenaica; Tahir Bin Mohamed, Fezzan; and Yahya Mas'ud Bin Issa, Tripolitania). Together, these six officers formed the Bureau of the Assembly.[20] Subsequently, Sulayman al-Jerbi became responsible for compiling the records of the Proceedings.

After a brief suspension, the meeting resumed with a suggestion by the President that the Assembly now discuss its agenda. This was adopted in the following form:

1. Nature of the state and form of government;
2. Establishment of the monarchy;
3. Appointment of a [committee] to draw up a constitution on the two above mentioned bases.[21]

From this moment, to an even greater extent than after the decision on rule 2 of the Rules of Procedure, it became clear that the majority in the National Assembly intended to settle without delay a number of basic political and constitutional issues before embarking upon a detailed study of the constitution itself.

Without further ado, the President opened a discussion on item 1 of the agenda. The following quotation from the Proceedings shows how the decision to give Libya a federal form of government was made:

20. More usually known as a Steering Committee.

21. *Proc. NCAL,* Stewart-Jackson Translation, 3rd Meeting, 2 December 1950.

The Vice-President Muh. Othman said that the nature of the government must be federal. The Hon. Mem. Abdul Aziz Zagalai' proposed that the Libyan state be independent and united within its natural boundaries; Egypt to the East, Tunis to the West, and the Sudan in the South. The Hon. Mem. Munir Burshan arose and emphasized the word "federal," since this would ensure the rights of each region. He added that he would prefer the addition of the phrase "federal and just." The Vice President Muh. Othman added "on a basis of equality." The Hon. Mem. Munir Burshan requested that the words "on a basis of equality" be changed. The Hon. Mem. Mahmoud al Muntasser requested that the aim of establishing a constitution be to prepare the way to complete unity. The Vice-President explained the word "federal" as meaning that each territory would manage its own affairs. The Hon. Mem. Munir Burshan explained that the expression "federal and just" was added because of the fears of certain of the members, and he asked that it be accepted. The Hon. Mem. the Secretary Yahia Massoud ben Issa then rose and asked what made the Assembly prefer federalism to a completely unitary organization. He explained that the economic state of the country did not allow every area to be a completely independent entity, and that he therefore wanted a single government for them all. His Hon. the President observed that if each of us could not exist independently, then we would have to co-operate. He went on to say that complete unity would at some time in the future replace federalism. The Vice-President Omar Shennaib said that this organization (i.e. federalism) was a temporary phase. His Hon. the President resumed his speech, and mentioned what had been said in the letter of congratulation sent by the representatives of America, to the effect that American federalism had made a single state out of the United States. On this he based his conclusion that federalism would not prevent us from becoming a single nation in the future. The Hon. Mem. the Secretary Yahia Massoud ben Issa showed that there were certain differences between Libya and the United States and went on to insist on the importance of the foundation that the N.C.A.L. would lay. His Hon. the President said that it was the constitution that would decide the matter.

The Hon. Mem. the Shaykh Muh. al Hankari said, "I think this problem, considered from a distance, will be seen to be internal. We want to avoid external dangers, and the only thing that will save us from them is federalism."

The Hon. Mem. Munir Burshan emphasised the importance of federalism at which some members applauded . . . and said, "We do not want anyone who impedes it." The Hon. Mem. Abdul Aziz Zagalai' said

"We do not want to set up obstacles, but merely to close the ranks to ward off dangers." The Hon. Mem. Mabrouk Geibani arose and said, "Once we have formed a government on a federal basis we shall demand the surrender of authority over us into our own hands." This was received with applause.

The Assembly now agreed that the form of the state should be federal. . . . His Hon. Mem. Munir Burshan asked that the word "just" be added to the statement as to the form of the state, so that it would become "federal and just." This request was granted.[22]

Looking back at this part of the record from a distance of fifteen years, its most noteworthy feature is perhaps that the President, a Tripolitanian, supported by the Vice-President, a Cyrenaican, should have declared his conviction that complete unity would at some time in the future replace federalism. This was verily foresight.

Still at the same meeting, the Assembly turned to the second item on its agenda. It took even less time to reach a decision on this than on item 1.

The Hon. Mem. Mahmud al Muntasser proposed that the Assembly resolve to appoint Muh. Idris al Muhdi al Sanussi as King. The members agreed to this unanimously by acclamation.

The Hon. Mem. Munir Burshan requested that the two resolutions be read out. The Secretary Suleiman Jerbi read them. His Hon. the President then read the text of the two resolutions in the form he himself had cast them in.

The wording of the resolutions was amended to read as follows:

1. That Libya is to be an independent, sovereign state, and that the form of the state is to be federal and just.
2. That the government is to be a constitutional monarchical representative democracy, under the crown of King Muh. Idris al Mahdi al Sanussi.
3. That the Assembly should present to H. M. the King its historic resolution, and that it should deem him henceforth lawful King of Libya.[23]

It was moreover decided to dispatch the following telegram to Benghazi:

H.M. Muh. Idris al Mahdi al Sanussi
First King of Libya.

The Libyan National Assembly is honoured to present to Your Majesty its historic resolution, passed unanimously at noon on Saturday 22 Safar 1370/2 December, 1950, proclaiming Your Majesty lawful King of

22. Ibid.
23. Ibid.

> Libya within its natural boundaries. Please accept the loyalty and devotion of the Assembly, together with its heartfelt congratulations. Long may you be preserved for your faithful nation, and long may Libya retain her beloved monarch.[24]

All the members of the Assembly signed the telegram.

Before the meeting closed, it was decided to discuss at succeeding meetings the establishment of a committee of eighteen members (six from each territory) to finalize the wording of the communication conveying the resolutions proclaiming the Amir King of Libya, and to draft a Constitution for the Libyan State. (This body was known indifferently as the Committee of Eighteen or the Committee for the Constitution. See pp. 509–10.) The fact both tasks were entrusted to the same committee indicated the special constitutional importance the NCAL attached to the terms of the letter which was to constitute its formal act of homage to the future King. The third meeting had indeed been momentous for Libya and its people, opening up as it did a new chapter in history.

In the meantime, the Commissioner, still held up at Lake Success, constantly urged by his Council and by some of his staff to return to his post where so many important developments were taking place, began to realize that his position, and probably the Council's too, was becoming disagreeably complicated. There he was, bound by his undertaking to the General Assembly that he would consult the Council on certain advice to be proffered to the NCAL, which the latter clearly did not want to receive. It was practically certain that that undertaking had induced a number of delegations at the General Assembly to vote against, or at any rate to abstain from voting for, the Egyptian proposal calling for an elected Libyan National Assembly. The Commissioner was personally on record as having declared his preference for such an elected body. Having lost on that issue in the Council, he had fallen back on the second best solution, namely, the preparation of a draft Constitution that would be subject to approval or amendment by an elected parliament. He had supported his suggestion by expressing grave doubts whether the NCAL, precisely because it had been appointed and not elected, would carry the necessary moral and political weight to elaborate a final, definitive Constitution. And now, a fortnight after his pledge had been given, and before he had had time to consult the Council, the NCAL had made it plain that it was not going to wait for advice. Moreover, in the face of strong opposition in Tripolitania, as well as from the Arab League, it had formally decided that Libya should be a federal State. In all likelihood, the members of the NCAL would argue that it had the right to do so under paragraph 3 of Resolution 289 (IV).

24. Ibid.

Altogether, these various developments had created an awkward immediate situation and in all probability would also cause trouble at the Sixth Session of the General Assembly in the autumn of the following year.

To make things even worse, the Commissioner's personal position and feelings caused him acute embarrassment. Earlier in the year he had been repeatedly obliged in his conversations with Libyans to stress that it was neither his nor the United Nations' responsibility, but that of the representatives of the Libyan people, to draft the Constitution. In those days, many a Libyan had been reluctant to assume such a responsibility. Now, on the contrary, the NCAL seemed eager to push ahead with the task; its sense of independence and initiative was heartwarming. It was certainly proof of a development to be rejoiced in, but it put the Commissioner in a difficult position, inasmuch as it was now incumbent upon him to advise the NCAL to act less precipitately in dealing with basic political issues that were capable of dividing the people.

Neither could he forget that the promise he had given the General Assembly covered certain important points which the NCAL might still like to consider incorporating in the Constitution.

Having thus weighed all aspects of the situation, the Commissioner decided to send an urgent message (dated 7 December 1950) to the Amir of Cyrenaica, Ahmed Bey Seif al-Nasr, and the President of the NCAL, which each received in the form of a letter transmitted by the Acting Chief of the Mission in Libya. After expressing his regrets for his continued enforced absence from Tripoli, he invited their attention to subparagraph 3 (b) of Resolution 387 (V), in which the establishment of a Provisional Libyan Government by 1 April 1951 was recommended. He assumed that this could be done only after a Constitution had been agreed upon. Subsequently, powers would have to be transferred to the Provisional Government, presumably in accordance with a program drawn up by himself in consultation with the Council and in cooperation with the Administering Powers.

The Commissioner also pointed out that he intended to ask the Council's advice on matters of constitutional development in the light of the recent discussions in the General Assembly. He suggested therefore that the NCAL, while naturally reserving its freedom of action, might find it in the interest of the future Libyan State to suspend for the time being its debate on matters of basic constitutional importance. If it did not, it might experience unpleasant repercussions at the Sixth Session of the General Assembly. Hinting that the criticisms voiced by the Arab States might well be repeated more forcefully, he expressed the fear that the validity of the decisions, past and future, of the NCAL and the Provisional Government might be questioned. Hence, he urged the President to use his influence to limit current discussions to questions related to the NCAL's program of work.

The reactions in Tripoli and Benghazi to the Commissioner's communication were most unfavorable, members of the NCAL considering it to be in complete contradiction with the Commissioner's earlier position. They deeply resented this change of face, the reason for which they failed to understand. No less a personage than Mahmud Muntasir, a Tripolitanian leader usually noted for the moderation of his views, wanted the Commissioner to know that the NCAL was determined to go ahead as a constituent body, regardless of the consequences. The Commissioner was accused of taking sides in a domestic issue and warned that Libya would not tolerate interference in its internal affairs, even from other Moslem States.

The Amir and the Mufti, although less agitated, nonetheless felt uneasy pending an explanation of the Commissioner's volte-face. The former asked the British Chief Administrator in Cyrenaica to inquire through London what might have happened. The Mufti approached the senior members of the Mission in Tripoli for clarification, undertaking to pacify his colleagues so far as possible.

At the NCAL's sixth meeting, held on 14 December 1950, the President informed the House that a special message had reached him from the Commissioner; the text was then read out to them. Thereupon a long and rather involved debate ensued on various procedural points. Should consideration of the letter be added to the agenda? What was its status—personal or official? Was the President obliged under the Rules of Procedure to submit the text of the letter, and that of any reply he might make, to the Assembly for its formal approval, or was simple conveyance enough? Finally, the Assembly having in the meantime resolved to visit Benghazi to lay the Act of Homage at the Amir's feet, it was decided to defer examination of the Commissioner's letter until its return.

The Act of Homage drafted by the Committee for the Constitution (the Committee of Eighteen) was now brought in, and after it had been solemnly read out, all members were invited to sign it. All did so, in alphabetical order. However, Abd al-Aziz al-Zaqalla'i, a member from Tripolitania, asked that the following reservation be written into the record in his name:

> I continue to maintain my previous position as regards the form of government, i.e. while agreeing to the enthronement of H. H. the Amir Muh. Idris al Sanussi as King of Libya, I retain my reservations concerning the federal system of government: I am a supporter of unity.[25]

25. *Proc. NCAL,* Stewart-Jackson Translation, 6th Meeting, 14 December 1950.

The NCAL's decision to defer its debate on the Commissioner's letter did not, however, prevent the President from sending him next morning the reply he had already prepared. In it he thanked the Commissioner for the efforts he had made in defense of the Libyan cause. Stating that the NCAL had decided that Libya should be a united kingdom under the Crown of His Highness the Amir, he expressed the opinion that this decision violated neither the spirit nor the letter of Resolutions 289 (IV) and 387 (V). On the contrary, he felt that the NCAL had simply exercised a right conferred on it by the United Nations itself. At the same time, he gave an assurance that it did not intend to ignore the Commissioner's advice.

On 19 December, the Commissioner at last got back to Tripoli. A few days later, His Eminence the Mufti came to see him, and in the course of a long talk the Commissioner gave the Mufti a detailed account of events at Lake Success, explaining at the same time how he had come to give his undertakings to the General Assembly. The Mufti did not omit to point out that it was the Council for Libya itself which had recommended that the members of the Committee of Twenty-One be appointed and not elected, and that it had similarly recommended that the three territories be represented on the Committee on an equal basis. These decisions, he argued, had made it very difficult for the Committee to act otherwise with regard to the composition of the NCAL. He personally considered that it was not equitable, for instance, to put Tripolitania and the Fezzan on the same footing; but in a spirit of conciliation and in order not to delay the setting up of the NCAL, the principle had been agreed.

He was convinced that, despite their criticisms on the election issue, the Arab delegations at Lake Success wanted to serve Libya's best interests; but they were ill-informed about the country's internal problems. He asserted, moreover, that the large majority of the population in the three territories had full confidence in the NCAL and that the main opposition came from a group of malcontents in Tripoli town, and not from the interior. Some of these malcontents had hankered after membership in the NCAL, and when these hopes had been dashed because of the small size of the House, they had added their voices to the criticisms emitted by the Congress Party.

The Commissioner raised the question of the nature of the Constitution, expressing his conviction that one ratified by an elected Parliament would enjoy more authority than a text prepared and proclaimed by an appointed body.

The Mufti then mentioned the possibility of writing amending provisions into the Constitution, to which the Commissioner again ventured the view that it might be better to submit a provisional text of the Constitution to an elected Parliament for review. The Mufti stuck to his point that, even though merely appointed, the NCAL should be considered as having been legally constituted, and that the Constitution it produced should accordingly be regarded as definitive. Any other procedure could not fail to cause postponement of independence.

On 8 January, the NCAL held its seventh meeting. On its agenda stood the examination of the Commissioner's letter. This gave rise to a prolonged discussion, as the following extract from the Proceedings shows:

> The Hon. Mem. Munir Burshan said that it seemed to him that Mr. Pelt was asking the Assembly to delay taking any step towards a constitution until it had heard Mr. Pelt's advice. The President answered that Mr. Pelt was only requesting that the Assembly listen to the advice that would be advanced by him or by his Council; that he wanted the Assembly's activities to be based on a firm foundation while at the same time leaving it complete freedom of action. The same Hon. Mem. asked if the President had understood from conversations with Mr. Pelt whether he wanted to hold up the Assembly's activities, or whether, on the contrary, he wanted it to continue them. The President observed that his conversations with Mr. Pelt would be examined afterwards. At the moment it was only the letter that was under examination. The Hon. Mem. Munir Burshan said that since the two examinations concerned the same subject it would be best to unite them. The Hon. Mem. Ahmed as Sari now rose, and said that it was to be understood from Mr. Pelt's letter that he wanted the Assembly to lay down a draft constitution. The Hon. Mem. Omar Shennaib objected to this, saying that Mr. Pelt simply wanted to be present when the constitution was being drafted, so that his views could be consulted [*sic*]. The Hon. Mem. Ahmed as Sari said that the constitution should be presented for a Parliament, chosen on the basis of free elections, to agree to. The Hon. Mem. Omar Shennaib answered that the Parliament was still to come and that it was the constitution that would create it. After the Secretary had read another section of the letter, the Hon. Mem. Abdul Aziz Zagalai' drew the attention of the President to the fact that Mr. Pelt advised the Assembly to limit itself to internal activities, and said that speaking for himself he considered it desirable to accept this advice. The Hon. Mem. Abdel Gawad Freites observed that what was to be understood from this section was that Mr. Pelt did not want the Assembly to have complete independence in drafting the constitution, and did not want it to act in his absence. "And we can say that we accepted this advice, since we were away in Cyrenaica, and the Assembly did not begin its activities until after Mr. Pelt's return to Tripoli.

The [Committee for the Constitution] met in Mr. Pelt's office, where the steps to be taken were examined one by one. It is therefore the U.N. office that provides us with the constitutional studies; if we find it difficult to understand something in these studies, then we ask Mr. Pelt's office to explain it. It is he who advises us, and we are continually guided by Mr. Pelt. We have proceeded on the basis of his recommendations, but without following them slavishly; we have acted rather in accordance with what seemed best all round." The Hon. Mem. Abdul Aziz Zagalai' observed that Mr. Pelt had said that after his consultations with H. M. the King and other personages he would refer back to his Council to ask its advice. The Hon. Mem. Abdel Gawad Freites answered that this did not prevent the Assembly from carrying out preliminary research in Mr. Pelt's office. The Hon. Mem. Ahmed as Sari then asked for a vote on his proposal, and requested that the Assembly accepted [*sic*] Mr. Pelt's view and draw up a draft constitution. The Hon. Mem. Abdul Majeed Ku'bar opposed him, saying that the Assembly should draw up a constitution since that was what had been resolved previously. The Hon. Mem. Ahmed as Sari expressed his ignorance of this, and the Chairman explained that this resolution had been taken in his absence. After the Secretary had read another section of the letter, the Hon. Mem. Abdul Aziz Zagalai' said that the word *minhaj* in Mr. Pelt's letter referred to the Rules of Procedure [and not to the working plan]. . . . The Hon. Mem. Munir Burshan reaffirmed his view that the letter and the President's discussion with Mr. Pelt should be examined at the same time. The Hon. Mem. Abdul Aziz Zagalai' then said that he thought that Mr. Pelt had sent this letter in order to explain the point which said that the National Assembly did not represent the nation; and that he had given the U.N. General Assembly an undertaking that he would advise the Assembly to draw up a draft constitution. The Hon. Mem. Khalil Gellal objected that the question concerned the very nature of the Assembly, since Mr. Pelt had not said that the Assembly was not recognised. The Hon. Mem. Abdul Aziz Zagalai' explained that he had said that Mr. Pelt had been asked to do this, "and he had not said that the Assembly was not recognised." The Hon. Mem. Khalil Gellal answered that the duty of the Assembly made it imperative that it carry out this task, which was within its competence, and for which it had been created; and that there was nothing to be lost by gaining Mr. Pelt's advice. After a short discussion between the President and the Hon. Mem. Abdul Aziz Zagalai', concerning the question of recognition of the Assembly, the Hon. Mem. Ahmed as Sari rose and asked whether the contents of Mr. Pelt's letter had been agreed on after it had been read in the first place. The President answered that the letter was not there to be discussed and commented on, and that he had simply wished to inform the Assembly of its contents. The same Hon. Mem. insisted on a straight reply to his question. The President repeated his statement that the letter was not an item to be agreed to by the Assembly. The same Hon. Mem. then asked why, in that case, had it been placed on the agenda?

The Hon. Mem. Abdul Aziz Zagalai' then rose and asked whether the letter was addressed to the President personally or to the Assembly as a whole. He asked for a vote on this point. The President said that the phrase "I request you to use your influence" showed that the letter was addressed to him personally; and that he had thought it best to let the Assembly know of any news that reached him concerning the Assembly. The Hon. Mem. Abdel Gawad Freites said that it did not so much matter to us that we should know whether the letter was personal or official as that we should understand it exactly and do as it requests, so long, that is, as this did not conflict with Libya's best interests. On the basis of what we have seen of Mr. Pelt's sincere devotion to the interests of the country we should believe that he would not propose anything likely to harm it; so let us fully accept it. In general we have understood it, and have compared it with the Assembly's resolution, with which we find it to be in complete agreement. We can see that Mr. Pelt is offering us sound advice in suggesting that we pass no resolutions in his absence; and in fact the Assembly has not so far passed any resolutions having practical consequences. The Hon. Mem. Khalil Gellal observed that the Assembly was agreed to continue its activities and those of the [Committee for the Constitution], and that it would not be a bad idea to ask Mr. Pelt's advice before doing so. At this point the Hon. Mem. Abdul Aziz Zagalai' asked for a vote on the question as to whether the letter was personal or concerned with the Assembly as a whole. The Hon. Mem. Khalil Gellal observed to him that the letter was addressed to the President, and that it therefore concerned the Assembly. The Hon. Mem. Ali Tamir added that the letter had arrived a long time ago, and that it contained advice about constitutional questions given by Mr. Pelt to the Assembly. Now that Mr. Pelt has gone so far and come to an understanding with the President, I do not think it necessary to examine the matter.

The Hon. Mem. Ahmed as Sari said that whether the letter was sent to the Assembly or to the President, the question was: did the members agree to it or not? The Hon. Mem. Khalil Gellal answered him that the Assembly, having read the letter, had decided to do as it suggested; that is to say, it would continue with its working plan. . . . There was no harm in listening to Mr. Pelt's advice once the Assembly had prepared its resolutions. The Hon. Mem. Munir Burshan added that having been informed of Mr. Pelt's letter the Assembly decided to follow it as far as possible, insofar as it did not conflict with the national interest. The President advanced the view that to set up a committee to draft a constitution would be to continue our activities, and that when we begin to examine the committee's proposals we will ask for guidance from Mr. Pelt. The Hon. Mem. Khalil Gellal proposed that the Assembly adopt a resolution to the effect that the [Committee for the Constitution] should continue its studies, at the same time taking advantage of Mr. Pelt's advice.

. . . The Assembly then turned to a consideration of the third item on the agenda. The President informed the members that Mr. Pelt wished the Assembly success in its efforts; that as U.N. Commissioner he was glad to proffer his advice, after having studied the question in his council; and that he—Mr. Pelt—had begun to work on another matter—his contacts with London, Paris and other places, after which he would contact the Assembly. The President then told the members that he had answered Mr. Pelt that the Assembly would draw on Mr. Pelt's advice and ideas, as well as those of others; that the Assembly thanked Mr. Pelt for his views, and that it would give his suggestions careful consideration. The Hon. Mem. Munir Burshan rose and asked the President the following question: Did Mr. Pelt tell you whether he thought the Assembly should suspend its activities or not? The President answered that Mr. Pelt said that the Assembly had freedom of action, and that he requested that it listen to his advice.

. . . The Hon. Mem. Abdul Aziz Zagalai' then asked for a vote on his proposal which was that the Assembly discontinue its activities until Mr. Pelt's return. A vote was taken on this proposal. It was supported only by its proposer and by the following [members]: Ali el Kaloush; Ali ben Saleem and Ahmed as Sari. It was thus agreed by 51 votes to 4 that the Assembly continue its activities.[26]

The situation was now perfectly clear. Courteously, but firmly, the NCAL had decided to go ahead with its work without waiting for the advice the Commissioner and the Council might be preparing about further constitutional development. It did not mean that in future it would not listen to any advice at all. It simply meant that it would listen to any advice the Commissioner, with or without previously consulting the Council, might find it appropriate to offer, provided it was not in the nature of an ultimatum.

26. *Proc. NCAL,* Stewart-Jackson Translation, 7th Meeting, 8 January 1951.

The NCAL still had a very important, and from its point of view very urgent, matter to settle, namely, the formal implementation of the decision to proclaim the Amir King of Libya. To make this decision effective, a simple telegram, even if signed by all the members of the Assembly, would obviously be inadequate and inappropriate. Arab custom requires the submission of the Act of Homage in writing and by submission in person. That is why the NCAL had unanimously decided to embark upon a journey of 1,000 kilometers by bus along the coastal road, under conditions which, even by local standards, were not exactly comfortable.

Meanwhile, the NCAL's plan to invite the Amir to ascend the throne of the future State had given rise to an exchange of telegrams between His Highness in Benghazi and the Commissioner in Lake Success. Both recognized that the Assembly's decision was of great political significance, not only for the future, but also because it would help to consolidate the immediate situation. On the other hand, if the Amir prematurely agreed to ascend the throne—that is to say, before the proclamation of Libya's independence, before a constitution had come into force and even before a Provisional Government had been established—the authority of the future Monarch might be impaired by what some might consider unbecoming haste. Not only would he for another twelve months be a King without effective royal powers or prerogatives; elevation to the throne too soon might induce Libyan and foreign public opinion to look upon him as a figurehead acting at the behest of the Administering Powers. Indeed, until the transfer of powers had been completed and an independent Libya thereby established, the Monarch would have found himself in a delicate position. With no real power (except, of course, in Cyrenaica), but with great political authority, constantly asked for advice but as yet unable to make legally enforceable decisions, having to make his way through a minefield sown with explosive issues, the King would truly have been walking where angels would fear to tread.

In view of all these circumstances, His Highness dispatched the following message to the President of the Assembly:

> I have received your telegram of 2 December 1950, informing me of the historic decision taken by your distinguished Assembly to invite me to accede to the throne of the united Libyan State.
>
> In reply to your invitation, I send you my sincere thanks and assure you of my gratitude for the confidence the Assembly over which you preside has shown in me.
>
> I hereby declare that I am willing to accept the Assembly's invitation to accede to the throne of the Libyan State. I consider, however, that it is

better for me to postpone the official proclamation of my accession to the throne until such time as the steps which have to be taken in the political, administrative and constitutional field have reached a stage where I am in a position to exercise royal powers. At this happy moment in the history of our beloved nation I am pleased to assure our noble people that I will always serve our country faithfully, striving to help its inhabitants to live in happiness and prosperity. I am pleased, moreover, to send your Assembly my best wishes and my sincere congratulations. I pray Almighty God to help you to succeed in your efforts.

(Signed) Amir of Cyrenaica.[27]

While waiting for the draft of the Act of Homage to emerge from the Committee of Eighteen, the NCAL decided on the design and colors of the Libyan flag. The record of the fourth meeting describes the event as follows:

The Hon. Mem. Omar Shennaib rose and presented the design of a flag drawn on a sheet of paper; it was composed of three colours, red, black and green, with a crescent and a white star in the middle of the black portion. At the same time the Hon. Mem. informed those present that this was the flag design chosen by H. M. the King. The members agreed to the flag design presented to them.[28]

The NCAL also decided that once the actual drafting of the Constitution had started, it would in principle meet once a week to consider, section by section, the draft articles submitted to it by the Committee of Eighteen. This timetable was chosen to enable it to study groups of interconnected articles together.

The reservation in the Amir's reply to the NCAL at first caused some misunderstanding among members, which gave rise to the following exchange of views:

27. Translation from the Arabic made for internal purposes by the language staff of the United Nations Mission in Libya. United Nations Archives. Typescript.

28. *Proc. NCAL,* Stewart-Jackson Translation, 4th Meeting, 4 December 1950. The King's choice had been inspired by the following symbolic considerations: the red stood for the blood of those who had fallen in the cause of freedom; the green was the traditional green of Islam; the black was the color of war, which would be waged against those who might be so bold as to attack Libya. The crescent and star is the traditional emblem of Islam. The Amir's own flag was black, with the crescent and star superimposed. It was the war flag he used in 1923 when the struggle against Italian fascism began. It was also the flag under which, from 1940 onward, the Senussi legion (Libyan Arab Force) fought with the British forces against the German and Italian armies in the Western Desert.

The Hon. Mem. Muh. al Hankari asked that the telegram of H. M. the King be re-read; when this had been done he asked whether the fact that H. M. was prepared to accept his appointment could not be considered the equivalent to accepting the homage paid to him. The Hon. Mem. Suleiman Jerbi answered that in saying that he was prepared to accept the throne His Majesty only meant that if the Assembly came to him with their homage he would accept it. The act of paying homage cannot be carried out by telegram. The Hon. Mem. Abdul Gawad Freites denied that H. M. the King's telegram implied any hesitation accepting homage. His Hon. the President observed that H. M. the King had already accepted with thanks, and that His Majesty had merely thought it best on his part to hope that this would be announced once the constitutional developments in the country had come to an end. The Hon. Mem. Munir Burshan said that the Assembly had in that case been precipitate in passing the resolution, and that it would be better to consult H. M. the King's opinion first. He proposed that the previous resolution be amended, or else that its dispatch be postponed. The President again emphasized that there was no need for any change in the resolution. The Hon. Mem. Abdul Gawad Freites supported the President's statement. He said that it was necessary to present the document doing homage because, firstly, homage was the most important basis on which the constitution would be raised, and, secondly, because it would permit H. M. the King to ask the nations who supervised the administration to hand over power to a local government. The Hon. Mem. Mahmoud al Muntasser explained that the point in dispute was the question of sovereignty, and especially the mention of the phrase "from henceforth" in the resolution. There was no disagreement as to H. M. the King's acceptance of the proffered homage. The Hon. Mem. Suleiman Jerbi added, however, that by the phrase "designating H. M. the King as lawful King of Libya from henceforth" the Assembly had not meant that His Majesty should take power immediately, since that was not possible until a government was established. The intention had been the Libyans should immediately start to consider H. M. the King in their relations to him, but that His Majesty would only come to exercise his power once the constitutional developments in the country had come to an end. The Hon. Mem. Muh. al Hankari then proposed that the presentation of the document proffering homage be delayed. After a brief debate on the subject the members agreed to re-affirm the previous resolution, considering any changes in it unnecessary. The Hon. Mem. Abdul Gawad Freites proposed that the document proffering homage begin with "In the name of Allah &c."

(Verily, those who do homage to you, do homage only to Allah: *Translator.*) The other members agreed to this.[29]

The Committee of Eighteen submitted to the NCAL the following draft act of homage:

> We are the representatives of the Libyan people from Cyrenaica, Tripoli and Fezzan meeting in Tripoli in Libya in the National Constituent Assembly by the Will of God.
>
> And we are endowed with full powers whose validity and whose fulfilment of legal form is acknowledged.
>
> And we are resolved upon the composition of unity between us and upon the creation of a sovereign democratic unified State, the system of rule in which will be constitutional and monarchical.
>
> We shall start on our work with praise and thanks to God for His gracious favour towards us in liberating our country and in granting it its independence.
>
> And we acknowledge the loyalty of His Highness Mohamed Idris al Mahdi as Sanusi the Great, Prince of Cyrenaica and his long, fruitful struggle for the good of Libya and her peoples;
>
> In fulfilment of the peoples' wishes and in confirmation of the earlier legal arrangements which issued from the legal representatives of the people to His Highness and in solicitation for the well-being of our country and its unity under the Crown of the King in whom we find ideals corresponding with those required by his lofty position.
>
> We hereby proclaim and do homage to His Highness the Prince Mohamed Idris al Mahdi as Sanusi, the great Prince of Cyrenaica, as constitutional King of the United Kingdom of Libya and we hope that His Highness will condescend to accept that.
>
> And we have decided on transporting the National Constituent Assembly and its whole organisation to Benghazi to submit this historic decision to His Majesty the great King and receive his acceptance of our homage.
>
> Tripoli in Libya, Saturday, the 22nd of Safar 1370 corresponding to the 2nd December, 1950.[30]

This draft gave rise to a discussion which is not recorded in detail in the Proceedings; but comparison of the text with the final version suggests that there was a considerable amount of redrafting, though the substance was not affected.

29. *Proc. NCAL,* Stewart-Jackson Translation, 5th Meeting, 7 December 1950.

30. *Proc. NCAL,* Committee for the Constitution, Stewart-Jackson Translation, 1st Meeting, 6 December 1950.

There is no doubt that the final text was more in keeping with the nature of the document than the original draft. It read as follows:

In the name of God, the Merciful, the Compassionate, surely those who swear allegiance to you do but swear allegiance to God; the hand of God is above their hands.

Therefore, whoever breaks his faith, he breaks it only to the injury of his own soul, and whoever fulfills what he has covenanted with God, He will grant him a mighty reward.

WE, THE REPRESENTATIVES OF THE LIBYAN PEOPLE of Cyrenaica, Tripolitania and the Fezzan, meeting in the City of Tripoli by the grace of God in a National Constituent Assembly invested with full powers found to be in good and due form,

DETERMINED to create unity among us and to establish a democratic, federal, independent and sovereign State, its form of government being a constitutional monarchy,

INITIATE our work by rendering praise and thanks to God for the blessings He has granted us in the liberation of our country and its independence,

AND IN RECOGNITION of the devotion of His Highness El Sayed Mohamed Idris El Mahdi El Senussi, the exalted Amir of Cyrenaica, and his long and fruitful struggle for the weal of Libya and its people,

AND IN FULFILLMENT of the universal wishes of the people and in confirmation of the previous lawful proclamations of His Highness by the lawful representatives of the people,

AND IN OUR DESIRE to ensure the happiness of our country and its unity under the crown of a King in whom we find embodied to the highest degree the attributes required for these high functions,

WE THEREFORE PROCLAIM His Highness El Sayed Mohamed Idris El Mahdi El Senussi, the exalted Amir of Cyrenaica, and acknowledge him as the constitutional King of the United Libyan Kingdom, and we beg His Majesty to deign give acceptance thereto,

AND WE HAVE DECIDED that the National Constituent Assembly as a whole shall proceed to Benghazi to submit this historic decision to His Majesty, the Exalted King, with a view to securing His Majesty's acceptance to this proclamation.

Tripoli, Saturday, 2 December 1950
22 Safar 1370 [31]

31. Translation from the Arabic made for internal purposes by the language staff of the United Nations Mission in Libya. United Nations Archives. Typescript.

The Amir replied in the following terms:

Cabinet of the Amir,
The 7th day of Rabi'al-Awal 1370,
17 December 1950.

"In the name of God, the Merciful, the Compassionate,
Thanks be to God, the Supreme.
The most truthful word is the book of God and the best advice is that of our prophet Mohamed. May the blessings of God be upon him.

To the Honourable President and Members of the Libyan Constituent Assembly—May peace and the blessings of God be with you.

We have received with the greatest pleasure the important historic document signed by all the members of your legitimate body, which is fully representative of the Libyan people and was established for the purpose of determining the form of the future Libyan State. We understand from the substance of your document that your esteemed body has decided:

Firstly: that the Libyan State shall be an independent sovereign constitutional monarchy, comprising three territories, Cyrenaica, Tripolitania and the Fezzan, within their natural boundaries.

Secondly: that the three territories, Cyrenaica, Tripolitania and the Fezzan shall unite into a federal State, under the name of the United Libyan Kingdom.

Thirdly: that We are invited by unanimous decision to ascend the throne of the United Libyan Kingdom as its crowned King.

Having examined your historic document, and in reply to your unanimous resolution, We are pleased to give a favourable answer to your request, to accede to your wishes and to accept your generous invitation, which decision We shall formally make public in due course.

We sincerely thank your honourable body for its resolution, in which We see the greatest proof of and the most important testimony to the valuable confidence which you place in our person in these happy historic circumstances, and We wish to assure you that, as in the past, We shall spare no effort in proving to our beloved Nation that We are a devoted servant of our country, working for the happiness and prosperity of its cherished sons.

On this joyful occasion, We offer your honourable body our sincerest greetings and best wishes, praying Almighty God that He may guide us on the right path for the weal and bliss of our country, shower His blessings on the work of your Assembly and crown your endeavours with full success.

Mohamed Idriss el-Mahdi el-Senussi [32]

The Commissioner summarized this important episode in Libyan history in the following brief passage in his second annual report:

> The National Assembly then discussed the form of the future Libyan Government. On the proposal of one of the Tripolitanian members, it decided unanimously and amid the applause and acclamations of the Assembly, that Libya should be a monarchy with His Highness the Amir Mohammed Idris al Senussi as King. It resolved to communicate this decision to him, and to inform him that it considered him King as from that day. . . .
>
> On 7 December 1950, the President of the Assembly [received] a message from the Amir in reply to the message inviting him to accept the throne. The Amir accepted the invitation, but preferred to postpone the proclamation of his acceptance until the accomplishment of the political, constitutional and administrative measures which would enable him effectively to exercise his royal prerogative. Therefore, he was known as the King-Designate.[33]

The title of "King-Designate" was never officially proclaimed, but from this time on until independence it was customary to use this style when speaking formally of the Amir. At the same time, Libyans used the styles "Your Majesty" and "His Majesty." [34]

Thus, in less than a month, the National Assembly had determined the form of the State, proclaimed the Monarchy, designated the King, and adopted the national flag. Although the first of these fundamental decisions was vehemently contested at the time, future developments proved that it was the sole solution capable of ensuring the unity of the country.

PART 2. POLITICS AND THE CONSTITUTION

By the time the Commissioner returned to Tripoli from Lake Success, he had been away for three months; far too long, given the tasks that required

32. Ibid. It is interesting to compare the terms of this exchange between the NCAL and Sayed Idris with those of the Act of Homage addressed to the Sayed by the leaders of the Tripolitanian Republic, and his reply thereto, as described in the Historical Background, pp. 23–26.

33. *Second Annual Report of the United Nations Commissioner in Libya,* paras. 38–40.

34. See also Chapter 8, p. 620, fn. 13.

his attention on the spot. Several members of the Council were getting impatient. However, the Mission staff had kept him informed of developments by regular and frequent cables. Thus he knew that the recommendations of the Committee of Twenty-One, and to an even greater extent the way in which the Tripolitanian members of the NCAL had been appointed and the latter itself convened, had aroused a storm of protest, seemingly spontaneous, but in fact organized by the National Congress Party. These protests had been whipped up into a tempest by the NCAL's decisions of 2 December 1950. Khalidi sums up the situation thus: "From that moment the Congress Party, supported by Pakistan and Egypt, came into conflict with the National Assembly over the constitutional development program." [35]

This of course implied that the Council for Libya would be divided internally, because several of its members were actively in favor of the NCAL. Vociferous demonstrators against the latter paraded the streets of Tripoli town, and the Commissioner found his desk in the Grand Hotel piled high with petitions signed by thousands of people, mostly from the Tripolitanian coastal cities, but not a few from the interior as well. The majority were protests against the federal form of State and the numerical equality of representation in the NCAL. Others, though admittedly less numerous were, on the contrary, in favor of the National Assembly as planned by the Committee of Twenty-One. These came particularly from the interior of Tripolitania and from the Fezzan.

What was remarkable was that not one of all these petitions, not even the most violent, said one word against the proclamation of the Amir as future King of Libya; indeed, many expressed joy and satisfaction at the prospect.

A separate pile of petitions related to Resolution 388 A (V) which set out economic and financial provisions for Libya (see the preceding chapter). They demanded the immediate restitution of former Libyan property confiscated or expropriated by the Italian authorities during the occupation, the signatories having clearly failed to grasp the General Assembly's true purpose.

Having been kept so well informed, the Commissioner felt that he was adequately acquainted with the facts of the situation. But that was not at all the same thing as being personally attuned to the new political climate that had developed during his absence. Hence a reconnaissance in depth and a reappraisal of the terrain and of the forces deployed over it were an urgent necessity if a program of work for the coming months was to be produced in good time.

The Commissioner's first concern was how to present a request for advice on further constitutional development to the Council for Libya in such a

35. Khalidi, *Constitutional Development in Libya,* p. 35.

way as to keep his promise to the General Assembly, to secure maximum support for his plans in the Council, and, above all, to make a salutary impact on the NCAL. Other matters, such as the timetable for the transfer of powers and the organization of technical assistance, also called for prompt attention, but it was obvious that constitutional development must come first.

So it was decided to make a systematic yet rapid survey of the political situation. A series of consultations was arranged between the Commissioner, the Principal Secretary and other members of the Mission staff, and practically all the leading personalities within, as well as outside, the NCAL, the Amir, Ahmed Bey Seif al-Nasr, the Chief Administrators of the three territories, and the members of the Council. Lastly, Arabic-speaking members of the staff were sent on individual trips throughout Tripolitania to interview local leaders not available in Tripoli town. The Commissioner himself made a few quick flights between 21 December 1950 and 16 January 1951 to discuss the new situation with the Governments of the United Kingdom, France, Italy, and Egypt, as well as with the Secretary-General of the Arab League.

In London and Paris, it became clear that the two Administering Powers would be reluctant to go along with the advice for which the Commissioner intended to request the Council's support. They realized that his policy aimed at giving the federal Libyan Government a substantial number of real functions in both the parliamentary and the executive sectors. The Commissioner was convinced not only that such a policy was in Libya's best interest, but also that it came closer to the current Libyan way of thinking than the British and French Governments cared to admit.

Those in London and Paris responsible for framing their Governments' policy toward Libya, on the other hand, wanted to restrict the federal Government's powers to a few matters such as foreign affairs and defense. This seemed to be the hard core of their opposition to the Commissioner's plans. Moreover, they feared the precedent that would be created if he were to give advice to the Libyans independently of the Council, as the latter might then react by tendering advice of its own without going through him. Another objection raised—in particular by the British—was the high cost of a bicameral Parliament. The Commissioner agreed that the greatest possible economy should be practiced, but believed that it would be more practical, and politically wiser, to discuss the cost of Parliament as constitutional functions came up for discussion one by one, rather than to decide in advance to limit the cost of the future federal structure.

Both Governments also expressed the fear that the plan for a draft Constitution subject to subsequent review by an elected Parliament might introduce an element of instability into the State-to-be. The Commissioner, on the other hand, feared—as he had explained to the General Assembly—that a Constitution drawn up under protest from part of the population by an appointed National Assembly would carry no weight, and might thus become a source of political instability both in Libya's domestic affairs and in her foreign relations. Remembering vividly the criticisms just voiced in the General Assembly, he was apprehensive about what might happen at the Sixth Session, unless in the meantime something was done to forestall potential objections to a Libyan State based on a contested Constitution. At the end of his talks with the British and French Governments he therefore made it clear that, whatever attitude their representatives on the Council might take, he was under a personal obligation to request advice along the lines he had indicated to the General Assembly, adding that the Council would be free to give it or to refuse it. The NCAL was likewise free to accept, to reject, or to adapt any advice he might give it. Naturally, the Commissioner concluded, he would far prefer to act in harmony with both the Council and the NCAL, and had not abandoned hope of achieving that consummation.

During his visit to Rome, he found the Italian Government but little interested in political questions; its attention was sharply focused on Tripolitanian problems and in particular on the future status and interests of the Italian minority there. The Commissioner also tried to find out whether the Italian Government still wanted one or more seats for its nationals in the NCAL or the future Libyan Parliament. This issue was, of course, linked with the deal arranged between the Italian member of the Council and his colleagues from Pakistan, Egypt, and Tripolitania in early June.[36] This was an important matter, affecting as it did the balance of power in the Council. However, the Commissioner left Rome for Cairo not much the wiser for his visit, except that he sensed some signs of disillusionment among his interlocutors.

In Cairo the situation was quite different. Both the Egyptian Foreign Minister and the Secretary-General of the Arab League continued to press the case for an elected National Assembly and a unitary State. However, when they learned that the Amir of Cyrenaica was favorably disposed toward a federal government with substantial powers, they indicated their willingness to consider a compromise. The Commissioner, for his part, warned Egypt that, by intervening too persistently in Libya's domestic affairs, particularly on the issue of federalism versus unitarism, it was courting a deterioration in relations between the two countries. This in turn would drive certain Libyan leaders into the arms of the British and the

36. For an account of these transactions, see Chapter 3, p. 244.

French, who were strongly opposed to the very form of Libyan unity the Egyptians wanted to see. Despite its logic, this argument did not seem to cut much ice.

When he returned to Tripoli the Commissioner decided that the only chance of improving the situation was to request the Secretary-General to take up the matter with the Permanent Delegations at United Nations Headquarters of the Powers interested in the Libyan question. Trygve Lie, who had been kept regularly informed of recent developments, undertook to do so with the aim of bringing about a better atmosphere between the Commissioner and the Council.

When, in the second half of January, the Commissioner and his staff compared notes, a picture emerged that suggested that agreement would not easily be reached on his proposed advice to the NCAL.

In his second annual report, the Commissioner summed up the situation in the following words:

> The leaders of [the National] Assembly and other political figures in Libya had expressed serious misgivings about the opportuneness of giving such advice unless it was requested; and both Administering Powers maintained that, in the first instance, the Assembly was fully and solely competent to take decisions on the matters in question and that the sense of the Commissioner's suggestions was moreover questionable. It was held that even to advise that the Constitution should be ratified by a Parliament to be subsequently elected would undermine the authority of the National Assembly and create instability where, above all things, stability was needed. Doubts were also expressed as to the cost and complexity of the proposed bi-cameral legislature as well as to the apportionment of competence between two Chambers. On the other hand, an opinion tenaciously held in some Libyan quarters, and supported by the Egyptian Government and the Secretary-General of the Arab League, characterized the National Assembly as an unlawful body within the context of the General Assembly's resolutions and so unfitted to receive the recognition which the giving of advice would imply.[37]

The Commissioner nonetheless decided that, in view of the position he had taken on 16 November before the General Assembly, he could not but submit to the Council a request for advice reproducing the gist of his statement there. However, he decided to make one concession to his many critics, namely, the omission of the vexatious words "should be considered as a draft" (relating to the Constitution).

37. *Second Annual Report of the United Nations Commissioner in Libya,* para. 17.

Appreciating that the General Assembly, or at least one group of delegations, would hold him accountable for any deviation from his original statement, he explained the change as follows:

> in the consultations with authorities both inside and outside Libya, which had preceded the formulation of the request, this terminology appeared to have conveyed a particular disparagement of the authority of the National Assembly, and since it was not essential to the purpose of the Commissioner's suggestions, he therefore, withdrew it in the hope of obtaining unanimous agreement more easily.[38]

Thus, his request for advice, dated 23 January 1951, was submitted to the Council in the following terms:

> In the light of the comments below, the Council is kindly requested to advise the Commissioner whether he should advise the Libyan National Assembly in the following sense:
>
> 1. The constitution to be prepared by the National Assembly should be enacted in a provisional form, would require final approval, and amendment, if necessary, by a parliament to be elected by the Libyan people as a whole.
> 2. Provision should be made in the constitution for a parliament consisting of two chambers, a small senate composed of elected representatives of the three territories on a basis of equality and a popular chamber to be elected by the people of Libya as a whole.
> 3. The popular chamber should have amongst its competencies the sole control over the State budget.
> 4. The Libyan government, that is the Libyan Cabinet, should be responsible to the popular chamber.[39]

In the comments accompanying his request, the Commissioner, following his interpretation of paragraphs 3 and 4 of Resolution 289 (IV), noted that:

> any advice the Commissioner, after having consulted the Council for Libya, may tender to the National Assembly is in the nature of a recommendation which that body, in view of the competence granted to it, may either accept or reject, either in whole or in part. It may be expected that the National Assembly would not reject in whole or in part an advice of the Commissioner unless it had good and serious reasons

38. Ibid., para. 18.
39. Ibid., Annex III, p. 74.

for doing so, in particular when such an advice previously had the support of the Council for Libya.[40]

With regard to the particularly sensitive point 1 of his request for advice, the Commissioner commented on his position in the following terms:

The first point is whether the constitution now under preparation by the National Assembly should be enacted only in a provisional form and require final approval, and if necessary amendment by a parliament to be elected by the Libyan people as a whole, or whether that constitution, from the moment of its adoption by the present National Assembly, should be considered as final subject to a revision or amendment clause as generally contained in constitutions.

. . . This grave question would not have arisen, or at least not with the same degree of acuteness either in Libya or in the debates of the General Assembly, if the present National Assembly had been an elected body. Since the history of the Assembly and its initiation are still fresh in the minds of all concerned, it seems needless to recall here how it came to be an appointed body.

. . . Since, however, the primary constitutional body established under paragraph 3 of resolution 289 (IV) was, in the event, appointed and not elected, the Commissioner, as he explained in his address to the General Assembly on 16 November 1950, would feel seriously concerned about the stability of the future Libyan State unless the basic law under which it must live were to be supported by the freely expressed consent of the Libyan people through their elected representatives.

. . . If the Libyan people are expected to accept and to respect their constitution as the law under which their existence as an independent nation is to be conducted, then each and every Libyan citizen should be made to feel that through his vote he has had an opportunity to make his views known.

. . . Hence the Commissioner's suggestion that the constitution, as it will be elaborated by the present appointed National Assembly, should be considered as provisional, subject to approval and, if so desired, amendment by an elected parliament. For what period of time the constitution should remain provisional is both a matter of political wisdom and a practical problem of establishing an electoral organization. It seems obvious that the sooner a final constitution is approved by an elected body the sooner will the country find its political stability.

. . . In various quarters, fears have been expressed that a procedure as

40. Ibid., pp. 74–75.

suggested above risks introducing an element of considerable instability into the Libyan political scene. It has been argued, also, that if a provisional constitution, in order to become final, has to be approved and possibly amended, by an elected parliament, the basic principles on which the provisional constitution is to be founded might be radically changed. This would particularly be true, it is argued, if the elected parliament was composed in direct proportion to the number of population of each of the three territories. It would be so much the more dangerous, it is added, since one of the most important of these principles is the federal form of the State on which presently, and probably for some years to come, Libyan unity is, and will continue to be based.

. . . No one with a realistic view of Libyan conditions can altogether deny the existence of this danger. However, the alternative of having a constitution drawn by an appointed body enacted as the final and definitive constitution raises a greater risk of creating political instability because it would lack authority with considerable parts both of Libyan and international opinion. The alternative is, in the Commissioner's opinion, the more dangerous one for Libyan unity and for Libya's standing in the community of nations.[41]

On point 2 of his request, the Commissioner observed:

The nature of the parliament should reflect the two political conceptions in existence in Libya, one favouring a federal, the other a unitarian, form of State. . . . the Commissioner strongly feels that the gap between these two conceptions of federalism and unitarianism cannot be bridged by continuing the rather harmful battle of words which has been raging for already too long a time. It is obvious that a balanced solution must be reached by bringing the discussion down to facts, *i.e.,* to a definition of the powers and functions actually to be exercised respectively by the central organs on the one hand, and by the local organs, on the other hand. It will also be necessary to define by what kind of organs, both central and local, these powers and functions will be exercised and how these organs are to be established and composed." [42]

The comment on point 3 read:

Even the earliest democratic constitutions contained the principle of "no taxation without representation." The Commissioner therefore feels that if a Libyan tax system were to be established, the control over that system should be vested in the chamber which will represent the people

41. Ibid., p. 75.
42. Ibid.

who will be called upon to pay taxes. Whether this competence should be solely vested in the lower chamber or whether the senate should also have a share in it will, of necessity, require a decision by the National Assembly. The Commissioner is of the opinion that the primary competence should be laid in the hands of the popular or lower chamber.[43]

Finally, in submitting point 4, the Commissioner observed that:

> Two dangers are to be avoided in this connexion. One is the establishment of an autocratic government which unavoidably would come about if the constitution were to omit any form of governmental responsibility. The other danger would arise if the principle of responsibility were to be so broadly defined and applied as to result in governmental instability. It therefore seems indicated to recommend a restricted form of responsibility.[44]

Seeing pretty well what was coming to him, the Commissioner wound up with a strong appeal to the Council to give him unanimous advice. Divided counsel, he warned, would do more harm than good to the Libyan people, their unity, and their independence.

At the time, this appeal for unanimous advice went unheeded, and a new round of consultations had to be initiated. It was then that a slight change for the better became perceptible in the attitude of the British and French members, which in time affected their colleagues from the United States of America, Cyrenaica, and the Fezzan. (The position of the members for Italy and for the minorities remained problematical.) It seemed that the combined efforts of the Secretary-General and the Commissioner were beginning to take effect, with the result that London and Paris had instructed their representatives on the Council to meet the Commissioner part way. They were still not prepared to support him fully. But they would agree to his advising the NCAL on his sole responsibility, either along the lines of his request, or following a slightly different though analogous approach. They also gave it to be understood that this rapprochement might evolve were the NCAL to *seek* the Commissioner's advice. In addition, the representatives of the Administering Powers were willing to give him time to try to resolve existing differences.

In the NCAL, by now considerably better informed about the General Assembly debates, leading members, including the President, were ready to consider any advice the Commissioner might tender. Some members even seemed eager for advice, going so far as to imply that if the Commissioner's advice was to serve any useful purpose, it should be forthcom-

43. Ibid., p. 76.
44. Ibid.

ing promptly. Others were against hasty decisions. Suspicions were voiced about advice emanating from the Council. On the other hand, the criticisms which had been leveled against it, both inside and outside Libya, had made the NCAL feel that its prestige was involved; it was therefore unlikely formally to ask for advice.

The questions of the NCAL's "legality or nonlegality," and whether the Constitution to be drafted by it would be provisional or definitive, on which widely differing views were held, were matters of deep concern to several people, both on the Council and in the NCAL. They in particular exercised the minds of certain Council members. These issues reflected, indeed, opposing positions in the long-standing controversy over the form of State and government.

Those hostile to the NCAL—generally speaking, those opposed to federalism—wanted the Constitution to be considered as a provisional instrument, so as not to forfeit their chance of getting the form of State changed at some time in the future.

They were faced by those, generally in favor of federalism, who insisted on the legality of the NCAL and hence on the finality of the Constitution. This side's object was to prevent "the opposition" from changing the form of State once it had been decided upon.

Looking at the situation from this angle, it was clear that a solution to the immediate problems might be found if agreement could be reached on the form of State, in particular with regard to the distribution of powers between the central (federal) government and the territorial administrations, as well as on the composition of the Libyan Parliament.

If no such accommodation could be reached within the NCAL, the Commissioner feared that he might have to refer the matter back to the General Assembly; indeed, in such an event, the vital paragraph 3 of Resolution 289 (IV) would become unworkable, and deadlock would ensue. But lack of agreement within the Council and consequent inability to formulate advice, like lack of agreement between the Commissioner and the Council, would cause no deadlock, since both acted only in an advisory capacity. Hence, the NCAL became the cynosure of attention in a critical situation.

Fortunately, this second round of consultations revealed that ideas about the distribution of powers between the federal and territorial governments showed signs of converging. Agreement on this point might come within reach provided all concerned could be diverted from an arid disputation about the meaning of terms like "federalism" and "unitarism" to a fruitful exchange of views on the practical definition of central and local powers. As it happened, this very issue was at the time under discussion in the Committee of Eighteen, and it did not seem out of the question that constructive conclusions would be reached. In this connection, it is worth mentioning that in the course of the consultations, members of the Mission staff were frequently told that the discussions were being affected by foreign pressure, brought to bear to control the degree of centralization. The pressure in question was exerted by the Administering Powers and by Libya's Arab friends alike, though in opposite directions.

Another matter that took up a great deal of time in the course of the consultations was the composition of Parliament. Among members of the NCAL, and to a certain extent in the Council also, four possible solutions were being canvassed:

1. Parliament should consist of a single chamber elected on a basis of proportional representation and possessing full legislative powers.

   This was the solution preferred by most of the Tripolitanians whom the Commissioner consulted, including certain Tripolitanian members of the NCAL. It was unacceptable to the Cyrenaicans and the Fezzanese because it would have given the Tripolitanians an overwhelming majority.

2. Parliament should consist of a single chamber elected, directly or indirectly, on a basis of equal representation of the three territories. The chamber would again possess full legislative powers.

   This solution was advocated in particular by the Fezzanese members of the Assembly and by the Fezzanese member of the Council; it was also the one preferred by the Administering Powers. It would have implied a very loosely federated State. Among the Cyrenaicans, too, many liked this solution; others were prepared to compromise on it if doing so would promote agreement with the Tripolitanians and Fezzanese. To the Tripolitanians, it was utterly unacceptable, since it would have opened up the possibility of a joint Cyrenaican-Fezzanese majority, which would have denied Tripolitania what it considered to be its right, as the largest and most progressive of the three territories, to play the leading part in the future political life of the country.

3. A few of those consulted had proposed a Parliament consisting of a single elected chamber made up of numbers of representatives from each of the three territories so fixed as to produce a predetermined balance of membership; for instance, the number of Cyrenaican and Fezzanese deputies together to be equal to that of the Tripolitanian members.

   This solution was turned down almost unanimously on the grounds that it would require lengthy, and probably unsuccessful, negotiations. It was, moreover, strongly felt that, even if the negotiations proved successful, the result would be an unstable, and therefore inevitably temporary, composition.

4. Parliament should consist of two chambers, a house of representatives

elected by the people as a whole on a fully proportional basis; and a senate elected or appointed on a basis of equal representation of the three territories. This was the solution tentatively mooted by the Commissioner at Lake Success.

> An increasing number of Libyan personages from all three territories seemed to be in favor of such a bicameral system, since they realized that no unicameral system would produce Libyan unity.

The Mission staff got the impression that the fourth variant was gaining ground, especially among the more moderate Tripolitanians and the more progressive Cyrenaicans. The Amir was understood not to view a parliamentary structure of this kind with disfavor. A few Fezzanese also were, privately, inclined to regard it benevolently. However, there was as yet no agreement either on the division of competence between the two chambers or on the procedure for settling any disputes that might arise between them. The Tripolitanians were disposed to leave the ultimate power of decision to the lower house, whereas the Cyrenaicans tended to the opposite procedure. It followed that if a bicameral Parliament proved to be the only practical solution, a mutually acceptable reconciliation procedure would have to be devised.

Viewing the outcome of the consultations *grosso modo,* particularly with regard to the composition of Parliament, it seemed that both outside, and particularly within, the NCAL there was a growing recognition of the need to reach an agreement if the three territories were to be united in any practical sense. No such awareness was as yet noticeable in the Council for Libya to any similar degree. The difference in political maturity between the two bodies thus reflected was, perhaps, not unnatural. The sixty members of the NCAL had now been meeting regularly for nearly two months. They had made appreciable progress in grasping one another's point of view and, however much they might still differ, they were bound by bonds of a common heritage. In the Council, six governmental representatives, not always sure of one another's intentions, called upon to defend different national viewpoints and interests, were competing for the support of four Libyan members who had their own internal differences to contend with. It was therefore not surprising that the Council should find it much more difficult to reach agreement than did the NCAL.

It was now up to the Commissioner to devise an approach offering the best chances of achieving the largest possible area of agreement.

In the meantime, well over a month had passed since the submission of his request for advice, and if any advice were to move the NCAL, it could not be much longer delayed. In the circumstances, the Commissioner informally suggested a compromise, the essence of which was that, on the Council's advice, he should advise the NCAL to the following effect:

(a) That the Libyan Constitution should provide for a Parliament of two Chambers, of which the upper Chamber should consist of an equal number of elected members for each territory and the lower Chamber of representatives elected on a proportionate basis for the inhabitants of all three territories;

(b) That the National Assembly should elaborate the details of the electoral system for each Chamber as well as the details of the division of legislative powers as between the two Chambers, assuming that the two Chambers should exercise such powers primarily on an equal basis and that any legislation would require the assent of both Chambers;

(c) That the National Assembly should devise a procedure for the settlement of any possible disputes between the two Chambers, taking into consideration the possibility of forming a joint body;

(d) That the Constitution might appropriately contain provision for the amendment of individual articles of the Constitution by means of normal legislative decisions of the Libyan Parliament, such constitutional amendments being approved by a special majority, such as two-thirds of the two Chambers or with such conditions as two separate readings, the approval of the King being required to give final effect to such amendments;

(e) That the Cabinet should be responsible to the two Chambers of Parliament, subject to such conditions as might assist in avoiding governmental instability owing to minor or transitory differences, and that the Cabinet should be required to answer criticism in Parliament at all times; that the National Assembly should prepare detailed provisions in this regard; that consideration be given to such provisions for votes of censure against the Cabinet as, for example, the requirement of special majorities in each Chamber or of a delay between the tabling of the motion and the vote;

(f) That, in accordance with democratic principles, both Chambers should have supervision over budgetary and financial matters, with the lower Chamber having primary competence; that the budget should be presented in the first instance to the lower Chamber, and in the event of any dispute between the two Chambers reconciliation should be sought as recommended in sub-paragraph (c) above.[45]

An informal meeting of the members of the Council was called at the Commissioner's residence to consider this compromise, but no agreement

45. Ibid., para. 19.

could be reached. The Council remained divided between a majority unwilling to endorse the request for advice before them, preferring not to give any advice at all, and a minority that insisted on giving advice in strict conformity with the terms of the Commissioner's statement before the General Assembly on 16 November 1950.

The Commissioner felt that he had done his utmost to bring the parties together, and that the time had come to let the Council face up to its responsibilities, well knowing that subsequently he would have to face up to his own.

PART 3. DIVIDED COUNCILS—RELUCTANT ADVICE

The consultations carried out by the Secretary-General in New York simultaneously with the Commissioner's negotiations in his own bailiwick proved, first, that the Governments of the Powers directly interested followed events on the spot with close attention and kept their Permanent Delegations in New York well informed. Within a few weeks, word came back from Headquarters to the effect that the Commissioner was on the right track in trying to narrow the areas of divergence both between himself and certain members of the Council and in his relations with leading members of the NCAL. In the course of February and early March 1951, the former became a little less reluctant to give advice on the outstanding, detailed questions of constitutional development, while the latter developed an increasing readiness to listen to it. At the same time, the Secretary-General felt strongly that it would be undesirable for the Council to tender formal advice as it had done in the past, since a majority in the NCAL would probably resent such an approach. This coincided with the Commissioner's own views. He realized that the NCAL feared that its prestige would be impaired by acceptance of advice gratuitously proffered by the Council and officially transmitted by himself. Conversely, if advice were tendered and rejected, the Council would lose much face. In particular, any impression that advice or suggestions were in reality a way of bringing foreign governmental pressure to bear on the NCAL had to be carefully avoided. The news from New York confirmed in the second place that the United States Government was in general agreement with the detailed proposals the Commissioner was preparing for Libya's constitutional structure, and that the Administering Powers were coming round to them, without, however, wishing to assume formal responsibility for them. In brief, a majority in the Council, including the representatives of Cyrenaica and the Fezzan, seemed ready to be consulted on suggestions the Commissioner might subsequently make to the NCAL on his own responsibility and not by way of formal advice. It could hardly be called a compromise, but if some such understanding could be reached, few feelings would be hurt, save, unfortunately, those of the members for Egypt, Pakistan, and Tripolitania.

The Commissioner was not the only one who had been racking his brains for a solution capable of disengaging the feuding factions. The United States representative on the Council, true to the task he had set himself, with his Government's approval, of acting as mediator whenever possible within the limits of his instructions, had also been trying to find some common ground on which the conflicts of prestige and interests, as well as the genuine differences of opinion, could be reconciled. The outcome was a United States draft resolution submitted to the Council at its seventy-fourth meeting on 12 March 1951.

A lengthy preamble recorded that the Commissioner's request for advice had been considered by the Council, which, however, had deferred a decision to give him a chance of carrying out private consultations; that the Council had heard the Commissioner's account of these consultations and taken note of the NCAL's decision regarding the form of State; and that the Council, while recognizing that final determination of the constitution rested with the NCAL, yet considered that Commissioner and Council had the responsibility under the two General Assembly resolutions on Libya of assisting the National Assembly in that task. The operative part of the proposal stated:

[*The United Nations Council for Libya*]

Advises The Commissioner that he might appropriately offer the following suggestions to the National Assembly with the idea that these suggestions, modified as the National Assembly may deem necessary to care for the particular needs of Libya, may prove to be acceptable to a majority of the Libyan people:

(1) That the Libyan Constitution provide that there shall be a Libyan Parliament consisting of two Chambers, the upper Chamber to be composed of representatives of the three territories on a basis of equality, such representatives either to be elected, or should the National Assembly prefer, be designated by the Government of each territory and appointed by the King; or the National Assembly might find it desirable that a limited portion of such representatives be nominated by the King on his own initiative, the others being designated by the Government of each territory and appointed by the King; and the lower Chamber to be elected on a proportional basis that will assure just and balanced representation to the population of the three territories.

Where the National Assembly determines that elections shall be held, the system to be employed, whether by direct or indirect suffrage, should be elaborated by the National Assembly:

That similarly the distribution of legislative functions between the two Chambers should be elaborated by the National Assembly, having in mind a basic principle of the federal system, that the two Chambers should, in principle, share that competence on a basis of equality, and that the concurrence of both Chambers and approval by the King would be required for the enactment of legislation;

That there should be elaborated by the National Assembly a procedure for reconciliation of possible conflicts between the two Chambers.

(2) That the Constitution might suitably contain provisions for its amendment by decision of the Libyan Parliament in accordance with its legislative procedures, and that the Constitution as a whole might be reviewed by the Libyan Parliament in the light of experience after a minimum period of, say, five years. That, in accordance with general constitutional practices, a special majority, such, for example, as a two-thirds or three-fourths vote of both houses, or some other exceptional voting procedure, should be required for approval of constitutional amendments.

(3) That members of the Libyan Cabinet should be required to appear before the lower Chamber or both Chambers of Parliament, give an accounting of their stewardship, and answer questions of members of Parliament;

That detailed provisions regarding the responsibilities of the Cabinet, whether to Parliament or to the King or to both, and means by which the Cabinet may be removed from office should be elaborated by the National Assembly.

(4) That control over Libyan State revenue and expenditure, and over State financial matters generally, should be within the competence of Parliament in accordance with democratic procedure;

That initiative in such matters should rest with the lower Chamber to which the State budget should be submitted in the first instance;

That differences in budgetary matters between the two Chambers should be reconciled in accordance with the procedure mentioned in point (1) above. The National Assembly might wish to provide against the possibility that reconciliation of such differences may not have been achieved before the close of a fiscal year, in which case expenditures on the scale of the previous fiscal year should be automatically authorized monthly until the differences shall have been reconciled.[46]

46. For full text of the draft resolution, see ibid., para. 20.

The Council devoted four consecutive meetings, all public, to the subject. Public interest was great, and the gallery of the Council's meeting room in the Grand Hotel was full to overflowing at all times.[47]

From the outset it was plain that the United States proposal stood no better chance of commanding unanimous approval than the Commissioner's original request for advice, or even his later, informal, compromise proposals. Nevertheless, there was a difference in that the Commissioner had no support whatsoever, whereas the United States member was at least sure of a majority. On the other hand, the two had it in common that they were opposed by the same minority "[characterizing] the National Assembly as an unlawful body within the context of the General Assembly's resolutions and so unfitted to receive the recognition which the giving of advice would imply." [48] At the same time, all members of the Council were conscious of the fact that the crux of the Libyan problem had been reached; hence, the debate was particularly tense.

The Commissioner opened the discussion

> by reviewing the causes of the delay to which his request for advice had been subjected: the opinion of a majority in the Council that no advice should be given to the National Assembly except at its request, and the fear entertained in some Libyan circles that such spontaneous advice might cast doubts upon the competence of the National Assembly. He affirmed that the suggestions he had outlined to the General Assembly still represented his views on the question under consideration and he expressed surprise that, although they had met with no criticism at the time, they should now give rise to such strong opposition.[49]

Reviewing the components of the United States draft resolution and the informal compromise he himself had suggested, he found that there was substantial agreement between the two in spite of important differences.

Indeed, on the whole the similarities far outweighed the differences of detail. In particular, both solutions were based on a bicameral Parliament and on the notion of possible review and amendment of the Constitution in the light of experience and in conformity with the will of the people ex-

47. During one meeting, the gallery became so overcrowded that the United Nations guard on duty, mindful of the needs of ventilation and the fire safety regulations, asked those for whom there were no seats to leave. They politely refused, explaining that, having been paid by the National Congress Party to attend, they were obliged to stay, and stand. For details of this debate, see Summary Records of 74th–77th Meetings, United Nations Doc. A/AC.32/COUNCIL/SR.74–77, 12–13 March 1951. Mimeographed.

48. *Second Annual Report of the United Nations Commissioner in Libya,* para. 17.

49. Ibid., para. 21.

pressed through freely elected representatives. In concluding his introductory statement, the Commissioner declared that

> he would consider accepting advice which resembled his original proposals in substance and which had the support of the majority of the Council. He reserved his right, however, to amend that advice as his judgment might dictate. . . . he urged the importance of unanimity within the Council, as an example to the Libyans.[50]

The United States member, introducing his proposal, said that "his resolution made it clear that the Council had no intention of interfering with the work of the NCAL or questioning the competence of its members." [51] Lewis Clark went on to say that, in his Government's opinion, it would be inappropriate, not to say impertinent, for the Council to presume that the NCAL was unable to meet the obligation imposed upon it by the General Assembly resolutions, or to offer unsolicited advice that it might or might not need.

In the opinion of the Egyptian member, federation was at the root of all the trouble; it was also the reason why there had been so much insistence on the principle of equality of representation between the three territories regardless of their population. The Egyptian delegation

> had felt it advisable temporarily to accept the principle of equal representation in order to bring the representatives of the three territories together to perform one simple task, namely, to prepare a plan. It had never thought for one moment that the Council was setting a precedent or making a ruling to be maintained. It had thought that once the Libyans could meet together, in any shape or form, it would be for them to decide the matter. It had never realized at that time that federation was the fundamental policy of the United Kingdom, France and the United States; that dramatic truth had only become apparent in the light of subsequent events. . . . The federal principle was quite clearly revealed in the composition of the National Assembly which, in his opinion, was contrary to the wording of the General Assembly resolutions.[52]

Questioning the merits of federalism as a suitable form of government for Libya, Selim Bey went on to say that

> Federal constitutions and governments, [the Egyptian] Government was convinced, were not in the best interests of Libya. In that opinion, his

50. Ibid.
51. Ibid., para. 22.
52. Ibid., para. 23.

Government had the support of all the members of the Arab League which had Libya's interest at heart. A population of a little more than a million Arabs having the same language, religion and customs, should be welded together by the sympathetic bonds of a unitary system, not divided by a loose, cold federal system which merely paved the way to foreign exploitation; federation, in fact, had never been meant for a people like the Libyans. The very word "federation" had no equivalent in Arabic because federation had never at any time existed in any Arab country. Was it conceivable that the Fezzanese who, in their desert isolation, knew nothing about federation should demand it? Or that the Cyrenaicans should insist on it to protect them against their Tripolitanian brothers? No, federation had been smuggled into Libya from abroad.[53]

The French member considered that

The National Assembly was truly representative of the three territories and the various trends of opinion in Libya. The French Government considered that, in offering advice to the National Assembly without that body having requested it, the Commissioner and the Council would be intervening in the internal affairs of the country and would be usurping constituent powers. They were only entitled to intervene if any decisions of the National Assembly were contrary to the provisions of the General Assembly resolutions or if any clauses in the Constitution conflicted with the general principles of the United Nations Charter or the Universal Declaration of Human Rights. It was on that point of principle that the representative of France objected to the Commissioner's request for advice in the form in which it had been presented. The United States draft resolution, however, offered a compromise in that it did not request the Commissioner to tender advice to the National Assembly but simply to offer it suggestions on the constitutional development of the country.[54]

The member for Cyrenaica, upholding the legality of the NCAL, declared that

Cyrenaica and the Fezzan had chosen their own solution to the constitutional question and, if a different solution were imposed on them, the desired results would not be achieved.[55]

53. Ibid. This was a somewhat astonishing statement, coming as it did from a governmental representative on the Council for Libya, who supposedly had studied the records of the General Assembly debates at the Fourth Session in 1949 on the future of the Italian colonies, and who in 1950 had himself attended, on behalf of the Council, the debates on Libya at the Fifth Session.

54. Ibid., para. 24.

55. Ibid., para. 25.

He was prepared to accept the United States draft resolution in a spirit of compromise since it was not mandatory or binding on the NCAL.

The member for the Fezzan [56] also defended the legality of the NCAL, considering it fully competent to draw up a constitution and to set a provisional government. He also outlined some points which he considered essential to a federal constitution, stressing in particular that "The members of the House of Representatives should be elected in such proportion that the Fezzan had its share of responsibility in the work of the Parliament." [57]

The representative of the United Kingdom affirmed

> that his Government considered the National Assembly to be the body envisaged in the General Assembly resolution of 1949 and as such to be fully competent to deal with any advice the Commissioner might offer it. . . . Generally speaking, he considered that the Commissioner should tender no formal advice to the National Assembly unless requested to do so by that body, whose competence to determine the Constitution had been so clearly recognized by the General Assembly that it might be unwise to trespass upon it uninvited. Should the Commissioner approach

56. Hajj Ahmed Sofu, the original Council member for the Fezzan, having resigned for reasons of ill health (see Chapter 2, p. 195, fn. 58, and Chapter 5, p. 354), the Commissioner, upon his return from New York in December 1950, had been obliged to start the procedure he was required to follow for the appointment of a successor. This went not without some difficulties. The French Administration in the Fezzan had proposed a member of the National Assembly by the name of Mohamed Bin Othman, well known to the Commissioner as having testified in 1948 before the Four Power Commission of Investigation for the Former Italian Colonies in favor of a united, independent Libya under the Senussi crown. At the same time, however, he had received a petition, dated 5 December 1950, signed by 159 "sons of Ghadames" residing in Tripoli, requesting the appointment of Sheikh al-Barquli. The Commissioner would have preferred to nominate two or three candidates, one of whom should have been Sheikh al-Barquli. However, the latter, having made his peace with Ahmed Bey Seif al-Nasr, now supported Mohamed Bin Othman's candidature. Under these circumstances Mohamed Bin Othman was appointed a Member of the Council. The Commissioner announced the appointment on 25 January 1951, and the new member took his seat the same day, after resigning from the NCAL, the two functions having been deemed incompatible.

Mohamed Bin Othman was born at Zoueyya, Shati, Fezzan, in 1919, son of the Qadi of Brach. He had studied at the Koranic School of Zawia and for five years continued his religious studies under the guidance of his father, to whom he subsequently became assistant. He later acted as an adviser to the Moslem (Shari'a) Court at Brach. In 1950 he had been one of the seven Fezzanese representatives on the Committee of Twenty-One. At the time of his appointment to the Council he was head of the Fezzanese delegation to the NCAL and one of the two Vice-Presidents of that body.

57. Ibid., para. 26.

the National Assembly informally, however, with suggestions of the type proposed in the United States draft resolution, the Assembly would no doubt be willing to take advantage of his help.[58]

The United Kingdom representative emphasized that

> the General Assembly had given the National Assembly authority to "determine" the Constitution; any attempt to undermine that authority and to reduce the National Assembly to the status of a drafting committee could not but lead to chaos. It might, however, be possible to recommend, as did the United States draft resolution, that provision should be made for a review of the Constitution after a given number of years.[59]

The representative for Pakistan maintained that

> while in November the Commissioner had given the General Assembly a solemn and considered undertaking, thereby gaining its confidence, he was now asking the Council for advice on proposals that differed materially from that earlier assurance. The Commissioner's implication that the competence of the National Assembly was limited had persuaded the General Assembly to dispense with elections in order to avoid loss of time, and it was now his duty, in spite of the known position of a majority in the Council, to redeem his pledge. . . . He therefore hoped that the Commissioner would revise his request for advice, to bring it into conformity with the promises he had made to the General Assembly.[60]

The Pakistani delegation found the United States draft resolution unacceptable, and therefore intended to submit amendments that would bring it into line with the obligation the Commissioner had assumed on 16 November 1950 at Lake Success.

The Italian member observed that

> Just as it had been necessary to grant equal representation to the three territories in order to bring them together in the Committee of Twenty-One, so . . . the same principle had had to be adopted in order to secure the participation of all three territories in the National Assembly.[61]

As to the issue of an elected versus an appointed National Assembly, Baron Confalonieri reminded the Council that, during the debate on Libya at the

58. Ibid., para. 27.
59. Ibid.
60. Ibid., para. 28.
61. Ibid., para. 29.

Fifth Session of the General Assembly, he had advocated the election of members of the National Assembly, adding that he was

> still of the opinion that that solution would have simplified the present situation. The National Assembly had begun its work, however, and it was too late to demand elections. Moreover, the National Assembly's decision to invite the Amir of Cyrenaica to accept the crown of Libya appeared to have met with general approval even among those in Tripolitania who were most hostile to the National Assembly. That was an important guide; and the Amir had accepted the National Assembly in its existing form. This fact was of some importance since the future King of Libya would have been unlikely to accept a solution which would have raised as much opposition as opponents of the National Assembly now claimed to exist, for fear of placing himself in a very delicate situation. It would therefore be wise . . . for the Council to await the final results of the work of the National Assembly before passing judgment. . . . [At the same time he] refused to believe that the National Assembly would not take into consideration the fundamental necessities of Tripolitania, since it was obvious that a Constitution which ignored those needs would be without practical effect, having been rejected by the great majority of Tripolitanians.[62]

Although he felt in great sympathy with the United States draft resolution, Baron Confalonieri stated that he "would withhold judgment until due time on the results of the very important decisions which the National Assembly was called upon to take." [63]

The member for Tripolitania, considering that the Committee of Twenty-One had been illegally constituted and that its work should therefore be considered null and void, declared that, to conform with the terms of Resolution 289 (IV), the following procedure should be followed:

> First, the Libyan people should elect their representatives; secondly, the United Nations should recognize the legality of that representation; finally, the trust should be handed over to the legitimate representatives of the people.[64]

In his opinion, the work of the National Assembly was also invalid: the people of Libya had chosen neither their own representatives nor their own constitutional system. To redress the situation, the promise given by the Commissioner to the General Assembly must be kept. He warned all those

62. Ibid.
63. Ibid.
64. Ibid., para. 30.

"who disregarded the rights of the people of Tripolitania against the repercussions which their attitude would have on public opinion in Libya and throughout the world." [65]

The representative of the minorities, who at the time, under the system of rotation, was Chairman of the Council, speaking last in the debate, declared that

> the fundamental choice before [the great majority of Libyans] was between federation and a unitary State. That, he believed, was a political question to be decided by the Libyans themselves according to their own interests and desires. Had the Minorities been regarded as an integral part of the population, they might have participated in that decision; the General Assembly, however, had failed to make an explicit pronouncement upon their status, while the Libyans in the Committee of Twenty-One had unanimously agreed to exclude them from participation in the National Assembly, despite the contrary view expressed earlier by the majority of the Tripolitanian political parties. The two Council representatives of the Arab people of Libya had agreed, at the Geneva meetings, that the Minorities could not be considered to be inhabitants of Libya within the meaning of the General Assembly resolution and had added an observation to that effect to the first annual report of the Commissioner. The Minorities were thus in the difficult position of desiring to co-operate and yet at the same time to refrain from intervening in a purely political question. He, as the representative of the Minorities in Libya, had therefore been instructed to abstain from voting.[66]

At this point Abdur Rahim Khan, the representative for Pakistan, introduced his counterproposal, which the United States representative found entirely unacceptable. Although the proposal was couched in the form of amendments to the United States draft resolution, these were of so far-reaching a nature that their adoption would have resulted in a different text requesting the Commissioner to tender the same advice that he had informed the General Assembly he would ask the Council to give, and for which there was no majority.

The votes on the two proposals were taken by roll call, at the instance of the member for Tripolitania. First, the Pakistani amendments were rejected by 5 votes (the Fezzan, France, the United Kingdom, the United States, and Cyrenaica) to 3 (Egypt, Pakistan, and Tripolitania), the members for

65. Ibid.
66. Ibid., para. 31.

Italy and the Minorities abstaining. The United States proposal was then carried by the same margin in reverse order.

The Commissioner thereupon recalled the position he had taken the previous year when his relationship with the Council was under discussion, namely, that as a general rule he would follow the Council's advice while fully reserving the right to change or amend that advice as circumstances might in his best judgment require.[67]

While the outcome of the debate clarified the situation to some extent, many of the arguments used had, wittingly or unwittingly, been based on false premises. A few comments will soon set the record straight.

First, the Commissioner had never questioned the legality of the NCAL. He had simply told the General Assembly that he very much doubted whether it enjoyed the necessary moral and political authority to produce a definitive constitution.

Second, he had not promised to give the NCAL advice, he had simply said that he intended to suggest to the Council that certain advice be given, expressing the hope that the Council would unanimously support him. This hope having been disappointed, he now had to consider on his own responsibility whether, and if so what, advice or suggestion he should convey to the NCAL.

Third, the case argued by the majority, that the Commissioner was not entitled to give advice to the NCAL unless it requested him to do so, was a misinterpretation of Resolution 289 (IV). The fact that paragraph 3 thereof provided that a constitution, including the form of government, should be determined "by representatives of the inhabitants of Cyrenaica, Tripolitania and the Fezzan, meeting and consulting together in a National Assembly" did not, in his view, conflict with the terms of paragraph 4, that "for the purpose of assisting the people of Libya in the formulation of the Constitution and the establishment of an independent Government, there shall be a United Nations Commissioner in Libya appointed by the General Assembly and a Council to aid and advise him." [68] On the contrary, for him the two provisions were complementary, implying that it was the responsibility of the Commissioner and the Council to assist the people of Libya in achieving the aims defined in paragraph 3. It followed that it was the NCAL's responsibility to draft the Constitution and determine the form of government. From all this, he could draw only one, oft-repeated conclusion, namely, that both he and the Council were at all times entitled to give advice, which the NCAL was free to accept or reject, in whole or in part.

67. See Chapter 4, pp. 303–35, passim.

68. For full text of General Assembly Resolution 289 (IV), 21 November 1949, see Annex I, pp. 891–93.

Fourth, the Council's resolution was, procedurally speaking, neither fish, flesh, nor good red herring. The cautious language of the last paragraph of the preamble hedged the operative part with so many qualifications that it constituted neither formal advice to the NCAL, nor a refusal to advise that body. The Council, in short, wanted to have its cake and eat it. It really wanted to evade its obligation to give advice without incurring odium for shirking its responsibilities. So it passed the buck to the Commissioner.

However, the substantive provisions of the resolution came fairly close to those which the Commissioner had promised the General Assembly to submit to the Council for advice. Even the position taken on the status of the Constitution was in essence identical with the amending provisions in the Commissioner's formal compromise proposal.

The recommendations did not carry great political weight, having been supported by only half the Council members—all partisans of federation. Hence, they would probably not satisfy the Arab delegations at the General Assembly; on the contrary, they might nourish the latter's hostility. This was an important consideration, given that the King-Designate and all leading figures of the country anticipated joining the Arab League after independence.

On the other hand, Libyan unity was the Commissioner's prime political concern, and if the Council's suggestions could help the NCAL—and in particular its Tripolitanian and Cyrenaican members—to reach agreement on the basic issue that divided them, it might be wise to go along with them. The differences between the ideas expressed in the draft resolution and the Commissioner's own views on future constitutional development could, he hoped, be reconciled fairly easily by adding a number of observations. So, on 3 April 1951, he addressed a long and detailed letter to the President of the NCAL, informing him that he regarded the advice given to him by the Council as helpful and constructive, and thought it might usefully be considered by the National Assembly. He found it appropriate to add, in consultation with his legal adviser, some comments on each of the four operative paragraphs of the resolution.

There is no need to do more than summarize these comments: the reader interested in detail will find the verbatim text of the Commissioner's letter in Annex IV (pp. 77–80) to his second annual report.

Paragraph 1. Having recognized that, given the NCAL's decisions on the form of the future State, it would be more democratic if both chambers were to be elected, the Commissioner pointed out that it might, nonetheless, be to Libya's immediate advantage, in view of its lack of experience of parliamentary government, to follow the example of a number of other newly independent States by providing for the appointment by the Head of

State of a limited number of members of the upper chamber. In this way, eminent citizens with particular experience in public or private administration or with modern professional training, who might not have the time or the inclination to take governmental office, or wish to get embroiled in the hurly-burly of day-to-day politics, would be enabled to place their knowledge at their country's disposal. Moreover, such a system would enable the Crown to appoint to the Senate representatives of ethnic or religious groups which, for one reason or another, had not benefited by the normal electoral processes. All nominated members ought, however, to be Libyan citizens.

Having quoted the relevant provisions of the constitutions of a number of federal States, most of them Moslem, and pointed out that upper chambers with a preponderance of appointed members usually enjoyed less power than the corresponding elected lower chambers, the Commissioner expressed the view that the Libyan Constitution should provide for the appointment of a minority of the Senators.

The terms "proportional basis" and "just and balanced representation" used to describe the desirable composition of the lower chamber were susceptible of a variety of interpretation. In particular, the second phrase might suggest that the representation of the three territories in the House of Representatives should be based on an agreed formula other than strict proportional representation in the accepted sense of the term.

Assuming that all three territories would be equally represented in the upper chamber, the Commissioner thought it essential that the lower chamber be elected by unqualified proportional representation based on either the total population of or the total number of voters in each territory. Not only would this accord with the provisions of most federal constitutions; it would also avoid the almost unsoluble difficulties with which negotiations to reach agreement on some other proportional formula were bound to be fraught.

Paragraph 2. Here the Commissioner was at pains to explain the differences between the procedure for changing the Constitution by amendment and that for doing so by review.

He pointed out that the amendment procedure would come into effect at the same time as the Constitution, i.e. that it would become operative on the date of promulgation of the latter. But it would allow only of changes of limited scope.

The review procedure, on the other hand, would become operative only after the lapse of a period of years to be specified in the Constitution itself. Its purpose would be to allow the Libyan people, if they so wished, to revise their Constitution systematically in the light of experience, perhaps through the instrumentality of the two chambers sitting jointly as a national congress. If this were considered insufficiently stringent, other provisions, which the Commissioner described in some detail, could be added which would make the revision procedure more democratic and ensure that the Constitution could not be frivolously modified.

No matter which procedure was chosen, amendments would require a two-thirds majority in each of the two chambers and subsequent approval by the Crown.

The amendment procedure was common to most national constitutions. The review procedure was foreign to them, but featured in the Charter of the United Nations. However, it seemed to be indicated in the case of Libya, because: (a) the present constitution was being drafted not by an elected, but by an appointed body; and (b) Libya had no experience of constitutional government in the modern sense of the term, and might therefore, after the passage of a few years, find its Constitution defective in some respects.

Paragraph 3, second paragraph. The Commissioner was convinced that the Constitution should embody the principle of ministerial responsibility before Parliament. But experience elsewhere had shown that too rigid application of the principle could lead to abuse, and hence to governmental instability, which would be unhealthy for a young country such as Libya. In its case, therefore, the integrity of the principle must be safeguarded by adequate restraints on abuse. After describing the ways in which such safeguards were made effective in various constitutions, and after suggesting that the NCAL might usefully consider adopting one or other of them, the Commissioner went on to point out that the NCAL would also have to decide whether the Cabinet should be responsible to both chambers or to the lower house alone. The choice depended to some extent on whether the upper chamber was elected or appointed; but even where it was elected, the principle of dual responsibility might create confusion and hence again make for instability.

Since a number of recently adopted bicameral federal constitutions made the Cabinet responsible only to the lower chamber, the Commissioner believed that, in the light of the foregoing considerations, Libya would be well advised to follow suit.

Paragraph 4. The only uncertain point here was whether the budget, and money bills generally, should require the approval of the upper chamber after they had passed the lower house. In the Commissioner's opinion, the NCAL having decided that Libya should be a federal State, and despite the fact that in principle the last word in financial matters must rest with the House of Representatives, the NCAL would have to look into the particular competence of the upper house in these matters.

When the President seized the NCAL of the Commissioner's letter, the NCAL unanimously decided to refer it to the Committee of Eighteen for "study and attention." [69] It will be seen in the next chapter that its contents gave rise to protracted discussion on a number of occasions.

The Commissioner had weathered yet another storm.

PART 4.
THE NATIONAL ASSEMBLY AND THE ARAB LEAGUE

Soon after the Committee of Twenty-One had finished its work, at the end of October 1950, the Arab press and radio launched a violent campaign, out of Cairo, against the NCAL and the way it had been constituted. The National Assembly was called an illegitimate institution, and the arguments advanced in support of this charge curiously resembled those heard earlier, first at Lake Success and later in Tripoli.

This time it was Cyrenaican public opinion that was quick to react. As early as 9 November 1950, the President of the Cyrenaican Assembly of Representatives, Rashid al-Kikhia, sent a telegram to the Secretary-General of the United Nations, with a copy to the Commissioner. He referred to dispatches published by Arab press agencies and broadcasting stations, according to which the Secretary-General of the Arab League, at a meeting of the delegations of the Arab States to the General Assembly held on 5 November 1950 in New York, had asked them strongly to oppose the way in which the NCAL was to be organized. The President also alleged that the Egyptian Minister for Foreign Affairs had made a similar appeal.

Kikhia complained that the authors of these appeals did not appreciate the realities of the situation in Libya, and that their action amounted to objectionable interference in the domestic affairs of the Libyan people. He therefore protested strongly on behalf of the Cyrenaican Assembly, adding that the Libyan people expected support and blessings from their Arab neighbors, not hostility. This widely publicized appeal did not produce the desired result, as was clear from the many stories reported in the *Arab Press and Radio Review* which the Mission received weekly from the United Nations Information Centre in Cairo. On the contrary, the campaign continued unabated through December and January; indeed, it grew more vehement. On 12 January 1951, a fresh protest was received from the same source, this time complaining that Azzam Pasha had once again interfered with Libya's internal affairs by making a statement to the Rome

69. *Proc. NCAL,* Stewart-Jackson Translation, 22nd Meeting, 17 April 1951.

newspaper *Il Tempo,* published on 5 January, and repeating the allegation that the NCAL was an illegal body. This time he added the information that he had told the United States Department of State that the Arab League could not tolerate in its midst a State founded illegally.[70] Kikhia pointed out that the Secretary-General of the Arab League was criticizing something which the United Nations had decided and the Libyan people had accepted; such interference in Libya's internal affairs was highly regrettable.

The fact that Azzam Pasha had made his statement to an Italian newspaper added insult to injury in the eyes of many members of the NCAL, among whom the feeling was gaining ground that something must be done to counter the hostile propaganda that was being disseminated both at

70. In reply to the question whether Libya would be admitted to membership in the Arab League, Azzam Pasha replied: "There is a fundamental issue in the way which cannot be overcome. For Libya to enter into the union of Arab States, it is necessary that she becomes a really independent State and not a satellite of other countries."

Recalling the favorable attitude of the Arab countries in the United Nations to the establishment of true independence in Libya, he stated:

> The foundation of a new State should emanate from a freely elected and representative assembly of the entire population of Libya, otherwise the new State would be founded on a false basis and we could not recognize it. The present Libyan Constituent Assembly, as it has been constituted from the various regions is absolutely out of proportion to the number of the inhabitants and can only represent an assembly of individuals. We cannot recognize it as being a representative organ of the people of Libya, so we cannot recognize the legality of its decisions. This is an illegal assembly and I have stated, even recently in Washington to the American State Department, that the Arab League cannot accept as a member a State created on an illegal basis.
>
> It is the duty of the people of Libya to build a state morally and legally on a democratic basis. The independence of the country is now a recognized fact in international circles, since the United Nations has agreed and confirmed it. Now it is only necessary to organize independence in such a way that it cannot be endangered by democratic methods but only by the use of illegal means as some people would like to adopt in founding the new State.
>
> The Arab League will fight with all its might to prevent the creation of a false free State and to make the will of the people of Libya prevail.

Translation provided by the Italian Association for International Relations, Rome, from *Il Tempo,* 5 January 1951.

The precise meaning of the words "legal," "illegal," and "unlawful" or "illegitimate," all of which were bandied about in the course of this controversy, was not always clear. The status of the NCAL was viewed not only in the light of the relevant United Nations resolutions, but also in that of the agreements reached between Tripolitanian and Cyrenaican leaders, hence the importance attached to the two documents dealt with later in this part.

home and abroad. As a result, a special meeting of the NCAL was called on 18 January 1951. Point 2 of the agenda read: "Reading the protest telegram to be sent to Mr. Pelt"; and point 3: "Review of the present situation with regard to the national question and the measures it demands." [71] The telegram received by the Commissioner repeated the gist of the Cyrenaican protests.

In the course of the debate on the second point, one of the Cyrenaican members, Khalil Qallal, proposed that a statement be issued confirming the legality of the NCAL and its representative character. A Tripolitanian member, Abd al-Majid Ku'bar, wanted to know whether there was documentary proof that people who had formerly approved federalism and an appointed NSAL were now alleging that the latter was not representative. Khalil Qallal replied in the affirmative, whereupon the leader of the Cyrenaican delegation, Omar Shenib, requested the Secretary of the NCAL to read out two documents. These turned out to be the letter of 17 June 1950 addressed by Selim Bey and Abdur Rahim Khan to the Amir, and handed to the latter by Beshir Bey Saadawi, and the accompanying *"Explanatory Memorandum Concerning the Constitutional Developments Anticipated in Libya,"* both of which have already been discussed in detail in this study.[72] The memorandum was neither dated nor signed; it bore, however, the initials "Sh," presumably those of Fuad Shukri (Beshir Bey's Egyptian adviser), by whom it had been written in the presence of Omar Shenib, so the latter assured the NCAL.

Up to that moment, both documents had been considered as strictly confidential both by their authors and by the Amir. The Commissioner had heard of their existence through the "desert wind," as the local saying goes, but had never seen them; nor had he tried to obtain copies. Experience had taught him that in Libya the best way of getting confidential information of interest to him was not to demand it; it had a way of reaching him in due time through channels of its own.

For various reasons, both the letter and the memorandum, which, as already related, were published the next day in the Tripoli newspaper *Tarablus al-Gharb* (19 January 1951),[73] were most revealing. Comparing dates, it will be seen that they had been written a few days after the adoption on 14 June by the Council for Libya of the Pakistani draft resolution establishing the Committee of Twenty-One.[74] The letter briefly explained the circumstances in which the Commissioner's original plan for a prepara-

71. *Proc. NCAL,* Stewart-Jackson Translation, 9th Meeting, 18 January 1951.
72. See Chapter 3, pp. 263–65.
73. Ibid.
74. See Chapter 3, p. 253.

tory committee had been rejected and the Pakistani proposal adopted in its stead. It then went on, as we know, to justify the bargain between Selim Bey and Abdur Rahim Khan on one side and Baron Confalonieri and Giacomo Marchino on the other, whereby the former, in return for two Italian votes in the Council for the Pakistani draft resolution, agreed to a resolution implying that an Italian should have a seat on the Committee of Twenty-One. It was alleged that the Tripolitanian leaders were prepared to pay this price, and that the Cyrenaican member of the Council and the Commissioner had opposed the transaction on the ground that the Amir would on no account accept an Italian on any Libyan constitutional body. In short, it was an attempt to wear the Amir's opposition down with specious arguments.[75]

Shukri's memorandum, written for Beshir Bey (it will be remembered that it was subtitled "The Difficulties Facing Elections in Tripolitania alone"), was intrinsically of much greater importance because it was clearly the product of an astute political mind. The Commissioner recognized it as the outcome of prolonged consultations with the Amir, with himself, with members of the Council, and probably, though to what extent it is difficult to say, with leading personages in Tripolitania and Cyrenaica. Its author had worked out a compromise solution based largely on Cyrenaican views, and clearly intended to meet them on the issue of the form of State and government. The memorandum also dealt in detail with the procedure to be followed in implementing the compromise.

The memorandum started out by summing up the "advantages of forming a Constituent Assembly on the same principles as the Committee of Twenty-One,"[76] meaning thereby appointment of the members on the basis of equality of representation among the three territories. In the matter of practical suggestions, however, it diverged notably from the method of organizing the Committee of Twenty-One in that it proposed that the political parties in Tripolitania should submit lists of their candidates without indicating who was to make the final selection. Reading between the lines, and recalling many conversations with him, the Com-

75. For full text of the letter, see Chapter 3, pp. 263–65; for details of the "deal," see Chapter 3, p. 244.

76. The NCAL delegation to the Arab League which visited Cairo in January and February 1951, of which more later, appended a copy of the memorandum to its report to the Assembly, which, as explained in footnote 2 to this chapter, was translated into English for the author by Frank H. Stewart. For the sake of consistency with quotations from the delegation's report, the quotations from the memorandum (direct or indirect) in the next few pages of this study have been taken from Stewart's translation, and not from that made for internal purposes by the language staff of the Mission (see Chapter 3, p. 263, fn. 27).

missioner had little doubt that Beshir Bey had intended to assign this task to himself.

Under the heading "measures to be taken in forming the new state," the author of the memorandum proposed that Cyrenaica and Tripolitania should immediately conclude an agreement "as regards the measures that must be resolved by the Constituent Assembly when it is created." These measures were in fact those actually taken by the NCAL at its third meeting on 2 December 1950 (though placed in a different order), namely:

1. Proclamation of His Highness the Amir as King of Libya.
2. Announcement that the new State is to be a federal one.
3. Immediate formation of a sub-committee of the Constituent Assembly to prepare a draft constitution on a federal basis.

The memorandum was vaguer and less incisive in dealing with the transfer of the powers held by the British and French Administrations. It left the reader with the impression that the author's idea was that the transfer should be effected before the declaration of independence by the establishment of "national" [77] governments in the three provinces to take over full powers.[78] With regard to Tripolitania, the author of the memorandum suggested that: "H. M. the King will charge the majority leader in Tripoli—this is a democratic procedure—to form a local national government or administration in Tripoli immediately." As Beshir Bey was in the habit of considering himself as the local majority leader, since he was President of the largest Tripolitanian party, it may safely be assumed that he saw himself in the role of deus ex machina.

In the Fezzan, His Majesty would confirm Ahmed Bey Seif al-Nasr as head of the local administration, while in Cyrenaica it was suggested that he might confirm the existing Government or, if he so wished, form a new one. It was also suggested that, again if he so wished, the King might form a supreme advisory council, made up of the heads of the local national governments or administrations under his chairmanship (the Arabic text says literally "supervision").

According to Shukri, this system of government would remain in force until the Constituent Assembly had finished drawing up a constitution,

77. Stewart points out that the term "National Government" has been used to render the Arabic *hukuma wataniya,* meaning a government of Libyans as opposed to a foreign administration. "Indigenous government" might have been better, but "national" has been used throughout the translation of *Proc. NCAL.*

78. In the case of Cyrenaica, the memorandum (in translation) speaks of the transfer of "full power"; in that of the Fezzan, of "extensive powers"; and in the case of Tripolitania, it merely refers to "power" without qualification.

when the formation of an independent Libyan Government would be proclaimed.

As one of the advantages of the plan, its author predicted that it would meet with no serious opposition in the Council for Libya; it would certainly be accepted by the majority and agreement might even be unanimous.

Looking back on the memorandum, particularly in the light of events between the time at which it was written and the proclamation of independence on 21 December 1951, nothing is easier than to pick out its weak points and lacunae; indeed, if the plan had been implemented, there is little doubt that the outcome would have been a looser federation than that finally established. The idea of transferring powers to local governments or administrations without insisting on the absolute necessity for making a final retransfer to the federal government is almost incomprehensible, especially coming from a man who always maintained that "unity" was his ideal. Provision for an elected National Assembly or for an elected Parliament after independence was also notable only by its absence. This reconfirmed the Commissioner's earlier impression that Beshir Bey, more than uncertain of the outcome of an election in the politically deeply divided province of Tripolitania, had come to prefer an appointed body in order to leave himself a freer hand.

An explanation current at the time of the self-contradictory fluctuations in Beshir Bey's tactics was that, having been convinced for a long time of the need for reaching a basic agreement with the Cyrenaicans and their leaders, he had swallowed their federal ideas hook, line, and sinker, confident that, once firmly in the saddle as Prime Minister of Tripolitania, he would be able to impose a more highly centralized form of State. If this reading of Beshir Bey's political thinking was correct, it revealed a serious misapprehension on his part of Libya's primary political difficulty, i.e. the difference in outlook and interests between Tripolitania and Cyrenaica. But it is hard to believe that a man so familiar with his country's problems could have been so mistaken. Or were those right who considered that Beshir Bey, besides overrating his own influence in Tripolitania, had also always underrated that of the Senussi leader in Cyrenaica, a miscalculation which might have led him to believe that in the last instance he would be able to shape Libya's future along his own lines? The Commissioner, in the course of his acquaintance with Beshir Bey, had sometimes asked himself that very question.

Another less plausible explanation was that the Tripolitanian leader, having always realized that a federal State under the Amir was the only possible way of bringing the three territories together in a single sovereign

State, but dependent for support on the Arab League and the Tripolitanian nationalists, had been forced to pay lip service to the concept of unity of which his backers were ardent advocates. For those in close contact with Beshir Bey during Libya's formative years, this machiavellian explanation is difficult to accept. All in all, the first explanation, though still open to doubt, appears the most likely.

Whatever Beshir Bey's private intentions may have been in approaching the Amir, and whatever the shortcomings of his plan, it is only fair to recognize that at the time it had the merit of proposing a solution to Libya's main constitutional problem which, barring an elected constituent assembly, came closer to practical politics than any alternative conceivable in the circumstances prevailing. The best justification for this view is that from June through November 1950 the plan provided the basis for agreement between the inner circle of Tripolitanian Congress Party leaders and their Cyrenaican opposite numbers led by the Amir. It was an ominous sign, however, that it should have been kept dark, at Beshir Bey's own request, leaving the Cyrenaican delegation to the NCAL to reveal its existence in order to prove that body's legitimacy and the validity of its decisions.[79]

To revert to the discussion in the NCAL, as soon as the Secretary had finished reading the two documents, Khalil Qallal made the following statement:

> We have had read to us the document by Muh. Kamil Salim Bey and Abd al-Rahman Khan, as also the recommendations of Fuad Shukri, acting in this matter on behalf of Sa'dawi Bey. All this shows that federalism is nothing new, but that it was the result of a long debate, and

79. When the author revisited Libya in the winter of 1964–65, he had an opportunity to talk over these events with friends there who had taken an active part in them. They gave him an explanation of Beshir Bey's political behavior in the summer of 1950 which had not occurred to him. In their view Saadawi's strategy for achieving unity had indeed been based on a transfer of powers to local governments. Once this had been completed, and the British and French had departed, the three territories would have entered into a union under the Amir as Head of State, a union which in the circumstances would have been dominated by Tripolitania. Saadawi himself would have become Prime Minister, first, of Tripolitania, then in the first union government, under which a true unitarist State would have been formed. Again, it seems incredible that so intelligent a man could have been so naïve. Yet this explanation cannot be lightly written off, as some of these ideas found expression not only in Beshir Bey's conversations with the Commissioner, but also in the memorandum which he submitted to the latter and to the British Chief Administrator in Tripolitania in connection with the British plan to set up an Advisory Council in that territory (see Chapter 2, pp. 135–37).

that it was an idea that ripened in the mind of Bashir Bey al Sa'dawi. It also shows that what the Assembly has done was in accord with what Bashir Bey al Sa'dawi, Kamil Selim Bey and Abd al-Rahman Khan had agreed on. Since Bashir Bey is head of the Conference, we consider his statements as being issued in its name. From this you may realize that the line followed in the resolution of the N.C.A.L. is in every way in accord with what was previously agreed on; and that the propaganda at the moment being issued against the Assembly must beyond all doubt be the result of a new change of outlook on the part of Bashir al-Sa'dawi and others. This being so we must issue a statement saying that the Assembly does not represent itself alone, but the whole nation, and that such resolutions as it has passed have been based on previous consultations." [80]

On the morning of 19 January, *Tarablus al-Gharb* commented editorially in the following terms:

In these difficult and critical circumstances surrounding the development of the national cause . . . we find that some of the leaders, supported by some representatives of . . . countries upon which we used to set great hopes and aspirations, are working not in order to facilitate our task and help us to proceed towards our objective and achieve unity, but in order to obstruct our action.[81]

There followed a rather confused debate in the NCAL, in the course of which embarrassed Tripolitanian members gave varying versions of their leader's position, and of their own interpretation of that position, leaving the impression that within the leadership of the National Congress Party there was a rift between adherents and opponents of Beshir Bey's policies; some of them accepted his concept of federalism, others were for unitarism. A few members of the Assembly tried to pour oil on the stormy waters and to reconcile the two points of view. One of the latter, Mohamed al-Hinqari, observed that two important points had to be clarified in the proposed statement. They were: "1. The legality of the Assembly's creation. 2. That the Assembly was trying to choose a form of federalism extremely close to unity. He said that this would gain general agreement." [82]

The contradiction between the leader's original plan and the attacks he launched five months later against the very National Assembly established

80. *Proc. NCAL,* Stewart-Jackson Translation, 9th Meeting, 18 January 1951. By "head of the Conference," the speaker meant "President of the National Congress Party of Tripolitania."

81. See Chapter 3, p. 263, fn. 27.

82. Ibid.

in conformity therewith passed tactfully unexplained. Understandably, the Tripolitanians were not keen on washing their dirty linen in public, and the Cyrenaicans wisely did not insist. They knew the answers anyway.

When the Secretary proposed that the NCAL start drafting the statement, Khalil Qallal handed him a prepared text which was read out. Some critical comments were made, a Tripolitanian member observing that he had not noticed in the statement any expression of the intention to arrive at a federal form of the State close to unity. Another Tripolitanian thought that the adverse remarks about the party leaders should be toned down, obviously with those about Beshir Bey in mind. Finally, as the Council of the Arab League was to meet in the Egyptian capital on 20 January, and the Libyan question was on its agenda, Khalil Qallal proposed that a delegation be sent to Cairo to present the NCAL's views. The proposal was unanimously approved. It was further decided that the delegation should consist of the President, representing Tripolitania, and the two Vice-Presidents, representing Cyrenaica and the Fezzan respectively. The Vice-President for the Fezzan having intimated that he could not go for personal reasons, Bubakr Bin Ahmed Bubakr was nominated in his place. The President added Khalil Qallal in view of his "special qualifications," so that, in fact, the delegation included two Cyrenaicans. In Benghazi, the four members were joined by Salim Bin Yasir as press adviser, Awni Dajani as legal adviser, and Wahbi Buri as an expert.[83]

As to the text of the statement to be submitted to the Council of the League, the substance of Khalil Qallal's text was tacitly approved, the delegation being left discretion to modify the wording in the light of the circumstances it encountered in Cairo.

On 12 February, the NCAL met to hear a report on the journey of its delegation to Cairo. It had become known through the press and the radio that it had run into difficulties; hence members were impatient to hear the report, and the atmosphere was tense.

The report was in two sections: (a) an account of constitutional developments in Libya, as given for the information of members of the Arab League; and (b) an account of the delegation's activities and discussions in Cairo given for the information of the NCAL.

In addition, the delegation submitted a separate report giving more detailed information on specific points. These documents were read into the record, and copies distributed to the members of the Assembly.

According to the report, the delegation arrived in Cairo in the evening of 22 January. The next morning, it had a meeting of about ninety minutes

83. Awni Dajani was at the time the Amir's legal adviser.

with the Egyptian Minister for Foreign Affairs, Muhamed Salah al-Din Pasha. During the next few days members made contact with those taking part in the meeting of the Arab League Council. Subsequently they had other discussions with the Minister, and with the leaders of several other Arab delegations. On 26 January the delegation was told that the Libyan question had suddenly been raised in the Political Committee of the Council, which had passed a resolution charging Egypt to keep an eye on the situation to ensure that resolution 289 (IV) was carried out within the appointed time. From the Cairo morning papers of 27 January it appeared that the Political Committee had taken up the matter without prior notice and disposed of it without preliminary study. The delegation complained that the proceedings had obviously been prejudiced, and that it had not been consulted. It had therefore decided to send forthwith the following telegram to the heads of the Arab delegations to the Council:

> We learn with surprise from today's newspapers that the Political Committee has passed certain specific resolutions on the Libyan question, although it has not yet either listened to the views of the Libyan delegation or even received its memorandum. Any action of this sort can only create the worst possible impression in Libya, and Libya wishes to announce that at no time in future will she be bound either to execute or recognize this resolution. The delegation came here to elucidate the Libyan question for you, and it hopes that the Political Committee will form no opinion on the matter before having heard what the delegation has to say and having studied its memorandum." [84]

In the evening of the same day the delegation presented its memorandum to the Political Committee; it was also distributed to the local press and news agencies and to all those in Cairo concerned with the Libyan question.

Apart from giving a factual account of Libyan constitutional development as already dealt with in this study, the memorandum expressed the hope that "the Arab delegations will exhibit a fitting concern for a fellow Arab nation which is advancing towards independence and the creation of a new Arab State. The delegation lays high hopes on the duties of brotherhood and on the lasting historical bonds which unite our Arab nation to its Arab brethren." [85]

Referring to the attempts made by the Arab delegations at Lake Success in October and November 1950 to modify the terms of General Assembly Resolution 387 (V) (see pp. 362–68), the memorandum observed that: "There is no doubt that if—God forbid—the Arab delegation's plan had

84. *Report of the NCAL Delegation to Arab League*, Stewart Translation, pp. 2–3.
85. Ibid., p. 3.

succeeded it would have represented a real, though unintentional, obstacle in the way of all the constitutional developments directed towards unification of Libya in accordance with the U.N. resolution. In fact the whole enterprise would have been seriously endangered."[86]

The memorandum contained the following paragraph, an obvious attempt to meet the critics of federalism:

> The N.C.A.L. aims (*muttajiha*) to produce a federal system closer to unity than to federation. This is to be done by forming a central government in which the ministries of Foreign Affairs, Finance, Defence, Communications, Education, Currency and Justice will be centered. Local administrations will be formed in Cyrenaica, Tripoli [*sic*] and the Fezzan. Each will have its own local legislative body and local administrative system, concerned with purely local matters, in accordance with the details that will be laid down by the constitution. There will be a central Parliament composed of two chambers. One of them will represent the inhabitants of the country on a numerical basis. The other will be for senators representing the [three] territories on a basis of equality. This will be on the pattern of the democratic Parliaments in the existing federal states. . . .
>
> At this, the first stage of national independence, there can as yet be no question of a single central government to rule a country whose area reaches 700,000 sq. miles and which has a little over a million inhabitants. In the past neither Italy nor Turkey was able to concentrate all power in a single government. There are, moreover, other internal political factors which demand that none of the three provinces be denied a local administration, at least at this first stage of independence. Take the example of Cyrenaica. It was the scene of the fiercest desert fighting of the Second World War, and there was a bitter and bloody struggle between its inhabitants and the Italians. The Cyrenaicans believe that if a centralized Libyan government were established the Italians who fled to Tripoli would gain the right to return to Cyrenaica and settle there; and at the moment the return of the Italians could only mean the revival of every sort of conflict between the two elements. The Cyrenaicans can only be guaranteed that the Italians will not settle in their country by being granted the right to pass legislation referring to their locality [*sic*] which will be in accord with their internal situation and their psychological needs. We do not think that the existence of such local powers or guarantees will detract from the country's independence or act invidiously against any particular group. Federalism is a modern form of

86. Ibid., p. 9.

government, employed in 17 independent nations, none of which, to the best of our knowledge, has rejected this system or claimed that it has detracted from its sovereignty.[87]

The NCAL's opposition to the suggestion made by the Commissioner in his statements to the General Assembly at Lake Success on 16–17 November 1950, to the effect that the Constitution being drafted should subsequently be submitted to a Parliament elected on a proportional basis for ratification and possible amendment, was justified in the following terms:

> [If the constitution produced by the N.C.A.L. were presented to a proportionately representative body] the single province with a majority in the Libyan chamber of representatives would be given the power to abrogate the constitution and to nullify the resolutions of the new constituent assembly, which were agreed on by representatives of all three provinces. This would bring the whole affair back to its beginning again, prevent the implementation of the U.N. decree [*sic*] and mean wasting the single opportunity we have been granted of establishing a Libyan state. The Libyan delegation knows more about the situation in Libya than do the Arab states, and it hopes that the present circumstances of the country will be properly appreciated. It must be borne in mind that at the most no more than two months remain in which to form a Libyan central government [i.e., until 1 April 1951, the deadline set by the General Assembly in Resolution 387 (V). *Author*], and that the N.C.A.L. has already made great progress in its work and has passed the most important of the historic resolutions concerning the form of government—a resolution whose provisions cannot be called into question in any other body. It gives us great pleasure to present this document to our brethren the Arab delegations in the name of a Libya that has proclaimed itself an independent, sovereign, monarchical state, and which now implores you not to adopt a position which will impede its efforts or nullify its resolutions—resolutions determined on by the Libyan nation, and which now represent a tangible reality impossible to ignore or deny. We hope that you will respect the desire of this nation to follow the road which seems most likely to bring it safely to its destination, and we hope that this nation will be given the opportunity to prove to the whole world that it has attained full independence, established its national life on democratic foundations and become one of the factors working for peace, security, and stability among the Arab peoples.
>
> It is incumbent upon us in this memorandum to record our protests

87. Ibid., pp. 10–12.

and objections to the destructive statements repeatedly issued by the Secretary General of the Arab League in Italy and elsewhere. These statements wounded the susceptibilities of the Libyan nation and of its king; they also encouraged the hopes and desires of the Italians in Libya, and this will always be a cause of conflict and a stumbling block to Libya's progress.

At this delicate stage of our national life it is our patriotic duty to tell you frankly that the N.C.A.L. is continuing its work with resolution and decision, and that there is nothing that will turn it from its consecrated task; and if those in the Arab League who oppose the Assembly succeed in hampering its work, then we charge you before God, history and the Arab conscience with the responsibility for preventing the implementation of the U.N. resolution, dismembering the country of Libya, consolidating colonialism in it, and creating a second Palestine.[88]

On 28 January, the Political Committee of the League Council devoted more than two hours to discussion of the memorandum. The Libyan delegation was invited to express its views. The report asserted that the delegation's arguments were strong and logical and that they met with general approval from the members of the Arab delegations; even the Egyptian Foreign Minister, whose opposition to the Libyan views was stronger than anyone else's, went no further than to maintain his reservations about the matter.

The report went on to complain that the secretariat of the Arab League was blatantly partisan and that it spared no expense in fighting the delegation by every possible means, including the enlistment of Libyan opposition elements living in Egypt. Because of all this, the delegation was forced to issue a lengthy statement, setting forth yet once more the NCAL's policies and views; this ended with the following warning:

The Libyan nation is not prepared to be a sacrificial lamb, or a plaything in the hands of politicians who change their views from one day to the next without paying any attention to the dangers that encompass the country's future, to the lack of time, or to the determination of the nation to establish the state within the appointed period.

So let those who play with fire beware! They must realize that the Libyan state is now an indisputable reality. Half the Libyan nation died in the struggle for freedom. They are not a people to be the object of scepticism and haggling. They are not prepared to allow any interference in their internal affairs. These affairs are entirely their own business, to be decided according to their best interests and wishes. They are not

88. Ibid., pp. 13–14. The first square brackets are the translator's.

> prepared to sacrifice their nation and their country, nor will they in the present tense international atmosphere waste their time in futile debate. Palestine is a sanguine warning that has not been forgotten. They will establish their state in spite of the obstacles, and personal ambitions, and the insincere opinions, all of which can lead to nothing but regret at having stood in the way of a nation fighting nobly for its independence.
>
> And finally: Long live Libya the free and the independent, and long live her King Idris I! [89]

The separate report submitted by the delegation was appended to the record of the NCAL's tenth meeting; it contained some interesting additional information.

On the subject of the delegation's first meeting with the Egyptian Minister for Foreign Affairs, the statement says:

> The delegation reached the Egyptian capital fully aware of the difficulties and adverse circumstances that would face it in a country whose government has persistently opposed the Assembly, and in which the influence of the head (*amin*) of the Arab League is so strong. He represents in fact the largest obstacle that the Assembly faced in carrying out its task. . . . [The delegation] then went to the Ministry of Foreign Affairs, where they were received by the Foreign Minister, H. E. Muh. Salah al Din Pasha. When the delegation asked His Excellency to appoint a time for their discussions, he suggested that they should begin to examine the Libyan question immediately. The delegation then explained, in brief, the procedure by which the N.C.A.L. was founded. They pointed out that Kamil Salim Bey, Mr. Abd al Rahim Khan, Mr. Mustafa Mizran and Mr. Bashir Bey al' Adawi had all taken part in laying the foundations of the Assembly whose legality they were now contesting. The Minister said that he would listen to what they had to say with great care, and that if he was in the wrong he would withdraw; but that if the delegation were

89. Ibid., p. 17. The assertion that half the Libyan nation died in the struggle for freedom must be an overstatement, cruel though the losses must have been. The population of the three territories under the Italian occupation was estimated at just over one million. The first postwar census, largely supervised by a United Nations expert, showed the total population in 1953–54 to be 10 percent above this figure (see Chapter 3, p. 221, fn. 12). The natural increase could not possibly have added 600,000 to the population in the space of fifteen years. Even counting total losses since the beginning of the guerrilla fighting at the time of the Italo-Turkish war in 1912, and allowing for concomitant losses by famine and the general disruption of what economy the country possessed, 500,000 dead seems a very high figure. The author's researches suggest that the total death roll from all causes except natural death between 1912 and 1943 was in the region of 250,000 to 300,000.

in the wrong, then it should withdraw. He proceeded to speak in an emotional fashion about Egypt's aims and those of the Arab States. He spoke of the dangers that faced the country from establishing federalism and opening the door to foreign influence. He said that in its present form the Assembly would be the object of continual attack and criticism because the rights of the majority were not respected in it. He added that it was strange that the Arab States should want Libya to reach maturity and be finally freed from the noose of colonialism while at the same time there were others who wanted to follow a policy that would not lead to this objective.[90]

The delegation refuted the Minister's charges with the arguments put forward in the memorandum, laying particular stress on the NCAL's intentions regarding the powers of the central government. At the end of the meeting, Salah al-Din Bey said, according to the statement: "I had been unaware of this portion of your aims. So long as these continue to be your objectives, I shall not oppose them.[91]

In the course of subsequent visits to heads of other delegations, it became clear that, as was to be expected, not all of these shared the Egyptian point of view.[92]

In the Political Committee, the debate on Libya had been long and acrimonious. Some delegations, in particular those of Iraq and Lebanon, had been against interference by the League or by any other Arab State in Libya's internal affairs. Egypt had clung to its point of view. The resolution requesting Egypt to keep an eye on the Libyan situation had been opposed by the Secretary-General of the League himself, who did not want to be bound by the date fixed by the United Nations for Libya's independence, saying that he saw no reason why it should not be put back.

The statement then related that Azzam Pasha invited the delegation to his house on the evening of 2 February:

> He reviewed his history and his achievements in Libya, and said that he would not fall short in helping any Tripolitanian or Cyrenaican. He regretted the attacks that had been made on him from Libya. He acknowledged the statement he had made in Italy, and said that it would be desirable to gain the support of Italy and of the Vatican, so that the Latin states would be on the side of the Arabs. He admitted that in 1940

90. *Proc. NCAL,* Stewart-Jackson Translation, 10th Meeting, 12 February 1951.

91. Ibid.

92. In particular, the delegation had meetings with the Prime Ministers of Egypt, Iraq, Lebanon, and Transjordan, and with the Ministers for Foreign Affairs of Egypt and Saudi Arabia.

he had advised the Tripolitanians not to join the Senussi army, since he had been convinced that the Axis powers would win. The discussion lasted some [four] hours, during which Azzam made various mutually contradictory statements. He did not concentrate his opposition on any single, specific area. Finally he said that if the delegation approved of it, he would announce to the papers that he would cease to intervene in the Libyan question.[93]

The statement ended by asserting that the efforts of the delegation had been crowned by complete success.

As might have been expected, the delegation's report and additional statement gave rise to a lively debate in the NCAL. The main bone of contention was the assertion that the Assembly's aim was a federal system closer to a unitary State than to a federation. A Cyrenaican member observed that the paragraph in question dealt with a matter on which the Assembly had as yet come to no conclusion. The President, supported by Khalil Qallal, pointed out that the memorandum did not mention a resolution; it merely spoke of the general direction in which the Assembly was moving. However, the NCAL was unable to make up its collective mind whether or not the delegation should have made such a statement.

On the other hand, it endorsed the delegation's expressed opposition to the submission of the Constitution it was engaged in drafting to an elected body for ratification and eventual amendment.

On another plane, complaints were voiced about the presence of two Cyrenaicans on the delegation, it being argued that there should have been a second Tripolitanian also.

When it became clear that the discussion would not produce a meeting of minds, a Cyrenaican member, Mabruk Geibani, submitted the following proposal: "The N.C.A.L. thanks the delegation for its praiseworthy activity, and confirms its report on its journey to Egypt, excepting only those parts of the report concerned with constitutional details, as to which the Assembly has as yet passed no resolution." With little further discussion, the proposal was adopted by 44 votes to 3, 7 members abstaining.[94]

Looking back to the origin of this series of clashes which, as mentioned before, had started with the Egyptian criticisms of the NCAL, it appears that Beshir Bey at first intended to carry out his part of the agreement with the Amir, the Cyrenaican counterpart consisting of the acceptance of a federal government with fairly extensive powers. During the summer of 1950, he repeated in a private conversation (see pp. 284–86) that he

93. *Proc. NCAL*, Stewart-Jackson Translation, 10th Meeting, 12 February 1951.
94. Ibid.

considered himself committed—and that he was known to be committed—to a loosely federated Libya—loose from his unitarist point of view—under a Senussi Prince; his policy, he said, was that of the Cyrenaicans and the Amir. Even as late as December 1950 he still seemed to support the plan. Later, as we know, he retreated, under pressure from his more extreme nationalist friends, both Egyptian and Tripolitanian. Why did he change his mind? The question is of real importance, for implementation of the agreement would have smoothed the course of Libya's constitutional development.

This time, it is not so difficult to fathom the mystery, though it is still not clear what actually took place behind the scenes. In one important respect, events had gone off the course charted by the Tripolitanian Congress Party and its leader: the selection of the twenty Tripolitanian members of the NCAL. Beshir Bey had planned to tour the various districts of the province himself to select them on a proportional population basis, so many for each district and so many from Tripoli town. Instead, as related on pages 296–97 above, following a proposal put forward unanimously by the Tripolitanian representatives in the Committee of Twenty-One, a preselection had been made by its Chairman, the Mufti. The latter's critics later accused him of yielding to pressure exerted by the British Administration and there is little doubt that he listened to its advice and to some extent followed it. The Mufti himself told the Commissioner that his principal aim had been to draw up a list of names as representative as possible of all shades of opinion: urban, rural, and tribal. Moreover, he had made a point of including not only members of the different political parties, but also independents. The author, knowing the Mufti as he did, and recalling his own experience when entrusted with the selection of the seven Tripolitanian members of the Committee of Twenty-One, believes this explanation to be truthful.

The Committee's eventual approval of the Mufti's list was not to Beshir Bey's liking, since the Congress Party was less strongly represented than he had wished.[95]

95. The situation has been succinctly summed up by an observer of the postwar Libyan scene in the following terms:

> The Advisory Council [for] Libya, it will be recalled, had discussed the manner in which the National Assembly would be composed and it was on the recommendation of the leaders of political parties, including the National Congress Party, that the principle of appointing, rather than electing, the Tripolitanian members was adopted. The National Congress Party, under the leadership of Bashir al-Saadawi, was satisfied that since four out of the seven Tripolitanian members of the Committee of Twenty-One were members of the National Congress, the appointment of the Tripolitanian representatives in the National Assembly would

This turn of events was deeply resented both in Tripolitania and by the secretariat of the Arab League and the Egyptian Government. It must be remembered that many politically conscious men in Tripoli town and Cairo, still suffering from the shock of the Bevin-Sforza plan, genuinely believed that a loose federation would make Libya vulnerable to foreign influence and intrigue. That this fear was not wholly unjustified has been shown more than once in the present study. Moreover, the sophisticated Arab nationalists in the towns found great difficulty in understanding the particularistic tribal mentality of the rural population, for the most part seminomads or settled farmers of seminomadic origin. The townsman is too readily disposed to look down on the "poor Bedouin," underrating the latter's attachment to his rude, desert way of life and the strength of character he derives from it. In Libya, the political misunderstanding between Tripolitanians, Cyrenaicans, and Fezzanese was in part due to this difference in outlook. (This also explains what the NCAL meant by saying that interference by the Arab League in the country's domestic affairs was mainly the result of lack of understanding of the realities of the internal situation.) The resentment of the nationalists against the composition of and policies pursued by the NCAL expressed itself in various ways. At the Fifth Session of the General Assembly, the Arab delegations had been against an appointed and for an elected Libyan National Assembly, thereby implying the dissolution of the NCAL. The Arab press and radio launched the anti-NCAL campaign described at the beginning of this part of the chapter. In Tripoli town, a number of public demonstrations were organized by the National Congress Party. On 15 January, a deputation of forty to fifty, led by Beshir Bey Saadawi and Mustafa Mizran, came to the Commissioner's office at the Grand Hotel to present a petition. The Commissioner being at the time in Cairo, the petition was received by a member of the Mission staff. The petition sought a single, democratic, constitutional State under King Idris, with one government and one freely elected Parliament proportionally representative of all the inhabitants of Libya. It added, however, that the Congress Party was not opposed to the establishment of a local administration in each of the three territories, provided no local parliament or government was established in any of them.

---

meet with the prior approval of the National Congress Party. When, however, the Mufti of Tripolitania submitted a list of representatives to the Committee of Twenty-One which did not meet with the approval of the National Congress Party, the National Assembly was denounced on the premise that it was appointed rather than elected.

Majid Khadduri, *Modern Libya: A Study in Political Development* (Baltimore: Johns Hopkins Press, 1963), p. 164.

On 23 January, a crowd of several hundred carrying placards denouncing federalism and the NCAL gathered in front of the Grand Hotel, and asked to be received. The Commissioner received thirty of the demonstrators, headed by Mustafa Mizran, who explained that they represented the Executive Committee of the National Congress of Tripolitania and came from different parts of the interior. Several of those who spoke repeated what had been said by the earlier deputation. The Commissioner answered that he had not yet met one person in Libya who was not genuinely in favor of unity, adding that in his opinion the question of federalism versus unitarism was not an academic semantic issue, but a practical problem of distributing powers among the different bodies to be established under the Constitution.

A few days later, the Commissioner received another communication expressing the opposite view, signed by about sixty sheikhs and notables, announcing their withdrawal from the National Congress Party and their support of the NCAL. More significant still was a visit from three elderly, dignified tribal chiefs, who had come more than one hundred miles from the Jebel Nefusa to Tripoli to offer the Commissioner the support of "five hundred rifles" if he considered he was in need of them. The Commissioner could not refrain from expressing his appreciation of the offer, while tactfully pointing out that it ought rightfully to have been made to the British Resident and that in any case he did not think that the situation warranted a show of force. All the same, the incident was symptomatic of the tension that prevailed everywhere between town and country.

To return to the mission to Cairo, subsequent developments suggested that the NCAL delegation had not been as successful in reconciling the conflicting points of view as its members had fancied. For instance, in March, the National Congress Party instructed its members in the NCAL to leave that body. Two out of nine of them obeyed, giving personal reasons as the motive for their withdrawal. In the course of its Seventeenth Session (22 March 1951), the NCAL accepted their resignation with a vote of thanks for services rendered. During the nineteenth meeting (29 March 1951), the Tripolitanian delegation invited by majority vote the President of the Assembly, in his capacity as chairman of their group, to appoint two successors. The President did so in the course of the same meeting, whereupon the National Assembly unanimously approved his decision.

A more serious sign that political sniping between the Arab League and the Congress Party on one side and the NCAL on the other was not only still going on but also causing increasingly bitter feeling, was an unpleasant incident that occurred in the Council for Libya. At the seventy-fourth meeting, held in the morning of 12 March, while the Council, with Marchino in the Chair, was discussing the Commissioner's request for advice on certain aspects of Libyan constitutional development,[96] the Egyptian member, who not infrequently allowed his emotions to get the upper hand, had in strong terms criticized Cyrenaica and praised Tripolitania for the views they held on federalism. He had also once more expressed the opinion that the NCAL was an illegal body. He had even gone so far as to declare:

> The federal principle was quite clearly revealed in the composition of the National Assembly which was contrary to the wording of the General Assembly resolutions. It had been still more clearly revealed at the first meeting of the National Assembly when, in the same breath and without any discussion, His Highness the Amir El Senussi had been proclaimed King and federation had been proclaimed the future form of the Libyan State; perhaps the latter had been the price for the former.[97]

In the course of the afternoon (seventy-fifth) meeting, the member for Cyrenaica, Ali Bey Jerbi, defending the legality of the National Assembly, had referred to the Egyptian statement as "a most unconstructive speech [that] could only serve to create fresh tension in Libya. If the Egyptian representative had wanted to sow the seeds of disunity and of civil war, he could not have made a speech more calculated to do so." Ali Bey went on to say that the Egyptian statement had produced a very painful impression on him and on all the Cyrenaicans who had heard it; and he "regretfully noted that the Egyptian representative apparently wished to create a rift between Egypt and Libya, when he should have wished to bring together two countries which had the same language, customs and religion. Mr. Jerbi deplored that attitude and hoped that it would not have such grave consequences as he feared."

The member for Pakistan immediately intervened on a point of order, asking the Cyrenaican representative "if he had really meant to imply that if a federation were not forthcoming, there would, in fact, be civil war in Libya," and seeking clarification of this remark.

Ali Bey Jerbi replied that

> the entire sense of the Egyptian representative's statement at the previous meeting necessarily led to the conclusions which he [Ali Bey] had expressed. . . . Cyrenaica and the Fezzan had chosen their own solution to the constitutional question and if a different solution were imposed on them, the desired results would not be achieved. When he had mentioned

96. See Chapter 4, pp. 314–35, passim.

97. For a complete account of this unhappy exchange, see passim Summary Records of 74th and 75th Meetings, from which all the relevant quotations are taken, United Nations Docs.A/AC.32/COUNCIL/SR.74–75, 12 March 1951. Mimeographed.

separation and civil war, he had not meant to say that the Egyptian representative actually wanted those things; he had been speaking purely hypothetically and in the conditional tense.

Selim Bey thereupon repeated that "very serious accusations had been leveled at him. The Cyrenaican representative had failed to produce any proof of his assertions which could only be termed thought-up and unfounded allegations, if he did not prove them." This was the tactful language of the précis-writer; in fact, the Egyptian member used the word "liar," whereupon his Cyrenaican colleague left the Council Chamber.

At this moment, at what looked like a prearranged signal, people in the public gallery demonstrated loudly in favor of the Egyptian representative. The Chairman immediately suspended the meeting and had the gallery cleared. Subsequently, the Commissioner arranged a truce so that meetings could proceed with both members in attendance, but the incident continued to rankle in the Council. Moreover, it had repercussions outside. The Cyrenaican Assembly of Representatives, in a cable of protest, demanded that the Egyptian Government recall Selim Bey. He, on his own initiative, left Tripoli for Cairo, telling the Commissioner that he was going to recommend that his Government withdraw from the Council, on the ground that the imperialist Powers were now in control of it. The Commissioner strongly advised him not to suggest any such action and informed the Secretary-General in Lake Success of the incident, so that he could cope with an Egyptian demarche, should need arise. However, no reaction came from Cairo. In Tripoli, a number of members of the NCAL, infuriated by the discourtesy to their Assembly, proposed at its fifteenth meeting that a formal protest be made.

A few days later, on 27 March, the Commissioner received by way of information from the President of the Assembly a copy of a protest approved by the NCAL on 22 March. After quoting the relevant parts of Selim Bey's statement in the Council, the text summed up the Assembly's feelings in the following words:

> Consequently, the Libyan National Assembly strongly protests against H. E. the representative of Egypt on the Council for Libya. It resolutely condemns his attempt to involve the Holiest of the holies of the Libyan people, his aggressiveness against the National Assembly which is legally representative of the people of Libya, and his insult to the Eastern part of Libya in the Council, by the use of unbecoming language.[98]

98. Translation from the Arabic made for internal purposes by the language staff of the United Nations Mission in Libya. United Nations Archives. Typescript. The text of the protest does not appear in *Proc. NCAL.*

From that moment, the atmosphere in the Council became distinctly less congenial. Tempers were constantly on edge, and throughout 1951 the Council's work suffered accordingly. As for the prevailing political atmosphere. Khalidi has neatly summarized it in the following terms:

> The revelation of the Sadawi and the Pakistani-Egyptian documents created a sensation in Libyan political circles and strongly bolstered the confidence and prestige of the National Assembly, while seriously undermining the position of the opposition.[99]

99. Khalidi, p. 44.

CHAPTER 7

The Making of the Constitution

PART 1. THE WORKSHOP

Notwithstanding the major political discussions which took up most of the NCAL's time during the initial months of its existence, members did not forget that its principal duty was the drafting of the Constitution. As early as 4 December 1950, therefore, in the course of its third meeting, the NCAL established a committee for this purpose.

The record of this meeting reveals that although there were no differences of opinion about applying the principle of equality of representation to the composition of the Committee, members disagreed about the number of representatives per territory. The Tripolitanians, having as usual to express a variety of opinions representing different shades of policy, demanded a larger number of representatives than the Fezzanese, who found it difficult to muster a sufficiently large number of persons capable of legal drafting. Finally, agreement was reached on six members per territory, and the Committee was thereafter known as the Committee of Eighteen or the Committee for the Constitution (see p. 446). After a brief suspension of the meeting, the members were designated on the spot, though the Fezzanese continued to protest that the number of six was too high.

The Committee's method of work also was the subject of discussion. Should it submit each article separately to the NCAL for examination, or would it be better to present groups of interconnected articles? The President was in favor of the second method, and the Assembly agreed. It was also decided that, time permitting, each group of articles would pass three readings at each drafting stage. In practice, this procedure could not always be applied; but in the large majority of cases it was adhered to.

A Tripolitanian member proposed that the document to be debated by the National Assembly should be called "Draft Constitution" and not "Constitution." That, of course, was a delicate point. A Cyrenaican member opposed the proposal, and the President tactfully disposed of it by remarking that it was of a "formal and unnecessary" nature. Furthermore, it was decided to meet in principle every Monday and not on Sunday as originally proposed; this decision was made for the sake of the members of the United Nations Mission, whose secretarial and supporting staff, though not the professional staff working directly with the Committee, were mostly Christians.

A member proposed that each meeting should henceforth be opened in the name of Allah and in that of the King, and that a picture of His Majesty be hung in the Assembly Hall. This was unanimously agreed. The President then adjourned the meeting and announced that the following morning a procession would form in front of the Senussi Mosque in the old city and move to the NCAL's seat (the Balbo Palace) to express joy over the enthroning of Sayed Idris as King of Libya. He suggested that all members be present to receive the congratulatory greetings of the procession. As related in footnote 35 on page 13 of the Commissioner's second annual report,[1] this procession ran into trouble, as it was challenged and broken up by a crowd of counterdemonstrators calling for the dissolution of the NCAL and expressing hostility toward federalism. The footnote, which was inserted at the request of the representative of Tripolitania, particularly stresses, however, that the demonstration was directed against the NCAL and federalism and not against the proclamation of His Highness the Amir as future King of Libya.

The incident, while once more illustrating the tension prevailing in Tripoli between partisans and opponents of federalism, also showed the unchallenged acceptance of the Amir as the personification of Libyan unity.

On 6 December, the Committee of Eighteen held its first meeting for the traditional purpose of drawing up the solemn act of homage to the Amir, the Bay'a,[2] the drafting of which was entrusted to a Sub-Committee of Six, once more composed on a footing of equality, that is, two members per territory. As this procedure proved effective, the Committee of Eighteen, during its second meeting on 9 December, decided to perpetuate the subcommittee in view of the very considerable amount of primary drafting that would have to be prepared for consideration by the full committee. Con-

1. *Second Annual Report of the United Nations Commissioner in Libya,* GAOR: Fifth Session, 1951, Supplement No. 17 (A/1949).

2. The Bay'a, according to Islamic tradition, is the formal act of homage or allegiance by which the people proclaim their ruler. The act is performed in three stages: the offer, its acceptance, and the Bay'a itself. For more particulars, see Ali Chaygan, *Essai sur l'Histoire du Droit Public Musulman aux Premiers Siècles de sa Formation* (Paris: Les Editions Domat-Montchrestien, F. Loviton et Cie, 1934). See also pp. 457–60 for the text of the Bay'a and the Amir's reply; and pp. 23–26 for the Bay'a submitted by the leaders of the Tripolitanian Republic in 1922.

sequently, the Committee of Six became the principal working instrument of the NCAL during the preparatory drafting stage.

The Working Group, as the Committee of Six came to be called, met on 11 December and decided to begin its labors by studying first the question of the distribution of powers between the future Libyan federation and its three component territories. This was a decision of fundamental importance. It demonstrated that the members of the Working Group had come round to the opinion that, rather than continue the vain discussion on the theoretical difference between federalism and unitarism, it was preferable to examine the issue on specific points. The Working Group of course realized that the problem of the distribution of powers had already arisen in the course of the preparation of every other federal constitution in the world. Recognizing its own lack of knowledge on the matter, it therefore requested the secretariat of the United Nations Mission in Libya to provide translations into Arabic of the relevant chapters of the Constitutions of Argentina, Australia, Brazil, Burma, Canada, the Federal Republic of Germany, India, Indonesia, Mexico, Switzerland, the United States, and Venezuela, later adding those of the Netherlands and the Union of South Africa. The legal adviser of the Cyrenaican delegation, Awni Dajani (see p. 495), moreover made available the constitutions of all the Arab States. From that moment onward, until the second half of March, the Working Group held sixteen meetings, practically turning itself into a class on constitutional law, each member taking home with him a mass of documentation to be studied. Moreover, in order to facilitate the work of the Group, the Commissioner had placed at its disposal and that of the NCAL in general all the legal and technical assistance that the personnel of the United Nations Mission was able to provide. This meant that the services of the Commissioner's legal adviser, Amar Loutfi, were constantly available to the Assembly and its subordinate organs, while another member of the staff, Ismail Raghib Khalidi, helped in particular the secretariat of the Group and Committee. Subsequently financial experts were also called in for advice. The United Nations legal adviser attended virtually all meetings.

Besides giving legal and technical assistance to the Working Group, the Commissioner also had to make up his mind as to the nature of his personal and political relationship with it. In order not to give its members the impression that he intended to impose himself upon them, he decided not to attend their meetings unless specially asked to do so. At the same time he assured them that his door, whether at home or at the Mission, would always be open to them whenever they wanted his advice. After a while they frequently did. Thus the road was paved to a smooth relationship, which soon developed into an agreeable one into the bargain and proved to be particularly fruitful when delicate matters of substance arose, as they could and did not fail to do. Moreover, it helped relations in another way. At Group meetings, with only the Mission's legal adviser and Assistant Secretary present, members could talk freely in Arabic, unhampered by the presence of the non-Arabic-speaking Commissioner. As soon as differences of opinion arose, either among themselves or with the adviser, they would call in the Commissioner or call on him. More often than not such a meeting would be for the purpose of drafting a compromise text, and doing this simultaneously in Arabic and English with the assistance of a professional United Nations interpreter helped to promote mutual understanding and to produce a clearer text.

With regard to matters of constitutional substance, the Commissioner, after having felt the pulse of the country and taken into account the conclusions reached by the Committee of Twenty-One, had elaborated a plan, the broad outline of which he had originally intended to submit to the Council for Libya for advice and subsequently to the NCAL. As related in Chapter 5 (pp. 364–65), for political reasons he was obliged to give priority to the General Assembly, making his statement to it on 16 November 1950. This statement, having been conceived for the specific purpose of dissuading the General Assembly from belatedly imposing upon the Libyan people the election of a National Assembly to replace the existing appointed one, was more detailed and precise than its author had intended it to be. He would have preferred to leave the Libyan people and its National Assembly more liberty to work out its destiny than was actually envisaged in the request for advice he had promised to submit to the Council. Fortunately, in a way, the Council had been divided and even reluctant to give any advice at all, with the result that its resolution of 14 March had been conceived in a subdued tone permitting the Commissioner to comment on it by making a variety of suggestions for the choice of the NCAL (letter of transmittal, 3 April 1951).[3] At first the NCAL's reaction both to the Council's advice and the Commissioner's comments was decidedly reserved. Subsequently this attitude changed for the better as the remainder of this chapter will show.

Nevertheless the episode served as a lesson to the Commissioner, who had learned that in the exercise of his advisory functions he would occasionally have to reckon with refusal to follow his advice. In such cases he should not feel hurt or vexed, even if in the eyes of the bystanders he might seem to lose face. This was part of the normal duties of any international official. At the same time his attitude could never be a passive one. His advice must always be of a positive character.

3. *Second Annual Report of the United Nations Commissioner in Libya,* Annex IV, pp. 77–80.

As to the nature of the Constitution, it would have to be democratic. He was dealing with people who had never been allowed to gain much practical experience in self-government, either under Ottoman or under Italian rule. Membership of the advisory councils of Turkish vilayets and of municipal councils with very limited powers under the Italian occupation, had been about all the experience a small number of Libyans ever had acquired in the field of administration. At the same time there existed an age-old system of rudimentary self-government in the internal functioning of the Arab tribes. Wherever there had been Senussi *zawiyas,* administrative practices had generally improved, until first the French, during the period of their penetration into northern Central Africa and the Sahara, and subsequently the Italians in Northern Libya, particularly in Cyrenaica, destroyed these centers. Even at its best, all past administrative experience had been parochial. Now a State had to be organized out of the three territories, capable of administering its people and maintaining itself in the world of today. It was bound to be poor because its economic resources were small. It had to be more or less decentralized because of the country's geography and demographic structure: a small population living an islandlike existence in a huge ocean of sand. Conditions of this nature were not conducive to a centralized autocratic form of government. Other reasons pointed in the same direction. One was that educated Libyans, particularly in Tripolitania, were imbued by a nineteenth-century spirit of democratic nationalism. Another was that, though the King-Designate had been proclaimed as such because he was, for historic reasons, the one person recognized by the people at large as a symbol of national unity, he would not have been accepted as an autocratic ruler without opposition, even in his native Cyrenaica. Apart from that, and notwithstanding the personal prestige he enjoyed, he possessed too much political wisdom and experience to be desirous of exercising his new royal powers in an autocratic manner. One more consideration was that the whole Arab world, some parts more rapidly than others, was painstakingly evolving from a feudal to a more democratic form of life. Last but not least, the Libyan State was being born as a child of the United Nations, which was bound to inject a certain democratic concept of its own.

But there was another side to the picture. While the internal situation momentarily required a fairly high degree of decentralization, considerations of an external nature called for a structure that, with the years and in the interest of international peace and security, could grow into a body politically coherent and economically strong enough to act as an element of stability in the Mediterranean, particularly on the southern coast of the Ancient World's sea. Egypt had already become an independent State; Libya was about to follow suit. In these circumstances it was to be expected that within the foreseeable future Tunisia, Algeria, and Morocco also would gain their independence. This was the Commissioner's line of reasoning, and not his alone, in 1950–51. Hence, Libya would occupy a central position in a string of five independent North African States stretching from the Near East to the Atlantic, which together would form the western wing of the Moslem world, facing the European continent vigorously at work rebuilding its economic, social, and political structure. At the same time the Mediterranean would remain an important seaway from West to East and vice versa with an additional outlet to, but also an inlet from, the Black Sea.

Looking at the map of the world as a whole, it was becoming clearer every day that the United States and the Soviet Union were to be the two dominating and conflicting great Powers, each trying to enlist a clientele among the small and medium-sized nations, including the members of the Arab League.

In the Mediterranean area the United States was making its influence more strongly felt, but Soviet pressures were becoming increasingly noticeable, particularly in the eastern basin. In the United Nations General Assembly, the fate of Libya had been decided under blasts of cold war.

What was to be Libya's position in these circumstances? Obviously it would not be strong enough to rely exclusively on its own forces to maintain its independence. It would always have to steer a middle course, as its King-Designate had clearly foreseen, a course that might have to be corrected with every major shift of the competing cyclones and anticyclones on the geopolitical weather chart of the world. But there were two political objectives of secondary importance it might try to achieve by its own means and through the political wisdom of its leaders. One was to keep its balance, at least within the limits of practical possibilities, between the interests of the big and medium-sized Powers that were constantly competing for influence in Libya. The other was not to provide foreign Powers with pretexts for intervening in its internal affairs because of civil strife or bad management. Obviously these two objectives were closely interlinked.

To sum up, while Libya's internal conditions required a federal form of government, its international position made it necessary to arm the central Government with such powers as foreign policy and defense, and with the means to exercise them.

Hence, the Libyan Constitution would inevitably have to represent a compromise between decentralizing and centralizing factors. The two Administering Powers, and to a certain extent the United States, together with Cyrenaica and the Fezzan, supported the first tendency; Tripolitania and its friends in the Arab League were predominantly on the centralizing side; and the Council was divided between the two policies. The Commissioner was therefore forced into the position of an arbiter. Personally he had a preference for as much centralization as was politically obtainable without impairing the chances of achieving unity among the three territories.

As the drafting went on, a growing sense of national community gradually became apparent among the members of the NCAL. The question of their country's future international position also began to exercise the minds of thoughtful Libyans. The time had not yet come to formulate a Libyan foreign policy, but a first outline of it was on the drawing board.

It was at about this time that the King-Designate, discussing one day the form of State with the Commissioner, who today repeats his words from memory, said: "Mr. Commissioner, you must never forget that Libya besides firstly being an Arab country also borders on the Mediterranean. It has always been in touch with Latins and Greeks. Spiritually and politically our face is, of course, turned toward the East and in particular to the Holy Places of Islam, but materially we will always have close relations with the West. This means that of necessity our policies will have to travel the middle of the road."

It was not unusual in those days to find Libyan politicians expressing and applying this concept of policy; for instance, it was clearly noticeable among those who drew up the Constitution. For one thing this meant that while they wanted a constitution of a Western democratic type, they intended at the same time, by clinging to Arab traditions, to protect themselves against certain pitfalls of parliamentary democracy, e.g., governmental instability under a cabinet system, as practiced by certain European States.

The Commissioner, whose duty it was to advise the Libyan people without making their decisions for them, therefore came to the conclusion that the best he could do was to help them in elaborating an appropriate democratic constitution, adapted to the country's particular traditions and needs. He was convinced that the best way of making a people familiar with the democratic system of government, its institutions, its rules, and the particular turn of mind to make it work, was to let them take their own responsibilities and decisions. This was the best training school, even if it meant making occasional mistakes.

This was one of the reasons why the drafting of the Constitution took longer than had been anticipated by the Working Group and the Committee of Eighteen. As a result, the preparation of the Commissioner's second annual report, in consultation with the Council for Libya, had to be done somewhat hastily if it was to be submitted in time to the General Assembly. As part of this report, a summary and brief history of the Libyan Constitution, promulgated on 7 October 1951, also had to be prepared. In these circumstances, Chapter 1 of the report, "Constitutional Development," had to be limited to a broad outline, leaving out a great deal of important detail and background information.

In the present study the Commissioner would have liked to make good these omissions by writing a full analytical account, article by article, of the discussions and drafts from the first rough concepts up to the final text. Ideally such an account should have included precise references to the origin and sources on which the Constitution was based. It should also have described the individual parts played by the principal members of the NCAL and their advisers, as well as by its secretariat.

For various reasons the writing of such a complete account has proved impossible. As far as the author knows, there is no Libyan participant in the drafting work who possesses a complete set of records in either English or French including all the discussions in the Working Group, the Committee of Eighteen, and the plenary meetings of the NCAL, together with all the drafts and amendments thereto which were finally included in the Constitution. In 1964–65 the author unsuccessfully tried to obtain from the Royal Diwan, from Libyan Government departments, and even from the relevant United Nations Archives, then still in Tripoli, a complete set of these documents. Provided no more time is lost in setting up Libyan national archives, it ought still to be possible to build up such a collection. Meanwhile the United Nations Archives contain by far the most comprehensive series available.

With regard to the records on the writing of the Constitution available to the author in 1964–66, the situation was as follows: the typescript records of the Working Group in the United Nations Archives were (and still are) considered classified material under current United Nations regulations. They are really internal file notes and memoranda compiled by the Mission staff in the discharge of official duties. The notes were not given to members of the Group to review and approve, as would be the case with official United Nations records, and the author used them only to refresh his memory. Even if these notes and memorandums could be published, many are brief summaries, sometimes relating in no more than a few paragraphs what was said and done during many hours of laborious discussion. Others are more detailed, but only too often refer to drafts of articles or chapters, the text of which is not included or annexed. Moreover, the agreed texts, alternatives for unresolved points, and an account of the discussions were frequently given orally and *in extenso* in the meetings of the Committee of Eighteen and often also in the NCAL in public session. The records of both these bodies have been published (see pp. 429–30, fn. 2).

An additional complication arises from the fact that in a number of cases Working Group drafts were written in French while the discussion was recorded in English, or vice versa. The reason for this is that the United Nations legal adviser preferred drafting in French or Arabic, whereas the Assistant Secretary provided by the Mission preferred English, a situation not unusual in international teamwork. This also explains why some archival notes on the deliberations of the Working Group were kept in English and others in French.

Since the discussions were actually held, and records kept, in Arabic, it is possible that there exist somewhere complete sets of records and drafts in that language. Even then, however, the difficulty would remain that a number of them, at least several drafts, were translations from English or French, sometimes even from French via English, into Arabic. To retranslate them back into their original language would probably not greatly clarify matters.

Most of the foregoing remarks apply equally to the United Nations archival records of the Committee of Eighteen. These remarks are not to be taken as criticism of the Mission staff responsible for assisting the Libyan groups. The Commissioner is only too well aware of the heavy pressure and the continuous strain, including a considerable amount of work at night, under which they accomplished their task; ninety-six Working Group meetings, twenty-five Committee of Eighteen meetings, and forty-three plenary meetings of the NCAL were held in less than a year. Frequently there was no time to prepare a full report, record, or translation, and on many occasions the Commissioner had to be satisfied with a brief written account supplemented by a lengthier oral report. It must also be noted that some of the most controversial issues regarding the Constitution were discussed in private and separate conversations among the Commissioner, the legal advisers, members of the NCAL, and, on important occasions, the King-Designate, and that the records of these conversations too, insofar as they exist, are still classified.

Fortunately for the author there are three sources of information on the writing of the Constitution which are available to research workers.[4] One consists of the printed records in Arabic published after the election of the

4. As mentioned in the Preface p. xx, during the writing of this study, permission was granted to the author to make free use of the mimeographed documents of the Council for Libya, summary records of its meetings, and also its working papers. It is to be noted, however, that the Council, for lack of time, never made a detailed examination of the draft constitution which was communicated to it only on 1 October 1951 (United Nations Doc. A/AC.32/COUNCIL/R.158), after the draft had been approved by the Committee of Eighteen in Arabic on 16 September. The final draft then had to be translated from Arabic into English and French. On the other hand, the Council documents contain a considerable mass of information on the political background to the writing of the Constitution.

first Libyan Parliament in 1952 by the Registrar of that body. The volume contains the records of the Committee of Eighteen, session by session, as well as those of the plenary meetings of the NCAL. Unfortunately, it includes no working papers or records of the Working Group. The report of the delegation sent by the NCAL in January–February 1951 to Cairo to explain the Libyan situation to the leaders of the League of Arab States was published in a separate volume. Thanks to the cooperation of the Libyan Government, the printed records were translated into English for the use of the present writer, and he cannot be grateful enough for the support thus afforded to him (cf., pp. 429–30, fn. 2). Even these records, however, have a shortcoming in that they frequently do not contain full texts of the draft articles and amendments with which they deal. This is the text which, with some amendments to be referred to later, became the Libyan Constitution as adopted by the NCAL on 7 October 1951. The definitive text is to be found as Annex I to the Commissioner's second annual report.[5] For convenience, it is repeated as Annex II to the present study (pp. 902–21). There is a slight difference in the numbering of the Articles between the draft and the final text, the former containing 214 Articles, the latter 213. For purposes of reference, the numbering of the final text has been followed.

The second public source available is the two annual and three supplementary reports submitted by the Commissioner to the Secretary-General of the United Nations in consultation with the Council for Libya and communicated by the latter to the General Assembly. (For the record, it should be added that the first two brief supplementary reports, presented in 1950, were *not* submitted to the Council for lack of time.) A summarized account of the drafting of the Constitution is to be found in the second annual report.[6]

The third source consists of a number of mimeographed progress reports and documents concerning Libyan constitutional development submitted by the Commissioner to the Council for Libya for its information. The most important of these are annexed to the annual reports. Others have been deposited in the United Nations Archives and Libraries as well as in those of the Governments represented on the Council for Libya. Finally, there must be a fairly large number of copies in the hands of Libyan Government departments and private citizens.

A comparison of these various records, public and confidential, reveals certain discrepancies, mainly in the dates of meetings and sometimes even

5. *Second Annual Report of the United Nations Commissioner in Libya,* pp. 61–71.

6. Ibid., pp. 1–15. The brevity of this account is offset by the freshness of memory of the author and his assistants and consultants at the time of writing.

in content. Differences in the recording of matters of substance are probably to be attributed to varying degrees of appreciation by different recorders of the importance of particular subjects.

Nevertheless, the following account of the history of the Libyan Constitution is more complete and gives considerably more background information than that which appeared in 1951 in the second annual report. On the other hand, it is less detailed than it would have been had the writer been allowed to quote directly from typescript memoranda in the United Nations Archives. Still, no point of importance has been skipped. At some time, a historian who knows Arabic and who is also well versed in public law may be able to compile a more detailed version.

The author believes that this account throws new light on the underlying trends that governed and inspired the debates, as well as on those chapters and articles which gave rise to substantial controversy. Moreover, it attempts to bring into focus the particular difficulties that arose from the system by which the General Assembly had decided to promote the transformation, under its auspices, of the former Italian colony of Libya into an independent State, as well as from the different ways in which the United Kingdom, France, the Commissioner, the Council for Libya, and above all, the Libyans themselves interpreted and sought to implement that system in drawing up the Constitution.

To round off this description of the method followed in tracing the elaboration of the Libyan Constitution, the author must also mention with gratitude and thanks the fact that with the cooperation of the late Omar Loutfi's family he was fortunate enough to gain access to a considerable volume of personal notes and papers of the man who contributed so much to the writing of Libya's basic law.[7]

There are a few men who, if still alive, could have added reminiscences important for the present account. After Omar Loutfi, they all must be counted among the principal architects of the Libyan Constitution, which served the country well for the initial decade of its independence and in large measure does so still. They were: Sheikh Mohamed Abul Is'ad al-Alim (Tripolitania), Grand Mufti of Libya and President of the NCAL; Omar Shenib (Cyrenaica), Vice-President of the NCAL and Chairman of the Committee of Eighteen; and Khalil Qallal (Cyrenaica), Chairman of the Working Group.

7. See Chapter 1, p. 80, fn. 63. The following works, already cited frequently, also proved most helpful in this connection: Ismail Raghib Khalidi, *Constitutional Development in Libya* (Beirut, Lebanon: Khayat's College Book Co-operative, 1956); and Majid Khadduri, *Modern Libya: A Study in Political Development* (Baltimore: Johns Hopkins Press, 1963).

A few other members of the Working Group or the Committee of Eighteen, some dead, others still alive, deserve mention for the important contributions they made:

Sulayman al-Jerbi (Cyrenaica), Principal Secretary of the NCAL; Munir Burshan (Tripolitania), Rapporteur of the Committee of Eighteen; Abu Bakr Bin Ahmad (Fezzan), Assistant Rapporteur thereto; Sheik Mohamed al-Hinqari (Tripolitania), member of the Working Group; and Abd al-Jawad al-Furaytis (Cyrenaica), member of the Working Group. In addition, Awni Dajani, legal adviser to the Cyrenaican delegation, deserves mention.

One further observation, concerning the order in which the material in Part 2 of this chapter has been arranged, may be useful to the reader. Owing to the procedure adopted whereby all chapters of the Constitution were submitted to three readings at each of the three stages of discussion, which was followed insofar as time permitted, hardly any subject was ever disposed of in one continuous debate. It also happened that the Working Group interrupted its discussion of a particular subject in order to seek the Committee of Eighteen's political guidance; or the latter sometimes returned a text to the Working Group for redrafting. On other occasions, a discussion was interrupted for consultations with the King-Designate or with the Commissioner and his legal adviser, or simply in order to permit members to discuss a problem privately. Whatever the actual cause, breaks in the discussions were the rule rather than the exception.

Moreover, the Working Group, which virtually determined the order of work, followed a program which differed considerably from the order in which it finally decided to group the subject matter, chapter by chapter, in the Constitution. For example, the "Preamble" was discussed several months after the chapters on the distribution of powers and the rights of the people simply because these last two subjects were considered to be of a more urgent nature.

In the circumstances the author had to decide on the order in which he would present the subject matter. It would have been confusing to the reader to relate the discussions in the chronological order followed from meeting to meeting with frequent changes of subject. It would have been equally confusing and, moreover, contrary to the historical course of events had the subject matter been dealt with in the order in which it eventually appeared in the Constitution.

To solve the problem the author was obliged to adopt an order which is neither factually chronological nor in strict accordance with that of the Constitution. This explains why Part 2 of this chapter is divided into sections which deal with the subject matter in the overall order used by the

Working Group. On the other hand, he has tried to disregard as much as possible the breaks that occurred in the discussions of any one topic, though, because of the date set for Libya's independence, he could not avoid frequently referring to the time factor. Thus the contents of each section correspond to what was finally to become a chapter of the Constitution.

For the reader's convenience, the (Roman) number of the corresponding chapter of the Constitution is given in parentheses after the title of each section.

PART 2. THE STRUCTURE

A. DISTRIBUTION OF POWERS
(Chapter III of the Constitution)

(Powers of the Federal Government and Joint Powers)

In conformity with instructions received from the Committee of Eighteen, the Working Group started off by examining the fundamental problem of all federal constitutions: the distribution of powers between the central and provincial or state governments. (In Libya, the latter were sometimes called local or territorial administrations. Terminology on the point was undecided for a long time, in part for political reasons.)

After having devoted several weeks to a close study of the systems practiced in other federations, the members of the Working Group had a general discussion on the subject, which was introduced by the Legal Adviser of the United Nations Mission in Libya. Some members thought that there should be a list of powers assigned to the federal government and another list of powers to be exercised by the provinces. A Tripolitanian member proposed that one single list of powers to be exercised by the provincial administrations be drawn up, all powers not mentioned therein coming within the competence of the central government. A Fezzanese member, on the contrary, preferred a single list enumerating the powers of the central government, leaving the residual powers to the local administrations. From these positions it was clear that the battle between federalists and antifederalists was to be fought all over again in the Working Group, and probably also in the Committee of Eighteen as well as in the NCAL itself. The Cyrenaican members supported the view of their Fezzanese colleagues. The United Nations legal adviser pointed out that under the special conditions prevailing in Libya, two lists might have advantages, but at the end of a long exchange of views, the Group decided in favor of a single list of federal powers, all residual powers to be left to the competence of the local administrations. At the same time, they decided that the nature of the central powers would, in general, be in accordance with the system mentioned in the memorandum which the NCAL delegation had submitted to the League of Arab States in Cairo, as described in Part 4 of Chapter 6. It was on the basis of this understanding that the Group began to elaborate a detailed list of powers. On many occasions the discussion gave rise to lively differences of opinion, practically always in connection with the degree of centralization of power in the hands of the federal state. For instance, the social insurance system inherited from the Italian Administration became one of these points of divergence. A Tripolitanian member, appreciative of this system, wanted to extend it to the whole of Libya, whereas the Cyrenaicans were of opposite opinion. The Working Group ended by declaring the item within the competence of the provinces, a decision that was later to be partially reversed, following technical advice from an expert of the International Labour Office in Geneva. Other questions like jurisdiction in matters of public education and public health were left in abeyance until a later reading because immediate agreement appeared to be out of reach.

One subject that gave rise to a particularly thorough debate was the financial impact of certain powers to be granted to the federal government. The members of the Group, having become budget-minded as a result of lengthy discussions with United Nations economists and finance experts, began to ask themselves seriously how the functions of the federal government, as described in the draft list of powers (which meanwhile had reached a total of seventy), should be financed. This question took on special importance in connection with customs administration and revenues, which several members wanted to leave within the competence of the provinces. The discussion of this subject was repeatedly reopened until the very end of the NCAL's labors. While this particular point, together with a few others, was left in suspense for the time being, it was decided in principle that, for reasons of economy, certain powers on the list would be placed within the sole legislative competence of the federal government, while the provinces would be responsible for the application of the relevant laws under the supervision of the central authority. At first sight this looked like a wise and reasonable arrangement. In fact, of course, it meant a weakening of the central government and as such had to be looked at again, both from the administrative and from the political angle. At the same time it proved a useful device for reconciling federal and unitary points of view.

Notwithstanding these sometimes serious disputes, there was a strong desire to reach unanimous conclusions, since the danger of divided opinions was fully realized.

It was on the basis of the foregoing provisional understanding that on 19 March 1951 the Working Group submitted for examination by the Committee of Eighteen a report containing a first plan for the distribution of powers.

Looking at the plan as a whole, it was clear that the Working Group intended all powers connected with foreign affairs, national defense, finance, currency, communications, justice, public education, health, and various other important matters of national interest, to be exercised either directly by the federal government, or by the provincial administrations under its supervision. However, at this stage no distinction had as yet been made, item by item, between these two methods of administration.

While this drafting had been going on, closely followed by the Commissioner and his staff, the former had simultaneously been obliged to pay attention to his other general duties. One particularly important point that could not be much longer delayed was the preparation of a detailed plan for the transfer of powers by the Governments of the United Kingdom and France, to a "duly constituted Libyan Government," as required by Resolution 387 (V). Obviously such a plan was directly related to that for the distribution of federal and territorial powers under discussion in the NCAL. On 6 February 1951, therefore, the Commissioner had convened a committee, known as the Coordination Committee, the composition and functions of which are described in detail in Chapter 10 (cf. pp. 744–53). One of the first preoccupations of this Committee was to establish a close working relationship with the NCAL. With this desideratum in view, the Commissioner wrote to the President of the NCAL on 30 March 1951 that he had learned with great satisfaction that a list of federal powers had been drawn up by the Working Group and would be submitted for further examination to the Committee of Eighteen. He suggested, however, that the NCAL might find it advisable not to take final decisions regarding the distribution of powers between the federal and local governments until it had had an opportunity to study its administrative and budgetary implications. Technical advice on the subject was being prepared by members of the Commissioner's staff. The size of the federal and local budgets would largely depend on the functions they would have to discharge. For this reason, a few days later, the Commissioner, acting in his capacity as Chairman of the Coordination Committee, invited the NCAL to be permanently represented on the Committee for the sake of closer mutual understanding.

The members of the Committee of Eighteen declared themselves in full agreement with these suggestions, deciding to undertake immediately the examination of the Working Group's recommendations on the distribution of powers. To a large extent they accepted the Group's proposals, though on a number of points there was disagreement. Discussion of some items, it was felt, should be postponed because of lack of adequate information. This was the case, for instance, with regard to customs, on which legal and technical advice from the Commissioner's office was requested; the important point was the issue of to whom customs revenues would go, the federal government or the provinces.

At the same time, the Committee, accepting the principle that for certain powers a distinction should be made as to who would be responsible for their legislative and executive aspects respectively, began to consider how to implement that principle. Thus they agreed that income tax ought to come within the legislative competence of the central government, but deferred consideration of the executive aspect of the question until a later stage.

Another matter over which provisional autonomy versus federal authority proved to be a sensitive issue was the stationing of federal troops in the provinces. One member argued that since a Libyan army did not exist there was no sense in discussing the point. Another member insisted that sooner or later the federation would have to have an army. Agreement was reached by determining that matters of this nature would require consultation between the federation and the provinces.

Rather unexpectedly, a lively discussion developed over ruins, historical sites, museums, and libraries—sources of cultural value, and also of tourist revenue, that were expensive to maintain and repair. Once again the question was whether the matter should come within the federal or the provincial sphere. In the absence of agreement the debate was postponed. Nor could immediate agreement be reached on such items as jurisdiction over the sale of drugs and medicines or the question of which authority should be empowered to organize a population census. Behind this last deadlock lay the fear that such a census would too clearly show up the considerable differences in population between the provinces, which might well strengthen the position of the opponents of equal representation. On many other points, however, such as, for instance, weights and measures, agreement was fairly easily reached.

A proposal to the effect that "intensification of agricultural production" should be a federal power was amended to read "the promotion of agricultural and industrial production and commercial activities and the ensuring to the country of essential foodstuffs." The new text could not have reflected more eloquently the unremitting anxiety of the Libyan people to protect themselves against the country's frequent droughts and the sufferings that follow in their train.

Once more the list came back to the Working Group, this time mainly for the purpose of dividing its items into functional categories to be assigned ultimately to particular federal government departments, but also for reconsideration of certain points left in abeyance by the Committee of Eighteen. In view of the progress being made, and also because time was beginning to press, the Commissioner, on 18 April 1951, addressed another letter to the President of the NCAL suggesting that the Committee of Eighteen might now resume its study of the distribution of powers, so that the Coordination Committee could formulate its observations on the financial, budgetary, and administrative aspects of the various problems. The proposals of the Committee of Eighteen, together with the observations of the Coordination Committee, should then be submitted as soon as possible to the NCAL for final consideration and decision.

The list reviewed by the Working Group was again submitted to the Committee of Eighteen in mid-May. This time it had been subdivided into three parts:

A. A list of items falling within the competence of the federal government, both from the legislative and from the executive point of view.
B. A list of items which were to come exclusively within the legislative competence of the federal government; the local governments to be responsible for their execution under the supervision of the central government.
C. A list of items on which the Group had been unable to reach agreement.

1. Posts, telegraphs, telephones, broadcasting, and other similar forms of communication
2. Customs
3. Regulation of imports and exports
4. Stamp duty
5. Organization and registration of companies and the taxes imposed on them
6. Income tax
7. Monopolies and concessions
8. Taxation necessary to meet the expenditure of the federal government
9. Subsoil wealth, mining, and prospecting

When the Committee of Eighteen started reconsidering the list of powers returned by the Working Group, its attention was drawn to an item which had been there from the outset, referring to foreign troops passing through the country and remaining therein temporarily when necessary in time of war. The item had never been discussed before nor had the Commissioner ever been consulted on it. Subject to reservations by a Fezzanese member, it had been inserted by the Working Group because at the end of hostilities foreign troops (British, American, and French) had indeed remained in the country and the Group had felt that something should be included in the Constitution to determine their status.[8]

This time Tripolitanian and Cyrenaican members of the Committee considered that to maintain this item might create a wrong impression, namely, that the NCAL had the intention of granting to the Libyan Government the constitutional power of authorizing the passage of foreign troops over its territory. It was therefore proposed to delete reference to the matter, which members considered should, if necessary, later be the subject of a treaty or treaties with the Governments whose troops were involved. The Legal Adviser of the United Nations Mission, having been asked for his opinion, suggested that if the Committee so wished the point might just as well be deleted. He suggested, however, that the reason for such action should be mentioned in the record of the meeting. This was done, the reason given being that the article in question was withdrawn because it fell within the scope of item 5 of the list of powers in Group A (p. 525), relating to the federal power of entering into and implementing treaties and agreements with other countries.

Looking back, it appears that it was at this moment that the idea of regulating the presence of foreign troops based on Libyan soil by international treaty was first mentioned, at least in writing.

After approving the first and second lists of powers, the Committee turned to the nine items left in abeyance by the Working Group. The outcome of the deliberations was that two items—"Posts, telegraphs, telephones, broadcasting, and other similar forms of communication" and "regulation of imports and exports"—were provisionally transferred to the second group (Joint Powers). The PTT services were finally again transferred to the first list (Article 36, item 24).

The remaining seven items in suspense were returned to the Working

8. In reply to a query from the author, Ismail Raghib Khalidi kindly supplied the following information from memory in a letter from New York, dated 29 June 1966: "with regard to foreign troops passing through the country, I recall that there was an off-the-record discussion in the Working Group, and it was felt by the Tripolitanian representative of the Group, that some provision be made to the effect that foreign troops could be stationed and pass through the country only in wartime. Whereas during peacetime such stationing of troops should be governed by a Constitutional provision subject to approval by Parliament. That is why probably Point 7 was never taken up at the subsequent meetings of either the Working Group or the Committee on Constitution." In the original list, item 7 was "The presence of foreign troops."

Group for reconsideration, but no agreement was reached. It was therefore decided to inform the Coordination Committee of this state of affairs, and on 17 May 1951, the Chairman of the Committee of Eighteen addressed the following letter to the Commissioner, in the latter's capacity as Chairman of the Coordination Committee:

> With reference to your letter of 18 April 1951, I have the honour to enclose herewith a copy of the list prepared by the Committee on the Constitution of the National Assembly, giving the functions of the Central Government of the Federal Libyan Kingdom, in order that the Co-ordination Committee may have a general idea to guide its work. The Committee on the Constitution divided the list of powers of the Central Government into two parts. The first part comprises 36 subjects, all of which fall within the legislative and executive competence of the Federal Government; the second part comprises 22 subjects, which are exclusively within the legislative competence of the Federal Government, to ensure that that policy is co-ordinated and unified between the territories. The local governments will carry out this policy under the supervision of the Central Government. All subjects which are not included in those two lists are within the competence of the local governments.
>
> The Committee [of Eighteen] was unable to take any decision on seven subjects, all of which concern financial matters and which are included in the third list attached to this letter. This was due to a lack of sufficient information.
>
> The required information concerns the present budgets of the three territories and the budgets of the Central Government as estimated in view of the distribution of powers between it and each of the local governments in the Libyan State.
>
> The Committee . . . will be obliged to Your Excellency if you will kindly supply it with the afore-mentioned information, together with the comments of the experts and their views on the seven subjects which are pending, so that the Committee may be able to take a decision on these subjects. Meanwhile, I should like to inform you that the lists which have been prepared by the Committee . . . will not finally be incorporated into the Constitution until such time as the pending subjects have been added and the list has been approved by the National Assembly.[9]

Most items in the first and second parts of the list will be found with a few changes in the final draft of the Constitution (Articles 36–39) as submitted to and approved by the NCAL. One or two amendments of

9. United Nations Doc. A/AC.32/CC/C.1/8, 22 June 1951. Mimeographed.

substance were introduced, however, at the last moment by the NCAL itself. And the seven matters still pending (Nos. 2, 4, 5, 6, 7, 8, and 9 in the list, Group C, on p. 525) gave rise to a great deal of discussion, the outcome of which had important effects on the final text.

It was not a simple task to supply the information asked for by the Chairman of the Committee of Eighteen, and it took the United Nations experts until the beginning of August to put the required memorandum into the hands of the Working Group.[10] Even then their reply did not cover all the information requested. The information relating to the existing budgets of the three provinces was given in the *General Economic Appraisal of Libya*—prepared by John Lindberg, then Chief Economist of the Technical Assistance Mission for Libya—a copy of which had been forwarded separately to the Working Group.[11] On the other hand, the memorandum did set forth the comments, views, and proposals the experts offered on the seven subjects still pending on the list of federal powers, although suggestions for federal budget procedures were still lacking, as the draft budget of the federal government was still under discussion in the Coordination Committee.

The memorandum further contained a study of the attribution of powers concerning financial matters as well as of the division of various sources of revenue between the central government and the local administrations. The study was of a purely technical character and was not concerned with political considerations.

The following is a summary:

Customs

The experts pointed out that customs revenues constituted one of the major sources of revenue for Tripolitania and Cyrenaica, the percentage relationship, based on existing rates, that they bore to the total estimated current revenues of each territory for 1951–52 being: Tripolitania 21 percent, Cyrenaica 41 percent, and the Fezzan 9 percent. Hence their disposal under the federal state was a matter which deserved special consideration. Accordingly, the subject of customs was dealt with by the experts under three heads: the legislative aspect; the executive aspect; and the disposal of customs revenues.

The importance of a uniform customs tariff for the whole country, with its connected common rules and regulations, could not be overemphasized.

10. "Memorandum Containing the Comments and Views of United Nations Experts in Libya, regarding the financial and budgetary aspects of some revenue and other items." United Nations Doc. A/AC.32/SEC.6, 6 August 1951. Mimeographed.

11. John Lindberg, *A General Economic Appraisal of Libya,* United Nations Publication Sales No. 1952.II.H.2 (ST/TAA/K/LIBYA/1, 22 September 1952). See also Chapter 9, p. 674 ff., in particular fn. 9.

If the provinces framed their own customs legislation, this would inevitably tend to produce competitive tariffs, which could not but prove ruinous to the economy of each of the three provinces and to the economic unity of the country as a whole.

The experts recommended that, to ensure a sound customs administration in Libya, and having regard to the practical aspects of the problem, the powers relating to the implementation of customs legislation should be vested in the federal government. They further recommended that the Constitution should provide that full powers be assigned to the federal government for instituting the country's customs administration. As regards revenues, it was recommended that they be treated as part of the general revenues of the federal government. The Constitution could provide for grants-in-aid to the provinces by the federal government from such general revenues. The procedure for making grants, and the formulas by which they might be determined, were discussed under the head "Taxation necessary to meet the expenditure of the Federal Government."

Stamp duty

In line with the practice followed in other countries and in view of the fact that local conditions in Libya varied considerably from place to place, it was recommended that stamp duty be placed within the legislative and executive competence of the provincial administrations.

Organization and registration of companies and the taxes imposed on them

At the outset the experts pointed out that organization and registration of companies, and the taxes imposed upon them, comprised two entirely different subjects. It was therefore suggested they should be dealt with separately in the Constitution.

The need for capital formation in Libya was so great that it was essential that a common national policy be laid down to encourage commercial enterprises to help in the development of the country's natural resources. The federal government was in the best position to evolve such a common policy and to produce uniform legislation on the subject. It was therefore recommended that the legislative aspect of the subject be assigned to the federal government, and that the executive aspect (which would comprise the arrangements for the registration of companies and the enforcement of federal company law) be placed within the competence of the provincial governments.

On the other hand, the experts suggested that company taxation should be treated as a separate subject in the Constitution. The most important taxes which companies would be required to pay were a business income tax on profits and a capital gains tax. Other taxes included property taxes, excise duties, license fees, etc. Company taxes were therefore dealt with under the next head, "Income tax."

Income tax

Income tax, the experts proposed, should be defined as follows: taxes on wages, salaries, and professional fees, and on business and agricultural profit in all its forms.

Income tax, they explained, constituted an important instrument in stabilizing a country's fiscal position. It could be used to prevent inflation where this was caused by large expenditures on public works and economic development over a short period. A uniform tax levied at one source not only accorded just and fair treatment to all inhabitants of a country, but also helped to promote the development of a country along natural lines and to foster economic unity. For this and other reasons, it was recommended that "income tax and the tax on business and agricultural profits" should come within the competence of the federal government both legislatively and executively.

The placing of income tax within the full competence of the federal government would automatically make the federal government responsible for its administration and collection. The experts also recommended that as in the case of customs revenues, the proceeds from income tax be treated as part of the general revenues of the federal government. The procedure for utilizing the general revenues as a whole was discussed under the head "taxation necessary to meet the expenditure of the Federal Government."

Monopolies and concessions

As the subject of monopolies and concessions was closely bound up with the organization of companies just discussed, the experts recommended that it too should fall within the legislative competence of the federal government. The enforcement of federal legislation on monopolies and concessions could, they suggested, be placed within the competence of the provincial administrations, it being understood that the federal government would have the right to exercise overall supervision.

The profits of, and fees or royalties paid by, monopolies and concessions should be treated as part of the general revenues of the federal government just as proposed in respect of taxes on personal income and business profits.

Taxation necessary to meet the expenditure of the federal government

It followed from the experts' previous recommendations that the revenues from customs, income tax, and monopolies and concessions should be treated as the general revenues of the federal government. The experts also advised providing in the Constitution for powers for the federal government to introduce such additional taxation as it might consider proper.

In their opinion the question of the procedure to be followed by the federal government for making grants-in-aid was one which would have to remain under continuous review by the federal government. They therefore recommended that whereas the Constitution should provide for the federal government to make grants-in-aid out of its general revenues to the provinces for the purpose of covering the latter's budgetary deficits, no specific formula for calculating such grants should be included in the Constitution.

Subsoil wealth, mining, and prospecting

Finally, the experts considered it desirable in the national interest that the exploitation of subsoil wealth, mining, and prospecting should be subject to national legislation. It was therefore suggested that whereas the legislative aspect of the subject be placed within the competence of the federal government, the executive aspect should be entrusted to the provincial administrations.

As soon as the members of the Working Group had studied the experts' memorandum, the Chairman invited two of its authors, a Polish economist and a Pakistani budget officer, to participate as advisers in the discussion. A lively and instructive exchange of views ensued. Generally speaking, the Working Group adopted the suggestions put forward by the experts, including the controversial one on customs, though not the recommendation regarding income tax. While the experts kept entirely to technical ground, the discussion on the Libyan side soon took on a political color. The principal speaker for Tripolitania said he preferred the system recommended in the experts' memorandum. His colleague from Cyrenaica, on the contrary, although agreeing that there should be uniform federal legislation on income tax, urged that the provincial administrations should enforce the law and collect the revenue, allocating it as they deemed fit. As might have been expected, the debate really turned around the issue of economic and political unity, as depending on a more or less centralized fiscal administration.

Finally, the Group decided to give the federal government the right to legislate on income tax, leaving to the territorial administrations the application of the relevant laws and the disposal of the revenue produced by that tax.[12]

12. In his progress report for August 1951 to the United Nations Technical Assistance Administration in New York, the Chief Economist of the technical assistance mission in Libya, Benjamin Higgins, who had succeeded John Lindberg (see Chapter 9, Pt. 1), commenting on this decision, said that the situation thus created was some-

The provincial approach was even more marked when, soon afterward, the seven items on finance came up once more for discussion in the Committee of Eighteen. While the Committee reluctantly agreed to let customs come within the competence of the federal government, both legislatively and executively, several members wanted to know how that government would come to the assistance of the provincial administrations that would be deprived of part of their revenue by such a provision. It was pointed out that the same question arose in the case of PTT revenue. Other members asked by what method the federal government would make available to the provinces money from grants-in-aid it might receive from foreign countries. Another crucial point was: by which authority would federal subsidies be determined—by the Federal government or by the provincial administrations, and according to what formula or principle? On this subject widely divergent opinions were expressed, the prevailing one being that the provinces ought not to be financially worse off after independence than before; indeed, they ought to be better off, as soon as the state of federal finances permitted. It was finally agreed that the matter would be regulated by federal law, according to a formula still to be defined in the chapter in the Constitution dealing with federal finance.

With regard to customs, it was wisely decided to propose that this service should remain within the jurisdiction of the provinces until 31 March 1952, so that its transfer to the federal regime would coincide with the beginning of the fiscal year 1 April 1952–1 April 1953. The provincial administrations would meanwhile subsidize the federal treasury under a transitional arrangement. As to the remaining recommendations of the experts, the Committee readily agreed to them, except the one regarding income tax. On this item there was the same clash of views as in the Working Group. Finally the Committee decided in favor of the Group's recommendation against that of the experts. At the request of a Fezzanese member, the minutes recorded by way of interpretation that tax on immovable property was to be considered as distinct from income tax.[13]

After one more reading, the Committee finally adopted, on 16 August

---

what anomalous, but not serious. The fiscal awkwardness entailed could, he felt, be overcome by an appropriate grant-in-aid formula. He moreover considered, and the Commissioner agreed, that perhaps fewer political problems would arise under this anomalous system than if both the executive and the legislative powers regarding income tax had been left in the hands of the federal government.

13. For particulars of the Fezzan fiscal system, see "Annual report of the French Government to the General Assembly concerning the administration of the Fezzan," GAOR: Fifth Session, 1950, Annexes, Agenda item 21 (A/1387, 22 September 1950), pp. 1–33.

1951, the distribution of powers between the federal government and the provincial administrations.

Having come to the end of their labors on this cardinal point, the Cyrenaican members, anxious lest in the eyes of their countrymen they might have gone too far on the road toward centralization, proposed the insertion at the end of the list of the following provisions:

> All questions which have not been included in the two lists of powers shall be within the competence of the Provinces

and

> The Federal Government shall delegate to the Provinces any of its powers as it may deem fit.

In a much shortened and more precise form, these provisions appear as Article 39 of the Constitution.

By letter of the same day the Commissioner, acting in his capacity as Chairman of the Coordination Committee, asked the NCAL to render a decision on the distribution of powers, so that the Committee could complete its preparation of the plan for their transfer. The NCAL did so on 18 August, unanimously and without amendment, reserving the right, however, to make any drafting changes later that might prove necessary.

At that moment all concerned with this key point of constitutional drafting heaved a sigh of relief. It soon proved, however, to be premature. The reservation just referred to turned out to be the cause of quite a few troublesome complications when the Working Group began to draw the final draft of the Constitution.

It was at about the same time that a new legal adviser, Sir Harry Trusted, joined the meetings of the Working Group.[14] Sir Harry, who had been Chief

14. Sir Harry Herbert Trusted, Q.C., was born on 27 June 1888. After overseas service from 1914 to 1919 in World War I, he completed his legal studies in England, and was appointed Puisne Judge of the Supreme Court of the Leeward Islands in 1925. From 1927 to 1929, he was Attorney General of this territory, an appointment which was followed by the Attorney Generalships of Cyprus (1929–32) and Palestine (1932–37). Sir Harry became Chief Justice in Palestine in 1937. He held this appointment until 1941, in which year he went to the Federated Malay States in the same capacity. In 1947 he was appointed Chairman of the Malayan Union and Singapore Salaries Commission, and in 1948, Commissioner to inquire into disturbances at Aden. He was attached to the Foreign Office for special duties from 1951 to 1953, and one of his first assignments was that of Legal Adviser to the Provisional Libyan Government. It will be seen that he brought many years of experience in administering the law in underdeveloped territories, and an excellent knowledge of conditions in the Middle East, to this task. Sir Harry completed a long and distinguished career by serving as a Divorce Commissioner in the Queen's Bench Division of the United Kingdom Courts from 1953 to 1959.

Justice in Palestine, and was on loan from the Foreign Office to the Provisional Libyan Government, was an able lawyer and a pleasant personality to work with. His relationship with Omar Loutfi was on a professionally friendly basis, and there is no doubt that in the final stage of the preparatory drafting he made some valuable suggestions for improving and clarifying the texts of several articles of the Constitution. However, as might have been expected, some of his advice, leaning to the British policy in favor of a loose federation, went too far in that direction and so occasionally gave rise to differences of opinion with the Commissioner and his legal adviser. Had Sir Harry arrived earlier, his influence might have seriously reduced the degree of centralization agreed to in the Working Group and the Committee of Eighteen. The possibility of achieving compromise solutions between federalists and unitarists also might have been endangered, or at least complicated. Fortunately for the future of Libyan unity, the agreements reached within these bodies on the main issues of federation had already hardened too much to be seriously affected by Sir Harry's suggestions in favor of increased provincial autonomy. A typical instance of these suggestions follows.

Item 10 of the list of federal powers (Article 36) had been worded: "Immigration into Libya after consultation with the Provinces and emigration from Libya."

Item 11 regulated: "Admission into and residence of foreigners in Libya and their expulsion."[15]

These two texts had been the subject of much discussion between the Libyans, whose main preoccupation in this connection was the coming and going of Italian subjects, both from and to Italy and within Libya. They had finally reached a compromise, the main point of which was that under item 10 the federal government would have to consult with the provinces, whereas this was not required under item 11. Sir Harry Trusted proposed that the phrase "after consultation with the Provinces" be inserted also into the text of item 11. Immediately the old controversy was revived. Sir Harry's proposal appeared on the surface perfectly logical, but he apparently had not understood that in the back of the Libyan mind immigration and emigration were specially connected with the coming and going of former Italian settlers, whereas under item 11 other categories of foreigners were included. The Cyrenaicans, being, as we have seen, obsessed by the fear that the federal government, under foreign pressure, might allow former Italian farmers—including those who had fled to Tripolitania—to reoccupy their properties in Cyrenaica, had insisted on subjecting immigration to provincial control through consultation. In Tripolitania the situa-

15. United Nations Doc. A/AC.32/COUNCIL/R.158, 1 October 1951. Mimeographed.

tion was more complicated and the general attitude toward it more liberal, yet the Tripolitanian representative also wanted his provincial administration to have its say in the matter.

With regard to the admission and residence of foreigners in general, the positions of the two Provinces were different inasmuch as Cyrenaica wished to be able to put Italians and certain other foreigners on a footing of equality, whereas Tripolitania wanted to have the possibility of treating them differently, if convenient. The difference was a subtle one, but had to be grasped. The Cyrenaican members of the Working Group supported Sir Harry's proposal whereas the Tripolitanians, together with the Fezzanese, opposed it on the ground that all matters concerning external relations must be within the executive and legislative competence of the federal government. The attitude of the Fezzanese was explained by their wish to see their liberty of movement into and out of Tripolitania, as well as their right of residence in that territory, unhampered by the restrictions the French authorities had imposed.

After a short debate, it was decided to leave item 11 unchanged.

Sir Harry had more success when, together with the United Nations legal adviser, he proposed to alter the text of the old draft Article III, which ran as follows:

> All questions which have not been included in the two lists of powers shall be within the competence of the Provinces [16]

He suggested that the much more realistic and clearer text of a new Article 39 be substituted:

> The Provinces shall exercise all powers connected with the matters which have not been assigned by this Constitution to the Federal Government.[17]

On the same day, the United Nations legal adviser, after consultation with the Commissioner, also made a gesture to allay the growing fears of the Cyrenaican delegation that in the eyes of their countrymen the federation was going to be overcentralized, by proposing a new Article 37, reading as follows, to be added at the end of the list of powers of the federal government:

> The Federal Government may with the agreement of any Province delegate to it or to its officers the executive power concerning any matter which is within its competence under this Constitution.[18]

16. *Second Annual Report of the United Nations Commissioner in Libya,* Annex XII, p. 96.

17. Text proposed orally during the course of the discussion. See Annex II, p. 907.

18. Ibid., and p. 906.

The Tripolitanian delegation wisely, though reluctantly, agreed to the proposal, on condition, however, that the new article should be completed by the words:

> . . . provided the Federal Government will bear the expense of the execution.[19]

The distribution of powers between the Federation and its component parts had thus virtually been decided, and it could be confidently asserted that the cornerstone of the Constitution had been laid.

B. RIGHTS OF THE PEOPLE
(Chapter II of the Constitution)

In the middle of April 1951, the Working Group began to study the people's fundamental rights and freedoms, or, as subsequently they were to be called in the Constitution, "Rights of the People." The latter title was preferred as it described more clearly the difference in the people's status between past and future. The Group used as its basic documentation the relevant chapters of the Constitutions of Egypt, Transjordan, Iraq, Lebanon, and Syria, as well as the Universal Declaration of Human Rights. Both the United Nations legal adviser and his colleague in the Cyrenaican delegation had, moreover, prepared draft texts, the first of which was ultimately used also during the discussion.

In the course of ten meetings, and after three thorough readings, the Group agreed, without much difficulty, on a draft set of rights which subsequently were to be almost identically incorporated as Chapter II, Articles 11 to 35, of the Constitution.

Of course, as the reader will have already grasped within this context, a crucial issue was the rights to be granted to the Italian minority, the residual group from the former colonial regime. The concern of this group was understandable. At that time, a return to Italy was not likely to hold prospects of a happy economic future (a situation which changed basically a few years later with a burgeoning Italian economy). At the same time there was concern lest a new Arab State would decline to grant religious freedom and the associated freedoms of civil status for marriage, inheritance, and other civil status positions, or the perpetuation of European codes of law and procedure.

It will be remembered that the Committee of Twenty-One, when recommending that "nonnational minorities" should not be allowed to participate

19. Ibid.

or to be represented in the National Assembly, had also said: "There is, however, a genuine intention and a general feeling that all civil, religious and social rights of all minorities and foreigners should be fully safeguarded in the future Constitution of Libya."[20]

The time had now come to carry out that intention. With that end in view the Working Group was fairly easily persuaded that it should adopt a United Nations-sponsored declaration, ensuring to all inhabitants of Libya, including members of the minorities and other foreigners, the enjoyment of the fundamental rights proclaimed in the Universal Declaration of Human Rights, such as personal liberty, and freedom of religion, speech, meeting, petition, and association.

Nevertheless, a legal distinction had to be drawn between Libyans and non-Libyans. Jews living in Libya and having no other nationality had always been considered as Libyans, though under Italian fascist rule a legal distinction based on racial considerations had been introduced. The Working Group did not want to perpetuate that distinction. In colonial Libya, Italians had enjoyed a privileged status; but this, under the British and French occupation, had for all practical purposes come to an end. Forced by circumstances of war, many Italians had returned to Italy; but a large number stayed on in the hope of being able to continue making a living in what many of them now considered their country of adoption. It was to the interest of the new State that, as skilled workers and technicians, they should do so. It was equally in the Libyan interest that members of the Greek and Maltese minorities should remain, just as it was a definite economic loss when, after 1948, many thousands of Jews emigrated to Israel.

It will be remembered that during the first year of the United Nations Mission's activities, difficulties had been caused by the Italian demand that Italian inhabitants of the country should be granted political rights. This the Committee of Twenty-One had refused, though there was no objection on the Libyan side to the grant of such rights, including the right of active and passive representation, to Italians and other foreigners once they had become naturalized Libyan citizens. Since, however, this was legally a complicated matter, the Working Group, wishing to get on with the drafting of the Constitution, had originally proposed that the definition of Libyan nationality and relevant questions, such as naturalization, be incorporated in a separate law. The rights of the people, on the other hand, including the rights of foreigners and members of minorities, were to be written into the Constitution, except for a few reasonable restrictions such as the prohibition of the establishment of secret associations and paramilitary organiza-

20. *Second Annual Report of the United Nations Commissioner in Libya,* Annex II, p. 73.

tions for political purposes.[21] This ended the first reading. Altogether the Working Group's proposed draft Bill of Rights turned out to be a liberally minded piece of work.

When the draft came up for discussion in the Committee of Eighteen, one meeting sufficed for approval of the whole of the proposed text on first reading, with the exception of the suggestion that the question of Libyan nationality be determined by a separate law. This item was returned to the Working Group for further study with the specific instruction that the latter formulate the principles defining Libyan nationality and prepare a draft covering the procedure for naturalization of foreigners. A Tripolitanian member of the Working Group proposed that all residents of Libya, regardless of their national origin, who had been continuously resident in Libya for ten years or more as from May 1943, should be considered as Libyan citizens provided that certain requirements were met. The purpose of this proposal, which had the Commissioner's full support, was to facilitate the acquisition of Libyan nationality in particular by those members of minority groups, Italian in the first place, who had vested interests in the country and intended to remain there.

A Cyrenaican member tabled a more detailed proposal according to which the conditions for acquiring Libyan citizenship were to be defined by law. The provisions would include special facilities to be accorded to Libyans residing outside the country; and similar facilities would be granted to citizens of Arab countries. Finally, he proposed that foreigners who had resided permanently in the country from 1940 until the promulgation of the Constitution should also enjoy the facilities, provided that they had important economic interests there and that their behavior had been beyond suspicion or doubt.

The mention of Libyans residing outside the country referred to the several thousands who had fled from the Italian occupation to find a haven, mostly in neighboring Arab countries. Their return and that of their offspring was of primary importance to the future Libyan State, which was badly in need of Libyans educated and trained abroad.

A few days later the matter came up again in the Committee of Eighteen. The Tripolitanian delegation proposed that two drafts be prepared: one defining the principles of Libyan citizenship, the second spelling out the conditions on which a foreigner could obtain Libyan nationality.

The following quotation from the minutes of the twelfth meeting of the Committee, held on 12 June, clearly shows the various tendencies prevailing amongst the members:

21. This restriction was inspired by fear of a recrudescence of fascism among the Italian minority in Tripolitania.

(v) The Hon. Member Mr. Mohamed al Mansouri put forward the idea that the period of residence should begin from 1943 and run from then on. After a discussion of what constituted a sufficient length of time for granting a foreigner Libyan nationality discussion moved to how far a naturalised person should be allowed to acquire political rights which a Libyan citizen enjoyed. The Hon. Members Mr. Omar Shennaib, Mr. Khalil al Gellal and Mr. Munir Burshan decided that a foreigner should have the right of enjoying whatever a Libyan citizen enjoyed merely by obtaining Libyan nationality.

(vi) Then the Hon. Member Mr. Mohammed bu Rahim suggested that it would be necessary to specify conditions for those who wished to take Libyan nationality. The Hon. Member Mr. Khalil Gellal opposed him saying that that should be within the special competence of the Law itself. The Hon. Member Mr. Mohammed bu Rahim replied that it was necessary to be circumspect in giving Libyan nationality to foreigners so as to prevent foreigners exercising their political rights without caution. The Hon. Members Mr. Munir Burshan and Mr. Abdul Majeed Ku'bar answered that it was a commonly acknowledged thing in the world and a thing prescribed in Constitutions that a foreigner who had become naturalised should enjoy the full political rights of his new nationality. The Hon. Member Mr. Khalil Gellal supported them saying that giving nationality had no meaning unless it was linked with the enjoyment of political rights.

(vii) After a discussion on the subject the Hon. Member Sheik Mohamed al Hankari observed the necessity of limiting the number of naturalised foreigners so that they could not gain ascendency over the local inhabitants.

(viii) Then the Committee moved to reflection on the drafting of a form which would define Libyans and the most important basic principles upon which the nationality law would stand. The Hon. Member Mr. Khalil Gellal offered once more the two first forms after they had been changed and they became as follows:

1. Every person who resided in Libya and has no other nationality, or is not the subject of any other State, shall be deemed to be a Libyan if he fulfils one of the following conditions:

(a) That he was born in Libya.

(b) That either of his parents was born in Libya.

(c) That he has had his normal residence in Libya for a period of not less than 10 years.

2. The wife of a Libyan citizen shall be considered a Libyan.

3. The Law shall define the conditions and special rules for acquiring

> nationality with regard to foreigners and it shall grant facilities to Libyans who have emigrated, to their children, to those from the Arab countries who apply for it and to the foreigners who apply for it and have lived in Libya continuously from 1st January 1943 up to the time of the issue of the Constitution. These last should have important economic interests in Libya and should have during the time of their residence a clean record of behaviour.
>
> The Committee confirmed these two forms and agreed upon them.[22]

Subject to a number of drafting changes, the texts agreed by the Committee were in substance to become Articles 8 and 9 of the Constitution.

The Committee proceeded to discuss, paragraph by paragraph, the Working Group's draft, paying particular attention to such questions as whether a specific right would apply to "Libyans" or to "everyone," or to some other specific category, but making hardly any changes of substance.[23]

An important decision, however, was that the words "for Libyans and foreigners" should be added at the end of the paragraph which was to become Article 28 of the Constitution, thus guaranteeing the right of foreigners to have their own schools. This was of particular importance to the Italian, Jewish, and in later years certain European and American, communities.

The second reading of the schedule of the rights of the people was thereby completed.

While these deliberations had been going on in the two subsidiary organs of the NCAL, triangular contacts had been constantly maintained between Khalil Qallal, the Chairman of the Working Group, Giacomo Marchino, the representative of the minorities on the Council for Libya, and the Commissioner, with the object of reaching, insofar as possible, all-round agreement on the issue of Libyans and "inhabitants." Marchino's position was never easy, but at this juncture it was especially delicate. Since the previous year's crisis over the Italo-Pakistan deal (see pp. 244–45) he had done his utmost to steer a noncommittal course between the various tendencies that divided both the Council and the Libyan people. This was, indeed, the best way in which he could serve the cause of the minorities he was so ably representing. He was fortunate in enjoying the confidence of the Jews, Greeks, Maltese, and a large number of the Italians, though the rightist elements amongst his own countrymen remained suspicious of what they

22. *Proc. NCAL,* Committee for the Constitution, Stewart-Jackson Translation, 12th Meeting, 12 June 1951.

23. See Articles 8–35 of the Constitution as adopted. See also *Second Annual Report of the United Nations Commissioner in Libya,* paras. 65–66.

called his pro-Arab and leftish tendencies. In his dealings with the Libyan political parties and their leaders, he had, of course, to be extremely careful and tactful. Most of them continued to trust him, but there were hotheads among the younger Libyan nationalists who began to have doubts, and said so openly. They criticized him for the neutral attitude he had adopted in the course of the Council debates since their resumption in December, fearing that one day his vote might go to the "colonial bloc." They were also afraid that he might support the policy of his Italian colleague instead of representing the minorities which, as a Tripolitanian weekly paper put it in an article directly addressed to him, "should give you your instructions and directives. But if you take instructions from your colleague, the representative of Italy, . . . your behaviour is that of a fifth columnist." [24]

Fortunately the Chairman and the members of the Working Group were intelligent men who wished to apply, as far as possible, the principles of the Universal Declaration of Human Rights to the minority issue. In this, they naturally were assisted by the members of the United Nations Commissioner's staff with day-to-day responsibility for these questions. Indeed, there was no hostility, in principle, to the non-Libyan minority claim for a status based on the Universal Declaration, barring, however, all political rights. At the same time it was clear that if the minorities obtained satisfaction on a bill of rights integrally written into the Constitution, they would become staunch supporters of a final and rigid basic law, difficult to amend. The Cyrenaican and Fezzanese members of the NCAL were not unaware of this position and the repercussions it might have on the international political scene—for instance, on the Latin-American vote on the Libyan question at the Sixth Session of the General Assembly of the United Nations in 1951. In a way this suited them, of course.

The position was awkward, however, for those Tripolitanians who preferred a provisional or draft Constitution, easily amendable. For reasons already referred to in Chapter 3, they had in the summer of 1950 supported the minority claims. Now it was difficult for them to change their stand, not only because practically the whole minority population was living in their province, but also, and by no means least, because of the special value to them of the minority vote in the Council where Marchino was sitting on the fence—if not comfortably, at least in good balance.

Altogether it was a complex situation. The reason for its analysis here at some length is that its particular form of complexity largely explains the relative smoothness of the negotiations on minority rights and their outcome as finally included in Chapter II of the Constitution. This should not be taken as meaning, however, that no difficulties at all were encountered,

24. *Liwa al-Hurriya,* 12 January 1951, over the signature of Usuf Mescherghi.

or that there were no sharp clashes between the parties. On most of these issues the Commissioner's legal adviser, or, occasionally, the Commissioner himself, was called upon to mediate. The results of their efforts were not always as they would have wished, but in a number of cases they succeeded in bringing the parties together.

In the course of June, Marchino, in consultation with the Advisory Committee of minorities representatives, of which he was Chairman, and with the assistance of the Commissioner's legal adviser, prepared an able memorandum setting out the fundamental principles underlying the status the minorities claimed for themselves in the new State. It suffered from too much detail and exceeded the measure of liberality which the Libyans could politically grant. However, together with the Working Group's draft, it provided an excellent basis for discussion, enabling the minorities to make a number of concessions and allowing the Libyan negotiators to do a considerable amount of face-saving, thus gaining leeway for themselves in their subsequent dealings with their more conservative compatriots, which were often to prove difficult.

The memorandum was accompanied by a draft entitled "Statute of the Rabbinical Tribunal" put forward by the Jewish community, in which the Libyan Government was asked to recognize and guarantee the juridical functions of the Tribunal within the limits, and according to the principles, laid down in the draft.

Most of July was taken up by minority talks between the personalities directly interested on both sides, most of the time in the presence of the United Nations legal adviser or the Commissioner. During these talks a close comparison was made between the draft "Rights of the People" prepared by the Working Group and the memorandum submitted by the minorities. Besides the Universal Declaration of Human Rights, account was also taken of the Minority Treaties ancillary to the Peace Treaty of Versailles [25] as well as of a draft resolution [26] discussed by the United

25. A summary by Oppenheim of the protection afforded by these treaties reads:

(i) For the *inhabitants,* protection of life and liberty and the free exercise of religion without distinction of birth, nationality, language, race or religion;
(ii) In general, for *certain inhabitants,* automatic acquisition, or just facilities for the acquisition, of the nationality of the contracting State;
(iii) For the *nationals,* equality before the law and as to all civil and political rights, and as to the use of any language. (The Permanent Court of International Justice repeatedly laid down that the prohibition of non-discrimination must operate in fact as well as in law and that a measure general in its application but in fact directed against members of a minority constitute a violation of the Minorities Treaty);
(iv) Freedom of organisation for religious and educational purposes; and

Nations Commission on Human Rights at its Sixth Session, held at Lake Success from 27 March to 19 May 1950. This draft resolution was considered to be of particular importance by the Libyan minorities because of its recommendation on the use of minority languages in the courts and in schools.

Other issues at stake in these talks concerned the length and the starting date of the period during which a foreigner would have to be permanently resident in Libya before being entitled to acquire Libyan nationality, as well as the question of the expulsion of foreigners from the country, and of their contractual rights and other interests. In this latter connection, the minorities attached great importance to a resolution adopted by the General Assembly on 2 December 1950, concerning the federation of Eritrea with Ethiopia and stipulating inter alia that "No one shall be deported except in accordance with the law." [27]

A specific Jewish claim, namely the right to emigrate to the new State of Israel, forcefully put forward by various Jewish organizations, had partially solved itself, or rather was largely being disposed of with the liberal co-operation of the British Administrations, before Libya became independent.

The requests and petitions of Jewish organizations, apart from claiming the traditional minority rights recognized by international law, now in-

---

> (v) State provision for the elementary instruction of their children through the medium of their own language in districts where a particular minority forms a considerable proportion of the population.

L. Oppenheim, *International Law: A Treatise,* ed. H. Lauterpacht (7th ed.; London: Longmans, Green and Co., 1952), Vol. I, *Peace,* Chapter XI, "The Protection of Minorities," p. 652.

26. The text of the relevant part of the draft resolution reads:

> [The General Assembly] . . . *Recommends* that, in the interest of enabling recognized minority groups to maintain their cultural heritage when they desire to do so, Member Governments should provide *as a minimum,* adequate facilities, in districts, regions and territories where they represent a considerable proportion of the population, for:
>
> (1) The use (in judicial procedure) *before the courts* of languages of such groups, *in those cases where the member of the minority group does not speak or understand the language ordinarily used in the courts;* (2) The teaching in State-supported schools of languages of such groups, provided that such groups request it and that the request in reality expresses the spontaneous desire of such groups;
>
> *Affirms* that such groups shall possess these or other rights so long as they are not used for the purpose of threatening or undermining the unity or security of States.

ESCOR: Eleventh Session, 1950, Commission on Human Rights Report, Supplement No. 5 (E/1681), pp. 10–11, fn. 9.

27. Resolution 390 A (V). For text, see GAOR: Fifth Session, 1951, Supplement No. 20 (A/1775), pp. 20–22.

sisted, however, on emigration *together with their belongings* as a right to be recognized in the Constitution. In the circumstances, this appeared a justified demand in particular with regard to personal effects and movable property. Article 13 (2) of the Universal Declaration of Human Rights provides that "Everyone has the right to leave any country, including his own, and to return to his own." Article 17 (2) further provides that "No one shall be arbitrarily deprived of his property."

In the course of history, both under Turkish and under Italian rule, relations between Arabs and Jews in Libya appear to have been generally good. However, in 1948, the year in which the State of Israel was founded, ugly anti-Jewish riots had occurred, mainly in the old part of Tripoli Town, the immediate causes of which have never been explained to the author's satisfaction. When the new independent State of Israel opened its frontiers to all Jewish immigrants, Libyan Jews started leaving by the thousands. It was estimated that between 30,000 and 34,000 Jews had been living in Libya, the great majority of them in Tripolitania. In 1950, shortly after the arrival of the United Nations Mission, the British authorities estimated that the number had gone down to just over 20,000. In May 1950, the same authorities stated that this figure had further declined, to approximately 16,000. They estimated that the number of Jews remaining in Libya in May 1951, when Jewish emigration to Israel was expected to be completed, would be only about 4,000. Subsequent developments proved this estimate to be roughly correct.

In the summer of 1951, Libyans were complaining that there was hardly a Jewish artisan left, and that they were obliged to turn to Italian craftsmen to have their hair cut or their shoes repaired. The same was true of many other trades. The Jews who remained behind were mostly those who owned immovable property, merchants, and, generally speaking, people belonging to the more well-to-do classes. Nevertheless a day might come when this rearguard of the old community too might wish to leave the country; and the same might apply some day to members of other minorities. It was therefore not a surprise when in June 1951 Marchino, after lengthy deliberations with his Committee, submitted to the Chairman of the Working Group, with a copy to the Commissioner, the aforementioned memorandum of fundamental principles of minority claims, including a paragraph stating that everyone should be free to emigrate to any other country without the loss of property, and with the power to transfer family or personal effects and equipment.

In the course of the elaborate and sometimes passionate negotiations between Marchino and the representatives of the Working Group, no agreement could be reached on the question of freedom to emigrate with belongings. On the Libyan side it was argued that such a right was inherent in democratic citizenship and should be regulated by law. To write it into the Constitution would imply an infringement of the sovereign authority of the State. Marchino argued that freedom of emigration had been recognized by many Constitutions, including the Statute of the City of Jerusalem approved by the General Assembly of the United Nations.

The real difficulty from the Libyan point of view, however, was that if freedom of emigration with belongings was introduced as a principle into the Constitution, it would apply without discrimination to all minorities, including the Italians, with whom much larger problems of a similar nature were still to be negotiated on the basis of the Peace Treaty and General Assembly Resolution 388 (V) on economic and financial provisions relating to Libya. However different the two problems might be in many respects, they also had points in common. The Libyans, wishing to keep their hands free, therefore would not meet the wishes of Marchino and the Jewish minority on this particular issue.

Another question of specific interest to all minority religions also gave rise to differences of opinion. The draft "Rights of the People" prepared by the Working Group contained an article (later to become Article 21 of the Constitution) declaring that the State would respect all religions and faiths and would ensure to Libyans and foreigners residing in its territory, freedom of conscience and the right freely to practice religion as long as it was not a breach of public order and was not contrary to morality. Marchino, invoking this principle, wanted the Constitution, in addition, to empower the State to regulate by law more detailed rules guaranteeing its implementation. The traditional relationship of the Moslem religion to the State, he reasoned, made it possible for Moslem religious sects to enjoy the right to organize themselves according to their own statutes. Their relations with the State were regulated on the basis of agreements concluded by their respective representatives. In Moslem States such agreements are in the nature of things, since Islam is the religion of the State (cf. Libyan Constitution, Article 5). State and religion have always been interwoven to the extent of being inseparable.

What Marchino was asking on behalf of the minority religions was practically tantamount to the right of concluding with the State similar agreements, guaranteeing not only freedom of religion and the right to practice it, but also freedom of religious instruction as well as the free practice of any form of religion. He demanded that the ecclesiastical nature or the religious or cultural aim of any association or institution should not give rise to special legislative restrictions or to special fiscal measures relating to its establishment, to its juridical capacity, or to any form of its activities.

It was in this spirit, for instance, that the draft Statutes of the Rabbinical Tribunal, just referred to, had been conceived.

The Libyan negotiators, though fully recognizing the principle of religious freedom underlying the minority demands, could not agree to the additional demands made by Marchino. In particular they raised two objections.

First, they could not accept the inclusion in the Constitution of a stipulation according to which the relations with the State of religions or faiths other than the Moslem religion would be regulated by law on the basis of agreements similar to those concluded by the representatives of Moslem sects. From their point of view, such a stipulation was redundant, since under the Constitution the State would grant all religions and faiths the right to organize themselves in accordance with their own statutes, provided always that these were not in contradiction with the Constitution, which granted a special position to Islam.

Second, they objected that acceptance of this particular minority demand would in fact amount to sanctioning the right of every religion to practice proselytism. Such practices would in all probability provoke acute Moslem reactions, harmful to the peace of the realm. As a matter of fact, they insisted, that was so true that all Moslem States had prohibited all forms of proselytism.

A large measure of understanding having been reached by the middle of August, Marchino enumerated the principal questions still outstanding in a letter to the Chairman of the Working Group, a copy of which was sent to the Commissioner. One more principle had been added, namely that of "freedom of economic initiative" (free enterprise). This problem was considered important by the minorities because of the influx of foreign capital it would in their opinion encourage. To the Libyans this was a controversial issue. On the one hand, they were well aware of the need to attract foreign capital if the country's economy were to be developed. On the other hand, they were afraid that foreign investment might easily be attended by economic and political interventions and pressures.

The Working Group, in the course of its subsequent discussions, went a long way to meet these final minority wishes. However, not all of them were satisfied.

In September, the Committee of Eighteen, when finalizing its work, made one more change of substance by inserting in Article 18 the words "or prohibited from moving in Libya." This obviously was a reflection on regulations introduced by the three British and French Administrations for the purpose of controling movements of travelers and goods between their respective territories. At the same time it revealed a fear that the provincial administrations of the future might apply travel restrictions not only to foreigners, as Cyrenaica planned to do with regard to Italian subjects, but also to Libyan citizens.

In the Committee of Eighteen there was opposition, both from the Cyrenaican and from the Tripolitanian side, to the use of minority-group languages in official transactions, but the majority agreed to it, and the relevant article was adopted after the Chairman of the Working Group had argued

> that their Constitution would be something of a target for discussion and argument in the United Nations Organisation and that there were nations to whom the interests of some foreign communities which were living with them in Libya were important; and that perhaps their attitude of neglect for that Article would have an influence on international public opinion. . . . in his opinion, the Article would be in their interest on a number of counts, since they were not fanatics nor were they rancorous. . . . therefore it would be to their advantage to leave the Article sound particularly since they had confined it to cases of necessity.[28]

From this moment onward the articles concerning the rights of the people were virtually left untouched except for minor drafting changes. This meant that in the end a compromise was reached which, though leaving several minority wishes unfulfilled, nevertheless, judged by United Nations standards, gave proof on the Libyan side of a broad-minded spirit of tolerance and a realistic understanding of both national and international requirements. Judging by the average conditions under which minorities generally live today in the newly born States of the postwar world, those dwelling in Libya apparently have no serious ground for complaint, provided, of course, that the relevant articles of the Constitution are observed both in letter and in spirit, even in times of international tension.

The general interests of the Greek and Maltese minorities were adequately covered by the "Rights of the People" and the "General Provisions"; but both groups had special problems requiring a solution: the Greeks in connection with sponge-fishing in Libyan territorial waters, and the Maltese in connection with restitution for the requisitioning or loss of their fishing boats through acts of war. However, these questions belong rather to the history of Libya after independence.

28. *Proc. NCAL,* Committee for the Constitution, Stewart-Jackson Translation, 20th Meeting, 27 August 1951.

C. THE KING
(Chapter V of the Constitution)

The King-Designate paid his first official visit to Tripolitania as future Head of State from 13 to 29 May 1951. It was an eventful occurrence, a brief account of which will be found in Part 1 of Chapter 8 (pp. 610–12). In the present context mention will be made only of the repercussions the royal presence had on the country's constitutional development. They were of considerable portent, because, for the first time, the Provisional Libyan Government, in existence since 29 March (see Chapter 10, p. 727); the members of the NCAL; the leaders of the opposition; the British Administration and the Council of Regency in Tripolitania, in existence since 8 March; the Commissioner; and the members of the Council for Libya found themselves in company with the future Head of State for consultations on matters of common national, not provincial, concern. To all participants these proved useful, to many they were an eye-opener on wider political and constitutional horizons than they had perceived up to that moment.

The King-Designate himself took the lead in giving expression to this new national consciousness in delivering a speech at the Royal Palace on the closing day of his visit. Speaking on the crucial issue of blending federalism and unity, he said:

> Great sons of Tripolitania,
> The federal system of Government decided upon by the National Constituent Assembly, which was set up in accordance with the decision of the United Nations and with the agreement of the [Council for Libya] after the advice offered by the Commissioner together with the leaders and prominent personages in the three territories, is not a new invention, as certain people depict it. Neither is Libya the first state to follow this system, for we have precedents in the new states which arose after the war and others among the great powers which followed this system for ages past. We consider that the attacks of certain countries which inveigh against this system are the result of immaturity and lack of knowledge as to the true state of Libya and the wishes of its inhabitants. We hold no doubt that the people of Libya are more solicitous than anyone else for their own interests in this matter and the security of their future. In this connection, we wish to point out that we understand from the Libyan Constituent Assembly that its work is in accordance with the wishes of my noble people, and that the constitution being drawn up by the said Assembly will include the establishment of one State and one Cabinet.

> When this occurs, the regimes in the three territories: Cyrenaica, Tripolitania and the Fezzan will be adjusted immediately the Constitution is proclaimed, from governments to administrations of provinces [vilayets] with internal legislative powers in those matters prescribed by the constitution.[29]

He also expressed the hope that the "provisional Libyan Government will undertake the conduct of parliamentary elections at the earliest opportunity in accordance with the provisions of the constitution." [30]

Speaking of the minorities, and once again addressing the Tripolitanians in particular, His Highness declared:

> There live in your midst foreign communities. In the past and in the present, you have been known for the way in which you have respected them and guarded over their interests in various fields, and there have existed and still exist between you and them good relations pervaded by mutual affection and joint assistance and co-operation towards the good of the country and the general interest. This is neither strange nor to be wondered at in you, for it is a characteristic of the Arabs to respect their guests, and the guest has the right of protection from his host. Therefore, let our guests in Libya rest fully assured, for in our religion, traditions and laws, they have the best guarantee, and we offer to them our esteem and sincere thanks for the way in which they have co-operated with you in this great welcome and fine reception.[31]

The royal attempt to sound a conciliatory note on the main controversial issues at stake was obvious and, psychologically, made at the very moment when the country was most in need of it. Coming from the supreme leader who had fortunately escaped the bomb attack made upon his arrival in Tripoli (pp. 611–12), the speech carried additional weight, though the convinced enemies of federalism never relaxed their hostile attitude, even after independence.

Another fruit of the numerous consultations held during these eventful days was that both the Provisional Government and the NCAL became aware of the need for a timetable. However, if such a schedule were to be drawn up and adhered to, the necessary guidance would have to come from the highest authority, the King-Designate himself.

In the course of a lengthy conversation between His Highness and the

29. Extract from translation of the Arabic text of the Amir's speech made for internal purposes by the language staff of the United Nations Mission in Libya. United Nations Archives. Mimeographed.

30. Ibid.

31. Ibid.

Commissioner, and after legal advice had been taken, it was agreed that the "duly constituted Libyan Government," to which by 1 January 1952 all powers were to be transferred under the terms of Resolution 387 (V), should preferably emanate from a parliament elected in accordance with the Constitution. Taking the elections held in Cyrenaica the previous year as a guide, it was considered that at least three to four months would be required to prepare and carry out elections for a federal parliament in the three provinces. Hence, the drafting of the Constitution would have to be finished by mid-August. Meanwhile the preparation of the plan for the transfer of powers should go ahead at the same pace. The adoption of the Constitution by the NCAL and the initiation of the transfer of powers by the British and French Administrations to a still provisional Libyan Government should, in the Commissioner's view, occur simultaneously, provided London and Paris were prepared to cooperate. Thus the four last months of the year would be available for the drafting of a federal electoral law by the NCAL, the setting up of the necessary electoral machinery, the actual holding of the elections, the establishment of a "duly constituted Libyan Government," and the formation of a federal administration. The second half of December was to be reserved for the final transfer of powers, the proclamation of independence, and the launching of the new State. This was admittedly an extremely tight schedule, a fact of which everybody concerned was aware, but nobody was willing to take the responsibility of openly opposing it. Even when, three months later, its implementation proved impossible for reasons of force majeure, and a very awkward situation ensued, the dominating will to reach independence before 1 January 1952 was nevertheless strong enough to overcome all obstacles. But that is another story, to be told later in this study.

At the end of May, however, it still looked as if bold planning and hard work would be sufficient to carry the day. The King-Designate, fulfilling his role in the plan, called in the leading members of the NCAL, including the six members of the already heavily burdened Working Group, and asked them to work even harder. The time was the eve of Ramadan, the month of fasting. In a Moslem country like Libya, where the prescriptions of the Koran are generally followed with the utmost strictness and devotion, the abstention from dawn to sunset from water as well as food in the long hot days of June saps human endurance after a few days.[32]

32. The Koran decrees: "eat and drink until a white thread can be distinguished by you from a black one at dawn. Then fulfil the fast until the night, and go . . . ye at your devotions in the mosques the while." *The Koran,* II (The Chapter of the Heifer (Medina)), 175–185, trans. E. H. Palmer, with an introduction by R. A. Nicholson and Geoffrey Cumberlege (Oxford: Oxford University Press, 1949), p. 24.

Some non-Moslems on the Mission staff, who in a spirit of solidarity with their Libyan colleagues tried to follow the same regime, soon found out how it frayed their nerves. When, therefore, the Chairman of the Working Group announced that the Group had promised the King-Designate to hold daily morning meetings during the month of Ramadan, while the members of the Committee of Eighteen would hold daily evening meetings, public opinion was properly impressed.

Soon after this new work schedule had come into force, the Group started to consider what they initially called the prerogatives of the King. Ultimately, the group of articles governing this subject was to become Chapter V of the Constitution under the title "The King." There is no reason to assume that there was a link between the King-Designate's visit to Tripoli and the fact that the Working Group put the definition of his powers on its agenda at this particular time. While the Constitution was being drafted, the King-Designate made a practice of closely following progress through information he regularly received from the NCAL's principal officers. He also occasionally asked for information from the Commissioner, who, anyway, made a point of flying periodically to Benghazi to render detailed oral reports, and who asked His Highness for advice whenever a serious problem arose. Sometimes these meetings took on a wider scope with several persons present discussing opposing views, the King-Designate listening attentively, rarely intervening except to ask for clarification. At the end he would more often than not request his visitors to reconsider the issue and come back with an agreed solution. If he gave an opinion, it always was in the form of personal advice, never as an order. This was in conformity with the position he strictly maintained of not pretending to exercise a function with which he had not yet been formally invested. Thus the NCAL was left to bear its own responsibilities as laid down in paragraph 3 of Resolution 289 (IV). With regard to the internal affairs of Cyrenaica, his position was at the same time, of course, that of reigning Prince.

After the establishment by the NCAL of the Provisional Libyan Government, whose members considered themselves de facto but not de jure responsible to that body, and who looked toward the King-Designate as their real though not yet enthroned sovereign, the latter began very prudently and unostentatiously to extend his personal authority to cover all Libyan affairs. Constitutionally speaking, it was admittedly an ambiguous situation, a form of transition of powers that allowed of no clear definition. It served the country well during the nine months it lasted, though occasionally it was the object of criticism. The practice of this period pragmatically laid the foundation for a relationship between King, Cabinet, and

Parliament that, on the day of independence and subsequently, following the election of the first lower house on 19 February 1952, was formalized without having to suffer a period of difficult transition.

During this unobtrusive evolution from the Senussi's Cyrenaican Amirate to his Libyan Kingship, the Working Group was quietly drafting the chapter of the Constitution on the royal prerogatives. The debates were facilitated by the personal attitude of the King-Designate, who wanted less, rather than more, power to be granted to him. The motive he gave for this policy was that in a modern State the people must learn to carry their own responsibilities instead of being governed from above as in olden times.

In conversation with the Commissioner on this subject, commenting at the same time on the traditional Arab concept of royal powers,[33] the King-Designate pointed out that, while personally he was in favor of a constitutional monarchy, he was obliged to take into account the tribal mentality, particularly strong in Cyrenaica, which regarded him for all practical purposes as an absolute monarch. Among the more emancipated elements of the Tripolitanian coastal belt there was, on the contrary, a greater realization of the present-day need to impose certain limitations on the royal prerogatives. Hence, the differences of opinion that occurred in the course of the debates once more followed the line of a Cyrenaican-Tripolitanian cleavage of thought.

As was now its custom, the Working Group began its study of the subject by reading through the relevant chapters of constitutions that might serve as models, in the first place, of course, those of Moslem countries, specifically Afghanistan, Egypt, Iran, Iraq, and Transjordan. It also asked for translations of the chapters concerning the royal powers in the constitutions of Belgium, Greece, and the Netherlands. Members also had before them two lists of royal prerogatives adapted to Libyan conditions, prepared respectively by the Cyrenaican and the United Nations legal advisers. It was decided to give priority to the Cyrenaican list without, however, losing sight of the other.

The question of national sovereignty and its source gave rise to little debate. Following ancient usage as codified in other Arab constitutions, it was agreed that the sovereignty of the Kingdom of Libya was vested in the Nation. By the will of God, the people entrusted the sovereignty to King Mohamed Idris al-Mahdi al-Senussi and after him to his male heirs, the oldest after the oldest, degree after degree. This wording became the first article of the chapter on the King (Article 44 of the Constitution). It will be observed that the text contains an element of choice; it is the people who

33. For an account of this concept, see Ali Chaygan.

decide to whom the sovereignty of the Kingdom is to be entrusted. Hence, it is surprising to note that the same article, amplified by the following one (45), declares that the succession to the throne shall be hereditary. However, in Article 46 the Constitution reintroduces a notion of choice by declaring that "In the event of the King's death and the Throne remaining vacant owing to the lack of a successor to the King or to no successor having been appointed, the Senate and the House of Representatives shall at once hold a joint meeting without convocation to appoint a successor within ten days." According to competent authors, this combination of elective and hereditary notions in matters of royal succession goes back to the very origins of Islamic public law.[34]

If nevertheless the question of the succession to the throne gave rise to some discussion among the authors of the Libyan Constitution, this was not for reasons of principle; it was rather that a choice had to be made between limiting the succession to the throne to the direct family line of the King-Designate, and extending it to cover all the descendants of the founder of the Senussi family, Sheikh al-Sayed Muhamed Bin Ali el-Senussi, the Grand Senussi (1787–1859).[35]

The Working Group decided to defer its decision on this matter until it had been made aware of the views of the King-Designate himself, though it at the same time considered that the choice of the Crown Prince should be left to the King. This explains why in its final form Article 45 of the Constitution states that "the order of succession to the throne shall be determined by Royal Decree promulgated by King Idris I within a year of the date of the Promulgation of this Constitution." This tactful manner of handling a delicate problem took into account both the fact that the King-Designate had no living male issue and the fact that in private younger men from a collateral branch of the family were laying claim to the succession.[36]

34. For origins of the elective and hereditary elements in Moslem public law on the problem of succession, see ibid., Chapter III, "Calife," pp. 42–55. On page 46 the author states that "les sunnites acceptent la légitimité des deux systèmes de transmission de pouvoirs, l'élection pour les quatre premiers califes et la succession pour les califes postérieurs." It is to be noted in this connection that the Senussi are Sunni Moslems.

35. See genealogical tree of the Senussi family in E. E. Evans-Pritchard, *The Sanusi of Cyrenaica* (Oxford: Oxford University Press, 1963), p. 20.

36. An account of the cause of these difficulties was published in the Benghazi weekly *Az-Zaman,* 27 January 1955, and may also be found in Muhammed Khalil, *The Arab States and the Arab League, An Encyclopaedic Review in two volumes,* Vol. I (Beirut, Lebanon: Khayat's College Book Co-operative, 1957), p. 207, under the heading *Memoirs of King Idris: A Definite Clarification of the Political History of Libya.*

After independence the following Royal Orders or Decrees were issued with regard

It took a few more meetings to finish the draft of the future Chapter V, most of the articles of which were approved with no, or practically no, discussion. With regard to the succession, it was decided to propose that it be limited to the dynasty of King Idris I (Article 44). The articles (59 and 60) absolving the King from all responsibility and stipulating that he shall exercise his powers through responsible ministers were approved without much discussion.

The question of to whom the ministers themselves were to be responsible proved to be more intricate.[37] To the King? To Parliament? Or to both? Each of these solutions had its supporters and its opponents. The discussion was further complicated by the need for viewing the problem from three different angles: the royal prerogatives; the duties and responsibilities of ministers; and the functions of Parliament. A clear picture became possible only when the various bits and pieces of constitutional drafting had been finally put together in one homogeneous text. During the preparatory stage it was the decisions of principle that counted. Thus it was decided that the King should have the prerogative of appointing the Prime Minister, or removing him from office, and of accepting his resignation. The same procedure was to apply to ministers, but on the proposal of the Prime Minister (future Article 72). Subsequently it was agreed that the House of Representatives should dispose, subject to certain restrictions, of the right to censure (vote of no confidence), thus enabling it to compel ministers to resign, either collectively or individually (future Articles 84–87). The restrictions (Article 87) consisted of a qualified majority vote and the observance of two intervals between the various stages of the process. The subject will be dealt with in more detail in the next section of this chapter. By Western parliamentary standards this was a somewhat unusual system of ministerial responsibility, but in the opinion of the Libyan legislators and foreign observers it was well adjusted to the needs of a people who were about to experience their first taste of parliamentary democracy.

A not dissimilar problem of balancing royal and parliamentary powers

to the succession to the throne: Order of 1 Muharran al-Haram 1372 (21 September 1952); Regulation relating to the Constitution of the Royal House, of 11 Muharran al-Haram 1372 (1 October 1952); Order of 14 Rabi Ath-Thani 1373 (21 December 1953); Order of 22 Safar 1374 (20 October 1954); and Decree Law on *Amendment of the Privy Council Law,* promulgated on 21 Rabi Thani 1376 (24 November 1956).

37. See extract from the Commissioner's letter to the President of the NCAL of 3 April 1951, based on the Council's advice of 13 March 1951, United Nations Doc. A/AC.32/COUNCIL/R.129, 14 March 1951. Mimeographed. For full text of these passages, see *Second Annual Report of the United Nations Commissioner in Libya,* Annex IV, pp. 77–80.

arose in connection with the sanctioning of laws by the King after they had been voted by Parliament. Should the King have the right to withhold his assent when he disagreed with a particular law? The question was discussed at great length by the Working Group, a few members of which were of the opinion that in view of the foreseeable lack of experience of the first parliaments to be elected after independence, the King in his wisdom should have the right to withhold his assent to a law where he thought it necessary to do so in the national interest. Others argued, on the contrary, that if the King did not sanction a law voted by Parliament, he would find himself in conflict with the representatives of the nation, a situation which, it was feared, might have serious consequences for the political stability of the future State. The Commissioner and the Legal Adviser, following a precedent provided by the Egyptian Constitution then in force (Articles 35 and 36), suggested that in case of disagreement the King should have the right to suspend the enactment of a bill and send it back to Parliament for reconsideration. This was accepted, provided that Parliament then would have the right to pass the law a second time, in which case the royal assent could no longer be withheld. The details of this procedure, as finally voted, will be found in Article 136 of the Constitution (Chapter VII, Part III, "Provisions Common to the two Chambers"). Thus, Parliament, if it insisted, would have the last word in matters of legislation, but not before it had been obliged to consider the King's objections. Before this agreement was reached, however, the question was discussed several more times. In particular the question of the second vote became the subject of a heated debate.

In the same context it was decided, following another article (37) of the Egyptian Constitution, that in making regulations for carrying out the laws the King should neither modify, suspend, nor exempt them from execution. In somewhat clearer language, this was to become Article 63 of the Libyan Constitution.

Members of the Working Group were also anxious to avoid abuses they had noticed in certain Arab and other countries made possible by failure to distinguish clearly between state property and the royal purse. Although nothing of this kind was to be feared from the King-Designate, whose integrity was proverbial, a suitable article was nevertheless proposed making a clear distinction between State and Crown property. It did not prove easy to reach agreement on the wisdom and suitability of such an arrangement. Subsequently a compromise was approved, later to become Article 57 of the Constitution, to the effect that the judicial procedure to be followed in cases brought by the Royal Estate or against it should be regulated by a federal law.

Many other aspects of the royal prerogatives came up in the course of the discussion as, for instance, the composition and powers of the Council of Regency, but none of them gave rise to much debate.

There remained, however, a few important issues, one of which concerned the King's right to conclude treaties with foreign powers, under traditional Moslem public law an undisputed royal prerogative. Some members, particularly on the Tripolitanian side, expressed the view that the approval of Parliament should be required, at least for important treaties, a view that tallied with the opinion expressed by the United Nations legal adviser. Other members, mainly in the Cyrenaican delegation, considered that the conclusion of foreign treaties should be one of the King's exclusive prerogatives.

After much discussion a compromise text was finally submitted to the Committee of Eighteen, which left to the King the power to declare war, conclude peace, and make treaties, provided that he informed Parliament as soon as the interest and security of the State permitted him to do so. Certain categories of treaty, however, such as those surrendering sovereign rights, imposing additional expenditures upon the public treasury, or affecting the private and public rights of citizens, were not to enter into force without the consent of Parliament. In no circumstances were secret articles to be contradictory to the published ones. When this draft came up for discussion in the Committee, it once more gave rise to intense controversy. This time a member of the Tripolitanian delegation insisted on adding "treaties of alliance" [38] to those requiring parliamentary approval. In the end, after a heated debate, the proposal was adopted; but this was not the end of the matter. It was not until the last plenary meeting of the NCAL in October that an unexpected solution was proposed by the King-Designate himself. It simply stated that "The King shall declare war and conclude peace and enter into treaties which he ratifies after the approval of Parliament" (Article 69). The implications of this amendment will be appreciated later.

Other draft articles went repeatedly back and forth between the Working Group and the Committee of Eighteen for further study and reconsideration; one of them, dealing with the composition of the Senate and in particular the King's right to appoint the members of the upper chamber in whole or in part, proved to be a specially hard nut to crack. It will be dealt with in more detail below in the section on the Parliament.

Another matter worth mentioning at this stage is the King's right to

38. The author has good reason to believe that in tabling this proposal the member in question had in mind "treaties of alliance" that might be proposed to Libya at the moment it was to become independent or just before.

proclaim martial law and declare a state of emergency. This time it was the United Nations legal adviser who suggested that such action should be subject to parliamentary approval. He proposed, moreover, that if Parliament were in recess, it should immediately be convened in special session. Opinions were greatly divided on this proposal, not least in the Committee of Eighteen. Many members feared that Parliament would not be able to reach a decision quickly enough, leaving the Government without special powers at the very moment when they were essential. Others, on the contrary, were convinced that the proclamation of martial law was too grave a measure to leave, unchecked, in the hands of King and Government. Looking at the issue in the light of Libya's rather special conditions—no lack of potentially critical issues, long distances, slow communications, and hence delays in assembling Parliament—the Commissioner realized that a practical way out had to be found. Valid arguments could be advanced on both sides. The solution finally reached was that the King would have the right to proclaim martial law and declare a state of emergency. At the same time he would have to present the proclamation of martial law—though not the one on a state of emergency—to Parliament, which would decide whether it would be maintained or repealed. If the proclamation were issued at a time when Parliament was not in session, Parliament must be urgently convened (Article 70).

One more controversial issue must be recorded because it provides a typical illustration of the main political dispute dividing the country. At the outset of the debate on the royal prerogatives it had been proposed that, before ascending the Throne, the King should take an oath before a joint session of the two chambers of Parliament, to the effect that he would observe the Constitution and the laws of the country and devote all his efforts to maintaining its independence and defending the safety of its territory. A Tripolitanian member proposed the addition of the words "and the preservation of national unity," in itself a perfectly innocuous and perhaps not entirely pointless completion of the oath. On the other side of the table, however, it was looked upon as a depreciation of federalism. The proposal was dropped.

D. THE MINISTERS
(Chapter VI of the Constitution)

The debate on the ministers was greatly facilitated by the fact that their position, functions, and responsibilities had, at least in part, already been discussed in connection with the royal prerogatives. One aspect of the question had, however, been left unresolved, namely the principle and the nature of ministerial responsibility to Parliament. In the event, this issue became the subject of heated debate from the moment it was raised in the Working Group, all through the Committee of Eighteen, until the time when it was finally settled by the NCAL itself. Its evolution is of interest.

The original draft that served as a basis for the discussion was that prepared by the legal adviser to the Cyrenaican delegation.

From the outset it had been unanimously agreed that no ministerial countersignature would be required when the King appointed or removed a Prime Minister, or accepted his resignation, thus making the Head of the Cabinet responsible to the Head of State.

This was indeed considered, in accordance with Arab tradition, to be one of the King's principal prerogatives. It was, moreover, looked upon as a condition for stable government. Other members, while not contesting the importance of governmental stability, argued, however, that the Council of Ministers collectively and individually, including the Prime Minister, should also be responsible to Parliament to ensure that the future State was established on a truly constitutional, parliamentary basis. They insisted in particular that royal decrees appointing ministers or relieving them from office should be countersigned by the Prime Minister. By the same token they proposed that the King's signature concerning the affairs of State must have the countersignature of the Prime Minister and of the competent ministers. This important principle was later to be incorporated in Article 85. No agreement could be reached on these issues, and several days were spent in vain negotiations behind the scenes. When the Working Group's meetings were resumed, some members were still of the opinion that in the appointment of ministers the power of the King should be paramount. Those in favor of a compromise considered, however, that a system of dual responsibility—the Prime Minister responsible to the King and the Cabinet as a whole responsible to Parliament—was the best solution for guaranteeing the stability of the State on the one hand and for satisfying the needs of parliamentary democracy on the other.

The United Nations legal adviser reminded the Working Group of the paragraph in the Commissioner's letter of 3 April based on the Council's advice of 13 March recommending the principle of ministerial responsibility to the lower chamber (cf. fn. 37 in this chapter). At the same time he suggested a parliamentary procedure to mitigate the possible harmful effects that ministerial responsibility might have under Libyan conditions, by introducing certain restrictive measures. A motion of censure would have to be signed by at least fifteen members of the House. A period of eight days would have to elapse from the day on which the motion was tabled before it could be discussed. This became known as the "cooling-off" period.

Again, two days would have to elapse between the discussion of the motion and the vote on it. In this way the Commissioner and his legal adviser hoped to make their suggestion more palatable to its opponents, but they succeeded only in part. A few members of the Working Group proposed an additional procedure providing that should the House of Representatives adopt a motion of censure, it must address a petition to the King requesting him to take such measures as he might deem useful. Only if the motion were twice reintroduced, that is, adopted three times in all, the King remaining passive, would the Cabinet or the relevant minister have to resign or be removed. Alternatively, the House might be dissolved. One more debate was devoted to the subject, and in the end the proposal was unanimously approved in a slightly different form, the principal change being that the King, instead of receiving a petition, would be informed by the House of the motion it had adopted. The result was still an unusual procedure, but at least it allowed the principle of ministerial responsibility to be introduced into the Constitution.

However, the Commissioner and his legal adviser, convinced that the approved procedure would in practice prove unworkable, continued to raise objections. Their arguments can best be summarized by quoting from the Commissioner's second annual report.

> The Working Group finally proposed that the principle of ministerial responsibility to the House of Representatives should be accepted. Nevertheless, in the case of a vote of no confidence in the Government, the House of Representatives was to inform the King that the Government no longer enjoyed its confidence. That procedure was to be repeated twice and only after the third vote of censure was the Government to resign. The Commissioner and his legal adviser drew the attention of the members of the Group to the disadvantage that such a system would oblige the King to intervene immediately a motion of censure was voted by the House and might create conflict between the King and the majority on each occasion. After attentively considering the merits of that argument, the Group changed its opinion and decided that the Ministers should be responsible to the House of Representatives, with the restriction that in the case of votes of censure a special majority of two-thirds of the members of the House of Representatives should be required. The Commissioner, however, advised the Group against this new formula, too, on the ground that the two-thirds majority required for a vote of censure might enable a Government that did not enjoy the confidence of the simple majority in the House of Representatives to stay in power. Such a situation would not only be contrary to the most ele-

mentary principles of the parliamentary system but it might also lead to the interruption of all governmental activities, since the simple majority could reject any legislative measure, including the vote on the budget. Nevertheless, the Working Group adopted the article in the form outlined above, a majority of the members fearing that if a motion of censure could be adopted by a simple majority, ministerial instability would ensue, with grave consequences for the future of a country which had only just espoused democracy.[39]

No other article on the ministers turned out to be as passionately controversial as that determining their responsibilities, which was finally submitted to the Committee of Eighteen for decision. However, a few others also touched on important aspects of ministerial status and functions.

It was decided, for instance, that "no non-Libyan may be a Minister" (later Article 81 of the Constitution), a restriction of considerable importance in the Arab world where, owing to community of language, religion, and custom, the interchangeability of political, civilian, and even military personnel is so much easier than between Western countries. The motive behind the article was admittedly the fear of foreign influence being exerted through nationals of other Arab countries, including Egyptians and Palestinian Arabs who, being stateless, might seek Libyan nationality; and, of course, fear of Italians who might have acquired Libyan nationality.

Another provident decision, later incorporated as Article 82, was that "no member of the Royal family may be a Minister," a stipulation inserted with the full consent of the King-Designate. It was one more indication of the latter's policy of not claiming more power than a correctly conceived and properly functioning constitutional monarchy should allow.

After considerable debate requiring a vote, it was decided that a minister might at the same time be a member of Parliament (Article 83).

On the proposal of the United Nations legal adviser, and without opposition, three more articles were added to the list in order to clarify certain situations and prevent possible abuses which, as experience teaches, may occur in any State, but tend to occur particularly in States that are still young in political and administrative experience. Thus, one article (Article 90 in the final text) determined a number of acts, functions, favors, and the like incompatible with ministerial office. It was a little too rigid in the light of Libyan conditions, but this was considered preferable to inadequate precaution. Another article (91) stipulated that the salaries of the Prime Minister and his colleagues should be determined by federal law, and a third article (92) provided for a federal law defining the civil and criminal re-

39. *Second Annual Report of the United Nations Commissioner in Libya,* para. 71.

sponsibilities of ministers with respect to offences committed by them in the exercise of their duties, and regulations as to how they should be charged and tried.

When the chapter on ministers was discussed in the Committee of Eighteen, all the articles passed without difficulty except the one on ministerial responsibility. The principle itself had by now been generally accepted, apparently with full recognition of its necessity. However, the Committee was deeply divided over the type of the majority—two-thirds or absolute—needed in the House for a vote of no confidence in the Council of Ministers or any of its members.

The record of the meeting contains a concise and accurate account of the various opinions expressed on this point:

> (xxvi) Article 87: Mr. Khalil Gellal explained the modification that had happened to it after consultations with Mr. Pelt and the legal adviser.
>
> The Hon. Member Mr. Munir Burshan turned the attention of the Committee to Mr. Pelt's recommendation which suggested that there should be an absolute majority of the House of Representatives instead of a two-thirds majority.
>
> The Hon. Member Mr. Abdel Gawad Freites followed him saying that he confirmed Mr. Pelt's advice in the case of a country which was mature and ready for the democratic system of government in all senses of the word, but as far as they were concerned since they were in the very early stages he said that he believed that Mr. Pelt's recommendation would probably not be good, but even harmful.
>
> Mr. Munir Burshan opposed him saying that his observation would be very worthy of approval if they were drafting their Constitution as they wished and as they pleased, but they were drafting a constitution which had to be offered to the United Nations Organisation which would examine it and compare it with such democratic systems as pleased them.
>
> The Hon. Member Mr. Abdul Majeed Ku'bar commented on that, saying that he confirmed the opinion of his colleague Mr. Burshan, and he added to it saying that they were drafting a constitution for future generations and for several centuries, and that therefore they could not consider the present draft as a base for the future of Libya from the point of view of maturity and progress, since it was not to be imagined that a patriot would attack a Ministry haphazardly or out of quarrelsomeness.
>
> Mr. Abdel Gawad said again that Mr. Pelt was fully conversant with their situation and that it was up to him to advise the United Nations

Organisation in that. But as regards what they had been so kind as to say, namely that there was no patriot who would attack a Ministry save on an understandable basis, the fact of the matter contradicted this in the majority of occasions. The President asked for a postponement of this Article until the meeting of the National Assembly so that they could consider it with the remainder of the other reservations.

Mr. Abdul Majeed suggested that the postponement of this should be mentioned in the resolution which would be sent by the President to the President of the National Assembly. His suggestion was accepted.[40]

This exchange of views gave the Commissioner and his legal adviser a good deal to ponder. Both were well aware of the responsibility they had taken upon themselves by pressing so persistently for the adoption of the principle of ministerial responsibility. Neither of them had any illusions that its application could not but run up against many obstacles, even setbacks. It might well take some generations before this principle could function as a well-oiled cogwheel in the parliamentary machinery. At the same time both were convinced that the political mentality and customs that are inseparable from the practice of ministerial responsibility provide perhaps the best schooling in the difficult art of parliamentary democracy. Furthermore, considering that the General Assembly, the Council for Libya, the NCAL, and the Libyan people themselves had apparently all presumed that Libya would be a democratically oriented State, a certain number of calculated risks had to be taken. Article 87 with its built-in safeguards covered one such risk. Moreover, it was a safeguard which the members of the NCAL instinctively seemed to want themselves. On the one hand they were attracted by the idea of living under a democratic system like their Egyptian neighbors; on the other, they realized only too well that their new liberty would have to be kept within bounds if it were not to destroy them.

The Commissioner had to consider what his own position would be when he had to give an account to the next session of the General Assembly of the United Nations of the way in which he had carried out his mission. The conflicting interests of the four great Powers had prevented them from reaching a settlement on the future of the strategically and politically vitally important space the war had left open on the southern shores of the Mediterranean Sea. The General Assembly, asked to find a solution to that problem, had decided that the gap should be filled by an independent State capable of occupying an otherwise dangerously unbalanced area. The new State had to be built with the materials available on the spot, by the in-

40. *Proc. NCAL,* Committee for the Constitution, Stewart-Jackson Translation, 23rd Meeting, 15 September 1951.

habitants themselves, according to their wishes. At the end of the war, Libya was the most backward of the five North African countries. Without unduly forcing the pace of its growth, it should be enabled to reach as soon as possible a level of development in harmony with that of its immediate neighbors. In this context, the form of its government might prove to be of considerable importance, not only from the national, but also from the international, point of view. Within the machinery conceived by the General Assembly, the Commissioner and his staff members were mere advisers. Were they giving the right kind of advice? This was the duty the Commissioner was answerable for, and as the end of his mission drew nearer, he himself, the Principal Secretary, the Legal Adviser, and other senior staff members and experts became more and more preoccupied by what answer they could give to that question. To argue that in the last instance the Libyan National Assembly and government would be responsible for their actions and decisions was not good enough, as that was not quite the way in which the General Assembly would look at it. As a whole, the Mission felt that it had done what it could within its terms of reference; but it also realized that on several points it might well be open to criticism. The question of ministerial responsibility, as it went unsolved to the NCAL, was one such point.

E. THE PARLIAMENT
(Chapter VII of the Constitution)

Although certain aspects of the basic organization, such as the general competence and procedure, of a federal, bicameral, parliamentary system had already been agreed upon during the first half of 1951, it was only toward the end of June of that year that the Working Group started to draft a comprehensive chapter on this knotty subject. Knotty, because it was in this chapter that the still much-contested federal structure of the State—which was not always clearly understood, even by its warmest supporters—would have to be spelled out in black and white.

The United Nations legal adviser had prepared a draft to serve as a basis for discussion, a draft inspired in part by those federal constitutions which the members of the Working Group had already studied and in part by precedents created by Arab constitutions with regard to the composition and functioning of the two chambers.

Started in June and finished in September, the articles relating to Parliament proved to be the most complicated section of the Constitution, giving rise to the largest number of controversial issues. Draft articles were transmitted from the Working Group to the Committee of Eighteen and vice versa time after time before a compromise could be reached. On no other subject were the Commissioner and the Legal Adviser asked so frequently for advice; on no other topic did they so often consider it their duty to tender advice on their own initiative. This was particularly so with regard to the House of Representatives, which was a type of institution unfamiliar to most members of the NCAL. A few older Libyans, for instance Omar Shenib, had been members of the Parliament in Constantinople at the time of the Young Turks in the first decade of the twentieth century. Other elders had been members of advisory councils in the vilayets of the Turkish Administration, and a somewhat younger generation had sat on the equally advisory municipal councils under the Italian Administration of Tripolitania. Others had gained experience in the administration of the Senussi Zawiyas. But none had been prepared for the kind of approach normally required in drawing up the constitutional provisions for a representative lower chamber. Fortunately, their common sense and marked political feeling for compromise to a large extent compensated for their lack of knowledge and experience. By tradition they were more familiar with a body of elders like the Senate, since it basically dealt with matters of provincial representation, though as a federal organ it was a novelty.

The Senate

In discussions concerning the Senate, it soon appeared that the principal point on which opinions were divided was whether members of the upper chamber were to be elected or appointed. In his letter of April, the Commissioner had recommended that provision be made in the Libyan Constitution for the possibility of enabling the Crown to appoint a limited number of members of the upper chamber. He had added that in order to safeguard the principles of democracy, it would seem preferable to constitute the upper chamber in major part of elected members, so that the appointed members would always be in the minority.[41]

The Legal Adviser had translated this recommendation into constitutional language by inserting in his draft the following article:

> The King appoints half or two-fifths of the members amongst those who enjoy the confidence of the people and who in the past have distinguished themselves in the service of the State and the country. The local legislative Councils in each province will elect the other members in conformity with the electoral law.[42]

41. *Second Annual Report of the United Nations Commissioner in Libya,* Annex IV, pp. 77–80.

42. Loutfi Papers.

As an alternative, he proposed the following briefer text:

> The King appoints the Senators amongst those who enjoy the confidence of the people and who have distinguished themselves in the past in the service of state and country.[43]

It will be noted that both drafts left open for discussion the most sensitive issues: whether the majority would be elected or appointed; whether all members should be appointed or elected; whether the local councils or the people should be consulted; and—a consideration of great importance—whether such election should be governed by a federal or local law.

In the course of the opening discussion in the Working Group, it became clear that the Cyrenaican delegation was in favor of a Senate wholly appointed by the King. The Tripolitanians took a more moderate line by suggesting a Senate composed of an elected majority, the remaining seats to be filled by royal appointment. The Fezzanese said that they needed more time to study the problem. Questions such as whether the Royal Decree appointing a Senator would require the countersignature of the Prime Minister, of the Minister of the Interior, or of both, were not raised at this stage. It soon became obvious that the Group first wanted political advice from its parent body. Hence, the issue was referred to the Committee of Eighteen.

When the Committee embarked upon its first reading of the chapter on Parliament, a discussion ensued which clearly demonstrated the differences at stake. After a few members had pointed out that senatorial elections would be held in accordance with electoral laws varying from one province to another, the following exchange took place, according to the minutes:

> Then the Hon. Member Mr. Abdul Gawad Freites arose and opposed the principle of forming the Senate by the two methods of election and appointment. He began to point out the preferability of the principle of appointment for all of the elders. Both the Hon. Members Mr. Mohamed al Mansouri and Mr. Mohammed Rahim supported him in this saying that those who were respectable and were of distinguished personality were above the pushing and shoving which took place in electoral battles, and would be averse to exposing themselves to the commotion and currents of party politics. They contended that they would keep far away from the din and clamour of the propaganda merchants in due consideration of their nobility and that they would disdain to expose themselves to the sallies of the fools who assist those who compete in electoral districts. The Hon. Member Mr. Munir Burshan opposed him saying that

43. Ibid.

> they had decided that sovereignty should be with the nation, and that this sovereignty should be exercised through election since their Law was on the most modern pattern and was a draft for the life of the nation which would extend through several generations and that there were those before them who were waiting to attack that Constitution of theirs. He was therefore of the opinion that election of half the Senate was necessary to avoid any attack which could be launched against them by someone who was looking for weakness. The Hon. Member Abou Baker ben Ahmad was of the same opinion as Mr. Munir Burshan. The Hon. Member Mr. Abdul Majeed Ku'bar followed them saying that the 3rd Article was quite frank and open in giving the King the right of choosing those who were capable of holding office without recourse to the currents of party politics, provided that the other half were elected by the Legislative Councils. He said that therefore there was not the least fear in this case of a lack of suitability in those who were elected. The Hon. Member Mr. Khalil Gellal replied saying that the Legislative Assemblies were the ones which would be elected and that they should none of them forget that nomination for them was popular. After considerable scrutiny of the various points of view and reference to what had been in Mr. Pelt's letter, the majority were of the opinion that appointment was preferable to election.[44]

The debate continued for a while along the same lines. The Commissioner's suggestion in favor of an elected majority found little support, let alone his original proposal for a fully elected Senate; and in view of the prevailing antagonism, it was perhaps better that way. The Committee, feeling that no consensus appeared possible at the moment, agreed to put a decision off until later. Virtually the matter was returned to the Working Group, where, meanwhile, the fifty-fifty solution had been making headway in the minds of members, partly thanks to numerous discussions behind the scenes with the King-Designate and with the Commissioner, as well as among the members themselves. However, to give practical effect to this solution, one particular difficulty had to be overcome. In the course of earlier deliberations, the Group, discussing the numbers of Senators, had fixed it at twenty-one (seven per province), defeating a minority which, for reasons of economy, had been in favor of eighteen. Considering that the compromise solution for the appointment issue required an even number, the debate on the size of the Senate was reopened. The final decision was

44. *Proc. NCAL,* Committee for the Constitution, Stewart-Jackson Translation, 16th Meeting, 31 July 1951.

in favor of twenty-four (eight per province, four to be appointed by the King, four to be elected by the local legislative councils). It was recommended, moreover, that the President of the Senate be appointed by the King, that the two Vice-Presidents be elected, and that the result of this election be subject to the King's approval. Thus the possibility was created of having all three provinces represented among the officers of the Senate.

During the final revision of the draft Constitution in August-September, the Working Group realized that the fifty-fifty solution for the composition of the Senate required the consideration of a few more unsolved problems. One was that under the system adopted the qualifications for appointed and elected Senators would almost certainly differ, not only between the two categories, but also from province to province. Another was that, except for matters such as age of eligibility, general qualifications for members of the two chambers ought to be identical. This question arose with regard to the conditions under which a member of Parliament might forfeit his membership. It had therefore been agreed that these conditions should be determined by federal electoral law, the necessity for which had, meanwhile, been recognized, after much discussion, in connection with the organization of the House of Representatives—a subject that is dealt with later in this section. In fact, the Group had found in the course of its work that, although dealing with each chamber separately, it could not avoid making provisions common to both. The result was that in the end Chapter VII of the Constitution was subdivided into three parts: Part I, the Senate; Part II, the House of Representatives; Part III, Provisions Common to the Two Chambers. This last part went a long way toward making conditions of membership uniform for the two chambers, while also regulating their respective competence and relationship.

The chain of events just described was a good example of an outcome more and more often experienced by the NCAL, namely, that a policy-decision system has a series of logical consequences. This was a phenomenon that members of the NCAL had not foreseen. At the very outset of its labors, the NCAL had adopted federalism as the fundamental principle for the form of State. When federalism had to be translated into constitutional articles and chapters, it required more consistency, and hence more centralization, than its Cyrenaican proponents in particular had expected. The organization of the House of Representatives forced the NCAL even further in this direction. The opponents of federalism remained dissatisfied, but even they, at least the more moderate among them, had to recognize that the Libyan State was going to be a less loose structure than they had feared. The two Administering Powers also did not fail to note what was happening, and it was at about this time that a senior British official, in conversation with the Commissioner, expressed the hope that centralization would not go much further.

Along with a number of questions of lesser importance, the issue of appointed versus elected senators continued to agitate the legislators. By the end of August the Working Group's compromise of a half-appointed, half-elected Senate had not yet been approved by the Committee of Eighteen, where the Cyrenaican members still opposed it. Moreover, an obstacle of timing had arisen with regard to the elected half of the first Senate: in late 1951 or early 1952, would all three provinces have elected legislative councils competent to elect their respective senators? Nothing was more unlikely.

It was against this background that during the twenty-first meeting of the Committee of Eighteen, on 27 August, a Tripolitanian member asked how long it would take to establish the first Senate and how long its term of office would last, proposing that if the Senate were to be appointed, the terms of office should be halved. This was related to a proposal previously adopted in the Working Group that the term of office be eight years and that half the members be replaced every four years. The Cyrenaicans then accepted a compromise providing that the King would appoint all members of the first Senate for four years, after which the elective provisions for half the Senate would enter into force. This was a statesmanlike solution, although it was not perfect and did not satisfy everybody. The Fezzanese delegation, which did not like the idea of having the first Senate wholly appointed by the King, asked for the following reservation to be entered in the record.

> Half the Senate shall be elected and the other half appointed, or at least if election should prove impossible His Majesty the King should appoint one half and the Governors of the provinces appoint the remaining half.[45]

This incident proved once again that in the Libya of those days, provincialism would creep in where it could not boldly tread.

The House of Representatives

The history of the provisions for a lower chamber, and of how in a few months' time the subject evolved from a state of confusion, involves an even more complicated but also more fascinating narrative than that concerning the Senate. It is more necessary than ever to limit this part of the story to the essential issues. That these were the more controversial ones goes without saying.

45. *Proc. NCAL,* Committee for the Constitution, Stewart-Jackson Translation, 21st Meeting, 27 August 1951.

When the Working Group turned to the study of the mode of composition of the lower chamber, by election or by appointment of its members, and by whom, it soon appeared that this issue was going to be the main source of controversy, exactly as it had been in the case of the Senate, and for similar reasons.

Once again the United Nations legal adviser had submitted a carefully prepared draft, taking into account the known differences of opinion, but at the same time taking care to ensure consistency with the Commissioner's statement before the General Assembly (cf. pp. 363–65) and the Council for Libya's advice of 13 March 1951; the Lower Chamber should be elected on the basis of universal and proportional suffrage so as to represent the whole of the Libyan people.[46]

The first reaction of the members of the Working Group was to propose that the members of the House of Representatives should be elected for four years by each provincial legislative council from among its own members, whether elected or appointed, in the ratio of one member to every 20,000 inhabitants and with a minimum of five members per territory. This last stipulation was the result of a demand by the delegation of the Fezzan which feared that Fezzanese representation in the House would otherwise be too feeble. The Commissioner and his legal adviser pointed out that a chamber which had been chosen in that way would, in fact, represent the provinces. The Working Group considered, however, that this objection could be overcome by adopting another article of the Legal Adviser's draft which declared that each member of Parliament represented the people as a whole. This, of course, was inconsistent with the system of locally elected deputies and no solution to the problem. During a large part of a hot Ramadan night, lively discussions went on at the Commissioner's residence. The rather disappointing result was that the next morning, when the Working Group met again, the previous day's decision was formulated:

> The local Legislative Assemblies shall elect from among their own members, who will be elected in accordance with their local electoral laws, the members of the House of Representatives.[47]

Still, on one point at least some progress had been made: for it was emphasized that the choice of federal legislators should be made from among the *elected* members of the local assemblies. Hence by implication

46. See GAOR: Fifth Session, 1950, 306th Plenary Meeting, 16 November 1950, pp. 411–12; and *Second Annual Report of the United Nations Commissioner in Libya,* Annex IV, pp. 77–80.

47. Minutes of the Working Group of the Committee for the Constitution of the NCAL. United Nations Archives. Typescript.

appointed members of the assemblies would not be eligible for election to the lower chamber.

At this stage the Working Group was forced to interrupt its work for more than a fortnight, as some of its members had been invited to participate in the meetings of the Coordination Committee.

This interval gave the Commissioner a welcome opportunity to examine the several unresolved constitutional problems in a quieter and more thoroughgoing manner than had been possible for some time. A visit to Benghazi, with the Legal Adviser, proved particularly helpful and did not fail to have a constructive effect on the deliberations of the Working Group. At the Group's next meeting a revised text was approved:

> Each province shall elect its Deputies to the Federal House of Representatives by universal suffrage, in accordance with the electoral law of the Province.[48]

Subsequently this text was confirmed by the Committee of Eighteen.

The Commissioner, however, continued to argue that certain disadvantages were still inherent in that solution. In his second annual report he recorded his objections:

> Instead of having a single Federal electoral law throughout Libya for the organization and regulation of elections, there would be three probably different laws. Furthermore, the lower Chamber would not really represent the Libyan people as a whole, in accordance with the spirit usually underlying a federal Constitution, but, rather, each of the Provinces separately. On several occasions, therefore, the United Nations Commissioner and the Legal Adviser tried to persuade the members of the Working Group and the Committee on the Constitution once again to change their opinions on this fundamental issue.[49]

Once more the matter was debated at a series of private meetings. From the records it is not quite clear at exactly what moment the idea of a federal law for the election of the House of Representatives began to supplant the concept of using provincial laws, but it must have been early in August. At first sight it looks as if the suggestion of a federal electoral law was made rather for reasons of expediency than out of conviction that in a federal system the lower chamber must be elected by the people as a whole in order to balance the Senate representing the provinces. However, this impression is only partly correct. The Tripolitanians, realizing that a popularly elected

48. Ibid.; and *Second Annual Report of the United Nations Commissioner in Libya,* para. 75.

49. *Second Annual Report,* ibid.

lower chamber would represent a unifying force, were genuinely in favor of a federal electoral law. But when the Cyrenaicans reluctantly came round to the Tripolitanian point of view, they did so for very different reasons.

It so happened that by the middle of August the Working Group was discussing the transitory dispositions of the draft Constitution (later Chapter XII, "Transitory and Provisional Provisions"). By that time, implementation of the program of constitutional development had reached a critical stage. Four and a half months were left if independence was to be proclaimed not later than 1 January 1952. It was beginning to dawn upon all concerned that if, before independence could come about, the Constitution had to be voted and promulgated, federal elections organized, a Parliament elected, the Constitution approved or amended, and the Provisional Federal Government replaced by a "duly constituted Libyan Government," more time would be required. The possibility of putting back the date of independence nobody would admit. Hence, some shortcut, legally satisfactory and politically defensible, would have to be found. One of the most time-consuming operations would be the preparation and holding of the elections for the lower chamber, particularly if this had to be done under three differing provincial electoral laws, all yet to be written by three legislative councils all yet to be elected. Under the pressure generated by this time factor, the concept of a federal electoral law rapidly gained ground. However, so strong was the opposition to this solution, particularly from the Cyrenaicans, that a suggestion was tabled by them that only the first House of Representatives should be elected on a federal law basis; for future elections the principle, already included in the draft Constitution, of allowing each province to elect its own representatives should be maintained. The United Nations legal adviser, when consulted, supported the Tripolitanian point of view. Once more the matter had to be taken to Benghazi, and it was only on 15 September that the Committee of Eighteen, without debate, approved the compromise recommended by the Working Group. The record merely states laconically, with regard to Articles 100 and 101: "Mr. Khalil Gallal explained the simple modification which had been introduced into them." [50] The modification consisted of making Article 100 read as follows:

> The House of Representatives shall consist of members elected in the three Provinces in accordance with the provisions of a federal electoral law.[51]

50. *Proc. NCAL,* Committee for the Constitution, Stewart-Jackson Translation, 23rd Meeting, 15 September 1951.

51. *Second Annual Report of the United Nations Commissioner in Libya,* p. 75.

Article 101 provided that:

> The number of Deputies shall be determined on the basis of one for every twenty thousand inhabitants or fraction of that number exceeding half, provided that the number of Deputies in any of the three Provinces shall not be less than five.[52]

Since Article 101 only fixed a proportion, it was necessary to insert a provisional Article 206 in Chapter XII, "Transitory and Provisional Provisions":

> In the first elections to the House of Representatives and until a census of the Libyan people has been made, the Province of Cyrenaica shall have fifteen Deputies; the Province of Tripolitania thirty-five Deputies; and the Province of the Fezzan five Deputies.[53]

Other transitory and provisional provisions affecting the House of Representatives were:

> *Article 204,* determining that the Provisional Federal Government would draw up the first electoral law for Parliament to be approved by the National Assembly and to be promulgated within a period of thirty days from the date of promulgation of the Constitution;

and,

> *Article 205,* making it obligatory to hold the first elections to the lower house within a period of three and a half months from the date upon which the electoral law was promulgated.

A remnant of provincialism in the electoral domain, proposed by Sir Harry Trusted, was that a voter for the lower chamber must be inscribed on one of the electoral rolls of the province in which he resides (Article 103 [2]). Apart from the fact that the text is not clear as to the number of rolls in each province, it implies that there is no federal electoral roll.

In comparing the provisions for the two chambers, there are a few more points to be noted. One is that a member of the Royal Family may be appointed to the Senate but may not be elected to it (Article 96), whereas a member of the Royal Family may not be elected a member of the House of Representatives (Article 103 [3]). A wise measure.

Articles 106 and 107 are also noteworthy since both are meant to protect the lower chamber against the danger of possible arbitrary policies of the Executive. The first prevents successive parliaments being dissolved on account of the same issue, while the second makes it imperative, after

52. See Annex II, p. 912.
53. Ibid., p. 920.

dissolution of the House of Representatives, to elect within three months a new chamber, which would then have to meet within twenty days.[54]

The minimum age of senators (40 Gregorian) and voters (21 Gregorian) did not give rise to much discussion, but the minimum for deputies provoked a lively debate—so much the more remarkable in that the most progressive point of view was defended by the representatives of the reputedly most backward province.

The United Nations legal adviser had suggested that a deputy must be at least twenty-five years of age, to which the Working Group had agreed. A majority in the Committee of Eighteen decided to raise the age to thirty. The members from the Fezzan held to the opinion that the age of twenty-five was to be preferred. The minutes of the Committee's sixteenth meeting read:

> The Article concerning the age of a deputy: The Committee confirmed it with a simple modification and that was the raising of the age of a deputy to 30, notwithstanding the Hon. Members of Fezzan who held to the opinion that the Article should remain as it was without modification. Mr. Abdul Gawad Freites demanded that those who required the age of a deputy to be reduced from 30 years to make their point of view clear. The Hon. Member Abou Baker ben Ahmad arose and said that the young men of the day were more mature in knowledge and education than the elders, because these others had lived in an atmosphere of imperialism and ignorance, and also because of the facilities for education and study for one group of young people rather than another. Mr. Burshan followed him and said that he should not forget that both experience and wordly wisdom had a great effect on thought and that study had no meaning if it were not accompanied by practice and experience: and that therefore he was of the opinion that the age of 30 would herald maturity and steadiness, and that these two things were the things most necessary in a deputy. After a discussion the modification was thrown open to the vote. 9 votes were cast for it, 5 votes against it, and one member abstained from voting.[55]

In fact, the significance of this vote was political. The fixing of the minimum age at thirty meant that the younger members of parties like the former Omar Mukhtar Club in Cyrenaica and the National Congress Party in Tripolitania would be precluded from entering Parliament for some years to come.

54. For full text of these Articles see ibid., p. 913.

55. *Proc. NCAL,* Committee for the Constitution, Stewart-Jackson Translation, 16th Meeting, 31 July 1951.

Provisions Common to the Two Chambers,
including Chapter IX of the Constitution (Federal Finance)

Of the three parts composing Chapter VII (Parliament), the third part containing the provisions common to the two chambers was by far the longest and most detailed. This was in part because, with the exception of a few important provisions like those relating to the budget and to ministerial responsibility, the legislative competence of the two houses was very much alike; and in part also because a considerable number of articles of a procedural nature were included. Thus Part I (Senate) contains only six Articles and Part II (House of Representatives) eight, whereas Part III has thirty-three.

The vast majority of these have been borrowed from other constitutions and have no special significance, but some unusual provisions demand attention. The most important of these is Article 136 concerning the sanctioning and promulgation of laws, the substance of which has already been examined in connection with the Royal prerogatives. Procedurally, the key point in this article is the regulation governing voting. Originally the Working Group had proposed that, whereas in the first instance a law should be voted in each chamber by simple majority, it should require an absolute majority after having been reconsidered at the King's request. Subsequently it was suggested that the second vote should be taken by a two-thirds majority. Members taking an opposing view argued that this proposal virtually transformed the King's right to sanction and promulgate the laws (Article 62) into a suspensive veto—an objection supported by the Commissioner. The debate was long and arduous, but finally the fear that an as yet inexperienced Parliament might be inclined to vote excessive legislative measures prevailed, and the two-thirds majority rule was approved.

Another important subject is dealt with in Article 138, which lays down the principle that the right to initiate laws shall be vested in the King, the Senate, and the House of Representatives. At the outset of the discussions on this fundamental issue of parliamentary democracy, opinions were wide apart. It was understood, however, that the King would exercise his power through his ministers, and that the responsibility would rest with them (Article 60). Thus the effect of Article 138 was balanced by the mechanism of ministerial responsibility, regulated by Articles 84–87. While these procedures applied to both chambers, it will be remembered that, in accordance with advice given by the Commissioner and the Council for Libya, the House of Representatives was to be given priority in matters of a budgetary and fiscal nature. This made it necessary to insert in Article 138 the words: "except when they concern the budget or the imposing of new taxes or the modification of taxes or exemption or part exception from taxes or their abolition, when the right to initiate such laws shall be vested in the King and the House of Representatives."

Budgetary and fiscal procedures are further covered in the Constitution under Chapter IX, "Federal Finance" (cf. pp. 604–07), from which it results that, notwithstanding the greater authority enjoyed by the lower chamber, the Senate is not without influence in these matters. Although Article 160 stipulates that the budget "shall be discussed and approved in the first instance by the House of Representatives," Article 171 lays down that "any dispute between the Senate and the House of Representatives concerning the approval of a head of the budget shall be settled by a decision taken by an absolute majority of the two Chambers meeting in Congress." Thus the Constitution grants the Senate the right to say its word on behalf of the provinces in federal financial matters; but, with the numerical difference in membership, the lower chamber remains the decisive authority.

Chapter IX of the Constitution is almost entirely based on proposals formulated by United Nations financial experts collaborating with some of their British professional colleagues on the Provisional Libyan Government staff and in the Tripolitanian Administration. Apart from a few political issues already referred to elsewhere in this study, the chapter deals mainly with questions of federal budgetary and financial administration. Both the Working Group and the Committee of Eighteen agreed with these proposals except on the thorny problem of customs revenues, which, as we have seen, continued to plague the NCAL almost to the last day of its work on the Constitution. The final decision was taken only in October in Benghazi and will be referred to in the next chapter.

Two more rights that members of the two chambers have in common must be mentioned here: to address questions and interpellations to ministers (Article 122); and to investigate specific questions within the competence of each chamber (Article 123).

Both articles, in particular the second one, caused some lively exchanges. Several members feared that the exercise of these rights would belittle the authority of ministers, or even that of the Government as a whole, in the eyes of the public. The right to raise an interpellation therefore is qualified by the requirement that at least eight days must pass between the tabling of a question and its discussion, except in cases of emergency and then only with the consent of the person addressed.

Parliament's right to investigate specific questions in accordance with the rules of procedure of each chamber caused a deadlock within the Working Group, which finally referred the issue to the Committee of Eighteen. Some members were opposed because it would reduce the authority of ministers.

Others considered that Parliament would be unable to do its duty of controlling the Executive without having the right to investigate the latter's actions. However, following a series of private discussions, by the time the Committee of Eighteen took them up they had ceased to be controversial and were approved without further debate.

F. THE JUDICIARY
(Chapter VIII of the Constitution)
(Federal Supreme Court)

When, in the second half of July, the Working Group started to draft the chapter of the Constitution relating to the judiciary, it followed its by then well established practice of first studying a number of foreign constitutions that might serve as models or examples. In this particular case the federal constitutions chosen were those of Argentina, Australia, Brazil, and India. After an initial examination, the members of the Group decided to invite the legal adviser of the Cyrenaican delegation to prepare a draft for purposes of discussion, to be based on these four texts, paying particular attention to the Indian Constitution. (The United Nations adviser was on leave at the time.)

From the outset it was recognized that Libya would need a Supreme Court. It was also realized that the country, being poor in lawyers possessing the qualifications appropriate to a Supreme Court judge—with the exception of Koranic law—would for some considerable time have to depend upon judges of foreign nationality. Hence, one of the first questions that arose in the discussions was the method of appointing judges. It was considered natural that they should be appointed by the King, subject to due process of ministerial responsibility, which at that time had not yet been approved. It also was virtually understood, though somewhat prematurely, that the President of the Court, starting with the first one, would always be of Libyan nationality. Following this line of thought, it became a major question whether the King, before filling a vacancy on the Supreme Bench, should consult the President alone or the Court as a whole. After much discussion it was agreed that only the President of the Court should be consulted, the principal argument for this decision being that consultation of the full Court would in all likelihood cause divided counsels leading to a recommendation approved by majority vote.

With regard to the retiring age of judges, the Working Group considered, contrary to what was proposed in the Cyrenaican draft, that in view of the Libyan climate and way of living, sixty-five was to be preferred to seventy (Gregorian). Perhaps it is not going too far to assume that in the more intimate discussions of the Working Group the consideration that a lower age of retirement would be instrumental in speeding up the gradual Libyanization of the Court carried a good deal of weight.

A much more important question was that of the permanent tenure for members of the Supreme Court and the procedure to be followed in the exceptional case where a judge had to be impeached because of proven misbehavior or incapacity. The Cyrenaican draft proposed that the procedure for investigating such a case would be regulated by federal law. Where the investigation led to proof of guilt, it would be for the two chambers of Parliament to recommend by a majority of not less than two-thirds of the members present and voting that the judge in question be removed by Royal Decree.

In the eyes of the Working Group it was not in harmony with Oriental concepts of propriety that cases of such a delicate nature should be treated by Parliament. Hence it adopted a text which, with some slight drafting changes, became Article 147 of the Constitution, reading as follows:

> The President and judges of the Court may not be removed from office; nevertheless, if it appears that for reasons of health, or because he has lost the confidence or respect which his office requires, one of them can no longer exercise his functions, the King, with the approval of the majority of the members of the Court, excluding the member concerned, shall relieve him of his office.[56]

Several other articles, some of them regulating highly important matters, were approved practically without discussion.

One of them, the future Article 152, granted the King the right to refer important constitutional and legislative questions to the Supreme Court for an opinion. The article further stipulated that "the Court shall examine such questions and inform the King of its opinion taking into account the provisions of this Constitution." This appeared a most useful provision in a young country where the Crown, ruling over a complicated federal structure and having but little experience of federal and democratic procedures, might frequently find itself confronted with delicate issues of a legal nature, possibly holding political implications and repercussions.

This was particularly so in view of the preceding (151) and the succeeding (153) articles. Article 151 introduced Libyans to the completely novel concept for them that "The Supreme Court exclusively shall be competent to hear disputes which may arise between the Federal Government and one or more Provinces or between two or more Provinces." Under both Turkish

56. For text of the Articles on the Judiciary, see Annex II, pp. 916–17.

and Italian rule, public disputes had been settled by administrative decision, except, of course, for litigation subject to Koranic law. It might be supposed that in the new Libya many disputes of a political nature would be settled by the personal intervention of the King; but under the new Constitution legal disputes of a nature as yet unforeseen would, no doubt, arise. That such disputes should be judged and settled by a juridical body with nationwide competence was an idea to which the Libyan people would only in time get accustomed.

Article 153 introduced yet another legal concept new to Libyans by stipulating that:

> An appeal may be lodged with the Supreme Court, in accordance with the provisions of the federal law, against any judgment by a provincial court in civil or criminal proceedings if such judgment included a decision in a dispute concerning this Constitution or the interpretation thereof.[57]

Article 154 went on to prescribe that the kinds of cases in which an appeal could be lodged would be determined by a federal law.

So far the discussions in the Working Group had been difficult enough; yet the members, conscious of the country's need for a tribunal acting in the dual capacity of a High Court of Appeal in civil and criminal cases and of a Supreme Bench in constitutional disputes, had nevertheless been able to reach agreement in the best interest of national unity.

A major snag arose, however, when the Working Group reached a draft proposal to the effect that rulings of the Supreme Court would be binding on all Courts within the United Kingdom of Libya. In the eyes of the proponents of provincial autonomy, this went too far. Two opinions were expressed. One, advanced by the majority, held that the Supreme Court's jurisprudence should be binding on the provincial courts only in cases when an interpretation of the Constitution was involved, the members concerned feeling that the provincial tribunals should have jurisdiction in all other cases. A minority maintained that the binding authority of the Supreme Court's jurisprudence over the provincial courts should be all-inclusive, so as to promote the development of a nationwide body of juridical doctrine both in civil and in criminal law. The majority opinion carried the day, but, before completing their first reading of the articles on the judiciary, the Working Group decided to add one new provision (Article 157) making it possible by federal law to confer other functions on the Supreme Court, as long as they were not contrary to the provisions of the Constitution. In this way the competence of the Court could be broadened if need arose.

57. Ibid.

One week later, early in September, it was the turn of the Committee of Eighteen to examine the draft provisions on the judiciary. Once more the age limit for judges was debated; retirement at sixty-five was generally preferred to retirement at seventy. The remaining articles were left virtually unchanged, though their order of presentation was slightly rearranged. When, however, the Committee came to discuss the binding nature of the Supreme Court's jurisdiction, opinions were divided along the same lines and just as deeply as in the Working Group. It was decided to defer a decision to a later meeting in order to allow more time for reflection, but during the interval the conflicting opinions hardened rather than softened. In these circumstances it was agreed to return the question to the Working Group after one member had formulated two drafts between which, in his opinion, a choice had to be made. According to the first, the article would read: "With regard to the interpretation of this Constitution, the legal principles embodied in the decisions of the Supreme Court shall be binding on all Courts within the United Kingdom of Libya." [58]

In the second version the article would simply read: "The legal principles embodied in the decisions of the Supreme Court shall be binding on all Courts within the United Kingdom of Libya," leaving out the reference to the interpretation of the Constitution.[59]

When it became clear that the Working Group could not agree any more than could the Committee, the United Nations and British legal advisers jointly proposed that the words "with regard to the interpretation of this Constitution" be deleted from the first draft above. The Working Group agreed, and so subsequently, did the Committee.

In fact this was a happy compromise, since by limiting the reference to "the legal principles," those resulting from interpretations of the Constitution by the Supreme Court were neither expressly included nor expressly excluded from the decisions binding on the lower courts. Hence, the latter remained free to decide whether or not to take into consideration in their judgments the Supreme Court's interpretations of the Constitution.

G. THE PROVINCES
(Chapter X of the Constitution)

It will be remembered that when, at one of the early meetings of the Working Group, a decision had to be taken on a subject that was to become the cornerstone of the future constitutional structure, the majority was in

58. Minutes of the Working Group of the Committee for the Constitution of the NCAL. United Nations Archives. Typescript.

59. Ibid.

favor of drawing up a list of federal powers, all residual powers being left within the competence of the provinces; the minority would have preferred to start the other way round (see pp. 521–36). Considering that the majority consisted of federalists while the minority was made up of supporters of a unitary form of State, one wonders, in retrospect, what the motives of each side could have been. The author cannot remember having seen or heard them clearly articulated; nor do the records of the three NCAL orgaus or his own papers do much to clarify the arguments for or against one or the other system. No doubt the study of certain foreign constitutions played a part, but in the minds of members, homebred political considerations must have held sway. It is a fair guess, in all the circumstances, that the majority of federalists must have been convinced that by first drawing up a limited list of federal powers they could best serve the cause of provincial autonomy. It is an equally fair guess that when the unitarists in the NCAL bodies accepted the majority system, without putting up much of a fight, they must have felt that their case would be strengthened by first drawing up the longest possible list of federal powers they could obtain. Looking back, it appears that there was a good deal of political shrewdness in both positions, insofar as the system preferred by each party permitted them together to reach a compromise by first drawing up a single list of federal powers, and subsequently splitting it up into two parts: the powers of the federal government; and joint powers. The whole was followed by a short chapter (IV) on general federal powers.

How much more difficult, both politically and constitutionally, it would have been to reach the same or an equivalent result if at the beginning of the discussions there had been a list of provincial powers obliging the provinces to make concessions to the federation. A most helpful circumstance in this respect was that the supporters of the unitary State outside the NCAL never showed much of a preference for one method of discussion or the other. Their leaders realized only too well that their chances of opposing the NCAL as such would have been considerably lessened had they become involved in the detailed issues attendant upon the distribution of powers. The system originally chosen also had a practical advantage in that it did not make it necessary to specify the "residual" powers left to the provinces. It was appreciated, of course, that a system of this kind might occasionally give rise to difficulties of constitutional interpretation as well as to administrative clashes, but that was one of the reasons why provision had been made for a Supreme Court.

The outcome of this approach to the problem was that when, at the end of July, the Working Group started drafting the chapter on the provinces it asked the United Nations legal adviser to prepare for it a simple text limited to matters of local interest and organization. Indeed, the main aspects of the relationship between the federation and the provinces had already been settled ad hoc, or were on the way to being settled in the chapters dealing with general provisions (Chapter XI) or transitory and provisional provisions (Chapter XII) in the Constitution. Hence the first article (176) of Chapter X merely states that "the Provinces shall exercise all powers which have not been assigned to the Federal Government under the provisions of this Constitution." Admittedly the time factor, too, was playing a part; there simply was no time left to start organizing in detail the internal constitutional and administrative structures of the provinces. What existed in this sector had been established by the Administering Powers and was in good part a residue of Italian procedures; it was not always to the satisfaction of the local people but was good enough to last until independence and for some time thereafter.

Last but not least, the Commissioner could not fail to perceive that at the back of the minds of even his closest Libyan friends there was a growing and perfectly understandable desire to see him and the Council, and above all the British and the French Administrators, out of the country by the appointed time. Thereafter, the Libyans would be free to settle among themselves what remained to be settled—in particular what was still closest to their hearts, namely, their provincial affairs.

Whether this state of mind was in the best national interest is still an open question to many observers of the Libyan scene, including the author. From a perfectionist point of view, there was much to be said for prolonging the transitory period so that all the loose ends in the rigging of the new ship of state could be made fast. However, such a course was out of the question. Nobody would have stood for it, and in any case it would have been in flat contradiction with the Commissioner's own principle of leaving to the Libyan people as much responsibility as possible. Moreover, there was the categoric prescription that independence would become effective *not later than* 1 January 1952. The idea of putting independence off until 1 January 1953, although sometimes discussed in private, remained theoretical. Even when, after independence, foreseeable difficulties arose as a result of unfinished business, they were not such as would have justified a delay, to the writer's way of thinking.

This is by no means to say that when the Working Group got down to the essence of the problem the internal organization of the provinces proved as simple as many Libyans had expected. In first and second reading everything went smoothly. The article, later to become Article 178 in the Constitution, expressing a basic federal concept, failed to provoke debate, even though it stated: "the Provinces shall be bound to observe the provisions of this Constitution and to enforce the federal law in the manner prescribed in this Constitution." Thus it deliberately confirmed the understanding, more solemnly stated in the Preamble, that the provinces, of their own free will and as equals, had entered into a Union called the United Kingdom of Libya.

Then the Fezzanese delegation entered a reservation to the effect that the Provincial Governor, or *Wali* as his title would be, appointed by the King, should always be chosen from among the people of his province. This proposal was opposed on two grounds; first, that it would reduce the royal powers; and second, that a local man would not necessarily be a better Wali than a candidate selected by the King from another province for his personal qualities. After a long discussion, the Fezzanese delegation, defeated but not convinced, and obviously having in mind the feelings of those in their distant territory where a "foreigner" would not be easily accepted as the highest authority, withdrew the motion.

The Working Group agreed that each province would have its own executive and legislative councils, but the question whether the latter should be elected in its entirety by universal suffrage, or in part appointed, aroused heated controversy which made agreement impossible. It was therefore decided to refer the matter to the Committee of Eighteen for instructions or guidance. Moreover, since it had been realized in the meantime that the provincial provisions might cause other unforeseen headaches, the Working Group dropped the whole subject for a time.

Three weeks later, in late August 1951, it was taken up again in the Committee of Eighteen. Once more the Fezzanese argued that their Wali should be a native of their province, this time adding that the King should only appoint him or relieve him of office after consultation with the appropriate local authorities. It was rumored, in usually well-informed Fezzanese circles, that this further amendment was prompted by French wishes in the matter. Again the proposal was defeated.

The Committee then came to the problem of the provincial executive and legislative councils, their composition, and their responsibilities. A Cyrenaican proposal, according to which the federal Constitution should simply stipulate that these two councils should deal with the internal affairs of the provinces and that their composition and competence should be determined by organic laws to be elaborated by each province separately, left many members dissatisfied and raised a host of new questions. One member asked on what authority the organic laws would be drawn up. Another wanted to know whether the three organic laws should be identical or whether they might vary, provided their provisions did not contradict the federal Constitution. This last question was of special importance in connection with the composition of the legislative councils which eventually would have to elect the provincial members of the federal Senate. Furthermore, in the absence of a federal electoral roll, and notwithstanding the provision for a federal electoral law—still to be written—the question might also have a bearing on the provincial rolls, and hence on the elections for the federal House of Representatives.

Several more points were raised. Would the Wali and the executive council be responsible to the legislative council, and if so, to what extent? Would the executive councils be composed of heads of local government departments? If the legislative councils were to include a number of appointed members, who would appoint them? Would the appointed members have the same right to legislate on behalf of the people as the elected members? Would the organization of the local judiciary come within the scope of the local organic law? Each of these questions was debated, most of them at great length. After two meetings it became evident that the majority of the problems were too important, too sensitive, and the available time too short, to enable well-considered conclusions to be reached. At one moment, indeed, it looked as if the debate would take a critical turn, when a Tripolitanian member, Munir Burshan, point blank asked his Cyrenaican colleague, Khalil Qallal, whether the Constitution of Cyrenaica would remain in force after the proclamation of the federal Constitution. The answer was that "the Cyrenaican Constitution would become null and void as soon as the Federal Constitution took effect." [60] This was a courageous assurance for a Cyrenaican to give, considering the strong autonomous feelings still prevalent in certain influential circles in his territory.

A few weeks were taken up by other subjects before the Working Group resumed its deliberations on the many queries raised about the provincial provisions, both its own and those of the Committee of Eighteen, most of which remained unresolved. However, in the meantime, a great deal of private consultation had been going on that helped to clear the air. On some questions agreement had been reached, but the internal organization of the provinces as such was substantially left to be determined by the organic laws. With regard to these laws themselves, it was resolved that each province should formulate its own on condition that its provisions were not contrary to those of the federal Constitution. A sentence, proposed by the British legal adviser, was added to the effect that "the formulation of [these] laws and their promulgation" would take place within a period not exceeding one year from the promulgation of the Constitution. These decisions were subsequently incorporated into Article 177. However, this

60. *Proc. NCAL,* Committee for the Constitution, Stewart-Jackson Translation, 21st Meeting, 27 August 1951.

article does not specifically determine by what procedure or body the organic laws would be drawn up, approved, and promulgated. Various suggestions were proffered, for instance a Cyrenaican proposal to the effect that the administration of each province should prepare a draft organic law to be submitted for approval to the elected legislature of that province, but there was no majority for it.

The British legal adviser, rightly considering this an unsatisfactory situation, proposed at one of the last meetings of the Working Group that there be inserted a temporary provision determining a uniform procedure to be followed by the provinces, namely: the governments of the three territories would enact the necessary electoral legislation and then hold elections for the legislative councils. Each council, when established, would pass the organic laws for its province, providing for an executive and a legislative council. The United Nations legal adviser supported this part of the proposal, explaining the advantages to be derived from a certain degree of uniformity in matters of provincial organization. All was of no avail.

The British proposal also contained a suggestion, perhaps unfortunately, to the effect that until the provincial administrations had been established in accordance with the provisions of their organic laws, the government of each territory would exercise the powers vested in the provinces under the Constitution, on the coming into force of the latter. This suggestion apparently aroused a double suspicion in the minds of members to the effect that on the one hand it might delay or complicate the transfer of powers, while on the other it might temporarily deprive the provinces of their share of the joint powers. Whatever the reason, the members of the Working Group unanimously announced that they had decided to leave the provinces full freedom of action in determining their internal administration and that they were not prepared to change their minds. It was at about this time, when the preparatory stage of the drafting of the Constitution was drawing toward its end, that a feeling seemed to grow among the legislators that they had gone as far as they safely could in sacrificing provincial interests and feelings to the new federal authority and the need for unity it represented. While the work had been going on, all of them had kept in close touch with those from whom they derived their powers, and they knew that there was a line they could not overstep. This even applied to a certain extent to Tripolitania, with the exception, of course, of the Congress Party leaders. As subsequent events showed, the Cyrenaican members, in their desire to accommodate their opposite numbers from Tripolitania, had, on a few points, gone further than they could afford.

Agreement was reached in principle on the position of the Wali as representative of the King within the province and as supervisor of the implementation of the federal Constitution and federal laws (Article 181). Nevertheless, Article 184 stipulated that, subject to the provisions of Article 181, the functions of the Wali would be determined by the organic law in each province. Here is one more of those typical Libyan compromises between federalists and unitarists: in this particular case between the desire of conservative circles in Cyrenaica to grant the King as much power as possible, and a Tripolitanian—and Fezzanese—tendency to impose certain limitations on his prerogatives, particularly where they encroached on their local affairs.

Yet another controversy was brought to a happy end when it was agreed that "Each Province shall have a Legislative Council, three-quarters of the members of which at least shall be elected" (Article 183). It is noteworthy that the article contains no reference to the appointed members, or to the appointing authority, or to the procedure to be followed. Appointment by the King, or by the Wali, or by cooption of the elected members? All these possibilities, and others, remained open, to be regulated by the organic laws.

Lastly, an important principle found expression in Article 185, which stipulated that judicial power would be exercised by the local tribunals in the provinces in accordance with the provisions of the Constitution, that is to say, that such exercise would be governed by the provisions of Article 155 concerning the binding character of the legal principles embodied in decisions of the Supreme Court. This too was a compromise between a unitary juridical system and a certain degree of provincial autonomy in this field. The details were left to be worked out in the respective organic laws which, as one Tripolitanian member of the Committee of Eighteen remarked, would be formulated according to the "environment and the capabilities of each Province." [61]

H. GENERAL PROVISIONS
(Chapter XI of the Constitution)

Once the main structure of the Constitution had been erected and the principal organs of the State given their appropriate place and function therein, the NCAL was called upon to settle a variety of problems left over from earlier discussions. It was by then early August, and some of the problems were of political importance. Others had already been solved, and agreed upon in the form of draft articles, but their place in the Constitution had yet to be determined. It was therefore decided to draft a chapter of General Provisions, comprising Articles 186–200 in the final text.

61. *Proc. NCAL,* Committee for the Constitution, Stewart-Jackson Translation, 20th Meeting, 27 August 1951.

In particular, this chapter deals with two issues on which agreement had been reached only after they had gone through stormy weather in the Working Group, the Committee of Eighteen, and even plenary meetings of the NCAL, not to mention endless private discussions. They were: the choice of a federal capital for the new State, and the clauses governing revision of the Constitution. (The problem of the use of a foreign language in official transactions, dealt with in Article 187, has already been referred to on page 547.)

Though the question of the site of the capital was perhaps the more controversial, and the more vital in terms of administrative efficiency, the clauses governing changes in the Constitution were, politically speaking, more important in terms of the national interest, present and future. When the matter came up for the first time in the Working Group, the Chairman, in order to place the problem in its proper historical setting, opened the discussion by rereading the Commissioner's letter of 3 April addressed to the President of the NCAL. This reminded members of the author's statement on provisions for constitutional change made to the General Assembly of the United Nations at its three hundred and sixth meeting, of the Council for Libya's advice of 13 March 1951, and of the Commissioner's comments thereon.

The Commissioner, it will be remembered, had recommended two procedures for changing the Constitution: one by amendment; the other by review after a fixed period of years (see pp. 485–86).

The Commissioner continued:

> With regard to these two procedures, it is to be noted that the amendment procedure, . . . is normally found in the constitutions of practically all countries since it is generally recognized that no constitution should be inalterable.[62]

In defense of the general review procedure, the Commissioner went on to say that:

> The general review procedure normally does not occur in national constitutions but it does occur in the Charter of the United Nations. The reason for which the National Assembly might consider the latter procedure as useful in the case of Libya is twofold. Firstly, the fact that the constitution now being elaborated will be the work not of an elected but of an appointed body; secondly, that Libya, having no precedent of constitutional government in the modern sense of the word, might wish to

62. *Second Annual Report of the United Nations Commissioner in Libya,* Annex IV, p. 79.

give itself an opportunity, after a fixed number of years, to look back over its recent experiences and to determine through a democratic procedure whether the state requires structural changes.[63]

In proposing the second procedure, the Commissioner also had in mind the forthcoming session of the General Assembly, where he hoped to avoid the criticisms that had come close to upsetting Libya's constitutional development in 1950.

It soon became apparent that the Commissioner and the NCAL were at cross purposes.

Provisions for change in the Constitution were basically a political question, not only from an internal Libyan point of view, but also in the international context. Domestically, the question was how to translate into constitutional language the wish of the federalists that the Constitution should be protected as securely as possible against any attempt on the part of a unitarist majority in an elected Parliament to change the form of State and Government after independence, which led them to favor inserting in the Constitution itself rigid provisions governing its revision and eventual amendment. The opposition, correspondingly, was in favor of an easy amendment procedure.

The United Nations legal adviser prepared a set of draft articles in the sense just indicated. The discussion in the Working Group showed unanimous opposition to the idea of a general review after a fixed term. The proposal never stood a chance, the main obstacle being that, according to Resolution 387 (V), the NCAL was the sole body competent to draw up the Libyan Constitution, on which basis it was argued that it made no sense to determine beforehand what period should elapse before its general review. This was, of course, not the real objection; but it served to cloak the intention of protecting federalism.

The Working Group was prepared to consider a conventional amendment clause, similar to those in the constitutions of Belgium, Egypt, India, and Iraq. However, the dominant desire was to make the amendment procedure as rigid as possible. Some suggested that the two chambers should first decide in principle, by absolute majority, to amend the Constitution, and that this decision should be sanctioned by the King. Subsequently the two chambers would have to determine on exactly what subject amendments should bear. A quorum of two-thirds of the members would be required in each chamber, and each decision would require a two-thirds majority.

Moreover, if an amendment aimed at changing the federal form of the State, the powers of the federal government, or those of the judiciary, the

63. Ibid.

approval of at least two provincial legislative councils also would be required. After the United Nations legal adviser had pointed out the difficulties that might arise in applying so complicated a procedure, the members of the Working Group decided to think the matter over.

At the next meeting it soon became apparent that the attitude of the majority had become even harder, obviously under Cyrenaican influence. Indeed, the Group decided that in addition to the conclusions reached on the previous occasion, the following points should be inviolate: the monarchical form of government; the order of succession to the Throne; the representative form of government; and the principles of liberty and equality. Once more the United Nations legal adviser tried to convince the Group that it was going too far in its attempts to make the most essential parts of the Constitution practically immutable, explaining that this was in contradiction with the opinion of several authoritative constitutional lawyers. A few, mostly Tripolitanian, members supported him. Finally, the Chairman proposed, by way of compromise, that the requirement of the King's sanction for the first stage of the review procedure should be dropped. Agreement was reached on this basis. At the request of the Group, the Legal Adviser reluctantly prepared a draft along these lines, for submission to the Committee of Eighteen.

This draft contained a provision according to which the consent of at least two provincial legislative councils would be required if the federal form of government, the powers of the Libyan Union, or those of the judiciary were to be changed. This provision became one of the main bones of contention. A Cyrenaican member suggested, evidently again by way of compromise, that the list of federal powers and the chapter on the judiciary should not be subject to the proposed restrictive procedure, but that the consent of all three provincial legislative councils instead of at least two should be required for a change in the federal form of government. The record is not quite clear on this point. Apparently there was a majority of speakers in favor of the Cyrenaican proposal, but a formal decision was postponed until a later date, and in the meantime the chapter was returned to the Working Party for final drafting. There the discussion became heated. Most of the arguments adduced earlier by the United Nations legal adviser were this time supported by the British adviser to the Provisional Libyan Government, Sir Harry Trusted, who strongly criticized the exclusion of specified matters from any possibility of review. To this, a Cyrenaican member retorted that only a revolution could bring about a change on those points. This was strong language voicing strong feelings.

The United Nations legal adviser considered that the proposal to raise from two to three the number of provincial legislative councils whose approval would be required for review of the provisions concerning the federal form of government was undemocratic, and inconsistent with the federal system. The Cyrenaican reaction to this argument was that the agreement to create a federal form of government, having been secured by unanimous consent of the three provinces, could only be abrogated by their common consent. Hence the issue was to determine whether a change in the federal form of government would require the unanimous consent of all three provinces or could be decided by a majority of two. A Tripolitanian member proposed as a more democratic solution approval by a three-fourths majority in each chamber and by two provinces. The majority did not accept this proposal, the Cyrenaicans and Fezzanese insisting on the most rigid protection of the federal principle. Finally, the provision was included in the Constitution as Article 199, even more strongly worded than it had been originally, providing for prior approval by all three legislative councils.

Looking at the review clauses (Articles 196–99) as a whole, the reader will probably be struck, as the author was at the time of their drafting and adoption, by the fact that Article 196 is in contradiction with the three that follow.

Indeed, taken together with Article 41, which stipulated that the legislative power should be exercised by the King in conjunction with Parliament, Article 196 allows both the King or either of the two chambers to propose the revision of the Constitution. There then follow a number of restrictions, concerning substance as well as procedure, and applicable to the review powers both of the King and of Parliament. At the same time both Articles 198 and 199 require the royal sanction for the resolutions voted by Parliament. However, Article 136 grants the King only a limited right of veto in the matter of promulgation of laws. Indeed, Parliament can, under the same article, overrule the King by revoting the law in question by qualified majority. Does Article 136 also apply to parliamentary resolutions relating to a review of the Constitution? This question was not answered at the time. The principle of ministerial responsibility also comes into play, though this too is subject to restrictions (Article 87). The procedure as a whole amounts to a carefully elaborated system of royal, ministerial, parliamentary, and, where the federal form of government is concerned, provincial checks and balances, the King playing the central part without necessarily having the last word.

The most remarkable thing about these arrangements is that neither in the records nor in any private papers is there any indication that the system was conceived as an entity. The writer, though as Commissioner he followed every stage of the work of the NCAL and frequently participated in it by giving assistance or advice, has no recollection of ever having heard of a comprehensive examination of the subject.

The fact is that, contrary to the fears of the Commissioner and his legal adviser, as reflected in their warnings to the Libyan drafters, the review clauses of the Constitution proved their worth during the early years of Libyan independence, because they were suited to conditions then prevailing, and also because they helped to bring about a much needed stability in relationships between the three provinces.

The choice of a capital was a very different proposition. On several occasions the question had come up for discussion in the Working Group, and each time it had run into an impasse. The same thing had happened in the Committee of Eighteen, but there, at least, the opposing positions had been frankly and fully explained. The quotation of a few paragraphs from the records of these debates may help the reader to understand in what kind of atmosphere the problem was ultimately solved a month later in the NCAL itself.

In the Committee, the debate was opened by a leading Cyrenaican member, who commented on the draft article proposing Benghazi as the federal capital:

> Mr. Khalil Gellal said . . . that the Hon. Members fully realised that the tragedies which had smitten Benghazi had destroyed very much of her and that she had not been left with the means of restoration by which she could be certain of a shining future unless she were made a centre for the Government since that perhaps would have an effect on her resurgence. If, however, his colleagues were to withhold this gesture of affection then hopes of her being regenerated would come to nought.[64]

Munir Burshan, of the Tripolitanian delegation, then suggested that discussion on the subject be postponed until the Tripolitanian members had met together and studied the article fully after mutual consultation among themselves.

A few weeks later the debate was resumed:

> The Hon. Member Mr. Abdul Majeed Ku'bar arose and he explained the difficulties which were in the way of rendering Benghazi a capital by pointing out that the emergent State was burdened with excessive expenses which it could only bear with difficulty while it was still in the process of formation, whereas Tripoli was in a complete state of cultivated preparedness. For historical, social and other reasons of cultural development it would not be easy to transfer the capital from Tripoli to anywhere else.
>
> The Hon. Member Mr. Mohamed bu Rahim arose and drew the Com-

64. *Proc. NCAL,* Committee for the Constitution, Stewart-Jackson Translation, 20th Meeting, 27 August 1951.

mittee's attention to the transference of the Turkish capital from Istanbul [Constantinople] to Ankara despite the existence of disparities between the two towns which were very similar to the disparities which his Hon. colleague Abdul Majeed Ku'bar had pointed to particularly. He also pointed out that Benghazi was then solely Arab and that therefore it was safer than other places because of its freedom from the intrigues and activities of foreigners.

The Hon. Member Mr. Khalil Gallal followed the observations of the Hon. Member Mr. Abdul Majeed Ku'bar by saying that, were they to adopt the observation of his honourable colleague, they would find that Benghazi could be more easily reached from the outlying parts of the Kingdom of Libya than Tripoli, for it was placed in the middle of the Libyan territory and half way along the Libyan shore; and he said that this was quite apart from the fact that he called upon his Tripolitanian brethren to evince a spirit of mutual solidarity and assistance which would compensate Cyrenaica which had sustained fearful destruction and terrible disruption. He said finally that he hoped especially that his brothers would reflect once more on the considerations which he had mentioned earlier.[65]

The next morning the Committee agreed to deal with the other articles of the general provisions before resuming the debate on the site of the capital. When they did return to the issue,

the Hon. Member Khalil Gallal put once again his point of view of approving Benghazi as a capital. He adduced geographical and political evidence for this together with the observation of the priority of Cyrenaica in view of its sacrifice and its losses.

The Hon. Member Mr. Munir Burshan opposed him saying . . . that [the] opposition would take advantage of the opportunity and launch against them an attack which would destroy the edifices which they had built up. . . .

The Hon. Member Mr. Khalil Gallal answered that if they were to attach any importance to the opposition it would truly be a great danger, but that they should not attach any importance to it; and that in any case it had as its intention the complete destruction of the draft so that it was a matter of indifference to them whether they decided to have Benghazi as their capital or Tripoli. He said that therefore they should not pay any attention to it.

The Hon. Member Mr. Mohamed al Hankari arose and said that the

65. *Proc. NCAL,* Committee for the Constitution, Stewart-Jackson Translation, 23rd Meeting, 15 September 1951.

natural historical position and the position as regards civilisation emphasised that the capital had always been Tripoli.

The Hon. Member Mr. Khalil Gallal said that the natural situation called upon them to make the capital Benghazi because of its being in the middle of Libya and he said that the transport of capitals from one place to another was a feasible proposition.[66]

At this juncture the records note that:

> The discussion grew fierce, argument broke out and there were divergent opinions. It was finally decided that it would be more appropriate to put off discussion and study of this to another opportunity namely the meeting of the National Assembly.[67]

As developments will show (see Chapter 8, pp. 636 ff.), this postponement of the discussion was a wise move.

I. TRANSITORY AND PROVISIONAL PROVISIONS
(Chapter XII of the Constitution)

As briefly mentioned in the section on the Parliament, above, more particularly in connection with the method of election to the House of Representatives, it was becoming clear by the middle of August that the timetable originally drawn up for the drafting of the Constitution and consequent developments could not be kept (p. 571). The NCAL could not be blamed for the delay. If less time had been lost the previous year over the selection of the representative of the minorities on the Council for Libya, and subsequently over the terms of reference, composition, and competence of the Committee of Twenty-One, the NCAL might well have met earlier in 1950 and a number of time-consuming complications avoided. But it is more realistic to recognize that difficulties of the kind described must be accepted as normally inherent in such an operation as that which forms the subject of this study, and in particular that the period of two years (in practice somewhat less) allowed for the implementation of Resolutions 289(IV) and 387(V) was too short.

The dilemma can best be summarized in the following terms: if the two General Assembly resolutions were to be implemented within their time limits, all powers held by the United Kingdom and France would have to be handed over to a "duly constituted independent Government," Resolution 289 (IV), or a "duly constituted Libyan Government," Resolution 387

66. *Proc. NCAL,* Committee for the Constitution, Stewart-Jackson Translation 24th Meeting, 15 September 1951.

67. Ibid.

(V), not later than 1 January 1952. A government could not be duly constituted under the terms of the Constitution being drafted until the latter had been adopted by the National Assembly and formully promulgated. At the same time it must be noted, as the Commissioner observed in his second annual report:

> no Libyan electoral law could be drafted until the Constitution had defined the bodies to be elected as well as the basic principles of the electoral system to be followed. Subsequently, sufficient time had to be left for the drafting of the electoral law itself, for its consideration and approval by the National Assembly and, last but not least, for the building up of a Libyan electoral mechanism in a country where such a mechanism had never previously existed.[68]

In addition, time would have to be allowed for the elections themselves. Circumstances being what they were, the NCAL had no choice but, with the tacit agreement of the Administering Powers and the consent of the Commissioner, to draw up a set of transitory and provisional provisions, including a new time table, to apply during the interval between the transfer of powers and the proclamation of independence at the end of 1951 and the moment at which the first elected Parliament could meet and a Government be formed in conformity with the letter and spirit of the Constitution. Needless to say, the interval had to be as short as possible, particularly in view of the fact that the Libyan question was on the agenda of the Sixth Session of the General Assembly, due to open in the late fall of 1951.

Meanwhile, it was becoming imperative for both legal and political reasons to clarify the meaning of "duly constituted Libyan Government" as used by the General Assembly. The Commissioner, though pressed for time, decided to ask the Council for Libya for advice. This matter will be dealt with in greater detail in Chapter 10.

Pending receipt of the Council's advice, the Working Group began to consider in first reading a draft for the transitional provisions prepared by the legal adviser to the Cyrenaican delegation, which was the result of numerous consultations. It had no difficulty in adopting two fundamental provisions: the full Constitution would come into force upon the declaration of independence, but Article 8, on Libyan nationality, and the transitory and provisional articles (Articles 201–13), would enter into force earlier, on the date of its promulgation. The distinction proved to be important, since the promulgation took place on 7 October 1951, well before

68. *Second Annual Report of the United Nations Commissioner in Libya,* para. 312.

the declaration of independence on 24 December. Activation of Article 8 was necessary for the electoral preparations, especially to determine who would be eligible to vote and stand for office.

The next two articles dealt with the crux of the matter, that is, what were the minimum requirements for a Government entitled to receive transferred powers (later Articles 202 and 203). This point was governed both by Resolution 289 (IV) and by Resolution 387 (V). The earlier resolution laid down that the Administering Powers, in cooperation with the United Nations Commissioner, should "(a) initiate immediately all necessary steps for the transfer of powers to a duly constituted independent government." The later resolution called upon the authorities concerned to take all necessary steps to ensure the early, full, and effective implementation of Resolution 289 (IV) and particularly "the transfer of power to an independent Libyan Government." At the same time Resolution 387 (V) provided for the establishment of a "Provisional Government of Libya," specifying that "powers shall be progressively transferred to the Provisional Government by the Administering Powers in a manner which will ensure that all powers presently exercised by them shall, by 1 January 1952, have been transferred to the duly constituted Libyan Government." Obviously the General Assembly had presumed that when independence was proclaimed a government duly constituted in accordance with the Constitution would be standing by to assume the powers already transferred to the Provisional Government and any residual powers still held by the United Kingdom and France. Now that the time table for this sequence of events had become impracticable, the question was how to find an alternative likely to be acceptable to the General Assembly.

The Working Group—after careful study of the problem, and well aware of the criticisms that might be leveled against its proposed solution both in the Council and in the General Assembly—conceived the following schema, which, although it later appeared in the Constitution in a somewhat different order and wording, remained unchanged in substance:

1. Until the establishment of a duly constituted Government, the Provisional Federal Government would exercise all the powers concerning the matters transferred to it by the Governments of the United Kingdom and France and the existing provincial governments;
2. The first King of the united Kingdom of Libya would begin to exercise his constitutional powers upon the declaration of independence provided that he took the oath prescribed in Article 47 before Parliament at its first session in a joint meeting.
3. Upon the declaration of independence the King would appoint the duly constituted Government.

In due course and without much discussion, the paragraphs of this schema became respectively Articles 202, 209, and 203 of the Constitution. As will be seen later, this stopgap arrangement gave rise to a considerable controversial debate, particularly in the Council for Libya. Yet it enabled the transfer-of-power machinery to operate as prescribed in Resolusion 387 (V). The plan was attractive to the NCAL and many other Libyans as it permitted the date set for independence to be maintained. It met with opposition because there were still a number of people, particularly within the Congress Party of Tripolitania, who would have liked to reopen the Libyan issue during the Sixth Session of the General Assembly, for reasons similar to those which had motivated the delegations of Arab States at the Fifth Session. Preference for a unitary form of State remained the driving motive behind this opposition. They hoped elections *before* the declaration of independence would produce a Parliament prepared to revise the draft Constitution.

Hence, from the NCAL's point of view, it was essential to round off the schema by adding watertight provisions for the election of the House of Representatives even though the elections were to be held after 1 January 1952. This proved to be one of the most difficult aspects of the procedure envisaged.

The Working Group proposed that the drafting of the electoral law for the lower chamber be entrusted to the Provisional Federal Government. Subsequently it should be ratified by the National Assembly and promulgated not more than thirty days after promulgation of the Constitution; the first elections should be held within four months (later shortened to three and a half months) of the date of promulgation. In drawing up this time table, and later the electoral law, the advice of an expert on electoral methods, G. P. Cassells, who was made available to the Provisional Libyan Government by the British Administration, proved of great help. The year before he had effectively helped the Cyrenaican Government to organize the elections to the Assembly of Representatives.

As already recorded, no census having been taken recently, it was decided, for the first elections, to allot fifteen seats to Cyrenaica, thirty-five to Tripolitania, and five to the Fezzan. (One of Cyrenaica's elder statesmen, Mansur Bey Kikhia, told the Commissioner that approximately the same proportions had applied within the much smaller Libyan representation in the Turkish Parliament at Constantinople in 1908.) Lastly, the first Parliament was to be convened not more than twenty days after the final electoral results were announced. The relevant provisions appeared in the final text of the Constitution as Articles 204, 205, 206, and 211.

In order to avoid any doubt about the continuity of existing laws, the

Working Group, on the advice of its legal advisers, also proposed that under certain conditions and limitations existing laws and decrees would continue to be effective provided they were consistent with the Constitution (ultimately Article 210). This was an indispensable provision covering laws and regulations of all origins—British, French, Italian, and even Turkish.

Chapter XII of the Constitution enjoyed plain sailing through the Committee of Eighteen, whose main contribution, as mentioned in the section on federal finance, was the addition of Article 212, leaving customs revenues at the disposal of the provincial treasuries until 1 April 1952 following a recommendation of the Coordination Committee (see also Chapter 8, p. 638).

Difficulties of an unexpected kind arose when the Working Group started finalizing the text of the Constitution for submission to the NCAL. When the discussion reached Article 202, the British legal adviser—exceptionally, and formally, speaking on behalf of His Majesty's Government—warned that the residue of sovereign powers to be handed over last would not be transferred except to a "duly constituted government." In this connection he stated that, in his opinion, the time limit for the holding of elections prescribed in Article 205 was far too short and would prevent the completion of the transfer of powers by 1 January 1952. He further declared that His Majesty's Government had no desire to delay the declaration of independence; on the contrary, it wished to accelerate it. A scheme somewhat different from the one conceived by the Working Group, which had already been approved by the Committee of Eighteen, would have to be devised. He therefore proposed the addition of a provision to the effect that upon the declaration of independence the Provisional Federal Government would for all purposes become the duly constituted Federal Government until elections had been held and Parliament established. In his opinion, the NCAL was the only competent body to take a decision of this nature.

At this point the United Nations legal adviser declared that he wished to reserve his position pending consultations with the Commissioner. In his opinion, the United Kingdom proposal, involving political principles, represented only one of several interpretations of Resolution 387 (V). In discussing it, he argued, the Working Group was not on purely legal ground.

According to his own interpretation, the General Assembly Resolution meant that, upon the declaration of independence, the Provisional Government would have to resign, whereupon the King, exercising his powers under the Constitution, would appoint a new Government.

After this statement the Working Group decided to suspend further discussion until the Commissioner's views were known.

It took a full week of private consultations, including some between the Commissioner and the British legal adviser in the presence of his United

Nations colleague, before agreement could be reached. In the end, the following text was agreed upon by all concerned: "That upon the declaration of independence the King shall establish the duly constituted Government." With the sole difference that the word "establish" was replaced by the word "appoint," this text became Article 203 of the Constitution; thus the United Nations legal view prevailed. However, it must be acknowledged that the British legal adviser's intervention had helped to clarify a situation which might have given rise to serious misunderstanding.

The question has been frequently asked why the British formally proposed that, despite the provisions of Resolution 387 (V), the Provisional Federal Government on the declaration of independence should become the duly constituted Federal Government. The United Kingdom Government must have had weighty reasons for such a last-minute move. There is good reason to believe that, as a result of expert discussions on monetary and financial matters (see Chapter 9, Part 2), as well as of the conclusions reached by the Coordination Committee (see Chapter 10), in all of which representatives of the Libyan Provisional Government had participated, unofficial talks had been initiated concerning certain financial and military agreements to be negotiated between the United Kingdom and Libya after independence. Of course, the Provisional Government had no power to bind the country in these matters. At the same time Libya had every interest in knowing, before independence, on what financial support it could count for the twofold purpose of covering the future budget deficit and financing the country's economic development. Similar considerations applied in Libyan-French and Libyan-American postindependence relationships.

On the other side of the fence, the three powers directly interested were anxious to know what military and other advantages they might obtain in exchange for the financial support they were expected to give to the future Libyan State to ensure its viability. In this context, it was understandable that they should prefer to go on officially negotiating after independence with the team with which they had previously had unofficial talks. At least, this seemes a plausible explanation. On the Libyan side, it was similarly understandable that on the day of independence, when the Provisional Government had tendered its resignation and the King summoned the outgoing Prime Minister and entrusted him with the task of forming a new Government, the composition of the latter should be the same as that of the Provisional Government. This is, indeed, what occurred, with the exception of one portfolio.[69]

The reasons suggested above were not the only explanation of the simi-

69. See *Supplementary Report to the Second Annual Report of the United Nations Commissioner in Libya,* GAOR: Sixth Session, 1951–52, Supplement No. 17A (A/1949/Add.1), para. 17.

larity between the two Cabinets. Mahmud Muntasir, the Prime Minister, had domestic political reasons for continuing with the team of men who had worked with him throughout the preparatory period, and who had become responsible for implementing the plans prepared with their collaboration and consent.

In retrospect, this seems to the writer the most logical explanation of a complicated sequence of events of which, at the time, as Commissioner, he was only partly aware. In fact his official position at that juncture—and even more so in the following months—was so delicate that he sometimes preferred not to be informed about certain matters, at least not officially. On the one hand he was fully within his powers in advising the Provisional Government in matters of a budgetary, monetary, and economic nature. Since the United Nations experts whose advice was available to him had confirmed the existence of serious deficits both in the three provincial budgets and in their balances of payments, it was indeed his duty to find ways of closing these gaps, an aim that it would take Libya many years to achieve unaided. He had been obliged reluctantly to admit that in the absence of any disinterested governmental offer to help Libya through a United Nations-controlled financial assistance fund (see Chapter 9, Part 2), the country's sole asset was its faculty to confer rights to maintain military bases, desirable for their geographical and strategic importance, and that the best policy to follow was to "sell" these rights for the best price it could get. He had even gone so far as to advise the King, the Provisional Government, and leading members of the NCAL in this sense, but it was obvious that this was the extreme limit to which he could go. To offer advice on the substance of these matters was far beyond his competence. He might be taken to task anyway in the General Assembly for having gone as far as he had. Hence it appeared sound policy to take a few precautions. One was not to keep his opinion secret; it would be better tactics to let people know privately how he felt about the issue, without making an official statement. He was constantly asked for his opinion on a problem that could not possibly be eluded, however painful it was to Libyan patriots to realize the necessity of having to tolerate the continued presence of foreign military forces on their soil after independence. At the end of August, moreover, he considered it both fair and wise to inform, privately and in detail, the chief of the opposition, Beshir Bey Saadawi, of the financial and economic situation which, in his opinion, would compel the new Libyan State to accept foreign military bases to pay for the financial support it so urgently needed. It was obvious from his reaction that Beshir Bey was extremely loath to accept the logical consequences of the state of affairs disclosed to him, even though he already knew of it in broad outline. In the light of the then world political situation, he was no more able than was the Commissioner to see any other way out than that Libya should side with the Western Powers, although Beshir Bey felt little enough sympathy with them. Libya should therefore, he admitted, be ready to consider any Western request for strategic bases and to enter into agreements concerning them after regular negotiations conducted by a legally established Libyan Government. However, the Libyan people, whose sole concern was to safeguard their country's independence, could not allow foreign powers to do as they liked with the country. He felt that undue haste had been shown in discussing these financial-military plans as early as the summer of 1951. He would have preferred them to be discussed only after the legal Libyan Government had been established, after independence. He said that his party would not recognize any decisions that were taken before the establishment of such a Government, and he therefore reserved its rights in this respect. On this particular point Beshir Bey came close to the Commissioner's own views, for the latter also believed that no Libyan Government was entitled to conclude any binding agreement with any foreign power until independence had been achieved. Moreover, in accordance with Article 69 of the Constitution, as it read at that moment (see pp. 556–57), such agreements would have to be laid before Parliament for its consent. On the other hand, the Commissioner felt that his interlocutor lacked a sense of reality in insisting that even private and preparatory talks between the future parties should be excluded at that stage.

A separate problem the Commissioner had to consider was whether he should formally ask the Council for Libya for advice on how to provide for the solution of the country's future budgetary, economic, and monetary difficulties. Council members had been fully informed about the prevailing situation, both orally and through official memoranda.[70]

Several expert reports on relevant matters had also been made available to them. No reactions or suggestions had been forthcoming from Council members with regard to these admittedly highly technical subjects. Asking them formally for advice accordingly would have caused serious embarrassment to everybody concerned, since such a request would have implied that the problems concerned came within the terms of reference of Commissioner and Council, and, hence, of the General Assembly. On the other hand, in talking privately to members, the Commissioner had never hidden under a bushel his personal belief that independent Libya's only way out of its financial difficulties, at least during the first years of its life, would be to make money out of the strategic position it had to offer.. Hence, he refrained from submitting a request for advice. Neither was he asked for one.

When it seemed that the Working Group had completed its task, the British legal adviser made one last effort, on 7 September, to undo a key

70. See *Second Annual Report of the United Nations Commissioner in Libya*, Annexes XVII–XXI, pp. 140–57.

part of the work, declaring that it would be wise to consult the representatives of the provinces in the NCAL before presenting the proposal that the Provisional Government should temporarily handle matters transferred to it by the two Administering Powers and the three provinces (Article 202). The move was doubtless intended to encourage Cyrenaican and probably Fezzanese opposition to the agreement. In fact, the proposal looked very much like an attempt to grant the provinces a last-minute opportunity to say their word and possibly delay the transfer of powers to the Federal Government, in particular those powers which they themselves had previously received and were already exercising. Cyrenaican as well as Tripolitanian adverse reactions came quickly and sharply. One of the Cyrenaican leaders remarked that if the Working Group had to consult somebody every time it was about to adopt an article, the Constitution could hardly be ready by the date required. One of his Tripolitanian colleagues wanted to know whether the British proposal meant that the whole Constitution should be submitted to the provinces for consultation and approval, or whether it applied only to the article under discussion. The United Kingdom spokesman replied that his suggestion was limited to conducting consultations only on the transfer of powers. Nevertheless, he apparently did not entirely rule out the possibility that a similar procedure might be followed with regard to the Constitution as a whole, adding, however, that that was a matter to be decided by the Working Group and the Committee of Eighteen. The same Tripolitanian member retorted that the NCAL was the only body competent to deal with the drafting of the Constitution and that the representatives of the three territories therein were fully empowered to take any course they wished to follow. The British suggestion was not discussed further.

After thorough examination by the Committee of Eighteen, the transitory and provisional provisions were approved, substantially as they appear in the final text of the Constitution.

As noted at the beginning of this section, Chapter XII raised one serious danger: the Council for Libya, and perhaps the General Assembly also, might not agree with the procedure by which the "duly constituted Libyan Government" was to come into being. The risk was accepted on the ground that there was no alternative except delaying the date of independence, a course even more open to criticism.

J. PREAMBLE

Several months after the NCAL had taken its preliminary decisions on the form of the State, and when such fundamental questions as the distribution of powers, the rights of the people, and the executive and legislative organization of the State had been practically solved, the Working Group invited the legal adviser of the Cyrenaican delegation to prepare a draft Preamble to the Constitution. They also asked the United Nations legal adviser for drafts of Chapter I, "Form of the State and the System of Government," and Chapter IV, "General Federal Powers." It was as late as the middle of June 1951 before the draft was discussed, not because it was considered to be lacking in importance—on the contrary, it was looked upon as an essential part of the work in hand—but because it was thought that it was unlikely to give rise to serious differences of opinion. Nevertheless, it had required a great deal of consultation *in camera,* in particular with the King-Designate.

This careful preparation explains why there is but little difference between the Cyrenaican legal adviser's draft of the Preamble and the text finally approved. There was merely some debate as to whether it should say that the representatives of the people of Libya "adopt, approve and determine the present Constitution" or "prepare and resolve this Constitution." Preference was finally given to the latter wording, which also, it was argued, sounded better in Arabic.

Two specific omissions may be noted: there is no reference in the Preamble to General Assembly Resolution 289 (IV) of 21 November 1949, which legally and politically was the basis of Libyan independence. Reference to it, if only to mark the existence of an umbilical cord between the United Nations and the fruit of its womb, might have been expected. Reference to Libya's ties with the United Nations appears only in Article 201, determining the ultimate date for independence set by the Resolution.

The author remembers that there was a moment when he seriously asked himself whether he should suggest that some reference be made in the Preamble to the United Nations background. Probably his suggestion would have been accepted. In other contexts, then and later—for instance when Libya was in need of United Nations assistance—its leaders never forgot to invoke the special link between the two. The Commissioner nevertheless decided not to raise the point. Nations do not like to be reminded that they received their independence as a gift, albeit a gracious gift, from an outsider—even when that outsider is the United Nations and not a colonial Power. Their nascent nationalism is psychologically in need of the belief that they owe their new status to an effort of their own, usually a revolt or a war of liberation. In the case of Libya there was a historical background of struggle, defeats, suffering, and exile with always flickering hopes of eventual delivery from Italian rule, even if the facts had not led directly to independence. Memories of resistance were an important unifying factor.

The second omission is that there is no provision for secession or dissolution of the Union. The thought apparently never occurred to any Libyan concerned. The explanation must be sought in the concept of unity peculiar to the Arabs. It is also implicit in the Preamble that to guarantee national unity is the first purpose of the State.[71]

K. FORM OF THE STATE AND THE SYSTEM OF GOVERNMENT (Chapter I of the Constitution)

The draft for this chapter of the Constitution, prepared by the United Nations legal adviser, was passed by the Working Group with practically no comments. Its substance being based on decisions taken unanimously by the NCAL at the outset of its work, there were hardly any political issues involved.

The Committee of Eighteen, on the contrary, introduced a significant change. The original draft of Article 1 stated: "Libya is a free independent sovereign State. Its sovereign rights are indivisible and inalienable. No part of its territory may be alienated." Although there is no record of any discussion or any indication of motive in the minutes of the meeting, it was decided to delete the word "indivisible" and to redraft the article to read: "Libya is a free independent sovereign State. Neither its sovereignty nor any part of its territories may be relinquished." [72]

Considering that what was at stake was nothing less than the Federation's sovereignty, it was not without importance to determine whether that sovereignty was deemed divisible. The Commissioner, therefore, asked for clarification. No fully authoritative answer was forthcoming, but he was told by a reliable source that the deletion of the mention of indivisibility was attributable to the wish of certain Cyrenaican leaders to ensure that the King-Designate would retain his sovereign rights over Cyrenaica should the Federation prove unworkable. Whether this is a correct version of what really happened remains an open question. If it is correct, it is indicative of the mentality that even as late as the summer of 1951 still prevailed in some Cyrenaican circles. There is no evidence whatsoever that the King-Designate himself shared this preoccupation, or that he was consulted about this particular drafting change.

The only other changes of any importance consisted in transferring the article declaring Arabic to be the official language of the State from Chapter

71. For text of Preamble, see Annex II, pp. 902–03.

72. *Proc. NCAL,* Committee for the Constitution, Stewart-Jackson Translation, 14th Meeting, 24 June 1951.

I to Chapter XI (Article 186) and in modifying the order in which the Libyan frontiers were defined, starting with the north instead of the east. This was done, according to the minutes, in order to preserve the Arabic order of the four points of the compass.

In August, the Working Group, while reviewing the final text of the draft Constitution, rejected a proposal put forward by the United Nations legal adviser that the system of government be described in Article 2 as "parliamentary representative" instead of merely "representative." The argument of the opponent, a member from Cyrenaica, was that "representative" and "parliamentary" were virtually synonymous. In fact there was still a tendency in conservative Cyrenaican circles to play down the parliamentary form of government.

The Working Group approved a proposal by the British legal adviser to the effect that the State emblem and anthem should be prescribed "by *a federal* law" and not simply "by law," as prescribed in the original text. In addition, the word "anthem" was to be preceded by the word "national" (Article 6).

L. GENERAL FEDERAL POWERS
(Chapter IV of the Constitution)

On first reading, both the Working Group and the Committee of Eighteen passed the draft text of Chapter IV, prepared by the United Nations legal adviser, without any substantial change.

However, when, in August, the text came once more before the Working Group, several modifications were made and other suggested changes rejected.

At the suggestion of the United Nations legal adviser, the first article of the original draft reading "sovereignty is vested in the nation" was completed by adding the words "and the nation is the source of powers" (Article 40).

The British legal adviser proposed the deletion of the second article which stated that the legislative, executive, and judiciary powers would be exercised in the manner established by the Constitution. These words were indeed redundant.

When the same person proposed, however, that the words "and legislative councils" be inserted after the words "the legislative power is exercised by the King in conjunction with the Senate and the House of Representatives" in the third article of the draft (finally Article 41), he was opposed by his United Nations colleague, who objected that the chapter under discussion dealt with the general powers of the Union and that a separate section (Chapter III, Part II) was devoted to the powers of the provinces and their constitutional position within the Union. The British legal adviser, while deferring to the objection, suggested that the heading of Chapter IV ought in that case to read "General Federal Powers." This the Group accepted.

The last article of the chapter, dealing with the judicial power, as originally drafted, simply stated that this power was exercised by the Courts. The British legal adviser suggested that mention of the "Supreme Court" would be more apposite. The Working Group agreed. In its final form, the text became Article 43 of the Constitution; it is to be read in conjunction with Articles 155 (Chapter VIII, "The Judiciary") and 185 (Chapter X, "The Provinces").

M. FEDERAL FINANCE
(Chapter IX of the Constitution)

Whereas, from the earliest stage of its work, the Working Group had given priority to the distribution of powers between the federal government and the provinces, showing a particular interest in financial powers, almost no attention had been paid to the manner in which the federal budget was to be administered. By the middle of the summer of 1951, however, this attitude was rapidly changing under the influence of a number of factors. The most important of these, no doubt, was the slowly growing realization that the federal government would both need and have at its disposal much larger revenues than the lawmakers had initially visualized. In itself, the belatedness of their interest was not so surprising, since the whole concept of federal financial administration was, along with the implication of other federal functions, new to them.

In this respect, the report of the United Nations experts on the seven financial subjects on which the Committee of Eighteen had been unable to take a decision (cf. pp. 525–26) had been a real eye-opener. The oral exchanges of views between the experts and the members of the Working Group had, moreover, greatly helped to clarify the picture. So had the discussions in the Coordination Committee, which had brought home to the Libyan members the relationship between federal finance and the transfer of powers. Similarly, the Libyans had discovered that in the future, as was inherent in the federal system, foreign grants-in-aid would be paid to the federal government and not directly to the provinces.[73] It was also a

73. It will be remembered that the Administering Powers had operated each of the territories as a separate entity, covering budget deficits by direct grants to Cyrenaica, Tripolitania, and the Fezzan, and within the latter, again separately to Ghudamis and Ghat.

surprise that the revenue from certain direct and indirect taxes which used to flow into the provincial treasuries would in the logic of federal arrangements become revenue for the center. Federal resources would be allocated in part to the provincial administrations as grants-in-aid. In the light of all of these factors, which, together with the need for a unified monetary system, were recognized as unavoidable if the Libyan federation was to develop into an economic unit, the previously underrated question of federal finance took on an unforeseen importance. As a result, Chapter IX of the Constitution was a series of compromises on the distribution of financial powers, parliamentary budget procedures, fiscal principles, and even broad treasury rules. The first of these matters has already been dealt with earlier in this chapter (pp. 526–36).

In the last week of August, a few days after the approval of the chapter on the distribution of powers by the Committee of Eighteen, the Working Group, using its privilege to suggest drafting changes in order to make the lists of powers consistent with other chapters, took a fresh look at both the financial powers included in Chapter III, part I of the Constitution, "Powers of the Federal Government," and those in Chapter IX, "Federal Finance." A draft for the latter had been prepared by the Legal Adviser in collaboration with the Principal Secretary and a group of United Nations financial experts. This draft had previously been examined by leading members of the Working Group and agreement in principle had been reached. It included an article to the effect that receipts from customs would be allocated to the federal government. Still worried, however, about the impression the loss of revenue to the provinces might make on those whom they represented, the members of the Group preferred two separate and specific stipulations, defining more clearly, first, the nature of all revenues and, second, which were to go into the federal and which into the provincial coffers. The first stipulation, referring to Article 36, determined that all taxes and duties relating to matters within the legislative and executive competence of the federal government should be paid to that government. The second, referring to both Articles 38 and 39, expressed the same principle with regard to the provinces. Subsequently the two provisions were included as Articles 172 and 173 in Chapter IX, both redrafted in more precise terms. It may be argued that both were redundant, but their insertion was considered necessary to reassure the supporters of federalism, to protect the members of the NCAL against criticism, and thus to disarm the opposition.

It was for similar reasons that the Committee of Eighteen completed Chapter IX by adding a further safeguard embodied in a new Article 175. This had its origin in Article 36, item 28, which empowered the federal government to introduce taxation necessary to meet its expenditure "after consultation with the Provinces." Several members were of the opinion that these five words did not adequately protect provincial finances. The new article therefore provided that the provinces should be consulted *before* the bill relating to such taxes was submitted to Parliament. An amendment to the effect that such legislation should be subject to approval was rejected as going too far in the direction of provincial autonomy.

As mentioned earlier, the Committee of Eighteen had decided in principle to insert in the chapter on federal finance an additional clause to strengthen the protection already offered by Article 176 to federal grants-in-aid to the provinces. So far nothing had been done in that direction.

When the Working Group had almost reached the end of its work, the British legal adviser made an attempt to implement this decision. At this stage of drafting, Article 176 read:

> The Federal Government must allocate annually to the Provinces from its receipts sufficient funds to enable them to discharge their obligations subject to the condition that their financial capacity is not less than it was before independence. The method and amount of such allocations shall be determined by federal law.[74]

This reflected a rather pessimistic view of the future of the new country's public finances; on the other hand, the British adviser justly remarked that there was a danger in having the needs of the provinces tied to the financial standards prevailing before independence, instead of relating them to a possibly improving situation. Probably he also considered it desirable not to weaken the provinces financially vis-à-vis the federal government, which might be expected to grow in strength with foreign support. He therefore proposed that the following phrase be added at the end of the Article:

> in a manner that will guarantee continuous prosperous advancement to the Provinces, proportionate to the increased revenues of the Federal Government, provided the amounts to be allocated by the Federal Government to the Provinces shall be increased in case of improvement in the federal revenue.[75]

Not all members agreed with this proposal, in which some saw the shadow of an attempt to establish in the future fixed percentages governing the financial relationships between the federal government and the provinces. This, in turn, they feared, might hamper the Federation's growth.

74. Minutes of the Working Group of the Committee for the Constitution of the NCAL. United Nations Archives. Typescript.

75. Ibid.

Others saw advantages in such a harmonious growth, the principal one being the possibility of forestalling exaggerated claims by the provinces on the federal treasury. In the end, with assistance from the British financial adviser to the Provisional Libyan Government, C. Pitt-Hardacre, whose wisdom and experience again proved a great asset (cf. pp. 718–19), agreement was reached on the following text, which later appeared as part of Article 174 of the Constitution:

> in a manner that will guarantee to the Provinces an increase in the amounts to be allocated to them by the Federal Government, such increases to be proportionate to the growth of the federal revenue and such as will guarantee to them a constant economic progress.[76]

This addition helped greatly in making the proposed federal finance system more palatable to the advocates of provincial autonomy, and later facilitated the unanimous approval of the Constitution. At the same time it avoided the establishment of fixed percentages, which would have resulted in a rigid and unworkable financial relationship between the federal State and the provincial administrations.

The remaining articles making up Chapter IX deal with current budget procedures. Simple as they may look, their drafting nevertheless raised some peculiar difficulties owing to the fact that they had to serve a Parliament and an administration without experience in this field. As a result the chapter contains a few safeguards not usually found in constitutions, such as, for instance, the one in Article 161 that "the Parliamentary session may not be terminated before the budget has been approved."

Although the main task of drafting the Constitution had been brought successfully to an advanced stage, the next chapter will show that there remained several basic issues to be resolved before the work could be completed.

76. Annex II, p. 918.

CHAPTER 8

The End of the Road

PART 1. THE POLITICAL CLIMATE

While the drafting described in Chapter 7 was going on, a great many other things had happened. Some of them will be related in greater detail in Chapter 9, others in Chapter 10; some, although they appeared important at the time, were only of ephemeral interest. But all in their different ways affected the evolution of the political situation in Libya between January and October 1951.

These events must therefore be briefly mentioned at this juncture to help the reader to understand the atmosphere in which the NCAL began the final reading of the completed draft of the Constitution.

An account has already been given in Chapter 6 of the state of affairs which the Commissioner found upon his return to Libya from Lake Success in mid-December 1950 (cf. p. 460). The line he had been obliged to take before the General Assembly had given rise to a great many misunderstandings, some genuine, some intentionally magnified for specific political purposes. It had taken many private interviews, statements in the Council for Libya, and press releases to redress the genuine ones. The intentional ones were irredeemable. Nevertheless, by the middle of March the Commissioner felt that he had succeeded in clarifying his personal position to the point where he could once more, within the limits of his terms of reference, resume his role as adviser to and mediator between the feuding parties.

This was the more necessary as relations between the NCAL and the National Congress Party in Tripolitania, mutually inimical from the outset, had in the meantime been rapidly deteriorating. Several incidents, such as Azzam Pasha's statement of 5 January 1951 to a correspondent of the Italian newspaper, *Il Tempo* (see pp. 487–89), the revelation of the Egyptian-Pakistani-Italian-National Congress bargain for Council votes to bring a minority member into the Committee of Twenty-One (p. 244), followed by the visit of protest to Cairo of an NCAL delegation in early February (p. 495), and a clash between the Egyptian and Cyrenaican members of the Council for Libya over the federalist issue and its repercussions in the NCAL (pp. 505–08), had all added fuel to the fire.

On the higher level of constitutional development the rift between federalists and unitarists continued to widen as the opposition saw the determination with which the NCAL was forging ahead, drafting a Constitution federal in form and nature but at the same time providing for a central government with fairly strong powers. The Congress Party continued to criticize the NCAL's legislative work without making any constructive counterproposals.

Another cause of political friction, particularly within the Council, was the institution by the Commissioner of the Coordination Committee, whose task it was to prepare a plan for the transfer of powers from the Administering Powers to the Libyan Government. The establishment of local governments by the British Administration in Tripolitania and its French counterpart in the Fezzan, more or less on the lines of the Cyrenaican Government set up on 16 September 1949, also provoked the opposition to criticism, although early in 1950 the Congress Party itself had asked for such local institutions. However, the fact that what had been claims were becoming part of a federal system following the pattern laid down by the NCAL, soon to be followed by the creation of a provisional federal Libyan Government, tended to increase rather than to reduce tension. Attempts by the King-Designate and the Commissioner to bring about some kind of reconciliation failed. However, in the NCAL, where the voice of a moderate opposition did make itself heard, repeated efforts to compromise on particular issues were increasingly successful. Unfortunately, these compromises were far from adequate in the eyes of the extreme unitarists. The opposition had, unwisely, been given no seat either in the Provisional Libyan Government or in the Tripolitanian Council of Regency, which was another cause of much bitter feeling on its side. On the other hand, the Cyrenaicans, and to a somewhat lesser extent the Fezzanese, were profoundly irritated by the Tripolitanian Congress Party's claim to represent the whole of the Libyan people, whereas, in fact, it did not even represent a major part of the population of its own province. By the time spring came, the Commissioner had the impression that the political situation in Tripolitania was going from bad to worse.

There was another indication of the rising emotional voltage in early March, when the local press broke the news that the Commissioner had been receiving letters threatening him with assassination such as had befallen the United Nations mediator, Count Folke Bernadotte, in Jerusalem a few years before. Fortunately, he was spared that fate, though as a symptom of the feelings harbored by certain elements the news was significant. In Cyrenaica, as events will show, other difficulties—less serious in nature than those of the western province—were brewing. In the Fezzan, it was difficult to judge the state of public opinion; as so often in that territory, the situation looked deceptively quiet on the surface.

Other factors making for unrest were the Near Eastern radio and press campaigns, emanating in particular from Cairo, which were mostly hostile to the NCAL and generally propagated the Arab League's objections to the Assembly's nonelective origin and to its composition on a basis of provincial equality.

When, in March, the Secretary-General of the United Nations planned a series of official visits to a number of Balkan and Near Eastern capitals, it was at first intended that on his way back from Cairo he would visit Benghazi to be received in audience by the King-Designate and also to meet the local Government. Thereafter, he was to spend two days in Tripoli to see the local authorities, including the Prime Minister of the Provisional Libyan Government, the United Kingdom Resident, the President of the NCAL, and the leader of the opposition there.[1] However, when it became known that the Congress Party planned to organize a mass demonstration against federalism and against the NCAL to mark the occasion, the visit to Libya was reluctantly deleted from Trygve Lie's itinerary. Indeed, it would have been wrong to allow the Secretary-General to become the focus of what, strictly speaking, was an internal Libyan political affair, though one which might have had international repercussions likely to come into the open during the next session of the General Assembly. Moreover, there was a security problem. The local Tripolitanian Administration, primarily responsible for law and order, had at its disposal only a small—even if effective—British-officered police force. Had the Congress Party demonstration got out of hand, the authority carrying the highest responsibility, the British Resident, might have been obliged to call out British troops, a measure that obviously would have harmed the cause of Libya and the United Nations, not to mention British interests themselves.

Soon afterward, the situation came to a dramatic climax with the first official visit of the King-Designate to Tripolitania (cf. pp. 548–49). It was quite understandable that both the Libyan and the local governments, as well as the British authorities, should feel nervous. The Libyan authorities—the Provisional Government and the Tripolitanian Council of Regency

1. This appeared in every respect an appropriate gesture for the Secretary-General to make while he was in the area, considering that Libya's independence was one of the United Nations' major concerns at the time.

—were rather inclined to be a little rough with their opponents, not only to protect the Amir but also to prevent a possible bloody clash between the mass of young urban demonstrators and several hundred Cyrenaican and Tripolitanian tribal supporters of the illustrious visitor who had come into town, all well armed, trigger-happy, and mounted on high-spirited Arab steeds. On the face of it they certainly looked a little too ready to act as a kind of self-appointed bodyguard.

On 14 March, the Tripolitanian authorities, no doubt on the advice of the British Administration, passed a law on the prevention of crime, designed to protect the public from irresponsible and dangerous agitation.[2] According to the opponents of the Council of Regency, the purpose of the law was to suppress opposition. Under this law, on the eve of the arrival of the King-Designate, a number of persons were exiled to the interior; house arrest, either in their own homes or in specified hotels, was imposed on others, and a few were actually imprisoned. According to the leaders of the opposition, approximately 850 people, all members of the Congress Party, were thus taken out of circulation. They were released immediately after the King-Designate's departure. According to the local Government, the numbers were considerably lower, as the following passage from the Commissioner's second annual report shows:

> The Prime Minister of Tripolitania stated . . . [that] on the occasion of the visit of the King-Designate, 105 persons, whom the Government believed likely to cause trouble, were held in preventive detention, of whom only thirty-six were detained longer than seventy hours. Of the latter, all but eight were lodged under supervision in hotels rather than prisons. A further forty persons were arrested on criminal charges after disorder which took place during the visit. In view of the attempt which had been made on the King-Designate's life, it was probable that more arrests would have betokened greater prudence. The Prime Minister added that if these persons were members of the National Congress Party, as its President had alleged, it was nothing of which to be proud. He also stated that the law which had been the subject of objection had never been invoked.[3]

That the law in question had not been invoked did not make much difference from the point of view of an excited public opinion, except that it did raise the question, on what legal basis had the Council of Regency acted?

2. *Second Annual Report of the United Nations Commissioner in Libya,* GAOR: Sixth Session, 1951–52, Supplement No. 17 (A/1949), para. 48.

3. Ibid., para. 50.

It is always difficult to judge in cases like these whether the measures taken were effective or not, much less whether they were too severe or too lenient. In the event, they did not prevent five small hand grenades of wartime vintage from being thrown; only two exploded, one near the Amir's car, one near the Senussi Mosque. The other three were aimed respectively at the Prime Minister, at a minister's house, and at the procession. A shot was also fired at the editor of a pro-government newspaper, but fortunately missed. Nobody was killed, and only a few people were slightly wounded. Apparently the affair was intended more as a show of disaffection than as a serious attempt at assassination. However that may be, the Congress Party denied all responsibility, though many people were inclined to see the hand of the Arab League behind it. No one was charged with throwing the grenades, although a few suspects were seized on the spot but released later for lack of evidence.

In Cyrenaican circles indignation was intense, and the Tripolitanian police were immediately reinforced by constabulary from Benghazi, a measure which had the additional advantage of keeping certain tribal elements under control.

Throughout the excitement, the King-Designate, unlike his entourage, remained calm and unruffled, and the general public, which at the outset had been rather apathetic, began to warm to him. The change in attitude was particularly evident when, after having spent a few days receiving in audience a large number of local leaders and notables, including the head of the opposition, he visited the interior. His progress there gave rise to spontaneous demonstrations of loyalty, and when numerous deputations were announced from the deep south of Tripolitania, the King-Designate decided to prolong his stay by two days.

The speech he delivered the day before his departure (pp. 548–49), was constructive and conciliatory, and was an act of sagacious statesmanship. It gave the impression of a man who, knowing himself to be the symbol of national unity, was above party strife and above criticism of his own person. Nevertheless, it was a speech in favor of federalism and, although it contained certain passages that reassured the growing number of moderate unitarists in Tripolitania, it meant for that very reason a defeat for the extremists. The latter were practically all urban by domicile and mentality, and the visit brought home forcefully to them the extent of rural support for federalism which for a long time they had preferred to ignore.

From an all-Libyan point of view, the incidents during the royal visit naturally led to some deterioration in relations between the two coastal provinces, while the Fezzanese felt increasingly attracted both to the Cyrenaican and to the Tripolitanian federalists. The friendly assurances given to the minorities had the desired effect, first in facilitating the negotiations concerning the human rights clauses in the Constitution, and, seven months later, in easing the passage of the Libyan question through the General Assembly.

In the long run the Congress Party was the loser, a setback which might have been avoided to national advantage had it seized the opportunity of the Amir's presence to seek a compromise. Unfortunately the meeting of the Party's leader with the Amir was not satisfactory, according to the latter's advisers. In this context it must, however, be added that the attitudes of the Provisional Libyan Government and of the Tripolitanian Council of Regency were not helpful. Nor was that of the British authorities, who were still suspected, not entirely without reason, of working for a loose federation.

When, after the departure of the King-Designate, political tension in Tripoli continued to mount, the Commissioner decided to take the unusual step of writing "Dutch uncle" letters both to the Prime Minister of the Provisional Libyan Government and to the leader of the opposition. In doing so, he took the precaution of disclaiming any right to interfere in administrative matters. At the same time, he pointed out that on the maintenance of law and order depended, to a large extent, both the success of constitutional development and the establishment of a "duly constituted Government" competent to receive sovereign powers from the United Kingdom and France, without which the achievement of independence might be delayed, or even miscarry. He therefore felt justified, in view of the prevailing political situation, in tendering advice as to how law and order could best be kept in a democratic state. In the letter to the Prime Minister he insisted on the necessity of ensuring that all action to that end be strictly within the law and free from unduly harsh treatment. On the political level, he pointed out that the opposition was entitled to express its views, provided it did so in an orderly manner, and that it would be wise policy to take those views into account if the Constitution were to command the maximum respect of the people. He moreover recommended respect for the rights of the individual and expressed the hope that the Provisional Government would do its utmost to hold general elections at the earliest possible date.

In his letter to the leader of the opposition the Commissioner emphasized that democracy could function properly only if the whole community behaved democratically. If a group of citizens acted in violation of the established rules, then it was the Government's duty to uphold those rules, if necessary by the use of force, always provided that the Government's forces themselves kept within the law. To the opposition, that should mean that attempts to organize unauthorized demonstrations, the use of intimidation to oblige shopkeepers to close their shops, and, last but not least, political murder, must be avoided as highly undemocratic.

While fully recognizing the opposition's right to differ from the Government on the great national issues under discussion, the Commissioner expressed the opinion that the prevailing situation could be radically improved by using factual arguments and constructively criticizing the policy of the NCAL and the governments, national and provincial, in office.

Copies of both letters were communicated to the British Resident for his information. Whether they had much effect was doubtful. In the course of the summer, one had the impression that the NCAL was gaining in prestige, thanks to increasing support from the moderates in the Congress Party, who formed their own party under the name of the General Libyan Congress, taking the King's speech in Tripoli as the basis for their program. On the other hand, the extremist wing of the Congress Party appeared more and more disposed to violence, at least in the choice of its political vocabulary. It also attempted to establish new branches, which the Government tried to prevent. Tension remained high, and the standard of democratic behavior correspondingly low. However, there were no more open acts of violence during the summer, and the authorities maintained law and order in a reasonably licit manner.

Nevertheless, shortly before the NCAL approved the draft Constitution, an unpleasant incident occurred that touched federalist opinion on a highly sensitive point. The Tripolitanian administration mouthpiece, *Tarablus al-Gharb,* reported on 3 August 1951 a statement alleged to have been broadcast by Beshir Bey Saadawi from a Middle East radio station to the effect that he had requested the Egyptian Government to ask the General Assembly at its Sixth Session to delay the proclamation of Libyan independence in order that it might be acquired "in accordance with the wishes of the people." [4] The broadcast went on to say that the Egyptian Government had agreed to do so. The story emanated from the Benghazi correspondent of the radio station.

Another paper, *Shu'lat al-Hurriya,* which supported the Congress Party, denied this news on 6 August under the headline "Flagrant lies propagated by stooges of imperialism." [5] Soon all the cafés in Tripoli were buzzing with heated arguments between those who believed the story and those who did not.

The following day the incident was raised at the twenty-fourth meeting

4. Quotation taken from an English translation of the Arabic article in *Tarablus al-Gharb* made for internal purposes by the language staff of the United Nations Mission in Libya.

5. Ibid. (mutatis mutandis).

of the NCAL. Most members found it difficult to believe that a Libyan-born leader like Beshir Bey Saadawi could have made such a request to a foreign government, but knowing the stand taken by the opposition on the problem, they did not believe it altogether impossible. The President's office was therefore instructed to inquire into the matter, through the Provisional Libyan Government, by checking the Egyptian papers and by questioning the author of the story as to its veracity. If it were found to be correct, a note of protest would be sent to the Secretary-General of the United Nations and to the Commissioner. This proposal was approved by all members present with the exception of two Tripolitanians.

To the best of the present author's knowledge, the inquiry never led to any clear conclusion. Later in the month Beshir Bey himself, on his return from Cairo, firmly denied having demanded the postponement of independence. In the NCAL nothing more was said about the incident; but that should not be interpreted as meaning that it failed to produce any effect on the members. For one thing, it greatly speeded up recognition of the need for transitory arrangements as laid down in Chapter XII of the Constitution. It also helped to make certain members who were still hesitant understand that general elections at the national level must be held as soon as possible, and that the preparation and adoption of an electoral law would have to be undertaken immediately after the proclamation of the Constitution. For, if this purpose were achieved and elections could be scheduled for shortly after independence, a proposal to delay the latter would lose a great deal of its force.

At this point, by way of counterattack, the Congress Party launched a campaign throughout the Tripolitanian coastal belt in favor of free elections under United Nations supervision. Beshir Bey Saadawi wrote to this effect to the Commissioner, and followed up his letter with a personal visit to push his Party's proposal. Cables were dispatched to the Secretary-General in New York and to the then President of the Council for Libya, Lewis Clark. Local party branches addressed letters and appeals to the Commissioner, declaring that a freely elected Parliament was the only way in which a legal government approved by the people could be formed. The people, it was argued, could not accept elections supervised by the British Administration. They therefore demanded the resignation of the "present government"—apparently meaning the Provisional Federal Government—and the formation of a government enjoying the people's full confidence.

There is no denying that politically this was a clever move, and one which, moreover, might have proved legally defensible had it been made at the right time by way of possible interpretation of Resolution 289 (IV). Indeed, it will be remembered that in April 1950, the Commissioner, in his first request for advice on constitutional development to the Council for

Libya, had proposed that the National Assembly should be elected, though the Resolution did not explicitly prescribe that it should be an elected body.[6] Had the Tripolitanian Congress Party supported the proposal at the time, the Council would probably have given advice in the sense requested. Unfortunately, the Party was then in favor of an appointed National Assembly, and remained so until the Fifth Session of the General Assembly in the autumn of 1950, when it turned half circle under pressure from the Arab League, led by Egypt. Then it was already too late to arrange for an elected National Assembly before independence, and this was so a fortiori in September 1951.

One more consideration had to be reckoned with. If 1 January 1952 were maintained as the ultimate date for the declaration of independence, and if the general election were scheduled to take place after that date, Resolution 289 (IV) would have ceased to be valid by the time the elections were held. The Commissioner, the Council, and the Administering Powers would no longer be functioning, and the Libyan Government would be left as the sole authority competent to supervise elections.

For all of these reasons, the Commissioner felt obliged to inform Beshir Bey Saadawi that he could not support his request, advising him to approach the Prime Minister of the Provisional Government with a proposal that a voluntary agreement be concluded between that Government and the political parties to ensure impartial and fair conduct of the elections to Parliament. At the same time, just before leaving for Benghazi, he gave Beshir Bey a full picture of the constitutional situation as he then saw it, to ensure that the latter was at least fully aware of his views on the matter.

Such, then, was the political situation and atmosphere when in September the Committee of Eighteen, after having given its approval to the draft Constitution article by article, submitted it to the NCAL for final discussion and assent. The situation was confused and complicated, the atmosphere was tense, protagonists were torn by divided loyalties. From the Commissioner's point of view this was not at all an appropriate state of affairs in which to proclaim the Constitution of a State that in three months was to enter the community of nations as a new and independent member. There was no choice but to carry on, however, for time was running short.

PART 2. CHANGE OF SITE AND ATMOSPHERE

On 10 September 1951, the NCAL received the first four Chapters of the draft Constitution, on 17 September the remaining eight. It was

6. First *Annual Report of the United Nations Commissioner in Libya,* GAOR: Fifth Session, 1950, Supplement No. 15, (A/1340), Annex V, pp. 45–46.

decided that the first reading should be held in open session, to give the public a chance to familiarize itself with the contents of the document. This was, indeed, becoming increasingly desirable, as until then the content had been known only through short news bulletins, supplemented by widespread rumors which were one of the causes of the prevailing unrest.[7] The public gallery was chock-full.

From the outset, the President made it clear that the draft Constitution was by no means final and that during the general debate that was about to start every member would have the right to submit any amendment or make any proposal he might deem necessary. Legally and procedurally this was a proper statement, but events were to prove that, given the prevailing political situation, it lent itself to abuse and loss of valuable time.

Previously there had been some discussion about a recess during the Islamic Feast of the Immolation, starting on 9 September and lasting for four days, which the Fezzanese members would have liked to celebrate at home with their families. A motion in this sense was defeated, however, after Khalil Qallal, the Chairman of the Working Group, had addressed the following moving appeal to his colleagues, who reacted enthusiastically to it:

> I ask my colleagues to bear something of a sacrifice and to make every effort, so that we can finish the Constitution as quickly as possible; the highest motives impel us to do so. . . .
>
> I oppose the vote, since the general good demands that we all work on without pause. We have accepted the responsibility of drawing up a constitution, and we must see the task out. We must pay no attention to other considerations. *Our* festival will be the day when we finish our task and bring our constitution into being. Let those among us who long for their families imagine that they are on a business trip, when they pass the festivals far from their families without this preventing them from carrying out their commercial enterprises. How much more so, then, should they be prepared to devote themselves to the constitution for a whole nation, on which the life of the nation, and that of generations to come, will be built.[8]

On 17 September, after the full draft had been read in public, the NCAL went into private session in order to consider a telegram received from the King-Designate asking for a copy of the draft Constitution and proposing that the NCAL should move to Benghazi to complete its deliberations. Although nobody said so openly, it was generally recognized that this in-

7. The *Weekly Information Bulletin* put out by the United Nations Mission dealt solely with Mission activities, of which those of the NCAL were no part. The Secretariat of the Assembly issued brief press communiqués of its own.

8. *Proc. NCAL,* Stewart-Jackson Translation, 27th Meeting, 5 September 1951.

vitation was much more than a simple act of convenience or courtesy. Its intention obviously was to remove the NCAL from the emotional atmosphere of Tripoli to the more sober-minded environment of the Cyrenaican capital, where, moreover, foreign pressure was less strongly felt.[9] It also meant, however, that in the last instance the draft Constitution would be reviewed under the influence of local pressure groups predominantly favorable to federalism, and in a city where the unitary concept of the State was held only by a small urban minority, barely tolerated by the authorities, and openly opposed by influential tribal elements. Hence it was possible that the change in atmosphere might create new kinds of problems, less dangerous perhaps for the final success of the operation than those in Tripoli, but no less harmful. At the same time the presence of the King-Designate as a highly respected element behind the scenes promised to be of great advantage.

Already in the course of the summer, the Cyrenaican Government had lodged a complaint with the Commissioner, through the intermediary of the British Resident, to the effect that they were not being kept adequately informed of what was going on in the NCAL and its two subordinate bodies. It had been easy for the United Nations Mission to prove that the members of the Government in Benghazi had received exactly the same documentation in Arabic as their Tripolitanian colleagues. Moreover, on each of the numerous occasions when the Commissioner or the Legal Adviser had flown to Benghazi to inform or consult the King-Designate, they had also made it a point to see the Cyrenaican Prime Minister. On the financial clauses of the Constitution, the Cyrenaican Minister of Finance had been fully consulted. It appeared, however, that the Cyrenaican delegation had kept the King-Designate more fully informed than his Government, some members of which were living in constant dread that their representatives in Tripoli might be yielding to the unitarist pressures of their Tripolitanian colleagues. Admittedly, the position of the Cyrenaican members of the NCAL had been a delicate one. Commanding jointly with the Fezzanese a majority on most issues, and frequently tempted to take advantage of that

9. Khalidi has the following to say on the subject: "in view of Cyrenaica's longer history of struggle and resistance against Italian colonization, its people and the Amir felt that they were entitled to a fuller share in the shaping of the Constitution than had hitherto been accorded them. As long as the Assembly was meeting in Tripoli, the Cyrenaicans felt themselves in a less favored position in the formulation of the Constitution; hence the convening of the Assembly in Benghazi fulfilled an age-old desire of the Cyrenaicans to be treated on an equal footing with their brothers, the Tripolitanians, in the affairs and destiny of Libya." Ismail Raghib Khalidi, *Constitutional Development in Libya* (Beirut, Lebanon: Khayat's College Book Co-operative, 1956), p. 59.

situation, their leaders, Khalil Qallal and Omar Shenib in particular, had had the wisdom to make certain concessions to the Tripolitanian minority of unitarist moderates. On the Tripolitanian side, a few men like Munir Burshan [10] had found themselves in a more or less comparable position with regard to the Congress Party, but, being on home ground, they had the possibility of giving day-to-day explanations of their policies to their more extreme political friends. These mutual attempts at understanding had finally produced a document including numerous compromises that were about to be put to the test in the very different atmosphere of an extremely proud, almost arrogant, provincial patriotism, a mixture of Arab nationalism and profound loyalty to Sanusiyah, peculiar to Cyrenaica. That the NCAL met in the Chamber of the Cyrenaican Assembly of Representatives almost seemed an omen.

From the time of his first visit to the territory, it had been clear to the Commissioner that Cyrenaica (like the Fezzan) would only join in a Libyan union if that union were built on a foundation of federalism. What now remained to be tested was the degree of federalism acceptable to the Cyrenaicans. Confronted with the draft Constitution elaborated in Tripoli, the first reaction of the conservative elements was one of reluctance, almost of revulsion. At the time, the Commissioner summarized his views on the situation as follows in his second report to the General Assembly:

> the Commissioner noted that a certain tendency to sectionalism was developing in Cyrenaica, where in some quarters it was apparently not expected that the Constitution would give such wide powers to the Federal Government as was in fact proposed. In particular, the proposal to transfer to the central Government a large number of the important powers exercised by the Government of Cyrenaica caused some resentment and a wish to reconsider certain articles of the Constitution with a view to their amendment in the opposite sense.[11]

In transmitting the draft Constitution to the President of the NCAL, the Chairman of the Committee of Eighteen had taken care to indicate, article by article, the points on which no agreement had as yet been reached, as

10. Munir Burshan resigned from the National Congress of Tripolitania in the summer of 1951.

11. *Second Annual Report of the United Nations Commissioner in Libya,* para. 96. While the Commissioner was in Benghazi attending the final phase of constitutional development, the Principal Secretary of the Mission was attending—as his personal representative—the Council for Libya which, in none too friendly a mood, had assembled in Geneva to examine both the second annual report and the plan for the transfer of powers, while waiting for the Constitution to be adopted.

well as those which had been approved subject to reservations by individual members who had placed on record in the Proceedings their intention of reasserting their objections in plenary session.

No agreement had been reached on provisions concerning the succession to the Throne (Articles 44 and 45), and the final decision thereon had been left to the King-Designate. The decision on the site of the capital (Article 188) had also been left open.

Reservations had been entered with regard to:

Article 36 (10)—Immigration into and emigration from Libya

Article 47—The royal oath

Article 87—Vote of no confidence by the House of Representatives

Article 95—Appointment of senators

Article 187—Use of foreign languages in official transactions

In addition to these eight outstanding issues, the Cyrenaican deputation, under pressure from its Government, wanted to reopen a few more questions, although agreement on them had previously been reached in Tripoli in the Committee of Eighteen. The most important of them was the disposal of customs revenue.

The reactions of the Cyrenaican and Tripolitanian members of the NCAL to the royal invitation to meet in Benghazi naturally differed. One Cyrenaican member (Khalil Qallal) said:

> The Committee for the Constitution intended to inform H. M. the King of the constitution, since he is a party to it, but we were delayed by the holiday. Since his Majesty has asked to be informed, we shall send it now with great pleasure, and comply to his request, which we consider an authoritative command.[12]

On the Tripolitanian side, it was first proposed that a delegation be sent from the three provinces to present the Constitution to His Majesty.[13] The same delegation could, moreover, provide any explanations requested. When, thereupon, it was suggested that the delegation might be composed of the three principal officers of the Committee of Eighteen, the President observed:

> The intention is not that those who drew up the constitution should defend their work. The intention is simply to present it to H. M. Discussing the constitution is a matter for the Assembly. Discussions and

12. *Proc. NCAL,* Stewart-Jackson Translation, 29th Meeting, 17 September 1951.

13. It should be noted at this point that although officially the King still bore the title of King-Designate, he was already generally addressed as H. M. the King, the title that will be used henceforward in this study.

debates are not to be held with H. M. the King. If H. M. graciously offers some direction to the Assembly, that direction will be studied, and its guidance follows [*sic*].[14]

It was finally decided that the delegation to be sent to present the Draft Constitution to the King would comprise the President and the two Vice-Presidents of the NCAL. It would be followed to Benghazi by the Assembly as a whole, the intention being to finish the final reading of the Constitution and enact its proclamation there.

The first two meetings in Benghazi (the thirtieth on 29 September and thirty-first on 30 September) were devoted to an exchange of courtesies and civilities between the Prime Minister of the host Government, the President of the Cyrenaican Assembly of Representatives, and the President of the NCAL. Members then listened to the second reading of the draft. Subsequently the President proposed that the Working Group be given time to study the articles in abeyance and prepare the necessary drafts so that the NCAL could have a complete text in front of it when it started the third reading. Meanwhile, the Working Group accompanied by the President and the two Vice-Presidents of the NCAL were received in ceremonial audience by the King.

On 2 October, the NCAL embarked upon the third and final reading of the Constitution, article by article, at its thirty-second meeting. During the interval, the Commissioner, who had accompanied the Assembly to Benghazi, paid a visit to the King, together with the federal Prime Minister, Mahmud al-Muntasir, to give him their joint views on the situation and to ask for his cooperation in solving the problems that, no doubt, would arise.

In the course of this audience all controversial questions were reviewed, and it was agreed that should any serious difficulties come up on any article, they would be considered outside the NCAL by a small Joint Committee, consisting of the King himself, when necessary, and of the federal Prime Minister and the Commissioner, assisted by the three officers of the National Assembly, each representing one of the three provinces. It was also agreed that if possible the final reading of the Constitution and its proclamation should be completed within one week. The King made it clear that his general attitude would be that of guide and counselor, since he had no wish to issue instructions to the NCAL. He emphasized that the Constitution should truly reflect the agreed opinions of the members of the National Assembly, and expressed the hope that it would be unanimously approved.

During the debates which followed, many articles were approved as they stood in the draft, or with only minor amendments not affecting matters of

14. *Proc. NCAL,* Stewart-Jackson Translation, 29th Meeting, 17 September 1951.

substance. These articles will not be referred to in what follows; mention will be made of only those that gave rise to substantive differences.

Disputes arose in the first instance over a few items in Chapter III, "Powers of the Federal Government and Joint Powers." A Tripolitanian member, Munir Burshan, pointed out that the chapter had already been approved on 18 August and transmitted to the Coordination Committee, which had taken it as the basis for its plan for the transfer of powers. Moreover, the Council for Libya, meeting in Geneva, had approved that plan on 28 September, by 7 votes to none with 2 abstentions.[15] He therefore opposed the reopening of the discussion. The majority of the NCAL agreed to this approach, but the Cyrenaican delegation opposed it, proposing a change in the wording of the relevant item of the agenda.

The question was whether the agenda item in question (2) should read "Discussion on the sections of the Constitution," [16] as proposed by the Secretary of the NCAL, or "Discussions of the sections of the Constitution with the exception of the third section" as proposed by a member from Tripolitania.

After an intervention by a member from Cyrenaica, it was finally agreed that item 2 of the agenda should read: "Discussion of the sections of the Constitution, with the exception of the sections in which only the verbal

15. The member for Cyrenaica, Ali Bey Jerbi, had resigned on being appointed Minister for Foreign Affairs in the Provisional Government. During the Council session held in September 1951 in Geneva, he was represented by Ali Mourridine Unayzi in his personal capacity. Unayzi, under the Council's rules of procedure, had accordingly no right to vote. Otherwise the vote would have been 8 votes for, with 2 abstentions (Egypt and France). On 1 October, the Commissioner, in conformity with the procedure prescribed in paragraph 7 of Resolution 289 (IV), appointed Unayzi member of the Council for Cyrenaica. Unayzi was born at Benghazi in 1904. After having attended elementary school at his place of birth, he specialized in agricultural subjects at secondary schools in Italy, receiving a degree in colonial agriculture from the Institute of Colonial Agriculture at Florence in 1923. From 1923 to 1930 he continued his studies at the University and Oriental School in Naples where in 1930 he received his Ph.D. in economics. Upon his return to Cyrenaica he was appointed First Secretary of Land Registry at Benghazi, and in 1935 Director of Waqf (Pious Endowment) Administration. He also acted as adviser on local political affairs to the Italian Administration. In 1941, after the first British occupation of Cyrenaica, he left for Cairo to resume his studies. From 1945 to March 1950 he served as member of the Arab League Secretariat. Upon his return to Benghazi he served as member of the Provisional Currency Committee and as alternate delegate for Cyrenaica on the Coordination Committee.

16. Groups of related articles that were sometimes called "sections" at the drafting stage became "chapters" in the later stages and in the final text. See also Chapter 6, p. 429, fn. 2.

amendments added by the Committee for the Constitution will be examined." [17]

Since it is always difficult in the course of a public debate to maintain a clear distinction between verbal emendations and substantive amendments to a text, this wording could for all practical purposes be interpreted as a victory for the Cyrenaican conservative group, enabling its members to reopen the debate on every feature of the Constitution that they deemed went too far toward centralized federalism or not far enough in the grant of royal powers.

The Preamble and Chapter I, "Form of the State and the System of Government," were approved without difficulty.

When the discussion reached Chapter II, "Rights of the People," Articles 8 and 9 (particularly the latter, regarding the acquisition of Libyan nationality) were, by common agreement, but more specifically to meet Cyrenaican wishes, set aside for separate examination. Most of the other articles comprising this chapter were approved without debate. However, there were two exceptions, each of which gave rise to some interesting exchanges of views.

Article 21 of the draft read:

> Freedom of conscience shall be absolute. The State shall respect all religions and faiths and shall ensure to Libyans and foreigners residing in its territory, freedom of conscience and the right to practice freely religion so long as it is not a breach of public order and is not contrary to morality.[18]

The record relates:

> The Hon. Mem. Munir Burshan asked how the phrase "contrary to morality" was to be understood. "Will it be defined by law? If so, we should add a clause to that effect."
>
> The Hon. Member Khalil Gellal said that it was understood that order and common morals were acknowledged matters and an effective convention, and that they came under the State.
>
> But the Hon. Member Ali Tamir observed that common morals were an ethical order generally applicable in the world and commonly acknowledged among the human race; and he said that there were special traditions which one city rather than another observed, and which it was essential be preserved by law.

17. *Proc. NCAL,* Stewart-Jackson Translation, 32nd Meeting, 2 October 1951.
18. Ibid.

The Hon. Member Munir Burshan repeated his suggestion, which was that the sentence "in accordance with the stipulations of the law" be added to the Article.

The Hon. Member Khalil Gellal objected to that, saying that it was not possible to draft a law defining morals and public order because the totality of order in the State was the effective law.

The Hon. Member Abdul Majeed Ku'bar arose and said that the Article was sound and that he hoped that members would confirm it. It was confirmed and agreement was reached upon it without further alteration.[19]

The next provision that gave rise to discussion was Article 30, which prescribed that:

Elementary education shall be compulsory for Libyan children of both sexes; elementary and primary education in the public schools shall be free.[20]

The following exchange ensued:

The Hon. Member Munir Burshan arose and said that this Article stipulated that it was the Government's job to apply the compulsory education law and that it would not be possible to carry this out. He therefore asked whether a further phrase should be added "within the bounds of possibility."

The secretary of the Assembly, the Hon. Member Suleiman Jerbi said that this was, of course, understood, even if it hadn't [*sic*] been mentioned in the Article. On this point the Chairman supported him, saying that if divine commands were to be observed within the bounds of possibility this was all the more reason that conventional commands should be so observed and that this was necessarily understood.

The Hon. Member Mahmoud al Maslati commented upon it saying that he believed that the interpretation of compulsory education should be that the people were to be looked to not to leave their children without education, but as for compelling the Government to open schools, this would depend upon its budget.

The secretary, Suleiman Jerbi then said that the Article remained sound. He went on to read the remainder of the Articles of Section 2 up to Article 35, and the members confirmed them and agreed upon them.[21]

19. Ibid.
20. Ibid.
21. Ibid.

These two examples are representative of the approach of many members of the NCAL to the new problems with which they were faced.

So far the debate had been sedate, but as soon as the secretary began to read Chapter III, "Powers of the Federal Government and Joint Powers," the atmosphere became tense and the old Cyrenaican-Tripolitanian antagonism raised its ugly head. The representatives of the host province argued that the distribution of powers had been settled in haste and on a wave of enthusiasm to enable the Coordination Committee to go ahead with its planning on the transfer of powers, and that at the same time it had been agreed that modifications of form and shape might be introduced later. Hence, the chapter should be reread, incidental changes being looked at "so that everybody could perceive them." [22]

Indeed, at the twenty-sixth meeting:

> The Hon. Mem. Khalil Gellal had requested that a note be made in the minutes to the effect that debating the list of powers now and passing a resolution about it would not prevent its being re-examined when the various sections of the constitution were co-ordinated.[23]

The Tripolitanian representatives countered by pointing out that on the contrary Chapter III had been discussed article by article, and that a reopening of the substantive discussion was accordingly precluded.

The President ruled that, the chapter having been previously approved by the NCAL, it could not be reviewed. Only its formal shape could be rediscussed.

In the course of the debate it transpired that the Secretary of the NCAL had indeed introduced "verbal" changes in the draft, and a Tripolitanian member asked the Chairman of the Working Group to explain such "modifications of language."

As the reading of Chapter III proceeded, it became clear that the Cyrenaican delegation was divided into two schools of thought. Some of its members were content to limit the discussion to verbal changes, whereas others wanted to go much further, proposing, for instance, that item 4 ("matters relating to war and peace") and item 5 ("the conclusion and implementation of treaties and agreements with other States") be transferred to Chapter V, "The King." One of the latter group complained that

> he and his Cyrenaican colleagues were being suppressed as regards freedom of speech and that no scope had been left for them for discussion.
>
> The President answered that they had been given in the Working

22. Ibid.
23. *Proc. NCAL,* Stewart-Jackson Translation, 26th Meeting, 18 August 1951.

> Committee sufficient time for discussion and study, and that therefore there was no meaning in asking for broadness of heart, breadth of mind and opportunity for further discussion, and that they were in a Libyan Assembly and not a Regional Assembly. . . . After its [the Libyan Assembly's] composition there was to be no distinction between delegates, rather that all were adorned with the common name of Libyan and that they had begun working together for the common good of Libya without neglecting the regions." [24]

At this point it was wisely decided to suspend the meetings for a quarter of an hour to allow members to calm down.

When the debate was resumed it soon appeared, not for the first time, that item 10 of Article 36 ("Immigration into Libya after consultation with the Provinces and emigration from Libya") was a highly sensitive issue with the Cyrenaicans, who wanted to make immigration subject to the agreement of the provinces instead of merely to consultation with them. It was not for nothing that they had made a reservation on this point in the Committee of Eighteen. At the same time, the Tripolitanians, upon reflection, had come to the conclusion that item 10 might after all have been worded too loosely. Their province too had its interest in possible Italian immigration into Libya. Moreover, the item as drafted also dealt with emigration from Libya, which affected both those Italians who might wish to leave Libya with their possessions and the Libyan Jews, whose massive exodus to Israel at the time was creating similar problems.

On the other hand, the Tripolitanians greatly hesitated to agree to substantive amendments to Chapter III, which might easily serve as a precedent for other parts of the Constitution where the Cyrenaicans wanted to introduce changes. Thus, they were reluctant to accept even the insertion of the word "mutual" between "after" and "consultation," although the Working Group had considered that, immigration and emigration being within federal and provincial competence, there must be consultation between the two administrations; and such consultations would of necessity have been "mutual." A simple way out of the difficulty would have been to transfer item 10 from Part I ("Powers of the Federal Government") to Part II ("Joint Powers"), but that too was considered by the Tripolitanians as a substantive change, and in any event it did not meet the Cyrenaicans' demands. It was in these circumstances that a new idea was put forward by members from both provinces to the effect that item 10 should by "verbal" change be restored to its original scope (immigration into Libya and emigration from Libya) and left where it was; a new article being inserted else-

24. *Proc. NCAL,* Stewart-Jackson Translation, 32nd Meeting, 2 October 1951.

where in the constitution to meet Cyrenaican wishes. In order to allow the Working Group to prepare a suitable draft of such an article, further discussion on item 10 was deferred.

The remaining items of Article 36 (with the exception, of course, of that on customs) did not give rise to much debate, the changes proposed being of a purely verbal nature. Nevertheless, one Cyrenaican member complained yet again that the Working Group and the Committee of Eighteen had been too much inclined to narrow the powers of the provinces, and announced his continued opposition to that policy.

Chapter IV, "General Federal Powers," was passed without any discussion of real importance, though there was one incident, typical of a certain Cyrenaican way of thinking. Salem al-Atrash, a Cyrenaican deputy, proposed in a prepared statement that Chapter IV should open with the following new article:

> The King of the Federal State of Libya, Mohammed Idris 1st should preserve for himself and for such of his progeny as should succeed him to the Throne of the Kingdom of Libya the title of Amir of Cyrenaica and the rights and distinctions which would result from this title in addition to the titles, rights and distinctions which he has as King of United Libya.[25]

The record goes on:

> A moment of silence reigned over the Assembly, and after it the Hon. Member Munir Burshan arose and said in a vigorously angry outburst that the King had risen from being an Amir to the rank of Majesty and he did not see that Mr. Idris al Mahdi al Sanusi should be reduced from the title of King to the title of Amir, and that he protested against this request. Cries of long live the King of Libya then arose, and a wave of clapping spread through the hall. During this the Hon. Member Mabrouk Geibani arose and raised his voice saying that they had acknowledged His Highness the Prince Mohamed al Mahdi Idris al Sanusi as King over Libya, and that they wished that the next day he should become Emperor, and he asked whether they wished to retreat from that position. This speech of his was approved in a wave of clapping and acclamation and thus the suggestion of the Hon. Member Salem el Atrash was rejected. But he asked, despite its refusal that it be recorded in the Minutes. The Article [40] was thus confirmed.[26]

25. Ibid.
26. Ibid.

The draft of Chapter V, "The King," gave rise to an exchange of views showing that the transition from the traditional Arab concept of kingship to that of a constitutional and parliamentary monarchy was not readily acceptable to all members. The clash between the two concepts is best illustrated by quoting further from the minutes of the same meeting:

> the Hon. Member Abdel Gawad Freites arose and delivered a long statement in which he said that the Articles which had passed were concerned with the King, and that from Article 58 onwards they were concerned with the King's authority, and he asked whether it was preferable that they should build their Constitution on observation of the power of the King's authority as an actual power against which they had no recourse, pointing out that that was for the interest of the people and for their relief in so far as their people were still in the course of understanding democratic systems and becoming used to them. He also asked whether they should build their Constitution on the premise that power in the hands of the King should be symbolic or actual, and said that he felt that if they looked to the common interest they would gain strength from the King's authority and increase in it.
>
> The President said that had they been left to their own devices they would have for themselves one of the greatest constitutions of the world, in that that was the noble Qur'an and the Sunna, and that they would have in the moderation and the intelligence and the skill of His Majesty their Lord something which would enable them to dispense with the drafting of that constitution, but that in so far as their independence was something which had come to them by way of the U.N. organisation, which desired of them that they draft a constitution after the manner of the constitutions of the world, they were for this reason drafting that representative constitution so that it would be tantamount to a passport for their entry into the group of the independent nations. He also said that their King, may God preserve him, was a moderate and constitutional man, and it was important to him that his commission be a fine and constitutional commission.
>
> The Hon. Member Munir Burshan then arose and said that he thought that the existing laws in the world prescribed that domination should be with the people and not with the King and that if they wished to load their King with many responsibilities he would recoil from the burden of them. He also said that when they drafted their Constitution they had taken care that it should be far from any possibility of being described as a dictatorship or an autocracy, and that they did not wish to leave any loophole to their enemies to attack them on it. He added that if they had

been certain that Mr. Muhammad Idris al Mahdi al Sanusi were immortal then they would have had done with that Constitution.

The Hon. Member Mr. Abdel Gawad al Freites said that these considerations which his honourable colleague had brought forward were worthy of being taken into account but it was abundantly clear that they were far more concerned with democracy than had been the great democratic nations notwithstanding the vast difference between them.[27]

Articles 44 and 45, both dealing with the succession to the Throne, were once more sent back to the Working Group, with instructions that the latter approach "the persons whom they ought to contact so that their opinion might be taken." [28]

Five days later, at the thirty-fourth meeting, the two articles were re-tabled in considerably different form.

The draft of Article 44 had read:

The constitutional sovereignty of the United Kingdom of Libya is vested in the nation. By the will of God the people entrust it to King Mohamed Idris al Mahdi Al Senussi and after him to his male heirs. The Throne of the Kingdom is hereditary in the dynasty of King Idris I. The order of succession to the Throne shall be determined by Federal law.[29]

The new text read simply:

The sovereignty of the United Kingdom of Libya is vested in the nation. By the will of God the people entrust it to King Mohamed Idris al Mahdi Al Senussi and after him to his male heirs, the oldest after the oldest, degree after degree.[30]

The draft of Article 45 had read:

The heir presumptive to the Throne shall be the eldest son of the King; in the event of the King having no son, the heir presumptive shall be appointed by the King. No one may accede to the Throne unless he is of sound mind, a Libyan and a Moslem born of Moslem parents.[31]

The new text ran as follows:

The Throne of the Kingdom is hereditary. The order of succession to the Throne shall be determined by Royal Decree promulgated by King Idris I within a year of the date of the promulgation of this Constitution.

27. Ibid.
28. Ibid.
29. *Proc. NCAL,* Stewart-Jackson Translation, 34th Meeting, 7 October 1951.
30. Ibid.
31. Ibid.

> No one may accede to the Throne unless he is of sound mind, a Libyan and a Moslem born of Moslem parents legally wedded. The Royal Decree which shall regulate the succession to the Throne shall have the same force as an article of this Constitution.[32]

The minutes relate that Munir Burshan asked his colleagues whether they considered that these articles should be drafted by the King.

The record goes on:

> The reply came that there were constitutional precedents similar to this.
>
> He asked whether they approved that royal affairs should be put before Parliament. The Hon. Member Mohamed al Hankari replied that this was not a law which should be submitted for that reason. The President then said that the Assembly had the right of drafting the Constitution and that this Article in so far as it was the special sphere of the King, had been placed by the Assembly in his hands to be formulated and set in order. After this discussion the Article was confirmed and approved.[33]

This was a courteous and respectful way of saying that the final drafting of these articles was left to the King himself.

It would be unfair to the NCAL and historically incorrect to leave the impression that during this final stage of the drafting of the Constitution its members spent all their time in political bickering. At the opening of the thirty-third meeting on 3 October, the Working Group submitted a new text for the much contested first paragraph of Article 87 in Chapter VI, "The Ministers," in which the two-thirds majority originally prescribed for a vote of no confidence in the Council of Ministers by the House of Representatives was replaced by a "majority of all its members." The new text was the outcome of long discussions between the officers of the Assembly and the Working Group, and the Commissioner and his legal adviser. What had carried the day was the realization that the King and the Cabinet should not be put in the position of having to govern with only minority support, reinforced by fear of criticism in the General Assembly of the United Nations. The King's personal influence behind the scenes had also been of great help.

32. Ibid. With reference to the last sentence of Article 45 as finally approved, it should be remembered that Article 197 in Chapter XI, "General Provisions," lists the order of succession to the Throne among the four subjects on which no proposal may be made to review the Constitution.

33. Ibid.

In the course of the same meeting a number of articles were substantively clarified. For instance, the draft of Article 102 had stipulated that to exercise voting rights a Libyan citizen had to be of the male sex. Upon reflection, it was decided to transfer this provision from the Constitution to the electoral law so as to facilitate change at whatever time in the future this might prove desirable; a remarkable case of foresight in an orthodox Moslem country.[34]

Another improvement was introduced in the case of Article 111, which in draft would have allowed each Chamber to decide upon the validity of the election of its members in accordance with its own rules of procedure. In the final stage it was decided to add a rider that a decision to the effect that the "election of a member was invalid" would require a majority of two-thirds of the members of the Chamber. Thus the risk of an arbitrary vote on such an issue was reduced. The record notes that the NCAL thought that this was "a good idea." Undeniably, the members knew the tendencies of their colleagues.

A curious discussion took place on Article 120, which prescribes that "Every bill adopted by one of the two Chambers shall be transmitted by the President of that Chamber to the President of the other Chamber." A Cyrenaican member proposed that the initiation of legislation be left exclusively to the House of Representatives, so that the "Council of Elders" (the Senate) could check on it before approving it. To one accustomed to a tribal way of life, the habit of trusting the wisdom of the elders is, indeed, a perfectly commendable way of handling public affairs. Even in Western countries it has not quite yet been lost, although it is slowly dying out. A few of the proposer's colleagues hastened to explain to him that, under a parliamentary system, taking the right of legislative initiative away from the Senate would reduce its power and authority. The matter was accordingly dropped.

No serious difference of opinion disturbed the calm until Article 136 was reached. This was a compromise text elaborately drafted by the Working Group in order to balance the respective powers of the Crown and Parliament while at the same time leaving the last word with the representatives of the people. One Cyrenaican member, *plus royaliste que le Roi*, proposed that instead of saying "the King may refer the law back to Parliament for reconsideration," the article should stipulate that "the King shall have the right of issuing laws or rejecting them." A Tripolitanian member reacted by pointing out that this meant the negation of Parliament. A long debate

34. Libyan women were enfranchised in 1961.

followed, during which the Chairman of the Working Group, Khalil Qallal, himself a Cyrenaican, said:

> the laws did not apply to the King except after they had gone through two stages in the Chamber of Representatives and the Chamber of Elders, and that the final approval had to be by a majority of two-thirds of the two Chambers together. The King, he said, was democratic by his very nature and that in this case the King had a right and the people had a right, but that the King was unable to oppose the opinion of the majority.[35]

To find a solution without hurting members' feelings by resort to a vote, the meeting was briefly suspended. When it resumed,

> The President resumed the discussion saying that Article 137 [136 in the final text] had been drafted by the Working [Group] and studied by the Committee for the Constitution, and they had made such modifications as they wished until they were of the opinion that they had reached a sound draft. But, he said, his brother and colleague Abdel Gawad Freites was full of love and loyalty for the King and careful for preserving his rights, and he had observed what anxieties had beset him on this Article; and he went on to say that it was for him to show what he felt was appropriate in the section on the rights of the King which they had confirmed and agreed upon. He did say, however, that if his honourable colleague could see his way to refraining from his insistence he would make the difficult parts of their discussion considerably more easy and he would secure much time for them.
>
> The Hon. Member Abdel Gawad Freites answered him saying that he was a devoted disciple of his Honour the President, and a member of the Assembly of which he was the President, and that therefore he had no contention with his Honour, that he retracted what he wished to say at their pleasure, and that he withdrew his request, thanking them for their graciousness and their direction. The Hon. Members thanked him unanimously and the Article was confirmed, remained sound and was agreed upon.[36]

It is difficult to imagine—or to find—a more courteous way of settling a difference of opinion occurring in the course of a parliamentary debate. Hence, all was well again until the Assembly came to Articles 173, 174, and 175, all in Chapter IX, "Federal Finance," and notoriously controversial.

35. *Proc. NCAL,* Stewart-Jackson Translation, 33rd Meeting, 3 October 1951.
36. Ibid.

In order to avoid a debate which in all likelihood would have been as stormy as it would have been inconclusive, it was decided once again to send these articles, together with Articles 171, 172, and 176, back to the Working Group for further reworking.

Thanks to its careful preparation, Chapter X, "The Provinces," went through without much difficulty, interventions being limited to requests for explanatory information on some of the articles.

When it came to Chapter XI, "General Provisions," the NCAL chose the easy path of first approving all the noncontroversial articles, while holding in suspense Article 188 (on the capital). It also sent back to the Working Group Article 199, which prescribed the conditions under which the provisions of the Constitution concerning the federal form of government might be reviewed. This was a question on which there existed a difference of opinion between the majority of the NCAL and the Commissioner, as well as between Cyrenaicans and Tripolitanians. Since, moreover, it had been decided in principle to add a new article, on immigration, to the general provisions, Chapter XI as a whole was left in abeyance for the moment.

As to Chapter XII, "Transitory and Provisional Provisions," it will be remembered that a politically fraught question arose with regard to the timetable for the proclamation of the Constitution, the declaration of independence and the holding of the first general election. Agreement had been reached on the principle of their order, but a few not so simple details still had to be determined. The first was the reference to Libyan nationality to be added to Article 201, to enable the NCAL to start drafting the electoral law. The Working Group had proposed introducing references both to Article 8 and to Article 9, the first of which defined Libyan nationality as such whereas the second determined, among other things, the conditions on which certain categories of foreigners might opt for Libyan nationality. The principal category of foreigners involved in this context were members of minorities, among them Italian settlers with not less than ten years of residence on Libyan soil. The conditions in question were to be regulated by law. It will also be remembered that this part of Article 9 was meant to offset the refusal to grant political rights to the Italian section of the population, and, though no formal promise had been made, the Working Group, following a broad suggestion made by the Committee of Twenty-One, had nevertheless undertaken to guarantee this right of option in the Constitution.

When the question came up for discussion in Benghazi, a Cyrenaican member, Salem al-Atrash, opposed the insertion in Article 201 of a reference to Article 9 because "it was connected with race unless it were modified." [37] His stand was arguable. Admittedly, the right of option had, in principle, been recognized in Article 9. However, failure to refer to it in Article 201 would for all practical purposes have meant that the conditions on which the right could be exercised would not be established soon enough to allow members of minorities with ten or more years of residence to opt for Libyan nationality, thereby enabling themselves to register as voters for the first general election. The Commissioner did not hesitate to make this point clear, not only for the sake of principle, but also because he feared that, if this impediment were allowed to persist, Libya would lose Latin American votes of which it might badly be in need in the course of the Fifth Session of the General Assembly. His arguments did not carry much weight, however, and a reference to Article 8 alone found a place in Article 201. The Tripolitanians were not prepared to put up a fight. By now their principal concern was to reach agreement with their eastern brethren on the approval of the Constitution.

Once more the timetable provoked a lively debate, this time in connection with Article 204, covering the period prescribed for the promulgation of the electoral law, and Article 205, relating to the interval between the promulgation of the law and the date of the election.[38] On both points the Cyrenaicans were unanimously in favor of the shorter periods, whereas the Tripolitanians were divided. What was at stake was the weighing of an external interest against an internal one. Most of the Tripolitanian members, with an eye on the political situation in their territory, wanted to give the first Government of independent Libya as much time as possible to prepare and supervise the electoral campaign. The main concern of the other side was to appear before the General Assembly armed with a guarantee in the Constitution that a general election would be held at the earliest possible moment after the declaration of independence. On this particular issue, the Commissioner, who considered it important to cushion as much as possible the impact of the criticism to be expected from Egypt and the Arab League, was definitely in favor of the shorter procedure. After a long debate, and in the face of the Commissioner's advice, it was agreed that the period of twenty days originally stipulated in Article 204 should be increased to thirty. On Article 205, no agreement could be reached. The draft provided for a period of three and a half months between the promulgation of the law and the holding of the elections. The Cyrenaicans, and one or two

37. Ibid.

38. The proposed timetable had been based on technical advice given by the British expert on electoral practices, Cassels, who early in 1950 had prepared the Cyrenaican electoral law and was now assisting the Provisional Government in drafting the federal one.

Tripolitanians, wanted to reduce this to three months. Most of the Tripolitanians were in favor of a longer, and some even of an indefinite, period. The Fezzanese sided with the Cyrenaicans. There was no other way out than a vote, a procedure the President did not like and always tried to avoid whenever possible. The result was 47 votes for the period of three and a half months proposed by the Working Group, 10 votes for a longer period, and 2 abstentions.

Apart from the eleven articles still in abeyance, there was one more important point to be decided, namely, Article 213, which in its draft form stipulated that the National Constituent Assembly would remain in existence until the declaration of independence. Most members felt that this provision might have to be reviewed. It was therefore sent back to the Working Group.

Thus, after three plenary meetings in Benghazi, twelve articles were still not approved, compared to eight unapproved when the NCAL left Tripoli. It was obvious that something had to be done rapidly to narrow the widening gap between opinions in order to bring the proceedings to an end. With this object in view, the date for the next meeting was fixed for 7 October, thus allowing three days for private discussions.

PART 3. THE COMPLETION OF THE CONSTITUTION

From the beginning, all the Benghazi meetings of the NCAL were held in public. From all over the Province notables and political leaders, both town and tribal, flocked to the capital. For the first time Cyrenaicans heard the draft Constitution read aloud to them. For the first time also they heard members of the NCAL from the three provinces discussing controversial questions of common interest. In a country without a national press, where in those days even the local press was underdeveloped, and which lacked a national broadcasting station, so that the few people with receiving sets were entirely dependent on foreign programs for Libyan news, the impact on the public of directly watching a great national event was profound. In Benghazi this was naturally more apparent than in the more sophisticated atmosphere of Tripoli.

The effect was twofold. On the one hand, the conservative elements led by the Prime Minister of Cyrenaica, Muhamed Saqizli, seemed to grow in strength as the debate developed, while on the other hand the King, the federal Prime Minister, and the Commissioner found themselves under increasing pressure from people both in and outside the NCAL who wanted to see the debate cut short and the Constitution adopted within a few days. At the same time, a mounting feeling of irritation drove the Tripolitanian and Fezzanese members to form a solid voting bloc against the Cyrenaicans, less and less willing to compromise with the latter on more and more issues. Not only was this a bad omen for the birth of Libyan unity; it also put the King in a most embarrassing position. Fully recognizing the danger of the situation, he authorized the Commissioner to make it known that he wished the NCAL to take the final vote on the Constitution before the week was out, if at all possible. To make it possible, he further agreed that, the problem of Article 87 having been solved, outstanding controversial questions should be limited to two: the capital (Article 188) and the system of federal grants-in-aid (Article 174). Both should be taken in hand by a joint committee consisting of the officers of the Assembly and the Working Group, the Commissioner and his legal adviser acting as mediators. If this procedure were followed, any other controversial question that might be raised would be automatically out of order, subject to the agreement of the President of the NCAL. Lastly, the King promised that if the Assembly reached a deadlock, he would personally come to the Commissioner's assistance.

The Joint Committee began by taking up the matter of the site of the federal capital. The Tripolitanians and the Fezzanese jointly proposed Tripoli; the Cyrenaicans fought hard for Benghazi. It soon became plain that no agreement could be reached along these lines. To shift the tussle to a different corner of the field, the Commissioner intimated to the Committee that it had the choice either of deleting all reference to the capital from the draft Constitution, mentioning the seat of the federal government alone, or of trying to work out a compromise. All present agreed that the first alternative was no solution, and that an accommodation must therefore be reached. Thereupon, the Commissioner submitted as a possible basis for discussion that Tripoli and Benghazi and—if so desired by the Fezzanese—Sabhah too might all be given the status of capital, the seat of the federal government being provisionally established in Tripoli. A more precise decision on the latter point could be taken after the federal government had been functioning for a time and some experience had been gained. In fact, Benghazi had suffered so much war damage that it could not become a suitable place to house a government for several years to come. Hence, Tripoli was the sole practical possibility. Yet at the same time the Cyrenaicans understandably feared that unless their first city was definitely designated as capital and seat of government, it would never be rebuilt.

At this point, the atmosphere grew so tense that the Commissioner considered it advisable to adjourn the meeting; he also had it in mind to forestall the Tripolitanians and Fezzanese from deciding the issue by an outright majority vote. Such a decision would have hardened Cyrenaican opposition and sapped the Province's willingness to join the Union.

By now, the situation was considered truly critical by all outsiders and by most Libyans.[39] Most of the foreign Consuls had come from Tripoli to Benghazi and were exercising influence on the Libyans to get them to settle their differences in the sense desired by the King, the Government, and the Commissioner. In particular, the assistance proffered by the British Resident and by the United States Consul General was most helpful.

Once more, on Saturday morning, 6 October, the Commissioner went to the King for advice. They agreed that the time had come to cut the Gordian knot. In the course of the audience, all possible compromise solutions were examined.

From a practical point of view, the best way out would have been to name both Tripoli and Benghazi as capitals, with the former as the normal seat of government. This would have allowed Parliament to be convened in Benghazi for special reasons. However, even the most conciliatory Cyrenaicans turned this solution down, proposing instead that both cities be designated as capitals, with the seat of government alternating year by year. The Tripolitanians and Fezzanese refused to accept this, using both financial and administrative arguments.

Finally, the King undertook to have a talk with the federal Prime Minister and subsequently to receive separately the Mufti, Omar Shenib, and Ahmed Abu Bakr. The four audiences took place in the course of the same morning.

His Majesty proposed the solution he personally preferred: two capitals, Tripoli and Benghazi, without specifying in the Constitution which of the two would be the seat of the government. This solution, too, proved unacceptable to the Tripolitanians and the Fezzanese, so that deadlock persisted. Accordingly, at the King's request, the Commissioner called a meeting that afternoon in the principal drawing room of the Manar Palace (now the home of the University of Libya) of the full Tripolitanian delegation, which was subsequently joined by leading members of the Fezzanese delegation. He pointed out to them that there was now but a single choice: no solution at all, with patently grave consequences; or the King's proposal, which the Cyrenaicans did not like, but might accept. The Commissioner appealed to them to sacrifice their provincial preferences for the sake of unity, and left them to discuss the matter among themselves. A long period of suspense ensued that he will not soon forget. When he was invited to

39. At the same time, there was a growing impression that, if the question of the capital could be settled, the other outstanding issues would be debated less acrimoniously.

rejoin the meeting, it was to learn that the King's proposal had been accepted on the express condition and understanding that during the following morning's plenary meeting of the NCAL, at which it was intended that the Constitution would be definitely adopted, the question of the seat of government would not be mentioned. The meeting had lasted three hours. Late that evening a group of Cyrenaican members of the NCAL, who in the meantime had also been holding a meeting, interspersed with consultations with the King, called on the Commissioner and announced their reluctant agreement to the two-capital solution and their acceptance of the Tripolitanian condition.

There was still the problem of the distribution of customs revenues to be settled. Admittedly, this was essentially a technical budgetary question; but it was complicated by a marked political undertone directly bound up with the issue of federalism. For that reason, it had aroused considerable suspicion in the minds of those Cyrenaicans who were in favor of a loose federation.

Reference has been made earlier to the opinion of the United Nations experts on the subject. Originally, the issue was whether customs revenues should be federalized or not. After a great deal of argument, the principle was approved, readily by the Tripolitanians and the Fezzanese, but only with great reluctance by the Cyrenaicans, who saw in it a derogation from their economic autonomy. In part to meet their fears, it had been agreed to insert in the Constitution an article (Article 174; see p. 604 ff.) providing for a system of federal grants-in-aid to the provinces with assurances that these would at least not result in a diminution of income. Furthermore, to provide the time necessary for the organization of a federal customs administration and for the practical consideration that it would be better to start with a new fiscal year in implementing Article 174, it was decided to include in the Constitution Article 212 (see Chapter XII, "Transitory and Provisional Provisions"), providing that Article 36, item 27 (customs) and Article 174 would not come into operation until 1 April 1952.

Nevertheless, the conservative elements in Cyrenaica, wanting further guarantees, reopened the issue. They even asked the King to support their case, arguing that, by their reckoning, they would lose approximately half of the revenue from customs they had hitherto enjoyed, and that the allocation system prescribed in Article 174 might well prove unreliable in practice.

A favorite Cyrenaican idea was to bring customs tariff policy within federal competence while learning the actual customs administration, including the receipt and disposal of revenue, in the hands of the provinces.

The Commissioner and his experts saw the problem in the following light. Revenue from customs for all three territories for the year 1952 was estimated at £1,100,000. The Coordination Committee had estimated that federal government expenditure would amount to rather less than £300,000 in the same year, leaving approximately £800,000 to be allocated to the three territories, in proportion to the revenue they had previously received, by the federal government under Article 174. At the time, the budgets of all three territories showed deficits, which were made good by the Administering Powers. Hence, when customs became an exclusively federal matter, each province's overall deficit would be further increased. To that extent, the Cyrenaicans were, of course, right, but it was precisely for that reason that the experts had recommended that the deficits in the territorial budgets should be covered by grants from the federal government.

The Cyrenaican counterargument, in part inspired by British and French advice, was that if customs revenues were left to the provinces, the latter would be in a position to make a joint grant to the federal government to which they would each contribute in proportion to their respective receipts.[40] It was at this point that the political undertone began to make itself heard.

The Commissioner held the view that under existing arrangements there were already three provincial deficits covered by the Administering Powers. If these arrangements were continued, the independent federal government would have practically no income, with the result that a fourth deficit would be incurred. This, too, would have to be met by France and the United Kingdom, which, however, by this time would no longer be Administering Powers but foreign Powers in the proper sense of the term. Hence, foreign influence would not only continue to bear on each of the three territories, but would also make itself felt at the federal level. Besides, if the federal government had no revenue of its own, it would perforce be a weak government, financially dependent not only on the provinces, but also on foreign aid. Conversely, under the system proposed by the United Nations experts, the federal government would be able to carry the weight of the territorial deficits out of the surplus from customs revenues on the one hand and foreign grants-in-aid on the other. This would not only reduce the four deficits to one; it would also preclude the provinces from maintaining direct financial relations with foreign powers, which would be contrary to the

40. Following a suggestion made by the Coordination Committee, it had already been agreed to apply this system for the purpose of financing the federal government during the transitional period between the declaration of independence and 1 April 1952.

Constitution, under Article 36 of which the conduct of all foreign relations was reserved to the federal government. Last, but not least, the federal government would find itself in a much stronger position.

The Commissioner's Cyrenaican opponents, highly suspicious of the proposed new system, asked him what would happen if the federal government failed to discharge its obligations. In reply, he reminded them that the federal government would be under a constitutional obligation to cover the territorial deficits. Moreover, according to Article 174, the method by which this was to be done, and the size of the allocations, would be determined by federal law in such a manner as to guarantee to the provinces an increase in their allocations proportionate to the growth of federal revenue. Hence the federal government would be under parliamentary control. The Cyrenaicans then asked: "Why not say so explicitly in the Constitution?" The Commissioner pointed out that control of customs revenues was already part of the general budget control to be exercised both by the House of Representatives and by the Senate.

At long last, the Cyrenaicans were convinced that a watertight control system was indeed provided for all foreseeable contingencies. They accepted it, and accordingly renounced their demands for additional transitional provisions and safeguards.

After a recess of four days, the NCAL resumed its work in plenary session on 7 October. Item 2 of the agenda was a discussion of the "suspended" articles, which, following the numbering of the final text of the Constitution, were 44, 45, 172, 173, 174, 175, 188, 201, and 212. A final article (213) was added stipulating that the NCAL would continue in existence until the declaration of independence. By that time it would have accomplished the task assigned to it under paragraph 3 of General Assembly Resolution 289 (IV). Moreover, several of its members were anxious to regain their liberty of action so that they could take part in the electoral campaign shortly to open. It will be noted that Article 199, on the review procedure for the constitutional provisions concerning the federal form of government, no longer appeared on the list; it had been settled in accordance with Cyrenaican wishes. The Tripolitanian members, who had always wanted to limit to two the number of legislative provincial councils whose consent would be required for such a review, had for the sake of peace bowed to the joint position of the Cyrenaicans and Fezzanese, who insisted on the consent of the three councils (the final text used the word "all").

Articles 44 and 45, dealing with the succession to the Throne, had been settled, as we have seen, a few days earlier.

Solutions had also been found for all the other articles; at least, such was the general belief. It soon became apparent, however, that agreement on certain points was not yet as complete as had been hoped the evening before. This emerged as soon as the question of the federal capital came up for discussion, and the Chairman of the Working Group announced that an agreement had been reached on the following text for this touchy provision: "The United Kingdom of Libya has two capitals, Benghazi and Tripoli."

Immediately, two Tripolitanian members protested that the agreement reached the day before had not referred to the two capitals as "Benghazi and Tripoli," but as "Tripoli and Benghazi." The Chairman replied that in putting Benghazi before Tripoli he had merely been keeping to the strict alphabetical order. Nevertheless, one Tripolitanian member, Mohamed al-Hinqari, insisted that Tripoli be placed before Benghazi. On this matter of prestige agreement was reached without ado, and Article 188 was approved.

In pursuance of the earlier agreement not to refer in any way to the seat of the federal government, it was also decided without further discussion that the two articles determining the seat of Parliament and that of the Supreme Court should be deleted.

Articles 172, 173, 174, and 175, in the chapter on federal finance, were left as drafted by the Working Group and definitively approved, thus putting an end to the differences over customs revenues. Article 212, precluding the coming into force of the new federal customs administration before 1 April 1952, was also adopted.

The Cyrenaicans won their battle over immigration by securing the insertion of a new Article 200, reading:

> Immigration into Libya shall be regulated by a federal law. No immigration shall be permitted into a Province without the approval of the Province having been secured.[41]

Article 201, concerning the coming into force of the Constitution, was approved as proposed by the Cyrenaicans, that is to say, with a reference to Article 8 but without mentioning Article 9.

At this point in the debate, the NCAL was taken completely by surprise by an announcement made on behalf of the King by the Chairman of the Working Group in connection with Article 69.

In the draft before the Assembly, this Article had read:

> The King shall on behalf of the Libyan people declare war and conclude peace and enter into treaties with foreign States and he shall communicate them to Parliament with appropriate statements and explanations when the interest and safety of the State permit. Treaties of alliance and those

41. Annex II, p. 920.

> which entail any reduction of the sovereign rights of the State or any expense to the public treasury or which are prejudicial to the public and private rights of Libyans shall have no effect until they have received the consent of Parliament. In no case may the secret articles be contradictory to the published articles.[42]

Khalil Qallal now announced that His Majesty the King did not wish to exercise this right, nor did he wish to practice it without the agreement of Parliament. His Majesty accordingly requested that the draft article be replaced by the following words: "The King shall declare war and conclude peace and enter into treaties which he ratifies after the approval of Parliament." [43]

The minutes describe the scene that ensued in the following terms:

> A storm of clapping and acclamation, with cries of "Long Live the democratic Monarch" arose in which those who were there purely to listen also took part. The King's observations were accepted with pleasure and approval. The aforementioned Article was modified to that [effect] and the modification was confirmed.[44]

The change as proposed and approved was undoubtedly democratic inasmuch as it granted Parliament the power to approve matters of war and peace before their ratification by the Executive. It was entirely in line with a tendency the Commissioner had time and again perceived in the King's attitude toward the Constitution, of wishing to reduce rather than to increase his prerogatives. At the same time, the change in Article 69 had an immediate bearing on an important question of foreign policy. For some months not only the King and the Provisional Libyan Government, but all well-informed Libyans, including the leaders of the opposition, had known that Libya's finances and its economy were in the red. They had also understood that the Administering Powers, as well as the United States of America, were prepared to provide assistance. The price would be acceptance of the presence of foreign troops and military installations on Libyan soil. Agreements to this end could be negotiated and concluded only by an independent Libyan Government. Under the original text of Article 69 this would have been primarily the responsibility of the King, unless the agreements in question were considered as treaties of alliance entailing a reduction of the sovereign rights of the State, in which case they would have needed the consent of Parliament.

42. United Nations Doc. A/AC.32/COUNCIL/R.158, 7 October 1951. Mimeographed.

43. *Proc. NCAL,* Stewart-Jackson Translation, 34th Meeting, 7 October 1951.

44. Ibid.

Apparently the King considered that even this provision failed to determine with sufficient precision the conditions under which parliamentary consent would be required. He had therefore put forward a much simpler text making Parliament responsible for approving the conclusion of treaties before he could ratify them.

To the best of the Commissioner's knowledge, the future Head of State had not consulted anyone about this important amendment, which, therefore, took completely by surprise not only the Libyan audience in the NCAL and the United Nations officials present, but also the representatives of the three countries which had undertaken to grant support in exchange for military facilities. They were abruptly confronted with the fact that in their future negotiations they would have to reckon not only with the King but also with Parliament. Thus the change in Article 69 affected to a considerable degree, if not the substance at least the political nature of future relations between the independent Libyan State and the Governments prepared to lend it financial support. It did not, of course, alter the fact that without foreign financial and economic support Libyan independence was likely to remain a hollow concept, at least for some time, and that the presence of foreign troops was therefore an inescapable necessity. Much more important, however, than its immediate effect were the long-term repercussions of Article 69. In the light of Libya's special geopolitical position in the Mediterranean basin and within the Arab world, this was of the greatest national significance. When, years later, Libya became an oil-producing country on a large scale, this significance was even more deeply appreciated than it was at the moment when the royal amendment to the article was acclaimed on democratic grounds. The King's initiative was an act of the highest political foresight and wisdom.

The enthusiasm aroused by the change in Article 69 had hardly died down, when, Arabs being linguistic perfectionists, a Tripolitanian member proposed some linguistic changes. When the President accepted them, a Cyrenaican member took advantage of the situation to assert his right to reopen the debate on matters of substance, in particular on Article 9, which dealt with the procedure for acquiring Libyan nationality. Fortunately, the majority wisely supported the President in overruling this attempt. However, the danger remained, and the Chairman of the Working Group accordingly suggested the adoption of a resolution recording the formal adoption of the Constitution and its proclamation. At this point, he was interrupted by yet another Cyrenaican member wishing to reopen the debate on points of substance. But the scene changed dramatically, as the record relates:

> the members of the Assembly and those present suddenly burst out with great shouts and acclamations which echoed throughout the hall crying,

"Long live His Majesty the King." They were startled because of it and they only stopped when His Majesty the King appeared before them accompanied by the President of the Libyan Government, Mahmoud Bey al Muntasser and the senior officer of the Guard. They all rose in honour of him, and shouts and clapping re-echoed. A wave of enthusiasm and joy at this unexpected visit overwhelmed those present and His Majesty was beaming with joy and graciously replied to those surrounding him. He then sat down in the place of the President of the Assembly in the midst of acclamation and clapping which continued until His Majesty indicated to the whole company that they could take their places.[45]

The King then declared:

I come to you to offer you my congratulations at your having succeeded in drafting this Constitution, and I desire success for you in such of your work as remains, and I thank you for your service which has had at heart happy and successful life for the Libyan people.[46]

After the Prime Minister of the Provisional Government and the President of the Assembly had made extemporaneous speeches, His Majesty rose, but before leaving the Hall to enthusiastic cheering, he made one more statement:

I thank . . . the President of the Government for his eloquent speech just as I thank His Honour the Mufti for his eloquent and comprehensive speech, and I hope that this day may be the day on which the Constitution is issued so that we may gain time.[47]

It was indicative of the King's ideas that his last recommendation was intended to end petty disputation.

Immediately after his departure, the NCAL resumed the debate on the clause on the promulgation of the Constitution which, after a brief discussion, was agreed upon in the form in which it appears as the Epilogue to the Constitution.

The record ends on the following note:

At the termination of the session the President said that they ought to consider that day a day of official national festival. The assembled company congratulated him on this and the session was adjourned in an atmosphere of joy and intense emotion, and those members who were

45. Ibid.
46. Ibid.
47. Ibid.

present and those who were there to listen began to embrace one another and to exchange congratulations on this great triumph.[48]

The Commissioner noted for the record:

On 18 October 1951, the President of the National Assembly informed the Commissioner that the Constitution was promulgated in Benghazi on 7 October 1951 over the signatures of the President and the two Vice-Presidents and that he had requested the Prime Minister of the Provisional Libyan Government to publish it in the first issue of the [Libyan] Official Gazette.[49]

This quotation concludes the account of the way in which the Libyan Constitution came into being after 317 days of hard work, the brunt of which had been borne by the Working Group under the able chairmanship of Khalil Qallal. The Commissioner is well aware of the part played in this performance by the staff of the United Nations Mission, including himself and, more especially, the legal advisers. It must however be stressed, when determining the respective responsibilities of the NCAL and the Mission, that the former had always taken full responsibility for all decisions, including those implying acceptance or rejection of United Nations advice.

Looking back at the work accomplished, the Commissioner has been fascinated to realize that the Constitution had grown, by way of piecemeal compromise, out of subtle Arab ways of negotiating pragmatically, sometimes illogically, but in the last instance always by agreement. Of course, the opposition of the Congress Party was always there, constantly making itself felt and, often indirectly or through its sympathizers in the Tripolitanian delegation, influencing the deliberations and votes in the NCAL. In this way, it played a larger part in the drafting of the Constitution than it probably realized or was prepared to admit.

The Commissioner has often been asked to give a rational—in the Western sense of the word—explanation or interpretation of the Libyan Constitution. He has always refrained from doing so because the Arab way of thinking does not lend itself to analysis by the methods of Western rationalism. All he can say looking back today is that for nearly ten years the Constitution was followed, not always to the letter, but at least in the spirit in which it was conceived. By the end of that period, political thought had evolved to the point at which a majority of the people, particularly the younger generation, were prepared to accept a more unitary form of State. Had the initiative for such a reform been taken in Parliament, it would

48. Ibid.

49. *Second Annual Report of the United Nations Commissioner in Libya,* para. 108.

probably have failed if only for lack of the consent of the legislative councils of the three provinces. Since, however, under Article 196, the right of proposing a revision of the Constitution also belonged to the King, this approach peacefully succeeded.

Since 1963 Libya has been a unitary State. Events may show that the changeover from the one system to the other was somewhat too rapid, rather too radical. Had the review clauses of the Constitution been less rigid, the evolution might have been more gradual. There is no doubt, however, that the tendency toward a unitary State had been strong from the outset and was bound to gather momentum. But that is another story, calling for a separate study.

PART 4. THE ELECTORAL LAW [50]

With the adoption and proclamation of the Constitution, an important part of the duties assigned to the Commissioner and to the Council for Libya under paragraph 4 of General Assembly Resolution 289 (IV) had come to an end. There remained, however, one aspect of these duties about which the competence of the Commissioner and the Council was not quite clear. On the one hand it could be argued that assisting the people of Libya in drawing up a federal electoral law was part of their duties, in the sense that this was a primary condition for the holding of elections and the establishment of an independent and sovereign State. On the other hand, Article 204 of the Constitution specifically instructed the Provisional Federal Government to draw up the first electoral law for Parliament and to submit its draft to the National Assembly for approval and promulgation. It will, moreover, be remembered that further articles in Chapter XII of the Constitution, "Transitory and Provisional Provisions," laid down a precise timetable covering a period of 155 days from the promulgation of the Constitution (7 October 1951) until the convocation of Parliament (11 March 1952), thus exceeding by seventy days the ultimate date set by the General Assembly of the United Nations for the proclamation of independence (1 January 1952), on which date the Commissioner and the Council would cease to function. In these circumstances, there was practically no time left for recourse to the usual procedure of requesting the Council for advice. Moreover, considerations of a psychological nature had to be taken into account. The Libyan people, their Provisional Government, and their

50. For the final text of the Electoral Law for the election of the Libyan Federal House of Representatives, see Annex III, pp. 922–40.

National Assembly were all beginning to breathe the air of independence and developing an increasing reluctance to accept foreign advice.

The Commissioner, who after the meeting of the NCAL in Benghazi had gone to Geneva between 16 and 30 October 1951 to consult the Council on his second annual report, returned to Tripoli on the evening of 28 October. On his desk he found a copy of the draft electoral law for his information and study. During his absence, a special Working Group of the NCAL [51] had been working hard on this draft under instructions to submit a report to the full session of the NCAL by 1 November. The NCAL itself, under the terms of the timetable, had to examine, approve, and promulgate the law not later than 7 November. For all these reasons, the Commissioner decided to invite the Working Group to meet him informally on 31 October. In the meantime, a second legal adviser having joined the Mission (cf. p. 744 and fn. 30), the two United Nations advisers had carefully studied the draft, and it was on the basis of their comments that the Commissioner and the Working Group together examined the very detailed text that was to be submitted to the NCAL in the evening of the following day.

At the outset the Chairman of the Working Group pointed out that, in preparing Libya's first electoral law, the Provisional Government had borne in mind its people's lack of experience in electoral practice. The law should not, therefore, be judged from a perfectionist point of view. Moreover, the draft had to take into account certain peculiar prevailing conditions, such as, for instance, the existence of seminomadic tribes with customs of their own. Indeed, at the time, the Libyan population was made up largely of seminomads, true nomads living only with and from flocks and herds, and townsfolk. The seminomadic tribes were, moreover, spread over a vast area. It could happen that a man born in a seminomadic tribe later settled in an oasis, while others settled down permanently in a village or city of the coastal belt. Hence, as subsequent events will show, the problems of place of residence and origin in relation to the identification of both electors and candidates proved difficult to solve.

The Commissioner assured the Working Group that, while he fully appreciated these conditions, he and his advisers nevertheless felt that on certain points the law was susceptible of improvement.

He went on to make a few suggestions, which were summarized as follows in the supplementary report to his second annual report:

51. This was a variant of the Working Group set up by the Committee of Eighteen to do the brunt of the work on the drafting of the Constitution (see Chapter 7, p. 510). The composition of the new body was varied from time to time, according to the subject matter before it, to enable it to make the best use of the specialist knowledge of members of the NCAL. It was, however, always chaired by Khalil Qallal.

(a) It appeared to him that the draft electoral law gave too much power to the Supervisor-General, the Provincial Supervisors and the Registering Officers whose decisions were to be final. He recognized that under prevailing circumstances it was difficult to provide for a system of judicial appeal against decisions of Supervisors and Registering Officers, but he suggested that instead these officers might be assisted by committees of at least three persons, amongst whom there should be one or two magistrates and a notable locally known for his impartiality. To these committees could be trusted the duty of exercising the powers granted under the draft electoral law to the Supervisor and his assistants.

(b) The Commissioner also pointed out that the power given under the law to the Supervisor-General to declare an election invalid did not seem to him to be in conformity with article 111 of the Constitution, which provided that the House of Representatives was itself to decide upon the validity of the election of its members. He therefore suggested that this section of the draft law should be deleted.

(c) The Commissioner further pointed out that the draft electoral law made certain distinctions between the electoral procedure to be applied in rural and urban districts and that he would prefer to see, whenever possible, the same procedure adopted in both kinds of districts. If such similarity were found impracticable he suggested that the National Assembly should at least endeavour to amend the text of the law in such a way as to allow each member of a tribe the right to present his candidature in the same way as had been provided for in urban districts, without granting the tribal chiefs the power to intervene.

(d) The Commissioner expressed the view that the amount of fifty Libyan pounds which each candidate was required to deposit might prove somewhat excessive.[52]

After having discussed these suggestions, the Working Party assured the Commissioner that in reporting to the NCAL they would take them into account as far as possible. In the event, as will be seen, some of them were accepted, in whole or in part; others were not. In particular, the suggestion made in (d) was not taken up. It had appeared to the Commissioner that, in a country where, in the years 1950 and 1951, the national annual income per head of population was estimated at $35, it was unreasonable to ask a

52. *Supplementary Report to the Second Annual Report of the United Nations Commissioner in Libya,* GAOR: Sixth Session, 1951–52, Supplement No. 17A (A/1949/Add.1), para. 27.

candidate for Parliament to deposit 50 Libyan pounds.[53] It meant in fact that no poor man, and hardly any middle-class man, could hope to enter Parliament unless a number of his supporters helped him by putting up—and therefore shared the risk of losing—the deposit required by law. It also meant that, for economic reasons, urban candidates would enjoy an advantage over candidates from rural districts, a situation which might engender corruption. The Commissioner therefore proposed that the deposit required be reduced from 50 to 20 Libyan pounds; his case was refuted by the not very convincing argument that in Egypt at that time the required deposit was £E 150. This was true enough, but meant, of course, nothing more than that Egypt had a rich man's Parliament. Admittedly, one had to take into account the low average standard of education—in the Occidental sense of the word—of the Libyan population. On the other hand, the Commissioner had seen enough of the degree of education conferred by Koranic schools, coupled with the inborn common sense of the average Bedouin and city dweller, not to fear an invasion of Parliament by incompetent people were the deposit of 50 pounds in fact reduced. Nevertheless it was, and still is, one of his deep regrets that his advice was not followed.

When the draft of the electoral law came up for discussion for the first time at the thirty-sixth meeting of the NCAL on 22 October, it was, in accordance with standing practice, referred to the Working Group, the Chairman of which, being a hard worker with little time left for the job, was inclined to keep matters close to his chest until they were ripe for discussion in a wider circle. This practice had occasionally been the subject of complaint by members of the NCAL. On the present occasion, Khalil Qallal was asked to keep the Assembly better and more regularly informed.

One week later, on 1 November, the Working Group made its report to the NCAL at its thirty-seventh meeting. The Chairman of the group referred to the unofficial meeting the Group had had with the Commissioner, and also gave an account of a meeting with the British expert on electoral matters, Cassels, who had originally assisted the Provisional Government in preparing the bill. Both meetings had led to last-minute changes.

Section 1,[54] based on Article 8 of the Constitution governing Libyan

53. As will be seen from the final text of the Electoral Law, Articles 25(2) and 69 prescribe that, pending the coming into force of all the provisions of the Libyan Currency Law, a Libyan pound would for the purposes of the law mean in Tripolitania 480 Military Authority lire, in Cyrenaica £ Egyptian 0.975, and in the Fezzan 980 Algerian francs.

54. To avoid confusion between Constitution and Electoral Law, the latter was subdivided into parts and sections instead of chapters and articles. However, the translators of *Proc. NCAL* have stuck to the word "article."

nationality, provoked no discussion, but Section 2, defining "residence," gave rise to considerable debate. As explained earlier in this study, the issue was whether a man's place of residence or his place of origin should prevail in identifying him for electoral purposes.

The record brings out the arguments adduced in favor of each of the two points of view. (In many respects, the same arguments also applied to the nomination of candidates.)

The first pertinent passage from the proceedings reads as follows:

> The Hon. Member Khalil al Gallal explained the place of residence and he said that many laws prescribed that if someone had dwelt in some country for three or four years he was considered a resident in it. He said therefore the question was a wide one, and furthermore Article 2 was not definitive in its present prescriptions.
>
> Then the Hon. Member Munir Burshan suggested that the place of a person's residence be considered the place in which he was himself registered.
>
> The Hon. Member Miftah 'Urayqib opposed him when he said that many of the people had moved from their towns within the province to the metropolis for private reasons, and they had registered themselves there for food supplies or for some other reason. He said that they were unable to give their votes to a candidate in the capital since they did not know its people so well as to be able to decide on those whom they trusted and those upon whom they could rely because they were in the position of foreigners.
>
> Then the Hon. Member Abdel Gawad Freites observed that the Article was too elastic, and to remove ambiguities they should say: The elector votes in the electoral district in which he is normally resident.
>
> The Hon. Member Belkasem Bouguila supported the proposal of the Hon. Member Munir Burshan.
>
> Then the Hon. Member Abu Baker ben Ahmad observed that it was necessary that a person's place of residence be within his province and that since it was not possible for a resident in Cyrenaica to nominate himself for membership of the Chamber of Deputies of Fezzan or Tripoli for special circumstances or the contrary, it should not be possible for him to vote for anyone else outside his province either.
>
> Then discussion broke out on the question and the Hon. Member Miftah 'Urayqib, who was supported by the Hon. Members Munir Burshan and Mohammed Ali Sifaat bu Farwa, said that in his opinion it was necessary for the elector to be given the right of voting and the candidate to be given the right of candidature in the town of his origin. Since, as

> had been said, there were people who had been compelled by special circumstances to move from the towns in which they originated and to settle in other ones, they then, if they were to nominate themselves in the town in which they had settled, could not be elected because they were strangers in that town and perhaps not known to the majority of the people there. Similarly they would not be able to elect one person rather than another in a town in which they had no interest.
>
> The other group at the head of which was the Hon. Member Mahmoud al Maslati, clung to the first view of the Hon. Member Munir Burshan in which he had said that the place in which a person was registered should be regarded as his place of residence.[55]

It was finally proposed that the relevant clauses of the Electoral Law of Iraq should be used as a model, Section 2 being referred back to the Working Group for final phrasing. In the end, this section was approved in a form which included both the place of residence and place of origin:

> For the purpose of the elections, the residence of a person shall be the place in which he normally resides, or the place of origin, within his Province, of his family.[56]

It will be noted that the section contains an important restriction to the effect that the place of residence or place of origin of an elector had to be "within his Province."[57] This was the renaissance of a difference of opinion already mentioned. Originally the problem had consisted in deciding between one single federal electoral law or three separate provincial laws for the election of the members of the House of Representatives. Agreement had been reached in favor of a federal law (Article 100 of the Constitution), but already at that stage Article 103 (2) restricted the selection of a deputy by stipulating that a candidate must "be inscribed on one of the electoral rolls of the Province in which he resides." Now a similar but even more precise restriction was being imposed on electors at the very moment when the concept of their residence was being broadened. For the sake of clarity, it must be noted that this limitation was not merely a victory for the Cyrenaican idea of loose federalism. It also was largely the result of geographical conditions and tenuous communications which prevented people in one province from maintaining regular intercourse with people in the others. Admittedly, there had been a fair amount of internal migration;

55. *Proc. NCAL,* Stewart-Jackson Translation, 38th Meeting, 3 November 1951.

56. *Proc. NCAL,* Stewart-Jackson Translation, 43rd Meeting, 6 November 1951.

57. This despite the fact that, in the English translation, the phrase "within his Province" qualifies only the "place of origin." There is no ambiguity in the original Arabic, where it qualifies also the phrase "the place in which he normally resides."

for instance, in time of drought, or for other reasons, Tripolitanians had migrated to Cyrenaica. Fezzanese also had migrated in considerable numbers to Tripolitania, in particular to the coastal cities, in most cases to improve their living standards by finding better-paid work. However, these migrations had not reached the point where it would have been realistic to merge the whole of the population of Libya into one single electoral body, when human relations were still much closer within each province.

Since only qualified electors could stand as candidates (Article 103 of the Constitution), it was logical for Section 4 to be worded in the following manner:

> Subject to the provisions of sections 5 and 23 of this law, every male person who has completed his thirtieth year (Gregorian) and who is inscribed upon the electoral rolls of a District within his Province shall be qualified to be a member of the House of Representatives.[58]

It might have been assumed that with that the issue was closed, but the debate flared up again in connection with Section 23, dealing with a procedural aspect (nomination papers) of the same question. After the original text of this section had been amended by bringing it into line with Sections 2 and 4, the Hon. Member Ali Tamir observed "that the candidate should have to nominate himself in the place of residence in which he was registered."[59]

In the final drafting of the law the text of this last decision was slightly amended; the substance was unchanged.

Section 3 (qualifications of electors) caused one of the fiercest controversies of the debate. This section, in its original form, disenfranchised lunatics, undischarged bankrupts, and persons convicted of and sentenced for a criminal offence.

The nature of the controversy will be apparent from the following quotations:

> The 3rd Article: When the Article was read the Hon. Member Salem al Atrash suggested a modification in it so that it should become: no person under sentence of judicial law passed upon him or who may possibly be sentenced can have the right to vote. The Hon. Member Khalil al Gellal debated this with him and asked him whether someone accused of an administrative or political offence should in his opinion be deprived of the right to vote.

58. See Annex III.
59. *Proc. NCAL,* Stewart-Jackson Translation, 40th Meeting, 4 November 1951.

The Hon. Member Salem al Atrash replied that all sentences would involve deprivation of the right to vote regardless of their form.

The Hon. Member Khalil Gellal commented that that was not possible in all democratic laws in the world and that there was unfairness in this [*sic*].

The Hon. Member el Munir Burshan suggested that the right of election be withdrawn from every person who was under sentence for a crime detrimental to honour, such as theft and forgery and similar crimes, even if sentence had not already been carried out upon him.

. . . There then took place a fierce discussion and the Hon. Members el Munir Burshan and Salem al Atrash demanded a vote on their proposal. The Hon. Member Suleiman Jerbi said that civil rights [*Translator's note:* "civil rights" here used to refer to all rights of a normal citizen, not only electoral rights] should be restored to everyone under sentence and that if the right to vote was taken away from somebody under sentence then perhaps it would be a long time before he could regain his civil rights. He also said that they did not know when such a person would regain his civil rights. The Hon. Member Munir Burshan replied that in every case a time was specifically mentioned in which the person in question would regain his civil rights. The Hon. Member Khalil Gellal commented on that saying that in the Courts of Law there was no time specified for the restoration of civil rights, since the restoration of civil rights applied especially to those declared bankrupt and this merely meant that it was essential for the person under sentence to take his request to a higher Court in which his behaviour and character would be set forth as being good; if this were proven, the Court then had to pass sentence that civil rights be restored to the person in question.

. . . The Hon Member Abdel Gawad Freites suggested the incorporation of the two suggestions together and a vote upon them both. The Hon. Member Munir Burshan said that if the Hon. Member Salem al Atrash was prepared to have his suggestion altered by the addition of the phrase "that it should not be possible for someone under sentence in a case of a crime detrimental to honour" he would be prepared to withdraw his request for a vote on his suggestion. The two suggestions were conjoined so that they became: "and that he shall not be one who is under sentence of legal punishment detrimental to honour and whose civil rights have not been restored." There then broke out a fierce discussion and while the Hon. Members Salem al Atrash, Munir Burshan, Mohammed Ali Sifaat bu Farwa and others approved the modification of the Article with the suggested addition, another group, at the core of which were the Hon. Members Mahmoud al Maslati, Mohamed al

> Hankari, Miftah 'Urayqib and His Honour the President, was of the opinion that this judgment was cruel and that sentence passed by previous Courts contained injustices.
>
> . . . Then the Hon. Member Mabrouk Geibani demanded that a vote first be taken on the suggestion of his colleague al Atrash, and secondly on the suggestion of his colleague Munir Burshan, and after a discussion the Hon. Member Salem al Atrash presented his suggestion for voting with this text "provided that he is not under sentence of legal punishment" and it was defeated by 36 votes against as compared with 4 votes in support and 13 abstentions.
>
> Then the suggestion of the Hon. Member Munir Burshan was put forward in its modified form from the Egyptian Electoral Law and it became: "and if he is not one who has been sentenced to jail for theft, bribery, betrayal of trust, forgery, trickery or any other crime in any way detrimental to honour, and whose civil rights have not been restored." This suggestion obtained the support of 37 votes, 4 votes were cast against it, and 12 members abstained from voting.[60]

Unfortunately this was not the end of the dispute. To understand what lay behind it, it is necessary to refer to a discussion at a later meeting of the NCAL.

The true roots of this passionate difference of opinion lay in the President's bald observation that sentences passed by previous courts contained injustices.

When, at the forty-third meeting, on 6 November, the Working Group submitted Section 3 in its newly adopted form, several speakers, and in particular the President, expressed their views more explicitly, as will be seen from the following quotation:

> Article 3: His Honour the President observed that the modification which had been drafted for this Article was harsh because the Laws originating from the time of the English were unjust in view of the non-existence of appeal Courts to which a sentenced person could have refuge at a time when it was possible to appeal against the judgment and the innocence of the accused was quite possible; and what was more there was no harm in considering this Article again so as not to deprive some of the people of the opportunity of candidature merely by reason of judgments which might perhaps have been erroneous.
>
> The Hon. Member Mahmoud al Maslati observed that exactly the same things were stipulated as regards an elector as were stipulated as regards a candidate except for the question of age.

60. *Proc. NCAL,* Stewart-Jackson Translation, 38th Meeting, 3 November 1951.

The Hon. Member Khalil Gellal commented on that by saying that the elector was not the candidate and the elector was the person who wished to elect someone to represent him. He pointed out that this was a personal right which he had and that it was not possible to deprive him of it without having an effect on the nation. It was the candidate who would know affairs and it was necessary that he should be above reproach. He said that in this there was another point of view and the person who would put that forward would say that despite the fact that the candidate should necessarily be of unblemished record very many people had been sentenced in the military Courts and that these had been sentenced by means of proclamations which were published on authority; and that at that time there were no Courts of Appeal which would enable the accused to defend himself by appealing to them so that they could review whether or not the sentence was just and approve it, or affirm the innocence of the accused. He said that in addition some tolerance should be shown in a first round of elections so that national Courts could be formed to preserve the rights of citizens with all justice and probity. He said that this point of view might be acceptable if the Assembly decided that [*sic*] but it would not be legal to change the Article or take action concerning it with the absence of some of the Hon. Members. He said that it was up to them to protest especially since the author of the modification himself was among them and the session was not to be put off until the morrow.

The Hon. Member Ali Sifaat bu Farwa said that they had finished with the Law, that they had agreed upon its Articles, and that there was no need to return to what they had decided and agreed upon.[61]

After a recess, controversy over Article 3 broke out again:

The Hon. Member Mabrouk Geibani arose and put forward a suggestion that discussion be resumed on the Article once more for the purpose of voting according to the prescriptions of the Rules of Procedure. The Hon. Members Salem al Murayyed, Ahmed Agheila al Kizza, and the Hon. Member Salem al Atrash opposed him in that. The Hon. Member Salem al Atrash said that it would be a pity if they were to see in the House of Representatives people who had not got a completely unblemished record just as it would also be a pity to deprive people who had been injured by false judgments of their right of candidature, and therefore he suggested the modification of the Article on terms which would guarantee both points of view; and that would be that

61. *Proc. NCAL,* Stewart-Jackson Translation, 43rd Meeting, 6 November 1951.

> every person who had been sentenced in a Court which was not a national one should have the right to bring forward an appeal against the judgment which had been given against him, to a national Court which would be formed with the object of looking into this.
>
> The Hon. Member Abdul Gawad Freites put forward a suggestion for the addition of a paragraph to the Article prescribing that somebody who had had judgment passed against him by a national Court should be disgraced and prevented from having the right of candidature.
>
> The Hon. Members Khalil Gellal, Mahmoud al Maslati and Mabrouk Geibani opposed him in that because no such Court existed.
>
> Then the suggestion to study the Article again was put to the vote, and the suggestion obtained 28 votes in agreement as opposed to 6 votes against, and 15 members abstained from voting.
>
> Then the Hon. Member Salem al Murayyad withdrew from the session giving as his reason the decision to resume study on the Article.
>
> The modification was cancelled in view of the agreement of the majority upon that. Then the Hon. Member Mohamed al Hankari asked whether the Article was to remain in its first form or be modified. The Hon. Member Suleiman Jerbi suggested that the Article be read in its form before modification and that then it would be possible to have a vote on whether to leave it as it was or change it.
>
> The Hon. Member Mabrouk Geibani opposed that but the Hon. Member Suleiman Jerbi convinced him on the point. The Article was then put to the vote and it was agreed that it should be left as it was in its first form.[62]

That is to say, as it finally appears in the law.

It was a great pity that the National Assembly, at its last session, after having succeeded in reaching compromise solutions on so many controversial issues, was unable to come to a unanimous conclusion on this point, which was not only of a legal but also of a moral nature.[63] Subsection 3 (c) as it remained provided simply that: "Every male Libyan who has completed his twenty-first year (Gregorian) shall be entitled to vote unless he is a person who: (a) . . . ; (b) . . . ; or (c) Is serving a term of imprison-

62. Ibid.

63. Although no explicit reason was given in the course of the debate for the opposition to the text as voted at the thirtieth meeting, there is reason to believe that its inclusion in the Electoral Law might have caused embarrassment to persons who had collaborated with the enemy in the days of the Italian occupation. At the same time, it must be noted that collaboration of this kind was looked upon less severely than in Western European countries, unless it had caused direct and grievous harm to the Libyan people.

ment."[64] The failure to arrive at a more satisfactory solution did not go unnoticed. When the Electoral Law came up for discussion on 7 January 1952 in the Council for Libya, the representatives of Egypt, Pakistan, and Tripolitania requested the insertion of the following footnote to paragraph 27 of the Commissioner's supplementary report:

> The representatives of Egypt, Pakistan and Tripolitania, during consultations on this report at Geneva, urged the Commissioner to convey, in an appropriate form, to the Government of Libya, their views that the present Electoral Law suffered from two serious defects which should be removed.
>
> Firstly, it permitted persons convicted of most heinous offences such as murder, dacoity, robbery and rape to become members of the Parliament, and
>
> Secondly, the arrangements for preventing tampering with ballot boxes, after the voting was over, were most unsatisfactory.
>
> As the Commissioner did not accept this request, the above representatives wish to draw the attention of the General Assembly to these defects in the Electoral Law.[65]

The representatives of Cyrenaica, the Fezzan, France, Italy, the United Kingdom, and the United States requested the addition to the footnote of the following comment:

> The representatives of Cyrenaica, the Fezzan, France, Italy, the United Kingdom and the United States of America, have the utmost confidence that the Libyan Government will, by due process of Libyan law, take any action it may deem desirable in the premises in order to ensure free elections in Libya.[66]

In fact, the first objection raised by the critics, although couched in exaggerated terms, was in substance justified. The second objection, as a study of the Electoral Law will show, was far less to the point. Admittedly, the precautions to be taken against tampering with ballot boxes could have been more effective, but it cannot be said that they were "most unsatisfactory."

It would take the author too far if he were to attempt to examine in detail the debates on the Electoral Law, but the following issues must be recorded.

64. See Annex III.

65. *Supplementary Report to the Second Annual Report of the United Nations Commissioner in Libya,* p. 5, fn. 27.

66. Ibid.

Section 8 imposed upon the Minister of Justice of the federal government the duty of specifying the names and boundaries of the urban electoral districts of Libya. Section 54 imposed upon him the same duty regarding the rural electoral districts (or corresponding tribal units). Doubts were expressed whether any person holding the federal portfolio of Justice could be expected to be sufficiently familiar with local political conditions to discharge these duties in a satisfactory manner. During the ensuing debate, two conflicting opinions were advanced. One was that the determination of electoral districts should be the prerogative of the federal Minister of Justice in his capacity of supreme authority in all electoral matters. The other was that he could not fulfil these particular duties without the assistance of the head of the provincial Department of Justice concerned. By way of compromise between these two schools of thought, it was decided by 32 votes in favor, 12 against, and 6 abstentions, to leave the decision in the last instance to the federal authority "after seeking guidance from the Provinces." [67]

The vote was significant for two reasons: first, because of its recognition of the Federation as the higher authority in a matter of considerable interest; second, because the division was not on a province versus province basis.

Section 16, dealing with proof of objection made to the inclusion of names in the electoral registers, originally gave the right of decision to the Supervisor General and his assistants, the Provincial Supervisors and the Registering Officers. At the Commissioner's suggestion, the section was amended by the addition of subsections (3), (4), and (5), the most important of which was subsection (4):

> (4) The decision of objections shall be the responsibility, in every case, of a committee to be appointed by the Minister of Justice. It shall consist of the Registering Officer, a judge and one notable of the district. In the event of disagreement between members of the committee, the opinion of the majority shall prevail.[68]

The introduction of this procedure affected, directly or indirectly, various other sections of the law. The power to deal with objections to the inclusion of names in the electoral registers having been entrusted to a committee, it was deemed consistent to make the same committee responsible also for dealing with objections to nomination papers. Section 30 lays down both the principle of this additional competence and the executive pro-

67. *Proc. NCAL,* Stewart-Jackson Translation, 39th Meeting, 3 November 1951.
68. See Annex III.

cedure to be followed. In fact, as the discussion of the Electoral Law proceeded, the part to be played by the committee established under Section 16 was extended to several more phases of the electoral procedures —Sections 32, 33 (1), 34 (3), 43 (2), 46 (2), 47 (b) and (c), and 48.

When Section 34 ("Presiding Officers at elections") came up for discussion, it was proposed that one more committee be appointed to supervise and guarantee the smooth running of the electoral proceedings. This proposal provoked some misunderstanding because it was feared that the members of such a committee might try to exercise political pressure on electors, particularly where the latter were illiterate or men of simple education. When, however, it was explained that the sole intention was that such committees should simply watch over the proceedings, and aid such electors as did not know how to discharge their electoral duties, it was decided to add to Section 34 a clause reading as follows:

> (3) The Committee appointed for the hearing of objections under Section 16 (4) shall assist the Presiding Officer to supervise the proceedings in the polling station on election day in order to facilitate the conduct thereof.[69]

Another important issue was whether police should be stationed within or outside the polling stations. The original text of Section 35 mentioned as one of the duties of the Presiding Officer the exclusion from the polling station of all persons other than: (1) candidates, or representatives of candidates; (2) election officials; (3) police officers on duty; (4) any person officially employed at the polling station.

The Chairman of the Working Group proposed in the course of the forty-first meeting that police officers should remain outside the polling station, but near enough to it to enable them readily to be called in, should need arise. He gave as his reason for making this proposal that the presence of police officers in the station would make electors feel that they were not entirely free. Several other members supported the Chairman, but the President had interpreted the words "on duty" as meaning that the Presiding Officer would already have called the police officers inside the polling stations because he had been obliged by conditions to summon them to keep order. Moreover, when it was noted that during the provincial elections in Cyrenaica the year before police officers had been present in the polling stations, members felt that prevention was better than cure; it was therefore decided to leave the section unchanged. Thereupon the President remarked that Section 35 should be read in conjunction with Section 34,

69. Ibid.

and in particular with Section 36, which dealt with the misbehavior of voters in the polling station and authorized the Presiding Officer to "call upon any police officer in or near the polling station to remove [any person misconducting himself] from the station."[70] The section added that no person thus ejected would be allowed to reenter the polling station without the permission of the Presiding Officer.

Another question that provoked lively discussion, and to which the Commissioner had previously drawn the attention of the Working Group, was the power given in the draft electoral law to the Supervisor General to declare an election invalid, whereas Article 111 of the Constitution provided that the two Chambers of Parliament alone were competent in this matter. The question arose in connection with the counting of votes, the declaration of results, the disposal of election papers, and the various irregularities which might occur during this phase of the electoral proceedings both in urban and in rural districts.

The President declared that a distinction should be made between the right of the Supervisor General to declare invalid electoral proceedings before the result of the vote had been announced, and the right of the House of Representatives to declare invalid the mandate of a member after his election had been declared valid by the Supervisor General. The distinction was an important one, since a decision of the kind to be made by the Supervisor General would be an administrative one, whereas a decision by the House or the Senate in pursuance of Article 111 of the Constitution would almost certainly be of a political character. Agreement in principle was easily reached. There nevertheless remained the necessity of defining the procedure to be followed by the Returning Officer when declaring the result of the poll, the competence of the Supervisor General in ordering a fresh election where discrepancies or irregularities were brought to light, and any elector's right to object to the validity of the election in his constituency. All three matters were satisfactorily settled respectively in Sections 51, 62, and 63.

The Commissioner having also suggested that the distinction between the electoral procedure to be applied in rural and urban districts should, wherever possible, be the same throughout the country, the NCAL decided to insert two sections (57 and 61) according to which a considerable number of rules for urban elections laid down in the Law were to apply mutatis mutandis to rural electoral districts. The principal improvement consisted in granting each member of a tribe the right to present his own candidature without the intervention of his tribal chief. An exception was made, how-

70. Ibid.

ever, in the case of nomination papers and written declarations which, in rural districts, would not need to be completed; while, analogously, objections against names appearing on registers and objections to the nomination of candidates would not have to be laid in writing in such areas.

The foregoing is a summary of the principal controversial points in the Electoral Law which necessitated debates taking up eight consecutive plenary meetings of the NCAL between 22 October and 6 November. So far as the law's general characteristics are concerned, these follow the basic principles laid down in Chapter VII, "Parliament," of the Constitution. In its technical aspects, the law bore the unmistakable mark of its English draftsman.

The Commissioner's supplementary report to his second annual report, which was also his last, contains the full text of the Electoral Law and an account of the way in which the elections themselves were organized and conducted.[71]

The elections were held on 9 February, and Parliament met for the first time on 25 March 1952 in Benghazi, only a fortnight later than foreseen in the timetable, and two months after the Royal Proclamation of Independence.

71. *Supplementary Report to the Second Annual Report of the United Nations Commissioner in Libya,* Annex VIII, pp. 35–45, and Chapter II, paras. 23–69, respectively. As already noted, the text of the Electoral Law is appended to this study as Annex III.

CHAPTER 9

Development, Financial Institutions, and Foreign Aid

PART 1. TECHNICAL ASSISTANCE AND LIBYAN DEVELOPMENT

The Commissioner's broad findings on the obvious economic facts of Libyan life have been described at various points in this study, in particular in Chapter 5, Part 3 (pp. 392–414). There was no secret about this—the Four Power Commission of Investigation for the Former Italian Colonies, and the Administering Powers in their annual reports to the General Assembly on the territories for which they were responsible, had made the outlines clear. No one doubted that, whatever it might have been in ancient times, Libya in 1950 was a very poor country, lacking natural resources and at a low level of development, whose problems had been aggravated by the ravages of war.

The General Assembly had acknowledged, not only in its discussions but also by one paragraph in the resolution deciding that Libya should become independent, that there were problems of economic development to be taken into account; but no definitive recommendations were made.[1] In effect, within the United Nations framework, the consideration of economic development was passed to the Commissioner, first to make an analysis of the problems with which the new country would be faced, and then to suggest solutions for them, both tasks to be carried out in collaboration with the Secretary-General and the specialized agencies. It was obvious, but never admitted in so many words, that solutions could be found only with the help of capital-exporting countries, which at the time primarily meant the then Administering Powers—the United Kingdom and France—and the United States. Italy, though understandably greatly wishing to keep a foot in the stirrup, did not at the time belong to this group. Libya's chief asset at the time of independence was its strategic position on the southern shores of the Mediterranean, which, by coincidence, was of interest to the

1. General Assembly Resolution 289 (IV), 21 November 1949, para. 9.

same three great Powers for well-known reasons. Libya could therefore count on their help. The nature, amount, terms, and specific details of assistance, however, had to be worked out. The Commissioner realized early in his assignment that it would be incumbent upon him to spark a program which he hoped to make as international as possible, and preferably United Nations based. At the same time, he was very much aware of the need to establish, insofar as possible, an all-Libyan economy to replace the three territorial economies, in terms of which the Libyans, as well as the Administering Powers, were still too prone to envisage the future.

This chapter is intended to give a detailed description of the multiple activities that resulted successively in the initial analysis of the problems on an all-Libyan basis, in the recommendations of technical experts as to how a Libyan program to cope with them could best be organized, and in the foreign aid needed to translate these recommendations into practical projects.

The sporadic discussion of these questions with the Council for Libya have also been described in Chapter 5, Part 3, and elsewhere in this study. The members of the Council were not personally greatly interested in economic development problems. As to the Administering Powers, their team working on financial and development problems was entirely different from that concerned with political affairs. In particular, the United Kingdom had a very major interest in subsidizing the future Libyan State in return for the right to maintain military facilities there as part of its overall strategic plans. The United States, too, had important interests in Libya, not only in the broad sense, but in the specific sense that at Mellaha, a suburb of Tripoli, it maintained a major air base—Wheelus Field—dating back to World War II but of great strategic significance in the cold war era of the 1950s.[2] In return for continued use of this facility, the United States was prepared to make a contribution to Libya's development.

On a smaller scale, the involvement of France in the Fezzan provided the basis for some form of continuing subsidy and development aid to meet at least that territory's needs.

In order to offset to some extent the preponderating influence of the United Kingdom and France, the Commissioner did his best to generalize and internationalize the aid-to-Libya program on a United Nations basis. He received unstinting support from the Executive Heads and Secretariats of the United Nations family of agencies, within their operational limits—indeed, sometimes far beyond their normal limits, as will be seen. He received pragmatic support from the Administering Powers, and somewhat

2. See Chapter 4, p. 315 and fn. 15.

more generous help from the United States in respect of pledges for aid to Libya at the technical level. The final arrangements for helping Libya's development turned out to be much more international than might have been expected, since the country's eventual development institutions—the Libyan Public Development and Stabilization Agency (LPDSA) and the Libyan Finance Corporation (LFC), of both of which much more is said later in this chapter—were supported by a kind of consortium of the United Kingdom, France, Italy, and the United States, the first plan having been prepared by an international United Nations team of experts. These institutions included on their respective boards of directors a United Nations official in the person of the Resident Representative in Libya of the Technical Assistance Board (TAB).

What follows summarizes three successive stages, each carried out by a different technical assistance team: a preparatory mission (June–July 1950) to define the terms and limits of the United Nations effort, locally known as the Goodrich mission, headed by Carter Goodrich;[3] a larger team of fourteen experts and technical personnel headed by a Chief Economist, John Lindberg,[4] to draw up an appraisal, or balance sheet, of the Libyan economy (December 1950 to June 1951), and finally a team of no less than twenty-seven members, headed by Benjamin Higgins[5] as Chief

3. See Chapter 5, pp. 399 ff.

4. John Lindberg was born in Stockholm, Sweden, in 1901. After studying economics at Stockholm University, where he received his doctor's degree (1920–25), he studied migration problems in the United States of America (1925–28). He subsequently returned to his home country as Associate Secretary to the Royal Commission of Unemployment. From 1930 to 1936 Lindberg was a member of the Statistical Section of the International Labour Office (Geneva), and from 1936 to 1946 he worked as a member of the Economics Section of the League of Nations (Geneva) in charge of studies on world production, etc. After spending the year 1946–47 in Princeton, N.J., as a member of the Institute of Advanced Studies, and the year 1948–49 as a Visiting Associate Professor in Economics at Swarthmore College in Pennsylvania, Lindberg served as a member of various United Nations technical assistance missions (Bolivia, 1950; Libya, 1951; Jordan, 1952–54). He is the author of many books, reports, and articles, including the United Nations report *A General Economic Appraisal of Libya,* United Nations Publication Sales No. 1952.II.H.2 (ST/TAA/K/LIBYA/1, 22 September 1952).

5. Benjamin Higgins was born in London, Ontario, in 1912. After studying economics at the University of Western Ontario and at the London School of Economics, and public administration at Harvard, he received his Ph.D. from the University of Wisconsin in 1941, the year in which he became a naturalized United States citizen. His varied career included teaching economics and public administration at various United States, Canadian, and Australian universities, as well as advisory and administrative functions in various countries. After his tour of duty in Libya, which culminated in the presentation of the report *The Economic and Social Development of*

Economist (July 1951 to January 1952). This last team prepared a six-year plan for the economic and social development of Libya which was submitted as a recommendation to the Libyan Government, and accepted by it, shortly after independence.

Thus, through a United Nations effort at the expert and administrative level, a State created by a United Nations decision already had, when it became independent, a workable blueprint for its economic and social development. It also had at its disposal, thanks to the sterling efforts of United Nations staff, both at the technical and the political level, the basic arrangements for a new common currency and for the necessary institutions for financing its development.

THE GOODRICH MISSION: AN INVENTORY

The principal recommendations of the Goodrich mission were that "a balance sheet" of the Libyan economy should be drawn up, followed by a plan for economic development. The report went on to recommend a strengthening of the staff of the United Nations Mission in Libya; to define the timing of technical assistance; and to make specific proposals as to what technical assistance ought to be provided immediately and what might be left until later, provided there was a reasonable assurance of continuity over a number of years.

The essence of the recommendations was that, as a first step, there should be prepared within about three months a comprehensive inventory of Libya's economic position and potential; this should be followed by a study of the possibilities of progressive economic development, based on better utilization of Libya's resources and property and on public and private investment. The second study should estimate the cost of the improvements suggested, recommend priorities, and indicate the timing of successive stages. It should be the point of departure for seeking the financial assistance required, whether from public or from private sources. Goodrich pointed out that experience in other developing countries had shown that money could be raised, if at all, only on the basis of carefully prepared, specific plans.

Libya, United Nations Publication Sales No. 1953.II.H.8 (ST/TAA/K/LIBYA/3, 12 October 1953), he served as monetary, fiscal, and economic adviser in various technical assistance missions in Indonesia, Lebanon, the Philippines, Greece, and Brazil. From 1959 to 1967 Higgins was Professor of Economics at the University of Texas. In September 1967 he became Head of the Department of Economics at the University of Montreal. He has published several books on economic development problems and policies.

The Goodrich mission's recommendations, in short, were framed in terms of the needs of Libya as an underdeveloped country and the special responsibility which the United Nations had assumed toward it.[6]

The mission emphasized that there was a need for a chain of technical assistance projects adapted to particular immediate as well as long-term requirements. One of the most important aims should be to help the new government to build up its administrative, social, and economic services, though it was recognized that it would be difficult to embark upon all these tasks while the Constitution was still being drafted. Nevertheless, there were a number of "obvious" subjects which could be studied.

The need for a general economic survey was rightly called "obvious." The per capita income was undeniably low (the Lindberg team arrived at a figure of $35 per annum), and the services provided by the local administrations, particularly in the educational and social fields, were very much below the levels demanded in more highly developed countries. Yet even such services as existed had in part been built up during the Italian occupation on capital expenditure holding but slender prospects of an economic return. On the eve of independence, the Administering Powers were still carrying a considerable share of the cost of government which substantially exceeded local public revenues. An objective and realistic assessment by impartial experts of the country's existing economic situation and immediate

6. Viewing matters from a different angle, the United Kingdom Government tended rather to look upon Libya as an overdeveloped country. In its first annual report to the General Assembly on the administration of Cyrenaica and Tripolitania, it stated:

> Economically these territories are not undeveloped lands with a considerable potential capacity for improved agriculture or prospects of mineral discovery and industrial development, but areas that supported a considerable colonial population from Phoenicia, Greece and Rome over a period of 1,000 years (from roughly 500 B.C. to 500 A.D.), and are now exhausted and largely infertile by reason of the exploitation they then suffered and the neglect to maintain the wells, cisterns, tanks, terraced fields, trees and so on (which were the essential basis of the agricultural prosperity of that earlier period) since the time of the Arab invasion, which brought in a largely pastoral economy and permitted extensive and indiscriminate grazing. The territories, therefore, need very substantial amounts of initially unproductive expenditure on investigations into such items as water resources, soil fertility, and in kindred fields, as well as the provision of cheap and easily accessible power for pumping water from subterranean storage. This sort of development is in hand on a scale limited by the finance available.

"Annual report of the Government of the United Kingdom to the General Assembly concerning the administration of Cyrenaica and Tripolitania," GAOR: Fifth Session, 1950, Annexes, Agenda item 21 (A/1390, 29 September 1950), p. 35.

As will be seen, whether the country was considered to be under- or overdeveloped made little difference to the assistance furnished to Libya. See also Chapter 5, pp. 392–94.

economic prospects was essential if Libya's future was to be planned as that of a single State rather than three separate territories. Such an assessment would be of help to the Commissioner, the Council for Libya, and the leaders of the emergent State.

Even greater importance was attached by the Goodrich mission to the need for the next survey team to examine and report on the most promising lines for increasing productivity in Libya in the broadest sense, on the basis of the economic unification of the country and the progressive improvement of techniques in agriculture and animal husbandry and other occupations; and to frame prudently and accurately cost plans for new capital investment.

The economic appraisal should indicate clearly and unmistakably the directions in which Libya's leaders might most hopefully look for the improvement of the economic position of the country and its people.

The mission recommended the recruitment of the following experts to carry out the general economic survey it proposed: a chief economist, to be assisted by a specialist in balance-of-payments studies, by an economist specializing in public finance, by a senior agricultural adviser, and by an adviser on currency and banking. Corresponding recommendations for the appointment of experts in specific fields included: a team of three for a water and soil resources survey in Tripolitania; an expert on irrigation and water projects for Cyrenaica; two or three experts for extension work in the Fezzan to promote the proper use of the newly opened artesian wells there; an expert to help devise schemes for long-term agricultural credit; an expert in the marketing of wool; and experts in rural electrification, viticulture, and the agricultural processing industries. In the social welfare field, it was recommended that an adviser be appointed to work out an appropriate long-term program for social development and ways and means of meeting relevant needs. In addition, a social adviser on questions relating to homeless children and juvenile delinquents should be provided, and it was suggested that the possibility of organizing a social welfare training center be explored.

Education had already been looked at by the United Nations Educational, Scientific and Cultural Organization (UNESCO), and the mission therefore limited itself to endorsing UNESCO's proposals that a training center be set up and a program of fellowships and scholarships established.

Similarly, in the field of public health, the mission endorsed the comments of the World Health Organization (WHO) consultant, and subsequently agreed about the need for appointing an experienced public health consultant to help the new government to draft a set of regulations and a public health administration scheme.

Finally, the mission recommended that an expert be appointed to work out a scheme for keeping reasonably up to date the salient vital statistics needed for the proper administration of the new State.[7]

Turning to the medium-term requirements, the mission recommended that, after a provisional Libyan government had been formed, a team of experts in various branches of public administration should be brought in for approximately three months to help to set up administrative services in such fields as the budget, overall organization, the civil service, fiscal administration, health, social welfare, and the essential statistical services. It further recommended that at the proper time experts from the International Monetary Fund (IMF) should be called upon to assist in the establishment of the currency and monetary system of the new State, a matter with which the Commissioner was already busy (see p. 687, fn. 20).

For longer-term projects, the mission suggested that the possibility be considered of appointing an agricultural expert for the improvement of date palms in the Fezzan, and of starting a center to train some fifteen to twenty social workers specialized in rural welfare.

As to the strengthening of the staff of the United Nations Mission in Libya, it was recommended that a Deputy Principal Secretary be provided to deal with technical assistance and economic and social development affairs. This officer was appointed in November 1950, and thereafter was concerned with advising the Administering Powers in the formulation of technical assistance requests to be submitted to the United Nations and the specialized agencies (cf. pp. 397–99), helping to arrange for their implementation, coordinating the activities of the experts, and generally keeping an eye on all matters relating to economic development. The Goodrich mission also endorsed the view expressed by the Commissioner and the Principal Secretary that the United Nations Mission should have technical staff qualified in the fields of currency, banking and exchange, public administration, and questions relating to former Italian property.

The Goodrich mission's report having been reviewed and approved by the Technical Assistance Board (TAB) in September 1950,[8] there remained the problem of negotiating an agreement with the two Administering Powers. Neither had envisaged as large a team of experts as was suggested; but on examining the report they, particularly the United Kingdom, were agreeable to its recommendations. Provision for a larger team

7. The UNESCO and WHO projects have been dealt with in more detail in Chapter 5, pp. 401–03.

8. "Report of the Preparatory Mission on Technical Assistance to Libya," United Nations Doc. TAB/R.57, 24 August 1950, and Adds. 1–4. Mimeographed. See also Chapter 5, p. 401, fn. 66.

was the more easily arranged because TAB, when it considered and approved the makeup of the team for Libya, gave sympathetic consideration to the view of the United Kingdom Government that it should not have to bear the full costs of local technical assistance expenditure, as was normally required of the requesting country, on the ground that it would soon cease to bear responsibility for the administration of Tripolitania and Cyrenaica. Looking to the future, it was clear that if the new Libyan State had to bear these expenses, it could do so only at the cost of increasing its deficit or curtailing essential disbursements in other directions. "Local" expenses comprised such items as office space and supplies, local transportation, interpretation, translation and stenographic services, and part of the subsistence allowances paid to the experts (at that time 12 percent of their total cost). TAB considered it reasonable that a substantial share of such costs should be met from United Nations technical assistance resources in view of the United Nations' special responsibility for promoting the establishment of an independent and viable Libya.

In negotiations conducted later by the Principal Secretary and United Nations Headquarters officials with the United Kingdom Government, it was agreed that the United Nations would provide, through its Mission in Libya, all facilities for the experts, while the United Kingdom would bear the cost of subsistence allowances and medical facilities.

Thus, on 15 December 1950, a basic technical assistance agreement was signed between the United Nations agencies represented on TAB and the United Kingdom Government in respect of Tripolitania and Cyrenaica. A supplementary agreement between the United Nations Food and Agriculture Organization (FAO) and the United Kingdom provided for the appointment of experts to work in Tripolitania and Cyrenaica as recommended by the Goodrich mission.

THE SECOND TEAM: AN ECONOMIC APPRAISAL

The United Nations and the specialized agencies had already been lining up experts for the appointments foreseen in the agreements signed with the United Kingdom, and by the end of January 1951, thanks to a "forced draft" approach, the chief economist and six experts were on duty in Libya, and five other posts were under active recruitment. For the purposes of this study, it will be sufficient to review the findings of the group as a whole, as expressed in the *Economic Appraisal,* a summary of which will be found on pages 674–79.

Meanwhile, a number of other practical, although small, beginnings were made in technical assistance. Among them were the collection from the

Italian Institute of Colonial Agriculture in Florence of a considerable amount of data and studies, and the results of agricultural experiments undertaken by the Italian Administration. In some cases these were of considerable value; for example, an analysis of soil conditions on the Barce Plain in Cyrenaica disposed of the Goodrich mission's tentative recommendation that a soil survey be carried out there.

As also recommended by the Goodrich mission, endorsing an earlier proposal, the United Nations Mission made arrangements through the French Residency in Tunisia for a group of seventeen farmers and officials of the Agricultural Departments of Tripolitania, Cyrenaica, and the Fezzan to visit Tunisia in October 1950 with the Mission's agricultural adviser. Visits to olive plantations, olive-oil mills, sheep-raising areas, irrigated plots, and orchards took in areas that were worked by tribes collectively as well as by individual Tunisians and French settlers. Experimental livestock stations raising horses, mules, donkeys, sheep, and goats were visited, as well as cooperative marketing associations. The group also observed examples of forest conservation and development.

The cost of the trip was shared three ways: the United Nations Mission furnished surface transport within Libya, as did the Government of Tunisia within its territory, all other expenses being defrayed by the British and French Administrations.

A similar tour was arranged in Egypt in February 1951 for another seventeen Libyan agronomists and officials of the three agricultural departments. Again, visits to experimental farms, to irrigation works, and to the government horticultural services, agricultural school, and agricultural museum proved of great interest to the Libyan group. In this case, transport expenses were entirely met by the United Nations, the participants' subsistence allowance being borne by the British and French Authorities.

Further study by the FAO mission staff and the British Administration led to the conclusion that a large-scale drilling program for water in Tripolitania would be beyond the resources of the United Nations program. The United States authorities, who had been kept well informed about the development of the latter, since they themselves were planning early initiation of a Point Four program in Libya, thereupon agreed, at the request of the United Kingdom, to assume responsibility for this project.

A small technical training center in Tripoli already had been opened by the British Administration to train clerical staff for government offices, and technicians such as carpenters, artisans, and electricians. Under a technical assistance agreement signed with UNESCO, a large center was opened on 1 January 1951 to take 232 boys, the principal and five teachers being provided by UNESCO. The original plan provided for fourteen teachers, but recruitment of qualified staff who could teach in Arabic proved difficult. Not until the second half of 1951 could an additional group of teachers be recruited.

Again in collaboration with UNESCO and FAO, a modest fellowship program was launched that provided for twenty-nine grants—including seven for Cyrenaica and seventeen for Tripolitania—in the first instance in local government (9), forestry (3), veterinary services (2), customs administration (2), education, or teacher training (7), police (3), and accountancy (3). Subsequently, ten UNESCO grants were made to enable Fezzanese students to study at the elementary-school level in Tunisia and Algeria, and five fellowships were granted early in 1950 under the United Nations Fellowship Program. Thus, during the first year of technical assistance for Libya, there were forty-four fellows studying abroad with United Nations agency help.

Such totals may seem puny to the reader, but in a country where in 1950 there was some argument whether there were sixteen or eighteen university graduates in all, and where secondary schools for Arabs were virtually nonexistent, they were significant. The problem was not to find funds for training abroad, but to find candidates who had the qualifications for advanced studies. Libyans with secondary education were practically limited to those who had completed it before 1939, and thus the majority were in the twenty-five to forty age group, and married, so that family responsibilities hampered their further education. Nevertheless, a secondary education was considered a basic requirement for entry at most levels of public service. Moreover, the poverty of the country meant that few Libyans were able to send their sons abroad. At the same time, the Arabic-language secondary schools established under the British Administration in 1950 would soon begin to produce educated youths, more prepared for further training. Nonetheless, an effort had to be made, and through intensive recruitment by the Administering Powers and relaxation of the normal academic standards required in the United Nations fellowship and scholarship program, the placements mentioned above were made at an estimated cost of $32,482 to the United Nations specialized agencies.

Participation by Libyans in a series of United Nations seminars financed out of technical assistance funds began with the attendance of three Libyans at a seminar on rural social welfare held in Cairo in November 1950. However, it is to be noted that all their expenses were paid by the respective administrations.

A request from France for technical assistance for the Fezzan having been lodged in February, a basic agreement was signed, on the same lines as that for Tripolitania and Cyrenaica, between the French Government and the specialized agencies represented on TAB on 23 March 1951, together with a supplementary agreement which provided that the senior economist, the public finance experts, the agronomist, and the social welfare expert who figured in the United Kingdom agreement should extend their activities to the Fezzan. In addition, three experts in agricultural extension and one in the improvement of date palms were to be provided.

The reluctance, and the ostensible reason therefor, of the United Kingdom and France to meet "local" technical assistance costs have already been discussed. One cannot help wondering whether this attitude was but a mask for their disinclination to accept United Nations experts of other than English or French nationality. However, in 1950 a compromise was reached, as described on page 669. For his part, the Commissioner requested the Secretary-General, as Chairman of TAB, to waive all payments of local subsistence assessments in the three territories until Libya attained independence, in view of the special responsibility of the United Nations to assist its economic and social development. The Commissioner likewise invoked the studies of the experts, still in draft, which confirmed Libya's great need for technical assistance and its deficitary position. Accordingly, for the first time in its admittedly short history, TAB, at its meeting on 22 June 1951, decided to waive the requirement that Libya pay such "local" costs. The pattern thus established was later applied as standard procedure to most of the new States that emerged in Africa and Asia.

In July 1951, another agreement, concluded with the United Kingdom—this time on behalf of WHO—provided for a team comprising a public health administrator, a sanitary engineer, and a public health nurse. On 21 July 1951, an agreement between UNESCO, the British Administration in Tripoli, and, for the first time, the Prime Minister of the Provisional Libyan Government, provided for a project in the field of teacher training to comprise a chief of project (who also served as chief of the UNESCO technical assistance mission) and six other experts to serve in two teacher-training colleges in Tripoli, in the Education Materials Production Center, and in the development of two model primary schools. The chief of the UNESCO mission was to discharge yet a third duty as a general adviser to the Minister of Education in the Provisional Government.

As the fruits of the labors of the Lindberg team began to take shape in a draft report, it became clear to the Administering Powers and the Commissioner, to the experts concerned, and to the participating agencies that a special effort would have to be made to get together the third and final team to draft an economic and social development plan for Libya.

An agreement was duly signed on 27 August between the United Nations, FAO, the International Labour Office (ILO), and the United Kingdom

Government covering the services of eighteen experts to advise the Administering Powers on the drafting of such a comprehensive plan. In addition to the chief economist and the senior agricultural expert, there were to be specialists in the following subjects: statistics, development financing, subsoil minerals, subsoil water, salt processing, tanning, manpower training, handicraft industries, range management and livestock, agricultural credit and cooperatives, marketing and grading of agricultural products, wool processing, agricultural processing industries, esparto grass conservation, forestry, and sponge fishing. Subsequently, an educational specialist was added by UNESCO.

At the request of the French Government, a corresponding agreement prolonging the work of the experts in the Fezzan was signed on 18 October 1951.

It will be noted that several sectors were already being studied by experts in the Lindberg team, recruited at the beginning of 1951, so that the new assignments were primarily extensions of the initial ones. This meant that the team was able to go into action unusually quickly. The chief economist, Benjamin Higgins, arrived to take over leadership for this last phase of the planning at the beginning of July.

The agreement foresaw that the draft development plan would be completed in from three to five months. As will be seen, this was unduly optimistic, even though many of the experts already in the country were given expanded terms of reference and continued their work without interruption. Even with assistance from the supporting services of the United Nations Mission, and with the collaboration of the Administering Powers and the Provisional Libyan Government, it proved impossible to finish the job by the end of 1951.

A request to the United Nations International Children's Emergency Fund (UNICEF) and WHO to implement the recommendations made as a result of a survey of tuberculosis problems and needs they had conducted in March 1951 (and which was submitted by the United Kingdom on 21 August and by France on 12 September), produced assistance to the amount of $60,000 for a BCG vaccination program and an allocation of $40,000 for motor vehicles for the rural public health services. The agreements were signed early in 1952.

The United Kingdom asked for technical assistance to develop an existing agricultural research station (set up by the Italians) at Sidi al-Misri in the suburbs of Tripoli as a national and international research center for the arid zones. This request sprang from a recommendation of the UNESCO Standing Committee on Arid Zones, which held its first meeting from 5 to 7 April 1951 at Algiers. TAB authorized a joint UNESCO and FAO team to study the possibilities, which led to a recommendation that aid should be furnished by FAO, at Libya's request, for a national agricultural research center staffed by nine scientists. It was recommended that the international aspects should be considered after the center had become firmly established on a national basis. When independence came, such a request was made within the context of the agricultural assistance sought as part of the agricultural development program.

The *General Economic Appraisal of Libya,* prepared for the United Nations Technical Assistance Administration (TAA) by Lindberg, was completed in draft form in late June, at which time it was communicated to the Administering Powers and the Provisional Libyan Government, and, in summary, to the Council for Libya. The final report, after review by the United Nations and the specialized agencies, was circulated in mimeographed form late in September. It was printed about a year later.[9]

As was to be expected, the *Economic Appraisal* confirmed Libya's extreme poverty and the limitations of its economy. The findings were not surprising, but the document was the first all-Libya study made, since other studies carried out by the Italian, British, or French Administrations had related either to the individual provinces or to narrow sectoral problems. The Italian studies in particular were concerned only with those parts of the economy which were State-controlled, directly or indirectly, or primarily intended for the benefit of the Italian colonists.

Lindberg pointed out that agriculture was the mainstay of the Libyan economy and was likely to remain so for a long time to come. It was clear that cereals were of the greatest importance in terms of the local diet, and that livestock was the most important source of income. For the purposes of future development, the Italian forms of static and irrigated farming were described as essential elements, particularly when combined with dry crops. Productivity, measured by manpower output, was unusually low among the Arab farmers. Consequently, Libya was barely able to grow an adequate diet for its people, and drought often brought real hardship and famine conditions.

The weakness of the economy was strikingly illustrated by the fact that, as already mentioned, national income was estimated at $35 per head per annum. Even this figure was somewhat misleading, because Libya's large balance-of-payments deficit obscured true income arising from its own productivity. The balance of payments for the four immediately pre-

9. John Lindberg, *A General Economic Appraisal of Libya,* United Nations Publication Sales No. 1952.II.H.2 (ST/TAA/K/LIBYA/1, 22 September 1952). The *Economic Appraisal* was also issued (summarized) in both draft and final form as United Nations Docs. A/AC.32/COUNCIL/R.14, 20 July 1951, and A/AC.32/COUNCIL/R.143/Rev.1, 24 September 1952. Mimeographed.

ceding years, i.e. 1947–50, had been in chronic and heavy deficit, covered only by foreign aid. By and large, grants-in-aid from the Administering Powers covered 85 percent of the adverse balance. The situation is revealed in all its starkness by the figures for 1950, when Libyan exports brought in $6,347,600, whereas imports cost $14,190,400. The gap was closed by military expenditure ($6,736,800) and by grants-in-aid ($3,738,000). At that, 1950 was a year which showed some improvement in the terms of trade, but income from exports covered only 45 percent of the cost of imports. On the credit side, military expenditure amounted to 40 percent and grants-in-aid to another 20 percent of that cost. This shows just how dependent Libya was on help from foreign Powers and their military expenditure.[10]

This budgetary deficit, coupled with a currency needing strong external support, was to have a major influence on the monetary arrangements that had to be made prior to Libya's acquisition of independence (see Part 2 of this chapter).

As for the possibilities of industrial development, Lindberg pointed out that, despite the advantages offered by sea transport, Libya's lack of fuel, industrial raw materials, and domestic skills was so great that industrial development would inevitably be hampered, although there was some chance of expansion in the agricultural processing sector. Thus, again, it was agriculture that would in the final analysis have to produce the export goods needed to pay for imports of the manufactured goods, fuel, and raw materials essential to economic development and a rising standard of living.

It was further pointed out that Cyrenaican industry had been virtually destroyed during the war, and had not been replaced except for some public utilities temporarily patched up by the British Administration. In Tripolitania, a good deal of industrial plant was still left, though important branches, particularly in the construction sector, proved to be too big for the territory's needs when Italian development was cut short. Public utilities were kept going only by the subsidies of the British Administration. The other industries, small in terms of numbers employed or output, were chiefly intended for satisfying simple local consumption needs, or for the processing of fish and agricultural products for export or local consumption. There was no industry in Fezzan.

Dealing with public finance, the *Economic Appraisal* presented a con-

10. See Stanislaw Kirkor, *Balance of Payments of Libya,* United Nations Publications Sales No. 1953.II.H.6 (ST/TAA/K/LIBYA/2, 7 August 1953). This study was also issued in mimeographed form as United Nations Doc. A/AC.32/COUNCIL/R.160, 12 September 1951. It is a supplement to the *Economic Appraisal.* Although its author's general conclusions were clear before the completion of the appraisal, his final detailed calculations were made only subsequently.

solidated statement of the Libyan budget, which indicated that the total estimated deficit in the years 1951–52 would be $4,870,339, or about 30 percent of the total expenditure of $16,550,531. The deficits in each of the three territories were: Tripolitania, $1,351,467 (15 percent of the estimated total expenditure there); Cyrenaica, $3,308,872 (47 percent); and the Fezzan, $210,000 (61 percent).

The foregoing figures were characteristic of Libya's deficitary position from the end of World War II until the time when the *Economic Appraisal* was compiled. The only exception related to Tripolitania, where, in three of the eight years, exceptionally good crops had resulted in a surplus.

It was further pointed out that, with the need for increased federal expenditure in the future and the expected increase in administrative expenditure at provincial levels also, and with the small hope of substantially increasing revenue, because of the low level of income, budget deficits would be bound to increase. This would mean an increase in grants-in-aid until such time as economic development and a rise in national income per head allowed the level of taxation to be raised, and until other sources of revenue became more productive.

In the light of these findings, read in conjunction with the balance-of-payments figures, the authors of the *Economic Appraisal* declared that foreign subsidies were a condition sine qua non of the viability of a Libyan State. Should foreign grants-in-aid cease, standards of living already close to the subsistence level would fall, and government activity and services, which also were at minimum or subminimal level, would have to be curtailed.

However, grants-in-aid must be regarded as a temporary expedient; foreign financial assistance should not be regarded as a permanent feature of the country's economy. Such assistance must be a means of helping Libya to help itself. In time, national income savings should increase to the point where outside aid became superfluous. Economic independence, insofar as the term still had any meaning, and a really viable economy required that domestic income should gradually rise to a level where it could stand the costs of the country's administration and at the same time provide a surplus for essential investment to maintain economic and social progress.

The *Economic Appraisal* expressed concern at the rate of population increase, estimated at more than 4 percent gross,[11] though, because of high infant mortality, still only slightly over 1 percent net, per annum. However,

11. The third (Higgins) team gives a figure of 5.3 percent per annum. See Benjamin Higgins, *The Economic and Social Development of Libya,* United Nations Publication Sales No. 1953.II.H.8 (ST/TAA/K/LIBYA/3, 12 October 1953), p. 4.

with the improved and expanded public health services that an independent State would surely find necessary, it was nearly certain that infant mortality would decline. Accordingly, a major problem loomed on the horizon in that an increase in national income at a rate substantially in excess of the potential population increase would be difficult to achieve. A growth rate for national income lower than the populaiton growth rate would, from the point of view of economic and social development, mean wasted effort, as it would lead only to a larger population subsisting at even lower levels of living. Economic development, therefore, hinged on the possibilities of increasing the national income faster than the population grew. Should studies, then, be centered on the circumstances determining the growth of national income rather than on those related to the improvement of the infant mortality rate? This was a grave problem, not only economically or demographically, but also from the moral and religious point of view. To the Commissioner and many of his collaborators it became a real matter of conscience as to whether any and, if so, what, recommendations should be made to the Libyan Government. Requests for advice addressed to religious leaders did not prove very helpful; the answers were either so contradictory as to be useless, or they indicated that the matter must be left in the hands of Allah. In an orthodox Moslem country, the easy way out was obviously to leave matters in Allah's hands; but the need to concentrate on increasing the national income was just as obvious and unavoidable. The Commissioner must confess that he lacked the moral courage to make up his mind one way of the other, so that in the end the recommendation made to the Libyan Government on this particular point was inconclusive. As matters turned out, it was years before infant mortality began to decline, and by the time the decrease became appreciable, oil had been discovered, national income was rising steeply, and the problem had radically changed.

From the economic point of view, savings are a basic condition of progress, but with the data available it had not been possible to determine what rate of gross savings would be necessary in Libya to provide for an early increase in national income at any given rate. During the early years of independence, capital requirements might be relatively limited, and the country might be in a position gradually to set up domestic savings institutes and a system of banking and finance, and to inculcate the general habits of saving and thrift essential to an accelerated rate of economic growth.

To create the conditions for higher income and savings, it was necessary not only to attract capital from abroad, but also to exercise strict economy in the use of the resources available at home. Yet savings for economic development could not be the only goal of Libyan economic activity. The prevailing standards of living in Libya must also slowly be raised, though mostly in those ways which served directly to increase productivity. Administrative costs or expenditure on regular budget account ought to be kept to the minimum compatible with effective administration. Savings should be as high as was compatible with the other needs; in particular, they should have priority for the use of the additional national income per head created by economic development.

In discussing the directions which economic development should take, the *Economic Appraisal* commented that, since the mainstay of the Libyan diet was cereals, it was obviously desirable to expand their production.[12] This might frequently be possible even without new capital investment. Cultivated areas could be extended, and increased yields per acre obtained through better methods of tillage and water use, and the introduction of better tools and improved strains of wheat and barley.

An increase in livestock production was equally desirable, both for increased home consumption and for export. Development of animal husbandry called for selective breeding of animals, better range management, the organization of marketing, the grading of wool, and the establishment of cold-storage facilities. The Lindberg team believed that results could be obtained relatively quickly.

The *Economic Appraisal* said that extensive new planting of olive trees, which flourished over large areas of Libya, was another solution recommended by most authorities. Citrus fruits were considered the most promising of capital-intensive tree crops, since they could carry the cost of full irrigation. The conviction was also expressed that conservation measures for esparto grass—a wild grass used at the time for high-grade paper production—could raise the income derived from an important source of foreign exchange.

Other, though more limited, possibilities lay in the further development of fisheries, especially for sponges, tuna, and sardines, all products with a ready export market.

Small local industries, it was thought, could be built up for the processing of agricultural and fisheries products, for example, olive-oil mills and refineries; tuna, sardine, fruit, and vegetable canneries; and sponge processing and grading plants.

Finally, a tourist industry was thought to have some prospects.

The *Economic Appraisal* suggested that in considering development and its priorities, immediate attention should be given to the problems of compensation for war damage and reconstruction, particularly in Cyrenaica (see

12. Lindberg, pp. 43–45.

Chapter 5, Parts 1, 2, and 3 passim). Reconstruction, it was argued, was not only an economic problem but also a moral responsibility. There was also a need for overhauling infrastructure investments, such as ports and power facilities, as a prerequisite for further development. Once these immediate necessities had been assured, the key to development lay in increased agricultural productivity and the solution of cognate questions of the processing, marketing, and distribution of agricultural products. But the physical possibility of increasing production only did not mean that any given project was economically sound or would promote a viable economy. Owing to the nature of the country and the level of skills of its people, sound development projects were likely to be small, with prosperity flowing from a number of minor projects rather than from a few major ones.

Moreover, expansion of the country's capacity to absorb capital would depend on the progress made in education, which, although costly, must be regarded as an essential element in any balanced program of economic improvement. However, the authors of the *Economic Appraisal* pointed out, first, that an inventory of sound investment projects, based on actual calculations of costs and prices, and estimates of precise needs for technical assistance and investment, required much more study and research; and second, that it would be feasible for technical assistance to set off a process of economic development where it would not occur spontaneously. The United Nations bore a special responsibility for seeing that Libya received the help necessary to make the country economically independent, but no amount of foreign aid would assure a lasting improvement in the people's lot unless development were supported by their own endeavors. The people must be prepared to subordinate minor needs to the overriding aim of development, to be thrifty in public expenditure, to change their habits and institutions, and to show restraint in respect of levels of consumption. Economic development was no simple matter; it would fail without a moral and spiritual leadership in Libya capable of rising to the occasion and of diverting the energies of the people into the creative channels of economic development rather than into the morasses of political and factional strife.

EFFECTS OF THE APPRAISAL

Circulation of the *Economic Appraisal* brought about a distinct change in the attitudes of the representatives of the Administering Powers, both on the spot and in London and Paris, and of the Provisional Libyan Government, toward technical assistance programs and activities. It also made a profound impression on the Libyan leaders. Among the latter, the Tripolitanians were perhaps the most deeply impressed; in private conversations with the Commissioner and members of his staff, several of them had expressed their conviction that the gloomy assessment of Libya's economic position made earlier by the British and French Administrations was intended to justify their opposition to independence—or at least their desire to delay it—rather than to paint a true picture (cf. Chapter 10, Part 5, p. 757). Now they were confronted with a sober analytical appraisal drawn up by a team of highly qualified experts, whose chief was a Swede, and which had few British or French members. It became very difficult for them in these circumstances to continue to nurse their suspicions. Competent observers thought this change was in part due to the fact that Libyan leaders generally had come to have confidence in the impartiality of the work of the Commissioner and his staff in political matters and, having had many opportunities to meet the experts from the United Nations and the specialized agencies, had similarly gained confidence in their integrity and lack of bias.

The Provisional Libyan Government, which was only just beginning to get an inkling of what it was up against in the economic sector, felt a great deal better when it saw the problems with which it was faced objectively analyzed and explained; and although the picture was far from rosy, at least the *Economic Appraisal* opened up new vistas.

As related in Chapters 7 and 8, the NCAL, at the Commissioner's informal suggestion, had delayed drafting constitutional provisions relating to financial, economic, and social matters pending the appearance of the *Economic Appraisal.* These provisions were accordingly more realistic than they would have been had the balance sheet not been available to them. Moreover, the report's data and findings, though no great surprise to the Commissioner, helped him effectively in tackling the problems of the transfer of powers and in the subsequent discussions on currency and foreign aid, as we shall see.

On the part of the Administering Powers, there was a distinct warming toward technical assistance, which they had earlier viewed with considerable skepticism, once they had sight of the draft of the report. In a way, their earlier reserved attitude was hardly surprising, since in 1950–51 technical assistance, though fairly widely known to colonial administrations under different names and in different forms, took on an entirely new appearance when administered by experts of various nationalities working for international organizations. British and French officials who had been dealing for years with Libyan economic and social problems had understandably been skeptical about foreign advisers coming to Libya to tell them things which they claimed to know much better, but at which they had generally looked piecemeal, in terms of each of the three provinces. Moreover, at the back of their minds, particularly in London, there lurked an uneasy feeling that the United Nations experts would propose overambitious development schemes. When they saw the team's realistic, modest, and practical approach and recommendations, they realized that the technical assistance experts, far from being ogres, were in fact, quite inadvertently, reliable allies, in that they advised the Libyans not to embark on projects which were impracticable or would require greatly increased subsidies, or would at the least lead to demands for larger subsidies. They also appreciated the way in which the team viewed Libya's economic problems against the overall background—a new angle for many of them.

It is fair to say also that some senior officials in the British and French Administrations, and particularly the British, recognized that the quality of the work of the international experts was distinctly superior to many of the earlier studies and reports, though no invidious comments had been made in any United Nations document.

It must be added that the *Economic Appraisal* and the detailed reports which began to become available in mid-1951 also silenced the prevalent background criticism to the effect that, although the United Nations had had a considerable number of people in Libya since December, few practical results beyond some training facilities and fellowships had come of their presence. Such criticism, while quite unfair considering the short time involved and the difficulties of mounting an international aid program, was nevertheless frequently heard in the Council for Libya and in the street. The translation of the reports into Arabic, the serialization of them in the Arabic edition of the Mission's newsletter (see p. 413, fn. 78), and the series of conferences with Libyan leaders about to be described all helped to counter this carping.

It must be admitted, however, that for a long time many Libyans continued to voice their disappointment that the United Nations had no means of providing development loans and grants or budget subsidies. The Commissioner's efforts to establish a fund to be fed from United Nations sources are recorded elsewhere, but, as is well known, the United Nations had then, and still has, no facilities for providing investment capital or cash grants-in-aid.

COMMISSIONER, COUNCIL, AND TECHNICAL ASSISTANCE: A CONSTITUTIONAL ISSUE

The relationship between the Commissioner and the Council for Libya on the one hand and the technical assistance activities carried out by the United Nations and its specialized agencies on the other was a new and unique feature of United Nations life, which calls for some explanation. It must be remembered that the Expanded Programme of Technical Assistance (EPTA) was approved by the General Assembly only a few months before the Commissioner took up his duties in Libya, so that the organizational structure had not yet been developed; nor were funds as yet available. There was a relatively small program of technical assistance financed from the regular budget of the United Nations and largely devoted to training in public administration. As has been repeatedly stressed in this study, the very decision that independence should be granted to Libya carried with it a moral obligation on the United Nations family of agencies and on Member States themselves to help the country to stand on its own feet by providing aid, either internationally or nationally. Although the matter was but little discussed in the General Assembly, there was never any opposition to the idea of helping Libya to improve its economy until such time as it was able to support itself and offer its people a reasonable standard of living. It could well be said that, had there been no technical assistance program to make this possible, some such facility would have had to be created in microcosm. In practice, before the formalities for launching a technical assistance program could be completed, the Secretary-General, at the request of the Commissioner, had appointed some technical staff to the Libyan Mission; at a later date, they would more likely have been paid for out of technical assistance funds from the outset.[13]

But an important constitutional issue was involved in the relationship between the Commissioner and the Council on the one hand and experts working either for the United Nations or for the specialized agencies on the other. In the first place, the Commissioner, as an elected agent of the General Assembly, was not responsible to the Secretary-General. Conversely, technical assistance experts were responsible to the Secretary-General or to the Executive Head of the specialized agency for which they happened to be working within the framework of EPTA. Strictly speaking, the staff of the United Nations Mission in Libya was under the administrative control not of the Commissioner, but of the Secretary-General, and hence under that of the Principal Secretary as the latter's personal representative on the spot.[14] In practice, this was a distinction without a difference and never created difficulty between the Commissioner and the Principal Secretary. The Commissioner did not pretend to know the technical answers to Libya's economic and social problems; his aim was to get the soundest possible advice or the best course to follow, by mobilizing not only the knowledge

13. For a more detailed treatment of these considerations, see Chapter 5, pp. 397 ff.

14. For a detailed description of the administrative setup of the United Nations Mission in Libya, see Chapter 2, pp. 113–24.

and skills of the experts assigned to Libya but also those of their parent organizations. This would obviously help him in his negotiations with the Administering Powers and the emergent Libyan authorities on such matters as the transfer of powers and the concomitant legislation, the establishment of LPDSA and LFC, the Libyan currency and civil service, and the long-term arrangements for grants-in-aid and foreign assistance.

In practice, the arrangements for providing technical assistance to Libya, which United Nations officials usually thought of as advice to be conveyed to the Libyans through the intermediary of the Commissioner, went through two stages. The first, already described, when the experts were financed out of the Mission budget; the second, from December 1950 onward, when the technical assistance agreements with the United Kingdom and France provided for teams of experts serving under EPTA rules. The position of the experts was clearly defined by Economic and Social Council Resolution 222 A (IX), Annex I, which set out EPTA's guiding principles. The latter stipulated that technical assistance should not be a means of foreign economic and political interference in the internal affairs of the country concerned, and should not be accompanied by any considerations of a political nature; that it should be given only to or through governments; that it should be designed to meet the needs of the receiving country, be provided as far as possible in the forms which that country desired, and, in other respects, generally be nonpolitical, nonpartisan, nondiscriminatory, and based on sound technical considerations; lastly, it should be within the financial capacities of the United Nations.[15] The Commissioner was well aware of these limitations, but the Council members for Egypt and Pakistan, and occasionally others, as recorded elsewhere in this study, maintained that the Council should not only review the work of the experts, but also advise and direct them, and they held this view despite many reminders of the pertinent General Assembly resolutions, which were specifically reproduced in the Council's documentation.[16]

The Commissioner, with the help of the Principal Secretary, kept the Council informed of the progress not only of the technical assistance programs, but also of the discussions on currency, of the drafting of the statutes of LPDSA and LFC, and of foreign aid possibilities and related matters. He would have welcomed constructive suggestions, but in fact the

15. For full text of ECOSOC Resolution 222 A (IX), 15 August 1949, and Annexes I and II thereto, see ESCOR: Ninth Session, 1949, Supplement No. 1 (E/1553), pp. 4–14.

16. See *Supplementary Report to the Second Annual Report of the United Nations Commissioner in Libya,* GAOR: Sixth Session, 1951–52, Supplement No. 17A (A/1949/Add.1), paras. 70 ff.

majority of the Council was satisfied with the way in which the United Nations experts went about their work. As usual, the antagonism of the Egyptian and Pakastani members, in which they were joined by their Tripolitanian colleague, was politically motivated. To a lesser extent, the same could be said of the representative of Italy. However, as important reports of substantial interest having great bearing on Libya's future were produced and circulated to the Council in the summer and fall of 1951, the critics of technical assistance appeared to be totally uninterested in the findings or in the implicit or explicit recommendations. Some time later, it became quite clear either that the representatives of Egypt and Pakistan had not reported to their Governments on the economic and social aspects of the Libyan question, or that their reports had gone unheeded, since, during the discussions on currency and on long-term financial aid to Libya, the Ministries of Foreign Affairs of the two countries professed ignorance until the matter was brought to their attention by the Commissioner or the Principal Secretary.

On the other hand, as already described, the Administering Powers, which had given a cool reception to the new idea that an international team should analyze Libyan problems, chiefly because this seemed to be at variance with their political leanings toward a loose federation, changed their views as soon as they had an opportunity of appreciating the spirit in which the international experts approached their tasks, and of assessing their professional ability.

The facilities available from the United Nations Mission in Libya, both on the political and on the administrative plane, were also unusual in the annals of technical assistance. In addition to the new Deputy Principal Secretary, the staff of the Commissioner's office was strengthened by a staff officer for agricultural matters, who also stood in for the Deputy Principal Secretary as required. There were also the linguistic, transport, communications, and general administrative services described in Chapter 2 (see pp. 113–24). Hence, far from being plagued by inadequate logistic support, a common fate for experts working in developing countries, those sent to Libya were able to concentrate closely on their professional work. Those familiar with technical assistance activities, where financial stringency usually imposes severe limitations on supporting services, will appreciate the value of such backstopping.

As regards the substantive work of the United Nations Mission, while it was essential that the Commissioner have the information assembled and advice provided by the experts, it was equally important that the experts should be informed of the general features of the political and administrative structure being planned for the future State, to which their recommendations would obviously have to be geared. As in the political sphere, the question turned on the extent of authority, particularly in financial and administrative matters, that the future central government would enjoy. Without prejudice to the final decision on this point, the Commissioner and his staff could give intelligent guidance to the experts, for there were a number of broad issues the outcome of which was already certain, such as that, although there would be no strong central ministries in the fields with which technical assistance was concerned, it was clear that grants-in-aid, or other forms of foreign aid, would have to be channeled through the central authorities after independence.

There were many other ways in which the Commissioner was able to facilitate the experts' work. We have already seen (p. 400) how meetings were arranged between two members of the Goodrich mission, senior officials of the Administering Powers, and Libyan personages. This procedure was repeated in the case both of the Lindberg and of the Higgins teams, when the local contacts ranged from village heads to the future King, and were extended to take in members of the Provisional Libyan Government and the NCAL. These consultations were sometimes rather informal. The Goodrich mission, for example, as already related, visited Libya during the fasting month of Ramadan, so that the meetings had to be held in the Commissioner's residence after the postsunset meal, which broke the day's fast, and that meant, in effect, after 10 P.M. These meetings, which were attended by representatives of the local administration and political parties, and by prominent members of the commercial, agricultural, and business communities, marked the beginning of a process whereby Libyans were brought into close association with the studies and recommendations of the United Nations experts. This was the Libyan groups' first encounter with any kind of planning procedure. They had as much to learn from the experts as the latter had to learn about Libyan reactions to their proposals.[17]

Meetings of the kind described were held from time to time during 1951, and in the later months were organized systematically, so that the Higgins team was able to meet with Libyans regularly (and usually during normal working hours) to discuss specific topics. These meetings took place with the full knowledge and approval of the Administering Powers in the first place, and later with that of the Provisional Libyan Government. Key officials from the administrations in turn were encouraged to, and in fact did,

17. Goodrich, already much experienced in international organization affairs, and having shortly before been on a technical assistance mission to Bolivia, confessed to the Commissioner that he was astonished at the intensity of political feeling generated in the technical assistance sphere. He therefore appreciated being piloted around the shoals of political issues. His astonishment was to be shared by many other experts.

attend them. Key members of the NCAL were also invited to take part, and accepted. All these meetings were serviced by the staff of the United Nations Mission.

As the experts' reports became final—i.e. as they were approved by the specialized agencies concerned—they were translated into Arabic and widely distributed, sometimes in as many as 500 copies, to ensure that they reached the entire interested official body and the nonofficial reading public. In addition, a fortnightly Arabic newsletter was issued by the Mission to give an account of United Nations technical assistance activities; the newsletter provided summaries, or in the case of the reports of more general interest, full translations, of reports on these activities (see p. 413, fn. 78).

The practice of associating Libyans with the discussion of their country's problems and the remedies suggested therefor persisted to a limited extent after independence, but before long operations became so highly technical that the Libyan groups were restricted to those directly concerned—for example, citrus growers, exporters, or officials from the technological departments of the Government. The publication of regular information about technical assistance activities through the Arabic language newsletter continued for several years after independence, until the Government's press services were able to take over.

It is certainly fair to say that the close knowledge of the analysis of the country's problems and of the recommendations made for coping with them thus acquired by the leaders and the people greatly enhanced the importance attaching to the experts' recommendations, particularly those relating to the six-year plan for Libya's economic and social development.[18]

THE THIRD TEAM: PRELIMINARIES TO THE PREPARATION OF THE ECONOMIC AND SOCIAL DEVELOPMENT PLAN

A description of the operation of the team brought together to produce an economic and social development plan for Libya may be of some interest. The Goodrich mission's recommendations had to be modified when it became clear that, for reasons of time and staffing, the *Economic Appraisal* would have to be regarded as the end of the first phase, and as the basis for the second phase of drafting a plan that could be transmitted to the Libyan authorities shortly before or at the time of independence. As mentioned (p. 673), it was estimated in July 1951, with what turned out to be undue optimism, that the chief economist and his colleagues would be able to draw up an economic development plan in three to five months.

18. Higgins, pp. 146–70.

It was recognized that there would not be time to work out costed investment schemes, but it was believed that recommendations could be formulated for the specialized agencies which could then carry out further experiments and make more detailed studies on lines deemed to be fruitful in the longer run. Specifically, it was desired to have a plan and projects ready for implementation after independence by LPDSA, the creation and statutes of which were under discussion with the Administering Powers, the experts, and the Provisional Libyan Government. However, a number of factors made it impossible to keep to this timetable. Although TAB and the specialized agencies represented on it made an extraordinary effort and gave top priority to the recruitment and dispatch to Libya of experts, there was the inevitable delay inseparable from the mobilization of an international professional team. Very few experts could be spared from the permanent staff of the United Nations family, and other experts often had commitments that could not be broken off overnight.

Moreover, the inherent difficulties of Libya's problems meant that more time was required for analysis and recommendations than had been expected. The agricultural sector was the most difficult to analyze in depth, and the most difficult in which to find reasonable prospects, yet it was the most important, since it was clear that Libya's potential and needs were greatest there. Moreover, the specialists found that existing agricultural reports were less reliable and less accurate than the Goodrich mission had thought.

Another time-consuming factor was that, as we have seen, the chief economist, the experts in public finance and public administration, and the agricultural economist were also acting as advisers to the Commissioner at various stages of the discussions on the future currency, financial clauses of the Constitution, budget preparation, grants-in-aid, and the development of financing institutions.[19] Meetings on these subjects took place in London and in Geneva, as well as in Tripoli, which encroached even more on the time available. Nonetheless, not only was the advice of these experts, and that of the two experts provided by the International Monetary Fund,[20] essential for the Commissioner in his negotiations, but, conversely, such

19. See also Chapter 7, Pt. 2, pp. 521–36 and 604–07; Chapter 8; and Chapter 10, Pts. 4, 6, 7, and 8, all passim.

20. Early in 1951, the Commisisoner had asked IMF for expert assistance in solving Libya's currency problems (see Chapter 10, p. 747 and fn. 33). The Fund sent two of its then staff members: G. A. Blowers, a special adviser in the Exchange Restrictions Department, later Governor of the Saudi Arabian Monetary Agency; and A. N. McLeod, an economist in the Latin American Division (North), also associated subsequently with the Saudi Arabian Monetary Agency, and, at the time of writing, Governor of the Central Bank of Guyana.

basic arrangements themselves had great influence on the nature of the institutional arrangements for planning and carrying out development.

A rough outline of the plan was drawn up in August and discussed with the territorial governments, the Provisional Libyan Government, and the Administering Authorities. However, not until November was the chief economist able to produce a final, detailed outline, which he discussed with the Amir as well. This outline had been thoroughly discussed within the team, the strength of which had risen to twenty-seven by late in the year, and with the Commissioner; it was accepted by all parties without difficulty.

In pursuance of the policy of associating Libyan leaders as closely as possible with the formulation of the team's recommendations, six working parties were set up, whose members, with the approval of the Provisional Libyan Government and the Administering Authorities, discussed matters with the Chief Economist and the appropriate experts at a series of meetings held in November and December. The working parties dealt respectively with: agriculture and animal husbandry; social development; the timing and financing of economic development; trade, commerce, industry, and public works; water supply, irrigation, power, public utilities, and housing; and tourism.

Many of those who attended these meetings, which were an extension of and served the same purposes as those organized earlier by the Goodrich and Lindberg missions, were later to hold important political and administrative appointments in the Government of Libya, and their participation in the preparation of what came to be known as the "Higgins Report" undoubtedly contributed substantially to its acceptance and to much of its implementation.

However, on Independence Day, only a rough outline of the plan was available; there were no precisely costed agricultural projects, for the agricultural chapters of the report were still under review at the Food and Agricultural Organization (FAO) headquarters in Rome. Nevertheless, as will be seen in more detail later, there was an outline of a budget for priority items in 1952–53 estimated at $3,360,000, and another for priority expenditure averaging $3,920,000 for the next five years.

Total development expenditures for each of the six years 1952–53 to 1957–58 was targeted at $6,000,000; this figure included funds to be provided by foreign governments for LPDSA and LFC, as well as expenditure by the Libyan-American Technical Assistance Service, which had come into being in June 1951, and which it was understood would be prepared to make $1,500,000 available from Point Four funds for 1952–53. It was also assumed that there would be substantial contributions from the United Nations Agencies through their technical assistance programs and their limited medical and nutritional supply programs, such as that of UNICEF. The target of $6 million had been informally accepted by the United Kingdom authorities, as the principal underwriters, as practicable both in the sense of raising such a sum and in that of Libya's absorptive capacity.

The final report was distributed on 1 July 1952, but most of the information was in the hands of the competent central and provincial authorities in Libya before that.[21] Thus, the fact that the report was not available in print on Independence Day was not a serious matter. The projects and programs for the first year (1952–53) had been thoroughly discussed and agreed to with the Provisional Libyan Government, and were included in the new State's first budget, or projected in that of LPDSA. As will be seen in the next chapter, the agreements with the United Kingdom Government covering a budget subsidy and development aid were concluded conditionally before independence, and subsequently formally confirmed.

The recommendations for an economic and social development program for Libya, as presented by the experts in the Higgins Report, followed the pattern which had emerged in the *Economic Appraisal* and from the discussions in the international group of experts on the establishment of a new currency, the development of financing institutions, and the arrangements for the subsidy to the budget.[22] Higgins succinctly summarized the recommendations thus: "The emphasis in the plan is . . . on teaching the Libyans to do better what they are already doing."[23] There could be no comparison with Western economic development, which has usually been synonymous with industrialization, accompanied by a sharp decline in the relative importance of agriculture and other primary industries and a marked growth in manufacturing, in trade and commerce, and in transport and other services. No such process was envisaged during the first six years of Libya's

21. The full text of the report was issued, in Libya only, under the title "The Economic and Social Development of Libya," by Benjamin Higgins, Chief Economist, United Nations Mission of Technical Assistance to Libya, assisted by a United Nations and Specialized Agencies team of experts provided under the United Nations Expanded Programme of Technical Assistance, in the technical assistance documents series of the Council for Libya. United Nations Doc. A/AC.32/TA.16, 1 July 1952, 421 pp. Mimeographed. A condensed version was published in print under the same title (see p. 664, fn. 5). This version, which ran to 170 pages, gave the same data, statements, and conclusions as the full text. But much of the explanatory material, which was of more interest to Libyan officials than to a broader public, was omitted.

22. The Meeting of Experts on Libyan financial, monetary, and development problems. See fn. 20 and Pt. 2 of this chapter.

23. Higgins, United Nations Doc. A/AC.32/TA.16, p. 325. Except where otherwise stated specifically, the descriptive text and figures that follow (pp. 689–98) are taken from the full (mimeographed) version of the Higgins Report, not from the condensed version cited in footnote 5.

development plan. The recommendations included no proposals for completely new industries, for new modes of transport, for new public utilities, or for large-scale investment projects of any other kind. Rather than promoting urban concentration, as would be normal in the case of industrialization, the plan consisted of projects and programs for the improvement, expansion, or restoration of existing plant, skills, and undertakings, and it deliberately emphasized projects for rural areas, which would work against migration to the towns.

Such a development budget seemed rather unusual in 1951. Looking back on it in the light of the experience of other basically agricultural countries which have since acquired independence, it no longer seems so strange. Two features peculiar to Libya were of paramount importance: first, the country had no known natural resources of any kind, either untapped or underexploited, with the possible exception of underground water in certain limited areas. (As is well known, in 1958 an enormous pool of petroleum was tapped, which has made Libya one of the largest oil producers in the world; but in 1951–52 this untold wealth was but a chimera in the minds of prospectors, oil companies, and Libyans alike, on which no development plan could be founded.) Second, the Italian occupation had brought in its train large-scale development in the shape of transport facilities, public utilities, and public buildings, many of which, however, had been damaged during the war. Although some of the development was too advanced for Libya's state of economic evolution at the time of independence, much of it was needed, and more would be, as the economy expanded. Thus the maintenance, repair, and restoration of existing plant had to feature largely in the plan merely to prevent retrogression.

It was pointed out in the report, however, that in the long run industrialization would have to be contemplated for Libya. New opportunities would have to be created, for instance, in processing industries, not only to increase productivity but also to provide jobs for the manpower that would become redundant once labor-saving devices had been introduced into agriculture and handicrafts and the reconstruction projects completed.

Observing that Libya had but one major untapped source of wealth—the latent skills of its people—the authors of the plan emphasized the importance of education, including training in agriculture, light industry, and handicrafts. To support such specialized training, a solid foundation of general education was needed, which meant an attack on illiteracy, improved facilities for elementary education, and, generally speaking, the development of the Libyan minds and bodies as top priority projects.

The proposed development budget therefore provided for the following education program: general education, including teacher training, $149,800 for the first year and $98,000 for each of the next five years; agricultural training, $37,800 for the first year and $12,600 for each of the next five years; and other technical training, $168,000 for the first year and $19,600 for each of the next five years. The first requirement was to increase the number and improve the quality of Libyan teachers. The existing men's and women's teacher-training centers in Tripoli were to be improved, and a new teacher-training course started at Benghazi. In both towns, library books, textbooks, laboratories, sports equipment, and model schools for teaching practice were needed, and in addition Benghazi wanted buildings.

Agricultural training was conceived as having two facets: the introduction of an agricultural bias into the instruction given in primary schools; and the establishment of agricultural training centers and in particular the expansion and improvement of existing facilities in each province.

With regard to technical and vocational training, it was pointed out that the existing schools in Tripoli and Benghazi needed more, and better qualified, staff, equipment, and space. The training of instructors should be given high priority.

Reverting to the agricultural sector, education in the broad sense lay at the heart of the plan. Experimental work to determine the most fruitful lines for agricultural improvement, demonstration programs, and extension work were given top priority with the object of teaching Libyan farmers better farming methods. Great importance was attached to the establishment under FAO's auspices of an agricultural and forestry institute at the Sidi al-Misri experimental farm near Tripoli, mentioned on page 673; which would be concerned not only with the foregoing activities, but also with investment projects, reforestation, resettlement, range improvement, and the provision of agricultural credit.

In addition, action projects of high priority were recommended for the planting of olive and almond trees, reforestation, and the import and breeding of pure seeds. Other projects were related to the improvement of small implements, the importation of livestock for breeding purposes, and a campaign against animal diseases. Second priority was given to range reseeding and regeneration. Improved methods of handling and marketing agricultural products, including the grading and packaging of fruits and vegetables and the control of insect pests such as the Mediterranean fruit fly, were regarded as of fundamental importance. Wool, being one of the most promising of Libyan products, merited a program for improving shearing, baling, scouring, and sorting techniques.

The recommended appropriations for such agricultural activities were $644,000 for the first year and $1,078,000 for each of the succeeding five years.

While the report was being written, a survey of underground water resources raised doubts as to how far irrigation from shallow wells could be extended without seriously lowering the already sinking water table. However, improvements in the water supply could be made by staggering irrigation hours and by pumping water around the clock instead of only during daylight hours. A case could also be made for increasing the number of cisterns, as well as for building check dams and other water-spreading devices to conserve winter rain. It was stressed, however, that a deep-drilling water prospecting program, which, as mentioned above, was in fact being contemplated by the Libyan-American Technical Assistance Service, was essential. The report recommended the expenditure of $140,000 in the first year, followed by an average of $252,000 a year over the next five years for water supply and irrigation projects.

Arguing that projects intended to keep things from getting worse were more important than those which would make the existing situation but little better, the authors of the report gave high priority to repairing the more essential public utilities and transport equipment damaged during the war. Even though, as has been said, some of these facilities were larger than Libya needed at the time, it was clear that, given the capital that had been invested in them and the fact that a minimum was required for the very process of economic and social development itself, they could not be allowed to deteriorate to the point of total unserviceability. However, it was recommended that a careful distinction be drawn between those that could be restored at fairly small cost and would be of use in the near future, and those that would cost too much to put into order in view of the obvious limits to their potential development.

In the light of these criteria, it was recommended that harbor facilities at Tripoli and Benghazi, highways, municipal water supplies, power plants, and the like be put into good working order, whereas railways should be written off. The proposed development budget for such purposes included project expenditures of $128,800 for the first year, and $4,370,800 for additional projects, spread over the next five years. This disproportionate emphasis on public works was a problem that troubled the experts exceedingly, and was recommended only after the most careful consideration. The reader will, of course, observe the close connection between this and the Libyan view, recorded so often in this work, that a large share of the available resources must be devoted to making good war damage. As will be seen, this onerous burden of repairs and reconstruction proved to be a thorny problem in Libya's postindependence development.

The team considered at length the problem of replacing the Tripoli power plant, which was an important installation in terms not only of urban supply but also of pumping power for the irrigated farms in the area. Generating costs at the antiquated plant were so high that both the Italian and British Administrations had been obliged to subsidize agricultural consumers. Plant capacity, too, was so inadequate that rationing was necessary and breakdowns frequent, often with disastrous effects on irrigated crops. However, the cost of replacement would have been so great as to absorb the entire resources of LPDSA for at least one year. Moreover, it was difficult to determine the desirable capacity for a new plant, since the rate of industrial expansion was extremely difficult to forecast, and not even the amount of irrigation—a major consumer of power—that would be economically desirable and feasible could be clearly foreseen in 1951. There was, moreover, some debate as to whether small, individual diesel generating plants might not be a more economical way of meeting irrigation pumping needs than expansion of the Tripoli grid. Accordingly, for the early stages of the program, the team recommended a rather limited expansion of irrigation, economies in the use of power, replacement of worn-out pumps, and more efficient distribution of the water pumped, as well as special credit facilities and low tariffs for farmers prepared to pump by night. For the longer run, it was suggested that Libya should apply for membership of the International Bank for Reconstruction and Development (IBRD) and negotiate a loan from it to build a new power plant.[24]

The lack of mineral and energy resources, and the scarcity of labor and managerial skills, gave little hope for any significant expansion of Libya's industry and commerce. However, one of the few surprises turned up by the experts' studies was that there was room for substantial expansion of fisheries, including sponge fishing. The coastal waters were found to abound in commercial species of fish hardly touched by the fishing methods then practiced. It was accordingly recommended that such expansion should be aided by LFC through loans totalling $28,000 in 1952 and $84,000 in each year thereafter, to finance the purchase or construction of boats, a refrigerated warehouse, trucks, and canneries.

It appeared that the tanning industry, too, which had some export po-

24. Over the years 1956–58, LPDSA and the Libyan Government spent slightly more than $4,000,000 on repairs and a modest expansion of the Tripoli plant. On 24 December 1961, the tenth anniversary of independence, a new power station was put into operation with United States assistance to the amount of $12,148,550, under an arrangement with the Italian Corporation which owned the old plant, whose assets were taken over against compensation by the Libyan Government. It is interesting to note, in the light of the warnings issued by the Higgins team, that in 1959 an IBRD team estimated that the expansion had cost the extraordinarily high figure of $700 per kw installed, transmitted, and distributed. The cost of generating and distributing power in Tripoli in 1958 was 6.2 cents per kwh—a very high figure.

tential, might be expanded at little cost by improving flaying and hide-processing techniques. In fact, a number of small-scale, pilot projects had already been put into successful operation, under the supervision of an FAO tanning expert, by the time of independence. The plan accordingly provided that two FAO experts should be recruited for this branch.

Realizing that Libya could offer the tourist beautiful beaches, romantic oases, mysterious deserts, Roman and Greek ruins, modern hotels, and the Arab world, the authors of the report pointed out that the hotels needed refurbishing and tourist transport facilities improvement. There were possibilities to be explored; but the tourist industry should be financed by the private sector.

A degree of industrialization in the raw-materials processing industries was suggested, including the freezing of fruit and vegetables, the packaging and freezing of meat and fish, and the pressing and refining of olive oil. Throughout this sector, handling and processing methods would have to be greatly improved. Finally, as these and related industries would depend on marketing possibilities for their viability, provision was made in the plan for an expert in the marketing of agricultural products as a most important technical-assistance post.

The team reluctantly came to the conclusion that Libya could not afford to divert any of its immediately foreseeable development funds to public assistance programs, i.e. to projects designed to raise living standards by public and private relief unrelated to increased productivity. On the other hand, essential development in such fields as education, public health, housing, the training of the blind, the rehabilitation of juvenile delinquents, and the treatment of orphans could be undertaken on the grounds that they would contribute indirectly to the present or potential productivity of Libya's labor force. In other words, the team believed that the only way of achieving the aims of public assistance programs—which were undoubtedly morally justified—was to raise the per capita income by increasing productivity, and then redistribute the extra wealth thus brought in, through taxation, social security legislation, and similar measures. Since an Italian social security system existed, it was recommended that it be retained, and extended, on a voluntary basis, to Libyans as well. Although such an undertaking would normally be too advanced for a State at Libya's stage of development, abandonment of the system would have been an unacceptable step backward.

The main public health problem being malnutrition, a school meals program was recommended, accounting for half of the social development program. It was recognized that even this was on too limited a scale to make a massive impact, but it was hoped that voluntary agencies and surplus food disposal programs might be associated with the operation later.

The recommended social development budget was $562,800 for the second through the sixth years. The only project recommended for the first year was a modest subsidy of $700,000 to help slum clearance.

Finally, a Stabilization Fund amounting to 25 percent of the resources of LPSDA, as required by Article 3 (3) of its Statute, was earmarked for drought relief programs. In the light of experience, it was anticipated that at least one year in four would be one of severe drought. It was considered that the projects envisaged should have lower priority and be labor-intensive, such as: forestation; range improvement; the sinking of livestock-watering wells; range reseeding; the building of check dams and other irrigation works; and similar activities that would provide employment for the rural population. The chief economist and his colleagues expressed concern about the prospects of raising sufficient funds to carry out these projects rapidly enough to build up the essential momentum and to produce results dramatic enough to convince the Libyans that progress was possible and thus overcome the initial inertia of a stagnant economy. Concern was also expressed whether the current pace of development would raise productivity more quickly than the death rate fell, thus allowing an increase in output per head and an improvement in the standard of living.

The plan also included a set of recommendations concerning technical assistance to be provided by the United Nations agencies. It was pointed out that successful implementation of the plan would call for a great deal of skilled administration and much further planning. There was a distinct shortage of skills of this kind in Libya, and the cost of engaging top-level planners and administrators abroad would fall very heavily on the Libyan budget. The logical source of such experts was thought to be the specialized agencies.

The continued presence of a Resident Representative of TAB, with extensive and substantial duties both in harmonizing and coordinating the work of the foreign experts and in advising the Libyan Government was endorsed; and this was in fact provided for in an agreement signed with the Libyan Government on Independence Day. It was further suggested that a Deputy Resident Representative, who would serve also as chief economist, should be appointed with special responsibility for directing planning research for the United Nations team. It was expected that he would produce an annual report, making and justifying recommendations for revising and adjusting the basic plan. It was also envisaged that the large team, comprising more than eighty experts, would form an integrated whole, headed by senior experts in the main fields, such as agriculture, health, and education, one of whose major duties would be to keep the Resident Representative informed about the situation of various programs, so as to simplify coordination and planning.

Another suggestion was that integrated planning by all the interested agencies could be furthered by a more formal grouping of the principal foreign officials concerned with development planning, and that the several working parties which had helped the Higgins team to draw up the report should be reconvened, and appropriately enlarged, with most of their members drawn from the Libyan administrative services.

It was also suggested that the General Manager and the Deputy General Manager of LPDSA should in the first place be appointed as United Nations officials, receiving emoluments on the Libyan civil service salary scale, plus an allowance from United Nations funds, but serving as officials of the Libyan Government—an arrangement more or less on the lines of what later became the United Nations OPEX program.[25] This was intended primarily to reduce LPDSA's administrative overheads.

Yet another long-term recommendation was that experts should be provided in public administration and public health to advise the newly established government services at federal and provincial level on operational problems, and also to carry out a survey on staff-training and improved working procedures and on the more efficient utilization of materials and equipment. Similarly, a public finance expert would be required to continue studies on taxation and budgetary legislation and procedures, and on balance-of-payments problems and foreign trade policy.

Considerable emphasis was laid on the need for improving the statistical services of the new government for the compilation of both general and vital statistics. In particular, the creation of a small central statistical office, headed in the first instance by a United Nations expert, was recommended. It was also recommended that a population census be taken with United Nations assistance, to be followed, later, by an agricultural census.

The estimated cost of the experts to be provided under EPTA in 1952 on the above lines was $1,537,000, including $252,000 for TAB's office and administrative staff. The United Nations itself would be asked to provide thirteen experts at an estimated cost of $200,000; ILO, twelve experts and instructors at an estimated cost of $90,000; FAO, twenty-four experts at an estimated cost of $600,000, including $100,000 for equipment; UNESCO, twelve experts, technicians, and lecturers at $185,000, including $22,000 in the first year for technical and other equipment and books; WHO, three experts at $50,000; and WMO, two fellowships, and a survey

25. Program for the provision of operational, executive and administrative personnel (part of EPTA), introduced in 1959–60. Briefly, under OPEX, experts are recruited by United Nations agencies to serve as civil servants of a developing country at its normal pay scales, but they receive a supplement from the agency to bring their emoluments up to international levels.

of Libya's needs in meteorology, at $10,000. Furthermore, the award of fifty fellowships and scholarships, spread over the entire program, was recommended, at a cost of $150,000.

In actuality, United Nations expenditure against these targets in 1952 was $700,000 for experts and approximately $200,000 for the TAB office and services, total expenditure rising to slightly above $1,000,000 in the following years. The principal reasons for the shortfall were recruitment delays and delays in negotiating detailed project plans and terms of reference. Moreover, some proposals were carried out under the Point Four program. In fact, the ceiling for the Libyan United Nations agency program leveled off at above $1,000,000, making it the largest per capita of such United Nations programs during those years.

The reader may be curious to know to what extent the recommendations were adopted and implemented after the period covered by this study. The six-year plan was approved in principle by the Government of independent Libya at Cabinet level and taken as the basis for LPDSA's activities. In practice, the Government relied upon it during the next four years to provide the guidelines, as well as an indication of the priorities to be accorded, for the country's development. However, it never proved possible to carry out the plan on the scale recommended. The main reason for this was that funds failed to materialize to the extent for which it was believed that assurances had been given. To make matters worse, LPDSA took over a number of projects originally begun under British administration, including the building of the new waterworks and the power station at Benghazi, and the reconstruction of the quays in Tripoli harbor. Prior commitments for such unfinished works did not leave LPDSA enough money to carry out fully the Higgins program. The substantial increase in United States aid to Libya made it necessary in late 1955 to recast development activities in a new five-year mold, covering the period 1956–61, in which the initial program was radically revised upward, though, again, the second five-year plan was never fully carried out.[26]

The resources available to Libya for development in its first year of independence comprised technical cooperation (Point Four) funds from the United States totaling $1,551,200; a grant to LPDSA and LFC from the United Kingdom of $1,064,000; a contribution from France of $610,400; one from Italy of $28,000; and assistance from the United Nations, including the maintenance of the Resident Representative's office, amounting to $900,000—making a total of $4,153,600. In addition, the United Kingdom provided a grant-in-aid of $6,608,000.

26. See *The Economic Development of Libya* (Baltimore: Johns Hopkins Press, for the International Bank for Reconstruction and Development, 1960), pp. 47–49.

Financial assistance from the United States rose sharply after 1954, and in the final financial agreement with the United Kingdom the development assistance grant was increased to $2,800,000 a year from 1953 to 1958, while the contribution from France was cut back to $280,000. Over the years 1954–59, the United Arab Republic and Turkey each pledged $28,000 a year to LPDSA, although in fact not all of this was received. Pakistan contributed $28,000 in 1958–59.[27] The whole development financing picture of course changed completely after 1958 with the discovery of oil.

ARRANGEMENTS FOR THE CONTINUATION OF TECHNICAL ASSISTANCE AFTER INDEPENDENCE

As we saw in Part 3 of Chapter 5 (pp. 413–14), TAB, ECOSOC, and the General Assembly had in turn passed resolutions to the effect that Libya, in view of its special relationship with the United Nations, should be eligible to receive technical assistance without interruption from the time it achieved independence until it became a member of the United Nations or of one of the specialized agencies, when it would be able on its own account to submit requests for technical assistance. TAB had also agreed that the waiver of local costs mentioned on page 672 should be extended for at least the first year following independence.

The Provisional Libyan Government, being well acquainted with these matters, filed its formal request for the continuation of technical assistance on these terms in November 1951. In doing so, the Prime Minister wrote to the Secretary-General, Trygve Lie, as Chairman of TAB: "I wish to express our particular thanks for the technical assistance which has been afforded Libya. We look forward, and materially depend upon, the continuation and enlargement of such help in the future." [28]

On Independence Day the resulting agreements with the United Nations were the first to be signed by the Government. Simultaneously, the Government addressed letters to the United Nations and the specialized agencies, seeking membership in these international bodies. The basic agreements which had been concluded separately with the United Kingdom and France as the Administering Powers (see respectively pp. 669 and 671) lapsed on independence, being immediately replaced by the new Basic Agreement with Libya. This Agreement was exceptional, for it contained the unusual and generous provision that TAB would bear the major share of the "local"

27. Ibid.

28. United Nations Doc. TAB/R.144, 6 December 1951. Mimeographed. The letter was dated 27 November 1951.

costs of technical assistance under the terms of the waiver. All the Libyan Government was required to do was to provide office accommodation, to pay postal, telephone, and telegraph charges, and to meet medical expenses for the experts—none of which meant spending foreign exchange.

The first supplementary agreement met the Libyan request of 27 November 1951 (which had been approved by TAB at its December meeting) that a Resident Representative should be appointed and that he should also act as Personal Representative in Libya of the Secretary-General and as a member without voting rights of the boards of directors of LPDSA and LFC (p. 664).

As will be seen in Part 2 of this chapter and in Chapters 10 and 11, the Commissioner had originally suggested the establishment of a development fund, drawing contributions not only from the former Administering Powers, but also from other members of the United Nations, with a United Nations official acting as the principal adviser to the Libyan Government on its utilization. This suggestion could not be realized when the agreements covering the British and French grants-in-aid and the arrangements for LPDSA and LFC were concluded. During the negotiations, the United Kingdom in particular had made it very clear that they could not agree that a United Nations official should give guidance to the Libyan Government that might result in its embarking upon projects that would call for an increase in the United Kingdom subsidies to the administrative or development budgets. For this reason, the Resident Representative's terms of reference made no mention of his giving the Libyan Government advice on current account, i.e. the regular, Libyan budget. Nevertheless, the range of activities considered appropriate for the Resident Representative, and his seat on the boards of directors of LPDSA and LFC, gave broad scope for coordinating the United Nations' programs with other development activities in the country, and an opportunity for him to take a leading part in helping the Libyans.

The request that the Resident Representative be simultaneously named Personal Representative of the Secretary-General had a political background. A number of prominent Libyans had suggested that the United Nations presence there be continued on some basis broader than that of technical assistance pure and simple. However, the Commissioner and the Provisional Libyan Government agreed that the presence of an international official with no clearly defined responsibilities might induce some political figures to regard him, mistakenly, as a sort of court of appeal from actions of the Government. This would be incompatible with Libyan sovereignty and a potential source of confusion and embarrassment. However, the Provisional Libyan Government did wish to maintain its special relationship with the United Nations in some form. When it became virtually certain that the Soviet Union would veto Libya's application for membership in the United Nations, as other applications were being vetoed, the Libyans became concerned at the prospect of remaining outside the United Nations at a time when they were faced with the negotiation of agreements for continuing military-base rights with France, the United Kingdom, and the United States, and of the longer-term financial arrangements with the first two countries. Negotiations with Italy on a broad range of topics deriving from General Assembly Resolution 388 (V) (economic and financial provisions for Libya) were also in prospect. The Libyan leaders wanted to have recourse to the United Nations if they found that unreasonable terms or conditions were being forced on them by the Powers concerned. Since under Article 99 of the United Nations Charter the Secretary-General may draw the attention of the Security Council to any matter which in his opinion may threaten the maintenance of international peace and security, the Libyans decided, so as to have a channel of communication should the need arise, to ask for the appointment of a personal representative of the Secretary-General, who, in order to get around the internal political difficulty, should combine his functions with those of Resident Representative.

In fact, it was never necessary for the Resident Representative to step outside the economic and development sphere. The dual designation was dropped in 1955, when the first Resident Representative, Thomas F. Power, Jr., who had earlier served as Principal Secretary of the United Nations Mission in Libya, completed his assignment.

A second agreement, also signed on Independence Day, extended the assignment terms of seven of the experts in the team working on the development plan for periods of two to six months, to give them time to finish their work.[29] In addition, provision was made for experts in esparto grass, salt processing, and public health nursing, all posts that had been included in the agreement, but for which it had proved impossible to find suitable candidates.

Further supplementary agreements provided for the continuation of UNESCO assistance to the Clerical and Technical Training Centre and to the Educational Training and Production Centre, on the understanding that it was open to decision whether to transfer the project in whole or in part to ILO in 1952.

Thus the technical assistance operation in independent Libya, one of the

29. The experts concerned were working on statistics, subsoil mineral resources, public finance, public administration, social welfare, public health administration, and sanitary engineering. The last two were later extended for one year in anticipation of a longer-term WHO project for Libya.

most intensive and most successful ever mounted by TAB, was launched in company with the Libyan ship of state.

PART 2.
MONETARY ARRANGEMENTS AND FOREIGN FINANCIAL AID

Not least among the problems to be solved in the establishment of an independent State and, later, of a basis for development, was that of creating a new Libyan monetary system.

Once again, Libya presented an unusual case in that there could be no question of reestablishing the Italian monetary system, which had come to an end with the British and French military occupation. Other States which acquired independence during the 1950s were as a rule able to remain within the currency and banking systems of the former colonial Power or to introduce, on the basis of their known resources, a new currency strong enough to command international recognition and to meet their own basic needs.

During the period examined by this study, each Libyan territory had its own currency. Egyptian currency circulated in Cyrenaica; it had arrived with the British Forces, and maintained its position, partly because the Allied Forces were paid in Egyptian pounds during the war, partly because, after the flight of the Italians, the Cyrenaicans would not touch Italian money—indeed, they would not even accept Military Administration Lire (MAL), the currency circulating in Tripolitania. MAL had been instituted as an occupation measure, local currency having been repatriated by the Italians when they fled the country; it was fully backed by sterling. The amount in circulation was equivalent to about $6,300,000, that of £E in Cyrenaica being estimated at $3,412,500. In the Fezzan, both Tunisian and Algerian francs circulated, apparently more or less interchangeably. However, the oasis of Ghudamis, which lies near the Tunisian border, apparently used only Tunisian francs.[30]

The monetary and financial problems attendant upon the establishment of an independent Libya had been brought to the notice of the Council for Libya early in 1950, and work on them proceeded simultaneously with the technical assistance and development studies as from September 1950,

30. A curious postal situation also existed in the Fezzan, for there were three distinct series of stamps: one for the Fezzan itself, a second for the oasis of Ghudamis, and a third for the oasis of Ghat. These separate systems were brought to an end in late 1951 with the introduction of a unified Libyan series.

when the two experts provided by IMF arrived in Libya.[31] Even before this, there had been some preliminary discussions, in particular with the United Kingdom authorities, who had prepared draft proposals for a new Libyan currency and had even, as the Commissioner discovered in early 1951 during talks at the Foreign Office, begun informal preliminary talks with the Amir and the Tripolitanian Administrative Council. Technical as well as policy considerations made it important that Libya should take an early decision in the matter and make essential arrangements for the conversion, which, it was at first hoped, could be effected before Independence Day.

The Commissioner therefore invited the Governments of Egypt, France, Italy, the United Kingdom, and the United States, all of which had direct monetary and economic interests in the Libyan currency and in future technical and development assistance to the country, to appoint experts in these subjects to meet with him.[32] The purpose of this Meeting of Experts on Libyan Financial, Monetary, and Development Problems would be to formulate recommendations for the Provisional Libyan Government. The IMF experts and the Principal Secretary had at various times during visits to the capitals of the countries in question collected some information and exchanged data and views on the problems involved. Against this background, a set of preliminary recommendations had been presented to the Commissioner, who had also been made aware of the views of the United Kingdom.

The British proposals for handling the problems of conversion and of budget assistance were expounded to the Commissioner, the IMF experts, and the senior technical assistance experts during conversations in London at the end of February 1951. To the Commissioner, it was obvious that the Foreign Office had been preparing its proposals for some time, but had waited to see the outcome of the discussions on the Libyan question at the Fifth Session of the General Assembly before explaining them to him in detail with all their implications.

The British position changed but slightly during the succeeding months of negotiation. The Commissioner was told that the United Kingdom Government was ready to provide the main support for the Libyan budget, taking care of the balance-of-payments deficits, if the currency were soundly

31. See p. 687, fn. 20. For a condensed version of the experts' report, see G. A. Blowers and A. N. McLeod, *Currency Unification in Libya,* IMF Staff Papers (Washington, November 1952), pp. 439–67.

32. See p. 689, fn. 22. See also *Second Annual Report of the United Nations Commissioner in Libya,* GAOR: Sixth Session, 1951–52, Supplement No. 17 (A/1949), paras. 207–50. For reports of the various sessions of the meetings, see ibid., Annexes XVII, XVIII, XX, and XXI, pp. 140–50 and 151–57.

established and if there were adequate budget controls. Note issues would be made by a currency authority, which should operate simply and virtually automatically, exchange controls being handled separately under government control. Libya would be free to join the sterling area if it so wished. It was the British view that the arrangements contemplated would ensure the viability of the currency and economy and give advantages not otherwise forthcoming.

Other States that might be interested in Libya's future—the British had in mind chiefly Italy—should provide assistance for development, not for the regular administrative budget. The British view here was that if any international body or its agents became concerned with the normal budget, undesirable complications would ensue.

The Commissioner was not happy about these proposals, and argued from the outset that, given Libya's geographical and hence political situation, an exclusively British subvention with its concomitant budget control was bound to provoke opposition. Control of the budget meant virtual control of the State, thought the Commissioner. Other interested States would probably not agree, though they might be willing to accept the position that the main subvention and the main influence should remain British. There would undoubtedly be a tendency to spend more in the new State, but if the check on that tendency, desirable though it might be in many ways, were to be exercised by a single foreign State, suspicions would certainly be aroused and give rise to criticism of the United Kingdom in the General Assembly. The Commissioner therefore hoped that a satisfactory agreement providing for some kind of international control could be reached. The British would not agree, either at that time or later, to any internationalization of support for the Libyan budget.

On currency, the United Kingdom approach was much the same. Although the Commissioner felt that he could agree that a major part of the currency backing should be in sterling, and redemption be solely in sterling, with a currency authority made up exclusively of experts, he still urged that Libya be accorded a special status authorizing it to retain its hard-currency earnings. He envisaged the latter as coming mainly from the United States military installations in the country, both from government expenditure and from the personal spending of the military personnel and their families. It seemed to him only just that the Libyan economy should benefit directly by the accident of strategic geography that had resulted in a considerable volume of dollar spending in the country, and that in large part accounted for the unusual interest shown by the United States in Libya's future and development.

The unwavering British reply to this was that the sterling pool would give Libya access to all the currencies it might need, and that no special arrangements were required. It was obvious that the United Kingdom had no intention of establishing a precedent in the case of Libya that might encourage similar requests from other sterling-area countries where there was major United States military spending. The Commissioner repeatedly pressed his point but always ran up against determined opposition.

At this stage, the United Kingdom officials were equally reluctant to accept a suggestion made by United Nations and IMF experts that Libya should be free to hold reserves in currencies other than sterling.

Nonetheless, it was recognized that some flexibility could be introduced to meet political objections. The Commissioner's original idea had been that the currency authority should be made up only of British and Libyan nationals, with, possibly, an expert designated by IMF. It was common ground that the functions of such an authority would be automatic, and that IMF might therefore find it difficult to justify the dispatch of a staff member to attend its meetings. But the Commissioner remained convinced that such representation would do much to reassure the Libyans as to the authority's independence and neutrality.

The Commissioner welcomed the United Kingdom's agreement that other countries might take part in financing Libyan development, having in mind in particular the potentialities of French, Italian, and United States aid.

There was some difference of opinion about the domicile of the currency authority. The British wanted its seat to be London, whereas the Commissioner felt that it should be Tripoli, with a committee of the whole meeting in London to conduct routine business—a view which the Libyans subsequently made their own. The United Kingdom authorities agreed to reconsider the matter, and in the end the Commissioner won.

In February 1951 he reserved his position on the currency backing, largely because he was still waiting for the studies on the balance of payments and related questions, and also because at that time there was no Libyan authority that could take a decision in the matter. He had come to realize during his conversations in London that the British proposals envisaging unilateral currency and development financing had been approved up to Cabinet level. However, the United Kingdom authorities had refrained from communicating the details of their proposals either to the Libyans or to the members of the Council for Libya until they knew the Commissioner's reactions.

As the Meeting of Experts was to be convened only a fortnight later, the Commissioner presumed that, as a matter of diplomatic routine, the British would have made their position clear at least to the very directly concerned French and American Governments, and probably also to the Italian,

Egyptian, and Pakistani Governments as members of the Council, as well as to the experts with whom the technical discussions had been held. Surprisingly, it transpired at the first meeting, as described below, that there had been no such preparation through diplomatic channels. Only after the British views had been set forth at the first Meeting of Experts was there apparently a diplomatic follow-up.

The Commissioner and the United Kingdom authorities were unable to achieve a meeting of minds on budgetary controls, which, under the British scheme, would in effect rest in the hands of the senior financial adviser, who was to be British. The Commissioner still hoped to get financial support for Libya from a number of countries, preferably under United Nations auspices. The British maxim was "he who pays the piper calls the tune"; for them, a subsidy and control of its expenditure went together. The Commissioner warned them that they were laying themselves open to a charge of exploiting financial controls to run Libya's entire economy, and suggested that some procedure such as a centrally administered fund for Libya as a whole should be devised that would avoid having a financial adviser for each contributing power—as would be necessary if, for instance, France made a contribution to assist the Fezzan and, possibly, Italy made one for Tripolitania alone.

During these talks the Commissioner discovered that the United Kingdom was definitely opposed to tying its subvention explicitly to the grant of military-base rights. Again, the United Kingdom, like the United States, feared that this would set an expensive precedent for analogous arrangements elsewhere. Implicitly, however, a tie there was. In the event, the simple and pragmatic view of the Libyans—that there should be a rental fee for bases—was to prevail, but this was the outcome of negotiations conducted well after independence.

Early in 1951, the Commissioner had endeavored to persuade the United States authorities that some sort of consideration for the base rights enjoyed at Wheelus Field should be paid into an account to support the regular Libyan budget, and also to LPDSA, then in the blueprint stage. Without any pretense at precision, a figure of at least one million dollars a year was mentioned. But high-level United States officials were adamant that they would not pay "rent" for bases. On the other hand, they were prepared to recommend a sizable Point Four technical assistance program and, if things went well, investment support for the follow-up. In the light of United States initial support for technical assistance of the order of $1,500,000 in 1952, and the increase in technical assistance and grants to a level around $30,000,000 in 1959—rather more than 20 percent of Libyan national income from all sources—it is clear in retrospect that the Commissioner was too modest in his approach and the United States authorities too sanguine in believing that they would not have to pay heavily to maintain their bases. But he decided that it would be wiser to accept for a start a small amount which could subsequently be increased, rather than risk jeopardizing the arrangements by insisting on a higher figure.

At the first session of the Meeting of Experts, held in London from 14 to 16 March 1951, the preliminary and still informal proposals put forward by the IMF experts, and another set of proposals put forward by the United Kingdom, were examined. The IMF experts recommended that a currency with a unit equivalent to four shillings, or $0.56, should be administered by a currency authority domiciled in Libya and made up of Libyan and foreign experts; that it should be on an exchange standard with 100 percent reserves in foreign exchange; and that the currencies of reserve and redemption should be determined by the authority itself. Finally, they recommended the creation of a bank drawing capital from the interested governments to enable adjustments necessary in years of drought to be made.

The United Kingdom proposed that the sterling cover of MAL be transferred to a Libyan Currency Board to cover a unified Libyan currency managed by the Board by automatic exchange against sterling, the Board's discretion being limited to the investment of reserves. Libya would be admitted to membership in the sterling area if it applied for it. If a stable currency were thus established, and if adequate, acceptable budgetary and import controls were introduced, the United Kingdom would make an annual contribution covering Libya's deficits both in the regular budget and in the balance of payments. Lastly, the United Kingdom advocated the establishment of a development and stabilization fund, rather than a bank, to which interested Governments might make contributions in the form of grants to finance development and to enable extraordinary measures to be taken to counteract the effects of drought.

This exchange of proposals clearly illustrated the interconnection and complexity of the problems of a monetary system, of development financing, of the provision of reserves against drought, and of foreign aid in the form of technical assistance; and the added difficulties of arranging these matters within a tight timetable while the relevant provisions of the Libyan Constitution were still under discussion in the NCAL, and while the transfer of powers and its inherent problems were still being discussed in the Coordination Committee.[33]

Both the French and the Italian experts immediately criticized the British proposals on the ground that they shut out currencies other than sterling,

33. For details of the establishment, composition, and functions of the Coordination Committee, see Chapter 10, pp. 744–53.

expressing their preference for the establishment of a bank authorized to issue debentures and to lend money privately. Thereupon, the United Kingdom expert offered to modify his Government's original proposals by accepting up to 25 percent of the reserves in currencies other than sterling, and by broadening the membership of the currency authority to include representatives of the Central Banks of other interested powers.[34]

In the course of these talks, the Commissioner summarized his position by recalling the United Nations' special responsibility toward Libya at the time and for any further period during which the new State might still need guidance and help in the shape of technical assistance. It followed that the United Nations specialized agencies should participate in the arrangements under consideration. Specifically, he believed that IMF should be represented on the Libyan currency authority and that IBRD should be represented in the proposed development corporation. Lastly, in the matter of foreign contributions to Libya's regular budget, a United Nations official should be appointed to advise the Libyan Government on their use. Such funds should be deposited in a special account to be opened in the name of the Libyan Government. The last proposal was vigorously opposed by the United Kingdom authorities, on the ground that the official in question might well recommend expenditure that would have the effect of increasing the deficit in the regular budget.

No conclusions were reached at the first session. The second took place in Geneva, from 11 to 28 April. The Commissioner understood that matters had been discussed among the countries concerned through diplomatic channels in the interim. His IMF and technical assistance advisers had also studied the complex problems involved.

This second session, which was attended by the Libyan Minister of Finance as an observer (his travel expenses were paid from the budget of the United Nations Mission), unanimously agreed to convey to the Provisional Libyan Government, through the Commissioner, a number of technical recommendations on currency matters. The fundamental differences still had to be reconciled, and the problems of financing economic development and of a stabilization fund were not on the agenda; nor were they discussed in specific terms. The recommendations were: that the currency unit should be 4 shillings sterling, or $0.56, to be divided into 100 parts; and that the initial monetary law should provide for 100 percent cover for the notes in foreign exchange, it being understood that, like any other Libyan law, the act could be amended or otherwise modified by the future Libyan Government in consultation with the currency authority when the development of the Libyan economy called for such a course of

34. *Second Annual Report of the United Nations Commissioner in Libya,* para. 214.

action. The composition of the reserve was not mentioned. Suggestions were also made about the denominations of the note and coin issues. It was agreed that the name of the currency should be decided by the Provisional Libyan Government, and that the latter, in consultation with the Administering Powers, should go ahead and establish a provisional Libyan currency authority made up of a British chairman, two Libyan members, two British nationals, a French national, and an Italian national. The five foreign members, appointed by their countries' Central Banks, would sit as independent experts. It was further recommended that IMF be asked to provide, on request, advice to the currency authority on matters within the purview of IMF's Articles of Agreement. It was understood that the initial approach to IMF would be made by the Commissioner, and that the arrangements would be renewed by the future Libyan Government after independence.

As no agreement on the composition of the currency reserve and related matters could be reached, it was recommended that a preparatory currency committee should be set up, with the same composition as that suggested for the provisional currency authority, and with the limited task of arranging for the printing of notes and the minting of coin.

At the end of the session, the delegations restated their positions.[35] Virtually all differences were focused on the composition of the currency reserve and on whether Libya should join the sterling area. The Egyptian expert argued that responsibility for note issue should lie with the issue department of a Libyan national bank, which would also serve as Government banker, deriving its capital from Libyan Government-guaranteed loans. While agreeing that a foreign exchange standard was best suited to Libya's circumstances and that 100 percent cover should be provided for the currency, he argued that as much convertible currency as possible should be included in it, and that the balance should be made up of currencies from countries with which Libya carried on a substantial trade. Nevertheless, in a spirit of conciliation, and to allow preparations to go ahead with all speed, the Egyptian delegation agreed to the proposals concerning the currency authority and to confining the cover for the note issue to convertible currencies and those of the United Kingdom, France, Italy, and Egypt.

The French delegation argued that it was for the Libyan Government to decide whether Libya should join the sterling area. It expressed the hope that Libya would adopt a currency system reflecting its international origins and refrain from discriminating among the States represented on the Council for Libya. As for the reserve, the French delegation wanted gold, convertible currencies, sterling, Egyptian pounds, French francs, and Italian lire to be included—although it did not wish the percentages to be de-

35. Ibid., Annex XVII, pp. 141–43.

termined in advance—and it wanted the possibility of a periodic redistribution of the reserves in agreed proportions to be left open.

The Italian delegation believed that other solutions than those proposed by the British and French could be found, and undertook to circulate suggestions for study before the next session of the Meeting of Experts. These never materialized.

The United Kingdom restated its point of view, emphasizing that the arrangements proposed were best fitted to create a stable currency simply, inexpensively, and quickly. It would, albeit reluctantly, agree to modify the 100 percent sterling cover to allow the currency authority to place up to 25 percent in other currencies. However, the authority would be legally obliged to redeem Libyan currency against sterling alone; it could have no discretion to redeem in any other currency, as suggested by the French delegation. It was argued that this procedure would have the considerable advantage of allowing the authority to maintain liquidity in sterling only, thus leaving the greater part of the cover available for investment.

Libya's foreign exchange needs would be met through membership in the sterling area, since Libya's foreign trade was predominantly with its member countries, or with others in the Mediterranean area which freely accepted sterling. Libya would be able, both then and in the future, to trade automatically in sterling throughout the area and could rely upon London to meet automatically such commitments in currencies other than sterling as it might have. It would be expected to maintain a normal exchange control system and to limit drawings of foreign currencies to what was necessary to meet its reasonable needs.

If these arrangements found favor, the United Kingdom would make available to the currency authority the requisite amount of the sterling backing then held in London against MAL presented for conversion into the new currency.

The United Kingdom delegation finally observed that in its view any substantial departure from or changes in its proposals along the lines suggested by the Egyptian, French, and Italian experts would involve a serious risk of loss of confidence in the stability of the Libyan currency, both at home and abroad, and might oblige His Majesty's Government to reconsider the whole position. Loss of confidence would be a severe handicap for the new State and inconsistent with membership in the sterling area; and if Libya were not a member, it would either have to rely on its own earnings in foreign currencies to finance its trade and internal requirements or become dependent upon ad hoc assistance from abroad to meet its deficit.

The United States delegation thereupon suggested that the various alternatives should be submitted to the Provisional Libyan Government for its consideration. The British proposals seemed to constitute a practical and beneficial solution. The United States expert added that it seemed desirable, no matter what currency arrangements were finally made, that Libya should be able to procure its essential dollar requirements and to have the use, over a reasonable period of years, of dollar earnings accruing to it.

The last assertion gave the Commissioner a short-lived hope that the United States Government would support his proposal that Libya be granted a special status—perhaps transferable-account status—to ensure that dollar-earnings from United States military expenditure remained entirely within the control of the Libyan authorities. But the United States authorities did not pursue the hinted change in their general support for the British proposals, and, as will be seen, later accepted the United Kingdom contention that Libya's dollar requirements could be adequately met out of the sterling pool. The Commissioner was never formally told the reasons for this hardening of the United States position, but he could well imagine that they were political, not technical.

The third round of discussions was held in Geneva from 29 May to 9 June 1951. This time the Libyan Minister of Finance attended, not as an observer, but as a full participant of the Meeting of Experts. Meanwhile, the Commissioner had transmitted to the Provisional Government, as requested, the recommendation that a preparatory currency committee be set up, and this had been done in cooperation with the Administering Powers. The Committee, comprising representatives of the Provisional Libyan Government, Egypt, France, Italy, and the United Kingdom, met at the European Office of the United Nations in Geneva (now the United Nations Office at Geneva) on 31 May and 1 June 1951. They decided that the new currency should be called the Libyan pound, should be equal in value to the pound sterling (the Libyan Government's stated preference), instead of the four-shilling unit recommended previously, and should be subdivided into 100 piastres and 1,000 milleims. It was also decided that Barclays Bank should be appointed as the agent of the currency authority, the Bank to provide the necessary office space in Tripoli and London; and that the seat of the authority should be in Libya with the possibility of meeting elsewhere as might be found appropriate for the proper conduct of its business. Other administrative and housekeeping decisions related to note designs; the appointment of a secretary; the quantities of notes to be printed (£7,850,000) and coin to be struck (£190,000); the provision of strong-room accommodation; the appointment of currency officers; and arrangements for the distribution of the new notes in preparation for their eventual issue.[36]

36. For full text of the Preparatory Committee's report, see ibid., Annex XVIII, Appendix I, p. 146.

The Libyan Finance Minister, Mansur Bey Qadara, without any previous intimation to the Commissioner, took the floor at the opening of the session to announce that the Provisional Libyan Government had decided to join the sterling area and to have 100 percent cover in sterling for its currency. Thereupon, the experts from the United Kingdom, the United States, and Italy expressed in turn their agreement with this decision; and the French expert said that he had no objection to it. The Egyptian representative reserved his Government's position. It was thus made plain that the British had been markedly successful in the diplomatic discussions that had been going on over the preceding four weeks.

The United Kingdom representative, speaking immediately after the Libyan Finance Minister, gave a concise account of the advantages Libya would derive from membership in the sterling area.[37] He gave assurances in the terms of the statement he had made at the close of the second session. In particular, Libya, as a fully independent member of the sterling area, would be entitled to draw automatically from the central reserves all the United States and Canadian dollars it might require to meet essential needs; conversely, it would be expected to pay into the central reserves all earnings in those two currencies over and above the essential working balances of Libyan banks. By the same token, neither the country's trade with its neighbors nor its readiness to accept capital investment from them would be adversely affected by its membership in the sterling area.

In what was obviously an attempt to respond to the efforts persistently made by the Commissioner in his negotiations with the United Kingdom, the latter's expert conceded that over the first few years Libya might be expected to contribute to the central reserve of the sterling pool more United States and Canadian dollars than it drew. This was a reference to the spending of United States military personnel at Wheelus Field and to the financial aid the Libyans were seeking in compensation for military-base rights. The United Kingdom expert emphasized that such a situation was not expected to persist, so that after the initial period Libya might be drawing more than it contributed, with the result that after a relatively few years, its net drawings would offset net earnings in the initial period. As with so many other predictions, this understandably failed to reckon with the totally changed situation that arose when Libya suddenly became a major producer of oil eight years later.

As to what had gone on behind the scenes, the Commissioner had the impression that the British monetary experts had brought pretty strong pressure to bear on the Libyan Government. How else could the sudden

37. Ibid., p. 147.

decision to join the sterling area, which, as was only too well known, was not popular among Libyan leaders, be explained? The Government's failure to discuss the matter with the Commissioner beforehand was so unexpected a breach of the confidence that normally prevailed between them that the event took on a quite exceptional character. Even today, eighteen years later, it is not possible to say with any degree of certainty what actually did happen.

For the only time in his tenure of office, the Commissioner, at a meeting the record of which was later made public, found himself obliged to criticize the wisdom and timing of an action taken by the Provisional Libyan Government. Noting that it had not yet had an opportunity to study the full reports of the IMF experts, and hence no opportunity of assessing the possibilities of securing a special status for its foreign exchange earnings in United States dollars, the Commissioner said, "While still reserving my position as to substance, I must consider that the statement by the Libyan Government was ill-timed. Hence I must consider that the decision of the Libyan Government, taken with the apparent support of one of the Administering Powers, but without the co-operation of or consultation with the Commissioner, was premature from every point of view." [38]

While acknowledging that there was much to be said for the sterling area machinery, the Commissioner pointed out that Libya still had not been granted special status for its potential dollar earnings. Moreover, there were political implications affecting Libya's neighbors that could not be overlooked. Finally, being well acquainted with the findings and recommendations of the technical assistance experts, shortly to be released in the draft *Economic Appraisal* (pp. 674–79), he argued that, the conclusions of the Lindberg team not being known to the Libyan delegation to the Meeting of Experts, the decision as to Libya's adherence or nonadherence to the sterling area should be deferred and possible alternatives examined. One such possibility was transferable-account status coupled with current utilization of hard currency earnings for development purposes or accumulating them in a Libyan currency reserve. The Commissioner concluded:

> I feel bound to point out that although this group is working on the expert level, its labours are governed by the over-riding necessity of taking into account the expressed special interest of the General Assembly in and the recognized special responsibility of the United Nations for Libya's future. In brief, this means that, in the opinion of the General

38. For full text of the Commissioner's statement, see ibid., Annex XIX, pp. 150–51.

Assembly, Libya should become truly independent and should receive disinterested international assistance to achieve this end.[39]

Commanding no support from the capital-exporting countries in the Council for Libya or in the Meeting of Experts, and especially in view of the Libyan Government's formal declaration of satisfaction with the arrangements negotiated with the United Kingdom Government, with the agreement of the French, Italian, and United States Governments, the Commissioner found himself in the awkward position of seeming to be *plus royaliste que le Roi.* In any event, the major issue of the currency and the allied issues of budget support and development financing machinery were now settled, and it only remained to fix the modalities.

To meet the concern expressed by the Italians and the minorities, the Libyan delegation gave categorical assurances that a policy of nondiscrimination would be pursued in foreign exchange and trade matters. This statement was welcomed by all members of the Meeting, which extended it to include investment policy and recommended that Libya consider entering into formal agreements to that effect.

In the light of the prevailing situation, the Meeting endorsed the recommendations that initially the currency should be backed 100 percent in sterling, but that the currency authority might, at its discretion, and with the consent of the competent authorities of the other countries concerned, invest up to 25 percent of its reserves in other currencies, and that banks operating in Libya might hold non-sterling working balances. Again, to meet Italian wishes in particular, it was agreed that equal commissions for all operations in foreign currencies should be fixed in Libya without discrimination and that the countries concerned should agree to consider admitting reciprocal transferability of their respective currencies in the accounts held with them by Libyan residents. All such transactions would have to conform to Libya's exchange regulations. The United Kingdom expert observed that this was the current practice among members of the European Payments Union.

It was further agreed that if, for any reason, transfer between sterling and other currencies in the reserves became impossible, even in cases where the Libyan exchange control was prepared to permit remittances in such other currencies, the currency authority should have discretion to sell them from its cover against tender of Libyan currency, and to buy them for its cover, up to the 25 percent limit specified, against issue of Libyan currency.

39. Ibid.

Finally, the harmony between the United Kingdom and the other powers was sealed when all but the Egyptian expert, who merely reserved his position, agreed that the Libyan currency authority should be entitled to redeem Libyan currency in sterling only.

The Meeting of Experts also considered and approved, without argument, a number of provisions for Libyan currency legislation regulating the technical functions of the currency authority, which were commended to the Libyan Government.[40]

At the end of the session, the Commissioner, more in sorrow than in anger, repeated his conviction that the unexpected and unconditional decision of the Libyan Provisional Government to join the sterling area, while defensible on technical grounds as in Libya's interest, was premature. He feared its possible repercussions on the hoped-for contributions to the Libyan budget, reminding the Meeting that during the recent discussions France had withdrawn its offer to meet up to 20 percent of the deficit, stating that it would limit its contribution to specific technical assistance projects.[41] He hoped that the assurances given by the Libyan delegation regarding foreign trade and exchange operations would be honored, and that they would be accepted by Libya's neighbors. Noting that it seemed that no offers of financial aid to redress the regular budget deficit would be forthcoming but that of the United Kingdom, he expressed concern lest Libya find itself in the delicate position of having to rely on one State alone to balance its budget. He therefore felt even more obliged than before to urge upon Libya and the General Assembly the necessity of establishing international controls to protect the country against the paramount influence of a single foreign Power. That was no reflection on the United Kingdom; he would have reacted in the same way had the predominance of any other single Power threatened, because the principle, as well as the dangers involved, would have been identical.

Subsequent work on the new Libyan currency was more or less routine, though for the staff of the Provisional Libyan Currency Authority, the printers and minters, and the officials responsible for handling the mechanics of the conversion, it was a very busy time. The Currency Law was enacted on 24 October 1951 by the Provisional Libyan Government, to which enabling powers had been transferred earlier (see pp. 800 ff.). The new notes and coin were put into circulation in February 1952.[42]

40. Ibid., Annex XVIII, Appendix IV, pp. 147–50.

41. Ibid., para. 220. In the event, France later contributed both to LPDSA and to the regular budget.

42. For the record of the currency discussion in the NCAL, see *Proc. NCAL*, Stewart-Jackson translation, 24th Meeting, 24 July 1951. The Currency Authority

SUBSIDIES TO THE REGULAR BUDGET

During the third session of the Meeting of Experts, the question of subsidies to Libya's regular budget again arose, since it was all part of one package with currency and economic development financing, with the military-base issue always looming large in the background.

The question was thoroughly examined: whereas the United Kingdom was prepared to underwrite the regular budget, no other capital-exporting Power would follow suit. The French Government's attitude has just been described. The Italian delegation, too, withdrew an earlier offer to help close the gap. The Egyptian delegation, while prepared to ask its Parliament for an appropriation, said that the amount of the contribution would depend on the size of the deficit, its causes, and other (unspecified) factors. The United States made it clear once more that it would provide assistance only within the framework of the Point Four program, not to cover budget deficits.

The cumulative effect of these negative or quasinegative reactions was that the United Kingdom, finding itself alone, decided to reserve its position. The Commissioner could not help thinking that this time the diplomatic pourparlers had been at best inconclusive. His fears about the unilateral nature of support for the Libyan budget were thus borne out.

The entire fourth session of the Meeting of Experts, which took place from 5 to 8 July, again in Geneva, was devoted to this problem. As will be apparent from what has just been said, the outcome was virtually a foregone conclusion.

The participants [43] were well aware of the deficitary state of the territorial budgets, totaling $4,870,339: $1,351,467 in Tripolitania, $3,308,872 in Cyrenaica, and $210,000 in the Fezzan for the current year. No one doubted that this condition would persist for some time, for no fresh revenue was in sight, and services could not be much curtailed without causing hardship.

The United Kingdom expert repeated his Government's offer to seek parliamentary sanction for covering the residual deficit of the Libyan budget by means of annual grants-in-aid, subject always to the maintenance of adequate safeguards to ensure prudent and economical budgeting. The size

lasted until March 1957, when the National Bank of Libya was created and took over issue functions. The Bank's capital came from part of the $12 million grant-in-aid made that year by the United States Government.

43. The Government of Egypt did not send a representative on this occasion. For a report of this session, see *Second Annual Report of the United Nations Commissioner in Libya,* Annex XX, pp. 151–52.

of such grants-in-aid would be fixed in relation to Libya's essential needs, as reflected in its budget, taking into account the foreign trade and balance-of-payments position. The acceptance of such aid and the nature of the safeguards would be a matter for direct negotiation and agreement between the two Governments, although it was emphasized that the offer did not bar other Governments from helping also. This willingness to accept help from other nations in meeting the Libyan deficit was a relaxation of the United Kingdom position as set forth to the Commissioner earlier in the year; however, that position remained unchanged in other respects.

The representatives of France, Italy, and the United States all made it clear once again that their Governments intended only to contribute to limited development projects and programs, not to balance the regular budget. All stated that in their opinion the United Kingdom proposals constituted an acceptable scheme for financial assistance to Libya not incompatible with their own Governments' offers. The Libyan representative, speaking personally, said that the United Kingdom proposals seemed in principle to be in Libya's interest. They would be commended to the Provisional Libyan Government. The Libyan Finance Minister also expressed the view that foreign financial aid should be channeled through the federal government, in the expectation that this would be in conformity with the Libyan Constitution as promulgated. This commanded unanimous agreement, although the United Kingdom expert made it clear that his Government's offer stood, and that its contributions would be made to whatever government institution proved to be appropriate under the Constitution.

APPOINTMENT OF A TECHNICAL ASSISTANCE RESIDENT REPRESENTATIVE

We have already seen in Part 1 of this chapter that the Commissioner was anxious that the future Libyan Government should enjoy the advice of a United Nations official on the administration of any funds that might be contributed by foreign Governments, and that the United Kingdom's immediate reaction to this suggestion was an adverse one (pp. 699–700). At the fourth session of the Meeting of Experts, the United Kingdom's argument was supported by the representatives of France, Italy, and the United States, seemingly in concert; but each country must have had its undivulged reasons for dropping the idea of an international solution for Libya's financial problems.

The Commissioner's first idea had been that the United Nations official in question should, for reasons made clear in Part 1, be the Resident Representative of TAB in Libya. Given the budgetary arrangements that were now virtually certain to apply, he now suggested that the future Resident Representative should, in addition to his functions as such, play a leading part in coordinating all the programs of the United Nations family of agencies, as well as sit on the Boards of Directors of LPDSA and LFC, and advise the Government generally on development matters (cf. p. 664). This had the advantage that the appointment and terms of reference of such an officer would be purely a matter for the future Libyan Government and TAB and no concern of other Governments. In 1951, the institution of Resident Representative was so new—less than a year old—that the members of the Meeting of Experts had no instructions on the matter, which may account for their attitude at the relevant session, as described in Annex XX, paragraphs 14–20, to the Commissioner's second annual report (p. 152 thereof). The Libyan Government's relevant request, including the appointment of the Resident Representative, eventually went through without difficulty as described at the beginning of this chapter.

INSTITUTIONS FOR FINANCING ECONOMIC DEVELOPMENT

The reader will by now be well aware that from the moment work started on the problems of Libya's economic and social development, United Nations personnel in Libya and the foreign Powers concerned realized that special arrangements of some kind would have to be made for financing development projects in Libya. The United Kingdom and Italian authorities in particular, though for very different reasons, were thinking in terms of managed investment, whereas the United States authorities at first had technical assistance projects alone in mind. The hard truth was that, since there were virtually no investment projects in Libya in a bankable sense, grants-in-aid were essential. The present-day concept of long-term fifty-year loans with ten-year periods of grace and bearing less than 1 percent interest, such as those made in recent years by the IBRD's subsidiary, the International Development Agency (IDA), and by the United States, United Kingdom, and Canadian Governments, were then but the pipe dreams of economists.

The United Kingdom authorities, not being without experience in these matters, had very early on intimated to the Commissioner that they favored the establishment in Libya of an investment agency, to the initial capital of which the United Kingdom Government would be prepared to contribute. The United Nations experts collaborated with local officials of the Administering Powers in developing these proposals, which were first brought into focus at the third session of the Meeting of Experts, following a series of draft exchanges at the expert level, including the studies made by the IMF experts, suggestions put forward by the United Nations and FAO secretariats, and the findings of the economists in the Lindberg and Higgins teams. It must again be emphasized that in 1950–51 the range of international and bilateral financing agencies available to developing countries in the mid-1960s was nonexistent. Looking back, the tools that were hammered out, mainly by United Kingdom treasury officials and United Nations experts, compare very favorably with today's more sophisticated development financing machinery—inadequate to needs as that remains.

The fifth and final session of the Meeting of Experts, held in Geneva from 24 to 29 September 1951, was devoted to consideration of recommendations for setting up the necessary institutions for financing Libyan economic development.[44] By this time there was a considerable amount of documentation before the experts, including the *Economic Appraisal,* supplemented by the *Balance of Payments of Libya,* and numerous monographs. The Chief Economist and his FAO colleague had prepared papers on problems of general development and on those of agricultural financing, together with proposals for institutions modifying those discussed at the third session. Of course, as was the case throughout the Libyan venture, and indeed is the case in international operations generally, it would have been better if all concerned had had more time to read and ponder the reports and studies.

It must be noted here that collaboration between staffs of the United Nations and the specialized agencies in the field of development financing, and indeed over the whole range of related topics, was greatly helped by the assignment to Libya early in 1951 of experienced, mature, and highly specialized British experts with a Treasury and development background. C. J. Pyke, the Treasury representative at the Meeting of Experts, and C. Pitt-Hardacre, Adviser to the Libyan Minister of Finance, brought to the problems of devising acceptable financing arrangements a wealth of experience and understanding, both of Libyan and international problems, which revealed them as men of vision and understanding. There were many occasions when Pyke's views conflicted fundamentally with those of the Commissioner, but he showed himself to be able and willing to appreciate the views of his colleagues, Libyan and international, and to strive to reach sound solutions in the common interest, while never forgetting his first allegiance. Pitt-Hardacre was a shrewd, perspicacious, and eminently practical adviser who became wholly absorbed in the task of putting Libya's finances into good order. He was assigned first to the British Administration

44. For a report of this session, see ibid., Annex XXI, pp. 153–57.

in Tripolitania, then to the Provisional Libyan Government. He had seen long service in British Pacific territories, more particularly in Sarawak. He had nearly become an expatriate in his years of service in Australia, held a distinguished war record as an Australian officer, and had a good working knowledge of seven oriental languages. He was a tower of strength to the United Kingdom of Libya from the moment the Provisional Government was formed. He soon established a professional rapport with the United Nations experts which was of mutual benefit, and in the Libyan interest.

To revert to the proceedings at the Meeting of Experts, it will be remembered that it had been agreed at the third session that the Provisional Libyan Government should be advised to set up two institutions, one for financing public works and basic economic and social development projects, the second to finance development by granting medium and long-term loans to private and corporate persons.

Starting from this base, the team of technical assistance experts and the specialists from the United Kingdom, French, and Italian Governments had reached an agreement which had been approved by the Ministers of the Provisional Libyan Government. Draft statutes for the two organizations had been drawn up by the technical assistance experts and members of the staff of the United Nations Mission in Libya, and the drafts served as the basic documents for the discussions in Geneva. At this session the Principal Secretary took the chair, the Commissioner being engaged in discussions with the NCAL in Benghazi on the closing stages of the drafting of the Constitution.[45]

Before describing the proposals in detail, the Commissioner may perhaps be allowed to remark on the change in the attitude of the British authorities since July 1950, when certain senior British officials in Libya, and even in the Foreign Office, had objected to the introduction of IMF experts to advise the Commissioner, and since September 1950, when the Commissioner was handed in London a draft currency law on the assumption that he would agree to its promulgation in the fall of 1950. Fortunately, wiser counsels prevailed in Whitehall once the United Nations experts had proved themselves. The United Kingdom delegation at the fifth session was pleased to receive professionally prepared drafts for the statutes of the two agencies. It must again be emphasized that all concerned were still experimenting with what might be described as the prototype of development financing units on a national basis later established all over the world as new countries came into being and as developing countries sought to achieve their

45. The Government of Egypt was again not represented.

aims and aspirations. The specialized agencies were similarly groping their way toward viable solutions. Libya was once again the testing and proving ground, a kind of pilot project.

It is fair to say that, having regard to the original analyses of the Libyan economy, to the agreement on sterling currency backing, and to the later series of economic studies, it was not difficult to reach agreement on the form and shape of the financing agencies.

At the risk of repetition, the recommendations can best be summarized in the form in which they eventually became law: [46]

The purposes of LPDSA would be to promote the economic and social development of Libya by investigating, formulating, financing, and carrying out programs and projects for technical assistance; to develop Libya's resources with a view to an expansion of production, especially that of food and raw materials; to help to maintain stability in periods of drought; and to assist the long-range balanced growth of Libya's foreign trade and the achievement and maintenance of equilibrium in the balance of payments. The Agency's funds should be allocated three-quarters to a development fund and one-quarter to a stabilization fund until the latter reached an amount of £ Libyan 1 million ($2,800,000).

LPDSA should have the power not only to investigate and formulate projects and programs designed to promote economic and social development, but also to finance and carry out, or to help in the financing and carrying out of, such programs and projects either through other Libyan Government agencies or other bodies, or through persons acting in that connection under its control and supervision. It was provided that stabilization fund activities, intended to relieve distress caused by drought, might include the buying and storing of foodstuffs and disposing of them in lean times, and the giving of assistance during famine periods to the inhabitants of Libya on a loan or relief basis.[47]

Under its statute, LPDSA was to be guided solely by economic and social considerations, due attention being paid, however, to economy and efficiency; it was to coordinate its planning activities with those of other agencies concerned with Libya's development, giving due consideration to the overall economic and social development plans of the Libyan Government. It was not empowered to borrow money or to raise loans. Member-

46. For full texts of the Statutes of LPDSA and LFC, see *Supplementary Report to the Second Annual Report of the United Nations Commissioner in Libya,* Annex IX, pp. 45–51.

47. In the event, LPDSA was faced, during the early years of independence, with a more or less severe drought every year, so that more than 25 percent of its annual intake of funds had to be allocated to what were essentially job-creating relief works.

ship on the Board of Directors required a minimum contribution of £ Libyan 10,000 ($28,000) from the government concerned. This requirement was waived in the case of the Resident Representative of TAB and the Libyan director. Each member had one vote for every £ Libyan 10,000 it contributed in any one year, the Libyan Government having a vote equal to that of the largest contributor. The General Manager and Deputy General Manager were to be appointed by the Board subject to the approval of the Libyan Government. The Board was to approve the yearly economic development plan after consulting the latter. Finally, there were the normal provisions for budget accounting, and for audit by the Auditor-General of Libya.

The statute, which was enacted by the Provisional Libyan Government on 20 December 1951, was approved by the Meeting of Experts without much difficulty because by late 1951 all three parties around the table—the Libyans, the Administering Powers, and the Commissioner and his advisers—were thoroughly acquainted with the facts and conditions of Libyan economic life. The Libyans had not been so well informed when the talks opened early in 1950.

The basic aim of the Italian sponsors of LFC was that it should provide some kind of credit for Italian farmers in Tripolitania. The need for this was recognized by the United Kingdom, French, and United States members of the Meeting of Experts, and on the political plane the scheme was considered to be necessary. One may fairly say that, throughout the discussions, the proposal was a minor factor, never opposed, but never strongly supported by any but the Italian delegation.

The Meeting—having heard the Italian Government's argument that LFC could operate on bankable arrangements without primary concern for profit-making, concentrating rather on Libya's economic and social development—somewhat reluctantly accepted the Italian proposals as modified by the United Nations experts. The latter had grave doubts whether there were in fact bankable loan possibilities on the Libyan scene—which, in effect, meant in Tripolitania.

Finally, the experts recommended to the future Libyan Government—the Libyan member reserving his position—that it establish a Libyan finance corporation, on condition that it should not interfere in political affairs, that it should coordinate its activities with others in the development field, and that it should be effectively under the operational control of the Libyan Government.[48] They also approved the corporation's draft statute.

48. For the report of the session, see *Second Annual Report of the United Nations Commissioner in Libya,* p. 156. In fact, although LFC was duly established, its interest rate of 5 percent to 7 percent was unrealistic, and it withered within a few years. At

At the fifth meeting of the session, the Italian representative announced his Government's intention of continuing the privileged treatment accorded to Libyan imports. Italy would request the States signatory to the General Agreement on Tariffs and Trade (GATT) to accept such a provision.[49] The Libyan representative expressed his appreciation of this gesture, but his United Kingdom colleague pointed out that, to benefit from the proposed arrangement, which must be reciprocal, Libya would have to join GATT. Although the meeting recognized that this would normally be a matter for Italy, Libya, and the members of GATT, it was agreed, without comment, that the Commissioner should transmit the Italian offer to GATT.[50] The extent of the concessions may be judged by the fact that Italian duty on imports from Libya was 11 percent for such commodities as tuna, olive oil, barley, and livestock, compared with rates of 25 to 40 percent for the same commodities imported from other countries. Considering the volume of trade involved—40 percent of Tripolitanian exports and 36 percent of Cyrenaican exports were going to Italy at the time—this was a real boon, especially for the Italian farmers in Libya.

When discussions opened on the United Kingdom subsidy for the regular budget and the contribution to the development budget (see Chapter 10, Part 6), it had been expected that everything would be tied up by the beginning of April 1952. It was soon realized that this date could not be met, for there would not be time between Libya's acquisition of independence and the date on which Parliament at Westminster had to pass the money bills for the United Kingdom fiscal year 1952–53 to negotiate, not only the financial agreement, but also that on the maintenance of military bases implicitly attached thereto. His Majesty's Government accordingly

---

the time it was still not realized by Italians in Rome and in Tripolitania how small a role such banking institutions could play in Libya or, conversely, how much credit was needed on nonbankable terms. See also Benjamin Higgins, *Economic Development* (New York: W. W. Norton, 1959), p. 708.

49. GATT is an integrated set of more than one hundred bilateral trade agreements first negotiated at Geneva, Switzerland, in 1947. It covers some 50,000 commodities and provides for substantial reductions in tariff duties between the members, known collectively as the Contracting Parties to GATT. Privileged treatment, such as that proposed by the Italian Government for Libyan imports, is subject to the prior assent of all other signatories to the agreement.

50. On 27 October 1951, the Contracting Parties to GATT, having received advice, both from the Commissioner and from the Government of Italy, agreed that Italy could continue to extend special low tariff duties on Libyan products until 30 September 1952. Thereafter, a fresh privileged position for Libya was negotiated, but within the framework of the European Common Market, where it was not so exceptional an arrangement.

extended the initial financial period to fifteen months, i.e. until 1 April 1953. On 13 December 1951, the Provisional Libyan Government and the United Kingdom concluded a temporary arrangement for financial assistance to Libya, as foreseen in the transfer of powers arrangements.

The purposes of the main agreement were: to ensure that Libya enjoyed conditions of financial stability and orderly economic development; the United Kingdom, provided that it was fully informed about Libya's means, would contribute to LPDSA and LFC up to £500,000 ($1,400,000) in 1952; the United Kingdom would also provide 100 percent sterling backing for the initial Libyan currency issue, and, until 31 March 1952, financial assistance to the administrations in Cyrenaica and Tripolitania, which in turn would finance the Libyan Federal Government by transferring to it funds from this assistance.

As from 1 April 1952, if, without prejudice to the undoubted right of Libya to determine its own budget after having taken the advice of the United Kingdom-nominated officials in Libya, there was agreement between the two Governments, and provided the central and provincial budgets had been drafted prudently, economically, and in accordance with the main purpose of the agreement, the United Kingdom would, at the request of the Libyan Government, contribute an amount equal to the deficits of the combined budgets. Should no agreement be reached between the two Governments, the United Kingdom still undertook to contribute a sum essential to support the Libyan economy, again provided the Libyan Government put in a request to that effect.

The agreement provided that Libya, in consultation with the United Kingdom, should appoint a chief financial and economic officer and an auditor-general, both to be servants of the Libyan Government serving under its civil service laws. The former was to have direct access to the Prime Minister and the Minister of Finance, and was to be the principal financial and economic adviser to the Government.

A parallel temporary agreement was concluded between the Provisional Libyan Government and France by means of an exchange of letters dated 13 and 14 December 1951. The French Government undertook to provide direct financial assistance to ensure the functioning of the administrative services in the Fezzan and for that territory's economic and social development, and to meet its budget deficit for the period up to 30 March 1952. For the following year, France agreed to provide the central government with financial assistance for the last two purposes only. Part of this aid might be in the form of a contribution to LPDSA (see p. 714, fn. 41). The amount of such assistance was to be determined by separate agreement. The Libyan Government undertook to appoint an official of French nationality to be primarily concerned with economic and financial questions concerning the Fezzan. He would serve on precisely the same conditions as his British counterpart, whom, moreover, he was required to keep informed of his proposals in order that they could be considered in the framework of the economic and financial position of Libya as a whole.

With the conclusion of these two agreements, the Libyan Government was assured that the deficit in its regular budget would be covered until 1 April 1953, and that at least £500,000 ($1,400,000) would be available for its initial development program.[51]

As had been tacitly foreseen on both the British and the Libyan sides, a treaty of friendship and alliance between Libya and the United Kingdom signed in 1953 gave the latter air- and land-base facilities, in return for which for the following five years the United Kingdom was to pay £1,000,000 ($2,800,000) a year to Libyan development organizations and £2,750,000 ($7,700,000) to the Libyan budget.[52] An agreement concluded in 1958 provided for payments of £3,250,000 ($9,100,000) in the form of budgetary aid for the next five years; but in that case there was no contribution to development.

An agreement for assistance from the United States over and above Point Four technical aid, which was extended when Libya became independent, was concluded in 1954. It gave the United States the right to occupy certain areas in Libya for military purposes, in particular at Wheelus Field. The quid pro quo was an initial payment of $7,000,000 (together with some food grain), followed by grants of $4,000,000 a year for six years running from July 1954, and of $1,000,000 a year for the eleven years after 1960.[53]

51. For full texts of the United Kingdom and French Temporary Agreements, see *Supplementary Report to the Second Annual Report of the United Nations Commissioner in Libya,* Annexes IV and V, pp. 29–31.

52. See Chapter 10, fn. 117, item 1, p. 831.

53. See Chapter 10, fn. 117, item 2, p. 831. Actual assistance from the United States substantially exceeded the amounts envisaged in the agreement. Loans, as well as grants, were made, together with special shipments of wheat and other cereals to meet shortages caused by drought. By 1959–60, assistance from the United States had risen to a level of $12 million, of which the greater part was earmarked for specific development projects, although assistance to Libya's regular budget had become a feature of United States aid by that time.

CHAPTER 10

The Transfer of Powers

PART 1. GENERAL CONSIDERATIONS

From the very beginning of its efforts to solve the Libyan question, the General Assembly had realized the need not only for cooperation between the Administering Powers and the Commissioner, but also for cooperation and coordination between the Administering Powers themselves. Subparagraphs 10 (a) and (b) of Resolution 289 (IV) bear witness to this conviction, which must have been inspired, at least in part, by the report of the Four Power Commission of Investigation for the Former Italian Colonies. Indeed, the factual situation in 1948 as described by the Commission was still very much the same when the Commissioner made his own reconnaissance tour during the first three months of 1950 (see pp. 172–201). The French and United Kingdom Governments had consulted one another on overall policies of common interest, which were pursued along more or less parallel lines, but cooperation between the three territorial administrations on the spot was limited to what was strictly necessary. This was in part due to geographical conditions, but in part also to differences in local conditions, interests, language, and administrative methods. Each of the three territories was in fact dealt with as an isolated entity. Cyrenaica and Tripolitania were separately administered from London, their administrators not even always receiving their instructions from the same metropolitan authorities. Contacts between the British Administrations in Tripolitania and Cyrenaica and their French counterpart in the Fezzan were channeled through the French Consul General in Tripoli and the French Consul in Benghazi respectively.

The adoption of Resolution 289 (IV) did not at first greatly change the situation. The Commissioner, watching Anglo-French policy working for a loose federation, soon became convinced that a change in the administrative setup was neither desired nor envisaged by the interested Powers, at any rate not in 1950. Only in 1951 did the change of mind and method required by the General Assembly resolutions begin to become perceptible.

Meanwhile the Commissioner, when trying to plan the course of action to be followed in the light of the experience he had gained through the work of the Committee of Twenty-One, increasingly felt the need for closer interterritorial cooperation. How else would it be possible to achieve Libyan unity in the various administrative sectors?

It was this realization that prompted him to state in the concluding remarks to his first annual report the following opinion:

> When the Libyan National Assembly has adopted a constitution, including the form of government, the Administering Powers should proceed to take all the necessary steps for the progressive transfer of functions to a provisional Libyan administration. As more detailed measures have to be taken, both within the territorial spheres and on the over-all Libyan level, the co-ordination of the activities of the Administering Powers will become progressively more necessary, particularly in the fields of administration, finance, currency and economy. The Commissioner may have to suggest at a not too distant date the establishment of a standing co-ordination committee, comprising officials of the Administering Powers and perhaps also of the Cyrenaican Government and the Fezzanese Administration, together with an appropriate representative of Tripolitania.[1]

When this paragraph of the report came up for consultation in the Council, only the question of Tripolitanian representation in the proposed coordination committee provoked comment. The substance of the Committee's duties was not even mentioned. It was therefore somewhat surprising that a few months later the setting up of the Committee caused one of the most heated debates that ever raged in the Council arena.

The delegates dealing with the Libyan question at the Fifth Session of the General Assembly in 1951 (see Chapter 5 above) were quicker to understand both the necessity of promoting the establishment of a Provisional Libyan Government (Resolution 387 [V] subparagraph 3 [b]) and the need to prepare and implement a program for the progressive transfer of powers to that Government (subparagraphs 3 [c] and [d]).

For the establishment of the Provisional Government, 1 April 1951 was suggested as a target date, and 1 January 1952 was confirmed as the date by which "all powers at present exercised by [the Administering Powers] shall . . . have been transferred to the duly constituted Libyan Government."[2]

1. First *Annual Report of the United Nations Commissioner in Libya,* GAOR: Fifth Session, 1950, Supplement No. 15 (A/1340), para. 258.

2. See Annex I, pp. 893–94.

Thus, by January 1951 not much time remained to do what was needed to achieve these objectives.

PART 2. THE ESTABLISHMENT OF A PROVISIONAL LIBYAN GOVERNMENT AND THREE LOCAL NATIONAL PROVISIONAL GOVERNMENTS

Seen from New York, the establishment of a Provisional Government must have looked very easy to those who had voted for it. On the field of action, it was not easy at all, and it was only through the NCAL resolution of 29 March 1951 that the Provisional Government came into being.

The cause of the delay was entirely political. When, on 2 December 1950, the NCAL had decided unanimously, and by acclamation, that the Libyan State should be federal in form, it was, of course, understood that the three provinces would be governed by more or less autonomous governments or administrations, which would enter into a common union by voluntary consent. The nature of that union and its degree of federalization were the NCAL's main preoccupations from early 1951 onward. Hence its decision to determine, as its first step in drafting the Constitution, the distribution of powers between the Federation and the Provinces. It followed from this concept of building up the State that, in the light of the Cyrenaican precedent, the provinces would have to be organized before the union could come into existence. This view of the sequence of events was shared by the Cyrenaicans and Fezzanese.[3] It was also in line with British and French policy, though early in 1950 neither Power had been in a hurry to establish a Provisional Libyan Government.

As to the Tripolitanians, originally they too had agitated for a local government through which in particular the National Congress Party had hoped to dominate Libya's further constitutional development. Later, they switched to a more direct unitarist approach, according to which the establishment of a Libyan Government should have had precedence over that of local governments.

So far the practical implications of this problem had been ignored, except, of course, for the partly successful British and French attempts to set up territorial governments. The adoption of Resolution 387 (V) made it a matter of immediate urgency.

3. In apparent contradiction to this way of thinking, the NCAL's Working Group had started by drawing up a list of *federal* powers. The reason for this has been explained in Chapter 7, pp. 521–36.

One item appeared on the agenda at the eleventh meeting, the wording of which was a political program in itself. It read: "Request that local governments be formed for Tripoli [*sic*], the Fezzan and Cyrenaica." [4] It soon became clear that the request was meant to be addressed to the King, and it was equally obvious that the wording of the item had been drafted by the federalist majority of the NCAL's officers. A Tripolitanian member immediately asked that discussion of the item be deferred, while one of his colleagues proposed that it be deleted altogether, because, he argued, the Assembly had been asked to form a temporary government for Libya and not governments for the three territories. Although several other Tripolitanian members also expressed disagreement with the agenda as it stood, it was nevertheless adopted.

When, however, a Cyrenaican member asked why Cyrenaica was mentioned in the request, and whether it was intended to confirm the government already existing there, or to replace it by another, the President adroitly changed the subject by consulting members on a convenient date and time for the twelfth meeting.

Two days later the item again appeared on the agenda in the same terms. This time the meeting was held in private, with the result that opposing points of view were stated more frankly. The President opened the debate:

> His Hon. the President then said that since the Assembly's task was to found a Libyan state and a central government; and since the government was to be set up after power had passed into the hands of the inhabitants of the country—which meant that power would have to be handed over in the Fezzan, Cyrenaica and Tripoli by founding [three] governments headed by the Libyan government; and since Tripoli and the Fezzan had no national government in them;—in view of this he thought we should first of all examine how best to transfer power in these two places with the support of the Cyrenaican government. He was inclined to believe that H. M. the King should intervene and examine how best to establish the apparatus for transferring power in Tripoli and the Fezzan. We hope that the question will be examined in the light of the national interest, since there were only a few days to exercise power between now and the date appointed for the foundation of a Libyan government.[5]

After the agenda had been approved, in the face of Tripolitanian opposition, a representative of that province, Abd al-Aziz al-Zaqalla'i, expressed the view that:

4. *Proc. NCAL,* Stewart-Jackson Translation, 11th Meeting, 19 February 1951.
5. *Proc. NCAL,* Stewart-Jackson Translation, 12th Meeting, 21 February 1951.

> the question of forming [three] governments in Tripoli, Cyrenaica and the Fezzan fell outside the competence of the Assembly, since the U.N. resolution demanded the formation of a provisional Libyan government before 1 April; and that it was the provisional Libyan government which was to examine the question of taking over power before establishing the constitution.[6]

The Tripolitanian objections placed the NCAL in a quandary. There was no doubt that Resolution 387 (V) spoke only of the establishment of a Provisional Government of Libya and of powers to be progressively transferred to that Government. The program for that transfer was to be drawn up by the Commissioner, aided and guided by the advice of the members of the Council for Libya, and in cooperation with the Administering Powers. Nowhere did the Resolution suggest that this program should include any transfer of powers to the provincial governments; neither did the earlier Resolution—289 (IV)—which left the entire responsibility for drawing up the Constitution to the NCAL. It could be argued, of course, that the General Assembly had not *precluded* a transfer of powers to three local governments. It had even tacitly recognized the transfer of powers in Cyrenaica in 1949, and had never said a word about undoing that transfer; nor had it criticized the Commissioner for allowing a limited and conditional measure of provincial autonomy in Tripolitania and the Fezzan the previous year. Nevertheless, the NCAL seemed to be in a confused state of mind, as transpires from the following exchange of views:

> The Hon. Member Khalil Gellal rose and explained that there was no doubt that the General Assembly of the U.N. had given the National Assembly of Libya the power to form a provisional central government. Since the National Assembly had decided on a federal system, it would not be easy to form the Libyan government now; in fact, preparations would be necessary. Because of this it had become necessary to establish an official body to take over power in the country. In view of this, it was necessary to form territorial governments to take over power, so as not to delay forming a central government until after the date fixed by the U.N. The Hon. Mem. added that this step was necessary to avoid losing time, and to avoid nullifying the resolutions that had been passed. The Hon. Mem. Abdul Aziz Zagalai' now said that since this fell outside the competence of the Assembly he proposed asking for the U.N.'s decision on the matter. The Hon. Mem. Suleiman Jerbi said that the question did not fall outside the Assembly's competence, since it had previously re-

6. Ibid.

solved the form of the state—which was to be federal—and it was impossible to set up a central government except on this basis. In order to carry this out we must first of all form territorial governments. The Hon. Mem. Khalil Gellal explained that the request that U.N. advice be sought was definitely in contradiction to the U.N. resolution. The U.N. had passed its resolution and could not now go back on it. In any case, the National Assembly had no need to ask the U.N. for advice. This power should belong to H. M. the King until it was possible to form a central government. The Hon. Mem. Abdul Aziz Zagalai' expressed the belief that the U.N. Council for Libya had been formed to help the Libyans in their constitutional development. Since this was an extremely important step, we should ask for advice, after which we can pass whatever resolutions we wish. The Hon. Mem. Ali Tamir added that since the Assembly had passed a resolution on Dec. 2 last which set up H. M. the Amir of Cyrenaica as King of Libya, it was fitting that His Majesty should be requested to do this; and that the Assembly could not consult with any other body since its only concern was to establish a constitution.[7]

The Tripolitanian members maintained their opposition. One of them, Salem al-Murayyid, reminded his opponents of a passage in the memorandum presented to the Political Committee of the League of Arab States in Cairo only a few weeks before, on 27 January (cf. Chapter 6, Part 4), in which an assurance was given that the provinces would be endowed with "administrations" and not with "governments." A Cyrenaican member replied that the memorandum had been drawn up with political considerations in mind. It represented a general intention, and nothing more. He further argued that such provincial governments would only be temporary.

The Tripolitanian member, Abd al-Aziz al-Zaqalla'i, then rose to say "that since his colleagues had started to consider putting a request to H. M. the King about forming provincial governments, he himself suggested that His Majesty be requested to set about forming a provisional Libyan Government." [8] This suggestion was opposed, however, by another Tripolitanian member, Munir Burshan, who pointed out that the formation of such a government fell within the competence of the NCAL.

Meanwhile, the officers of the Assembly had prepared the following draft resolution, which the President proposed be put to the vote:

> Inasmuch as we representatives of the Libyan nation in the N.C.A.L. resolved on the second day of December 1950 to found a federal state of Libya which would include the three territories, Cyrenaica, Tripoli and

7. Ibid.
8. Ibid.

the Fezzan, and proclaimed and did homage to the Sayyid Muh. Idris al Mahdi al Sanussi, Amir of Cyrenaica, as constitutional monarch of the united Libyan Kingdom, and inasmuch as this resolution and this act of homage demand the formation of temporary local governments in Tripoli, Cyrenaica and the Fezzan to take over power from the two existing administrations, the N.C.A.L. requests the King to agree to this and having consulted whatever bodies and persons he wishes, to be so good as to choose suitable persons for this purpose. His Majesty is also requested to ask the two powers at present controlling the administration of Tripoli [*sic*] and the Fezzan to help those persons chosen to take over and exercise their powers, preparatory to the creation of the federal Libyan state at the time fixed by the U.N. resolution.[9]

The vote was taken by roll call, the resolution being adopted by 47 votes to 3, with 3 abstentions. It was clear from these figures that several Tripolitanian members had voted for the resolution.

To this request, H. M. the King replied by the following telegram which was read out at the thirteenth meeting of the National Assembly on 5 March:

"His Hon. the President of the N.C.A.L.,
Tripoli.

We have received the telegram of Your Honour dated 21.2.1951, which announced the resolution of your honourable body requesting our agreement to the formation of local governments in Tripoli and the Fezzan on the model of the local government in Cyrenaica, preparatory to carrying out the resolution of your honourable body as to the formation of a federal Libyan state at the time fixed by the U.N. We agree to this, and have informed the English administration in Tripoli and the French in the Fezzan of the fact that we have agreed. This we did with all speed in order to allow the local governments to take over local power and responsibility from the two above mentioned administrations.

Muh. Idris Al Mahdi al Sanussi.[10]

It was further announced that the Coordination Committee would speed up its work on the distribution of powers. When a Tripolitanian member asked to whom the local government in Tripoli would be responsible, the President replied that this government was to be a temporary one and that its sole purpose was to take over powers. In fact the situation proved to be considerably more complicated than this answer implied.

9. Ibid.
10. *Proc. NCAL,* Stewart-Jackson Translation, 13th Meeting, 5 March 1951.

On 15 March there appeared on the agenda of the National Assembly an item entitled: "Request for the formation of a provisional government for the united Libyan State." [11]

The discussion that ensued was marked by much hesitation. Some members wondered whether even a provisional federal government could be established as long as no Constitution had been adopted. Others agreed that it would be necessary first to determine at least the powers of the King and the provincial governments, as well as the distribution of powers between the federal and local executives.

Another important question was, who should set up the Provisional Government, the King or the NCAL? Or should the King form the Government and the Assembly determine its powers?

A leading delegate from the Fezzan, Abu Bakr Bin Ahmed, supported by others, maintained that no federal government could be established as long as there was no local government in his province. On this score no news of any kind had reached Tripoli, where on 8 March a Council of Regency had been appointed by the British Resident.[12]

A draft resolution submitted by Omar Shenib proposed that the King be requested to announce his accession to the Throne, to form a provisional federal government, and to draw up rules for the election of the Libyan Parliament. The motion was not even discussed, and after a long and confused debate it was decided to defer the whole matter until 22 March. On that date there still was no news about the formation of a local government in the Fezzan, and the item was postponed once more until 24 March.

At the opening of the eighteenth meeting, the President made the following statement:

> Since the right to create the Libyan government belongs to the N.C.A.L.; and since the Assembly resolved on 2 Dec. 1950 to call H. H. the Amir to the throne of Libya; and since it was customary for the task of appointing ministers to fall to the king of a nation; and since H. M. the King has not yet exercised his constitutional powers the Assembly has the right to appoint members of the government, while H. M. possesses the honorary rank . . . which the Assembly has determined; I therefore think it best that the Assembly appoint the government after consultation with H. M. the King.[13]

This proposal having been tacitly approved, a delegation of nine members, three per territory, was appointed to wait upon the King. Since time

11. *Proc. NCAL,* Stewart-Jackson Translation, 15th Meeting, 15 March 1951.

12. See *Second Annual Report of the United Nations Commissioner in Libya,* GAOR: Sixth Session, 1951–52, Supplement No. 17 (A/1949), paras. 41–50.

13. *Proc. NCAL,* Stewart-Jackson Translation, 18th Meeting, 24 March 1951.

was running out, the Commissioner was asked to make the United Nations plane available, which he gladly did. A last-minute discussion as to whether the delegation should be given instructions—and if so, what—led to no conclusion.

The minutes of the nineteenth meeting contain the following report made on behalf of the delegation by the President of the Assembly:

> His Hon. explained to the members that in accordance with the Assembly's resolution the delegation had travelled to Cyrenaica to contact H. M. the King. They were honoured by a meeting with His Majesty, at which they discussed the formation of a Libyan government. His Majesty said that he thought that the resolution of the General Assembly of the U.N. had determined the formation of the Libyan government as a prerogative of the Constituent Assembly. After some talk his Majesty was informed of the names of the persons chosen and the offices that would be assigned to them in the new government. They gained the confidence of His Majesty.[14]

The President added that a draft resolution on the subject would be read by the Secretary. Before it came to this, various questions were put to the President. From his answers it emerged that certain members of the proposed Provisional Libyan Government, who were already holding portfolios in the Tripolitanian Council of Regency, would retain both posts. More important was an assurance given by the President to the effect that the Provisional Government would be responsible to the NCAL.

As to the question whether the Assembly had the right to dismiss the Government, various and differing opinions were expressed. According to the minutes, the general consensus appears to have been: "As for the dismissal of ministers, that will depend on what the law prescribes in such cases; but it seems reasonable to assume that the body or person that has the right to appoint should also have the right to dismiss." [15]

The draft resolution was then read out. After a lengthy preamble of *consideranda,* the operative part read as follows:

> *Therefore* the National Assembly decides:
> (1) To establish as from this day, the 21 Jamad al Tani 1370 Hagera, corresponding to 29 March 1951, the provisional Federal Government, whose functions shall include the following:
> (a) To establish contact with the United Nations Commissioner regarding the preparation of the plan provided for by the United Nations General Assembly resolution of 17 November 1950 concerning the

14. *Proc. NCAL,* Stewart-Jackson Translation, 19th Meeting, 29 March 1951.
15. Ibid.

transfer to it of the powers from the two administering Powers in Libya; (b) To receive the powers progressively transferred from the two administering Powers in Libya in a manner that will ensure the transfer of all powers from the two existing Administrations before 1 January 1952, in accordance with the United Nations General Assembly resolution of 17 November 1950, provided that its exercise of such powers would be in conformity with the provisions of the constitution, with particular regard to the distribution of powers between the Federal Government and the local governments, when that matter has been determined by the National Assembly.

(2) To appoint the following persons, whose consent has been obtained, to the offices of State as given below:

Sayed Mahmud Al Muntasser	Prime Minister, Minister of Justice and Minister of Education
Sayed Ali Jerbi	Minister of Foreign Affairs and Minister of Health
Sayed Omar Shanneib	Minister of Defence
Sayed Mansour Ben Qadara	Minister of Finance
Sayed Ibrahim Ben Sha'aban	Minister of Communications
Sayed Mohammed Ben Othman	Minister of State

(3) That His Eminence the President of the National Assembly shall communicate this resolution to the authorities concerned.

Issued at the headquarters of the National Assembly in Tripoli on Thursday, 21 Jamad Al Tani 1370, corresponding to 29 March 1951.[16]

It is to be noted that of the six ministers, three were Tripolitanians, two Cyrenaicans, and the sixth a Fezzanese. Hence the composition of the Government made a break with the principle of territorial equality. Five ministers were to be responsible for eight ministries (counting the Prime Minister's Office as one such), the sixth being a minister without portfolio.

After the second reading, a member from Tripolitania wanted to know how the Commissioner could draw up plans for the transfer of powers as long as he did not know how the NCAL would distribute powers between the federal and the local governments. This was indeed a very pertinent question, to which the Chairman of the Working Group replied that the Coordination Committee would soon be able to put forward a draft proposal on this point which, after approval by the NCAL, would be communicated to those concerned.

16. *Second Annual Report of the United Nations Commissioner in Libya,* Annex X, pp. 87–88. Translation from the Arabic made for internal purposes by the language staff of the United Nations Mission in Libya.

After a third reading the resolution was unanimously approved. The minutes record that on this happy occasion the Assembly stood in silence for five minutes "in memory of the souls of the pious martyrs." [17]

Indeed it was a happy occasion. For the first time in history the Libyan people had a national government of their own, appointed by their own representatives and authorized to take over powers from the two States temporarily administering the country. An elderly member from Tripolitania, Mahmud al-Maslati, rose to make a moving speech, recalling his memories of the Tripolitanian Republic of more than thirty years earlier, thus linking past with present.

The establishment of the Provisional Libyan Government was marked by messages of congratulation from the Governments of France, the United Kingdom, and the United States, from the President of the General Assembly, from the Secretary-General of the United Nations, and from the King-Designate and the Prime Minister of Cyrenaica.

In retrospect it is even more evident than it appeared at the time that the first three months of 1951 represent a critical episode in the country's constitutional development. Having decided in principle that Libya would be a federal state, the NCAL, as the preceding quotations from its records clearly show, was for a while of two minds, wavering between a loose and a more centralized federation. The federalist elements backed by the Administering Powers would, no doubt, have thrown their weight on the side of the provinces, had it not been for Resolution 387 (V) which so clearly limited the transfer of powers to a Provisional *Libyan* Government. As from 29 March, the date on which the latter came into being, at least a structural balance between the two tendencies was established. It remained to be seen how the final distribution of powers would turn out. Chapters 7 and 8 tell how the matter was handled and solved on the constitutional level. The rest of this chapter will show how the actual transfer of powers was organized from the legal, administrative, and budgetary points of view. As the two processes interacted, no clear picture emerged until the adoption of the Constitution by the NCAL on 7 October 1951.

PART 3.
CONSTITUTIONAL DEVELOPMENT IN THE PROVINCES

To help the reader to understand the complexity of the transfer operation that had to be planned and implemented in the course of 1951, it is neces-

17. *Proc. NCAL,* Stewart-Jackson Translation, 19th Meeting, 29 March 1951.

sary to remind him briefly of certain constitutional developments, already described in detail in earlier chapters, that had occurred in 1949–50.[18]

As the reader is by now well aware, Cyrenaica had enjoyed internal autonomy since the promulgation by the British Chief Administrator of Transitional Powers Proclamation No. 187 of 16 September 1949. It had a constitution of its own, enacted by the Amir, and a Cabinet assisted by an administration which included a strong element of British staff. On the other hand certain powers were still reserved to the British Resident, whose post replaced that of Chief Administrator when the Proclamation took effect. A plan based on British long-term policy was drawn up at the request of the Cyrenaican Government for the purpose of transferring to the Amir the reserved powers also. This plan was suspended in March–April 1950 on the advice of the Commissioner, who considered the existence of an independent Cyrenaica prejudicial to the future unity of Libya; it was never revived. On 31 December 1949, a Cyrenaican nationality law was enacted, for the purpose, the Commissioner was told, of determining the qualifications of those who would be entitled to participate in the elections for a local Assembly of Representatives. Elections actually took place in June 1951, and the Assembly met later the same month.

In Tripolitania, the situation was entirely different because of both external and internal factors. In January 1950 the Commissioner had received a memorandum from the United Kingdom Government, informing him of its intentions to establish, by progressive steps, an autonomous Tripolitanian Government, whose competence would be limited to that territory's domestic affairs. As a result of his remonstrations, certain changes were introduced into the British plan, but its *pièce de resistance,* the establishment of an administrative council, was maintained. This Council held its first meeting on 15 May 1950. Other parts of the plan were postponed, but at the beginning of 1951, the United Kingdom Government returned to the charge, its position having meanwhile been facilitated by the NCAL's decision of 2 December 1950 that the Libyan State should be federal in form, thus presuming the existence of local administrations.

From this point on, the developments need to be treated in somewhat greater detail.

During December 1950 and January 1951, the Commissioner held informal conversations with the United Kingdom Government about the establishment of a Tripolitanian Government along the lines of the one existing in Cyrenaica. His position, strengthened by experience, was in principle the same as the one he had taken the previous year. He was pre-

18. For the Commissioner's official accounts of these events, see first *Annual Report of the United Nations Commissioner in Libya,* paras. 38–49 and 60–89; and *Second Annual Report of the United Nations Commissioner in Libya,* paras. 41–50.

pared to recognize the usefulness and even the necessity of territorial governmental institutions in a federal system, provided they in no way hampered the freedom of action, granted to the NCAL by paragraph 3 of Resolution 289 (IV), to determine the form of government in accordance with the wishes of the inhabitants. It was in accordance with this principle that he advised the United Kingdom Government that the following four points should be brought out in the proclamation by which the new local organs were to be set up:

(a) That the final allocation of powers to the Tripolitanian Administration should be subject to the decisions of the National Assembly with regard to the distribution of powers between the Central Government and the local administrations;
(b) That the Tripolitanian Administration should be competent to hold elections for a local legislative body;
(c) That the organ to be established should be termed "administration" not "government," so as to make clear the local nature of its functions as distinct from those of the Provisional Libyan Government;
(d) That its principal members should be designated by a lesser term than "minister," in order again to emphasize the limited scope and to hold expenditure at a prudent level. The Commissioner also made known his contention that the proposed administration should be established after elections to a legislative body had been held.[19]

The Commissioner took the same line in his talks with Tripolitanian politicians.

During the early months of 1951, and after the Commissioner had discussed the matter in Paris, measures similar to those taken in Tripoli were carried through in the Fezzan. It became evident that the French Government was anxious not to lag behind the United Kingdom in granting increasing powers of local government to the territories under its administration. For both Powers, the ultimate purpose was plainly to weaken the future federation by strengthening the position of the provinces. Thus, in the Fezzan, by Decree No. 5, issued by the French Resident on 29 March 1951, the "counselors" to the Chef du Territoire were replaced by "ministers." Subsequently, the Chef du Territoire himself issued Decree No. 4 reappointing as ministers his erstwhile counselors. At the same time, their administrative prerogatives were somewhat expanded.[20] It is true that

19. *Second Annual Report of the United Nations Commissioner in Libya,* para. 42.

20. See "Annual report of the French Government to the General Assembly concerning the administration of the Fezzan," GAOR: Fifth Session, 1950, Annexes, Agenda item 21 (A/1387, 22 September 1950), pp. 1–33. See also United Nations Doc. A/1970 and Add. 1, 10 September 1951. Mimeographed.

Ahmed Bey Seif al-Nasr had sent his brother Omar to Benghazi to consult with the King before these measures became law. Nevertheless a unique opportunity of consulting the inhabitants through their traditional representatives (by summoning a *jemaa*) had been lost. In Tripolitania, the leaders of the political parties and various notables had at least been consulted before the relevant proclamation was issued. In the Fezzan nothing of the kind was done.

It goes without saying that the Commissioner, too, consulted the King on these developments of such great importance to the future of the Kingdom. His Majesty was not in agreement with the Commissioner's four points, but in the interest of harmonious evolution "preferred that local governments in Tripolitania and the Fezzan should be organised in the same way as the Government of Cyrenaica, using the same designations. After the establishment of the State, these might be reviewed." [21] The United Kingdom Government, on the other hand, was unwilling to incorporate in its proclamation matters with which the King disagreed. It was difficult not to perceive a certain reasonableness in both attitudes; the Commissioner therefore ceased to argue the point, at least for the moment. Indeed, he feared that difficulties might arise in the not too distant future as a result of inconsistencies between the autonomous powers prematurely granted to the territories and the distribution of powers between the Federation and the provinces to be determined by the NCAL. It was to be feared in particular that, for lack of timely coordination between these two operations, the future transfer of powers would be unnecessarily complicated. This explains why the Commissioner felt thoroughly dissatisfied with the obvious lack of collaboration between the Administering Powers and himself.

Admittedly, as he reported to the Secretary-General and the General Assembly, he had been "consulted on several occasions on this subject throughout the months of January and February, though in general terms, but on 1 March, while in London for the first talks on monetary questions, he was shown a copy of the Draft Transitional Powers Proclamation No. 219, which was submitted to the Administrative Council in Tripoli and published on 5 March. He remarked that little time had been left for him to study the text, but repeated his wish that it should take account of the four matters [already] mentioned." [22]

Upon reflection, he decided that the matter was sufficiently serious to justify his lodging a complaint with the British Resident in Tripoli and the French Resident in Sabhah, though it was unlikely that they were personally responsible. In point of fact, by this time the Commissioner had established

21. *Second Annual Report of the United Nations Commissioner in Libya,* para. 43.
22. Ibid., para. 44.

mutual confidence with the two Residents; but both were obliged to act in accordance with their instructions. More than likely, the Foreign Office and the Quai d'Orsay feared that, in distributing powers between the Federation and provinces, the NCAL would attribute less influence to the latter than the United Kingdom and France wished. Consulting the troublesome Commissioner on the actual text of the British Proclamation and the French Decision would have taken time, and might have allowed the NCAL to forestall the issuance of the two documents.

In order not to undermine the local authority of the two Residents, the Commissioner decided not to communicate his letters to the Council for Libya. On the other hand, he could not but publish them six months later as Annexes VIII and IX to his second annual report.

The letter to the British Resident in Tripolitania, dated 10 April 1951, after having recalled the course of the consultations, noted that:

> On 2 March I [the Commissioner] therefore presented to the Foreign Office a few preliminary observations on the draft under reservation that upon my return to Tripoli I would study it in more detail and forward my definite comments at a later date. I then also observed that the co-operation of His Majesty's Government with me in this matter had not been as close as I had expected. Indeed, the resolution of 21 November 1949 [289 (IV)] and my earlier experience of such consultations indicated both the need for and the possibility of a more timely and effective collaboration.[23]

The letter continued:

> while the normal process of federation consists in the agreement of a number of sovereign States to relinquish certain powers in favour of a federal government, the stipulation of resolution 289 (IV) concerning "an independent and sovereign State" presumed eventual Libyan sovereignty without requiring a sovereign act of accession or federation by the territories. The same resolution established the organ competent to constitute that State, while the resolution of 17 November 1950 further enabled that organ, s.c., the Libyan National Assembly, to establish a provisional government of Libya competent to receive powers from the British and French administrative authorities. It seemed to me therefore that the transfer of powers would be made to the Provisional Libyan Government which would then transfer to regional authorities such powers as might be prescribed by the Constitution. Paragraph 3 (c) of the later resolution, when interpreted in the light of the earlier resolution,

23. Ibid., Annex VIII, pp. 83–85.

does not, I believe, exclude intermediate transfers of powers, but it may well be argued that the most straightforward interpretation of its wording indicated an instruction to transfer powers exclusively to the Provisional Libyan Government. Indeed if circumstances had been different, I should have maintained this view.[24]

Having recalled the position he had taken at the beginning of 1950 on problems of constitutional development, the Commissioner went on to say:

I am not convinced that Proclamation 219 in its present form will serve the purpose which His Majesty's Government attributed to it, namely the preparation of Tripolitanians for their rapidly approaching independence as a part of the federal State.

In the first place, I notice that the proclamation does not provide that elections shall be held under the auspices of the Council of Regency. In Cyrenaica elections were foreseen in the local constitution which itself evolved from the Transitional Powers Proclamation of 16 September 1949; in Tripolitania, quite properly, no constitution has been enacted, but it would have seemed to me both legitimate and constructive to empower the Council of Regency to hold elections for a legislative Council.

You will recall that since the early stages of our discussions on constitutional development in Tripolitania, I have consistently advised the holding of elections before the establishment of a governmental body, whether the latter was called Executive Council or Council of Regency. You agreed, I believe, with the desirability of such a procedure but insisted that because much time had been lost and because the interval before independence was thus even shorter than had once been foreseen, it was necessary to establish a local administration without further delay; since it would moreover take up to four months to prepare and hold elections, the procedure of elections could not be honoured. I agreed reluctantly, because the arguments seemed valid, but advised at the same time that it should be clearly within the competence of the local administrations to hold elections as soon as possible. I held and still hold that the political situation in Tripolitania could be considerably clarified and most of the present internal disputes brought to an end by the normal process of elections. Yet the Proclamation, although it refers both in its preamble and in one of its operative paragraphs to the establishment at some future time of a democratic, representative and permanent government in Tripolitania, does not specifically confer powers upon the new Council of Regency to hold elections.

24. Ibid.

In these circumstances, I am surprised that the wishes of the National Assembly were not more carefully followed in the matter of establishing the Government of Tripolitania. They were, in effect, that the Amir of Cyrenaica should select the members after consulting with such organizations and persons as he might choose and should then request the Administering Powers to enable such persons to "receive and exercise their powers." I am not satisfied that His Highness was in fact allowed full liberty of selection and I am inclined to doubt whether the powers of appointment and dismissal of the President and the members of the Council of Regency given to the British Resident in article 3, "in full consultation with His Highness and with the advice of His Highness" are strictly compatible with the consideration given in the Preamble to the National Assembly resolution of 21 February 1951.[25]

Finally, after having made some critical remarks about the limitation set by the Proclamation to the value of the new system as an instructional exercise in administrative responsibility, the Commissioner ended by respectfully suggesting

> that it might be appropriate to envisage a revision in the sense of liberalization of Proclamation 219 in a not too distant future and in any case as soon as the National Assembly's decision regarding the distribution of powers and the plan for the transfer of powers to the Provisional Government will have clarified the overall picture of constitutional development.[26]

The letter to the French Resident in the Fezzan was sent eight days later, on 18 April 1951. Since many of the general comments on the British Proclamation also applied to French Decision No. 5, the Commissioner sent a copy of his letter of 10 April to the French Resident, and vice versa. By the same token, he hoped to facilitate coordination of policies between the two Administering Powers on the spot; such coordination was still deficient while becoming more and more urgent as the time for planning the progressive transfer of powers to the Provisional Libyan Government approached.

After an introduction along these lines, the letter to the French Resident proceeded:

> The first [comment] concerns the way in which the new Government of the Fezzan has been established. The resolution adopted by the Libyan National Assembly on 21 February 1951 provides for the necessity of

25. Ibid.
26. Ibid.

establishing a local provisional government in each of the three territories and contains *inter alia* the following paragraphs:

"(begs His Majesty) after consultation with the organizations and personalities he himself may choose, to be gracious enough to select suitable persons for this purpose,

"and to request the Administering Powers in Tripolitania and the Fezzan to enable those persons to receive and exercise their powers as a preliminary measure towards the establishment of the federal Libyan State by the appointed date, in accordance with the resolution of the United Nations."

It is to be noted that reference is made in the preamble of Decision No. 5 to the National Assembly resolution. It is, moreover, a fact that Omar Bey Seif El Nasr went to Benghazi, on behalf of his brother, to confer with the Amir on the subject of the establishment of the Fezzanese Government. Nevertheless, it is my impression that neither Decision No. 5 nor Ahmed Bey Seif El Nasr's Decree No. 4 are in full accordance with the resolution of the Libyan National Assembly. Decree No. 4, signed by the Chief of Territory, indicates that it was Ahmed Bey Seif El Nasr himself who appointed the members of his Government; no mention is made of any kind of consultation with the Amir. Thus Decree No. 4 gives the impression that Ahmed Bey Seif El Nasr took the place of the Amir in the selection and appointment of the Ministers, a function which the National Assembly had recognized as the prerogative of the Amir. I would have thought that the Chief of Territory should have consulted the "Consultative Assembly composed of elected representatives of the *Jemaas* and the councils of nomad tribes" which was established by Decision No. 3 of 12 February 1950 and which forms part of the "transitional régime for the Fezzan."

I know that it is difficult to convene the Consultative Assembly, owing to the long distances between the different populated areas of the Fezzan and the paucity of local means of transport. I would have thought, however, that an occasion of such significance as the establishment, for the first time in history of the territory, of a local government would have fully justified a special convocation of the Assembly. The annual report on the administration of the Fezzan, dated 13 September 1950, which the French Government submitted to the last session of the United Nations General Assembly, emphasizes, on page 20, that one of the purposes of the Assembly of *Jemaas* is to supervise the activities of the *mudirs*. That is an essential democratic element of the constitutional development of the Fezzan and it seems to me that when it was a matter of selecting the members of the local government—that is to say, the *mudirs* of the highest rank—it would have been both wise and in keeping with the intention of the French Government to give the Assembly of *Jemaas* an opportunity to give their advice on the choice of the persons to be entrusted with the management of the local affairs of the Territory. Such a procedure would have been more in keeping with the spirit of the National Assembly's resolution of 21 February 1951.[27]

The Commissioner continued:

With regard to the representative system which has been operating in the Fezzan since February 1950, I wonder whether the time has not come to reorganize it on the lines of the electoral law promulgated in Cyrenaica on 5 April 1950, at the same time retaining the traditional character it has possessed from time immemorial. The application of that law in June of this year has furnished ample proof of the practical possibility of holding duly organized elections, with the participation of he nomad tribes, for the purpose of forming a representative Assembly on a democratic basis. Without going into details, for the moment, of the mechanism of that law, I would like to point out that the French Administration in the Fezzan might with advantage, perhaps, take it as an example in instituting an electoral reform which seems to me all the more desirable in that the whole constitutional development of Libya points to the necessity of organizing elections in the near future both for a federal parliament and for local assemblies.[28]

The letter ended with the following suggestions:

To sum up, the constitutional problem in Libya, as it develops for the whole of the country and as it will shortly affect the Fezzan in particular, makes it desirable, in my opinion, that the present transitional régime should be re-examined, particularly with regard to the powers and the method of election of the "Assembly of the *Jemaas* and the councils of the nomad tribes." It seems to me equally desirable that new elections for that Assembly should be considered, so that the Fezzanese population may have an opportunity to give their views on the election of Ministers to form the local government.[29]

27. Ibid., Annex IX, pp. 85–87. The English translation of the quotation from the National Assembly resolution of 21 February was made for internal purposes by the language staff of the United Nations Mission in Libya, and therefore differs slightly from the Stewart-Jackson version quoted on pp. 730–31.

28. Ibid.

29. Ibid.

In short, by the time Proclamation No. 219 in Tripolitania and Decision No. 5 in the Fezzan had been promulgated, the administrative situation in Libya looked more like an exercise in decentralization than the realization of the General Assembly's wish to establish a United Libya. It was indeed high time to start planning Operation Transfer at the federal level.

PART 4. THE COORDINATION COMMITTEE

Experience shows that the transfer of powers from one State to another is never a simple operation, whether or not the parties concerned have equal or unequal administrative capacity and approximately equal actual or potential resources. In the case of Libya, on the one side were two highly organized administrations; on the other, an administration still to be created in a country that as yet had never known one run and staffed by its own people. To complicate matters even more, powers were to be transferred to the Federal Government on two levels: (a) by the United Kingdom and France; and (b) by the provinces, especially Cyrenaica, in respect of part of the powers already received by them. The second transfer might have been avoided had it been feasible to coordinate with the policies of the Administering Powers and those of the political leaders in the three territories, at an early stage, the distribution of powers to be decided by the NCAL. Such simplification, however desirable in itself, had clearly proved to be impracticable, if only for political reasons, both internal and external. To cap all, seven different administrations would be involved in the final exercise: two British; one French; three provincial; and one federal.

When, in the autumn of 1950, at the time of drafting his first annual report, the Commissioner had first announced his intention of establishing a standing Coordination Committee, he had been sufficiently well aware of the complications ahead to ask the Secretary-General to appoint a second legal adviser for the Mission.[30] Looking back, however, he must admit that he underrated the difficulties of an administrative, budgetary, economic, and monetary nature that would have to be straightened out before the first powers could be transferred.

30. The adviser made available was Marc Schreiber, a member of the Office of Legal Affairs at United Nations Headquarters. Schreiber, a Belgian, received his degree of Doctor at Law specializing in constitutional law at the University of Brussels. He practiced law in Belgium, served with the Belgian Government-in-Exile in London, was seconded to the Secretariat of the Preparatory Commission for the United Nations in 1945, and from 1946 on was a member of the Office of Legal Affairs, becoming Deputy-Director of the General Legal Division in 1953. In 1966 he was appointed Director of the Division of Human Rights.

On his return to Tripoli from the Fifth Session of the General Assembly, the Commissioner found that an immediate decision had to be taken on a problem of tactics also. At what stage was the Council for Libya to be consulted on the matter?

The terms of reference for this particular area of the Commissioner's duties had been laid down in subparagraphs 3 (c) and (d) of General Assembly Resolution 387 (V). Aided and guided by the advice of the members of the Council for Libya, and in cooperation with the Administering Powers, he was to proceed immediately to draw up a program for the progressive transfer of powers to the Provisional Libyan Government in a manner ensuring that by 1 January 1952 all powers would have been transferred to the duly constituted Libyan Government. In its definition of purpose this instruction was clear enough; but as regards implementation it could be interpreted in different ways. Literally, it could be read as meaning that from the outset of the drafting process the Council should be asked for aid and guidance in preparing the program. Quite obviously such a course would have entailed an extremely complicated procedure, even had the Council been the most reasonable body ever to advise a commissioner. But, adding a grain of common sense, the Resolution could also be interpreted as instructing the Commissioner to request the Council's advice on a properly elaborated program while keeping it fully informed about progress during the preparatory stage. Taking into account the Council's habit of rarely seeing things unanimously, to put it mildly, the intricate character of the problem of transfer, and the short time in which it had to be unraveled, the Commissioner elected to rely upon the second interpretation, fully realizing that he would be criticized for so doing. He knew from experience that the criticism of certain Council members, unfair and demagogic as it was at times, could be exasperating. But a long international career teaches one the wisdom of staying, within the limits of human endurance, *au-dessus de la mêlée,* as long as one's conscience is clear about serving the cause in hand to the best of one's ability.

The General Assembly's reaction to his first annual report had, moreover, strengthened his belief that a man in the position in which it had put him could get away with a good deal of independent initiative and unconventional action by giving his critics full opportunity of expressing their feelings to their hearts' content, and by answering them honestly and reasonably without beating about the bush. Hence the long extracts from Council debates in his annual reports and the numerous footnotes on controversial points therein.

As neither the General Assembly nor the Council for Libya had expressed any criticism of or even doubt about the Commissioner's proposal for setting up a Coordination Committee, he proceeded to discuss its composition and broad terms of reference with the Administering Powers through an oral exchange of views followed by an exchange of letters. Subsequently, he paid brief visits to Benghazi, Cairo, London, Paris, Rome, and Sabhah to settle matters of practical detail.[31]

The result was agreement that the Coordination Committee should meet in Tripoli on 6 February 1951. It would be composed of the British Chief Administrator of Tripolitania, the British Resident in Cyrenaica, the French Resident in the Fezzan, the Prime Minister of Cyrenaica, and a representative of the Chief of Territory of the Fezzan. Since there was no indigenous administration in Tripolitania, the Chief Administrator of that territory was asked by the Commissioner to appoint a Libyan to represent it on the Committee. Finally, the legal adviser to the British Administration on transfer of powers was also to be a member of the Committee, as was the Commissioner himself.

On 20 January 1951, the Commissioner announced to the Council the setting up and the composition of the Committee. He furthermore expressed the opinion that:

> he did not believe it desirable or feasible to draft the precise terms of reference for the Co-ordination Committee at this time. Broadly speaking, the Committee should work out a plan which would provide for the progressive transfer of powers to the provisional government of Libya of those functions now carried out by the governments of the United Kingdom, France and the Cyrenaican Administration which the Libyan National Assembly has by that time decided, or appears likely to decide, should be exercised by the future Libyan government. The plan should include recommendations on such matters as the organization of the administration, its required civil service establishment, including conditions of service, budgetary requirements, relationship to local authorities and related matters. The Committee should meet regularly in Tripoli and in other places in Libya as frequently and for as long as may be required.
>
> The Commissioner also informed the governments and authorities concerned that in accordance with the provisions of the General Assembly resolutions, he would ask the advice of the Council for Libya on the recommendations which the Coordination Committee will [*sic*] develop before recommending them to the provisional Libyan government.

31. To his regret, he was unable, because of lack of time, to visit Karachi. Fortunately, during the Fifth Session of the General Assembly, there had been several opportunities to discuss the Libyan situation with the Head of the Pakistani delegation and Minister of Foreign Affairs, Sir Zafrullah Khan.

> The Commissioner believed that it would be preferable that he ask the advice of the Council on specific plans and programmes rather than attempting to initiate discussion to formulate such plans and programmes in the Council in the first instance, particularly in view of the many operational and technical aspects of the questions which will [*sic*] be involved.[32]

It will be noted that, at variance with the Commissioner's original intentions, as expressed in paragraph 258 of his first annual report, the broad outline of the Committee's task no longer included economic or currency questions. Indeed, the Coordination Committee's burden appeared heavy enough as it was; moreover, the other two categories of problem required a different type of expert. In view of this division of labor, the Commissioner, through the intermediary of the Secretary-General, requested the International Monetary Fund (IMF) to assist by providing him with experts to make recommendations regarding the establishment of a unified Libyan currency.[33] The IMF assigned two of its staff for this purpose. Besides the United Kingdom and France, the Commissioner also invited the governments of countries with direct monetary, economic, or other interests in Libya—including Egypt, Italy, and the United States—to appoint experts who could be consulted on these questions. The work of this group has been described in Part 2 of Chapter 9 of this study. It went without saying that the tasks of the two bodies were closely interconnected and that in the end their recommendations had to be integrated as components of a single overall program for consideration by the Libyan Provisional Government.

On 9 and 12 February the Commissioner's informative memorandum on the Coordination Committee was critically examined by the Council at open meetings. The statements made by the members for Egypt, Pakistan, Tripolitania, and even by the representative of the minorities, all amounted to one long complaint that the Council had been confronted with a fait accompli. The members for France, the United Kingdom, and the United States defended the Commissioner's plan as a normal and logical program which, in their opinion, should be carried out. The remaining members unfortunately kept silent—unfortunately, because the listeners in the public gallery got the impression that they were watching a manifestation of East-

32. United Nations Doc. A/AC.32/COUNCIL/R.106, 20 January 1951, pp. 2–3. Mimeographed.

33. See Chapter 9, pp. 687 and 702 and fn. 20 and 31. The Foreign Office was not too pleased about this appeal for advice to IMF. They apparently would have preferred to handle the matter unilaterally through the Treasury and the Bank of England. The Commissioner, on the other hand, totally lacking in technical knowledge of currency matters, felt the need for disinterested expert advice.

West antagonism. In fact, the basic issue at stake once more consisted in a conflict of opposing views about the respective duties of the Commissioner and the Council, complicated by a deep-seated suspicion, on the Middle Eastern side, of the Administering Powers' intentions. Admittedly, there were grounds for these suspicions; the Bevin-Sforza plan still rankled. The fact that one of the Commissioner's duties was to keep the balance between these two Powers and their detractors was little appreciated by either side. In the eyes of the Commissioner's constant critics in particular, things could not be right as long as he could not be put in the wrong. A curious instance of that mentality was brought out in an intervention by the member for Egypt. Recalling that the coordination program was to be drawn up by the Commissioner "aided and guided by the advice . . . of the Council for Libya," Selim Bey expressed the view that the Commissioner

> was to collect the necessary information from the Administering Powers, draw up a plan and submit it to the Council for advice, and finally carry out, in co-operation with the Administering Powers, a programme that would be the result of the teamwork of those three bodies—the Commissioner, the Council and the Administrations." [34]

The Commissioner asked whether this was not precisely what he was proposing. His question went unanswered. Under such conditions, the debate could clearly lead to no conclusion. No motion was tabled, and the Chairman declared the meeting closed.

Looking back, the opening meeting of the Coordination Committee on 6 February is of comparable importance in the history of Libya's emancipation to the first meeting of the Committee of Twenty-One on 27 July 1950. On the earlier occasion the Libyan people started organizing their political unity. Now, the Administering Powers and the provinces, recognizing that, thanks to the NCAL, unity and independence were in the offing, actually started organizing the framework of the State to be born.

It was a remarkable day for another reason also. The two British Residents met their French counterpart for the first time. For the few thousand Fezzanese in Tripoli in particular, French participation in this meeting was an important indication that their wish to become an integral part of the future union was to be realized.

It was a sober and businesslike meeting. The Commissioner provisionally took the Chair to deliver a factual statement recalling the circumstances in

34. Summary Records of 69th and 70th Meetings, United Nations Docs. A/AC.32/COUNCIL/SR.69, 11 February 1951, pp. 11–12, and A/AC.32/COUNCIL/SR.70, 12 February 1951, p. 15. Mimeographed.

which the Committee had come into being, and the general nature of the task it would be called upon to fulfill. To propose a detailed agenda would have been premature, but suggestions regarding the internal organization and the conduct of the Committee's business were clearly called for, to avoid loss of time. As a result it was unanimously decided to take a decision on the chairmanship at the next meeting, to appoint the Deputy Principal Secretary of the United Nations Mission, Alberto Gonzales-Fernandez, Secretary of the Committee, and to make its records and documents confidential. The next forty-eight hours were actively spent in private talks, to enable a considerable number of formal decisions to be taken at the second and last of the first round of meetings without a dissenting voice being raised. Thus it was resolved that the Commissioner or one of his deputies should be permanent Chairman of the Committee. This proved to be a particularly helpful arrangement as it permitted him or the Principal Secretary of the Mission to act as stimulator—an important function in view of the mass of work that had to be got through in a relatively short time—and as a go-between at the service of all parties concerned.

It was also proposed, against the Commissioner's advice, to communicate no decisions to the Council for Libya until the plan for the transfer of powers had been finally agreed upon and presented to the Commissioner. This proposal was as significant as it was unwise. The Commissioner could not leave the Council in the dark for months at a time about what was going on in so important a field. The same consideration applied to the NCAL, and later also to the Provisional Libyan Government. It was therefore finally agreed that no communication would be made to the Council without the Committee's consent. In point of fact, the Commissioner made a brief oral statement to the Council in April, and in July submitted for its information three papers by way of progress reports, which gave rise to a lively discussion, an account of which will be given later. In April also the Commissioner, in consultation with the Administering Powers and acting in his capacity as Chairman, found it necessary to invite representatives of both the Libyan Provisional Government and the NCAL to participate in the Committee's work. This not only appreciably improved contacts between all parties concerned; it also had the psychological and political advantage of increasing Libyan influence in the Committee, and, consequently, of enhancing the prestige of the two Libyan bodies in the eyes of the people. It was equally desirable in view of the fact that the opposition elements in Tripolitania were watching all that was going on with an eagle's eye. It is now clear that the principal advantage of this arrangement was that it made the Libyan members familiar with the Committee's work, thus making possible maximum agreement with them, and so ultimately facilitating the acceptance of the Committee's recommendations by the Provisional Government.

An important decision taken at the Committee's second meeting was the appointment of an Establishment Committee with two sub-committees, one for financial and the other for legal matters. Its main task was to draw up an establishment and departmental organization, and a budget for the federal government. It was made up of one representative from each of the Administering Powers and three Libyan representatives, one from each territory. The two sub-committees consisted of three members each, respectively British, French, and Libyan. However, it was understood that each of the three bodies was free to co-opt any person who could, by his technical advice, assist it. In practice this meant that any expert, whether British or French or from the United Nations—and, as events proved, even Libyans because of their knowledge of local affairs—could be called on for help. As to working methods, the Establishment Committee itself was left a large measure of freedom and flexibility.

Thanks to the United Nations aircraft, the Committee could be convened at short notice. The facts that its members and those of the sub-committees were interchangeable and that the United Nations Mission provided a common secretariat, professional and clerical, and, last but not least, meeting-room facilities at the Mission's headquarters, all made for a high degree of efficiency. Looking back, it is astonishing to see how much was accomplished in barely six months (March to August). This is particularly noteworthy as the Establishment Committee was not able to start its main work until the NCAL had determined what were to be the responsibilities of the federal government. As related in Chapter 7, Part 2, Section A, this proved less simple than it had looked originally. So, in order not to lose valuable time, the Coordination Committee instructed its working bodies to prepare plans for transferring powers in respect of the following matters, which were almost certain to come in whole or in part within federal competence:

1. Communications (postal, telegraph and telephone services, railways, ports and lights, aviation and roads);
2. Public health regulations in ports and airfields, quarantine arrangements, and other related matters;
3. A unified customs tariff and a customs law governing imports and exports;
4. A civil service law and draft service contracts requiring the unification, for federal purposes, of the civil service legislation applicable in each territory; and
5. A civil service pension and provident fund.

The provincial administrations were requested to supply the secretariat of the Committee with the relevant documentation, including budgetary information, on each of these subjects. Finally, the Financial Sub-Committee was instructed to examine financial implications in each of the five sectors, and to study methods by which the federal government could be financed in the absence of any federal revenue. This last task was a tall order for which, if taken literally, there was no solution. It will be remembered that it had caused many headaches in the Committee of Eighteen and the Working Group. It did so again in the Coordination Committee.

At the end of its second meeting, the Coordination Committee decided to hold its next session in Benghazi, at a date to be fixed by the Chairman as soon as the NCAL had taken a decision on the responsibilities of the federal government.

From the foregoing general account, one thing emerges with particular clarity: the change in the general approach of the Administering Powers as compared to their attitude one year earlier. They had gradually come to realize that, despite their original skepticism, Libya was in fact going to become an independent State. This did not mean, however, that they had changed their minds about the degree of looseness they wished to see in the forthcoming federation. On the contrary; not only had this policy recently been given tangible expression in the formation of the Tripolitanian and Fezzanese "governments," it was also demonstrated by the attitude adopted, by the United Kingdom in particular, toward the problem of how the federal Libyan Government was to be financed. In this connection it must be appreciated that, politics apart, considerations of a technical financial nature played a substantial part. These were orally explained to the Commissioner and his experts as early as January 1951, and subsequently confirmed in writing and repeated by statements in the Coordination Committee and its subsidiary organs.

Indeed, the United Kingdom Government had stated formally that the grants-in-aid made by it to the Government of Cyrenaica and to the British Administration in Tripolitania for the British financial year ending on 31 March 1952 were earmarked for specific purposes and could not be diverted to any other uses without the express authorization of Parliament in London. (Similar restrictions applied to the French grant-in-aid to the Fezzan.) To change this situation would have taken too long, especially as Parliament was then in recess. Moreover, had special authorization been sought, the transfer of powers might well have been substantially delayed. Other means of financing the Provisional Libyan Government therefore had to be found if it were to begin to receive powers by the middle of September. A suggestion by the Commissioner that Parliament be requested to provide funds for the dual purpose of covering both the expenditures of

Tripolitania and Cyrenaica and those of the federal government was turned down, even though the total amount involved would not have exceeded that already voted for the two territories individually.

As time went on, and the drafting of the Constitution progressed, the Administering Powers, particularly the United Kingdom Government, became more and more uneasy as they watched the tendency to increase the number of federal powers and hence to broaden the competence of the federal government. Not only was this development objectionable to them from a political point of view, but, as a British Treasury official remarked, it was only to be feared that with each additional federal power, federal expenditures would rise and with them the bill for grant-in-aid which the British taxpayer would be expected to foot; in reply to which the Commissioner was in duty bound to point out that the right granted to the Libyan people by the United Nations to determine their own Constitution, including the form of government, must not be fettered by financial considerations. Any attempt to do so would undoubtedly provoke criticism at the next session of the General Assembly in view of paragraph 3 and subparagraphs 10 (a) and (b) of Resolution 289 (IV) and subparagraph 3 (c) of Resolution 387 (V). He was therefore obliged to resist a suggestion which reached him from London in the course of March to the effect that federal functions should be divided into two categories: "existing services" and "new services." Separate lists would be prepared for each category, and each list costed separately. As this would mean a great deal of work, an official would be seconded from the United Kingdom to undertake this particular task. As regards financial cover, it was further suggested that "existing services" be financed from appropriations less grants-in-aid; funds would, however, be made available immediately as an advance, pending legislative action by Parliament at Westminster. As regards "new services" —for instance the Ministry of Foreign Affairs or the federal Parliament— the federal government, it was suggested, would have to find its own means of financing them. Needless to say this suggestion, particularly in the form in which it was put forward, was unacceptable either to the Libyans or to their United Nations advisers. It looked too much like an attempt to bring political pressure to bear through financial devices. No similar proposals were made on the French side, and in the end the British did not insist.

At the same time, the Commissioner himself could not help feeling uneasy about staff costs and other financial implications of the growing list of federal powers.[35] Hence, he advised the Provisional Government to restrain

35. From the Libyan point of view, overstaffing would, of course, mean a large number of foreign specialists or experts employed by the Government, as a result of which Libyan civil servants would feel discriminated against and belittled. At the same

its tendency to seek the transfer of powers before it was properly equipped to exercise them. Its prestige would undoubtedly have suffered from a premature assumption of power. He also discouraged such plans as those for setting up an ambitious foreign service staffed by persons inexperienced in diplomacy, who already saw themselves at the head of Libyan diplomatic missions. But for the same reason he also opposed a British suggestion that all powers be transferred en bloc, at one and the same time. Obviously, from the point of view of British parliamentary procedure and Treasury accountancy, it was the easier course to follow, but seen from the Libyan angle, it was impracticable and unreasonable. Was it reasonable, the Commissioner asked his British interlocutor, to expect the Provisional Government, with its unavoidable inexperience in matters of administration and its initial lack of organization and trained staff, to assume simultaneously all the functions of government? He believed that the answer to this question could not be in doubt, even if a carefully prepared organizational plan were elaborated by the Coordination Committee in the few months left. He also believed that, pending the deliberations of that Committee and the NCAL's decisions on the distribution of powers, it would be premature to suggest when and how powers might be transferred. For all these reasons, he thought that it would be more logical to plan for a series of transfers geared to the ability and readiness of the Provisional Government to accept authority and effectively exercise it. It was not for nothing that Resolution 387 (V) recommended a "progressive" transfer of powers, in order to enable the Provisional Government to set up, piece by piece, the administrative machinery it would need to carry out its future duties, machinery of which, after independence, the "duly constituted Libyan Government" would stand in even greater need. To assist the Administering Powers, the Commissioner, and the Libyan Government in this vast preparatory task was the very raison d'être of the Coordination Committee, and the time available for carrying it out was only too short.

The responsible authorities in London slowly came around to this idea of a phased transfer of powers.

PART 5. SETTING UP THE MACHINERY

The Establishment Committee met on the date fixed by its parent body, 28 February, in a mood that at first did not strike the United Nations Mission staff as very promising. The French member, very courteously,

---

time, foreign grants-in-aid out of proportion to the Federal Government's own revenue would debase its authority and demean its independence.

proposed that his British colleague be elected Chairman; whereupon the latter, contrary to the secretariat's advice that one French and one Libyan candidate be nominated, proposed two of his fellow-countrymen as chairmen of the sub-committees. Quite understandably, the French considered this rank bad manners, while the Libyans, suspicious of British intentions, feared some sort of double-crossing. The Commissioner thought it rather to be the stirrings of an obsolete colonial tradition. An informal chat between the Commissioner and the British Resident was sufficient to redress the situation in good time, but an unfortunate impression lingered.

Worse was a tendency which soon became noticeable, particularly among the British members, to fall behind schedule in carrying out the duties assigned to the Committee. Admittedly, excuses could be found for this lack of zeal. In March, the NCAL was still far from a decision on the distribution of powers, a decision required, at least in provisional form, before the Committee could get down to its main task of planning the framework for the federal administration, at the same time making suggestions for a staff establishment and a draft budget. In the case of their secondary duties, the European members had another excuse for sluggishness in that the provincial administrations were slow in furnishing the necessary documentation. However, some documentation was available on ports and lights, quarantine, aviation, and roads. The obvious course would have been to study this material thoroughly, call for what was still lacking, and after its submission draw up a set of conclusions. Instead, the British and French members, without properly studying the documentation available, without discussing it with, or even consulting, their Libyan colleagues, reached a series of conclusions mainly slanted in the direction of provincial autonomy except for a self-evident proposition that provincial policies in matters of trunk roads linking the three territories be coordinated. They then proposed to adjourn pending the submission of further information. The most objectionable feature of this approach was the tendency to take policy decisions. The terms of reference of the Establishment Committee did not empower it to determine which services should be federal or local, or how far federal supervision should go. Its duty was to produce a general picture of the various services, and to suggest objectively the cheapest and most effective way of fitting them into a federal administrative system. The Commissioner had therefore to intervene once more, still informally, but this time a little more forcefully, presenting at the same time a program of work that could usefully have been undertaken. His remonstrations were of no avail. On 9 April the Establishment Committee proposed that it suspend its work until it received a final list of powers from the Committee of Eighteen. To complete the disorder, two members, one Libyan and one

British, were away at one of the Meetings of Experts on Libyan financial, monetary, and development problems in Geneva (Chapter 9, Part 2), and others intended to go to Benghazi to consult the King. In fact it happened more and more frequently that work came to a standstill because of lack of time and staff caused by conflicting timetables and priorities.

Other means had therefore to be found of keeping the Committee at the conference table. So in early April the Commissioner talked the situation over with the President of the NCAL, asking him whether a copy of the provisional and tentative list of federal powers prepared by the Working Group, then under discussion in the Committee of Eighteen, could be made available to the Establishment Committee to help it in its work. For the reasons given in Chapter 7, Part 2, Section A, this list was far from final; nevertheless, it was sufficiently advanced to enable a tentative assessment of its administrative and budgetary implications to be made. On the same occasion, the Commissioner suggested to the President that final decisions regarding the distribution of powers between the federal government and the provincial administrations be put off until the NCAL itself had had an opportunity of studying the budgetary consequences of such measures. (It was also at this time that, as mentioned on page 749, he invited the Provisional Government and the NCAL to be represented on the Coordination Committee. Both accepted, though not without having first obtained the agreement of the King, who had been forewarned by the Commissioner.)

By the middle of May, the Committee of Eighteen had produced a second draft list of powers still incomplete, but already much more precise. In conformity with the Commissioner's request, this list had not been forwarded to the NCAL for final decision. In particular, seven items dealing with financial matters were still in suspense pending advice from United Nations experts (pp. 525–27).

Now the boot was on the other foot. The Coordination Committee was no longer waiting for the NCAL—just the opposite; the Committee no longer had any excuse to wait and see. From this moment, the Establishment Committee became a much more effective tool, spurred on in particular by its Financial Sub-Committee, whose members had a special interest in finding out, in exact monetary terms, the total cost of the future federal government.

Meanwhile, the British authorities in Tripoli made no secret of their dislike of the way the distribution of powers was developing. In their eyes, too much power was being given to the federal government and not enough to the provincial administrations. Attempts were therefore made privately to persuade leading members of the NCAL to reverse this tendency, though without much success. Hence the delaying tactics in the Establishment

Committee which had irritated the Mission staff. The British authorities also made it known to the Commissioner that they did not favor the idea of Libyan ministers sitting jointly with members of the Establishment Committee to study the question of federal powers; they would have preferred separate studies by each side, followed by negotiations. The Commissioner took the opposite view, not only in the interests of time, but also in order from the outset to lay the foundations for agreed settlements on the staffing and costing of future government departments and services. Such settlements, he believed, would later provide a useful basis for determining the grants-in-aid to which in the end the United Kingdom and France would have to commit themselves.

Working on this hypothesis the Mission staff, several of the experts and key members of the Financial Sub-Committee, notably the British Financial Adviser to the Provisional Libyan Government, working at great speed, produced most of the key recommendations and estimates. This task formed an essential part of the planning described in Part 2 of Chapter 9.

This account would be too long and overburdened by administrative details were the author to give a complete list of all the recommendations made by the Coordination Committee in connection with the transfer of powers.[36] To keep this chapter within bounds, therefore, the reader is referred to Chapters II and III of the Commissioner's second annual report and Annexes XI–XXI thereto, as well as to the Supplementary Report to his second annual report, Chapter I and Annexes II–VII and IX thereto.

However, the story of Libya's independence would be incomplete without a narrative account of the principal features of the closing stages, and in a few instances paragraphs from the two reports are quoted or paraphrased in what follows.

The month of August 1951 proved to be eventful, critical, and decisive. From May to August a working group of the Establishment Committee (set up under the co-option procedure mentioned on page 750), with the assistance of the Mission secretariat, had been preparing preliminary recommendations on the basis of the list of powers transmitted by the NCAL to the Commissioner on 17 May. The Mission staff, in particular, had been

36. On 31 August, the Coordination Committee submitted to the Provisional Libyan Government no less than thirty-seven recommendations regarding the initial organization and the ordinary budget for the period 1 September 1951 to 31 December 1952, accompanied by eight appendixes each containing the complete staff establishment and itemized budget for seven ministries, as well as a summary thereof. On the same date the Committee submitted the recommended texts of a civil service law, a provident fund law, and a form of contract for specialists in Libyan Government service. See *Second Annual Report of the United Nations Commissioner in Libya*, Annex XII, Sections 7 and 8, pp. 96–124.

doing a great deal of detailed preparatory work, in constant consultation with members of the working group of the Establishment Committee on the one side and members of the Provisional Government on the other. It was at this stage that the first plans were drawn up for the administrative organization of the federal government, together with an estimate of the funds and staff required for each of the federal ministries. On the basis of the provisional list of federal powers, it was assumed that the federal government would number six ministers, of whom four would hold one office each —Finance, Health, Communications, and Defense—and two would hold two portfolios each: the Prime Minister's Office and Education; and Foreign Affairs and Justice. Alternatively, it was suggested that for economy's sake Health and Education might be combined to form a single ministry, and the Prime Minister's Office fused with Defense or Foreign Affairs, at least for the first few years. Suggestions were also made for staffing on a very economical scale, and for grading, salary scales, and representation and other allowances. Other sections of the draft plan dealt with office space and equipment, official cars, travel, and subsistence rates. Full account was taken of the fact that the budgets of all three provinces were deeply in deficit, a total of £1,700,000, 30 percent of the total budgets, being covered by grants from the Administering Powers.

As already mentioned, twelve months earlier Libyans had generally disbelieved these figures, or had even suspected the British and French authorities of having created deficits artificially in order to justify indefinite prolongation of the occupation. Now, thanks to the United Nations experts, these doubts had been removed, and the Provisional Government was cooperating to the best of its ability in trying to make savings wherever possible. One suggestion to this end, prompted by the lack of experienced Libyan administrators, was to combine federal ministerships with the top executive post in a provincial administration. On the same grounds, the Commissioner shared the reluctance of the Administering Powers to make budgetary provision for a federal army, a plan especially and not understandably cherished by Omar Shenib, the Minister of Defense. He and his friends felt this would be in the best traditions of the Libyan Arab Force that had fought in World War II alongside the Allied Armies, under its own flag, helping to liberate the homeland from the Italian colonial rulers and their German allies (p. 39). However, a conservative estimate showed that the initial cost of a simple police striking force, or mobile constabulary of one thousand men, all ranks included, would be £360,000. At the same time, it was difficult to deny that in a country as large as Libya, where tribal blood feuds still broke out occasionally, quite apart from the question of defense against a foreign invader and the inescapable factor of prestige, the federal government would need a police force of its own. The first provisional estimate of federal expenditures (without a police force) gave a total for all ministries of £208,150. This meant that, counting on the continuation of the annual £35,000 revenue from communications services, an amount of £122,800 would be required each year over and above available revenues. In addition, in the first year £50,350 would be required in respect of nonrecurrent expenditure required for the initial installations of the new central government.

At the end of June, the Commissioner transmitted the first version of the plan to the Prime Minister for comment, thus fulfilling an undertaking made some time earlier that he would not submit any proposal concerning the budget and organization of the federal government to the Coordination Committee without first showing it to the Libyan Cabinet.

Within a week, the Commissioner received the Provisional Government's comments, which revealed a number of differences of opinion and appreciation. Leaving salary scales and similar problems aside, he found that the Provisional Government objected to the suggested combination of the Prime Minister's Office with other portfolios. It was also against the proposal to give federal ministers additional functions as heads of provincial administrations, for fear that such cumulation of office might create conflicts of interests. The Commissioner and staff had reluctantly gone along with such a suggestion in the first place, mainly in an effort to economize. Above all, the Libyans insisted on the creation of an army of limited size for the maintenance of internal security, and drew attention to the need for providing funds for a delegation of five or six members to represent Libya, after independence, at the Sixth Session of the General Assembly, to be held in the winter of 1951–52 in Paris. They finally suggested that the Civil List, which in the plan had been maintained at its existing level, might have to be reexamined. On the whole, these comments were reasonable enough, but as the British, French, and United Nations financial experts did not fail to point out, they all tended to increase the already very considerable deficit. A suggestion made by the Committee of Eighteen that taxes be increased had been advised against by the head of the United Nations technical assistance team on economic grounds.

It was in these circumstances that a fortnight later the Establishment Committee met to consider both the Commissioner's draft plan and the Prime Minister's comments thereon. All that need be said here of these proceedings is that when, on 24 July, the Coordination Committee met for the third time at the Commissioner's office, in the presence of the Federal Minister of Finance representing the Libyan Prime Minister, the Commissioner as Chairman was in a position to state that

Agreement had been reached on the majority of points but a divergence of views persisted with regard to the number of Ministers in the Federal Government and the distribution of portfolios, and the question whether the Federal Director of Education should be a Libyan or a non-Libyan. Those questions had been left to the Co-ordination Committee to decide, though the final decision would, of course, rest with the Provisional Libyan Government.

The question whether there should be a separate Ministry of Defence —to meet the wishes expressed by the Provisional Government—and the question of the Royal Civil List had been deferred because the necessary documentation was not available. Those questions would be discussed by the Establishment Committee as soon as the documentation was forthcoming.[37]

He further submitted a memorandum dealing with the organizational and legal aspects of the transfer of powers.[38]

This was a new aspect of the problem for the Coordination Committee. Since the document described four possible methods of transferring powers, and the representatives of the Administering Powers and the Provisional Libyan Government had to seek instructions, it would indeed have been premature to go further. On the Libyan side of the table there was an evident preference for transfer by one single proclamation at the earliest possible date, but after an exchange of views it was agreed that a gradual and progressive transfer would be more workable.

Another point on which the Chairman asked for the Committee's advice was the transfer of powers from the provincial governments to the central government. This lay outside the competence of the Administering Powers. Should it be left to the four interested parties, or should the Legal Sub-Committee be asked for help? It was finally agreed to ask that body to draft a formula for submission to the federal government and the provincial governments as a basis for discussion. When the Committee took up the timing proposed for the progressive transfer of different groups of powers, the discussion became quite lively, particularly in the case of such sensitive issues as immigration and emigration, so much so that the Chairman was obliged to remind members that the Committee was engaged only in a preliminary reading.

At the next meeting, held in the afternoon of the same day, the Chairman asked for opinions on the two main questions on which the Establishment

37. Coordination Committee, Summaries of Discussions, United Nations Doc. A/AC.32/CC/MIN.3, 24 July 1951, p. 2. Mimeographed.

38. United Nations Doc. A/AC.32/CC.5, 21 July 1951. Mimeographed.

Committee had been unable to reach agreement. The first was that of the number of ministers in the federal government and the distribution of portfolios between them. Originally, the Provisional Government had intended to recommend a Cabinet of six—the same as the NCAL had fixed for the Provisional Government itself, in agreement with the King (three from Tripolitania, two from Cyrenaica, and one from the Fezzan) (see p. 734). Now, apparently, there was a propensity toward increasing the number to seven so as to achieve equality between the two larger provinces. From the Fezzanese side came a warning that such a change would mean trouble. The Cyrenaican member of the Committee expressed his personal view that the matter should be left to the NCAL and the Provisional Government in consultation with the King. The same course, he felt, ought to be followed in the distribution of portfolios, which should be governed by political considerations and the competence of individual ministers. Unfortunately, the question also had a budgetary aspect. It was finally decided, on the Chairman's proposal, to transmit the Coordination Committee's recommendation in favor of six ministers to the Provisional Government, together with the final text of the budget document, which the Committee had not yet seen.

The second question on which the Establishment Committee had disagreed was of a very different nature. It had arisen as a result of the way in which the draft budgets of the individual ministries had been drawn up, involving a distinction between posts to be occupied by Libyans, and those (marked "S") reserved for "specialists," by which was meant "non-Libyan" experts, the latter epithet having been considered untactful. The budget of the Ministry of Health and Education provided for a federal director of education, a post which, it was proposed, should be filled by a specialist. The basic scale of pay being the same for the two categories, the difference of opinion was not influenced by financial considerations. It really was a matter of qualifications. There was general agreement that the director should be a highly qualified educationist of great experience, with Arabic as his mother tongue. The point at stake was whether the appointee could be found in Libya, or whether a national from another Arab country would have to be brought in. The matter had been referred to the Coordination Committee for a recommendation on the understanding that the final decision would lie with the federal government. To the Libyan members it was an issue of particular importance. Not only were they deeply conscious of the general backwardness of their people in areas other than religious education; they were also convinced that only a Libyan could conceive an educational program capable, during the years to come, of inspiring the younger generation with the sense of national unity, within the Arab world, that all Libyan patriots, whatever their province of origin and whatever their views on the form of the State, wanted to instil into their children.

None of the European members present challenged that concept; they simply doubted whether a candidate with the required qualifications could be found in Libya or among Libyan refugees educated abroad. After a long and very frank discussion, it was decided that the secretariat should be asked to formulate a new recommendation on the Director of Education to be considered by the Committee at its next meeting. As a result, there appeared in the draft budget for the Ministry of Health and Education two posts, one for a federal Director of Education, the second for a technical assistant. A footnote explained that "Either the Director or the Assistant Director will be a specialist." Thus the Government was given elbowroom for various choices.[39]

While all this preparatory work was going on, the Commissioner had also to pay attention to other fields. Not only did the NCAL's progress have to be closely watched; its relationship with the Coordination Committee had also to be kept in proper trim. The Government, on the other hand, began to feel frustrated, as it was under constant fire from the opposition on the ground that it was not yet exercising any real power, while at the same time, as a result of its participation in the Committee's work, it knew only too well why this was so. Similar criticisms also began to irk the NCAL.

Lastly, the Council for Libya, or at least several of its members, if not eager to be consulted on the transfer of powers, expected at least to be informed about it. As usual, the Council was divided. The British, French, Cyrenaican, and Fezzanese members knew all there was to know about the transfer puzzle; the others—not without reason, and inclined to criticize anyway—felt that they were being kept in the dark. The United States member, well informed from a variety of sources, was ready to mediate if necessary.

The Commissioner had constantly to think of what his position would be when he came to defend his final report against the attacks that were bound to be made on it at the Sixth Session of the General Assembly. In all the circumstances, he decided to give the Council precedence, and, as things turned out, this proved to be good tactics.

In the light of the prevailing state of affairs, it would have been premature to ask the Council for advice on a plan that was still in preparation. It seemed useful, however, to ask members of the Council for their individual reactions to the progress made so far, in order to find out whether in their opinion events were moving in the right direction. This was so much the more desirable inasmuch as, for reasons already given, preparations were running behind the timetable the Commissioner had announced to the

39. *Second Annual Report of the United Nations Commissioner in Libya,* Annex XII, Appendix VI, p. 111.

Council at its seventy-eighth meeting on 17 April. He had then said that he hoped the plan would be ready for the Council's consideration by the end of June or early in July. In the event, the Coordination Committee had reached only tentative conclusions by July. Still, those conclusions were sufficiently substantive to be communicated by way of information. The Commissioner therefore submitted three papers to the Council: the draft list of federal powers prepared by the Committee of Eighteen; the draft program for the transfer of powers, still under consideration by the Coordination Committee; and an informative summary of the tentative conclusions arrived at by the Committee regarding the administrative organization and budget of the federal Libyan government. Together these papers represented a fairly complete forecast of the probable—and as it turned out actual—outcome of the Committee's work.[40]

The first of these documents reproduced the list of powers transmitted to the Commissioner on 17 May 1951, and dealt with in Chapter 7, Part 2, Section A above. (The seven financial items on which no decision had been taken were still in abeyance when the list was submitted to the Council.)

The second document was the text of a memorandum containing a draft program for the transfer of powers, presented by the Commissioner to the Coordination Committee. It started off by summarizing the constitutional situation in each of the three provinces, and was based on the assumption that "In order to avoid a breach of continuity detrimental to the future of the Libyan state, no powers should be transferred in specific fields until after the Provisional Government has organized its services in a sufficiently adequate manner and has available the necessary financial resources." [41] Attached to the memorandum was a list of powers divided into three groups: matters with respect to which powers would be transferred to the Provisional Government at the initial stage (between 15 August and 30 September); [42] matters with respect to which powers would be transferred to the Provisional Government during the intermediate stage (between 15 October and 15 November); and matters with respect to which powers would be transferred to the Provisional Government during the final stage (between 1 and 31 December). The third list was followed by a note to the effect that

40. United Nations Docs. A/AC.32/COUNCIL/R.144, 24 July 1951; A/AC.32/COUNCIL/R.145 and Corr. 1, 21 July 1951; and A/AC.32/COUNCIL/R.146, 25 July 1951, respectively. Mimeographed.

41. United Nations Doc. A/AC.32/CC.5, 21 July 1951, p. 2, annexed to United Nations Doc. A/AC.32/COUNCIL/R.145, 21 July 1951. Mimeographed.

42. The date of 15 August was selected as it was the target date fixed by the NCAL for the completion of its work.

The other powers at present exercised by the British or French Residents would also be given up before the end of the year. They would include powers at present exercised in relation to the territorial governments, powers listed in the residual list of the various proclamations not referred to [in the list], including those relating to property in Libya referred to in the United Nations General Assembly Resolution 388 (V) dated 15 December 1950.[43]

In making this classification of powers, careful thought had been given to the sequence of transfer and the related timetable. This obviously brought administrative, financial, and political factors into play. The list, like its subdivisions, was therefore of a tentative nature, put forward simply as a basis for discussion. It rested on the further assumption that all powers which would finally belong to the central government, whether currently exercised by the Administering Powers or by the provincial governments, would be transferred to the Provisional Government not later than the end of 1951. The Commissioner's suggestions regarding the organization and budget of the Libyan federal government had also to be taken into account.

The third paper gave an overall, but nonetheless fairly detailed, picture, ministry by ministry, of how the federal government should be organized; what staff would be required, including foreign "specialists"; and the corresponding cost estimates. Although it did not give details of the ministerial budgets, which the Provisional Government had decided should be kept confidential for the time being, it contained the following summary of the first provisional estimates of federal government expenditure:

Table 3. [*Draft*] *Summary of Expenditures of the First Provisional Estimates of the Federal Government*

Head	*Ministry*	*Personnel Emoluments*	*Other Charges*	*Special Expenditure*	*Total*
I	Civil List	£ —	—	—	—
II	Prime Minister	13,020	3,500	1,000	17,520
III	Communications	7,550	2,500	1,400	11,450
IV	Defense	4,500	800	700	6,000
V	Finance and Economics	15,200	2,600	1,800	19,600
VI	Foreign Affairs	9,600	29,800	4,615	44,015
VII	Health and Education	6,800	2,000	1,400	10,200
VIII	Justice	15,580	3,000	1,000	19,580
IX	Miscellaneous	—	17,920	31,000	48,920
		£72,250	62,120	42,915	177,285

43. United Nations Doc. A/AC.32/CC.5, 21 July 1951, p. 10, annexed to United Nations Doc. A/AC.32/COUNCIL/R.145, 21 July 1951. Mimeographed.

The document ended with a statement that the Coordination Committee was still examining these estimates and was also devoting attention to the problem of meeting federal expenditure either by contributions from the provincial budgets—which would entail retrenchment or increased taxation —or, alternatively, by an increase in grants-in-aid from foreign Governments.

The Council considered these papers at its eightieth and eighty-first meetings on 27 and 28 July. The Tripolitanian representative refused to discuss the subject, contending that:

> since the question under discussion was that of the transfer of powers to the Provisional Libyan Government, a government set up by an Assembly that was not in any way the National Assembly provided [*sic*] in the United Nations General Assembly resolution 387 (V), he would refrain from taking any part in the discussion and would withhold his agreement from any such transfer of powers.[44]

The member for Egypt recalled that the draft list of powers was based on the assumption that the form of the future Libyan State would be federal. The views of the Egyptian delegation on that subject were well known. He emphasized that it was hopeless to build on a false foundation. He also maintained his former charge that the Council had been confronted with a fait accompli. Nevertheless he would put on record his opinion that the draft plan was unsatisfactory, and that, based as it was on wrong premises and a wrong approach, its solutions must be wrong too.

The United Kingdom representative's belief was that, although the documents under discussion were only tentative, much useful work had been done. Since, however, the program would require his Government's study and approval, he was not in a position to approve it or to express a definite opinion on it; but the Commissioner's approach to the problem and the procedure proposed by him seemed to be in conformity with Resolution 387 (V).

The French member took a similar line, observing that it was not for him at that intermediate stage to express an opinion on a matter which was still being studied by other representatives of the French Government.

The Italian representative, stating that he was unable to associate himself with any general approval of the Commissioner's suggestions, reproached the Commissioner for not seeking the Council's advice on the documents he had submitted.

44. Summary Records of 80th Meeting, United Nations Doc. A/AC.32/COUNCIL/SR.80, 27 July 1951, pp. 3–4. Mimeographed.

The Cyrenaican member considered the steps so far taken by the Commissioner to be fully in harmony with the General Assembly Resolution.

The member for the minorities declined to discuss the documents on the ground that they were too vague. However, he emphasized that any procedure that would ensure the prompt transfer of power to Libya would be acceptable to those he represented.

The Pakistani representative repeated his accusation, made earlier in the session, that the Commissioner had failed to seek the Council's aid and guidance. He also complained about the slowness of the Coordination Committee's work, which had been complicated, in his opinion, by the participation of the Provisional Libyan Government without warrant from the General Assembly. He finally maintained that the Council could not consider the documents before it since it lacked the necessary complementary information, e.g. as to why defense and foreign affairs had been relegated to the last group of powers to be transferred.

The United States representative, too, believed that the Commissioner's approach to the problem was in conformity with Resolution 387 (V). Nevertheless, he found difficulty in commenting on the documents before him without having heard the views of the British, French, and Libyan members. He strongly urged that the process of transfer be speeded up, and asked the Commissioner to arrange for the initial transfer of powers to be made between 15 August and 30 September.

Finally, the representative of the Fezzan expressed the view that the Commissioner's actions were in conformity with the General Assembly's instructions; but he, too, reserved his substantive comments.

The Commissioner, replying, observed that no program for the transfer of powers could be complete unless it provided not only for the cession of powers by the one party but also for their assumption by the other party. A break in the exercise of powers could only create chaos.

Altogether, from the Commissioner's point of view, the Council's attitude had been disappointing in the sense that even those members who agreed with his general approach had refrained from making any constructive suggestions, or even derogatory or laudatory comments, about the details of the plan. They had been given an opportunity of doing so, but had not seized it. Even the criticisms he had heard expressed were so general as to be of very little help.

On adjourning after the two-day session, the Council decided to meet again in Geneva on 14 September 1951, expecting to start consulting with the Commissioner on his second annual report on 25 September. The Commissioner, wishing to avoid any further delay, suggested that it should meet in Tripoli toward the end of August, or about 6 September, to give him its advice on the final program for the transfer of powers. This date and place of meeting proved unacceptable to several members, including the Chairman of the Council for September, Ambassador Lewis Clark. Finally, it having been ascertained that a meeting on 14 September was ruled out by lack of conference facilities at Geneva, the majority, consulted by cable and letter, decided that the Council should meet there on 25 September.

On 8 September the Commissioner transmitted to the Council the Coordination Committee's detailed documentation, followed on 10 September by a formal request for the Council's advice on the draft program for the transfer of powers. This request, and the way in which the Council dealt with it, will be gone into later. First it is necessary to revert to events which had in the meantime been taking place in the NCAL.

The NCAL's impatience with the Coordination Committee's slow progress, fully shared by the Provisional Government, was due to considerations different from those which had motivated the criticisms expressed by the opposition in the Council. The latter originally wanted a "simple and straightforward" transfer of powers to "the 'people' of Libya" (as the member for Pakistan liked to say), or later from the United Kingdom and France to a central Libyan government, uncomplicated by any trace of federalism. They shut their eyes to the unrealistic nature of such a course. For their part, the members of the NCAL and the Provisional Federal Government, heckled by their own opposition for being powerless, and restlessly waiting for the powers promised to them, did not always fully appreciate the complications of a situation in which large budgetary deficits and lack of experienced staff had to be reconciled with a transfer of powers on two levels in less than twelve months' time.

At the twenty-fourth meeting of the NCAL, held on 24 July, this feeling of impatience, bordering on revolt, broke out into the open during a debate which showed that many members were unwilling, or more often unable, to appreciate the true state of affairs; fortunately, a few did, and said so.

It was a member for Cyrenaica who, at the opening of the meeting, proposed that an item on the transfer of powers be added to the agenda. He wanted to know whether agreement had been reached between the Provisional Libyan Government and the Commissioner on the preparation of the plan, and urged all concerned to act with the greatest possible speed. Another member opposed the proposal, arguing that it was ludicrous to address a request of this kind to the Commissioner before it was known what the powers of the federal government would be. He, too, urged that the Committee of Eighteen and its Working Group be enjoined to work faster. This opposition notwithstanding, the majority decided to place the new item on the agenda, after which the Chairmen of the Committee of

Eighteen and the Working Group were invited to give an account of the progress they had made in defining the federal powers.

During the ensuing debate, it became clear that there was some confusion in the minds of certain members as to the distinction to be made between the transfer of powers to the provincial governments and to the federal government respectively. It was also asked whether it was necessary that the entire Constitution be approved before the transfer of powers could begin, or whether adoption of the chapter on the distribution of powers would be enough. Since there was a generally recognized need for speedy action and the situation did not seem to be very clear to the Assembly, the President's proposal that the Commissioner and the Provisional Government be asked for information was approved.

The President, who was personally well aware of the difficulties, therefore wrote forthwith to the Commissioner, informing him that "the National Constituent Assembly is concerned at the delay in executing the program of transfer of powers." The letter went on:

> The Assembly and I myself fully appreciate the fact that this programme entails necessary complicated studies and preliminary steps; it does however appear essential that the work should be completed and the necessary action taken soon, so that the Government may be able to deal with the heavy duties with which it will be faced after the enactment of the constitution, which—as you are no doubt aware—is about to be completed. Since the Assembly decided at the conclusion of the discussion to contact you and to ask you for a reply on this question, I will be obliged to Your Excellency if you will inform us of the developments and of the approximate date—which we hope will be soon—upon which the transfer of powers to the Libyan Government is expected to begin.[45]

It will be noted that the President himself was somewhat overoptimistic in stating that the enactment of the Constitution was about to be completed.

The Commissioner would have replied immediately, in pursuance of his usual cooperation with the President, had it not been for the reserved attitude shown by the representatives of the two Administering Powers on the Council for Libya, who had privately given him to understand that he should not take it for granted that their respective Governments would approve his draft plan. At the same time, he had the feeling that, in informed Libyan circles, opposition to a number of points in the plan was stiffening. In these circumstances he preferred to put off answering the President's letter until the situation became clearer. He apologized per-

45. United Nations Archives. Typescript.

sonally to the President for the delay, broadly indicating the reasons for it, and met with full understanding.

At the meetings of the Coordination Committee held in Tripoli on 7 and 8 August, the Commissioner's forebodings were largely borne out. When, in his introductory statement, he suggested that the Committee should first take up the program of the transfer of powers, in order to reach agreement on it with the least delay, the British Resident in Tripolitania expressed a preference for the opposite procedure, i.e. that the Committee should first complete its study of the organization and budget of the future federal government. He emphasized the danger of fixing definite dates for the transfer of any given group of powers. One of his fears evidently was that, in organizing its own services, the federal Provisional Government might dislocate and thereby weaken the provincial administrations by recruiting some of their administrative staff.

The Commissioner very well understood this fear, which had both political and administrative origins. On the other hand, his duty was to help the central government to build up its services, taking into account the intimate interdependence between the timetable for the transfer of powers on the one hand and its administrative organization and budget on the other. In the circumstances, and especially in view of the paucity of available funds and staff, a certain antagonism between the two sides was unavoidable. In his own mind, he was clear about what ought to have been done. First, a program for the progressive transfer of powers should have been drawn up, accompanied by a timetable and a global budget. Then, but only then, and therefore within the agreed framework of the timetable and budget, negotiations should have been opened on detailed staffing and costing, ministry by ministry, post by post. In theory, this looked sound. In practice, the preparatory work had already gone too far to make it a workable proposition at so late an hour. Moreover, the fact that the United Kingdom and France—mainly the former—would have to cover the federal deficit, proved the determining factor.

Immediately after the British Resident had spoken, the representative of Cyrenaica, Ali Nourridine Unayzi, asked for the floor, stating that he was speaking under instructions from the King, and urging on his behalf the Coordination Committee and all other bodies concerned with Libyan independence to do everything within their power to make quicker progress. All through the day the discussion went on, the Committee examining the Commissioner's draft plan for administration and budget paragraph by paragraph, and becoming more and more deeply involved in detail. Agreement was reached on most points, at least provisionally, but at the same time the British representatives repeatedly reserved their position.

When the Committee came to the problem of the legal instrument, or instruments, by which the transfer of authority from the Administering Powers to the Libyan Provisional Government would be effected, the legal adviser to the two British Administrations, Sir Harry Trusted, drew attention to the important point that the Provisional Government, under the NCAL resolution establishing it, had been authorized to receive powers, but not to exercise them except in accordance with the Constitution.[46] Consequently, he argued, the Provisional Government could not de facto exercise the powers transferred to it until the Constitution had been finally approved. The difficulty, he continued, might be overcome in one or two ways:

> The Proclamation transferring powers might give the Provisional Government authority to exercise the powers in question and it might state what the Provisional Government could do; the Provisional Government would then have delegated power, as the local Governments in Tripolitania and Cyrenaica now had. Or the National Assembly might insert a transitory provision in the Constitution enabling the Provisional Government to exercise power until a Libyan Government enjoying full powers under the Constitution had been established.
>
> . . . While the proclamation transferring power would vary according to which solution was adopted, in neither case would there be any need for the Provisional Libyan Government formally to accept the powers in question.[47]

The Chairman then informed the Committee that the NCAL had just begun to consider the transitory provisions, which would in any case have to be included in the Constitution. In the light of what Sir Harry Trusted had said, he suggested that the Commissioner's legal advisers should study the question and submit a draft text which he, as Commissioner, would recommend to the NCAL for inclusion in the Constitution. This suggestion was accepted.

Sir Harry had, in fact, given the NCAL an important piece of advice, which was not lost on its members.

Another weighty problem which was equally thoroughly debated was: should there be one single proclamation or agreement containing a timetable for the progressive transfer of all three groups of powers, or should there be a series of proclamations or agreements, one for each group? It was finally agreed that:

46. See text of NCAL resolution on p. 734, operative paragraph 1 (b).

47. Coordination Committee, Summaries of Discussions, United Nations Doc. A/AC.32/CC/MIN.6, 8 August 1951, pp. 3–4. Mimeographed.

the legal advisers of the parties concerned should be invited to draft appropriate legal instruments on the basis of the following recommendations: that there should be a series of separate proclamations for the transfer of each group of powers, the total transfer to be completed by the end of the year and that in each case there should be three simultaneous proclamations, identical in purpose, two by the United Kingdom and one by France.[48]

The transfer of certain powers from the provincial governments to the federal government had already been discussed in the course of the Committee's meeting on 24 July, when it had been decided to ask the Legal Sub-Committee to draft a formula which could be submitted to the federal Prime Minister and his colleagues from the three provinces as a basis for discussion (pp. 759–60). Admittedly, the exact powers could not be determined until the Constitution had been approved, but at least the legal form of transfer, even if it varied from territory to territory, could usefully be drawn up, to save time. Nevertheless, the British legal adviser, arguing that the federal government would not be able to exercise certain of these powers so long as it did not dispose of the necessary legislative machinery, expressed doubt about the usefulness of preparing such instruments. The Chairman, reminding the Committee that the federal government would have to draft a number of legislative texts, and that the transfer of certain powers would entail reorganization of the territorial governments and raise administrative and budgetary questions, argued that the sooner the transfer of those powers could be initiated the better it would be from every point of view. He therefore suggested that the Committee should adhere to its previous decision, and so it was agreed.

A lengthy discussion ensued when the Committee reached the Commissioner's list of powers tentatively placed in three groups in order of transfer, but not yet accompanied by a timetable.[49] The intention of its author and his advisers was that this list should serve as the basis for an exchange of views on the desirability of classifying powers in one group or another in the light of various administrative, financial, and political considerations. It was also hoped that some agreement might be reached on a timetable, notwithstanding the uncertainty about the date of promulgation of the Constitution. Most of the suggestions for transferring items from one group to another, generally by bringing them forward into an earlier one, came from the representative of Cyrenaica, who continued to speak with

48. Ibid., p. 5.

49. United Nations Doc. A/AC.32/CC.5, 21 July 1951, pp. 6–10, annexed to United Nations Doc. A/AC.32/COUNCIL/R.145, 21 July 1951. Mimeographed.

the royal authority behind him. Sometimes he carried the day; sometimes he did not. For instance the Committee agreed to transfer item 21 ("Currency, the printing of notes and the minting of coins") from group III to group I, provided that the national government decided that currency was to be within the competence of the federal government. It also agreed to transfer items 21 ("Banking") and 22 ("Regulation of imports and exports") from group II to group I, provided that the necessary specialists were available in time to assist the Provisional Government.

On the contrary, for reasons already given at length in Chapter 7, Part 2, Section A, no agreement could be reached on transferring item 10 ("Immigration and emigration") or item 11 ("Admission into, and the residence of foreigners in Libya, and their expulsion") from group III to group I, as the representative of Cyrenaica had insistently urged.

Tahir Bekir, representing Tripolitania, received satisfaction when he proposed the transfer of item 5 ("Development of agricultural, industrial and commercial production and the measures necessary to ensure the country's essential foodstuffs in consultation with the governments of the territories") and item 18 ("Antiquities, etc.") from group II to I; but he had no such luck on items 11 ("All forms of insurance") or 17 ("Labour and social insurance matters") these being too complicated to allow of early transfer. Further discussion on the placing of items in the various groups did not affect the overall picture.[50]

The Committee next turned its attention to another important aspect of the matter, namely, the timing of the transfers. The question was closely bound up with the date on which the Constitution would be adopted, or at least that part of it which was to determine the distribution of powers between the Federation and the provinces. Unfortunately, as we know, the drafting took much longer, mainly for political reasons, than members of the NCAL and the Commissioner had expected, creating a situation that fast became awkward for all concerned. The Administering Powers, while still wary of a binding and rigid timetable, were not anxious to find themselves toward the end of the year in a position where they might be accused of having delayed the declaration of independence. The Libyans were so eager to gain their independence by 1 January 1952 that at this point no hurdle was too high for them to clear.

The Commissioner, perhaps, was in the most difficult position of all. Indeed, the dates he had proposed for the transfer of powers in the document before the Committee were based on the assumption that the NCAL would be able to finish with the Constitution by 15 August. Now 15 Septem-

50. *Proc. NCAL,* Stewart-Jackson Translation, 19th Meeting, 29 March 1951, pp. 9–10.

ber, or even later, seemed a more likely date. Furthermore, there was the question of elections. Subparagraph 3 (c) of Resolution 387 (V) provided for powers to be "progressively transferred to the Provisional Government by the administering Powers in a manner which will ensure that all powers at present exercised by them shall, by 1 January 1952, have been transferred to a duly constituted Libyan Government." The General Assembly had not made an elected Parliament a sine qua non for the establishment of a duly constituted Government, but in pursuance of the Constitution then being elaborated, elections would have to be held before such a Government could be set up. However, there was no time left for preparing elections. This was the main reason why the Working Group, with the help of its legal advisers, had been busy on a set of transitional provisions whereby, among other things, the Provisional Government, subject to certain conditions, would be authorized to exercise the powers transferred to it pending the establishment of the duly constituted Government. The Commissioner wondered, not without misgivings, how first the Council and subsequently the General Assembly would look upon such a procedure. Whatever the answer, a provisional decision had to be taken there and then. It was therefore agreed: first, that the Coordination Committee would unanimously appeal to the NCAL to speed up its work as much as possible; and second, on a suggestion put forward by the British Resident in Tripolitania and adopted by the Chairman, that the timetable for the transfer of powers should come into effect on D-Day, viz. the date on which the Constitution was finally adopted and promulgated. Thus the powers in group I were to be transferred by D-Day plus 30, those in group II by D-Day plus 50, and those in the final group not later than 15 December 1951. It was felt that by adopting this military form of timetable the pressure of time would be brought home to the NCAL more forcefully than before. From the Commissioner's point of view, the outcome was undoubtedly much better than anything he had dared to hope for. At the same time, he was unhappy at having been forced to include in his plan a condition which made even the beginning of the transfer of powers dependent on the final approval of the Constitution in its entirety, when what really mattered was final approval of the chapter on the distribution of powers. Indeed, several other chapters, which in early August were still in abeyance, had no direct connection with the transfer problem; though admittedly, from a strictly legal standpoint, it could equally well be argued to the contrary, namely, that no article or chapter of a constitution can be considered as validly in force unless the whole instrument is effective. It was a delicate point, but his Libyan experiences had long since taught the Commissioner that, in carrying out the General Assembly's instructions, he should not take too legalistic an approach, though always holding himself ready, if necessary, to meet legal criticism by common sense backed by legal arguments. Not being a lawyer himself, it was fortunate that the Secretary-General had provided him with such excellent and reliable advisers, neither of whom was lacking in political judgment.

He did not feel happy either about the insistence with which the three Residents had argued that, prior to any transfer of powers, the federal government must be provided with adequate administrative services and financial resources. Of course, in principle this condition was indisputably correct, and the Commissioner himself had always regarded it as an indispensable requirement for the proper functioning of an independent Libyan Government. But, looking at the practical aspect of the problem, he did not believe that this meant that every government department must necessarily be in perfect working order before any powers at all could be transferred. The very aim of transferring powers progressively was to permit the step-by-step organization of the services that were to exercise them. It was precisely for this reason that the members of his staff, together with United Nations and British and French experts, had worked out in great detail the functional organization of each ministry and its cost. These proposals, approved by the Establishment Committee, were now before the Coordination Committee.[51]

On 24 July, the Committee had already taken a first look at the proposals, and copies had been sent to London and Paris for study there. Now the Residents had received detailed instructions, and the proposals were about to be examined much more thoroughly. On the Libyan side, too, there had been more time to look at them with a critical eye, though the Government had been made aware of their contents and general nature through its representatives on the Coordination Committee and its sub-committees. As things turned out, the discussion took two meetings, and the going was heavy, not to say leaden. It is never simple when setting up a bureaucracy to discuss with those directly interested questions of competence, establishment, and grading of staff, salary scales, ministerial emoluments and allowances, office equipment in general—and office cars in particular—not to mention countless other items. The discussion becomes even more tricky when, by common agreement, decisions must be taken on such problems as whether senior posts are to be occupied by local people or by foreign "specialists," and in what hierarchical order. If, on top of all this, the discussions are overshadowed by paucity of financial resources, one side of the table, the foreigners, having undertaken for a price to subsidize the other, the

51. United Nations Doc. A/AC.32/CC/C.1/9/Rev. 2, 1 August 1951. Mimeographed.

future rulers of the country, the situation requires a degree of self-control and courtesy far beyond normal standards of human behavior in international relations. The fact that no hard words were spoken and a constructive atmosphere prevailed is a splendid compliment to the wisdom and good manners of all concerned.

Once more, lack of space forbids a detailed account of the negotiations of those two days. Appreciable progress was made, but the agenda was far from exhausted when the session ended. By common consent, the sensitive items, like the number of ministers in the Cabinet, the Libyan police force, and the Civil List, were held over until the next session, when the Prime Minister himself would be present. Moreover, the meetings would be held in Benghazi, thus making consultations with the future Head of State considerably easier. In this connection, it is important to note that the part played by the King, and his influence on current events, were steadily growing.

The British Resident in Tripolitania made a reservation about the proposed new grading and salary scales for civil servants of the federal government which, if adopted, would also be applicable to officials in the service of the territorial governments.

The representative of Cyrenaica proposed no less than sixteen amendments or additions to points of detail in the Commissioner's proposals, most of which related to specific senior posts in the administration or items in the budget. For instance, he wanted it to be stipulated that the chef de cabinet to the Prime Minister and the director of personnel should both be Libyans. In both cases a compromise was found. Others, however, were of a more general nature, as for example the Government's right to review the position of "specialists" in its service. The Commissioner had proposed that such review should be periodical. Unayzi considered that this did not go far enough; he wanted the Government to have the right of review "at its discretion." After a close comparison of texts, it was found that this demand could be satisfied by amending the Arabic text only.

Another recommendation in the Commissioner's proposals, introduced at the request of the British Administration, was to the effect that the financial and economic adviser (a "specialist") would be responsible for the administration of the entire Ministry of Finance and Economics. The representative of Cyrenaica wished this paragraph to be deleted since, he argued, it was obvious that such a responsibility rested with the Minister and with the Minister alone. A solution was found by amending the text to read: "He [the Adviser] would be a specialist responsible to the Minister for the administration of the entire Ministry." [52]

52. Coordination Committee, Summaries of Discussions, United Nations Doc. A/AC.32/CC/MIN.8, 9 August 1951, pp. 4–5. Mimeographed.

Agreement was also reached on a request for increased staff in the Ministry of Finance and Economics, especially as it now seemed likely that customs and a few related questions would be transferred to federal competence. In addition, it was decided that there ought to be two secretaries, instead of one, for currency, banking, and exchange, one of whom would be a Libyan.[53]

So, in the course of a protracted meeting, thanks to much patience and tact displayed by both sides, the Chairman occasionally acting as mediator, solutions were found for practically all such problems. On one point—diplomatic representation abroad—no compromise could be reached for financial reasons. In one or two cases Unayzi withdrew his amendments, as for instance in the matter of the assistants to the director of civil aviation who, under international agreements negotiated under the auspices of the International Civil Aviation Organization, require special technical qualifications, which at the time no Libyan possessed.

When, at long last, the deliberations came to an end, the Chairman wanted to know whether the document he had submitted could be considered to have the approval of the Committee, with the exception, of course, of the three outstanding questions specified above. The British Resident in Tripolitania thought the proposals very reasonable, but was still unable to give a categorical assurance that his Government would agree to everything therein. The Acting Resident in the Fezzan reserved the position of the French Government until it had been able to study the documents in their final form.

Since, however, the Commissioner had still to work out a program, it was agreed that he would submit the two documents to the Provisional Libyan Government, together with a covering letter drawing attention to the points upon which no recommendations had yet been formulated and making the position of the Administering Powers quite clear. Before adjourning, the Committee decided to issue an informative press release, without going into too great detail, the purpose of which was to silence criticism by informing the public of the progress being made in preparing for the transfer of powers, and that its completion was only awaiting the adoption of the Constitution. This, it was hoped, would also impel the NCAL to proceed more quickly.

Altogether the meeting had been constructive, but it was clear that there were still many difficulties ahead, whereas time was fast running out.

The Commissioner's first duty now was to transmit to the Provisional Government the Preliminary Conclusions reached by the Coordination Committee on the draft program for the transfer of powers. He did so by

53. Ibid., p. 5.

letter of 13 August 1951 to the Prime Minister,[54] to which were also attached the documents communicated earlier to the Council and already privately made known to the Prime Minister and the President of the NCAL. He made it clear that the draft was meant to serve as the basis for discussions with the Provisional Government and that it had also been referred to London and Paris by the British and French Residents. The plan would therefore have to be examined again at the forthcoming meeting of the Coordination Committee in Benghazi when, he hoped, the Prime Minister would be present. The crucial paragraph in the letter reiterating the essence of paragraph 2 (i) in the Preliminary Conclusions, read:

> However, I should like to draw your attention to the fact that the programme of transfer of powers can only be finalized after the National Assembly has finally approved the Libyan constitution and particularly has taken a definite decision regarding the question of the respective competence of the Federal Government and the provincial administrations.[55]

By stressing the distinction between final approval of the Constitution in its entirety and a definite decision by the NCAL on the sole chapter thereof dealing with the distribution of powers, the Commissioner, with the tacit approval of the Committee, hoped to avert a clash between the Government and the Assembly on the one hand the Administering Powers on the other. With the same objective in mind he had not reproduced in his letter a paragraph from the Preliminary Conclusions which, when read in the light of the previous one, almost sounded like a threat:

> 2 . . . (ii) No powers should be transferred in specific fields until after the Provisional Libyan Government has organized federal services in a sufficiently adequate manner and has available the necessary financial resources and personnel.[56]

The categorical prohibition implied in such a provision, which was suggested by the Administrative Powers, could have endangered the implementation of the transfer program within the time limits set; moreover, it carried the risk of upsetting the relationship between Libya and the Administering Powers, which was of such importance for the future. In any case, the Commissioner did not like using pressure of this kind in a program for which he, in the last instance, as the representative of the United

54. See *Second Annual Report of the United Nations Commissioner in Libya*, Annex XII, Sections 1–2, pp. 89–92.

55. Ibid., p. 92.

56. Ibid., p. 90.

Nations, would have to shoulder the responsibility. He felt certain that better results could be obtained by trying to bring the parties together on the basis of a compromise.

Similar feelings prompted him to write, the same day, a second letter to the Prime Minister transmitting the latest draft of the paper on the organization and budget of the federal government.[57] After referring to previous consultations that had taken place on these subjects, he drew the Prime Minister's special attention to the few points on which the views of the Provisional Government and the Coordination Committee had differed, or which had been left in suspense. He invited the Prime Minister's comments.

The next morning the Prime Minister and the Commissioner consulted one another about the measures to be taken to maintain the effective relationship between the Provisional Government and the Coordination Committee that had prevailed from the first contact between them. The Prime Minister was adamant in refusing to accept the two conditions which, in the opinion of the Committee, must be fulfilled before power could be transferred. On the other hand, he proved most helpful in offering to request the NCAL to adopt, with the least possible delay, the chapter of the Constitution on the division of powers, together with the transitory and provisional provisions required to bridge the intervals between the proclamation of independence, the holding of elections, and the coming into being of a duly constituted Libyan Government. The following day he wrote to the President of the NCAL to that effect.

PART 6. CONTESTED ADJUSTMENTS

The Government's reaction was not slow in coming; neither was that of the NCAL. Both were negative in the first instance; yet positive, insofar as both bodies attempted to meet the Administering Powers halfway.

On 15 August, the Prime Minister informed the Commissioner that the Council of Ministers had discussed the Coordination Committee's Preliminary Conclusions, adding:

> As a first conclusion of this discussion, the members of the Government have decided to inform you promptly that they do not approve of the contents of sub-paragraph (ii) of paragraph 2, which states that no powers should be transferred until after the Provisional Libyan Government has organized its services and has made available the necessary financial resources and personnel.

57. United Nations Doc. A/AC.32/CC/C.1/9/Rev. 3, 10 August 1951; see also fn. 51, p. 773.

> What the Government desires is that the transfer of power shall be completed at the first available opportunity. In accordance with your recommendation to me during our meeting on 14 August, I have today written to the President of the National Assembly requesting him to convene a meeting of the National Assembly to discuss and approve the chapters of the constitution relating to competences and elections so that powers may be received and elections held as soon as possible. I have also requested the President of the National Assembly to inform me of the latest date for receiving the powers and of the dates when elections will be initiated and completed.[58]

He ended by giving an assurance that the Council of Ministers would submit both the document on the transfer of powers and that on the organization and budget of the federal government to further study.

On receipt of this letter, the Commissioner, fearing that his and the Coordination Committee's motives might have been misunderstood, sent the following explanation to the Prime Minister on 16 August:

> I fully agree with the desire of the Government that the transfer of powers should be undertaken and completed as soon as possible. As a matter of fact, I consider it essential that the Administering Powers should start progressively transferring these powers in the near future. However, I am also anxious that this transfer of powers should be real and not illusory or disappointing. The Federal Government should be in a position actually to exercise the powers to be transferred to it from the moment it receives them. Otherwise, that Government would be in the embarrassing position of having legally received powers, but being unable to exercise them. Indeed, if precautions to this effect were not taken, the Libyan Federal Government would receive powers the exercise of which would remain for a considerable time to come in the hands of the local governments. Alternatively, such powers would not be exercised effectively by anyone and essential government services might cease to function. This would not be compatible with the dignity of the Government, nor would it be in the interests of the country because such a situation could easily lead to confusion and difficulties.
>
> For these reasons, I am most anxious that the transfer of powers should be undertaken not only quickly but effectively, in order that the Government can actually deal with the many problems which will inevitably confront it. The Co-ordination Committee had such considerations in mind when they expressed the opinion to which you refer.

58. *Second Annual Report of the United Nations Commissioner in Libya,* Annex XII, Section 3, p. 92.

In practical terms, the statement to which you refer means that, in advance of the transfer of powers, there must be designated or recruited the necessary minimum staff to assist the ministers in discharging their functions. This can probably best be done, at least at the outset, by transferring a limited number of officials from local government service to the federal service. Obviously, this staff must be paid, have basic office and other equipment, and funds to discharge its functions. Funds and supplies will be obtained only on the basis of a plan. It was precisely to meet this problem that the Co-ordination Committee and its sub-committees have devoted considerable study to recommendations regarding the federal budget and establishment, which were transmitted to you in my letter of 13 August as document A/AC.32/CC/C.1/9/Rev.3.

I believe that it will be found in practice that such planning and a transfer on the basis of a carefully prepared budget and establishment plan, will facilitate and make effective, rather than delay, the transfer and the actual exercise of powers.[59]

The Provisional Government, conscious of the need for haste, wasted no time; on 21 August the Prime Minister addressed another letter to the Commissioner on behalf of the Council of Ministers, commenting in greater detail on the two parts of the latter's draft plan.

Referring once more to the position taken in his letter of 15 August, he reiterated that it should not be necessary for the whole Constitution to be approved by the National Assembly prior to the transfer of powers: "it should be enough for the National Assembly to approve the chapters of the constitution relating to the powers of the Federal Government and elections." [60] Neither should the transfer of powers be delayed until the Provisional Libyan Government had organized federal services in a sufficiently adequate manner and had available the necessary financial resources and personnel. The Council of Ministers accordingly demanded that subparagraphs 2 (i) and (ii) of the Preliminary Conclusions be amended; and, having declared itself in entire agreement with the suggestion that a transitory provision should be inserted in the Constitution enabling the government to exercise power until a duly constituted government had been established, gave as its opinion that the latest date for the transfer of powers should be 15 November 1951.

With regard to the Commissioner's revised suggestions for the organization and budget of the federal Libyan government, the Cabinet declared its entire approval of the proposal that the number of ministries should be

59. Ibid., Section 4, p. 93.
60. Ibid., Section 5, p. 94, para. 2 (i).

eight, to be held by six ministers. They insisted, however, that the distribution of portfolios be left to whoever was called upon to form the Government.

Among other points of importance, the Cabinet expressed the view that the Parliamentary Affairs Department foreseen in the Prime Minister's Office should be responsible to the Prime Minister only until a Parliament had been elected, after which it would be responsible to the President of the House.

It also rejected the suggestion that the Secretary to the Cabinet should be a specialist. In its view, he should be a Libyan. However, the appointment of a specialist as an adviser attached to the Prime Minister's Office, and directly responsible to him, was not excluded. Lastly, the Cabinet supported the views already expressed by the Libyan representatives in the Coordination Committee in favor of the appointment of a Libyan as Director of Education, adding the suggestion that the Assistant Director of Education should have the title "technical assistant."

For its part, the NCAL held a special session on 18 August in response to the Prime Minister's request. The Preliminary Conclusions had quite clearly created a most unpleasant impression in the NCAL. In part, apparently, because they were regarded as an oblique criticism of the pace at which the NCAL was proceeding. One Cyrenaican member asked whether the meeting could not pass a resolution protesting against the Coordination Committee's desire to make the transfer of power dependent on the adoption of the Constitution in its entirety. A Tripolitanian member said:

> Anyone who has read the Co-ordination Committee's plans for transferring power will realize that there is an organized conspiracy. We should therefore finish the constitution as quickly as possible, and hold meetings even at night, so as to thwart this conspiracy by meeting.[61]

The Chairman of the Working Group, who, after the President, felt the greatest measure of personal responsibility for the NCAL's work, took a more moderate line, explaining that:

> the Assembly had previously sent a letter to Mr. Pelt requesting him to speed up the work of the Co-ordination Committee in preparing plans to transfer powers in accordance with the U.N. resolution. The Co-ordination Committee, however, had thought that the constitution should be completed before beginning to transfer power. This would take a good deal of time, in spite of the fact that the Co-ordination Committee had already obtained the list of federal powers, which in itself was sufficient

61. *Proc. NCAL,* Stewart-Jackson Translation, 26th Meeting, 18 August 1951.

> to take over the powers since it listed them. It became clear to us, however, that the Co-ordination Committee would insist on the completion of the constitution, or at least of the list of federal powers; and although we cannot agree to this principle, it seems to us that there would be no harm in it if the Assembly were to examine the list in order to simplify matters and save time.[62]

The NCAL responded to this last appeal, but insisted on going through the list item by item; and those issues which had given rise to heated debates on earlier occasions did so again. The meeting ended with the adoption of two resolutions, one on the transfer of powers, the other approving the powers allotted to the federal government and to the provincial administrations respectively. In the first, the NCAL considered:

> 1. That it will not be necessary to make the approval of the constitution in its entirety a prior condition for the transfer of powers if the National Assembly has approved the competences of the Federal Government and each of the provincial administrations and if the Provisional Libyan Government is vested with the authority to exercise the powers transferred to it during the interval between the date of approval of the list of powers and the date of the enactment of the Constitution.
> 2. That, while the organization of the federal services is undoubtedly necessary for the proper functioning of the governmental work after the transfer of powers, the completion of the administrative organization as a whole cannot be a basic condition for the transfer of powers and it would be sufficient if that organization could develop step by step with the transfer itself.[63]

In the light of these considerations, the NCAL resolved to convey its point of view to the Commissioner requesting him "to place [it] before the Co-ordination Committee and endeavour to obtain its acceptance or, alternatively, to persuade the Committee to reconsider the plan for the transfer of powers." [64] This was not the kind of language the Commissioner would have chosen himself had he been consulted. It sounded too much as though the NCAL was entrusting him with a mission on its behalf instead of working through its own representatives on the Committee. On the other hand, it facilitated his task as mediator, a role his chairmanship of the Committee was increasingly obliging him to play.

In its second resolution the NCAL resolved:

62. Ibid.

63. *Second Annual Report of the United Nations Commissioner in Libya,* Annex XII, Section 6, p. 95.

64. Ibid.

> To approve, by the unanimous vote of its fifty-four members present, the chapter on the powers of the Federal Government and of the provincial administrations attached to this resolution, reserving its right to rearrange this chapter at the appropriate time in order to bring it into harmony with the remaining chapters of the Constitution.[65]

The list of powers referred to in this resolution was essentially the same as that which was finally approved on 7 October as Chapter III of the Constitution. However, the NCAL, exercising its right to rearrange, had in the meantime considerably revised the wording of the various items, as well as, to a certain extent, their serial order (particularly in the case of the joint powers).

Thus the Provisional Government and the NCAL had given in on certain points of secondary importance, while sticking to their guns on the basic issues that separated them from the Coordination Committee. It will be remembered that they had acted similarly on earlier occasions, when they had rejected suggestions put forward by the Commissioner who, after all, was no more than their adviser. This time, however, they had opened up a rift between themselves and the Administering Powers, on whom they depended, and would continue to depend, for financial support. This step was the more noteworthy in that the language used reflected a sense of calm self-confidence and authority without which no government that wishes to command respect can survive.

It was in this atmosphere of divergent policies that on 22 August the Coordination Committee opened its last series of meetings in the Benghazi Parliament building. If tension pervaded the air, it was not so much for fear of failure, as because the time for definitive decisions had arrived, and everyone realized it. There was no more room for postponements and reexaminations. As to the final outcome, it was generally recognized by now that the point of no return had been passed and that events were moving inexorably toward the goal set by the General Assembly in November 1949 in Resolution 289 (IV). Yet the road ahead was blocked by many obstacles that still had to be removed.

The attendance at the first meeting demonstrated the particular importance that all concerned attached to the work in hand.[66]

65. Ibid.

66. Apart from the regular members, the Commissioner noted the presence of: the Prime Minister of the Provisional Libyan Government, Mahmud al-Muntasir; the Prime Minister of Cyrenaica, Mohamed Saqizli; the Minister of the Interior of the Fezzan, Hajj Hamuda Bin Tahir, representing the Government of that Province; the representative of the Tripolitanian Government, Tahir Bekir; the British Resident in Tripolitania; the British Resident in Cyrenaica; the Acting French Resident in the

In his opening remarks, the Chairman stated that he personally shared the opinion of the Provisional Government and the NCAL that there was no need for all sections of the Constitution to be approved before the transfer of powers could take place in accordance with a sound plan providing for the necessary financial resources and staff.

It took five lengthy meetings of intensive discussion to reach a set of conclusions acceptable to both sides and to the Commissioner, who was ultimately responsible for recommending them to the Libyan Government in the form of a comprehensive plan. He also had to keep in mind that not only would he have to obtain, at least by majority vote, favorable advice on it from the Council for Libya, but also that he would in all probability have to defend it before the General Assembly of the United Nations.

In fact the Coordination Committee, with the help of the Mission staff, had elaborated a voluminous program that went much further than a mere plan for a transfer of powers. By now it will be clear to the reader that the Commissioner and the Administering Powers had, for obvious reasons, always been in agreement on the basic concept that the Libyan Government, whether provisional or duly constituted, should not only receive powers but be in a position to exercise them effectively. As a result, as is apparent from Part 5 of this chapter, the initial setup of the federal administration, the way in which it was to be organized, staffed, and financed, had almost become a greater preoccupation than the transfer problem itself, though the latter remained the main target. At first, the Coordination Committee's work had been hampered by ignorance of precisely what powers the federal government was to exercise. Once that point had been cleared up, it became increasingly plain that the transfer-of-power operation, as such, would be largely dependent on the administrative and budgetary organization of the Government and, preeminently, on the way in which the federal State was to be financed. This last problem was itself affected by the NCAL's decision that customs should be included among the functions of the federal government. This had not been a hasty decision, and meant, of course, that customs revenues would no longer flow into the provincial

---

Fezzan; and Sir Harry Trusted, Legal Adviser to the two British Administrations in Libya on the transfer of powers. Also present were: Omar Shenib, Minister of Defense in the Provisional Libyan Government; Dutheil of France, Assistant to the French Resident in the Fezzan; C. Pitt-Hardacre, the British-nominated Financial Adviser to the Provisional Libyan Government and Member of the Finance Sub-Committee; and Munir Burshan, Rapporteur of the NCAL Committee for the Constitution. The Commissioner was assisted by the Principal Secretary of the United Nations Mission in Libya; by his legal adviser (Marc Schreiber); and by the Secretary of the Coordination Committee.

treasuries, but would become the major source of income for the central government.

As far back as May 1951, at a time when the Establishment Committee had begun to discuss the organization of the federal government,[67] but before the United Nations experts had been able to express an opinion on its financial prospects, the Amir had paid his first official visit to Tripolitania in his then new style of King-Designate (see pp. 548–49 and pp. 610 ff.). On that occasion the Commissioner had sought an audience with him, in the course of which, among other things, the matter of federal revenue was discussed. Neither the one nor the other was an expert, but both realized that to any government, and especially to a federal government, financial independence was of paramount importance politically. In the case of Libya, such a status was clearly out of the question for a long time to come, and foreign aid would be unavoidable; but at least ways and means ought to be found of making the Government as independent as possible vis-à-vis its own provinces. The King was keenly aware of this, and asked the Commissioner whether he had any views on the subject. There was only one answer. The largest stable, internal, and immediately available source of income was customs revenue. The main question was, however, whether the provinces would be willing to forfeit their current income from that source, and how, eventually, they could be compensated for their loss. They would almost certainly vigorously oppose such a radical change. In the Working Group a feeling prevailed that the Cyrenaican Government in particular, proud as it was of its recently won internal autonomy, would adopt a negative attitude whenever the question was raised. As has been shown in Chapter 7, Part 2, Sections A and M, later developments proved this assumption to be correct. Up to the last moment, until the final approval of the Constitution, Cyrenaica continued to raise objections. It must be admitted that the question was a difficult one for the provincial politicians and administrators, especially for the extreme federalists. From the point of view of the convinced protagonists of a unitarist State there was no problem, since all revenue would go to the central government. The convinced federalists, however, had to answer the awkward questions of how strong they wanted the federal government to be, and to what extent they were willing to sacrifice provincial interests. The Commissioner insisted on an early decision, as so many other matters depended on it. The King said that he wanted time for reflection. A few days after his return to Benghazi, an oral message from him to Omar Shenib, Chairman of the Committee of Eighteen, reached

67. The Committee at that moment had before it the provisional list of federal powers transmitted to it on 17 May, as described in Part 5 of this chapter.

Tripoli and was relayed to the Commissioner by the Cyrenaican member of the Council for Libya, Ali Bey Jerbi. It was to the effect that His Majesty was in favor of including customs among the federal powers, provided that the NCAL saw fit to take the responsibility for such a decision. The Assembly, however, was still waiting for expert advice on the seven financial items, including customs, on which decision had been deferred, advice which became available only at the end of July. It finally recommended that, on economic, financial, and administrative grounds, customs should be included amongst the federal powers.

During this long interval of more than two months, the Coordination Committee, too, had been left in suspense, a situation that had further complicated its labors. The Chairman, the Libyan members, and the United Nations Mission staff had been inclined to assume that in the end customs would be federalized. The British and French members, without definitely expressing the opposite opinion, were not in a position to share their colleagues' assumption. As a result, the key question of how to finance the federal government had virtually been left unbroached, though privately an agreement had been reached as to the alternative measures to be taken on whichever side the NCAL might come down.

Looking back on this episode, the Commissioner cannot help feeling that the responsible authorities in London and Paris, somewhat guilty of wishful thinking, but sustained in their hopes by the attitude of the Cyrenaican Government, were expecting to continue, even after the proclamation of independence, their grants-in-aid to the provinces, which would then have been called upon to subsidize the federal government. This, at least, was the way some responsible officials in those capitals were still looking at the situation in the late winter and spring of 1951, and, as matters turned out, it was the method that had to be used initially. Needless to say, had these expectations been realized on a continuing basis, Libya would indeed have been a very loose federation. It was this danger that the King had clearly foreseen and tried to prevent by showing his hand early. Measured in terms of political consequences, the stand he adopted in favor of federal customs was of an importance equal to that which he had taken in seeking, in March 1950, the Commissioner's advice on whether immediate Cyrenaican independence would be compatible with General Assembly Resolution 289 (IV) (pp. 157–72). In both cases, he put Libyan above Cyrenaican interests.

Working relationships within the Coordination Committee would have been decidedly unpleasant in that summer of 1951 had the British and French Administrators on the spot been as reluctant to recognize the shape of things to come as were their masters at home. Their position was not an easy one. Most of them clearly realized which way the wind was blowing, but apparently were not allowed to admit it; they were even supposed officially to discourage the inevitable solution from taking its natural course. On the other hand, the Commissioner and his collaborators would have been guilty of a gross want of tact had they tried to force the issue. While hopeful, not to say confident, that their advice on the customs question would be followed, they carefully stuck to the only correct line, namely, that the decision lay with the NCAL. In short, all concerned respected the rules of the game, and collaboration within the Committee remained cordial and effective.

However, as soon as the NCAL, by its decision of 18 August, had decided to classify customs as an exclusively federal power, the Coordination Committee had to revise certain of its conclusions with regard both to the organization and budget of the federal government and to its financing. On 22 August, the Chairman drew attention to this necessity. He was immediately followed by the British Resident in Tripolitania who recalled yet again that for constitutional reasons the allocation of certain sums, voted by Parliament at Westminster to the Cyrenaican Government and the British Administration in Tripolitania for specific purposes, could not be diverted to other uses without the express authorization of the United Kingdom Parliament. He said:

> If, therefore, the provincial administrations to which those grants had been allocated wanted to use them towards the financing of the Federal Libyan Government, there would have to be a special agreement on the subject between the United Kingdom Government and the Libyan Government.
>
> He hoped it would be possible for such an agreement to be concluded in the very near future but he pointed out that it would be necessary for him to convince his Government of the financial desirability of such an agreement rather than of its political urgency. The main difficulty lay in the decision of the National Assembly to place customs within the competence of the Federal Government: the transfer of powers with regard to customs created a financial problem and hence the constitutional difficulties to which he had referred. He hoped, however, that it would be possible for the United Kingdom Government to conclude the necessary financial agreement which would facilitate the transfer of powers during the transition period before Libya achieved independence.[68]

68. Coordination Committee, Summaries of Discussions, United Nations Doc. A/AC.32/CC/MIN.9, 4 September 1951, p. 5. Mimeographed.

Pitt-Hardacre helpfully enlarged on the subject in the following terms:

> the powers to be transferred fell into three categories: those whose transfer would have no financial implications, those whose financial implications need not stand in the way of their immediate transfer, and those whose transfer to the Federal Government would affect the grants-in-aid which had been made to the Libyan territories for specific purposes. If the Provinces were to be deprived of the large revenue they obtained from customs, they would not be able to meet their current expenses except by the grants-in-aid allocated to them by the United Kingdom Government. They could not do that without the specific authorization of the British Parliament. Parliament was at present in recess and would not meet again until October, when it was doubtful whether the question of Libyan finance could be the first item on its agenda. It was obvious, therefore, that it would be to Libya's advantage to avoid any action that would give rise to constitutional problems.
>
> On the other hand, the sum needed to finance the organization of the federal services was comparatively small. Each territory would be called upon to contribute a given proportion and all that would be necessary in the case of Cyrenaica and Tripolitania would be an agreement between the United Kingdom Government and the Libyan Government, which could be in the form of a simple exchange of letters. Thus it would be seen that there was a great advantage in choosing that solution and in not transferring powers with regard to customs to the Federal Libyan Government until the end of the present financial year, when the British Parliament would be able to consider a request from the British Government for the allocation of a new grant-in-aid to Libya.[69]

Thanks to the earlier preparatory talks, an understanding was reached on 23 August 1951 between the Provisional Libyan Government, the governments of the three provinces, and the Administering Powers, whereby it was agreed that the cost of the Provisional Government and of the succeeding duly constituted Government from 1 September 1951 to 31 March 1952 would be borne by the three provinces in the following proportions; Tripolitania 60 percent, Cyrenaica 30 percent, and the Fezzan 10 percent. In order to enable the Cyrenaican Government and the British Administration in Tripolitania to make these contributions without infringing British constitutional procedures, a financial agreement would be concluded between the Government of the United Kingdom and the Provisional Libyan Government. A similar temporary agreement would be concluded with France.

69. Ibid.

Negotiations with the United Kingdom were in fact started shortly afterward, those with France later in the autumn.[70]

It would be redundant to relate in any detail the discussions that took place during the six meetings held by the Coordination Committee in Benghazi. All points of any importance were included in the Committee's conclusions which, as the reader knows, were subsequently transmitted to the Prime Minister of the Provisional Libyan Government and also published as Annex XII to the Commissioner's second annual report, where, together with the concomitant correspondence, they take up more than forty pages. It may be enough to state that the conclusions were virtually final and that agreement on them was unanimous. They dealt with three main subjects: the Commissioner's program for the transfer of powers; thirty-seven recommendations regarding the initial organization and the first ordinary budget of the federal government for the year 1952; and recommended texts for the Libyan civil service law, the draft Libyan provident fund law, and the draft form of contract for specialists in Libyan Government service (cf., p. 756, fn. 36).

The second of these documents also contained an estimate for a supplementary regular budget for the period 1 September through 31 December 1951 (recommendations Nos. 35–37), during which period, as originally planned, the Provisional Government would be receiving powers progressively transferred and would be beginning to exercise the functions of government. Without false modesty, it can be confidently asserted that these recommendations and related documents represented a carefully prepared piece of work, which, having been elaborated in full partnership with the Provisional Government, constituted an agreed administrative foundation for the new Libyan State.

For the general sequel, a summary will have to suffice, more or less following that issued at the time as Part C (pages 24–29) of Chapter II, "Work of the Coordination Committee," of the Commissioner's second annual report. This can now be completed by the addition of certain details which it would have been premature to make public in 1951, or which, looking back, seem more important than they did then.

In his covering letter transmitting the recommendations of the Coordination Committee, the Commissioner specifically replied to the two objections raised by the Provisional Government in the Prime Minister's letters of 16

70. Details of the agreements and the negotiations that led up to them will be found in Chapter 9 and in Part 8 of this chapter. The texts of the agreements are given in *Supplementary Report to the Second Annual Report of the United Nations Commissioner in Libya,* GAOR: Sixth Session, 1951–1952, Supplement No. 17A (A/1949/Add.1), Annexes IV and V, pp. 29–31.

and 21 August, and in the NCAL's resolution of 18 August. With regard to the Coordination Committee's original suggestion that no powers should be transferred in specific fields until after the Provisional Government had organized its services in a sufficiently adequate manner or until it disposed of the necessary financial resources, the Commissioner was by this time in a position to let the Prime Minister know that if recommendations Nos. 23–27 [71] were accepted by the Provisional Government and acted upon promptly, the federal services would in his and the Committee's opinion be sufficiently well organized to warrant a start being made with the transfer of powers. The recommendations referred to in particular related to the appointment of the director of personnel and the beginning of the organizational work for the establishment of the ministries and their installation at least fifteen days before powers affecting their respective departments were transferred to them. Consequently, the Prime Minister's office and the Ministries of Finance and Economics, Communications, Health and Education, and Justice should come into being as early as possible in September. The Ministry of Foreign Affairs should be organized as from October so that it would be ready to assume its functions in December. The Ministry of Defense should be organized by 1 December. The Commissioner insisted that it was absolutely essential that the Director of Personnel be appointed at the earliest possible moment.

With regard to the other point that had caused a difference of opinion, namely, the Coordination Committee's preliminary conclusion to the effect that no powers should be transferred until the Constitution had been approved in its entirety, the Committee had in the meantime reconsidered its position. Both the Government and the NCAL had argued that it would be sufficient if the list of federal powers alone had been adopted and the federal government vested with authority to exercise the powers transferred to it during the interval between the date of approval of the list and that of the enactment of the Constitution. The Commissioner had shared this opinion and was now able to inform the Prime Minister that the Coordination Committee, too, had accepted the Libyan point of view. The transfer of powers could therefore begin on the basis of the NCAL's decisions of 18 August regarding federal powers.

In this way the Committee, and more particularly the Administering Powers, handsomely deferred to a reasonable Libyan claim.

Writing to the President of the NCAL in early September, the Commissioner furthermore suggested, at the Committee's request, that two transitional provisions be inserted in the Constitution, one enabling the Pro-

71. *Second Annual Report of the United Nations Commissioner in Libya,* Annex XII, Section 7, pp. 103–13.

visional Libyan Government to exercise power until such time as a duly constituted Government had been established, the other to the effect that federal powers with regard to the collection and disbursement of customs revenues should become operative only as from 1 April 1952.

On 5 September, at its twenty-seventh meeting, the NCAL adopted the following resolution

> . . . giving the provisional Libyan government the right to exercize the powers it will receive in accordance with the section of the constitution devoted to federal powers. In view of the first article of the N.C.A.L.'s resolution issued on 29 March, which was concerned with the establishment of the provisional Libyan government, and in view of the necessity of transferring power from the two administering powers as specified in the U.N. resolution issued on 17 Nov. 1951, and of exercizing it in accordance with the provisions of the constitution, in particular those concerned with the division of power between the federal government and the local governments, once this had been decided by the National Assembly,
>
> And in accordance with the resolution of the National Assembly issued on 18 August 1951, which was concerned with agreement on the prerogatives of the Libyan federal government and of the provinces (*wilayat*) respectively; And inasmuch as the Co-ordination Committee, in answer to the Assembly's request, has on 24 August 1951 recommended the Libyan federal government and the provinces to take the section of the constitution devoted to federal powers as the basis for the transfer of power from the two administering powers, and to begin the transfer not later than 15 September 1951; And since the Constitution has not yet been published, and inasmuch as it is necessary that the provisional Libyan government immediately exerçise the powers it will receive,
>
> The National Constituent Assembly resolves:
>
> 1. To grant the provisional Libyan government the right to exercize power in all the questions which will fall within its competence, in accordance with what was decided in the section of the constitution devoted to federal powers on which the Assembly agreed on 18 Aug. 1951.
> 2. That the President of the National Assembly is to communicate this resolution to those concerned, so that they may act in accordance with it.[72]

As described in Chapter 7, Part 2, Section A, the customs question was finally settled only in Benghazi the day before the Constitution was approved in its entirety.

72. *Proc. NCAL,* Stewart-Jackson Translation, 27th Meeting, 5 September 1951.

In making its recommendations on the administrative organization and regular budget of the Libyan Government for the year 1952, the Coordination Committee, in full agreement with the Commissioner, was guided by certain considerations which it considered fundamental. These considerations are so characteristic of the circumstances prevailing at the time as to provide historical warrant for quoting them in detail:

(a) The greatest frugality should be observed in the expenditure of the Federal Government, particularly in view of the existing deficits and of the pressing needs of Libya for economic development and for expanded social services in the fields of education and public health.
(b) At present, only the foundations of a central administration should be laid down and the senior posts provided together with the essential secretarial staff. The expansion to full establishment of each Ministry would be worked out gradually by the Federal Government after it had assumed powers. The task of co-ordinating the provincial administrations and eliminating overlapping services and administrative functions was also left to the Federal Government after the transfer of powers.
(c) The Federal Government should have eight ministries, as was the case for the Provisional Libyan Government, the portfolios to be held by six Ministers, as had been determined by the National Assembly. The distribution of the eight portfolios between the six Ministers would be decided by the Prime Minister on being asked to form a government. The eight Ministries would be: Office of the Prime Minister, Ministry of Foreign Affairs, Ministry of Defence, Ministry of Finance and Economics, Ministry of Health, Ministry of Education, Ministry of Communications and Ministry of Justice. The Co-ordination Committee, however, recommended that, in order to ensure a better co-ordinated policy in two important departments of the Federal Government, the Ministries of Health and Education should be amalgamated or, at any rate, held by one Minister. Furthermore, it recommended that the Minister of Justice should not hold any other portfolio, so that he could devote his entire time to the substantial task of codification which will have to be undertaken by the Federal Government.
(d) Since Libya is not, in the opinion of the Committee, at present in a position to provide, from among its nationals, enough trained and experienced technical and civil service personnel to hold all the top-level technical posts in the federal ministries, it is unavoidable that, until such Libyan personnel is available, such posts should be held by qualified officials of non-Libyan nationality to be known as specialists. The latter, however, would be servants of the Libyan Government, and wherever possible, each should have a Libyan deputy who should be trained with

a view to eventually assuming the duties of his chief. The question of specialists should be periodically reviewed by the Federal Government in order to ascertain if some of the posts held by them could not be filled by equally competent Libyan civil servants.

(e) Libyan and specialist officials of the Federal Government should receive the same basic salaries and the same increments. The Co-ordination Committee also recommended that conditions of service under the Federal Government and the provincial administrations should, as far as circumstances permitted, be similar and uniform. The Co-ordination Committee envisaged a Libyan Civil Service in which Federal and provincial officials would be interchangeable.[73]

In the light of Libya's present circumstances (1969), such preoccupations sound ridiculous; but they are eloquent testimony of the extremely

73. *Second Annual Report of the United Nations Commissioner in Libya,* para. 129. The following tentative schedule for grades and salaries of officials was recommended by the Coordination Committee (ibid., Annex XII, Section 8, p. 124):

Number of Grade	*Commencing Salary per Annum* £	*Annual Increment* £	*Maximum Salary* £
I	1,200	35	1,375
II	900	30	1,050
III	700	25	825
IV	550	20	650
V	400	15	475
VI	325	15	400
VII	244	12	304
VIII	175	10	235
IX	144	10	164
X	96	10	136

A separate schedule for specialists' allowances applying to grades I–V was the following:

	Married Accompanied £ Stg. p.a.	*Married Unaccompanied* £ Stg. p.a.	*Single* £ Stg. p.a.
Accommodated rates:			
Special grade and grades I–V	—	325	160
Unaccommodated rates:			
Special grade and grades I–V	530	385	220

The rate of specialists' allowance shown above were liable to review from time to time.

precarious financial conditions in which the United Kingdom of Libya was born.

In such circumstances, it was not surprising that the Coordination Committee continued to advise against the establishment of an army, even one of very limited strength and purpose intended to help local police forces to maintain internal security. It will be clear from what has been said earlier on the subject that even a tiny army only one thousand strong would have more than doubled the original federal budget estimates. In the opinion of the Coordination Committee, the defense of Libya could best be guaranteed through the collective security system established under the Charter of the United Nations and by the conclusion of treaties of peace and friendship with neighboring States. This sounded a pretty compliment to the United Nations, but there is little doubt that for the security of Libya and the protection of their own interests the Administering Powers put their faith in the treaties of friendship, including military clauses, which they themselves hoped to conclude with the new State after independence, rather than in the collective system of the Charter. However, in order not to rule out completely the future creation of an army, a token appropriation of $200 was put into the budget of the Defense Minister for preliminary studies on the subject. Only with the greatest reluctance did the Provisional Government agree to this solution; but they very well understood that they had no interest in increasing, for an objective for which there was no immediate need, a deficit which could then be covered only by even more extensive foreign aid, thus undermining the country's independence. In any event, the United Kingdom refused to raise its grant-in-aid, and that was the end of it, at least for the time being.

As a result of these highly conservative considerations, the estimates for the ordinary Libyan budget for 1952 showed total expenditure amounting to £292,150, made up as follows: [74]

A comparison with the table on page 763, giving the estimates of federal expenditure included in the Coordination Committee's Preliminary Conclusions, shows an increase of £114,865, in part the result of the Committee's desire to meet certain Libyan wishes, in part due to increases proposed by the Administering Powers themselves, e.g. in the Civil List. Expenditure under head IX, *Miscellaneous,* also shows a substantial increase.

The recommended initial establishment of the federal ministries was fifty-six, of whom twenty were to be specialists, plus a secretariat of forty.

In the original plan, the Provisional Government was expected to begin to exercise governmental functions on 1 September, the first transfer of

74. Ibid., Annex XII, p. 113.

Table 4. *Summary of Expenditures of the First Provisional Estimates of the Federal Government*

Head	*Ministry*	*Personal Emoluments*	*Other Charges*	*Special Expenditure*	*Total*
I	Civil List *	£ —	75,000	—	75,000
II	Prime Minister	15,050	3,500	1,000	19,550
III	Communications	7,550	2,500	1,400	11,450
IV	Defense	4,500	800	900	6,200
V	Finance	18,950	2,600	1,800	23,350
VI	Foreign Affairs	9,600	32,600	6,200	48,400
VII	Health and Education	6,700	2,000	1,400	10,100
VIII	Justice	15,600	3,000	1,500	20,100
IX	Miscellaneous	—	17,000	61,000	78,000
		£77,950	139,000	75,200	292,150

Revenue was estimated at:

I	Communications (net surplus)	£ 35,000
II	Additional funds required in respect of recurring items	181,950
III	Additional funds required in respect of non-recurring items	75,200
		£292,150

* The matter is still being discussed between the Federal Prime Minister and the King-Designate.

powers having been planned for 15 September. Hence, as just mentioned, a supplementary ordinary budget was required for the last four months of 1951. Total supplementary expenditure was estimated at £63,600. Although the date of 15 September was subsequently put back because of certain difficulties encountered in staffing and organization, the supplementary budget was left as it stood. Personally, the Commissioner could not help feeling that this delay, too, might well have been due to the old Anglo-French tactics of holding up the first transfer of powers until after the promulgation of the Constitution, as well as to a desire to bring pressure to bear on the Libyans to speed up the negotiations on the temporary financial agreements, which had just opened. As matters turned out, the first transfer of powers took place only on 12 October, five days after the promulgation of the Constitution.

It has already been explained that the federal budget was to be financed during the transitional period, from 1 September 1951 to 31 March 1952, by allocations paid by the provincial treasuries out of the United Kingdom and French grants-in-aid of which they were in receipt. Under the plan recommended by the Coordination Committee, the situation would be reversed as from 1 April 1952, from which date the several deficits, federal and provincial, would be consolidated. In the meantime, new grants-in-aid, of which the principal was the residual guarantee of the United Kingdom, would have been voted at Westminster. Thus the grant to Libya of foreign financial aid would be brought into harmony with the Constitution, by virtue of which the federal government was the sole instance authorized to accept such grants, which naturally involved relations with foreign Powers. Moreover, from the same date the federal government would begin to receive revenue from the federalized customs administration and start making grants to the provinces through the machinery provided for in Article 174 of the Constitution.

All this having been settled, or being well on the way to settlement, it remained to draw up a timetable for the progressive transfer of powers. To justify the complex procedures that had to be used, it may be useful to recall the manner in which, on 1 September 1951, functions of government in the three still independent provinces of Libya were exercised by no less than six different authorities. In his second annual report, paragraphs 138 and 139, the Commissioner summarized the situation on that date as follows:

> (a) In Cyrenaica, since the enactment of Proclamation No. 187 of 16 September 1949 on the Transitional Powers in Cyrenaica, executive, administrative and legislative powers with respect to internal matters had been conferred upon the Cyrenaican Government, which was set up under the Constitution proclaimed by the Amir on 18 September 1949; other powers had been retained by the United Kingdom as the Administering Power and were exercised by the British Resident.
>
> (b) In Tripolitania, executive and legislative powers with respect to internal matters were transferred to the Council of Regency by Proclamation No. 219 of 5 March 1951 on the Transitional Powers in Tripolitania, which set up that body; other powers had been retained by the United Kingdom as the Administering Power and were exercised by the British Resident.
>
> (c) In the Fezzan, the Transitional Régime established by Decision No. 3 of 12 February 1950 (superseded by Decision No. 5 of 29 March 1951) gave competence to the Government of the Fezzan set up under the *Chef du Territoire* to deal with a number of subjects affecting internal policy and administration; other powers were retained by France as the Administering Power and were exercised by the French Resident.
>
> . . . The powers to be transferred to the Federal Government were initially distributed among all these authorities, and therefore, in addition to transfers of power from the Administering Powers to the Provisional Government, as envisaged by General Assembly resolution 387 (V),

certain transfers were required as between the Libyan territorial governments and the Provisional Government of Libya.[75]

The Commissioner and the Coordination Committee had therefore been obliged, in preparing their plans, to seek solutions to three major problems:

1. The grouping and the sequence of the sixty-four powers to be transferred, and the proposing of the approximate date when the transfer of each group would take place;
2. The method and the legal instruments by which the transfer of powers from the three provincial governments to the Provisional Libyan Government should be effected; and
3. The method and the legal instruments by which the transfer of reserved powers from the Administering Powers to the Provisional Libyan Government and to the duly constituted Libyan Government which would succeed it should be effected.[76]

Furthermore, it must not be forgotten that the schedule for transfer was largely governed by the financial implications of the transfer of given groups of powers.

The sixty-four powers to be transferred to the Provisional Government, were, with its consent, finally divided into four groups. As mentioned in the second annual report, paragraphs 142–45, they respectively included the following powers and would be transferred according to the following timetable.

Group I comprised only the power relating to currency, the printing of notes, and the minting of coins. The United Kingdom indicated its readiness, after agreeing with the French Government, to transfer, in the first two weeks of September, such powers as would enable the Provisional Libyan Government to enact the necessary legislation for the establishment of a Provisional Currency Authority under Libyan law.

Group II, comprising twenty-four powers, would be transferred as soon as the necessary legal instruments could be drafted, the target date being 15 September. The powers in this group were:

Questions relating to nationality;
Stock exchanges;
Inquiries and statistics pertaining to the federal government;
Questions relating to the employees of the federal government;
Properties of the federal government;
Cooperation between the federal government on the one hand, and the provinces on the other, with regard to the work of the criminal police,

75. Ibid., paras. 138–39.
76. Ibid., para. 140.

the establishment of a central bureau for the criminal police, and the pursuit of international criminals;

Education in universities and other institutions of higher education and provisions regarding degrees;

Weights and measures;

All forms of insurance;

General judicial organization of the State;

Civil, commercial, and criminal laws;

Civil and criminal procedure;

Regulation of the legal profession;

Literary, artistic, and industrial copyright, inventions, agents, patents, trade marks, and merchandise marks;

Newspapers, books, printing presses, and broadcasting;

Infringements of the law on any subject within the legislative competence of the Federation, except with regard to matters falling within the competence of the Supreme Court;

All matters relating to the national flag and national anthem;

Public holidays;

Conditions for practicing the liberal, scientific, and technical professions;

General policy for education;

Antiquities and archaeological sites and any museum, library, and other institutions declared to be of national importance by federal law;

Public health and coordination of questions relating thereto;

Quarantines and their hospitals; and

Licences for practicing the medical professions and other professions connected with public health.

Group III, comprising eighteen powers, having considerable financial implications, was to be transferred upon the conclusion of the financial agreements. The powers in this group were:

Meteorology;

Posts and telegraphs, telephones, wireless, federal broadcasting, and similar forms of federal communications;

Federal roads and other roads declared by the federal government, after consultation with the provinces, not to be exclusively territorial roads;

Construction and control of federal railways, subject to the approval of the provinces which they would cross;

Customs;

Taxation necessary to meet the expenditures of the federal government, after consultation with the provinces;

Federal Bank;

Public debt;

Exchange;
Development of agricultural, industrial, and commercial production and the measures necessary to ensure the country essential foodstuffs in consultation with the provinces;
Organization of companies;
Income tax;
Monopolies and concessions;
Subsoil wealth, mining, and prospecting;
Expropriation;
Labor and social insurance matters;
Banking; and
Regulation of imports and exports.

The fourth and last group, group IV, comprising twenty-six powers, mostly concerned with foreign affairs and defense, were to be transferred on the day of proclamation of Libyan independence. The powers in this group were:

Diplomatic, consular, and trade representation;
Questions regarding the United Nations;
Participation in international conferences and bodies and the implementing of decisions made thereat;
Declaration of war and conclusion of peace;
Entering into and implementing of treaties and agreements with other countries;
Regulation of foreign trade;
Foreign loans;
Extradition and receiving of fugitive offenders;
Passports for traveling outside the Libyan federation, and visas;
Immigration and emigration;
Admission into and residence of foreigners in Libya, and their expulsion;
All matters relating to foreign affairs;
The recruiting, equipping, training, maintenance of land, sea, and air forces, and employment thereof for the defense of the State;
Defense industries;
Military, navy, and air force arsenals;
Delimitation of power in cantonment areas; appointment of powers of cantonment authorities within such areas; regulation of house accommodation within such areas and their delimitation, in consultation with the provinces;
Arms necessary for national defense, including fire arms, ammunition, and explosives;
Martial law;

Atomic energy and mineral resources essential to its production;
All other matters relating to national defense;
Airways;
Maritime shipping and navigation;
Major ports considered by the federal government to be of importance to international navigation;
Aircraft and air navigation; construction of airports;
Regulation of air traffic and administration of airports; and
Lighthouses, including lightships, beacons, and other provisions for the safety of sea and air navigation.

In the course of this final stage of transfer, the Administering Powers would also relinquish all such governmental powers, other than those relating to matters listed above, as they still possessed with respect to Libya, including all remaining powers of the Residents of the three territories then included in the "reserved list" and all other powers of the Residents relating to the approval of, or consultation with respect to, legislative or administrative acts of appointment by the Libyan authorities whether federal or territorial, and including also any remaining powers of the Administering Powers under General Assembly Resolution 388 (V) on the economic and financial provisions relating to Libya.[77]

While the members of the Coordination Committee had been laboring over these administrative and budgetary problems, the Legal Sub-Committee had been hard at work determining the form in which powers were to be made over.

With regard to the transfers to be made by the two Administering Powers, it was recommended that they be effected by formal instruments, separate for each province, identical in purpose and issued simultaneously. The transfer of powers with respect to matters within the competence of the territorial governments, and which had become federal powers by decision of the NCAL, would be made to the Provisional Libyan Government by means of formal instruments indicating the assent of the provincial governments and of the respective British and French Residents.[78]

77. In the event, the dates set above for the transfer of powers were delayed by about one month (see pp. 771 ff.).

78. The full text of Transfer of Powers Proclamations Nos. 1 and 2 issued on 12 October 1951 by the British Resident for Tripolitania and by the French Resident for the Fezzan will be found in *Second Annual Report of the United Nations Commissioner in Libya,* Annex XVI, pp. 137–40.

Transfer of Powers Proclamations Nos. 1 and 2 issued on 12 October 1951 by the British Resident for Cyrenaica will be found in *Supplementary Report to the Second Annual Report of the United Nations Commissioner in Libya,* Annex III, pp. 28–29.

Transfer of Powers Proclamation No. 3 issued on 15 December 1951 by the British

PART 7.
THE COUNCIL FOR LIBYA AND THE TRANSFER OF POWERS

When, in the course of its sixty-ninth and seventieth meetings held on 9 and 12 February 1951 in Geneva, the Council for Libya considered the Commissioner's memorandum on the establishment of the Coordination Committee, the Commissioner had assured the Council that any plan for the transfer of powers emerging from that Committee and accepted by him would be a draft, which could be discussed and, if necessary, amended. On 17 April, at its seventy-eighth meeting, the Council had been informed by the Commissioner that he hoped that the plan would be ready for the Council at the end of June or early in July. However, as we have seen in Part 4 of this chapter, the delays that marked the NCAL's deliberations on the distribution of powers meant that the Committee had by then been able to reach only tentative conclusions, which the Commissioner duly submitted to the Council for information. The latter, despite the fact that it had devoted two meetings to the subject, had not examined in detail the docu-

---

Residents for Tripolitania and Cyrenaica and by the French Resident for the Fezzan will be found in ibid., Annex VI, pp. 32–34.

Transfer of Powers Proclamation No. 4 issued on 24 December 1951 by the British Residents for Tripolitania and for Cyrenaica and by the French Resident for the Fezzan will be found in ibid., Annex II, pp. 25–27, and in Annex V to this study. The United Kingdom, moreover, issued at the Court of Buckingham Palace, on 4 December 1951, an Order entitled *Cyrenaica and Tripolitania (Termination of Administration) Order in Council, 1951,* the text of which will be found in ibid., Annex VII, p. 35, and in Annex VI to this study.

In order to simplify somewhat a complicated procedure, references to transfers of powers held by and made with the consent of the respective provincial authorities were included in Proclamations 2, 3, and 4. In this connection the following paragraph in Transfer of Powers (No. 2) Proclamation for Cyrenaica, following the signature of the British Resident, is particularly noteworthy:

Transfer of powers to the Provisional Libyan Government

IRADAH

We, Mohammed Idriss el Mahdi el Senussi, Amir of Cyrenaica, in accordance with the provisions of Article 14 of the Transitional Powers Proclamation No. 187 hereby signify our consent to the transfer of powers to the Provisional Government of Libya set forth in the Transfer of Powers (No. 1) Proclamation No. 191 and the Transfer of Powers (No. 2) Proclamation No. 192 made by the British Resident in Cyrenaica on the 12th day of October 1951.

(*Signed*) MOHAMMED IDRISS EL MAHDI EL SENUSSI

Made at Our Court of Al Manar this 14th day of October, 1951, equivalent to the 13th day of Muharram, 1371.

ments before it or made any specific recommendations. Although three members had raised objections, four had expressed the opinion that the plan was in harmony with the intent of General Assembly Resolution 387 (V), and that the Commissioner should continue along the lines he had laid down. For his part, the latter had promised that the final recommendations of the Coordination Committee would be submitted to the Council with a formal request for advice when it met again in Geneva in September (cf. pp. 764–65).

Unfortunately, the situation rapidly degenerated into a race against time. The Coordination Committee had agreed upon its final conclusions on 25 August. It took a week of hard work before these documents, including translations into Arabic, could be communicated to the Provisional Government (31 August). Another week passed before all the documents were ready for distribution in the Council's three working languages.[79]

As we have seen, the plan for the transfer of powers provided for a single power (currency, the printing of notes and the minting of coins) to be transferred between 1 and 15 September, and for a much larger group to be transferred by 15 September. It looked therefore as if, after all, the Commissioner, despite all his promises, would have to confront the Council yet again with a fait accompli—a most embarrassing situation, particularly since the members for Egypt and Pakistan seemed to suspect him of trying deliberately to deprive them of an opportunity of adequately examining the plan. To complicate matters even more, it proved extremely difficult to agree on a date and place of meeting convenient to all concerned.[80] The Commissioner was obliged to stay in Libya, where the NCAL was entering the critical final stage of its labors. The Council had adjourned on 28 July after having decided to reassemble in Geneva on 25 September. The agenda was heavy: two requests for advice: one regarding the program for the transfer of powers, the other on the meaning of the expression "duly constituted Libyan Government." Furthermore, the Commissioner had to consult the Council about his second annual report. Last, but not least, there was the

79. For texts of the documentation, see *Second Annual Report of the United Nations Commissioner in Libya,* Annex XII, pp. 89–129. For text of the request for advice on the draft program for the transfer of powers, see ibid., Annex XIII, pp. 129–32.

80. For a detailed statement of events, see "Statement regarding the Request of the United Nations Commissioner in Libya for Advice concerning a Draft Programme for the Transfer of Powers to the Provisional Libyan Government from the Administering Powers and the Libyan Territorial Governments, made by the Personal Representative of the United Nations Commissioner in Libya at the 85th meeting of the Council for Libya—28 September 1951," United Nations Doc. A/AC.32/COUNCIL/R.156, 28 September 1951. Mimeographed.

problem of the Constitution, which would have passed through its final stage without the Council having had sight even of a draft.

It was in these circumstances that on 27 August, as related on page 765, the Commissioner asked the Chairman of the Council—at that time the member for the United Kingdom—to convene the Council in Tripoli around 6 September for the specific purpose of giving him advice on the plan for the transfer of powers. This deadline could have been met, though not without difficulty, by shifting staff from the preparation of the annual report to that of the request for advice. However, the United States representative, who, by rotation, was to be Chairman for the month of September, supported by several of his colleagues, rejected this suggestion on grounds of convenience and insisted on the Council's meeting in Geneva in September. There ensued a half factual, half emotional clash which, if not carefully handled, could easily have become explosive. The scene was set for it. In Tripoli there was a grossly overworked staff, sweating it out in sultry, subtropical summer weather, nerves frayed to tatters.[81] Several members of the Council were enjoying leave in Europe. The Libyans were pressing for the transfer of powers to be put into motion, fearing that the Commissioner's request for advice might mean further delay. The Administering Powers, in their heart of hearts, were not at all keen on yet another debate which might well result in questions they considered settled being reopened. Finally, the Commissioner, anxious to have the Council's reaction to his plan and well aware of the blame he might incur if the transfer of powers were initiated before the Council had had time to comment on the plan, was sorely tempted to accuse his advisory body of shirking its primary duty. But, he asked himself, what advantage could he hope to derive from quarreling with people with whom he still had to cooperate for another four months and who might complicate the winding-up of his mission at the forthcoming session of the General Assembly? He therefore decided not to insist on an earlier meeting in Tripoli (see p. 766), consoling himself with the reflection that this postponement made work easier for his staff and that he could hardly be accused of dragging his feet after having taken the initiative. So the request for advice was finally considered by the Council at its eighty-fourth and eighty-fifth meetings, held in Geneva on 27 and 28 September 1951, in the absence of the Commissioner, who had gone with the NCAL to Benghazi. The decision to leave for Benghazi had been difficult to take, but it appeared to the Commissioner that for the good of

81. It was during this period that a medical expert of the World Health Organization, a member of the technical assistance team, considered it his duty to warn the Principal Secretary that he was driving the staff of the Mission beyond the limits of endurance.

the cause, and in all the circumstances, his role as adviser to the NCAL should take priority over his duty to attend the Council meetings, at which he could be replaced by the Principal Secretary, who was familiar with all the issues at stake and fully empowered to act as his personal representative. Several Council members, including the Chairman, agreed to this substitution.

To the understandable dismay of the Provisional Libyan Government, the transfer of powers was delayed. The first two groups were handed over only on 12 October. This enabled the Principal Secretary to assure the Council in all honesty that it was still in a position to recommend amendments to the transfer program. Had the Council seized this opportunity, the Commissioner would have been obliged to reconvene the Coordination Committee for the sole purpose of submitting the Council's recommendations to it; the Committee would then have been free to adopt or reject them. In either eventuality, it would have been for the Commissioner to decide whether to make a recommendation of his own to the Provisional Government, or, according to the subject matter, to the NCAL. In the final instance, it would have been within the competence of either of these two bodies to take a definite decision—individually or, and more probably, in consultation with one another. Admittedly, such a course might have created a delicate situation, and would certainly have wasted precious time, but at least the Council could no longer have complained that it had been confronted with a fait accompli. However, no amendment was even proposed.

The very fact that the possibility of a clash with the Provisional Libyan Government had to be reckoned with, illustrated a trend that was becoming more and more perceptible. That Government, three months away from the proclamation of independence, and, legally speaking, still without power, was nevertheless gaining in authority: authority by anticipation. Commissioner and Council, especially the latter, were slowly beginning to fade out of the picture, a development that some of its members seemed to resent. The Administering Powers saw themselves exchanging the position of responsible administrators for that of advisory though influential backers. Thus it was the opposition, both within and outside the Council, that was gradually finding itself faced with an accomplished situation. The crucial issue was whether the outside critics would prove capable of playing the role of a loyal, constitutional opposition in the new Libyan State.

When, on 25 September, the Council finally got down to business in Geneva, it was soon made plain that the Commissioner's absence was a sore point, particularly with the members for Egypt, Pakistan, and Tripolitania, who had apparently wanted to call him to task. Even the Italian representative joined in the chorus of protest. The Commissioner, foreseeing this situation, which was only to be expected, had attempted to forestall it by addressing an identical message to each of the ten Council members on 19 September. Invoking possible delay in the completion of the Constitution because of complications on vital issues which he feared might arise in Benghazi, he expressed regrets for his absence and asked the Council to choose between two procedures: either to continue its meetings in Geneva with the assistance of the Principal Secretary until the Constitution had been approved, when the Commissioner would immediately join them; or to move to Tripoli where, thanks to the United Nations plane, the Commissioner could be with them for half days while also carrying on his mission in Benghazi.

Rereading the text of this message after so many years, the Commissioner is bound to agree that the situation could not but have been obscure to any Council member not fully aware of what was going on in the NCAL. Indeed, with the exception of the representatives of the United Kingdom, France, Cyrenaica, the United States, and the Fezzan, none knew much about the subject, for the simple reason that the NCAL did not want them to be any better informed on constitutional matters than was the general public. It was understandably jealous of its prerogative of determining the country's Constitution, including the form of government, and had stubbornly refused to keep the Council in the picture. It had not forgotten the Commissioner's attempt earlier in the year to give advice opposed to the views held by the majority of its members about the nature of the Constitution being drafted. Subsequently, it had overcome its reluctance to listen to the Commissioner, but it still mistrusted the Council. This distrust in turn prevented the Commissioner from keeping the Council officially informed of the Assembly's progress. It had also made it difficult for him to explain clearly the reasons why he felt obliged to go to Benghazi for the NCAL's final meetings. To have told the Council more would have been a betrayal of the good faith of the Assembly's leaders, who had confided in him at length about their last-minute troubles.

As a result, there began to circulate among the members of the Council, some of whom were downright suspicious and all of whom were jealous of their right to know what was going on, the most extraordinary batch of rumors and half-truths about the Constitution. Some of them were, in all likelihood, simply put about for argument's sake; others were genuine beliefs rooted in ignorance. Generally speaking, however, it must be admitted that the Council knew far less about the drafting of the Constitution than it did, for instance, about the work of the Coordination Committee. One of the worst overt misunderstandings, apparently based on genuine conviction, was to the effect that the Constitution had originally been drafted in English by the British legal adviser. The member for Egypt, who advanced this thesis, gave the following version of the procedure:

> The drafting of the Constitution had been completed by the Committee the National Assembly had appointed for that purpose. That Committee had been composed of the most prominent members of the National Assembly and had been assisted by a British legal adviser. Selim Bey knew that adviser personally and could assure the members of the Council that it was the latter who had drawn up the Constitution in English. It had then been translated article by article into Arabic. The Egyptian legal adviser to whom [the Principal Secretary] had referred had prepared nothing, he had merely helped the Committee to understand what had been prepared for it. Since the Committee was composed of the most prominent men in the National Assembly, it was certain that its draft Constitution would be accepted by the Assembly; the Amir had been constantly informed of every step in the drafting of the Constitution and Selim Bey was sure that he, too, was satisfied with it, as were the British authorities.[82]

To anyone familiar with the true course of events this was a ludicrous distortion of the facts; but it is not surprising that in the minds of men poisoned by suspicion it should sound eminently plausible. To such it was unbelievable that constitutional issues should have arisen at the last moment, presumably among Libyans, of so vital a nature as to delay the completion of the Constitution and warrant the Commissioner's absence from Geneva. They therefore insisted on being told what the issues were and who had raised them. Had the NCAL formally asked the Commissioner for advice, or had he gone to Benghazi on his own account? Unless they were given a reply to that question, how could they judge whether they should go back to Tripoli or stay in Geneva? They also wanted to know why they had not yet seen the draft of the Constitution, and why the Commissioner had not sought their advice on it. The member for Pakistan stated that:

> [he] was convinced that the Commissioner and [the Principal Secretary] had seen the Libyan draft Constitution. They contended, however, that it could not be transmitted to the members of the Council, despite the fact that the Council was composed of responsible men who held very high positions both in their own countries and in the United Nations. Ob-

82. Summary Records of 83rd Meeting, United Nations Doc. A/AC.32/COUNCIL/SR.83, 27 September 1951, p. 5. Mimeographed.

> viously, the Commissioner feared that those members of the Council who were apt to voice criticisms would become rather a nuisance, were they allowed to see the draft Constitution; consequently, he had decided to withhold it from them. Was that a friendly or co-operative attitude or the way in which the Council should be treated?[83]

Their desire to see the draft Constitution was in itself entirely reasonable, not only because of the advisory functions the Council was called upon to discharge; not only because members were entitled to expect the Commissioner to consult it on such an important document before it was finally approved; but also and in particular because they had been informed that in the next few days the Council was going to be asked for its advice on the meaning of the expression "duly constituted Libyan Government." How could it give advice on this sensitive question without having previously studied the relevant provisions of the draft Constitution?

The Principal Secretary had a difficult two days trying to answer all the questions and criticisms addressed to him; he had to defend the Commissioner, while at the same time being careful not to commit the NCAL to the point where the Council could legitimately encroach upon its prerogatives. The record shows that he enjoyed support from other Council members, especially from the Cyrenaican representative, who even went so far as to say, later in the debate, that

> [he] understood the desire of the Egyptian representative that the Commissioner should join the Council in Geneva as soon as possible. He himself realized, however, that the presence of the Commissioner was far more necessary in Libya at the moment, for reasons which he was not in a position to explain to the Council.[84]

The Principal Secretary made the best of a bad job; but it was plain that he did not succeed in silencing his critics, partly because they did not want to be satisfied on the substance, partly also because they had firmly made up their minds not to give in to the Commissioner unless he could put an absolutely watertight case—from their point of view—to them.

When, on the second day of the discussion, the subject seemed to be exhausted, the member for Pakistan proposed the following passage as a summary of the situation, to be reported to the Commissioner:

> This Council, having considered the Commissioner's communication contained in document A/AC.32/COUNCIL/R.153 and having heard the statements of the representative of the Commissioner, requests the Chair-

83. Ibid., p. 7.
84. Ibid., p. 20.

> man to inform the Commissioner by cable that the information at the disposal of the Council is insufficient to enable the Council to decide on either of the two alternatives mentioned in the last paragraph of the Commissioner's communication. The Council considers that it is essential that the Commissioner should meet the Council in Geneva at the earliest possible date and assist it to reach a decision on the alternatives suggested by the Commissioner.[85]

The Council decided so to inform the Commissioner.

Following a suggestion made by the Chairman, the representative of the United States, it was also agreed that the Principal Secretary should inform the Commissioner that the Council had expressed a formal desire to study a copy of the draft Constitution as soon as he could obtain it from the NCAL.

On 28 September, the Chairman received the following reply from the Commissioner:

> I profoundly regret that primary duties laid upon me by General Assembly resolution of 21 November 1949 oblige me to stay with National Assembly at the very moment it may most require my aid and advice. At same time I entirely agree with Council desire I should join them soonest possible in Geneva. I will therefore arrive Geneva as soon as my presence here no longer necessary.[86]

On 1 October the Principal Secretary informed the Council that

> the Commissioner had discussed with the Bureau of the National Assembly and the Chairman of the National Assembly Sub-Committee on the Constitution the question of communicating to the Council the draft Libyan Constitution. They had agreed that the text of the Constitution should be distributed to the members of the Council on the understanding that it would be made quite clear that the text was the text drafted by the Committee on the Constitution, and that it had not yet been approved by the National Assembly, which was quite free to accept, amend, or reject it.[87]

This somewhat emotional interlude over, the Council at last settled down to the first substantive item on its agenda, which was the Commissioner's request for advice on the transfer of powers. On this issue the Council had

85. Ibid., p. 18.

86. Summary Records of 85th Meeting, United Nations Doc. A/AC.32/COUNCIL/SR.85, 28 September 1951, p. 22. Mimeographed.

87. Summary Records of 86th Meeting, United Nations Doc. A/AC.32/COUNCIL/SR.86, 1 October 1951, p. 2. Mimeographed.

not only been kept well informed; it was also fully documented. The request put to the Council was to advise the Commissioner:

> whether the draft programme for a transfer of powers to the Provisional Libyan Government and the duly constituted Libyan Government . . . , considered in the light of the explanation furnished hereunder and the supporting documentation furnished to the Council, is in conformity with the provisions of General Assembly resolution 387 (V), paragraph 3.[88]

The contents of document A/AC.32/CC.19 and "the explanation furnished hereunder" have already been extensively summarized. An extract and a factual summary of the discussion that followed can also be found in the Commissioner's second annual report, Chapter II, paragraphs 167–79 (pp. 31–34).

Nonetheless, the Principal Secretary, as personal representative of the Commissioner, took care to recount in an opening statement the history of the transfer of powers operation, reminding the Council of each occasion on which it had been informed about it, and pointing out that no powers had as yet been transferred, so that no charge of presenting the Council with a fait accompli could be made. His effort was of no avail. Even more insistently than in July, the opposition maintained its point of view, namely, that the submission of a detailed plan, including a timetable, was in itself an accomplished fact, whether or not the actual transfer of powers had started. Theoretically, they had a case. But then it would have been necessary to consult the Council on every detail at every stage of the plan from the day on which the Coordination Committee had been set up in January until the adoption of its final conclusions in August. Such a procedure, which would have resulted in constant clashes, all sorts of complications, and loss of time to an extent incompatible with the General Assembly's wishes, would clearly have been unworkable.

Another question that loomed large in the discussion was the NCAL's resolution of 5 September 1951, vesting the Provisional Libyan Government with authority to exercise the powers to be transferred to it (pp. 789–90). The member for Egypt, supported—without much conviction—by his colleague from Pakistan, argued at length that the General Assembly had not given the National Assembly carte blanche to grant the Provisional Libyan Government the right to exercise the powers it was to receive. The NCAL was not entitled to do so, he claimed, first, because it had not been elected but appointed, and second because it was responsible to no one. This last point was not entirely without weight. Indeed, the responsibility of

88. *Second Annual Report of the United Nations Commissioner in Libya,* Annex XIII, p. 129.

the Provisional Government to the NCAL had never been formally determined. It certainly was not responsible to the King. Nor was it responsible to the Administering Powers, as the member for the United Kingdom had claimed in the course of the debate, only to retract his claim shortly afterward. It would have been more to the point to recall—though nobody thought of doing so—a statement made by the President of the NCAL in reply to a question put to him by a Tripolitanian member at its nineteenth meeting on 29 March 1951 to the effect that he considered the Provisional Government to be responsible to the NCAL. What was even more important was that in fact the Government itself appeared to feel responsible to the NCAL, and that the latter had occasionally called upon the former to explain to it certain executive actions, for instance, in connection with the currency question.

Whatever the exact nature of this preconstitutional relationship might have been, several members of the Council were evidently intrigued by the question of what could have moved the Egyptian representative to argue that the Provisional Government was not competent to exercise power. Could it be part of a tactical attempt to delay the proclamation of independence by arguing that powers could only be exercised by the "duly constituted Libyan Government," and that this in turn could only be established after an elected Parliament had been brought into being? Or could it even be a more far-reaching attempt to reopen the whole Libyan problem at the Sixth Session of the General Assembly of the United Nations? Whatever the answer to these questions, the other members of the Council took the line that the drafters of Resolution 387 (V) could not have intended that powers should be transferred to the Provisional Government without its also being empowered to exercise them. Only the members for Pakistan and Tripolitania declined to share this opinion, the latter, as previously, refusing to take part in the debate.

Not a word of substantive comment was uttered on the content, merits, or demerits of the plan and its concomitant documentation. A majority expressed their general approval of it. In particular, the United States member deemed that the manner in which the question of the transfer of powers had been dealt with was in conformity with the provisions of the General Assembly Resolution, and that the proposed program appeared to be calculated to achieve the General Assembly's wishes in a most efficient manner. He accordingly tabled the following draft resolution:

> *The United Nations Council for Libya,*
>
> *Having considered* the Commissioner's request for advice concerning the draft programme for the transfer of powers to the Provisional Federal Libyan Government by the Administering Powers . . . ,

Having examined the supporting documentation furnished to the Council by the Commissioner, and in particular the provisions of the resolution of the Libyan National Assembly of 18 August 1951, determining the powers of the Libyan Federal Government and of the Provincial Administrations,

Noting with satisfaction the decision of the Governments of Cyrenaica, Tripolitania and the Fezzan to contribute to the expenses of the Federal Government until 31 March 1952 in a manner which will enable the Federal Government to exercise its powers,

Noting the conclusions reached by the Co-ordination Committee, with the participation of the representatives of the Administering Powers, the Provisional Federal Government and the territorial Governments,

(a) That the powers exercised in Libya on behalf of the Governments of the United Kingdom and France will be fully relinquished by these Governments before the end of 1951 or on such an earlier date as may be decided for the proclamation of Libyan independence; and

(b) That the powers which are at present exercised by the Governments of Cyrenaica, Tripolitania and the Fezzan, and which, in accordance with the decisions of the National Assembly, are to become federal powers under the Libyan Constitution, will be transferred to the Federal Government before the date of independence,

1. *Considers* that the programme of transfer of powers drawn by the Commissioner in co-operation with the Administering Powers conforms to the provisions of General Assembly resolution 287 (V), paragraph 3;

2. *Expresses* its confidence that the programme will be fully and effectively implemented within the time period prescribed by the General Assembly and calls upon the United Nations Commissioner, the Administering Powers, the Provisional Libyan Government and the Governments of Cyrenaica, Tripolitania and the Fezzan to co-operate and mutually co-ordinate their activities toward that end.[89]

Further discussion followed, during which the Principal Secretary warmly welcomed the United States draft resolution. The members for Egypt, Pakistan, and Tripolitania seemed unmoved. During the last few minutes, however, all three, who had been sailing so close to the wind, decided to allow themselves a little more sea room. The representative of Pakistan announced that if, in the first line of the second operative paragraph, the word "confidence" were replaced by "hope," he would have no objection to voting for the United States draft resolution. The amendment was accepted. His Egyptian colleague said that he had reached the conclusion that

89. Ibid., para. 176.

it would make no difference whether the United States draft resolution was adopted or rejected. He could not bring himself to vote on such a resolution and would therefore abstain, but he wished it to be clearly understood that he was not doing so because he was in any way opposed to the transfer of powers to the Libyan people. His one desire was to see all powers in the hands of Libya as soon as possible.[90]

The Tripolitanian member followed the same course, without explaining his vote. Clearly none of the three was prepared to take a stand which could have been interpreted by Libyan public opinion as hostile to independence by the end of 1951. And so it came to pass that the United States draft resolution was at last adopted by 7 votes to none, with 2 abstentions (Egypt and Tripolitania).[91]

It looked like a peaceful ending to a bitter debate, but, in fact, those who thought that all was to be plain sailing from then on were gravely mistaken. Such illusions were shattered when on 1 October the debate opened on the Commissioner's further request for advice concerning the meaning of the expression "the duly constituted Libyan Government."

The issue would probably never have arisen had it been agreed in 1950 that both the Committee of Twenty-One and the NCAL should be elected, not appointed. It might also have been avoided if, in 1951, the latter had finished its work early enough in the year to allow a general election to be held and an elected parliament to be convened before or at the moment when independence was proclaimed. That this was not the case was no reason for crying over spilled milk, but it could not be denied that a problem had been created which was unforeseen in General Assembly Resolutions 289 (IV) and 387 (V). Indeed, Libyan constitutional development had taken longer than anticipated by the authors of those resolutions or by the Commissioner himself. This was in part due to the Cyrenaican and Fezzanese preference for a federation, with its inherently complicated structure, and to the original Tripolitanian opposition to elections; in part to the British and French policy of giving priority to the transfer of powers to the provinces over that to a central government. Admittedly, the Pakistani member had repeatedly warned the Council to beware of such a delay; but

90. Summary Records of 85th Meeting, United Nations Doc. A/AC.32/COUNCIL/SR.85, 28 September 1951, p. 21. Mimeographed.

91. When this vote was taken, the Cyrenaican chair technically was vacant. Unayzi was only sitting in for Ali Bey Jerbi, following the latter's resignation, and was therefore not entitled to vote. At the beginning of the eighty-seventh meeting (2 October), he was formally installed as the member for Cyrenaica and thenceforward exercised his voting rights.

he had never proposed a practical way of preventing it. The Committee of Eighteen, advised by the Commissioner and the Coordination Committee, had found a way out of the difficulty by including in the Constitution the transitional and provisional provisions governing the formation of a duly constituted Government and laying down a legally binding timetable for drafting an electoral law and holding elections. It had been hoped for a while that this timetable might have been kept before the deadline set for the proclamation of independence, that is, not later than 1 January 1952. But with the chances of this growing dimmer day by day, the Commissioner began to fear that a state of confusion would ensue, dangerous enough to compromise the timely achievement of Libyan independence in the eyes of the General Assembly. It was one thing to attempt to avert such a development by writing certain precautionary measures into the Constitution; it was quite another to convince the General Assembly that this was the *right* thing to do. This, he felt, was a typical situation on which the Council's advice should be sought, for to appear before the General Assembly without having done so might well expose him to justified censure. So on 24 September he submitted a request for advice.[92]

In stating his need, after having explained the situation in which he found himself, and having emphasized that the draft Constitution provided for an elected Parliament, he formulated the issue as follows:

> Technical factors with respect to the establishment of the electoral machinery have governed the fixing of the above-mentioned periods of time. It appears from these time periods that, although they establish deadlines, the possibility cannot be excluded that the election for the House of Representatives may not be constituted before 1 January 1952. In that eventuality, the question would arise whether the King and the Cabinet constituted by him could be considered as the duly constituted government envisaged by the General Assembly, or whether, alternatively, the establishment of all principal governmental organs, King, Council of Ministers, both Houses of Parliament, and Supreme Court, would be necessary in order that there may be "a duly constituted Libyan Government." [93]

The argument continued:

> This question is linked to that of transfer of power. Can all powers of government be transferred under paragraph 3 (c) of resolution 387 (V)

92. For the full text of the request, see *Second Annual Report of the United Nations Commissioner in Libya,* Annex XIV, pp. 132–35.

93. Ibid., pp. 133–34.

to the Provisional Government? Or must the final stages of the transfer of powers, those pertaining in particular to foreign affairs and defence, be effected between the administering States and "the duly constituted government"? In case the second assumption is correct, in the absence of "a duly constituted government" before 1 January 1952, would the postponement of the date of the final transfer of power and consequently of the date of independence have to be envisaged until such time as the House of Representatives is constituted and assumes its responsibilities with respect to legislation and in relation to the Council of Ministers?[94]

Having noted, moreover, that neither the General Assembly's Resolutions nor the official records of its deliberations provided any specific definition of the expression "a duly constituted . . . Government," the Commissioner asked the Council kindly to advise him on the following points:

1. Can a Libyan Government, consisting of the King and of a Council of Ministers appointed by Him upon the declaration of Libyan independence and in accordance with the constitution, be considered as the "duly constituted Libyan Government" referred to by the General Assembly, with the understanding that the constitution which is to come into effect on the date of proclamation of independence will contain provisions for an elected House of Representatives, that the elections will take place within a time period specified in the constitution, and, in all likelihood, shortly after 1 January 1952?
2. In case the answer to the first question is in the negative, what course of action, consistent with the General Assembly resolutions, would the Council advise the Commissioner to take?
3. Can all functions of government, including foreign affairs and defence, be transferred to the Provisional Federal Government, subject to that Government's transferring those functions in its turn to the government constituted in accordance with the provisions of the constitution?
4. In case the answer to the third question is in the negative, what course of action consistent with paragraph 3 (c) of General Assembly resolution 387 (V) would the Council advise the Commissioner to take.[95]

As might have been expected, the representative for Pakistan opened the debate by recalling his earlier warnings and accusing the Commissioner of having made a serious mistake in not raising the question earlier; the hour at which he had finally done so was indeed late.

The ominous consequence of that mistake, he argued, was that the Coun-

94. Ibid., p. 134.
95. Ibid., pp. 134–35.

cil was confronted with two alternatives: either it could agree to consider the Provisional Government as the "duly constituted . . . government" so that powers could be transferred to it and Libyan independence proclaimed before 1 January 1952; or it could postpone the date of Libyan independence until a "duly constituted . . . government" had been established. By refusing to subscribe to the theory that a "duly constituted . . . government" was a government established in conformity with the Constitution, the Pakistani representative refuted the solution adopted by the Committee of Eighteen. At the same time, he insisted that it was the duty of the Commissioner and the Administering Powers to establish a duly constituted Government in Libya before 1 January 1952, and accordingly rejected the argument that the NCAL itself claimed that it would take three and a half months to organize elections in Libya; it was inconceivable that it should take so long, given the people's desire for independence at the earliest possible moment.

In his opinion, a duly constituted Government was:

> a Government which derived its power from the people of the country, as the result of elections in which they were able freely to express their views, and which was based on democratic principles that were recognized as an integral part of modern civilization. Regardless of whom the people concerned had chosen as their leader and so long as popular opinion had been freely expressed, the Government resulting from the election could be considered "duly constituted" if it had the attributes of democracy, if it was responsible to the people, through the King or Parliament, and if it recognized that all its citizens had equal rights. No Government which failed to fulfil those conditions could ever be called a "duly constituted Government." [96]

This point of view was quite defensible on general principles; but its application to the case under consideration would in fact have led to a situation contrary to the aims of the General Assembly, which had recommended in Resolution 289 (IV) that the independence of Libya should "become effective as soon as possible and [*in any case*] not later than 1 January 1952." The member for Pakistan asked for a quick legal opinion on the issue, a demand that was supported by several other members of the Council.

The member for Egypt spoke along very much the same lines. According to him the correct procedure would be the following:

96. Summary Records of 86th Meeting, United Nations Doc. A/AC.32/COUNCIL/SR.86, 1 October 1951, pp. 11–12. Mimeographed.

> once the elections had been held and the Parliament set up, the King would take the oath before the representatives of the people and would appoint the Council of Ministers; the latter would appear before Parliament, which would take a vote of confidence in it. Only then would Parliament and King together declare the independence of their country. If it were declared in those circumstances, it would indeed be true independence, for it would be based upon the setting up of all the mechanism necessary for the smooth functioning of a State." [97]

He at least frankly faced the fact that the Commissioner would be obliged to ask the General Assembly for an additional two months, to make up lost time; that interval would allow elections to be held and a duly representative constitutional Government to be set up.

The Chairman, speaking as representative of the United States, was of an entirely different opinion:

> In his opinion, there was no legal question involved in the interpretation of the phraseology used by the General Assembly. That body had not attempted to conceal its meaning beneath a mass of verbiage. It had meant exactly what it said: namely, that the powers to be transferred should be transferred to a duly constituted Government. A duly constituted Government could only be a Government established in conformity with the laws of the land, in the case in question in conformity with the provisions of the Constitution.
>
> By the terms of the General Assembly resolutions, the Libyan National Assembly was to determine the Constitution, including the form of government. The National Assembly had been convened, had set up a Provisional Libyan Government and was about to complete its determination of the Libyan Constitution. It seemed to him, therefore, that the answer to the Commissioner's request for advice should be that if the Libyan Constitution, as determined by the National Assembly, authorized the King and a Council of Ministers appointed by him to function as a duly constituted Libyan Government, such a Government was indeed the "duly constituted Libyan Government" envisaged by the General Assembly; if the Constitution did not contain that authorization, such a Government would not be the "duly constituted Libyan Government." The question, therefore, was one to be determined by the Libyan Courts of Justice and was not the concern of the Council.[98]

97. Ibid., p. 19.

98. Summary Records of 87th Meeting, United Nations Doc. A/AC.32/COUNCIL/SR.87, 2 October 1951, p. 6. Mimeographed.

Hence, he concluded, his answer to the first half of the Commissioner's first question was decidedly in the affirmative. The proviso contained in the second half of the question seemed to him quite irrelevant, because he believed that: "Whether the Constitution contained provisions for an elected House of Representatives or whether elections were to take place within a specified period did not in any way affect the major question of what constituted a "duly constituted Libyan Government." [99]

Having answered the first question in the affirmative, he did not need to reply to the second question in the Commissioner's request for advice.

With regard to the third question, he repeated what he had said earlier, namely:

> that whether the functions referred to could in fact be transferred to the Provisional Federal Government and thence to the Government constituted in accordance with the provisions of the Constitution was a question which could be determined only by the Libyan Constitution, as interpreted by the Courts of Libya. That being so, there was no answer to be given to question 4.[100]

The United States representative ended his intervention by tabling a draft resolution worded as follows:

> *The United Nations Council for Libya,*
> *Having considered* the Commissioner's request for advice concerning the meaning of the expression "the duly constituted Libyan Government," as used in General Assembly resolutions 289 (IV) and 387 (V) . . ,
> *Is of the opinion*
> (1) That by "duly constituted Libyan Government" it was the intention of the General Assembly to mean a government established under provisions of the Libyan Constitution; and
> (2) That all functions of government may appropriately be progressively transferred to the Provisional Libyan Government in a manner which will ensure that all powers which, in accordance with the Libyan Constitution come within the competence of the duly constituted Libyan Government, will be transferred by 1 January 1952 to such a government established under the provisions of the Libyan Constitution.[101]

From this point on the discussion became a duel between two schools of thought: one affirming that a duly constituted Government should be based on general elections to be held before the declaration of independence; the

99. Ibid., p. 7.
100. Ibid.
101. *Second Annual Report of the United Nations Commissioner in Libya,* para. 188.

other affirming that a Government established in conformity with the provisions of the Constitution would be a duly constituted Government.

The United Nations legal adviser, when invited to express an opinion on the legal aspects of what was meant by the expression "duly constituted Libyan Government," submitted the following conclusions, with problems of the transfer of powers in particular in mind:

> It may first be noted that under the proposed text of the Libyan Constitution, the elected Chamber would not immediately possess the same degree of power and influence in the process of the formation of a Council of Ministers as is enjoyed by Parliaments in certain other countries which have adopted and practiced the system of constitutional monarchy. The Libyan Council of Ministers does apparently not require an affirmative vote of confidence of the House of Representatives before assuming the exercise of its constitutional functions. The initiative of a proposal of a vote of non-confidence must be taken by fifteen members of the House of Representatives on conditions provided in Article 87 of the Constitution. It seems correct to assume that until such a motion of non-confidence is approved, the Council of Ministers would remain in power and would continue to exercise validly its functions as long as it would retain the confidence of the King (article 72).
>
> The provisions of article 64 of the Constitution may also be mentioned. Under the draft Constitution Parliament is to meet in regular session and it may also meet in extraordinary sessions. With respect to intervals between such sessions, article 64 provides that
>
> > "If, when Parliament is not in session, exceptional circumstances arise which necessitate urgent measures, the King may issue decrees in respect thereof which shall have the force of law provided that they are not contrary to the provisions of this Constitution. Such decrees must be submitted to Parliament at its first meeting; if they are not approved by either of the Chambers they shall cease to have the force of law."
>
> Although this article does not apply to the case under consideration, it is significant to note that the proposed Libyan constitutional system envisages the contingency of certain legislative functions of Parliament being exercised temporarily and subject to confirmation by Parliament, by the King and the Ministers.
>
> Such constitutional situations are not unknown in democratic countries, whether in normal times or during periods of emergency when it is not possible to call a session of Parliament. . . .
>
> The constitutional history of new States having gained independence shows many examples of transitional periods during which until Parlia-

mentary organs could be elected, legislative as well as executive powers were concentrated provisionally in the hands of the Government. The specific assurance inserted in the draft Libyan Constitution that the Libyan Parliament will be constituted and in a position to exercise its constitutional functions within a specific period, is significant in this respect.

In the light of these considerations and placing oneself on purely legal grounds, it would seem therefore possible to conclude, that under the provisions of the General Assembly resolutions with respect to Libya, a Government constituted in accordance with the transitory provisions proposed by the Constitutional Committee [*sic*] for the approval of the National Assembly, could be considered as the duly constituted government for the purposes provided in paragraph 10 (a) of General Assembly resolution 289 (IV) and 3 (c) of resolution 387 (V).[102]

The members for Pakistan and Egypt were critical of this legal opinion, the former contending that too much emphasis was placed on the fact that the expression "the duly constituted . . . Government" had not been specifically paraphrased or determined in the General Assembly Resolutions or in its discussions. They considered that the Legal Adviser should have paid more attention to the Commissioner's statements at the three hundred and sixth and three hundred and seventh meetings at the Fifth Session of the General Assembly about the nature of the National Assembly and the Constitution it was to prepare.[103]

One objection advanced by the member for Egypt was that the opinion just submitted to the Council was not legal but political in nature.

The member for the United States stated that, on the contrary:

United States Government lawyers had studied the same material as that quoted by the Pakistani representative and had come to exactly the same conclusions as [the legal adviser to the United Nations Mission], namely, that according to the provisions of the General Assembly resolution a Government constituted in accordance with the transitory provisions of the draft Constitution as submitted to the National Assembly by its Committee could be considered the duly constituted Libyan Government. They had in fact gone further and had said that it *should* be considered the duly constituted Government.[104]

102. For the full text of this legal opinion, see Annex IX, pp. 953–57.

103. See GAOR: Fifth Session, 1950, 306th Plenary Meeting, 16 November 1950, pp. 411–12; and 307th Plenary Meeting, 17 November 1950, pp. 421–22.

104. Summary Records of 89th Meeting, United Nations Doc. A/AC.32/COUNCIL/SR.89, 6 October 1951, p. 20. Mimeographed.

In the course of the debate the member for Pakistan had raised another point of interest relevant to the question under discussion. He had drawn attention to it before, but never so incisively as on this occasion. The Commissioner had always held that his advice was not binding on the Libyan people or, ipso facto, on either the NCAL or the Provisional Government, whether or not that advice was supported by the Council. The Pakistani representative, strongly supported by his Egyptian colleague, thought otherwise:

> if it was conceded that the Commissioner and Council had been sent to Libya to assist the Libyans to draw up their Constitution, it followed logically that any action that was taken against their advice—and the disinterested and judicial character of that advice, which would be in conformity with the principles and purposes of the United Nations Charter, could not *a priori* be questioned—could not be right. By appointing a Commissioner and setting up a Council for Libya, the General Assembly had implicitly indicated that it expected the representatives of the Libyan people to respect the advice they would be given. He did not think, therefore, that the freedom of action claimed for the Libyan people could be admitted to quite such an extent as the United States representative seemed to think.[105]

Obviously, had this point of view been recognized from the outset as legally valid—which it was not—the relationship between the Council, the Commissioner, and the National Assembly would have been radically different. In fact, such an approach might well have led to open hostility. This was indeed the very point which had made the NCAL so deeply suspicious of the Council. Had the issue never been raised, relations between the two bodies would in all likelihood have been more mutually trustful. The Council's advice would have carried more weight, and the Commissioner would have found himself less often between the devil and the deep blue sea.

Thus the battle swayed backward and forward for almost five lengthy meetings, speakers becoming increasingly repetitious. The United States representative refused to accept a Pakistani amendment that the words "based on elections" be inserted after the word "Government" in the first paragraph of his draft resolution. Had his amendment been incorporated, the Pakistani representative would have voted for the resolution. As it was, he abstained.

On the other hand, the United States representative agreed to an amendment proposed by the new member for Cyrenaica who, like his colleague

105. Summary Records of 88th Meeting, United Nations Doc. A/AC.32/COUNCIL/SR.88, 3 October 1951, p. 19. Mimeographed.

from the Fezzan, was firmly opposed to any attempt to postpone independence beyond 1 January 1952, for which he saw no valid reason. Unayzi fully agreed with the Legal Adviser's conclusions, and warmly defended the Constitution adopted the day before in Benghazi, which, he stressed, provided for a democratic parliamentary State, including an elected House of Representatives. The only problem was *when* the elections would take place; that was purely a technical and practical question. In no case could elections be considered an essential prerequisite to independence. Using the argument advanced the year before by the Tripolitanian Congress Party against holding elections under the watchful eye of the Administering Powers, he urged that:

> it was absolutely essential that all powers, without exception, should be transferred by the Administering Powers before the elections took place, in order to avoid any possibility of foreign interference in the conduct of the elections; otherwise, even if the Administering Powers did not influence the electors in any way—and he was sure that they would not—there would always be criticism that the elections had not been free.[106]

As to the United States draft resolution, he objected to the second operative paragraph, which appeared to envisage a transfer of powers in two stages. He proposed, therefore, that it be amended to read:

> (2) That all functions of government may appropriately be progressively transferred to the Provisional Federal Libyan Government in a manner which will ensure that all powers which, in accordance with the Libyan Constitution come within the competence of the duly constituted *Federal* Libyan Government, will be transferred by 1 January 1952, to a government established under the provisions of the Libyan Constitution.[107]

The Cyrenaican representative concluded by stating that:

> the expression "the duly constituted Libyan Government" meant the Libyan Government constituted after the promulgation of the Constitution and in accordance with its provisions. His delegation therefore replied in the affirmative to the Commissioner's first and third questions, which meant that there was no need for it to reply to the second and fourth questions.[108]

When at last the Chairman took the vote, the outcome was 6 for the United States draft resolution as amended by Cyrenaica (Cyrenaica, Fez-

106. Summary Records of 90th Meeting, United Nations Doc. A/AC.32/COUNCIL/SR.90, 8 October 1951, pp. 6–7. Mimeographed.

107. Ibid.

108. Ibid., p. 8.

zan, France, Italy, United Kingdom, and the United States) 2 against (Egypt and Tripolitania), with 2 abstentions (Minorities and Pakistan).

One more crisis had been weathered, and, although the majority was the smallest possible under the Council's rules of procedure, and although the Libyan Parliament would only be elected in February 1952, the decision carried enough weight to remove any lingering doubts about the legality of declaring Libya independent before the end of the year.

PART 8. THE DAWNING OF INDEPENDENCE

One of the attractions of the United Nations Mission was that there was never a dull moment. After the promulgation of the Constitution on 7 October, the Commissioner hurried from Benghazi to Geneva, with a brief stopover in Tripoli, where, on the surface, the political situation was unusually quiet. From conversations with local political leaders he gained the impression that the parties were reconsidering their positions in the light of the new situation resulting from the imminence of the transfer of powers, the preparation of the electoral law, and the forthcoming declaration of independence. The public was coming to know the details of the Constitution, and as a whole seemed satisfied. A good many members of the public asked the United Nations Information Officers in Tripoli and Benghazi for copies of the Constitution. The press, even the opposition newspaper, *Shu'lat al-Hurriya,* published on 15 October 1951 large extracts prepared by these same officers. Nevertheless, Beshir Bey Saadawi, in an interview with the editor of the local English newspaper, *The Sunday Ghibli,* published on 28 October, declared that he considered the Constitution as a draft, the last word on which should be left to Parliament. He would not say whether the Constitution was good or bad, only that a freely elected Government should have the power to alter it if necessary. He made some conciliatory remarks about Great Britain, saying that he would be happy to see Libya conclude an alliance with her, and, indeed, with other Western powers. However, such alliances ought, he felt, to be left to be negotiated by a Government freely elected by and from all the people of the country. Libya was a poor country, and he for one would be happy to see Britain help her in every possible way. The Congress Party intended to participate in the coming elections, but he wanted safeguards in view of possible falsification of the results. All this sounded as if the opposition party was revising its policies; but it also revealed that public opinion was aware of the fact that financial agreements were being negotiated, at least with the United Kingdom.

This time, the principal criticism of the Constitution came from the Benghazi paper, *al-Istiqlal,* authorized by the Cyrenaican Government to reappear after having been prohibited for six months. On 6 October, its leading article bore the title "We had been promised federalism; we are given unitarism."

Another complaint of a different nature was voiced by the Jewish community in Tripoli, to the effect that the Constitution did not specifically recognize the right of emigration. This was an important matter for the Libyan Jews at that moment, in view of their exodus to Israel. At the Commissioner's request, the Prime Minister gave an assurance that no obstacles would be put in the way of these mass departures.

From the outset of the financial negotiations, the Commissioner was kept in the picture, both sides asking him for advice and comments. It soon appeared that the negotiations would not be easy. They were, moreover, technically complicated by the fact that whereas the Prime Minister and his Finance Minister were negotiating with the British Resident in Tripoli, who depended on London for instructions, the Commissioner had to deal with the British member of the Council for Libya in Geneva, where at the same time rather tense consultations were being conducted on his second annual report. Fortunately, the United Nations radio network and its capable staff provided a fast day-and-night service. Furthermore, the United Nations DC-3 and its indefatigable crew were available for rapid journeys from Geneva to Tripoli and back whenever the situation could not be handled by cable.

The problem had one rather special and somewhat ironical aspect. When it had been decided in the Coordination Committee to divide the powers to be progressively transferred into four groups, it had been considered natural, not only on legal and political grounds, but also for practical reasons, to relegate to the fourth and last group all powers connected with defense and foreign relations; that is to say, all those powers which make a State master of its own fate, or, to use the hallowed term, a sovereign and independent State. Hence these powers were to be handed over on the day of independence itself. However, there was a snag. The plan also provided for the negotiation and conclusion of financial agreements between Libya and the Administering Powers prior to the transfer of the powers in the third group. In fact, this particular operation was subject to the conclusion of the agreements. Yet at that juncture the Provisional Libyan Government would not technically be entitled to enter into negotiation with foreign Governments. Hence, it had to be specially empowered to that effect. A special and identical clause was therefore included in all three Transfer of Powers (No. 2) Proclamations, issued on 12 October, 1951; it read as follows:

Power to make and implement certain Agreements

. . . Power is hereby transferred to the Provisional Government of Libya to conclude financial agreements with the Administering Powers in order to enable the transfer of further powers and to take any executive or legislative action appropriate for the implementation of any such agreement.[109]

Nobody felt entirely happy about this stratagem, least of all the Provisional Government, which realized that it put into the hands of the Administering Powers an instrument through which they could exert pressure to enforce their terms. However, as no alternative was in sight, and Libya could not achieve independence without financial support, the Council of Ministers reluctantly gave in. There was, of course, one way of lessening the pressure, namely, by delaying the transfer of powers and the declaration of independence until shortly before 1 January 1952, when both sides would be under equal pressure to meet the ultimate deadline set by the General Assembly. But this conflicted with other Libyan views and interests, as will emerge.

At the time at which these various factors had to be weighed one against the other, it was assumed that the Libyan item would come up for discussion in the General Assembly well before Christmas.[110] But nothing definite had yet been decided, one reason being that, owing to circumstances already explained, the consultations between the Council and the Commissioner on the latter's second annual report had started late. He knew even less when he would be able to draft and submit his final report. The Provisional Libyan Government naturally wanted independence to come before the debate opened in the General Assembly. Underlying this desire, shared by all who wanted to see the emancipation of Libya brought to a happy ending before the end of the year, was the idea of self-proclaimed independence as opposed to independence conferred by the General Assembly. Not only would the Libyan delegation then appear in a more dignified and stronger position, taking its seat in the Assembly Hall as an equal among equals; it would also be better placed to counteract possible maneuvers to make its independence subject to conditions proposed by certain meddlesome friends. This danger was not wholly imaginary. Indeed, the Arab Press, in

109. See *Supplementary Report to the Second Annual Report of the United Nations Commissioner in Libya,* Annex III, p. 29.

110. The Sixth Session of the General Assembly was held in Paris and opened later than usual—on 6 November 1951—in the Palais de Chaillot. After a break over Christmas and the New Year, it resumed its work in January 1952, closing on 5 February.

particular that in Cairo, was heavy with rumors that the Government of Egypt, together with those of other Arab States, intended to table a proposal that parliamentary elections under United Nations control be imposed upon the Libyan people. Some of these reports referred, by way of justification, to the suggestions made by the Commissioner in the course of his statement at the three hundred and sixth plenary meeting of the General Assembly.[111]

Their authors omitted to mention, however, that on that occasion the Commissioner had been speaking in terms of *advice* to be given to the NCAL after consultation with the Council; this advice, if accepted, was to be implemented before the last date set for independence. Hence, its acceptance would have been an *internal* Libyan affair. To certain Arab circles, on the contrary, in the autumn of 1951, the measure under consideration looked very much like a condition to be imposed by the General Assembly upon Libya and to be accepted by it before independence could be granted or recognized. There was nothing precise, far less official, about these rumors, but they were persistent and suggestive enough to give many a Libyan the jitters. A remark like that made by Beshir Bey Saadawi in *The Sunday Ghibli* about the provisional nature of the Constitution could not fail to add fuel to the fire. In their imagination, the Libyans foresaw last-minute foreign intervention seeking to make their independence subject to the transformation of the Constitution from a federal into a unitary instrument. It was because of this fear that the Provisional Government had, as early as August, proposed 15 November as the latest date for the declaration of independence. At the time, the Coordination Committee had refused to agree, being convinced that the Government would not be ready to exercise power effectively until well into December. The Commissioner had shared that view, and still did so.

The British position changed almost overnight following events in Egypt, as a result of which the latter's relations with the United Kingdom suddenly deteriorated. On 8 October the Egyptian Government submitted to Parliament for approval four decrees abrogating its 1936 Treaty with the United Kingdom as well as the Sudan Condominium Agreement of 1899. The British Government refused to recognize what it considered a unilateral denunciation, claiming the maintenance of its full rights in both the Suez Canal zone and the Sudan. Anti-British demonstrations and riots broke out in Egyptian cities, especially in Cairo and Alexandria. British troops in the Canal Zone had their leave canceled. His Majesty's Government announced new proposals for Middle East defense to be presented to Egypt. The

111. See GAOR: Fifth Session, 1950, 306th Plenary Meeting, 16 November 1950, pp. 411–12.

French and United States Governments supported the United Kingdom. The Arab League stood firm behind Egypt.

These events are not part of the story of Libyan independence; but they naturally affected it. For one thing, the Provisional Libyan Government was now more eager than ever to achieve independence at an early date, so as to face the General Assembly with an accomplished fact. It feared—not without reason—that its interests might become a pawn in the larger game the General Assembly would have to play. Hence it wanted to sign the financial agreements as quickly as possible, thus bringing forward the date on which independence could be proclaimed.

The United Kingdom Government itself was now also in favor of early independence. Having its hands full with the Middle East problem, it apparently did not want to deal simultaneously with the Libyan question, or if it had to, only in the form of an issue no longer the subject of controversy.

The Foreign Office nursed the hope that during the Sixth Session of the General Assembly the powers directly involved in the Middle East crisis, including the Arab States, would have no time to pay much attention to Libya, as long as it could be argued that its independence had been achieved in accordance with the General Assembly's wishes. Thus, between 20 and 30 October, while the Commissioner and the Principal Secretary were still in Geneva, the British Resident in Tripoli, talking to the officer in charge of the United Nations Mission, unexpectedly volunteered the opinion that the principal Libyan Government departments had made sufficient progress in staffing and organization to allow independence to be proclaimed at the beginning of November. The Consuls General of France and the United States used much the same language. All three were careful to add that any decision in this sense should be taken only with the Commissioner's full consent. Meanwhile, the Provisional Government was on its way to Benghazi to obtain the King's consent to the prompt signing of the financial agreements, this to be followed forthwith by the transfer of the third and fourth groups of powers. The King was also asked to fix the Day of Independence for early November. Thus it very much looked as if this time it would be the Commissioner's turn to be confronted with a fait accompli.

While fully appreciating the United Kingdom's desire to free itself of its Libyan worries, the Commissioner viewed with mixed feelings the Provisional Government's rush toward independence before it was properly prepared for it. Neither did he care for the idea of its signing financial agreements containing provisions which he did not believe were to Libya's advantage. He, moreover, no longer shared the fear that during the forthcoming debate in the General Assembly Libya would be threatened by attempts to interfere in its internal affairs. It rather looked to him as if

Libya would enjoy a friendly reception, barring, perhaps, some criticism from one or two Arab States. Pleading with the Prime Minister by cable from Geneva for a less impetuous approach to independence, he referred in particular to the transfer of powers program, the complete text of which would be annexed his second annual report and in the hands of delegates to the General Assembly within a few weeks. He pointed out that, apart from the Constitution, the effectiveness of Libyan independence would be judged by the standards set by that program, which deliberately proposed 15 December as the earliest possible date for independence, a date, moreover, that was already widely known in and outside Libya. He recalled that it was equally widely known that the British Residents, acting on instructions from London and fully supported by the Commissioner, had insisted that the final transfer of powers be put off until such time as the federal government was able effectively to exercise them. The Libyan Government had accepted the program, and that fact, too, was well known. It was largely because of such considerations, and in the light of the timetable, which was an inherent part of the plan, that the Council for Libya had agreed to it. If at this stage the British and Libyan positions were seen to change unexpectedly and suddenly, many people might become suspicious, and explanations satisfactory to the General Assembly would have to be provided. The Commissioner, for one, did not feel that he would be in a position to assure the Assembly that the Libyan Government would be able to function satisfactorily by early November. Admittedly, good progress in staffing and in administrative organization had been made, but it was equally true that not everything would be in proper running order even by mid-December. Furthermore, this lapse of time would substantially enhance the administration's efficiency. He further argued that any deviation from the program would cause speculation as to what hidden motives the British and Libyan Governments might have in so radically advancing the date of independence. Machiavellian designs could easily be imputed to them. One such, which was already current and which might be credible even to Libya's genuine friends, was that the United Kingdom and France were urging premature independence upon a still inadequately organized Libyan Government in order to enable the three more highly organized territorial governments to continue to function quasi-independently under an illusory federation. Suspicions of this kind would put the Libyan Government as well as the Administering Powers and, last but not least, the Commissioner himself in an awkward position vis-à-vis all those delegations in the General Assembly which had unremittingly insisted on genuine Libyan unity.

One of the Commissioner's primary anxieties at this stage was the extent to which the Provisional Libyan Government, as yet unable to account for its actions to an elected Parliament, could bind the future duly constituted Government. This question was of considerable significance both with regard to the form and content of the agreements to be signed by the Prime Minister and with regard to their duration. In this context, it appeared to the Commissioner that it was of the utmost interest to the two contracting parties to avoid at all costs any possible inconsistency between the agreements and the Libyan Constitution. Caution in this respect would, he emphasized, protect the position of the Provisional Government while at the same time strengthening that of its successor which, under Article 69 of the Constitution, would have to obtain Parliament's approval before the King could ratify the agreements. He therefore suggested that the Provisional Government, while assuming full responsibility for all measures necessary during its period in office to build up federal governmental machinery, should limit its other obligations to the strictest minimum, so as to leave as much liberty of action as possible to the Government that would take office on the declaration of independence. Given this line of argument, the period for which the agreements were to be valid was naturally of particular importance.

At the time of the discussions in the Coordination Committee at Benghazi in August, the Commissioner's understanding had been that two financial agreements would be concluded, the first covering the period from 1 September 1951 until the end of the current United Kingdom fiscal year on 31 March 1952, the second the period beginning on 1 April 1952. The first was to be negotiated and signed by the Provisional Government; the second was similarly to be negotiated by that Government, but would have to be signed by and take effect under the authority of the duly constituted independent Government, established and exercising power in pursuance of the Constitution. This notion of the sequence of events in the financial sector had been described in the following passage in the Commissioner's covering letter of 31 August, transmitting the Coordination Committee's conclusions to the Provisional Libyan Government:

> The method of the financing of the Provisional Libyan Government and the succeeding duly constituted Libyan government until 31 March 1952 by contributions by Tripolitania, Cyrenaica and the Fezzan, has solved that question in a manner which should greatly facilitate the transfer of powers. However, a pre-requisite of the transfer to the Provisional Libyan Government of those powers which would affect the grants-in-aid made to Cyrenaica and Tripolitania is the conclusion of a financial agreement between the United Kingdom Government and the Provisional Libyan Government for the remaining period of the British financial

> year, that is, until 31 March 1952. Such an agreement could be in the form of an exchange of letters. I hope that this can be concluded without difficulty in the very near future. For the next British financial year beginning on 1 April 1952, the British Parliament would be able to consider a request from the United Kingdom Government for the allocation of a new grant-in-aid to the Federal Government of Libya.[112]

However, the Commissioner had subsequently been informed that the requirements of parliamentary procedure in the United Kingdom for the approval of grants to the federal Libyan Government in due time made it impossible to proceed in this way. London therefore contemplated a single interim financial agreement covering the period up to 31 March 1953, instead of 1952, thus fusing the two agreements originally intended to be separate. Knowing that it was His Majesty's Government's intention to replace this interim agreement by one of longer duration, covering among other things the military facilities it intended to ask for in exchange for its financial support, the Commissioner thought it not unlikely that the prolongation of the interim agreement by one year was also meant to give more time for negotiating the permanent agreement.

Admittedly, the British authors of the draft agreements had made an appreciable effort to avoid subjecting the grant of contributions to Libya to conditions which might appear inconsistent with the latter's status as an independent State, and to refrain from imposing extensive obligations on its Government. At the same time, it was obvious and understandable that the British taxpayer had to be given reasonable guarantees that his money was being spent for the purposes for which it had been voted.

Nevertheless, the Commissioner, constantly thinking of the account he would have to render to the General Assembly, proposed a few amendments inspired by the preoccupations just described. Most of these were editorial emendations, but one touched on a specific point of substance. It will be remembered that, with regard to the organization of the Ministry of Finance and Economics, the Coordination Committee had made a recommendation (No. 16) to the effect that:

> (a) There should be a very senior official to act as Financial and Economic Adviser to the Minister. He would control and ensure adequate direction of all the activities of the Ministry and would be responsible to the Minister for the administration of the entire Ministry.[113]

112. *Second Annual Report of the United Nations Commissioner in Libya,* Annex XII, Section 9A, p. 126, para. 5.

113. Ibid., Annex XII, Section 7, p. 100.

This particular formula represented a British-Libyan compromise reached in the course of the Committee's deliberations. The Commissioner accordingly proposed that the words "He shall be the principal financial and economic adviser of that Government and shall be responsible to the Minister of Finance" should be textually inserted in the agreement. To his and its regret, the Libyan Government did not obtain satisfaction on this point. Instead, Article 6 (a) of the temporary agreement reads as follows:

> The Chief Financial and Economic Officer shall have access to the Prime Minister and the Minister of Finance of the Libyan Government. He shall be the principal financial and economic officer of that Government.[114]

The crucial issue of his responsibility, therefore, was not properly defined. His authority, as well as that of the Minister himself, could only suffer from such lack of clarity.

While this three-cornered consultation between Geneva, London, and Tripoli was going on, the Council, at its ninety-third meeting, held in Geneva on 12 October, had on its agenda Libya's monetary and financial problems. As far as the currency question was concerned, the debate, based on four reports and a statement by the Commissioner concerning the Meetings of Experts on Libyan financial, monetary, and development problems, related to events which had reached the stage of implementation.[115] The financial problems, on the contrary, were eminently topical, and the discussion might have been of a highly constructive nature had only the members who were critical of the relevant passages in the transfer-of-powers plan come forward with workable alternative solutions. None did, however. It was no wonder, therefore, that the Provisional Government showed little interest in what was being said in Geneva.

The Prime Minister, supported by the British Resident, continued to press for early signature of the agreements and an early declaration of independence. The Commissioner as steadfastly continued to advise against this course of action. Negotiations dragged on and decisions were put off from one day to the next. Then an easy way out presented itself, as the result of circumstances which, on the surface, were irrelevant to the substance: in early November it became apparent that, because of the planning of the General Assembly's agenda on the one hand and the lateness of the

114. *Supplementary Report to the Second Annual Report of the United Nations Commissioner in Libya,* Annex IV, p. 30.

115. The Commissioner had kept the Council periodically and fully informed about these problems. However, in view of their technical nature, he had not asked the Council for advice on them. Nor did it ever attempt to give such advice.

Commissioner's reports on the other, the general feeling in Paris was that the debate on the Libyan question should be deferred until December, or even later.

When the Sixth Session of the General Assembly finally opened, the debate on the adoption of the agenda of the *Ad Hoc* Political Committee was not exclusively procedural. Eight items had been referred to that Committee, among them the Libyan question. When, on 19 November, it discussed the order in which these items should be taken, the Netherlands delegation proposed that Libya be placed sixth. This proposal was generally supported by the Western Powers, whereas the Arab and socialist States expressed a preference for an earlier debate. Though none of the speakers touched on the substance of the matter, it was obvious that the true issue at stake was whether the question should come up before or after the declaration of Libyan independence, in other words, before or after the Christmas recess. In the event, the Netherlands motion was adopted by 32 votes to 16, with 9 abstentions. Thus the Libyan delegation could feel fairly certain of coming to the Assembly table as the representatives of an independent State; the transfer of powers could be carried out according to plan; and, last but not least, the preparation of the general election would be sufficiently well advanced to make a proposal in the Assembly for a general election under United Nations control virtually pointless. Sighs of relief were to be heard all around, except, of course, in opposition circles.[116]

The Commissioner, by then back in Tripoli, took advantage of this period of relative détente to discuss in detail with the Prime Minister and the United Kingdom representatives the British draft financial agreements. Apart from the point of substance mentioned a little earlier, his main preoccupation was that the draft should be so amended as to make it, insofar as possible, a technical and nonpolitical instrument. There existed in Libya and abroad a widespread belief that the agreements under negotiation were nothing but a deal by which the United Kingdom would pay a certain sum in exchange for military bases and other facilities. There is no doubt that the two parties had in principle agreed to sign, after Libya had achieved independence, a treaty governing their financial, economic, and political (including military) relations. The United Kingdom desired such an alliance as an important link in its chain of strategic ties in the Mediterranean. Libya required such a treaty out of sheer financial need. Furthermore, many Libyans, though far from all, believed that their country needed the support of a strong and friendly foreign Power. Plans to this effect had,

116. For an account of the procedural debate, see GAOR: Sixth Session, 1951–52, *Ad Hoc* Political Committee, 1st Meeting, 19 November 1951, pp. 2–5. See also Chapter 11, passim.

indeed, been under consideration from the time the United Kingdom had first envisaged granting quasi-independence to Cyrenaica. Talks on the subject had been suspended, pending the conclusion of action in the General Assembly of the United Nations. Later, they were reopened. In the autumn of 1951 this was no secret. Neither was it a secret that immediately after the declaration of independence an interim agreement would be signed between the United Kingdom and the duly constituted Libyan Government provisionally regularizing the presence of British troops on Libyan soil; or that collateral agreements would have to be signed in respect of the United States and French military forces in the country.

It was obvious, however, that the United Nations could have no truck with treaties of this kind, whether provisional or permanent, even though one of their purposes was to grant financial support to a State to whose creation it had so largely contributed. This was so much the more pertinent because Arab nationalism, the Libyan brand not excepted, looked on such treaties with a critical eye, while military bases and similar matters had become one of the hottest issues in the cold war. Hence it was important to draw a clear distinction between the financial agreements to be concluded with the United Kingdom and France before independence and the treaties of alliance to be negotiated and signed after Independence Day.[117]

It was with this in mind that the Commissioner suggested orally that, in order to bring out the difference between the interim financial agreements

117. Three treaties were signed after independence, with the United Kingdom, with the United States, and with France (chronological order):

1. *Treaty of Friendship and Alliance (with exchange of Notes regarding the operation of the Treaty and Military and Financial Agreements before the exchange of the instruments of ratification) between Her Majesty in respect of the United Kingdom of Great Britain and Northern Ireland and His Majesty the King of the United Kingdom of Libya.* Signed at Benghazi, 29 July 1953. Ratified by the Libyan Parliament, 7 December 1953. For text, see *United Nations Treaty Series, 186* (1954), No. 2491, pp. 185–283.

2. *Exchange of letters constituting an Agreement between the United States of America and Libya relating to Economic Assistance to Libya.* Signed at Benghazi, 9 September 1954. Ratified by the Libyan Parliament, 30 October 1954. For text, see ibid., *238* (1956), No. 3365, pp. 218–26.

3. The treaty with France was signed at Benghazi on 10 August 1955, and ratified by the Libyan Parliament on 10 April 1956. This treaty also provided for the final rectification of Libya's frontiers in favor of the French territories in Africa. For text, see ibid., *300* (1958), No. 4340, pp. 263–95.

For an account of the negotiations leading up to the conclusions of the three treaties, see Majid Khadduri, *Modern Libya: A Study in Political Development* (Baltimore: Johns Hopkins Press, 1963), pp. 226–31 (United Kingdom); pp. 252–58 (United States); and pp. 258–61 (France).

and the lasting treaties, Article 3 of the former be amended to read: "The purpose of this agreement is to ensure that the Libyan State shall enjoy conditions of financial stability and to contribute to the orderly economic and social development of Libya." As will be seen from Annex IV to the supplementary report to the second annual report, words to this effect did indeed find their way into the text signed on 13 December 1951.

Another suggestion made by the Commissioner, also adopted, was prompted by British insistence that the interim agreement should be extended to cover the financial year 1 April 1952 through 31 March 1953. Considering that the agreement would require the approval of the Libyan Parliament, and in order to give the Government some freedom of action at the time, he proposed the insertion at two places in Article 4 (d) of the words "provided the Libyan Government requests such a contribution." [118] Of course, every member of Parliament know that the Government had no option but to make such a request. However, the mere provision of the possibility of not doing so would, in case of objections from the floor of the House, enable the Minister of Finance to retort by asking where else could he find the money to cover the deficit?

In November the Commissioner was asked by the Libyan Minister of Foreign Affairs, writing on behalf of the Prime Minister, for advice on the drafts for a proposed exchange of letters between the Government of France and the Provisional Government relating to French financial assistance. The period to be covered by the French agreement was the same as that specified in the British agreement, but there was an important difference in purpose. While nominally the French contribution purported to serve the harmonious development of the Libyan economy as a whole, it was in fact meant to cover the deficit in the Fezzanese administrative budget and to ensure the economic and social development of that province. For the remainder of the fiscal year—i.e. until 31 March 1952—this was in accordance with the agreement arrived at during the meetings of the Coordination Committee in Benghazi in August 1951.

The French Government's concern that the province for which it had borne administrative responsibility for so many years should be adequately provided for in the future, so that the appreciable improvements it had introduced in that territory might not be lost, was in itself understandable; and in view of the current state of Libyan finances, both federal and provincial, it was in Libya's interest to accept a French contribution. However, from 1 April 1952 it would be contrary to the Constitution and detrimental

118. *Supplementary Report to the Second Annual Report of the United Nations Commissioner in Libya,* Annex IV, p. 30.

to Libyan unity to do so to meet the needs of one province exclusively. It would, moreover, be politically inadvisable, since such a contribution by a foreign Power would almost certainly arouse, both at home and abroad, suspicions of the donor's intentions. The Commissioner therefore advised the Provisional Government against such an arrangement. Instead, he recommended that the French Metropolitan Government should make a nonearmarked contribution to the Libyan Government, which in return might give assurances that it intended to give due attention to the particular needs of the Fezzan by fully carrying out, in respect of that territory, its obligations under Article 174 of the Constitution. This suggestion was accepted in principle by both parties, but it appeared in the text of the agreement signed on 14 December 1951 in too ambiguous a form to protect them effectively against the kind of criticism that was to be feared.[119]

The Commissioner furthermore suggested that the French Government might contribute the equivalent of £150,000 to the Libyan Public Development and Stabilization Agency (LPDSA) in accordance with the latter's statutes, i.e. for the benefit of Libya as a whole. Again the Libyan Government could assure the French that, in approving projects submitted to LPDSA, it would endeavor, as far as practicable, to maintain economic and social development in the Fezzan at not less than the rate at which it had been proceeding at the moment of independence. A provision more or less in that sense was included in the agreement, but the amount of the contribution was not specified. Instead it was left to be determined by agreement between the two Governments. (In the event, under the Treaty of 1955, see page 831, footnote 117, France promised to contribute 130 million francs in that year and 350 million in 1956 for the economic development of Libya.) Moreover, it was to form part of the assistance to be allocated to the Fezzan in pursuance of Article 174 of the Libyan Constitution.

The French Government's intention to limit its financial assistance to the Fezzan was also reflected in the way in which the functions of the French specialist to be appointed to the Libyan Ministry of Finance and Economics were defined. He was to be primarily responsible for economic and financial questions relating to the Fezzan. He would have access to the Prime Minister and the Minister of Finance, but would keep the Chief Financial and Economic Officer (a United Kingdom specialist) informed of his proposals so that the latter could consider them within the broader framework of Libya's general financial and economic position.

In brief, a comparison of the two agreements shows that at the end of

119. Ibid., Annex V, p. 31.

1951, contrary to the situation prevailing at the beginning of 1950, France seemed to regard most of Libya as being within the British zone of influence. It also appeared to recognize, as it had done earlier, the existence of a special Italian interest in Tripolitania. Whether such recognition was tacit or resulted from explicit agreements was not clear. Nevertheless, French policy toward Libya still gave the impression that France expected to enjoy in the Fezzan a privileged position similar to that granted to the United Kingdom in the other two provinces.

In November the Provisional Libyan Government discussed with the United States Government a proposal for a donation of funds for economic as well as technical assistance and asked the Commissioner for advice on the manner in which they could be utilized. Not wishing to prejudge subsequent recommendations by experts, the Commissioner expressed the opinion that the Government could do no better than use the United States donation for development purposes in a working capital budget, separate from its administrative budget. The same advice would apply equally to donations of a similar nature which might be made by other countries. He specifically agreed with the view expressed by the Prime Minister, that no opening should be given to the United Kingdom or French Governments to seize upon the United States contribution as a pretext for reducing the grants-in-aid they had themselves undertaken to make. Apparently the Prime Minister had fears of this kind and took the precaution of asking for support should they materialize.

As explained in Chapter 9, the Commissioner, though prepared to admit that they were sometimes unavoidable, never liked bilateral financial agreements covering aid to Libya or, for that matter, to any developing country. He preferred multilateral arrangements, less dangerous to the recipient and often more conducive to the maintenance of peaceful relations. However, beggars cannot be choosers. That old adage applied particularly to Libya. The Commissioner had therefore to be constantly on his guard to make it perfectly clear that, in advising the Provisional Libyan Government on the bilateral financial agreements with the United Kingdom and France, he was in no way implicating the United Nations in a financial-military bargain. So, when he sent his supplementary and final report to the Secretary-General for submission to the General Assembly, he included the following two paragraphs in the letter of transmittal:

> It will be noted that neither in the present report nor in my previous reports have I referred to the presence of foreign troops and military installations on Libyan soil. As long as the territories composing Libya were administered by the United Kingdom and Frence, that is to say, up

to the day that Libyan independence was proclaimed, these two Powers were responsible for Libya's foreign relations and defence which, therefore, did not come within my competence nor within that of the Provisional Libyan Government. The latter Government ceased to exist the moment the last powers, including foreign relations and defence, were transferred to it. It resigned on the morning of Independence Day, 24 December 1951, and was immediately succeeded by the duly constituted Government, appointed by His Majesty the King of Libya, in conformity with the provisions of the Libyan Constitution.

At the same moment, the Commissioner's functions, as defined by General Assembly Resolutions 289 (IV) and 387 (V), came to an end. These facts, as well as the fact that foreign relations and defence and, therefore, the conclusions of any treaties or agreements concerning the presence of foreign troops and military installations on Libyan soil, became the concern of the sovereign, independent, and duly constituted Libyan Government and of the Parliament to be elected after independence explains why these matters are not referred to in my report.[120]

The month of December was marked by dramatic changes in scene and atmosphere as Independence Day approached.

With the assistance of British and French officials, and in close cooperation with United Nations experts, the Provisional Libyan Government made good progress in staffing and organizing its ministerial establishments, while the provincial administrations were reorganized in accordance with their reduced responsibilities. On 15 December 1951, the day after the financial agreement with France was signed, the third group of powers was transferred to the Provisional Libyan Government. As in the proclamations on the transfer of the second group, the provincial governments signified their assent wherever powers were involved which, being exercised by them in pursuance of earlier transfers, had to be ceded to the federal government. In some cases, particularly in Cyrenaica, this did not always pass off without heart-burning. Nevertheless the Commissioner and his staff, when preparing the draft of his final report for consideration by the Council, noted with satisfaction that the process of transfer went like a well-oiled machine, not least thanks to the effective cooperation of the Administering Powers. As the federal government assumed more and more powers, so its authority grew.

At the same time the organization of the general elections (divided into five stages: preliminary arrangements; registration of electors; issue of writs and nomination of candidates; uncontested elections; and contested

120. Ibid., pp. v and vi.

elections) was moving ahead, not always without hitch, but, generally speaking, satisfactorily, as far as could be seen from Tripoli. By the time independence was declared, practically all measures relating to the first two stages had been implemented. More details about these preparations will be found in the Commissioner's supplementary report, Chapter II, Part B, paragraphs 32–69 (pp. 5–10).[121]

During the weeks preceding Independence Day, the Commissioner was visited by several leaders of political parties seeking assistance and advice in preparing their electoral campaigns. The National Congress Party continued to press for the election to be carried out under United Nations supervision. The Commissioner advised against such a course, expressing the view that in all probability the General Assembly would refuse to impose a control of this kind upon an independent State which was supposed to be able to look after itself. Moreover, the mounting of the control apparatus would be a costly and time-consuming affair in a country as large as Libya.[122] The same Party also proposed various changes in the Electoral Law which, admittedly, was not perfect, as has already been made clear. However, most of these changes were such as to require amendment of the law by the NCAL, a procedure for which there was obviously no time if the schedule were to be held to.

Leaders of the smaller parties, afraid of being crushed between the Government and the opposition, came to see the Commissioner even after independence, to ask for assistance in concluding coalition arrangements with one side or the other.[123] This was, of course, completely outside the

121. Election Day was 19 February 1952. The Government won forty-six out of the total of fifty-five seats. The National Congress Party won a sweeping victory in Tripoli town and its environs, but lost heavily in the rest of the country, though of the fifty-five constituencies, thirty-five were located in Tripolitania. See *Libya: Background Note* (London: Royal Institute of International Affairs, December 1954). Mimeographed. See also Khadduri, pp. 215–20. The latter mentions the disturbances in the tribal areas of Tripolitania after the elections. He also reports the expulsion from the country of Beshir Bey Saadawi on 22 February 1952—a procedure made possible by the fact that in earlier years Beshir Bey had acquired a Saudi Arabian passport and had never regained his Libyan citizenship (see p. 438, fn. 9, pp. 548–49, and pp. 610–12).

122. Altogether there were 226 polling districts and as many polling stations. On the assumption that an international control agency would be staffed by individuals belonging to neutral States and therefore, presumably, not speaking Arabic, this organization would have required the engagement of 452 persons—226 supervisors and 226 interpreters—not to mention clerical, transportation, and other supporting staff.

123. The leader of one of the smaller opposition parties explained his dilemma in the following terms: whether to participate in the elections, which would mean recognizing the existing state of affairs; or whether, alternatively, to continue opposi-

Commissioner's terms of reference, and would have been so even before independence. In order to make his position clear, and by way of a last piece of advice, he wrote both the Prime Minister and the Leader of the Opposition on 2 January 1952 in the following terms:

> I may be allowed to reiterate a personal opinion which I have repeatedly expressed to all concerned, whether inside or outside the Government, to whatever party they may belong and even to those who have not adhered to any party at all, namely that the interests of the country would best be served by conducting the elections with calmness and integrity in accordance with the letter and spirit of both the Constitution and the Electoral Law.[124]

This was asking a great deal from people in an emergent democracy on the verge of fighting their first electoral battle after two years of acrimonious political disputation. However, in politics, perhaps more than in any other walk of life, experience can only be earned by trial and error. This was best illustrated by the local papers, both in Benghazi and in Tripoli. Editors and political leaders clearly found it difficult to adjust themselves to the new situation. Most of them were still too deeply immersed in preindependence problems to suggest party programs for the future. Though the problem was no longer whether Libya would become independent or not, *Shu'lat al-Hurriya* nevertheless published on 3 December 1951 a telegram from Beshir Bey Saadawi, at that moment in Jidda, Saudi Arabia, to the effect that, having been informed of developments in Libya, he was returning to Tripoli, adding that he would, by the help of God, achieve freedom and realize the nation's aspirations.

He belonged with those in the Arab world who found it difficult to realize that their dream was coming true, and it was symptomatic of their mental approach that their skepticism was mainly due to their deeply rooted suspicions of the Administering Powers. The relegation of the Libyan question to a lowly place on the agenda of the *Ad Hoc* Political Committee of the General Assembly was taken as justification of this suspicion. The Paris correspondent of the Cairo newspaper *Al Ahram* reported that the Arab delegations at the General Assembly were getting restless over the postponement of the debate, a postponement which they considered was intended to

---

tion as long as the elections were based on an unlawful procedure and were unconstitutional. And what should he do after that, he asked. Was it not possible to form a neutral government for which he could vote without losing his self-respect?

124. United Nations Archives. Typescript. The Commissioner expressed a similar opinion in his final report to the General Assembly. See *Supplementary Report to the Second Annual Report of the United Nations Commissioner in Libya,* para. 134.

give the United Kingdom an opportunity to carry out its "plot" against Libyan independence. In other words, the United Kingdom, with the Commissioner and the United Nations Secretariat as accomplices, intended to face the General Assembly with the fait accompli of a treaty, which, it was argued, Libya had no right to conclude as long as it was under United Nations supervision, but which it would be entitled to sign, without objection on the part of the United Nations, as soon as it became an independent and sovereign State.

In situations like these, nothing is worse than a half-truth except a misconception based on a half-truth. Libya was not under the supervision of the United Nations. It was up to the Provisional Libyan Government to decide whether and why, rightly or wrongly, it was entitled to sign an agreement with a foreign power. Of course, any member of the General Assembly had the right to criticize Libya for having concluded agreements considered to be in conflict with the Charter, the relevant resolutions of the General Assembly, or the principles of international law. Whether such criticisms were made before or after Independence Day made not the slightest difference to the act of signature, except that in the first case Libya could not claim the right to defend itself at the bar of its peers, whereas in the second it could. The attitude of the Arab States was paradoxical. They had been the first to assert Libya's right to independence, but at the first sign of her acting independently they were up in arms against her, shutting their eyes to her terrible financial plight.

It is to the credit of the Egyptian Government that it was the first of the Arab States to look facts in the face. In its issue of 3 December 1951, *Al Ahram* reported the decision of the Egyptian Council of Ministers, officially confirmed on 20 December, to recognize the Libyan State on its acquiring independence and to exchange diplomatic and consular representatives with it.

At about the same time, the Pakistani member of the Council for Libya, in the course of an interview with the independent Tripolitanian paper *Al Libi*, published on 6 December, said somewhat unexpectedly that, as he had predicted earlier, the independence of Libya had been attained without difficulties and without disturbances, so that only a few were able to realize the greatness of what had already been achieved. He commended the King for the leading role he had played, with the assistance of the Libyan people and their leaders, in making such a successful outcome possible. Without that, no outside intervention could have helped Libya to attain her independence within so short a period. It was evident, he went on, that among an intelligent people such as the Libyans some were bound to be critical of the Constitution or the form of government. His sincere advice to them was not to expect perfection in all things. It was unwise to waste time and effort in attempting to pull down what had already been built. Instead, the Libyans should concentrate on electing competent and honest men to the future Parliament. In conclusion, he urged all Libyans to assist and cooperate with the Libyan Government and to follow the lead of the King and other leaders. This interview foreshadowed Rahim Khan's change of heart to be expressed so generously at the Sixth Session of the General Assembly (see pp. 849–51).

From this moment the last vestige of nervous pressure for early independence vanished, and all the Government's attention was focused on preparations for the great day. As to the date, there was still some uncertainty. The target originally envisaged by the Coordination Committee—15 December—remained valid, but on 14 December the United Kingdom delegation to the General Assembly in Paris, as well as the British Resident in Tripoli, urgently intervened in favor of a postponement until later in the month. The reason given in Paris was technical unpreparedness to make the last transfer of powers on 15 December. The explanation unofficially given on the spot was that the United Kingdom Ambassador-Designate to the Court of King Idris, Sir Alec Kirkbride, could not leave his post at Amman early enough. Anyway, 15 December was ruled out because it was only on that day that the temporary financial agreement with France would be signed. Another reason for putting the date back was that negotiations between the Libyan and Italian Governments about certain categories of Italian state property, which preferably should be terminated before Independence Day, were making but slow progress.[125]

On top of everything, the Libyan Government was asked by the Egyptian Government to agree that the credentials of the Egyptian Ambassador to King Idris be issued in the name of His Majesty the King of Egypt *and the Sudan,* a much contested matter at the time. The Commissioner having been asked for advice, recommended that United Nations procedural precedent be followed. Subsequently he was informed from Paris that the Credentials Committee of the General Assembly, faced with the same problem in respect of the Egyptian delegation to the Sixth Session, had recommended that the dual title be accepted, adding that acceptance did not necessarily imply recognition. The Libyan Government decided to follow this precedent, which caused some irritation in United Kingdom circles and was hailed as a victory by the Arab States. In fact, it was a first indication that the Libyan Government intended, insofar as possible, to take an independent line in its foreign policy. A spark of humor was not lacking from this nicety of diplomatic protocol, in that there was keen competition between the United Kingdom and Egyptian Ambassadors to be accredited first. This

125. See General Assembly Resolution 388 (V), 15 December 1950, Article I, paras. 3 and 5, and Chapter 5, Parts 1 and 2.

was not without importance, since the winner would become doyen of the diplomatic corps. Sir Alec triumphed.

Meanwhile, all the parties concerned were in constant consultation with the King and with one another to reach agreement on a date for independence convenient to all. Several suggestions were made, one as late as 29 December. Now it was the Commissioner, anxious to have some sea room in view of possible unforeseen events, who began to press for early independence. At last, 24 December was agreed as firm, barring weather hazards for the United Nations plane which would be ferrying those taking part in the ceremony between Tripoli and Benghazi.[126]

After all, the successive postponements of Independence Day had not been unwelcome to the Provisional Libyan Government, which had found time almost too short to complete all the necessary preparations. To mention only the most important, the sequence of events on Independence Day had to be determined in accordance with the Constitution and the usage prescribed by internal law and custom. The Royal Proclamation of Independence, to be read by the King from the balcony of the Manar Palace at Benghazi, had to be drafted and approved, as had also the letters officially announcing the birth of Independent Libya to the members of the United Nations, as well as requests for admission to membership of the Organization and its principal specialized agencies. In the domestic sector, too, there was much to be done, even though the organization of government departments was progressing steadily and the various ministries were beginning to exercise the powers that had been transferred to them. Laws were being enacted, subject to subsequent approval by Parliament, such as the Libyan Public Development and Stabilization Agency Law, 1951, and the Libyan Finance Corporation Law, 1951.

During December the program for the final and decisive transfer of powers and subsequent events had been carefully prepared in consultation with the King, the Provisional Government, the Administering Powers, and the United Nations Mission. When the time came it was carried out according to plan.[127] In describing the events the author cannot do better than

126. Western diplomats accredited to the Court of King Idris in later years often complained that 24 December, being Christmas Eve, was a most inconvenient date. At the time when the decision had to be made, however, no more convenient date could be found.

127. There was one incident that was not foreseen in the plan. A few minutes after the United Nations plane, with the Commissioner and several Libyan personalities on board, had left Wheelus Field near Tripoli, one of the two engines failed. The pilot immediately swung the disabled plane around and made a perfect emergency landing. Shortly afterward the journey was resumed in another aircraft made available by the base authorities.

follow the factual and unadorned account that appeared in the Commissioner's supplementary report:

> In the early hours of 24 December 1951, the remaining group of powers, namely, the fourth and last group listed by the Co-ordination Committee, were transferred by the three Residents to the Provisional Libyan Government, thus completing the transfer of all powers to the Federal Government.
>
> In Tripolitania, the British Resident enacted Transfer of Powers (No. 4) Proclamation No. 223, and identical Proclamations *mutatis mutandis* were simultaneously issued in Benghazi and Sebha. The proclamation in the Fezzan abrogated all the powers which the Government of France possessed in that territory.[128]

In the evening of 24 December, the King gave a reception for the Consular Corps and officials and notables in Benghazi. The same evening, in Tripoli, the Prime Minister received the Diplomatic and Consular Corps; this event was followed by a State dinner, the first in the life of independent Libya.

While the events just described were making history, the United Nations Mission, having come to the end of its task, was quietly winding up its political duties but transforming itself into a TAB Office maintaining continuity for a group of technical assistance experts with supporting secretarial language and administrative personnel. This new office was, of course smaller. The capable and devoted professional staff of the Mission, previously engaged in political matters and the servicing of Council meetings, was dispersed, some returning to United Nations Headquarters, others being transferred to other field missions, some returning to their national service from which they had been seconded, others going to new employment. The Principal Secretary was to organize and head the revised arrangements as the first Resident Representative, and was designated as the Personal Representative of the Secretary-General of the United Nations, an excellent example of continuity by which both sides benefited. A new chapter was opening in the relationship between Libya and the United Nations family.

It would be an exaggeration to pretend that all Libyans were happy on Independence Day. Two groups were not, the protagonists of unitarism in Tripoli and the extreme federalists in Benghazi. The first criticized the new State because it was insufficiently centralized and too much dominated by the country's traditionalist forces. The second deplored with nostalgia the

128. See *Supplementary Report to the Second Annual Report of the United Nations Commissioner in Libya,* paras. 11–12, and Annex II, pp. 25–27.

loss of the large measure of autonomy they had hoped to maintain in a loose federation, hating to see their way of life disturbed by the modernists from the western province. But even these two contending groups found it difficult not to rejoice that the dream of independence had come true, even though the form of the State might not be entirely to their liking. As for the mass of the people, they seemed satisfied with the new situation, as far as could be discerned in a large country with an underdeveloped press, no national radio network, and inadequate means of communication and transportation. The Fezzan, isolated in the vastness of the Sahara and still under French influence, needed more time to adjust itself than the two coastal provinces.

Apart from political preferences, there remained the question of whether a poor country like Libya would be able, financially and administratively, to support the burden of a federal structure. But that was a question that could only be answered by experience.

CHAPTER 11

Independent Libya at the Sixth Session of the General Assembly (1951–1952)

On 30 October 1951 the Commissioner submitted his second annual report; this was followed by a supplementary report dated 8 January 1952. Between these two dates, on 24 December 1951, one week earlier than the deadline fixed in operative paragraph 2 of Resolution 289 (IV), Libya, comprising Cyrenaica, Tripolitania, and the Fezzan, had been constituted an independent and sovereign State, as recommended in operative paragraph 1 of that Resolution. A Constitution, including the form of government, had been determined by representatives of the inhabitants of Cyrenaica, Tripolitania, and the Fezzan meeting and consulting together in a National Assembly, as prescribed in operative paragraph 3. Lastly, the Administering Powers had submitted their reports on the administration of the territories for which they were responsible.[1]

For reasons and in circumstances dealt with in Chapter 10, the Libyan question (item 20 on the General Assembly's agenda) had been put at the end of the list of subjects to be treated by the *Ad Hoc* Political Committee which finally took it up at its forty-eighth to fifty-fourth meetings, between 23 and 28 January 1952. At the same time the Committee also dealt sum-

1. *Second Annual Report of the United Nations Commissioner in Libya,* GAOR: Sixth Session, 1951–52, Supplement No. 17 (A/1949). *Supplementary Report to the Second Annual Report of the United Nations Commissioner in Libya,* GAOR: Sixth Session, 1951–52, Supplement No. 17A (A/1949/Add.1). "Annual Report of the French Government [to the General Assembly] on the Administrative of the Fezzan," United Nations Doc. A/1970, 10 September 1951. Mimeographed. "Supplement to the Annual Report of the French Government on the Administration of the Fezzan," United Nations Doc. A/1970/Add.1, 16 January 1952. Mimeographed. "Annual Report of the Government of the United Kingdom of Great Britain and Northern Ireland [to the General Assembly] concerning the Administration of Cyrenaica and Tripolitania," United Nations Doc. A/2024, 21 December 1951. Mimeographed. "Supplementary Report of the Government of the United Kingdom and Northern Ireland [to the General Assembly] concerning the Administration of Cyrenaica and Tripolitania," United Nations Doc. A/2024/Add.1, 12 January 1952. Mimeographed.

marily with the question of the appropriate adjustment of the frontiers between Egypt and the former Italian colony of Libya with particular reference to paragraphs 2 and 3 of Annex XI of the Treaty of Peace with Italy (item 22 of the Assembly's agenda). The problem of Libyan war damages (item 21) was dealt with by the Second Committee (see p. 859).

As these dates show, the General Assembly found itself confronted with the accomplished fact of Libyan independence. By letter of 24 December 1951, Libya had applied for admission to membership of the United Nations. Simultaneously, it applied for membership of the main specialized agencies.[2] Its Prime Minister, Mahmud al-Muntasir, had been invited by the Chairman of the *Ad Hoc* Political Committee to take a seat at the Committee table, as were also an observer for the Italian Government and the Commissioner.

That any delegation would formally contest the validity of Libyan independence seemed unlikely, though, as we shall see, a few took positions which came close to challenging it; but more or less virulent criticisms of the way in which Resolution 289 (IV) had been implemented by the Administering Powers, the Commissioner, and the Council for Libya were to be expected. Conversely, other delegations, which at the Fourth and Fifth Sessions of the General Assembly had expressed doubts or qualms about the course taken by Libyan events, might be prepared to accept the final outcome as an honorable, though not ideal, result of what remained in the history of the United Nations a unique exercise in decolonization, and therefore one to be judged solely on its specific merits and demerits. It was in this atmosphere of calculating expectation that the Libyan Government, the Commissioner and staff of the United Nations Mission in Libya, the members of the Council, and probably the Administering Powers, too, awaited the forthcoming debates and the Assembly's verdict.

Everyone realized, of course, that the prevailing international situation and the tense cold war atmosphere surrounding it were hardly conducive to reconciliation of the conflicting views and interests that had come to light during 1949 and 1950. Such pregnant political issues as the problem of the independence of Korea, threats to the political independence and territorial integrity of Greece, threats to the peace of the Far East, the question of Palestine, and a few others like them, all of which were on the agenda, could not fail to affect at least the tone, and in all probability the substance too, of the impending debate on Libya.

In accordance with the usual practice, the discussion began in the *Ad Hoc* Political Committee, which in turn reported to the plenary Assembly,

2. United Nations Doc. A/2032, 3 January 1952. Mimeographed.

where the debate was renewed. It would be repetitious to cover the same ground twice, so the author will briefly confine himself to the proceedings in the Committee, where many of the old arguments and controversies recounted earlier were again paraded, either for propaganda purposes, or to complete the record of a consistent policy. Nonetheless, feelings of satisfaction as to what had been achieved by all the parties concerned under the benevolent aegis of the United Nations, coupled with fears about the political and economic future of the new State, found expression, thereby leavening the reiteration of the traditional congratulatory statements.

Even to give a full account of the discussion in committee alone would require many lengthy quotations from the official records of the General Assembly. At this late stage in the work, the author feels that a more statistical treatment of this final debate may spare the general reader the pangs of boredom.[3]

Naturally, the analysis that follows makes no claim to statistical accuracy in the mathematical sense. The mere fact that a particular speaker did not specifically mention, for example, his delegation's support for Libya's aspirations to membership of the United Nations—or at least is not reported in the summary records as having done so—cannot be taken as proof that the delegation in question was indifferent to or opposed to such a development. The author does, however, believe that this approach will bring out the mixture of old and new ways of thinking that characterized the final discussions on the disposal of the first of the three former Italian colonies whose fate had been placed in the hands of the United Nations.

The general debate took the best part of seven meetings (forty-eighth to fifty-fourth). Disregarding, for analytical purposes, the statements and interventions of the representative of Libya, of the observer for the Italian Government, and of the Commissioner himself, no fewer than thirty-nine members of the Committee out of a total of sixty spoke in the debate. For our present purposes, those thirty-nine speakers can be grouped as follows, though the author must make it plain that no hard-and-fast political significance attaches to the classification:

Western and Commonwealth group	7 members	(Australia, France, Greece, New Zealand, Turkey, United Kingdom, United States)
Arab States	7 members	(Egypt, Iran, Iraq, Lebanon, Saudi Arabia, Syria, Yemen)

3. The specialist reader who wishes to study the matter more carefully should consult the full records of the discussions in GAOR: Sixth Session, 1951–52, *Ad Hoc* Political Committee, 48th–54th Meetings, 23–28 January 1952, pp. 263–307.

Latin American group	10 members	(Bolivia, Brazil, Chile, Dominican Republic, Ecuador, El Salvador, Haiti, Nicaragua, Uruguay, Venezuela)
East European group	5 members	(Byelorussian Soviet Socialist Republic, Czechoslovakia, Poland, Ukrainian Soviet Socialist Republic, Union of Soviet Socialist Republics)

The remaining ten members who spoke were Afghanistan, Burma, China, Ethiopia, India, Israel, Liberia, Pakistan, the Phillippines, and Yugoslavia; most of them had close links with one or other of the four main groups without actually belonging to them (at this time the idea of an uncommitted group of Member States had yet to take shape).

Of the thirty-nine members in question, no fewer than thirty-one welcomed the emergence of Libya as an independent sovereign State, and no member expressed dissatisfaction or disappointment with the overall result, though, as already mentioned, some members, in particular the East European group and Egypt, were lukewarm, to say the least. Pakistan was a special case, for after a long record in the Council for Libya of being highly critical, it ended up by expressing slight reservations but endorsing the final result.

Though not too much weight should be attached to laudatory or congratulatory phrases uttered on such occasions, the fact remains that thirty-four speakers paid glowing tributes to the people, the Sovereign, or the Government of the new State. Several of them paid a tribute to all three. In fact, the only delegations who refrained from offering congratulations were the members of the East European bloc. What is rather surprising is that no fewer than thirteen speakers expressed appreciation and admiration of the way in which the Administering Powers had cooperated with the Commissioner, with the Council for Libya, and above all with the Libyans themselves in seeing that the General Assembly's Resolutions on Libya were implemented fully and harmoniously within the prescribed time limits. It is even more surprising that two Arab States, Iraq and Syria, were among these thirteen. Five Latin American delegations also were among this group, again rather surprisingly, seeing that the final outcome was not so much to Italy's advantage as the Latin American States had originally wished.

The Council for Libya drew eleven tributes. Here we find that not one Arab State took the trouble to commend the Council—a not altogether warranted neglect; Afghanistan and Turkey were the only Moslem countries to do so.

Lastly, the author may perhaps be allowed the indulgence of placing on record the fact that no fewer than twenty-four speakers warmly commended the Commissioner on the way in which he had carried out his duties, in most cases extending these congratulations to the members of his staff, who had well earned them.

In the course of a statement made early in the debate, the Prime Minister of Libya, after having expressed his Sovereign's and his people's gratitude to the United Nations, spoke movingly of his country's desire to become a member of the organization as soon as possible. Thereafter, twenty-three speakers supported him hoping that this objective would be promptly reached.[4] There was also one expression of qualified support by the Israeli representative, whose statement will be described in rather more detail later. The East European group were ominously silent about membership.

Ten speakers dwelt on Libya's poverty and on the economic and social problems the new country would face, urging that everything possible be done to expand and speed up the technical assistance already being provided to Libya on a modest scale by the United Nations family of international organizations.

On the question of the presence of foreign troops and military bases on Libyan soil, eight delegations—those of the East European group plus Egypt, Syria, and Lebanon—expressed, with varying degrees of vehemence, their opposition to the maintenance of these forces in the country, and two—Saudi Arabia and India—indirectly voiced their disapproval of such arrangements (the Pakistani position will be dealt with separately).

Only one speaker mentioned the minorities in Libya: again it was the representative of Israel.

As an interesting aside to the foregoing rather dry recital of the feelings that prevailed in the Committee, it may be noted that two countries praised the Italians for the part they had played in the settlement. These were Bolivia, which praised the Italian settlers for what they had done for Libya in general and Tripolitania in particular, and Uruguay, which commended the Italian Government on the conciliatory attitude it had taken over the preceding two years. Thus, the strong Latin American sentiment in favor of Italy, so marked at the outset in 1948–49 (see Chapter 1, Part 3), was not so publicly evident as it had been previously. This probably is explicable by the fact that the Italian Government was generally satisfied with the outcome and expected to settle its remaining problems with Libya through the United Nations Tribunal in Libya or by diplomatic negotiation.

Its observer, Baron Confalonieri, who had also served as Italy's representative on the Council for Libya, indicated in the course of the general debate that

4. But see footnote 69 to Chapter 5, p. 403.

> Italy had been among the first countries to recognize the new State of Libya and hoped to enjoy relations of mutual confidence and true friendship with that country. The Italian delegation was sure that those friendly feelings were shared by the Libyan people, their Government and their Sovereign. [He] took the opportunity of expressing, further, his convictions that all the provisions adopted by the General Assembly in resolution 388 (V) of 15 December 1950 would soon be put into practice. Italy considered that in adopting that resolution, the General Assembly's intention had been to lay down the necessary solid foundation for the establishment of the best relations between the two countries.
>
> Furthermore, Italy was prepared to co-operate in any plan for technical assistance to Libya. Obviously such co-operation must be on a basis of mutual trust. There were many Italians who thoroughly understood the needs of the country and would be able to make a valuable contribution to its development.[5]

The representatives of the two Administering Powers, the United Kingdom and France, were naturally listened to with special interest. So was the delegate for the United States.

Selwyn Lloyd, representative of the United Kingdom, remarked that

> The most significant factor in Libyan independence was the part played by the Libyan people itself through its representatives in the national Assembly. They consummated the process of constitutional evolution in a remarkably short time under the wise and far-sighted guidance of King Idris. They had shown commonsense, a grasp of realities and the ability to profit from the constitutional experience of other countries. The Constitution they had framed was the highest tribute to their achievement. It was to be hoped that the spirit of the United Nations Charter, which it so clearly reflected, would continue to inspire future Libyan Governments.[6]

In his statement during the general debate, Charles de Beaumont, representative of France, gave emphasis to

> the bonds of friendship between France and Libya and paid a tribute to the new independent State for its heroic participation in the Second World War. He was glad to join in welcoming the Prime Minister of Libya to the Committee and he would not forget Ahmed Bey [Seif

5. GAOR: Sixth Session, 1951–52, *Ad Hoc* Political Committee, 52nd Meeting, 25 January 1952, p. 289, paras. 26–27.

6. GAOR: Sixth Session, 1951–52, *Ad Hoc* Political Committee, 48th Meeting, 23 January 1952, p. 264, para. 9.

> al-Nasr] of the Fezzan who, with his supporters, had afforded effective assistance to General Leclerc.

De Beaumont further noted that

> independence had in fact been achieved under King Idris el-Senussi even before the target date of 1 January 1952. France had participated in the surveys of technical assistance needs and had adopted the necessary measures to implement, in respect of the Fezzan, resolution 388 (V) which concerned the disposal of Italian property in Libya. France had therefore strictly honoured its commitments.[7]

John Sherman Cooper, representative of the United States, observed that

> the proclamation of Libya as an independent and Sovereign State marked the successful completion of a project of remarkable co-operation between the United Nations and the people of Libya . . . an achievement of which the United Nations could be proud.

He also noted the importance of keeping in mind that

> the successful fulfillment of the General Assembly resolution required decision which only the Libyans themselves could take in the exercise of their right of self-determination. . . . [This] success would not have been possible without the sincere efforts of the representatives of the three parts of Libya who had been able to reconcile differences and reach agreement without compromising or losing sight of their common objectives of unity and independence. . . . In the opinion of the United States delegation, the Libyan Constitution was soundly based upon liberal and democratic principles and under its free institutions would be able to develop as an essential basis of its national life.[8]

It is now necessary to deal with four more interventions: those of the representatives of Pakistan, Egypt, the USSR, and Israel. Two of them disrupted the agreeable atmosphere of praise and satisfaction in which the debate had, generally speaking, proceeded; another dealt with the special position of one delegation; the fourth, coming as it did from a member of the Council for Libya, who for nearly two years had been the most vociferous critic in that body, was unexpected, to say the least. Let us deal with this intervention first.

Abdur Rahim Khan (Pakistan) began by emphasizing the uniqueness of the problem and by recalling that many had believed that the General

7. Ibid., paras. 11 and 13.
8. Ibid., p. 265, paras. 19–26.

Assembly's original decision, embodied in Resolution 289 (IV), was not in keeping with Libya's political and economic conditions. However that might be, the responsibility for that decision was shared equally by all members of the United Nations. Having described the resolution's defects and omissions [9] and the difficulties to which they had given rise, he said that, to the great credit of the people of Libya, a National Assembly had been formed, a Constitution adopted, the form of government determined, and independence achieved. As for the presence of military bases and foreign troops in Libya, "he was able to assert that neither political leaders nor anyone occupying an important position in the country objected to the presence of those forces." [10] On the contrary, the advantages they brought that country, particularly in the economic field, were generally recognized there. (In this respect, Rahim Khan was being unduly optimistic. It is true that Beshir Bey Saadawi had fairly recently—28 August 1951—privately gone on record at a meeting at the Commissioner's residence to the effect that, provided a legally established Libyan Government and an elected Parliament agreed, he was reluctantly prepared to accept the need for tolerating foreign military bases on Libyan soil by way of compensation for foreign subventions; but it was no secret that, in their heart of hearts, he and his Tripolitanian Congress Party were hostile to such a presence. Such an assertion as Rahim Khan's therefore created a sensation, and a rejoinder was only to be expected.)

Rahim Khan then turned to Libya's provisional financial agreements with certain Powers, saying that, while his Government did not consider them perfect, neither did it believe that they encroached upon the country's independence or would be extended long enough to embarrass or fetter the future Libyan Government. Economic stability was nearly as important as political freedom. As regards the parliamentary situation, he hoped that the Libyan Government would set about remedying the unsatisfactory features of the electoral law, to which he had repeatedly drawn attention in the Council, in the light of what had been said about them at the General Assembly. He further hoped, in view of the forthcoming general elections, that the wisdom and ability recently displayed by the Libyan people would again be deployed to ensure that their wishes were fully and freely ex-

9. "The General Assembly resolution had left a number of important points to be decided; for example, it had not stated who was to convene the National Assembly, who were to sit on it as a representative of the people of Libya, how they were to be assisted by the Commissioner and the Council, what facilities were to be available to the members of the National Assembly in the accomplishment of their task and what was the extent of talent available in the country for that purpose." Ibid., pp. 265–66, para. 34.

10. Ibid., para. 35.

pressed. Rahim Khan ended by paying a very warm tribute to the King, adding that Pakistan was eagerly looking forward to Libya's admission to membership of the United Nations.

This chivalrous retreat by a former adversary from his once overcritical, at times even negative, approach to Libyan affairs to a sober, constructive position was much appreciated, and not by the Commissioner alone.

The opposition's heavy guns were really brought to bear when in the course of the forty-ninth meeting A. A. Soldatov spoke for the Soviet Union.[11] He opened by recalling that at the Fifth Session the USSR had, in the sole interests of the Arab population, unsuccessfully called for the withdrawal of all foreign troops from and the closing of all military bases on Libya's soil after independence, on the ground that their presence was a violation of the rights of the Libyan people and an infringement of Libya's sovereignty. The maintenance of troops and installations there was a threat to peace and security, and a means of bringing pressure to bear on Libya's Arab neighbors, by the Atlantic Powers. The activities of the Commissioner and the Administering Authorities in Libya had been inspired not by respect for the equality of peoples and for their right to self-determination, but by deference to vested interests in France, the United Kingdom, and the United States.

The Soviet Union, faithful to its principles, as it had been when the last vestiges of foreign occupation had been eliminated from Egypt, Lebanon, and Syria, would renew at the current (sixth) session its demand that the United Nations act forthwith to bring about the departure of all foreign forces and installations from Libya.

The representative of the Soviet Union was supported by his colleagues from Byelorussia, Czechoslovakia, Poland, and the Ukraine. None of these five statements contained any helpful suggestions or comments whatsoever about Libya's political, financial, economic, or social future.

When Mostapha Bey, for Egypt,[12] in a brief statement at the Committee's forty-eighth meeting, congratulated the Libyan people on their country's accession to independence, he paid a tribute to the work of the Commissioner and his staff, and expressed support for the USSR representative's demands. However, he also rather ominously, to the Commissioner's mind, reserved the right to comment later on the substantive issues. The Commissioner's forebodings were fully realized when, at the fifty-first meeting, he launched a blistering attack on what he considered to be the defects in

11. GAOR: Sixth Session, 1951–52, *Ad Hoc* Political Committee, 49th Meeting, 23 January 1952, pp. 269–70, paras. 2–13.

12. GAOR: Sixth Session, 1951–52, *Ad Hoc* Political Committee, 48th Meeting, 23 January 1952, pp. 267–68, paras. 50–53.

the Constitution and political institutions of the new State, which according to him were democratic in name alone, having been imposed by force on the Libyan people against their true feelings and wishes. The federal structure decided upon was designed to perpetuate the colonialism of the past and to clothe the imperialist plans of the occupying Powers with legality.

Mostapha Bey then assailed the way in which France, the United Kingdom, and the United States had exploited the resolutions on international economic and technical assistance to Libya, adopted by the General Assembly at its Fifth Session, to tighten their own grip on the country. But the unity and freedom so ardently desired by the Libyans could make sense only in a setting devoid of any form of foreign domination.

Recalling the criticisms voiced at the Fifth Session of the way in which the Libyan National Assembly had been established, and of the creation by the Administering Powers of local governments in the three provinces, Mostapha Bey made great play with the Commissioner's plans for an elected bicameral Parliament based on proportional representation and incorporating the principles of governmental and ministerial responsibility, and especially of his inability to keep his promise to the General Assembly to secure the unanimous support of the Council for Libya for these plans—an inability caused, in the speaker's view, by the hostile attitude of the Administering Powers. In the upshot, Libya's Constitution had been drafted by an appointed body without any pretense at democratic consultation of the people.

Mostapha Bey's last target was the agreement concluded between Libya and the United Kingdom. He stated that, despite the warnings of the Commissioner and the Tripolitanian member of the Council, there had been concluded an agreement whereby the United Kingdom had undertaken to cover Libya's budget deficit. The agreement would run until 31 March 1953, during which period the most senior official in the Libyan Ministry of Finance would be British. This was tantamount to placing Libya for the next eighteen months under United Kingdom tutelage in all financial matters, a position fraught with danger for Libya and its people.[13]

Thus one, at least, of the Commissioner's governmental critics on the Council showed that he had lost none of his intransigence!

The statement of the Israeli representative, Abba Eban, understandably differed from all the others. Israel's creation had been deeply resented by the Arab States surrounding it on all sides but the sea, and their resentment had persisted. The birth of yet another Arab State, and the consequent enlargement of the Arab League, could not have been unreservedly wel-

13. GAOR: Sixth Session, 1951–52, *Ad Hoc* Political Committee, 51st Meeting, 25 January, 1952, pp. 281–82, paras. 1–10.

come to Israel, especially in view of potential repercussions in North Africa even farther to the west. Lastly, there was the question of the Libyan Jews.

Though he did not specifically refer to them, none of the foregoing considerations could have been far from Eban's mind. He recalled, in order to illustrate Israel's policy in regional relations, that, contrary to the confident expectations of many delegations, his Government had in 1949 declined to support the Administering Powers' proposal for a ten-year trusteeship for Libya. It so happened that the proposal had been rejected by a single vote. This respite had given governments time for reflection, and by 1950 all Member States had favored speedy independence for Libya.

The conflicts which divided the Near East were acute but transient; they should not therefore be taken as a basis for international planning. The truth of regional cooperation would eventually prevail.

Rarely had a people inherited a richer patrimony or realized so many of its hopes so quickly as had the Arabs; but, Eban warned Libya, it must never forget that, far from being at the end of its struggles, it was barely at the beginning of them. Rapid political progress was of little value if apathy and inertia continued to plague social and economic advance. Hence the urgent need for expanding technical assistance to Libya.

Eban also emphasized his Government's deep concern that adequate provision be made for the protection of minorities in the new State; 15,000 Jews having already emigrated therefrom to Israel, the latter could not but interest itself in the conditions and well-being of those still there.

As for Libya's admission to the United Nations, Israel could support this on one condition: that, as required by the United Nations Charter, Libya desired to establish friendly relationships with all other Member States (cf. footnote 69 to Chapter 5).[14]

The rest of the fifty-second meeting and part of the fifty-third were devoted to replies, most speakers at the same time repeating their main arguments, though mercifully more briefly. In particular, the Pakistani representative replied to a comment made at the beginning of the fifty-second meeting by Soldatov, reproaching him (Rahim Khan) for his alleged defense of the retention of armed forces and military bases in Libya.

The USSR representative had said:

> Not one representative had spoken in favour of the retention of armed forces and military bases in Libya, with the single exception of the representative of Pakistan, who although he had spent two years in the country, seemed to be ignorant of the true state of affairs there. It was

14. GAOR: Sixth Session, 1951–52, *Ad Hoc,* Political Committee, 52nd Meeting, 25 January 1952, pp. 287–88, paras. 1–7.

incomprehensible that a member of the Council for Libya should be unaware of the existence of the National Congress Party. At the beginning of the year, the President of that Party had addressed an appeal to a number of delegations to the effect that the United Nations should set the seal on Libya's independence by fixing a date for the withdrawal of foreign troops which were interfering in the country's domestic affairs in order to carry out their imperialistic designs. The appeal further said that the Libyan people hoped that the United Nations would adopt a resolution as soon as possible calling for the withdrawal of foreign armed forces and for the taking of urgent steps to promote the holding of free and democratic elections within the shortest possible period, adding that the Libyan people expected the United Nations to help it in its struggle for the elimination of foreign influences. . . .

Those facts demonstrated the falsity of the allegations that the Libyan people had no objection to the presence of foreign troops on their soil. Such statements as that made by the representative of Pakistan could not be taken seriously.[15]

Rahim Khan pointed out that the alleged statement by the National Congress Party on foreign troops mentioned by Soldatov had apparently been made in January 1952, when he himself had been in Geneva. Perhaps he ought to have made it clear when he spoke at the forty-eighth meeting that no such statement had been made up to the end of 1951 while he was still in Libya and in a position to hear of it.[16]

On 28 January—three days after this exchange between the Pakistani and USSR representatives—the Egyptian representative addressed a letter to the Chairman of the Committee requesting him to circulate as a committee document a cable sent from Tripoli by Beshir Bey Saadawi (no date of dispatch of the cablegram appears in the document), asserting that the National Congress Party considered the continued presence of foreign troops in Libya incompatible with national sovereignty, and adding that such continuance would be a constant source of trouble and endanger peace and stability. Any treaty concluded under such conditions would be unavailing and worthless. In the same message Beshir Bey repeated his request for United Nations supervision of the forthcoming Libyan elections.

It will be noted that Beshir Bey Saadawi's position as reflected by this telegram was not in accordance with the statement he had made to the Commissioner earlier, when the latter had informed him of the need to turn to advantage the presence of foreign troops and installations as a source

15. Ibid., pp. 288–89, paras. 18–19.
16. Ibid., p. 292, para. 49.

of foreign financial aid to cover Libya's budget deficit and provide funds for its economic and social development.[17] (See this chapter, p. 850.)

In these circumstances, some comment was bound to be made by the representative of the Libyan Government when he came to reply, at the end of the debate at the fifty-third meeting, to what had been said earlier.

On this occasion, the Prime Minister was unable to attend in person, and the Deputy Prime Minister, Fethi al-Kikhia, spoke for him. He expressed his gratification that

> the great majority of the members of the Committee had followed the wise counsel of the representative of Pakistan and had dealt with the problem before them in a sympathetic and realistic spirit. He was also happy to note that almost all the Arab States had adopted the same benevolent attitude to the Libyan problem. Nevertheless, he was unable to subscribe to certain opinions put forward in the course of the discussion, which, in the view of the Libyan Government, related to a domestic matter with which the Libyan Government and Parliament were alone competent to deal . . . . He wished to reaffirm that Libya was in a better position than anyone else to protect and maintain its independence and sovereignty . . . . Libya was firmly determined to maintain and respect the principles of the United Nations Charter and the Universal Declaration of Human Rights. It hoped that the United Nations would have confidence in the ability of the democratic Government of Libya to maintain the independence and sovereignty of the United Kingdom of Libya. By strictly adhering to those principles the Libyan people could best testify its gratitude to the United Nations and deserve the aid it hoped to obtain from the Organization.[18]

In the meantime, a number of draft resolutions had been tabled. The first was introduced at the forty-ninth meeting by a group of twelve European, Asian, African, Commonwealth, and Latin American States, together with the United States, the only major Power among the sponsors. According to this proposal, the General Assembly would congratulate the people and Government of Libya on the establishment of Libyan independence; take note of the fact that national elections would be held in Libya in the near future; request the Secretary-General and the specialized agencies to continue to extend to Libya, at its request, such technical assistance as they

17. For text of the Egyptian representative's letter and Beshir Bey Saadawi's telegram, see GAOR: Sixth Session, 1951–52, Annexes, Agenda item 20 (A/AC.53/L.46, 28 January 1952), p. 2.

18. GAOR: Sixth Session, 1951–52, *Ad Hoc* Political Committee, 53rd Meeting, 28 January 1952, pp. 296–97, paras. 12–20.

might be in a position to provide, and, finally, consider that Libya, having become an independent, sovereign State and having applied for membership of the United Nations, should be admitted in accordance with Article 4 of the Charter.[19]

At the same meeting, the Soviet Union submitted a draft resolution to the effect that the General Assembly considered it essential that all foreign troops and military personnel be withdrawn from Libya, and all foreign military bases there be liquidated, within three months.[20]

At the fifty-first meeting, Egypt, Saudi Arabia, Syria, and Yemen jointly submitted amendments to the twelve-Power proposal: first, the insertion of the words "free and democratic" before the words "national elections"; second, the insertion after that paragraph of two new paragraphs, one calling upon Member States to provide Libya, as part of an integrated program channeled through United Nations institutions, with financial and technical assistance; the second requesting the Secretary-General to inform the Economic and Social Council (ECOSOC) and the General Assembly itself of economic and social programs to be undertaken in Libya, and to suggest measures for utilizing United Nations resources and governmental aid to promote Libya's development.[21]

At the same time, Egypt submitted a draft resolution similar to that tabled by the Soviet Union, but allowing six months for the withdrawal and providing for the military bases to be handed over to the Libyan authorities rather than dismantled.[22]

At the fifty-second meeting, the Soviet Union proposed that the whole of operative paragraph 4 of the twelve-Power draft resolution be deleted.[23] (This was tantamount to opposing the admission of Libya as a member to the United Nations.)

At the next meeting, the four Arab delegations submitted a revision of their original amendments. The main features of the new text were (a) a proposal that both Members of the United Nations and nonmembers should provide financial assistance to Libya by contributing to a special account,

19. For full text of the twelve-Power draft resolution, see GAOR: Sixth Session, 1951–52, Annexes, Agenda item 20 (A/AC.53/L.39, 23 January 1952), p. 1. See also Chapter 5, p. 403, fn. 69.

20. United Nations Doc. A/AC.53/L.40, 23 January 1952. Mimeographed. But see GAOR: Sixth Session, 1951–52, *Ad Hoc* Political Committee, 54th Meeting, 28 January 1952, p. 306, para. 34.

21. United Nations Doc. A/AC.53/L.41, 25 January 1952. Mimeographed.

22. GAOR: Sixth Session, 1951–52, Annexes, Agenda item 20 (A/AC.53/L.42, 25 January 1952), p. 2.

23. United Nations Doc. A/AC.53/L.43, 25 January 1952. Mimeographed.

and (b) a request to ECOSOC to study measures for administering and making use of these funds.[24]

Then the Chilean delegation, led by Hernan Santa Cruz, introduced a series of subamendments, presenting alternative texts for each of the three new paragraphs proposed by the four Arab States, namely: one requesting ECOSOC to study ways and means by which the United Nations, with the cooperation of all Member States and the appropriate specialized agencies, could lend more assistance in financing Libya's economic and social development, not overlooking the possibility of a special account for voluntary contributions; a second requesting the Secretary-General to provide ECOSOC with the facilities it needed to carry out this task, and also to examine, if Libya should so request, the feasibility of appointing a finance officer within the framework of the technical assistance program to coordinate the receipt and application of monies made available to Libya to meet deficits in its regular administrative budgets; and a third requesting the Secretary-General to give attention to Libya's economic problems in particular and to continue to report on economic development in Africa generally.[25]

During the ensuing discussion, the Chilean representative orally revised his subamendments, providing for due consultation with the Libyan Government, and dropping the suggestion regarding the appointment of a finance officer. Thus revised, the subamendments were accepted by the four sponsors of the Arab amendments.

There followed a lively debate which, as the reader can imagine from what precedes, centered on two main issues:

1. Foreign troops and military bases, the withdrawal of which from Libyan territory was demanded, though in different terms, by the USSR draft resolution and the Arab amendments to the twelve-Power proposal; both were defeated, but the former was reintroduced in plenary meeting;
2. The way in which future technical, and especially financial, assistance should be rendered to the new State. Should this mainly be done through bilateral agreements, as the former Administering Powers wished, or through international organs and institutions? The latter solution was favored by a number of States, most of whom were themselves still in need of assistance.

24. United Nations Doc. A/AC.53/L.41/Rev.1, 28 January 1952. Mimeographed. But see GAOR: Sixth Session, 1951–52, *Ad Hoc* Political Committee, 53rd Meeting, 28 January 1952, p. 298, fn. 1 to para. 23.

25. United Nations Doc. A/AC.53/L.45 and Rev.1, 28 January 1952. Mimeographed. But see GAOR: Sixth Session, 1951–52, *Ad Hoc* Political Committee, 53rd Meeting, 28 January 1952, p. 300, fn. 2 to para. 46.

The second solution was in essence very close to what the Commissioner had had in mind when, at the third session of the Meeting of Experts on Libyan financial, monetary, and development problems, he had suggested that "direct financial assistance to Libya from other Governments [that is, other than the United Kingdom, France, Italy, and the United States] should be paid into a special account of the Libyan Government, the expenditure of the funds to be supervised by an expert appointed by the Secretary-General of the United Nations within the framework of the Technical Assistance Programme." [26]

At the time, the proposal was rejected by the British, French, Italian, and United States experts, though supported by their Egyptian colleague. The Arab amendments in their final shape aimed at reviving it. Opposition came from the same side as it had six months earlier. It will also be remembered that later in 1951, on the recommendation of the Coordinating Committee and with the Commissioner's agreement, the Provisional Libyan Government, for lack of a better solution, had approved the foundation of a public development and stabilization agency (LPDSA) and a finance corporation (LFC). The issue before the *Ad Hoc* Political Committee therefore boiled down to a simple question: should all financial assistance to Libya be channeled through these two institutions, or should there also be an independent special account for voluntary contributions? This time the Arab-Chilean proposals carried the day.

This, however, was not the end of the fighting. When, on 1 February 1952, the draft resolution recommended by the Committee—the twelve-Power proposal as modified in the course of the debate—came up for discussion in the full Assembly, the battle over (1) and (2) above was refought on the same lines without producing a different outcome.

A Soviet Union draft resolution on the evacuation of foreign troops and bases from Libya, more or less identical with the one thrown out in the Committee, was rejected by the Assembly by 34 votes to 6, with 10 abstentions.[27] The passage of the Committee's draft resolution was then held up by a procedural debate provoked by the Powers opposed to the two paragraphs relating to additional financial assistance, the point being whether a two-thirds majority was required for the adoption of the controversial provisions and for that of the proposal as a whole. The General Assembly, following a challenged ruling by the President, decided by 29

26. *Second Annual Report of the United Nations Commissioner in Libya,* paras. 223–24, and Annexes XVIII and XIX, pp. 144–51.

27. See GAOR: Sixth Session, 1951–52, 370th Plenary Meeting, 1 February 1952, para. 203.

votes to 17, with 5 abstentions, that a simple majority would suffice. In the outcome, the draft resolution as a whole was adopted by 53 votes to none.[28]

It must be admitted that the two provisions that caused so much trouble had little practical effect.[29]

Before finally disposing of the Libyan question, the General Assembly passed two more resolutions. The first noted the intention of the Government of Egypt to enter into negotiations with the Libyan Government with a view to settling in a friendly and good-neighborly spirit the question of the adjustment of their common frontiers.[30]

The second resolution concerned the problem of compensation for war damage, which, as mentioned previously, was of particular interest to Cyrenaica.[31] Following a survey made by an expert appointed under instructions from the Secretary-General, the Second Committee had dealt with the matter at its one hundred and eighty-ninth and one hundred and ninetieth meetings. Acting on that Committee's recommendation, the General Assembly expressed the belief that the problem should be considered within the framework of the overall development plans for Libya. It also invited the Secretary-General and the Technical Assistance Board to give sympathetic consideration to Libyan requests for assistance which would strengthen the Libyan economy, including the repair or reconstruction of damaged property and installations.[32]

Comparing the debates on the Libyan question at the Fourth Session with those that took place at the Sixth, the reader will be struck by a significant change in the emphasis placed on various of its aspects. On both occasions

28. Ibid., paras. 196–202. The draft resolution as adopted became General Assembly Resolution 515 (VI), 1 February 1952. For full text, see Annex I, pp. 900–01.

29. The Secretary-General opened an account to receive contributions and for a number of years wrote annually to some Member States suggesting contributions, but none was made. As noted in Chapter 9, modest contributions to the LPDSA were made by Turkey, Egypt, and Pakistan for varying numbers of years. However, until oil royalties began to flow into the coffers of the Libyan Treasury after 1959, the bulk of the deficits on the administrative and the development budgets were met respectively by payments in various forms by the United Kingdom and United States Governments, the much smaller French subvention barely serving to redress the financial imbalance of the Fezzan.

30. General Assembly Resolution 516 (VI), 1 February 1952. For text, see GAOR: Sixth Session, Supplement No. 20 (A/2119), p. 13.

31. See *Supplementary Report to the Second Annual Report of the United Nations Commissioner in Libya,* Annex X, p. 52.

32. General Assembly Resolution 529 (VI), 29 January 1952. For full text, see p. 901.

the interests of delegations were divided between recognized political issues and those of a technical-administrative nature but having political undertones.

In both categories issues had radically changed. In 1949 the dominating political question had been that of the shape of Libyan unity, and the cognate problems of the form of State and government. The main technical-administrative issues related to the United Nations machinery required to implement General Assembly Resolution 289 (IV). In particular, Sub-Committee 17 had gone to great pains in putting that machinery together. At the Fifth Session of the General Assembly, in 1950, delegations had noted that for lack of a few components the movement had creaked and squeaked from time to time, and that no amount of the oil of goodwill could make it run perfectly smoothly. In 1952, therefore, one might have expected delegations to take stock of the way in which their work had stood the test of practical operation. With a few exceptions, of which Rahim Khan's statement summarized on pages 849–51 was the outstanding example, little of the kind happened. Naturally, many critical or laudatory remarks were uttered with an eye to the parts played by the principal actors, but little was said about the intricacies of the action itself. The most vital aspect of the question—whether the unique method of decolonization and emancipation devised for Libya by the Assembly might not be applicable to the many other countries on the threshold of independence at the time—aroused hardly any interest. The Syrian representative, Ahmad Choukayri, was virtually the only speaker to make constructive suggestions in this regard.[33] And not a word was said about the highly controversial question, considered as fundamental only a few months earlier: whether the Libyan Government, whose representatives had joined in the discussions at the Sixth Session, had or had not been "duly constituted." The minorities question too, once so knotty, was relegated to limbo.

Instead, the two questions that exercised the minds of the delegates were straightforward problems of power politics: the presence of foreign troops

33. Choukayri said: "It was a matter for congratulation that, when the four great Powers had failed to agree on the disposal of the former Italian colonies, they had referred the question to the General Assembly, which had decided in favour of Libyan independence. It would be well if the same procedure were applied and the same results obtained in the case of those countries which did not yet enjoy autonomy or independence." GAOR: Sixth Session, 1951–52, *Ad Hoc* Political Committee, 51st Meeting, 25 January 1952, p. 284, para. 42.

Also Jawaharlal Nehru said: "India realized that the liberation of Libya was not an isolated event but part of a vast movement which was today stirring the whole of the Arab and Asiatic world and leading it towards political emancipation and social progress." Ibid., p. 285, para. 53.

and military bases on Libyan soil, and the question of who should pay the piper and call the tune in the new State. Admittedly, the General Assembly is primarily a political body, so that it is only natural that its members should look at the items on its agenda through their political viewfinders. But, regrettably, the debate in January and February of 1952 suggested only too painfully that, collectively as well as individually, the members of the United Nations were still but little disposed to learn from the decolonization experience gained in Libya both by themselves and by the organization to which they belonged.

Afterthoughts

Having reached his journey's end, the author can no longer delay attempting an evaluation, or at least an appreciation, of the methods used and policies followed in the Libyan venture. To call such comments conclusions would be as pretentious as it would be premature. Pretentious, because to be valid conclusions must flow from a logical and reasoned analysis of causes and effects which, in turn, depend on a rational sequence of events. The reader who has so patiently followed happenings in Libya as chronicled in this study will have noted that only to a very limited extent were they the product of logic or reason, at least in the Western sense of these words. To analyze and recapitulate them by Cartesian methods would not only distort them, but also, and similarly, affect the conclusions reached. The risk appears that much the greater, inasmuch as not only did the events take place in the atmosphere peculiar to the Libyan condition; the General Assembly Resolutions that determined them were themselves the result of political compromise, and sometimes more pragmatic than rational. As subsequent developments showed in this case too, the language of compromise is seldom distinguished by clarity, and thus encourages differences in interpretation, which, more often than not, are intended to further specific views or aims. Even the Commissioner cannot plead complete innocence in this respect when United Nations or Libyan interests seemed to him to be threatened.

To draw conclusions would also be premature, because the conditions which basically affect the Libyan people and their State today are so different from those prevailing in 1950–51 as to make comparisons extremely hazardous. Both the Constitution and the economic and social development plan with which Libya started life as an independent State had been designed for a poor country, badly in need of internal consolidation, whose growth would be slow, and probably painful, and which certainly could not be expected, for many years to come, to play an active role in the economy or politics of the region of which it formed a part. Had these conditions, both internal and external, evolved along the anticipated lines, a comparative appreciation of Libya's position in 1951–52 and in 1966–67 would have been feasible. But, things being what they are now, the elements to be compared have changed so radically that a second inquiry into the wisdom and efficiency with which development has been managed would be required before valid opinions could be expressed.

Such a study would deal first with the Constitution, which, as revised and amended at the end of the first decade of independence, transformed Libya from a federal into a unitary State. Again, halfway through that decade, oil was struck in Libya in enormous and unexpected quantities; almost overnight, the country's income began to soar. Last but not least, the political and strategic situation in the Mediterranean has changed so profoundly over the past fifteen years as to oblige Libya, whether it likes it or not—though not in fact unwillingly, as far as the younger generation is concerned—to take a stand in a political context which the founding fathers of the country, many of whom are still alive, could hardly have imagined, let alone foreseen. Hence, conflict between the older and younger generations may well severely strain Libya's internal balance; indeed, it is apparently already doing so.

Such are the circumstances in and the reasons for which the author shies at presenting conclusions. Instead he prefers to indulge in a little soul-searching over what appears to be right or wrong in the methods and procedures applied by the General Assembly to Libya's emancipation, and in the actions and judgment of the Administering Powers, the Libyan leaders, the Council for Libya, and himself. As mentioned in the Foreword, he has also been tempted by the possibilities of drawing from this experience lessons that might prove useful in future cases of decolonization, or in earlier cases that may have to be reviewed.

Experience suggests that, before the author develops this theme, the reader may need to be reminded, redundant though this may seem, of the nature of the United Nations. The Organization is in no sense a world government, and possesses none of the attributes of sovereignty. Least of all has it, with one exception, either the authority or the means to enforce its recommendations or decisions. The exception is to be found in Chapter VII of the Charter, "Action with Respect to Threats to the Peace, Breaches of the Peace, and Acts of Aggression," the chapter meant by its drafters to put teeth into the United Nations system for the maintenance of peace; but, quite apart from the fact that this system has never successfully been put into practice, it would in no way have been applicable to Libya. It is especially necessary to emphasize this fundamental fact in the case of the disposal of the former Italian colonies. The onlooker might well conclude that the General Assembly was entitled as of right to decide on the future of these colonies; in fact it was not. The issue came before it only because the Governments of the Union of Soviet Socialist Republics, of the United Kingdom, of the United States, and of France had, in highly exceptional circumstances, referred the matter to the General Assembly for a *recommendation* (not, as one might have expected, a *decision*) which the Four Powers had agreed not only to accept, but also to put into effect. This meant that the implementation of Resolution 289 (IV) and its concomitant recommendations was an obligation which France and the United Kingdom in particular, as the Administering Powers concerned, had undertaken to carry out in cooperation with the representative of the United Nations in Libya. But it did not mean that any part or parcel of their rights and duties had been surrendered to the United Nations or its Commissioner.

Still, misunderstandings on this basic issue were so persistent that as late as January 1952 the Commissioner found it necessary to point out in his final report:

> A United Nations representative on a mission of the kind entrusted by the General Assembly to the Commissioner has no other source of influence and no other strength than that provided to him by the moral authority of the United Nations and has no means of action at his disposal other than those furnished by the Organization. It is to the extent to which the wishes of the United Nations are respected by the parties concerned that his action can be effective.[1]

These words have, in fact, a much wider bearing than their specific relationship to the Libyan case might lead one to believe. Every United Nations servant—or, more generally speaking, every international official—who has been on a mission of any importance for his organization, or who has been involved in some delicate negotiation on its behalf, knows from experience how much he depends on its moral authority. With the support of that authority, striking results can sometimes be obtained. Without it, failure is inevitable. In the last instance, that moral support depends on the

1. *Supplementary Report to the Second Annual Report of the United Nations Commissioner in Libya,* GAOR: Sixth Session, 1951–52, Supplement No. 17A (A/1949/Add.1), para. 117. Egypt and Pakistan requested the insertion of the following footnote: "The representative of Pakistan suggested to the Commissioner, who did not agree, that in the last sentence of this paragraph it would be more correct to say that 'It is to the extent to which the wishes of the United Nations are respected *by the Commissioner* and the parties concerned that his action can be effective.' " The Commissioner observed that, in his opinion, the phrase "parties concerned" is all-inclusive. Ibid., p. 19, fn. 101.

collective behavior of the States Members of the organization concerned. In the case in point, their behavior was worthy of the high aims of the United Nations, which largely accounts for the success of the operation.

In the light of the foregoing, the most important feature of Resolution 289 (IV) was its unconditional provision concerning the power of the Libyan National Assembly to determine the country's Constitution, including the form of government.[2] This provision was all the more remarkable in that it stood completely by itself. As has been seen, the relationships among the Administering Powers, the Council, and the Commissioner were controlled by an ingenious system of checks and balances. The National Assembly was not part of that system. The Pakistani member of the Council, speaking on 23 January 1952 in the *Ad Hoc* Political Committee of the General Assembly as his country's representative, though generously accepting the final outcome, nonetheless deplored the unfettered liberty of action left to the Libyan constituent body, which even extended to its composition, convocation, and internal organization.[3]

On reflection, the author, who has sometimes complained about the lack of precision of other paragraphs of the Resolution, considers that the NCAL's complete freedom of action as implied in paragraph 3 of General Assembly Resolution 289 (IV) proved to be an advantage to the Libyan people and to the United Nations alike. On the one hand, its independence engendered and stimulated in the former a sense of responsibility which it might otherwise never have had a chance of developing; on the other hand, it was the best possible protection against outside interventions and pressures which were certainly not lacking. This last remark does not refer to the Administering and other Powers alone; it applies equally to the United Nations, to the General Assembly, and hence to the latter's agents, the Commissioner and the Council. The story as unfolded in this study contains many examples of attempts to interfere with the drafting of the Constitution. At this late stage, it would be pointless to go into them in detail yet again, except perhaps with regard to the Commissioner himself.[4]

2. See Annex I, p. 891, para. 3.

3. GAOR: Sixth Session, 1951–52, *Ad Hoc* Political Committee, 48th Meeting, 23 January 1952, pp. 265–66. See also Chapter 11, pp. 850–51.

4. It will be recalled that one of the most surprising of the critical outside influences on the Libyans engaged in drafting their Constitution, and on the Commissioner advising them, ironically enough originated with the representatives on the Council for Libya of two states—Egypt and Pakistan—which had themselves only recently acquired independence. These two representatives, apparently working without precise instructions from their Governments, were the most prone to lecture the Libyans, to try to influence them politically. The common bonds of religion with the Libyans seemed to count but little with these gentlemen on the political plane. Both certainly

Although the Commissioner had been officially appointed to assist the people of Libya in the formulation of the Constitution and the establishment of an independent Government, it was sometimes difficult not to overstep the mark between help and pressure. On one occasion, as related in Chapter 6, Part 1 (pp. 446 ff.), he did (in suggesting that the Constitution should be considered as provisional and subject to review and possible amendment by an *elected* National Assembly), and was courteously but firmly reproved. However, the fact that the NCAL fortunately appreciated that his action was inspired not by personal interest or prejudice, but merely by too ardent a conviction that he was right about the issues at stake, ruled out the possibility of serious consequences.

The delicate balance among the Administering Powers, the Council, and the Commissioner has been dealt with often enough in earlier chapters, in all its aspects and contexts, to make its workings intelligible. True, the machinery did not always function to perfection, and sometimes failed to function at all, but this was due rather to human deficiencies than to defects in the system itself. The only question that it seems worthwhile to ponder now is whether the General Assembly could have devised a better system. To this question, the author's answer is, broadly speaking, in the negative, with the possible exception of a few debatable details.

Libyan leaders sometimes argued that the Commissioner should have been given the power to supervise the executive functions of the Administering Powers, or, alternatively, that the latter should have been replaced by a United Nations executive organ. Any such division of responsibilities could only have created confusion. Apart from the fact that it would have been exceedingly difficult to draw up workable financial and administrative arrangements (since, presumably, the United Nations would not have been able to pay the costs of administration), in practice a Commissioner with supervisory authority would have paralyzed the local British and French authorities in the effective discharge of their duties while at the same time he himself would have been placed in an ambiguous position and diverted, with his staff, from the main task of advising the Libyan people. One cannot act as an adviser on political and constitutional development to a people, and at the same time administer them; it is one thing or the other.

The alternative would probably have amounted to direct trusteeship exercised by the United Nations itself under Article 81 of the Charter. The

---

seemed to have a deep emotional antagonism to the British as a colonial power, despite personal and career ties with British culture, while at the same time giving the impression of having the lowest opinion of the Libyans' ability to tread the path to independence as their own countrymen had so lately done.

setting up of such a system would have raised a host of legal, financial, and administrative questions far beyond the organizational capacity of the United Nations as it stood in 1950–51. The direct administration of New Guinea (West Irian) by the United Nations for six months in 1962–63 can hardly be compared with the burden the Organization would have been obliged to shoulder had it been charged with the administration of a much more developed country like Libya for two years.[5]

Hence, the arrangements provided for in paragraph 10 of Resolution 289 (IV), by which the Administering Powers were to cooperate with the Commissioner in implementing the Resolution, were by far the most effective in the circumstances. The author has heard it suggested that the duties of the Administering Powers could have been defined more precisely. He doubts the validity of this suggestion. The terms of paragraph 10 were perfectly clear and sufficiently explicit in view of the aims to be achieved. No stricter wording would have compelled a reluctant sovereign Power to cooperate more closely with an advisory United Nations Commissioner whose only court of appeal in case of deadlock was the General Assembly. Since, however, such an appeal to the Assembly would only have been justified by a disagreement of the most serious nature, and as its outcome would have been problematical, it was obviously in the common interest of all concerned to refrain from pushing their differences to so extreme a point. And this in fact was how they understood and handled the situation.

As has been seen, the relationship between the Commissioner and the Council was of a more complex and sometimes more emotional nature. There is no reason to go into the matter further, though the former may perhaps seize the opportunity to admit that the Council members were not the only ones to occasionally let themselves go. The Commissioner, too, sometimes gave vent to feelings which, in retrospect, he realizes would better have been left unexpressed. Both sides may invoke as excuses for their behavior the nervous tension created by the unrelenting race against time, the often oppressive weather, and the only too frequent deep-seated conflicts of opposing views.

It is now clear that more important than these temperamental outbursts was the reconsideration of a basic issue raised and settled in November 1949 in Sub-Committee 17, namely: whether the Libyan people should be advised by a Commissioner alone, by a Council alone, or by a combination of the two; and in the last case what their respective duties and the relationship between them would be. In the end, the combination of a Commis-

5. Practically the whole of the costs of the West Irian operation were shared equally by the Indonesian and Netherlands Governments, the cost to the United Nations being only minor.

sioner and a Council prevailed. As early as September 1950, and notwithstanding the difficulties that had arisen between them, the Commissioner expressed the opinion that the General Assembly had chosen the right solution and that the Council had given him much valuable advice.[6] In subsequent reports, he confirmed that opinion, if sometimes adding a few disparaging remarks.[7] After sixteen years in which to reflect on the matter, it seems to him that a somewhat closer and cooler examination of the Commissioner-Council relationship, which, in some form or other, is bound to be a crucial part of any decolonization scheme for which the United Nations may become responsible in the future, is called for. Perhaps the best approach would be to examine the possible alternatives to the system adopted by the General Assembly at its Fourth Session.

First of all, one could imagine, at least in theory, a resolution similar in all respects to Resolution 289 (IV) except for the provision for a Commissioner and a Council. The General Assembly, and Sub-Committee 17 in particular, did not even envisage a solution of this kind, which would have left the Libyan people and the Administering Powers to settle the country's future without outside assistance. Apart from the fact that in such circumstances the United Nations could not have accepted responsibility for the solution of the problem entrusted to it, the three Libyan territories and the two occupying Powers, lacking a common clearing house for the settlement of their differences, would have found themselves in a state of conflict and confusion from which there would have been no way out. The three provinces, quite unconnected with one another, holding different views on their individual destinies as well as on their common destiny, would have been obliged to deal with two Governments, exercising their powers through three different administrations, for the purpose of constituting a single, independent, and sovereign State. Some new arrangement might conceivably have emerged from such a state of chaos, but Libyan unity and independence would certainly have been the least likely result.

One solution, put forward by several delegations and seriously considered by Sub-Committee 17, was to entrust the role of adviser to a committee or council constituted approximately as the Council for Libya eventually was, the Libyan members probably being co-opted by the six foreign member Governments. This was the solution favored by those Governments which, fearing the de facto dominant position of the Administering Powers, wanted to have a finger in the pie in order to be able to oppose the danger, as they

6. First *Annual Report of the United Nations Commissioner in Libya,* GAOR: Fifth Session, 1950, Supplement No. 15 (A/1340), para. 252.

7. *Supplementary Report to the Second Annual Report of the United Nations Commissioner in Libya,* para. 122.

saw it, of British and French imperialism. It was rejected; had it been approved, there is good reason to believe that the resulting Council would have been permanently divided into at least two groups, each giving the Libyan people advice. As experience with the Council proved, the voting power of each of these groups varied. As a rule, the Council rendered its advice by a majority, the composition of which changed from case to case. There were also tied votes. Only in the second part of 1951 did a more or less steady majority emerge; but for the greater part of the two transitional years the Libyan people and the NCAL would in all probability have been bewildered by contradictory advisory opinions. As to the Administering Powers, they would either have been just as bewildered as the Libyans, or, more likely, would have gone their own way, leaving the Council to its quarrels.

This is not to say that the Council was useless. On the contrary, its value becomes evident the moment one tries to imagine what would have happened had a Commissioner, without a Council to aid and advise him, been appointed to assist the people of Libya in their efforts to surmount the numerous obstacles they met along the road to unity and independence. He would have found himself without a sounding board to test his views, either in private or in public, on the many controversial questions with which he was bound to be faced. His contacts with the Administering Powers would have been much more difficult without the easy consultation available through their respective representatives on the Council. The same would have been true, and to an even greater extent, had he been deprived of the advantage of regular contacts with the leaders of the three territories and with those of the minorities through the same channel. Last, but by no means least, how could he have maintained effective relations with the most active opposition, which kept him so constantly on his toes?

The members of Sub-Committee 17 must have had a vision of the advantages of a two-stage advisory system when, after also having rejected a proposal that there be a Commissioner without a Council, they adopted the combination of a Commissioner assisted by a Council to aid and advise him. The fact that in paragraph 8 of Resolution 289 (IV) they added the rider that the former should consult and be guided by the advice of the members of the latter at once complicated and facilitated the interpretation of the Resolution as to their mutual relationship. In particular, the use of the word "guided"—which the Commissioner interpreted in the way Alpinists do—allowed him to consider that, having discharged his obligation to consult the Council, he was not necessarily bound to follow its advice. If he did, he was covered; if he did not, he went out on his own.

The experience of his two years in Libya fully bore out the hypothetical picture of the difficulties in which he would have found himself without the Council's aid and guidance. In practice, the system, broadly speaking, worked as follows.

Whenever the Commissioner found himself up against an almost unanimous Council—complete unanimity was virtually unknown—he knew that he would be wise to give way, or at least to make concessions. Whenever he was supported by a comfortable majority, he knew that he was traveling relatively safely, though never absolutely, as there always was a minority to be reckoned with, on which he might have to fall back on another occasion. Really delicate situations arose when the Council voted four to six, more so when it was evenly divided or, worst of all, when a roll-call vote produced a majority of less than five, owing to abstentions or absences. In such circumstances, especially in the early months of his collaboration with the Council, the Commissioner was sometimes tempted to ignore it and to go his own way. He soon learned, however, that in the interest of good relations it was better to seek a compromise, either by repeating his request for advice in a modified form which took reasonable objections into account, or by asking for supplementary advice on a particularly controversial part of the issue at stake. He also sometimes arranged informal meetings of Council members at his residence, but these were rarely successful, except where one of the members was prepared to act as mediator (not infrequently this turned out to be career diplomat Lewis Clark, the United States member) and provide the essential elements for a compromise text. All this goes to show that cooperation between the Commissioner and the Council, although not easy, was nevertheless well worth the time and trouble involved, in order to make the system work, and that the General Assembly had been right to adopt it.

Such would not have been the case, however, had paragraphs 4 and 8 of Resolution 289 (IV) been interpreted and implemented in accordance with the ideas of the Egyptian, Pakistani, and Tripolitanian members of the Council, who consistently held the view that the Commissioner should act as the Council's executive agent, and as such be obliged to carry out its decisions. This procedure would have thrown the machine completely out of gear, and, had the General Assembly approved it, which happily it never did, the Commissioner would have felt obliged to resign. Indeed, all the basic elements of his position, namely, his responsibility toward the General Assembly, the status and value of his advice to the people of Libya and the NCAL, his cooperation with the Administering Powers, and his freedom of judgment vis-à-vis the Council, would have been disrupted. A man carrying the responsibilities of an adviser cannot be free in his advice if at the same time he is required to act as the executive agent of another, so to speak superadvisory, body. The two functions are incompatible.

There are three more points about Resolution 289 (IV) worth looking at again.

First, paragraph 3 recommended that the Libyan Constitution and the form of the country's government should be determined by representatives of the inhabitants of Cyrenaica, Tripolitania, and the Fezzan meeting and consulting together in a National Assembly. The use of the word "inhabitants" in this context was unfortunate. The intention of those responsible for its inclusion was admittedly a praiseworthy one, namely, to protect the minorities in Libya. Why, then, did they not recommend in unambiguous terms that a clause or clauses be written into the Constitution, safeguarding the rights of the minorities in accordance with the relevant provisions of the Universal Declaration of Human Rights, at the same time clarifying the meaning of paragraph 3 by speaking of the "peoples" of the three territories? Reading between the lines of the official records, one gets the impression that the Arab States, supported by a few others, might have opposed such a proposal on the grounds that it was tantamount to interference in the domestic affairs of the future Libyan State: an argument of doubtful value when the issue was the protection of human rights, one of the Charter's most vital aims. Paragraph 3 would also have been made sufficiently plain had the General Assembly adopted the Israeli proposal that the word "all" be inserted before the words "the inhabitants"; but it did not, and the outcome was an imprecise and therefore confusing text. It is a great pity that this vital issue was not put to the test of a roll-call vote in plenary meeting. Instead, the would-be protectors of the minorities were satisfied, quite illogically and unrealistically, with a text that could be, and was, interpreted as meaning that aliens domiciled in Libya had the right to be represented in the country's constituent assembly. It is difficult to imagine a more flagrant example of an attempt at foreign interference in the domestic affairs of a State, an attempt that was all the more egregious in that that State was still in the making. Quite naturally, the Libyan people resented this provision, which was so much the more abhorrent to them in that its principal beneficiaries would have been citizens of the very colonial power which had at last been driven from the country. It is small wonder that this question of "inhabitants" became a stumbling block that not only held up Libyan constitutional development but, for a while, also complicated the grant of basic human freedoms and guarantees to the minorities in the Constitution.

The second point relates to paragraph 9, concerning the provision of economic and social aid to Libya. At the time at which paragraph 9 was drafted, the United Nations Expanded Programme of Technical Assistance was only just coming into being, while plans for preinvestment and capital investment for developing States on easy terms through international agencies had hardly reached even the academic stage. Today, the United Nations family of agencies, through the United Nations Development Programme and IBRD, especially in the case of the latter through its affiliate, IDA, has made considerable progress in this field. Had paragraph 9 been drafted under these conditions, it would certainly have worn a very different aspect—not only because new methods of combined technical and financial assistance are now available, but also because the process of decolonization is now looked upon, in the light of experience, from a less exclusively political angle, and with much more understanding of and sympathy for the economic and social implications, than in 1949.

The second reason why the author, rethinking Libya's economic and social problems, feels that his original views need reconsideration is that on one particular point he was not entirely fair to the Council. In his final report, after having praised that body for the valuable advice it had given him on political issues, he added the following observation:

> As the result of its composition, the Council was however inclined to take more interest in matters of a political and constitutional nature rather than to give technical advice on the many administrative, financial, economic and social problems which proved such important elements in the attainment of Libyan independence.[8]

It is hardly surprising that the United States member, supported by his Pakistani and United Kingdom colleagues, requested the inclusion of a footnote, on which the Commissioner and the Italian member in turn commented in further footnotes. To be brief, the plaintiffs alleged that the Commissioner's statement was not substantiated by the record.

This is perhaps the place to enlarge upon this particular problem. Indulging in the luxury of hindsight, the Commissioner must confess that his observation was out of focus. It was not the composition of the Council that was to blame, but rather a basic and widespread misapprehension on all sides that such a body could be expected to advise, within the rigid and exacting time limits allowed, not only on political and constitutional matters, but also on a wide range of topics covering public administration, including subjects as diverse as the drafting of a budget and a civil service law; and on economics, ranging from unusual balance-of-payments calculations involving four currencies, to problems of agricultural and educational development. The Commissioner never pretended to be an expert in such matters, but he had at his right hand an outstanding body of permanent staff and specially recruited technical experts, themselves backed by the

8. Ibid., p. 20, fn. 103.

technical resources of the specialized agencies which had seconded or recruited them. Not only were the Council members themselves not expected by their Governments to be technical aid experts; they were not backed by staff qualified to review the experts' work. Indeed, any such review procedure would have been an unnecessary, even undesirable, exercise, a wasteful reploughing of the ground, except insofar as a general evaluation by the Governments which would be asked to finance the recommended programs was concerned. In due course, but only after independence, i.e. after the Commissioner and the Council had left the stage, such a critical review of the projects and program proposals put forward in the Higgins Report was carried out by technical personnel from the United Kingdom, the United States, and, in the case of the Fezzan, France at the time when they were participating in Libyan development, as well as by Libyan officials and the Cabinet. The latter, who, in the final analysis, were most closely concerned, took the decision to seek implementation of the recommendations made by the Higgins team.

It was also unfair for other reasons to tax the members of the Council with not responding with more advice in the administrative and development fields. The Administering Powers themselves at first approached such problems at the provincial level. The members for Italy and the minorities also followed a parochial approach, geographically and sectorally, complicated by the personal interests of the Italian agricultural and commercial communities in Tripolitania, which were in a sense their constituents. The Administering Powers brought in a first-rate team of senior technical staff, fully qualified to look at Libya's problems as a whole and in depth, only when they came to realize that the United Nations had assigned a top-flight team to Libya. The need for such expertise was brought home to them by the terms of reference of the Coordination Committee and by the concurrent work of the Meeting of Experts on currency problems. Even so, the United Kingdom and France had no intention of discussing these problems outside the Meetings of Experts, the Coordination Committee, or ad hoc discussions at the technical level, where negotiations could be limited to a group comprising members of the Provisional Libyan Government, senior Libyan civil servants, and United Nations personnel. They had no intention of getting involved in essentially political and potentially demagogic public argument with the Egyptian, Pakistani, and Tripolitanian members, who would in all probability have used such occasions as springboards for political polemics. (As for the representatives of the other Governments on the Council, they had not been appointed for their technical qualifications or background to debate such questions. They were therefore not anxious to embark on such discussions.) In any case, their superiors in London and

Paris were well satisfied with the work of the United Nations staff, and endorsed the Commissioner's recommendations except on the key issues of sterling-area membership and the internationalization of financial aid. In those two cases, with the help of the United States and Libyan members, they overrode the Commissioner. In brief, in the one area of political importance, the Administering Powers won their point and imposed their will outside the Council, so that they had no need, let alone desire, to raise the issue again inside it.

Another very pertinent cause of the Council's inability to give advice on questions of administration and development was lack of time. All concerned underestimated the time factor for both the political and the developmental issues. The basic data were not so readily available as might have been thought from a perusal of the Report of the Four Power Commission of Investigation for the Former Italian Colonies or the annual reports of the Administering Powers, or from the overoptimistic predictions of Italian economists and agronomists. The capacity of the existing administrations to produce the data required for thorough studies on top of their normal workload was similarly overestimated even in the searching, though brief, investigation carried out by Goodrich and his colleagues, who charted the course of United Nations studies on Libya. No one had realized the delays that would ensue when the stormy seas of monetary arrangements had to be sailed against an adverse political wind. The Commissioner had assumed that the Administering Powers would have done more preparatory work on the shape of the administrative services of the future Libyan State than proved to be the case. Then, working quite literally night and day, the staff produced an enormous amount of documentation that was duly presented to the Council, whose members, other than the British, French, United States, Cyrenaican, and minorities representatives, had only the vaguest notion of what to expect, since they were quite unfamiliar with the complexities of modern administration and the problems of economic development. In fact, they could not begin to digest the material, let alone comment on it. Those prone to criticize might well have thought twice before exposing themselves to the embarrassment of a devastating barrage from the Commissioner's side, which not only could turn the documentation to the best advantage, but also draw on the professional knowledge of a highly expert team.

Nonetheless, the Commissioner was entitled to expect that Council members would respond to his requests for advice with more grace and effectiveness than they did. The Administering Powers could have made it clearer that their technical services had reviewed the experts' work, as they had, and the opposition might have recognized that their desire to forestall any politically motivated distortion of the analysis, or the planning, or the shaping of the administration of the new State, had been well served by the disinterested advice of the experts provided by the United Nations family of agencies. But perhaps this expectation was unrealistic.

It is worth repeating that at the time the technical assistance activities of the United Nations were in their infancy. No such effort had ever before been mounted in connection with a decolonization operation. Later General Assembly resolutions dealing with subjects known to have economic and social ramifications increasingly, indeed almost unfailingly, called on the Technical Assistance Board, or later on the Special Fund, or even more recently on the unified United Nations Development Programme, to help political bodies and missions and embryonic or newborn States. But none of them suggested that the concomitant advice or proposals should pass through a political filter such as the Council for Libya.

The problem of time, or rather the lack of it, is the subject of the author's third comment on Resolution 289 (IV). As will be remembered, at the Fourth Session of the General Assembly, the French delegation, for reasons of its own, opposed the prescription of any fixed period in which Libya was to be helped to get ready for independence. Failure to lay down such a time limit in Resolution 289 (IV) would have been a grave mistake. It is psychologically, and hence politically, highly unwise to allow a people to wait indefinitely for independence once it has been promised to them, or even where no such promise has been made. The General Assembly was practically unanimous on this point, though opinions differed greatly as to the appropriate length of the transitional period, proposals varying from immediate independence to independence in ten years. A compromise was reached to the effect that the putative independence should become effective as soon as possible and in any case not later than 1 January 1952. In practice, this meant within two years, a period dictated by political considerations rather than based on any serious attempt to estimate the time that would be required to finish the job. Admittedly, such an estimate could only have been approximate.

Accepting this, and recognizing that the general tendency was to speed up the attainment of independence, it would still have been preferable, in the author's opinion, if the target had been set at three years, the Commissioner being authorized to recommend to the General Assembly, after consulting the Council and ascertaining the views of the Libyan bodies concerned and those of the Administering Authorities, a somewhat earlier date. In practice, such a recommendation could have been considered only at a regular session of the General Assembly. Hence, when Resolution 289 (IV) was being drafted late in 1949, one could not have expected any recommendation to be taken up earlier than the fall of 1952. Moreover, since it would hardly have been the first item on the agenda, and since it could be adopted only after consideration of a report from the Commissioner, the probability is that such a procedure would have resulted in Independence Day being fixed for some date in November 1952. The additional ten months would not materially have affected the outcome, but at least all concerned, and especially the Libyans, would have had a better chance of assimilating the new ideas, of studying the problems, and of working out more complete, and possibly more effective, solutions. For the Administering Powers, the solution would have been neater, for the new currency could have been introduced under the aegis of the Provisional Libyan Government, the central structure of the latter could have been better organized for the transfer of responsibilities, and the procedure generally would have profited from a little more time for adjustments. Above all, an elected lower chamber would have been in session.

However, the author must in all honesty admit that there was also a possibility that toward the middle of the third year the Libyans, feeling that all was ready, would not have waited for the Commissioner to recommend and the General Assembly to sanction an earlier date, but would have made a unilateral declaration of independence. This was, of course, more or less what they did in December 1951, when they beat the gun by a week.

In brief, two years was too short a time; a little longer would have been better, provided it had been prescribed at the outset. It is unthinkable that the period could have been prolonged once the hawsers had been cast off and the voyage begun. Without unduly stressing the physical and nervous strain on the Mission staff, on the experts, on the hard-working officials of the Administering Powers, on the Libyans engaged in making the Constitution, and on the Provisional Libyan Government, the guillotine erected in the Resolution was at best a handicap, and perhaps even detrimental, to the accomplishment of certain parts of the task the United Nations had undertaken in Libya, which, in part or in whole, had to be left unfinished. It would serve no useful purpose to hold a detailed post mortem on the subject: one or two examples will make clear what the author has in mind.

Reverting to the Council, though this body was kept fully informed of the activities of the Coordination Committee, it had no time for a thorough examination and discussion of that body's intricate and vital report. The same applies to the four reports produced by the Meeting of Experts on Libyan financial, monetary, and development problems.[9] Nor was the Council able to carry out its most essential task of making a serious study of the

9. Although the experts held five sessions, no report was issued covering the first meeting.

draft Constitution and the Electoral Law before their adoption. It must be acknowledged that, had relations between the Council and the NCAL been more trustful, and had the members of the Council been prepared to forgo their summer holidays in 1951, the situation might have been more satisfactory.

It can be argued that the Commissioner himself was responsible for some of the shortcomings. It is true that, while systematically keeping the Council and others concerned, including the leaders of the Libyan opposition, fully informed of what was going on, he did neglect in the second half of 1951 to seek the Council's formal advice on some matters, or did so purely pro forma, well knowing that no substantial advice would be forthcoming. In all such cases the reason was that neither the Council, nor the Commissioner himself, nor the Mission staff would have had enough time to prepare and deal with the requests with the care they demanded. Consequently, the Council suffered from an understandable sense of frustration, which, fortunately, was at least in part dispelled by the Commissioner's request, submitted in October 1951, for advice about the fundamental issue of the meaning of the expression "duly constituted Libyan Government" as used in Resolutions 289 (IV) and 387 (V).

Nor had anyone thought of estimating how much time would be taken up by the essential rounds of consultations which the Commissioner was obliged to hold outside Libya with Governments represented on the Council on a variety of topics, including the unduly protracted discussions on the selection of the minorities representative, or in traveling between the capitals involved, and inside Libya. Lastly, the need for the Commissioner to attend each regular session of the General Assembly to present his successive reports, and the delays inseparable from the carrying out of what were essentially ground-breaking tasks for everyone involved, ought to have been reckoned with. No one foresaw the peripatetic element of the Commissioner's duties.

A little more time would also have enabled the Libyan authorities, with the help of the United Nations Mission, to make a better job of tying up other loose ends, such as, for instance, the drafting of the organic laws for the provinces, provided for in Article 177 of the Constitution. However, this might have looked like impracticable perfectionism, and in any case, toward the end of 1951 the Commissioner began to feel that he should not overstay his welcome without very cogent reason.

So much for the structure and practical implementation of Resolution 289 (IV) and the politically highly important Resolution 387 (V). The author is also aware that the reader will be awaiting an answer to the question asked on page xv, in the Preface, namely, whether "the international assistance given to Libya by the United Nations in cooperation with the Administering Powers, and with the Libyan leaders themselves, displayed any specific advantages or revealed any particular shortcomings vis-à-vis the more conventional bilateral process of decolonization." Or, in more general terms, and discarding the specifically Libyan context, to what extent will the decolonization procedure devised by the General Assembly in Resolution 289 (IV) and the way in which it was implemented prove applicable to more or less similar cases in future? In part, but in part only, the question was answered also in the Foreword. Subsequently, in successive chapters of this study, it has been shown how many problems were tackled and more or less successfully solved through collaboration between the Administering Powers, the United Nations Mission, the Council, and the Libyan people themselves, represented by the NCAL and the Provisional Government under the guidance of the King.

Since independence, insofar as fifteen years of trial and error by the Libyans themselves allow an opinion to be formed, United Nations assistance has been vindicated. This is not to say that the Libyan Constitution has functioned ideally, or that—despite the great resources derived in recent years from oil royalties—the country's economic and social development, including that of its administration, has produced all the results that might have been hoped for. Admittedly, the Libyans have successfully overcome many a difficulty, even surmounted many a crisis, and it may justly be claimed that this is due at least in part to the foundations of State and economy that the United Nations helped them to lay; but much remains to be done, to be improved, to be consolidated. Only the future will show whether they can keep up this pace. Fifteen years is too short a period to provide the final answer to certain long-term questions.

One such open question—and a fundamental one—is the viability of Libya's economy. By setting aside by act of Parliament, for development purposes, 70 percent of all royalties from the current very high oil production, the Libyan Government and Parliament have shown their awareness of this very important problem, the solution of which should envisage the building up of an economy, based perhaps on modernized agriculture, capable of sustaining a standard of living ensuring decent social conditions when the oil reserves are near exhaustion. There is as yet no sign of any substitute capable of thus sustaining the economy, but neither is there any but a very long-term prospect of falling oil production.

How much time will there be for a transition of such vast scope? Twenty-five, fifty, or a hundred years? No geologist seems to be able or willing to predict with any degree of certainty how long it will be before present reserves are exhausted. Nor does anybody know what new reserves may be concealed in Libya's soil. However, on the analogy of the dwindling coal reserves of many countries, it is likely that the day will come when Libya's oil reserves will be depleted. Moreover, nuclear or solar energy may come to compete with and to a considerable extent replace fossil fuels. Libya's proximity to industrial Europe gives it an advantage over oil-producing countries which must pay Suez Canal tolls or ship their products round the Cape, but this is only a relative advantage, not an insurance policy against the eventual exhaustion or decline of its oil resources.

But Libya is not the only country dependent on a single crop or a single mineral resource which must think far ahead. The manner in which it plans now for its economic future is fundamental not only for the material prosperity of its people but also for its continued independence.

Nothing is certain in this changing world except perhaps the resources above and below a country's soil and the actual and potential skills of its people. The Libyan Government has shown foresight in pushing ahead with schemes, and planning more, for irrigation and forestation, for modernizing agricultural methods and equipment, and for vitalizing an agricultural extension service and providing agricultural education facilities; it has also embarked upon a country-wide geological search for mineral resources and is pressing on with the development of water resources (the location of a substantial, though still not fully measured, quantity of deep aquifers has been a by-product of drilling for oil). In the not-too-distant future, inexpensive desalinization processes may revolutionize the agricultural potential of seaside desert countries.

However, the manpower budget rather than the availability of funds will be the most important factor in Libyan development. The most urgent need is still greater investment in human resources through education and vocational training. The progressive development of human productive skills in healthy bodies is fundamental: the more so since skilled labor has proved to be a bottleneck in Libyan development. The diversification of the nonoil sector over twenty years, visualized by the Government planning authorities, will be basically conditioned by the total manpower available, skilled and unskilled, both now in short supply. Productivity per man is even more important than total numbers. The temporary solution of bringing in foreign workers in both categories met only the short-term labor problem, although bringing in high-level technicians from abroad, particularly in the industrial sector outside the oil industry, could facilitate the establishment of new enterprises providing more job opportunities for Libyans. The untapped pool of womanpower will also have to be drawn upon.

Highest priority for education and training facilities will make it easier to realize the promise which lies both in diversification on the lines just mentioned and in government-sponsored programs for building roads, houses, and schools and for resettlement and the extension of public utilities. It will also benefit the food-processing and building-materials industries in the private sector, and help the development of a petrochemical industry. Lastly, the trade and services sectors, not to mention Government technical services themselves, need to be expanded and staffed to the maximum extent by Libyans.

Unremitting efforts must also be made to develop agriculture, though it must be recognized that growth of productivity here is bound to be slower than in other sectors. Rural development, widely and generously subsidized, is essential, both economically and politically.

The Libyan Government deserves a special tribute for the remarkably successful way in which, contrary to many dire predictions, it has controlled inflation during the oil boom, which is still going on, with its high growth rate coupled with shortages of supplies, including manpower and local goods and services.

On the other hand, the new wealth has not been spread so widely or so equitably as might have been hoped. Although, since all oil revenues go to the State, no individual has a direct share in them, as happens in some other oil-rich areas, some Libyans who have been in a position to provide services of one kind or another to the foreign oil companies have greatly benefited, while the urban poor, some of whom have been lured from their rural homes to the towns by stories of the riches awaiting them there, languish in the sub-subsistence-level poverty to which their lack of education and skills condemns them. However, the Government recognizes the need for achieving a more balanced distribution of income. There are many social welfare plans afoot, including subsidized housing, which are making thoughtful Libyans wonder whether the provision of such facilities on too generous a scale might not undesirably curb the incentive to work. However, it is probable that this danger will be averted by the creation of new jobs through diversification, provided always—and it is necessary to emphasize this point yet again—that vocational training, based on a system that will turn out trained workers by the thousand rather than by the hundred, is made available to young and old alike in both the industrial and the agricultural sectors.

The necessity for planning for diversity in the economy, though in the totally different context of escaping from the limitations of marginal agricultural productivity, was a fundamental consideration in the Higgins Report, which was submitted to the Libyan Government several years before oil entered the Libyan economic picture. The road to this goal as once recommended by a United Nations technical assistance mission will, even in its new form, produce a new challenge to and opportunities for the Organization's technical assistance activities and resources. The great difference is that Libya now can, and does, reimburse the United Nations family for making available the services of experts, under "Funds-in-Trust" arrangements.

Another long-term question, which can only be answered by future generations of Libyans is whether they will succeed in further developing and strengthening the sense of national unity and integration that is their very lifeblood as citizens of an independent State. Undeniably, considerable progress has been made in this direction. It may even be asked whether the attempt to achieve unification in the form of a State has not been pushed farther than the present stage of economic, social, and political integration warrants. On the other hand, it is understandable that in the light of the prevailing international situation in North Africa and the Near East, Libya should be anxious to consolidate its unitary form as soon as possible, even if this means doing away entirely with the much contested federal form of government.

The author has sometimes heard Arab friends maintain that the way in which Libyan unity came about—by a process of give and take, through mutual respect and tolerance for one another's interests and idiosyncrasies notwithstanding the large differences in size, numbers, and degree of development between the three territories, and by turning the valuable assets of a common religion, language, and culture to the greatest possible advantage—might serve as a small-scale model for Arab unity in the wider sense of the word. This is an attractive hypothesis, raising many absorbing questions; regrettably, it reaches too far into the future to allow it to be examined profitably within the present context. For one thing, the dramatic events in the Near East of June 1967, and their immediate and longer-term repercussions on both the internal and external relationships of the Arab world, make it difficult to forecast developments at the present juncture.

In one respect, posing these questions helps us to realize how much easier the United Nations' task in Libya was made by three fortunate circumstances.

First, that task was to help the people to achieve the very thing they desired above everything else—their independence.

Second, the two colonial Powers with which the United Nations had to deal, whatever their specific interests and policies in Libya may have been, had not been the country's original colonial masters. Had they been, the Organization's task might well have been much more difficult.

Third, the Libyan people had a leader whose guidance had for years been sought and accepted, not only for its intrinsic and religious value but also as an active catalyst of unity and independence. As the years of foreign rule drew toward their fateful end, the people rallied around him in increasing numbers. His eligibility for the highest position in the State was unquestioned; no rival ever came forward to claim the Throne. King Idris I exercised his royal prerogatives for more than fifteen years, unobtrusively weathering many a storm, always keeping the ship of state on an even keel, constantly adjusting his course to the changing winds of rapidly developing situations. His authority was uncontested, and it was an element of stability. It is the author's belief that King Idris' greatest achievement was to bring his people an image of nationhood and a growing sense of integration strong enough to create a lasting bond. Indeed, a rapidly increasing number of Libyans, particularly in the younger generation, are realizing that a setback in this process of integrating nationhood would not only endanger Libyan unity and independence so laboriously brought about but also might imperil the political stability existing on the southern shore of the Mediterranean. Indeed, the three principles underlying Resolution 289 (IV)—independence, unity, and self-determination regarding form of state and government—were meant not only to solve Libya's internal problems but even more to prevent a potentially dangerous state of disagreement between the victorious allies from developing into a major international dispute.

These considerations bring the author full circle. The question is not in fact whether Resolution 289 (IV) as it stands could be used for future decolonization operations. Not only, as pointed out in the Foreword, do circumstances vary widely from one case to another; the present state of the international community, its composition, the forces that make it act or prevent it from acting, and hence the nature of the United Nations itself, differ so much from those obtaining in 1949–52, that a simple repetition of the Libyan exercise is unthinkable. Must it then be concluded that the experience gained in that venture is of no further use whatsoever? On the contrary: the author believes that the Libyan operation provided certain lessons which, if genuinely applied, might have proven their value in certain cases where States which have comparatively recently acquired their independence are now running into grave internal political and economic structural difficulties. The lessons may prove equally useful in cases still to be dealt with, or in other countries that may in the future be in need of new forms of United Nations assistance.

In order of priority, these lessons may be summarized as follows:

1. Sincere acceptance and realistic application of the principles of the Atlantic and United Nations Charters, especially of that provision of the former which proclaims the right of all peoples to choose the form of

government under which they will live, are indispensable. It sounds so simple, but as a matter of practical politics the principle seems difficult to implement. The Libyan peoples were granted that right, and the United Nations, acting as their adviser, did its utmost to make sure that they were able to exercise it as they wished. Notwithstanding internal differences and external pressures about *how* they should do so, the fact remains that the Libyan peoples did freely exercise their right to self-determination. It is the writer's conviction that consciousness that a Libyan National Assembly wrote the country's Constitution on its home ground after full and frank debate will prove to be a potent source of national strength and consolidation.

2. Confidence in the organ that presides over the decolonization process during the transitional period is also essential. For reasons explained in the Foreword, the peoples of dependent territories—certain successful cases where independence has been attained through direct negotiation with the colonial Power notwithstanding—are generally inclined to place their trust in an international body rather than in the colonial overlord or another single Power. The story of Libyan independence as related here seems to bear out this thesis, which, however, is subject to one important proviso. Experience shows beyond doubt that the mere fact of being international is not enough to command this trust; it has to be earned, no matter who is involved. It must be earned by the disinterestedness and impartiality of the policies pursued and procedures used, and, last but not least, by the conduct of the staff chosen to carry them out. This may sound like perfectionism; and such perfectionism is certainly difficult, if not impossible, of achievement by organizations whose members are sovereign States capable of reaching agreement only by way of compromise. By its very nature, such agreement represents meetings of interests rather than meetings of minds, and hence, as a rule, is neither completely disinterested nor completely impartial. This is one of the reasons why, in the practical implementation of compromise decisions, so much depends upon the international staff in charge of the operation.

3. It would be nonsensical to pretend that international civil servants are inherently or by definition more honest or more capable than their national counterparts. Why should they be? But the former's outlook and approach must of necessity be different, the difference being in many respects comparable to that between federal officials and their state or cantonal colleagues in a federation or confederation. A wit has said that the difference between a diplomat and an international official is that the former thinks too well of his own government and not well enough of the one to which he is accredited, whereas the latter does not think well of

any of the member governments of the organization he serves. Neither of these two observations is absolutely true, but together they contain an element of truth, inasmuch as international staff judge the behavior of all governments by one and the same standard, namely, that laid down in the Charter, a product of the founding Member States' own making. Hence international officials are not impractical idealists, as some people believe. On the contrary, their profession makes of them realists who operate on the principle that the highest interests of one's own country are best served by promoting the security and welfare of the entire community of nations. To use technical language, their creed is that universal coexistence between States is more likely to be assured by multilateral (international) methods than through a multiplicity of competitive bilateral agreements. The author believes that this is particularly true in the delicate sphere of decolonization. That such inspired people not only exist, but are also capable of carrying out their work practically has often been demonstrated, but less frequently admitted by the interested parties. It was proved by the team of men and women who served the United Nations in Libya. Despite the many differences in their background and opinions, and regardless of the many nationalities among them, they were trusted both by the Libyan people and by the Administering and other interested Powers. At no time did the Secretary-General or the Commissioner receive a complaint to the contrary. In the few exceptional cases where members of the team failed to live up to the desired high standards, the Commissioner and the Principal Secretary were able to dispose of the matter by internal administrative action.

4. Another lesson learned is that no international civil servant may ever forget that he is at all times dealing with sovereign States, collectively his master, but only collectively. This is a fact of international life that imposes certain very obvious limitations. In the case in point it meant, for instance, that the Commissioner had to give way when the four most directly interested Powers unanimously rejected his proposal that financial assistance to Libya be channeled through a fund administered by the United Nations. It also meant that, even though he disagreed with them, he always had to reckon with British and French views on the form of the future Libyan State, for which, in collaboration with him, the Administering Powers carried their share of the responsibility all three owed to the General Assembly.

5. The final lesson was that, by judiciously taking local circumstances into account, the Commissioner could achieve results that were, speaking formally, beyond his competence. Constitutionally, his functions were

exclusively advisory; but, having to seek advice from, as well as render advice to, people who more often than not disagreed with one another, he found himself increasingly called upon to play the part of mediator, even of arbiter. This in effect meant that on a number of occasions, for want of a better alternative, his advice constituted the only acceptable solution. Thus he found, after a time, that he could wield more influence than he had expected at the outset, though this would, of course, have been impossible in the absence of mutual confidence.

To recapitulate, the success of the United Nations operation in Libya depended largely on the following factors, which might well apply elsewhere:

(a) The matter was placed in the hands of the General Assembly without reservations or binding instructions, and with a formal undertaking on the part of the interested Powers that they would carry out its recommendations;
(b) The ardent desire of the Libyan people to become independent even at the cost of sinking their internal dissensions, and their readiness to accept disinterested advice and assistance, while relying on their own judgment and accepting full responsibility for the final decisions, which were exclusively theirs;
(c) The presence in Libya of an international civil service team, capable of inspiring confidence, and instructed only to assist and advise, not to administer;
(d) The arrangement by which the head of this team was a commissioner, appointed by the General Assembly and solely and directly responsible to the latter, who was in turn aided and advised by, but not responsible to, a council comprising representatives both of the Powers directly interested and of the main Libyan population groups;
(e) The readiness, in the end, of the Administering Powers to cooperate constructively with the international team as well as with the Libyan people in the discharge of the obligations they had assumed;
(f) The constant support, in every respect, of the Secretary-General at Headquarters; and
(g) The fact that no one—not even the General Assembly of the United Nations—but the National Constituent Assembly of Libya itself was responsible for the decision about the form of State and Government. The last word lay with the Libyan people, through their King, the Provisional Government, and the NCAL. It should always be thus when the United Nations comes to the aid of new States.

Looking back, it is clear, as has been recognized by other writers, that Libya served as an important proving ground for the nascent technical assistance program of the United Nations family.

The lessons learned and experience gained in Libya in technical assistance and development planning techniques have long since been incorporated in the standard operational procedures of the United Nations system. These too have evolved and strengthened their capacity for such tasks over the intervening years. The United Nations and its specialized agencies have repeatedly demonstrated their concern and readiness to help emerging nations prior to and immediately upon achieving independence. As colony after colony in Africa and Asia has achieved independence during the years following Libya's freedom, there have been technical assistance teams on hand, though not often on such a large scale and with such broad terms of reference. Quite normally, surveys and analyses of the young nations' economic and social problems have been mounted and recommendations made for their solution. In some cases, especially where there were known to be important natural resources which could provide backing for loans and economies with promise of viability, such surveys have been undertaken by the International Bank for Reconstruction and Development. The leaders of these States, at both the putative and the independent stages, have shown their confidence in the quality and disinterestedness of the internationally recruited staffs by virtually automatically seeking assistance through United Nations channels. The former metropolitan Powers have better understood, and accordingly facilitated, this process than was the case in Libya when the assistance program was new and relatively unknown. It has become normal for the General Assembly and other United Nations bodies to recommend to the Executive Heads of the specialized agencies and of the United Nations Development Programme that special attention should be given to the needs of the emerging States. The device of making this easier for the treasuries of the new States by exempting them from paying the cash portion of local costs, initially used to help Libya, has been similarly applied for varying periods for nearly all of the States that have become independent in recent years. Thus, with regard to the technique of mobilizing available United Nations resources to meet technical problems and preinvestment work, the experience gained in Libya has not gone unheeded; the lessons have been drawn, and applied on subsequent occasions.

As to the question raised in the Foreword, whether the rendering of assistance in the process of decolonization should be entrusted to national or to international institutions, the Libyan experience suggests that the best results are obtained by calling on both. The average national civil servant who has devoted his career to administering colonial territories on behalf of his Government is not usually the right person to undertake what amounts to the dismantling of his life work. Indeed, it is unfair to expect him to do so. The international civil servant has the advantage over him of coming to the operation with a fresh and unbiased mind, though he generally lacks the intimate knowledge and experience of local conditions (of which, however, his national counterpart may have so much that he cannot see the wood for the trees). A system in which the two forces cooperate in helping a dependent people to achieve the independence which is in principle its right is clearly better, provided the dependent people themselves have the final say in the matter and provided also that the General Assembly of the United Nations—and not one of its subsidiary bodies—lays down the broad lines of the venture in conformity with the principles of the Charter, and keeps a watchful eye on all stages of its implementation.

The reader will not need to be told that in the author's opinion the United Nations intervention in Libya was a success. The best proof of the soundness of the course followed and the solutions found is that Libya—although it lies in a political and social fracture zone stretching from the Atlantic coast of Morocco through the Near, Middle, and Far East to the shores of the Pacific, a zone torn by strife and internal domestic upheavals during the past two decades—demonstrated a remarkable degree of political stability until the events of the Arab-Israeli conflict in 1967 set in motion a series of events leading to the overthrow of the King and the proclamation of a Republic. One cannot foretell the future course of the new regime, but from the outset it has talked only in terms of a united Libya.

The stability and determination of the Libyan governments over a period of seventeen years enabled the country to achieve some noteworthy economic, social, and constitutional progress, although the low starting point and the conservative approach of the persons charged with administration made some of the younger generation impatient.

Prior to the Revolution of 1969 there had been a major peaceful political change from a federal to a centralized form of state in 1963 by amendment of the Constitution. Furthermore, the emancipation of women in a country where they had long known a heavy veil, literally and figuratively; the rapid expansion of elementary and secondary education; the great expansion of public health facilities; the efforts to provide low-cost housing to relocate the people living in "bidonvilles" on the outskirts of the towns; as well as the efforts to improve the lot of the rural population by schemes for agricultural improvement, irrigation, and public works were all commendable efforts to use the oil resources for the benefit of the people. The potential dangers of a run-away inflation were avoided. There were, however, inequities in the distribution of the new-found wealth harvested by some in a position to work with and for the new, largely foreign, elements in the economy.

Yet those in the United Nations family of agencies and those who by their aid programs in the early years of Libyan independence assisted the people of Libya can take pride in their achievements. There are sound foundations upon which progress can hopefully be made, provided that the fundamental triad of unity, independence, and self-determination of the people is maintained.

Annexes

Annex I

TEXTS OF RESOLUTIONS REGARDING THE DISPOSAL OF THE FORMER ITALIAN COLONY OF LIBYA ADOPTED AT THE FOURTH (1949), FIFTH (1950), AND SIXTH (1951–52) SESSIONS OF THE GENERAL ASSEMBLY OF THE UNITED NATIONS.*

289 (IV): Question of the Disposal of the Former Italian Colonies

A

The General Assembly,

In accordance with Annex XI, paragraph 3, of the Treaty of Peace with Italy, 1947, whereby the Powers concerned have agreed to accept the recommendation of the General Assembly on the disposal of the former Italian colonies and to take appropriate measures for giving effect to it,

Having taken note of the report of the Four Power Commission of Investigation, having heard spokesmen of organizations representing substantial sections of opinion in the territories concerned, and having taken into consideration the wishes and welfare of the inhabitants of the territories, the interests of peace and security, the views of the interested Governments and the relevant provisions of the Charter,

A. *With respect to Libya, recommends:*

1. That Libya, comprising Cyrenaica, Tripolitania and the Fezzan, shall be constituted an independent and sovereign State;
2. That this independence shall become effective as soon as possible and in any case not later than 1 January 1952;
3. That a constitution for Libya, including the form of the government, shall be determined by representatives of the inhabitants of Cyrenaica, Tripolitania and the Fezzan meeting and consulting together in a National Assembly;
4. That, for the purpose of assisting the people of Libya in the formulation of the constitution and the establishment of an independent Government, there

* Only General Assembly resolutions dealing with matters of substance are included in this Annex. No such resolutions were adopted at the Third Session (1948–49), although the question of the disposal of the former Italian colonies appeared on its agenda. Resolutions on procedural matters have been omitted, with the exception of those referring to the procedure recommended for the delimitation or adjustment of the boundaries of the former Italian colonies, which in fact is a substantive issue. Resolutions adopted by the Economic and Social Council and certain specialized agencies have also been omitted.

shall be a United Nations Commissioner in Libya appointed by the General Assembly and a Council to aid and advise him;

5. That the United Nations Commissioner, in consultation with the Council, shall submit to the Secretary-General an annual report and such other special reports as he may consider necessary. To these reports shall be added any memorandum or document that the United Nations Commissioner or a member of the Council may wish to bring to the attention of the United Nations;

6. That the Council shall consist of ten members, namely:

(*a*) One representative nominated by the Government of each of the following countries: Egypt, France, Italy, Pakistan, the United Kingdom of Great Britain and Northern Ireland and the United States of America;

(*b*) One representative of the people of each of the three regions of Libya and one representative of the minorities in Libya;

7. That the United Nations Commissioner shall appoint the representatives mentioned in paragraph 6 (*b*), after consultation with the administering Powers, the representatives of the Governments mentioned in paragraph 6 (*a*), leading personalities and representatives of political parties and organizations in the territories concerned;

8. That, in the discharge of his functions, the United Nations Commissioner shall consult and be guided by the advice of the members of his Council, it being understood that he may call upon different members to advise him in respect of different regions or different subjects;

9. That the United Nations Commissioner may offer suggestions to the General Assembly, to the Economic and Social Council and to the Secretary-General as to the measures that the United Nations might adopt during the transitional period regarding the economic and social problems of Libya;

10. That the administering Powers in co-operation with the United Nations Commissioner:

(*a*) Initiate immediately all necessary steps for the transfer of power to a duly constituted independent Government;

(*b*) Administer the territories for the purpose of assisting in the establishment of Libyan unity and independence, co-operate in the formation of governmental institutions and co-ordinate their activities to this end;

(*c*) Make an annual report to the General Assembly on the steps taken to implement these recommendations;

11. That upon its establishment as an independent State, Libya shall be admitted to the United Nations in accordance with Article 4 of the Charter.

B. [Deals with Italian Somaliland]

C. [Deals with Eritrea]

D. With respect to the above provisions:

1. . . . .

2. *Authorizes* the Secretary-General, in accordance with established practices,

(*a*) To arrange for the payment of an appropriate remuneration to the United Nations Commissioner in Libya;

(*b*) To reimburse the travelling and subsistence expenses of the members of the Council for Libya, of one representative from each Government represented on the Advisory Council for Somaliland, and of one representative and one alternate from each Government represented on the Commission for Eritrea;

(*c*) To assign to the United Nations Commissioner in Libya, to the Advisory Council for Somaliland, and to the United Nations Commission for Eritrea such staff and to provide such facilities as the Secretary-General may consider necessary to carry out the terms of the present resolution.

[Annexure dealing with text proposed by the delegation of India]

B

The General Assembly, to assist it in making the appointment of the United Nations Commissioner in Libya,

Decides that a Committee composed of:

The President of the General Assembly, two of the Vice-Presidents of the General Assembly (Brazil and Pakistan), the Chairman of the First Committee, and the Chairman of the *Ad Hoc* Political Committee shall nominate a candidate or, if no agreement can be reached, three candidates.

C

The General Assembly,

Considering its recommendations regarding the disposal of the former Italian colonies,

Calls upon the Interim Committee of the General Assembly to study the procedure to be adopted to delimit the boundaries of the former Italian colonies in so far as they are not already fixed by international agreement, and report with conclusions to the fifth regular session of the General Assembly.

250th plenary meeting,
21 November 1949.

387 (V): Libya: Report of the United Nations Commissioner in Libya; Reports of the Administering Powers in Libya

The General Assembly,

Having resolved by its resolution 289 A (IV) of 21 November 1949 that Libya shall be constituted a united independent and sovereign State,

Having noted the report of the United Nations Commissioner in Libya, prepared in consultation with the Council for Libya, and those of the administering Powers, submitted in accordance with General Assembly resolution 289 A (IV), as well as the statements made by the United Nations Commissioner and the representative of the Council for Libya,

Having noted in particular the confidence expressed by the United Nations Commissioner that the aim of the General Assembly, namely, that Libya should become an independent and sovereign State, will be attained within the time-limit prescribed, with the increasing co-operation of the administering Powers with the United Nations Commissioner and the mutual co-ordination of their activities toward that end,

Having noted the statements in the above-mentioned report of the United Nations Commissioner regarding the needs of Libya for technical and financial assistance both before and after independence, if such assistance is requested by the Government of Libya,

1. *Expresses confidence* that the United Nations Commissioner in Libya, aided and guided by the advice of the members of the Council for Libya will take the necessary steps to discharge his functions toward the achievement of the independence and unity of Libya pursuant to the above-mentioned resolution;

2. *Calls upon* the authorities concerned to take all steps necessary to ensure the early, full and effective implementation of the resolution of 21 November 1949, and particularly the realization of the unity of Libya and the transfer of power to an independent Libyan Government; and, further,

3. *Recommends:*

(*a*) That a National Assembly duly representative of the inhabitants of Libya shall be convened as early as possible, and in any case before 1 January 1951;

(*b*) That this National Assembly shall establish a Provisional Government of Libya as early as possible, bearing in mind 1 April 1951 as the target date;

(*c*) That powers shall be progressively transferred to the Provisional Government by the administering Powers in a manner which will ensure that all powers at present exercised by them shall, by 1 January 1952, have been transferred to the duly constituted Libyan Government;

(*d*) That the United Nations Commissioner, aided and guided by the advice of the members of the Council for Libya, shall proceed immediately to draw up a programme, in co-operation with the administering Powers, for the transfer of power as provided in sub-paragraph (c) above;

4. *Urges* the Economic and Social Council, the specialized agencies and the Secretary-General of the United Nations to extend to Libya, in so far as they may be in a position to do so, such technical and financial assistance as it may request in order to establish a sound basis for economic and social progress;

5. *Reaffirms* its recommendations that, upon its establishment as an independent State, Libya be admitted to the United Nations in accordance with Article 4 of the Charter.

307th plenary meeting,
17 November 1950.

388 (V): Economic and Financial Provisions Relating to Libya

A

Whereas, in accordance with the provisions of article 23 and paragraph 3 of annex XI of the Treaty of Peace with Italy, the question of the disposal of the former Italian colonies was submitted on 15 September 1948 to the General Assembly by the Governments of France, the Union of Soviet Socialist Republics, the United Kingdom of Great Britain and Northern Ireland and the United States of America,

Whereas, by virtue of the above-mentioned provisions, the four Powers have agreed to accept the recommendation of the General Assembly and to take appropriate measures for giving effect to it,

Whereas the General Assembly, by its resolutions of 21 November 1949 and of 17 November 1950, recommended that the independence of Libya should become effective as soon as possible, and in any case not later than 1 January 1952,

Whereas paragraph 19 of annex XIV of the Treaty of Peace with Italy, which contains the economic and financial provisions relating to ceded territories, states that "The provisions of this annex shall not apply to the former Italian colonies. The economic and financial provisions to be applied therein will form part of the arrangements for the final disposal of these territories pursuant to article 23 of the present Treaty",

Whereas it is desirable that the economic and financial provisions relating to Libya should be determined before the transfer of power in that territory takes place, in order that they may be applied as soon as possible,

The General Assembly

Approves the following articles:

Article I

1. Libya shall receive, without payment, the movable and immovable property located in Libya owned by the Italian State, either in its own name or in the name of the Italian administration of Libya.

2. The following property shall be transferred immediately:

(*a*) The public property of the State (*demanio pubblico*) and the inalienable property of the State (*patrimonio indisponibile*) in Libya, as well as the relevant archives and documents of an administrative character or technical value concerning Libya or relating to property the transfer of which is provided for by the present resolution;

(*b*) The property in Libya of the Fascist Party and its organizations.

3. In addition, the following shall be transferred on conditions to be established by special agreement between Italy and Libya:

(*a*) The alienable property (*patrimonio disponibile*) of the State in Libya and the property in Libya belonging to the autonomous agencies (*aziende autonome*) of the State;

(*b*) The rights of the State in the capital and the property of institutions, companies and associations of a public character located in Libya.

4. Where the operations of such institutions, companies and associations extend to Italy or to countries other than Libya, Libya shall receive only those rights of the Italian State or the Italian administration which appertain to the operations in Libya. In cases where the Italian State or the Italian administration of Libya exercised only managerial control over such institutions, companies and associations, Libya shall have no claim to any rights in those institutions, companies or associations.

5. Italy shall retain the ownership of immovable property necessary for the functioning of its diplomatic and consular services and, when the conditions so require, of the schools necessary for the present Italian community whether such property is owned by the Italian State in its own name or in the name of the Italian administration of Libya. Such immovable property shall be determined by special agreements concluded between Italy and Libya.

6. Buildings used in connexion with non-Moslem public worship and their appurtenances shall be transferred by Italy to the respective religious communities.

7. Special agreements may be concluded between Italy and Libya to ensure the functioning of hospitals in Libya.

Article II

Italy and Libya shall determine by special agreements the conditions under which the obligations of Italian public or private social insurance organizations towards the inhabitants of Libya and a proportionate part of the reserves accumulated by the said organizations shall be transferred to similar organizations in Libya. That part of the reserves shall preferably be taken from the real property and fixed assets in Libya of the said organizations.

Article III

Italy shall continue to be liable for the payment of civil or military pensions earned as of the coming into force of the Treaty of Peace with Italy and owed by it at that date, including pension rights not yet matured. Arrangements shall be concluded between Italy and Libya providing for the method by which this liability shall be discharged.

Article IV

Libya shall be exempt from the payment of any portion of the Italian public debt.

Article V

Italy shall return to their owners, in the shortest possible time, any ships in its possession, or that of its nationals, which are proved to have been the property of former Italian nationals belonging to Libya or to have been registered in Libya, except in the case of ships acquired in good faith by Italy or its nationals.

Article VI

1. The property, rights and interests of Italian nationals, including Italian juridical persons, in Libya, shall, provided they have been lawfully acquired, be respected. They shall not be treated less favourably than the property, rights and interests of other foreign nationals, including foreign juridical persons.

2. Italian nationals in Libya who move, or who have since 3 September 1943 moved, to Italy shall be permitted freely to sell their movable and immovable property, realize and dispose of their assets, and, after settlement of any debts or taxes due from them in Libya, to take with them their movable property and transfer the funds they possess, unless such property and funds were unlawfully acquired. Such transfers of property shall not be subject to any import or export duty. The conditions of the transfer of this movable property to Italy will be fixed by agreement between the administering Powers or the Government of Libya upon its establishment on the one hand, and the Government of Italy on the other hand. The conditions and the time-periods of the transfer of the funds, including the proceeds of above-mentioned transactions, shall likewise be determined.

3. Companies incorporated under Italian law and having their *siège social* in Italy shall be dealt with under the provisions of paragraph 2 above. Companies incorporated under Italian law and having their *siège social* in Libya and which wish to remove their *siège social* to Italy shall likewise be dealt with

under the provisions of paragraph 2 above, provided that more than 50 per cent of the capital of the company is owned by persons usually resident outside Libya and provided also that the greater part of the activity of the company is carried on outside Libya.

4. The property, rights and interests in Italy of former Italian nationals belonging to Libya and of companies previously incorporated under Italian law and having their *siège social* in Libya, shall be respected by Italy to the same extent as the property, rights and interests of foreign companies generally. Such persons and companies are authorized to effect the transfer and liquidation of their property, rights and interests under the same conditions as may be established under paragraph 2 above.

5. Debts owed by persons in Italy to persons in Libya or by persons in Libya to persons in Italy shall not be affected by the transfer of sovereignty. The Government of Italy and the administering Powers or the Government of Libya after its establishment shall facilitate the settlement of such obligations. As used in the present paragraph, the term "persons" includes juridical persons.

Article VII

Property, rights and interests in Libya which, as the result of the war, are still subject to measures of seizure, compulsory administration or sequestration, shall be restored to their owners, and, in cases submitted to the Tribunal referred to in article X of the present resolution, following decisions of that Tribunal.

Article VIII

The former Italian nationals belonging to Libya shall continue to enjoy all the rights in industrial, literary and artistic property in Italy to which they were entitled under the legislation in force at the time of the coming into force of the Treaty of Peace. Until Libya becomes a party to the relevant international convention or conventions, the rights in industrial, literary and artistic property which existed in Libya under Italian law shall remain in force for the period for which they would have remained in force under that law.

Article IX

The following special provisions shall apply to concessions:

1. Concessions granted within the territory of Libya by the Italian State or by the Italian administration of Libya, and concession contracts (*patti colonici*) existing between the *Ente per la Colonizzazione della Libia* or the *Istituto della Previdenza Sociale* and the concessionaires of land to which each contract related shall be respected, unless it is established that the concessionaire has not complied with the essential conditions of the concession.

2. Land placed at the disposal of the *Ente per la Colonizzazione della Libia* and of the colonization department of the *Istituto della Previdenza Sociale* by the Italian State or the Italian administration of Libya and which has not been the object of a concession shall be transferred immediately to Libya.

3. Land, buildings and their appurtenances referred to in sub-paragraph (*d*) of paragraph 4 below shall be transferred to Libya in accordance with the arrangements to be made under that sub-paragraph.

4. Special agreements between Italy and Libya shall provide for:

(a) The liquidation of the *Ente per la Colonizzazione della Libia* and of the colonization department of the *Istituto della Previdenza Sociale*. the interim status of those institutions for the purpose of enabling them to fulfil their obligations towards concessionaires whose contracts are still in operation, and, if necessary, the taking over of their functions by new organizations;

(b) The repayment by those institutions to financial concerns of the quotas subscribed by the latter in the establishment of the *Ente per la Colonizzazione della Libia,* and, in the case of the *Istituto della Previdenza Sociale,* the reconstitution of that part of its reserves invested by that institution in its colonization department;

(c) The transfer to Libya of the residual assets of the institutions to be liquidated;

(d) Arrangements relating to land placed at the disposal of these institutions and to the buildings on and appurtenances to that land, in which, after their abandonment by the concessionaires, no further investment could be made by the institutions;

(e) Payments in amortization of the debts of concessionaires owed to those institutions.

5. In consideration of the renunciation by the Italian Government of its claims against those institutions, the latter shall cancel the debts of the concessionaires and the mortgages securing those debts.

Article X

1. A United Nations Tribunal shall be set up, composed of three persons selected by the Secretary-General for their legal qualifications from the nationals of three different States not directly interested. The Tribunal, whose decisions shall be based on law, shall have the following two functions:

(a) It shall give to the administering Powers, the Libyan Government after its establishment, and the Italian Government, on request by any of those authorities, such instructions as may be required for the purpose of giving effect to the present resolution;

(b) It shall decide all disputes arising between the said authorities concerning the interpretation and application of the present resolution. The Tribunal shall be seized of any such dispute on the unilateral request of one of those authorities.

2. The administering Powers, the Libyan Government after its establishment and the Italian Government shall supply the Tribunal as soon as possible with all the information and assistance it may need for the performance of its functions.

3. The seat of the Tribunal shall be in Libya. The Tribunal shall determine its own procedure. It shall afford to the interested parties an opportunity to present their views, and shall be entitled to request information and evidence which it may require from any authority or person whom it considers to be in a position to furnish it. In the absence of unanimity, the Tribunal shall take decisions by a majority vote. Its decisions shall be final and binding.

B

The General Assembly

Authorizes the Secretary-General, in accordance with established practice,

1. To arrange for the payment of an appropriate remuneration for the members of the United Nations Tribunal set up under article X above and to reimburse their travel and subsistence expenses;

2. To assign to the United Nations Tribunal such staff and provide such facilities as the Secretary-General may consider necessary to carry out the terms of the present resolution, utilizing the existing United Nations staff of the Libyan Mission in so far as possible.

326th plenary meeting,
15 December 1950.

398 (V): Technical Assistance for Libya after Achievement of Independence

The General Assembly,

Mindful of its resolution 289 A (IV) of 21 November 1949,

Having considered Economic and Social Council resolution 322 B (XI) of 15 August 1950, and the proposal of the Secretary-General as to the procedure which would enable Libya to continue to receive technical assistance after its independence has been achieved and before it has become a Member of the United Nations or of a specialized agency participating in the expanded programme of technical assistance,

Considering the special responsibility of the United Nations for the future of Libya,

Recognizing the need for continuing technical assistance to Libya without interruption, even after the attainment of its independence, for the development of its economy, for its social progress and for the improvement of its public administration,

Recognizing further the need for immediate study of a complete plan for the economic, social and cultural development of Libya,

1. *Requests* the Economic and Social Council and the specialized agencies concerned to consider Libya, as soon as it shall be constituted an independent State in accordance with General Assembly resolution 289 A (IV), as eligible to continue to receive technical assistance, in such form as the Government of Libya may request, from the expanded programme of the United Nations and in accordance with the fundamental principles and other provisions of Economic and Social Council resolution 222 A (IX);

2. *Instructs* the Technical Assistance Board, when giving technical assistance to Libya, to be mindful of the economic unity and independence of Libya in accordance with the aforesaid fundamental principles laid down in resolution 222 A (IX) of the Economic and Social Council and in resolution 304 (IV) of the General Assembly;

3. *Recommends* that the need for preparing a complete plan for the economic, social and cultural development of Libya shall be borne in mind by the appropriate authorities when requesting technical assistance for Libya or when considering requests for technical assistance for Libya.

308th plenary meeting,
17 November 1950.

515 (VI): Libya: Annual Report of the United Nations Commissioner in Libya; Annual Reports of the Administering Powers in Libya

The General Assembly,

Recalling its resolutions 289 A (IV) of 21 November 1949 and 387 (V) of 17 November 1950 resolving that Libya be constituted a united, independent and sovereign State, and providing for the adoption of certain measures to this end,

Recalling further its resolution 398 (V) of 17 November 1950 on technical assistance for Libya after achievement of independence,

Noting the report of the United Nations Commissioner in Libya of 30 October 1951, and his supplementary report of 8 January 1952, prepared in consultation with the Council for Libya, as well as the reports submitted by the Administering Powers in accordance with resolution 289 A (IV) of 21 November 1949,

Noting with appreciation the part played by the United Nations Commissioner, the Council for Libya and the Administering Powers towards the implementation of the above resolutions of the General Assembly within the time-limit specified in those resolutions,

Noting that on 24 December 1951 the United Kingdom of Libya was established as an independent and sovereign State, all authority in Libya having been relinquished by the Administering Powers to the Government of the United Kingdom of Libya,

1. *Congratulates* the people and the Government of the United Kingdom of Libya on the establishment of Libyan independence in accordance with the provisions of the pertinent General Assembly resolutions,

2. *Notes* that free and democratic national elections will be held in Libya in the near future in accordance with the provisions of the Constitution of the United Kingdom of Libya;

3. *Requests* the Economic and Social Council to study, in consultation with the Government of the United Kingdom of Libya, ways and means by which the United Nations, with the cooperation of all governments and the competent specialized agencies, and upon the request of the Government of Libya, could furnish additional assistance to the United Kingdom of Libya with a view to financing its fundamental and urgent programmes of economic and social development, giving consideration to the possibility of opening a special account of voluntary contributions to that end, and to report thereon to the General Assembly at its seventh session;

4. *Requests* the Secretary-General to give the Economic and Social Council any assistance necessary to enable it to carry out this task;

5. *Requests also* the Secretary-General to give in his studies special attention to the economic problems of the United Kingdom of Libya, and notes in that connexion Economic and Social Council resolution 367 B (XIII) of 14 August 1951 in which the Council requested the Secretary-General to continue to report, as part of the annual world economic report, on economic developments in Africa, with special attention to the measures being taken under the

technical assistance and other programmes of the United Nations and the specialized agencies;

6. *Requests* the Secretary-General and the specialized agencies to continue to extend to the United Kingdom of Libya, upon its request, such technical assistance as they may be in a position to render in accordance with the principles of their technical assistance programmes;

7. *Considers,* since the United Kingdom of Libya has been established as an independent and sovereign State and has applied for membership in the United Nations, that it should now be admitted to the United Nations in accordance with Article 4 of the Charter and the General Assembly's previous recommendations on this subject.

370th plenary meeting,
1 February 1952.

529 (VI): Libya: Problem of War Damages

The General Assembly,

Having examined and noted the report of the Secretary-General containing a general survey of the problem of war damages in Libya, submitted in accordance with resolution 389 (V) adopted by the General Assembly on 15 December 1950,

Having heard a statement made by a representative of the United Kingdom of Libya,

Believing that the problem of war damages should be considered within the general framework of the over-all economic development plans for the country,

Invites the Secretary-General, and the agencies participating in the Technical Assistance Board, to give sympathetic consideration to requests of the Libyan Government for assistance with economic development programmes which would strengthen the Libyan economy, including the repair or reconstruction of damaged property and installations, public and private, and in this connexion to appoint, as requested by the Libyan Government, any additional experts that may be required to collect the necessary data, to complete the survey of the problem of war damages and to make recommendations.

366th plenary meeting,
29 January 1952.

Annex II

CONSTITUTION OF THE UNITED KINGDOM OF LIBYA AS PROMULGATED BY THE NATIONAL CONSTITUENT ASSEMBLY ON 7 OCTOBER 1951*

Table of Contents

Preamble

In the name of God the beneficent, the merciful:

We, the representatives of the people of Libya from Cyrenaica, Tripolitania and the Fezzan, meeting by the will of God in the cities of Tripoli and Benghazi in a National Constituent Assembly:

Having agreed and determined to form a union between us under the Crown of King Mohamad Idris Al Mahdi Al Senussi, to whom the nation has offered the Crown and who was declared constitutional King of Libya by this the National Constituent Assembly:

And having decided and determined to establish a democratic independent sovereign State which will guarantee the national unity, safeguard domestic tran-

* Text from *Second Annual Report of the United Nations Commissioner in Libya,* prepared in consultation with the Council for Libya, General Assembly Official Records: Sixth Session, 1951–52, Supplement No. 17 (A/1949), Annex I, p. 61.

quillity, provide the means for common defence, secure the establishment of justice, guarantee the principles of liberty, equality and fraternity and promote economic and social progress and the general welfare:

And trusting in God, Master of the Universe, do hereby prepare and resolve this Constitution for the United Kingdom of Libya.

Chapter I

FORM OF THE STATE AND THE SYSTEM OF GOVERNMENT

Article 1. Libya is a free independent sovereign State. Neither its sovereignty nor any part of its territories may be relinquished.

Article 2. Libya is a State having a hereditary monarchy, its form is federal and its system of government is representative. Its name is "the United Kingdom of Libya."

Article 3. The United Kingdom of Libya consists of the Provinces of Cyrenaica, Tripolitania and the Fezzan.

Article 4. The boundaries of the United Kingdom of Libya are:

On the north, the Mediterranean Sea;

On the east, the boundaries of the Kingdom of Egypt and of the Anglo-Egyptian Sudan;

On the south the Anglo-Egyptian Sudan, French Equatorial Africa, French West Africa and the Algerian Desert;

On the west, the boundaries of Tunisia and Algeria.

Article 5. Islam is the religion of the State.

Article 6. The emblem of the State and its national anthem shall be prescribed by a federal law.

Article 7. The national flag shall have the following dimensions: Its length shall be twice its breadth, it shall be divided into three parallel coloured stripes, the uppermost being red, the centre black and the lowest green, the black stripe shall be equal in area to the two other stripes together and shall bear in its centre a white crescent, between the two extremities of which there shall be a five-pointed white star.

Chapter II

RIGHTS OF THE PEOPLE

Article 8. Every person who resides in Libya and has no other nationality, or is not the subject of any other State, shall be deemed to be a Libyan if he fulfils one of the following conditions:

(1) That he was born in Libya;

(2) That either of his parents was born in Libya;

(3) That he has had his normal residence in Libya for a period of not less than ten years.

Article 9. Subject to the provisions of article 8 of this Constitution, the conditions necessary for acquiring Libyan nationality shall be determined by a federal law. Such law shall grant facilities to persons of Libyan origin residing abroad and to their children and to citizens of Arab countries and to foreigners who are residing in Libya and who at the coming into force of this Constitution have had their normal residence in Libya for a period of not less than ten years.

Persons of the latter category may opt for Libyan nationality in accordance with the conditions prescribed by the law, provided they apply for it within three years as from January 1952.

Article 10. No one may have Libyan nationality and any other nationality at the same time.

Article 11. Libyans shall be equal before the law. They shall enjoy equal civil and political rights, shall have the same opportunities and be subject to the same public duties and obligations, without distinction of religion, belief, race, language, wealth, kinship or political or social opinion.

Article 12. Personal liberty shall be guaranteed and everyone shall be entitled to equal protection of the law.

Article 13. No forced labour shall be imposed upon anyone save in accordance with law in cases of emergency, catastrophe or circumstances which may endanger the safety of the whole or part of the population.

Article 14. Everyone shall have the right of recourse to the Courts, in accordance with the provisions of the law.

Article 15. Everyone charged with an offence shall be presumed to be innocent until proved guilty according to law in a trial at which he has had the guarantees necessary for his defence. The trial shall be public save in exceptional cases prescribed by law.

Article 16. No one may be arrested, detained, imprisoned or searched except in the cases prescribed by law. No one shall under any circumstances be tortured by anyone or subjected to punishment degrading to him.

Article 17. No offence may be established or penalty inflicted except by law. Only offences committed after the promulgation of a law shall be subject to the penalties specified therein for those offences; the penalty inflicted shall not be heavier than the penalty that was applicable at the time the offence was committed.

Article 18. No Libyan may be deported from Libya under any circumstances nor may he be forbidden to reside in any locality or compelled to reside in any specific place or prohibited from moving in Libya except as prescribed by law.

Article 19. Dwelling houses are inviolable; they shall not be entered or searched except in cases and according to the manner prescribed by law.

Article 20. The secrecy of letters, telegrams, telephonic communications and all correspondence in whatever form and by whatever means shall be guaranteed; they shall not be censored or delayed except in cases prescribed by law.

Article 21. Freedom of conscience shall be absolute. The State shall respect all religions and faiths and shall ensure to Libyans and foreigners residing in its territory freedom of conscience and the right freely to practise religion so long as it is not a breach of public order and is not contrary to morality.

Article 22. Freedom of thought shall be guaranteed. Everyone shall have the right to express his opinion and to publish it by all means and methods. But this freedom may not be abused in any way which is contrary to public order or morality.

Article 23. Freedom of the Press and of printing shall be guaranteed within the limits of the law.

Article 24. Everyone shall be free to use any language in his private transactions or religious or cultural matters or in the Press or any other publications or in public meetings

Article 25. The right of peaceful meetings is guaranteed within the limits of the law.

Article 26. The right of peaceful association shall be guaranteed. The exercise of that right shall be regulated by law but the establishment of secret associations and those which have as their purpose the realization of political objectives by means of organizations of a military nature shall be prohibited.

Article 27. Individuals shall have the right to address public authorities by means of letters signed by them in connexion with matters which concern them but only organized bodies or juristic persons may address the authorities on behalf of a number of persons.

Article 28. Every Libyan shall have the right to education. The State shall ensure the diffusion of education by means of the establishment of public schools, and of private schools which it may permit to be established under its supervision, for Libyans and foreigners.

Article 29. Teaching shall be unrestricted so long as it does not constitute a breach of public order and is not contrary to morality. Public education shall be regulated by law.

Article 30. Elementary education shall be compulsory for Libyan children of both sexes; elementary and primary education in the public schools shall be free.

Article 31. Property shall be inviolable. No owner may be prevented from disposing of his property except within the limits of the law. No property of any person shall be expropriated except in the public interest and in the cases and in the manner determined by law and provided such person is awarded fair compensation.

Article 32. The penalty of general confiscation of property shall be prohibited.

Article 33. The family is the basis of society and shall be entitled to protection by the State. The State shall also protect and encourage marriage.

Article 34. Work is one of the basic elements of economic life. It shall be protected by the State and shall be the right of all Libyans. Every individual who works shall be entitled to fair remuneration.

Article 35. The State shall endeavour to provide as far as possible for every Libyan and his family an appropriate standard of living.

Chapter III

PART I: POWERS OF THE FEDERAL GOVERNMENT

Article 36. The Federal Government shall exercise legislative and executive powers in connexion with the matters shown in the following list:

(1) Diplomatic, consular and commercial representation;
(2) Affairs of the United Nations and its specialized agencies;
(3) Participation in international conferences and bodies and the implementation of the decisions adopted by them;
(4) Matters relating to war and peace;
(5) The conclusion and implementation of treaties and agreements with other States;
(6) The regulation of trade with foreign States;
(7) Foreign loans;
(8) Extradition;
(9) The issue of Libyan passports and visas;

(10) Immigration into Libya and emigration from Libya;
(11) Admission into and residence of foreigners in Libya and their expulsion;
(12) Matters relating to nationality;
(13) All other matters relating to foreign affairs;
(14) Provision for the land, sea and air forces, their training and maintenance and the employment thereof;
(15) Defense industries;
(16) Libyan military, naval and air force arsenals;
(17) The limitation of powers in cantonment areas, the appointment of personnel for these areas and determining their powers and the regulation of residence therein. The boundaries thereof shall be delimited after consultation with the Provinces;
(18) Arms of all kinds for national defence, including firearms, ammunitions and explosives;
(19) Martial law;
(20) Atomic energy and materials essential to its production;
(21) All other matters relating to national defence;
(22) Air lines and agreements relating thereto;
(23) Meteorology;
(24) Posts and telegraphs, telephones, wireless, federal broadcasting and other forms of federal communication;
(25) Federal roads and other roads which the Federal Government, after consultation with the Provinces, decides do not belong to a particular Province;
(26) The construction and control of federal railways, after agreement with the Provinces which they cross;
(27) Customs;
(28) Taxation necessary to meet the expenditure of the Federal Government, after consultation with the Provinces;
(29) Federal Bank;
(30) Currency, the minting of coins and the issue of notes;
(31) Federal finances and public debt;
(32) Exchange and stock exchanges;
(33) Inquiries and statistics relating to the Federal Government;
(34) Matters relating to the officers of the Federal Government;
(35) In consultation with the Provinces, the promotion of agricultural and industrial production and commercial activities and the ensuring to the country of essential foodstuffs;
(36) Properties of the Federal Government, the acquisition, management and disposal thereof;
(37) Co-operation between the Federal Government and the Provinces in the work of the criminal police and the establishment of a central bureau for the criminal police and the pursuit of international criminals;
(38) Education in universities and other institutions of higher education and the determination of educational degrees;
(39) All matters assigned by this Constitution to the Federal Government.

Article 37. The Federal Government may, with the agreement of any Province, delegate to it or to its officers the executive power concerning any matter which is within its competence under this Constitution, provided the Federal Government will bear the expense of the execution.

PART II: JOINT POWERS

Article 38. In order to ensure a co-ordinated and unified policy between the Provinces, the legislative power relating to the following matters shall be within the competence of the Federal Government, while the executive power in connexion with the implementation of that legislation shall be within the competence of the Provinces acting under the supervision of the Federal Government

(1) Companies;
(2) Banks;
(3) Organization of imports and exports;
(4) Income tax;
(5) Monopolies and concessions;
(6) Sub-soil wealth and prospecting and mining;
(7) Weights and measures;
(8) All forms of insurance;
(9) Census;
(10) Shipping and navigation;
(11) Major ports which the Federal Government considers to be of importance with regard to international navigation;
(12) Aircraft and air navigation, the construction of airports, the regulation of air traffic and the administration of airports;
(13) Lighthouses, including lightships, beacons and other provisions for the safety of sea and air navigation;
(14) The establishment of the general judicial organization subject to the provisions of chapter 8 of this Constitution;
(15) Civil, commercial and criminal law, civil and criminal procedure, the legal profession;
(16) Literary, artistic and industrial copyright, inventions, patents, trademarks and merchandise marks;
(17) Newspapers, books, printing presses and broadcasting;
(18) Public meetings and associations;
(19) Expropriation;
(20) All matters relating to the national flag and the national anthem and official holidays;
(21) Conditions for practising scientific and technical professions;
(22) Labour and social security;
(23) The general system of education;
(24) Antiquities and archaeological sites and museums, libraries, and other institutions declared by a federal law to be of national importance;
(25) Public health and the co-ordination of matters relating thereto;
(26) Quarantine and quarantine stations;
(27) Conditions for licences to practise the medical profession and other professions connected with health.

Article 39. The Provinces shall exercise all powers connected with the matters which have not been assigned by this Constitution to the Federal Government.

Chapter IV

GENERAL FEDERAL POWERS

Article 40. Sovereignty is vested in the nation and the nation is the source of powers.

Article 41. Legislative power shall be exercised by the King in conjunction with Parliament. The King promulgates the laws when they have been approved by Parliament in accordance with the procedure prescribed by this Constitution.

Article 42. Executive power shall be exercised by the King within the limits of this Constitution.

Article 43. Judicial power shall be exercised by the Supreme Court and other courts, which shall give judgments within the limits of this Constitution, in accordance with the law and in the name of the King.

Chapter V

THE KING

Article 44. The sovereignty of the United Kingdom of Libya is vested in the nation. By the will of God the people entrust it to King Mohamad Idris Al Mahdi Al Senussi and after him to his male heirs, the oldest after the oldest, degree after degree.

Article 45. The Throne of the Kingdom is hereditary. The order of succession to the Throne shall be determined by Royal Decree promulgated by King Idris I within a year of the date of the promulgation of this Constitution. No one may accede to the Throne unless he is of sound mind, a Libyan and a Moslem born of Moslem parents legally wedded. The Royal Decree which shall regulate the succession to the Throne shall have the same force as an article of this Constitution.

Article 46. In the event of the King's death and the Throne remaining vacant owing to the lack of a successor to the King or to no successor having been appointed, the Senate and the House of Representatives shall at once hold a joint meeting without convocation to appoint a successor within ten days; three-quarters at least of the number of members of the two Chambers shall be present and the voting shall take place openly by a majority of two-thirds of the members present. If the choice cannot take place within the time specified, the two Chambers shall jointly proceed to make the choice on the eleventh day, in the presence of an absolute majority of the members of each of the two Chambers and by a proportionate majority. If the House of Representatives has been dissolved the old House shall immediately meet until the King has been chosen.

Article 47. Before assuming his constitutional powers, the King shall take the following oath before a joint session of the Senate and the House of Representatives: "I swear by Almighty God to observe the Constitution and the laws of the country and to devote all my efforts to the maintenance of the independence of Libya and to defending the safety of its territory."

Article 48. Whenever the King wishes to travel outside Libya or when circumstances prevent or delay him temporarily from exercising his constitutional powers, he may appoint one or more Deputies to perform such duties and to exercise such rights and powers as the King may delegate to such Deputy or Deputies.

Article 49. The King shall attain his majority upon the completion of his eighteenth lunar year.

Article 50. If the King is a minor, or if any circumstances prevent or delay him from exercising his constitutional powers and he himself is unable to appoint a Deputy or Deputies, the Council of Ministers shall with the consent of Parliament appoint a Regent or a Council of Regency to perform the duties of the King and to exercise his rights and powers until such time as he becomes of age or is capable of exercising his powers. If Parliament is not in session it shall be convened. If the House of Representatives has been dissolved the old House shall immediately meet until such time as the Regent or Council of Regency has been appointed.

Article 51. No person may be appointed a Deputy to the Throne or a Regent or a member of the Council of Regency unless he is a Libyan and a Moslem and has completed his fortieth year (Gregorian); however, a male of the Royal Family who has completed his twenty-first year (Gregorian) may be appointed.

Article 52. During the period between the death of the King and the taking of the constitutional oath by his successor to the Throne, by the Regent or by the members of the Council of Regency, the Council of Ministers shall, on its own responsibility, exercise the constitutional powers of the King in the name of the Libyan nation.

Article 53. The Regent or any member of the Council of Regency shall not assume office unless he has taken the following oath before a joint meeting of the Senate and the House of Representatives: "I swear by Almighty God to observe the Constitution and the laws of the country, to devote all my efforts to the maintenance of the independence of Libya and to defending the safety of its territory and to be loyal to the King".

A Deputy to the Throne shall take this oath before the King or some person designated by the King.

Article 54. A Minister or any members of a legislative body may not be Regent or a member of a Council of Regency. If a Deputy to the Throne is a member of any legislative body he shall not take part in the activities of that body during the time he is acting as Deputy to the Throne.

Article 55. If a Regent or a member of the Council of Regency, appointed in accordance with article 50, dies or is prevented by any circumstances from performing his duties as Regent or as a member of the Council of Regency, the Council of Ministers may with the consent of Parliament appoint another person to replace him, in accordance with the provisions of articles 51, 53 and 54.

If Parliament is not in session it shall be convened. If the House of Representatives has been dissolved, the old House shall immediately meet until such time as a Regent or a member of the Council of Regency has been appointed.

Article 56. The Civil List of the King and of the Royal Family shall be fixed by federal law; it may not be reduced during his reign but it may be increased by resolutions of Parliament. The law shall limit the salaries of Deputies to the Throne and of Regents which shall be paid from the Civil List of the King.

Article 57. The judicial procedure to be followed in cases brought by the Royal Estate or against it shall be regulated by a federal law.

Article 58. The King is the supreme head of the State.

Article 59. The King shall be inviolable. He shall be exempt from all responsibility.

Article 60. The King exercises his power through his Ministers and responsibility rests with them.

Article 61. The King shall not assume a throne outside Libya except after the consent of Parliament.

Article 62. The King sanctions and promulgates the laws.

Article 63. The King shall make the necessary regulations for carrying out the laws without modifying or suspending the laws or dispensing with their execution.

Article 64. If, when Parliament is not in session, exceptional circumstances arise which necessitate urgent measures, the King may issue decrees in respect thereof which shall have the force of law provided that they are not contrary to the provisions of this Constitution. Such decrees must be submitted to Parliament at its first meeting; if they are not submitted to Parliament or if they are not approved by either of the Chambers they shall cease to have the force of law.

Article 65. The King shall open the sessions of Parliament and close them, and shall dissolve the House of Representatives in accordance with the provisions of this Constitution; and he may, when necessary, convene a joint meeting of the two Chambers to discuss any important question.

Article 66. The King may, if he deems necessary, convene Parliament to meet in an extraordinary session; he shall also convene it upon the presentation of a petition signed by an absolute majority of the members of the two Chambers. The King shall pronounce the closure of an extraordinary session.

Article 67. The King may adjourn the session of Parliament but the adjournment may not exceed a period of thirty days nor may it be repeated during the same session without the consent of both Chambers.

Article 68. The King is the supreme commander of all the Libyan armed forces.

Article 69. The King shall declare war and conclude peace and enter into treaties which he ratifies after the approval of Parliament.

Article 70. The King shall proclaim martial law and a state of emergency provided that he shall present the proclamation of martial law to Parliament in order to decide whether it shall continue or be repealed. If that proclamation is made when Parliament is not in session, Parliament must be urgently convened.

Article 71. The King shall create and confer titles, ranks, decorations and all other signs of honour.

Article 72. The King shall appoint the Prime Minister, he may remove him from office or accept his resignation; he shall appoint the Ministers, remove them from office, or accept their resignation at the proposal of the Prime Minister.

Article 73. The King shall appoint diplomatic representatives and remove them from office at the proposal of the Minister of Foreign Affairs. He shall accept the credentials of the heads of foreign diplomatic missions accredited to him.

Article 74. The King shall establish the public services and appoint senior officials and remove them in accordance with the provisions of the law.

Article 75. Currency shall be issued in the name of the King, according to law.

Article 76. No death sentence imposed by any Libyan court shall be executed except with the consent of the King.

Article 77. The King shall have the right to grant pardon or to commute a sentence.

Chapter VI

THE MINISTERS

Article 78. The Council of Ministers shall consist of the Prime Minister and of the Ministers whom the King deems fit to appoint at the proposal of the Prime Minister.

Article 79. Before assuming office the Prime Minister and Ministers shall take an oath before the King.

Article 80. The King may appoint Ministers without portfolio in case of necessity.

Article 81. No non-Libyan may be a Minister.

Article 82. No member of the Royal Family may be a Minister.

Article 83. A Minister may at the same time be a member of Parliament.

Article 84. The Council of Ministers shall be responsible for the direction of all the internal and external affairs of the State, in accordance with the powers given to the Federal Government by this Constitution and in accordance with the provisions of this Constitution.

Article 85. For the signatures of the King concerning the affairs of State to be effective, they must have the counter-signature of the Prime Minister and of the competent Ministers, provided that decrees appointing the Prime Minister or relieving him of office shall be signed by the King alone and decrees appointing Ministers or relieving them of office shall be signed by the King and countersigned by the Prime Minister.

Article 86. The Ministers are collectively responsible to the House of Representatives for the general policy of the State and each of them individually is responsible for the activities of his Ministry.

Article 87. If the House of Representatives by a majority of all its members passes a vote of no confidence in the Council of Ministers, the Council of Ministers must resign. If the decision concerns one of the Ministers, he must resign.

The House of Representatives shall not consider the request for a vote of no confidence, whether such request be direct or implied, unless it has been presented by fifteen or more of the Deputies. Such request may not be discussed except after eight days from the date of its presentation and shall not be voted upon except after two days from the completion of the discussion thereon.

Article 88. Ministers shall have the right to attend the meetings of both Chambers and must be heard whenever they so request; they may not take part in the voting unless they are members. They may have the assistance of any officer they choose of their Ministry or may appoint any such officer as a deputy to represent them. Each Chamber may when necessary request any Minister to attend its meeting.

Article 89. In the event of the dismissal or resignation of the Prime Minister all the Ministers are considered thereby to have been dismissed or to have resigned.

Article 90. The Ministers may not while holding office assume any other public office, exercise any other profession or purchase or rent any property belonging to the State, and they may not directly or indirectly take part in the undertakings concluded and tenders invited by the public administration or the institutions falling under the administration or control of the State. They may not be members of the Board of Directors of any company nor may they take an active part in any commercial or financial enterprise.

Article 91. The salaries of the Prime Minister and the other Ministers shall be determined by federal law.

Article 92. A federal law shall prescribe the civil and criminal responsibilities of the Ministers and the manner in which they may be charged and tried in respect of offences committed by them in the exercise of their duties.

Chapter VII

PARLIAMENT

Article 93. Parliament shall consist of two Chambers, the Senate and the House of Representatives.

PART I: THE SENATE

Article 94. The Senate shall consist of twenty-four members; each of the three Provinces of the Kingdom of Libya shall have eight members.

Article 95. The King appoints one-half of the members. The other members shall be elected by the Legislative Councils of the Provinces.

Article 96. A Senator must be a Libyan and have completed the fortieth year of his age (Gregorian) and possess such qualifications as are provided in the federal electoral law.

Members of the Royal Family may be appointed to the Senate but may not be elected.

Article 97. The President of the Senate shall be appointed by the King. The Senate shall elect two Vice-Presidents; the result of the election shall be submitted to the King for approval. The appointment of the President and the election of the two Vice-Presidents shall be for a period of two years and the President may be re-appointed and the two Vice-Presidents may be re-elected.

Article 98. Membership of the Senate shall be for eight years. Half the appointed Senators and half the elected Senators shall be replaced every four years. Retiring Senators may be re-appointed or re-elected.

Article 99. The Senate shall meet at the same time as the House of Representatives; its sessions shall close at the same time as those of the House of Representatives.

PART II: THE HOUSE OF REPRESENTATIVES

Article 100. The House of Representatives shall consist of members elected in the three Provinces in accordance with the provisions of a federal electoral law.

Article 101. The number of Deputies shall be determined on the basis of one Deputy for every twenty thousand inhabitants or fraction of that number exceeding half, provided that the number of Deputies in any of the three Provinces shall not be less than five.

Article 102. A voter must be:

(1) A Libyan; and

(2) Shall have completed his twenty-first year (Gregorian), in addition to the conditions prescribed by the federal electoral law.

Article 103. A Deputy must:
(1) Have completed his thirtieth year (Gregorian);
(2) Be inscribed on one of the electoral rolls of the Province in which he resides; and
(3) Not be a member of the Royal Family, in addition to the conditions prescribed by the federal electoral law.

Article 104. The term of office of the House of Representatives shall be four years unless it is dissolved earlier.

Article 105. At the opening of every session, the House of Representatives shall elect a President and two Vice-Presidents, who shall be eligible for re-election.

Article 106. If the House of Representatives is dissolved on account of any matter, the succeeding House of Representatives may not be dissolved on account of the same matter.

Article 107. The order whereby the House of Representatives is dissolved shall call upon the electors to carry out new elections in the three Provinces within a period not exceeding three months. It must also provide for the new Chamber to be convened within twenty days of the completion of the elections.

PART III: PROVISIONS COMMON TO THE TWO CHAMBERS

Article 108. Each member of Parliament represents the whole people; his electors or the authority that appoints him may not make his mandate subject to any conditions or restrictions.

Article 109. No one may be both a Senator and a Deputy at the same time. No member of Parliament may at the same time be a member of a provincial Legislative Council or the holder of any public office. Other cases of incompatibility shall be determined by the federal electoral law.

Article 110. Before assuming his duties each Senator and each Deputy shall take publicly in the place of meeting of his Chamber the following oath: "I swear by Almighty God to be loyal to the country and to the King, to observe the Constitution and the laws of the country and to carry out my duties honestly and truthfully."

Article 111. Each Chamber decides upon the validity of the election of its members in accordance with its rules of procedure provided that, in order to decide that the election of a member is invalid, a majority of two-thirds of the members of the Chamber shall be required. This power may be delegated to another authority by virtue of a federal law.

Article 112. The King shall call Parliament annually to hold its regular meeting in the first week of November. Failing such convocation Parliament shall meet on the tenth day of the same month. Unless the Chamber of Deputies is dissolved, the regular session shall last for at least five months and the King shall pronounce the closure of the session.

Article 113. The period of sessions shall be common to both Chambers. If both Chambers meet, or either of them meets, at a time other than the legal time the meeting shall be unlawful and any resolutions taken shall be void.

Article 114. The meetings of the two Chambers shall be public but each Chamber shall, at the request of the Government or of ten of its members, go into secret session in order to decide whether the discussion on the question before it is to be held in public or in secret.

Article 115. During extraordinary sessions Parliament shall not discuss, except with the consent of the Government, questions other than those for which it has been convened.

Article 116. The meetings of either of the two Chambers shall not be valid unless the majority of the members are present at the opening of the meeting. Neither of the two Chambers may take a decision unless the majority of its members are present at the time of the decision.

Article 117. Except in cases where a special majority is required, decisions in each of the Chambers shall be adopted by a majority of the members present. If the vote is equally divided, the proposal in question shall be considered to have been rejected.

Article 118. Voting on questions under discussion in each Chamber shall take place in the manner prescribed in its rules of procedure.

Article 119. Neither Chamber may discuss a bill before it has been considered by the appropriate committees in conformity with its rules of procedure.

Article 120. Every bill adopted by one of the two Chambers shall be transmitted by the President of that Chamber to the President of the other Chamber.

Article 121. A bill which has been rejected by either Chamber may not be reintroduced at the same session.

Article 122. Every member of Parliament has the right, in conditions which shall be determined in the rules of procedure of each Chamber, to address questions and interpellations to Ministers. Discussion on an interpellation shall not take place until at least eight days after it has been presented, except in cases of emergency and with the consent of the person to whom the interpellation is addressed.

Article 123. Each Chamber shall have the right to investigate, in accordance with its rules of procedure, specific questions within its competence.

Article 124. Members of Parliament shall have immunity with regard to opinions they have expressed in either Chamber or in the committees thereof, subject to the provisions of the respective rules of procedure.

Article 125. Except in cases of *flagrante delicto,* no member of either Chamber may be prosecuted or arrested for criminal offences while Parliament is in session, without the authorization of the Chamber of which he is a member.

Article 126. Members of Parliament other than those who exercise governmental offices compatible with parliamentary membership may not be granted any title or decoration, with the exception of military ranks and decorations, during their term of office.

Article 127. The conditions under which a member of Parliament forfeits his membership shall be determined by the Federal electoral law and the decision of such forfeiture shall be taken by a majority of all the members of the Chamber to which such member belongs.

Article 128. If a seat becomes vacant in either of the Chambers, it shall be filled within three months by election or appointment in conformity with the provisions of this Constitution; the period of three months shall commence on the date on which the Chamber informs the Government of the vacancy. The term of office of a new Senator shall be limited to the term of office of his predecessor. The term of office of a new member of the House of Representatives shall expire upon the termination of the period of office of the Chamber.

Article 129. Elections for a new House of Representatives shall take place within the three months preceding the expiration of the period of office of the old House of Representatives. If it is not possible to carry out elections within the said period, the term of office of the old House of Representatives shall extend until elections are held, notwithstanding the provisions of article 104.

Article 130. The replacement of half the members of the Senate shall take place by means of election or appointment within the three months preceding the expiration of the terms of office of the retiring Senators. If it is impossible to effect the replacement within that period, the term of office of the Senators whose period of office has expired shall be prolonged until the election or appointment of the new Senators, notwithstanding the provisions of article 98.

Article 131. The remuneration of members of Parliament shall be fixed by federal law, provided that no increase in such remuneration shall take effect until after the expiration of the term of office of the House of Representatives which decided it.

Article 132. Each Chamber shall lay down its own rules of procedure and it shall specify therein the manner in which it will exercise its functions.

Article 133. The President of each Chamber shall be responsible for maintaining order in his Chamber; no armed force may enter either Chamber or be stationed near its doors except by request of the President.

Article 134. No one may present a request to Parliament except in writing. Each Chamber may transmit the petitions addressed to it to the Ministers. The Ministers shall be bound to give the Chamber necessary explanations regarding such petitions whenever the Chamber so requires.

Article 135. The King shall sanction the laws passed by Parliament and shall promulgate them within thirty days of the date of their communication to him.

Article 136. Within the period prescribed for the promulgation of a law, the King may refer the law back to Parliament for reconsideration, in which case Parliament must reconsider the law. If the law is passed again by a two-thirds majority of the members composing each of the two Chambers, the King shall sanction and promulgate it within the thirty days following the communication to him of the last decision. If the majority is less than two-thirds the bill shall not be reconsidered during that session. If Parliament in another session passes such bill again by a majority of all the members composing each of the two Chambers the King shall sanction and promulgate it within the thirty days following the communication of the decision to him.

Article 137. Laws which are promulgated by the King shall become effective in the United Kingdom of Libya after thirty days from the date of their publication in the official gazette. This period may be increased or decreased by a special provision in the law concerned. The laws must be published in the official gazette within fifteen days of their promulgation.

Article 138. The right to initiate laws shall be vested in the King, the Senate and the House of Representatives, except when they concern the budget or the imposing of new taxes or the modification of taxes or exemption or part exemption from taxes or their abolition, when the right to initiate such laws shall be vested in the King and the House of Representatives.

Article 139. The President of the Senate shall preside whenever the two Chambers meet together in Congress. In his absence the President of the House of Representatives shall preside.

Article 140. The meetings of the Congress shall be valid only when the absolute majority of the members of each of the two Chambers composing the Congress are present.

Chapter VIII

THE JUDICIARY

Article 141. The general judicial organization of the State shall be determined by federal law in accordance with the provisions of this Constitution.

Article 142. The judges shall be independent; in the administration of justice, they shall be answerable only to the law.

FEDERAL SUPREME COURT

Article 143. The Supreme Court shall consist of a President and of judges appointed by the King.

Article 144. Before taking office the President and members of the Supreme Court shall take oath before the King.

Article 145. Should the office of a judge fall vacant, the King, after consulting the President of the Court, shall appoint another judge.

Article 146. The President and the judges of the Court shall retire when they have completed the sixty-fifth year of their age (Gregorian).

Article 147. The President and judges of the Court may not be removed from office; nevertheless, if it appears that for reasons of health, or because he has lost the confidence or respect which his office requires, one of them can no longer exercise his functions, the King, with the approval of the majority of the members of the Court, excluding the member concerned, shall relieve him of his office.

Article 148. The basic salaries, allowances and provisions concerning leave of absence and pensions or provident fund of judges of the Supreme Court shall be determined by a federal law; no modification which would be prejudicial to a judge shall apply to a judge after he has been appointed.

Article 149. When the President of the Court is absent or otherwise unable to perform his duties the King may appoint a member of the Court to perform the duties of the President.

Article 150. When a judge is absent or otherwise unable to perform his duties the King may, after consultation with the President, appoint some person to replace him during his absence; the member thus appointed shall enjoy all privileges of the other judges of the Court while he is so acting.

Article 151. The Supreme Court exclusively shall be competent to hear disputes which may arise between the Federal Government and one or more Provinces or between two or more Provinces.

Article 152. The King may refer important constitutional and legislative questions to the Supreme Court for an opinion; the Court shall examine such questions and inform the King of its opinion, taking into account the provisions of this Constitution.

Article 153. An appeal may be lodged with the Supreme Court, in accordance with the provisions of the federal law, against any judgment by a provincial court in civil or criminal proceedings if such judgment included a decision in a dispute concerning this Constitution or the interpretation thereof.

Article 154. Subject to the provisions of article 153, the cases in which an appeal against the judgment of a provincial court or an appeal for cassation may be lodged with the Supreme Court shall be determined by a federal law.

Article 155. The legal principles embodied in the decisions of the Supreme Court shall be binding on all courts within the United Kingdom of Libya.

Article 156. All civil and judicial authorities in the United Kingdom of Libya shall give the Supreme Court any assistance it may require.

Article 157. Other functions may be conferred on the Supreme Court by federal law, so long as they are not contrary to the provisions of this Constitution.

Article 158. The Supreme Court, with the approval of the King, shall determine the rules regulating the practice and procedure in the Court and fixing the fees to be charged.

Chapter IX

FEDERAL FINANCE

Article 159. The general budget shall be submitted to Parliament for study and approval at least two months before the beginning of the financial year. The budget shall be approved head by head. The beginning of the financial year shall be determined by a federal law.

Article 160. The budget shall be discussed and approved in the first instance by the House of Representatives.

Article 161. The parliamentary session may not be terminated before the budget has been approved.

Article 162. In all cases where the budget has not been approved before the beginning of the financial year, provisional monthly credits shall be opened by Royal Decree on the basis of one-twelfth of the credits for the preceding year, and revenue shall be collected and sums expended in accordance with the laws in force at the end of the preceding financial year.

Article 163. Any expenditure for which provision has not been made in the budget or which exceeds the budget estimates must be authorized by Parliament and any transfer of funds from one head of the budget to another must also be so authorized.

Article 164. Between sessions or during the period when the House of Representatives is dissolved and in cases of urgent necessity, new expenditure for which provision has not been made in the budget may be approved or sums may be transferred from one head of the budget to another on condition that such action is taken by Royal Decree and submitted to Parliament within a period of not more than one month after the next meeting.

Article 165. A draft exceptional budget may in cases of necessity be drawn up for more than one year to provide for revenue and expenditure of an exceptional nature; such a budget shall not be put into force until it has been approved by Parliament.

Article 166. The Audit Office shall audit the Federal Government accounts and shall report to Parliament on the result of the audit. The powers of the Audit office and its constitution and the rules for exercising its auditing powers shall be determined by federal law.

Article 167. No tax may be imposed, modified or abolished except by law. No one may be exempt from the payment of taxes except in cases provided by law. No one may be asked to pay any amounts or fees except within the limits of the law.

Article 168. No pension, compensation, gratuity or payment from the provident fund may be approved for payment out of the Government Treasury except within the limits of the law.

Article 169. No public loan or undertaking that is likely to be a charge on the Treasury for one or more of the following years may be contracted without the consent of Parliament.

Article 170. The currency system shall be determined by federal law.

Article 171. Any dispute between the Senate and the House of Representatives concerning the approval of a head of the budget shall be settled by a decision taken by an absolute majority of the two Chambers meeting in Congress.

Article 172. The receipts from all taxes and fees relating to matters which are within the legislative and executive competence of the Federal Government under article 36 of this Constitution shall be paid to the Federal Government.

Article 173. Each Province shall have the revenue from taxes and fees accruing from matters within its competence in accordance with article 39 of this Constitution, and also from matters within its executive competence in accordance with article 38 of this Constitution.

Article 174. The Federal Government must allocate annually to the Provinces from its receipts sufficient funds to enable them to discharge their obligations subject to the condition that their financial capacity is not less than it was before independence. The method and amount of such allocations shall be determined by federal law in a manner that will guarantee to the Provinces an increase in the amounts to be allocated to them by the Federal Government, such increases to be proportionate to the growth of the federal revenue and such as will guarantee to them a constant economic progress.

Article 175. In cases of the imposition of federal taxes for which provision is made in article 36, paragraph (28), the Provinces shall be consulted before the bill relating to such taxes is submitted to Parliament.

Chapter X

THE PROVINCES

Article 176. The Provinces shall exercise all powers which have not been assigned to the Federal Government under the provisions of this Constitution.

Article 177. Each Province shall formulate its own Organic Law provided that its provisions are not contrary to the provisions of this Constitution. The formulation of such laws and their promulgation shall take place within a period not exceeding one year from the promulgation of this Constitution.

Article 178. The Provinces shall be bound to observe the provisions of this Constitution and to enforce the federal law in the manner prescribed in this Constitution.

Article 179. Each Province shall have a governor who shall be called the "Wali."

Article 180. The King shall appoint the Wali and may relieve him of office.

Article 181. The Wali shall represent the King within the Province and shall supervise the implementation of this Constitution and of the federal laws therein.

Article 182. Each Province shall have an Executive Council.

Article 183. Each Province shall have a Legislative Council, three-quarters of the members of which at least shall be elected.

Article 184. The functions of the Wali shall be determined by the Organic Law in each Province, subject to the provisions of article 181, and the functions of the Executive and Legislative Councils shall also be so determined.

Article 185. Judicial power shall be exercised by the local tribunals in the Provinces in accordance with the provisions of this Constitution.

Chapter XI

GENERAL PROVISIONS

Article 186. Arabic shall be the official language of the State.

Article 187. Cases in which a foreign language may be used in official transactions shall be determined by a federal law.

Article 188. The United Kingdom of Libya has two capitals, Tripoli and Benghazi.

Article 189. The extradition of political refugees shall be prohibited. International treaties and the federal laws shall prescribe the grounds for the extradition of ordinary criminals.

Article 190. Foreigners shall be deported only in accordance with the provisions of the federal law.

Article 191. The legal status of foreigners shall be prescribed by federal law in accordance with the principles of international law.

Article 192. The state shall guarantee respect for the systems of personal status of non-Moslems.

Article 193. General amnesty shall not be granted except by federal law.

Article 194. A federal law shall determine the manner in which the land, sea and air forces are established and regulated.

Article 195. No provision of this Constitution may be suspended under any circumstances except where such suspension is temporary in time of war or during the operation of martial law and is in accordance with law. In any event a parliamentary session may not be suspended when the conditions prescribed by this Constitution for the holding of such a session exist.

Article 196. The King or either of the two Chambers may propose the revision of this Constitution either by the amendment or deletion of one or more of its provisions or by the insertion of additional provisions.

Article 197. No proposal may be made to review the provisions relating to the monarchal form of government, the order of succession to the Throne, the representative form of government or the principles of liberty and equality guaranteed by this Constitution.

Article 198. For the purpose of reviewing this Constitution, each of the two Chambers shall, by an absolute majority of all its members, adopt a resolution stating the necessity for the review and prescribing the subject thereof. The two Chambers shall, after discussing the matters subject to review, adopt their decisions in respect thereof. Discussion and voting in each of the two Chambers shall not take place unless two-thirds of its members are present. The resolutions to be valid must be adopted by a majority of two-thirds of the members present in each of the two Chambers and must be sanctioned by the King.

Article 199. In the event of a review of the provisions concerning the federal form of government, such review must be approved, in addition to the provisions laid down in the preceding article, by all the Legislative Councils of the Provinces. Such approval shall be expressed by a resolution taken in this respect by the Legislative Council of each Province before the review is presented to the King for his sanction.

Article 200. Immigration into Libya shall be regulated by a federal law. No immigration shall be permitted into a Province without the approval of the Province having been secured.

Chapter XII

TRANSITORY AND PROVISIONAL PROVISIONS

Article 201. This Constitution shall come into force upon the declaration of independence, which must take place by 1 January 1952 in accordance with the resolution of the United Nations General Assembly dated 21 November 1949. Nevertheless the provisions of article 8 of this Constitution and of this chapter shall come into force on the promulgation of this Constitution.

Article 202. Until the establishment of a government constituted in accordance with the provisions of article 203 of this Constitution, the Provisional Federal Government shall exercise all the powers concerning the matters transferred to it by the two Administering Powers and by the existing Provincial Governments, provided that the provisions laid down by it shall not be contrary to the fundamental principles established by this Constitution.

Article 203. Upon the declaration of independence the King shall appoint the duly constituted government.

Article 204. The Provisional Federal Government shall draw up the first electoral law for Parliament, provided it is not contrary to the provisions laid down in this Constitution. The law shall be submitted to the National Assembly for approval and promulgation. The said law must be promulgated within a period not exceeding thirty days from the date of the promulgation of this Constitution.

Article 205. The first elections to the House of Representatives must take place within a period not exceeding three and a half months from the date upon which the electoral law is promulgated.

Article 206. In the first elections to the House of Representatives and until a census of the Libyan people has been made, the Province of Cyrenaica shall have fifteen Deputies; the Province of Tripolitania thirty-five Deputies and the Province of the Fezzan five Deputies.

Article 207. Notwithstanding the provisions of articles 95 and 98 of this Constitution, the King shall appoint all members of the first Senate. Its term of office shall be four years as from the date of the first session of Parliament.

Article 208. Articles 95 and 98 shall become operative as from the date of the expiration of the term of office of the first Senate.The members of the Senate who will retire at the end of the first four years in accordance with the provisions of articles 95 and 98 shall be selected by lot.

Article 209. Notwithstanding the provisions contained in article 47 of this Constitution, the first King of the United Kingdom of Libya shall exercise his constitutional powers upon the declaration of independence, provided that he shall take the prescribed oath before Parliament at its first session in a joint meeting.

Article 210. Unless they are inconsistent with the principles of liberty and equality guaranteed by this Constitution, all laws, subsidiary legislation, orders and notices which may be in operation in any part of Libya upon the coming into force of this Constitution shall continue to be effective and in operation until repealed or amended or replaced by other legislation enacted in accordance with the provisions of this Constitution.

Article 211. The first Parliament shall be convened within a period of not more than twenty days from the date on which the final results of the election are announced.

Article 212. Article 36, paragraph (27) and article 174 of this Constitution shall not come into operation before 1 April 1952.

Article 213. The National Assembly shall continue in existence until the declaration of independence.

*

* *

The Libyan National Assembly prepared and resolved this Constitution in its meeting held in the city of Benghazi on Sunday, 6 Muharram, Hagera 1371, corresponding to 7 October 1951, and delegated its President and [the] two Vice-Presidents to promulgate it and submit it to His Majesty, the Exalted King, and publish it in the Official Gazette in Libya.

*

* *

In fulfilment of the decision of the National Assembly, we hereby promulgate this Constitution in Benghazi on Sunday, 6 Muharram, Hagera 1371, corresponding to 7 October 1951.

President of the
National Assembly
MOHAMED ABULAHDAD AL ALEM

Vice-President of the
National Assembly
OMNER FAYEK SCHENNEIB

Vice-President of the
National Assembly
ABUBAKER BEN AHMED ABUBAKER

Annex III

THE ELECTORAL LAW FOR THE ELECTION OF THE LIBYAN FEDERAL HOUSE OF REPRESENTATIVES *

Part I

The Libyan

1. Every person who resides in Libya and has no other nationality or is not the subject of any other State, shall be deemed to be a Libyan if he fulfils one of the following conditions:

(a) That he was born in Libya;

(b) That either of his parents was born in Libya;

(c) That he has had his normal residence in Libya for a period of not less than ten years.

Definition of residence

2. For the purpose of the elections, the residence of a person shall be the place in which he normally resides, or the place of origin, within his Province, of his family.

Qualification of electors

3. Every male Libyan who has completed his twenty-first year (Gregorian) shall be entitled to vote unless he is a person who:

(a) Is a lunatic; or

(b) Has been declared to be a bankrupt and has not been discharged; or

(c) Is serving a term of imprisonment.

Qualifications of candidates for election

4. Subject to the provisions of sections 5 and 23 of this law, every male person who has completed his thirtieth year (Gregorian) and who is inscribed upon the the electoral rolls of a District within his Province shall be qualified to be a member of the House of Representatives.

Royal Family disqualified for election

5. All persons who are members of the Royal Family shall be disqualified for election as members of the House.

Number of elected members of the House

6. The number of Deputies shall be on the basis of one Deputy for every twenty thousand inhabitants or fraction of that number exceeding half; pro-

* Text from *Supplementary Report to the Second Annual Report of the United Nations Commissioner in Libya,* prepared in consultation with the Council for Libya, General Assembly Official Records: Sixth Session, 1951–52, Supplement No. 17A (A/1949/Add. 1), Annex VIII, p. 35.

vided that the number of Deputies in any of the three Provinces shall not be less than five; and provided that, in the first elections to the House of Representatives and until a census of the Libyan people has been held, the Province of Cyrenaica shall have fifteen Deputies, the Province of Tripolitania thirty-five Deputies, and the Province of the Fezzan five.

Electoral system

7. (1) The Provinces of Libya shall be divided up, as may be necessary, into Urban Electoral Districts and Rural Electoral Districts.

(2) Both Urban Electoral Districts and Rural Electoral Districts shall be sub-divided, as may be necessary, into constituencies or tribal units, each containing, as near as may be, twenty thousand inhabitants; provided that the Minister of Justice shall, in the case of the Province of the Fezzan, determine its five constituencies without any reservation regarding the aforesaid number of inhabitants.

(3) For purposes of voting, constituencies (or corresponding tribal units) will be sub-divided into polling-districts, in each of which a polling-station will be situated. No polling district shall contain more than 3,500 electors.

Urban electoral districts, constituencies and polling districts

8. (1) The Minister of Justice of the Federal Government shall, after seeking guidance from the Provinces, specify, by public notice, the names and boundaries of the Urban Electoral Districts, constituencies and polling districts of Libya. He may, if necessary, assign distinguishing letters to constituencies or polling districts.

(2) Subject to the provisions of sections 57 and 61 of this law, parts I, II and III of this law shall apply to elections in Urban Electoral Districts only.

Appointment of Supervisor of Elections

9. (1) The Minister of Justice shall appoint a person to be known as the Supervisor-General of Elections. The Minister shall have power to issue to all election officers such directions as he may deem necessary to ensure effective execution of the provisions of this law; and shall also have power either personally or by delegation, to administer any oaths required to be taken under this law.

(2) The Supervisor-General shall exercise general direction and supervision over the administrative conduct of elections to the House and enforce on the part of all election officers fairness, impartiality and compliance with the provisions of this law.

Appointment of Provincial Supervisors

10. The Minister of Justice shall, after consultation with the Supervisor-General, appoint Provincial Supervisors to represent the Supervisor-General, where necessary, in each of the three Provinces of Libya, and to assist him in the discharge of his duties.

Appointment of Registering and Returning Officers

11. (1) The Minister of Justice shall appoint by name or by office such number of officers as may be required to act as Registering and Returning Officers for each town electoral district.

(2) An appointment made by the Minister of Justice under this section may be revoked by him at any time.

Appointment of persons to assist Registering and Returning Officers

12. The Supervisor-General of Elections may appoint such persons as may be necessary to assist Registering Officers and Returning Officers in the discharge of their duties.

Registration of electors

13. (1) As soon as may be after the publication of the Urban Electoral Districts, constituencies and polling districts of Libya under section 8 of this law, the Minister of Justice shall cause a public notice to be published in each of the three Provinces of Libya calling upon each person who is qualified to be an elector in any one of the town electoral districts into which the country is divided, and who wishes to have his name included in the electoral register of that district, to forward his application to the Registering Officer of the polling district in which he resides so as to reach that officer within a period of three weeks from the date of such notice. Upon receipt of an application, the Registering Officer shall give a receipt for it to the applicant.

(2) Any such application may be in the form of schedule No. 1 to this law and shall be signed, or marked by the applicant, if he is unable to write, in the presence of a person able to read and write Arabic, of not less than twenty-one years of age, who shall sign the application as witness to the applicant's signature or mark.

(3) Upon the expiration of the period referred to in subsection (1) of this section and within one week from such expiration, the Registering Officer of each polling district shall prepare a separate electoral register of each polling district in such form as may be prescribed by the Supervisor-General.

(4) In preparing the aforesaid register, the Registering Officer shall include therein the name of every eligible person normally resident in his polling district from whom an application made in accordance with the requirements of sub-section (2) of this section has been received. The Registering Officer may also include in the Register the name of any person normally resident in his polling district who appears to him to be qualified for registration, even though such person has failed to make application as aforesaid, and the Registering Officer shall make such enquiries as he may think fit for this purpose.

(5) No person shall be registered in more than one constituency or in more than one polling district in any constituency.

Completion of Registers.

14. (1) On completion of the Register, the Registering Officer shall cause the aforesaid Register or copies thereof to be exhibitetd in one or more of the government offices in the district.

(2) The Registering Officer shall thereupon, by means of a notice to be posted in a conspicuous place on Government offices, etc., in his polling district, give notice that the aforesaid Register or copies thereof are open for inspection in the places referred to in sub-section (1) and that any person whose name appears in the Register may object to the inclusion of his own name or the name of any other person therein in accordance with the procedure prescribed hereunder; and that any person whose name has been omitted from the Register after he has submitted an application and obtained a receipt therefore may request that his name be entered in the Register.

Objections

15. Objections made under section 14 shall be in writing and shall reach the Registering Officer not later than two weeks from the date of publication of the Public Notice under section 14 (2).

Proof of objection

16. (1) Where objection is made to the inclusion of any name in the Register, the Registering Officer shall call upon the objector to give *prima facie* proof of the grounds of the objection.

(2) If such proof is given the Registering Officer shall require proof of the qualifications of the person in regard to whom objection has been made and may make such enquiries to this end as may appear to him necessary.

(3) If the qualification of such person is not proved, the name of such person shall be expunged from the Register. If the qualification of such person is so proved, the name of such person shall be retained on the Register.

(4) The decision of objections shall be the responsibility, in every case, of a committee to be appointed by the Minister of Justice. It shall consist of the Registering Officer, a judge and one notable of the district. In the event of disagreement between members of the committee, the opinion of the majority shall prevail.

(5) For the purpose of sub-section (4), the expression "judge" shall include a judge in the civil and penal Tribunal, or Court of Appeal, the Qadi of a Sharia Court and the President and members of an Ahliyya Court.

Certification of the Register

17. As soon as may be after the Register has been completed as provided in section 13, the Registering Officer shall certify the Register to be, to the best of his knowledge and belief, a true and correct Register of electors in his polling district.

Annual revision of Registers

18. (a) On or before the first day of January in each year following the year in which the Register for any electoral district is first certified under this law, the Minister of Justice shall cause a Notice to be published in the Gazette and in one or more newspapers calling upon every person who

(i) Being entitled to have his name entered on the Register, is not registered in any Register; or

(ii) Being already registered, is desirous of having his name entered in the Register of some other polling district by reason of change of residence.

To forward his application for registration to the Registering Officer of the constituency in which he resides so as to reach him not later than thirty days from the date of the publication of the aforesaid Notice in the Gazette.

(b) The provisions of sections 15 and 16 of this law shall apply *mutatis mutandis* to all applications for registration or change of registration under this section.

(c) The Registering Officer of each constituency shall expunge from the Register the name of any person who is proved to his satisfaction to be dead or disqualified under section 3.

Certification of revised Registers

19. As soon as may be after the annual revision of the Registers has been

completed, the Registering Officer shall certify the revised Register to be, to the best of his knowledge and belief, a true and correct Register of electors in his constituency.

Part II

ISSUE OF WRITS AND NOMINATION OF CANDIDATES

Number of members for each Constituency

20. Each Constituency shall return one Deputy to serve in the House of Representatives.

Writ of election

21. (1) For the purpose of every general election of members of the House of Representatives and for the purposes of the election of members to supply vacancies caused by death, resignation or otherwise, the Minister of Justice shall issue such number of writs as may be required addressed to the Returning Officers of the respective urban districts of which members are to be returned.

(2) Every such writ shall be, as nearly as may be, in the form shown in schedule No. 2 to this law.

(3) Upon the receipt of such writ every Returning Officer shall proceed to hold the election in the manner hereinafter provided.

Notice of times and place of nomination

22. Upon the issue of a writ the Returning Officer shall give information thereof by means of a notice to be posted up in a conspicuous place on government buildings in the town electoral district to which the writ relates, and shall likewise give notice of the day and place of nomination of candidates for election, at least ten clear days before the day fixed for such nomination.

Nomination papers

23. (1) Subject to the provisions of section 5, any person who possesses the qualifications set out in section 4 and who is qualified to vote in a Constituency and who is willing to stand for election, may be nominated as a candidate for that Constituency; provided that an elector registered in an Urban Electoral District may be a candidate in any Constituency in that Urban Electoral District or in any other Constituency in which he has his place or origin provided that it is situated in a district within the Province in which he is registered.

(2) No person may be nominated as a candidate for more than one Constituency.

(3) Each candidate shall be nominated by means of a nomination paper to be supplied by the Returning Officer on application therefore at his office. The nomination paper will be signed by two persons as proposer and seconder respectively and by not less than four other persons, all of whose names must appear in the register of electors for the Constituency for which the candidate seeks election. No person shall sign the nomination papers of more than one candidate. The written consent of the candidate must be endorsed on the nomination paper, which may be in the form set out in schedule No. 3 to this law.

(4) Each candidate shall, at the time of his nomination deliver to the Returning Officer a statement showing that he possesses the qualifications required for election as a member of the House of Representatives. This statement may be in the form set out in schedule No. 4 to this law. Should this statement not

be delivered to the Returning Officer, the nomination of such candidate shall be void.

Proceedings on nomination day

24. (1) The Returning Officer shall, by means of a notice to be posted in a conspicuous place on government buildings in the electoral district in question, notify the time and place at which nomination papers may be delivered to him, and shall attend at that place, at the time indicated, to receive nomination papers and the statement of the candidate's qualifications.

(2) The documents referred to above may be delivered to the Returning Officer at the time and place referred to in sub-section (1) of this section, by the candidate or by his proposer or seconder. If not delivered at the prescribed time and place they shall be deemed to be null and void.

(3) The Returning Officer shall forthwith cause a copy of the nomination paper to be posted up in a conspicuous position outside the place of nomination.

Deposits by candidates

25. (1) The candidate, or some person on his behalf, shall deposit with the Returning Officer between the date of the issue of the writ and mid-day on the day of nomination, the sum of *fifty* Libyan pounds, and in default of such deposit being so made the candidate shall be deemed to have withdrawn his candidature.

(2) Until the day of coming into force of all the provisions of the Libyan Currency Law, the Libyan Pound shall, for the purposes of this law, mean in Tripolitania : 480 Military Authority Lire; in Cyrenaica : 0.975 Pound Egyptian; in the Fezzan : 980 Algerian Francs.

(3) The Returning Officer shall forthwith give a receipt for the said sum and shall pay the same into the Treasury.

Return of deposit

26. The deposit paid to the Returning Officer shall be returned to the candidate or to the person who has paid the deposit on his behalf upon the occurrence of any of the following circumstances:

(a) If the candidate for election is not nominated;

(b) If the candidate withdraws his candidature within the specified period;

(c) If the candidate dies, in which case it shall be returned to his legal personal representative, or if not made by him, to the person by whom it was made.

Forfeiture of deposit

27. If a candidate who has made the required deposit or on behalf of whom the deposit has been made, is not elected and the number of votes polled by him does not exceed one-eighth of the total number of votes polled in his constituency the amount deposited shall be forfeited and paid to the general revenue.

Return of deposit to elected members

28. (1) In cases where the candidate is elected, the sum deposited shall be returned to him or to the person who has paid the deposit on his behalf, as soon as he has made affirmation as a member of the House of Representatives.

(2) In cases where the candidate has not been elected but has polled more than one-eighth of the total number of votes, the sum deposited shall be returned to him or to the person who has paid the deposit on his behalf, as soon as possible after the result of the election has been declared.

Objections to nomination papers

29. (1) Objection to the nomination of a candidate in a Constituency may be made within forty-eight hours from mid-day on the day of nomination by a person registered as a voter in that Constituency on all or any of the following grounds:

(a) That the description of the candidate is insufficient to identify the candidate;

(b) That the nomination paper does not comply with or was not delivered in accordance with the provisions of this law;

(c) That it is apparent from the contents of the nomination paper that the candidate is not capable of being elected a member of the House of Representatives;

(d) That the candidate is not eligible to stand for election for that Constituency in accordance with section 23;

(e) That the necessary deposit has not been paid in accordance with the provisions of section 25 of this law.

(2) No objection to a nomination paper shall be allowed unless made to the Returning Officer within the period specified in sub-section (1).

(3) Every objection shall be in writing signed by the objector and shall specify the ground of objection; provided that, if the objector is illiterate, it must bear his thumb-print and the signature of two witnesses.

Decision on objection

30. (1) The decision of objections to nomination papers shall, in every case, be the responsibility of a committee to be appointed by the Minister of Justice. It shall consist of the Returning Officer, a judge and one notable of the district.

(2) Upon receipt of an objection, the committee shall decide on its validity and inform the candidate of their decision and, if the objection is upheld, of the grounds of their decision. In the event of disagreement between members of the committee, the opinion of the majority shall prevail.

(3) The decision of the committee allowing or disallowing the objection shall be final and without appeal.

(4) For the purposes of sub-section (1), the expression "judge" shall include a judge of the civil and penal Tribunal, or Court of Appeal, the Qadi of a Sharia Court and the President and members of an Ahliyya Court.

Voluntary withdrawal of candidature

31. A candidate may before one o'clock in the afternoon on the day of nomination, but not afterwards, voluntarily withdraw his candidature by tendering to the Returning Officer a notice signed by him to that effect. Thereupon, the Returning Officer shall cause notice of such withdrawal to be posted in a conspicuous place outside his office.

Part III

THE CONDUCT OF ELECTIONS IN URBAN ELECTORAL DISTRICTS

Uncontested elections

32. If, after all objections which may have been lodged have been decided by the Returning Officer's Committee, no more candidates stand nominated for that

constituency than there are vacancies to be filled, the Returning Officer shall forthwith declare the nominated candidate or candidates to be elected, and shall forthwith make a return, which may be, in the form of schedule No. 5 to this law, to the Supervisor General who shall cause the name or names of the member or members so elected to be published.

Contested elections

33. (1) If, in any constituency after the decisions by the Returning Officer's Committee of any objections which may have been lodged, more candidates stand nominated for that district than there are vacancies to be filled, the Returning Officer shall forthwith take steps to enable an election to be held in accordance with the provisions of this law, and may allot to each candidate a symbol approved by the Supervisor General.

(2) Immediately after the decision of objections, the Returning Officer shall report to the Supervisor General that the election is contested, sending to him a statement showing:

(a) The symbol, if any, allotted to each candidate;

(b) The situation of each polling station in the electoral district.

(3) Upon receipt of this report, the Supervisor General shall cause to be published a notice specifying:

(a) The constituency in which the election is contested;

(b) The date on which the poll will be taken;

(c) The names of the candidates together with the symbols allotted to them;

(d) The situation of the polling station or polling stations in the constituency in question.

(4) If, in any constituency, a duly nominated candidate shall die before an election can be held, the Supervisor General shall cause the election in that constituency to be postponed for a period not exceeding fifteen days and shall arrange afresh for the nomination of a candidate for that constituency in accordance with part II of this law.

Presiding Officers at elections

34. (1) Each Returning Officer may, with the approval of the Supervisor General, appoint one or more persons, known as presiding officers, whose duty it shall be to preside at each polling station in the Returning Officer's electoral district. The Presiding Officer is responsible for ensuring that all proper arrangements are made for the conduct of the poll in his polling station. The Presiding Officer shall be supplied with a copy of that part of the register of electors containing the names of the electors assigned to his polling station.

(2) The Returning Officer may, if he thinks fit, act himself as the Presiding Officer.

(3) The Committee appointed for the hearing of objections under section 16 (4) shall assist the Presiding Officer to supervise the proceedings in the polling station on election day in order to facilitate the conduct thereof.

Duties of Presiding Officer

35. It shall be the duty of the Presiding Officer or of the Returning Officer when acting as a Presiding Officer:

(a) To ensure that a notice shall be fixed in a conspicuous place outside the polling station showing the name of each candidate and, where necessary, the symbol allotted to him;

(b) To provide at each polling station such facilities as will ensure that electors are enabled to cast their votes free from observation;
(c) To keep order in the polling station;
(d) To exclude all persons from the polling station save the following:
(i) Candidates or representatives of candidates;
(ii) Election officials;
(iii) Police officers on duty;
(iv) Any person officially employed at the polling station.

Misbehaviour of voters in the polling station

36. If any person misconducts himself in the polling station, or fails to obey the lawful orders of the Presiding Officer, the latter may call upon any police officer in or near the polling station to remove such person from the station, and the police officer shall thereupon remove the person, who may not, without the permission of the Presiding Officer re-enter the polling station.

Right to vote

37. Only such persons as are included in the election roll of the polling district in which the polling station is situated may vote at that polling station.

List of candidates to be displayed

38. A list of the duly nominated candidates shall be prominently displayed in the polling station.

Voting by ballot

39. Voting shall be by secret ballot by means of a voting token, which shall not be identifiable by individual mark, and which shall be issued direct to the voter in the polling station by the person in charge. It shall not be signed or marked by the voter.

Voting tokens

40. The person in charge of the polling station shall be given a number of voting tokens approximately equal to the number of voters on the roll in that polling district, and shall sign a receipt for them.

Voter's name to be checked with electoral roll

41. Before a voting token is issued to a voter, his name shall be checked with the electoral roll; and a mark shall be made against the name of every voter to whom a voting token is issued.

Voter to appear in person

42. No vote is valid unless the voter appears at the polling station and casts his vote in person. No one shall cast a vote on behalf of another person on any pretext whatever.

Ballot boxes

43. (1) In the voting room of each polling station there shall be placed a number of ballot boxes equal to the number of candidates; and the name of one of the candidates, together with such other mark of identification as the Returning Officer shall think fit, shall be prominently displayed on each of the ballot boxes. Each ballot box shall have an aperture large enough to receive a voting token.

(2) The Presiding Officer shall immediately prior to the opening of the poll

satisfy himself, in the presence of the Committee assigned to his polling station, that the ballot boxes are empty. He shall then lock them and place his seal upon them in such manner as to prevent them being opened without breaking the seal. Only the apertures shall be left open for the receipt of votes.

Procedure for voting

44. (1) After his name has been checked against the roll each voter shall be given one voting token only, and the procedure for voting shall be explained to him.

(2) The voter shall then enter the voting area alone and cast his vote by dropping his voting token into the ballot box of the candidate he favours.

(3) Any vote which is not recorded exactly as required by this rule shall be invalid.

Spoilt voting tokens

45. A voter who satisfies the Presiding Officer that he has inadvertently dealt with his voting token in such a manner that it cannot conveniently be used as a voting token shall upon surrendering the spoilt token to the Presiding Officer be given a fresh voting token, and the spoilt voting token shall immediately be cancelled by the Presiding Officer.

Closing of poll

46. (1) No voting token shall be delivered to a voter after the hour fixed for the closing of the poll. But if at the hour aforesaid there is in the polling station any voter to whom a voting token has been delivered, such voter shall be allowed to record his vote.

(2) Should it be found impracticable to proceed to the counting of the votes recorded on the same day as the poll, all unused and spoilt voting tokens, the register of electors and other documents, together with the sealed ballot boxes, shall be placed in a place of safety for the night by the Presiding Officer, in the presence of his Committee, and the votes shall be counted the next day at such time and place as the Returning Officer may prescribe, prior notice thereof being given to the candidates.

Counting of votes

47. At the counting of votes the following procedure shall be observed:

(a) Each candidate may appoint an agent to attend the counting of the votes;

(b) The Returning Officer, his committee, assistants and clerks, together with the candidates or their agents for counting, but no other person save with the sanction of the Returning Officer, may be present at the counting of the votes;

(c) The Returning Officer shall then, in the presence of the committee, open each ballot box, or boxes, place the voting tokens in one heap and then proceed to count the votes, marking as rejected any ballot paper found to be invalid in accordance with section 48 of this law.

(d) The Returning Officer shall take such steps as he may consider necessary to check the number of voting tokens in the ballot boxes against either the number of unused voting tokens or the number of voting tokens issued in each polling station as found in accordance with section 41.

Votes to be rejected

48. Any voting tokens which appear to be not properly authenticated or in any way irregular, shall be shown to the Returning Officer, who, with his com-

mittee shall decide whether it is valid or not. Any voting token found to be invalid shall not be included in the count.

Recount of votes

49. Should the candidate or his agent ask for a recount of the votes, the votes cast shall be counted again before the Returning Officer declares the result of the election.

Equality of votes

50. When the number of votes cast between any of the candidates is found to be equal and the addition of one vote would entitle any of the candidates to be declared elected, the determination of the candidate to whom the one additional vote shall be deemed to have been given shall be made by lots in the presence of the Returning Officer and his committee in such manner as they shall determine.

Declaring result of poll

51. When the counting of votes has been completed the Returning Officer shall, subject to the provisions of sections 49 and 50 hereof, forthwith declare the candidate to whom the greatest number of votes has been given to be elected, and shall, as soon as may be thereafter, inform the Supervisor General, who will cause the name or names of the member or members so elected, to be published.

Disposal of election papers

52. After the declaration of the result of the election the Returning Officer shall seal up the ballot papers and all other documents relating to the election (excepting the electoral rolls) and retain the same for a period of six months and thereafter shall cause them to be destroyed, unless otherwise directed by order of the Supervisor General.

Part IV

PROCEDURE IN RESPECT OF ELECTION OF REPRESENTATIVES IN RURAL DISTRICTS

Election procedure in rural districts

53. Notwithstanding anything to the contrary in the preceding sections of this law, the following provisions shall have effect regarding the procedure to be followed for the election of members to represent rural districts in the House of Representatives.

Rural Electoral Districts

54. The Minister of Justice of the Federal Government shall, after seeking guidance from the Provinces, specify by Public Notice, the names, and, where possible, the boundaries of the Rural Electoral Districts and Constituencies (or corresponding tribal units) and polling districts of Libya.

Appointment of election officials in rural districts

55. (1) The Minister of Justice shall appoint such number of literate persons acquainted with tribal customs and procedure, as may be required, to perform the duties of Returning Officers and Registering Officers in Rural Electoral Districts.

(2) Returning Officers and Registering Officers shall perform their duties

subject to the instructions of the Supervisor-General of Elections and of Provincial Supervisors.

(3) The Supervisor-General of Elections may also appoint such persons as may be necessary to assist Returning Officers and Registering Officers in the discharge of their duties.

(4) It shall be the duty of each Registering Officer, as soon as he shall receive instructions from the Supervisor-General of Elections to that effect, to draw up a list of male members normally resident in the polling district to which he is appointed possessing the qualifications referred to in section 3 of this law. A Registering Officer may make such enquiries as he may think fit for this purpose and his decision as to whether a member of his district is qualified to vote shall be final.

Issue of writs for elections by tribes

56. The Minister of Justice shall, for the purpose of every general election of members of the House of Representatives to represent rural electoral districts, and for the purpose of the election of members to supply vacancies caused by death, resignation or otherwise, issue such number of writs as may be required, which writs shall be, as nearly as may be, in the form shown in schedule 2 to this law, addressed to the Supervisor-General of Elections, who shall transmit them to the Returning Officers, and the Returning Officers shall thereupon explain the contents thereof, including the date, time and place of nomination and election of candidates, to the tribal chiefs and sub-chiefs, who in turn shall explain the same to the tribesmen. Returning Officers may employ the services of Registering Officers to assist them in these, and other duties.

Application of other sections

57. The provisions of sections 1, 2, 3, 4, 5, 6, 7, 9, 10, 13 (5), 15, 16, 17, 18, 19, and of 20, 23, 25, 26, 27, 28, 29, and 30 of this law shall apply *mutatis mutandis* to elections in Rural Electoral Districts; provided that, in the said Rural Electoral Districts, nomination papers (schedule 3) and written declarations (schedule 4) need not be completed; and provided also that, in the said Rural Electoral Districts, objections made under sections 15 and 29 need not be in writing.

Withdrawal of candidature

58. In Rural Electoral Districts, a candidate may withdraw his candidature within five days from mid-day on the day of nomination by notifying the appropriate Returning Officer to this effect, provided that no candidate elected to the House under section 59 may thereafter withdraw his candidature.

Uncontested elections in Rural Electoral Districts

59. If, in any Constituency or equivalent tribal unit, after the period allowed for objections has lapsed, no more candidates have been nominated than there are vacanies to be filled, the Returning Officer shall declare the candidature of candidates who have been nominated to be duly elected members of the House of Representatives.

Contested elections

60. If there are more candidates nominated than there are vacancies in any Constituency, or equivalent tribal unit, the following procedure shall be observed:

(1) The Returning Officer of the Constituency concerned shall furnish each Registering Officer in his Constituency with a list containing the names of the candidates nominated. Thereafter the Registering Officer shall, with the help, if necessary, of the chiefs or sub-chiefs of the tribe concerned, call together the electors, whose names are on the list prepared by him under section 55 (4), upon the day appointed for the election, and enquire from each of them in turn, in the presence of the Committee appointed under sections 16 (4) and 59, for whom they wish to vote. The Registering Officer shall thereupon in the presence of the aforesaid Committee, write down the name of the candidate for whom each tribesman wishes to vote opposite the name of the tribesman in question in the list aforesaid, and such entry shall be deemed a duly recorded vote as though the tribesman had completed a ballot paper under the provisions of section 44 of this law.

(2) At the counting of votes, the Committee set up in accordance with sections 30 (1) and 59 shall, in the presence of the Registering Officers and of the chiefs or sub-chiefs, count up the number of times the name of each candidate has been entered on the list, and the candidate obtaining the highest number of entries in the Constituency (or corresponding tribal unit), shall be declared by the Returning Officer to be the duly elected representative for the Constituency (or corresponding tribal unit) concerned.

Application of other sections

61. The provisions of sections 33 (4), 36, 37, 42, 46, 47 (a) and (b), 49, 50, 52 of this law shall apply *mutatis mutandis* to elections in Rural Electoral Districts.

Part V

Irregularities

62. If during the elections and before the counting of votes any discrepancy or irregularity has occurred which might in the opinion of the Returning Officer and his Committee have affected the result, they shall enquire into the matter and forward a full report to the Supervisor-General, who shall decide whether or not the election is valid. If it is not valid, he shall order a fresh election to be held. The decision of the Supervisor-General in this matter shall be final.

Validity of membership

63. The House of Representatives alone is competent to decide upon the validity of the election of its members, and any elector may object to the validity of the election in his Constituency by submitting a petition to the President of the House within ten days from the date that the House is convened.

Incompatibility of Senators and others

64. (1) No Deputy may, at the same time, be either a Senator, a "Wali", a member of a Provincial Executive Council, a mayor, a member of a Municipal Council or the holder of any public office. All such persons, if they are nominated as candidates for election to the House of Representatives, shall immediately resign their posts.

(2) For the purposes of this law, the expression "holder of a public office" shall be deemed to mean all persons who are in receipt of a regular monthly

salary from the Government, provided that this definition does not conflict with the provisions of sub-section I, and provided also that it shall not include the Prime Minister and Ministers of the Federal Government and also tribal Mustashars and Sheikhs.

Forfeiture of membership

65. Any member of the House of Representatives who is found not to possess the qualifications for membership or who ceases to fulfil the conditions for membership provided in sections 3 and 4 of this law, owing to circumstances which were either not discovered until after his election or have arisen during his term of office, shall forfeit his membership. The decision concerning such forfeiture of membership shall be taken by the majority of all the members of the House of Representatives.

Qualifications of members of the Senate

66. A Senator must possess such qualifications as are provided in Article 96 of the Constitution and in subsections (a), (b) and (c) of section 3 of this law.

Part VI

PUBLIC SECURITY DURING ELECTIONS

Public security

67. The Minister of Justice shall be empowered, to issue orders regarding public security during the holding of elections; and to forbid any person to carry a firearm, stick, knife or other object capable of being used as an offensive weapon within the vicinity of any polling station or other electoral office.

Misbehaviour in polling station

68. A person who:

(a) Enters the place set aside for the ballot without right of entry and does not leave the place when ordered to do so by the Presiding Officer;

(b) Misbehaves at the place set apart for the ballot and does not obey the orders of the Presiding Officer in any way;

shall upon conviction by a competent Court be liable to a fine not exceeding ten Libyan pounds. Until the day of the coming into force of all the provisions of the Libyan Currency Law, the Libyan Pound shall, for the purposes of this law, mean—in Tripolitania 480 Military Authority Lire; in Cyrenaica 0.975 Pound Egyptian; in the Fezzan 980 Algerian Francs.

Part VII

OTHER ELECTION OFFENCES

Election offences

69. Any person who:

(a) Intentionally enters a name in any electoral register or part thereof or strikes out a name therefrom in contravention of the provisions of this law or intentionally fails to enter a name therein or strike out a name therefrom, or

(b) By force or threats, directly or indirectly, prevents an elector from using his right to vote or compels him to vote contrary to his wishes;

(c) Restrains the liberty of an elector in any way, or causes or threatens him material or moral harm, injury or loss;

(d) Intentionally misleads an elector as to his free right of voting or to prevent him from using such right, or in any way personates an elector;

(e) Directly or indirectly gives, lends, offers or undertakes to give an elector money or benefit or any other thing to induce him to vote in a special manner or to refrain from voting;

(f) Directly or indirectly accepts or asks for any money, benefit or any other thing for himself or any other person whether before, during or after the election for the purpose of using his vote for any particular candidate, to abstain from voting or to induce to vote for any particular candidate or to abstain from voting;

(g) Votes at the election knowing that his name has been entered unlawfully or wrongly in any electoral register or part thereof;

(h) Knowingly votes in the name of another or in the name of a fictitious person;

(i) Uses his right to vote more than once in one election;

(j) Steals, conceals, damages, spoils or forges an electoral register or part thereof, or an election paper, or any other document relating to the conduct of the election, or changes or seeks to change the result of any election by any means whatsoever, or with the intention of causing a new ballot to be taken;

(k) Enters the place set aside for the ballot carrying arms of any kind;

(l) Interferes with the freedom of an election or with the orderly conduct thereof by the use of force, threats, or by taking part in any demonstration or by unseemly or riotous conduct;

(m) Removes any box of ballot papers, or damages or opens such box without legal authority;

shall on conviction by a competent Court be liable to imprisonment for a period not exceeding one year or to a fine not exceeding one hundred Libyan pounds or both. Until the day of coming into force of all the provisions of the Libyan Currency Law, the Libyan Pound shall, for the purpose of this Law, mean—in Tripolitania 480 Military Authority Lire; in Cyrenaica 0.975 Pound Egyptian; in the Fezzan 980 Algerian Francs.

Violating secrecy of ballot

70. Any person who:

(a) Infringes the secrecy of the ballot or the secret of an elector's vote without his permission;

(b) Publishes or spreads before or during the election false statements regarding the conduct of a candidate, or his character in order to affect the result of the election;

shall on conviction by a competent Court be liable to imprisonment for a period not exceeding six months or to a fine not exceeding one hundred Libyan pounds or both. Until the day of coming into force of all the provisions of the Libyan Currency Law, the Libyan Pound shall, for the purposes of this Law, mean—in Tripolitania 480 Military Authority Lire; in Cyrenaica 0.975 Pound Egyptian; in the Fezzan 980 Algerian Francs.

The Libyan National Assembly approved this law, which was prepared by the

Provisional Federal Government in accordance with article 204 of the Libyan Constitution and submitted for approval on the 20th October 1951; and, after making suitable amendments, issued it as a law and empowered their President to sign it and to forward it to the Government for publication in the Official Gazette and for implementation in respect of the election to the first House of Representatives.

Issued in Tripoli on Tuesday the sixth of Safr Al Kheir 1371 corresponding to the sixth of November 1951.

(Signed) Mohamed Abu Al Asaad Al Alim
President of the National Assembly

SCHEDULE NO. 1 (SECTION 13 (2))

TOWN ELECTORAL DISTRICT OF. . . .

Form of application to be forwarded in pursuance of a notification under Section 13 (2)

To the Registering Officer of the . . . . Polling District (give the name of the polling district for which applicant is qualified to vote)

I apply to have my name inserted in the Register of Electors for the named district.

1. My full name is . . . .
   (give name, Christian or other names in full, surname first)
2. My father's name is . . . .
3. All notices relating to this application should be sent to me at
   . . . .
   (give full postal address)
4. I declare in support of my application that:

(i) I am a Libyan

(ii) I have completed my twenty-first year (Gregorian) on the first day of . . . . in this year.

(iii) I have been ordinarily resident at . . . . (state exact address or addresses of residence in the elected district) in the above-named electoral district for a period of . . . . immediately prior to the first day of . . . . in this year.

5. I have not signed any previous application during the year to be registered for the above electoral district.

Dated the . . . . day of . . . . 19. . . .

. . . .
(Signature or thumb print of applicant)

N. B.: No person can be registered who is:

(a) Serving a term of imprisonment;

(b) Has been declared to be a bankrupt and has not been discharged;

(c) Is a lunatic.

(This application must be signed in the presence of a person over 21 years of age who is able to read and write Arabic.)

SCHEDULE NO. 2 (SECTIONS 21 AND 56)

WRIT OF ELECTION

By the Minister of Justice

. . . .

To the Returning Officer of the
Urban } Electoral District of . . . .
Rural }

Whereas by sections 21 and 56 of the Electoral Law of 1951, it is provided that for the purpose of every general election of members of the House of Representatives and for the purposes of the election of members to supply vacancies caused by death, resignation or otherwise, the Minister of Justice shall issue writs addressed to the Returning Officer, of the respective Urban/Rural electoral districts for which members are to be returned;

And whereas I think it expedient that writs should be issued for the election of members to serve in the House of Representatives;

And whereas the seat of the Electoral Member for the constituency of. . . . . . has become vacant in consequence of . . . . ;

Now, therefore, I . . . . , Minister of Justice as aforesaid, do hereby require that, notice of the time and place fixed for the nomination of candidates having been first duly given as required by law, you do on the . . . . day of . . . . at . . . . in the said Urban/Rural Electoral District, cause election to be made according to law, of a member to serve in the House of Representatives for the said constituency and that, if necessary, you do cause the name of such member when so elected to be certified to the Supervisor General of Elections not later than the . . . .

(Signed). . . . .
Minister of Justice

SCHEDULE NO. 3 (SECTION 23 (3))

URBAN ELECTORAL DISTRICT OF . . . .

Nomination paper

We, the undersigned, electors for the constituency of . . . . do hereby nominate the following person as a proper person to serve as member of the House of Representatives for the said constituency of . . . . and we certify that to the best of our belief he is qualified for election as a member of the House of Representatives under the conditions prescribed by sections 4 and 23 of the Electoral Law of 1951.

Surname	*Other names*	*Address*	*Occupation*

. . . . Signature . . . . district (if any).

Number on Register of Electors and distinctive letter of polling

Proposer . . . .
Seconder . . . .

We, the undersigned, electors of the constituency of . . . . hereby assent to the foregoing nomination:–

1. . . . .
2. . . . .
3. . . . .
4. . . . .
5. . . . .
6. . . . .
7. . . . .
8. . . . .

I, ... nominated in the foregoing nomination paper hereby consent to such nomination as candidate for election as a member of the House of Representatives for the constituency of . . . . and name as my address for serving of process and papers under the Electoral Law,

Address . . . .
Witness my hand this . . . . *day of* . . . . *19*. . . . . .
Signed by the said nominee . . . .
in the presence of . . . .

(Signature of witness) *(Signature of candidate)*
. . . .

SCHEDULE NO. 4 (SECTION 23 (4))

URBAN ELECTORAL DISTRICT OF . . . .

Declaration of a person nominated as a candidate for election as a member of the House of Representatives

I, ...
of . . . . in the . . . .
of . . . . do solemnly and sincerely declare:

That I am duly qualified to be elected a member of the House of Representatives for this constituency and that:

1. I am a Libyan of the full age of thirty years and am qualified to be registered as an elector for the election of members of the House;
2. I am not an undischarged bankrupt, nor a lunatic, nor serving a term of imprisonment.

(Signed) . . . .
Declared before me this . . . . day of . . . . 19. . . .
(Signed) . . . .

SCHEDULE NO. 5 (SECTION 32)

Return where there are no more candidates than members to be elected

I certify that the member elected for the constituency of .... is .... of .... (give address) (as in nomination paper) no other candidate having been nominated (or the other candidates having withdrawn, as the case may be).

Dated at .... this .... day of ....

(Signed) ....

Returning Officer

Annex IV

PROCLAMATION OF LIBYAN INDEPENDENCE
By KING MOHAMED IDRISS AL MAHDI AL SENUSSI
at Benghazi, on 24 December 1951

IN THE NAME OF GOD, THE MERCIFUL, THE COMPASSIONATE, TO OUR NOBLE PEOPLE

We joyfully proclaim to the noble people of Libya that in fulfilment of their endeavours and of the United Nations Resolution of 21 November 1949, our beloved country has, with the help of God, attained independence.

We offer to Almighty God our prayers of heartfelt praise and thanksgiving for His blessings, and rejoice with the Libyan people upon this happy and historic occasion.

We formally proclaim that Libya has, from today, become an independent Sovereign State, and, in compliance with the Resolution of the Libyan National Assembly of 2nd December 1950, we take to ourself henceforth the title of His Majesty the King of the United Kingdom of Libya.

We welcome also the coming into force at this moment of the Constitution of the Country, as drawn up and promulgated by the National Assembly on the 6th day of Muharram in the year 1371 (7 October 1951). It is our wish, as you well know, that the life of the country should conform to true constitutional principles, and we intend henceforward to exercise our powers in accordance with the provisions of this Constitution.

At this solemn moment of our country's history, we pledge ourselves before God and the Nations to direct our every endeavour towards the interests and prosperity of our noble people in order that our high aims may be achieved and that our beloved country may attain the place it deserves among the free nations.

It is our duty one and all to preserve what we have gained at so dear a price, and to hand it down carefully and faithfully to our posterity.

At this blessed hour, we are mindful also of our heroes of the past. We invoke the dew of God's mercy and reward upon the souls of our righteous martyrs, and we salute the sacred banner, the legacy of our fathers and the hard-earned symbol of our unity, in the hope that the new era which dawns today will be for our country an era of well-being and of peace. We pray God that He may help us in this—and may bestow upon us prosperity and guidance, for the source of all help, indeed, is God.

Annex V

TRANSFER OF POWERS PROCLAMATION No. 4

Issued on 24 December 1951 by the British Residents for Tripolitania and for Cyrenaica and by the French Resident for the Fezzan

(a) BRITISH RESIDENCY, TRIPOLITANIA

Transfer of Powers (No. 4). Proclamation No. 223

Whereas by resolutions adopted by the General Assembly of the United Nations on 21 November 1949 and 17 November 1950 respectively, provision was made that Libya, comprising Cyrenaica, Tripolitania and the Fezzan, should become an independent State, on the completion of the action prescribed by the resolutions:

And whereas the Constitution of Libya has been duly determined in accordance with the aforesaid resolution of 21 November 1949, and was promulgated on 7 October 1951:

And whereas it is provided by the aforesaid resolution of 17 November 1950 that powers shall be progressively transferred to the Provisional Government of Libya by the Administering Powers in a manner which will ensure that all powers at present exercised by them shall, by 1 January 1952, have been transferred to the duly constituted Government, and that the United Nations Commissioner, aided and guided by the advice of members of the Council for Libya, shall proceed to draw up a programme in co-operation with the Administering Powers, for the transfer of powers as aforesaid:

And whereas in accordance with the programme for the transfer of powers which has been drawn up certain powers have already been transferred and it is now desired to transfer all remaining powers:

And whereas the authority to effect such transfer is vested in the British Resident, but the Tripolitanian Government has been consulted as regards matters within its competence and has signified its agreement:

And whereas it is provided by the Cyrenaica and Tripolitania (Termination of Administration) Order in Council, 1951, that the authority of His Majesty in Cyrenaica and Tripolitania shall terminate on such date as shall be proclaimed in those territories by the respective British Residents therein as the date on which all action required to be taken in those territories in order that the independence of Libya may become effective has been completed:

And whereas all such action will be completed by the issue of this Proclamation:

Now therefore the British Resident hereby proclaims as follows:

Short title

1. This Proclamation may be cited as the Transfer of Powers (No. 4) Proclamation No. 223.

Final transfer of power

2. To the intent that the independence of Libya shall become effective in the manner provided for in the resolutions adopted by the General Assembly of the United Nations on 21 November 1949 and 17 November 1950 respectively, all powers which under the Libyan Constitution are to be exercised by the Federal Government of Libya, and which are not already possessed by the Provisional Government of Libya, are hereby transferred to the Provisional Government of Libya and all powers which under the Libyan Constitution are to be exercised by the Province of Tripolitania and which are not already possessed by the Province of Tripolitania, are hereby transferred to the Province of Tripolitania.

Termination of authority of His Britannic Majesty

3. The date of this Proclamation is hereby proclaimed, for the purposes of the Cyrenaica and Tripolitania (Termination of Administration) Order in Council 1951, to be the date on which all action required to be taken in those territories in order that the independence of Libya may become effective has been completed.

Dated at Tripoli this 24th day of December 1951.

(Signed) T. R. BLACKLEY
British Resident

(b) BRITISH RESIDENCY, CYRENAICA

Transfer of Powers (No. 4) Proclamation No. 194

Whereas by resolutions adopted by the General Assembly of the United Nations on 21 November 1949 and 17 November 1950 respectively, provision was made that Libya, comprising Cyrenaica, Tripolitania and the Fezzan, should become an independent State on the completion of the action prescribed by the resolutions:

And whereas the Constitution of Libya has been duly determined in accordance with the aforesaid resolution of 21 November 1949, and was promulgated on 7 October 1951:

And whereas it is provided by the aforesaid resolution of 17 November 1950 that powers shall be progressively transferred to the Provisional Government of Libya by the Administering Powers in a manner which will ensure that all powers at present exercised by them shall, by 1 January 1952, have been transferred to the duly constituted Government, and that the United Nations Commissioner, aided and guided by the advice of members of the Council for Libya, shall proceed to draw up a programme in co-operation with the Administering Powers, for the transfer of powers as aforesaid:

And whereas in accordance with the programme for the transfer of powers which has been drawn up certain powers have already been transferred and it is now desired to transfer all remaining powers:

And whereas the authority to effect such transfer is vested in the British

Resident but, under Article 14 of the Transitional Powers Proclamation, the prior agreement of His Highness the Amir is necessary as regards internal affairs:

And whereas His Highness the Amir has signified his agreement as aforesaid:

And whereas it is provided by the Cyrenaica and Tripolitania (Termination of Administration) Order in Council 1951, that the authority of His Majesty in Cyrenaica and Tripolitania shall terminate on such date as shall be proclaimed in those territories by the respective British Residents therein as the date on which all action required to be taken in those territories in order that the independence of Libya may become effective has been completed:

And whereas all such action will be completed by the issue of this Proclamation:

Now therefore the British Resident hereby proclaims as follows:

Short title

1. This Proclamation may be cited as the Transfer of Powers (No. 4) Proclamation No. 194.

Final transfer of power

2. To the intent that the independence of Libya shall become effective in the manner provided for in the resolutions adopted by the General Assembly of the United Nations on 21 November 1949 and 17 November 1950 respectively, all powers which under the Libyan Constitution are to be exercised by the Federal Government of Libya, and which are not already possessed by the Provisional Government of Libya, are hereby transferred to the Provisional Government of Libya, and all powers which under the Libyan Constitution are to be exercised by the Province of Cyrenaica and which are not already possessed by the Province of Cyrenaica are hereby transferred to the Province of Cyrenaica.

Termination of authority of His Britannic Majesty

3. The date of this Proclamation is hereby proclaimed for the purposes of the Cyrenaica and Tripolitania (Termination of Administration) Order in Council 1951, to be the date on which all action required to be taken in those territories in order that the independence of Libya may become effective has been completed.

Made by me at Benghazzi, Cyrenaica, this 24th day of December, 1951.

(Signed) E. A. V. de CANDOLE
British Resident

(c) FRENCH RESIDENCY

Proclamation Number Four

Whereas by resolutions adopted by the General Assembly of the United Nations on 21 November 1949 and 17 November 1950 respectively, provision was made that Libya, comprising Cyrenaica, Tripolitania and the Fezzan, should become an independent State on the completion of the action prescribed by the resolutions:

And whereas the Constitution of Libya has been duly determined, in accordance with the requirements of the aforesaid resolution of 21 November 1949 and was promulgated on 7 October 1951:

And whereas it is provided, by the aforesaid resolution of 17 November 1950, that powers shall be progressively transferred to the Provisional Government of Libya by the Administering Powers in a manner which will ensure that all powers at present exercised by them shall by 1 January 1952 have been transferred to a duly constituted Government and that the United Nations Commissioner, aided and guided by the advice of the members of the Council for Libya, shall proceed to draw up a programme in co-operation with the Administering Powers, for the transfer of powers as aforesaid:

And whereas in accordance with the programme for the transfer of powers which has been drawn up certain powers have already been transferred and it is now desired to transfer all remaining powers:

And whereas the authority to effect such transfer is vested in the French Resident in the Fezzan, but the Fezzanese Government has been consulted as regards matters within its competence and has signified its agreement:

And whereas the Governor General of Algeria has authorized the French Resident in the Fezzan to transfer to the Libyan Government the last group of powers which he is still exercising in the name of the Administering Powers:

Now therefore the French Resident in the Fezzan hereby proclaims as follows:

1. This proclamation may be cited as the Transfer of Powers (No.4) Proclamation.

2. To the intent that the independence of Libya shall become effective in the manner provided for in the resolutions adopted by the General Assembly of the United Nations on 21 November 1949 and 17 November 1950 respectively, all powers which under the Libyan Constitution are to be exercised by the Federal Government of Libya, and which are not already possessed by the Provisional Government of Libya, are hereby transferred to the Provisional Government of Libya, and all powers which under the Libyan Constitution are to be exercised by the Province of the Fezzan and which are not already possessed by the Province of the Fezzan, are hereby transferred to the Province of the Fezzan.

3. From the date of this Proclamation all powers retained by the Administering Power shall have been transferred in such manner that the independence of Libya shall become effective.

Dated at Sabha this 24th day of December 1951.

(Signed) CAUNEILLE
French Resident

Annex VI

CYRENAICA AND TRIPOLITANIA (TERMINATION OF ADMINISTRATION) ORDER IN COUNCIL, 1951

At the Court of Buckingham Palace, the 4th Day of December, 1951

Present: THE KING'S MOST EXCELLENT MAJESTY IN COUNCIL

Whereas by the Cyrenaica and Tripolitania (Administration) Order in Council, 1949 (hereinafter referred to as "the Principal Order"), provision was made for the exercise of the authority of His Majesty in each of the territories of Cyrenaica and Tripolitania by a Chief Administrator appointed for that purpose by, and responsible to, His Majesty's Principal Secretary of State for Foreign Affairs;

And whereas the Principal Order was amended in its application to Cyrenaica by the Cyrenaica and Tripolitania (Administration) (Amendment) Order in Council, 1949;

And whereas the Principal Order was amended in its application to Tripolitania by the Cyrenaica and Tripolitania (Administration) (Amendment) Order in Council, 1951;

And whereas provision was, *inter alia,* made by the two amending Orders in Council aforesaid that the title of the Chief Administrator in Cyrenaica and Tripolitania respectively should be changed to that of British Resident;

And whereas by resolutions adopted, in pursuance of the Joint Declaration which forms Annex XI of the Treaty of Peace with Italy signed on the 10th day of February, 1947 (*a*), by the General Assembly of the United Nations on the 21st day of November, 1949, and the 17th day of November, 1950, respectively, it was provided that Libya, comprising Cyrenaica, Tripolitania and the Fezzan, should become an independent and sovereign State on completion of the action prescribed by the said resolutions with a view to the independence of Libya becoming effective;

And whereas all such action will shortly be completed;

Now therefore, His Majesty, in exercise of all powers enabling Him, in that behalf, is pleased, by and with the advice of His Privy Council, to order, and it is hereby ordered as follows:

Short title

1. This Order may be cited as the Cyrenaica and Tripolitania (Termination of Administration) Order in Council, 1951;

Termination of authority

2. The authority of His Majesty in Cyrenaica and Tripolitania shall terminate

on such date as shall be proclaimed in those territories by the respective British Residents therein as the date on which all action prescribed to be taken in those territories in order that the independence of Libya may become effective has been completed.

(Signed) F. J. FERNAU

Annex VII

TEMPORARY AGREEMENT BETWEEN THE GOVERNMENT OF THE UNITED KINGDOM OF GREAT BRITAIN AND NORTHERN IRELAND AND THE LIBYAN GOVERNMENT REGARDING FINANCIAL ASSISTANCE TO LIBYA TO BE PROVIDED BY THE GOVERNMENT OF THE UNITED KINGDOM OF GREAT BRITAIN AND NORTHERN IRELAND

13 December 1951

Interpretation

ARTICLE 1

In this Agreement

"The United Kingdom Government" means the Government of the United Kingdom of Great Britain and Northern Ireland;

"The Libyan Government" means the Provisional Government of Libya until Libya becomes independent, and thereafter means the Federal Government of Libya.

"The Provincial Administrations" means the local Governments or Administrations of Cyrenaica, Tripolitania and the Fezzan;

"The Currency Commission" means the Currency Commission, the constitution, powers and duties of which are provided for in the Currency Law enacted by the Libyan Government in [*sic*] the 24th day of October 1951;

"The initial issue of Libyan currency" means all Libyan currency notes and coins issued by the Currency Commission against Military Administration lire notes, Egyptian currency notes and Algerian franc notes which are tendered in Libya within such period or periods from the date on which the Libyan pound becomes the standard of currency in Libya as the Currency Commission may in its discretion determine.

Coming into force and duration of Agreement

ARTICLE 2

This Agreement shall come into force upon signature and shall continue in force until 31 March 1953, unless previously replaced by an Agreement between the United Kingdom and Libyan Governments.

Purpose of Agreement

ARTICLE 3

This Agreement is made to ensure that Libya shall enjoy conditions of financial stability and orderly economic development.

Obligations of the United Kingdom Government

ARTICLE 4

In order to carry out the purpose set out in Article 3 of this Agreement, the United Kingdom Government will, provided Libyan financial affairs are being conducted in a manner appropriate for the achievement of that purpose and provided that the United Kingdom Government is informed fully of Libya's needs, give financial assistance to Libya as follows:

(a) The United Kingdom Government will contribute during the financial year beginning on 1 April 1952, to the Development and Stabilisation Agency which is to be established under Libyan Law, and may contribute during the financial year beginning on 1 April 1952, to the Finance Corporation which is to be so established, sums not exceeding £500,000 sterling in the aggregate for the purposes for which those organisations are to be established and in conformity with their statutes;

(b) The United Kingdom Government will provide one hundred per centum sterling backing for the initial issue of Libyan currency in accordance with arrangements acceptable to the United Kingdom and Libyan Governments;

(c) Until 31 March 1952, the United Kingdom Government will continue to give financial assistance to the Governments or Administrations of Cyrenaica and Tripolitania, it being the intention that the Provincial Administration will, out of their general revenues, finance the Libyan Government in order to enable the Libyan Government to exercise the powers progressively transferred to it;

(d) As regards the financial year beginning on 1 April 1952, if, without prejudice to the undoubted right of Libya to determine its own budgets, there is agreement between the United Kingdom and Libyan Governments that the budgets of the Libyan Government and the Provincial Administrations for that year have been framed prudently, economically and with regard to the purpose set out in article 3 of this Agreement, the United Kingdom Government will make a contribution to the Libyan Government of a sum equal to any deficiency in the combined Budgets provided the Libyan Government requests such a contribution. In the event that agreement is not reached, the United Kingdom Government will nevertheless make a contribution to the Libyan Government of any sum essential to support the Libyan economy provided the Libyan Government requests such a contribution.

Obligations of the Libyan Government

ARTICLE 5

In order further to carry out the purpose set out in article 3 of this Agreement, the Libyan Government agrees that there shall be a Chief Financial and Economic Officer and an Auditor General, who shall be officers of the Libyan Government and subject to the Civil Service Laws of Libya. All matters relating to their appointments shall be the subject of consultation between the United Kingdom and Libyan Governments.

Duties of the Chief Financial and Economic Officer and Auditor General

ARTICLE 6

(a) The Chief Financial and Economic Officer shall have access to the Prime Minister and the Minister of Finance of the Libyan Government. He shall be the principal financial and economic officer of that Government.

(b) The Auditor General shall be the principal auditor of the Libyan Government.

Signed at Tripoli, this 13th day of December 1951.

For the Libyan Government
(Signed) Mahmoud MUNTASSAR
Prime Minister

For the United Kingdom Government
(Signed) T. R. BLACKLEY
British Resident Tripolitania

Annex VIII

TEMPORARY AGREEMENT BETWEEN THE GOVERNMENT OF FRANCE AND THE LIBYAN GOVERNMENT REGARDING FINANCIAL ASSISTANCE TO LIBYA TO BE PROVIDED BY THE GOVERNMENT OF FRANCE

14 December 1951

Your Excellency,

I have the honour to acknowledge receipt of your letter of 13 December 1951, which states as follows:

"During the exchange of views which I have had with your Excellency, I have had occasion to inform your Excellency of the importance that my Government attaches to the harmonious development of the Libyan economy.

"It is in this development of Libya's resources and in the creation of the prerequisites for an administration adapted to the needs of a modern economy, that the Government of the Republic sees the best guarantees that Libya's progress and development in accordance with the very spirit of the United Nations resolution of 21 November 1949 will become increasingly marked. My Government has instructed me to inform Your Excellency that it will be happy to grant Libya financial assistance within the limits of the budgetary credits allocated by the Parliament of the Republic of France and in accordance with the following provisions:

"1. Until 31 March 1952, the French Government will continue to give direct financial assistance to ensure the functioning of the administrative services in the Fezzan and the economic and social development of that province, to the extent to which the expenses relating thereto cannot be met from the resources of the Provincial Administration of the Fezzan.

"2. With regard to the period from 1 April 1952 to 31 March 1953, the French Government, conscious of the needs which its representatives noted in the Fezzan during the time when France was responsible for the provisional administration of the province, and with a view to continuing the work undertaken by France will give the Libyan Government the financial assistance, which the latter may request and which in conformity with the provisions of article 174 of the Libyan Federal Constitution, it shall apply to the Federal budget to cover the deficit on the Fezzanese budget and to ensure the economic and social development of that province.

"Part of this assistance may be in the form of a contribution to the Development and Stabilization Agency to be established in Libya to meet the expenses which the aforesaid Agency incurs in the development of the country, such contribution being made in accordance with the Statutes of the said Agency.

"The amount of this assistance for the period in question shall be determined by agreement between the French Government and the Libyan Government.

"3. The Libyan Government shall appoint an official of French nationality who shall primarily be responsible for economic and financial questions relating to the Fezzan. The name of this official shall be put forward by the French Government. He shall be an officer of the Libyan Government and subject to the Civil Service Laws of Libya.

"The French official responsible for economic and financial questions relating to the Fezzan shall have access to the Prime Minister and the Minister of Finance but he shall keep the Chief Financial and Economic Officer informed of his proposals so that the latter may consider them within the framework of Libya's general financial and economic position.

"I would be grateful if you would inform me of your Government's acceptance, on the above conditions, of the financial assistance offered to it by the French Government.

"The provisional agreement thus hereby reached by exchange of letters shall come into force immediately. It shall continue in force until 31 March 1953, unless previously replaced by an agreement between the French and Libyan Governments".

I have the honour to inform you that the Provisional Libyan Government accepts the financial assistance offered by the French Government, on the conditions specified above.

The agreement thus reached by exchange of letters shall come into force immediately and shall continue in force until 31 March 1953, unless previously replaced by an agreement between the French and Libyan Governments.

I have the honour to be
Your Excellency,
Your obedient servant,
(Signed) Mahmoud MUNTASSER

M. Georges BALAY,
Ambassador of France,
Tripoli

Annex IX

TEXT OF A STATEMENT PROVIDED FOR THE COUNCIL FOR LIBYA BY THE LEGAL ADVISER TO THE UNITED NATIONS LIBYAN MISSION ON THE LEGAL ASPECTS OF THE QUESTION OF INTERPRETATION OF THE EXPRESSION "DULY CONSTITUTED LIBYAN GOVERNMENT," RAISED IN A REQUEST FOR ADVICE OF THE COMMISSIONER *

PRELIMINARY REMARKS

May I be permitted to preface my observations with a few preliminary remarks. The representative of Pakistan, who was the first at yesterday's meeting to request that a legal opinion be given to the Council, referred to a passage in the draft report of the Commissioner to the General Assembly, which indicates that the Commissioner had sought legal advice on the meaning of the expression "a duly constituted Libyan Government" and that the Commissioner had envisaged the possibility of submitting a legal opinion on that question to the Prime Minister of the Provisional Libyan Government and to the Council at its present session. That was the intention of the Commissioner at the time his report to the General Assembly was being drafted. Realizing, however, the complexity of the problem and its special political importance, the Commissioner decided to submit the matter for advice to the Council and no legal opinion has been formulated in a written form in the name of the Commissioner nor has it been transmitted to the Prime Minister of the Provisional Libyan Government.

I hope, nevertheless, that my observations may be of some assistance to the Council in formulating their opinion on the questions raised by the Commissioner. As stated already by the representative of the Commissioner and by various members of the Council, the question is not a purely legal one; it has many far-reaching political implications, and I trust that the Council will be aware that my situation in appearing before it on this occasion is a delicate one as I have to limit myself rigidly to the legal aspects of the problem and avoid any political aspects it may have. My position is not made any easier by the fact that several members of the Council have already expressed their views on the problem and supported them by an impressive argumentation, eloquently presented to the Council.

* This statement was to have been made at the eighty-seventh meeting of the Council for Libya but could not be delivered for lack of time. It was therefore circulated in typescript to the members of the Council on 3 October 1951, as United Nations Doc. A/AC.32/COUNCIL/R. 163.

May I in this connexion recall, although this is hardly necessary in the case of those of the members of the Council who, like the representative of Pakistan, have participated in the work of other important United Nations organs—but because this may correct an impression which might have been created by recent debates—that legal advisers of the United Nations Secretariat appearing before United Nations bodies are bound to observe the strictest impartiality and objectivity and base their reasoning on purely legal considerations. Like all other members of the Secretariat, they are specifically forbidden by the United Nations Charter to receive instructions from governments or authorities external to the Organization. In giving advice their only purpose is to assist the organs they serve and their views, although they are habitually given serious consideration, are not binding on the organs to which they are submitted.

In presenting usefully a legal opinion at this stage on the factors which the Council should take into consideration before arriving at a conclusion on the question of the "duly constituted Libyan Government" one has to consider the problem as it presents itself at this moment to the Council and not as to what it could have been if the resolution of the General Assembly had been implemented in a different way than has been the case. Nor can such an opinion presented on the basis of the situation described in the Commissioner's request for advice be necessarily applicable if that situation were to change in some important respects or if the responsibilities of United Nations organs other than the Council or the Commissioner were involved. The basis of an opinion given at the present juncture must necessarily be the text of the two relevant General Assembly resolutions in the light of the intentions of their authors as stated in the Official Records of the discussion in the General Assembly, and with the consideration given to the various stages reached up to date in the implementation of the resolutions. It is, for instance, not necessary at this time to examine from the legal point of view the question whether the National Assembly, which is now putting the final touches to a Libyan constitution is "the National Assembly duly representative of the inhabitants of Libya", to which reference is made in paragraph 3 (*a*) of resolution 387 (V). It is sufficient to note that this view is accepted by the administrative Powers, the United Nations Commissioner and the Council itself. (See in particular the advice of the Council to the Commissioner dated 13 March 1951.)

OBSERVATIONS

1. In examining the text of the two relevant General Assembly resolutions, one first notes the special emphasis in the text of paragraph 2 of resolution 289 (IV) which states that the "independence of Libya shall become effective as soon as possible and *in any case* not later than 1 January 1952". This may be considered in the light of the discussion in the General Assembly as the major decision of principle reached by the Assembly at its fourth session with respect to Libya and one does not find in the text of the resolution any explicit qualification to this decision or any condition directly attached to it.

It does not seem necessary to analyse at this stage what would the powers of the General Assembly be should it wish to alter at its sixth session this basic decision with respect to the date at which Libya is to be independent. Should it be considered that the Assembly has the power to modify its previous decisions with respect to Libya, it might possibly be open to the Commissioner or to a member or members of the Council to make the General Assembly appropriate suggestions in this respect. Under the present text of the resolution, however, such an eventuality cannot, in my opinion, be envisaged for the purpose of this opinion, unless it is felt that there are essential and insuperable obstacles to the fulfilment of the General Assembly's major purpose with respect to Libya.

2. Pursuing this examination of resolution 289 (IV), one notes that the second major decision of the Assembly is "that a constitution of Libya, including the form of government, shall be determined by representatives of the inhabitants meeting and consulting together in a National Assembly".

The intention of the General Assembly is therefore again clear that the general structure of the Libyan State, its "constitution" and its "form of government" should not be decided upon by the General Assembly itself, nor by any other authority other than the Libyan National Assembly, and that the role of the organs the General Assembly has created for Libya, the United Nations Commissioner and the Council, is to "assist, to aid and to advise" the Libyan people and not to "decide" on this matter on their behalf. Here again, it is not necessary to analyse what might be the powers of the General Assembly in this respect at its sixth session and to what extent it may or may not ascertain whether the Libyan National Assembly has given effect to its decisions and intentions. The Council and the Commissioner can only take into account the fact that, under the General Assembly resolution, it is the National Assembly which has been given the responsibility of deciding upon the form of government in Libya.

3. If these conclusions are accepted, one needs only to examine how do the decisions of the National Assembly affect the problem now under the Council's consideration.

One then notes the decision of the National Assembly of 2 December 1950 that Libya should become a federal, democratic, independent, and sovereign State, its proclamation of His Highness the Amir of Cyrenaica as the constitutional King of the United Kingdom of Libya, and the acceptance by the Amir on 17 December 1950 of the throne and the postponement by him of the official declaration thereof to the appropriate time.

There is, further, the decision of the National Assembly to establish, in pursuance of the United Nations resolution, a provisional federal government having, in particular, the right to receive progressively governmental powers from the two administering States; and the determination by the National Assembly on 18 August 1951 of the respective powers of the Federal Government and of the provincial administrations. There is finally the draft Libyan constitution prepared by the Constitutional Committee of the National Assembly.

Should this draft constitution be finally approved by the National Assembly, what would the situation be in relation to the problem of determining as to what would be the "duly constituted Libyan Government"?

4. During the consultations which the Commissioner had on this problem, one of the questions which was raised was whether the expression "government" should be taken in a broad sense as including all the principal organs established by the Constitution: the King, the Council of Ministers, the two Houses of Parliament and the Federal Supreme Court, or should it be understood in a narrower sense as meaning the executive branch of the Government, the one which in particular enters into relationship with foreign governments and more generally represents a country in its foreign relations.

It seemed to us that there were no conclusive grounds on which to base our interpretation on the broader meaning sometimes given to the expression "government" and that the duly constituted government could therefore be understood in its more generally accepted sense as being the executive branch, provided it was established and functioned in accordance with the constitution.

What factors are then to be taken into consideration in this respect on the basis of the draft constitution submitted for final approval by the National Assembly now assembling in Benghazi?

It shall not repeat the data already furnished to the Council . . . but simply try to supplement them as may be necessary in order to arrive at conclusions.

The executive power is to be exercised by the King within the limits of the constitution (article 42). It is true that it is provided in article 47 that, before assuming his constitutional powers, the King has to take an oath before a joint session of the Senate and the House of Representatives. This article, however, must be considered together with article 210, which is one of the transitory provisions which are to come into force on the date of promulgation of the constitution and which states that "Notwithstanding the provisions contained in article 47 . . . the first King of the United Kingdom of Libya shall exercise his constitutional powers upon the declaration of independence provided that he shall take the prescribed oath before Parliament at its first session in a joint meeting". It is, therefore, the declared intention of the Constitutional Committee of the National Assembly that the King should have the full exercise of his constitutional rights at the time of the declaration of independence, whether or not Parliament is constituted by that time.

Article 85 of the Constitution provides that all acts of the King except those relating to the appointment of Ministers can produce effect only if they are countersigned by the Prime Minister and the competent Ministers. The Prime Minister is appointed by the King and the other Ministers by the King upon the proposal of the Prime Minister. The Council of Ministers can, therefore be established immediately upon the declaration of independence. Article 204, to which reference was made in the Council, may only be understood as an affirmation by the National Assembly that under the constitution it will approve, the King will immediately upon independence have the powers of appointing members of the first Council of Ministers of independent Libya.

Under the proposed constitution, Parliament has certain powers in relation to the Council of Ministers. The most important is the power of the House of Representatives to pass a vote of no confidence in the Council of Ministers or one of the Ministers which results in their resignation (article 87); each member of Parliament may address questions or interpolations to Ministers (article 123) and each Chamber has the right of investigation (article 124).

The transitory provisions provide that the members of the first Senate shall be appointed by the King. The members of the House of Representatives are to be elected. It results, however, from the time limits fixed by the constitution and from the memorandum of the Commissioner that the first elections may not take place before the date fixed by the National Assembly for Libyan independence.

5. What are the conclusions to be drawn from a study of these provisions?

It may first be noted that under the proposed text of the Libyan constitution, the elected Chamber would not immediately possess the same degree of power and influence in the process of the formation of a Council of Ministers as is enjoyed by Parliaments in certain other countries which have adopted and practised the system of constitutional monarchy. The Libyan Council of Ministers does apparently not require an affirmative vote of confidence of the House of Representatives before assuming the exercise of its constitutional functions. The initiative of a proposal of a vote of non-confidence must be taken by fifteen members of the House of Representatives on conditions provided in article 87 of the Constitution. It seems correct to assume that, until such a motion of non-confidence is approved, the Council of Ministers would remain in power and would continue to exercise validly its functions as long as it would retain the confidence of the King (article 72).

The provisions of article 64 of the Constitution may also be mentioned. Under the draft constitution, Parliament is to meet in regular session and it may also meet in extraordinary sessions. With respect to intervals between such sessions, article 64 provides that "If, when Parliament is not in session, exceptional circumstances arise which necessitate urgent measures, the King may issue decrees in respect thereof which shall have the force of law provided that they are not contrary to the provisions of this Constitution. Such decrees must be submitted to Parliament at its first meeting; if they are not submitted to Parliament or if they are not approved by either of the Chambers they shall cease to have the force of law".

Although this article does not apply to the case under consideration, it is significant to note that the proposed Libyan constitutional system envisages the contingency of certain legislative functions of Parliament being exercised temporarily and subject to confirmation by Parliament, by the King and the Ministers.

Such constitutional situations are not unknown in democratic countries, whether in normal times or during periods of emergency when it is not possible to call a session of Parliament. Recent cases of complete impossibility of convening the House of Parliament are those experienced by governments of countries occupied by the Axis States during the last war and which sought refuge on allied territory and exercised functions of Government, both executive and legislative, until such time as their territory was liberated, and which sought confirmation of the legislation enacted during the period of emergency as soon as their Parliaments could resume the exercise of their functions.

The constitutional history of new States having gained independence shows many examples of transitional periods during which, until Parliamentary organs could be elected, legislative as well as executive powers were concentrated provisionally in the hands of the Government. The specific assurance inserted in the draft Libyan constitution that the Libyan Parliament will be constituted and in a position to exercise its consitutional functions within a specific period, is significant in this respect.

6. In the light of these considerations and placing oneself on purely legal grounds, it would seem therefore possible to conclude that under the provisions of the General Assembly resolutions with respect to Libya, a government constituted in accordance with the transitory provisions proposed by the Constitutional Committee for the approval of the National Assembly could be considered as the duly constituted government for the purposes provided in paragraph 10 (*a*) of General Assembly resolution 289 (IV) and 3 (*c*) of resolution 387 (V).

Annex X

UNITED NATIONS DOCUMENTATION *

The documentation of the Council for Libya and related and other bodies dealing with the Libyan problem, 1949–1952 *

1. The First, Second, Fifth, and Sixth Standing Committees of the General Assembly (GA) were, at different times and to differing degrees, called upon to deal with Libyan matters.

2. Two ad hoc committees of the GA were also called upon: The *Ad Hoc* Political Committee (A/AC.28/. . . . .) and the Interim Committee (A/AC.18/ . . . . . .).

3. Both the *Ad Hoc* Political Committee and the Political Committee itself set up, at one time or another, sub-committees to handle specific aspects of the problem: Sub-Committee 1, and Sub-Committees 15 and 17 respectively (A/AC.38/SC.1/. . . . . , A/C.1/SC.15/. . . . and A/C.1/SC.17).

4. The Advisory Committee on Administrative and Budgetary Questions (ACABQ) dealt with the budget of the UN Mission in Libya; its reports were issued in the Fifth Committee series (A/C.5/. . . . .).

5. The Council for Libya, being an ad hoc organ set up by the GA—i.e. one with a determined, even if indefinite life—was allotted a main symbol in the series reserved for such bodies. This, the key signature, so to speak, for the Libyan documentation, was A/AC.32/. . . . . To this was added the word COUNCIL/ for the latter's own documentation (A/AC.32/COUNCIL/. . . .). This series was further subdivided to meet specific needs, e.g. A/AC.32/COUNCIL/ CC/. . . . . , for the Coordination Committee. Branch series were also set up to cover certain ancillary fields, e.g. A/AC.32/COUNCIL/INF . . . . . , for documents put out by the Mission Information Officers, and A/AC.32/TA/. . . . . . , for technical assistance papers.

6. The final disposal of a UN document naturally depends on its importance. Thus the proceedings and main documentation of the GA and ECOSOC and their principal committees are finally published as the printed Official Records of the Assembly (GAOR) and of ECOSOC. Less important papers, including the great mass of the Council for Libya's documentation, never get beyond the mimeographed form, though bound collections of the documents in the A/. . . . and E/. . . . . which are not printed in the Official Records can be found in the UN Libraries at New York and Geneva. Ephemeral productions, such as press releases and other information documents, are not usually retained in the

* See also Preface, pp. xvi–xx.

United Nations Archives. Finally, such material as the Loutfi Papers, the notes of private meetings taken by members of the staff of the UN Mission in Libya, biographical notes on Libyan personalities, and the like, have usually, though not invariably, been preserved in the United Nations Archives.

7. The following enumeration, by no means exhaustive, gives information about the main documentation series referred to in *Libyan Independence and the United Nations:*

General Assembly (Fourth, Fifth, and Sixth Sessions)

GAOR, Supplements (A/..... series), Annual Reports of the Secretary-General; Annual Reports of the UN Commissioner in Libya

GAOR, Verbatim Records of Plenary Meetings (A/PV..... series)

GAOR, Summary Records of Plenary Meetings (A/SR..... series)

GAOR, Annexes, General Documentation (A/..... series), where not reproduced as Supplements

GAOR, First Committee, Summary Records of Meetings (A/C.1/SR..... series)

GAOR, First Committee, General documentation (A/C.1/..... series) Annexes to Summary Records of Meetings

(Similarly for: *Ad Hoc* Political Committee (A/AC.38/..... series)

Interim Committee	(A/AC.18/..... series)
Second Committee	(A/C.2/..... series)
Fifth Committee	(A/C.5/..... series)
Sixth Committee	(A/C.6/..... series)

United Nations Tribunal in Libya (Fifth Session of GA onward)

General documentation (A/AC.51/R..... series)

Note: Also published in A/AC.32/COUNCIL/Trib/..... series;

ECOSOC (Eleventh and Thirteenth Sessions)

Summary records of Council meetings (E/SR..... series)

General documentation (E/..... series)

Technical Assistance Committee records and documents (E/TAC/SR..... and E/TAC/..... series)

Official Records, ECOSOC, Supplement No. 1 (*Resolutions*)

United Nations Council for Libya

Note: All of this documentation is *mimeographed.*

	Series
Summary Records of Meetings	A/AC.32/COUNCIL/SR . . .
General documentation	A/AC.32/COUNCIL/R . . .
Working documents	A/AC.32/COUNCIL/W . . .
Council agenda	A/AC.32/COUNCIL/AGENDA
Council information	A/AC.32/COUNCIL/INF/R . . .
Council communications	A/AC.32/COUNCIL/R . . .
Coordination Committee:	
Minutes of meetings	A/AC.32/COUNCIL/CC/MIN/. . .
General documentation	A/AC.32/COUNCIL/CC/R . . .
Working documents	A/AC.32/COUNCIL/CC/W. . .

Establishment Committee:

Legal Sub-Committee A/AC.32/COUNCIL/CC/C.1/. . .

Financial Sub-Committee A/AC.32/COUNCIL/CC/C.2/. . .

Meeting of Experts on Libyan Monetary, Financial, and Development Problems Q/AC.32/MON/R . . .

Information documents A/AC.32/COUNCIL/INF . . .

Technical assistance documents A/AC.32/COUNCIL/TA . . .

Secretariat documents A/AC.32/COUNCIL/SEC . . .

UN Tribunal in Libya (see above) A/AC.32/COUNCIL/TRIB . . .

Other series:

UN Technical Assistance Mission to Libya (TAB/R . . . (TAB/INF/E/LIBYA R . . .

Note: All other sources directly connected with the Mission or with the Council for Libya are in manuscript or typescript in the United Nations Archives.

Annex XI

ITALIAN LEGISLATION RELATING TO NATIONALITY AND MINORITIES IN LIBYA, 1934–1950 [1]

A. The relevant Italian laws are the following:
Royal Decree No. 2012, 3 December 1934, on Libyan Nationality (this became Law No. 675 on 11 April 1935/XIV [*Ordinamento organico della Libia*])
Royal Decree No. 70, 9 January 1939/XVII, incorporating the four Libyan Provinces into the Kingdom of Italy
B. The following commentaries summarize the views of various bodies and authorities on this legislation.
C. The Commissioner, in his first annual report, observed:

> Legislation which was in force at the time of occupation remained valid, unless altered or over-ridden by proclamation of the Chief Administrator. In particular, laws of evident fascist ideology were revoked. Islamic and Jewish laws continued to apply for matters relating to the personal status of the members of the communities concerned.[2]

D. The modifications introduced by the British Administration were explained to the Commissioner as follows:
When the British Administration was established, the status of Tripolitania was that of an enemy-occupied territory, and under the provisions of international law it was, as the British Government understood the matter, incumbent upon the occupying Power to maintain in force, as far as possible, the existing laws. The British Military Administration therefore took over not only the *corpus* of law under which the people of the country lived, but also the system of administration established by the Italian Government, superimposing thereon British control. There were, of course, changes; in particular, the privileged position enjoyed by Italians was much modified. Italian law, however, continued to be administered where it had previously been applicable, but was modified and extended by proclamation as occasion demanded.
E. The Four Power Commission of Investigation for the Former Italian Colonies describes the judicial situation in Tripolitania as follows:

> In Tripolitania the following law is in force:
> (a) *British Law*: enacted in Proclamations and Regulations of the Chief Administrator.
> (b) *Italian Law*: issued prior to 23rd January, 1943, except that having an

1. See Chapter 4, fn. 38 and pp. 342 ff.
2. First *Annual Report of the United Nations Commissioner in Libya,* GAOR, Fifth Session, 1950, Supplement No. 15 (A/1340), para. 51.

obvious Fascist character; otherwise Italian laws have been amended only as necessitated by military circumstances.

(c) *Moslem and Jewish Law*: applied only by the Sharia Courts and the Rabbinical Courts respectively.[3]

There follows a description of the various courts: military (general and summary), Italian (civil and penal), Ahlya, Shari'a, and Rabbinical.

F. In Cyrenaica, the situation from 1943 onward was somewhat different. The Four Power Commission notes in the section headed *Administration of Justice*:

British Law

Enacted by means of Proclamations and Regulations made by the Chief Administrator under the authority of the Commander-in-Chief Middle East Land Forces.

Italian civil law

In accordance with a Proclamation by the Chief Administrator (No. 81 of 17th November, 1945) all laws of the territory which were in force at the time of the occupation have remained in force, except in so far as they are suspended by or inconsistent with any Proclamation issued by the British Military Administration, and except in so far as they may be necessarily modified by reason of the circumstances of the occupation. The Italian civil and commercial codes have remained in force, and are applied by the Civil Court. Although the Italian Penal Code technically remains in force, it has been almost entirely superseded by the Civil Offences Proclamation (No. 85), which is, however, largely based upon it.

Islamic or Sharia law

Applied by the Sharia Courts.

Rabbinical law

Applied by the Rabbinical Court.[4]

There follows a summary description of the Cyrenaican courts similar to the one relating to Tripolitania.

The situation in Cyrenaica changed again with the grant of internal autonomy to the territory on 16 September 1949. The personal status of the Arab inhabitants was determined by the Cyrenaican Nationality Law enacted on 31 December 1949.

G. In the case of the Fezzan, the Four Power Commission describes the judicial system as follows:

The following forms of law apply in the Fezzan.

Muslim Law: administered by the Qadis.

French Military Law.

Customary Law: Among the Tuaregs and in the region of Ghadames.

Italian law has not been officially abrogated but, according to the French authorities, is a dead letter, because no copies of Italian legislation remained in the territory at the time of the occupation. [According to the French Military Administration the Ordinances of the Military Governor are based as

3. Four Power Commission of Investigation for the Former Italian Colonies, *Report*, Volume III, *Report on Libya*, Part Two, *Tripolitania*, pp. 22 ff. Mimeographed.

4. *Ibid.*, Part Four, *Cyrenaica*, pp. 14–15.

far as possible on what appear to have been the regulations in force in the territory in the past.] *
* French/United Kingdom addition
U.S.S.R. remark—Article 43 of the Regulations under the Hague Convention is not respected.[5]

The report goes on to describe the courts, which, in the Fezzan, are local in character and differ from area to area.
H. It should be noted that neither in Cyrenaica nor in the Fezzan were there any minorities in the sense of the relevant provisions of General Assembly Resolution 289 A (IV).
I. Pending the enactment of a uniform legislative system, the Libyan Constitution contained, in Chapter XII, "Transitory and Provisional Provisions," an Article (210) which stipulated:

> Unless they are inconsistent with the principles of liberty and equality guaranteed by this Constitution, all laws, subsidiary legislation, orders and notices which may be in operation in any part of Libya upon the coming into force of this Constitution shall continue to be effective and in operation until repealed or amended or replaced by other legislation enacted in accordance with the provisions of this Constitution.[6]

J. The following works may also be profitably consulted:
(i) Enrico de Leone, *La Colonizzazione dell'Africa del Nord* (Padova: Cedam - Casa Editrice Dott. Antonio Milani, 1960), Tomo Secondo, Cap. IV, V, and VI, pp. 339–581; and
(ii) E. E. Evans-Pritchard, *The Sanusi of Cyrenaica* (Oxford: The Oxford University Press, 1949), *passim,* and more particularly pp. 212–17.

5. *Ibid.,* Part Three, *The Fezzan,* pp. 13–14.
6. See p. 921.

Annex XII

ADDITIONAL MATERIAL RELATING TO THE ELABORATION OF RESOLUTION 388 (V) ON ECONOMIC AND FINANCIAL PROVISIONS RELATING TO LIBYA, ADOPTED BY THE GENERAL ASSEMBLY ON 15 DECEMBER 1950 [1]

A. Excerpts from statements made in the Ad Hoc *Political Committee*

1. By the United Kingdom representative, Sir Gladwyn Jebb, at the Committee's seventh meeting on 9 October 1950. Having drawn attention to paragraph 42 of his Government's report on its administration of Cyrenaica and Tripolitania, quoted on pages 372–73, Sir Gladwyn went on:

> . . . The questions as a whole raised points of law and points of fact. A change of sovereignty in a territory immediately raised questions relating to the devolution of the rights and responsibilities of the former government. The provisions laid down in Annex XIV of the Peace Treaty with Italy did not apply to the former Italian colonies. It was nevertheless probable that some of those provisions might be applied by analogy. The position of Italian interests in the territories was as follows: there were, on the one hand, certain rights inherent in the ownership of State or parastatal property; there were, on the other hand, liabilities arising from the Italian public debt, some local contractual engagements entered into between the Italian metropolitan and local governments, and, finally, private property, such as concessions granted to private individuals.
>
> . . . The position as regards immovable property was extremely complex. Under Turkish rule the Ottoman Land Code and the Ottoman Civil Code had been applied, but the rights of the State under those Codes had been more or less modified throughout the territory by local custom. By decree No. 1207 of 3 July 1921, the Italian Government had introduced a new system of registration of immovable property. That system involved no fewer than nine different kinds of property. Certain difficulties had arisen, particularly when local customs had to be taken into account, and the solutions arrived at had not always been consistent, with the result that in certain regions there was a possibility of demands for adjustment of title.
>
> . . . In the same way the Italian Government had followed six different methods of acquiring land. Some of those methods had led to demands for restoration.

1. As explained in Chapter 5, p. 373, the following material is intended to provide for those interested a more detailed account of the legal technicalities and arguments that complicated the solution of the problem of the disposal of former Italian property in Libya.

. . . When the Italian Administration left Libya, the municipal system had broken down, though in many cases the old organisation had been restored. The new municipalities set up in Tripolitania had as yet acquired only part of the property which had belonged to their predecessors, the remainder having been returned to the State for purposes of administration. In Cyrenaica the new municipalities had been granted only the free use, and not the full ownership, of the former communal property.

. . . It was also necessary to distinguish between the rights of persons or undertakings resident in Libya and those of persons or undertakings not resident there, and between those whose property and activities had been confined entirely to Libya and those who had had interests or property in Libya but whose principal activities had been carried on outside the territory.

. . . As regards what had sometimes been called 'parastatal property' the situation was still more complicated because it was not easy to reach an agreement on the meaning of the term. In Libya under Italian rule there had been three different kinds of parastatal organizations, and a decision must be reached as to how far and in what cases the property of those organisations should pass to the State. Each case could be decided only on its merits.

. . . As regards the liabilities of Italy, Libya was obviously quite incapable of providing even part payment of the Italian public debt. But an agreement must be reached between the Italian Government and the future Libyan State concerning the contractual engagements of the Italian Government, in such cases as, for example, the payment of pensions. Finally, it was necessary to reach a decision as to the future of many concessions granted by the Italian administration to private individuals, particularly to foreigners, since a certain number of those concessions had lapsed.

. . . All those questions called for a very thorough examination and a certain number of legal decisions would have to be made. His Majesty's Government had concluded that the safest and most practical solution would be for the General Assembly to appoint a special United Nations court of arbitration . . . [to] go to Libya in order to examine the questions on the spot.

. . . The Government of the United Kingdom considered it desirable that the General Assembly should give the proposed court instructions in the form of general principles. For the rest, aside from the general principles of international law and procedure, it might be guided by provisions similar to those which already governed the Peace Treaty with Italy as regards the disposal of property in former Italian territories other than colonies." [2]

2. By Count Vitetti, the observer for the Government of Italy, at the Committee's eleventh meeting, on 12 October 1950.

Count Vitetti said that:

. . . the observations he was proposing to make were of a preliminary nature and he would be obliged to return to the question in greater detail at a later stage. At the present stage of the discussion, however, he would confine himself to indicating to what extent the problem of Italian rights and responsibilities in Libya was bound up with the clauses of the Peace Treaty with Italy.

2. GAOR: Fifth Session, 1950, *Ad Hoc* Political Committee, 7th Meeting, 9 October 1950, pp. 45–46.

. . . Paragraph 19 [of Annex XIV of the Peace Treaty with Italy] was . . . perfectly explicit and indicated beyond all possibility of doubt that the signatories to the Peace Treaty had decided that the economic and financial clauses of that Treaty were not applicable to the Italian colonies, for which other provisions would be framed. . . . although the United Kingdom Government had previously suggested that the rules of international law and procedure should be applied to the problem of Italian property in the former Italian colonies with due regard to the interest of all concerned, it was now declaring itself in favour of application, by analogy, of the provisions of the Peace Treaty concerning Italian property in territories other than the former Italian colonies.

. . . It was a well-known juridical principle that analogy consisted in the extension of the application of a juridical rule concerning a question for which that rule had been expressly laid down to another question for which no rule had been laid down and which was by nature analogous to the first question. The United Kingdom representative had himself expressed some doubt as to the possibility of extending the provisions of Annex XIV to the former Italian colonies . . . To have recourse to analogy in the case in point would be to modify the sense of Annex XIV of the Peace Treaty and to render its provisions worthless.

. . . the economic and financial obligations laid upon Italy . . . were an exception to the principles generally prevailing in international law, for they led to a very severe and restricted set of rules. He quoted as an example the question of the transfer to the successor States of all property belonging to the Italian Government, without any compensation to that Government. . . . Furthermore, it was a principle both of national and international law that a clearly established exception could not be extended either by analogy or by any other means of interpretation beyond a strictly limited field of application. Consequently, the provisions of Annex XIV, which were an exception, could not be applied to another exception, namely, the economic and financial clauses to be drawn up for the former Italian colonies.

It seemed, therefore, that if the principle of analogy were eliminated and paragraph 19 of Annex XIV were thus nullified, the United Kingdom draft resolution would no longer be founded upon juridical principles. If that text were founded neither upon the principle of analogy nor upon the general principles of international law, what would be its legal basis? That was the fundamental question which he wished to ask the United Kingdom delegation.

. . . In connexion with another juridical question he pointed out that under article XXIII of the Peace Treaty Italy had renounced all its rights and claims to Italian property in Africa. It was obvious that the renunciation applied to sovereignty and to all rights and claims relating to sovereignty. That was clear, both in Annex XI of the Treaty, and also, whenever property was ceded under the terms of other articles of that Treaty, as in the case of Albania (article 29), such cession had been stated explicitly. Therefore, as the question of Italian property was indissolubly bound up with sovereignty, that property was transferred at the same time as sovereignty. Thus, under Annex XI of the Treaty, the General Assembly of the United Nations was entitled to make recommendations to the four Powers in connexion with the final disposal of the former Italian colonies, while Italy, which [had] subscribed to the Peace Treaty, was required to accept any decision taken on the matter.

. . . As to Italian property and responsibilities in Libya, quite a different problem arose, and it was essential to define the juridical provisions. The Italian delegation considered that the problem could not be solved without consultation with the Italian Government. The provisions of Annex XIV of the Peace Treaty could not apply by analogy, and the solution proposed in the United Kingdom draft resolution would lead to all Italian desiderata being completely ignored, which would be neither just nor legal. On the one hand, that solution would be unjust. If it was applied, Italy, which had participated in drawing up strict provisions concerning its responsibilities, on the grounds that it possessed property in other territories, would be debarred from similar participation in connection with the territory of its former colonies. On the other hand, from the legal point of view, if Italy were denied the right to participate in drawing up those provisions, that would be tantamount to imposing upon it the indeterminate obligation of accepting any decision which might be taken without its consent. For the first time in history, a State would thus be burdened with such an indefinite obligation that all the legal principles of all the legislation of the world, especially British legislation, would consider it to be without any value. He was convinced that the United Kingdom delegation had never intended to introduce into international law the principle of the validity of an indefinite obligation; however, that principle was implied in the draft resolution.

. . . Before deciding, therefore, what Italian property should be transferred without compensation or what obligations Italy must assume, it should first be decided whether it was legitimate to impose on Italy new and quite exceptional burdens without its consent.[3]

B. Statement made by the United Nations Commissioner in Libya in Sub-Committee 1 of the Ad Hoc *Political Committee of the General Assembly at its Fourth Meeting, held on 2 November 1950 at Lake Success*

After some introductory remarks, relating to his status in the Sub-Committee, and the scope and purpose of his suggested changes to the United Kingdom draft resolution on economic and financial provisions relating to Libya (see C below), which have been referred to in Part 2 of Chapter 5 above (pp. 378–80), the Commissioner went on as follows:

The question with which the Sub-Committee is dealing is one of great importance to the Libyan State and the Libyan people. Until it is settled, the financial and economic future of the country will remain unstable. The rational exploitation of its resources will be handicapped because in the present uncertainty it is impossible to plan an agricultural economic development program. As the Committee is aware, former Italian State and parastatal property and considerable property belonging to Italian individuals is now held by the British and French Administrations as custodians. In practical terms this means that the properties can neither be turned over as assets to the Libyan State nor be exploited by individuals or corporations whether Libyan or foreign. Much of the best agricultural land of the country, particularly in Cyrenaica, is thus tied up. Although annual leases are given for this property, it is impossible for the State or an individual to put capital

3. GAOR: Fifth Session, 1950, *Ad Hoc* Political Committee, 11th Meeting, 12 October 1950, pp. 65–66.

investment into property of such uncertain status, to maintain or to develop it. The question is further complicated by the fact that a great deal of the property, including all the Italian settlements in Cyrenaica, was abandoned by the owners who were evacuated by the Italian Supreme Command shortly before the withdrawal of the Italian army.

The primary points which my suggested amendments [to the United Kingdom draft resolution] try to clarify are that all State property and all the Italian State or assimilated property interests should be transferred to Libya, as the successor State, without compensation, as was provided for other Italian territories ceded under the terms of the Italian Peace Treaty. A second guiding principle is that private property of Italian nationals shall remain in the hands of the present owners. Properties of a para-statal character in which the Italian State or any of its agencies, including the Fascist party, had an interest, should, in so far as State financial interest, not including managerial interest, is represented, be treated as State property and be turned over without compensation.

Further, my suggested amendments would make it quite clear that the decision of the Arbitral Tribunal shall be binding on all parties concerned. The Tribunal would be charged in particular with the responsibility for determining whether transfers of real property after the outbreak of the war were legal or fictitious.

It might be helpful, Mr. Chairman, if I explain the suggested revisions paragraph by paragraph.

The changes suggested in the preamble are merely drafting changes. . . .

Minor drafting changes are suggested in paragraphs 2 and 3 for purpose of clarity. It is suggested that paragraph 2 should refer to general principles of law as well as those of international law. The paragraph regarding expenses and a secretariat for the Tribunal [has] been made more specific in accordance with [United Nations] practice, and placed later in the draft.

The suggested addition to paragraph 4 provides that, should the Tribunal continue to function after the establishment of the Libyan State, the Government of Libya shall also be bound to submit to the Tribunal information regarding the properties involved.

A new paragraph 6 is suggested to provide specifically that the decisions of the Tribunal shall be binding on all governments concerned, both now and after the achievement of Libya's independence. I have suggested this in order to leave no doubt regarding the status of the Tribunal's decisions.

In paragraph 10 it is suggested that ships belonging to Libyan residents seized by Italy after 10 June 1940, and still held, should be returned. This date, which marks the entrance of Italy into the war, is suggested because after that date a number of fishing ships, particularly those belonging to the Maltese and perhaps Greek communities, were seized. At the same time, a large part of the Maltese community was taken to Italy and interned. The date of 3 September 1943 was the date used in Annex XIV of the Italian Peace Treaty, since [it] was the armistice day for the war on the Italian peninsula. However, this date has no significance in Libya, since the hostilities there had ceased long before that date. It would be equitable to provide that, in view of the special circumstances, these ships should be returned to their former owners so that they could be once more employed by them in the fishing industry which was severely crippled by these seizures. It is further suggested that these ships should be returned to all persons at present residing in Libya rather than those who acquire the nationality of Libya since it will not be possible to acquire such nationality until a Libyan State has been established. After further discussion with the legal advisers, I expect to submit a redraft of this paragraph since its present form is not entirely satisfactory.

A new paragraph 11 has been introduced following the provisions of paragraphs 9 to 13 of Annex XIV of the Italian Peace Treaty, to provide specifically that the property rights and interests of Italian nationals in Libya shall be respected, providing of course that those rights and interests have been lawfully acquired and do not conflict with the other provisions of this resolution. Such provisions should effectively protect the legitimate interest of the Italian inhabitants of the territory.

A new paragraph 13 is suggested to provide that the problem of compensation for war damages shall be studied by the Secretary-General, who shall submit a report on the subject to the next session of the General Assembly. The question of compensation for war damages is one which looms large in Libyan [preoccupations], particularly in Cyrenaica. I have been urgently asked by the Libyan leaders to draw this question to the attention of the General Assembly. The Libyans have frequently pointed out to me that their country was devastated by the ebb and flow of the armies during the last war, and that, as the victims of that destruction, they need assistance in rebuilding and replacing their capital equipment. Obviously, this question is a very difficult and complicated one with far-reaching ramifications. I am not in a position now to suggest a solution but I believe that because of the importance of the question it should be the subject of a special study by the Secretary-General.

The amendments suggested to the first paragraph of [the Annex] provide in the beginning of the first sentence that, pending the establishment of Libya as an independent State, the Administering Powers may act on behalf of Libya to receive without payment former Italian State property within Libya. Secondly, it provides that property commonly known as para-statal property belonging to Italian public institutions and publicly owned companies and associations as well as such property belonging to the Fascist party or its auxiliary organisations, shall be included among those properties to be transferred to the Libyan State without payment. This provision is, *mutatis mutandis,* similar to that in paragraph 1 of Annex XIV. It is further suggested that relevant archives and documents of a technical as well as an administrative character pertaining to Libya, shall be transferred to that State. This provision is designed to place at the disposal of the Libyan State archives and documents regarding its territory which will be helpful for an orderly administration and for the exploitation of its resources.

A new paragraph is suggested as No. 3 of the Annex to provide that transfer of property and interests having taken place after the entrance of Italy into the war shall be deemed null and void. This paragraph is similar to paragraph 3 of Annex XIV, except that, as in the case of the seized ships, which I mentioned a moment ago, the date has again been changed to 10 June 1940. This change is suggested because I have been informed by my Libyan advisers and others that in a number of cases para-statal properties were hastily and without proper legal justification transferred to individual owners just prior to the withdrawal of the Italian armies [from] North Africa. It is, however, provided that actions taken in the normal course of operations of the former para-statal organisations should be exempt from this provision.

In concluding, I would like to inform the Sub-Committee that with regard to the composition of the proposed Arbitral Tribunal I may have to make certain suggestions in the light of the discussion which is . . . about to begin.[4]

C. Written texts submitted by the United Kingdom delegation

1. Draft resolution on economic and financial provisions relating to Libya; introduced at the seventh meeting of the *Ad Hoc* Political Committee on 9 October 1950, and referred by the latter to Sub-Committee 1 for consideration.

Whereas annex XIV of the Treaty of Peace with Italy contained economic and financial provisions, relating to territories ceded by Italy,

Whereas paragraph 19 of that annex stated that its provisions should not apply to the former Italian Colonies, but that 'the economic and financial provisions to be applied therein will form part of the arrangements for the final disposal of these territories, pursuant to article 23 of the Treaty',

Whereas the four Powers were unable to agree upon their disposal by 15 September 1948 in accordance with article 23 of the Treaty, and therefore the matter was referred to the General Assembly of the United Nations in accordanace with annex XI to the Treaty of Peace with Italy,

Whereas the general disposal of the former Italian Colonies (excepting Eritrea) was effected by resolution 289 (IV) of the General Assembly adopted 21 November 1949, but the question of financial and economic provisions was left in abeyance,

Whereas it is desirable that before the transfer of the administration in Libya takes place in accordance with the above-mentioned resolution, the financial and economic provisions to be applied in connexion with the final disposal of Libya should be determined and that as far as possible their application to property in Libya should have been decided;

The General Assembly resolves:

1. That the economic and financial provisions to be applied in Libya, in accordance with Annex XIV, paragraph 19, of the Treaty of Peace with Italy, shall be those set forth in the annex to and in paragraphs 6 to 10 of the present resolution;
2. That a United Nations Arbitral Tribunal, composed of three persons selected by the Secretary-General on the grounds of their legal qualifications from the nationals of three different States not directly interested in the question, shall be entrusted with the task of deciding all questions relating to the application of the provisions in the annex, and that in deciding such questions the Tribunal should, in so far as the provisions of the annex afford no direct guidance, be inspired by the general principles of international law and practice;

4. United Nations Archives. Typescript. The text has been slightly amended to bring the orthography and other minor aspects into harmony with normal United Nations editorial practice.

3. That the above-mentioned Tribunal shall proceed to Libya as soon as possible, arrangements for accommodation and staff having been made by the Secretary-General of the United Nations. All the expenses of the Tribunal shall be borne by the United Nations;
4. That the administering Powers shall submit to the Tribunal as soon as possible all the information which they possess with regard to all property covered by the annex to this resolution, and shall request the directions of the Tribunal as to the disposition of the property. The Tribunal shall give immediate directions with regard to all property about which no reasonable doubt arises. The Tribunal shall then decide all cases where there is doubt or dispute and shall, before reaching a decision thereon, afford to all interested parties a reasonable opportunity of presenting their views;
5. That the Tribunal shall determine its procedure. It may take all decisions by a majority vote. It shall be entitled to submit demands for information which it requires for the purposes of deciding the matters submitted to it to any Government or authority which it deems to be likely to be in a position to furnish such information;
6. That the social insurance organizations operating in Libya shall be excepted from the provisions of the annex and special arrangements shall be concluded between Libya and Italy to govern the conditions under which the obligations of Italian public or private social insurance organizations towards the inhabitants of Libya and a proportionate part of the reserves accumulated by the said organizations shall be transferred to similar organizations in the successor State, together with all real property and fixed assets of the said organizations in Libya;
7. That the Government of Italy shall continue to be liable for the payment of civil or military pensions earned, as from the coming into force of the Treaty of Peace with Italy, for service under the Italian State, municipal or other local authorities, by persons who acquire Libyan nationality, including pension rights not yet matured. Arrangements shall be concluded between the Governments of Italy and Libya providing for the method by which this liability shall be discharged;
8. That the Government of Libya shall be exempted from the payment of any portion of the Italian public debt;
9. That Italy shall return to Libya in the shortest possible time any ships in Italian possession which were owned on 3 September 1943, by persons resident in Libya who acquire the nationality of Libya or by other nationals of Member States of the United Nations, except any ships which have been subject to a *bona fide* sale.
10. That if Libya grants compensation to its nationals for loss or damage sustained during, and as a result of, the Second World War, then it shall grant no less favourable treatment in this respect to nationals of Member States of the United Nations.

ANNEX

1. The Libyan State shall receive, without payment, the movable and immovable property, within the Territory of Libya, which formerly belonged solely to the Italian State or to local authorities under the Italian Administration, as well as all relative archives and documents of an administrative character

or historical value concerning the Territory of Libya or relating to property transferred under this paragraph.

2. The Libyan State shall receive, without payment, all Italian State interest (as it existed on the coming into force of the Treaty of Peace with Italy) in any undertakings, public companies and organizations within Libya. Where the operations of such undertakings, public companies and organizations extend to Italy or elsewhere, the Libyan State shall receive only such Italian State interest as appertains to the operations which are confined to Libya. In cases where the former Italian or Libyan Governments exercised only managerial control over any concerns, as distinct from possessing financial or property rights, the Libyan State shall not be entitled to have any interest in the concern transferred to it.

3. Concessions within the Territory of Libya which were granted to individuals by the Italian or former Libyan Governments shall be confirmed if it is shown that the concessionaire has carried out the terms of the concession in full.[5]

2. Statement amplifying the reasons underlying the submission of the draft resolution, issued by the United Kingdom delegation on 17 October 1950.

[1. . . .]

2. Annex XIV of the Treaty of Peace with Italy contained the economic and financial provisions relating to territories ceded by Italy. However, paragraph 19 of the Annex specifically said that the provisions of this Annex should not apply to the former Italian colonies, but that 'the economic and financial provisions to be applied therein will form part of the arrangements for the final disposal of these territories pursuant to Article 23 of the Treaty'.

3. According to Article 23, the disposal of the former Italian colonies was to be effected by the four Powers, but the onus was eventually placed on the United Nations because of the failure of the Council of Foreign Ministers to agree.

[4. . . .]

5.(*a*) . . . the Assembly should lay down the principles which are to govern the assumption by the Successor State of certain economic and financial rights of the former Italian Administration.

(*b*) . . . the Assembly should establish an Arbitral Tribunal to adjudicate in these matters.

6. The reasons for making the latter recommendation are simple, viz:

(*a*) Owing to the fact that no government existed in Libya at the time of the occupation, the Administrations of Tripolitania and Cyrenaica did not inherit complete records, and it has become clear that such records as have been compiled in subsequent years require extensive supplementation, for instance from Italy.

(*b*) In many cases where the records do appear to be complete there is an obvious need for legal appreciation of the facts and for arbitration based on the principles of international law and taking into account the interests of all concerned.

5. GAOR: Fifth Session, 1950, Annexes, Agenda item 21 (A/AC.38/L.9, 9 October 1950), pp. 45–46.

(*c*) Although His Majesty's Government are anxious to place their data and such local experience as they have acquired at the disposal of an internationally appointed Arbitral Tribunal, they feel quite unable to accept the position of sole arbiter in this matter.[6]

The statement continued with a paragraph-by-paragraph commentary on the United Kingdom draft resolution. This commentary has been summarized in Chapter 5, Part 2, pp. 376–77.

6. United Nations Doc. A/AC.38/SC.1/L.1, 17 October 1950. Mimeographed.

Annex XIII

STAFF OF THE UNITED NATIONS MISSION IN LIBYA, 1950–1952

Listed below are the internationally recruited personnel who served on the staff of the United Nations Mission in Libya during 1950–52. Periods of service varied. Expert personnel and consultants paid out of technical assistance funds are not listed.

United Nations Commissioner in Libya
Adrian Pelt

Principal Secretary
Thomas F. Power, Jr.

Deputy Principal Secretary
Alberto Gonzalez-Fernandez

Deputy Principal Secretary for Economic and Social Affairs
Jerome Pintos

Advisers
Syed H. Ahmed, Budget and Administration
Christopher Burney, Political
Paul Cremona, Political
Albert Grand, Political and Information Officer
Albert J. P. Le Bel, Agricultural
Omar Loutfi, Legal
Saleh Hahmoud, Political
Johann P. Mensing, Land Claims
Marc Schreiber, Legal

Arabic Information Officer
Yusuf Al-Khal

Administrative Officer
V. A. De Angelis

Finance Officers
Max Doerner
Leif G. Haug

Précis-Writers
Georgette Cohen
Elsa Haim
Constance Rolfe
Imogen Salter

Chief Languages Services
Georges Lambert-Lamond

Revisers
Raouf Kahil
A. Michelet

Interpreter-Translators
Fuad George Badawi
John G. Chackal
Yusuf El Bandak
Kamel Georges
Khemaïs Hajeri
I. Khalidi
S. Salameh
Taher Thabit
George Wakim

Documents Officer
Henriette Hartmann

Secretaries
Mohamed A. Aboul-Kheir
Magdeleine Allard
Alice Bidart
Jacqueline Bracciotti
Marthe Briand
Raissa El Sayed
Jenny Jones

Pauline Keller
Yehia Mohamed Mansour
Cora Moorer
Ida Paquin
Hanna Platz
Isis Ragheb
Lorraine Shea
Myriam Stevens
Helen Stokell
S. Taieb

Field Service Personnel

Brian Anscombe
Jasper Bloomfield
Edmond Bunny
Patrick Hanley
Jacob Hartland
Abdul Al Khattab
Einar Michalsen
Kaare Moksnes
Edward Muro
Nassib Nassar
Pierre Pichou
Mok Seng Tan

Telephone Operator

Mary Mantin

Mimeograph Operator

Yusuf Ghazla

Chauffeurs

Alberigo Dama
Mehdi Ben Freg
Domenico Guderzo
Vincenzo Micillo
Ali Tagiuri Suleman

Index

The following abbreviations or short titles, as well as the accepted abbreviations for the specialized agencies of the United Nations, are used within entries.

ACABQ	United Nations Advisory Committee on Administrative and Budgetary Questions
AP	Administering Power(s)
BCA	British Chief Administrator(s), Cyrenaica, Tripolitania
BMA	British Military Administration, Cyrenaica, Tripolitania
C-18	Committee of Eighteen (Committee for the Constitution)
C-21	Committee of Twenty-One
CC	Coordination Committee for the Transfer of Powers
CFM	Council of Foreign Ministers
CL	Council for Libya
FLG	Federal Libyan Government
FMA	French Military Administration
Four Power Commission	Four Power Commission of Investigation for the Former Italian Colonies
LFC	Libyan Finance Corporation
LPDSA	Libyan Public Development and Stabilization Agency
Meeting of Experts	Meeting of Experts on Libyan financial, monetary, and development problems
Minutes of C-18	*Minutes of the Committee of Eighteen*
NCAL	National Constituent Assembly of Libya
NCLL	National Council for the Liberation of Libya
PLG	Provisional Libyan Government
Preparatory Committee	Preparatory Committee for the National Assembly of Libya
Proc. NCAL	*Proceedings of the National Constituent Assembly of Libya*
R	United Nations Resolution (adopted by the General Assembly)
SC-1	Sub-Committee 1 of the *Ad Hoc* Political Committee, UNGA
SC-15	Sub-Committee 15 of the 1st Committee, UNGA

SC-17	Sub-Committee 17 of the 1st Committee, UNGA
TA	Technical assistance
TAB	Technical Assistance Board
UK	United Kingdom
UN	United Nations
UNCL	United Nations Commissioner in Libya
UNGA	United Nations General Assembly
UNML	United Nations Mission in Libya
US	United States of America
USSR	Union of Soviet Socialist Republics
WG	Working Group on the Constitution and Electoral Law (Committee of Six)